RAND McNALLY

TODAY'S WORLD

A NEW WORLD ATLAS

FROM

THE CARTOGRAPHERS

OF

RAND McNALLY

TODAY'S WORLD

A NEW WORLD ATLAS FROM
THE CARTOGRAPHERS OF RAND McNALLY

RAND McNALLY
CHICAGO • NEW YORK • SAN FRANCISCO

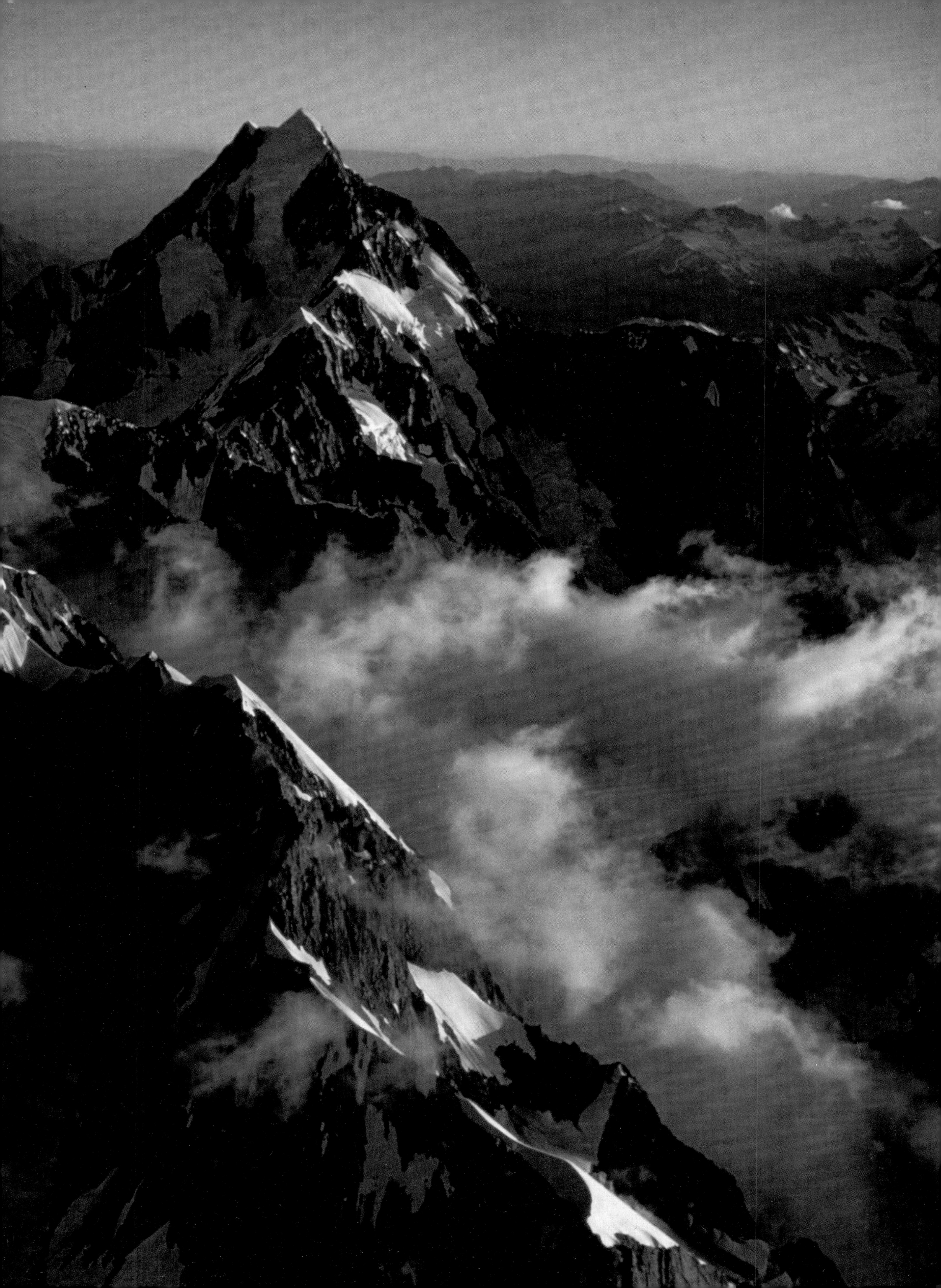

CONTENTS

USING THE ATLAS

Maps and Atlases v
Sequence of the Maps vi
Getting the Information vi
Finding Places vi
Measuring Distances vi
Determining Direction vii
Understanding Map Symbols vii
World Time Zones viii

REFERENCE MAPS

Map Symbols and Index Map 1
World 2-3

EUROPE 4-5
Northern Europe 6-7
British Isles 8-9
Central Europe 10-11
Belgium, Netherlands, and Luxembourg 12
Switzerland 13
France and the Alps 14-15
Spain and Portugal 16-17
Italy 18-19
Southeastern Europe 20-21
Baltic and Moscow Regions 22-23

ASIA 24-25
Northwest Asia 26-27
Northeast Asia 28-29
China, Japan, and Korea 30-31
Northeastern China and Korea 32-33
Eastern and Southeastern China 34-35
Japan 36-37
Southeastern Asia 38-39
Burma, Thailand, and Indochina 40-41
India, Pakistan, and Southwestern Asia 42-43
Northern India and Pakistan 44-45
Southern India and Sri Lanka 46
Southern Arabian Peninsula 47
The Middle East 48-49
Israel and Southern Lebanon 50-51

AFRICA 52-53
Western North Africa 54-55
Eastern North Africa 56-57
Southern Africa 58-59
Egypt and Sudan 60-61
Northern Africa 62-63
West Africa 64-65
Southern Africa and Madagascar 66-67

AUSTRALIA 68-69
Eastern Australia 70-71
New Zealand 72

ANTARCTICA 73

SOUTH AMERICA 74-75
Northern South America 76-77
Southern South America 78
Southeastern Brazil 79
Central Argentina and Chile 80-81
Peru, Bolivia, and Western Brazil 82-83
Colombia, Ecuador, Venezuela, and Guyana 84-85

NORTH AMERICA 86-87
Middle America and Caribbean 88-89
Mexico 90-91
Central America 92-93
Caribbean Region 94-95
Canada 96-97
United States of America 98-99
Alaska and the Yukon 100-101
Southwestern Canada 102-103
South-Central Canada 104-105
Southeastern Canada 106-107
Northeastern United States 108-109
Great Lakes Region 110-111
Southeastern United States 112-113
Mississippi Valley 114-115
Southern Great Plains 116-117
Northern Great Plains 118-119
Southern Rocky Mountains 120-121
Northwestern United States 122-123
California, Nevada, and Hawaii 124-125

PACIFIC AND INDIAN OCEANS 126-127

ATLANTIC OCEAN 128

INDEX 129-192

TODAY'S WORLD

Printed in the United States of America

Library of Congress Cataloging-in-Publication Data
Rand McNally and Company.
Today's world : A new world atlas from the cartographers of Rand McNally.
p. cm.
Includes index.
ISBN 0-528-83500-9
1. Atlases. I. Title.
G1021.R4867 1992 <G&M>
912—dc20 92-16250
CIP
MAP

Title page photo, Mount Cook, New Zealand, J. Amos/ SUPERSTOCK

USING THE ATLAS

MAPS AND ATLASES

Satellite images of the world (figure 1) constantly give us views of the shape and size of the earth. It is hard, therefore, to imagine how difficult it once was to ascertain the look of our planet. Yet from early history we have evidence of humans trying to work out what the world actually looked like.

Twenty-five hundred years ago, on a tiny clay tablet the size of a hand, the Babylonians inscribed the earth as a flat disk (figure 2) with Babylon at the center. The section of the Cantino map of 1502 (figure 3) is an example of a *portolan* chart used by mariners to chart the newly discovered Americas. Handsome and useful maps have been produced by many cultures. The Mexican map drawn in 1583 marks hills with wavy lines and roads with footprints between parallel lines (figure 4). The methods and materials used to create these maps were dependent upon the technology available, and their accuracy suffered considerably. A modern topographic map (figure 5), as well as those in this atlas, shows the detail and accuracy that cartographers are now able to achieve. They benefit from our ever-increasing technology, including satellite imagery and computer assisted cartography.

In 1589 Gerardus Mercator used the word *atlas* to describe a collection of maps. Atlases now bring together not only a variety of maps but an assortment of tables and other reference material as well. They have become a unique and indispensable reference for graphically defining the world and answering the question *where*. Only on a map can the countries, cities, roads, rivers, and lakes covering a vast area be simultaneously viewed in their relative locations. Routes between places can be traced, trips planned, boundaries of neighboring states and countries examined, distances between places measured, the meandering of rivers and streams and the sizes of lakes visualized–and remote places imagined.

FIGURE 1

FIGURE 4

FIGURE 2

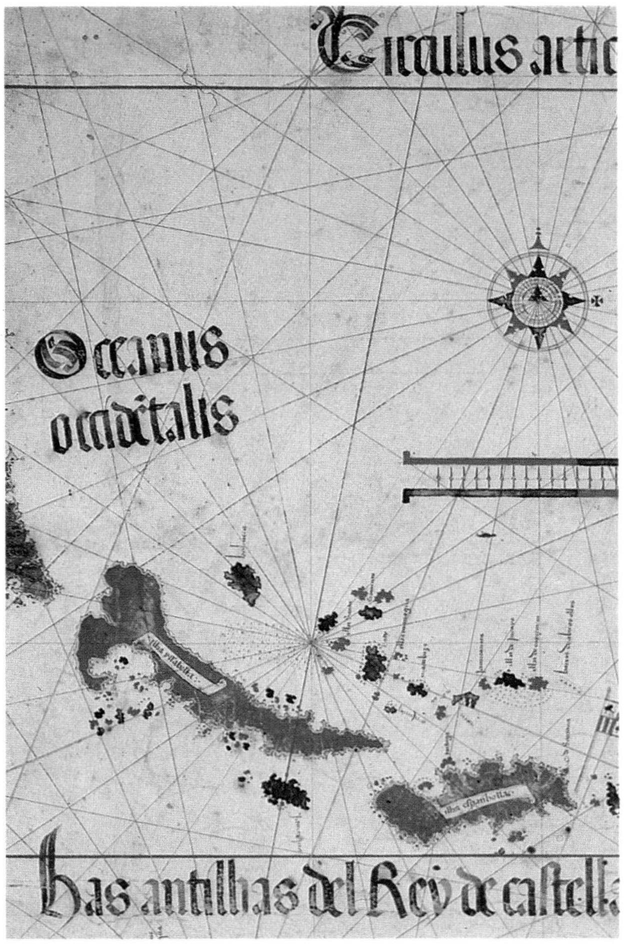

FIGURE 3

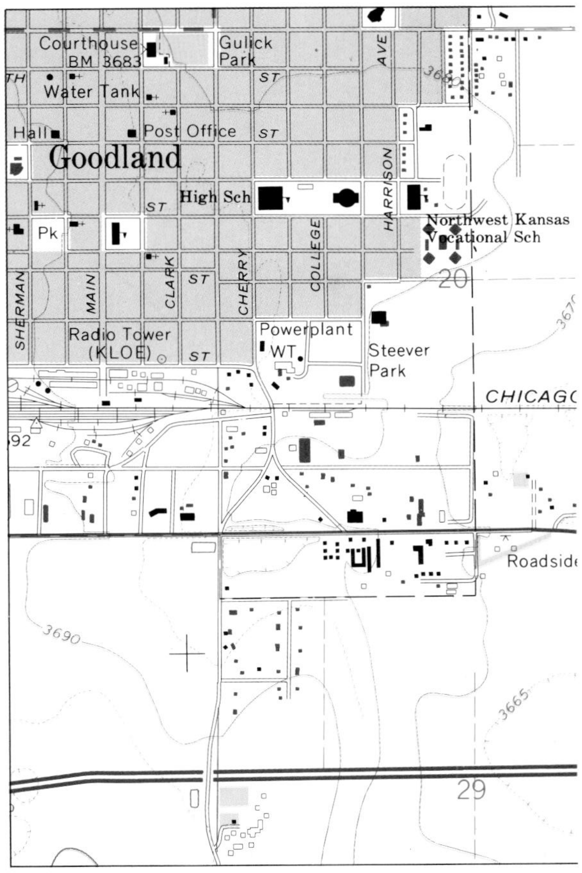

FIGURE 5

SEQUENCE OF THE MAPS

The world is made up of seven major landmasses: the continents of Europe, Asia, Africa, Antarctica, Australia, South America, and North America (figure 6). The maps in this atlas follow this continental sequence. To allow for the inclusion of detail, each continent is broken down into a series of maps, and this grouping is arranged so that as consecutive pages are turned, a continuous successive part of the continent is shown. Larger-scale maps are used for regions of greater detail (having many cities, for example) or for areas of global significance.

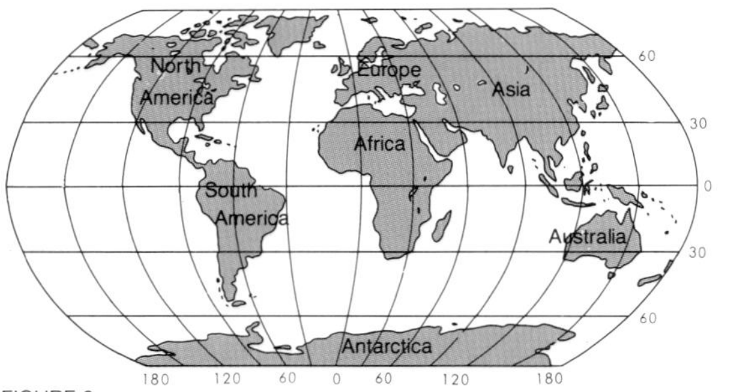

FIGURE 6

GETTING THE INFORMATION

An atlas can be used for many purposes, from planning a trip to finding hot spots in the news and supplementing world knowledge. To realize the potential of an atlas the user must be able to:

1. Find places on the maps
2. Measure distances
3. Determine directions
4. Understand map symbols

FINDING PLACES

One of the most common and important tasks facilitated by an atlas is finding the location of a place in the world. A river's name in a book, a city mentioned in the news, or a vacation spot may prompt your need to know where the place is located. The illustrations and text below explain how to find Yangon (Rangoon), Burma.

1. Look up the place-name in the index at the back of the atlas. Yangon, Burma can be found on the map on page 38, and it can be located on the map by the letter-number key *B2* (figure 7).

Yancey, co., N.C., U.S.	**f10**	140
Yanceyville, N.C., U.S.	**A3**	140
Yanchang, China	**D9**	30
Yancheng, China	**B9**	34
Yandoon, Burma	**F3**	40
Yangjiang, China	**G9**	30
Yangon (Rangoon), Burma	**B2**	38
Yangquan, China	**D9**	30
Yangtze see Chang, stm., China	**E10**	30
Yangzhou, China	**C8**	34
Yanji, China	**C12**	30
Yankton, S.D., U.S.	**E8**	148
Yankton, co., S.D., U.S.	**D8**	148
Yanqi, China	**C4**	30
Yantai (Chefoo), China	**D11**	30
Yantic, stm., Ct., U.S.	**C7**	114
Yapen, Pulau, i., Indon.	**F10**	38
Yaqui, stm., Mex.	**C5**	90
Yaraka, Austl.	**D8**	68

FIGURE 7

2. Turn to the map of Southeastern Asia found on page 38. Note that the letters *A* through *H* and the numbers *1* through *11* appear in the margins of the map.

3. To find Yangon, on the map, place your left index finger on *B* and your right index finger on *2*. Move your left finger across the map and your right finger down the map. Your fingers will meet in the area in which Yangon is located (figure 8).

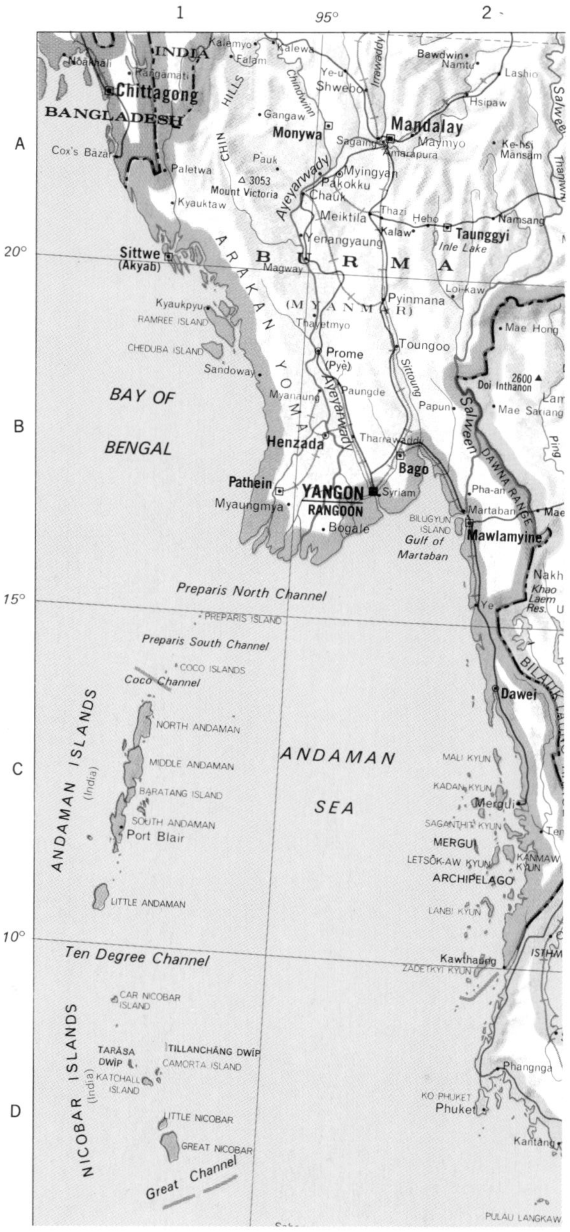

FIGURE 8

MEASURING DISTANCES

In planning trips, determining the distance between two places is essential, and an atlas can help in travel preparation. For instance, to determine the approximate distance between Paris and Rouen, France, follow these three steps:

1. Lay a slip of paper on the map on page 14 so that its edge touches the two cities. Adjust the paper so one corner touches Rouen. Mark the paper directly at the spot where Paris is located (figure 9).

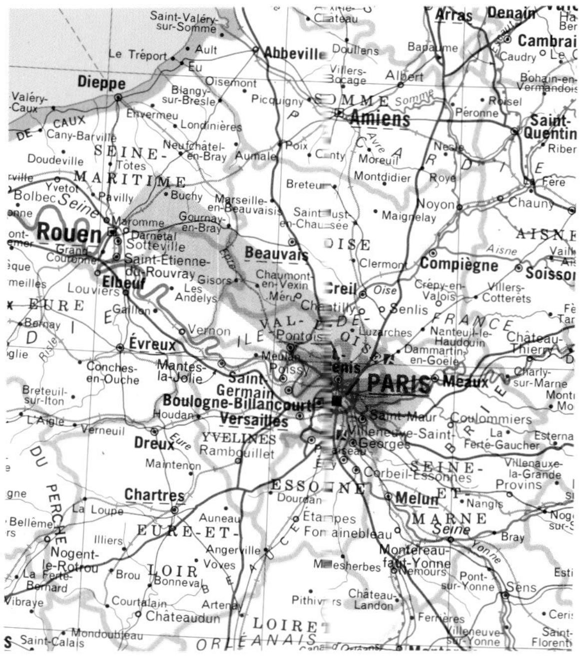

FIGURE 9

2. Place the paper along the scale of miles beneath the map. Position the corner at 0 and line up the edge of the paper along the scale. The pencil mark on the paper indicates Rouen is between 50 and 100 miles from Paris (figure 10).

3. To find the exact distance, move the paper to the left so that the pencil mark is at 100 on the scale. The corner of the paper stands on the fourth 5-mile unit on the scale. This means that the two towns are 50 plus 20, or 70 miles apart (figure 11).

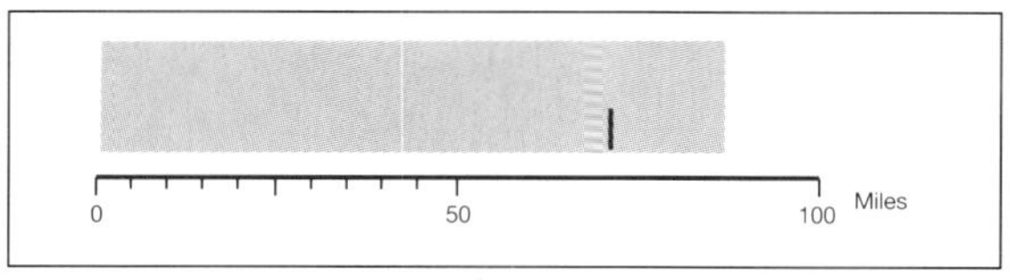

FIGURE 10

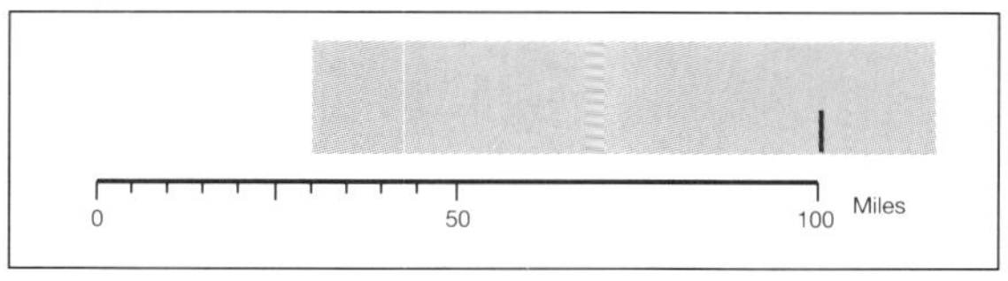

FIGURE 11

DETERMINING DIRECTION

Most of the maps in the atlas are drawn so that when oriented for normal reading, north is at the top of the map, south is at the bottom, west is at the left, and east is at the right. Most maps have a series of lines drawn across them–the lines of *latitude* and *longitude*. Lines of latitude, or *parallels* of latitude, are drawn east and west. Lines of longitude, or *meridians* of longitude, are drawn north and south (figure 12).

Parallels and meridians appear as either curved or straight lines. For example, in the section of the map of Europe (figure 13) the parallels of latitude appear as curved lines. The meridians of longitude are straight lines that come together toward the top of the map. Latitude and longitude lines help locate places on maps. Parallels of latitude are numbered in degrees north and south of the *Equator.* Meridians of longitude are numbered in degrees east and west of a line called the *Prime Meridian,* running through Greenwich, England, near London. Any place on earth can be located by the latitude and longitude lines running through it.

To determine directions or locations on the map, you must use the parallels and meridians. For example, suppose you want to know which is farther north, Bergen, Norway, or Stockholm, Sweden. The map in figure 13 shows that Stockholm is south of the 60° parallel of latitude and Bergen is north of it. Bergen is farther north than Stockholm. By looking at the meridians of longitude, you can determine which city is farther east. Bergen is approximately 5° east of the 0° meridian (Prime Meridian), and Stockholm is almost 20° east of it. Stockholm is farther east than Bergen.

UNDERSTANDING MAP SYMBOLS

In a very real sense, the whole map is a symbol, representing the world or a part of it. It is a reduced representation of the earth; each of the world's features–cities, rivers, etc.–is represented on the map by a symbol. Map symbols may take the form of points, such as dots or squares (often used for cities, capital cities, or points of interest), or lines (roads, railroads, rivers). Symbols may also occupy an area, showing extent of coverage (terrain, forests, deserts). They seldom look like the feature they represent and therefore must be identified and interpreted. For instance, the maps in this atlas define political units by a colored line depicting their boundaries. Neither the colors nor the boundary lines are actually found on the surface of the earth, but because countries and states are such important political components of the world, strong symbols are used to represent them. The Map Symbols page in this atlas identifies the symbols used on the maps.

FIGURE 12

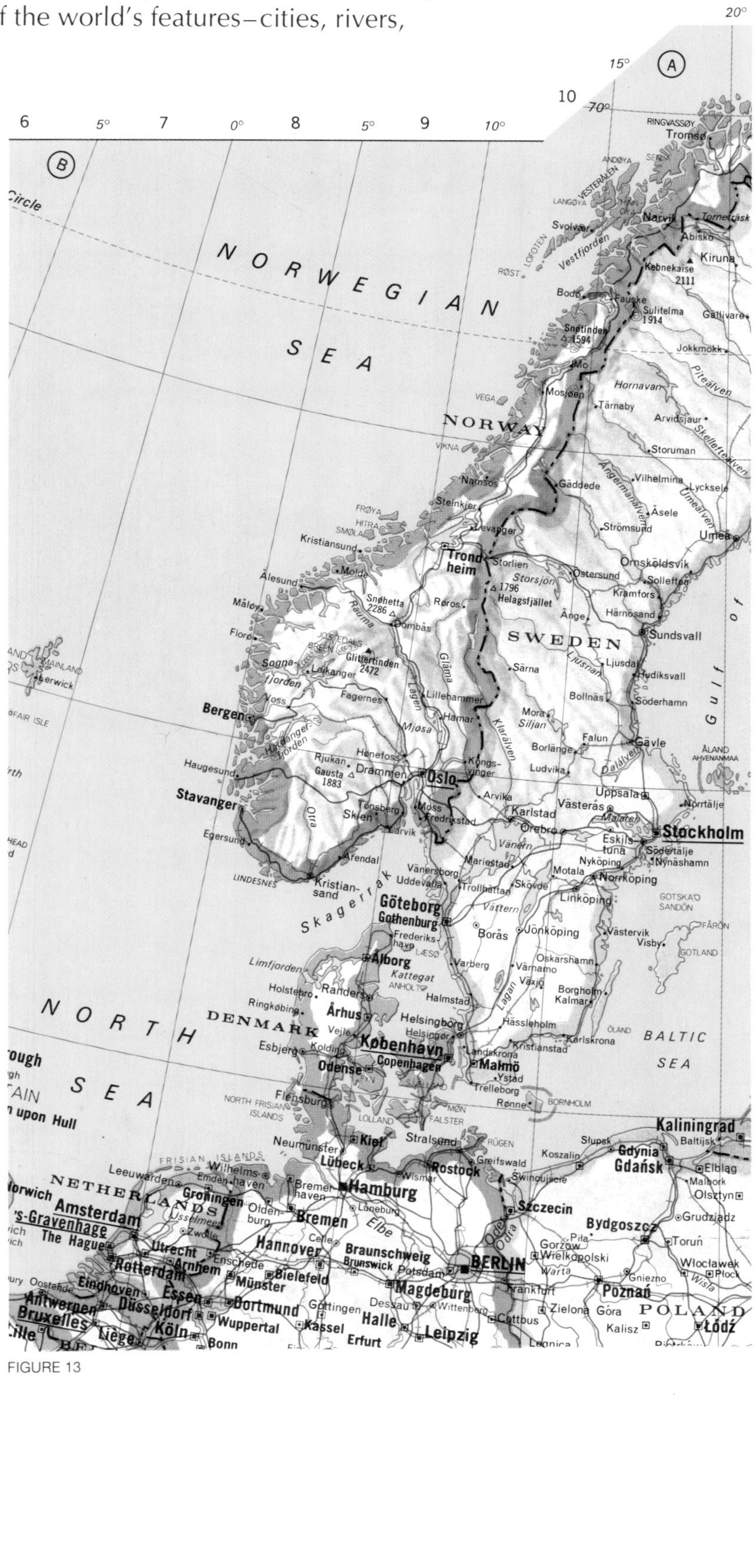

FIGURE 13

ARCTIC OCEAN
Beaufort Sea
GREENLAND
(Den.)
Baffin Bay
BAFFIN ISLAND
Thule
Godhavn
Godthåb
Davis Strait
Angmagssalik
Reykjavík
ICELAND
Norwegian Sea
FAEROE ISLANDS
(Den.)
RUSSIA
Bering Strait
UNITED STATES
Arctic Circle
Nome
Yukon
Fairbanks
Mount McKinley
6194
Anchorage
Bering Sea
Gulf of Alaska
ALEUTIAN ISLANDS
Inuvik
VICTORIA ISLAND
Yellowknife
Hudson Bay
Churchill
Juneau
ROCKY MOUNTAINS
CANADA
Edmonton
Calgary
Vancouver
Seattle
Winnipeg
Lake Superior
Lake Huron
Québec
Ottawa
Montreal
Toronto
Lake Ontario
Saint Lawrence
NEWFOUNDLAND
St. John's
Halifax
Portland
Minneapolis
NORTH AMERICA
CHICAGO
Lake Michigan
DETROIT
L. Erie
Boston
NEW YORK
PHILADELPHIA
Washington
APPALACHIAN MOUNTAINS
SAN FRANCISCO
Salt Lake City
Denver
UNITED STATES
St. Louis
LOS ANGELES
San Diego
Phoenix
El Paso
Dallas
Atlanta
Mississippi
Rio Grande
Houston
New Orleans
Gulf of Mexico
Miami
BAHAMAS
BERMUDA
(U.K.)
ATLANTIC OCEAN
Monterrey
MEXICO
CABO SAN LUCAS
Guadalajara
CIUDAD DE MÉXICO
MEXICO CITY
La Habana
CUBA
DOMINICAN REPUBLIC
HAITI
Port-au-Prince
Santo Domingo
PUERTO RICO (U.S.)
San Juan
JAMAICA
Kingston
GUADELOUPE (Fr.)
MARTINIQUE (Fr.)
BARBADOS
TRINIDAD AND TOBAGO
Port of Spain
GUATEMALA
BELIZE
HONDURAS
Tegucigalpa
Guatemala
San Salvador
EL SALVADOR
NICARAGUA
Managua
San José
COSTA RICA
Panamá
PANAMA
Caribbean Sea
ÎLE CLIPPERTON
(Fr.)
Caracas
VENEZUELA
GUYANA
Georgetown
Paramaribo
SURINAME
FRENCH GUIANA
Medellín
Santa Fe de Bogotá
Cali
COLOMBIA
Quito
ECUADOR
Guayaquil
ARCHIPIÉLAGO DE COLÓN
GALÁPAGOS ISLANDS
(Ec.)
Equator
Iquitos
Manaus
Amazon
Belém
Fortaleza
CABO DE SÃO ROQUE
Natal
Recife
Madeira
BRAZIL
Trujillo
ANDES
PERU
Lima
SOUTH AMERICA
Salvador
Arequipa
La Paz
BOLIVIA
Sucre
Goiânia
Brasília
Belo Horizonte
PARAGUAY
SÃO PAULO
RIO DE JANEIRO
Santos
Antofagasta
Asunción
Curitiba
ISLA SAN AMBROSIO
(Chile)
CHILE
Co. Aconcagua
6959
Córdoba
Paraná
Porto Alegre
Valparaíso
Santiago
Rosario
BUENOS AIRES
URUGUAY
Montevideo
ARCHIPIÉLAGO JUAN FERNÁNDEZ
(Chile)
ARGENTINA
Concepción
Mar del Plata
Bahía Blanca
FALKLAND ISLANDS
(U.K.)
Punta Arenas
CABO DE HORNOS
CAPE HORN
SOUTH GEORGIA
(U.K.)
Drake Passage
SOUTH ORKNEY ISLANDS
(U.K.)
ANTARCTIC PENINSULA
Bellingshausen Sea
Weddell Sea
Antarctic Circle
Ross Sea
ROSS ICE SHELF
MARIE BYRD LAND
Vinson Massif
4897
ANTAR
PACIFIC OCEAN
MIDWAY ISLANDS
(U.S.)
HAWAIIAN ISLANDS
(U.S.)
Honolulu
Tropic of Cancer
JOHNSTON ATOLL
(U.S.)
POLYNESIA
LINE ISLANDS
KIRIBATI
PHOENIX ISLANDS
TOKELAU
(N.Z.)
ÎLES MARQUISES
WALLIS AND FUTUNA
(Fr.)
W. SAMOA
AM. SAMOA
Apia
FIJI
ÎLES TUAMOTU
NIUE
(N.Z.)
COOK ISLANDS
(N.Z.)
FRENCH POLYNESIA
TONGA
Tropic of Capricorn
PITCAIRN
(U.K.)
ISLA DE PASCUA
EASTER ISLAND
(Chile)
International Date Line
PACIFIC OCEAN
CHATHAM ISLANDS
(N.Z.)
Porto
Madrid
PORTUGAL
Lisboa
SPAIN
AÇORES AZORES
(Port.)
GIBRALTAR
(U.K.)
Rabat
Casablanca
MOROCCO
ARQUIPÉLAGO DA MADEIRA
(Port.)
ISLAS CANARIAS
CANARY ISLANDS
(Sp.)
ATLAS
WESTERN SAHARA
MAURITANIA
Nouakchott
Tombouctou
CAPE VERDE
SENEGAL
Dakar
GAMBIA
Banjul
GUINEA-BISSAU
Bamako
GUINEA
Conakry
Freetown
SIERRA LEONE
IVORY COAST
Yamoussoukro
Monrovia
LIBERIA
Abidjan
IRELAND
Glasgow
Dublin
UNITED KINGDOM
LONDON
SAINT HELENA
(U.K.)
ATLANTIC OCEAN
Equator

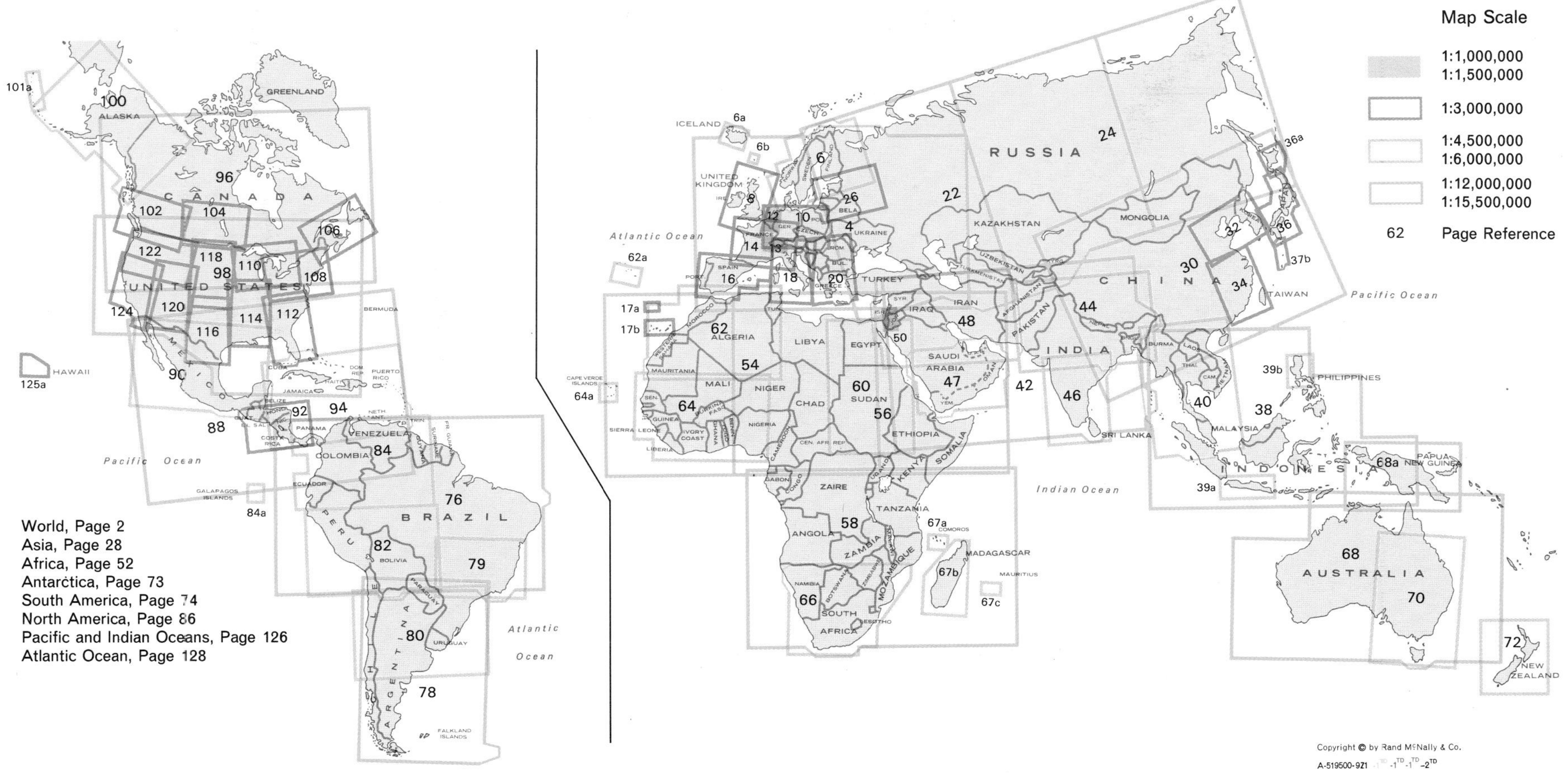

World Maps Symbols

Inhabited Localities

The size of type indicates the relative economic and political importance of the locality

Écommoy	Lisieux	**Rouen**
Trouville	**Orléans**	**PARIS**
Bi'r Safājah °	Oasis	

Alternate Names

MOSKVA
MOSCOW

Basel
Bâle

English or second official language names are shown in reduced size lettering

Volgograd
(Stalingrad)

Historical or other alternates in the local language are shown in parentheses

Urban Area (Area of continuous industrial, commercial, and residential development)

Capitals of Political Units

BUDAPEST Independent Nation

Cayenne Dependency (Colony, protectorate, etc.)

Recife State, Province, County, Oblast, etc.

Political Boundaries

International (First-order political unit)

- Demarcated and Undemarcated
- Disputed de jure
- Indefinite or Undefined
- Demarcation Line

Internal

- State, Province, etc. (Second-order political unit)
- *MURCIA* — Historical Region (No boundaries indicated)
- GALAPAGOS (Ecuador) — Administering Country

Transportation

- Primary Road
- Secondary Road
- Minor Road, Trail
- Railway
- *Canal du Midi* — Navigable Canal
- Bridge
- Tunnel
- TO MALMÖ — Ferry

Hydrographic Features

- Shoreline
- Undefined or Fluctuating Shoreline
- *Amur* — River, Stream
- Intermittent Stream
- Rapids, Falls
- Irrigation or Drainage Canal
- Reef
- *The Everglades* — Swamp
- RIMO GLACIER — Glacier
- *L. Victoria* — Lake, Reservoir
- *Tuz Gölü* — Salt Lake
- Intermittent Lake, Reservoir
- Dry Lake Bed
- *(395)* — Lake Surface Elevation

Topographic Features

- Matterhorn △ 4478 — Elevation Above Sea Level
- 76 ▽ — Elevation Below Sea Level
- Mount Cook ▲ 3764 — Highest Elevation in Country
- 133 ▼ — Lowest Elevation in Country
- Khyber Pass 1067 — Mountain Pass

Elevations are given in meters.
The highest and lowest elevations in a continent are underlined

- Sand Area
- Lava
- Salt Flat

ARCTIC OCEAN
Beaufort Sea
GREENLAND
(Den.)
Baffin Bay
BAFFIN ISLAND
VICTORIA ISLAND
UNITED STATES
Arctic Circle
RUSSIA
Bering Strait
Nome
Yukon
Fairbanks
Mount McKinley
6194
Anchorage
Inuvik
Mackenzie
Yellowknife
Thule
Godhavn
Godthåb
Davis Strait
Angmagssalik
Reykjavík
ICELAND
FAEROE ISLANDS
(Den.)
Norwegian Sea
Bering Sea
Gulf of Alaska
Juneau
Hudson Bay
Churchill
ROCKY MOUNTAINS
CANADA
Edmonton
ALEUTIAN ISLANDS
Vancouver
Calgary
Winnipeg
Seattle
Lake Superior
Lake Huron
Saint Lawrence
Québec
Montreal
Ottawa
Ontario
Toronto
NEWFOUNDLAND
St. John's
Halifax
Portland
Minneapolis
NORTH AMERICA
CHICAGO
Lake Michigan
DETROIT
L. Erie
Boston
NEW YORK
PHILADELPHIA
Washington
APPALACHIAN MOUNTAINS
ATLANTIC OCEAN
Salt Lake City
Denver
SAN FRANCISCO
UNITED STATES
St. Louis
LOS ANGELES
San Diego
Phoenix
El Paso
Rio Grande
Dallas
Mississippi
Atlanta
Houston
New Orleans
PACIFIC OCEAN
MIDWAY ISLANDS
(U.S.)
AÇORES AZORES
(Port.)
BERMUDA
(U.K.)
ARQUIPÉLAGO DA MADEIRA
(Port.)
ISLAS CANARIAS CANARY ISLANDS
(Sp.)
Tropic of Cancer
Gulf of Mexico
Miami
BAHAMAS
Monterrey
CABO SAN LUCAS
MEXICO
La Habana
CUBA
HAWAIIAN ISLANDS
(U.S.)
Honolulu
Guadalajara
CIUDAD DE MÉXICO
MEXICO CITY
DOMINICAN REPUBLIC
HAITI
Port-au-Prince
Santo Domingo
PUERTO RICO (U.S.)
San Juan
JAMAICA
Kingston
GUADELOUPE (Fr.)
BELIZE
GUATEMALA
Guatemala
HONDURAS
Tegucigalpa
San Salvador
EL SALVADOR
Managua
NICARAGUA
Caribbean Sea
MARTINIQUE (Fr.)
BARBADOS
TRINIDAD AND TOBAGO
Port of Spain
CAPE VERDE
JOHNSTON ATOLL
(U.S.)
San José
COSTA RICA
Panamá
PANAMA
Caracas
VENEZUELA
GUYANA
Georgetown
Paramaribo
SURINAME
FRENCH GUIANA
ÎLE CLIPPERTON
(Fr.)
Medellín
Santa Fe de Bogotá
Cali
COLOMBIA
LINE ISLANDS
Equator
Quito
ECUADOR
Guayaquil
ARCHIPIÉLAGO DE COLÓN
GALAPAGOS ISLANDS
(Ec.)
Manaus
Amazon
Belém
Fortaleza
CABO DE SÃO ROQUE
Natal
Recife
Iquitos
ANDES
PERU
Trujillo
Lima
Madeira
BRAZIL
SOUTH AMERICA
Salvador
ATLANTIC OCEAN
KIRIBATI
PHOENIX ISLANDS
TOKELAU
(N.Z.)
ÎLES MARQUISES
WALLIS AND FUTUNA
(Fr.)
W. SAMOA
AM. SAMOA
Apia
ÎLES TUAMOTU
POLYNESIA
FIJI
NIUE
(N.Z.)
COOK ISLANDS
(N.Z.)
FRENCH POLYNESIA
TONGA
Arequipa
La Paz
BOLIVIA
Sucre
Goiânia
Brasília
Belo Horizonte
SAINT HELENA
(U.K.)
Tropic of Capricorn
PITCAIRN
(U.K.)
ISLA DE PASCUA
EASTER ISLAND
(Chile)
Antofagasta
PARAGUAY
Asunción
SÃO PAULO
RIO DE JANEIRO
Santos
Curitiba
ISLA SAN AMBROSIO
(Chile)
CHILE
Co. Aconcagua
6959
Córdoba
Paraná
Porto Alegre
International Date Line
ARCHIPIÉLAGO JUAN FERNÁNDEZ
(Chile)
Valparaíso
Santiago
Rosario
BUENOS AIRES
URUGUAY
Montevideo
ARGENTINA
Concepción
Mar del Plata
Bahía Blanca
CHATHAM ISLANDS
(N.Z.)
FALKLAND ISLANDS
(U.K.)
Punta Arenas
CABO DE HORNOS
CAPE HORN
SOUTH GEORGIA
(U.K.)
Drake Passage
SOUTH ORKNEY ISLANDS
(U.K.)
Antarctic Circle
ANTARCTIC PENINSULA
Bellingshausen Sea
Weddell Sea
Ross Sea
ROSS ICE SHELF
MARIE BYRD LAND
Vinson Massif
4897
ANTAR
IRELAND
Glasgow
Dublin
UNITED KINGDOM
LONDON
Porto
Madrid
PORTUGAL
Lisboa
SPAIN
GIBRALTAR
(U.K.)
Rabat
Casablanca
MOROCCO
ATLAS
WESTERN SAHARA
MAURITANIA
Nouakchott
SENEGAL
Dakar
GAMBIA
Banjul
GUINEA-BISSAU
Bamako
GUINEA
Conakry
SIERRA LEONE
Freetown
Monrovia
LIBERIA
IVORY COAST
Yamoussoukro
Abidjan
Tombouctou
180° 165° 150° 135° 120° 105° 90° 75° 60° 45° 30° 15° 0°
1 2 3 4 5 6 7 8 9 10 11 12 13
A B C D E F G H I J K L
90° 75° 60° 45° 30° 15° 0° 15° 30° 45° 60° 75° 90°

DETERMINING DIRECTION

Most of the maps in the atlas are drawn so that when oriented for normal reading, north is at the top of the map, south is at the bottom, west is at the left, and east is at the right. Most maps have a series of lines drawn across them–the lines of *latitude* and *longitude*. Lines of latitude, or *parallels* of latitude, are drawn east and west. Lines of longitude, or *meridians* of longitude, are drawn north and south (figure 12).

Parallels and meridians appear as either curved or straight lines. For example, in the section of the map of Europe (figure 13) the parallels of latitude appear as curved lines. The meridians of longitude are straight lines that come together toward the top of the map. Latitude and longitude lines help locate places on maps. Parallels of latitude are numbered in degrees north and south of the *Equator.* Meridians of longitude are numbered in degrees east and west of a line called the *Prime Meridian*, running through Greenwich, England, near London. Any place on earth can be located by the latitude and longitude lines running through it.

To determine directions or locations on the map, you must use the parallels and meridians. For example, suppose you want to know which is farther north, Bergen, Norway, or Stockholm, Sweden. The map in figure 13 shows that Stockholm is south of the 60° parallel of latitude and Bergen is north of it. Bergen is farther north than Stockholm. By looking at the meridians of longitude, you can determine which city is farther east. Bergen is approximately 5° east of the 0° meridian (Prime Meridian), and Stockholm is almost 20° east of it. Stockholm is farther east than Bergen.

UNDERSTANDING MAP SYMBOLS

In a very real sense, the whole map is a symbol, representing the world or a part of it. It is a reduced representation of the earth; each of the world's features–cities, rivers, etc.–is represented on the map by a symbol. Map symbols may take the form of points, such as dots or squares (often used for cities, capital cities, or points of interest), or lines (roads, railroads, rivers). Symbols may also occupy an area, showing extent of coverage (terrain, forests, deserts). They seldom look like the feature they represent and therefore must be identified and interpreted. For instance, the maps in this atlas define political units by a colored line depicting their boundaries. Neither the colors nor the boundary lines are actually found on the surface of the earth, but because countries and states are such important political components of the world, strong symbols are used to represent them. The Map Symbols page in this atlas identifies the symbols used on the maps.

FIGURE 12

FIGURE 13

World Time Zones

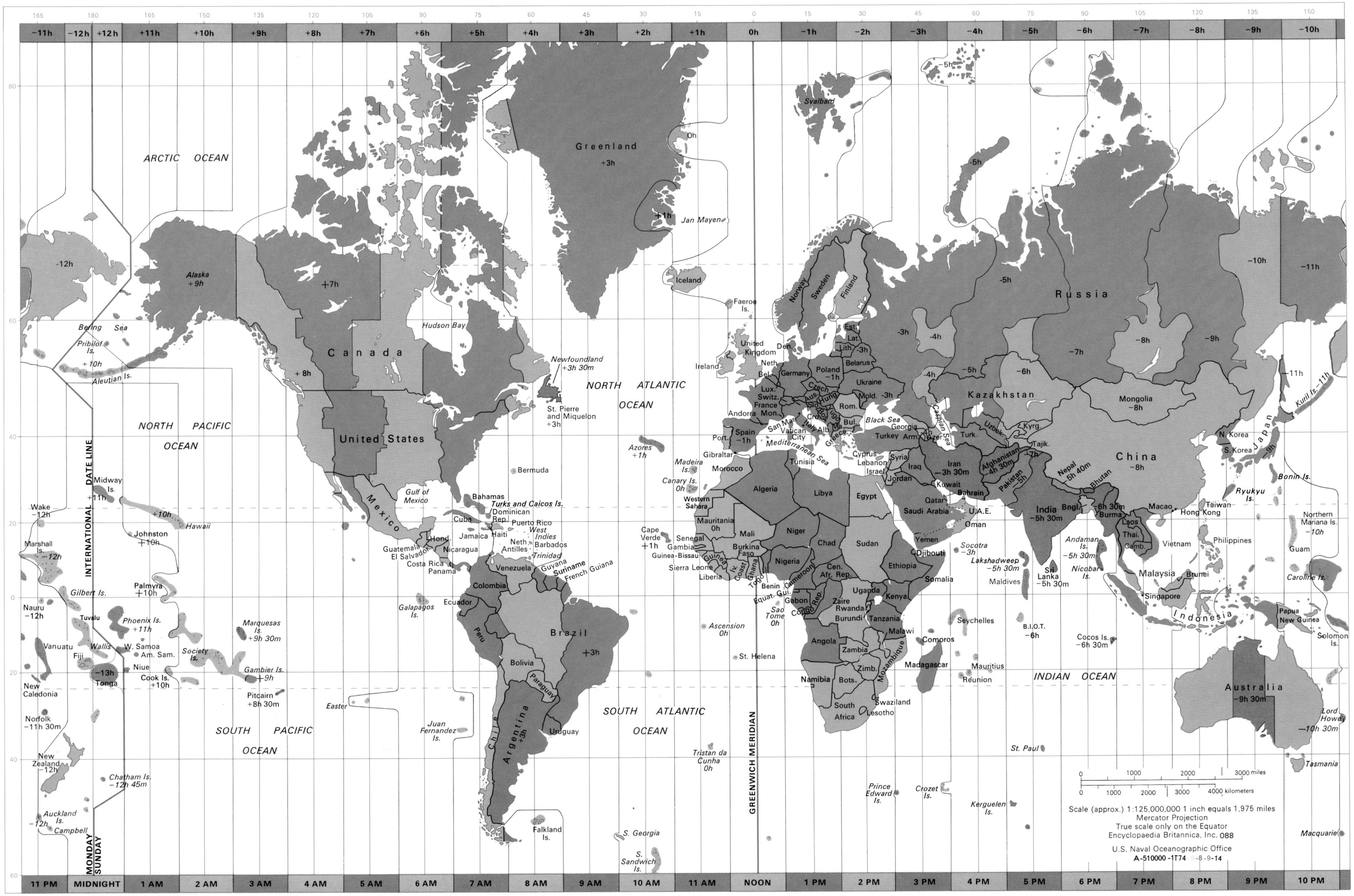

Time Zones

- Standard time zone of even-numbered hours from Greenwich time
- Standard time zone of odd-numbered hours from Greenwich time
- Time varies from the standard time zone by half an hour
- Time varies from the standard time zone by other than half an hour

h m hours, minutes

The standard time zone system, fixed by international agreement and by law in each country, is based on a theoretical division of the globe into 24 zones of 15° longitude each. The mid-meridian of each zone fixes the hour for the entire zone. The zero time zone extends 7½° east and 7½° west of the Greenwich meridian, 0° longitude. Since the earth rotates toward the east, time zones to the west of Greenwich are earlier, to the east, later.

Plus and minus hours at the top of the map are added to or subtracted from local time to find Greenwich time. Local standard time can be determined for any area in the world by adding one hour for each time zone counted in an easterly direction from one's own, or by subtracting one hour for each zone counted in a westerly direction. To separate one day from the next, the 180th meridian has been designated as the international date line. On both sides of the line the time of day is the same, but west of the line it is one day later than it is to the east.

Countries that adhere to the international zone system adopt the zone applicable to their location. Some countries, however, establish time zones based on political boundaries, or adopt the time zone of a neighboring unit. For all or part of the year some countries also advance their time by one hour, thereby utilizing more daylight hours each day.

Kilometers 0 1000 2000 3000 Km.
Statute Miles 0 1000 2000 3000 Mi.

One centimeter represents 750 kilometers.
One inch represents approximately 1200 miles.
Robinson Projection
Scale 1:75,000,000

Europe

ATLANTIC OCEAN
NORWEGIAN SEA
NORTH SEA
BALTIC SEA
MEDITERRANEAN SEA
Tyrrhenian Sea
Adriatic Sea
Ionian Sea
Bay of Biscay
English Channel
CELTIC SEA
Irish Sea
Skagerrak
Arctic Circle
ICELAND
Reykjavík
FAEROE ISLANDS (Den.)
Tórshavn
SHETLAND ISLANDS
ORKNEY ISLANDS
HEBRIDES
IRELAND
Dublin
Cork
Belfast
NORTHERN IRELAND
SCOTLAND
Glasgow
Edinburgh
Aberdeen
Dundee
UNITED KINGDOM
GREAT BRITAIN
ENGLAND
WALES
LONDON
Birmingham
Manchester
Liverpool
Leeds
Sheffield
Bristol
Cardiff
NORWAY
Oslo
Bergen
Stavanger
Trondheim
SWEDEN
Stockholm
Göteborg
Malmö
DENMARK
København
NETHERLANDS
Amsterdam
's-Gravenhage
Rotterdam
BELGIUM
Bruxelles
Antwerpen
LUXEMBOURG
GERMANY
BERLIN
Hamburg
München
Köln
Frankfurt
Stuttgart
Dresden
Leipzig
FRANCE
PARIS
Lyon
Marseille
Bordeaux
Toulouse
Nantes
Nice
Strasbourg
SWITZERLAND
Bern
Zürich
Genève
ALPS
AUSTRIA
Wien
ITALY
Roma
Milano
Torino
Napoli
Genova
Firenze
Venezia
CORSE
CORSICA
SARDEGNA
SARDINIA
SICILIA
SICILY
Palermo
Catania
MALTA
Valletta
SPAIN
Madrid
Barcelona
Valencia
Sevilla
Bilbao
Málaga
ANDORRA
PORTUGAL
Lisboa
Porto
ILLES BALEARS
BALEARIC ISLANDS
Gibraltar (U.K.)
POLAND
Gdańsk
Poznań
Łódź
Wrocław
Kraków
Szczecin
CZECHOSLOVAKIA
Praha
HUNGARY
Budapest
SLOVENIA
CROATIA
Ljubljana
Zagreb
BOSNIA AND HERCEGOVINA
Sarajevo
Beograd
ALBANIA
Tiranë
Kaliningrad
MOROCCO
Rabat
Casablanca
Fès
ALGERIA
El Djazaïr
Algiers
Oran
ATLAS MOUNTAINS
TUNISIA
Tunis
Copyright © by Rand McNally & Co.
Map prepared by Esselte Map Service AB, Stockholm.

Kilometers 0 200 400 600 Km.

Statute Miles 0 200 400 600 Mi.

Scale 1:12,000,000

One centimeter represents 120 kilometers.

One inch represents approximately 190 miles.

Miller Oblated Stereographic Projection

Northern Europe

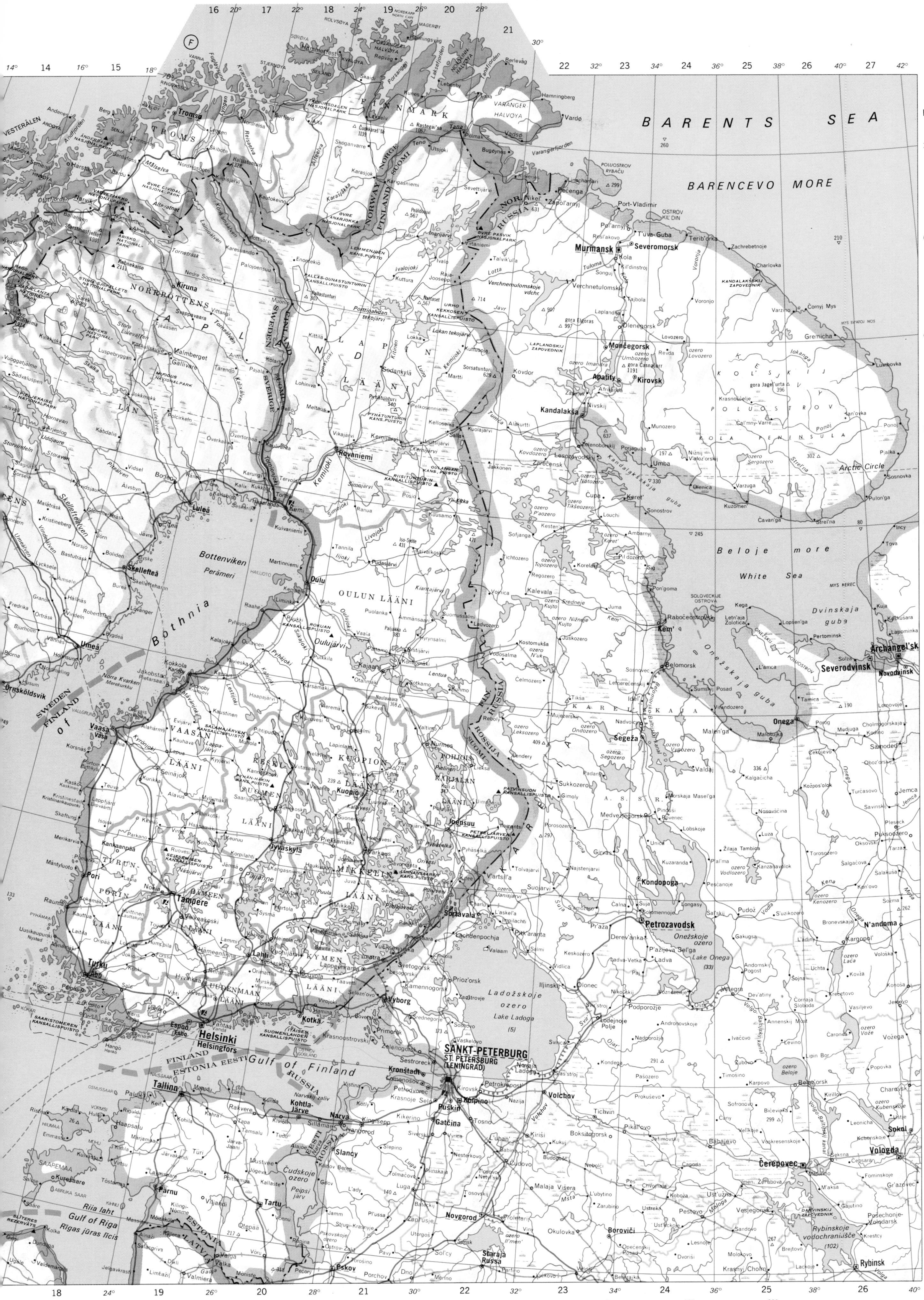

Kilometers 0 100 200 Km.

Statute Miles 0 100 200 Mi.

Scale 1:4,500,000 One centimeter represents 45 kilometers.
One inch represents approximately 71 miles.
Lambert Conformal Conic Projection

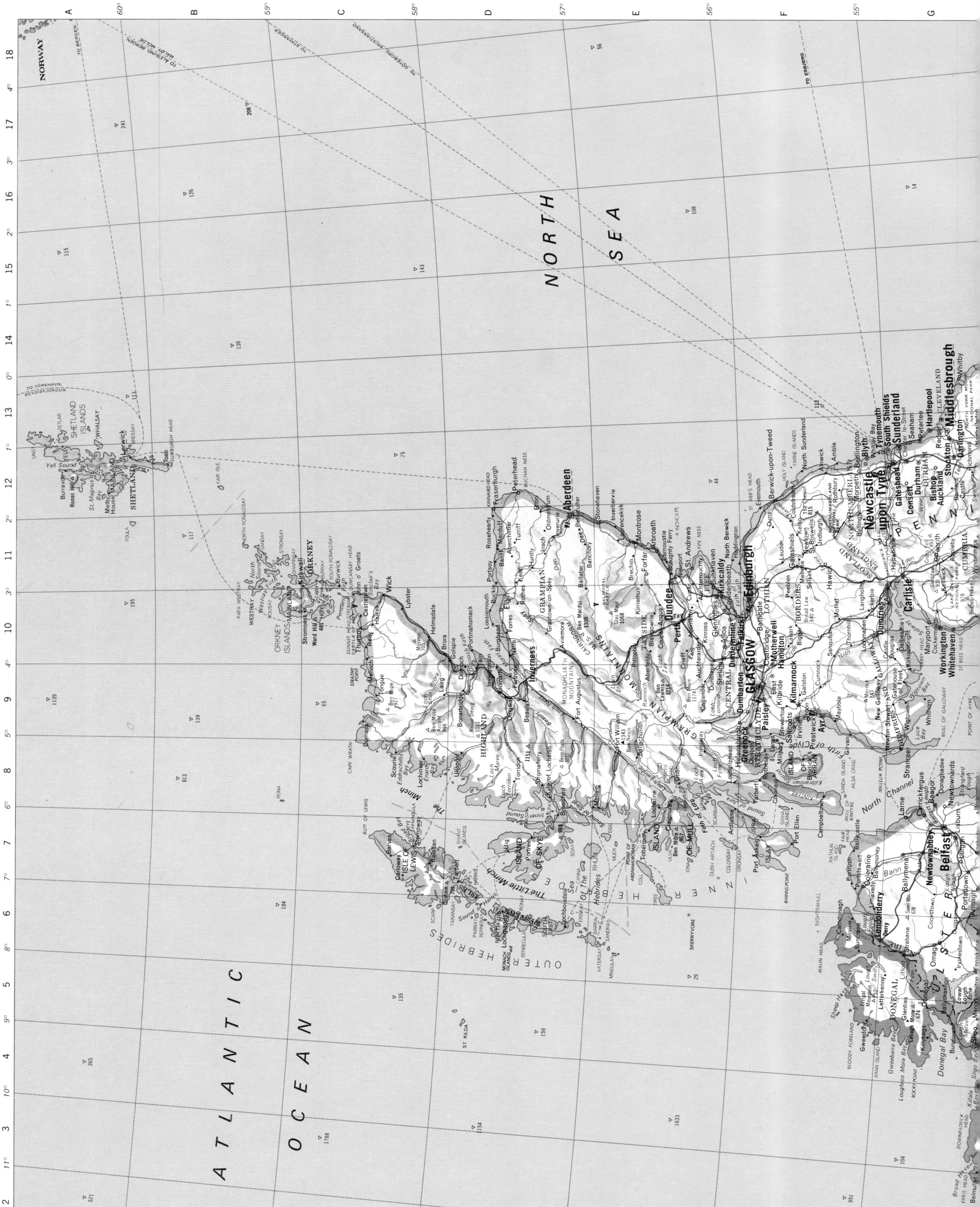
NORTH SEA
ATLANTIC OCEAN
NORWAY
SHETLAND ISLANDS
ORKNEY
OUTER HEBRIDES
HIGHLAND
GRAMPIAN
Aberdeen
Inverness
Dundee
Perth
Edinburgh
GLASGOW
Newcastle upon Tyne
Sunderland
Middlesbrough
Carlisle
Belfast
Londonderry
DONEGAL
Wick
Kirkwall
Lerwick
Stornoway
North Channel

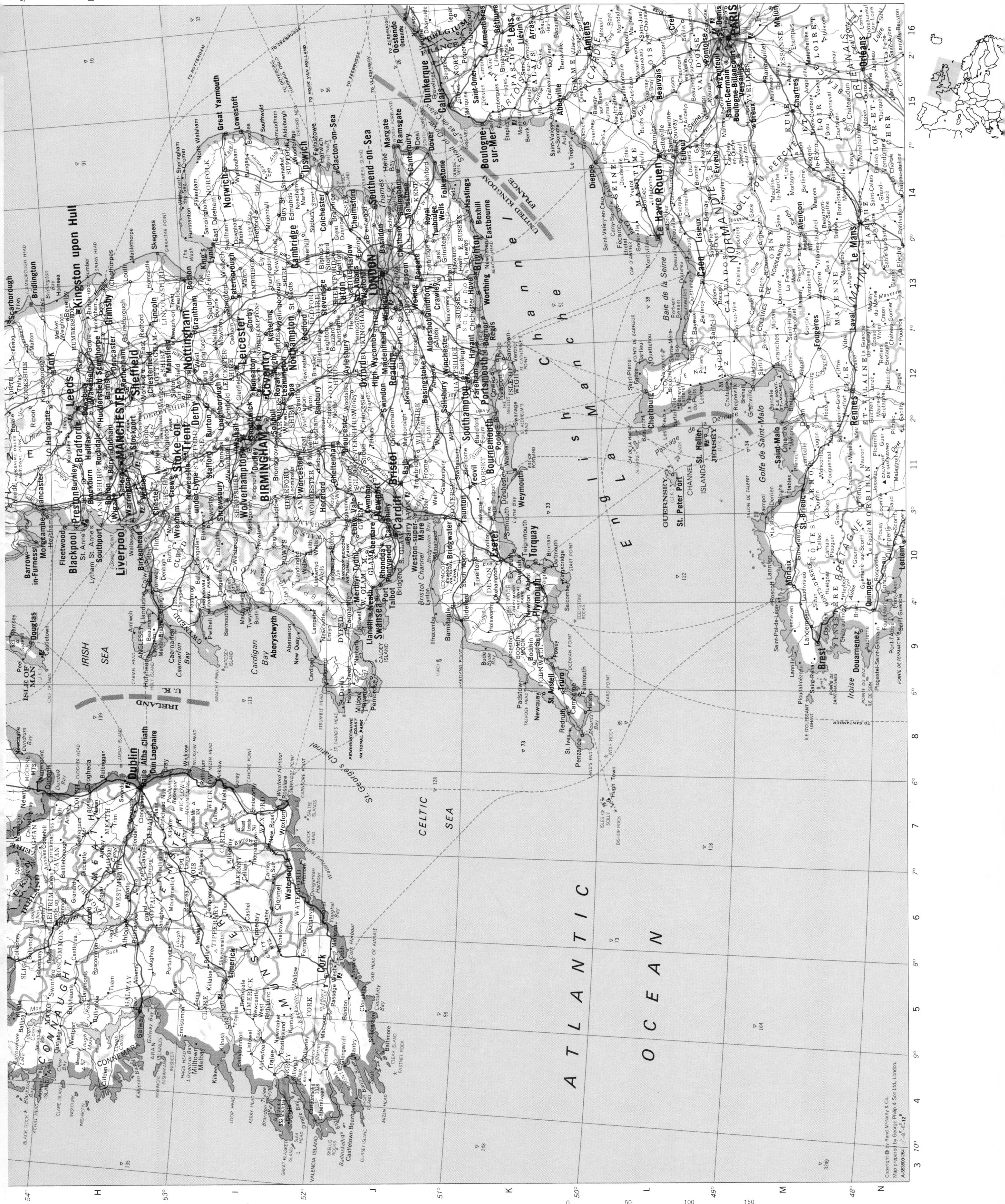

Kilometers 0 50 100 150 Km.

Statute Miles 0 50 100 150 Mi.

Scale 1:3,000,000

One centimeter represents 30 kilometers.

One inch represents approximately 47 miles.

Conic Projection, Two Standard Parallels

Central Europe

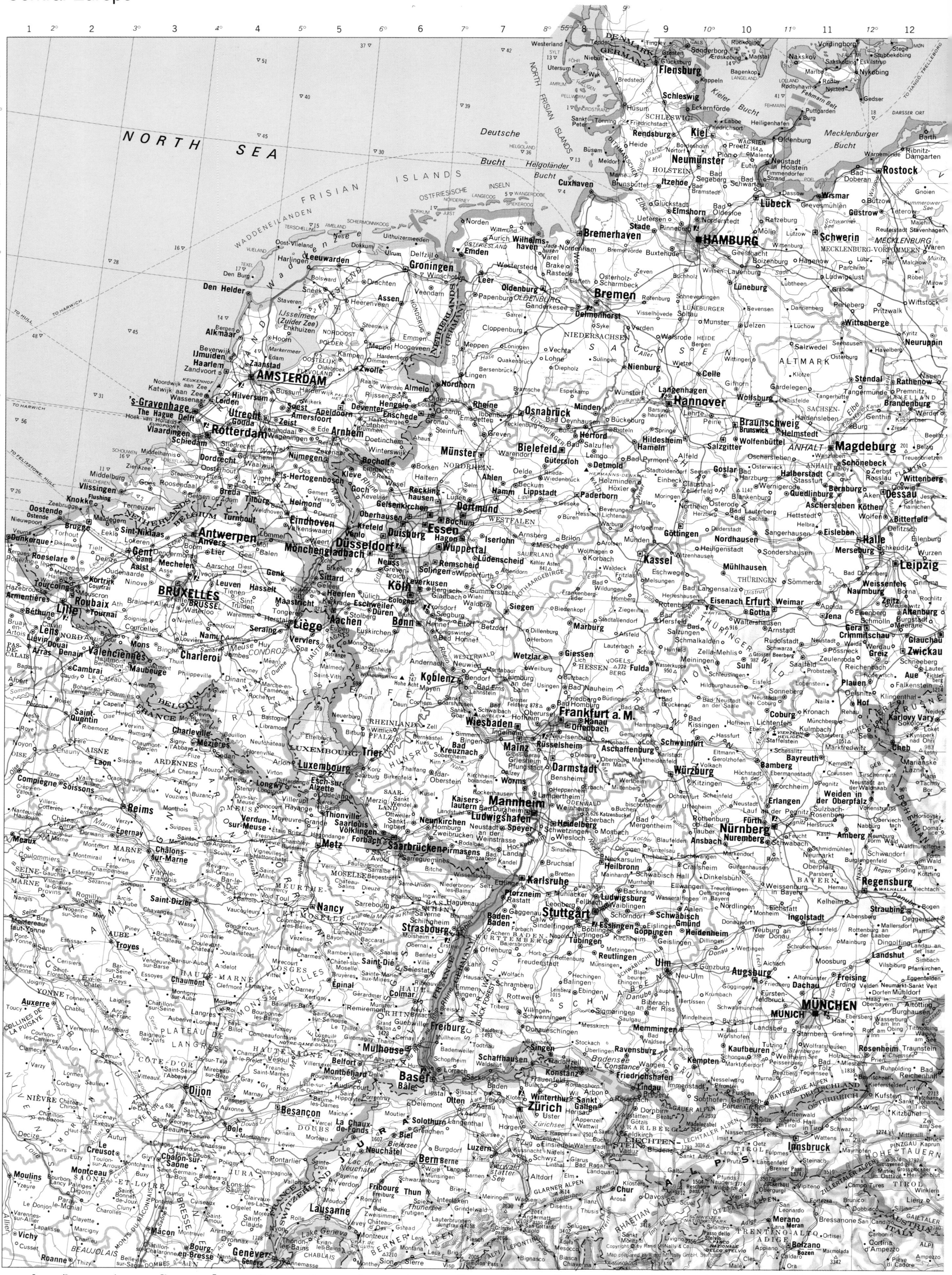

Kilometers 0 50 100 150 Km.
Statute Miles 0 50 100 150 Mi.

Scale 1:3,000,000

One centimeter represents 30 kilometers.
One inch represents approximately 47 miles.
Conic Projection, Two Standard Parallels.

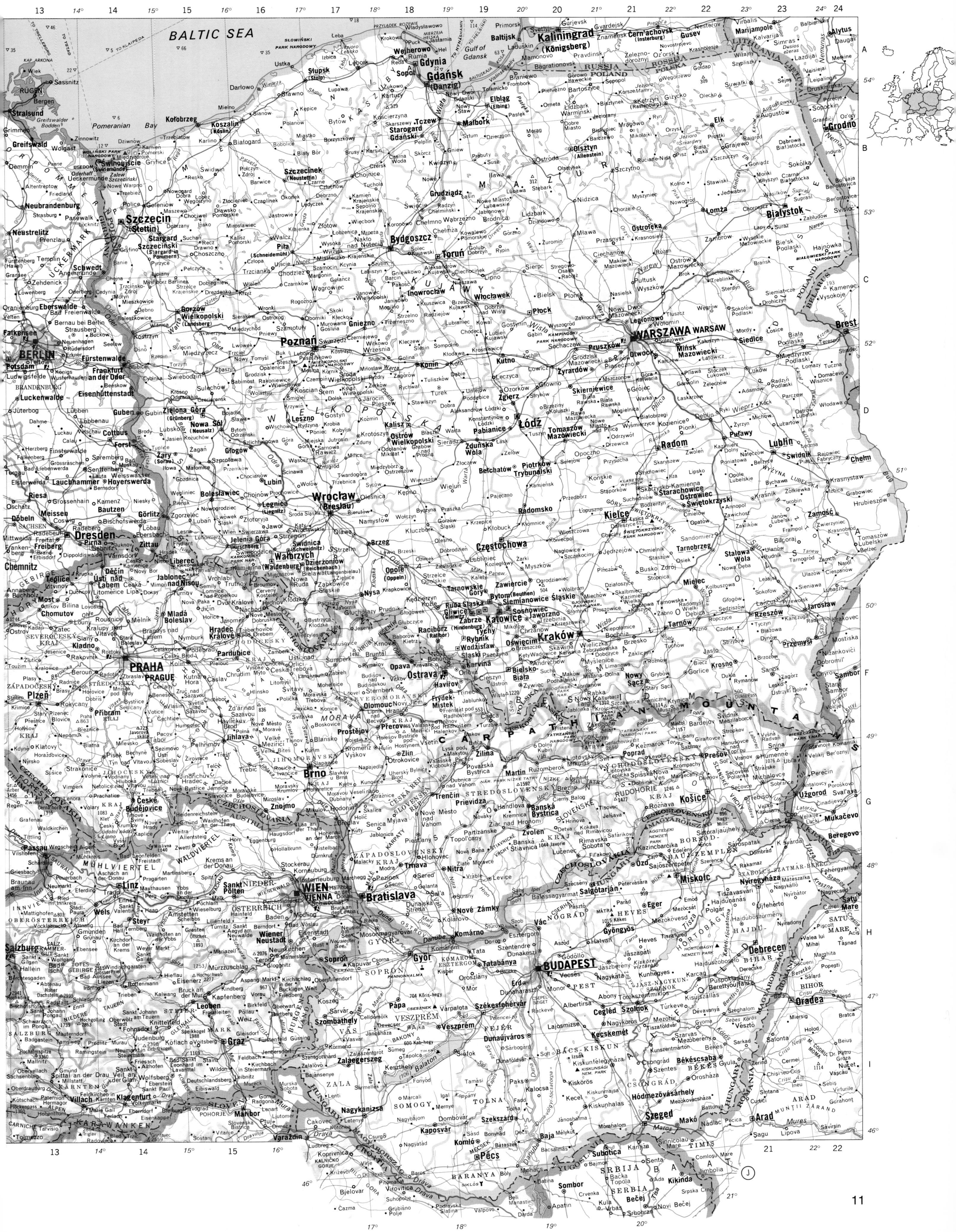
BALTIC SEA
Pomeranian Bay
Gulf of Gdansk
Kaliningrad (Königsberg)
Gdańsk (Danzig)
Gdynia
Szczecin (Stettin)
Bydgoszcz
Toruń
Białystok
WARSZAWA WARSAW
Poznań
Łódź
Wrocław (Breslau)
Lublin
Kraków
Katowice
Częstochowa
Kielce
Rzeszów
BERLIN
Dresden
PRAHA PRAGUE
Brno
Ostrava
CARPATHIAN MOUNTAINS
Košice
WIEN VIENNA
Bratislava
Linz
Graz
Salzburg
BUDAPEST
Debrecen
Miskolc
Szeged
Pécs
Győr
Oradea
Arad

Belgium, Netherlands, and Luxembourg

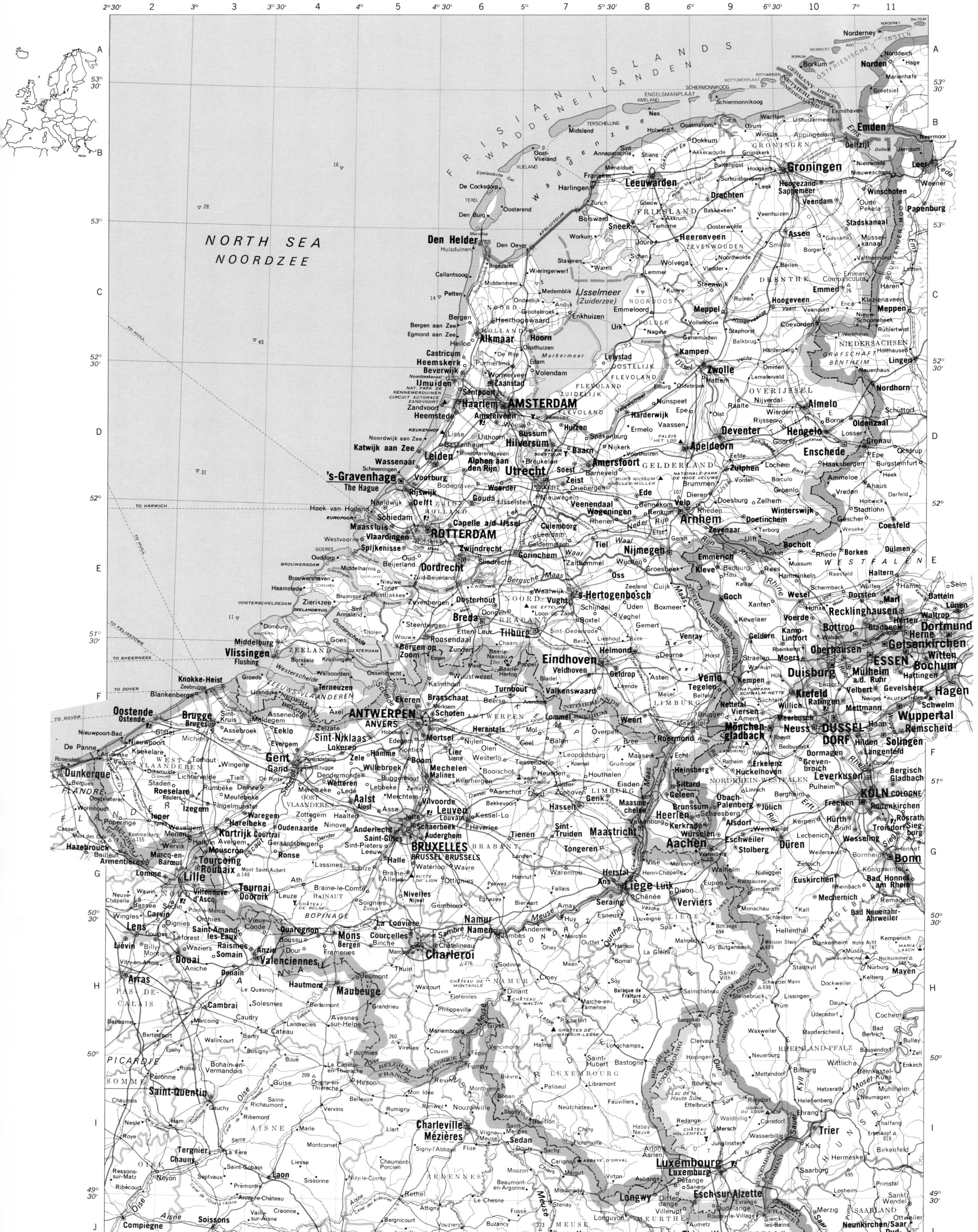

Scale 1:1,500,000

One centimeter represents 15 kilometers.
One inch represents approximately 24 miles.
Lambert Conformal Conic Projection

Kilometers 0 10 20 30 40 50 Km.
Statute Miles 0 10 20 30 40 50 Mi.

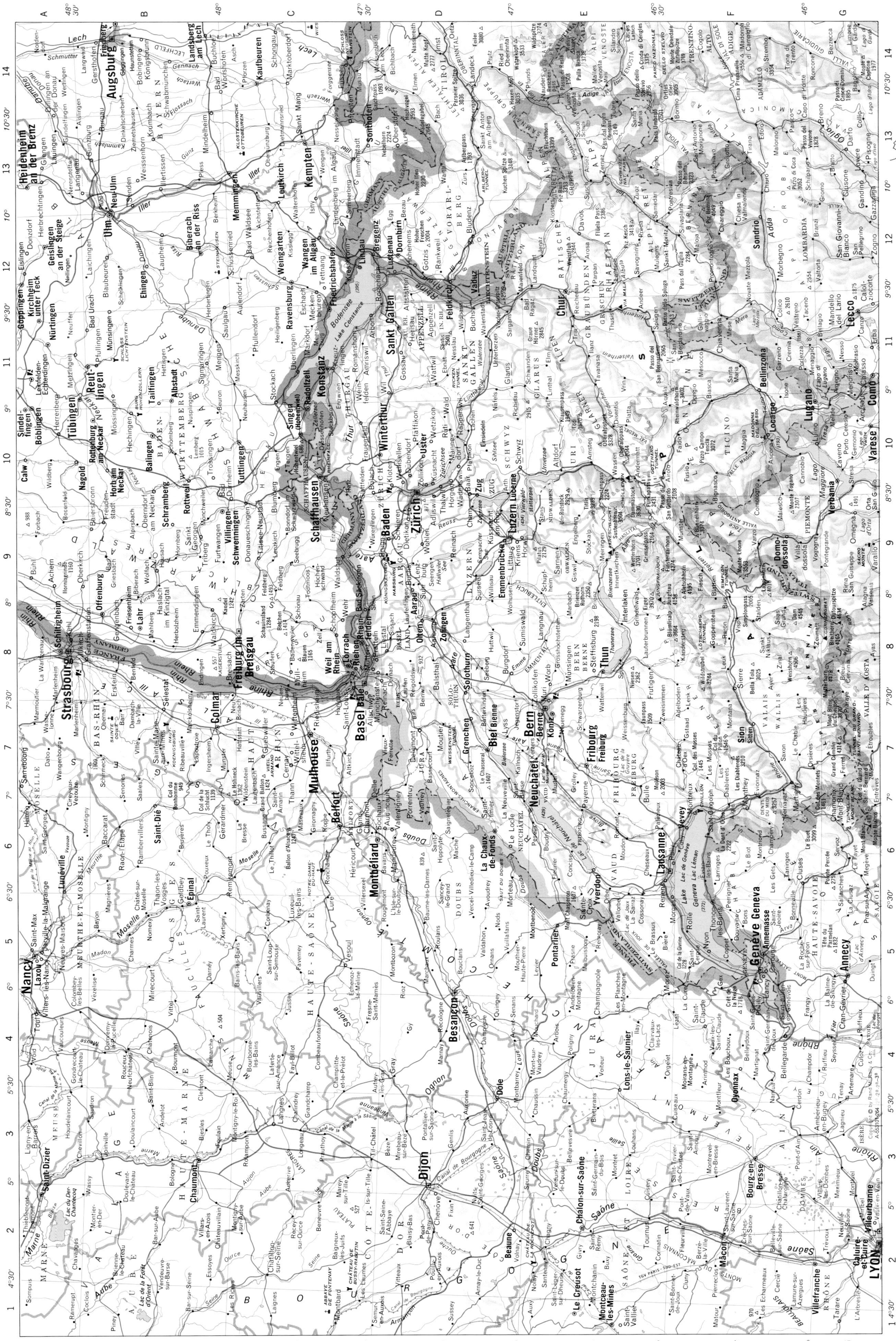

Scale 1:1,500,000
One centimeter represents 15 kilometers.
One inch represents approximately 24 miles.
Lambert Conformal Conic Projection

Kilometers 0 10 20 30 40 50 Km.
Statute Miles 0 10 20 30 40 50 Mi.

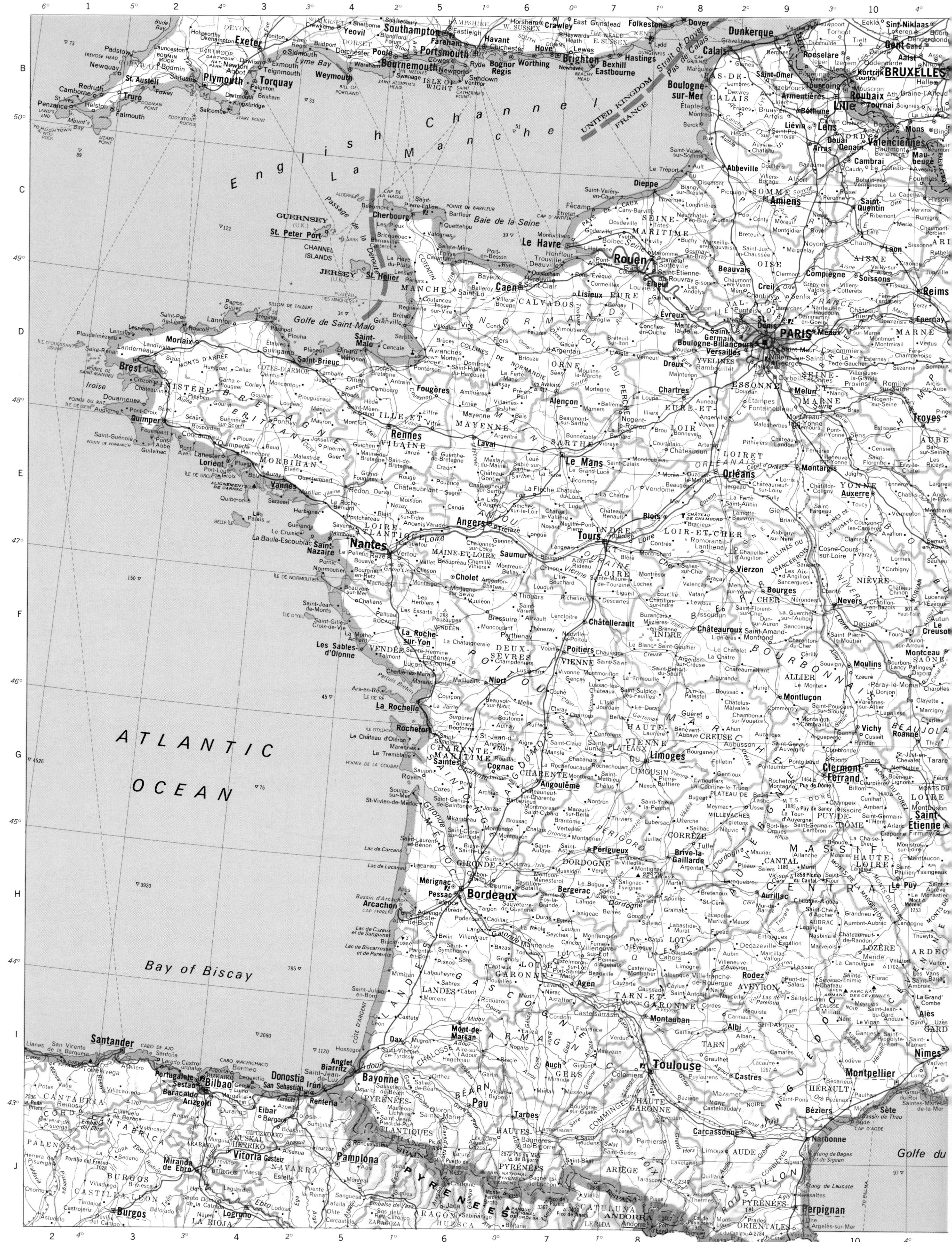
English Channel
La Manche
ATLANTIC OCEAN
Bay of Biscay
Golfe de Saint-Malo
Baie de la Seine
Strait of Dover
Pas de Calais
UNITED KINGDOM
FRANCE
PARIS
BRUXELLES
Lille
Rouen
Le Havre
Caen
Cherbourg
Rennes
Nantes
Brest
Quimper
Lorient
Vannes
Saint-Brieuc
Saint-Malo
Le Mans
Angers
Tours
Orléans
Poitiers
Limoges
La Rochelle
Bordeaux
Toulouse
Montpellier
Nîmes
Perpignan
Clermont-Ferrand
Saint-Étienne
Bayonne
Biarritz
Pau
Tarbes
Bilbao
Santander
Donostia
San Sebastián
Pamplona
Vitoria
Burgos
Logroño
Andorra
Southampton
Portsmouth
Brighton
Plymouth
Exeter
Bournemouth
Torquay
Dover
Folkestone
Calais
Dunkerque
Boulogne-sur-Mer
Amiens
Reims
Troyes
GUERNSEY
JERSEY
CHANNEL ISLANDS
St. Peter Port
St. Helier
PYRÉNÉES
MASSIF CENTRAL
BRETAGNE
NORMANDIE
POITOU
LIMOUSIN
AUVERGNE
LANGUEDOC
GASCOGNE
LANDES
Golfe du Lion

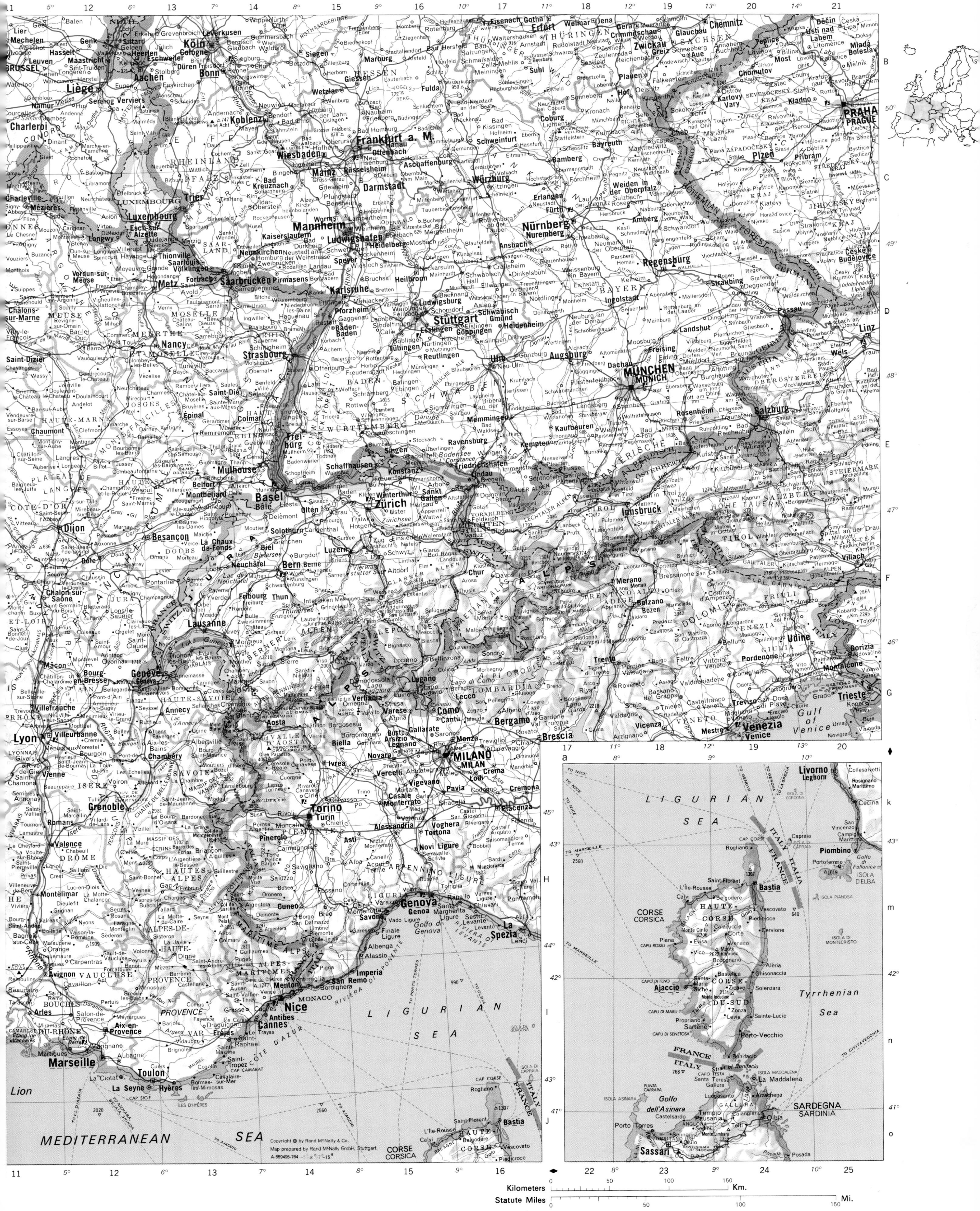

Kilometers 0 50 100 150 Km.

Statute Miles 0 50 100 150 Mi.

Scale 1:3,000,000

One centimeter represents 30 kilometers.

One inch represents approximately 47 miles.

Lambert Conformal Conic Projection

Spain and Portugal

Kilometers 0 50 100 150 Km.
Statute Miles 0 50 100 150 Mi.

Scale 1:3,000,000

One centimeter represents 30 kilometers.
One inch represents approximately 47 miles.
Conic Projection, Two Standard Parallels

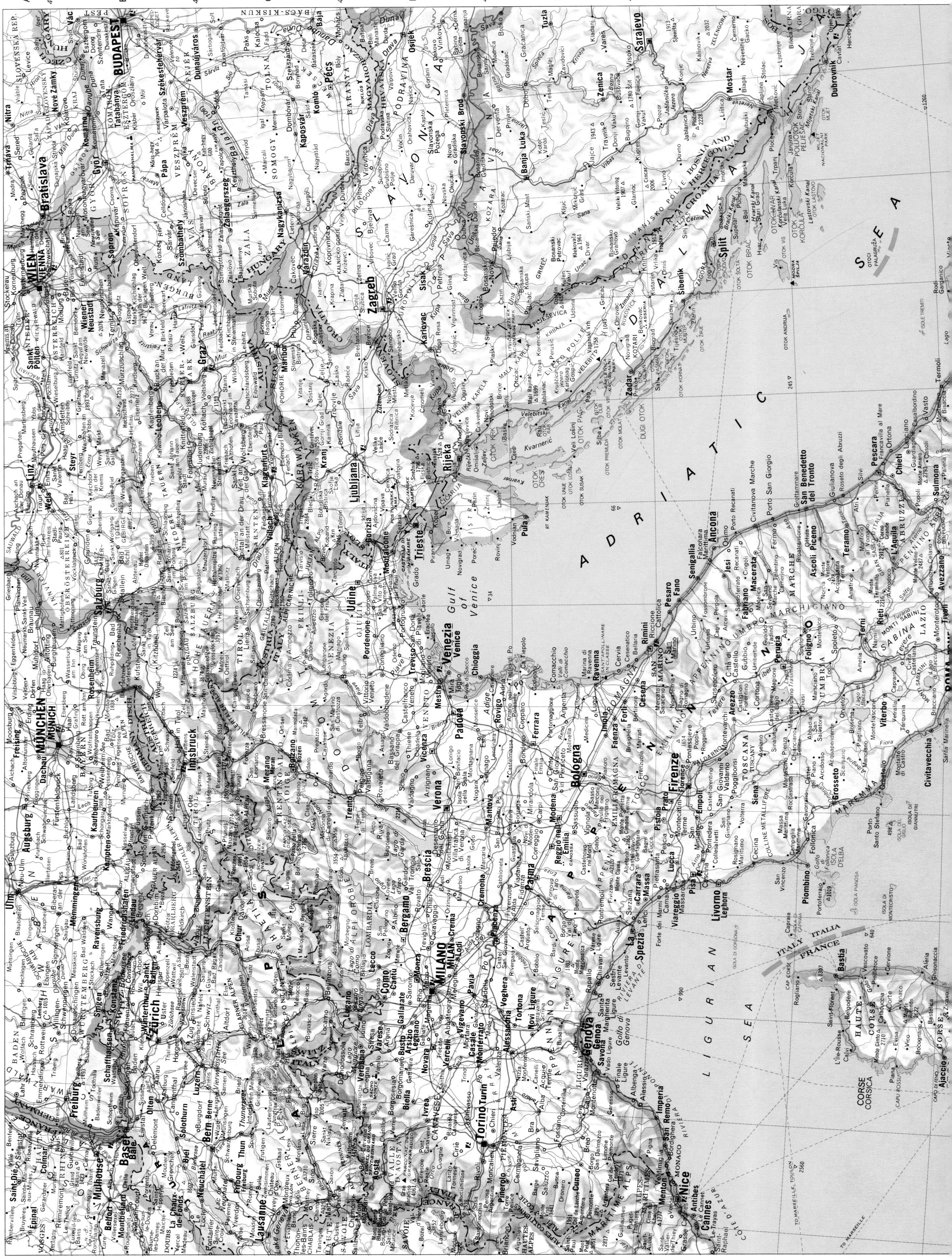
BUDAPEST
WIEN
VIENNA
Bratislava
Graz
Zagreb
Ljubljana
Sarajevo
Split
Rijeka
Trieste
Venezia
Venice
Gulf of Venice
A D R I A T I C
S E A
MILANO
MILAN
Torino
Turin
Genova
Genoa
Bologna
Firenze
Florence
Ancona
Pescara
LIGURIAN SEA
CORSE
CORSICA
Bastia
Ajaccio
Nice
MONACO
MÜNCHEN
MUNICH
Salzburg
Innsbruck
Zürich
Bern
Basel
Linz
Pécs
Zadar
Mostar
Dubrovnik

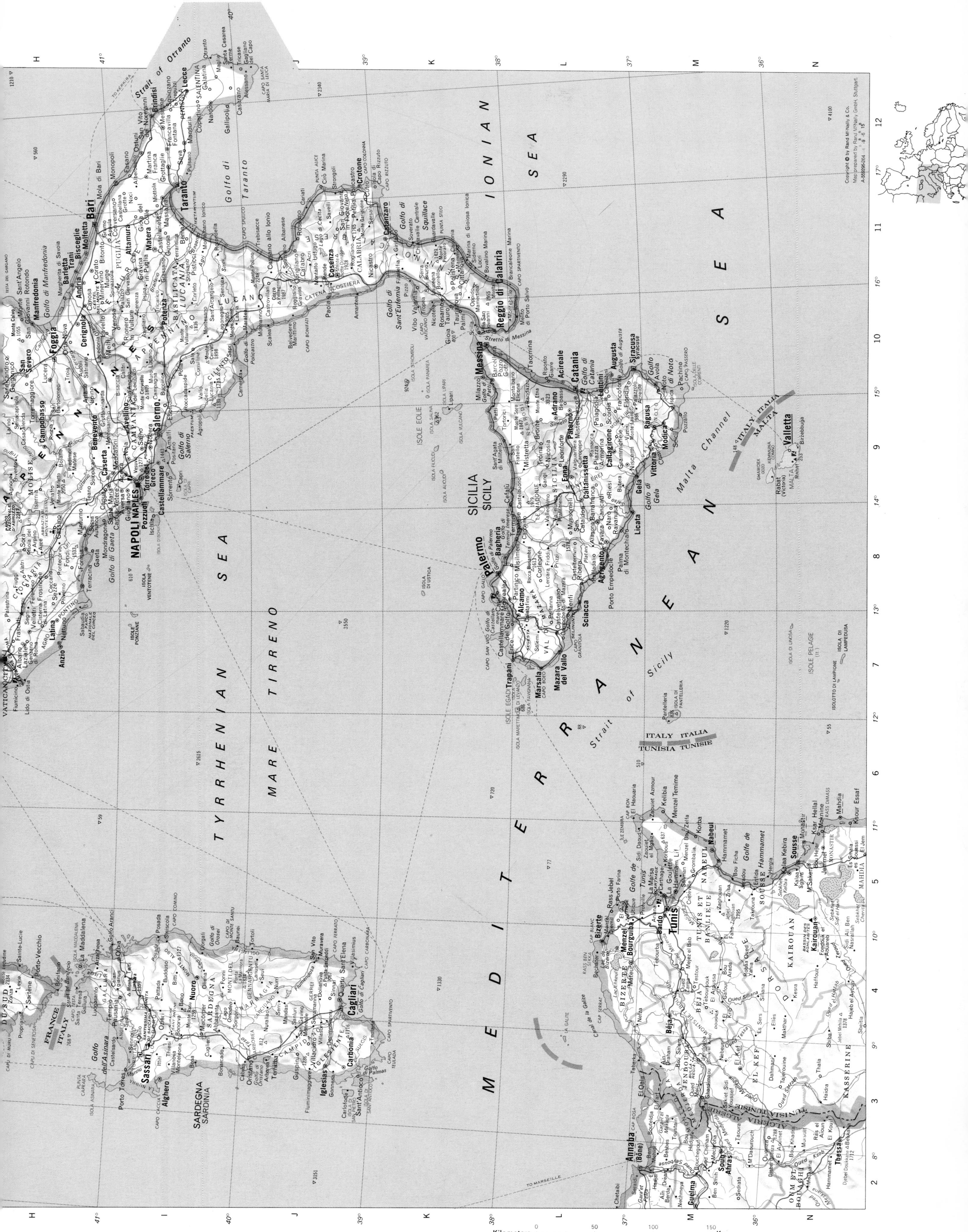

Kilometers 0 50 100 150 Km.

Statute Miles 0 50 100 150 Mi.

Scale 1:3,000,000

One centimeter represents 30 kilometers.
One inch represents approximately 47 miles.
Conic Projection, Two Standard Parallels

Southeastern Europe

Kilometers 0 50 100 150 Km.

Statute Miles 0 50 100 150 Mi.

Scale 1:3,000,000

One centimeter represents 30 kilometers.

One inch represents approximately 47 miles.

Conic Projection, Two Standard Parallels

Baltic and Moscow Regions

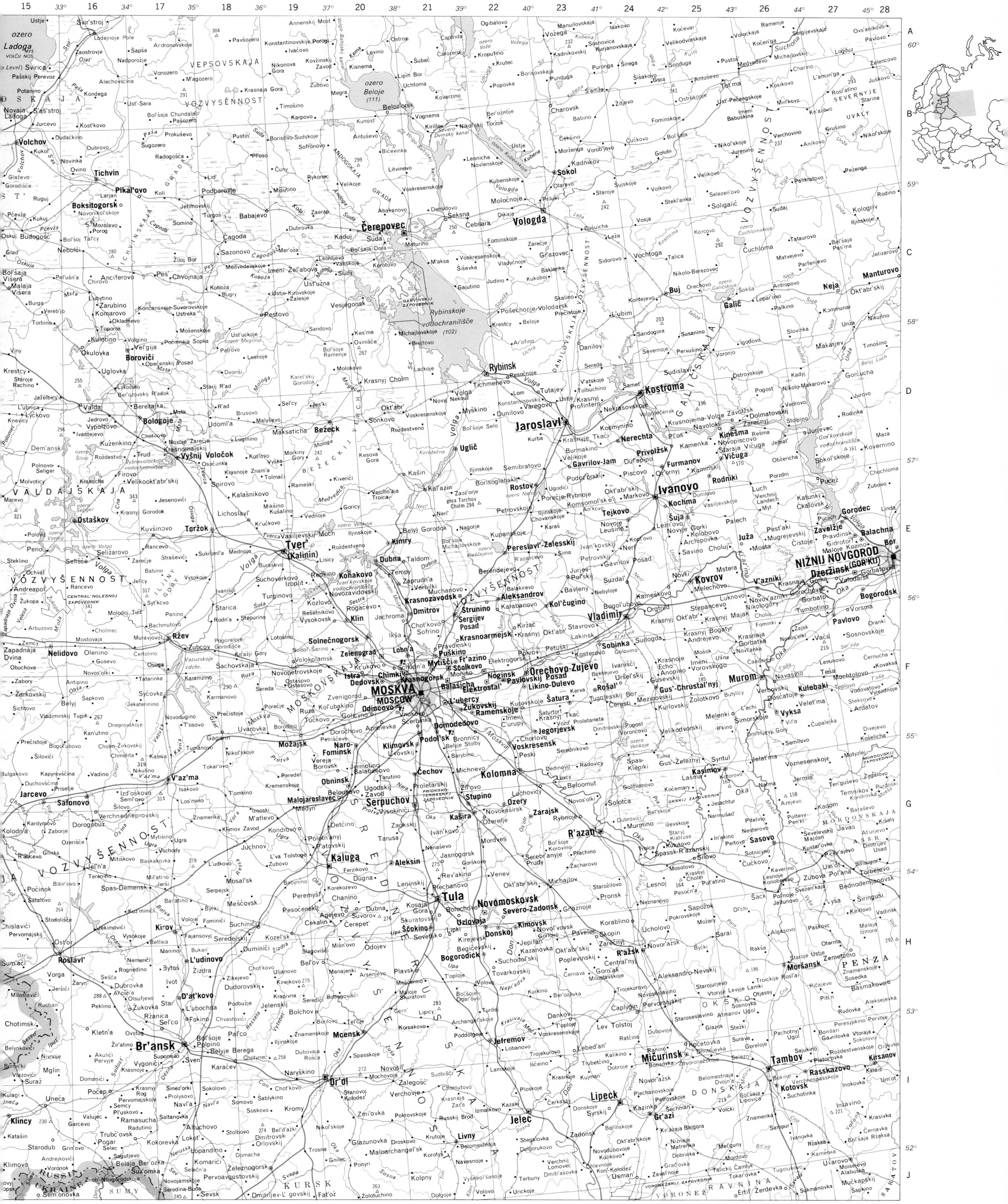

Kilometers 0 50 100 150 Km.
Statute Miles 0 50 100 150 Mi.

Scale 1:3,000,000
One centimeter represents 30 kilometers.
One inch represents approximately 47 miles.
Lambert Conformal Conic Projection

ARCTIC
OCEAN
North Pole
ATLANTIC
OCEAN
GREENLAND
(Den.)
ICELAND
Reykjavík
UNITED STATES
Bering Strait
Chukchi Sea
Bering Sea
ALEUTIAN BASIN
ALEUTIAN ISLANDS
Greenland Sea
GREENLAND BASIN
JAN MAYEN (Nor.)
Norwegian Sea
NORWEGIAN BASIN
LOFOTEN BASIN
FAEROE ISLANDS (Den.)
Arctic Circle
SVALBARD (Nor.)
Barents Sea
ZEML'A FRANCA-JOSIFA
FRANZ JOSEF LAND
SEVERNAJA ZEML'A
Kara Sea
Karskoje more
Laptev Sea
more Laptevych
Vostočno-Sibirskoje more
East Siberian Sea
OSTROV VRANGEL'A
NOVOSIBIRSKIJE OSTROVA
Sea of Okhotsk
Ochotskoje more
OKHOTSK BASIN
OSTROV SACHALIN
SAKHALIN
KURIL'SKIJE OSTROVA
KURIL ISLANDS
Sea of Japan
JAPAN BASIN
HOKKAIDO
HONSHU
KYUSHU
EAST CHINA SEA
Yellow Sea
IRELAND
UNITED KINGDOM
North Sea
NORWAY
SWEDEN
FINLAND
Baltic Sea
DENMARK
NETHERLANDS
BELGIUM
GERMANY
POLAND
CZECHOSLOVAKIA
AUSTRIA
HUNGARY
ROMANIA
BULGARIA
UKRAINE
BELARUS
EUROPE
RUSSIA
SIBERIA
ZAPADNO-SIBIRSKAJA RAVNINA
SREDNESIBIRSKOJE PLOSKOGORJE
URAL'SKIJE GORY
URAL MOUNTAINS
CHREBET ČERSKOGO
KAZAKHSTAN
UZBEKISTAN
TURKMENISTAN
KYRGYZSTAN
TAJIKISTAN
MONGOLIA
CHINA
ASIA
TIEN SHAN
ALTAI
GOBI
TARIM PENDI
KUNLUN SHAN
HINDU KUSH
PAMIR
AFGHANISTAN
IRAN
IRAQ
SYRIA
TURKEY
ASIA MINOR
SAUDI ARABIA
Black Sea
Caspian Sea
Aral'skoje more
Aral Sea
ozero Bajkal
Lake Baikal
ozero Balchaš
Lake Balkhash
NORTH KOREA
SOUTH KOREA
DA HINGGAN LING
SICHOTE-ALIN'
LONDON
Dublin
Amsterdam
Bruxelles
BERLIN
Hamburg
Warszawa
Praha
WIEN
BUDAPEST
Beograd
Bucureşti
Sofija
Stockholm
Oslo
København
Helsinki
Tallinn
Riga
Vilnius
Minsk
KIJEV
SANKT-PETERBURG
ST. PETERSBURG
MOSKVA
MOSCOW
Nižnij Novgorod
Kazan'
Samara
Saratov
VOLGOGRAD
Rostov-na-Donu
ODESSA
Char'kov
Perm'
JEKATERINBURG
Čel'abinsk
Omsk
Novosibirsk
Krasnojarsk
Irkutsk
Jakutsk
Magadan
Vladivostok
Ulaanbaatar
BEIJING
PEKING
TIANJIN
SHANGHAI
NANJING
WUHAN
XI'AN
Lanzhou
Seoul
P'yŏngyang
Sapporo
Ōsaka
Nagoya
Hiroshima
Fukuoka
Sendai
Niigata
ISTANBUL
ANKARA
TBILISI
Jerevan
BAKU
TEHRAN
BAGHDAD
DIMASHQ
DAMASCUS
Kābol
Taškent
Alma-Ata
Bišket
Dušanbe
Aščabad
Ürümqi
Kashi
Murmansk
Archangel'sk
Noril'sk
Vorkuta
Petropavlovsk-Kamčatskij
Volga
Ob'
Jenisej
Lena
Amur
Irtyš
Don
Dnepr
Huang
Chang

INDIAN OCEAN
ARABIAN SEA
Bay of Bengal
Andaman Sea
SOUTH CHINA SEA
Laccadive Sea
Gulf of Aden
Gulf of Oman
Gulf of Thailand
Gulf of Tonkin
Java Sea
Celebes Sea
Sulu Sea
Philippine Sea
INDIA
PAKISTAN
BURMA
THAILAND
LAOS
CAMBODIA
VIETNAM
MALAYSIA
INDONESIA
PHILIPPINES
SRI LANKA
BANGLADESH
NEPAL
BHUTAN
OMAN
YEMEN
SOMALIA
ETHIOPIA
DJIBOUTI
MADAGASCAR
AUSTRALIA
ARABIAN PENINSULA
AR-RUB' AL-KHALI
HIMALAYAS
GREATER SUNDA ISLANDS
SUMATRA
JAWA
BORNEO KALIMANTAN
MALDIVES
SEYCHELLES
MAURITIUS
REUNION
CHAGOS ARCHIPELAGO
COCOS ISLANDS
CHRISTMAS ISLAND
ANDAMAN ISLANDS
NICOBAR ISLANDS
NINETYEAST RIDGE
CARLSBERG RIDGE
MID-INDIAN RIDGE
MID-INDIAN BASIN
WHARTON BASIN
BROKEN RIDGE
JAVA TRENCH
MASCARENE PLATEAU
SOMALI BASIN
MADAGASCAR BASIN
ARABIAN BASIN
Tropic of Cancer
Tropic of Capricorn
Equator
New Delhi
Bombay
Calcutta
Madras
Karachi
Colombo
Dhaka
Rangoon
Krung Thep (Bangkok)
Kuala Lumpur
Singapore
Jakarta
Manila
Hong Kong
Taipei
Perth
Mugdisho
Antananarivo
Scale 1:24,000,000
One centimeter represents 240 kilometers.
One inch represents approximately 380 miles.
Lambert Azimuthal Equal-Area Projection
Kilometers
Statute Miles

BALTIC SEA
FINLAND
KARELIA
ESTONIA
LITHUANIA
LATVIA
POLAND
BELARUS
UKRAINE
ROMANIA
HUNGARY
CARPATHIAN MOUNTAINS
BLACK SEA
Azovskoje more
Sea of Azov
Beloje more
White Sea
KOL'SKIJ POLUOSTROV
KOLA PENINSULA
GEORGIA
CAUCASUS
KAVKAZ
TURKEY
IRAQ
KURDISTAN
CASPIAN SEA
(28 Meters Below Sea Level)
Kara-Bogaz-Gol
PRIKASPIJSKAJA NIZMENNOST'
PLATO USTJURT
TURKMENISTAN
KARAKUMY
UZBEKISTAN
KYZYLKUM
KAZAKHSTAN
KAZACHSKIJ MELKOSOPOČNIK
Aral'skoje more
Aral Sea
ozero Balchaš
Lake Balkhash
(342)
BETPAK-DALA
KYRGYZSTAN
TAJIKISTAN
AFGHANISTAN
PAMIR
TIEN SHAN
IRAN
DASHT-E KAVIR
DASHT-E LUT
ZAGROS
URAL'SKIJE GORY
SEVERNYJE UVALY
TIMANSKIJ KRAJ
OBŠČIJ SYRT
ERGENI
Moskva
MOSCOW
Sankt-Peterburg
Helsinki
Tallinn
Riga
Vilnius
Minsk
Kijev
Kiev
Kišinëv
București
Budapest
Odessa
Sevastopol'
Char'kov
Doneck
Rostov-na-Donu
Volgograd
(Stalingrad)
Saratov
Samara
(Kujbyšev)
Kazan'
Nižnij Novgorod
(Gor'kij)
Perm'
Jekaterinburg
Čel'abinsk
Ufa
Orenburg
Astrachan'
Machačkala
Tbilisi
Jerevan
Baku
Tehrān
Mashhad
Aşchabad
Taškent
Samarkand
Dušanbe
Biškek
Alma-Ata
Karaganda
Celinograd
Archangel'sk
Murmansk
Herāt
Kashi
H
I
J
K
L
1
9
10
20°
25°
30°
35°
40°
45°
55°
60°
65°
70°
75°
80°

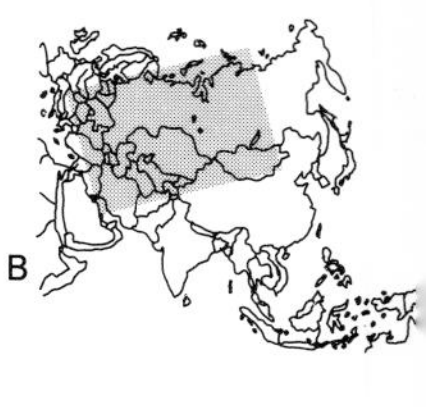

Kilometers 0 200 400 600 Km.

Statute Miles 0 200 400 600 Mi.

Scale 1:12,000,000

One centimeter represents 120 kilometers.

One inch represents approximately 190 miles.

Lambert Conformal Conic Projection

Kilometers 0 200 400 600 Km.
Statute Miles 0 200 400 600 Mi.

Scale 1:12,000,000
One centimeter represents 120 kilometers.
One inch represents approximately 190 miles.
Lambert Conformal Conic Projection

ALASKA
UNITED STATES
Chukchi Sea
Bering Strait
Bering Sea
VOSTOČNO-SIBIRSKOJE MORE
EAST SIBERIAN SEA
NOVOSIBIRSKIJE OSTROVA
OSTROV KOTEL'NYJ
OSTROV VRANGEL'A
proliv Longa
SAINT LAWRENCE ISLAND
NUNIVAK ISLAND
SAINT MATTHEW ISLAND
Arctic Circle
ČUKOTSKIJ POLUOSTROV
Anadyrskij zaliv
ANADYRSKOJE PLOSKOGORJE
KOR'AKSKOJE NAGORJE
JUKAGIRSKOJE PLOSKOGORJE
KOLYMSKAJA NIZMENNOST'
MOMSKIJ CHREBET
CHREBET ČERSKOGO
VERCHOJANSKIJ CHREBET
SIBERIA
CHREBET SUNTAR-CHAJATA
CHREBET SETTE-DABAN
CHREBET DŽUGDŽUR
ALDANSKOJE NAGORJE
STANOVOJ CHREBET
BUREINSKIJ CHREBET
SICHOTE-ALIN'
SREDINNYJ CHREBET
POLUOSTROV KAMČATKA
KAMCHATKA
zaliv Šelichova
SEA OF OKHOTSK
OCHOTSKOJE MORE
OSTROV SACHALIN
SAKHALIN
Tatarskij proliv
La Perouse Strait
KURIL'SKIJE OSTROVA
KURIL ISLANDS
KOMANDORSKIJE OSTROVA
PACIFIC OCEAN
SEA OF JAPAN
HOKKAIDŌ
JAPAN
HONSHŪ
CHINA
MANCHURIA
NEI MONGGOL ZIZHIQU
HEILONGJIANG
Lena
Aldan
Kolyma
Indigirka
Amur
Jakutsk
Magadan
Ochotsk
Petropavlovsk-Kamčatskij
Komsomol'sk-na-Amure
Chabarovsk
Blagoveščensk
Vladivostok
Nachodka
Južno-Sachalinsk
Harbin
Qiqihar Tsitsihar
Jiamusi
Sapporo
Hakodate
Habomai, Shikotan, Kunashiri, and Etorofu, occupied since 1945, are claimed by Japan pending a final peace treaty.

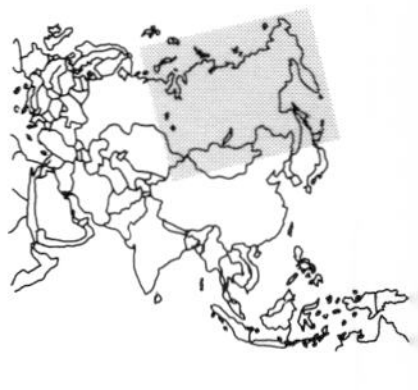

China, Japan, and Korea

Kilometers 0 200 400 600 Km.

Statute Miles 0 200 400 600 Mi.

Scale 1:12,000,000

One centimeter represents 120 kilometers.

One inch represents approximately 190 miles.

Lambert Conformal Conic Projection

Northeastern China and Korea

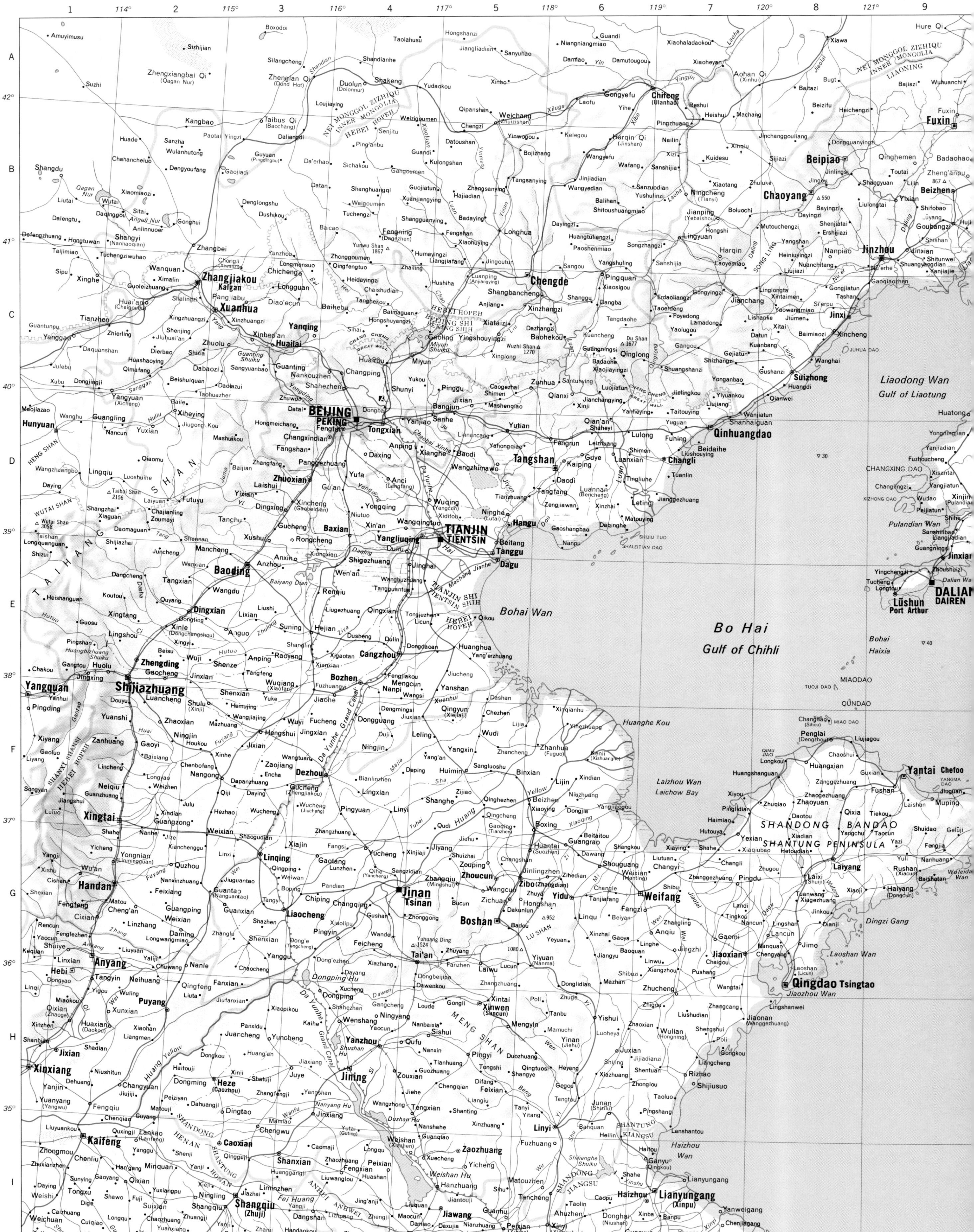

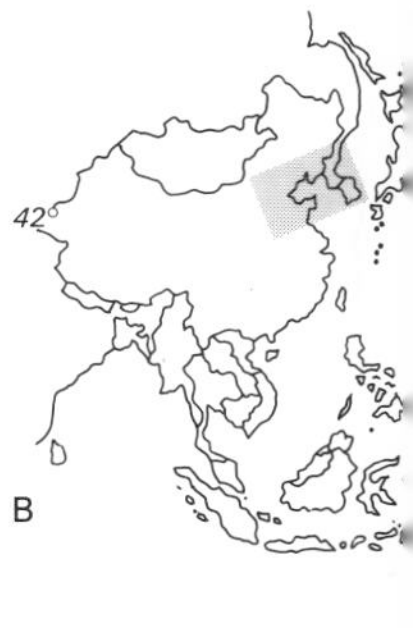

Kilometers 0 50 100 150 Km.

Statute Miles 0 50 100 150 Mi.

Scale 1:3,000,000

One centimeter represents 30 kilometers.

One inch represents approximately 47 miles.

Lambert Conformal Conic Projection

Eastern and Southeastern China

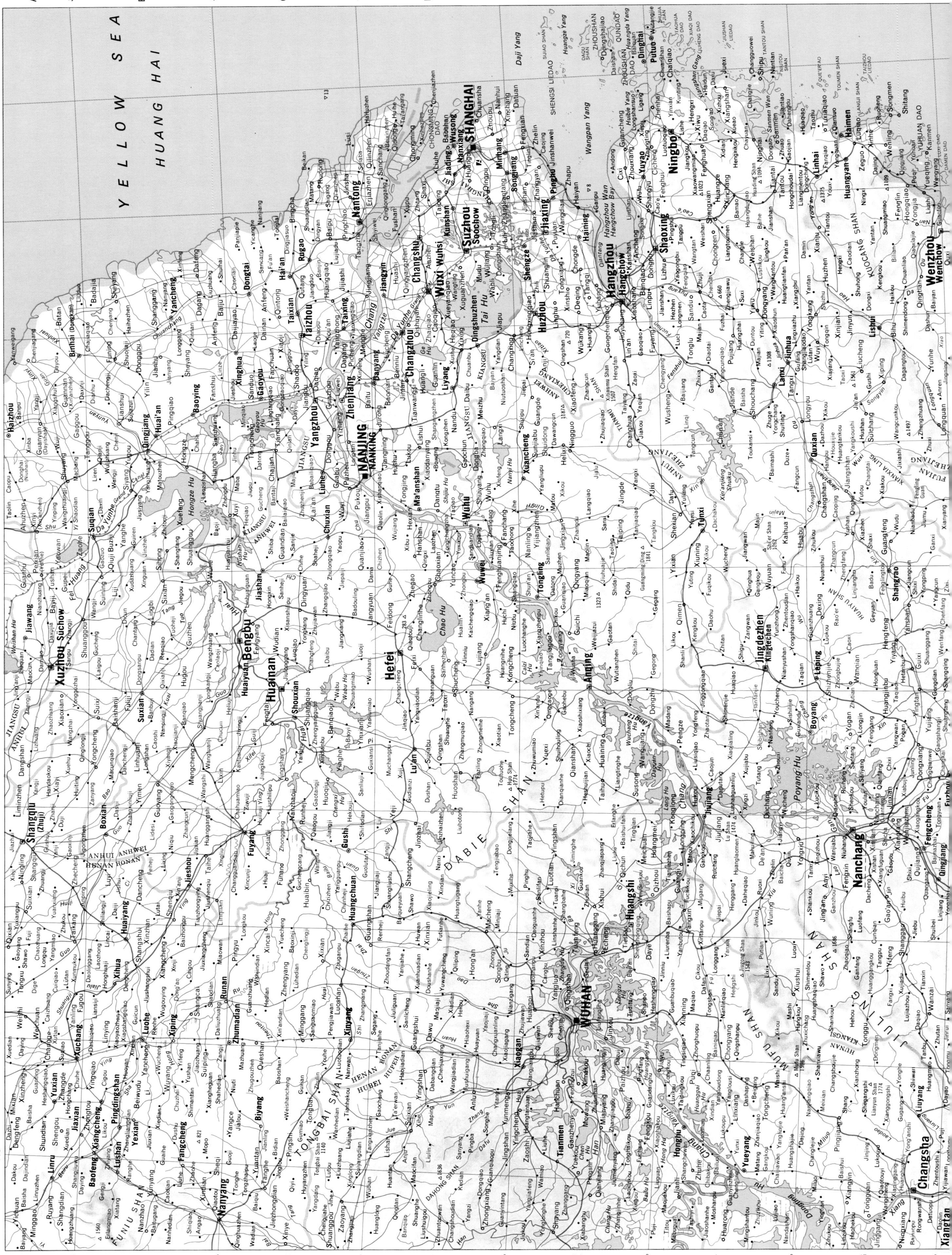

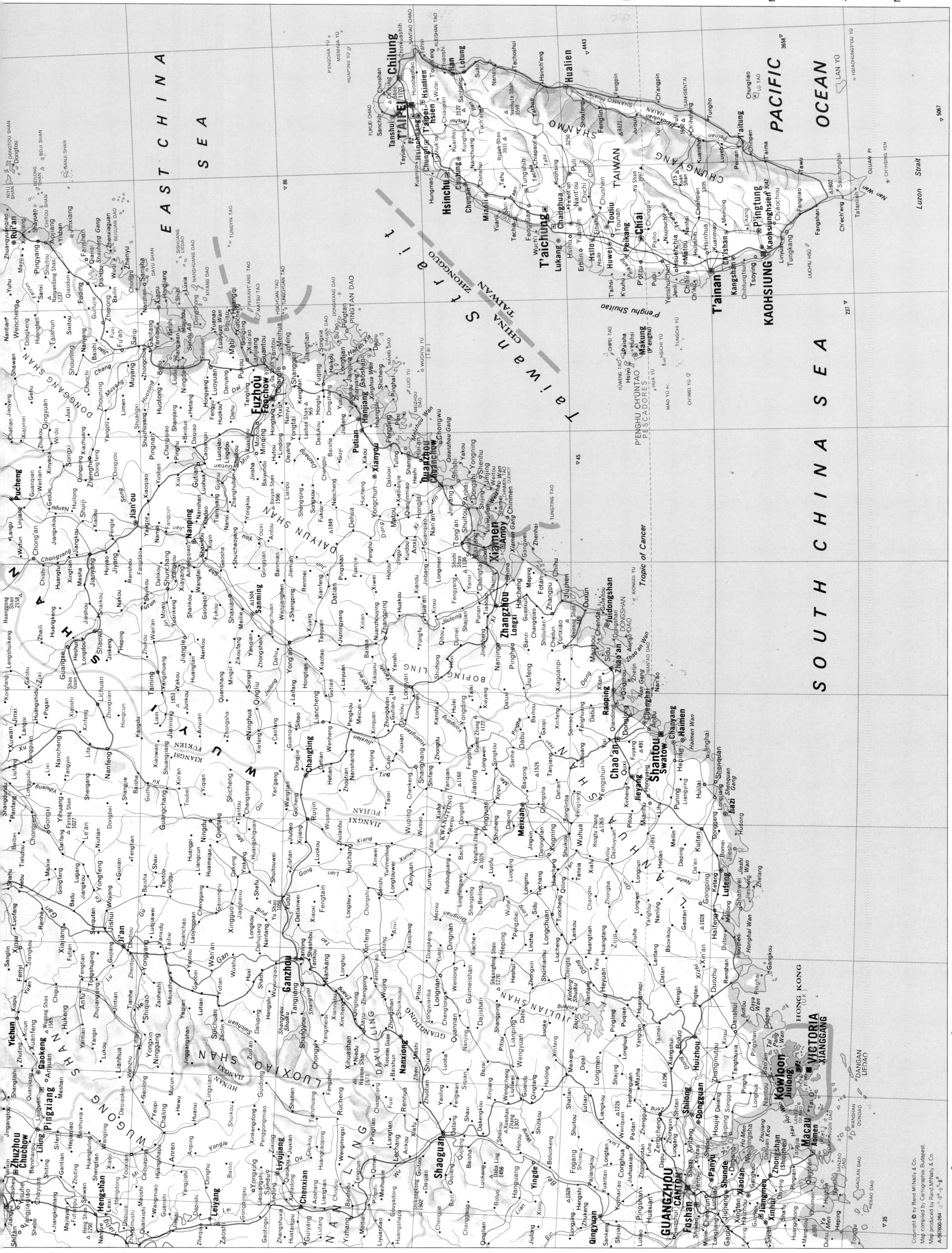

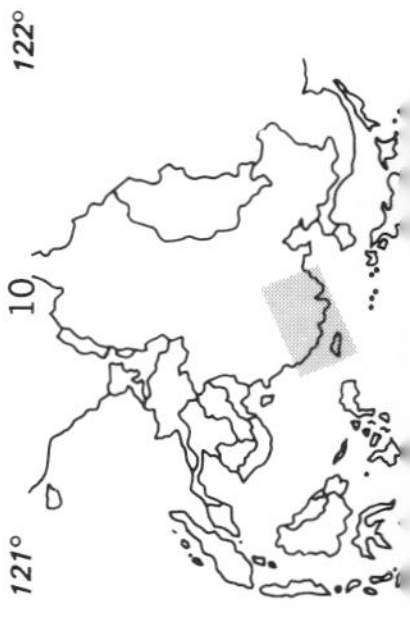

Kilometers 0 50 100 150 Km.

Statute Miles 0 50 100 150 Mi.

Scale 1:3,000,000

One centimeter represents 30 kilometers.

One inch represents approximately 47 miles.

Lambert Conformal Conic Projection

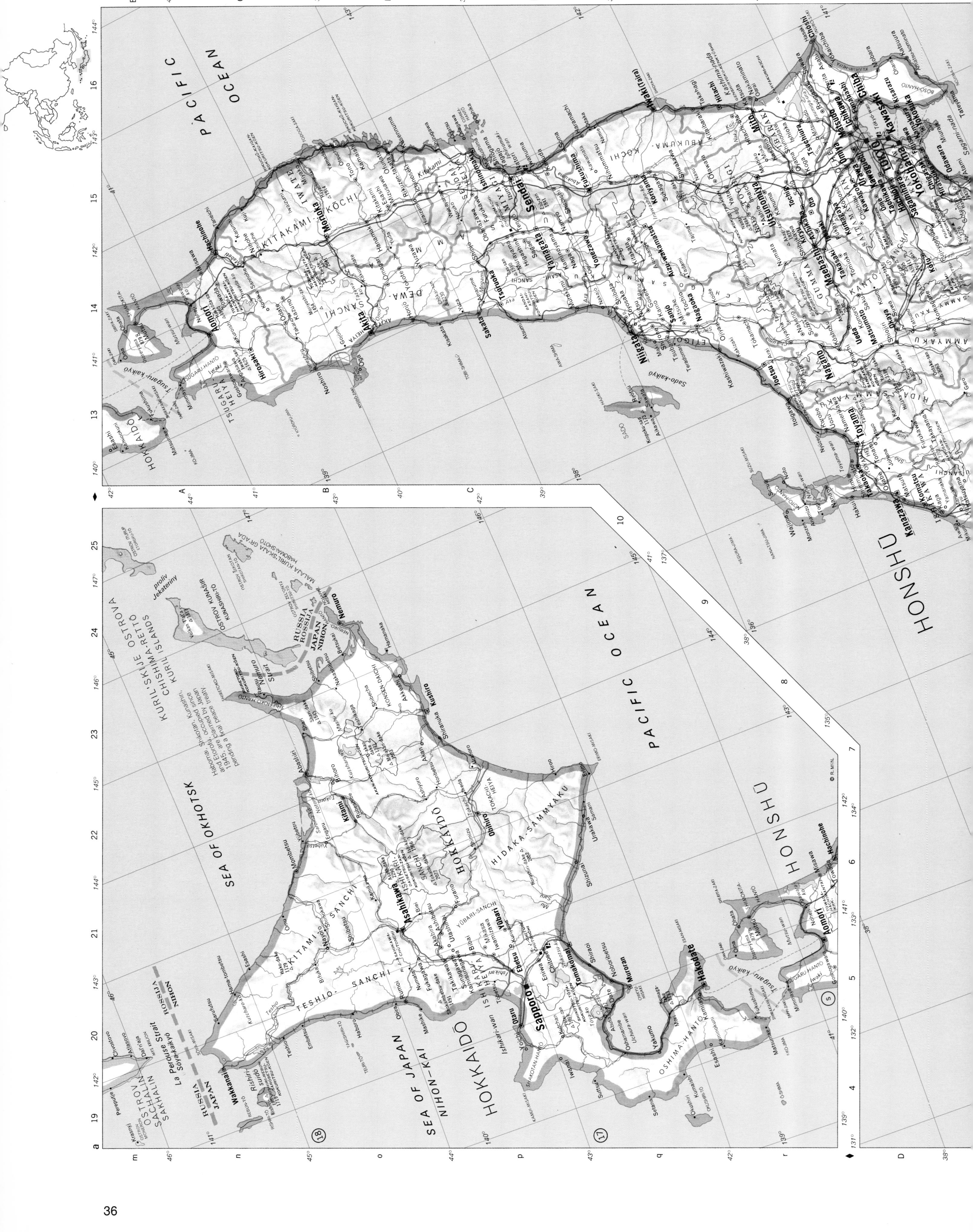
PACIFIC OCEAN
SEA OF OKHOTSK
SEA OF JAPAN
NIHON-KAI
HOKKAIDŌ
HONSHŪ
KURIL'SKIJE OSTROVA
CHISHIMA-RETTŌ
KURIL ISLANDS
OSTROV SACHALIN
SAKHALIN
La Perouse Strait
Sōya-kaikyō
RUSSIA
JAPAN
Sapporo
Asahikawa
Hakodate
Kushiro
Aomori
Sendai
Niigata
Akita
Morioka
Yamagata
Tōkyō
Kawasaki
Chiba
Yokohama
Toyama
Kanazawa
SADO

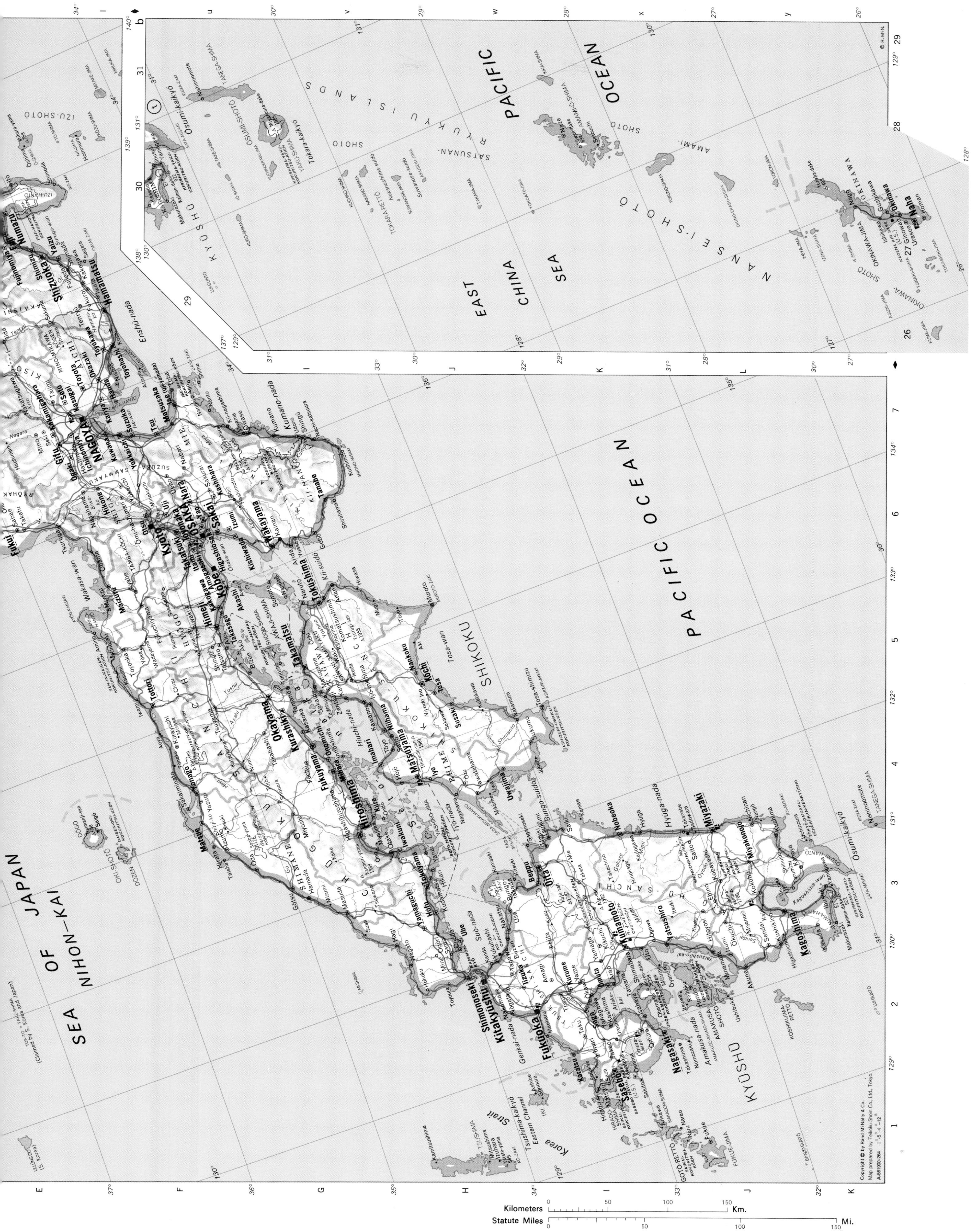

Kilometers 0 50 100 150 Km.

Statute Miles 0 50 100 150 Mi.

Scale 1:3,000,000

One centimeter represents 30 kilometers.
One inch represents approximately 47 miles

Lambert Conformal Conic Projection

CHINA
YUNNAN
GUANGXI ZHUANGZU
GUANGDONG
Nanning
GUANGZHOU (CANTON)
Foshan
Dongguan
Shantou
Swatow
Chao'an
New Kowloon
Xinjiulong
VICTORIA
XIANGGANG
HONG KONG (U.K.)
Aomen Macau
Zhanjiang
ZHIZIQU
Beihai
Haikou
HAINAN
HAINAN DAO
TUNGSHA TAO
PRATAS ISLAND
(claimed by China and Taiwan)
Taiwan Strait
BANGLADESH
Chittagong
INDIA
BURMA
MYANMAR
ARAKAN YOMA
Mandalay
Monywa
Sittwe (Akyab)
Taunggyi
Prome (Pye)
Henzada
Pathein
YANGON
RANGOON
Bago
Mawlamyine
Gulf of Martaban
BAY OF BENGAL
Preparis North Channel
Preparis South Channel
Coco Channel
ANDAMAN ISLANDS (India)
NORTH ANDAMAN
MIDDLE ANDAMAN
SOUTH ANDAMAN
Port Blair
LITTLE ANDAMAN
ANDAMAN SEA
MERGUI ARCHIPELAGO
Ten Degree Channel
NICOBAR ISLANDS (India)
CAR NICOBAR
LITTLE NICOBAR
GREAT NICOBAR
Great Channel
LAOS
Louangphrabang
Viangchan (Vientiane)
Savannakhet
Pakxe
THAILAND
Chiang Mai
Nakhon Sawan
Khon Kaen
Nakhon Ratchasima
Ubon Ratchathani
KRUNG THEP
BANGKOK
Chon Buri
Gulf of Thailand
ISTHMUS OF KRA
Surat Thani
Nakhon Si Thammarat
Phuket
Songkhla
Hat Yai
CAMBODIA
Phnum Penh
Kâmpóng Saôm
VIETNAM
Ha Noi
Hai Phong
Nam Dinh
Gulf of Tonkin
Vinh
Hue
Da Nang
Qui Nhon
Nha Trang
Buon Me Thuot
Bien Hoa
THANH PHO HO CHI MINH (SAIGON)
Can Tho
XISHA QUNDAO
PARACEL ISLANDS
(claimed by China, Taiwan and Vietnam)
SOUTH CHINA SEA
SPRATLY ISLANDS
PALAWAN
Balabac Strait
MALAYSIA
SEMENANJUNG MALAYSIA
George Town (Pinang)
Alor Setar
Kota Baharu
Kuala Terengganu
Ipoh
Kuantan
Kelang
Kuala Lumpur
Seremban
Melaka
Johor Baharu
SINGAPORE
Strait of Malacca
Kota Kinabalu (Jesselton)
Bandar Seri Begawan
BRUNEI
Kuching
Sibu
Sandakan
BORNEO
KALIMANTAN
Pontianak
Samarinda
Balikpapan
Banjarmasin
Selat Makasar
Makassar Strait
KEPULAUAN NATUNA BESAR
INDONESIA
GREATER SUNDA ISLANDS
SUMATERA
SUMATRA
Banda Aceh
Medan
Pematangsiantar
Padang
Pekanbaru
Jambi
Palembang
Bengkulu
Tanjungkarang-Telukbetung
Pangkalpinang
PULAU BANGKA
Karimata Strait
KEPULAUAN MENTAWAI
Equator
LAUT JAWA
JAVA SEA
JAKARTA
Bogor
BANDUNG
Cirebon
Semarang
Yogyakarta
Surakarta
SURABAYA
Malang
MADURA
JAWA
JAVA
BALI
Denpasar
LOMBOK
Mataram
SUMBAWA
INDIAN OCEAN
CHRISTMAS ISLAND (Austl.)
Copyright © by Rand McNally & Co.
Map prepared by Esselte Map Service AB, Stockholm.
A-569800-264

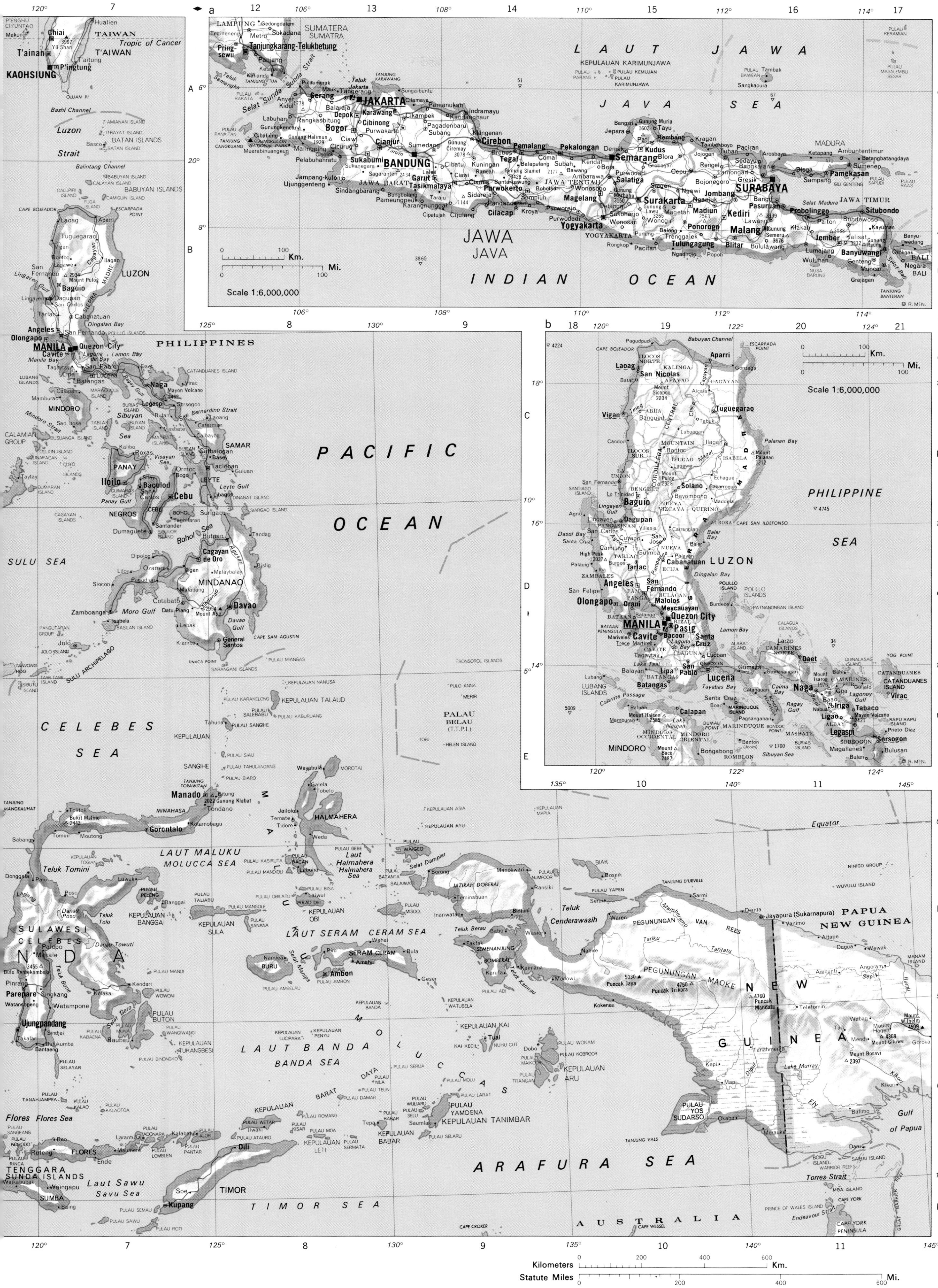

Kilometers 0 200 400 600 Km.

Statute Miles 0 200 400 600 Mi.

Scale 1:12,000,000

One centimeter represents 120 kilometers.
One inch represents approximately 190 miles.
Lambert Conformal Conic Projection

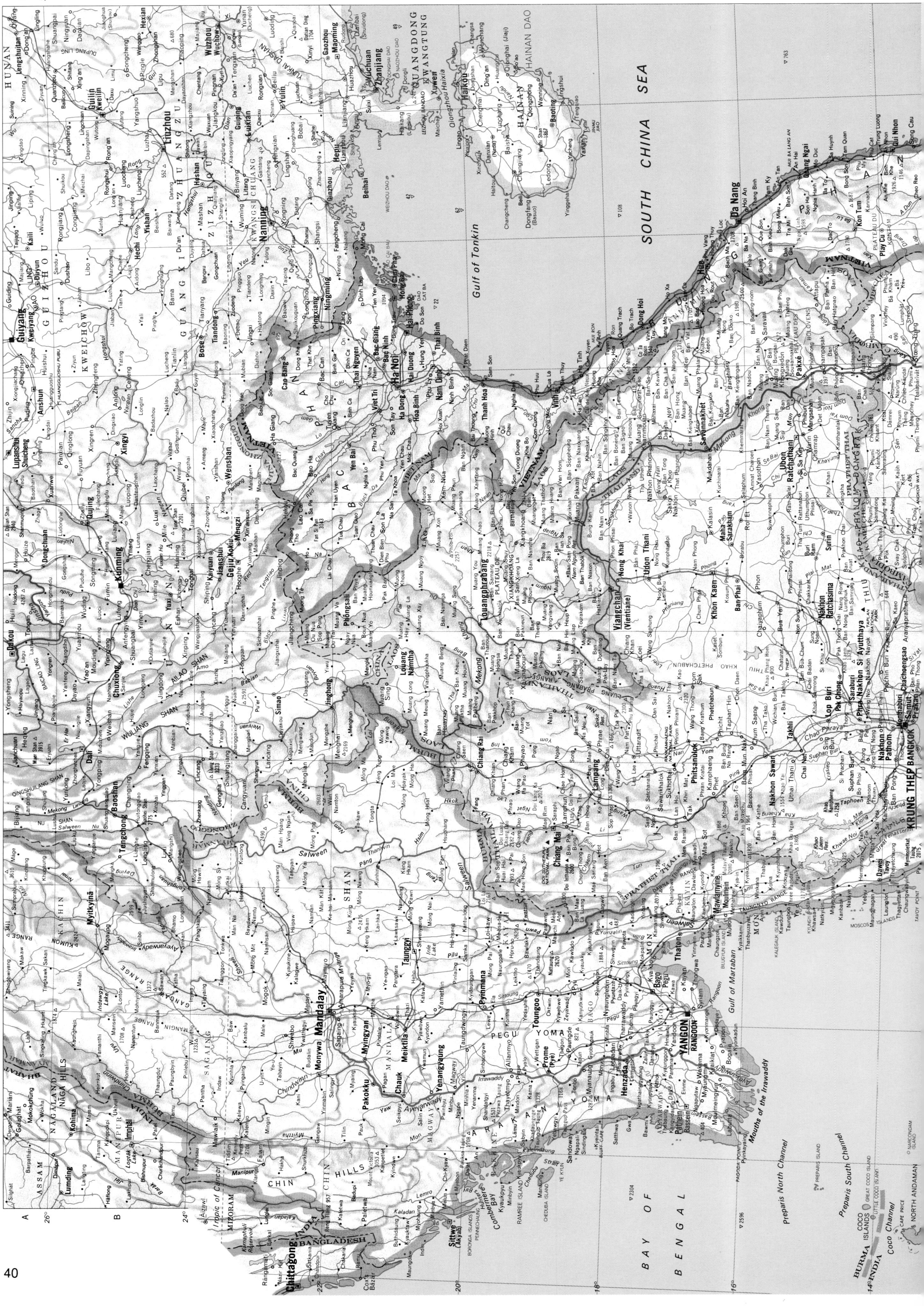
SOUTH CHINA SEA
Gulf of Tonkin
BAY OF BENGAL
Gulf of Martaban
Mouths of the Irrawaddy
Preparis North Channel
Preparis South Channel
Coco Channel
HAINAN DAO
Qiongzhou Haixia
Da Nang
Hue
Vinh
Ha Noi
Hai Phong
Nam Dinh
Thanh Hoa
Viangchan (Vientiane)
Louangphrabang
Udon Thani
Khon Kaen
Nakhon Ratchasima
Ubon Ratchathani
KRUNG THEP BANGKOK
Chiang Mai
Chiang Rai
Lampang
Phitsanulok
Nakhon Sawan
Mawlamyine
Moulmein
Thaton
YANGON RANGOON
Pegu
Bago
Bassein
Pathein
Henzada
Prome (Pye)
Toungoo
Pyinmana
Taunggyi
Meiktila
Mandalay
Monywa
Myingyan
Pakokku
Chauk
Yenangyaung
Myitkyina
Sittwe (Akyab)
Chittagong
Imphal
Kohima
Lumding
Kunming
Nanning
Guiyang
Liuzhou
Guilin
Zhanjiang
Haikou
Wenshan
Gejiu
Dali
Baoshan
Tengchong
Simao
Jinghong
Lincang
BANGLADESH
BURMA
CHINA
LAOS
THAILAND
VIETNAM
KAMPUCHEA
INDIA
NORTH ANDAMAN
COCO ISLANDS
Tropic of Cancer
Mekong
Salween
Irrawaddy
Chindwin
Sittoung
Red
Black
PLATEAU DU TRANH NINH
PLATEAU DES BOLOVENS
PLATEAU DU KONTUM
DÂNGRÊK
HAINAN
GUANGXI ZHUANGZU
YUNNAN
GUIZHOU
GUANGDONG
ASSAM
MANIPUR
MIZORAM
NAGALAND
NAGA HILLS
CHIN HILLS
ARAKAN YOMA
PEGU YOMA
SHAN
KACHIN
SAGAING
MANDALAY
MAGWAY
KAYIN
MON

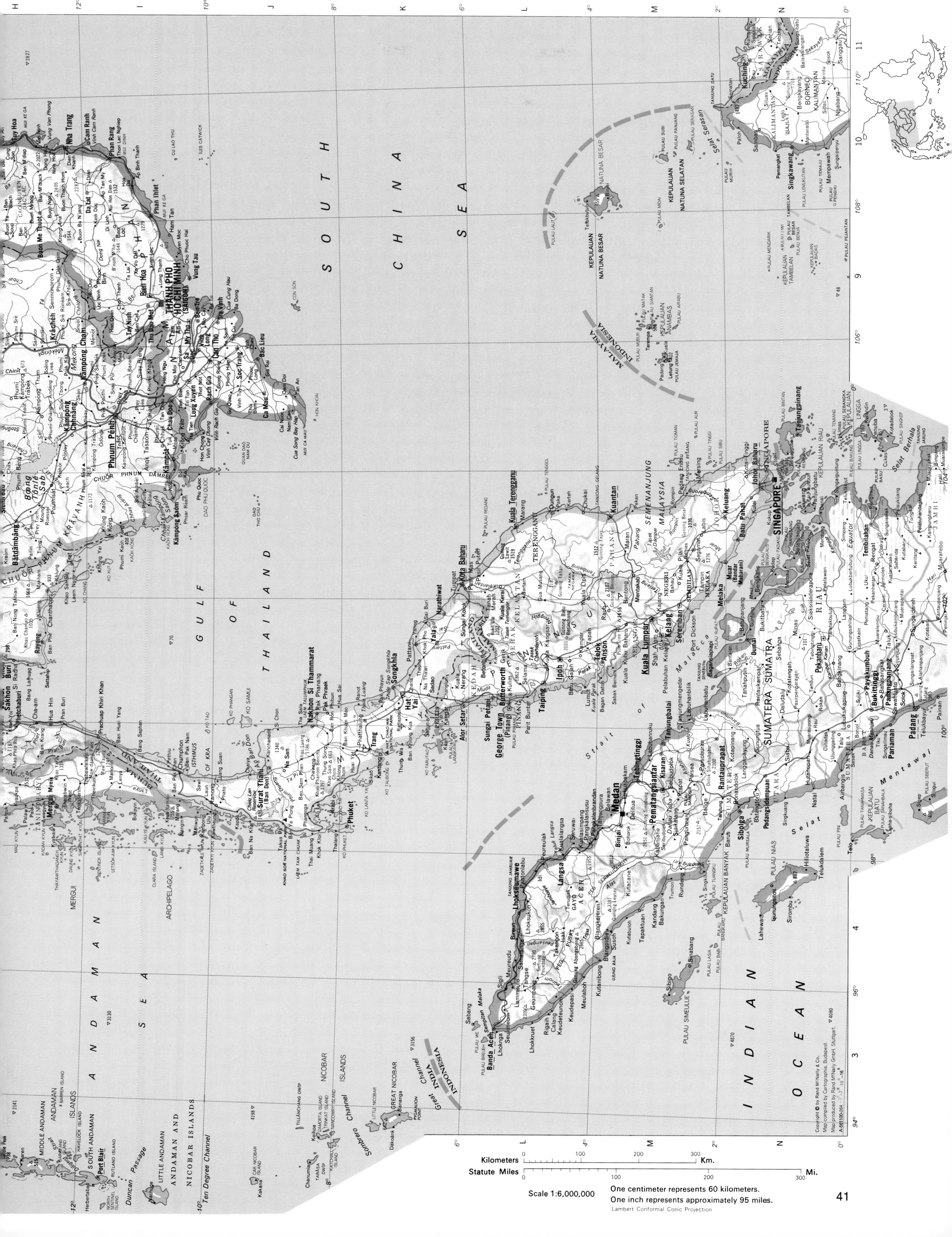

Kilometers 0 100 200 300 Km.

Statute Miles 0 100 200 300 Mi.

Scale 1:6,000,000

One centimeter represents 60 kilometers.
One inch represents approximately 95 miles.
Lambert Conformal Conic Projection

Kilometers 0 200 400 600 Km.
Statute Miles 0 200 400 600 Mi.

Scale 1:12,000,000
One centimeter represents 120 kilometers.
One inch represents approximately 190 miles.
Lambert Conformal Conic Projection

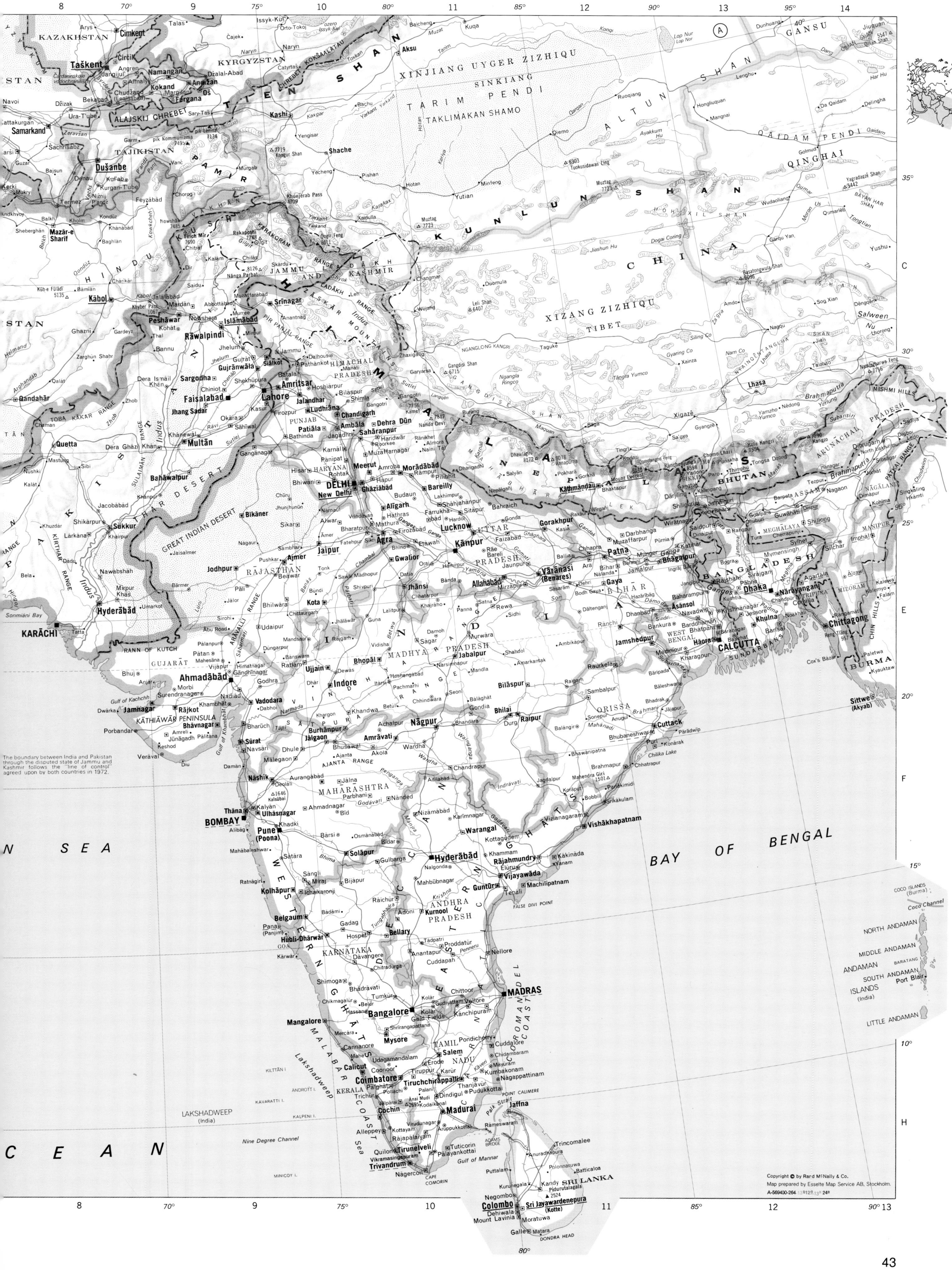
KAZAKHSTAN
KYRGYZSTAN
TAJIKISTAN
XINJIANG UYGER ZIZHIQU
SINKIANG
TARIM PENDI
TAKLIMAKAN SHAMO
TIEN SHAN
PAMIR
ALTUN
KUNLUN SHAN
QAIDAM PENDI
QINGHAI
GANSU
CHINA
XIZANG ZIZHIQU
TIBET
HINDU KUSH
KARAKORAM
JAMMU AND KASHMIR
HIMACHAL PRADESH
PUNJAB
HARYANA
UTTAR PRADESH
RAJASTHAN
THAR DESERT
GREAT INDIAN DESERT
PAKISTAN
NEPAL
BHUTAN
BANGLADESH
BURMA
INDIA
MADHYA PRADESH
BIHAR
WEST BENGAL
ORISSA
GUJARAT
KATHIAWAR PENINSULA
MAHARASHTRA
ANDHRA PRADESH
KARNATAKA
KERALA
TAMIL NADU
SRI LANKA
MEGHALAYA
ASSAM
ARUNACHAL PRADESH
NAGALAND
MANIPUR
MIZORAM
TRIPURA
SIKKIM
BAY OF BENGAL
ARABIAN SEA
INDIAN OCEAN
LAKSHADWEEP (India)
ANDAMAN ISLANDS (India)
NORTH ANDAMAN
MIDDLE ANDAMAN
SOUTH ANDAMAN
LITTLE ANDAMAN
COCO ISLANDS (Burma)
Coco Channel
Port Blair
Lakshadweep Sea
Nine Degree Channel
Gulf of Mannar
Palk Strait
ADAMS BRIDGE
CAPE COMORIN
DONDRA HEAD
POINT CALIMERE
FALSE DIVI POINT
RANN OF KUTCH
Gulf of Kachchh
Gulf of Khambhat
Sonmiani Bay
WESTERN GHATS
EASTERN GHATS
MALABAR COAST
COROMANDEL COAST
VINDHYA RANGE
SATPURA RANGE
AJANTA RANGE
ARAVALLI RANGE
SUNDARBANS
SULAIMAN RANGE
KIRTHAR RANGE
TOBA KAKAR RANGE
PIR PANJAL RANGE
DELHI
New Delhi
BOMBAY
CALCUTTA
MADRAS
KARACHI
Lahore
Islāmābād
Kābol
Taškent
Dušanbe
Samarkand
Kathmandu
Dhaka
Colombo
Sri Jayawardenepura (Kotte)
Lhasa
Hyderābād
Bangalore
Ahmadābād
Kānpur
Lucknow
Jaipur
Nāgpur
Pune (Poona)
Patna
Vārānasi (Benares)
Chittagong
Sittwe (Akyab)
The boundary between India and Pakistan through the disputed state of Jammu and Kashmir follows the "line of control" agreed upon by both countries in 1972.
Copyright © by Rand McNally & Co.
Map prepared by Esselte Map Service AB, Stockholm.

Northern India and Pakistan

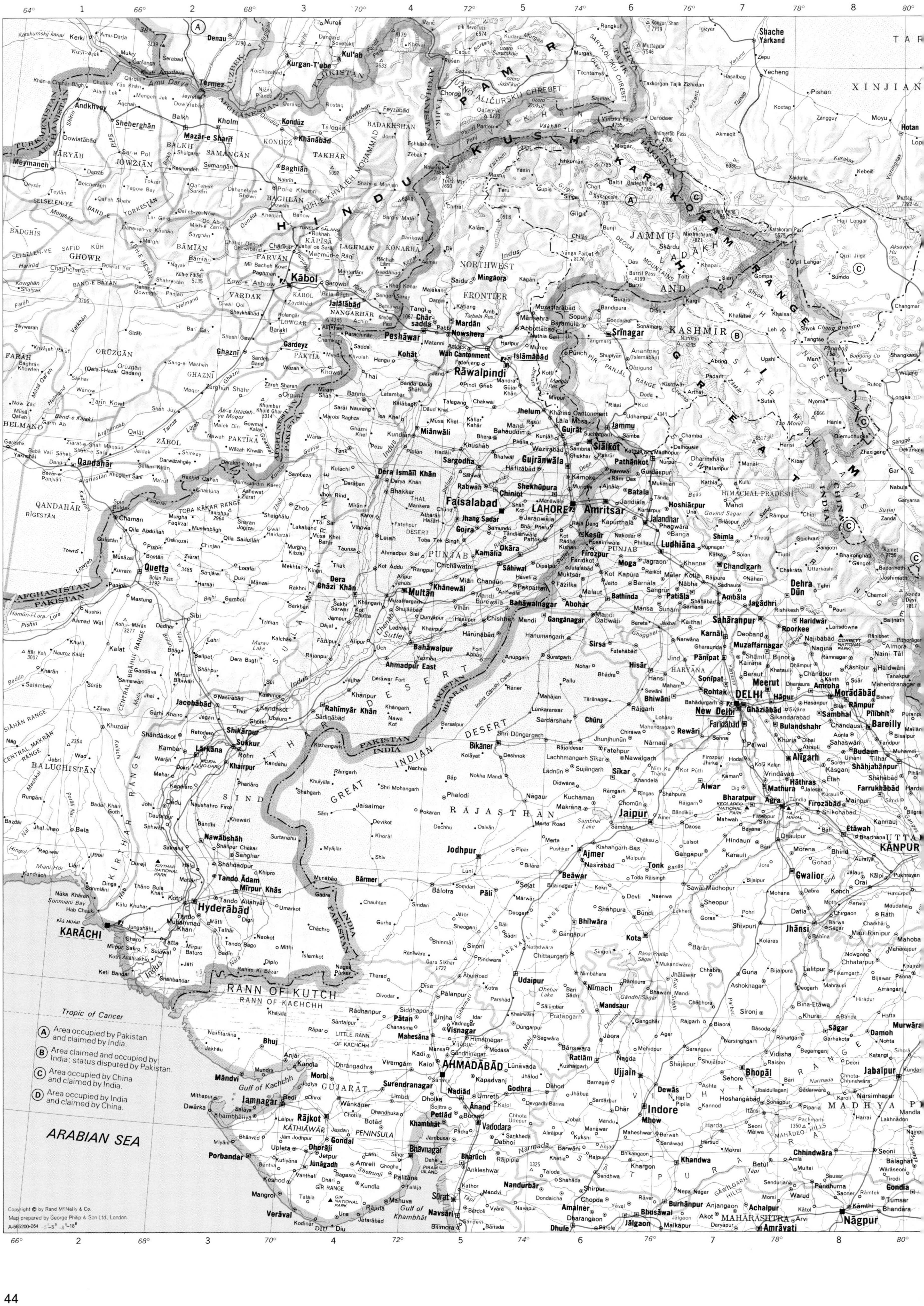

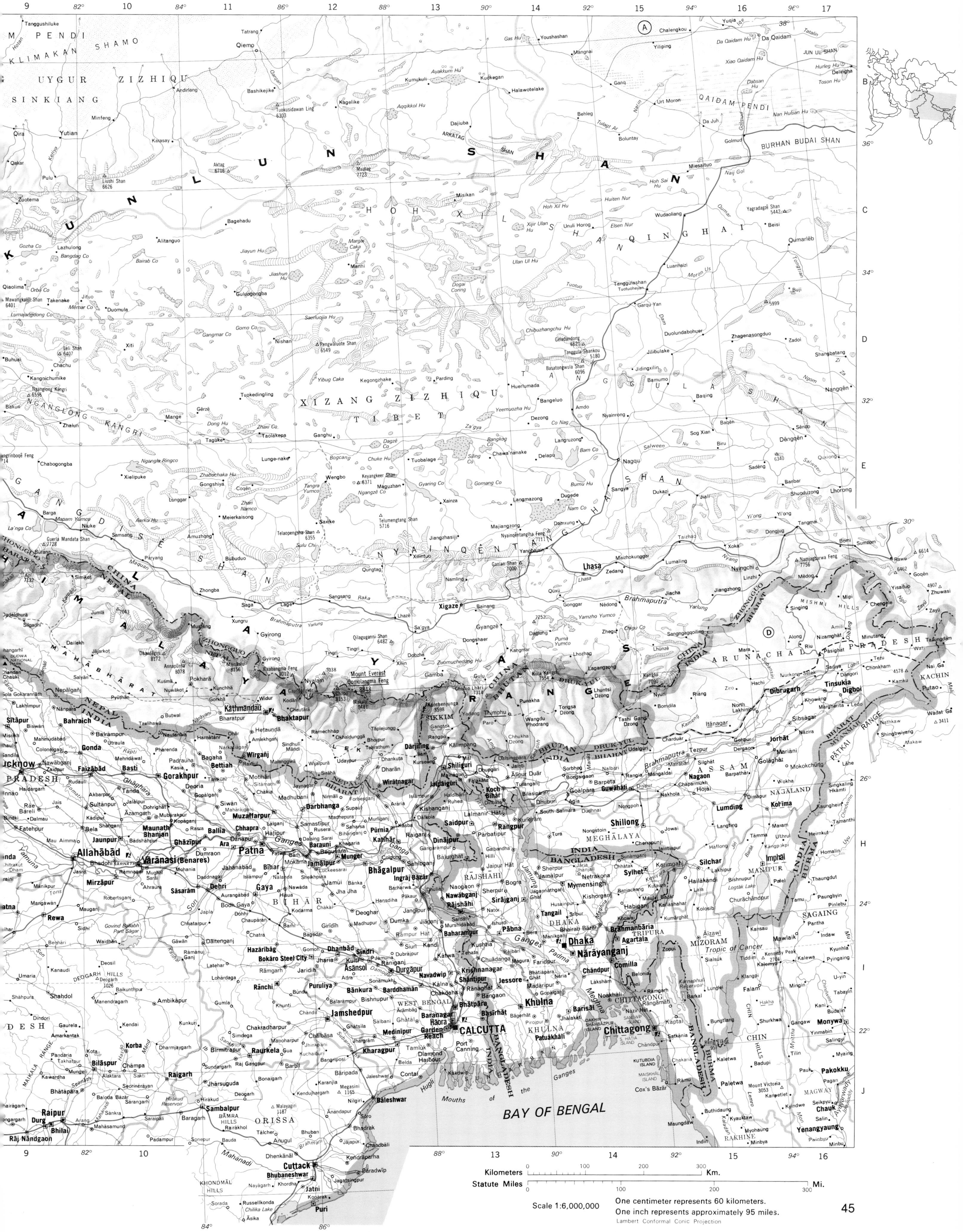

Scale 1:6,000,000

One centimeter represents 60 kilometers.
One inch represents approximately 95 miles.
Lambert Conformal Conic Projection

Southern India and Sri Lanka

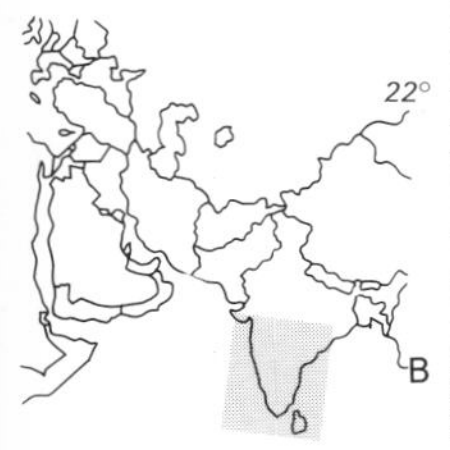

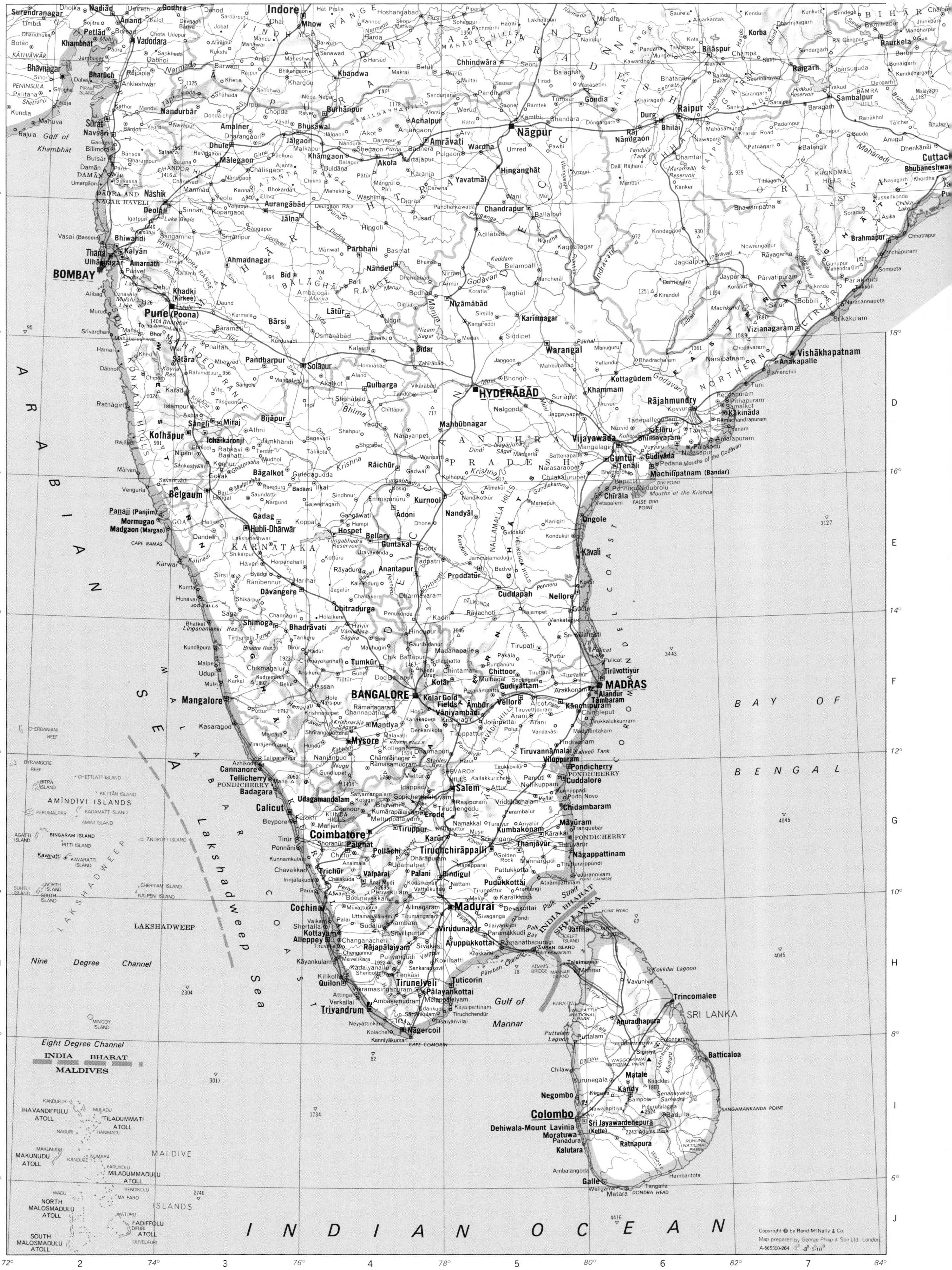

Kilometers 0 100 200 300 Km.

Statute Miles 0 100 200 300 Mi.

Scale 1:6,000,000

One centimeter represents 60 kilometers.

One inch represents approximately 95 miles.

Lambert Conformal Conic Projection

Southern Arabian Peninsula

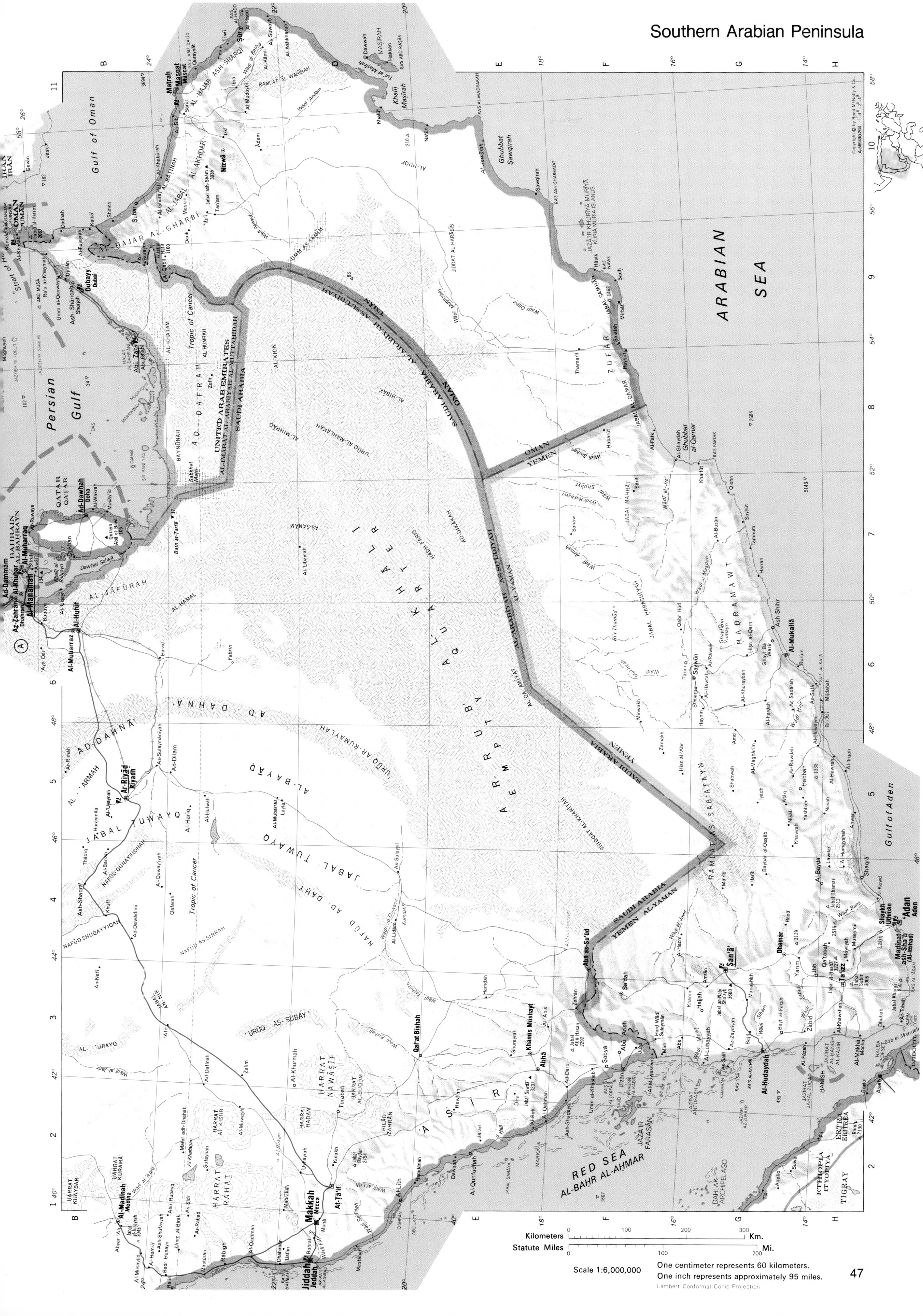

Kilometers 0 100 200 300 Km.
Statute Miles 0 100 200 Mi.

Scale 1:6,000,000

One centimeter represents 60 kilometers.
One inch represents approximately 95 miles.
Lambert Conformal Conic Projection

The Middle East

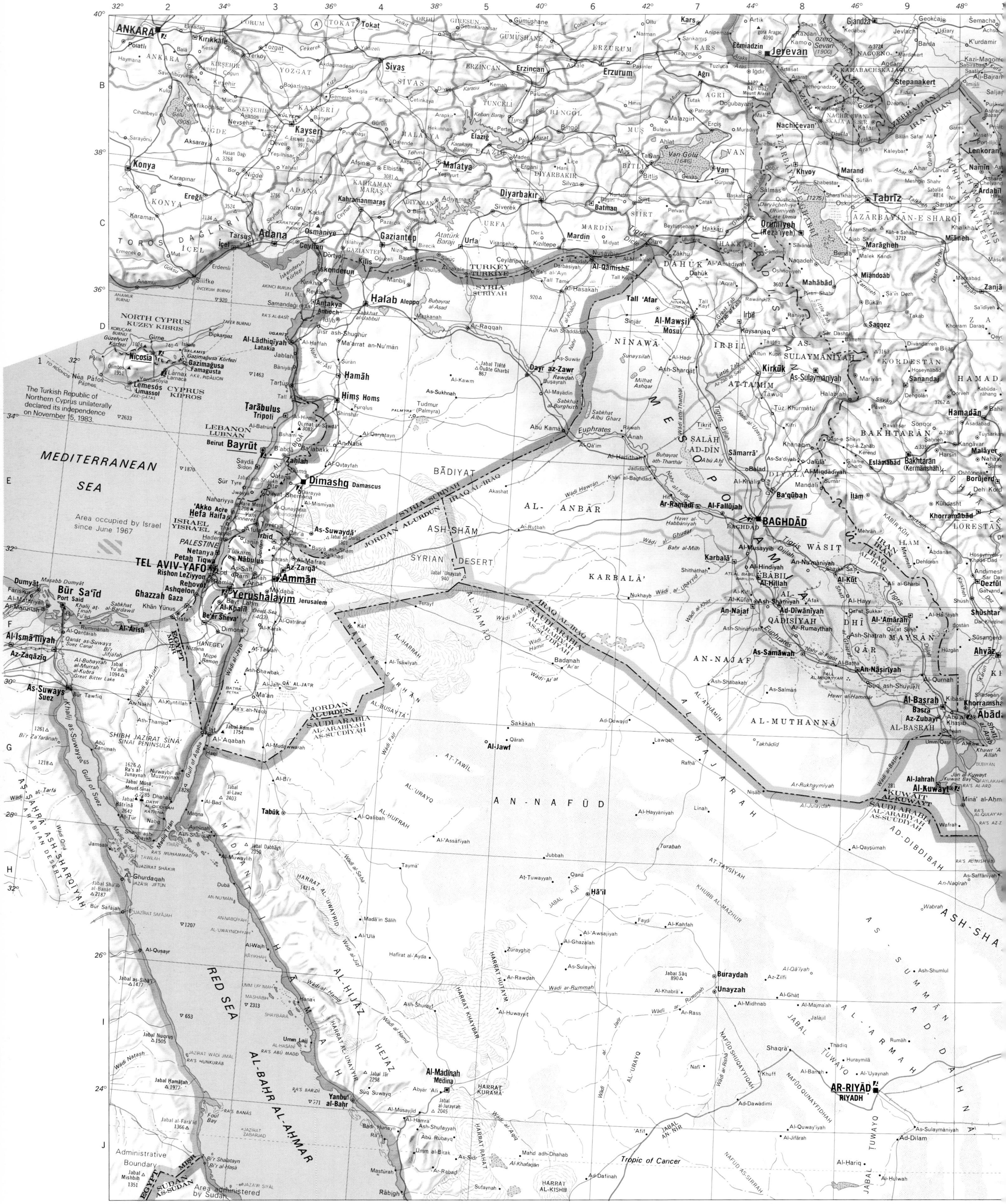

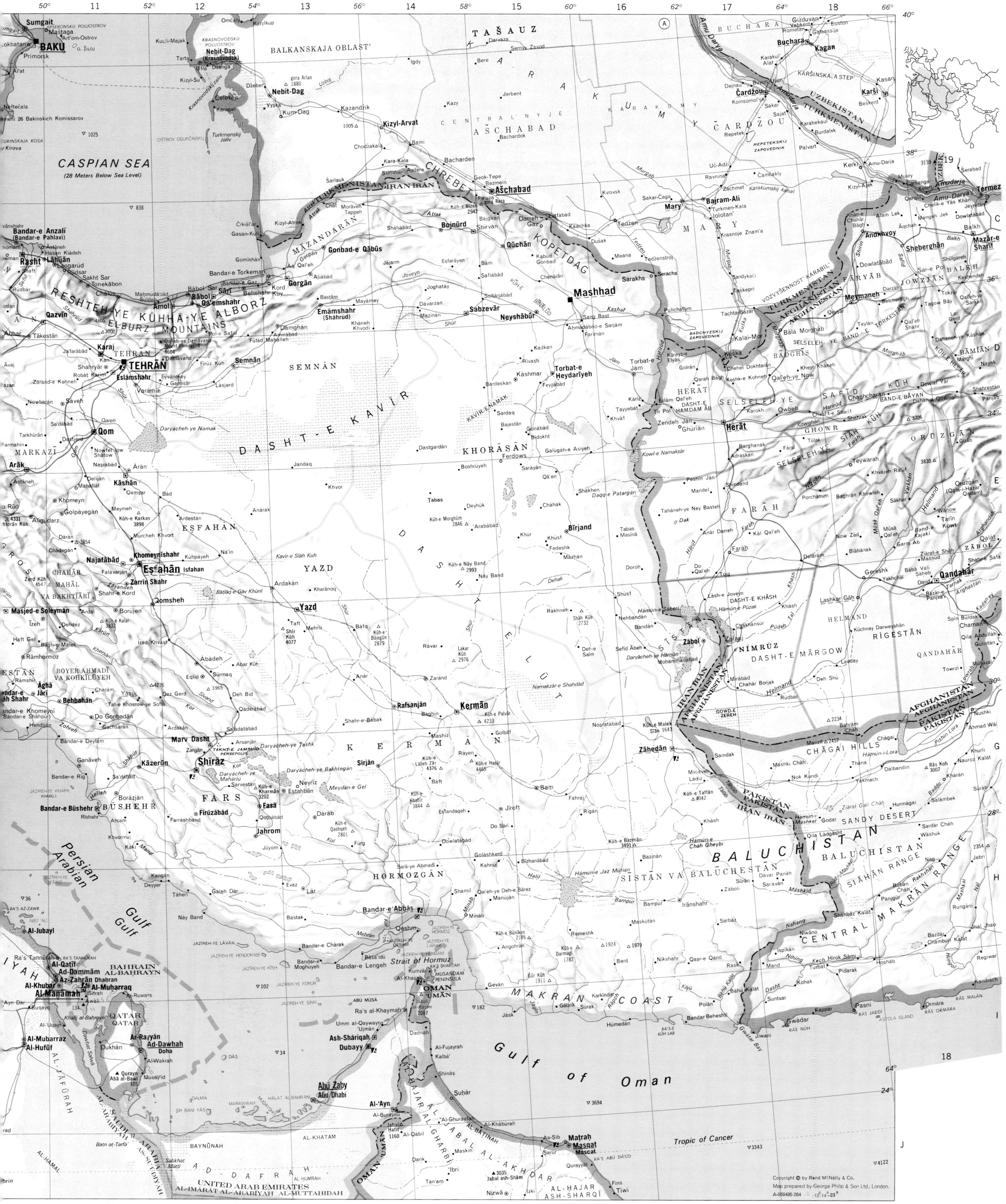

Kilometers 0 100 200 300 Km.

Statute Miles 0 100 200 300 Mi.

Scale 1:6,000,000

One centimeter represents 60 kilometers.
One inch represents approximately 95 miles.
Lambert Conformal Conic Projection

Israel and Southern Lebanon

Kilometers 0 10 20 30 40 50 Km.

Statute Miles 0 10 20 30 40 50 Mi.

Scale 1:1,000,000

One centimeter represents 10 kilometers.

One inch represents approximately 16 miles.

Lambert Conformal Conic Projection

ATLANTIC OCEAN
MID-ATLANTIC RIDGE
WEST EUROPEAN BASIN
LABRADOR BASIN
Labrador Sea
IRMINGER BASIN
REYKJANES RIDGE
ICELAND BASIN
ROCKALL RISE
NORWEGIAN BASIN
Norwegian Sea
LOFOTEN BASIN
GREENLAND BASIN
Greenland Sea
Barents Sea
Kara Sea
North Sea
Baltic Sea
Bay of Biscay
Mediterranean Sea
Black Sea
Caspian Sea
Red Sea
AZORES-GIBRALTAR RIDGE
CANARY BASIN
PLATEAU
CANADA
GREENLAND (Den.)
ICELAND
Reykjavík
FAEROE ISLANDS (Den.)
IRELAND
UNITED KINGDOM
LONDON
FRANCE
PARIS
SPAIN
MADRID
PORTUGAL
Lisboa
ITALY
ROMA
GERMANY
BERLIN
POLAND
WARSZAWA
NORWAY
Oslo
SWEDEN
Stockholm
FINLAND
Helsinki
DENMARK
København
CZECHOSLOVAKIA
Praha
AUSTRIA
WIEN
HUNGARY
BUDAPEST
ROMANIA
BUCUREŞTI
BULGARIA
Sofija
GREECE
Athínai
ALBANIA
Tiranë
BELARUS
Minsk
UKRAINE
KIJEV
RUSSIA
MOSKVA
SANKT-PETERBURG
EUROPE
ASIA
TURKEY
ANKARA
İSTANBUL
SYRIA
DIMASHQ
IRAQ
BAGHDĀD
IRAN
TEHRĀN
SAUDI ARABIA
EGYPT
AL-QĀHIRAH
LIBYA
Ṭarābulus
TUNISIA
Tunis
ALGERIA
EL DJAZAÏR
MOROCCO
Rabat
WESTERN SAHARA
MAURITANIA
Nouakchott
MALI
NIGER
KAZAKHSTAN
UZBEKISTAN
TURKMENISTAN
URAL'SKIJE GORY
URAL MOUNTAINS
ZAPADNO-SIBIRSKAJA RAVNINA
BOL'ŠOJ KAVKAZ
CAUCASUS
ATLAS MOUNTAINS
SAHARA
Arctic Circle
Tropic of Cancer

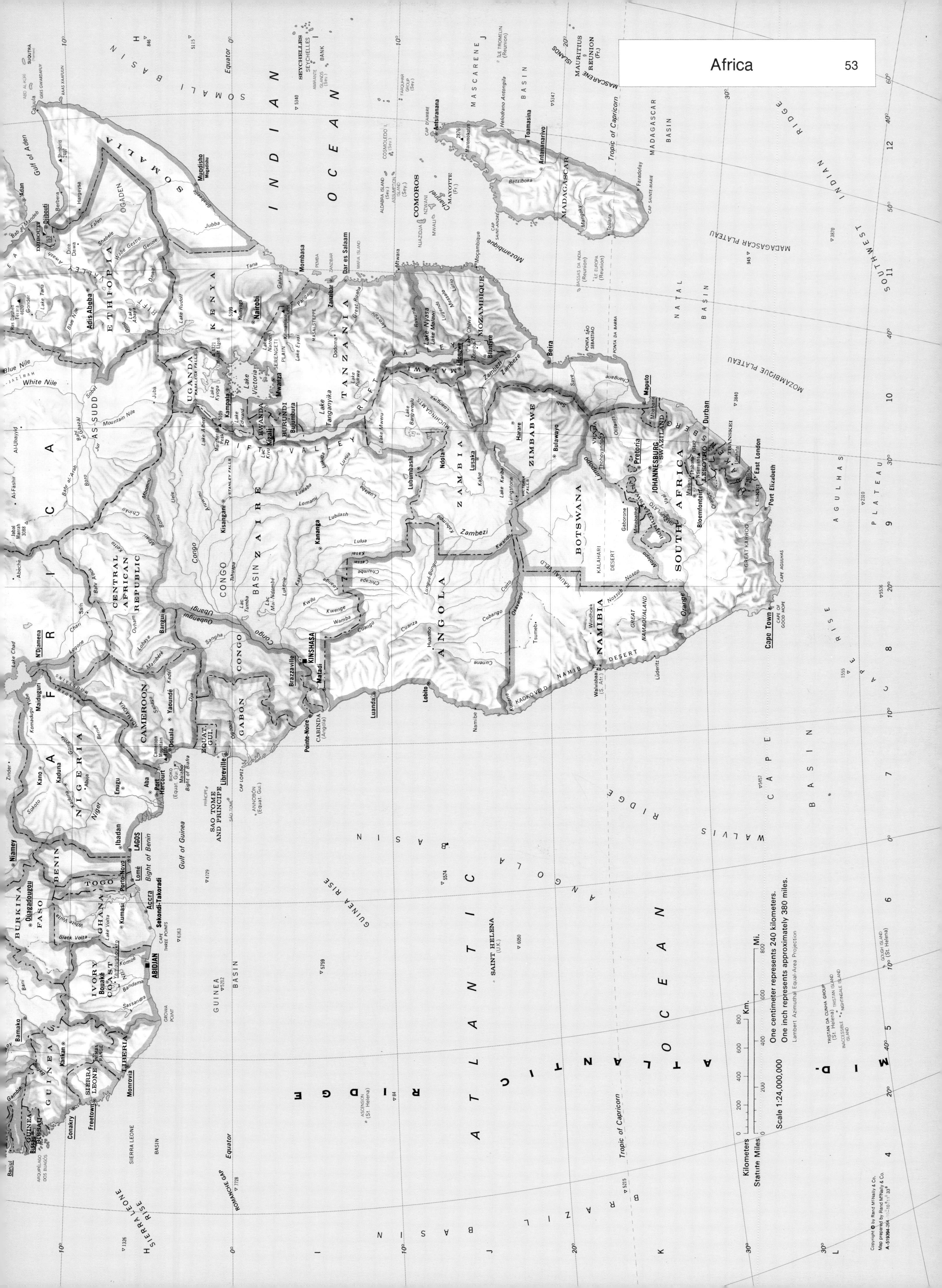
INDIAN OCEAN
ATLANTIC OCEAN
AFRICA
Gulf of Aden
Gulf of Guinea
Bight of Benin
Bight of Biafra
Mozambique Channel
Tropic of Capricorn
Equator
SOMALIA
ETHIOPIA
KENYA
UGANDA
TANZANIA
RWANDA
BURUNDI
ZAIRE
CONGO
GABON
EQUAT. GUI.
CAMEROON
NIGERIA
BENIN
TOGO
GHANA
BURKINA FASO
IVORY COAST
LIBERIA
SIERRA LEONE
GUINEA
GUINEA-BISSAU
CENTRAL AFRICAN REPUBLIC
ANGOLA
ZAMBIA
MALAWI
MOZAMBIQUE
ZIMBABWE
BOTSWANA
NAMIBIA
SOUTH AFRICA
LESOTHO
SWAZILAND
MADAGASCAR
COMOROS
SAO TOME AND PRINCIPE
SAINT HELENA (U.K.)
MAURITIUS
REUNION (Fr.)
SEYCHELLES
Mogadisho
Djibouti
Adis Abeba
Nairobi
Mombasa
Dar es Salaam
Zanzibar
Kampala
Kigali
Bujumbura
Kinshasa
Brazzaville
Luanda
Lobito
Lusaka
Harare
Bulawayo
Lilongwe
Blantyre
Beira
Maputo
Pretoria
Johannesburg
Durban
Cape Town
Port Elizabeth
East London
Bloemfontein
Windhoek
Gaborone
Antananarivo
Toamasina
Antsiranana
Lagos
Ibadan
Accra
Abidjan
Monrovia
Freetown
Conakry
Bamako
Niamey
Ouagadougou
N'Djamena
Bangui
Yaoundé
Douala
Libreville
Kano
Kaduna
Lake Victoria
Lake Tanganyika
Lake Nyasa
Lake Chad
Lake Volta
Congo
Zambezi
Orange
Limpopo
Niger
Blue Nile
White Nile
KALAHARI DESERT
NAMIB DESERT
Scale 1:24,000,000
One centimeter represents 240 kilometers.
One inch represents approximately 380 miles.
Lambert Azimuthal Equal-Area Projection
Kilometers
Statute Miles
Copyright © by Rand McNally & Co.
Map prepared by Rand McNally & Co.

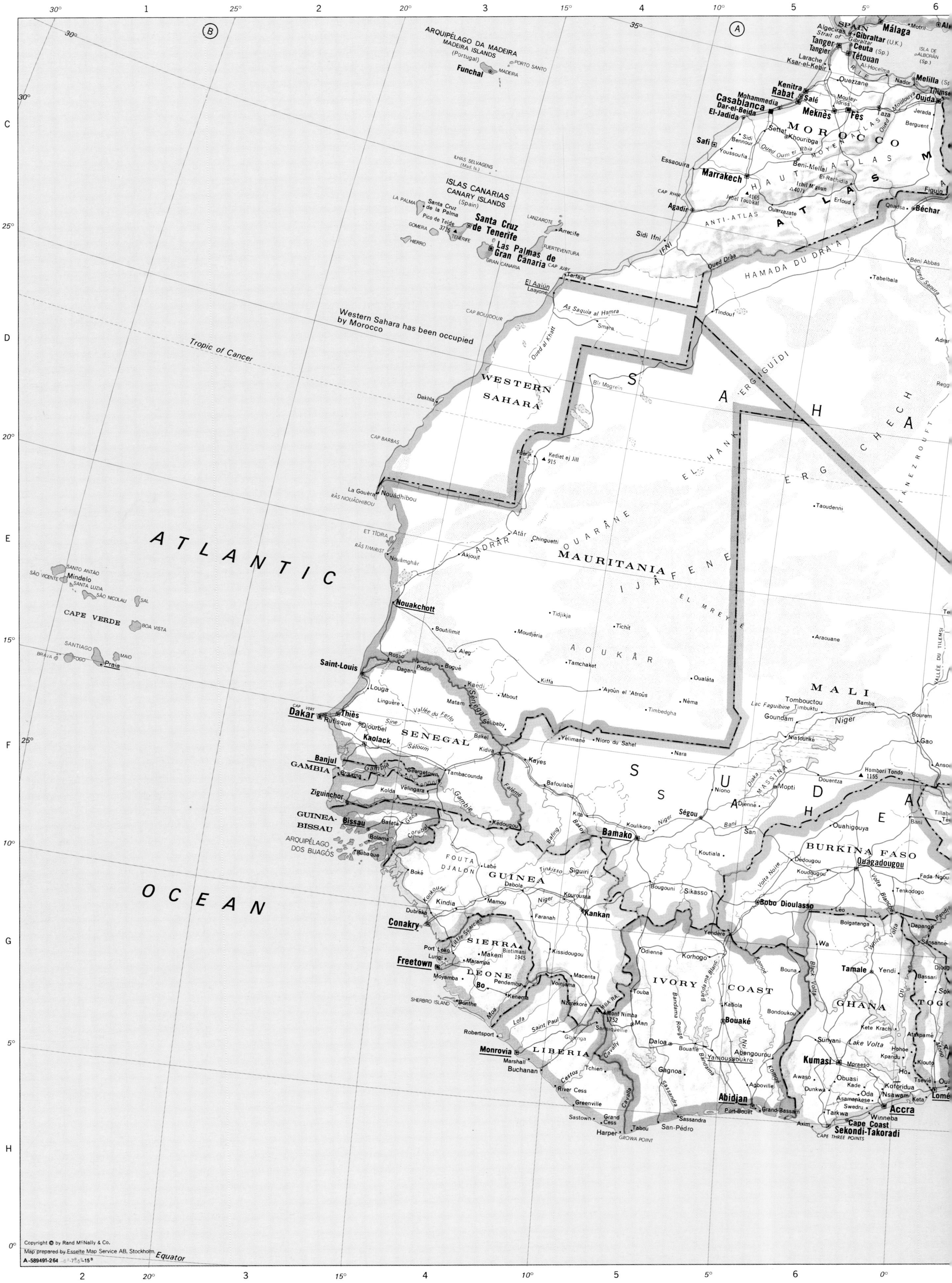
ARQUIPÉLAGO DA MADEIRA
MADEIRA ISLANDS
(Portugal)
Funchal
PORTO SANTO
ILHAS SELVAGENS
ISLAS CANARIAS
CANARY ISLANDS
(Spain)
Santa Cruz de Tenerife
Las Palmas de Gran Canaria
LANZAROTE
Arrecife
FUERTEVENTURA
CAP JUBY
Tarfaya
El Aaiún
Laayone
CAP BOUJDOUR
Western Sahara has been occupied by Morocco
Tropic of Cancer
WESTERN SAHARA
Dakhla
CAP BARBAS
La Gouèra
Nouâdhibou
RÂS NOUÂDHIBOU
ATLANTIC
OCEAN
CAPE VERDE
SANTO ANTÃO
SÃO VICENTE
Mindelo
SANTA LUZIA
SÃO NICOLAU
SAL
BOA VISTA
SANTIAGO
MAIO
BRAVA
FOGO
Praia
SPAIN
Málaga
Algeciras
Gibraltar (U.K.)
Strait of Gibraltar
Tanger
Tangier
Ceuta (Sp.)
Tétouan
Larache
Ksar-el-Kebir
Al-Hoceima
Melilla
Nador
Oujda
Kenitra
Rabat
Salé
Mohammedia
Casablanca
Dar-el-Beida
El-Jadida
Meknès
Fès
Taza
Safi
Settat
Khouribga
MOROCCO
Essaouira
Marrakech
Beni-Mellal
Er-Rachidia
HAUT ATLAS
MOYEN ATLAS
Agadir
CAP RHIR
ANTI-ATLAS
Ouarzazate
Erfoud
Sidi Ifni
IFNI
Oued Drâa
HAMADA DU DRA
Tindouf
Béchar
Tabelbala
Smara
As Saquia al Hamra
Bîr Mogreïn
ERG IGUIDI
ERG CHECH
SAHARA
Taoudenni
TANEZROUFT
Fdérik
Kediet ej Jill 915
Atâr
Chinguetti
OUARÂNE
ADRAR
Akjoujt
ET TÎDRA
RÂS TIMIRIST
Nouâmghâr
MAURITANIA
Nouakchott
Tidjikja
Tichit
Boutilimit
Moudjéria
AOUKÂR
Aleg
Tamchaket
Kiffa
Ayoûn el 'Atroûs
Oualâta
Néma
Timbedgha
Araouane
MALI
Tombouctou
Timbuktu
Goundam
Lac Faguibine
Bamba
Bourem
Gao
Niger
Saint-Louis
Rosso
Dagana
Podor
Bogué
Kaédi
Louga
Linguère
Matam
Mbout
Dakar
CAP VERT
Thiès
Rufisque
Diourbel
Kaolack
SENEGAL
Sélibaby
Bakel
Kidira
Kayes
Yélimané
Nioro du Sahel
Nara
Banjul
GAMBIA
Georgetown
Tambacounda
Ziguinchor
Kolda
Vélingara
Bafoulabé
GUINEA-BISSAU
Bissau
Bafatá
Bolama
Bubaque
ARQUIPÉLAGO DOS BIJAGÓS
Kédougou
Kita
Bamako
Koulikoro
Ségou
Mopti
Djenné
San
Niono
Douentza
Hombori Tondo 1155
FOUTA DJALON
Labé
Boké
GUINEA
Dabola
Siguiri
Kindia
Mamou
Kouroussa
Kankan
Faranah
Dubréka
Conakry
Koutiala
Sikasso
Bougouni
BURKINA FASO
Ouahigouya
Ouagadougou
Koudougou
Dédougou
Tenkodogo
Fada Ngourma
Bobo Dioulasso
Léo
SIERRA LEONE
Port Loko
Makeni
Bintimani 1945
Freetown
Lungi
Moyamba
Bo
Kenema
Pendembu
SHERBRO ISLAND
Bonthe
Kissidougou
Macenta
Voinjama
Nzérékoré
Mont Nimba 1752
Sanniquellie
Gbanga
Robertsport
Monrovia
LIBERIA
Marshall
Buchanan
River Cess
Greenville
Sastown
Grand Cess
Harper
GROWA POINT
Tchien
Odienné
Korhogo
IVORY COAST
Touba
Man
Katiola
Bouaké
Bondoukou
Bouna
Daloa
Bouaflé
Yamoussoukro
Abengourou
Gagnoa
Agboville
Abidjan
Port-Bouet
Grand-Bassam
Sassandra
Tabou
San-Pédro
GHANA
Wa
Tamale
Yendi
Bolgatanga
Sunyani
Lake Volta
Kete Krachi
Kumasi
Obuasi
Dunkwa
Koforidua
Accra
Tarkwa
Winneba
Cape Coast
Sekondi-Takoradi
Axim
CAPE THREE POINTS
TOGO
Equator
Copyright © by Rand McNally & Co.
Map prepared by Esselte Map Service AB, Stockholm.

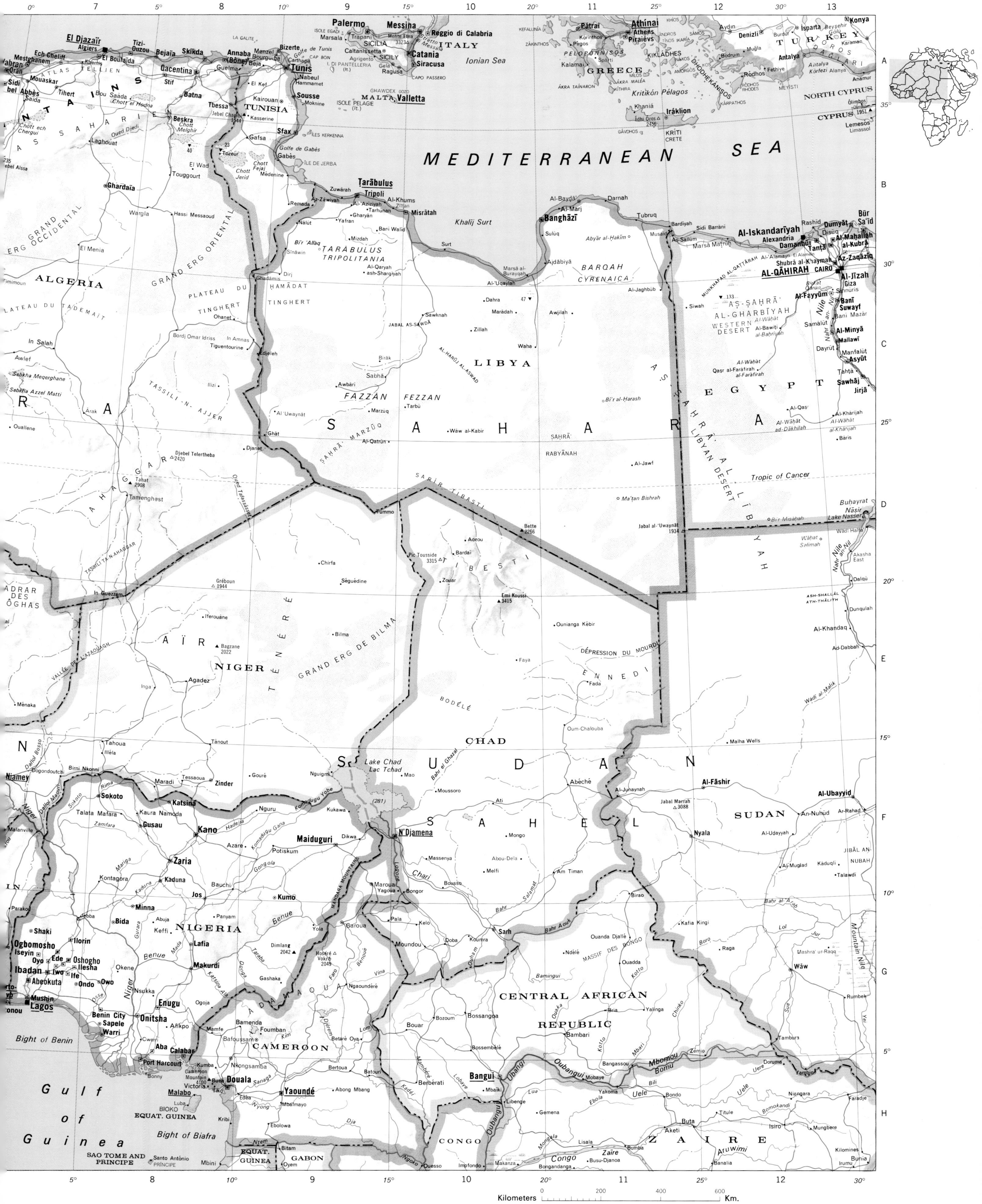

Kilometers 0 200 400 600 Km.

Statute Miles 0 200 400 600 Mi.

Scale 1:12,000,000

One centimeter represents 120 kilometers.

One inch represents approximately 190 miles.

Miller Oblated Stereographic Projection

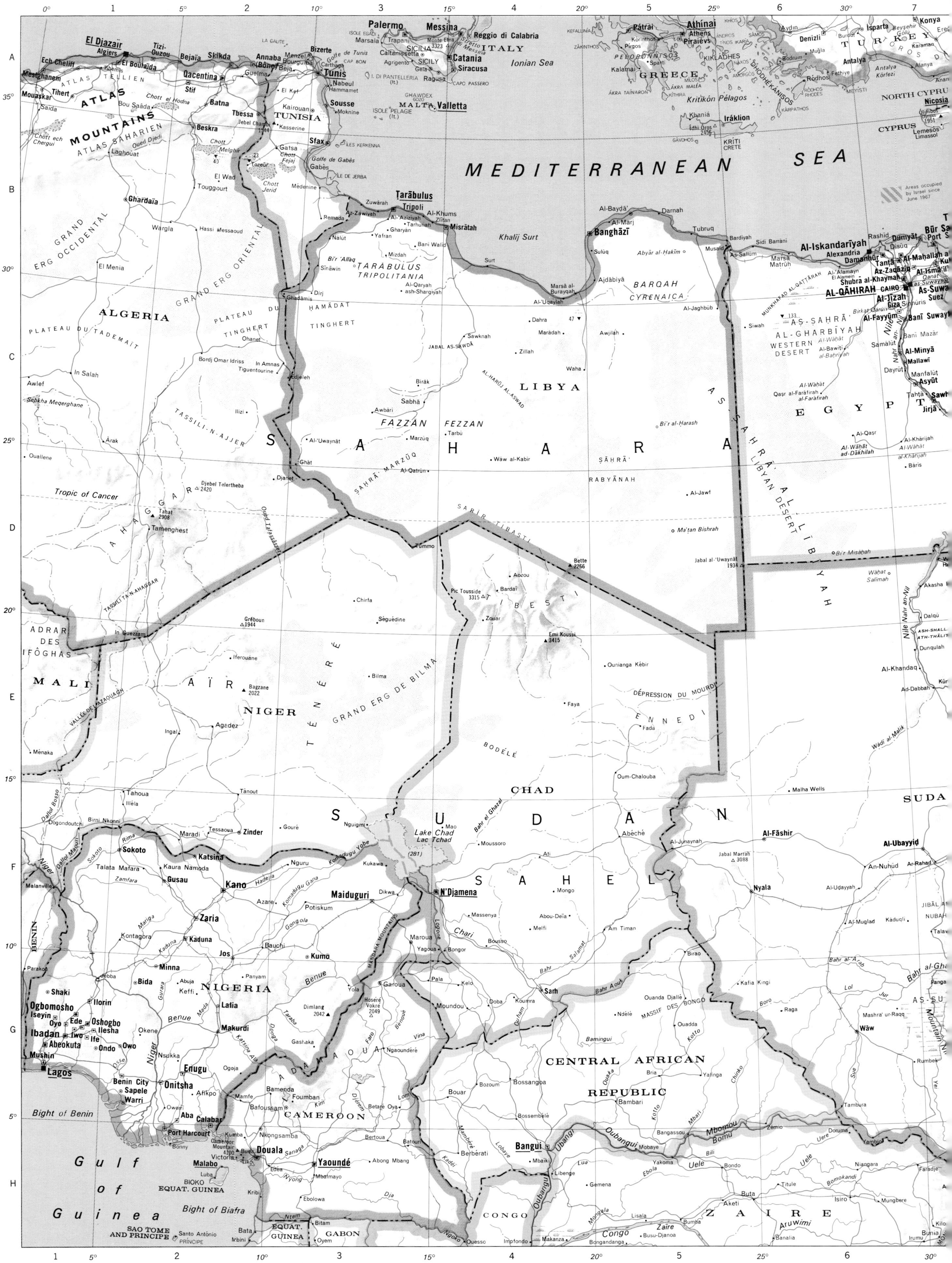
MEDITERRANEAN SEA
Ionian Sea
Khalīj Surt
Gulf of Guinea
Bight of Benin
Bight of Biafra
Tropic of Cancer
ALGERIA
LIBYA
TUNISIA
NIGER
CHAD
NIGERIA
CAMEROON
CENTRAL AFRICAN REPUBLIC
MALI
BENIN
CONGO
GABON
ZAIRE
EQUAT. GUINEA
SAO TOME AND PRINCIPE
EGYPT
SUDAN
GREECE
ITALY
TURKEY
MALTA
CYPRUS
SICILY
SAHARA
SUDAN
SAHEL
ATLAS MOUNTAINS
GRAND ERG OCCIDENTAL
GRAND ERG ORIENTAL
PLATEAU DU TADEMAÏT
PLATEAU DU TINGHERT
HAMĀDAT TINGHERT
TASSILI-N-AJJER
AHAGGAR
AÏR
TÉNÉRÉ
GRAND ERG DE BILMA
TIBESTI
ENNEDI
BODÉLÉ
DÉPRESSION DU MOURDI
FAZZĀN
FEZZAN
ṢAḤRĀ' MARZŪQ
SARĪR TĪBASTĪ
BARQAH
CYRENAICA
AṬ-ṢAḤRĀ' AL-LĪBĪYAH
LIBYAN DESERT
AS-ṢAḤRĀ' AL-GHARBĪYAH
WESTERN DESERT
ADAMAOUA
MASSIF DES BONGO
Lake Chad
Lac Tchad
El Djazaïr
Algiers
Tunis
Ṭarābulus
Tripoli
Banghāzī
Valletta
Athinai
Athens
Al-Qāhirah
Cairo
Al-Iskandarīyah
Alexandria
Niamey
N'Djamena
Lagos
Yaoundé
Bangui
Malabo
Kano
Maiduguri
Zinder
Agadez
Sabhā
Misrātah
Ghadāmis
Tamenghest
Ouargla
Ghardaïa
Palermo
Messina
Catania
Nicosia
Sfax
Gabès
Sousse
Qacentina
Annaba
Batna
Biskra
Zaria
Kaduna
Jos
Ibadan
Ogbomosho
Enugu
Port Harcourt
Calabar
Douala
Garoua
Maroua
Sarh
Abéché
Al-Fāshir
Nyala
Al-Ubayyid
Faya
Bilma
Djanet
Marzūq
Siwah
Asyūṭ
Al-Khārijah
Emi Koussi 3415
Pic Toussidé 3315
Tahat 2908
Bette 2266
Jabal al-'Uwaynāt 1934
Areas occupied by Israel since June 1967

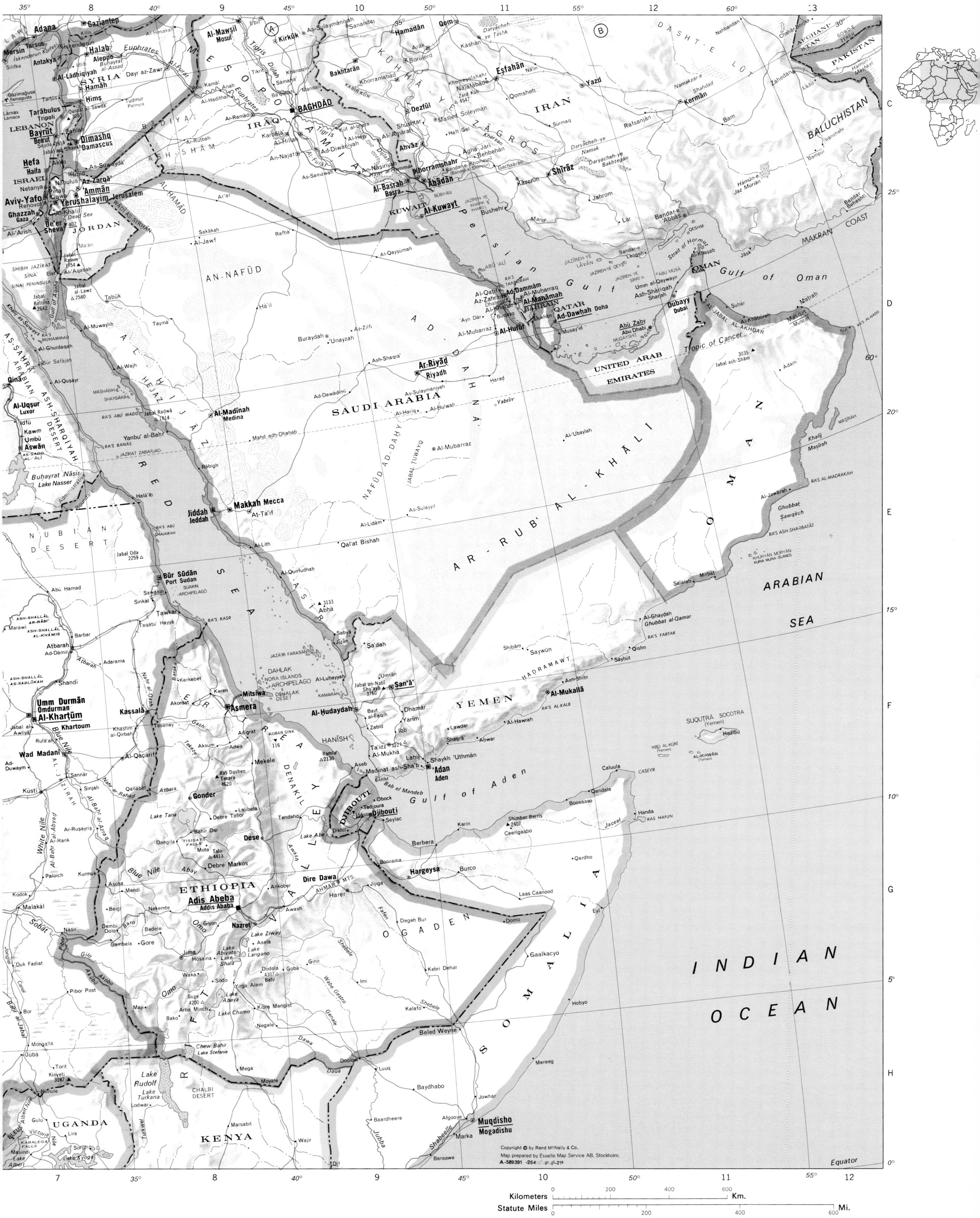

Kilometers 0 200 400 600 Km.

Statute Miles 0 200 400 600 Mi.

Scale 1:12,000,000

One centimeter represents 120 kilometers.
One inch represents approximately 190 miles.

Miller Oblated Stereographic Projection

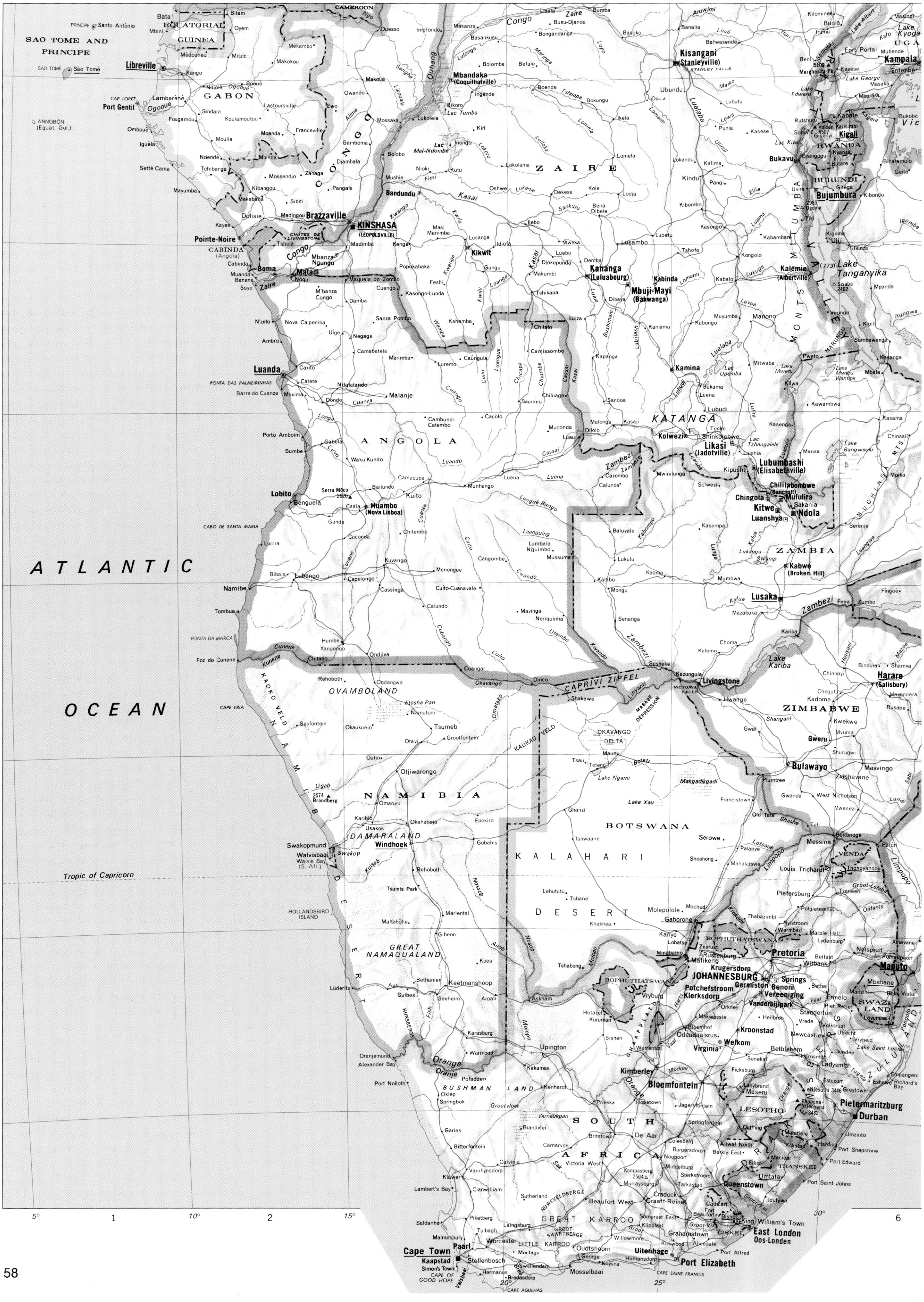
ATLANTIC
OCEAN
SAO TOME AND PRINCIPE
EQUATORIAL GUINEA
GABON
CONGO
ZAIRE
ANGOLA
NAMIBIA
BOTSWANA
ZAMBIA
ZIMBABWE
SOUTH AFRICA
LESOTHO
SWAZILAND
RWANDA
BURUNDI
KATANGA
OVAMBOLAND
DAMARALAND
GREAT NAMAQUALAND
BUSHMAN LAND
KALAHARI DESERT
NAMIB DESERT
KAOKO VELD
GREAT KARROO
LITTLE KARROO
CAPRIVI ZIPFEL
OKAVANGO DELTA
Tropic of Capricorn
Libreville
Port Gentil
Brazzaville
KINSHASA (LÉOPOLDVILLE)
Pointe-Noire
Matadi
Boma
Luanda
Lobito
Huambo (Nova Lisboa)
Kisangani (Stanleyville)
Mbandaka (Coquilhatville)
Bandundu
Kananga (Luluabourg)
Mbuji-Mayi (Bakwanga)
Kalemie (Albertville)
Lake Tanganyika
Bujumbura
Kigali
Kampala
Bukavu
Kolwezi
Likasi (Jadotville)
Lubumbashi (Elisabethville)
Ndola
Kitwe
Kabwe (Broken Hill)
Lusaka
Livingstone
Harare (Salisbury)
Bulawayo
Windhoek
Swakopmund
Walvisbaai Walvis Bay (S. Afr.)
Lüderitz
Keetmanshoop
Gaborone
Pretoria
JOHANNESBURG
Maputo
Mbabane
Kimberley
Bloemfontein
Maseru
Pietermaritzburg
Durban
East London Oos-Londen
Port Elizabeth
Cape Town Kaapstad
CAPE OF GOOD HOPE
CAPE AGULHAS
Congo
Zaire
Kasai
Cuanza
Cunene
Zambezi
Okavango
Limpopo
Orange
Lake Kariba
Lake Ngami
VICTORIA FALLS
5° 10° 15° 20° 25° 30°
0° 5° 10° 15° 20° 25° 30°
A B C D E F G H
1 2 3 4 5 6

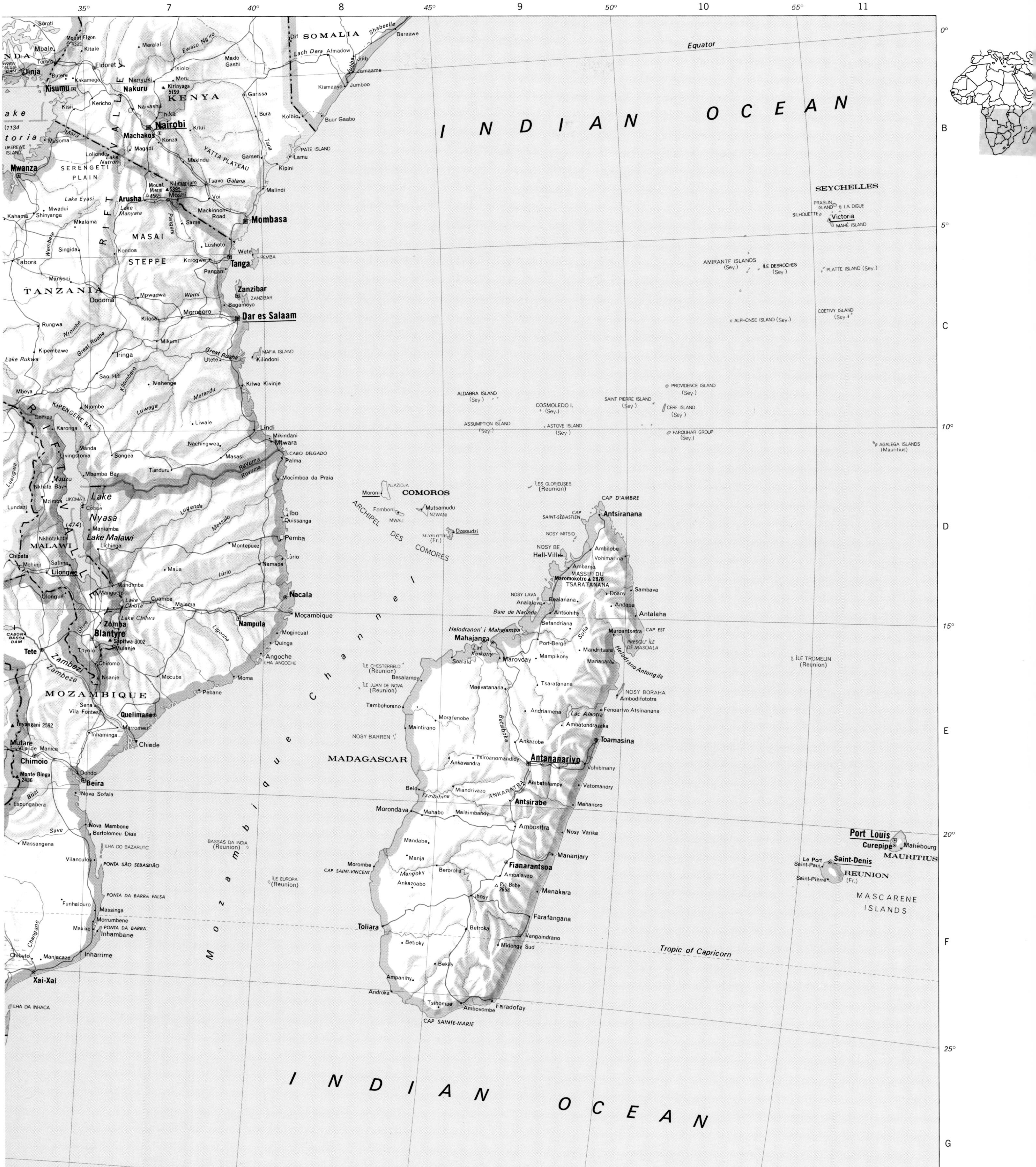

Kilometers 0 200 400 600 Km.

Statute Miles 0 200 400 600 Mi.

Scale 1:12,000,000

One centimeter represents 120 kilometers.

One inch represents approximately 190 miles.

Miller Oblated Stereographic Projection

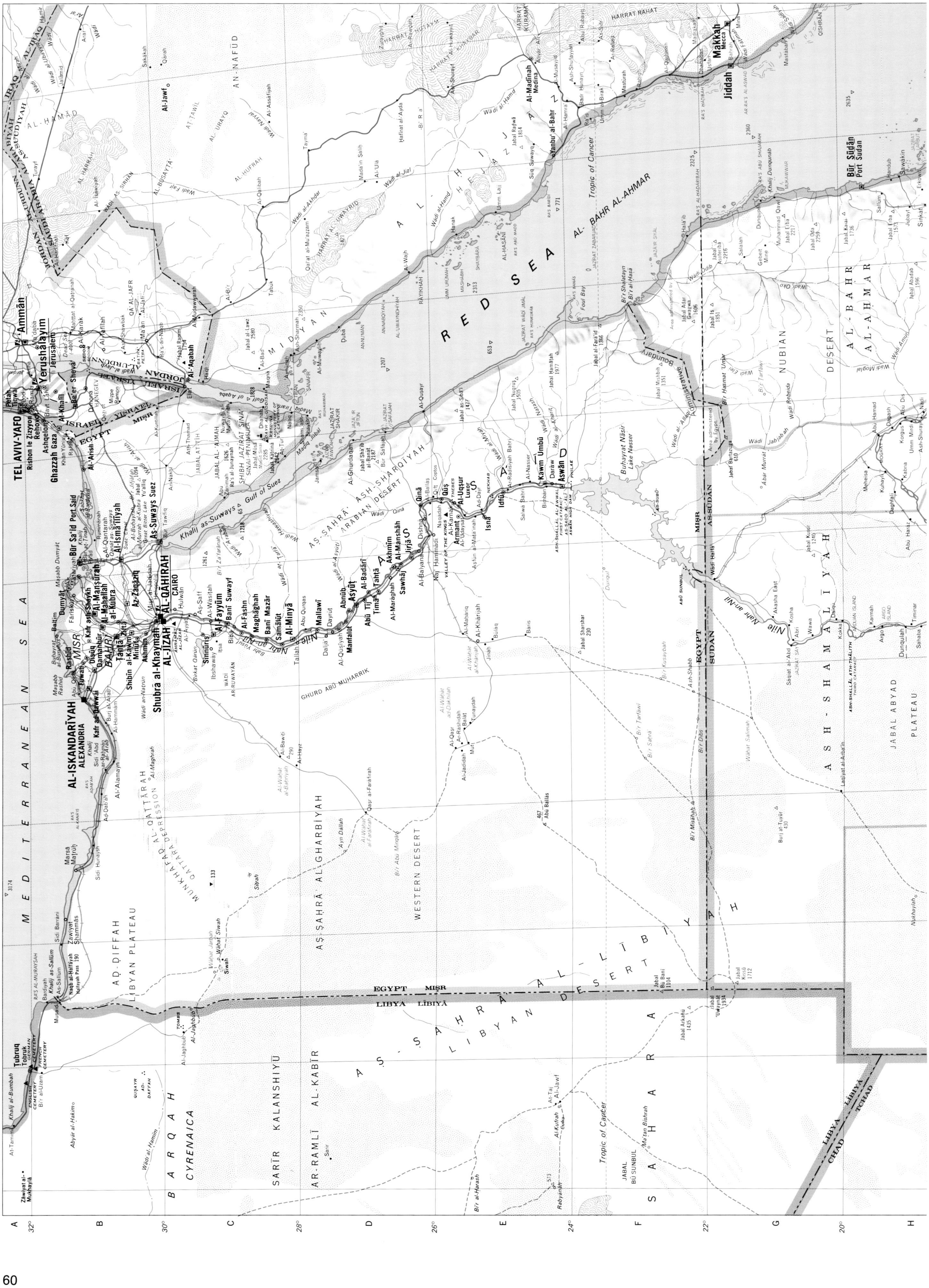
MEDITERRANEAN SEA
RED SEA
AL-BAHR AL-AHMAR
AL-ISKANDARIYAH
ALEXANDRIA
AL-QAHIRAH
CAIRO
AL-JIZAH
Shubra al-Khaymah
Bur Sa'id Port Said
As-Suways Suez
Al-Isma'iliyah
Al-Mansurah
Dumyat
Tanta
Az-Zaqaziq
Al-Fayyum
Bani Suwayf
Al-Minya
Asyut
Sawhaj
Qina
Luxor
Aswan
Isna
Idfu
Kawm Umbu
Wadi Halfa
Bur Sudan
Port Sudan
Jiddah
Makkah
Mecca
Al-Madinah
Medina
Yanbu' al-Bahr
Al-'Aqabah
'Amman
Yerushalayim
Jerusalem
TEL AVIV-YAFO
Ghazzah Gaza
ISRAEL
EGYPT
MISR
SUDAN
AS-SUDAN
LIBYA
LIBIYA
CHAD
TCHAD
JORDAN
IRAQ
SAUDI ARABIA
SHIBH JAZIRAT SINA'
SINAI PENINSULA
AS-SAHRA' ASH-SHARQIYAH
ARABIAN DESERT
AS-SAHRA' AL-GHARBIYAH
WESTERN DESERT
AS-SAHRA' AL-LIBIYAH
LIBYAN DESERT
NUBIAN DESERT
LIBYAN PLATEAU
AD-DIFFAH
MUNKHAFAD AL-QATTARAH
QATTARA DEPRESSION
CYRENAICA
BARQAH
SARIR KALANSHIYU
AR-RAMLI AL-KABIR
Buhayrat Nasir
Lake Nasser
Tropic of Cancer
Nile
Khalij as-Suways
Gulf of Suez
Gulf of Aqaba
Marsa Matruh
Siwah
Tubruq
Tobruk
JABAL ABYAD PLATEAU
AL-HIJAZ

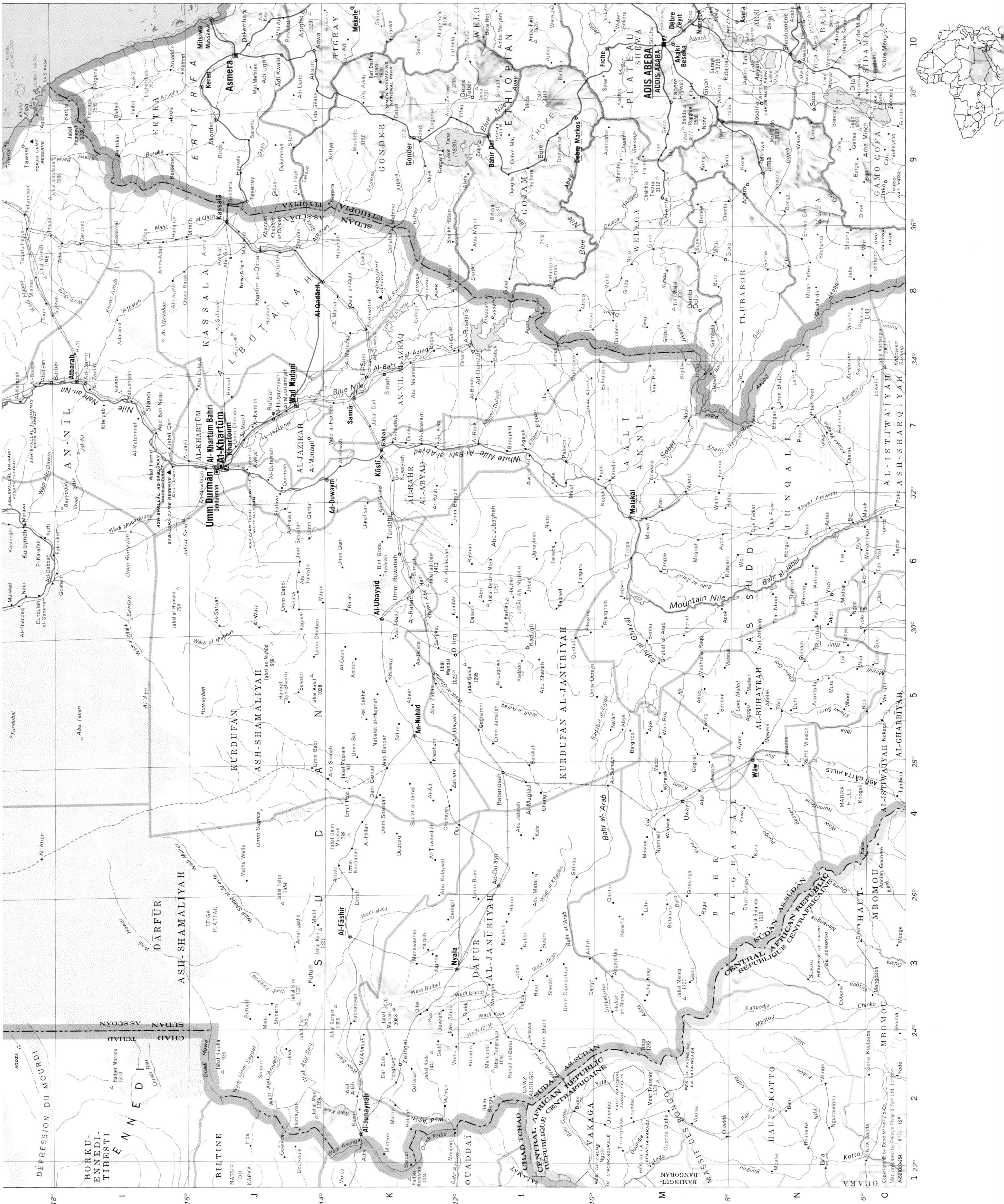

Kilometers 0 100 200 300 Km.

Statute Miles 0 100 200 300 Mi.

Scale 1:6,000,000

One centimeter represents 60 kilometers.
One inch represents approximately 95 miles.
Lambert Azimuthal Equal-Area Projection

Northwestern Africa

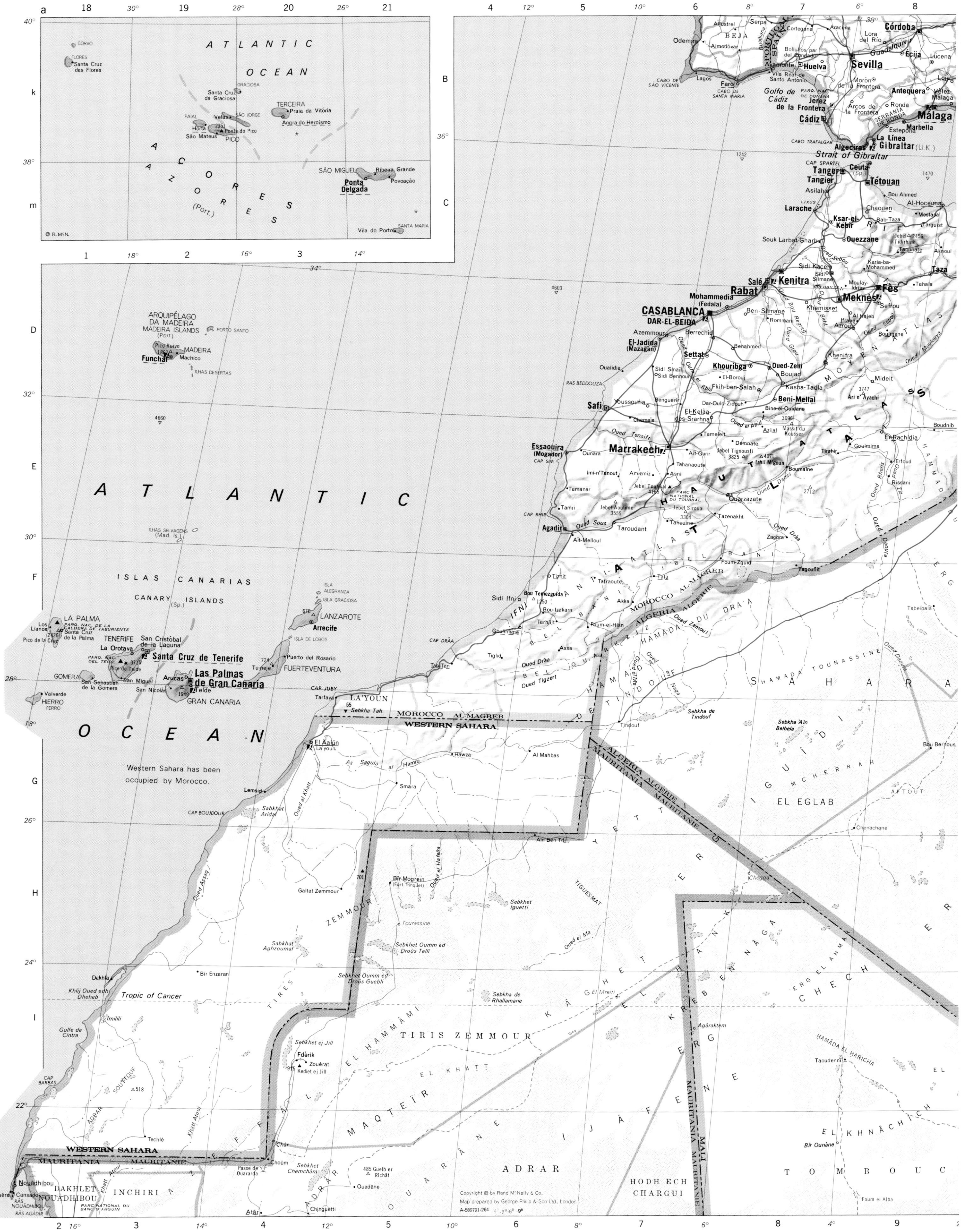

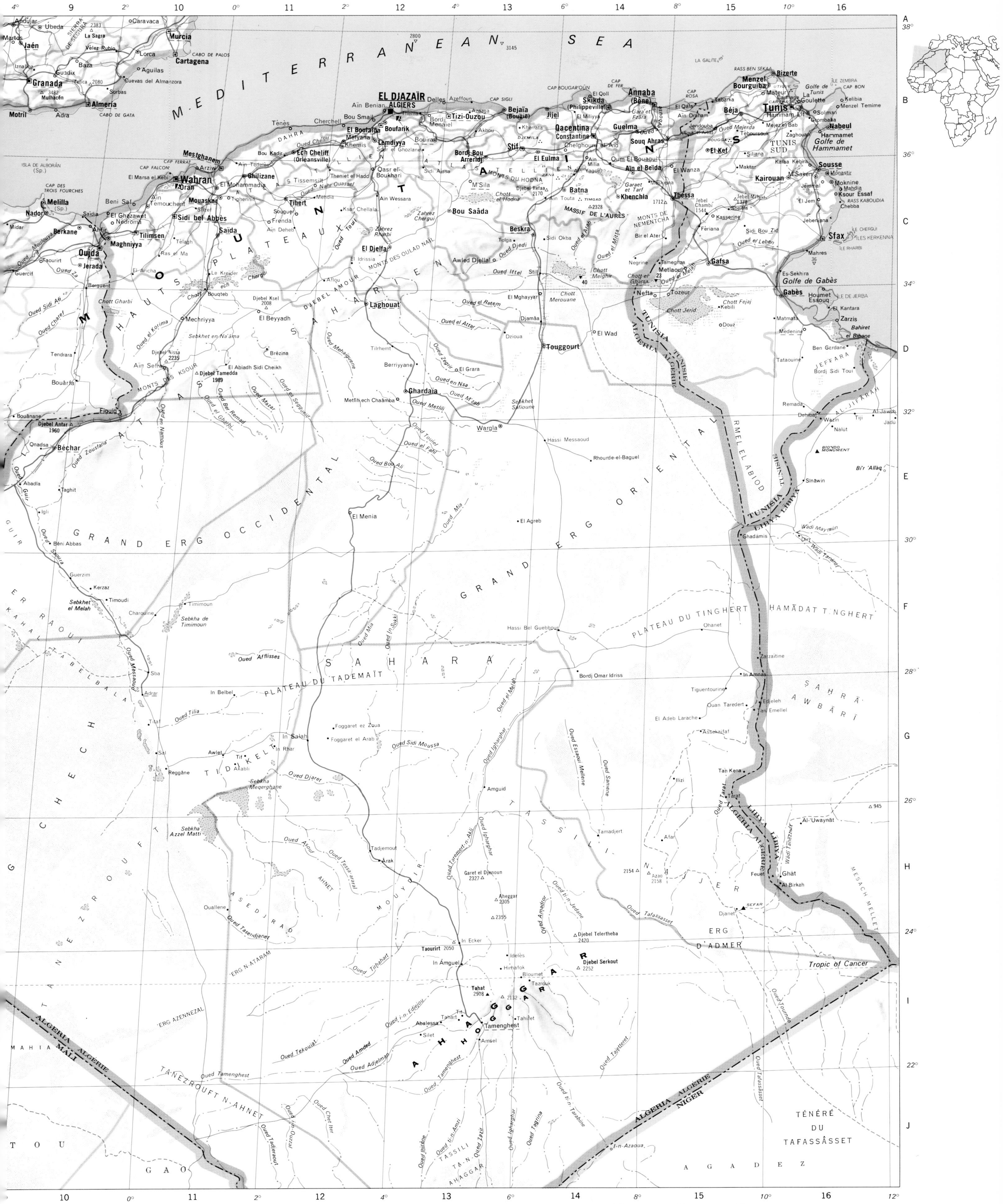

Kilometers 0 100 200 300 Km.

Statute Miles 0 100 200 300 Mi.

Scale 1:6,000,000

One centimeter represents 60 kilometers.
One inch represents approximately 95 miles.

Lambert Azimuthal Equal-Area Projection

West Africa

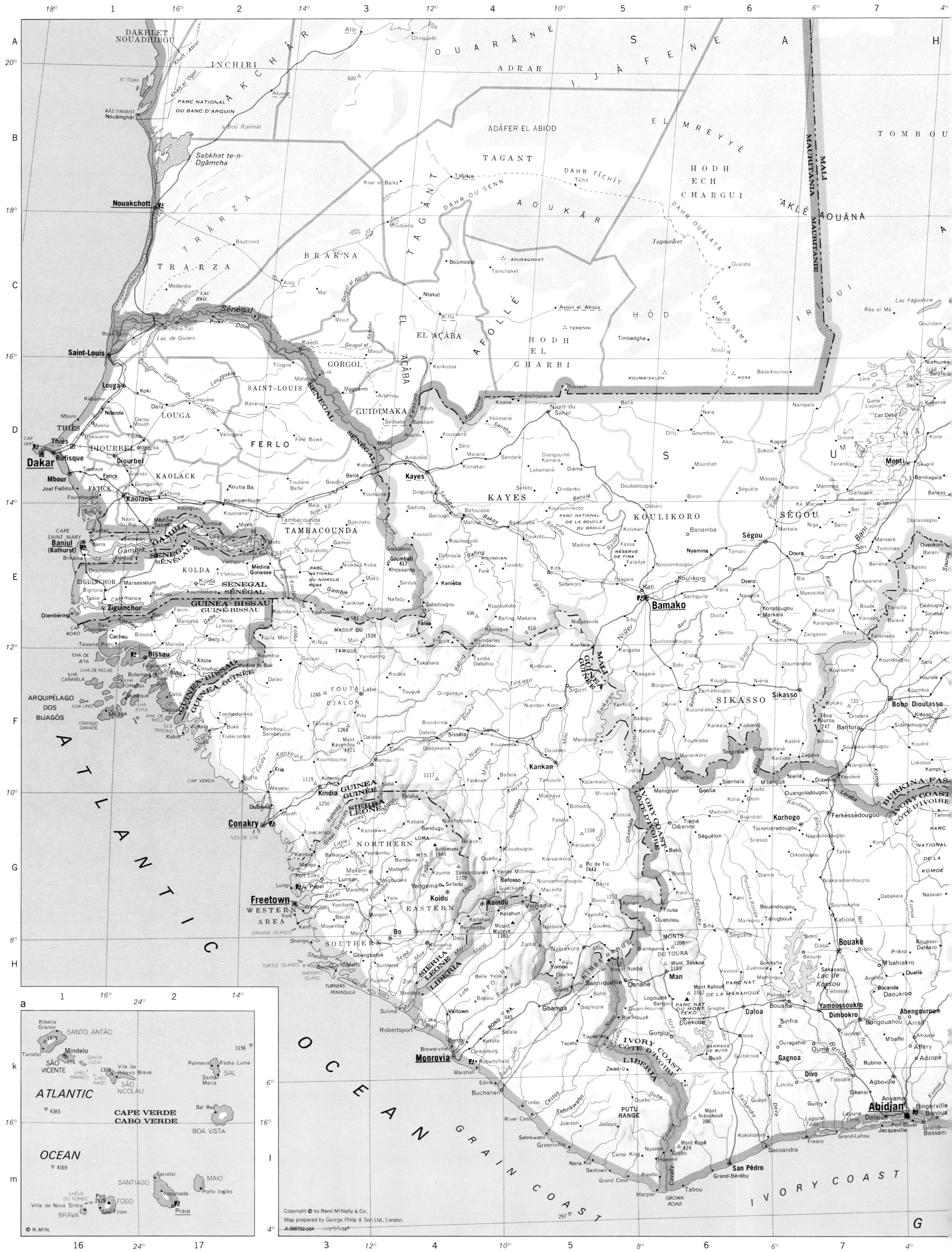

DAKHLET NOUADHIBOU
INCHIRI
PARC NATIONAL DU BANC D'ARGUIN
ADRAR
ADÂFER EL ABIOD
TAGANT
TRARZA
BRAKNA
GORGOL
GUIDIMAKA
HODH ECH CHARGUI
HODH EL GHARBI
MALI
MAURITANIA
MAURITANIE
Nouakchott
Saint-Louis
Louga
Thiès
Dakar
Rufisque
Mbour
DIOURBEL
KAOLACK
FERLO
SAINT-LOUIS
SÉNÉGAL
TAMBACOUNDA
KOLDA
Kayes
KAYES
KOULIKORO
Bamako
Ségou
SÉGOU
SIKASSO
Sikasso
Mopti
Banjul (Bathurst)
GAMBIA
GUINEA-BISSAU
GUINÉ-BISSAU
Bissau
Ziguinchor
ARQUIPÉLAGO DOS BIJAGÓS
GUINEA
GUINÉE
Conakry
Labé
Kankan
SIERRA LEONE
Freetown
WESTERN AREA
NORTHERN
EASTERN
SOUTHERN
Bo
LIBERIA
Monrovia
Buchanan
IVORY COAST
CÔTE D'IVOIRE
Abidjan
Bouaké
Yamoussoukro
San Pédro
ATLANTIC OCEAN
GRAIN COAST
IVORY COAST
CAPE VERDE
CABO VERDE
SANTO ANTÃO
SÃO VICENTE
SÃO NICOLAU
SAL
BOA VISTA
MAIO
SANTIAGO
FOGO
BRAVA
Praia
Mindelo
ATLANTIC
OCEAN
Copyright © by Rand McNally & Co.
Map prepared by George Philip & Son Ltd., London.

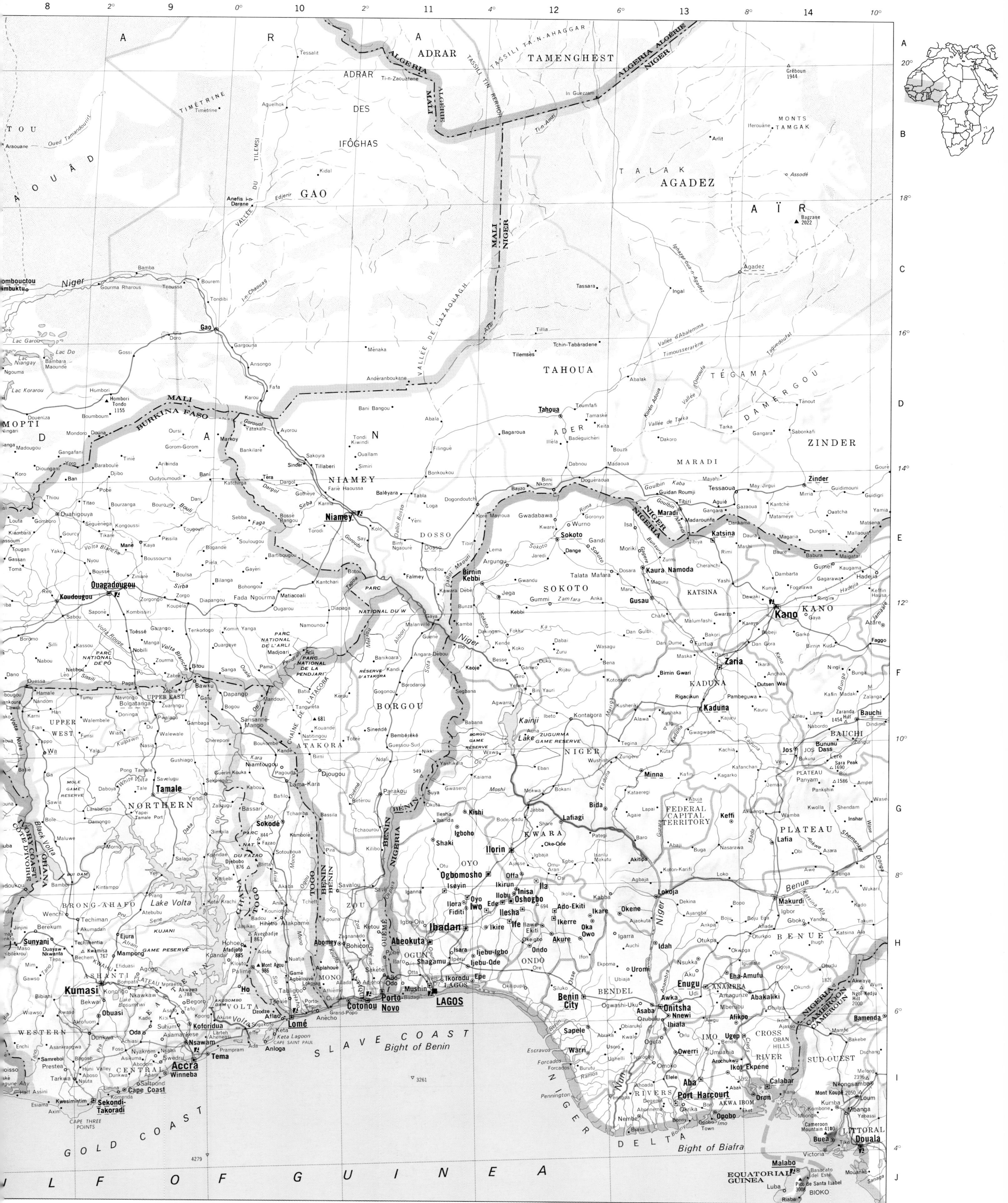

Kilometers 0 100 200 300 Km.

Statute Miles 0 100 200 300 Mi.

Scale 1:6,000,000

One centimeter represents 60 kilometers.

One inch represents approximately 95 miles.

Lambert Azimuthal Equal-Area Projection

Southern Africa and Madagascar

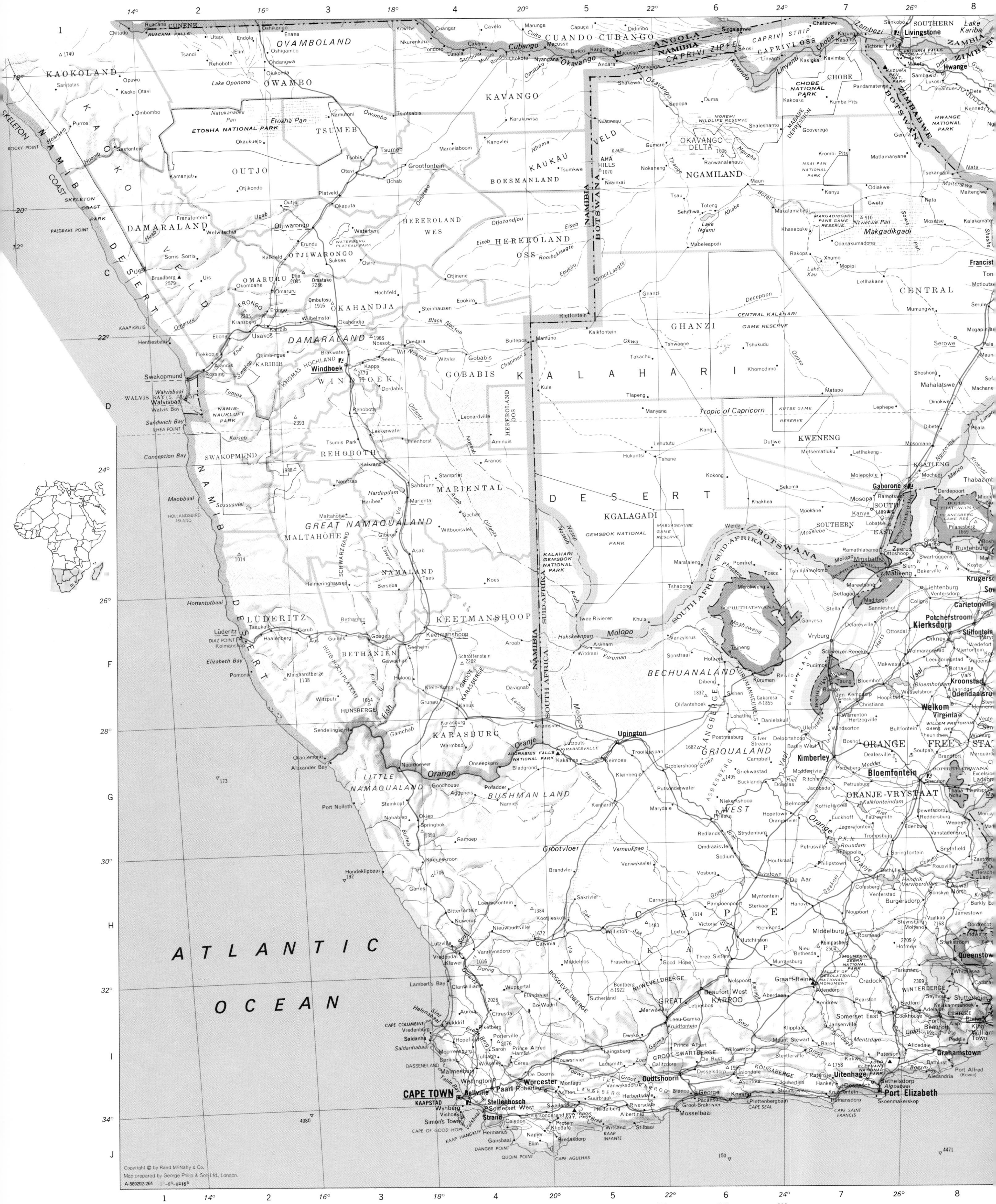

Kilometers 0 100 200 300 Km.

Statute Miles 0 100 200 300 Mi.

Scale 1:6,000,000

One centimeter represents 60 kilometers.
One inch represents approximately 95 miles.

Lambert Azimuthal Equal-Area Projection

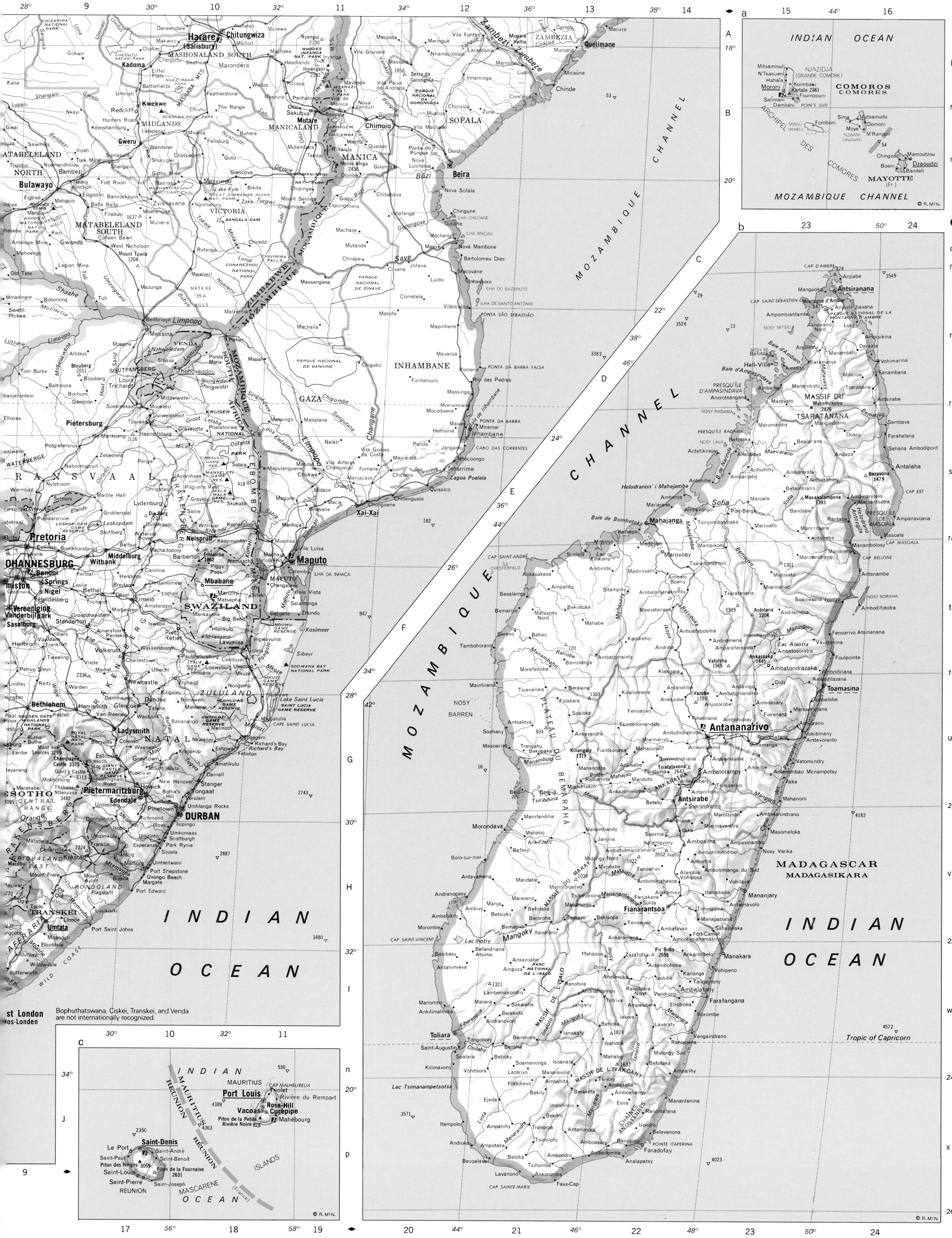

INDIAN OCEAN
MOZAMBIQUE CHANNEL
MADAGASCAR
MADAGASIKARA
Antananarivo
Toamasina
Mahajanga
Antsiranana
Fianarantsoa
Toliara
Antsirabe
MASSIF DU TSARATANANA
PLATEAU DU BEMARAHA
Tropic of Capricorn
CAP SAINTE-MARIE
CAP D'AMBRE
Harare (Salisbury)
Bulawayo
Beira
Maputo
Chimoio
Quelimane
Xai-Xai
Inhambane
Pretoria
Mbabane
SWAZILAND
DURBAN
Pietermaritzburg
Ladysmith
Umtata
TRANSKEI
NATAL
MANICA
SOFALA
GAZA
INHAMBANE
ZAMBEZIA
MASHONALAND SOUTH
MIDLANDS
MATABELELAND SOUTH
VICTORIA
MANICALAND
Limpopo
Zambeze
Save
COMOROS
COMORES
Moroni
Dzaoudzi
MAYOTTE (Fr.)
ARCHIPEL DES COMORES
MAURITIUS
Port Louis
RÉUNION (France)
Saint-Denis
MASCARENE ISLANDS
Bophuthatswana, Ciskei, Transkei, and Venda are not internationally recognized.
© R. McN.

PACIFIC OCEAN
Km.
Mi.
INDONESIA
NEW GUINEA
PAPUA NEW GUINEA
BISMARCK ARCHIPELAGO
NEW BRITAIN
Arafura Sea
Gulf of Carpentaria
Coral Sea
Torres Strait
Gulf of Papua
Port Moresby
Jayapura (Sukarnapura)
Puncak Jaya 5030m
Puncak Trikora 4750m
Mt. Giluwe 4368m
Mt. Wilhelm 4509m
Mount Ulawun 2334m
Equator
AUSTRALIA
©1979 R.M.&N.
Timor Sea
Savu Sea
Laut Sawu
TIMOR
Kupang
Joseph Bonaparte Gulf
Darwin
ARNHEM LAND
Arafura
MELVILLE ISLAND
BATHURST ISLAND
KIMBERLEY PLATEAU
KING LEOPOLD RANGES
DURACK RANGES
Wyndham
Kununurra
Lake Argyle
Derby
Broome
Fitzroy Crossing
Halls Creek
INDIAN OCEAN
EIGHTY MILE BEACH
Port Hedland
DAMPIER ARCHIPELAGO
BARROW ISLAND
Roebourne
Dampier
Karratha
GREAT SANDY DESERT
TANAMI DESERT
NORTHERN TERRITORY
Lake Gregory
Lake Mackay
Lake Disappointment
Lake Macdonald
MACDONNELL RANGES
Lake Amadeus
Mount Olga 1069
Ayers Rock 867
GIBSON DESERT
WESTERN AUSTRALIA
HAMERSLEY RANGE
Mount Bruce 1235
Mount Meharry 1251
Newman
Tropic of Capricorn
Carnarvon
Shark Bay
Lake Macleod
ROBINSON RANGE
Lake Carnegie
Wiluna
Meekatharra
GREAT VICTORIA DESERT
Geraldton
Lake Barlee
Kalgoorlie
Boulder
NULLARBOR PLAIN
Eucla
Forrest
DARLING RANGE
Wanneroo
Perth
Fremantle
Bunbury
Albany
Esperance
Great Australian Bight
SOUTHERN OCEAN
Copyright © by Rand McNally & Co.
Map prepared by Esselte Map Service AB, Stockholm.

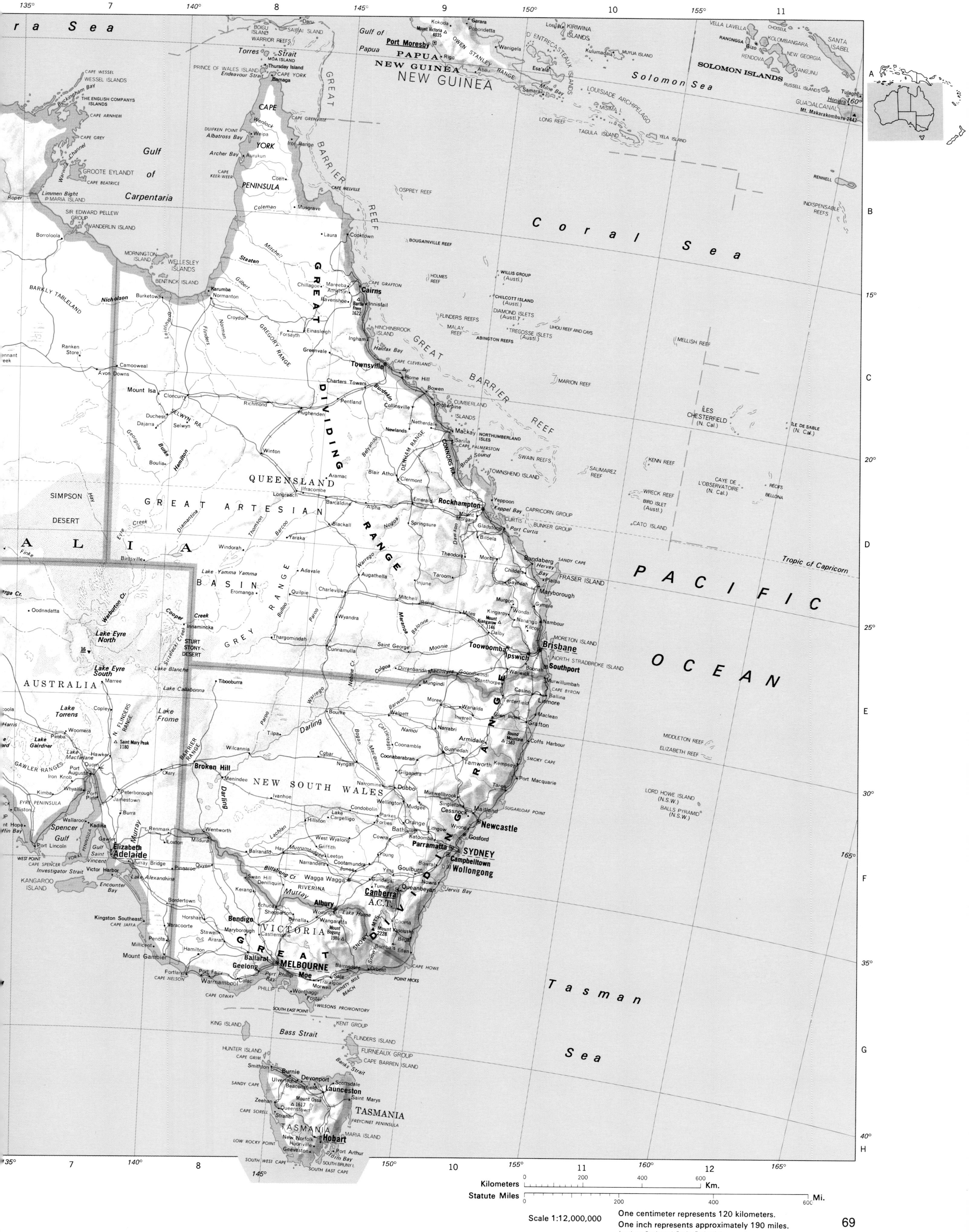

Kilometers 0 200 400 600 Km.

Statute Miles 0 200 400 600 Mi.

Scale 1:12,000,000

One centimeter represents 120 kilometers.
One inch represents approximately 190 miles.

Lambert Conformal Conic Projection

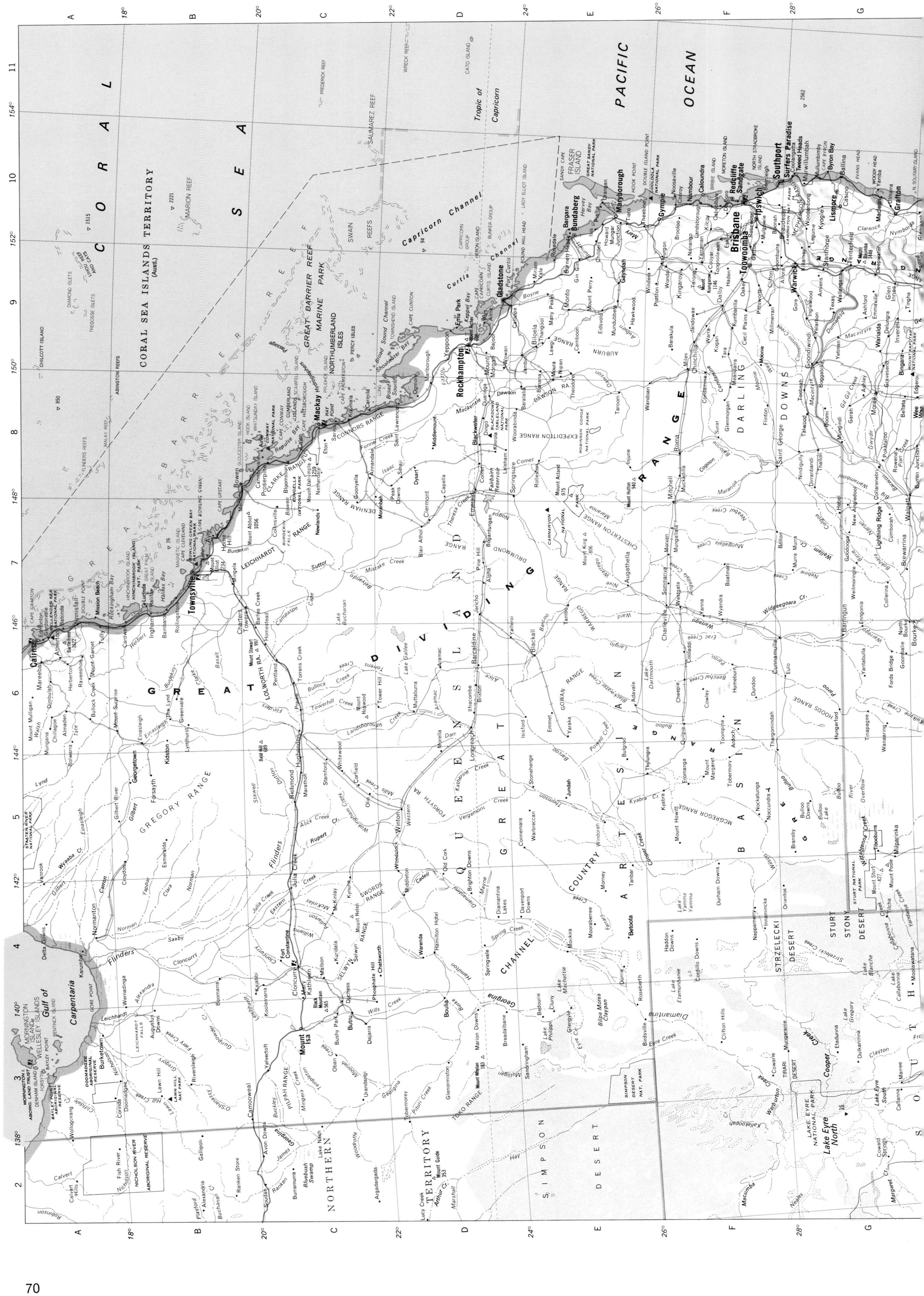
CORAL SEA
PACIFIC OCEAN
Tropic of Capricorn
CORAL SEA ISLANDS TERRITORY (Austl.)
GREAT BARRIER REEF
GREAT BARRIER REEF MARINE PARK
Capricorn Channel
SWAIN REEFS
MARION REEF
WILLIS ISLETS
FRASER ISLAND
Gulf of Carpentaria
MORNINGTON ISLAND
WELLESLEY ISLANDS
GREAT DIVIDING RANGE
GREAT ARTESIAN BASIN
QUEENSLAND
NORTHERN TERRITORY
SIMPSON DESERT
CHANNEL COUNTRY
DARLING DOWNS
GREGORY RANGE
STURT STONY DESERT
STRZELECKI DESERT
Cairns
Townsville
Mackay
Rockhampton
Gladstone
Bundaberg
Maryborough
Gympie
Brisbane
Ipswich
Toowoomba
Southport
Surfers Paradise
Warwick
Lismore
Grafton
Mount Isa
Cloncurry
Charters Towers
Hughenden
Longreach
Winton
Barcaldine
Emerald
Roma
Charleville
Cunnamulla
Birdsville
Boulia
Normanton
Burketown
Camooweal
Bowen
Proserpine
Ingham
Tully
Innisfail
Lake Eyre North
Lake Eyre South

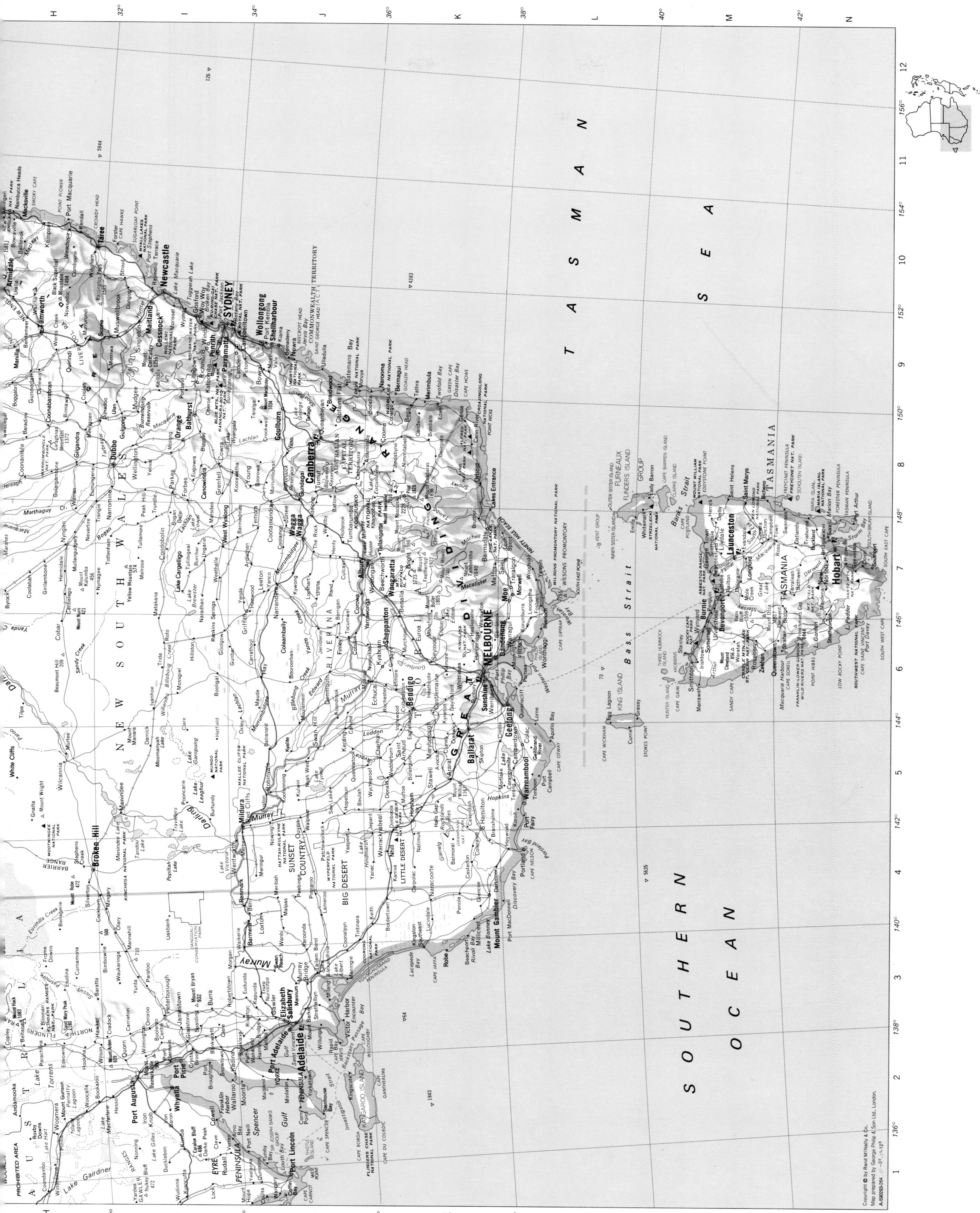

Kilometers 0 100 200 300 Km.

Statute Miles 0 100 200 300 Mi.

Scale 1:6,000,000

One centimeter represents 60 kilometers.
One inch represents approximately 95 miles.
Lambert Conformal Conic Projection

New Zealand

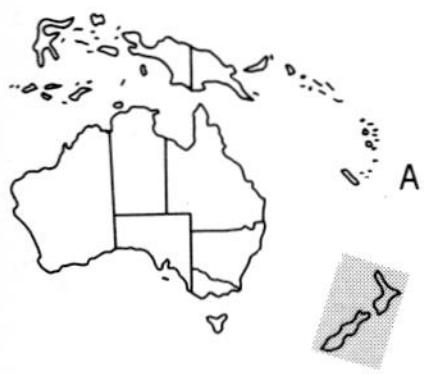

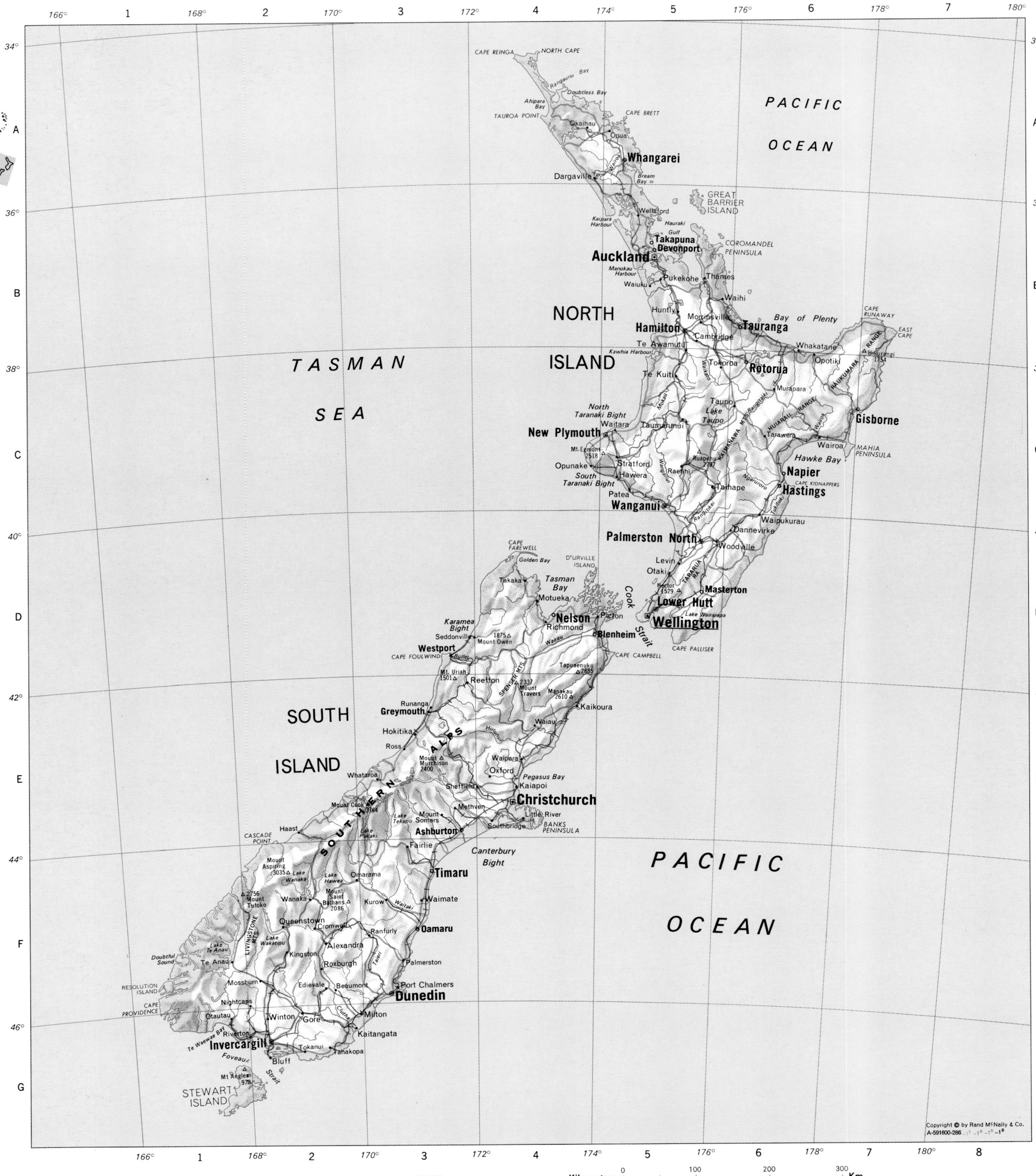

Scale 1:6,000,000

One centimeter represents 60 kilometers.
One inch represents approximately 95 miles.
Lambert Conformal Conic Projection

Kilometers 0 100 200 300 Km.
Statute Miles 0 100 200 300 Mi.

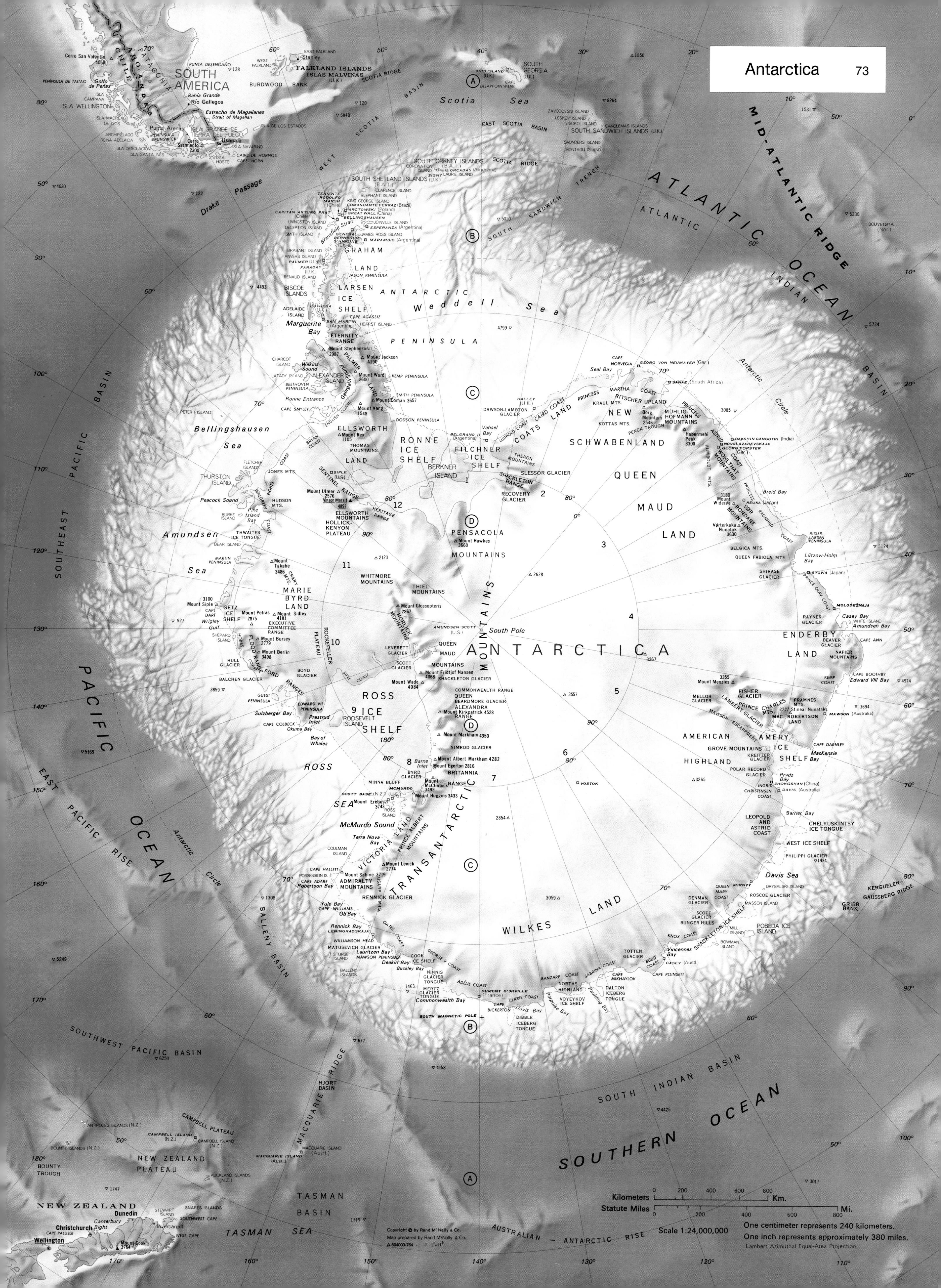
SOUTH AMERICA
FALKLAND ISLANDS
ISLAS MALVINAS
Scotia Sea
SOUTH GEORGIA
SOUTH ORKNEY ISLANDS
SOUTH SHETLAND ISLANDS
SOUTH SANDWICH ISLANDS
Drake Passage
MID-ATLANTIC RIDGE
ATLANTIC OCEAN
GRAHAM LAND
LARSEN ICE SHELF
ANTARCTIC PENINSULA
Weddell Sea
Bellingshausen Sea
ALEXANDER ISLAND
ELLSWORTH LAND
RONNE ICE SHELF
FILCHNER ICE SHELF
BERKNER ISLAND
COATS LAND
NEW SCHWABENLAND
QUEEN MAUD LAND
ELLSWORTH MOUNTAINS
Vinson Massif 4897
PENSACOLA MOUNTAINS
Amundsen Sea
MARIE BYRD LAND
WHITMORE MOUNTAINS
THIEL MOUNTAINS
South Pole
ANTARCTICA
TRANSANTARCTIC MOUNTAINS
ENDERBY LAND
AMERICAN HIGHLAND
AMERY ICE SHELF
ROSS ICE SHELF
ROSS SEA
McMurdo Sound
VICTORIA LAND
WILKES LAND
Davis Sea
SOUTH MAGNETIC POLE
PACIFIC OCEAN
SOUTHERN OCEAN
SOUTH INDIAN BASIN
SOUTHWEST PACIFIC BASIN
NEW ZEALAND PLATEAU
NEW ZEALAND
TASMAN BASIN
TASMAN SEA
AUSTRALIAN - ANTARCTIC RISE
Antarctic Circle
Kilometers 0 200 400 600 800 Km.
Statute Miles 0 200 400 600 800 Mi.
Scale 1:24,000,000
One centimeter represents 240 kilometers.
One inch represents approximately 380 miles.
Lambert Azimuthal Equal-Area Projection

NORTH AMERICA
UNITED STATES
ROCKY MTS.
APPALACHIAN MOUNTAINS
GREAT PLAINS
OZARK PLATEAU
EDWARDS PLATEAU
Omaha
Des Moines
CHICAGO
CLEVELAND
NEW YORK
PHILADELPHIA
Baltimore
WASHINGTON
Chesapeake Bay
Norfolk
Pittsburgh
Indianapolis
Cincinnati
Charleston
Louisville
Kansas City
ST. LOUIS
Denver
Cheyenne
Pikes Peak 4301
Wichita
Oklahoma City
Santa Fe
Albuquerque
Nashville
Chattanooga
Memphis
Little Rock
Birmingham
Atlanta
Richmond
Raleigh
Charlotte
Columbia
Charleston
Savannah
Montgomery
Jackson
Shreveport
Dallas
Fort Worth
Mobile
New Orleans
Jacksonville
Tampa
Miami
Houston
San Antonio
Laredo
Brownsville
El Paso
CAPE HATTERAS
CAPE LOOKOUT
CAPE FEAR
CAPE CANAVERAL
CAPE SABLE
Lake Okeechobee
LONG ISLAND
GEORGES BANK
BLAKE RIDGE
BLAKE PLATEAU
MEXICO
SIERRA MADRE ORIENTAL
SIERRA MADRE DEL SUR
Monterrey
Matamoros
Torreón
Tampico
Guadalajara
Laguna de Chapala
CIUDAD DE MEXICO
MEXICO CITY
Puebla
Veracruz
Pico de Orizaba 5610
Oaxaca
Acapulco
Villahermosa
Mérida
YUCATAN PENINSULA
Bahía de Campeche
CAMPECHE BANK
GULF OF MEXICO
MEXICO BASIN
Canal de Yucatán
Straits of Florida
BAHAMAS
GRAND BAHAMA
ABACO
ELEUTHERA
Nassau
ANDROS
CAT ISLAND
SAN SALVADOR
GREAT BAHAMA BANK
GREAT INAGUA
WEST INDIES
CUBA
La Habana
Havana
ISLA DE LA JUVENTUD
Santiago de Cuba
Guantánamo
CAYMAN ISLANDS (U.K.)
CAYMAN TRENCH
GREATER ANTILLES
JAMAICA
Kingston
Windward Passage
HISPANIOLA
HAITI
Port-au-Prince
DOMINICAN REPUBLIC
Pico Duarte 3175
Santo Domingo
Canal de la Mona
PUERTO RICO (U.S.)
San Juan
PUERTO RICO TRENCH
VIRGIN ISLANDS
LEEWARD ISLANDS
ANTIGUA AND BARBUDA
MONTSERRAT (U.K.)
GUADELOUPE (Fr.)
DOMINICA
MARTINIQUE (Fr.)
Fort-de-France
SAINT LUCIA
BARBADOS
Bridgetown
SAINT VINCENT AND THE GRENADINES
GRENADA
WINDWARD ISLANDS
LESSER ANTILLES
TRINIDAD AND TOBAGO
Port of Spain
ARUBA (Neth.)
CURAÇAO
BONAIRE
NETHERLANDS ANTILLES
VENEZUELAN BASIN
CARIBBEAN SEA
COLOMBIAN BASIN
BELIZE
Belize City
Belmopan
Gulf of Honduras
GUATEMALA
Guatemala
Volcán Tajumulco 4220
HONDURAS
Tegucigalpa
EL SALVADOR
San Salvador
NICARAGUA
Managua
Lago de Nicaragua
Bluefields
COSTA RICA
San José
Volcán Barú 3475
PANAMA
Panamá
Colón
Golfo de Panamá
ISTMO DE PANAMÁ
Golfo de Tehuantepec
MIDDLE AMERICA TRENCH
TEHUANTEPEC RIDGE
GUATEMALA BASIN
PANAMA BASIN
COCOS RIDGE
ISLA DEL COCO (C.R.)
ISLA DE MALPELO (Col.)
COLÓN RIDGE
CARNEGIE RIDGE
ARCHIPIÉLAGO DE COLÓN
GALAPAGOS ISLANDS (Ec.)
ISLA FERNANDINA
ISLA ISABELA
ISLA SANTIAGO
ISLA SANTA CRUZ
ISLA SAN CRISTÓBAL
Equator
SOUTH AMERICA
VENEZUELA
CARACAS
Maracaibo
Lago de Maracaibo
Golfo de Venezuela
Barquisimeto
Barcelona
Ciudad Bolívar
Ciudad Guayana
Pico Bolívar 5007
San Cristóbal
Orinoco
Apure
Meta
Arauca
Embalse de Guri
SALTO ANGEL ANGEL FALLS
Puerto Ayacucho
San Fernando de Atabapo
Cerro Marahuaca 2579
LLANOS
COLOMBIA
SANTA FE DE BOGOTÁ
Barranquilla
Cartagena
Pico Cristóbal Colón 5800
Cúcuta
Bucaramanga
Medellín
Manizales
Nevado del Tolima 5215
Cali
Buenaventura
CORDILLERA OCCIDENTAL
CORDILLERA ORIENTAL
Magdalena
Cauca
Guaviare
Mitú
Caquetá
Putumayo
GUYANA
Georgetown
Cuyuni
Essequibo
KAIETEUR FALL
Mount Roraima 2875
PAKARAIMA MTS.
SURINAME
Paramaribo
FRENCH GUIANA
Cayenne
CABO ORANGE
Oiapoque
TUMUC-HUMAC MTS.
ECUADOR
Quito
Cayambe 5790
Chimborazo 6310
Cuenca
Guayaquil
Golfo de Guayaquil
Esmeraldas
PUNTA GALERA
Tumaco
Loja
PERU
LIMA
Iquitos
Chiclayo
Trujillo
Huaraz
Nevado Huascarán 6746
Nevado Yerupaja 6634
Cerro de Pasco
Huancayo
Pucallpa
Cajamarca
Cuzco
Ica
Arequipa
Nevado Coropuna 6305
Volcán Misti 5822
Lago Titicaca
Puno
PUNTA PARIÑAS
PUNTA NEGRA
PUNTA CARRETA
Marañón
Ucayali
Napo
ANDES
PERU-CHILE TRENCH
BOLIVIA
La Paz
Nevado Illampu 6421
Cochabamba
CORD.
Riberalta
Guajará-Mirim
Trinidad
Beni
Mamoré
Madre de Dios
Puerto Maldonado
Cobija
Rio Branco
BRAZIL
SELVAS
Amazon
Amazonas
Negro
Japurá
Branco
Boa Vista
Pico da Neblina 3014
Represa Balbina
Manaus
Óbidos
Santarém
Porto de Moz
Fonte Boa
Içá
Solimões
Leticia
Javari
Yavari
Juruá
Purus
Madeira
Porto Velho
Aripuanã
Tapajós
Juruena
Iriri
Xingu
SA. DO CACHIMBO
São Manuel
SA. FORMOSA
Guaporé
Itenes
Mato Grosso
Cuiabá
Paraguai
PLANALTO DO MATO GROSSO
Jari
Amapá
ILHA DE MARACÁ
ILHA CAVIANA DE FORA
CABO MAGUARI
ILHA DE MARAJÓ
Macapá
Pará
Belém
Tocantins
Araguaia
Marabá
Carolina
CHAPADA DAS MANGABEIRAS
Porto Nacional
ILHA DO BANANAL
Brasília
Goiânia
São Luís
Parnaíba
Teresina
Fortaleza
Paulistana
Juàzeiro
Represa de Sobradinho
São Francisco
Barra
Pico das Almas 1836
Paraguaçu
Itabuna
Pardo
ESPINHAÇO
Montes Claros
Belmonte
Campina Grande
Caruaru
João Pessoa
PONTA DO SEIXAS
Natal
Recife
Maceió
Penedo
Aracaju
Salvador
ATOL DAS ROCAS
ILHA FERNANDO DE NORONHA (Braz.)
CABO DE SÃO ROQUE
ATLANTIC OCEAN
NORTH AMERICAN BASIN
BERMUDA (U.K.)
BERMUDA RISE
Sargasso Sea
Kelvin Seamount
Rehoboth Seamount 1235
Muir Seamount
Yakutat Seamount 1133
Great Meteor Tablemount 269
MID-ATLANTIC RIDGE
Tropic of Cancer
AZORES
AÇORES AZORES (Port.)
AZORES PLATEAU
FLORES
TERCEIRA
PICO
SÃO MIGUEL
SANTA MARIA
CAPE VERDE BASIN
GUIANA BASIN

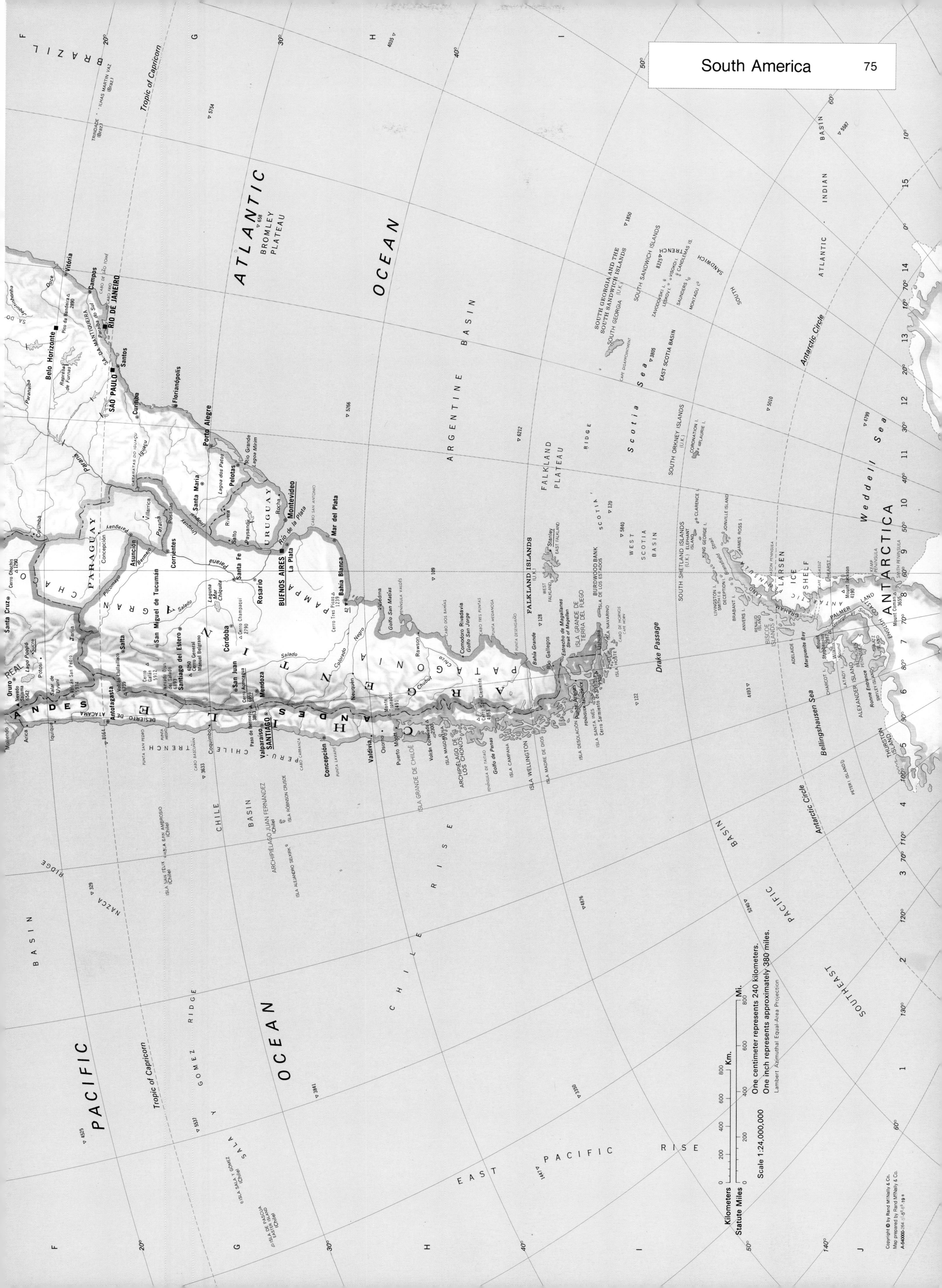
ATLANTIC OCEAN
PACIFIC OCEAN
ARGENTINE BASIN
CHILE BASIN
CHILE RISE
EAST PACIFIC RISE
SOUTHEAST PACIFIC BASIN
ATLANTIC - INDIAN BASIN
BROMLEY PLATEAU
FALKLAND PLATEAU
SCOTIA RIDGE
Scotia Sea
Weddell Sea
Bellingshausen Sea
Drake Passage
Antarctic Circle
Tropic of Capricorn
NAZCA RIDGE
SALA Y GOMEZ RIDGE
BRAZIL
PARAGUAY
URUGUAY
ARGENTINA
CHILE
ANDES
PATAGONIA
PAMPAS
GRAN CHACO
ANTARCTICA
LARSEN ICE SHELF
PALMER LAND
FALKLAND ISLANDS (U.K.)
SOUTH GEORGIA AND THE SOUTH SANDWICH ISLANDS (U.K.)
SOUTH ORKNEY ISLANDS
SOUTH SHETLAND ISLANDS
SOUTH SANDWICH ISLANDS
SOUTH SANDWICH TRENCH
ISLA GRANDE DE TIERRA DEL FUEGO
ARCHIPIÉLAGO JUAN FERNÁNDEZ (Chile)
ISLA DE PASCUA (EASTER ISLAND) (Chile)
ISLA SALA Y GÓMEZ (Chile)
TRINDADE (Braz.)
ILHAS MARTIN VAZ (Braz.)
ALEXANDER ISLAND
THURSTON ISLAND
PETER I ISLAND
RIO DE JANEIRO
SÃO PAULO
Belo Horizonte
BUENOS AIRES
Montevideo
Asunción
SANTIAGO
Valparaíso
Córdoba
Rosario
Mendoza
San Miguel de Tucumán
Salta
Porto Alegre
Curitiba
Florianópolis
Mar del Plata
Bahía Blanca
La Plata
Concepción
Valdivia
Puerto Montt
Comodoro Rivadavia
Río Gallegos
Stanley
Ushuaia
Antofagasta
Arica
Iquique
Oruro
Sucre
Potosí
Santa Cruz
Santos
Campos
Vitória
Pelotas
Santa Maria
Corrientes
Santa Fe
San Juan
Santiago del Estero
Neuquén
Rawson
Viedma
Kilometers 0 200 400 600 800 Km.
Statute Miles 0 200 400 600 Mi.
Scale 1:24,000,000
One centimeter represents 240 kilometers.
One inch represents approximately 380 miles.
Lambert Azimuthal Equal-Area Projection

Northern South America

Kilometers 0 200 400 600 Km.
Statute Miles 0 200 400 600 Mi.

Scale 1:12,000,000

One centimeter represents 120 kilometers.
One inch represents approximately 190 miles.
Oblique Conic Conformal Projection

ATLANTIC OCEAN
BARBADOS
Bridgetown
TOBAGO
GUYANA
Georgetown
SURINAME
Paramaribo
FRENCH GUIANA
Cayenne
TUMUC-HUMAC MTS.
ACARAI MTS.
AMAPÁ
Macapá
ILHA DE MARAJÓ
Equator
Belém
Amazon
Amazonas
Santarém
São Luís
Parnaíba
Fortaleza
Teresina
MARANHÃO
PARÁ
Represa de Tucuruí
Marabá
Imperatriz
SERRA DOS CARAJÁS
CEARÁ
PIAUÍ
RIO GRANDE DO NORTE
Natal
Campina Grande
João Pessoa
PARAÍBA
PERNAMBUCO
Recife
Olinda
Maceió
ALAGOAS
SERGIPE
Aracaju
Petrolina
Juazeiro
Represa de Sobradinho
TOCANTINS
B R A Z I L
ILHA DO BANANAL
BAHIA
Feira de Santana
Salvador
Vitória da Conquista
Ilhéus
Itabuna
SERRA DO CACHIMBO
MATO GROSSO
PLANALTO DO MATO GROSSO
Cuiabá
GOIÁS
Brasília
Goiânia
Anápolis
PLANALTO CENTRAL
MINAS GERAIS
Montes Claros
Belo Horizonte
Uberlândia
Uberaba
ESPÍRITO SANTO
Vitória
Vila Velha
MATO GROSSO DO SUL
Campo Grande
Corumbá
SÃO PAULO
Ribeirão Preto
Campinas
SÃO PAULO
Santos
RIO DE JANEIRO
Niterói
Tropic of Capricorn
ILHA FERNANDO DE NORONHA (Brazil)
ATOL DAS ROCAS
Presidente Prudente
PARAGUAY

Kilometers 0 200 400 600 Km.

Statute Miles 0 200 400 600 Mi.

Scale 1:12,000,000

One centimeter represents 120 kilometers.

One inch represents approximately 190 miles.

Oblique Conic Conformal Projection

Southeastern Brazil

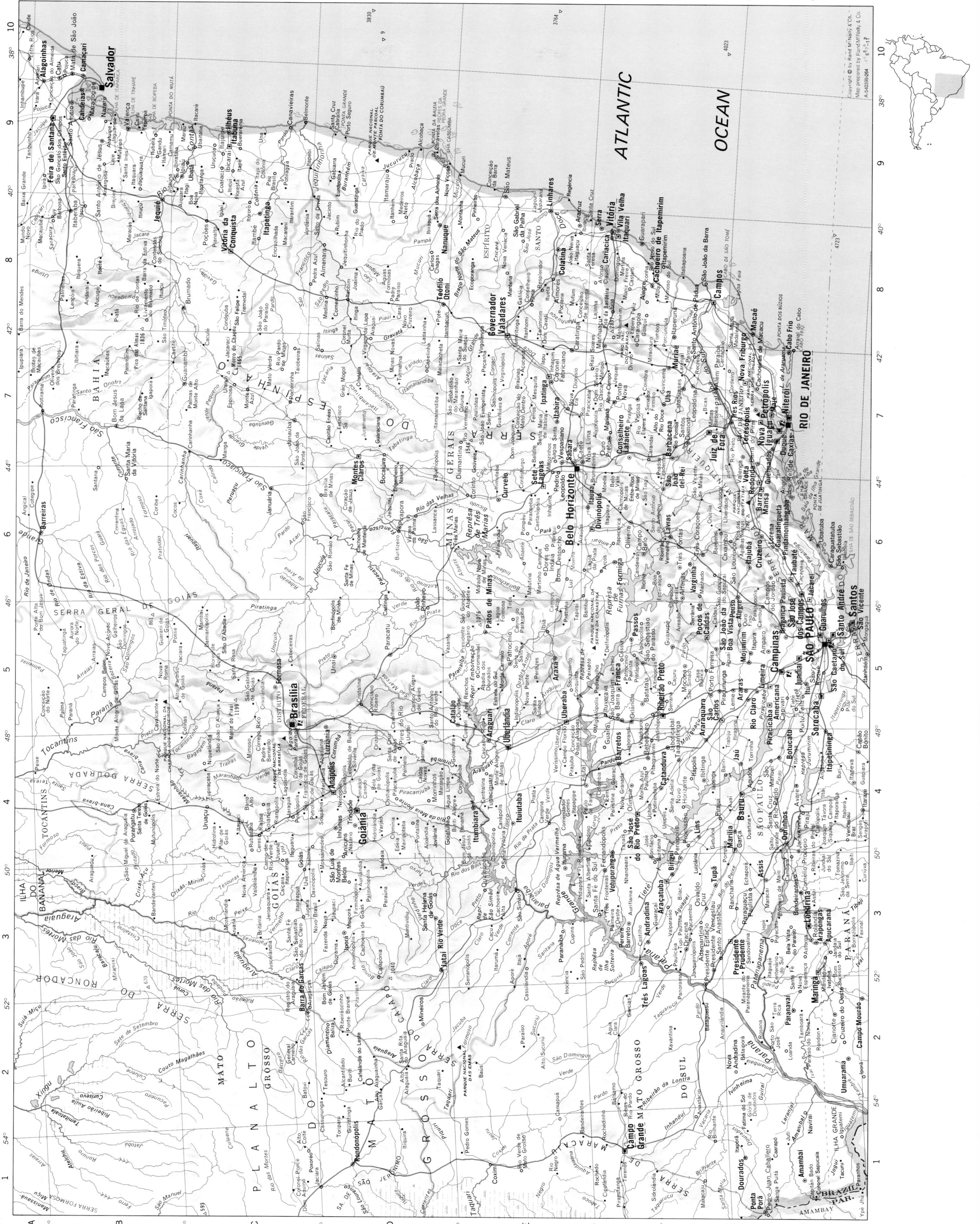

Kilometers 0 100 200 300 Km.
Statute Miles 0 100 200 300 Mi.

Scale 1:6,000,000
One centimeter represents 60 kilometers.
One inch represents approximately 95 miles.
Oblique Conic Conformal Projection

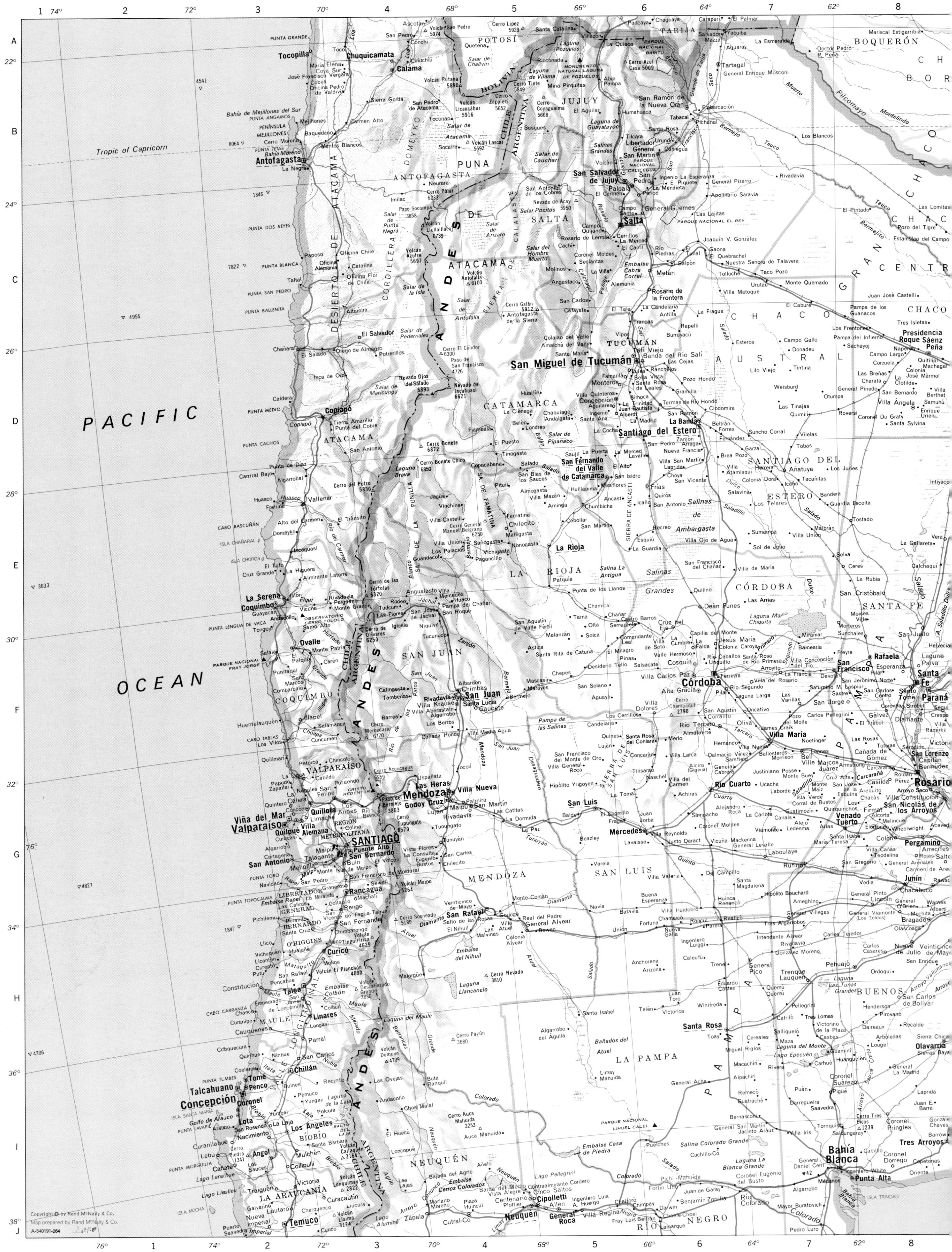
PACIFIC
OCEAN
Tropic of Capricorn
BOLIVIA
CHILE
ARGENTINA
ANDES
PUNA DE ATACAMA
DESIERTO DE ATACAMA
CORDILLERA DOMEYKO
GRAN CHACO
CHACO AUSTRAL
CHACO CENTRAL
PAMPA
BOQUERÓN
POTOSÍ
TARIJA
JUJUY
SALTA
ANTOFAGASTA
ATACAMA
CATAMARCA
TUCUMÁN
SANTIAGO DEL ESTERO
LA RIOJA
CÓRDOBA
SANTA FE
SAN JUAN
COQUIMBO
VALPARAÍSO
REGIÓN METROPOLITANA
LIBERTADOR GENERAL BERNARDO O'HIGGINS
MAULE
BIOBÍO
LA ARAUCANÍA
MENDOZA
SAN LUIS
BUENOS AIRES
LA PAMPA
NEUQUÉN
RÍO NEGRO
Tocopilla
Chuquicamata
Calama
Antofagasta
Taltal
Chañaral
Copiapó
Caldera
Vallenar
La Serena
Coquimbo
Ovalle
Viña del Mar
Valparaíso
SANTIAGO
San Antonio
Rancagua
San Fernando
Curicó
Talca
Linares
Chillán
Talcahuano
Concepción
Los Ángeles
Angol
Temuco
San Salvador de Jujuy
Salta
San Miguel de Tucumán
Santiago del Estero
La Banda
San Fernando del Valle de Catamarca
La Rioja
San Juan
Mendoza
San Luis
Córdoba
Río Cuarto
Villa María
Santa Fe
Paraná
Rosario
Pergamino
Junín
San Rafael
Santa Rosa
Neuquén
Cipolletti
General Roca
Bahía Blanca
Punta Alta
Cerro Aconcagua 6959
Ojos del Salado 6893
Copyright © by Rand McNally & Co.
Map prepared by Rand McNally & Co.
A-540191-264

Kilometers 0 100 200 300 Km.

Statute Miles 0 100 200 300 Mi.

Scale 1:6,000,000

One centimeter represents 60 kilometers.

One inch represents approximately 95 miles.

Oblique Conic Conformal Projection

Peru, Bolivia, and Western Brazil

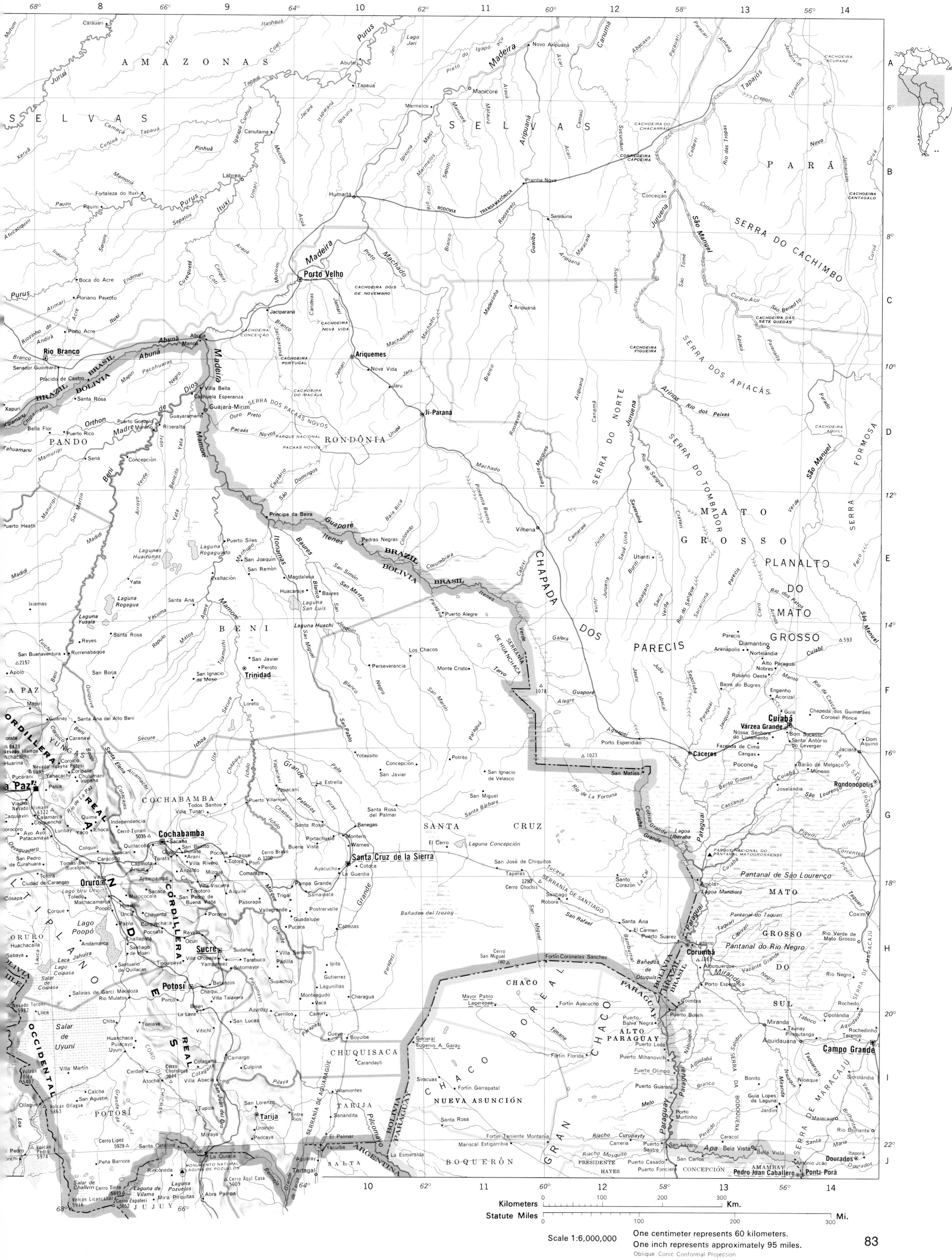

Kilometers 0 100 200 300 Km.

Statute Miles 0 100 200 300 Mi.

Scale 1:6,000,000

One centimeter represents 60 kilometers.
One inch represents approximately 95 miles.
Oblique Conic Conformal Projection

Colombia, Ecuador, Venezuela, and Guyana

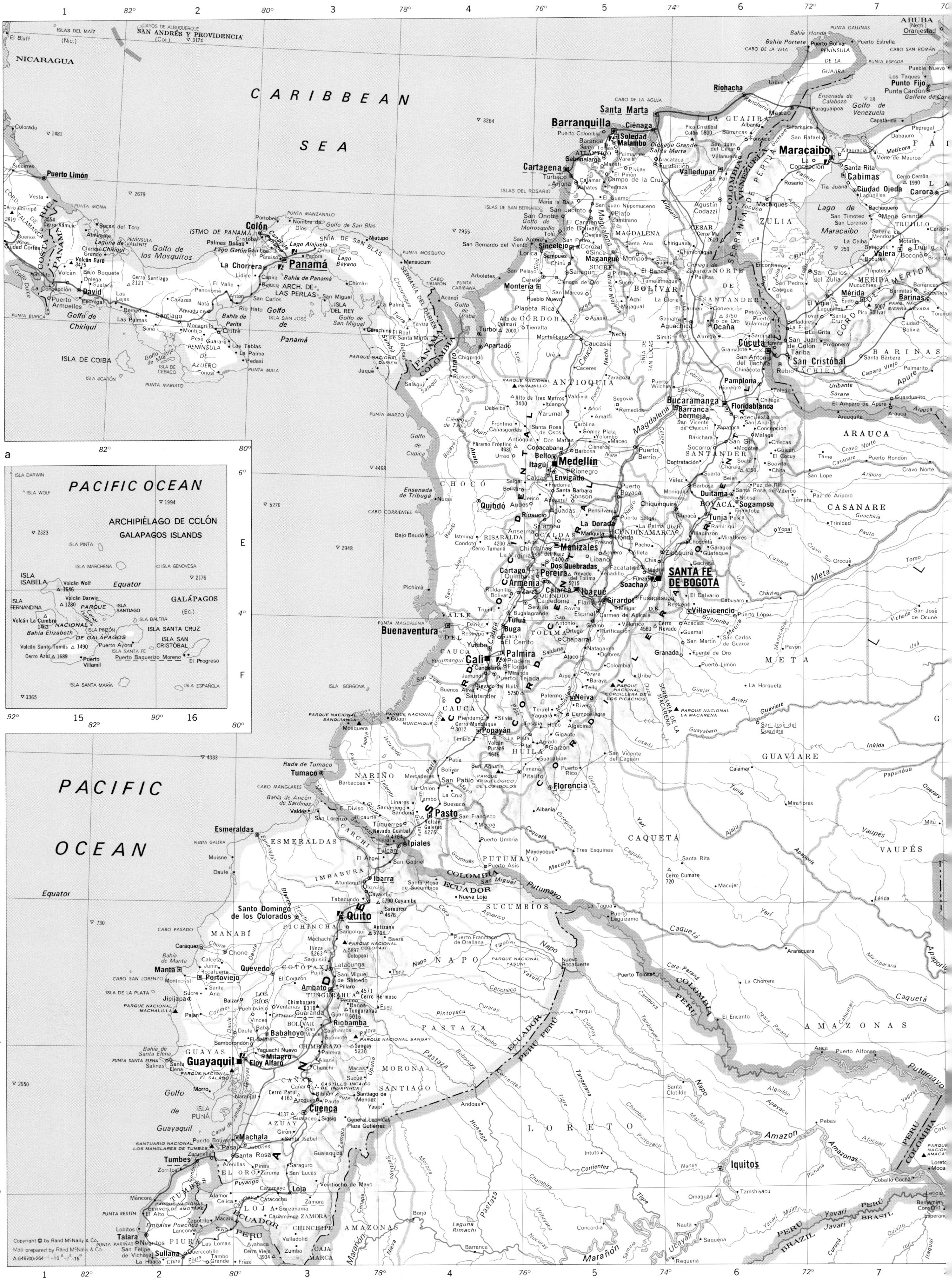

Kilometers 0 100 200 300 Km.
Statute Miles 0 100 200 300 Mi.

Scale 1:6,000,000 One centimeter represents 60 kilometers.
One inch represents approximately 95 miles.
Oblique Conic Conformal Projection

ARCTIC OCEAN
North Pole
ATLANTIC OCEAN
EUROPE
ASIA
RUSSIA
SIBERIA
CANADA
UNITED STATES
GREENLAND
ICELAND
FINLAND
SWEDEN
NORWAY
SVALBARD
Greenland Sea
Norwegian Sea
North Sea
Barents Sea
Karskoje more
Kara Sea
more Laptevych
Laptev Sea
Vostočno-Sibirskoje more
East Siberian Sea
Chukchi Sea
Beaufort Sea
BERING SEA
Sea of Okhotsk
Gulf of Alaska
Hudson Bay
Baffin Bay
Labrador Sea
Davis Strait
Denmark Strait
Bering Strait
QUEEN ELIZABETH ISLANDS
ELLESMERE
BAFFIN ISLAND
VICTORIA ISLAND
BANKS ISLAND
SOUTHAMPTON ISLAND
NOVAJA ZEMLJA
SEVERNAJA ZEMLJA
ZEMLJA FRANCA-IOSIFA
FRANZ JOSEF LAND
NOVOSIBIRSKIJE OSTROVA
ALEUTIAN ISLANDS
ALEUTIAN TRENCH
ALEUTIAN BASIN
LOFOTEN BASIN
NORWEGIAN BASIN
GREENLAND BASIN
ICELAND BASIN
IRMINGER BASIN
LABRADOR BASIN
REYKJANES RIDGE
MOHNS RIDGE
JAN MAYEN RIDGE
BARENTS TROUGH
ROCKY MOUNTAINS
MACKENZIE MOUNTAINS
BROOKS RANGE
ALASKA RANGE
URAL'SKIJE GORY
URAL MTS.
VERCHOJANSKIJ CHREBET
CHREBET ČERSKOGO
POLUOSTROV KAMČATKA
Arctic Circle
MOSKVA
MOSCOW
SANKT-PETERBURG
Stockholm
Oslo
København
Helsinki
Reykjavik
Murmansk
Archangel'sk
Noril'sk
Jakutsk
Magadan
Anchorage
Fairbanks
Edmonton
St. John's

NORTH AMERICA
UNITED STATES
ATLANTIC OCEAN
PACIFIC OCEAN
GULF OF MEXICO
CARIBBEAN SEA
Sargasso Sea
WEST INDIES
SOUTH AMERICA
MEXICO
COLOMBIA
VENEZUELA
BRAZIL
PERU
ECUADOR
PANAMA
COSTA RICA
NICARAGUA
HONDURAS
EL SALVADOR
GUATEMALA
BELIZE
CUBA
HAITI
JAMAICA
BAHAMAS
DOMINICAN REPUBLIC
APPALACHIAN MOUNTAINS
ROCKY MOUNTAINS
GREAT PLAINS
SIERRA MADRE OCCIDENTAL
SIERRA MADRE ORIENTAL
SIERRA MADRE DEL SUR
CHIHUAHUAN DESERT
SONORAN DESERT
BAJA CALIFORNIA
WASHINGTON
NEW YORK
PHILADELPHIA
BOSTON
CHICAGO
DETROIT
TORONTO
MONTRÉAL
OTTAWA
ST. LOUIS
LOS ANGELES
SAN FRANCISCO
CIUDAD DE MÉXICO
MEXICO CITY
La Habana
CARACAS
SANTA FE DE BOGOTÁ
Tropic of Cancer
Equator
Kilometers
Statute Miles
Scale 1:24,000,000
One centimeter represents 240 kilometers.
One inch represents approximately 380 miles.
Lambert Azimuthal Equal-Area Projection
Copyright © by Rand McNally & Co.
Map prepared by Rand McNally & Co.

UNITED STATES
MEXICO
GULF OF MEXICO
PACIFIC OCEAN
SIERRA MADRE OCCIDENTAL
SIERRA MADRE ORIENTAL
SIERRA MADRE DEL SUR
Golfo de California
BAJA CALIFORNIA
Tropic of Cancer
Bahía de Campeche
Golfo de Tehuantepec
PENINSULA YUCATAN
GUATEMALA
EL SALVADOR
BELIZE
ISLAS REVILLAGIGEDO
ÎLE CLIPPERTON (Fr.)
San Diego
Tijuana
Mexicali
Ensenada
Phoenix
Tucson
Albuquerque
El Paso
Ciudad Juárez
Amarillo
Oklahoma City
Tulsa
Dallas
Fort Worth
Shreveport
Austin
San Antonio
Houston
Galveston
Baton Rouge
New Orleans
Memphis
Little Rock
Jackson
Hermosillo
Chihuahua
Ciudad Obregón
Culiacán
La Paz
Mazatlán
Durango
Torreón
Monterrey
Saltillo
Nuevo Laredo
Laredo
Corpus Christi
Brownsville
Matamoros
Ciudad Victoria
Tampico
San Luis Potosí
Aguascalientes
Guadalajara
León
Querétaro
Morelia
CIUDAD DE MEXICO (MEXICO CITY)
Puebla
Veracruz
Acapulco
Oaxaca
Mérida
Campeche
Villahermosa
Tuxtla Gutiérrez
Guatemala
San Salvador
Tegucigalpa
Belize City
Copyright © by Rand McNally & Co.
Map prepared by Esselte Map Service AB, Stockholm.
A-530000-264

Kilometers 0 200 400 600 Km.
Statute Miles 0 200 400 600 Mi.

Scale 1:12,000,000
One centimeter represents 120 kilometers.
One inch represents approximately 190 miles.
Oblique Conic Conformal Projection

Kilometers 0 100 200 300 Km.
Statute Miles 0 100 200 300 Mi.

Scale 1:6,000,000
One centimeter represents 60 kilometers.
One inch represents approximately 95 miles.
Lambert Conformal Conic Projection

GULF
OF
MEXICO
Bahía de Campeche
Golfo de Tehuantepec
Gulf of Honduras
Tropic of Cancer
TEXAS
LOUISIANA
MISSISSIPPI
ALABAMA
TAMAULIPAS
NUEVO LEÓN
SAN LUIS POTOSÍ
GUANAJUATO
QUERÉTARO
HIDALGO
MÉXICO
MORELOS
PUEBLA
VERACRUZ
OAXACA
MICHOACÁN
GUERRERO
TABASCO
CHIAPAS
CAMPECHE
YUCATÁN
QUINTANA ROO
GUATEMALA
BELIZE
HONDURAS
EDWARDS PLATEAU
SIERRA MADRE ORIENTAL
SIERRA MADRE DEL SUR
SIERRA MADRE DE CHIAPAS
ISTMO DE TEHUANTEPEC
YUCATAN PENINSULA
PENÍNSULA DE YUCATÁN
Fort Worth
Dallas
Arlington
Abilene
Shreveport
Jackson
Waco
Austin
San Antonio
Houston
Galveston
Beaumont
Baton Rouge
New Orleans
Mobile
Corpus Christi
Laredo
Nuevo Laredo
Brownsville
Matamoros
Reynosa
McAllen
Monterrey
Saltillo
Ciudad Victoria
Tampico
San Luis Potosí
Aguascalientes
León
Querétaro
Pachuca
CIUDAD DE MÉXICO
MEXICO CITY
Toluca
Puebla
Cuernavaca
Veracruz
Xalapa
Orizaba
Córdoba
Oaxaca
Acapulco
Coatzacoalcos
Villahermosa
Tuxtla Gutiérrez
Ciudad del Carmen
Campeche
Mérida
Cancún
Chetumal
Belize City
Belmopan
Guatemala
San Pedro Sula
Río Grande
Rio Bravo
Mississippi
Colorado
Brazos
Trinity
Sabine
Usumacinta
102°
100°
98°
96°
94°
92°
90°
88°
32°
30°
28°
26°
24°
22°
20°
18°
16°
9
10
11
12
13
14
15
16
A
B
C
D
E
F

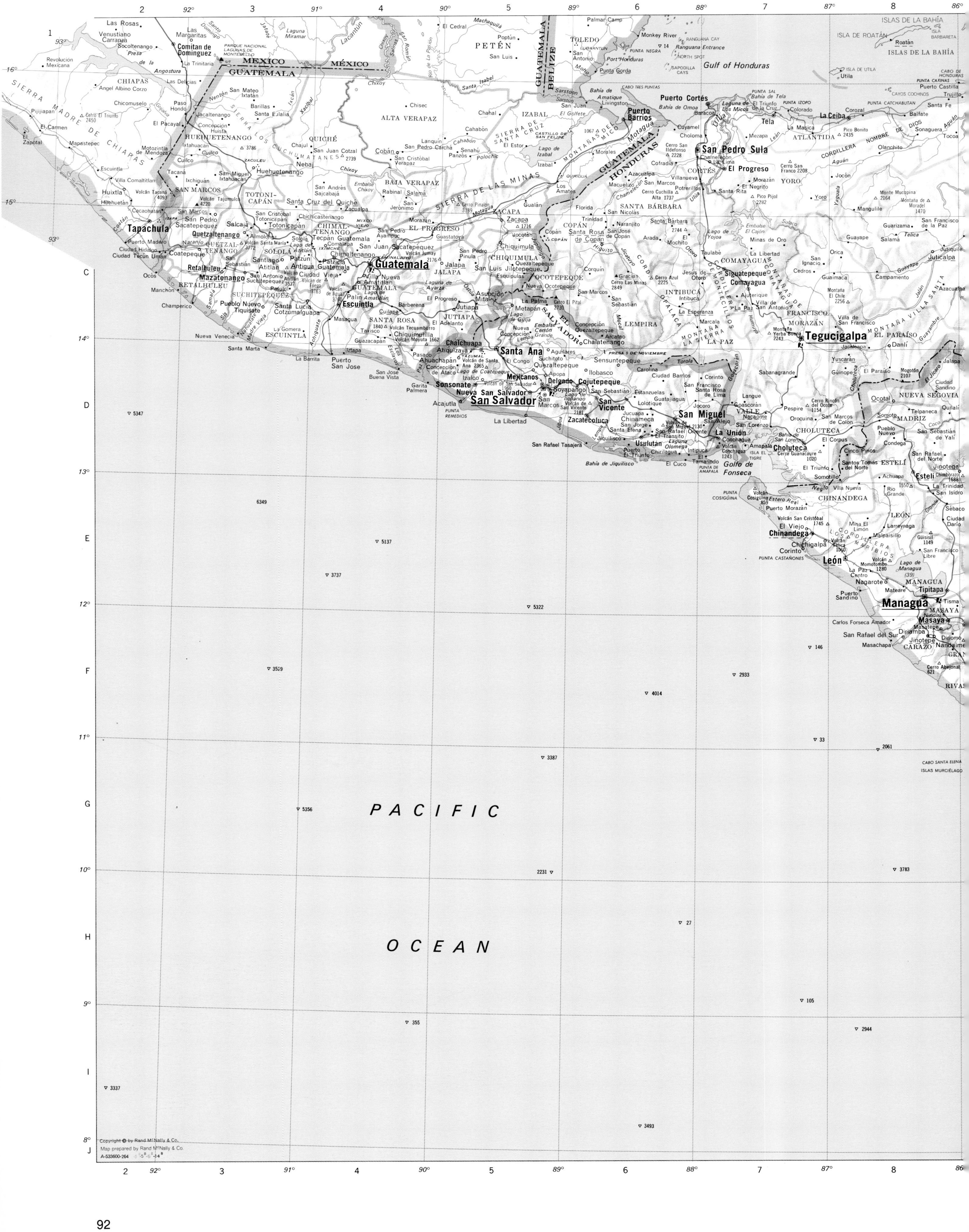
PACIFIC
OCEAN
Gulf of Honduras
Golfo de Fonseca
MEXICO
GUATEMALA
BELIZE
HONDURAS
EL SALVADOR
PETÉN
ALTA VERAPAZ
BAJA VERAPAZ
QUICHÉ
HUEHUETENANGO
SAN MARCOS
CHIAPAS
IZABAL
ZACAPA
CHIQUIMULA
JUTIAPA
JALAPA
SANTA ROSA
ESCUINTLA
RETALHULEU
SUCHITEPÉQUEZ
SACATEPÉQUEZ
COPÁN
OCOTEPEQUE
SANTA BÁRBARA
CORTÉS
ATLÁNTIDA
YORO
COMAYAGUA
INTIBUCÁ
LEMPIRA
LA PAZ
VALLE
CHOLUTECA
EL PARAÍSO
NUEVA SEGOVIA
MADRIZ
ESTELÍ
CHINANDEGA
LEÓN
MANAGUA
MASAYA
CARAZO
ISLAS DE LA BAHÍA
SIERRA MADRE DE CHIAPAS
SIERRA DE LAS MINAS
Tapachula
Quetzaltenango
Mazatenango
Retalhuleu
Escuintla
Guatemala
Antigua Guatemala
Cobán
Puerto Barrios
Puerto Cortés
San Pedro Sula
El Progreso
La Ceiba
Tela
Tegucigalpa
Comayagua
Siguatepeque
Santa Ana
San Salvador
Nueva San Salvador
Sonsonate
Acajutla
La Libertad
San Miguel
La Unión
Usulután
Zacatecoluca
San Vicente
Cojutepeque
Chalchuapa
Choluteca
Chinandega
León
Managua
Masaya
Estelí
Corinto
El Viejo
Comitán de Domínguez
Huehuetenango
Puerto San José
Copyright © by Rand McNally & Co.
Map prepared by Rand McNally & Co.
A-533600-264

Kilometers 0 50 100 150 Km.
Statute Miles 0 50 100 150 Mi.

Scale 1:3,000,000

One centimeter represents 30 kilometers.
One inch represents approximately 47 miles.
Lambert Conformal Conic Projection

Caribbean Region

Kilometers 0 100 200 300 Km.
Statute Miles 0 100 200 300 Mi.

Scale 1:6,000,000
One centimeter represents 60 kilometers.
One inch represents approximately 95 miles.
Lambert Conformal Conic Projection

Beaufort Sea
PACIFIC OCEAN
Gulf of Alaska
UNITED STATES
CANADA
ROCKY MOUNTAINS
COAST MOUNTAINS
MACKENZIE MTS
CASCADE RANGE
SIERRA NEVADA
ALASKA RANGE
BRITISH COLUMBIA
ALBERTA
SASKATCHEWAN
MANITOBA
WASHINGTON
OREGON
IDAHO
MONTANA
WYOMING
NORTH DAKOTA
SOUTH DAKOTA
MINNESOTA
NEBRASKA
IOWA
CALIFORNIA
UTAH
COLORADO
GREAT BASIN
VICTORIA ISLAND
BANKS ISLAND
MELVILLE ISLAND
PRINCE OF WALES ISLAND
BOOTHIA PENINSULA
Great Bear Lake
Great Slave Lake
Lake Athabasca
Lake Winnipeg
Anchorage
Fairbanks
Whitehorse
Vancouver
Victoria
Seattle
Tacoma
Portland
Spokane
Edmonton
Calgary
Saskatoon
Regina
Winnipeg
Lethbridge
Great Falls
Missoula
Helena
Butte
Billings
Boise
Salt Lake City
Ogden
Provo
Reno
Sacramento
SAN FRANCISCO
Oakland
San Jose
Fresno
Stockton
Modesto
Bismarck
Fargo
Grand Forks
Minneapolis
St. Paul
Duluth
Rapid City
Sioux Falls
Sioux City
Casper
Cheyenne
Yukon
Mackenzie
Peace
Athabasca
Churchill
Columbia
Snake
Missouri
1 2 3 4 5 6 7 8 9 10 11 12 13 14
8 9 10 11 12 13 14
D E F G H I

Scale 1:12,000,000

One centimeter represents 120 kilometers.

One inch represents approximately 190 miles.

Lambert Conformal Conic Projection

PACIFIC OCEAN
CANADA
UNITED STATES
MEXICO
WASHINGTON
OREGON
IDAHO
MONTANA
WYOMING
NEVADA
UTAH
COLORADO
ARIZONA
NEW MEXICO
CALIFORNIA
NORTH DAKOTA
SOUTH DAKOTA
NEBRASKA
KANSAS
OKLAHOMA
TEXAS
ALBERTA
SASKATCHEWAN
MANITOBA
BRITISH COLUMBIA
ROCKY MOUNTAINS
GREAT BASIN
VANCOUVER ISLAND
SAN FRANCISCO
LOS ANGELES
Copyright © by Rand McNally & Co.
Map prepared by Rand McNally & Co.
ARCTIC OCEAN
Beaufort Sea
Chukchi Sea
BERING SEA
ALASKA
BROOKS RANGE
ALASKA RANGE
Arctic Circle
Gulf of Alaska
ALEUTIAN ISLANDS
PACIFIC OCEAN
Kilometers
Miles
Copyright © by Rand McNally & Co.
OAHU
Honolulu
MOLOKAI
LANAI
MAUI
KAHOOLAWE
HAWAII
KAUAI
NIIHAU
PACIFIC OCEAN
Kilometers
Miles
Copyright © by Rand McNally & Co.

Kilometers 0 200 400 600 Km.

Statute Miles 0 200 400 600 Mi.

Scale 1:12,000,000

One centimeter represents 120 kilometers.

One inch represents approximately 190 miles.

Albers Conical Equal-Area Projection

Alaska and the Yukon

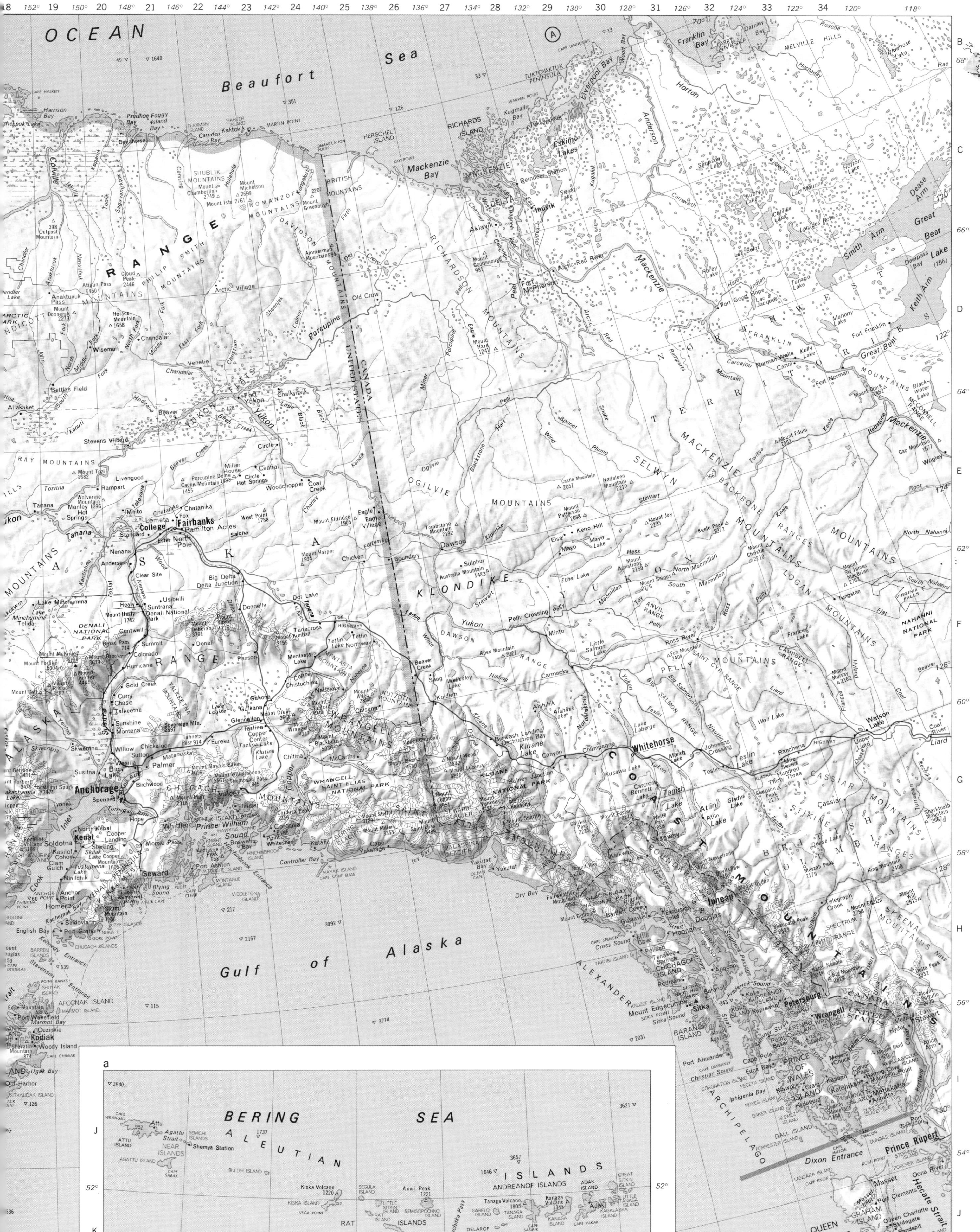

Kilometers 0 100 200 300 Km.
Statute Miles 0 100 200 300 Mi.

Scale 1:6,000,000
One centimeter represents 60 kilometers.
One inch represents approximately 95 miles.
Lambert Conformal Conic Projection

PACIFIC
OCEAN
Queen
Charlotte
Sound
Dixon Entrance
Hecate
Strait
U.S.
CANADA
CANADA
UNITED STATES
QUEEN
CHARLOTTE
ISLANDS
GRAHAM
ISLAND
MORESBY
ISLAND
VANCOUVER
ISLAND
COAST
MOUNTAINS
PACIFIC
RANGES
KITIMAT
RANGES
HAZELTON
MOUNTAINS
BABINE
RANGE
NECHAKO
PLATEAU
FRASER
PLATEAU
OMINECA
MOUNTAINS
TWEEDSMUIR
PROVINCIAL
PARK
Prince Rupert
Kitimat
Prince George
Quesnel
Williams Lake
Powell River
Nanaimo
Port Alberni
VANCOUVER
Victoria
Bellingham
Port Angeles
Everett
Mount Vernon
Smithers
Terrace
Strait of Georgia
Strait of Juan de Fuca
Copyright © by Rand McNally & Co.
Map prepared by Rand McNally & Co.
A-520220-264

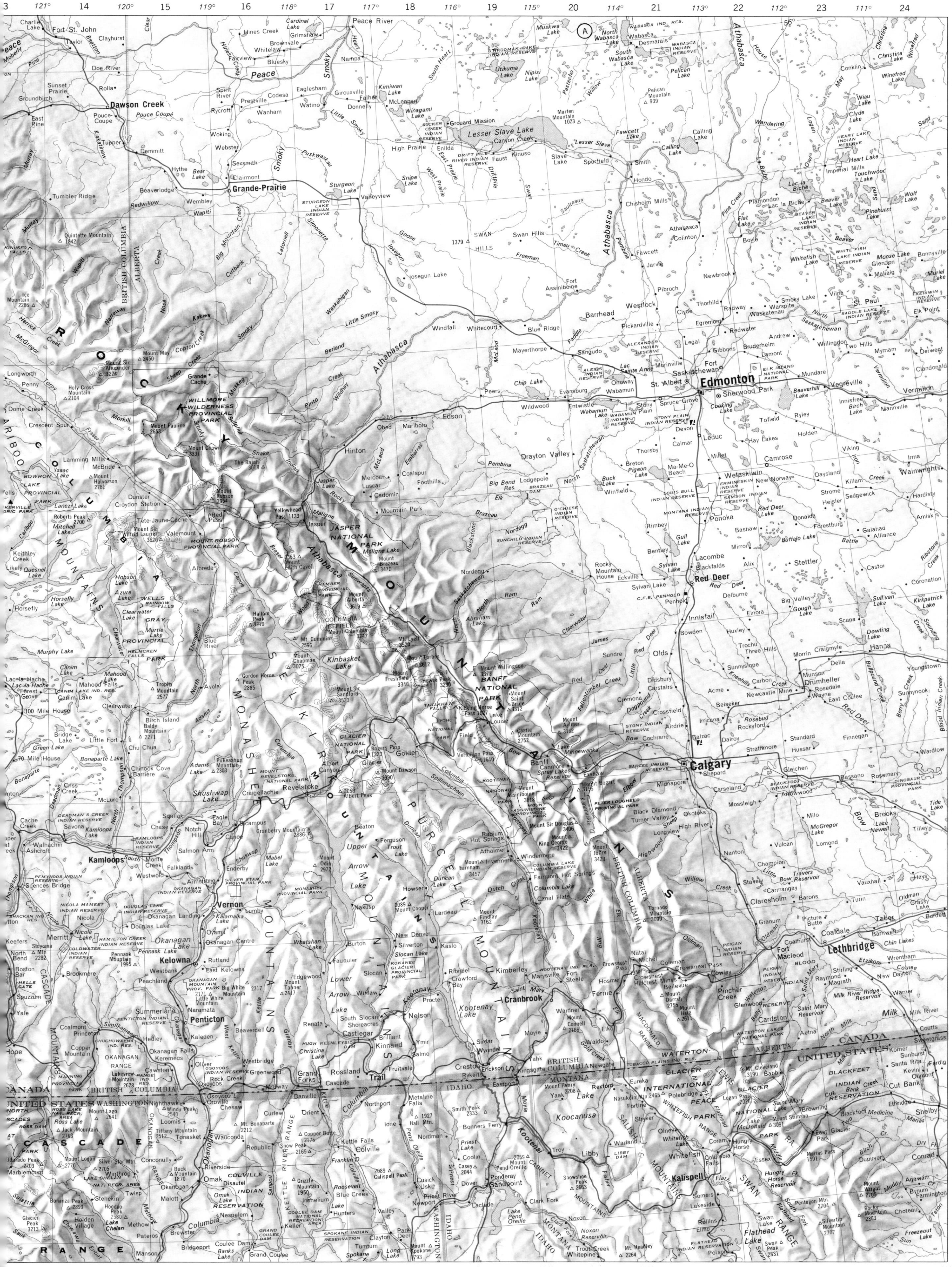

Kilometers 0 50 100 150 Km.

Statute Miles 0 50 100 150 Mi.

Scale 1:3,000,000

One centimeter represents 30 kilometers.

One inch represents approximately 47 miles.

Lambert Conformal Conic Projection

South-Central Canada

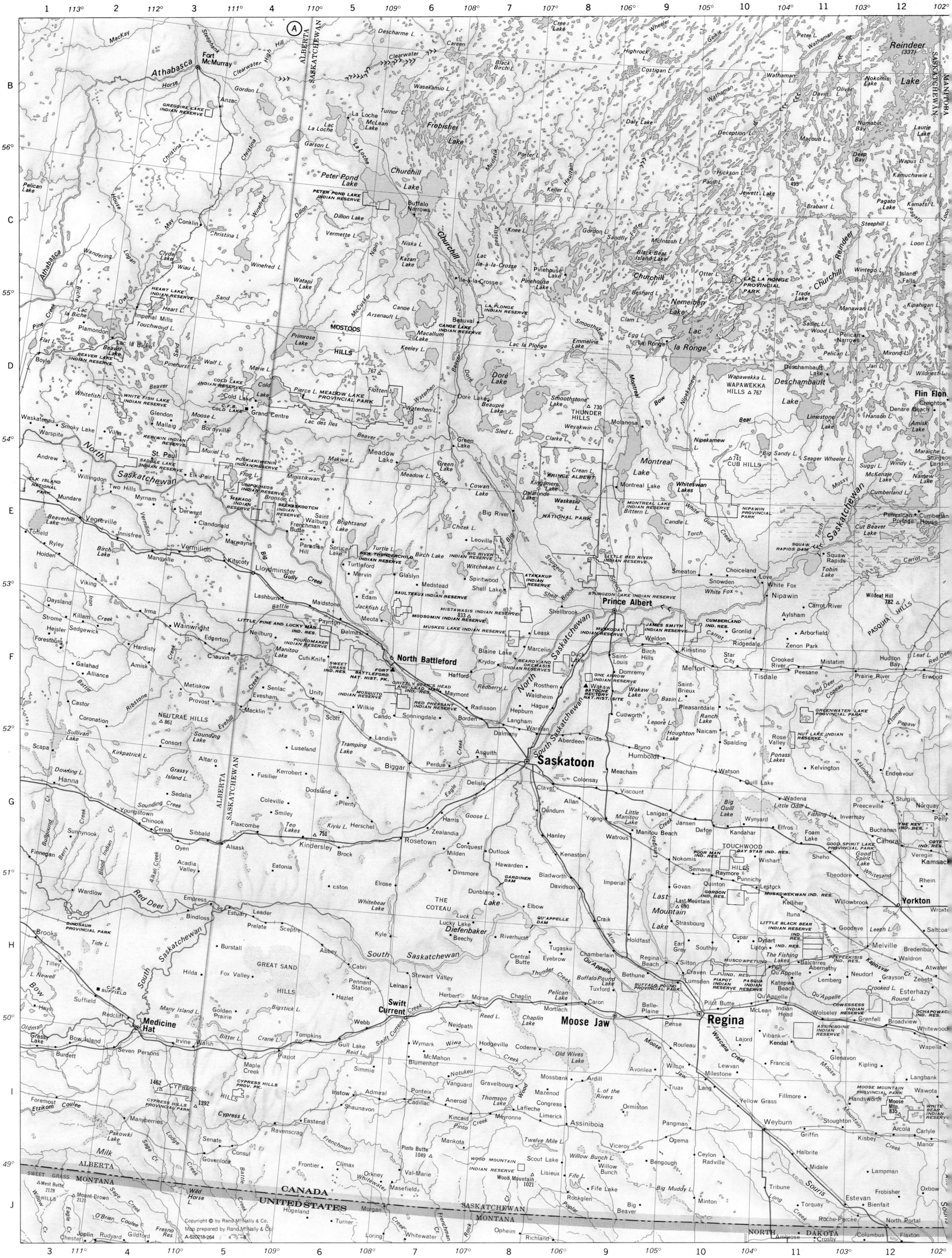

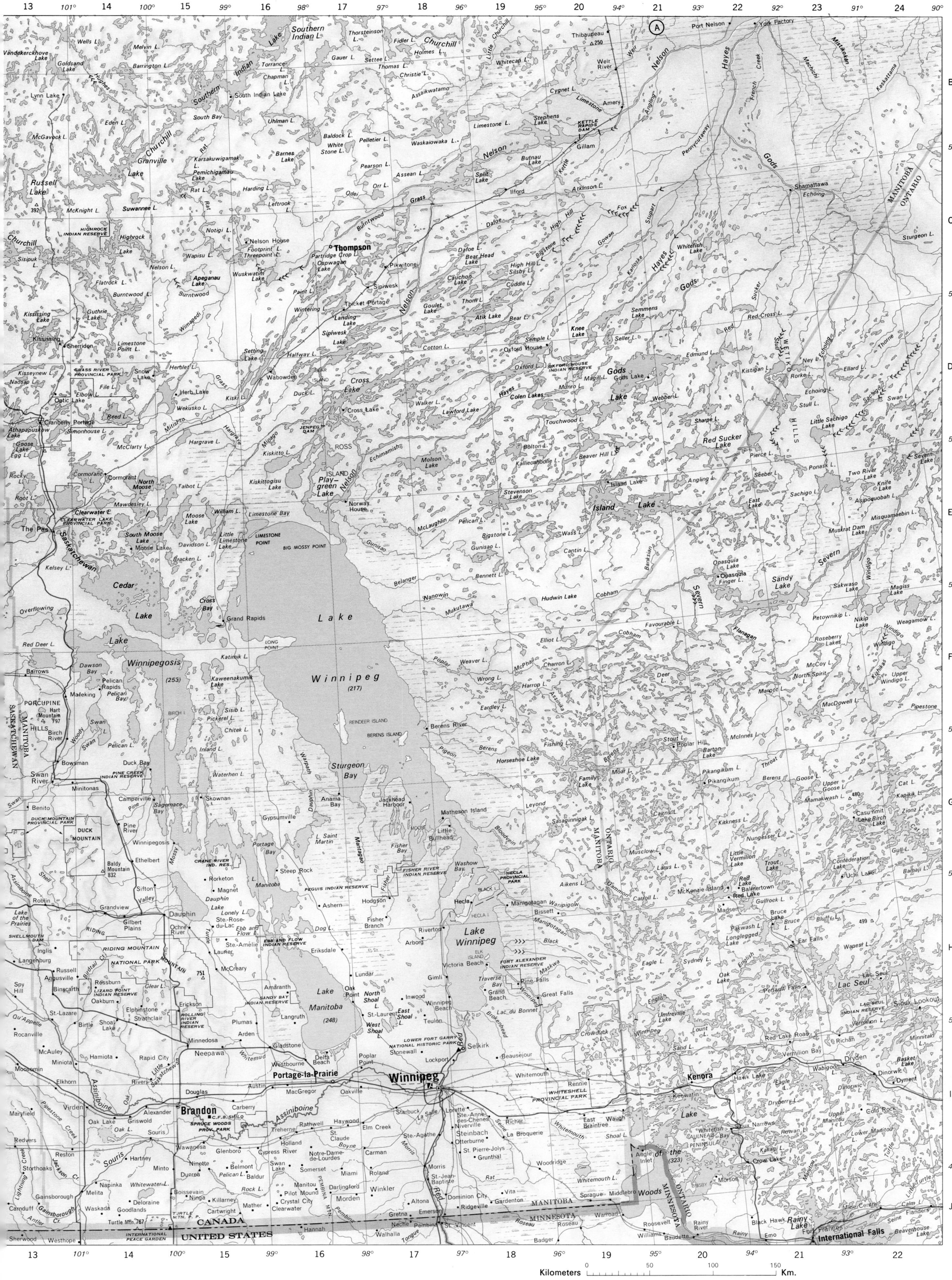

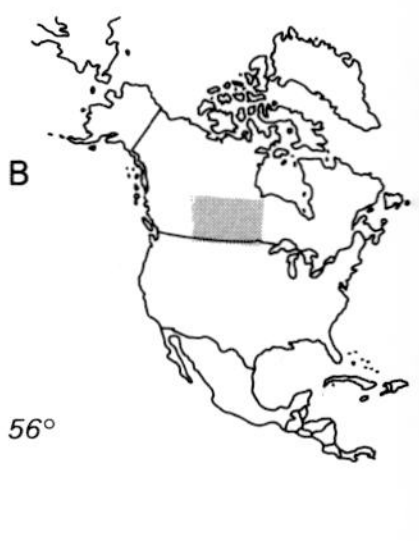

Kilometers 0 50 100 150 Km.

Statute Miles 0 50 100 150 Mi.

Scale 1:3,000,000

One centimeter represents 30 kilometers.
One inch represents approximately 47 miles.
Lambert Conformal Conic Projection

Southeastern Canada

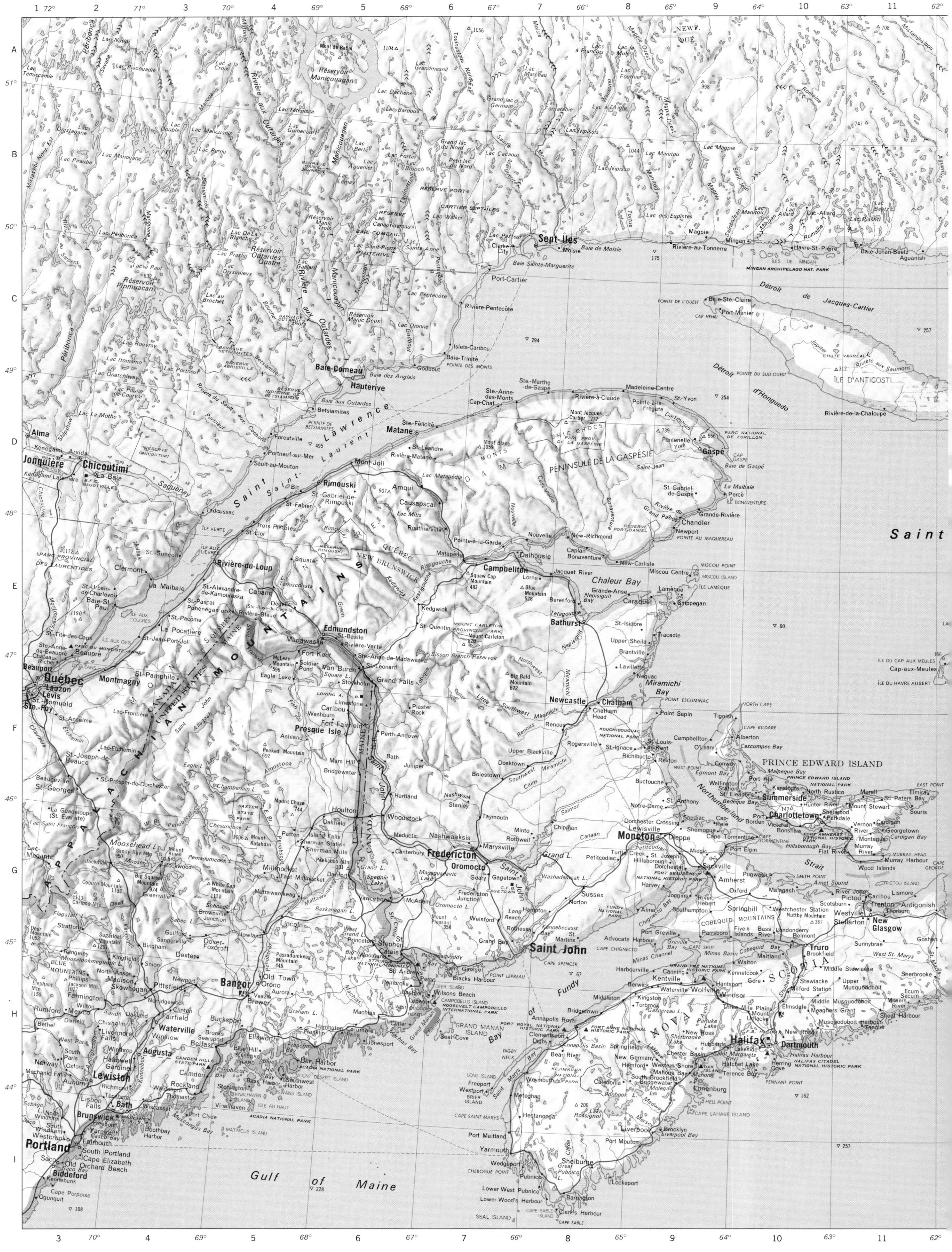

Kilometers 0 50 100 150 Km.

Statute Miles 0 50 100 150 Mi.

Scale 1:3,000,000

One centimeter represents 30 kilometers.

One inch represents approximately 47 miles.

Lambert Conformal Conic Projection

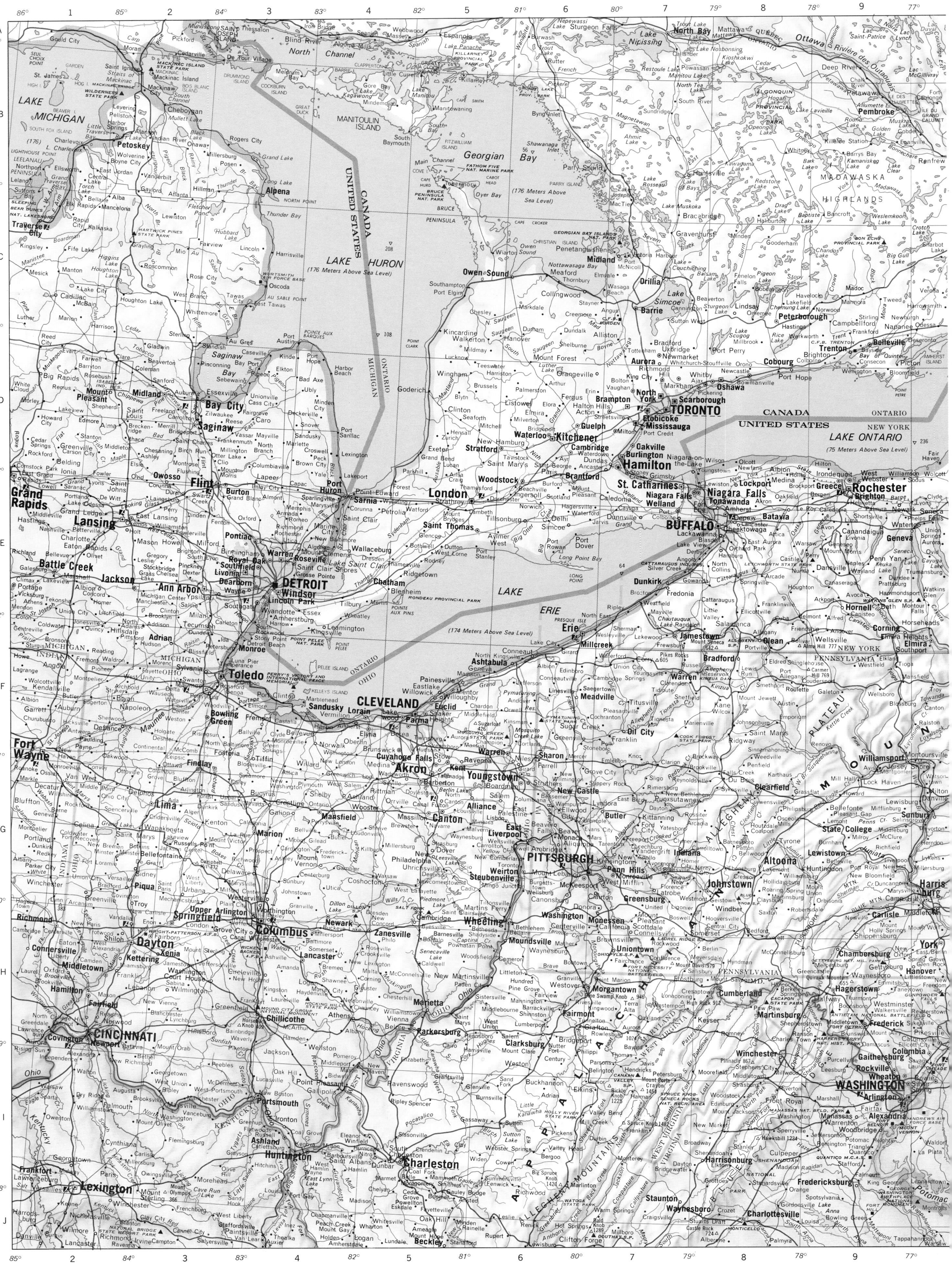
LAKE MICHIGAN
LAKE HURON
(176 Meters Above Sea Level)
Georgian Bay
LAKE ONTARIO
(75 Meters Above Sea Level)
LAKE ERIE
(174 Meters Above Sea Level)
CANADA
UNITED STATES
MICHIGAN
ONTARIO
NEW YORK
PENNSYLVANIA
OHIO
INDIANA
KENTUCKY
WEST VIRGINIA
VIRGINIA
MARYLAND
MANITOULIN ISLAND
BRUCE PENINSULA
North Channel
APPALACHIAN MOUNTAINS
ALLEGHENY MOUNTAINS
ALLEGHENY PLATEAU
BLUE RIDGE
TORONTO
DETROIT
CLEVELAND
BUFFALO
PITTSBURGH
CINCINNATI
WASHINGTON
Columbus
Toledo
Windsor
London
Hamilton
Rochester
Erie
Akron
Canton
Youngstown
Dayton
Lexington
Charleston
Grand Rapids
Lansing
Flint
Saginaw
Bay City
Fort Wayne
Ann Arbor
Kitchener
Niagara Falls
Harrisburg
Frederick
Johnstown
Altoona
Wheeling
Huntington
Alexandria

Kilometers 0 50 100 150 Km.

Statute Miles 0 50 100 150 Mi.

Scale 1:3,000,000

One centimeter represents 30 kilometers.

One inch represents approximately 47 miles.

Albers Conical Equal-Area Projection

Great Lakes Region

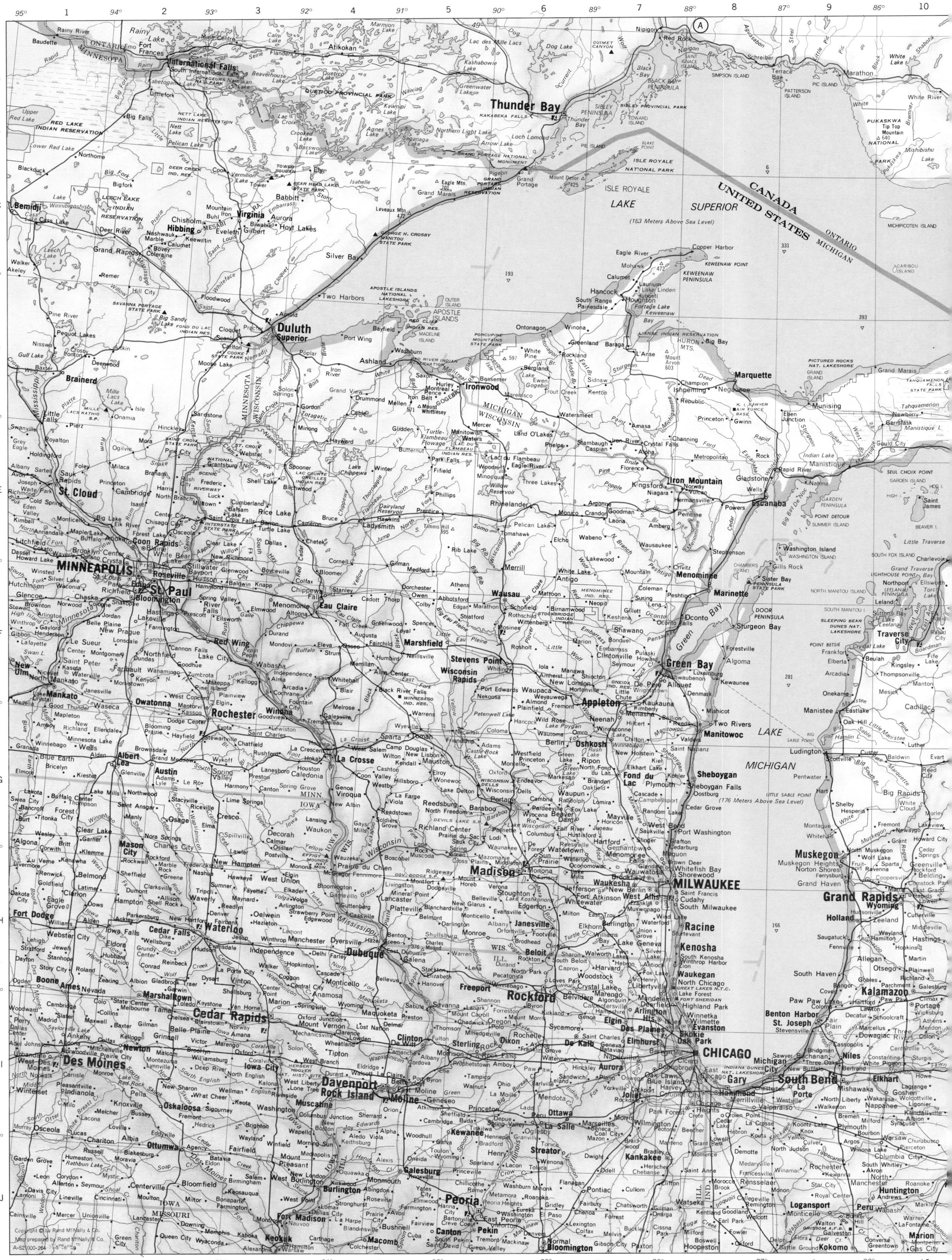

Kilometers 0 50 100 150 Km.

Statute Miles 0 50 100 150 Mi.

Scale 1:3,000,000

One centimeter represents 30 kilometers.

One inch represents approximately 47 miles.

Albers Conical Equal-Area Projection

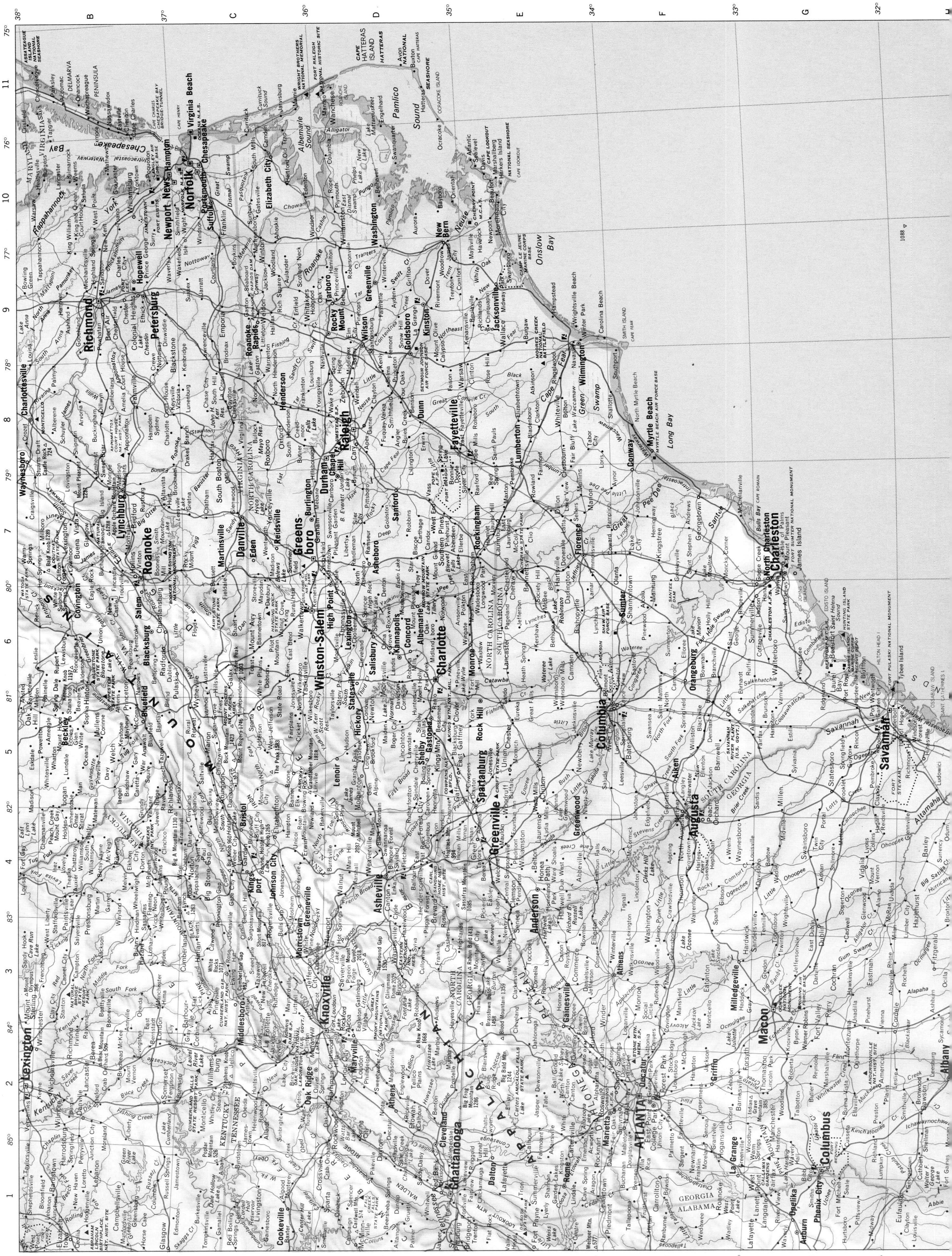

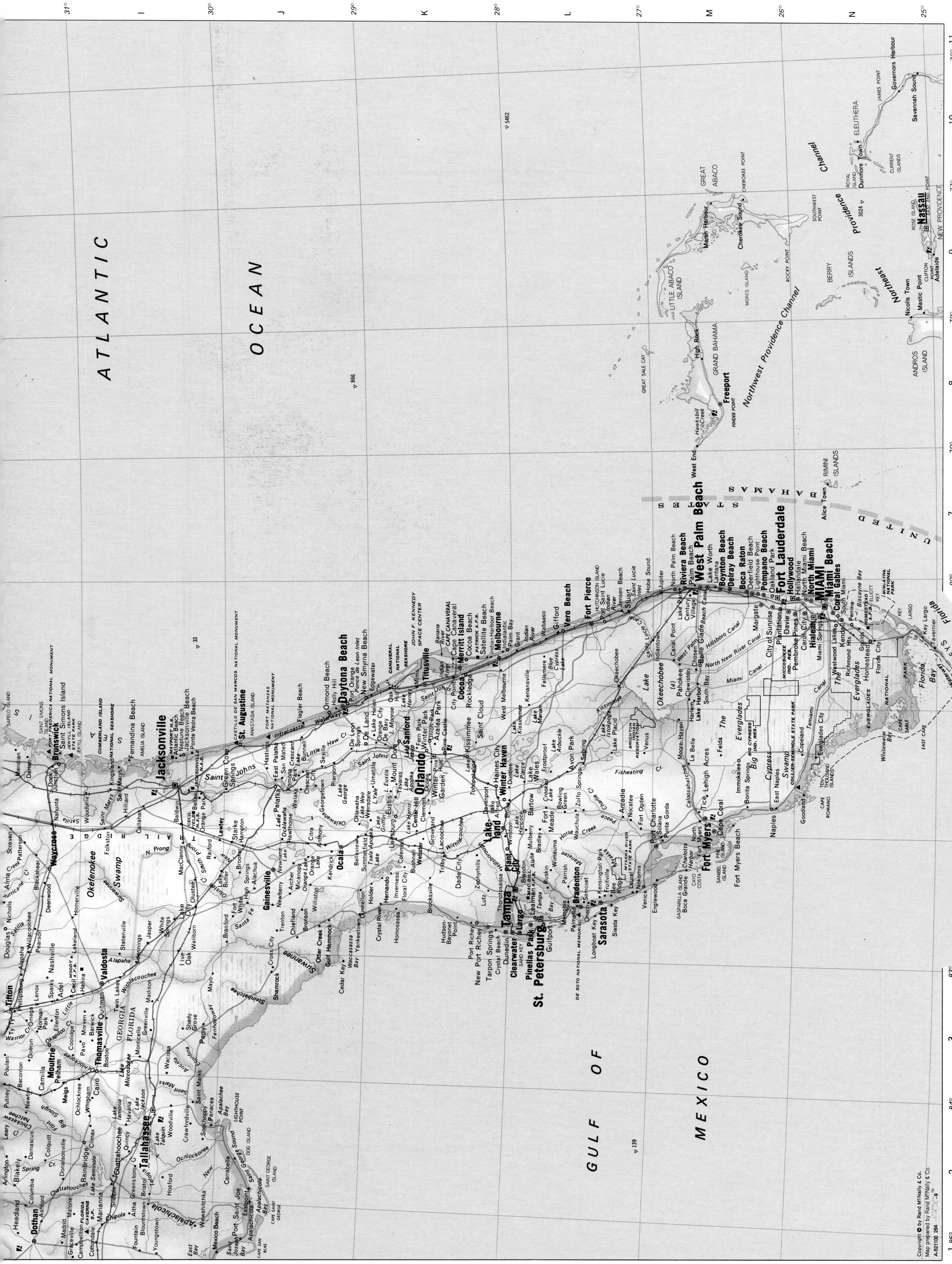

Kilometers 0 50 100 150 Km.

Statute Miles 0 50 100 150 Mi.

Scale 1:3,000,000

One centimeter represents 30 kilometers.

One inch represents approximately 47 miles.

Albers Conical Equal-Area Projection

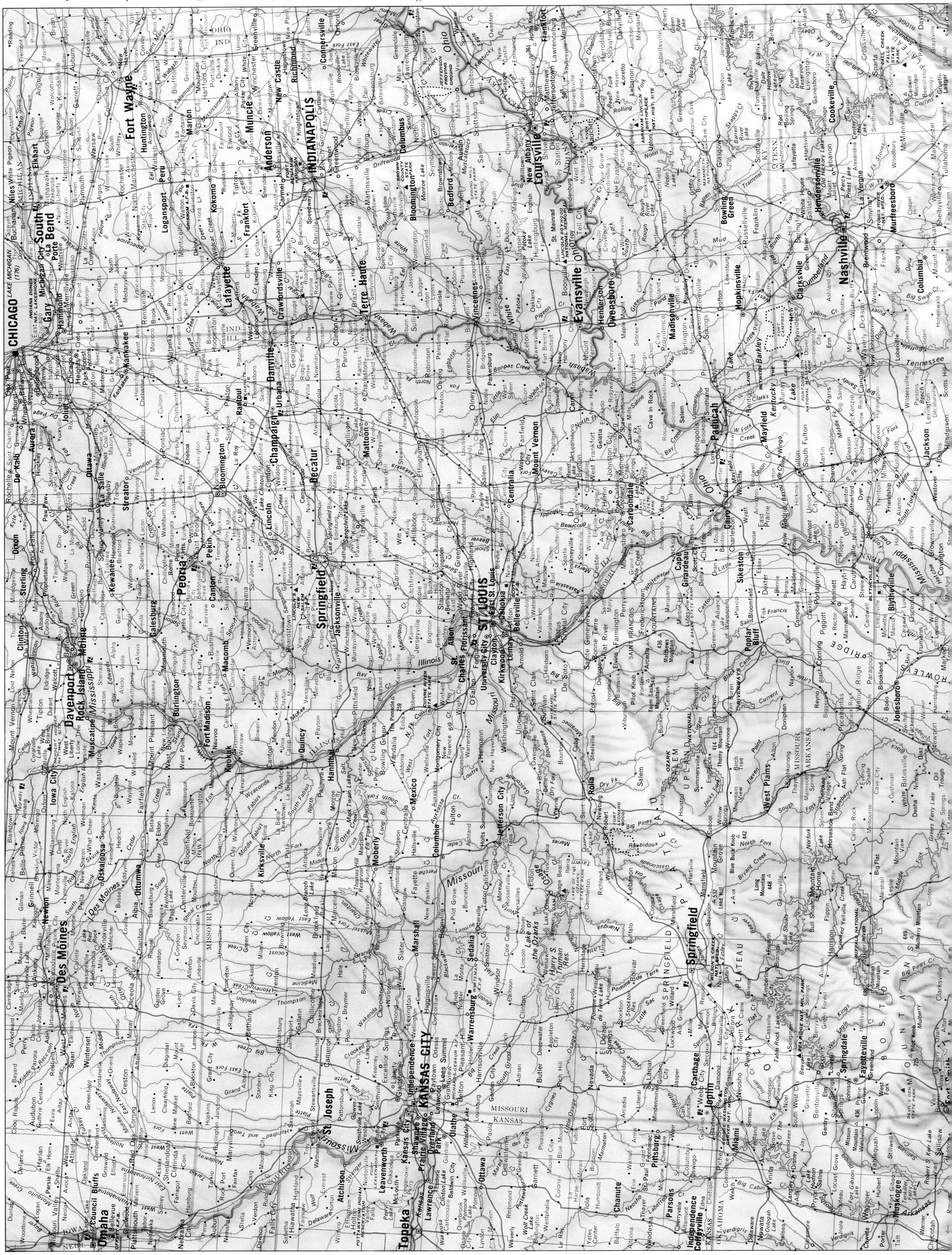
CHICAGO
INDIANAPOLIS
ST. LOUIS
KANSAS CITY
Louisville
Nashville
Evansville
Springfield
Peoria
Des Moines
Omaha
Topeka
Fort Wayne
South Bend
Terre Haute
Paducah
Joplin
MISSOURI
KANSAS
OKLAHOMA

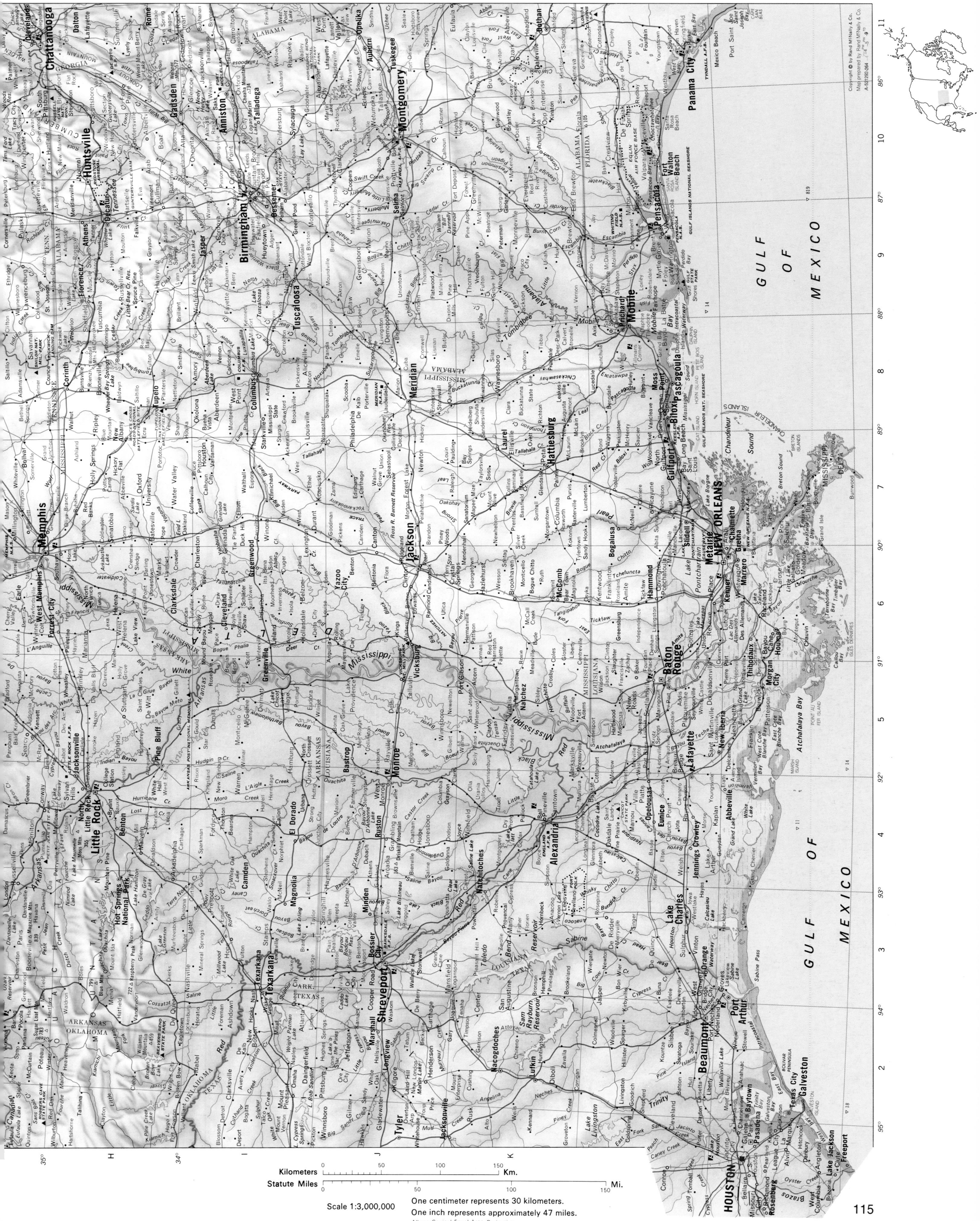

Kilometers 0 50 100 150 Km.

Statute Miles 0 50 100 150 Mi.

Scale 1:3,000,000

One centimeter represents 30 kilometers.
One inch represents approximately 47 miles.

Albers Conical Equal-Area Projection

Albers Conical Equal-Area Projection

WYOMING
IDAHO
COLORADO
UTAH
NEVADA
DENVER
Colorado Springs
Pueblo
Cheyenne
Laramie
Casper
Rock Springs
Salt Lake City
Ogden
Provo
Grand Junction
Pocatello
Idaho Falls
Twin Falls
Great Salt Lake
GREAT SALT LAKE DESERT
GREAT DIVIDE BASIN
WIND RIVER RANGE
BEAR RIVER RANGE
SAN JUAN MOUNTAINS

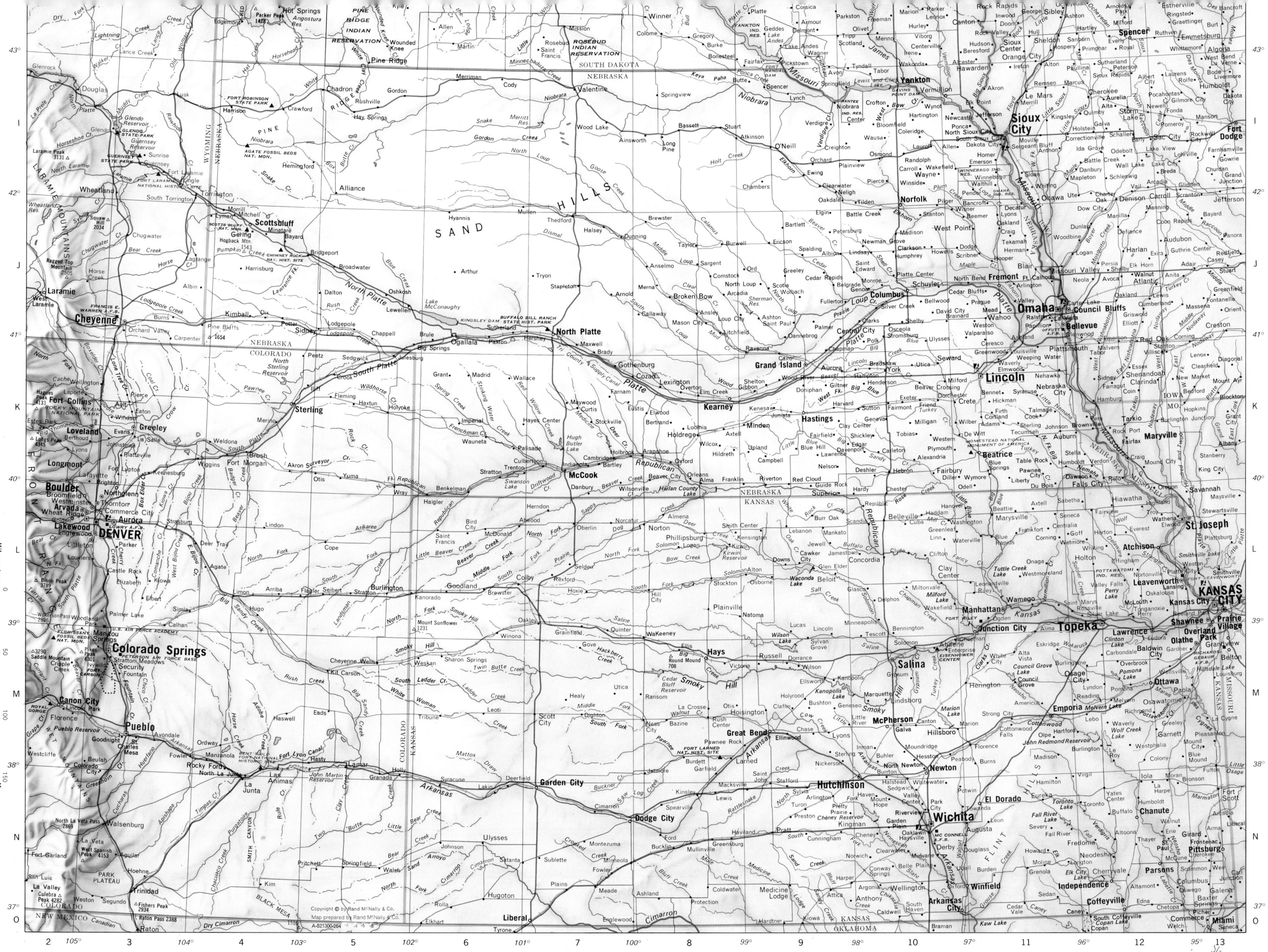

Kilometers 0 50 100 150 Km.

Statute Miles 0 50 100 150 Mi.

Scale 1:3,000,000

One centimeter represents 30 kilometers.

One inch represents approximately 47 miles.

Albers Conical Equal-Area Projection

Salt Lake City
Denver
Colorado Springs
Pueblo
Cheyenne
Laramie
Casper
Idaho Falls
Pocatello
Twin Falls
Ogden
Provo
Grand Junction
Rock Springs
Boulder
Fort Collins
Greeley
Lakewood
Longmont
Great Salt Lake
Great Salt Lake Desert
Great Divide Basin
Snake River Plain
Uinta Mountains
Wind River Range
Bear River Range
Wasatch Range
Sangre de Cristo Mts.
San Juan Mountains
Sawatch Range
Book Cliffs
Roan Plateau
Colorado Plateau
Bighorn Mts.
Laramie Mountains
Medicine Bow Mountains
Ruby Mountains
Schell Creek Range
Wyoming
Idaho
Utah
Nevada
Colorado

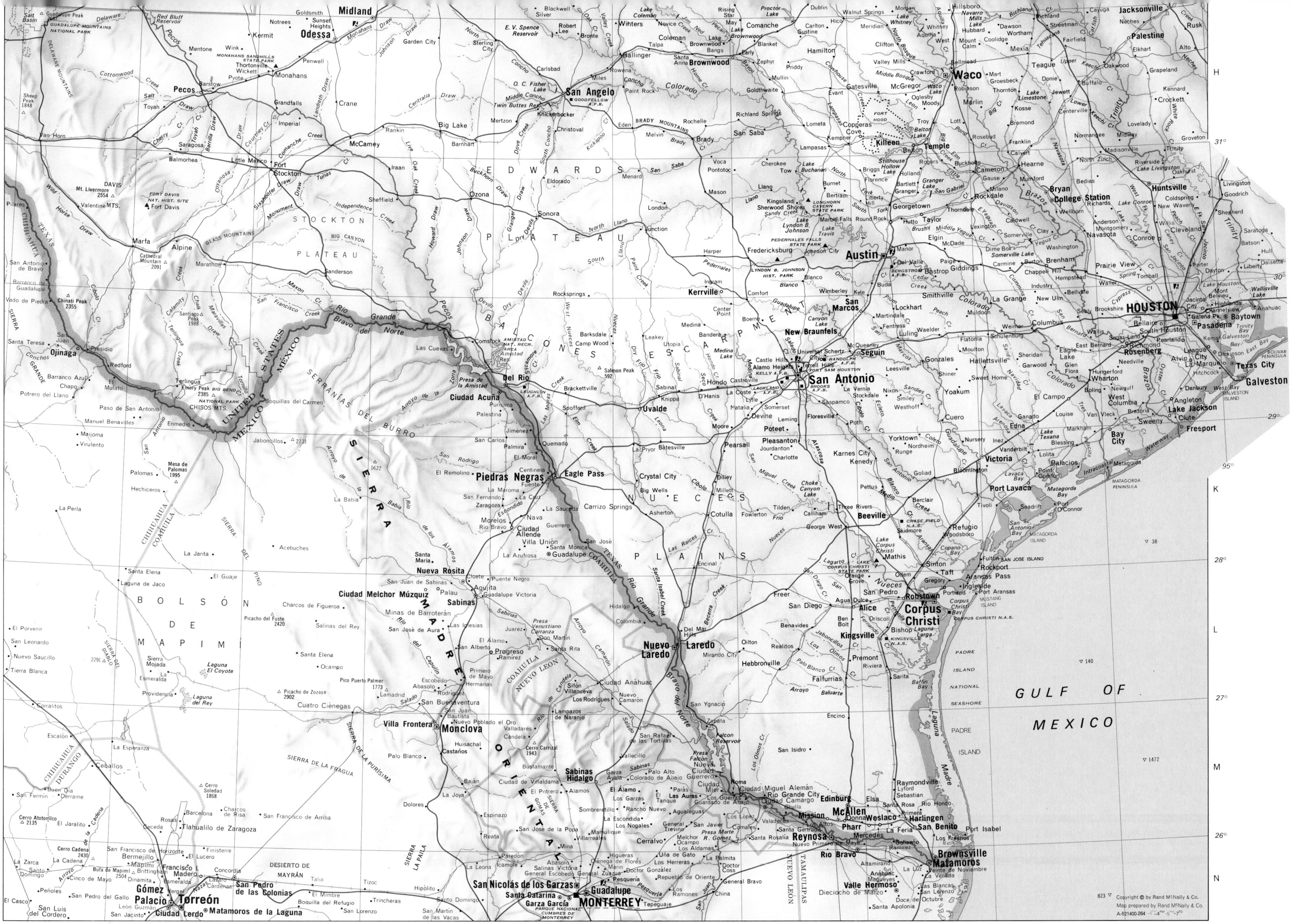

Kilometers
Statute Miles
0 50 100 150 Km.
0 50 100 150 Mi.
Scale 1:3,000,000
One centimeter represents 30 kilometers.
One inch represents approximately 47 miles.
Albers Conical Equal-Area Projection

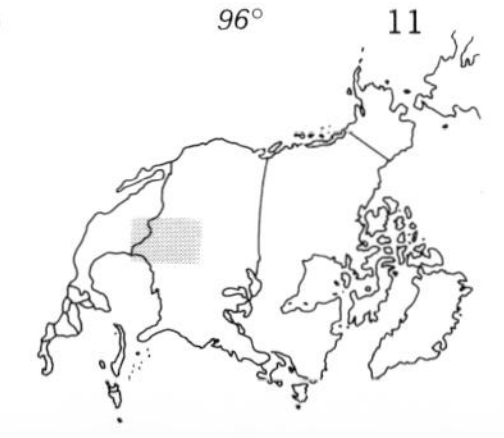

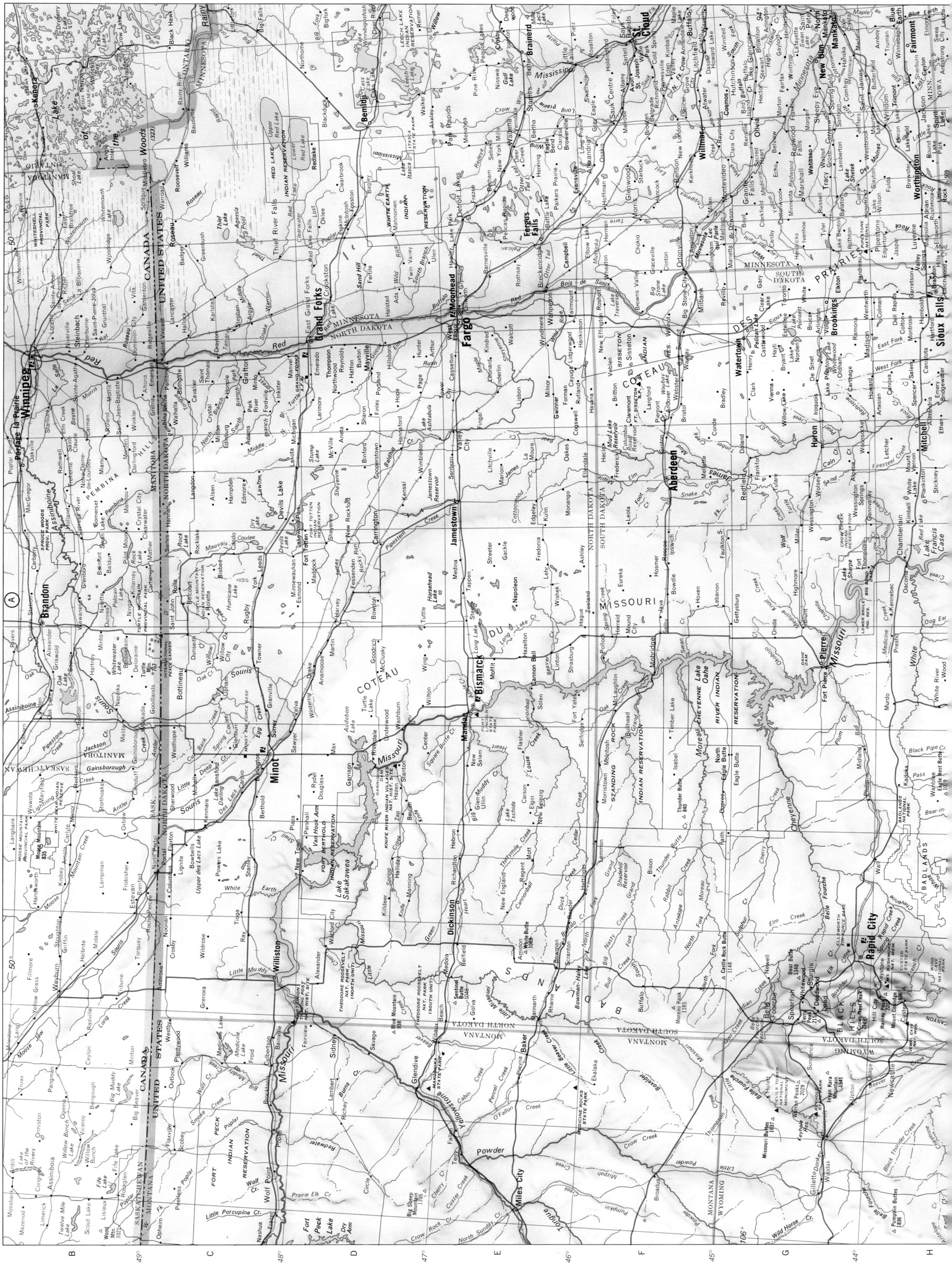
CANADA
UNITED STATES
MANITOBA
SASKATCHEWAN
ONTARIO
MONTANA
NORTH DAKOTA
SOUTH DAKOTA
MINNESOTA
WYOMING
IOWA
Winnipeg
Brandon
Portage la Prairie
Kenora
Lake of the Woods
Minot
Williston
Bismarck
Mandan
Dickinson
Jamestown
Fargo
Moorhead
Grand Forks
Devils Lake
Aberdeen
Pierre
Rapid City
Watertown
Brookings
Sioux Falls
Mitchell
Huron
Bemidji
Brainerd
St. Cloud
Fergus Falls
Willmar
Mankato
New Ulm
Worthington
Miles City
Glendive
Sidney
Wolf Point
Baker
Missouri
Yellowstone
Red
Souris
Lake Sakakawea
Lake Oahe
BADLANDS
BLACK HILLS
COTEAU DU MISSOURI
COTEAU DES PRAIRIES
FORT PECK INDIAN RESERVATION
FORT BERTHOLD INDIAN RESERVATION
STANDING ROCK INDIAN RESERVATION
CHEYENNE RIVER INDIAN RESERVATION
RED LAKE INDIAN RESERVATION
WHITE EARTH INDIAN RESERVATION
SISSETON INDIAN RES.
INTERNATIONAL PEACE GARDEN
THEODORE ROOSEVELT NAT. PARK

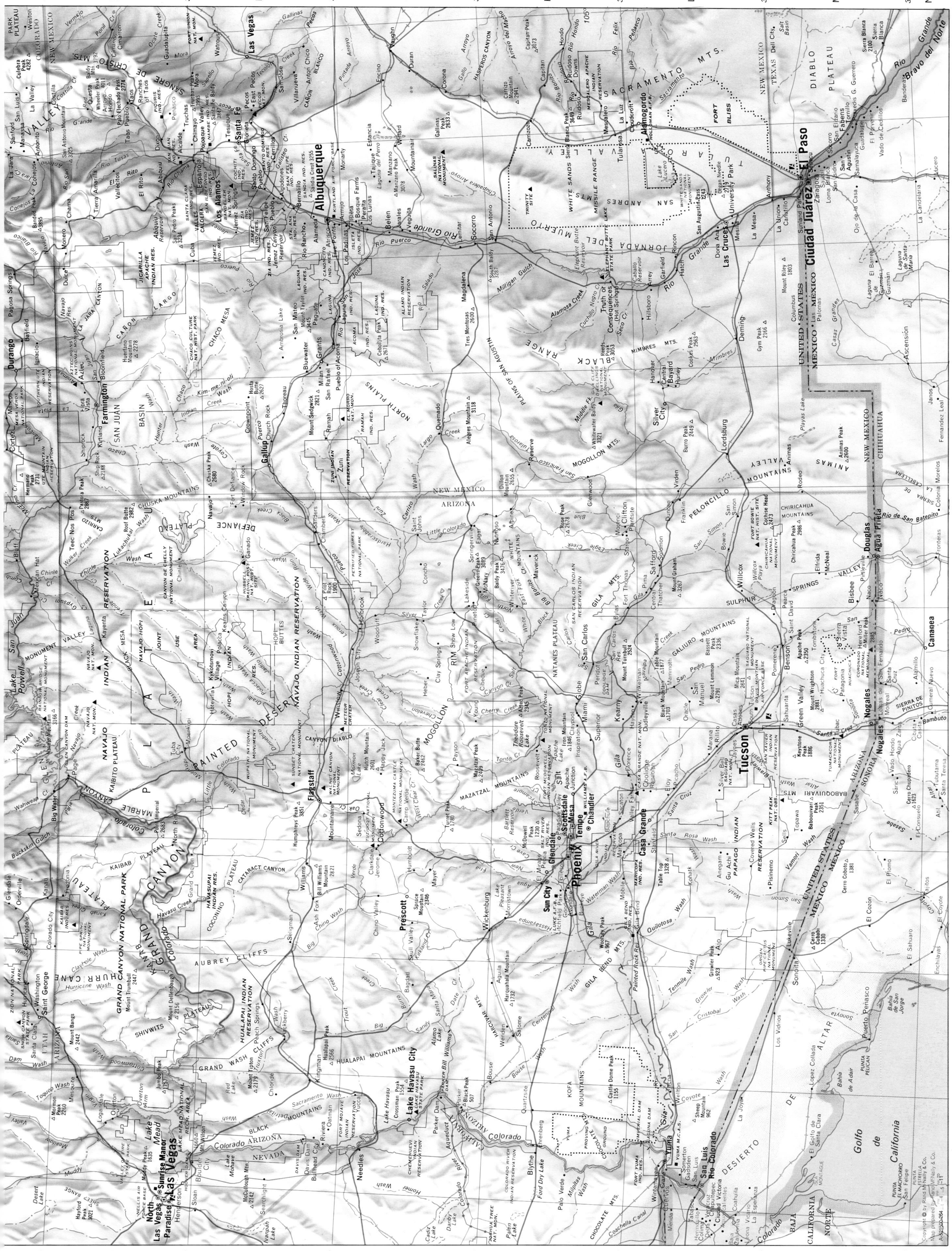

Kilometers 0 50 100 150 Km.

Statute Miles 0 50 100 150 Mi.

Scale 1:3,000,000

One centimeter represents 30 kilometers.

One inch represents approximately 47 miles.

Albers Conical Equal-Area Projection

Northwestern United States

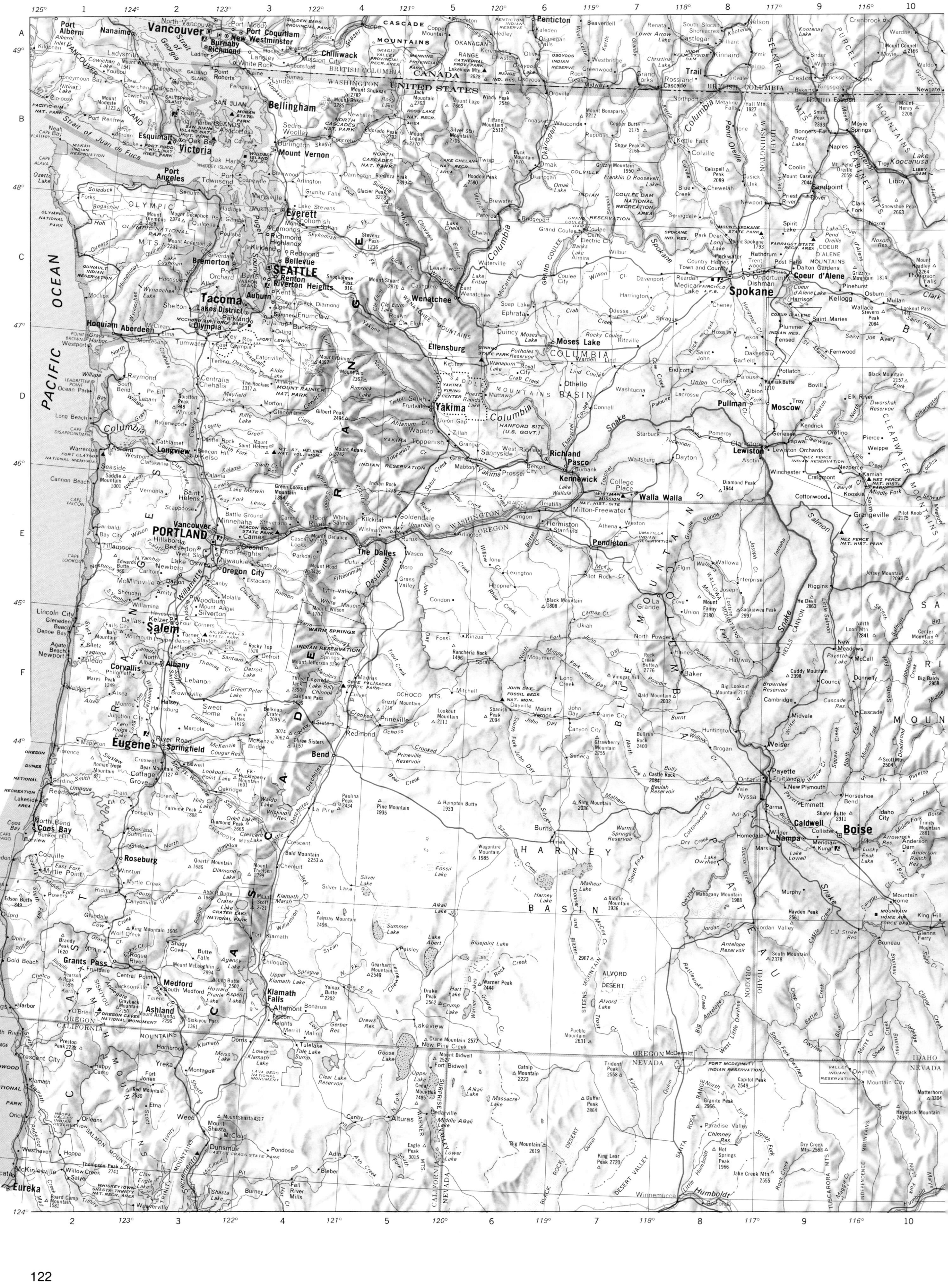

Kilometers 0 50 100 150 Km.

Statute Miles 0 50 100 150 Mi.

Scale 1:3,000,000

One centimeter represents 30 kilometers.

One inch represents approximately 47 miles.

Albers Conical Equal-Area Projection

SAN FRANCISCO
Oakland
San Jose
Sacramento
Stockton
Modesto
Merced
Santa Rosa
Reno
Sparks
Carson City
Eureka
Redding
Chico
Medford
Klamath Falls
Twin Falls
Elko
Winnemucca
COAST RANGES
CASCADE RANGE
KLAMATH MOUNTAINS
SIERRA NEVADA
GREAT BASIN
GREAT SALT LAKE DESERT
BLACK ROCK DESERT
COLUMBIA PLATEAU
SNAKE RIVER PLAIN
HARNEY BASIN
SACRAMENTO VALLEY
SAN JOAQUIN VALLEY
RUBY MOUNTAINS
SHOSHONE RANGE
TOIYABE RANGE
EGAN RANGE
SCHELL CREEK RANGE
WHITE MOUNTAINS
NELLIS WEAPONS RANGE

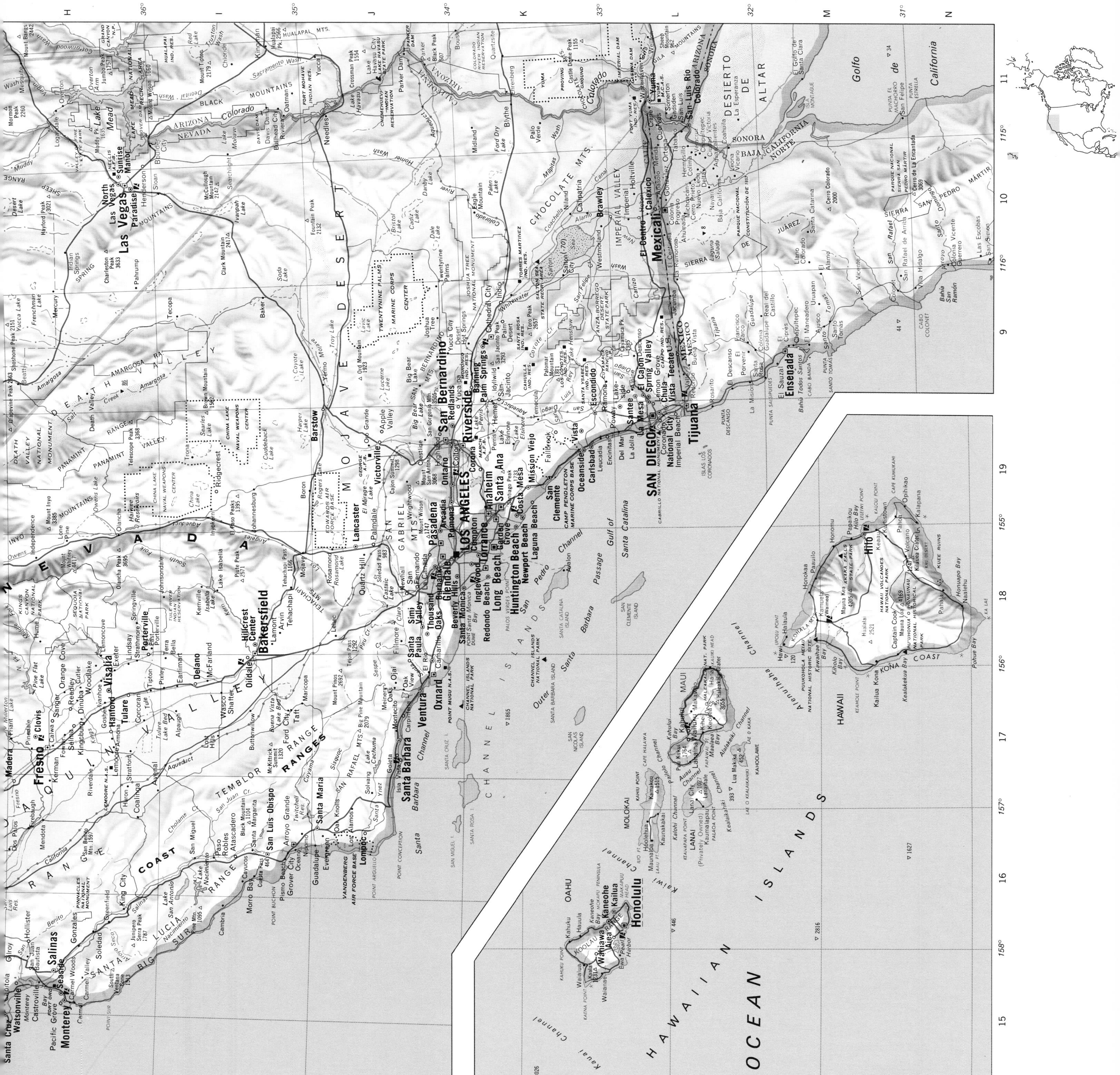

Kilometers 0 50 100 150 Km.

Statute Miles 0 50 100 150 Mi.

Scale 1:3,000,000

One centimeter represents 30 kilometers.

One inch represents approximately 47 miles.

Albers Conical Equal-Area Projection

GREENLAND
Greenland Sea
Barents Sea
Arctic Circle
ICELAND
Norwegian Sea
FINLAND
UNITED KINGDOM
IRELAND
North Sea
Baltic Sea
FRANCE
POLAND
GERMANY
UKRAINE
HUNGARY
ROMANIA
BULGARIA
ITALY
SPAIN
MEDITERRANEAN SEA
Black Sea
TURKEY
ASIA MINOR
SYRIA
IRAQ
IRAN
SAUDI ARABIA
ARABIAN PENINSULA
YEMEN
OMAN
EGYPT
LIBYA
SAHARA
Tropic of Cancer
SUDAN
ETHIOPIA
AFRICA
SOMALIA
KENYA
TANZANIA
ZAIRE
ZAMBIA
ZIMBABWE
MOZAMBIQUE
BOTSWANA
NAMIBIA
SOUTH AFRICA
MADAGASCAR
KAZAKHSTAN
Caspian Sea
AFGHANISTAN
PAKISTAN
INDIA
HIMALAYAS
NEPAL
BHUTAN
BURMA
THAILAND
MALAYSIA
Arabian Sea
ARABIAN BASIN
Bay of Bengal
SRI LANKA
MALDIVES
SEYCHELLES
MAURITIUS
REUNION
CHINA
MONGOLIA
GOBI
RUSSIA
SIBERIA
URAL MOUNTAINS
ZAPADNO-SIBIRSKAJA RAVNINA
SREDNESIBIRSKOJE PLOSKOGORJE
TIBET
KUNLUN SHAN
TIEN SHAN
Sea of Okhotsk
Sea of Japan
JAPAN
N. KOREA
S. KOREA
Yellow Sea
East China Sea
South China Sea
TAIWAN
PHILIPPINES
Philippine Sea
PHILIPPINE BASIN
VIET-NAM
BORNEO
INDONESIA
SUNDA SHELF
GREATER SUNDA ISLANDS
JAVA TRENCH
Arafura Sea
Timor Sea
NEW GUINEA
PAPUA NEW GUINEA
Coral Sea
Gulf of Carpentaria
AUSTRALIA
GREAT SANDY DESERT
GREAT VICTORIA DESERT
GREAT DIVIDING RANGE
Great Australian Bight
TASMANIA
INDIAN OCEAN
Tropic of Capricorn
MID-INDIAN BASIN
NINETY EAST RIDGE
WHARTON BASIN
NORTH AUSTRALIAN BASIN
PERTH BASIN
CHAGOS-LACCADIVE PLATEAU
CARLSBERG RIDGE
SOMALI BASIN
MASCARENE BASIN
MADAGASCAR BASIN
MID-INDIAN RIDGE
SOUTHWEST INDIAN RIDGE
SOUTHEAST INDIAN RIDGE
SOUTH INDIAN BASIN
CROZET BASIN
KERGUELEN PLATEAU
AGULHAS BASIN
ATLANTIC-INDIAN RIDGE
ATLANTIC-INDIAN BASIN
SOUTH AUSTRALIAN BASIN
SOUTHERN OCEAN
TASMAN BASIN
Antarctic Circle
ENDERBY LAND
AMERY ICE SHELF
AMERICAN HIGHLAND
WILKES LAND
ANTARCTICA

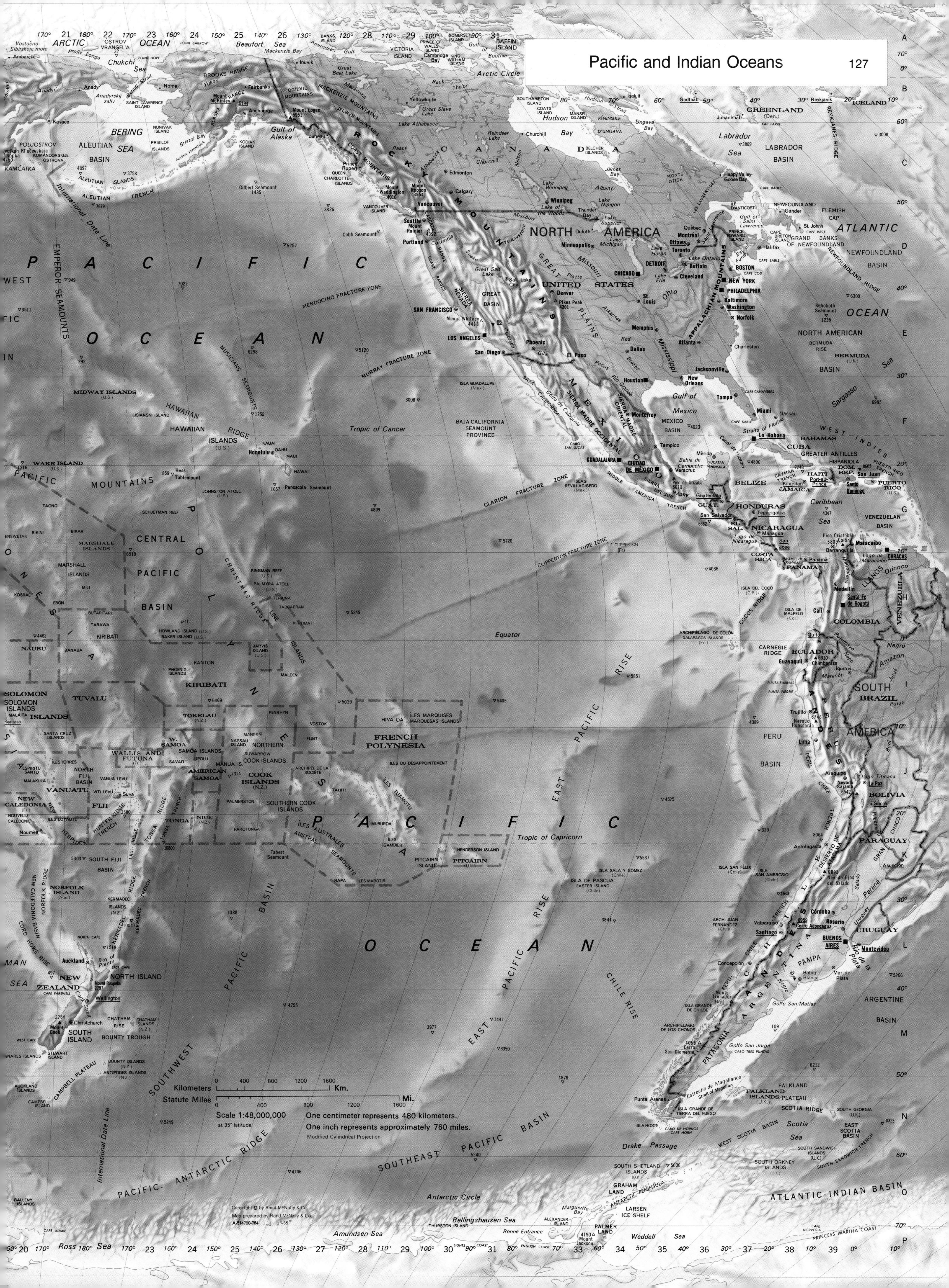
ARCTIC OCEAN
Beaufort Sea
Chukchi Sea
BERING SEA
Gulf of Alaska
ALEUTIAN BASIN
ALEUTIAN TRENCH
International Date Line
EMPEROR SEAMOUNTS
P A C I F I C
O C E A N
MENDOCINO FRACTURE ZONE
MURRAY FRACTURE ZONE
MUSICIANS SEAMOUNTS
MIDWAY ISLANDS (U.S.)
HAWAIIAN RIDGE
HAWAIIAN ISLANDS (U.S.)
Honolulu
Tropic of Cancer
BAJA CALIFORNIA SEAMOUNT PROVINCE
WAKE ISLAND (U.S.)
PACIFIC MOUNTAINS
CLARION FRACTURE ZONE
CLIPPERTON FRACTURE ZONE
MARSHALL ISLANDS
CENTRAL PACIFIC BASIN
CHRISTMAS RIDGE
LINE ISLANDS
KIRIBATI
NAURU
Equator
SOLOMON ISLANDS
TUVALU
TOKELAU (N.Z.)
W. SAMOA
AMERICAN SAMOA
COOK ISLANDS (N.Z.)
FRENCH POLYNESIA
VANUATU
FIJI
NEW CALEDONIA
TONGA
NIUE (N.Z.)
Tropic of Capricorn
PITCAIRN (U.K.)
SOUTH FIJI BASIN
NORFOLK ISLAND
NEW ZEALAND
NORTH ISLAND
SOUTH ISLAND
Wellington
Auckland
Christchurch
CHATHAM RISE
BOUNTY TROUGH
CAMPBELL PLATEAU
SOUTHWEST PACIFIC BASIN
EAST PACIFIC RISE
CHILE RISE
PERU BASIN
SOUTHEAST PACIFIC BASIN
PACIFIC-ANTARCTIC RIDGE
Antarctic Circle
Amundsen Sea
Bellingshausen Sea
Ross Sea
Weddell Sea
Drake Passage
Scotia Sea
ATLANTIC-INDIAN BASIN
NORTH AMERICA
CANADA
UNITED STATES
MEXICO
ROCKY MOUNTAINS
GREAT PLAINS
APPALACHIAN MOUNTAINS
Hudson Bay
Labrador Sea
GREENLAND (Den.)
LABRADOR BASIN
ATLANTIC OCEAN
NORTH AMERICAN BASIN
Gulf of Mexico
Caribbean Sea
CUBA
HAITI
DOM. REP.
JAMAICA
BELIZE
HONDURAS
GUAT.
EL SAL.
NICARAGUA
COSTA RICA
PANAMA
COLOMBIA
VENEZUELA
ECUADOR
PERU
BOLIVIA
BRAZIL
PARAGUAY
URUGUAY
ARGENTINA
CHILE
SOUTH AMERICA
ANDES
PATAGONIA
PAMPA
ARGENTINE BASIN
FALKLAND ISLANDS (U.K.)
SCOTIA RIDGE
SOUTH GEORGIA (U.K.)
SOUTH SANDWICH ISLANDS (U.K.)
SOUTH SHETLAND ISLANDS
SOUTH ORKNEY ISLANDS (U.K.)
GRAHAM LAND
ANTARCTIC PENINSULA
LARSEN ICE SHELF
PALMER LAND
Kilometers 0 400 800 1200 1600 Km.
Statute Miles 0 400 800 1200 1600 Mi.
Scale 1:48,000,000 at 35° latitude
One centimeter represents 480 kilometers.
One inch represents approximately 760 miles.
Modified Cylindrical Projection
Copyright © by Rand McNally & Co.
Map prepared by Rand McNally & Co.

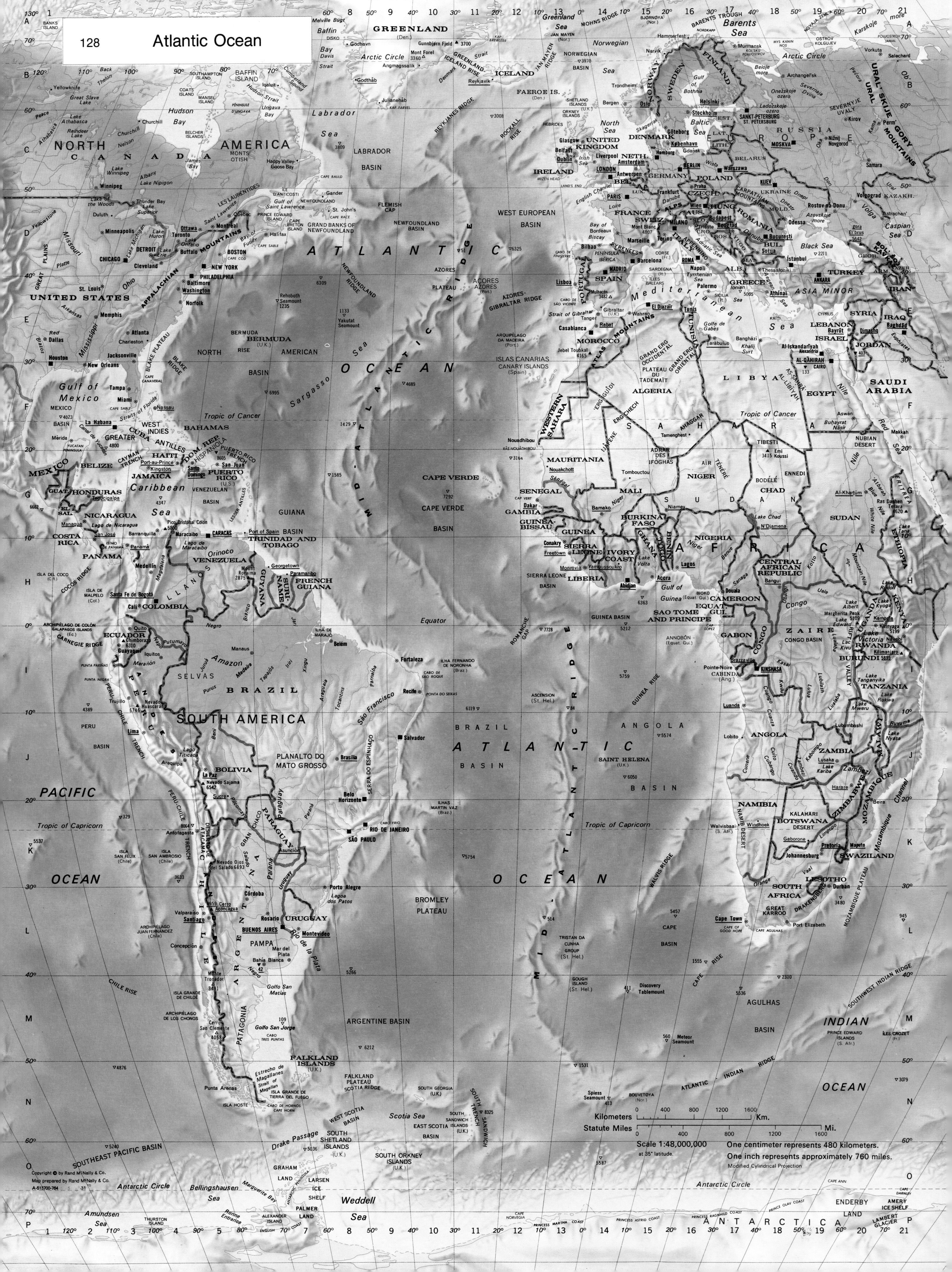
GREENLAND
Baffin Bay
Davis Strait
Labrador Sea
Hudson Bay
NORTH AMERICA
CANADA
UNITED STATES
Gulf of Mexico
Caribbean Sea
Norwegian Sea
North Sea
ICELAND
UNITED KINGDOM
IRELAND
FRANCE
SPAIN
PORTUGAL
EUROPE
Baltic Sea
Barents Sea
Mediterranean Sea
Black Sea
ATLANTIC OCEAN
NORTH AMERICAN BASIN
WEST EUROPEAN BASIN
MID-ATLANTIC RIDGE
Sargasso Sea
Tropic of Cancer
AFRICA
SAHARA
LIBYA
ALGERIA
EGYPT
SAUDI ARABIA
CAPE VERDE BASIN
Gulf of Guinea
Equator
SOUTH AMERICA
BRAZIL
BRAZIL BASIN
ANGOLA BASIN
PACIFIC OCEAN
Tropic of Capricorn
ARGENTINE BASIN
CAPE BASIN
AGULHAS BASIN
INDIAN OCEAN
Scotia Sea
Weddell Sea
Drake Passage
Antarctic Circle
ANTARCTICA
Kilometers 0 400 800 1200 1600 Km.
Statute Miles 0 400 800 1200 1600 Mi.
Scale 1:48,000,000 at 35° latitude.
One centimeter represents 480 kilometers.
One inch represents approximately 760 miles.
Modified Cylindrical Projection
Copyright © by Rand McNally & Co.
Map prepared by Rand McNally & Co.
A-613700-764

Name — Map Ref. — Page

Dja, stm., Afr. H9 54
Djakarta see Jakarta, Indon. J13 39a
Djamâa, Alg. D13 62
Djambala, Congo B2 58
Djanet, Alg. H15 62
Djedi, Oued, val., Alg. C13 62
Djema, Cen. Afr. Rep. N3 60
Djemila, hist., Alg. B13 62
Djénné, Mali E7 64
Djérem, stm., Cam. G9 54
Djibo, Burkina D9 64
Djibouti, Dji. F9 56
Djibouti, ctry., Afr. F9 56
Djokupunda, Zaire C4 58
Djougou, Benin G10 64
Djúpivogur, Ice. B6 6a
Djurås, Swe. K14 6
Dmitrija Lapteva, proliv, strt., Russia C20 28
Dmitrijevka, Russia I23 22
Dmitrijev-L'govskij, Russia I18 22
Dmitrov, Russia E20 22
Dmitrovskij Pogost, Russia F22 22
Dmitrovskij-Orlovskij, Russia I18 22
Dnepr, stm., Eur. H4 26
Dneprodzeržinsk, Ukr. H4 26
Dnepropetrovsk, Ukr. H4 26
Dneprovsko-Bugskij kanal, Bela. I7 22
Dnestr, stm., Eur. H3 26
Dnestrovskij liman, I., Ukr. C14 20
Dnieper see Dnepr, stm., Eur. H4 26
Dniester see Dnestr, stm., Eur. H3 26
Dno, Russia D12 22
Doaktown, N.B., Can. F7 106
Doany, Madag. O23 67b
Doba, Chad E4 56
Dobane, Cen. Afr. Rep. N3 60
Dobbiaco, Italy C7 18
Dobczyce, Pol. F20 10
Dobele, Lat. E6 22
Döbeln, Ger. D13 10
Doberai, Jazirah, pen., Indon. F9 38
Doboj, Bos. E2 20
Dobr'anka, Russia F9 26
Dobrič, Bul. F11 20
Dobrinka, Russia I23 22
Dobříš, Czech. F14 10
Dobromil', Ukr. F22 10
Dobrudžansko plato, plat., Bul. F11 20
Dobruja, reg., Eur. E12 20
Dobruš, Bela. I14 22
Dobson, N.C., U.S. C6 112
Doce, stm., Braz. E8 79
Doce, stm., Braz. E3 79
Dock Junction, Ga., U.S. H5 112
Doctor Arroyo, Mex. F9 90
Doctor Cecilio Báez, Para. C10 80
Doctor Pedro P. Peña, Para. B7 80
Dod Ballāpur, India F4 46
Doddridge, Ar., U.S. I3 114
Doddsville, Ms., U.S. I6 114
Dodecanese see Dhodhekánisos, is., Grc. M10 20
Dodge, Ne., U.S. J11 118
Dodge Center, Mn., U.S. F3 110
Dodge City, Ks., U.S. N7 118
Dodgeville, Wi., U.S. H5 110
Dodola, Eth. N10 60
Dodoma, Tan. C7 58
Dodsland, Sask., Can. G6 104
Dodson, La., U.S. J4 114
Dodson, Mt., U.S. B17 122
Dodson, Tx., U.S. E6 116
Doe River, B.C., Can. A14 102
Doerun, Ga., U.S. H3 112
Doetinchem, Neth. E9 12
Dogai Coring, I., China C13 44
Dog Creek, B.C., Can. F12 102
Dog Creek, stm., B.C., Can. F12 102
Dog Island, i., Anguilla E13 94
Dog Lake, I., Man., Can. G16 104
Dōgo, i., Japan K8 36
Do Gonbadān, Iran F11 48
Dogondoutchi, Niger E12 64
Dogpound Creek, stm., Alta., Can. F20 102
Doğubayazıt, Tur. B8 48
Doha see Ad-Dawhah, Qatar B7 47
Doiran, Lake, I., Eur. H6 20
Dois de Novembro, Cachoeira, wtfl, Braz. C10 82
Dokka, Nor. K12 6
Dokšicy, Bela. G10 22
Doksy, Czech. E14 10
Doland, S.D., U.S. G9 118
Dolbeau, Que., Can. G18 96
Dol-de-Bretagne, Fr. D5 14
Dole, Fr. E12 14
Dolega, Pan. C1 84
Dolgeville, N.Y., U.S. D12 108
Dolgoje, Russia I20 22
Dolgorukovo, Russia I21 22
Dolinsk, Russia H20 28
Dolisie, Congo B2 58
Dolj, co., Rom. E7 20
Dollard, b., Eur. B11 12
Dolmatovskij, Russia D25 22
Dolomites see Dolomiti, mts., Italy C6 18
Dolomiti, mts., Italy C6 18
Dolores, Arg. I10 80
Dolores, Col. F5 84
Dolores, Guat. I15 90
Dolores, Co., U.S. G8 120
Dolores, Ur. G9 80
Dolores, Ven. C8 84
Dolores, stm., U.S. F8 120
Dolores Hidalgo, Mex. G9 90
Dolphin and Union Strait, strt., N.W. Ter., Can. C9 96
Dolžak, Ukr. A10 20
Dom Aquino, Braz. C1 79
Domažlice, Czech. F12 10
Dombarovskij, Russia G9 26
Dombås, Nor. J11 6
Dombrád, Hung. G21 10
Dom Cavati, Braz. E7 79
Dome Creek, B.C., Can. D13 102
Domeyko, Chile E3 80
Domeyko, Cordillera, mts., Chile B4 80
Domfront, Fr. D6 14
Domiciano Ribeiro, Braz. D5 79
Domingo M. Irala, Para. C11 80
Domingos Martins, Braz. F8 79
Dominica, ctry., N.A. G14 94
Dominical, C.R. H11 92
Dominican Republic (República Dominicana), ctry., N.A. E9 94
Dominica Passage, strt., N.A. G14 94
Dominion, N.S., Can. F13 106
Dominion, Cape, c., N.W. Ter., Can. C18 96
Dominion City, Man., Can. I17 104
Dom Joaquim, Braz. E7 79
Domo, Eth. G10 56
Domodedovo, Russia F20 22
Domodossola, Italy C3 18
Domoni, Com. L16 67a
Dom Pedrito, Braz. F11 80
Domremy, Sask., Can. F9 104
Dom Silvério, Braz. F7 79
Domuyo, Volcán, vol., Arg. I3 80
Don, stm., Russia H6 26
Don, stm., Scot., U.K. D11 8
Dona Ana, N.M., U.S. L10 120
Donadeu, Arg. D7 80
Donald, Austl. K5 70
Donalda, Alta., Can. E22 102
Donaldson, Ar., U.S. H4 114
Donaldsonville, La., U.S. L6 114
Donalsonville, Ga., U.S. H2 112
Doñana, Parque Nacional de, Spain H5 16
Donaueschingen, Ger. H8 10
Donauwörth, Ger. G10 10
Don Benito, Spain G6 16
Doncaster, Eng., U.K. H12 8
Dondo, Ang. C2 58
Dondo, Moz. B12 66
Dondra Head, c., Sri L. J6 46
Dond'ušany, Mol. A11 20
Doneck, Ukr. H5 26
Donegal, Ire. G5 8
Donegal, co., Ire. G5 8
Donegal Bay, b., Ire. G5 8
Doneraile, S.C., U.S. E7 112
Donetsk see Doneck, Ukr. H5 26
Dong, stm., China L6 34
Donga, stm., Nig. G15 64
Dong'an, China B3 34
Dongara, Austl. E2 68
Dongba, China D8 34
Dongchuan, China A7 40
Dongdaoan, China E5 32
Dong'ezhen, China G4 32
Dongfang (Basuo), China E10 40
Dongfeng, China A13 32
Donggu, China I4 34
Dongguan, China L2 34
Dongguanyingzi, China B8 32
Donghai Dao, i., China D11 40
Dong Hoi, Viet. F9 40
Dongmen, China G3 34
Dong Nai, stm., Viet. I9 40
Dongshi, China K7 34
Dongtai, China C9 34
Dongting Hu, I., China G1 34
Dongyang, China F9 34
Dongzhi, China E5 34
Donie, Tx., U.S. H10 116
Doniphan, Mo., U.S. F6 114
Doniphan, Ne., U.S. K9 118
Donjek, stm., Yukon, Can. F25 100
Donji Vakuf, Bos. E12 18
Don Matías, Col. D5 84
Donna, Tx., U.S. M8 116
Donnelly, Alta., Can. B17 102
Donnelly, Id., U.S. F9 122
Donner, La., U.S. M6 114
Donner Pass, Ca., U.S. E5 124
Donner und Blitzen, stm., Or., U.S. G7 122
Donora, Pa., U.S. G7 108
Donostia (San Sebastián), Spain B10 16
Don Peninsula, pen., B.C., Can. E6 102
Donskoj, Russia H21 22
Donskoje, Russia I22 22
Doolow, Som. H9 56
Doomadgee, Austl. A3 70
Doon, Ia., U.S. H11 118
Doornik (Tournai), Bel. G3 12
Door Peninsula, pen., Wi., U.S. F8 110
Dora, Al., U.S. I9 114
Doraville, Ga., U.S. F2 112
Dorcheat, Bayou, stm., U.S. I3 114
Dorchester, N.B., Can. G9 106
Dorchester, Ont., Can. H14 110
Dorchester, Eng., U.K. K11 8
Dorchester, Ne., U.S. K10 118
Dorchester, Wi., U.S. E5 110
Dorchester, Cape, c., N.W. Ter., Can. C17 96
Dorchester Crossing, N.B., Can. F9 106
Dordogne, dept., Fr. G7 14
Dordogne, stm., Fr. H8 14
Dordrecht, Neth. E6 12
Dordrecht, S. Afr. H8 66
Doré, stm., Sask., Can. D7 104
Doré Lake, Sask., Can. D7 104
Doré Lake, I., Sask., Can. D7 104
Dorena, Or., U.S. G3 122
Dores do Indaiá, Braz. E6 79
Dornach, Switz. D8 13
Dornbirn, Aus. H9 10
Doro, Mali C9 64
Dorochovo, Russia F19 22
Dorog, Hung. H18 10
Dorogobuž, Russia G16 22
Dorohoi, Rom. B10 20
Dorrance, Ks., U.S. M9 118
Dorre Island, i., Austl. E2 68
Dorrigo, Austl. H10 70
Dorris, Ca., U.S. C4 124
Dorset, co., Eng., U.K. K11 8
Dortmund, Ger. D7 10
Dorton, Ky., U.S. B4 112
Dörtyol, Tur. C4 48
Do Rūd, Iran E10 48
Doruma, Zaire H6 56
Dos, Canal Numero, Arg. I6 80
Dosatuj, Russia G15 28
Dos Bahías, Cabo, c., Arg. E3 78
Doščatoje, Russia F25 22
Dos Hermanas, Spain H6 16
Dos Palos, Ca., U.S. H5 124
Dos Quebradas, Col. E5 84
Dossor, Kaz. H8 26
Dothan, Al., U.S. K11 114
Doting Cove, Newf., Can. C20 106
Dotnuva, Lith. F6 22
Douai, Fr. B10 14
Douala, Cam. I14 64
Douarnenez, Fr. D2 14
Double, Lac, I., Que., Can. B3 106
Double Island Point, c., Austl. E10 70
Double Point, c., Austl. A7 70
Double Springs, Al., U.S. H9 114
Doubletop Peak, mtn., Wy., U.S. G15 122
Doubs, dept., Fr. E13 14
Doubs, stm., Eur. E12 14
Doubs, Saut de, wtfl, Eur. D6 13
Doudeville, Fr. C7 14
Douentza, Mali D8 64
Douglas, Man., Can. I15 104
Douglas, I. of Man G9 8
Douglas, Ak., U.S. G27 100
Douglas, Az., U.S. M7 120
Douglas, Ga., U.S. H4 112
Douglas, N.D., U.S. D6 118
Douglas, Wy., U.S. B11 120
Douglas, Cape, c., Ak., U.S. G18 100
Douglas, Mount, mtn., Ak., U.S. G18 100
Douglas Channel, strt., B.C., Can. D5 102
Douglas Lake, B.C., Can. G14 102
Douglas Lake, res., Tn., U.S. C3 112
Douglas Lake Indian Reserve, B.C., Can. G14 102
Douglass, Ks., U.S. N10 118
Douglasville, Ga., U.S. F2 112
Doulaincourt, Fr. D12 14
Doulevant-le-Château, Fr. D11 14
Doullens, Fr. B9 14
Doumanaba, Mali F7 64
Doura, Mali E7 64
Dourada, Serra, plat., Braz. B4 79
Dourados, Braz. G1 79
Dourados, stm., Braz. G1 79
Dourdan, Fr. D9 14
Dourkoulé, Chad J2 60
Douro (Duero), stm., Eur. D4 16
Doushanhe, China D3 34
Douz, Tun. D15 62
Dove Creek, Co., U.S. G8 120
Dover, Austl. N7 70
Dover, Eng., U.K. J15 8
Dover, Ar., U.S. G3 114
Dover, De., U.S. H11 108
Dover, Id., U.S. B9 122
Dover, N.H., U.S. D16 108
Dover, N.J., U.S. G12 108
Dover, N.C., U.S. D9 112
Dover, Oh., U.S. G5 108
Dover, Ok., U.S. D9 116
Dover, Tn., U.S. F9 114
Dover, Strait of (Pas de Calais), strt., Eur. J15 8
Dover-Foxcroft, Me., U.S. B17 108
Dovre, Nor. K11 6
Dovsk, Bela. H13 22
Dowagiac, Mi., U.S. I9 110
Dowagiac, stm., Mi., U.S. H9 110
Dow City, Ia., U.S. J12 118
Dowlatābād, Afg. B1 44
Dowlatābād, Afg. B2 44
Dowlat Yār, Afg. C1 44
Dowling Lake, I., Alta., Can. F22 102
Downey, Id., U.S. H13 122
Downieville, Ca., U.S. E5 124
Downing, Mo., U.S. B4 114
Downingtown, Pa., U.S. G11 108
Downs, Ks., U.S. L9 118
Downs Mountain, mtn., Wy., U.S. G16 122
Downsville, N.Y., U.S. E12 108
Downton, Mount, mtn., B.C., Can. E10 102
Downton Lake, I., B.C., Can. G11 102
Dows, Ia., U.S. H2 110
Dowshī, Afg. C3 44
Doyle, Ca., U.S. D5 124
Doyles, Newf., Can. E14 106
Doylestown, Oh., U.S. G5 108
Doylestown, Pa., U.S. G11 108
Doyline, La., U.S. J3 114
Dōzen, is., Japan K8 36
Dozier, Al., U.S. K10 114
Dra'a, Hamada du, des., Alg. F7 62
Drâa, Oued, val., Afr. F5 62
Dracena, Braz. F3 79
Dracut, Ma., U.S. E15 108
Drăgășani, Rom. E8 20
Dragons Mouths, strt. B12 84
Dragoon, Az., U.S. L6 120
Draguignan, Fr. I13 14
Drain, Or., U.S. G2 122
Drake, N.D., U.S. D7 118
Drakensberg, mts., Afr. F9 66
Drake Passage, strt. J8 74
Drake Peak, mtn., Or., U.S. H5 122
Drakesboro, Ky., U.S. E9 114
Drakes Branch, Va., U.S. C8 112
Dráma, Grc. H8 20
Drammen, Nor. L12 6
Drang, stm., Asia H9 40
Draper, N.C., U.S. C7 112
Draper, Ut., U.S. D5 120
Drau (Drava) (Dráva), stm., Eur. C8 18
Drava (Drau) (Dráva), stm., Eur. D13 18
Drawno, Pol. B15 10
Drayton, N.D., U.S. C10 118
Drayton, S.C., U.S. E5 112
Drayton Valley, Alta., Can. D20 102
Drean, Alg. M2 18
Drenthe, prov., Neth. C10 12
Dresden, Ont., Can. H13 110
Dresden, Ger. D13 10
Dresden, Oh., U.S. G4 108
Dresden, Tn., U.S. F8 114
Dretun, Bela. F12 22
Dreux, Fr. D8 14
Drew, Ms., U.S. I6 114
Driftpile, stm., Alta., Can. B19 102
Drift Pile River Indian Reserve, Alta., Can. B19 102
Driftwood, B.C., Can. B8 102
Driftwood, stm., B.C., Can. B8 102
Driftwood, stm., In., U.S. C10 114
Driggs, Id., U.S. G14 122
Drin, stm., Alb. H3 20
Drina, stm., Eur. E3 20
Drinit, Gjiri i, b., Alb. H3 20
Driscoll, Tx., U.S. L9 116
Driskill Mountain, hill, La., U.S. J4 114
Drobeta-Turnu Severin, Rom. E6 20
Drogheda, Ire. H7 8
Drogičin, Bela. I8 22
Drogobyč, Ukr. H2 26
Drohiczyn, Pol. C22 10
Drokija, Mol. A11 20
Drôme, dept., Fr. H12 14
Droskovo, Russia I20 22
Druja, Bela. F10 22
Drumheller, Alta., Can. F22 102
Drummond, Mt., U.S. D12 122
Drummond, Wi., U.S. D4 110
Drummond Island, i., Mi., U.S. E12 110
Drummond Range, mts., Austl. E7 70
Drummondville, Que., Can. B14 108
Drumright, Ok., U.S. D10 116
Druskininkai, Lith. G6 22
Družba, Kaz. H14 26
Drvar, Bos. E11 18
Dry Bay, b., Ak., U.S. G25 100
Dryberry Lake, I., Ont., Can. I21 104
Dry Cimarron, stm., U.S. C3 116
Dry Creek Mountain, mtn., Nv., U.S. C9 124
Dryden, Ont., Can. I22 104
Dry Devils, stm., Tx., U.S. J6 116
Dry Fork, stm., Mo., U.S. E5 114
Dry Prong, La., U.S. K4 114
Dry Ridge, Ky., U.S. I2 108
Drysdale, stm., Austl. C5 68
Drysdale River National Park, Austl. B5 68
Dry Tortugas, is., Fl., U.S. O4 112
Dschang, Cam. I15 64
Du, Ghana F9 64
Duarte, Pico, mtn., Dom. Rep. E9 94
Duartina, Braz. G4 79
Dubā, Sau. Ar. H3 48
Dubach, La., U.S. J4 114
Dubai see Dubayy, U.A.E. B9 47
Dubawnt, stm., N.W. Ter., Can. D12 96
Dubawnt Lake, I., N.W. Ter., Can. D12 96
Dubayy (Dubai), U.A.E. B9 47
Dubbo, Austl. I8 70
Dübendorf, Switz. D10 13
Dubesar' (Dubossary), Mol. B13 20
Dublin (Baile Átha Cliath), Ire. H7 8
Dublin, Ga., U.S. G4 112
Dublin, Tx., U.S. G8 116
Dublin, Va., U.S. B6 112
Dublin, co., Ire. H7 8
Dubna, Russia E20 22
Dubois, Id., U.S. F13 122
Dubois, In., U.S. D10 114
Du Bois, Ne., U.S. K11 118
Du Bois, Pa., U.S. F8 108
Dubois, Wy., U.S. A7 120
Dubossarskoje vodochranilišče, res., Mol. B13 20
Dubossary, Mol. B13 20
Dubovka, Russia H6 26
Dubréka, Gui. G3 64
Dubrovka, Russia H16 22
Dubrovka, Russia B13 22
Dubrovnik, Cro. G2 20
Dubrovno, Bela. G13 22
Dubuque, Ia., U.S. H5 110
Duchcov, Czech. E13 10
Duchesne, Ut., U.S. D6 120
Duchesne, stm., Ut., U.S. D6 120
Duchess, Austl. C3 70
Duchovščina, Russia F15 22
Duck, stm., Tn., U.S. G9 114
Duck Bay, Man., Can. F14 104
Duck Hill, Ms., U.S. I7 114
Duck Lake, Sask., Can. F8 104
Duck Lake, I., Man., Can. D16 104
Duck Mountain, mtn., Man., Can. G13 104
Duck Mountain Provincial Park, Man., Can. G14 104
Duck Mountain Provincial Park, Sask., Can. G13 104
Du Couedic, Cape, c., Austl. K2 70
Duda, stm., Col. F5 84
Dudelange, Lux. J9 12
Duderstadt, Ger. D10 10
Dudinka, Russia D9 28
Dudleyville, Az., U.S. L6 120
Dudorovskij, Russia H18 22
Duékoué, I.C. H6 64
Duero (Douro), stm., Eur. C5 16
Due West, S.C., U.S. E4 112
Duffer Peak, mtn., Nv., U.S. C7 124
Dufourspitze, mtn., Eur. G14 14
Dufur, Or., U.S. E4 122
Duga-Zapadnaja, mys, c., Russia F21 28
Dugdemona, stm., La., U.S. J4 114
Dugger, In., U.S. C9 114
Dugi Otok, i., Cro. E10 18
Du Gué, stm., Que., Can. E18 96
Duhi, Sud. N5 60
Duida, Cerro, mtn., Ven. F10 84
Duisburg, Ger. D6 10
Duitama, Col. E6 84
Duiwelskloof, S. Afr. D10 66
Dukambiya, Eth. J9 60
Duke, Ok., U.S. E7 116
Duke of York Bay, b., N.W. Ter., Can. C16 96
Duk Fadiat, Sud. N6 60
Duk Faiwil, Sud. N6 60
Dukhān, Qatar B7 47
Duki, Pak. E3 44
Dukla Pass, Eur. F21 10
Dūkštas, Lith. F9 22
Duku, Nig. F8 64
Dulan, China D6 30
Dul'apino, Russia D23 22
Dulce, N.M., U.S. H10 120
Dulce, stm., Arg. F7 80
Dulce, Golfo, b., C.R. I11 92
Dulce Nombre de Culmí, Hond. B9 92
Dul'durga, Russia G14 28
Dulkaninna, Austl. G3 70
Dulovka, Russia D11 22
Dulovo, Bul. F11 20
Duluth, Ga., U.S. E2 112
Duluth, Mn., U.S. D3 110
Duma, Bots. B6 66
Dūmā, Syria A6 50
Dumaguete, Phil. D7 38
Dumaresq, stm., Austl. G9 70
Dumaring, Indon. E6 38
Dumas, Ar., U.S. I5 114
Dumas, Tx., U.S. D5 116
Dumayr, Syria A7 50
Dumbarton, Scot., U.K. F9 8
Dumei, China K6 34
Dumfries, Scot., U.K. F10 8
Dumfries and Galloway, prov., Scot., U.K. F9 8
Duminiči, Russia H18 22
Dumka, India H12 44
Dumont, Ia., U.S. H3 110
Dumraon, India H11 44
Dumyāṭ, Egypt B6 60
Dumyāṭ, Masabb, mth., Egypt F1 48
Dunaföldvár, Hung. I18 10
Dunaharaszti, Hung. H19 10
Dunajec, stm., Eur. E20 10
Dunakeszi, Hung. H19 10
Dunaújváros, Hung. I18 10
Dunbar, W.V., U.S. I5 108
Dunblane, Sask., Can. G8 104
Duncan, B.C., Can. I11 102
Duncan, Az., U.S. L7 120
Duncan, Ms., U.S. H6 114
Duncan, Ok., U.S. E9 116
Duncan, stm., B.C., Can. G17 102
Duncan Lake, res., B.C., Can. G18 102
Duncannon, Pa., U.S. G9 108
Duncan Passage, strt., India I2 40
Duncansby Head, c., Scot., U.K. C10 8
Dundaga, Lat. D5 22
Dundalk, Ont., Can. F15 110
Dundalk, Ire. G7 8
Dundalk, Md., U.S. H10 108
Dundas, Ont., Can. G16 110
Dundas, Mn., U.S. F2 110
Dundas Island, i., B.C., Can. C4 102
Dundas Peninsula, pen., N.W. Ter., Can. B10 96
Dundee, S. Afr. G10 66
Dundee, Scot., U.K. E11 8
Dundee, Fl., U.S. K5 112
Dundee, Mi., U.S. I12 110
Dundee, Ms., U.S. H6 114
Dundee, N.Y., U.S. E10 108
Dundurn, Sask., Can. G8 104
Dunedin, N.Z. F3 72
Dunedin, Fl., U.S. K4 112
Dunedoo, Austl. I8 70
Dunfermline, Scot., U.K. E10 8
Dungannon, Va., U.S. C4 112
Dungas, Niger E14 64
Dungog, Austl. I9 70
Dungun, Malay. L7 40
Dunhua, China C12 30
Dunhuang, China C5 30
Dunilovo, Russia D21 22
Dunkerque, Fr. A9 14
Dunkirk, In., U.S. B11 114
Dunkirk, N.Y., U.S. E7 108
Dunkirk, Oh., U.S. G3 108
Dunkirk see Dunkerque, Fr. A9 14
Dunkuj, Sud. K7 60
Dunkwa, Ghana I9 64
Dún Laoghaire, Ire. H7 8
Dunlap, Ia., U.S. J12 118
Dunlap, Tn., U.S. G11 114
Dunleary see Dún Laoghaire, Ire. H7 8
Dunmore, Pa., U.S. F11 108
Dunmore Town, Bah. B6 94
Dunn, N.C., U.S. D8 112
Dunnellon, Fl., U.S. J4 112
Dunning, Ne., U.S. J7 118
Dunnville, Ont., Can. H16 110
Dunqulah, Sud. H6 60
Dunqulah al-Qadīmah, Sud. H6 60
Dunqunāb, Sud. G9 60
Dunrea, Man., Can. I15 104
Duns, Scot., U.K. F11 8
Dunseith, N.D., U.S. C7 118
Dunsmuir, Ca., U.S. C3 124
Dunster, B.C., Can. D15 102
Dun-sur-Auron, Fr. F9 14
Dun-sur-Meuse, Fr. C12 14
Dunville, Newf., Can. E20 106
Duolun (Dolonnur), China A4 32
Duolundabohuer, China D15 44
Duomaer, China E2 30
Duomula, China E3 30
Duozhu, China M3 34
Du Page, stm., Il., U.S. I7 110
Dupree, S.D., U.S. F6 118
Duque de Caxias, Braz. G7 79
DuQuoin, Il., U.S. E7 114
Durack Ranges, mts., Austl. C5 68
Duran, N.M., U.S. J11 120
Durance, stm., Fr. I12 14
Durand, Il., U.S. H6 110
Durand, Mi., U.S. H12 110
Durand, Wi., U.S. F4 110
Durango, Mex. E7 90
Durango, Spain B9 16
Durango, Co., U.S. G9 120
Durango, state, Mex. E7 90
Durant, Ia., U.S. I5 110
Durant, Ms., U.S. I7 114
Durant, Ok., U.S. F10 116
Durazno, Ur. G10 80
Durban, S. Afr. G10 66
Durbe, Lat. E4 22
Durbin, W.V., U.S. I7 108
Đurđevac, Cro. C12 18
Düren, Ger. E6 10
Durg, India J9 44
Durgāpur, India I12 44
Durham, Ont., Can. F15 110
Durham, Ca., U.S. E4 124
Durham, N.H., U.S. D16 108
Durham, N.C., U.S. D8 112
Durham, co., Eng., U.K. G12 8
Durham Heights, mtn., N.W. Ter., Can. B8 96
Durleşty, Mol. B12 20
Durmitor, mtn., Yugo. F3 20
Durness, Scot., U.K. C9 8
Dürnkrut, Aus. G16 10
Durrell, Newf., Can. C19 106
Durrës, Alb. H3 20
Dursunbey, Tur. J12 20
D'Urville, Tanjung, c., Indon. F10 38
D'Urville Island, i., N.Z. D4 72
Dušak, Turk. C16 48
Dušanbe, Taj. J11 26
Dusetos, Lith. F8 22
Dushan, China B9 40
Dushanzi, China C3 30
Dusheng, China E4 32
Dushore, Pa., U.S. F10 108
Duson, La., U.S. L4 114
Düsseldorf, Ger. D6 10
Dustin, Ok., U.S. D10 116
Dutch Creek, stm., B.C., Can. G18 102
Dutch Harbor, Ak., U.S. J11 100
Dutch John, Ut., U.S. D7 120
Dutlwe, Bots. D6 66
Dutou, China M4 34
Dutton, Ont., Can. H14 110
Dutton, Mt., U.S. C14 122
Dutton, stm., Austl. C5 70
Dutton, Mount, mtn., Ut., U.S. F4 120
Duyun, China A9 40
Duze, China F7 34
Dvinskaja guba, b., Russia I26 6
Dvuch Cirkov, gora, mtn., Russia D25 28
Dvůr Králové [nad Labem], Czech. E15 10
Dwārka, India I3 44
Dwight, Il., U.S. I7 110
Dworshak Reservoir, res., Id., U.S. D10 122
Dyer, Tn., U.S. F8 114
Dyer, Cape, c., N.W. Ter., Can. C20 96
Dyersburg, Tn., U.S. F7 114
Dyersville, Ia., U.S. H4 110
Dyfed, co., Wales, U.K. J9 8
Dyje (Thaya), stm., Eur. G16 10
Dyment, Ont., Can. I22 104
Dynów, Pol. F22 10
Dysart, Sask., Can. H10 104
Dysart, Ia., U.S. H3 110
Džalal-Abad, Kyrg. I12 26
Džalinda, Russia G16 28
Džambejty, Kaz. G8 26
Džambul, Kaz. I12 26
Džanga, Turk. A12 48
Džanybek, Kaz. H7 26
Dzaoudzi, May. L16 67a
Dzavchan, stm., Mong. B5 30
Džebel, Turk. B13 48
Dzemul, Mex. G15 90
Dzeržinsk, Bela. H10 22
Dzeržinsk, Russia E26 22
Dzeržinskoje, Kaz. H14 26
Džetygara, Kaz. G10 26
Džezkazgan, Kaz. H11 26
Dzibalchén, Mex. H15 90
Dzibilchaltún, hist., Mex. G15 90
Dzierżoniów (Reichenbach), Pol. E16 10
Dzilam González, Mex. G15 90
Dzioua, Alg. D13 62
Dzitás, Mex. G15 90
Dzitbalché, Mex. G14 90
Džizak, Uzb. I11 26
Džugdžur, chrebet, mts., Russia F19 28
Džul'fa, Azer. J7 26
Dzungarian Basin see Junggar Pendi, China B4 30
Džungarskij Alatau, chrebet, mts., Asia H8 28
Džurin, Ukr. A12 20
Džusaly, Kaz. H10 26
Džüün Charaa, Mong. B8 30
Dzuunmod, Mong. B8 30
Dzygovka, Ukr. A12 20

E

Eads, Co., U.S. M5 118
Eagar, Az., U.S. J7 120
Eagle, Ak., U.S. D24 100
Eagle, Co., U.S. E10 120
Eagle, stm., Newf., Can. F21 96
Eagle, stm., Yukon, Can. C26 100
Eagle, stm., Co., U.S. E10 120
Eagle Bay, B.C., Can. G15 102
Eagle Bend, Mn., U.S. E12 118
Eagle Butte, S.D., U.S. F6 118
Eagle Creek, stm., Sask., Can. G7 104
Eagle Grove, Ia., U.S. H2 110
Eaglehawk, Austl. K6 70
Eagle Lake, Tx., U.S. J10 116
Eagle Lake, I., B.C., Can. F10 102
Eagle Lake, I., Ont., Can. H20 104
Eagle Lake, I., Ont., Can. I21 104
Eagle Lake, I., Ca., U.S. D5 124
Eagle Mountain, Ca., U.S. K10 124
Eagle Mountain, mtn., Id., U.S. D10 122
Eagle Mountain, hill, Mn., U.S. C5 110
Eagle Pass, Tx., U.S. K6 116
Eagle Peak, mtn., Ca., U.S. C5 124
Eagle River, Mi., U.S. C7 110
Eagle River, Wi., U.S. E6 110
Eagle Rock, Va., U.S. B7 112
Eaglesham, Alta., Can. B17 102
Eagleton Village, Tn., U.S. D3 112
Eagletown, Ok., U.S. H2 114
Eagle Village, Ak., U.S. D24 100
Eardley Lake, I., Man., Can. F18 104
Ear Falls, Ont., Can. H21 104
Earle, Ar., U.S. G6 114
Earl Grey, Sask., Can. H10 104
Earlham, Ia., U.S. A2 114
Earlimart, Ca., U.S. I6 124
Earlington, Ky., U.S. E9 114
Earl Park, In., U.S. B9 114
Earlville, Il., U.S. I7 110
Earlville, N.Y., U.S. E11 108
Early, Ia., U.S. I12 118
Early, Tx., U.S. H8 116
Earth, Tx., U.S. E4 116
Easley, S.C., U.S. E4 112
East Alton, Il., U.S. D6 114
East-Angus, Que., Can. B15 108
East Aurora, N.Y., U.S. E8 108
East Bay, b., Tx., U.S. J12 116
East Bend, N.C., U.S. C6 112
East Berbice-Corentyne, prov., Guy. E13 84
East Berlin, Pa., U.S. H10 108
East Bernard, Tx., U.S. J10 116
East Bernstadt, Ky., U.S. B2 112
East Brady, Pa., U.S. G7 108
East Braintree, Man., Can. I19 104
East Brewton, Al., U.S. K9 114
East Caicos, i., T./C. Is. D9 94
East Cape, c., N.Z. B7 72
East Carbon, Ut., U.S. E6 120
East Channel, mth., N.W. Ter., Can. B28 100
East Chicago, In., U.S. A9 114
East China Sea, Asia R3 37b
East Coulee, Alta., Can. F22 102
East Dublin, Ga., U.S. G4 112
East Dubuque, Il., U.S. H5 110
East Ely, Nv., U.S. E11 124
Eastend, Sask., Can. I6 104
Easter Island see Pascua, Isla de, i., Chile G4 74
Eastern Ghāts, mts., India F5 46
East Falkland, i., Falk. Is. G5 78
East Fayetteville, N.C., U.S. D8 112
East Flat Rock, N.C., U.S. D4 112
East Frisian Islands see Ostfriesische Inseln, is., Ger. B7 10
East Gaffney, S.C., U.S. D5 112
East Gallatin, stm., Mt., U.S. E14 122
East Glacier Park, Mt., U.S. B12 122
East Grand Forks, Mn., U.S. D10 118
East Grand Rapids, Mi., U.S. H10 110
East Greenwich, R.I., U.S. F15 108
Easthampton, Ma., U.S. E14 108
East Helena, Mt., U.S. D14 122
East Jordan, Mi., U.S. E10 110
East Kelowna, B.C., Can. H15 102
East Kilbride, Scot., U.K. F9 8
Eastlake, Mi., U.S. F9 110
Eastlake, Oh., U.S. F5 108
East Lake, I., Ont., Can. E21 104
Eastland, Tx., U.S. G8 116
East Lansing, Mi., U.S. H11 110
East Laurinburg, N.C., U.S. E7 112
East Liverpool, Oh., U.S. G6 108
East London (Oos-Londen), S. Afr. I8 66
East Lynn Lake, res., W.V., U.S. I4 108
Eastmain, Que., Can. F17 96
Eastmain, stm., Que., Can. F17 96
Eastmain-Opinaca, Réservoir, res., Que., Can. F17 96
Eastman, Ga., U.S. G3 112
East Millinocket, Me., U.S. B18 108
East Missoula, Mt., U.S. D12 122
East Moline, Il., U.S. I5 110
East Naples, Fl., U.S. M5 112
East Nishnabotna, stm., Ia., U.S. K12 118
East Olympia, Wa., U.S. D3 122
Easton, Md., U.S. I10 108
Easton, Pa., U.S. G11 108
Eastover, S.C., U.S. F6 112
East Palatka, Fl., U.S. J5 112
East Palestine, Oh., U.S. G6 108
East Pecos, N.M., U.S. I11 120
East Peoria, Il., U.S. J6 110
East Pine, B.C., Can. B13 102
Eastpoint, Fl., U.S. J2 112
East Point, Ga., U.S. F2 112
East Point, c., P.E.I., Can. F12 106
Eastport, Newf., Can. D20 106
Eastport, Id., U.S. A9 122
Eastport, Me., U.S. C20 108
East Porterville, Ca., U.S. H7 124
East Prairie, Mo., U.S. F7 114
East Prairie, stm., Alta., Can. B18 102
East Rockingham, N.C., U.S. E7 112
East Saint Louis, Il., U.S. D6 114
East Shoal Lake, I., Man., Can. H17 104
East Siberian Sea see Vostočno-Sibirskoje more, Russia C23 28
East Spencer, N.C., U.S. D6 112
East Stroudsburg, Pa., U.S. G11 108
East Tawas, Mi., U.S. F12 110
East Troy, Wi., U.S. H7 110
Eastville, Va., U.S. B11 112

Name — Map Ref. — Page

East Wenatchee, Wa., U.S. C5 122
East Wilmington, N.C., U.S. E9 112
Eaton, Co., U.S. D12 120
Eaton, In., U.S. B11 114
Eaton, Oh., U.S. H2 108
Eatonia, Sask., Can. G5 104
Eaton Rapids, Mi., U.S. H11 110
Eatonton, Ga., U.S. F3 112
Eatonville, Wa., U.S. D3 122
Eau Claire, Wi., U.S. F4 110
Eau Claire, stm., Wi., U.S. F4 110
Eau Claire, Lac à l', l., Que., Can. E18 96
Eau Galle, stm., Wi., U.S. F3 110
Eauze, Fr. I7 14
Eban, Nig. G12 64
Ebano, Mex. F10 90
Ebb and Flow Indian Reserve, Man., Can. G15 104
Ebb and Flow Lake, l., Man., Can. G16 104
Ebbw Vale, Wales, U.K. J10 8
Eben Junction, Mi., U.S. D9 110
Ebensburg, Pa., U.S. G8 108
Ebensee, Aus. H13 10
Eberbach, Ger. F8 10
Ebermannstadt, Ger. F11 10
Eberndorf, Aus. I14 10
Ebersbach, Ger. D14 10
Ebersberg, Ger. G11 10
Eberstein, Aus. I14 10
Eberswalde, Ger. C13 10
Ebetsu, Japan D16 36a
Ebinur Hu, l., China C3 30
Ebnat, Switz. D11 13
Eboli, Italy I10 18
Ebolowa, Cam. H9 54
Ebony, Nmb. D2 66
Ebro (Ebre), stm., Spain E12 16
Ebro, Embalse del, res., Spain B8 16
Eccles, W.V., U.S. B5 112
Echaporã, Braz. G3 79
Ech Cheliff (Orléansville), Alg. B11 62
Echimamish, stm., Man., Can. D17 104
Echo, Mn., U.S. G12 118
Echo Bay, N.W. Ter., Can. C9 96
Echoing, stm., Can. C23 104
Echoing Lake, l., Ont., Can. D22 104
Echt, Neth. F8 12
Echuca, Austl. K6 70
Écija, Spain H6 16
Eckernförde, Ger. A9 10
Eckville, Alta., Can. E20 102
Eclectic, Al., U.S. J10 114
Eclipse Sound, strt., N.W. Ter., Can. B17 96
Ečmiadzin, Arm. I6 26
Écrins, Barre des, mtn., Fr. H13 14
Ecru, Ms., U.S. H7 114
Ecstall, stm., B.C., Can. D5 102
Ecuador, ctry., S.A. D3 76
Ecum Secum, N.S., Can. H11 106
Ed, Eth. H2 47
Edam, Sask., Can. E6 104
Edam, Neth. C7 12
Eddystone Point, c., Austl. M8 70
Eddyville, Ia., U.S. I3 110
Eddyville, Ky., U.S. E8 114
Ede, Nig. H12 64
Edéa, Cam. H9 54
Edehon Lake, l., N.W. Ter., Can. D13 96
Edéia, Braz. D4 79
Edelény, Hung. G20 10
Eden, Austl. K8 70
Eden, Ms., U.S. J6 114
Eden, Tx., U.S. H7 116
Eden, Wy., U.S. B7 120
Edenburg, S. Afr. G7 66
Eden Lake, l., Man., Can. B14 104
Edenton, N.C., U.S. C10 112
Eden Valley, Mn., U.S. E1 110
Edenville, S. Afr. F8 66
Edeowie, Austl. H3 70
Eder, stm., Ger. D8 10
Edfu see Idfū, Egypt E7 60
Edgar, Ne., U.S. K10 118
Edgar, Wi., U.S. F6 110
Edgard, La., U.S. L6 114
Edgartown, Ma., U.S. F16 108
Edgefield, S.C., U.S. F5 112
Edgeley, N.D., U.S. E9 118
Edgemont, S.D., U.S. H4 118
Edgeøya, i., Sval. B3 24
Edgerton, Alta., Can. F4 104
Edgerton, Mn., U.S. H11 118
Edgerton, Oh., U.S. F2 108
Edgerton, Wi., U.S. H6 110
Edgerton, Wy., U.S. A10 120
Edgewater, Al., U.S. I10 114
Edgewater, Fl., U.S. K6 112
Edgewood, B.C., Can. H16 102
Edgewood, Il., U.S. D8 114
Edgewood, Ia., U.S. H4 110
Edgewood, Md., U.S. H10 108
Edgewood, Tx., U.S. G11 116
Édhessa, Grc. I6 20
Edina, Mn., U.S. F2 110
Edina, Mo., U.S. B4 114
Edinboro, Pa., U.S. F6 108
Edinburg, Il., U.S. C7 114
Edinburg, In., U.S. C11 114
Edinburg, Ms., U.S. J7 114
Edinburg, N.D., U.S. C10 118
Edinburg, Tx., U.S. M8 116
Edinburg, Va., U.S. I8 108
Edinburgh, Scot., U.K. F10 8
Edinburgh, Arrecife, rf., Nic. C12 92
Edinburgh Channel, strt., Nic. C12 92
Edincik, Tur. I11 20
Edirne, Tur. H10 20
Edison, Ga., U.S. H2 112
Edisto, stm., S.C., U.S. G6 112
Edisto Island, i., S.C., U.S. G6 112
Edith Cavell, Mount, mtn., Alta., Can. E16 102
Edjeleh, Alg. G15 62
Edmond, Ok., U.S. D9 116
Edmonds, Wa., U.S. C3 122
Edmonton, Austl. A6 70
Edmonton, Alta., Can. D21 102
Edmonton, Ky., U.S. F11 114
Edmore, Mi., U.S. G10 110
Edmore, N.D., U.S. C9 118
Edmund Lake, l., Man., Can. D21 104
Edmundston, N.B., Can. E5 106
Edna, Ks., U.S. N12 118
Edna, Tx., U.S. K10 116
Edna Bay, Ak., U.S. I28 100
Edolo, Italy C5 18
Edremit, Tur. J11 20
Edsbro, Swe. L16 6
Edsbyn, Swe. K14 6
Edson, Alta., Can. D18 102
Eduardo Castex, Arg. H6 80
Eduni, Mount, mtn., N.W. Ter., Can. D30 100
Edward, Lake, l., Afr. B5 58
Edwards, Ms., U.S. J6 114
Edwards, N.Y., U.S. C11 108
Edwards, stm., Il., U.S. I5 110
Edwards Plateau, plat., Tx., U.S. I6 116
Edwardsville, Il., U.S. D7 114
Edward VII Peninsula, pen., Ant. C9 73
Edziza, Mount, mtn., B.C., Can. H29 100
Eek, Ak., U.S. F13 100
Eeklo, Bel. F4 12
Eel, stm., Ca., U.S. D1 124
Eel, stm., In., U.S. B10 114
Eel, stm., In., U.S. C9 114
Effingham, Il., U.S. C8 114
Effingham, Ks., U.S. L12 118
Ega, stm., Spain C9 16
Egadi, Isole, is., Italy L7 18
Egaña, Arg. I9 80
Egan Range, mts., Nv., U.S. E11 124
Eganville, Ont., Can. E18 110
Egegik, Ak., U.S. G16 100
Eger, Hung. H20 10
Eger see Cheb, Czech. E12 10
Egeria Mountain, mtn., B.C., Can. D4 102
Egersund, Nor. L10 6
Eggenburg, Aus. G15 10
Egg Harbor City, N.J., U.S. H12 108
Egg Lake, l., Man., Can. D13 104
Egg Lake, l., Sask., Can. C9 104
Egilsstaðir, Ice. B6 6a
Egmont, Mount, mtn., N.Z. C4 72
Egmont Bay, b., P.E.I., Can. F9 106
Egremont, Alta., Can. C21 102
Éguas, Rio das, stm., Braz. B6 79
Egypt (Mișr), ctry., Afr. C7 56
Ehrenberg, Az., U.S. K2 120
Ehrhardt, S.C., U.S. F5 112
Eibar, Spain B9 16
Eichstätt, Ger. G11 10
Eidsvåg, Nor. J11 6
Eidsvold, Austl. E9 70
Eifel, mts., Ger. E6 10
Eiger, mtn., Switz. E9 13
Eight Degree Channel, strt., Asia I2 46
Eights Coast, Ant. C11 73
Eighty Mile Beach, Austl. C4 68
Eildon, Austl. K6 70
Eildon, Lake, res., Austl. K6 70
Eilenburg, Ger. D12 10
Einasleigh, Austl. B6 70
Einasleigh, stm., Austl. A5 70
Einbeck, Ger. D9 10
Eindhoven, Neth. F7 12
Einsiedeln, Switz. D10 13
Eiru, stm., Braz. B6 82
Eirunepé, Braz. B7 82
Eisden, Bel. G8 12
Eisenach, Ger. E10 10
Eisenberg, Ger. E11 10
Eisenerz, Aus. H14 10
Eisenhüttenstadt, Ger. C14 10
Eisenkappel, Aus. I14 10
Eisenstadt, Aus. H16 10
Eišiškės, Lith. G8 22
Eisleben, Ger. D11 10
Eitorf, Ger. E7 10
Eivissa, Spain G13 16
Eivissa (Ibiza), i., Spain G13 16
Ejea de los Caballeros, Spain C10 16
Ejeda, Madag. T21 67b
Ejido, Ven. C7 84
Ejido Jaboncillos, Mex. C8 90
Ejin Qi, China C7 30
Ejutla de Crespo, Mex. I11 90
Ekalaka, Mt., U.S. F3 118
Eket, Nig. I13 64
Ekibastuz, Kaz. G7 28
Ekpoma, Nig. H13 64
Eksjö, Swe. M14 6
Ekwan, stm., Ont., Can. F16 96
Ekwok, Ak., U.S. G16 100
Ela, Burma E4 40
El Aaiún (La'youn), W. Sah. G4 62
El Abiadh Sidi Cheikh, Alg. D11 62
El Adeb Larache, Alg. G15 62
El Adelanto, Guat. C5 92
El Agreb, Alg. E13 62
El Aguilar, Arg. B6 80
Elaine, Ar., U.S. H6 114
El Alamein see Al-ʿAlamayn, Egypt B5 60
El Alia, Tun. L5 18
El Alto, Arg. E6 80
El Alto, Peru J2 84
El Amparo de Apure, Ven. D7 84
Elandsvlei, S. Afr. I4 66
El Angel, Ec. G4 84
El Aouinet, Alg. N2 18
El Arahal, Spain H6 16
El Arco, Mex. C3 90
El Aricha, Alg. C10 62
El Aroussa, Tun. M4 18
Elat, Isr. I3 50
El Ávila, Parque Nacional, Ven. B9 84
Elazığ, Tur. B5 48
Elba, Al., U.S. K10 114
Elba, Isola d', i., Italy G5 18
El Banco, Col. C6 84
El Barco de Valdeorras, Spain C5 16
Elbasan, Alb. H4 20
El Baúl, Ven. C8 84
El Baúl, Cerro, mtn., Mex. I9 90
El Baúl, Cerro, mtn., Mex. I12 90
Elbe (Labe), stm., Eur. B9 10
Elbert, Co., U.S. L3 118
Elbert, Mount, mtn., Co., U.S. E10 120
Elberta, Mi., U.S. F9 110
Elberton, Ga., U.S. E4 112
Elbeuf, Fr. C8 14
El Beyyadh, Alg. D11 62
Elbistan, Tur. B4 48
Elbląg (Elbing), Pol. A19 10
El Bluff, Nic. F11 92
El-Borouj, Mor. D7 62
El Boulaïda, Alg. B12 62
Elbow, Sask., Can. G8 104
Elbow, stm., Alta., Can. G20 102
Elbow Cay, i., Bah. C4 94
Elbow Lake, Mn., U.S. F12 118
Elbow Lake, l., Man., Can. D14 104
El'brus, gora, mtn., Russia I6 26
Elbrus, Mount see El'brus, gora, mtn., Russia I6 26
El Cabezo, Arrecife, rf., Mex. H12 90
El Caburé, Arg. D7 80
El Caimanero, Laguna, b., Mex. F6 90
El Cajon, Ca., U.S. L9 124
El Cajón, Embalse, res., Hond. B7 92
El Calafate, Arg. G2 78
El Callao, Ven. D12 84
El Calvario, Col. E6 84
El Calvario, Ven. C9 84
El Campo, Tx., U.S. J10 116
El Capitan, mtn., Mt., U.S. D11 122
El Carmen, Arg. C6 80
El Cármen, Bol. H12 82
El Carmen, Col. C6 84
El Carmen, Peru E3 82
El Carmen, stm., Mex. B6 90
El Carmen de Bolívar, Col. C5 84
El Carricito, Mex. C8 90
El Carril, Arg. C6 80
El Castillo de La Concepción, Nic. F10 92
El Cedral, Guat. A4 92
El Cedrito, Mex. C9 90
El Centro, Ca., U.S. L10 124
El Cerrito, Col. F4 84
El Cerro, Bol. G11 82
El Chile, Montaña, mtn., Hond. C8 92
Elcho, Wi., U.S. E6 110
El Chorrillo, Arg. G5 80
El Cocuy, Col. D6 84
El Colorado, Arg. D9 80
El Cóndor, Cerro, mtn., Arg. D4 80
El Congo, El Sal. D5 92
El Corazón, Ec. H3 84
El Corpus, Hond. D7 92
El Coyote, stm., Mex. B3 90
El Cozón, Mex. B3 90
El Cuco, El Sal. D6 92
El Cuervo, Laguna, l., Mex. C7 90
Elda, Spain G11 16
El Dátil, Mex. B3 90
El Desemboque, Mex. C3 90
El Desemboque, Mex. B3 90
El'dikan, Russia E19 28
El Diviso, Col. G3 84
El Djazaïr (Algiers), Alg. B12 62
El Djelfa, Alg. C12 62
Eldon, Ia., U.S. J3 110
Eldon, Mo., U.S. D4 114
Eldora, Ia., U.S. H2 110
Eldorado, Arg. D11 80
Eldorado, Braz. C14 80
El Dorado, Mex. E6 90
El Dorado, Ar., U.S. I4 114
Eldorado, Il., U.S. E8 114
El Dorado, Ks., U.S. N11 118
Eldorado, Ok., U.S. E7 116
Eldorado, Tx., U.S. I6 116
El Dorado, Ven. D12 84
El Dorado Springs, Mo., U.S. E2 114
Eldoret, Kenya A7 58
Eldred, Pa., U.S. F8 108
Eldridge, Ia., U.S. I5 110
Eleanor, W.V., U.S. I5 108
Electra, Tx., U.S. E8 116
Electric City, Wa., U.S. C6 122
Elefante, Isla del see Elephant Island, i., B.A.T. B1 73
Elefantes, Rio dos (Olifants), stm., Afr. E11 66
Elei, Wādī, val., Afr. G8 60
Eleja, Lat. E6 22
Elektrogorsk, Russia F21 22
Elektrostal', Russia F21 22
El Encanto, Col. H6 84
El Encanto, Guat. I15 90
Elephant Butte Reservoir, res., N.M., U.S. K9 120
Elephant Island, i., B.A.T. K9 74
El Estor, Guat. B5 92
El Eulma, Alg. B13 62
Eleuthera, i., Bah. B6 94
Eleuthera Point, c., Bah. B6 94
Eleva, Wi., U.S. F4 110
Eleven Point, stm., U.S. F5 114
Elevsís, Grc. K7 20
El Fahs, Tun. M4 18
El Ferrol del Caudillo, Spain B3 16
Elfrida, Az., U.S. M7 120
Elfros, Sask., Can. G11 104
El Fuerte, Mex. D5 90
El Galpón, Arg. C6 80
El Ghazawet, Alg. C10 62
Elgin, Scot., U.K. D10 8
Elgin, Il., U.S. H7 110
Elgin, Ia., U.S. H4 110
Elgin, Mn., U.S. F3 110
Elgin, Ne., U.S. J9 118
Elgin, N.D., U.S. E6 118
Elgin, Ok., U.S. E8 116
Elgin, Or., U.S. E8 122
Elgin, Tx., U.S. I9 116
El Golfete, l., Guat. B6 92
Elgon, Mount, mtn., Afr. A6 58
El Grara, Alg. D13 62
El Grove, Spain C3 16
El Guaje, Mex. D8 90
El Guaje, Laguna, l., Mex. C8 90
El Guamo, Col. B5 84
El Guapo, Ven. B10 84
El Guayabo de Abajo, Mex. D6 90
El Hadjar, Alg. M2 18
El Hank, clf, Afr. D5 54
El Haouaria, Tun. L6 18
Elhovo, Bul. G10 20
El Huecú, Arg. I3 80
El Huisache, Mex. F9 90
Eliasville, Tx., U.S. G8 116
Elida, N.M., U.S. F3 116
El Ídolo, Isla, i., Mex. G11 90
El Idrissia, Alg. C12 62
Elim, Ak., U.S. D13 100
El Infiernillo, Canal, strt., Mex. C3 90
Eliot, Me., U.S. D16 108
Élisabethville see Lubumbashi, Zaire D5 58
Elisenvaara, Russia K21 6
Elista, Russia H6 26
Elizabeth, Austl. J3 70
Elizabeth, Co., U.S. E12 120
Elizabeth, Il., U.S. H5 110
Elizabeth, La., U.S. L4 114
Elizabeth, N.J., U.S. G12 108
Elizabeth, W.V., U.S. H5 108
Elizabeth City, N.C., U.S. C10 112
Elizabethton, Tn., U.S. C4 112
Elizabethtown, Il., U.S. E8 114
Elizabethtown, Ky., U.S. E11 114
Elizabethtown, N.Y., U.S. C13 108
Elizabethtown, N.C., U.S. E8 112
Elizabethtown, Pa., U.S. G10 108
El-Jadida (Mazagan), Mor. D6 62
El Jaralito, Mex. D7 90
El Jebel, Co., U.S. E9 120
El-Jebha, Mor. J7 16
El Jem, Tun. N5 18
El Jícaro, stm., Nic. D8 92
Ełk, Pol. B22 10
Elk, stm., Alta., Can. E19 102
Elk, stm., B.C., Can. H19 102
Elk, stm., U.S. G10 114
Elk, stm., Co., U.S. D10 120
Elk, stm., Ks., U.S. N11 118
Elk, stm., Mn., U.S. E2 110
Elk, stm., Mo., U.S. F2 114
Elk, stm., W.V., U.S. I5 108
Elk, stm., Wi., U.S. E5 110
Elkader, Ia., U.S. H4 110
El Kantara, Tun. D16 62
El-Karafab, Sud. H6 60
Elk City, Ok., U.S. D7 116
Elk Creek, Ca., U.S. E3 124
El Kef, Tun. M3 18
El-Kelâa-des-Srarhna, Mor. D7 62
El Kerma, Alg. J11 16
Elk Grove, Ca., U.S. F4 124
Elkhart, In., U.S. A11 114
Elkhart, Ks., U.S. N6 118
Elkhart, Tx., U.S. H11 116
Elkhart Lake, Wi., U.S. G7 110
Elkhead Mountains, mts., Co., U.S. D9 120
Elkhorn, Man., Can. I13 104
Elk Horn, Ia., U.S. J12 118
Elkhorn, Wi., U.S. H7 110
Elkhorn, stm., Ne., U.S. J10 118
Elkhorn City, Ky., U.S. B4 112
Elkhorn Mountain, mtn., B.C., Can. H9 102
Elkin, N.C., U.S. C6 112
Elkins, W.V., U.S. I7 108
Elk Island, i., Man., Can. H18 104
Elk Island National Park, Alta., Can. D22 102
Elkland, Pa., U.S. F9 108
Elk Mountain, Wy., U.S. C10 120
Elk Mountain, mtn., Wy., U.S. C10 120
Elko, B.C., Can. H19 102
Elko, Nv., U.S. D10 124
El Kouif, Alg. N3 18
Elk Point, Alta., Can. D24 102
Elk Point, S.D., U.S. I11 118
Elk Rapids, Mi., U.S. F10 110
El Krib, Tun. M4 18
Elk River, Id., U.S. D9 122
Elk River, Mn., U.S. E2 110
Elkton, Ky., U.S. F9 114
Elkton, Md., U.S. H11 108
Elkton, Mi., U.S. G12 110
Elkton, S.D., U.S. G11 118
Elkton, Va., U.S. I8 108
Elkville, Il., U.S. E7 114
Ellard Lake, l., Ont., Can. D23 104
Ellaville, Ga., U.S. G2 112
Ellef Ringnes Island, i., N.W. Ter., Can. B9 86
Ellen, Mount, mtn., Ut., U.S. F6 120
Ellendale, Mn., U.S. G2 110
Ellendale, N.D., U.S. E9 118
Ellensburg, Wa., U.S. D5 122
Ellenton, Ga., U.S. H3 112
Ellenville, N.Y., U.S. F12 108
Ellerbe, N.C., U.S. D7 112
Ellès, Tun. N4 18
Ellesmere Island, i., N.W. Ter., Can. A11 86
Ellettsville, In., U.S. C10 114
Ellice, stm., N.W. Ter., Can. C12 96
Ellice Islands see Tuvalu, ctry., Oc. G24 2
Ellichpur see Achalpur, India J7 44
Ellicott City, Md., U.S. H10 108
Ellicottville, N.Y., U.S. E8 108
Ellijay, Ga., U.S. E2 112
El Limón de Teachi, Mex. E6 90
Ellington, Mo., U.S. E6 114
Ellinwood, Ks., U.S. M9 118
Elliot, S. Afr. H8 66
Elliotdale, Transkei H9 66
Elliot Lake, Ont., Can. D13 110
Elliot Lake, l., Man., Can. F19 104
Elliott, Ia., U.S. J12 118
Elliott, Ms., U.S. I7 114
Elliott Key, i., Fl., U.S. N6 112
Ellis, Ks., U.S. M8 118
Ellisras, S. Afr. D8 66
Elliston, Newf., Can. D20 106
Elliston, Mt., U.S. D13 122
Ellisville, Ms., U.S. K7 114
Elloree, S.C., U.S. F6 112
Ellore see Elūru, India F11 42
Ellsworth, Ks., U.S. M9 118
Ellsworth, Me., U.S. C18 108
Ellsworth, Mi., U.S. E10 110
Ellsworth, Mn., U.S. H11 118
Ellsworth, Wi., U.S. F3 110
Ellsworth Land, reg., Ant. C12 73
Ellsworth Mountains, mts., Ant. C12 73
Ellwangen, Ger. G10 10
Ellwood City, Pa., U.S. G6 108
Elm, Switz. E11 13
Elm, stm., U.S. F9 118
Elm, stm., N.D., U.S. D10 118
Elma, Ia., U.S. G3 110
Elma, Wa., U.S. C2 122
El Mahdia, Tun. C16 62
El Malah, Alg. J10 16
El Maneadero, Mex. B1 90
El Manteco, Ven. D11 84
El Marsa el Kebir, Alg. C10 62
Elm City, N.C., U.S. D9 112
Elm Creek, Man., Can. I16 104
Elm Creek, Ne., U.S. K8 118
El Médano, Mex. E4 90
El Menia, Alg. E12 62
Elmer, N.J., U.S. H11 108
El Mghayyar, Alg. D13 62
Elmhurst, Il., U.S. I8 110
El Milagro, Arg. F6 80
El Miliyya, Alg. B14 62
Elmina, Ghana I9 64
Elmira, Ont., Can. G15 110
Elmira, P.E.I., Can. F11 106
Elmira, N.Y., U.S. E10 108
El Mirage, Az., U.S. K4 120
Elmira Heights, N.Y., U.S. E10 108
El Mochito, Hond. C6 92
El Mohammadia, Alg. C11 62
El Molinillo, Spain F7 16
El Monte, Chile G3 80
Elmore, Austl. K6 70
Elmore, Mn., U.S. G1 110
Elmore, Oh., U.S. F3 108
Elmore City, Ok., U.S. E9 116
Elmsdale, N.S., Can. H10 106
Elmshorn, Ger. B9 10
Elm Springs, Ar., U.S. F2 114
El Multe, Mex. I14 90
Elmvale, Ont., Can. F16 110
Elmwood, Il., U.S. J6 110
Elmwood, Ne., U.S. K11 118
Elmwood, Wi., U.S. F3 110
Elne, Fr. J9 14
El Negrito, Hond. B7 92
El Nihuil, Arg. H4 80
El Nopal, Cerro, mtn., Mex. C6 90
Elnora, Alta., Can. F21 102
Elnora, In., U.S. D9 114
El Ocote, Cerro, mtn., Mex. E6 90
Eloise, Fl., U.S. L5 112
Elora, Ont., Can. G15 110
Elora, Tn., U.S. G10 114
El Oro, prov., Ec. I3 84
Elortondo, Arg. G8 80
Elorza, Ven. D8 84
Eloy, Az., U.S. L5 120
Eloy Alfaro, Ec. I3 84
El Pacayal, Mex. J13 90
El Palmar, Bol. I10 82
El Palmar, Ven. D12 84
El Palqui, Chile F3 80
El Pao, Ven. C11 84
El Pao, Ven. C8 84
El Paraíso, Hond. D8 92
El Paraíso, dept., Hond. C8 92
El Paso, Spain O23 17b
El Paso, Il., U.S. J6 110
El Paso, Tx., U.S. M10 120
El Peñuelo, Mex. E9 90
El Perú, Ven. D12 84
Elphinstone, Man., Can. H14 104
El Pilar, Ven. B11 84
El Piñón, Col. B5 84
El Pintado, Arg. C8 80
El Piquete, Arg. C6 80
El Pital, Cerro, mtn., N.A. C5 92
El Portal, Ca., U.S. G6 124
El Port de Pollença, Spain F15 16
El Prat de Llobregat, Spain D14 16
El Progreso, Guat. C5 92
El Progreso, Hond. B7 92
El Progreso, dept., Guat. C4 92
El Puerto de Santa María, Spain I5 16
El Puesto, Arg. D5 80
El Qala, Alg. B15 62
El Qoll, Alg. B14 62
El Quebrachal, Arg. C6 80
El Quelite, Mex. F6 90
Elqui, stm., Chile E3 80
El Rastro, Ven. C9 84
El Real de Santa María, Pan. C4 84
El Reno, Ok., U.S. D9 116
El Rey, Parque Nacional, Arg. C6 80
El Rio, Ca., U.S. J6 124
El Rito, N.M., U.S. H10 120
El Rito, stm., N.M., U.S. H10 120
El Roble, Mesa, mtn., Mex. B2 90
El Rom, Isr. Occ. B5 50
El Rosarito, Mex. C2 90
Elrose, Sask., Can. G6 104
Elroy, Wi., U.S. G5 110
Elsa, Yukon, Can. D5 96
Elsa, Yukon, Can. E27 100
Elsa, Tx., U.S. M9 116
El Salado, Chile D3 80
El Salitre, Ec. H3 84
El Salto, Mex. F7 90
El Salvador, ctry., N.A. D6 92
El Samán de Apure, Ven. D8 84
El Sauz, Mex. C6 90
El Sauzal, Mex. B1 90
Elsberry, Mo., U.S. C6 114
El Seibo, Dom. Rep. E10 94
Elsie, Mi., U.S. G11 110
Elsinore, Ut., U.S. F4 120
Elsmere, De., U.S. H11 108
El Socorro, Ven. C10 84
El Sombrero, Ven. C9 84
Elst, Neth. E8 12
Elsterwerda, Ger. D13 10
El Sueco, Mex. C6 90
El Tagarete, Cerro, mtn., Mex. D7 90
El Tajín, hist., Mex. G11 90
El Tala, Arg. D6 80
El Tamarindo, El Sal. D7 92
El Tambo, Col. G4 84
El Tarf, Alg. M3 18
El Tecuán, Mex. E6 90
El Tigre, Ven. C10 84
El Tigre, Isla, i., Hond. D7 92
Eltmann, Ger. F10 10
El Tocuyo, Ven. C8 84
El Tofo, Chile E3 80
Elton, La., U.S. L4 114
El Tránsito, Chile E3 80
El Tránsito, El Sal. D6 92
El Trébol, Arg. G8 80
El Triunfo, Hond. D7 92
El Triunfo, Mex. F4 90
El Triunfo, Cerro, mtn., Mex. B2 92
El Triunfo de la Cruz, Hond. B7 92
El Tunal, Arg. C6 80
El Turbio, Arg. G2 78
Elūru, India D6 46
Elva, Est. C9 22
El Valle, Pan. C2 84
Elvas, Port. G4 16
El Vendrell, Spain D13 16
El Viejo, Nic. E7 92
El Vigía, Ven. C7 84
El Vigía, Cerro, mtn., Mex. G7 90
Elvins, Mo., U.S. E6 114
Elvira, Arg. H9 80
El Volcán, Chile G3 80
El Wad, Alg. D14 62
El Wanza, Alg. C15 62
Elwell, Lake, res., Mt., U.S. B14 122
Elwood, In., U.S. B11 114
Elwood, Ks., U.S. L13 118
Elwood, Ne., U.S. K8 118
Elx, Spain G11 16
Ely, Mn., U.S. C4 110
Ely, Nv., U.S. E11 124
El Yagual, Ven. D8 84
Elyria, Oh., U.S. F4 108
Emāmshahr (Shāhrūd), Iran C13 48
Emas, Parque Nacional das, Braz. E2 79
Emba, Kaz. H9 26
Emba, stm., Kaz. H9 26
Embarcación, Arg. B6 80
Embarras, stm., Alta., Can. D18 102
Embarras, stm., Il., U.S. D9 114
Embarrass, Wi., U.S. F7 110
Embarrass, stm., Mn., U.S. C3 110
Embarrass, stm., Wi., U.S. F7 110
Embreeville, Tn., U.S. C4 112
Embrun, Ont., Can. B11 108
Embrun, Fr. H13 14
Emden, Ger. B7 10
Emden, Il., U.S. B7 114
Emelle, Al., U.S. J8 114
Emerado, N.D., U.S. D10 118
Emerald, Austl. D8 70
Emerson, Man., Can. I17 104
Emerson, Ar., U.S. I3 114
Emerson, Ga., U.S. E2 112
Emerson, Ia., U.S. J12 118
Emerson, Ne., U.S. I11 118
Emery, S.D., U.S. H10 118
Emery, Ut., U.S. F5 120
Emet, Tur. J13 20
Emiliano Zapata, Mex. I14 90
Emiliano Zapata, Bahía, b., Mex. H16 90
Emilia-Romagna, prov., Italy E6 18
Emine, nos, c., Bul. G11 20
Eminence, Ky., U.S. D11 114
Eminence, Mo., U.S. E5 114
Emlembe, mtn., Afr. E10 66
Emlenton, Pa., U.S. F7 108
Emmaus, Pa., U.S. G11 108
Emmaville, Austl. G9 70
Emmeline Lake, l., Sask., Can. C8 104
Emmeloord, Neth. C8 12
Emmen, Neth. C10 12
Emmenbrücke, Switz. D9 13
Emmendingen, Ger. G7 10
Emmer-Compascuum, Neth. C11 12
Emmerich, Ger. D6 10
Emmet, Ar., U.S. I3 114
Emmetsburg, Ia., U.S. H13 118
Emmett, Id., U.S. G9 122
Emmiganūru, India E4 46
Emmitsburg, Md., U.S. H9 108
Emmonak, Ak., U.S. E12 100
Emo, Ont., Can. J21 104
Emory, Tx., U.S. G11 116
Emory, stm., Tn., U.S. C2 112
Emory Peak, mtn., Tx., U.S. J3 116
Empalme, Mex. D4 90
Empangeni, S. Afr. G10 66
Empedrado, Arg. D9 80
Empedrado, Chile H2 80
Empire, La., U.S. M7 114
Empire, Nv., U.S. D6 124
Empoli, Italy F5 18
Emporia, Ks., U.S. M11 118
Emporia, Va., U.S. C9 112
Emporium, Pa., U.S. F8 108
Empress, Alta., Can. H4 104
Empty Quarter see Ar-Rubʿ al-Khālī, des., Asia E5 47
Ems, stm., Eur. C7 10
Emsdetten, Ger. C7 10
Emure-Ekiti, Nig. H12 64
En (Inn), stm., Eur. F17 14
Encampment, Wy., U.S. C10 120
Encampment, stm., U.S. C10 120
Encantado, Braz. E13 80
Encarnación, Para. D11 80
Encinal, Tx., U.S. K7 116
Encinitas, Ca., U.S. K8 124
Encino, N.M., U.S. J11 120
Encino, Tx., U.S. M8 116
Encontrados, Ven. C6 84
Encounter Bay, b., Austl. J3 70
Encruzilhada, Braz. C8 79
Encruzilhada do Sul, Braz. F12 80
Encs, Hung. G21 10
Endako, B.C., Can. C9 102
Endako, stm., B.C., Can. C9 102
Ende, Indon. G7 38
Endeavor, Wi., U.S. G6 110
Endeavour, Sask., Can. F12 104
Endeavour Strait, strt., Austl. B8 68
Enderby, B.C., Can. G15 102
Enderby Land, reg., Ant. B4 73
Enderlin, N.D., U.S. E10 118
Endicott, N.Y., U.S. E10 108
Endicott, Wa., U.S. D8 122
Endimari, stm., Braz. C8 82
Endola, Nmb. A2 66
Ene, stm., Peru D4 82
Enewetak, atoll, Marsh. Is. G20 126
Enez, Tur. I10 20
Enfida, Tun. M5 18
Enfield, N.H., U.S. D14 108
Enfield, N.C., U.S. C9 112
Engaño, Cabo, c., Dom. Rep. E10 94
Engcobo, Transkei H9 66
ʿEn Gedi, Isr. F4 50
Engelberg, Switz. E9 13
Engelhard, N.C., U.S. D11 112
Engel's, Russia G7 26
Engen, B.C., Can. C10 102
Engenho, Braz. F13 82
ʿEn Gev, Isr. C5 50
Enggano, Pulau, i., Indon. G3 38
England, Ar., U.S. H5 114
England, ter., U.K. I12 8
Englee, Newf., Can. B17 106
Englefield, Cape, c., N.W. Ter., Can. C15 96
Englehart, Ont., Can. C16 110
Englewood, B.C., Can. G8 102
Englewood, Co., U.S. E12 120
Englewood, Fl., U.S. M4 112
Englewood, Ks., U.S. N8 118
Englewood, Tn., U.S. D2 112
English, In., U.S. D10 114
English, stm., Ont., Can. G14 96
English, stm., Ia., U.S. I4 110
English Bay, Ak., U.S. G19 100
English Channel (La Manche), strt., Eur. K12 8
English Coast, Ant. C12 73
English Harbour West, Newf., Can. E18 106
Énguera, Spain G11 16
Engure, Lat. D6 22
Engwilen, Switz. C11 13
ʿEn H̱arod, Isr. C4 50
Enid, Ok., U.S. C9 116
Enilda, Alta., Can. B18 102
eNjesuthi, mtn., Afr. G9 66
Enka, N.C., U.S. D4 112
Enkhuizen, Neth. C7 12
Enmedio, Cerro de, mtn., Mex. H9 90
Enna, Italy L9 18
Ennadai Lake, l., N.W. Ter., Can. D12 96
Ennedi, plat., Chad E5 56
Ennis, Mt., U.S. E14 122
Ennis, Tx., U.S. G10 116
Enniskillen, N. Ire., U.K. G6 8
Enns, Aus. G14 10
Enns, stm., Aus. G14 10
Enochs, Tx., U.S. F4 116
Enon, Oh., U.S. H3 108
Enosburg Falls, Vt., U.S. C14 108
Enrique Urien, Arg. D8 80
Enriquillo, Dom. Rep. F9 94
Enriquillo, Lago, l., Dom. Rep. E9 94
Enschede, Neth. D10 12
Ensenada, Arg. H10 80
Ensenada, Mex. B1 90
Enshi, China E8 30
Entebbe, Ug. A6 58
Enterprise, Guy. D13 84
Enterprise, Al., U.S. K11 114
Enterprise, Ca., U.S. E4 124
Enterprise, Ks., U.S. M10 118
Enterprise, Ms., U.S. J8 114
Enterprise, Or., U.S. E8 122
Enterprise, Ut., U.S. G3 120
Entiat, stm., Wa., U.S. C5 122
Entrée, Île d', i., Que., Can. E12 106
Entre Rios, Bol. I9 82
Entre Rios, Braz. A9 79
Entre Ríos, prov., Arg. F9 80
Entre Ríos, Cordillera, mts., Hond. C9 92
Entre-Rios de Minas, Braz. F6 79
Entroncamento, Port. F3 16
Entwistle, Alta., Can. D19 102
Enugu, Nig. H13 64
Enumclaw, Wa., U.S. C4 122
Envalira, Port d', Eur. C13 16
Envermeu, Fr. C8 14
Envigado, Col. D5 84
Envira, Braz. B6 82
Envira, stm., Braz. B6 82
Eo, stm., Spain B4 16
Eolia, Mo., U.S. C5 114
Eolie, Isole, is., Italy K9 18
Epe, Nig. H11 64
Epecuén, Lago, l., Arg. I7 80
Épéhy, Fr. H3 12
Épernay, Fr. C10 14
Epes, Al., U.S. J8 114
Ephesus, hist., Tur. L11 20
Ephraim, Ut., U.S. E5 120
Ephrata, Pa., U.S. G10 108
Ephrata, Wa., U.S. C6 122
Épinal, Fr. D13 14
Epirus see Ípeiros, hist. reg., Grc. J4 20
Epokiro, Nmb. C4 66
Epping, Eng., U.K. J14 8
Epping, N.H., U.S. D15 108
Epsom, Eng., U.K. J13 8
Epukiro, stm., Afr. C5 66
Eqlīd, Iran F12 48
Equality, Il., U.S. E8 114
Equatorial Guinea, ctry., Afr. H8 54
Erath, La., U.S. M4 114

Name — Map Ref. — Page

Erba, Italy D4 18
Erciş, Tur. B7 48
Erciyes Dağı, mtn., Tur. B3 48
Érd, Hung. H18 10
Erdaoliangzi, China C7 32
Erdene, Mong. C9 30
Erding, Ger. G11 10
Erebato, stm., Ven. E10 84
Erebus, Mount, mtn., Ant. C8 73
Ereğli, Tur. C3 48
Erenhot, China C9 30
Erepecuru, Lago do, l., Braz. H14 84
Eressós, Grc. J9 20
Erétria, Grc. K7 20
Erexim, Braz. D12 80
Erfoud, Mor. E8 62
Erft, stm., Ger. D6 10
Erfurt, Ger. E11 10
Erges (Erjas), stm., Eur. F5 16
Ērgļi, Lat. E8 22
Ergun (Argun'), stm., Asia A11 30
Er Hai, l., China B6 40
Erhlin, Tai. L9 34
Eriba, Sud. I9 60
Erice, Italy K7 18
Erichsen Lake, l., N.W. Ter., Can. B16 96
Erick, Ok., U.S. D7 116
Erickson, B.C., Can. H18 102
Erickson, Man., Can. H15 104
Ericson, Ne., U.S. J9 118
Erie, Co., U.S. D11 120
Erie, Il., U.S. I5 110
Erie, Ks., U.S. N12 118
Erie, Pa., U.S. E6 108
Erie, Lake, l., N.A. H15 110
Erie Canal see New York State Barge Canal, N.Y., U.S. D8 108
Eriksdale, Man., Can. H16 104
Erimo-misaki, c., Japan F18 36a
Erin, Ont., Can. G15 110
Erin, Tn., U.S. F9 114
Eritrea, hist. reg., Eth. E8 56
Erjas (Erges), stm., Eur. F5 16
Erjiazhen, China C10 34
Erkelenz, Ger. D6 10
Erkowit, Sud. H9 60
Erlangen, Ger. F11 10
Ermelo, Neth. D8 12
Ermelo, S. Afr. F9 66
Ermenek, Tur. C2 48
Ermineskin Indian Reserve, Alta., Can. E21 102
Ermoúpolis, Grc. L8 20
Erne, Lower Lough, l., N. Ire., U.K. G6 8
Erne, Upper Lough, l., Eur. G6 8
Ernée, Fr. D6 14
Erode, India G4 46
Eromanga, Austl. F5 70
Erongo, Nmb. C2 66
Erota, Eth. I9 60
Er-Rachidia, Mor. E8 62
Errol Heights, Or., U.S. E3 122
Erskine, Mn., U.S. D11 118
Erskine Inlet, b., N.W. Ter., Can. A12 96
Erstein, Fr. D14 14
Ertai, China B5 30
Ertil', Russia J23 22
Ertix (Irtyš), stm., Asia H9 28
Ertuğrul, Tur. J11 20
Erudina, Austl. H3 70
Eruwa, Nig. H11 64
Erval, Braz. G12 80
Erval d'Oeste, Braz. D13 80
Erwin, N.C., U.S. D8 112
Erwin, Tn., U.S. C4 112
Erwood, Sask., Can. F12 104
Eryuan, China A5 40
Erzgebirge (Krušné hory), mts., Eur. E13 10
Erzin, Russia G17 26
Erzincan, Tur. B5 48
Erzurum, Tur. B6 48
Esa'ala, Pap. N. Gui. A10 68
Esashi, Japan F15 36
Esashi, Japan H16 36
Esbjerg, Den. N11 6
Esca, stm., Spain J5 14
Escalante, Ut., U.S. G5 120
Escalante, stm., Ut., U.S. G5 120
Escalante, stm., Ven. C7 84
Escalante Desert, des., Ut., U.S. G3 120
Escalón, Mex. D7 90
Escalon, Ca., U.S. G5 124
Escambia, stm., Fl., U.S. L9 114
Escanaba, Mi., U.S. E8 110
Escanaba, stm., Mi., U.S. D8 110
Escárcega, Mex. H14 90
Escarpada Point, c., Phil. L20 39b
Escatawpa, stm., U.S. L8 114
Escaut (Schelde), stm., Eur. E3 10
Esch-sur-Alzette, Lux. I8 12
Eschwege, Ger. D10 10
Eschweiler, Ger. E6 10
Escobal, Pan. H15 92
Escobedo, Mex. C8 90
Escocesa, Bahía, b., Dom. Rep. E10 94
Escondido, Ca., U.S. K8 124
Escondido, stm., Nic. E11 92
Escudo de Veraguas, Isla, i., Pan. H13 92
Escuinapa de Hidalgo, Mex. F7 90
Escuintla, Guat. C4 92
Escuintla, Mex. J13 90
Escuintla, dept., Guat. C3 92
Escuminac, Point, c., N.B., Can. E9 106
Eşfahān (Isfahan), Iran E11 48
Esfarāyen, Iran C14 48
Eshkāshem, Afg. B4 44
Eshowe, S. Afr. G10 66
Esigodini, Zimb. C9 66
Esk, Austl. F10 70
Eskdale, W.V., U.S. I5 108
Eskifjörður, Ice. B7 6a
Eskilstuna, Swe. L15 6
Eskimo Lakes, l., N.W. Ter., Can. B28 100
Eskimo Point, N.W. Ter., Can. D14 96
Eskişehir, Tur. H14 4
Eskridge, Ks., U.S. M11 118
Esla, stm., Spain C6 16
Eslāmābād, Iran D9 48
Eslāmshahr, Iran D11 48
Eşme, Tur. K12 20
Esmeralda, Austl. B5 70
Esmeralda, Cuba D5 94
Esmeraldas, Ec. G3 84
Esmeraldas, prov., Ec. G3 84
Esmeraldas, stm., Ec. G3 84
Esmond, N.D., U.S. C8 118
Esneux, Bel. G8 12
Espada, Punta, c., Col. A7 84
Espalion, Fr. H9 14
Espanola, Ont., Can. D14 110
Espanola, N.M., U.S. I10 120
Esparza, C.R. H10 92
Espejo, Spain H7 16
Espera Feliz, Braz. F8 79
Esperança, Braz. J8 84
Esperance, Austl. F4 68
Esperance Bay, b., Austl. F4 68
Esperanza, Arg. F8 80
Esperanza, Mex. D5 90
Esperanza Inlet, b., B.C., Can. H8 102
Espinal, Col. E5 84
Espinhaço, Serra do, mts., Braz. C7 79
Espinho, Port. D3 16
Espinillo, Arg. C9 80
Espino, Ven. C9 84
Espinosa, Braz. C7 79
Espírito Santo, state, Braz. E8 79
Espíritu Santo, Isla, i., Mex. E4 90
Espita, Mex. G15 90
Espoir, Bay d', b., Newf., Can. E18 106
Espoo (Esbo), Fin. K19 6
Espumoso, Braz. E12 80
Espungabera, Moz. C11 66
Esquel, Arg. E2 78
Esquimalt, B.C., Can. I11 102
Esquina, Arg. F9 80
Esquina Negra, Arg. H9 80
Esquipulas, Guat. C5 92
Esquipulas, Nic. E9 92
Esquiú, Arg. E6 80
Essaouira (Mogador), Mor. E6 62
Es-Sekhira, Tun. C16 62
Essen, Bel. F5 12
Essen, Ger. D7 10
Essequibo, stm., Guy. E13 84
Essequibo Islands-West Demerara, prov., Guy. D13 84
Es Sers, Tun. M4 18
Essex, Ont., Can. H13 110
Essex, Ia., U.S. K12 118
Essex, Md., U.S. H10 108
Essex, Mo., U.S. F7 114
Essex, co., Eng., U.K. J14 8
Essex Junction, Vt., U.S. C13 108
Essexville, Mi., U.S. G12 110
Esslingen, Ger. G9 10
Es Smala es Souassi, Tun. N5 18
Essonne, dept., Fr. D9 14
Essoyes, Fr. D11 14
Es-Suki, Sud. K7 60
Est, Île de l', i., Que., Can. E12 106
Est, Pointe de l', c., Que., Can. C12 106
Estacada, Or., U.S. E3 122
Estacado, Llano, pl., U.S. F4 116
Estados, Isla de los, i., Arg. J8 74
Eşţahbān, Iran G13 48
Estância, Braz. F11 76
Estancia, N.M., U.S. J10 120
Estanislao del Campo, Arg. C8 80
Estanzuelas, El Sal. D6 92
Estats, Pique d', mtn., Eur. C13 16
Estcourt, S. Afr. G9 66
Este, Italy D6 18
Esteio, Braz. E13 80
Estelí, Nic. D8 92
Estelí, dept., Nic. D8 92
Estella, Spain C9 16
Estelline, S.D., U.S. G11 118
Estelline, Tx., U.S. E6 116
Estepa, Spain H7 16
Estepona, Spain I6 16
Esterhazy, Sask., Can. H12 104
Esteros, Arg. D7 80
Estes Park, Co., U.S. D11 120
Este Sudeste, Cayos del, is., Col. E13 92
Estevan, Sask., Can. I12 104
Estevan Group, is., B.C., Can. D5 102
Estevan Point, B.C., Can. H8 102
Estherville, Ia., U.S. H13 118
Estill, S.C., U.S. G5 112
Estiva, Rio da, stm., Braz. B6 79
Eston, Sask., Can. G6 104
Estonia (Eesti), ctry., Eur. C8 22
Estrela, Braz. E13 80
Estrela, mtn., Port. E4 16
Estrela do Norte, Braz. B4 79
Estrela do Sul, Braz. E5 79
Estremadura, hist. reg., Port. F3 16
Estuary, Sask., Can. H5 104
Esztergom, Hung. H18 10
Étables, Fr. D4 14
Etadunna, Austl. G3 70
Etah, Grnld. B12 86
Etah, India G8 44
Étain, Fr. C12 14
Étamaniou, stm., Que., Can. B13 106
Étampes, Fr. D9 14
Étaples, Fr. B8 14
Etāwah, India G8 44
Etchemin, stm., Que., Can. F3 106
Etchojoa, Mex. D5 90
Ethan, S.D., U.S. H10 118
Ethel, Ms., U.S. I7 114
Ethel, Mount, mtn., Co., U.S. D10 120
Ethelbert, Man., Can. G14 104
Ethel Lake, l., Yukon, Can. E26 100
Ethiopia (Ityopiya), ctry., Afr. G8 56
Ethridge, Mt., U.S. B13 122
Ethridge, Tn., U.S. G9 114
Etna, Ca., U.S. C3 124
Etna, Wy., U.S. A5 120
Etna, Monte, vol., Italy L10 18
Etobicoke, Ont., Can. G16 110
Etomami, stm., Sask., Can. F12 104
Etosha Pan, pl., Nmb. B3 66
Etowah, Tn., U.S. D2 112
Etowah, stm., Ga., U.S. E1 112
Étretat, Fr. C7 14
Ettelbruck, Lux. I9 12
Et Tidra, i., Maur. B1 64
Ettlingen, Ger. G8 10
Ettrick, Va., U.S. B9 112
Etzikom Coulee, stm., Alta., Can. I3 104
Etzná, hist., Mex. H14 90
Eu, Fr. B8 14
Euchiniko, stm., B.C., Can. D10 102
Eucla, Austl. F5 68
Euclid, Oh., U.S. F5 108
Eucumbene, Lake, res., Austl. K8 70
Eudistes, Lac des, l., Que., Can. B8 106
Eudora, Ar., U.S. I5 114
Eudora, Ks., U.S. M12 118
Eudunda, Austl. J3 70
Eufaula, Al., U.S. K11 114
Eufaula, Ok., U.S. D11 116
Eufaula Lake, res., Ok., U.S. D11 116
Eugene, Or., U.S. F2 122
Eugenia, Punta, c., Mex. D2 90
Eugenio Bustos, Arg. G4 80
Eugowra, Austl. I8 70
Eumungerie, Austl. H8 70
Eunice, La., U.S. L4 114
Eunice, N.M., U.S. G3 116
Eupen, Bel. G9 12
Euphrates (Firat) (Nahr al-Furāt), stm., Asia F9 48
Eupora, Ms., U.S. I7 114
Eure, dept., Fr. C7 14
Eure, stm., Fr. D8 14
Eure-et-Loir, dept., Fr. D8 14
Eureka, Ca., U.S. D1 124
Eureka, Il., U.S. J6 110
Eureka, Ks., U.S. N11 118
Eureka, Mt., U.S. B10 122
Eureka, Nv., U.S. E10 124
Eureka, S.C., U.S. E5 112
Eureka, S.D., U.S. F8 118
Eureka, Ut., U.S. E4 120
Eureka Springs, Ar., U.S. F3 114
Euroa, Austl. K6 70
Europa, Île, i., Reu. F8 58
Europa, Picos de, mts., Spain B7 16
Europa Point, c., Gib. I6 16
Europe C9 52
Europoort, Neth. E5 12
Euskal Herriko, prov., Spain B9 16
Euskirchen, Ger. E6 10
Eustace, Tx., U.S. G10 116
Eustis, Fl., U.S. K5 112
Eustis, Ne., U.S. K7 118
Eutaw, Al., U.S. J9 114
Eutsuk Lake, l., B.C., Can. D8 102
Eva, Al., U.S. H10 114
Evadale, Tx., U.S. L2 114
Evans, Co., U.S. D12 120
Evans, Lac, l., Que., Can. F17 96
Evans, Mount, mtn., Co., U.S. E11 120
Evansburg, Alta., Can. D19 102
Evans City, Pa., U.S. G6 108
Evansdale, Ia., U.S. H3 110
Evans Head, c., Austl. G10 70
Evans Strait, strt., N.W. Ter., Can. D16 96
Evanston, Il., U.S. H8 110
Evanston, Wy., U.S. C6 120
Evansville, Il., U.S. D7 114
Evansville, In., U.S. E9 114
Evansville, Mn., U.S. E12 118
Evansville, Wi., U.S. H6 110
Evansville, Wy., U.S. B10 120
Evant, Tx., U.S. H8 116
Evart, Mi., U.S. G10 110
Evarts, Ky., U.S. C3 112
Eveleth, Mn., U.S. C3 110
Evening Shade, Ar., U.S. F5 114
Everard, Lake, l., Austl. F7 68
Everard, Mount, mtn., B.C., Can. F9 102
Everest, Ks., U.S. L12 118
Everest, Mount (Qomolangma Feng), mtn., Asia G12 44
Everett, Pa., U.S. G8 108
Everett, Wa., U.S. C3 122
Everglades City, Fl., U.S. N5 112
Everglades National Park, Fl., U.S. N6 112
Evergreen, Al., U.S. K10 114
Evergreen, Ca., U.S. I5 124
Evergreen, Mt., U.S. B11 122
Everly, Ia., U.S. H12 118
Everman, Volcán, vol., Mex. H4 90
Evesham, Sask., Can. F5 104
Évian-les-Bains, Fr. F13 14
Evionnaz, Switz. F7 13
Evisa, Fr. G3 18
Évora, Port. G4 16
Évreux, Fr. C8 14
Évros (Marica) (Meriç), stm., Eur. H10 20
Évry, Fr. D9 14
Évvoia, i., Grc. K7 20
Ewa, Hi., U.S. p15 125a
Ewen, Mi., U.S. D6 110
Ewing, Ne., U.S. I9 118
Ewing, Va., U.S. C3 112
Ewo, Congo B2 58
Exaltación, Bol. E9 82
Excelsior Mountain, mtn., Ca., U.S. F6 124
Excelsior Springs, Mo., U.S. C2 114
Exeter, Ont., Can. G14 110
Exeter, Eng., U.K. K10 8
Exeter, Ca., U.S. H6 124
Exeter, Ne., U.S. K10 118
Exeter, N.H., U.S. E16 108
Exeter, stm., N.H., U.S. D15 108
Exeter Sound, strt., N.W. Ter., Can. C20 96
Exira, Ia., U.S. J13 118
Exmore, Va., U.S. B11 112
Exmouth, Austl. D2 68
Exmouth, Eng., U.K. K10 8
Exmouth Gulf, b., Austl. D2 68
Expedition Range, mts., Austl. E8 70
Experiment, Ga., U.S. F2 112
Exploits, stm., Newf., Can. D17 106
Exploits, Bay of, b., Newf., Can. C18 106
Exploits Dam, Newf., Can. D17 106
Exshaw, Alta., Can. F19 102
Extremadura, prov., Spain F5 16
Exuma Cays, is., Bah. B6 94
Exuma Sound, strt., Bah. B6 94
Eyebrow, Sask., Can. H8 104
Eyehill Creek, stm., Can. F4 104
Eyl, Som. G10 56
Eymoutiers, Fr. G8 14
Eyota, Mn., U.S. G3 110
Eyrarbakki, Ice. C3 6a
Eyre, Austl. F5 68
Eyre North, Lake, l., Austl. G2 70
Eyre Peninsula, pen., Austl. I1 70
Eyre South, Lake, l., Austl. G2 70
Eysturoy, i., Faer. Is. D8 6b
Ezine, Tur. J10 20

F

Fabens, Tx., U.S. M10 120
Faber Lake, l., N.W. Ter., Can. D9 96
Fábrega, Cerro, mtn., Pan. H12 92
Fabriano, Italy F7 18
Facatativá, Col. E5 84
Factoryville, Pa., U.S. F11 108
Fada, Chad E5 56
Fada Ngourma, Burkina E10 64
Fadd, Hung. I18 10
Faddeja, zaliv, b., Russia B13 28
Fadit, Sud. M7 60
Faenza, Italy E6 18
Faeroe Islands (Føroyar), dep., Eur. D8 6b
Fafa, Mali D10 64
Fafakourou, Sen. E2 64
Fafen, stm., Eth. G9 56
Faga, stm., Burkina E10 64
Făgăraş, Rom. D8 20
Fagernes, Nor. K11 6
Făget, Rom. D6 20
Faguibine, Lac, l., Mali C8 64
Fagurhólsmýri, Ice. C5 6a
Faido, Switz. F10 13
Fairbairn Reservoir, res., Austl. D8 70
Fairbank, Ia., U.S. H3 110
Fairbanks, Ak., U.S. D21 100
Fairbanks, La., U.S. L4 114
Fair Bluff, N.C., U.S. E7 112
Fairborn, Oh., U.S. H2 108
Fairburn, Ga., U.S. F2 112
Fairbury, Il., U.S. J7 110
Fairbury, Ne., U.S. K10 118
Fairchance, Pa., U.S. H7 108
Fairchild, Wi., U.S. F5 110
Fairfax, Al., U.S. J11 114
Fairfax, Mn., U.S. G13 118
Fairfax, Mo., U.S. B1 114
Fairfax, Ok., U.S. C10 116
Fairfax, S.C., U.S. G5 112
Fairfax, S.D., U.S. H9 118
Fairfax, Vt., U.S. C13 108
Fairfax, Va., U.S. I9 108
Fairfield, Al., U.S. I10 114
Fairfield, Ca., U.S. F3 124
Fairfield, Id., U.S. G11 122
Fairfield, Il., U.S. D8 114
Fairfield, Ia., U.S. I4 110
Fairfield, Me., U.S. C17 108
Fairfield, Mt., U.S. C14 122
Fairfield, Ne., U.S. K9 118
Fairfield, Oh., U.S. H2 108
Fairfield, Tx., U.S. H10 116
Fairgrove, Mi., U.S. G12 110
Fairhaven, Ma., U.S. F16 108
Fair Haven, N.Y., U.S. D10 108
Fair Haven, Vt., U.S. D13 108
Fairhope, Al., U.S. L9 114
Fairland, In., U.S. C11 114
Fairland, Ok., U.S. C12 116
Fairlie, N.Z. F3 72
Fairmont, Mn., U.S. H13 118
Fairmont, Ne., U.S. K10 118
Fairmont, N.C., U.S. E7 112
Fairmont, W.V., U.S. H6 108
Fairmont Hot Springs, B.C., Can. G19 102
Fairmount, Ga., U.S. E2 112
Fairmount, Il., U.S. B9 114
Fairmount, In., U.S. B11 114
Fairmount, N.D., U.S. E11 118
Fair Ness, c., N.W. Ter., Can. D18 96
Fair Oaks, Ca., U.S. F4 124
Fair Oaks, Ga., U.S. F2 112
Fair Plain, Mi., U.S. H9 110
Fairplains, N.C., U.S. C5 112
Fairplay, Co., U.S. E10 120
Fairview, Alta., Can. A16 102
Fairview, Ga., U.S. E1 112
Fairview, Il., U.S. J5 110
Fairview, Ks., U.S. L12 118
Fairview, Mi., U.S. F11 110
Fairview, Mt., U.S. D3 118
Fairview, Ok., U.S. C8 116
Fairview, Tn., U.S. G9 114
Fairview, Ut., U.S. E5 120
Fairview, W.V., U.S. H6 108
Fairview Park, In., U.S. C9 114
Fairview Peak, mtn., Nv., U.S. E7 124
Fairweather Mountain, mtn., N.A. G26 100
Faisalabad, Pak. E5 44
Faison, N.C., U.S. D8 112
Faith, S.D., U.S. F5 118
Faiyum see Al-Fayyūm, Egypt C6 60
Faizābād, India G10 44
Fajardo, P.R. E12 94
Fakfak, Indon. F9 38
Fakrinkotti, Sud. H6 60
Faku, China A11 32
Falaise, Fr. D6 14
Falam, Burma C2 40
Falāvarjān, Iran E11 48
Fălciu, Rom. C12 20
Falcón, state, Ven. B8 84
Falconara Marittima, Italy F8 18
Falconbridge, Ont., Can. D15 110
Falcon Heights, Or., U.S. H4 122
Falcon Reservoir (Presa Falcón), res., N.A. M7 116
Falémé, stm., Afr. F4 54
Falešty, Mol. B11 20
Falfurrias, Tx., U.S. L8 116
Falher, Alta., Can. B17 102
Falkensee, Ger. C13 10
Falkenstein, Ger. E12 10
Falkirk, Scot., U.K. E10 8
Falkland, B.C., Can. G15 102
Falkland Islands, dep., S.A. G5 78
Falkland Sound, strt., Falk. Is. G5 78
Falkville, Al., U.S. H10 114
Fall, stm., Ks., U.S. N12 118
Fallais, Bel. G7 12
Fallbrook, Ca., U.S. K8 124
Fall Creek, Wi., U.S. F4 110
Fallentimber Creek, stm., Alta., Can. F19 102
Falling, stm., Va., U.S. B8 112
Fallon, Mt., U.S. E2 118
Fallon, Nv., U.S. E7 124
Fall River, Ks., U.S. N11 118
Fall River, Ma., U.S. F15 108
Fall River, Wi., U.S. G6 110
Fall River Mills, Ca., U.S. C4 124
Falls City, Ne., U.S. K12 118
Falls City, Or., U.S. F2 122
Falls Creek, Pa., U.S. F8 108
Falmouth, Jam. E6 94
Falmouth, Eng., U.K. K8 8
Falmouth, Ky., U.S. I2 108
Falmouth, Me., U.S. D16 108
Falmouth, Ma., U.S. F16 108
Falmouth, Va., U.S. I9 108
False Divi Point, c., India E6 46
Falso, Cabo, c., Dom. Rep. F9 94
Falso, Cabo, c., Hond. B11 92
Falster, i., Den. N12 6
Fălticeni, Rom. B10 20
Falun, Swe. K14 6
Famaillá, Arg. D6 80
Famatina, Arg. E5 80
Famatina, Sierra de, mts., Arg. E5 80
Family Lake, l., Man., Can. G19 104
Fana, Mali E6 64
Fanado, stm., Braz. D7 79
Fanambana, Madag. N24 67b
Fanchon, Pointe, c., Haiti E7 94
Fanchuan, China C8 34
Fandriana, Madag. R22 67b
Fang, Thai. E5 40
Fangak, Sud. M6 60
Fangcheng, China B1 34
Fangdao, China H7 34
Fangxi, China G3 34
Fanipol', Bela. H10 22
Fanny, Mount, mtn., Or., U.S. E8 122
Fanny Bay, B.C., Can. H10 102
Fano, Italy F8 18
Fan Si Pan, mtn., Viet. C7 40
Fanxian, China H3 32
Faraday, sci., B.A.T. B12 73
Faradje, Zaire H6 56
Faradofay, Madag. T22 67b
Farafangana, Madag. S22 67b
Farāh, Afg. E17 48
Farahalana, Madag. O24 67b
Farā'id, Jabal al-, mtn., Egypt J3 48
Farallon Islands, is., Ca., U.S. G2 124
Faramana, Burkina E7 64
Faranah, Gui. F4 64
Farasān, Jazā'ir, is., Sau. Ar. F2 47
Faratsiho, Madag. Q22 67b
Farewell, Cape, c., N.Z. D4 72
Fargo, N.D., U.S. E11 118
Faribault, Mn., U.S. F2 110
Faribault, Lac, l., Que., Can. E18 96
Farīdkot, India E6 44
Farīdpur, Bngl. I13 44
Farīmān, Iran D15 48
Farina, Il., U.S. D8 114
Fāriskūr, Egypt B6 60
Farley, Ia., U.S. H4 110
Farmer City, Il., U.S. B8 114
Farmersburg, In., U.S. C9 114
Farmersville, Il., U.S. C7 114
Farmersville, Tx., U.S. F10 116
Farmerville, La., U.S. J4 114
Farmington, Il., U.S. J5 110
Farmington, Ia., U.S. J4 110
Farmington, Me., U.S. C16 108
Farmington, Mn., U.S. F2 110
Farmington, Mo., U.S. E6 114
Farmington, N.H., U.S. D15 108
Farmington, N.M., U.S. H8 120
Farmington, Ut., U.S. D5 120
Far Mountain, mtn., B.C., Can. E9 102
Farmville, N.C., U.S. D9 112
Farmville, Va., U.S. B8 112
Farnam, Ne., U.S. K7 118
Farnham, Que., Can. B14 108
Farnham, Mount, mtn., B.C., Can. G18 102
Farnhamville, Ia., U.S. I13 118
Faro, Braz. I14 84
Faro, Port. H4 16
Faro, stm., Afr. G9 54
Farquhar Group, is., Sey. D10 58
Farragut, Ia., U.S. K12 118
Farrāshband, Iran G12 48
Farrell, Pa., U.S. F6 108
Farrukhābād, India G8 44
Fārsī, Afg. E17 48
Farsund, Nor. L10 6
Fartak, Ra's, c., Yemen G8 47
Farvel, Kap, c., Grnld. D15 86
Farwell, Mi., U.S. G11 110
Farwell, Tx., U.S. I3 116
Fasā, Iran G12 48
Fasano, Italy I12 18
Fatehpur, India G6 44
Fathai, Sud. M6 60
Fathom Five National Marine Park, Ont., Can. E14 110
Fatick, Sen. D1 64
Fátima, Port. F3 16
Fatoto, Gam. E3 64
Fat'ož, Russia I18 22
Faulkton, S.D., U.S. F8 118
Faulquemont, Fr. C13 14
Fauquier, B.C., Can. H16 102
Fauske, Nor. H14 6
Faust, Alta., Can. B19 102
Fauvillers, Bel. I8 12
Faux-Cap, Madag. T21 67b
Favara, Italy L8 18
Faverges, Fr. G13 14
Favourable Lake, l., Ont., Can. F21 104
Fawcett, Alta., Can. C20 102
Fawcett Lake, l., Alta., Can. B21 102
Fawn, stm., Ont., Can. F15 96
Fawnie Nose, mtn., B.C., Can. D9 102
Fawnie Range, mts., B.C., Can. D10 102
Faxaflói, b., Ice. B2 6a
Faxinal, Braz. G3 79
Faxinal do Soturno, Braz. E12 80
Faya, Chad E4 56
Fayd, Sau. Ar. H7 48
Fayette, Al., U.S. I9 114
Fayette, Ia., U.S. H4 110
Fayette, Ms., U.S. K5 114
Fayette, Mo., U.S. C4 114
Fayette, Oh., U.S. F2 108
Fayetteville, Ar., U.S. F2 114
Fayetteville, Ga., U.S. F2 112
Fayetteville, N.C., U.S. D8 112
Fayetteville, Tn., U.S. G10 114
Fayetteville, W.V., U.S. I5 108
Fayl-Billot, Fr. E12 14
Fazenda de Cima, Braz. F13 82
Fazenda Nova, Braz. D3 79
Fāzilka, India E6 44
Fāzilpur, Pak. F4 44
Fazzān (Fezzan), hist. reg., Libya C3 56
Fdérik, Maur. I4 62
Fear, Cape, c., N.C., U.S. F9 112
Feather, stm., Ca., U.S. E4 124
Feathertop, Mount, mtn., Austl. K7 70
Fécamp, Fr. C7 14
Federación, Arg. F10 80
Federal, Arg. F9 80
Federalsburg, Md., U.S. I11 108
Fehérgyarmat, Hung. H22 10
Fehmarn, i., Ger. A11 10
Fehmarn Belt, strt., Eur. A11 10
Feia, Lagoa, b., Braz. G8 79
Feijó, Braz. C6 82
Feira, Zam. E6 58
Feira de Santana, Braz. B9 79
Feixiang, China G2 32
Fejaj, Chott, sw., Tun. D15 62
Fejér, co., Hung. H18 10
Felanitx, Spain F15 16
Felda, Fl., U.S. M5 112
Feldbach, Aus. I15 10
Feldkirch, Aus. H9 10
Felhit, Eth. I10 60
Feliciano, Arroyo, stm., Arg. F9 80
Felix, Cape, c., N.W. Ter., Can. C13 96
Felix, Rio, stm., N.M., U.S. K11 120
Felixlândia, Braz. E6 79
Felixstowe, Eng., U.K. J15 8
Felixton, S. Afr. G10 66
Félix U. Gómez, Mex. C4 90
Fellbach, Ger. G9 10
Felletin, Fr. G9 14
Fellsmere, Fl., U.S. L6 112
Feltre, Italy C6 18
Femund, l., Nor. J12 6
Femundsenden, Nor. K12 6
Fen, stm., China D9 30
Fenelon Falls, Ont., Can. F17 110
Fengcheng, China C12 32
Fengcheng, China G4 34
Fengdu, China F8 30
Fengfeng, China G2 32
Fenghuanjing, China D6 34
Fengjia, China F9 32
Fenglin, Tai. L10 34
Fengxin, China G4 34
Fengyang, China E10 30
Fengyüan, Tai. K9 34
Fengzhen, China C9 30
Feni, Bngl. I14 44
Fennimore, Wi., U.S. H5 110
Fennville, Mi., U.S. H9 110
Fenoarivo Atsinanana, Madag. P23 67b
Fenshui'ao, China J3 34
Fenton, Mi., U.S. H12 110
Fentress, Tx., U.S. J9 116
Fenwick, W.V., U.S. I6 108
Fenyang, China D9 30
Feodosija, Ukr. H5 26
Ferdinand, In., U.S. D10 114
Ferdows, Iran D15 48
Fergana, Uzb. I12 26
Fergus, Ont., Can. G15 110
Fergus Falls, Mn., U.S. E11 118
Ferguson, B.C., Can. G17 102
Ferguson, Ky., U.S. B2 112
Ferguson, Mo., U.S. D6 114
Fériana, Tun. C15 62
Ferkéssédougou, I.C. G7 64
Ferlo, Vallée du, val., Sen. D2 64
Fermo, Italy F8 18
Fermont, Que., Can. F19 96
Fernández, Arg. D7 80
Fernandina, Isla, i., Ec. J13 84a
Fernandina Beach, Fl., U.S. I5 112
Fernando de la Mora, Para. C10 80
Fernando de Noronha, Ilha, i., Braz. D12 76
Fernandópolis, Braz. F3 79
Fernando Póo see Bioko, i., Eq. Gui. J14 64
Fernán-Núñez, Spain H7 16
Ferndale, Ca., U.S. D1 124
Ferndale, Wa., U.S. B3 122
Fernie, B.C., Can. H19 102
Fernley, Nv., U.S. E6 124
Fern Park, Fl., U.S. K5 112
Fernwood, Id., U.S. C9 122
Ferolle Point, c., Newf., Can. A16 106
Ferrara, Italy E6 18
Ferreñafe, Peru B2 82
Ferreyra, Arg. F6 80
Ferriday, La., U.S. K5 114
Ferrières, Fr. D9 14
Ferris, Tx., U.S. G10 116
Ferro, stm., Braz. B1 79
Ferrol, Península de, pen., Peru C2 82
Ferron, Ut., U.S. E5 120
Ferros, Braz. E7 79
Ferryland, Newf., Can. E21 106
Ferrysburg, Mi., U.S. G9 110
Fertile, Mn., U.S. D11 118
Fès, Mor. C8 62
Feshi, Zaire C3 58
Fessenden, N.D., U.S. D8 118
Festus, Mo., U.S. D6 114
Fété Bowé, Sen. D3 64
Feteşti, Rom. E11 20
Fethiye, Tur. M13 20
Feuchtwangen, Ger. F10 10
Feuet, Libya H16 62
Feuilles, Baie aux, b., Que., Can. E19 96
Feuilles, Rivière aux, stm., Que., Can. E18 96
Feyzābād, Afg. B4 44
Fez see Fès, Mor. C8 62
Fiambalá, Arg. D5 80
Fianarantsoa, Madag. R22 67b
Fiantsonana, Madag. Q22 67b
Fiche, Eth. M10 60
Fichtelberg, mtn., Ger. E12 10
Fichtelgebirge, mts., Eur. E11 10
Ficksburg, S. Afr. G8 66
Fidenza, Italy E5 18
Fidler Lake, l., Man., Can. A18 104
Field, B.C., Can. F18 102
Fieldale, Va., U.S. C7 112
Fier, Alb. I3 20
Fiesch, Switz. F9 13
Fiesole, Italy F6 18
Fife, prov., Scot., U.K. E10 8
Fife Lake, Sask., Can. I9 104
Fife Lake, Mi., U.S. F10 110
Fife Lake, l., Sask., Can. I9 104
Fifield, Wi., U.S. E5 110
Figueira da Foz, Port. E3 16
Figueres, Spain C14 16
Figuig, Mor. D10 62
Fiji, ctry., Oc. H24 2
Filabusi, Zimb. C9 66
Filadelfia, C.R. G9 92
Filchner Ice Shelf, Ant. C1 73
File Lake, l., Man., Can. D14 104
Filingué, Niger D11 64
Fillmore, Sask., Can. I11 104
Fillmore, Ca., U.S. J7 124
Fillmore, Ut., U.S. F4 120
Finale Ligure, Italy E3 18
Finarwa, Eth. K10 60
Fincastle, Va., U.S. B7 112
Findlay, Il., U.S. C8 114
Findlay, Oh., U.S. F3 108
Findlay, Mount, mtn., B.C., Can. G18 102
Fingal, N.D., U.S. E10 118
Finger Lake, l., Ont., Can. E21 104
Fíngoè, Moz. E6 58
Finistère, dept., Fr. D2 14
Finisterre, Cabo de, c., Spain C2 16
Finke, Austl. E6 68
Finke, stm., Austl. E7 68
Finland (Suomi), ctry., Eur. C13 4
Finland, Gulf of, b., Eur. L20 6
Finlay, stm., B.C., Can. E7 96
Finley, Austl. J6 70
Finley, N.D., U.S. D10 118
Finmoore, B.C., Can. D11 102
Finn, stm., Eur. G6 8
Finnegan, Alta., Can. F22 102
Finnmark, co., Nor. F19 6
Fins, Oman C11 47
Finsteraarhorn, mtn., Switz. E9 13
Finsterwalde, Ger. D13 10
Fiora, stm., Italy G6 18
Fīq, Isr. Occ. C5 50
Firavitoba, Col. E6 84
Firebaugh, Ca., U.S. H5 124
Firenze (Florence), Italy F6 18
Firmat, Arg. G8 80
Firminópolis, Braz. D3 79
Firminy, Fr. G11 14
Firovo, Russia D16 22
Fīrozābād, India G8 44
Fīrozpur, India E6 44
Firth, Ne., U.S. K11 118
Firth, stm., N.A. C4 96
Firth, stm., N.A. B24 100
Fīrūzābād, Iran G12 48
Fīrūz Kūh, Iran D12 48
Fish (Vis), stm., Nmb. F3 66
Fish, stm., Al., U.S. L9 114
Fisher, Ar., U.S. G6 114
Fisher, Il., U.S. B8 114
Fisher, La., U.S. K3 114
Fisher, stm., Man., Can. G17 104
Fisher, stm., Mt., U.S. B10 122
Fisher Bay, b., Man., Can. G17 104
Fisher Branch, Man., Can. G17 104
Fisher Channel, strt., B.C., Can. E7 102
Fisher River Indian Reserve, Man., Can. G17 104
Fishers Island, i., N.Y., U.S. F15 108
Fisher Strait, strt., N.W. Ter., Can. D16 96
Fishing Creek, Md., U.S. I10 108
Fishing Lake, l., Man., Can. F19 104
Fishing Lake, l., Sask., Can. G11 104

Name — Map Ref. — Page

Fisk, Mo., U.S. F6 114
Fismes, Fr. C10 14
Fitchburg, Ma., U.S. E15 108
Fitzgerald, Ga., U.S. H3 112
Fitzgerald River National Park, Austl. F3 68
Fitz Hugh Sound, strt., B.C., Can. F7 102
Fitzroy, stm., Austl. C4 68
Fitzroy, stm., Austl. D9 70
Fitzroy, Monte (Cerro Chaltel), mtn., S.A. F2 78
Fitzroy Crossing, Austl. C5 68
Fiume see Rijeka, Cro. D9 18
Fiumicino, Italy H7 18
Five Islands, N.S., Can. G9 106
Five Points, N.M., U.S. I10 120
Fizi, Zaire B5 58
Fizuli, Azer. B9 48
Fjällåsen, Swe. H17 6
Fkih-Ben-Salah, Mor. D7 62
Flagler, Co., U.S. L4 118
Flagler Beach, Fl., U.S. J5 112
Flagstaff, Az., U.S. I5 120
Flagstaff Lake, res., Me., U.S. B16 108
Flambeau, stm., Wi., U.S. E4 110
Fläming, reg., Ger. D12 10
Flaming Gorge Reservoir, res., U.S. C7 120
Flanagan, Il., U.S. J7 110
Flanagan, stm., Ont., Can. F21 104
Flanders, Ont., Can. B3 110
Flanders (Flandre), hist. reg., Eur. G2 12
Flandes, Col. E5 84
Flandreau, S.D., U.S. G11 118
Flasher, N.D., U.S. E6 118
Flat, Tx., U.S. H9 116
Flat, stm., N.W. Ter., Can. F31 100
Flat, stm., Mi., U.S. G10 110
Flat Bay, Newf., Can. D15 106
Flatey, Ice. B2 6a
Flateyri, Ice. B2 6a
Flathead, stm., Mt., U.S. I20 102
Flathead Lake, l., Mt., U.S. C11 122
Flat Lake, l., Alta., Can. C22 102
Flat Lick, Ky., U.S. C3 112
Flatonia, Tx., U.S. J9 116
Flat River, P.E.I., Can. F11 106
Flat River, Mo., U.S. E6 114
Flat Rock, Al., U.S. H11 114
Flat Rock, Il., U.S. D9 114
Flatrock Lake, l., Man., Can. C14 104
Flattery, Cape, c., Wa., U.S. B1 122
Flatwood, Al., U.S. J10 114
Flatwoods, Ky., U.S. I4 108
Flaxcombe, Sask., Can. G5 104
Flaxton, N.D., U.S. C5 118
Flaxville, Mt., U.S. C2 118
Fleetwood, Pa., U.S. G11 108
Fleming, Co., U.S. K5 118
Fleming-Neon, Ky., U.S. B4 112
Flemingsburg, Ky., U.S. I3 108
Flensburg, Ger. A9 10
Fletcher, N.C., U.S. D4 112
Fletcher, Ok., U.S. E8 116
Fletcher Pond, res., Mi., U.S. F12 110
Fleurance, Fr. I7 14
Fleur-de-Lys, Newf., Can. B17 106
Fleurier, Switz. E6 13
Flevoland, prov., Neth. D7 12
Flinders, stm., Austl. A4 70
Flinders Island, i., Austl. M8 70
Flinders Reefs, rf., Austl. A8 70
Flin Flon, Man., Can. D13 104
Flint, Mi., U.S. G12 110
Flint, stm., U.S. H10 114
Flint, stm., Ga., U.S. I2 112
Flint, stm., Mi., U.S. G12 110
Flint Lake, l., N.W. Ter., Can. C18 96
Flintville, Tn., U.S. G10 114
Flippin, Ar., U.S. F4 114
Flisa, Nor. K13 6
Flize, Fr. C11 14
Flomaton, Al., U.S. K9 114
Flomot, Tx., U.S. E6 116
Floodwood, Mn., U.S. D3 110
Flora, Il., U.S. D8 114
Flora, In., U.S. B10 114
Flora, Ms., U.S. J6 114
Florac, Fr. H10 14
Florala, Al., U.S. K10 114
Floral City, Fl., U.S. K4 112
Floral Park, Mt., U.S. E13 122
Flora Vista, N.M., U.S. H8 120
Florence, Al., U.S. H9 114
Florence, Az., U.S. K5 120
Florence, Co., U.S. F11 120
Florence, Ks., U.S. M11 118
Florence, Or., U.S. G1 122
Florence, S.C., U.S. E7 112
Florence, Tx., U.S. I9 116
Florence, Wi., U.S. E7 110
Florence see Firenze, Italy F6 18
Florencia, Col. G5 84
Florencio Sánchez, Ur. G10 80
Flores, Braz. E11 76
Flores, i., Indon. G7 38
Flores, i., Port. k18 62a
Flores, Laut (Flores Sea), Indon. G7 38
Flores da Cunha, Braz. E13 80
Flores de Goiás, Braz. C5 79
Flores Island, i., B.C., Can. H8 102
Floresta Azul, Braz. C9 79
Florešty, Mol. B12 20
Floresville, Tx., U.S. J8 116
Floriano, Braz. E10 76
Floriano Peixoto, Braz. C8 82
Florianópolis, Braz. D14 80
Florida, Col. F4 84
Florida, Cuba D5 94
Florida, Hond. B6 92
Florida, Peru A3 82
Florida, Ur. H10 80
Florida, state, U.S. F10 98
Florida, stm., Co., U.S. G9 120
Florida, Straits of, strt., N.A. B4 94
Florida Bay, b., Fl., U.S. N6 112
Floridablanca, Col. D6 84
Florida City, Fl., U.S. N6 112
Florida Keys, is., Fl., U.S. O5 112
Floridia, Italy L10 18
Florido, stm., Mex. D7 90
Florien, La., U.S. K3 114
Flórina, Grc. I5 20
Florissant, Mo., U.S. D6 114
Florø, Nor. K9 6
Flotten Lake, l., Sask., Can. D6 104
Flower's Cove, Newf., Can. A17 106
Flowery Branch, Ga., U.S. E3 112
Floyd, N.M., U.S. E3 116
Floyd, Va., U.S. C6 112
Floyd, stm., Ia., U.S. I11 118
Floydada, Tx., U.S. F5 116
Floyds Fork, stm., Ky., U.S. D11 114
Fluchthorn, mtn., Eur. E13 13
Flushing, Mi., U.S. G12 110
Fluvanna, Tx., U.S. G5 116
Fly, stm. m15 68a
Foam Lake, Sask., Can. G11 104
Foča, Bos. F2 20
Foça, Tur. K10 20
Focşani, Rom. D11 20
Fodé, Cen. Afr. Rep. O2 60
Fodécontea, Gui. F2 64
Foggaret el Arab, Alg. G12 62
Foggaret ez Zoua, Alg. G12 62
Foggia, Italy H10 18
Fogo, Newf., Can. C19 106
Fogo, i., C.V. m16 64a
Fogo, Cape, c., Newf., Can. C19 106
Fogo Island, i., Newf., Can. C19 106
Fogolawa, Nig. E14 64
Fohnsdorf, Aus. H14 10
Foix, Fr. J8 14
Foix, hist. reg., Fr. J8 14
Fokino, Russia H17 22
Folakara, Madag. Q21 67b
Foley, Al., U.S. L9 114
Foley, Mn., U.S. E2 110
Foleyet, Ont., Can. B13 110
Foley Island, i., N.W. Ter., Can. C17 96
Foligno, Italy G7 18
Folkestone, Eng., U.K. J15 8
Folkston, Ga., U.S. I4 112
Follett, Tx., U.S. C6 116
Follonica, Italy G5 18
Follonica, Golfo di, b., Italy G5 18
Folsom, Ca., U.S. F4 124
Folsom Lake, res., Ca., U.S. F4 124
Fomboni, Com. L15 67a
Fonda, Ia., U.S. I13 118
Fonda, N.Y., U.S. E12 108
Fond du Lac, Sask., Can. E11 96
Fond du Lac, Wi., U.S. G7 110
Fond du Lac, stm., Sask., Can. E11 96
Fondi, Italy H8 18
Fondouk el Aouareb, Tun. N4 18
Fonni, Italy I4 18
Fonseca, Col. B6 84
Fonseca, Golfo de, b., N.A. D7 92
Fontainebleau, Fr. D9 14
Fontana, Arg. D9 80
Fontana, Ca., U.S. J8 124
Fontana Lake, res., N.C., U.S. D3 112
Fontanelle, Ia., U.S. J13 118
Fontarabie, Lac, l., Que., Can. A7 106
Fontas, stm., Can. E8 96
Fonte Boa, Braz. I9 84
Fonteneau, Lac, l., Que., Can. A12 106
Fontenelle, Que., Can. D9 106
Fontur, c., Ice. A6 6a
Fonyód, Hung. I17 10
Foochow see Fuzhou, China I8 34
Foothills, Alta., Can. D18 102
Footprint Lake, l., Man., Can. C16 104
Footville, Wi., U.S. H6 110
Foraker, Mount, mtn., Ak., U.S. E19 100
Forbach, Fr. C13 14
Forbes, Austl. I8 70
Forbes, Mount, mtn., Alta., Can. F18 102
Forchheim, Ger. F11 10
Ford, Ks., U.S. N8 118
Ford, stm., Mi., U.S. D8 110
Ford City, Ca., U.S. I6 124
Ford City, Pa., U.S. G7 108
Ford Ranges, mts., Ant. C10 73
Fordsville, Ky., U.S. E10 114
Fordville, N.D., U.S. C10 118
Fordyce, Ar., U.S. I4 114
Forel, Mont, mtn., Grnld. C16 86
Foreman, Ar., U.S. I2 114
Foremost, Alta., Can. I3 104
Forest, Ont., Can. G13 110
Forest, Ms., U.S. J7 114
Forest, Oh., U.S. G3 108
Forest Acres, S.C., U.S. E6 112
Forestburg, Alta., Can. E22 102
Forest City, Ia., U.S. G2 110
Forest City, N.C., U.S. D5 112
Forest City, Pa., U.S. F11 108
Forest Grove, B.C., Can. F13 102
Foresthill, Ca., U.S. E5 124
Forest Home, Al., U.S. K10 114
Forest Lake, Mn., U.S. E3 110
Forest Park, Ga., U.S. F2 112
Forestville, Que., Can. D4 106
Forestville, Wi., U.S. F8 110
Forfar, Scot., U.K. E11 8
Forgan, Ok., U.S. C6 116
Forillon, Parc National de, Que., Can. D9 106
Forked Deer, stm., Tn., U.S. G7 114
Forks, Wa., U.S. C1 122
Forlì, Italy E7 18
Forman, N.D., U.S. E10 118
Formentera, i., Spain G13 16
Formia, Italy H8 18
Formiga, Braz. F6 79
Formosa, Arg. D9 80
Formosa, Braz. C5 79
Formosa, prov., Arg. C9 80
Formosa, Serra, plat., Braz. D14 82
Formosa see Taiwan, ctry., Asia L9 34
Formoso, stm., Braz. B6 79
Formoso, stm., Braz. E2 79
Forney, Tx., U.S. G10 116
Fornosovo, Russia B13 22
Forres, Arg. D7 80
Forrest, Austl. F5 68
Forrest, Il., U.S. J7 110
Forrest City, Ar., U.S. G6 114
Forreston, Il., U.S. H6 110
Forsan, Tx., U.S. G5 116
Forsayth, Austl. B5 70
Forst, Ger. D14 10
Forster, Austl. I10 70
Forsyth, Ga., U.S. F3 112
Forsyth, Mo., U.S. F3 114
Forsyth, Mt., U.S. D19 122
Forsyth Range, mts., Austl. D5 70
Fort Adams, Ms., U.S. K5 114
Fort Albany, Ont., Can. F16 96
Fort Alexander Indian Reserve, Man., Can. H18 104
Fortaleza, Braz. D11 76
Fortaleza, stm., Peru D3 82
Fortaleza de Santa Teresa, Ur. G12 80
Fortaleza do Ituxi, Braz. B8 82
Fort Amherst National Historic Park, P.E.I., Can. F10 106
Fort Anne National Historic Park, N.S., Can. H8 106
Fort Assiniboine, Alta., Can. C20 102
Fort Atkinson, Wi., U.S. H7 110
Fort Battleford National Historic Park, Sask., Can. F6 104
Fort Beaufort, S. Afr. I8 66
Fort Beauséjour National Historic Park, N.B., Can. G9 106
Fort Benton, Mt., U.S. C15 122
Fort Bidwell, Ca., U.S. C5 124
Fort Bragg, Ca., U.S. E2 124
Fort Branch, In., U.S. D9 114
Fort Bridger, Wy., U.S. C6 120
Fort Calhoun, Ne., U.S. J11 118
Fort-Carnot, Madag. R22 67b
Fort Chipewyan, Alta., Can. E10 96
Fort Cobb, Ok., U.S. D8 116
Fort Collins, Co., U.S. D11 120
Fort-Coulonge, Que., Can. B10 108
Fort Covington, N.Y., U.S. C12 108
Fort Davis, Al., U.S. J11 114
Fort Davis, Tx., U.S. I3 116
Fort Defiance, Az., U.S. I7 120
Fort-de-France, Mart. G14 94
Fort Deposit, Al., U.S. K10 114
Fort Dodge, Ia., U.S. H1 110
Fort Duchesne, Ut., U.S. D7 120
Forteau, Newf., Can. A17 106
Fort Edward, N.Y., U.S. D13 108
Fort Erie, Ont., Can. H17 110
Fortescue, stm., Austl. D3 68
Fortezza, Italy C6 18
Fort Fitzgerald, Alta., Can. E10 96
Fort Frances, Ont., Can. B2 110
Fort Franklin, N.W. Ter., Can. D33 100
Fort Fraser, B.C., Can. C10 102
Fort Gaines, Ga., U.S. H1 112
Fort Garland, Co., U.S. G11 120
Fort Gay, W.V., U.S. I4 108
Fort Gibson, Ok., U.S. D11 116
Fort Gibson Lake, res., Ok., U.S. C11 116
Fort Good Hope, N.W. Ter., Can. C30 100
Forth, Firth of, b., Scot., U.K. E11 8
Fort Hall, Id., U.S. G13 122
Fortin, Lac, l., Que., Can. B6 106
Fortín Ayacucho, Para. H12 82
Fortín Coroneles Sanchez, Para. H12 82
Fortín Florida, Para. I12 82
Fortín Garrapatal, Para. I11 82
Fortín Teniente Montanía, Para. B9 80
Fortín Uno, Arg. J6 80
Fort Jones, Ca., U.S. C3 124
Fort Klamath, Or., U.S. H4 122
Fort-Lamy see N'Djamena, Chad F4 56
Fort Laramie, Wy., U.S. B12 120
Fort Lauderdale, Fl., U.S. M6 112
Fort Liard, N.W. Ter., Can. D8 96
Fort-Liberté, Haiti E9 94
Fort Loramie, Oh., U.S. G2 108
Fort Loudoun Lake, res., Tn., U.S. D2 112
Fort Lupton, Co., U.S. D12 120
Fort Macleod, Alta., Can. H21 102
Fort Madison, Ia., U.S. J4 110
Fort McMurray, Alta., Can. E10 96
Fort McMurray, Alta., Can. B3 104
Fort McPherson, N.W. Ter., Can. C27 100
Fort Meade, Fl., U.S. L5 112
Fort Mill, S.C., U.S. D6 112
Fort Mitchell, Al., U.S. G1 112
Fort Morgan, Co., U.S. K4 118
Fort Myers, Fl., U.S. M5 112
Fort Myers Beach, Fl., U.S. M5 112
Fort Nelson, B.C., Can. E8 96
Fort Nelson, stm., B.C., Can. E8 96
Fort Norman, N.W. Ter., Can. D32 100
Fort Ogden, Fl., U.S. L5 112
Fort Payne, Al., U.S. H11 114
Fort Peck, Mt., U.S. B19 122
Fort Peck Lake, res., Mt., U.S. C19 122
Fort Pierce, Fl., U.S. L6 112
Fort Pierre, S.D., U.S. G7 118
Fort Plain, N.Y., U.S. E12 108
Fort Portal, Ug. A6 58
Fort Providence, N.W. Ter., Can. D9 96
Fort Qu'Appelle, Sask., Can. H11 104
Fort Recovery, Oh., U.S. G2 108
Fort Resolution, N.W. Ter., Can. D10 96
Fortress Mountain, mtn., Wy., U.S. F16 122
Fortress of Louisbourg National Historic Park, N.S., Can. G14 106
Fort Saint James, B.C., Can. C10 102
Fort Saint John, B.C., Can. A14 102
Fort Saskatchewan, Alta., Can. D21 102
Fort Scott, Ks., U.S. N13 118
Fort-Ševčenko, Kaz. I8 26
Fort Severn, Ont., Can. E15 96
Fort Simpson, N.W. Ter., Can. D8 96
Fort Smith, N.W. Ter., Can. D10 96
Fort Smith, Ar., U.S. G2 114
Fort Steele, B.C., Can. H19 102
Fort Stockton, Tx., U.S. I4 116
Fort Sumner, N.M., U.S. E2 116
Fort Supply, Ok., U.S. C7 116
Fort Thomas, Az., U.S. K7 120
Fort Thompson, S.D., U.S. G8 118
Fort Totten, N.D., U.S. D9 118
Fort Towson, Ok., U.S. E11 116
Fortuna, Arg. H6 80
Fortuna, C.R. G10 92
Fortuna, Ca., U.S. D1 124
Fortuna, Río de la, stm., Bol. G12 82
Fortuna Ledge (Marshall), Ak., U.S. F13 100
Fortune, Newf., Can. E18 106
Fortune Bay, b., Newf., Can. E18 106
Fortune Harbour, Newf., Can. C18 106
Fort Valley, Ga., U.S. G3 112
Fort Vermilion, Alta., Can. E9 96
Fortville, In., U.S. C11 114
Fort Walton Beach, Fl., U.S. L10 114
Fort Washakie, Wy., U.S. A8 120
Fort Wayne, In., U.S. A11 114
Fort Wellington, Guy. D14 84
Fort White, Fl., U.S. J4 112
Fort William, Scot., U.K. E8 8
Fort William see Thunder Bay, Ont., Can. B6 110
Fort Worth, Tx., U.S. G9 116
Fort Yates, N.D., U.S. E7 118
Fortymile, stm., N.A. D24 100
Fort Yukon, Ak., U.S. C22 100
Foshan, China L2 34
Fossano, Italy E2 18
Fossil, Or., U.S. F5 122
Fosston, Mn., U.S. D12 118
Foster, Austl. L7 70
Foster, stm., Sask., Can. C9 104
Foster, Mount, mtn., N.A. G27 100
Fosters, Al., U.S. I9 114
Fostoria, Oh., U.S. F3 108
Fouesnant, Fr. E2 14
Fougamou, Gabon B2 58
Fougères, Fr. D5 14
Fouke, Ar., U.S. I3 114
Foul Bay, b., Egypt J3 48
Foulpointe, Madag. P23 67b
Foulwind, Cape, c., N.Z. D3 72
Foumban, Cam. G9 54
Foumbouni, Com. K15 67a
Foum-el-Hisn, Mor. F6 62
Foum-Zguid, Mor. E7 62
Foundiougne, Sen. D1 64
Fountain, Co., U.S. M3 118
Fountain, Fl., U.S. I1 112
Fountain City, Wi., U.S. F4 110
Fountain Green, Ut., U.S. E5 120
Fountain Inn, S.C., U.S. E4 112
Fountain Peak, mtn., Ca., U.S. J10 124
Fountain Place, La., U.S. L5 114
Fourche LaFave, stm., Ar., U.S. H4 114
Fourche Maline, stm., Ok., U.S. E12 116
Fourchu, N.S., Can. G13 106
Four Corners, Or., U.S. F3 122
Fouriesburg, S. Afr. G9 66
Fourmies, Fr. B11 14
Four Mountains, Islands of, is., Ak., U.S. J9 100
Fournier, Lac, l., Que., Can. A8 106
Four Oaks, N.C., U.S. D8 112
Fouta Djalon, reg., Gui. F3 64
Foux, Cap à, c., Haiti E8 94
Foveaux Strait, strt., N.Z. G1 72
Fowler, Ca., U.S. H6 124
Fowler, Co., U.S. M3 118
Fowler, In., U.S. B9 114
Fowler, Ks., U.S. N7 118
Fowler, Mi., U.S. G11 110
Fowlerton, Tx., U.S. K8 116
Fowlerville, Mi., U.S. H11 110
Fowman, Iran C10 48
Fox, stm., Man., Can. C20 104
Fox, stm., U.S. B5 114
Fox, stm., Il., U.S. D8 114
Fox, stm., Wi., U.S. F7 110
Foxe Basin, b., N.W. Ter., Can. C17 96
Foxe Channel, strt., N.W. Ter., Can. D16 96
Foxe Peninsula, pen., N.W. Ter., Can. D17 96
Fox Harbour, Newf., Can. E20 106
Fox Islands, is., Ak., U.S. J10 100
Fox Lake, Il., U.S. H7 110
Fox Lake, Wi., U.S. G7 110
Fox Mountain, mtn., Yukon, Can. F28 100
Foxpark, Wy., U.S. C10 120
Fox Valley, Sask., Can. H5 104
Foxworth, Ms., U.S. K7 114
Foyle, Lough, b., Eur. F6 8
Foz do Cunene, Ang. E2 58
Foz do Iguaçu, Braz. C11 80
Foz do Jordão, Braz. C6 82
Foz Giraldo, Port. E4 16
Foziling, China D5 34
Fraga, Arg. G6 80
Fraile Muerto, Ur. G11 80
Framingham, Ma., U.S. E15 108
Frampol, Pol. E22 10
Franca, Braz. F5 79
Franca-Iosifa, Zeml'a (Franz Josef Land), is., Russia A6 24
Francavilla Fontana, Italy I12 18
France, ctry., Eur. F8 4
Frances, stm., Yukon, Can. F30 100
Frances Lake, l., Yukon, Can. F30 100
Francés Viejo, Cabo, c., Dom. Rep. E10 94
Francesville, In., U.S. B10 114
Franceville, Gabon B2 58
Franche-Comté, hist. reg., Fr. F12 14
Francia, Ur. G10 80
Francis, Sask., Can. H11 104
Francis Case, Lake, res., S.D., U.S. H8 118
Francisco Beltrão, Braz. D12 80
Francisco I. Madero, Mex. E8 90
Francisco I. Madero, Mex. E7 90
Francisco Morazán, dept., Hond. C7 92
Francisco Murguía, Mex. E8 90
Francisco Sá, Braz. D7 79
Francistown, Bots. C8 66
Francofonte, Italy L9 18
François, Newf., Can. E17 106
François, Lacs à, l., Que., Can. A8 106
François Lake, B.C., Can. C9 102
François Lake, l., B.C., Can. C9 102
Francs Peak, mtn., Wy., U.S. G16 122
Frangy, Fr. F12 14
Frankel City, Tx., U.S. G4 116
Frankenmuth, Mi., U.S. G12 110
Frankford, Ont., Can. F18 110
Frankford, Mo., U.S. C5 114
Frankfort, S. Afr. F9 66
Frankfort, S. Afr. I8 66
Frankfort, In., U.S. B10 114
Frankfort, Ks., U.S. L11 118
Frankfort, Ky., U.S. D12 114
Frankfort, Mi., U.S. F9 110
Frankfort, N.Y., U.S. D11 108
Frankfort, Oh., U.S. H3 108
Frankfort, S.D., U.S. G9 118
Frankfurt am Main, Ger. E8 10
Frankfurt an der Oder, Ger. C14 10
Franklin, Az., U.S. L7 120
Franklin, Ga., U.S. F1 112
Franklin, Id., U.S. H14 122
Franklin, Il., U.S. C6 114
Franklin, In., U.S. C10 114
Franklin, Ky., U.S. F10 114
Franklin, La., U.S. M5 114
Franklin, Me., U.S. C18 108
Franklin, Ma., U.S. E15 108
Franklin, Mn., U.S. G13 118
Franklin, Ne., U.S. K9 118
Franklin, N.H., U.S. D15 108
Franklin, N.J., U.S. F12 108
Franklin, N.C., U.S. D3 112
Franklin, Oh., U.S. H2 108
Franklin, Pa., U.S. F7 108
Franklin, Tn., U.S. G10 114
Franklin, Tx., U.S. H10 116
Franklin, Va., U.S. C10 112
Franklin, W.V., U.S. I7 108
Franklin, Wi., U.S. H7 110
Franklin Bay, b., N.W. Ter., Can. C7 96
Franklin D. Roosevelt Lake, res., Wa., U.S. B7 122
Franklin Grove, Il., U.S. I6 110
Franklin Harbor, b., Austl. I2 70
Franklin Lake, l., N.W. Ter., Can. C13 96
Franklin Mountains, mts., N.W. Ter., Can. D31 100
Franklin Strait, strt., N.W. Ter., Can. B13 96
Franklinton, La., U.S. L6 114
Franklinton, N.C., U.S. C8 112
Franklinville, N.Y., U.S. E8 108
Frankston, Tx., U.S. G11 116
Frankton, In., U.S. B11 114
Frankville, Al., U.S. K8 114
Franz Josef Land see Franca Iosifa, Zeml'a, is., Russia A6 24
Frascati, Italy H7 18
Fraser, Co., U.S. E11 120
Fraser, stm., B.C., Can. G13 102
Fraser, stm., Newf., Can. E20 96
Fraser, stm., Co., U.S. D11 120
Fraserburg, S. Afr. H5 66
Fraser Island, i., Austl. E10 70
Fraser Lake, B.C., Can. C10 102
Fraser Lake, l., B.C., Can. C10 102
Fraser Plateau, plat., B.C., Can. E11 102
Frauenfeld, Switz. C10 13
Fray Bentos, Ur. G9 80
Fray Luis Beltrán, Arg. J6 80
Fray Marcos, Ur. H11 80
Frazee, Mn., U.S. E12 118
Frazer, Mt., U.S. B19 122
Fr'azino, Russia F21 22
Frederic, Wi., U.S. E3 110
Frederica, De., U.S. H11 108
Fredericia, Den. N11 6
Frederick, Md., U.S. H9 108
Frederick, Ok., U.S. E7 116
Frederick, S.D., U.S. F9 118
Frederick Reef, rf., Austl. C11 70
Fredericksburg, Ia., U.S. H3 110
Fredericksburg, Tx., U.S. I8 116
Fredericksburg, Va., U.S. I9 108
Fredericktown, Mo., U.S. E6 114
Fredericktown, Oh., U.S. G4 108
Frederico Westphalen, Braz. D12 80
Fredericton, N.B., Can. G7 106
Fredericton Junction, N.B., Can. G7 106
Frederikshavn, Den. M12 6
Frederiksted, V.I.U.S. F12 94
Frederik Willem IV Vallen, wtfl, Sur. F14 84
Fredonia, Col. E5 84
Fredonia, Az., U.S. H4 120
Fredonia, Ks., U.S. N12 118
Fredonia, N.Y., U.S. E7 108
Fredonia, N.D., U.S. E8 118
Fredrikstad, Nor. L12 6
Freeburg, Il., U.S. D7 114
Freeburg, Mo., U.S. D5 114
Freehold, N.J., U.S. G12 108
Freeland, Mi., U.S. G11 110
Freeland, Pa., U.S. F11 108
Freels, Cape, c., Newf., Can. C20 106
Freels, Cape, c., Newf., Can. F20 106
Freeman, S.D., U.S. H10 118
Freeman, stm., Alta., Can. C19 102
Freeport, Bah. A5 94
Freeport, N.S., Can. H7 106
Freeport, Fl., U.S. L10 114
Freeport, Il., U.S. H6 110
Freeport, Me., U.S. D16 108
Freeport, N.Y., U.S. G13 108
Freeport, Pa., U.S. G7 108
Freeport, Tx., U.S. K11 116
Freer, Tx., U.S. L8 116
Freetown, S.L. G3 64
Fregenal de la Sierra, Spain G5 16
Freiberg, Ger. E13 10
Freiburg [im Breisgau], Ger. H7 10
Freirina, Chile E3 80
Freising, Ger. G11 10
Freistadt, Aus. G14 10
Freital, Ger. D13 10
Fréjus, Fr. I13 14
Fremantle, Austl. F3 68
Fremont, Ca., U.S. G4 124
Fremont, In., U.S. A12 114
Fremont, Ia., U.S. I3 110
Fremont, Mi., U.S. G10 110
Fremont, Ne., U.S. J11 118
Fremont, N.C., U.S. D9 112
Fremont, Oh., U.S. F3 108
Fremont, Wi., U.S. F7 110
Fremont, stm., Ut., U.S. F6 120
French Broad, stm., U.S. D4 112
Frenchburg, Ky., U.S. B3 112
French Creek, stm., Man., Can. B22 104
French Guiana (Guyane français), dep., S.A. C8 76
French Island, i., Austl. L6 70
French Lick, In., U.S. D10 114
Frenchman Bay, b., Me., U.S. C18 108
Frenchman Butte, Sask., Can. E5 104
Frenchmans Cap, mtn., Austl. N6 70
French Polynesia, dep., Oc. H3 2
French Southern and Antarctic Territories, dep., Afr. M10 126
Frenda, Alg. C11 62
Fresco, stm., Braz. E8 76
Freshfield, Mount, mtn., Can. F18 102
Fresne-Saint-Mamès, Fr. E12 14
Fresnes-en-Woëvre, Fr. C12 14
Fresnillo, Mex. F8 90
Fresno, Col. E5 84
Fresno, Ca., U.S. H6 124
Fresno, stm., Ca., U.S. H5 124
Fresno Reservoir, res., Mt., U.S. B16 122
Frewsburg, N.Y., U.S. E7 108
Freycinet Peninsula, pen., Austl. N8 70
Freyre, Arg. F7 80
Fria, Cape, c., Nmb. E2 58
Friant, Ca., U.S. H6 124
Friars Point, Ms., U.S. H6 114
Frías, Arg. E6 80
Frías, Peru A2 82
Fribourg (Freiburg), Switz. E7 13
Fribourg (Freiburg), state, Switz. E7 13
Friday Harbor, Wa., U.S. B2 122
Fridley, Mn., U.S. E2 110
Fridtjof Nansen, Mount, mtn., Ant. D9 73
Friedberg, Aus. H16 10
Friedberg, Ger. E8 10
Friedberg, Ger. G10 10
Friedland, Ger. B13 10
Friedrichshafen, Ger. H9 10
Friedrichsort, Ger. A10 10
Friedrichstadt, Ger. A9 10
Friend, Ne., U.S. K10 118
Friendship, N.Y., U.S. E8 108
Friendship, Tn., U.S. G7 114
Friendship, Wi., U.S. G6 110
Fries, Va., U.S. C6 112
Friesach, Aus. I14 10
Friesland, prov., Neth. B8 12
Friguia, Gui. E4 64
Frío, stm., N.A. G10 92
Frio, stm., Tx., U.S. K8 116
Frio, Cabo, c., Braz. G7 79
Friona, Tx., U.S. E4 116
Frisco, Tx., U.S. F10 116
Frisco City, Al., U.S. K9 114
Frisian Islands, is., Eur. E9 4
Fritch, Tx., U.S. D5 116
Friuli-Venezia-Giulia, prov., Italy C7 18
Friza, proliv, strt., Russia H21 28
Frobisher, Sask., Can. I12 104
Frobisher Bay, b., N.W. Ter., Can. D19 96
Frobisher Lake, l., Sask., Can. B6 104
Frog Lake, l., Alta., Can. E4 104
Frohnleiten, Aus. H15 10
Froid, Mt., U.S. C3 118
Frolovo, Russia H6 26
Fromberg, Mt., U.S. E17 122
Frombork, Pol. A19 10
Frome, stm., Austl. G3 70
Frome, Lake, l., Austl. H3 70
Frontenac, Ks., U.S. N13 118
Frontera, Mex. H13 90
Frontera, Mex. D9 90
Frontier, Sask., Can. I6 104
Frontier, Wy., U.S. C6 120
Frontino, Col. D4 84
Frontino, Páramo, mtn., Col. D4 84
Front Range, mts., Co., U.S. D11 120
Front Royal, Va., U.S. I8 108
Frosinone, Italy H8 18
Frost, Tx., U.S. G10 116
Frostburg, Md., U.S. H8 108
Frostproof, Fl., U.S. L5 112
Frøya, i., Nor. J11 6
Fruges, Fr. B9 14
Fruita, Co., U.S. E8 120
Fruitdale, Al., U.S. K8 114
Fruitdale, Or., U.S. H2 122
Fruithurst, Al., U.S. I11 114
Fruitland, Id., U.S. F9 122
Fruitland, Md., U.S. I11 108
Fruitport, Mi., U.S. G9 110
Fruitvale, B.C., Can. H17 102
Fruitvale, Wa., U.S. D5 122
Fruitville, Fl., U.S. L4 112
Frunze see Biškek, Kyrg. I12 26
Frunzovka, Ukr. B13 20
Frutal, Braz. F4 79
Frutigen, Switz. E8 13
Frýdek-Místek, Czech. F18 10
Fryeburg, Me., U.S. C16 108
Fryingpan, stm., Co., U.S. E10 120
Fuchang, China E2 34
Fuchū, Japan M8 36
Fuchun, stm., China F8 34
Fuding, China H9 34
Fuego, Volcán de, vol., Guat. C4 92
Fuencaliente de la Palma, Spain O23 17b
Fuensalida, Spain E7 16
Fuente de Cantos, Spain G5 16
Fuente de Oro, Col. F6 84
Fuentesaúco, Spain D6 16
Fuerte, stm., Mex. D5 90
Fuerte Olimpo, Para. I13 82
Fuerteventura, i., Spain O26 17b
Fufeng, China E8 30
Fuhe, China L2 34
Fuhu, China F7 34
Fuji, Japan L13 36
Fujian (Fukien), prov., China F10 30
Fujieda, Japan M13 36
Fujin, China B13 30
Fujinomiya, Japan L13 36
Fuji-san (Fujiyama), vol., Japan L13 36
Fujisawa, Japan L14 36
Fujiyama see Fuji-san, vol., Japan L13 36
Fuji-yoshida, Japan L13 36
Fukagawa, Japan D17 36a
Fukou, China I6 34
Fukuchiyama, Japan L10 36
Fukue-jima, i., Japan O3 36
Fukui, Japan K11 36
Fukuoka, Japan N5 36
Fukushima, Japan J15 36
Fukuyama, Japan M8 36
Fulacunda, Gui.-B. F2 64
Fūlādī, Kūh-e, mtn., Afg. C2 44
Fulda, Ger. E9 10
Fulda, Mn., U.S. H12 118
Fulda, stm., Ger. D9 10
Fulechang, China B8 40
Fuling, China F8 30
Fullerton, Ca., U.S. K8 124
Fullerton, Ne., U.S. J10 118
Fulpmes, Aus. H11 10
Fulton, Al., U.S. K9 114
Fulton, Ar., U.S. I3 114
Fulton, Il., U.S. I5 110
Fulton, Ks., U.S. M13 118
Fulton, Ky., U.S. F8 114
Fulton, Ms., U.S. H8 114
Fulton, Mo., U.S. D5 114
Fulton, N.Y., U.S. D10 108
Fulton, Tx., U.S. K9 116
Fulton, stm., B.C., Can. C8 102
Fultondale, Al., U.S. I10 114
Fumay, Fr. C11 14
Fumel, Fr. H7 14
Fumintun, China A14 32
Funabashi, Japan L14 36
Funchal, Port. M21 17a
Fundación, Col. B5 84
Fundy, Bay of, b., Can. H8 106
Fundy National Park, N.B., Can. G8 106
Funhalouro, Moz. D12 66
Funing, China B8 34
Funk Island, i., Newf., Can. C20 106
Funtua, Nig. F13 64
Funza, Col. E5 84
Fuqikou, China F6 34
Fuquay-Varina, N.C., U.S. D8 112
Furano, Japan D17 36a
Fūrg, Iran G13 48
Furmanov, Russia D24 22
Furnas, Reprêsa de, res., Braz. F5 79
Furneaux Group, is., Austl. L8 70
Furnes (Veurne), Bel. F2 12
Furqlus, Syria D4 48
Fürstenfeldbruck, Ger. G11 10
Fürstenwalde, Ger. C14 10
Fürth, Ger. F10 10
Furth im Wald, Ger. F12 10
Furudal, Swe. K14 6
Furukawa, Japan K12 36
Furukawa, Japan I15 36
Fury and Hecla Strait, strt., N.W. Ter., Can. C15 96
Fusagasugá, Col. E5 84
Fushan, China D9 34
Fushuigang, China D2 34
Fushun, China B11 32
Fusilier, Sask., Can. G5 104
Fusui, China G8 30
Futianpu, China H1 34
Futuyu, China D2 32
Fuwah, Egypt B6 60
Fuxi, China J2 34
Fuxian, China D8 30
Fuxian (Wafangdian), China D10 32
Fuxian Hu, l., China B7 40
Fuxin, China A9 32
Fuyang, China C4 34
Fuyu, China B11 30
Fuzhai, China F9 34
Fuzhou, China G5 34
Fuzhou (Foochow), China I8 34
Fuzhuang, China I6 32

Name | Map Ref. | Page

Fyn, i., Den. N12 6

G

Gaalkacyo, Som. G10 56
Gabarus, N.S., Can. G13 106
Gabarus Bay, b., N.S., Can. G13 106
Gabas, stm., Fr. I6 14
Gabbs, Nv., U.S. F8 124
Gabela, Ang. D2 58
Gabès, Tun. D16 62
Gabès, Golfe de, b., Tun. C16 62
Gabiarra, Braz. D9 79
Gabir, Sud. M3 60
Gable Mountain, mtn., B.C., Can. C13 102
Gabon, ctry., Afr. B2 58
Gaborone, Bots. E7 66
Gabriel Strait, strt., N.W. Ter., Can. D19 96
Gabrovo, Bul. G9 20
Gacé, Fr. D7 14
Gachetá, Col. E6 84
Gachsārān, Iran F11 48
Gackle, N.D., U.S. E8 118
Gadag, India E3 46
Gadamai, Sud. I9 60
Gäddede, Swe. I14 6
Gadilovići, Bela. H13 22
Gadsden, Al., U.S. H10 114
Gadsden, Az., U.S. L2 120
Gaeta, Italy H8 18
Gaeta, Golfo di, b., Italy H8 18
Gaffney, S.C., U.S. D5 112
Gafour, Tun. M4 18
Gafsa, Tun. C15 62
Gagarin, Russia F18 22
Gage, Ok., U.S. C7 116
Gagetown, N.B., Can. G7 106
Gagetown, Canadian Forces Base, mil., N.B., Can. G7 106
Gaggenau, Ger. G8 10
Gaghamni, Sud. L5 60
Gagnoa, I.C. H7 64
Gagnon, Que., Can. F19 96
Gagra, Geor. I6 26
Gaibandha, Bngl. H13 44
Gail, Tx., U.S. G5 116
Gaillac, Fr. I8 14
Gaillard, Lac, l., Que., Can. B5 106
Gaillon, Fr. C8 14
Gainesboro, Tn., U.S. F11 114
Gainesville, Fl., U.S. J4 112
Gainesville, Ga., U.S. E3 112
Gainesville, Mo., U.S. F4 114
Gainesville, Tx., U.S. F9 116
Gainsborough, Sask., Can. I13 104
Gainsborough Creek, stm., Can. I13 104
Gairdner, Lake, l., Austl. F7 68
Gaital, Cerro, mtn., Pan. I14 92
Gaithersburg, Md., U.S. H9 108
Gaixian, China C10 32
Gajny, Russia E8 26
Gajutino, Russia C21 22
Gajvoron, Ukr. A13 20
Galaassija, Uzb. B18 48
Galahad, Alta., Can. E23 102
Galán, Cerro, mtn., Arg. G8 74
Galán, Cerro, mtn., Arg. C5 80
Galapagos Islands see Colón, Archipiélago de, is., Ec. J13 84a
Galashiels, Scot., U.K. F11 8
Galați, Rom. D12 20
Galați, co., Rom. D11 20
Galatia, Il., U.S. E8 114
Galatina, Italy I13 18
Galax, Va., U.S. C6 112
Gáldar, Spain O25 17b
Galdhøpiggen, mtn., Nor. K11 6
Galeana, Mex. B6 90
Galeana, Mex. E9 90
Galela, Indon. E8 38
Galena, Ak., U.S. D16 100
Galena, Il., U.S. H5 110
Galena, Ks., U.S. N13 118
Galena, Mo., U.S. F3 114
Galena Park, Tx., U.S. J11 116
Galeota Point, c., Trin. I14 94
Galera, stm., Braz. F12 82
Galera, Punta, c., Ec. G2 84
Galera Point, c., Trin. I14 94
Galesburg, Il., U.S. J5 110
Galesburg, Mi., U.S. H10 110
Galesville, Wi., U.S. F4 110
Galeton, Pa., U.S. F9 108
Galheiros, Braz. B5 79
Galič, Russia C25 22
Galicia, prov., Spain C3 16
Galicia, hist. reg., Eur. F12 4
Galilee, Lake, l., Austl. D6 70
Galilee, Sea of see Kinneret, Yam, l., Isr. C5 50
Galiléia, Braz. E8 79
Galion, Oh., U.S. G4 108
Galiuro Mountains, mts., Az., U.S. L6 120
Gallarate, Italy D3 18
Gallatin, Mo., U.S. C3 114
Gallatin, Tn., U.S. F10 114
Gallatin, stm., U.S. E14 122
Galle, Sri L. I6 46
Galliano, La., U.S. M6 114
Galliate, Italy D3 18
Gallinas, stm., N.M., U.S. D2 116
Gallinas, Punta, c., Col. A7 84
Gallinas Peak, mtn., N.M., U.S. J11 120
Gallipoli, Austl. B2 70
Gallipoli, Italy I12 18
Gallipoli see Gelibolu, Tur. I10 20
Gallipoli Peninsula see Gelibolu Yarımadası, pen., Tur. I10 20
Gallipolis, Oh., U.S. I4 108
Gällivare, Swe. H17 6
Galloway, Mull of, c., Scot., U.K. G9 8
Gallup, N.M., U.S. I8 120
Galougo, Mali E4 64
Galt, Ca., U.S. F4 124
Galtat Zemmour, W. Sah. H4 62
Galty Mountains, mts., Ire. I5 8
Galva, Il., U.S. I5 110
Galva, Ia., U.S. I12 118
Galva, Ks., U.S. M10 118
Galvarino, Chile J2 80
Galveston, In., U.S. B10 114
Galveston, Tx., U.S. J12 116
Galveston Bay, b., Tx., U.S. J12 116
Galveston Island, i., Tx., U.S. J12 116
Gálvez, Arg. G8 80
Galway, Ire. H4 8
Galway, co., Ire. H5 8
Galway Bay, b., Ire. H4 8
Gamagōri, Japan M12 36
Gamaliel, Ky., U.S. F11 114
Gamarra, Col. C6 84
Gambaga, Ghana F9 64
Gambela, Eth. M8 60
Gambell, Ak., U.S. E9 100
Gambia, ctry., Afr. F3 54
Gambia (Gambie), stm., Afr. F3 54
Gambi Aṭrash, Sud. L7 60
Gambier, Oh., U.S. G4 108
Gambier, Îles, is., Fr. Poly. K26 126
Gambo, Newf., Can. D19 106
Gamboa, Pan. C3 84
Gamboma, Congo B3 58
Gammon, stm., Can. G19 104
Gamoep, S. Afr. G4 66
Gamon, Sen. E3 64
Gan, stm., China A11 30
Gan, stm., China G4 34
Ganado, Az., U.S. I7 120
Ganado, Tx., U.S. J10 116
Gananoque, Ont., Can. F19 110
Ganāveh, Iran G11 48
Gancevići, Bela. I9 22
Gand (Gent), Bel. F4 12
Ganda, Ang. D2 58
Gandak (Nārāyani), stm., Asia G11 44
Gander, Newf., Can. D19 106
Gander, stm., Newf., Can. C19 106
Gander Bay, Newf., Can. C19 106
Gander Bay, b., Newf., Can. C19 106
Ganderkesee, Ger. B8 10
Gander Lake, l., Newf., Can. D19 106
Gāndhi Sāgar, res., India H6 44
Gandi, Nig. E12 64
Gandia, Spain G11 16
Gandu, Braz. B9 79
Ganfang, China G3 34
Gangānagar, India F5 44
Gangāpur, India G7 44
Gangaw, Burma C3 40
Gangdisê Shan, mts., China E9 44
Ganges, B.C., Can. I11 102
Ganges, Fr. I10 14
Ganges (Ganga) (Padma), stm., Asia I13 44
Ganghu, China D12 44
Gangi, Italy L9 18
Gangkou, China F4 34
Gangotri, India E8 44
Gangotri, India E8 44
Gangou, China C7 32
Gangoumen, China B4 32
Gang Ranch, B.C., Can. F12 102
Gangtok, India G13 44
Gangu, China E8 30
Gannett Peak, mtn., Wy., U.S. G16 122
Gannvalley, S.D., U.S. G9 118
Ganq, China B15 44
Gänserndorf, Aus. G16 10
Gansu (Kansu), prov., China D7 30
Gantt, Al., U.S. K10 114
Ganxi, China G7 34
Ganzê, China E7 30
Ganzhou, China J3 34
Ganzo Azul, Peru C4 82
Gao, Mali C9 64
Gaobu, China H6 34
Gaocun, China F10 32
Gaohe, China M1 34
Gaokeng, China H2 34
Gaoling, China C5 32
Gaona, Arg. C6 80
Gaoqiaozhen, China C9 32
Gaoshan, China J8 34
Gaotan, China E6 34
Gaotingsi, China I1 34
Gaoua, Burkina F8 64
Gaoxinji, China A4 34
Gaoya, China G6 32
Gaoyou, China C8 34
Gaoyou Hu, l., China C8 34
Gap, Fr. H13 14
Gar, China E3 30
Garachiné, Pan. C3 84
Garagoa, Col. E6 84
Garanhuns, Braz. E11 76
Garara, Pap. N. Gui. A9 68
Garber, Ok., U.S. C9 116
Garberville, Ca., U.S. D2 124
Garça, Braz. G4 79
Garças, Rio das, stm., Braz. C2 79
García, Mex. C5 90
García de Sola, Embalse de, res., Spain F6 16
Garcias, Braz. F2 79
Gard, dept., Fr. I11 14
Garda, Italy D5 18
Garda, Lago di, l., Italy D5 18
Gardelegen, Ger. C11 10
Garden City, Ga., U.S. G5 112
Garden City, Ks., U.S. N7 118
Garden City, Mo., U.S. D2 114
Garden City, Tx., U.S. H5 116
Gardendale, Al., U.S. I10 114
Garden Grove, Ca., U.S. K8 124
Garden Grove, Ia., U.S. J2 110
Garden Lakes, Ga., U.S. E1 112
Garden Peninsula, pen., Mi., U.S. E9 110
Garden Plain, Ks., U.S. N10 118
Garden Reach, India I13 44
Gardenton, Man., Can. I18 104
Gardey, Arg. I9 80
Gardeyz, Afg. D3 44
Gardiner, Me., U.S. C17 108
Gardiner, Mt., U.S. E15 122
Gardiner, Or., U.S. G1 122
Gardiner Dam, Sask., Can. G8 104
Gardiners Bay, b., N.Y., U.S. F14 108
Gardner, Ks., U.S. M13 118
Gardner, Ma., U.S. E15 108
Gardner Canal, b., B.C., Can. D6 102
Gardnerville, Nv., U.S. F6 124
Gardone Val Trompia, Italy D5 18
Garešnica, Cro. D11 18
Garfield, Ks., U.S. M8 118
Garfield, N.M., U.S. L9 120
Garfield, Wa., U.S. C8 122
Garfield Mountain, mtn., Mt., U.S. F13 122
Gargouna, Mali D10 64
Gargždai, Lith. F4 22
Garibaldi, Braz. E13 80
Garibaldi, B.C., Can. H11 102
Garibaldi, Or., U.S. E2 122
Garibaldi, Mount, mtn., B.C., Can. H11 102
Garibaldi Provincial Park, B.C., Can. G12 102
Garies, S. Afr. H4 66
Garissa, Kenya B7 58
Garita Palmera, El Sal. D4 92
Garko, Nig. F14 64
Garland, Al., U.S. K10 114
Garland, Tx., U.S. G10 116
Garland, Ut., U.S. C4 120
Garlasco, Italy D3 18
Garliava, Lith. G6 22
Garlin, Fr. I6 14
Garm, Taj. J12 26
Garmisch-Partenkirchen, Ger. H11 10
Garnavillo, Ia., U.S. H4 110
Garner, Ia., U.S. G2 110
Garner, N.C., U.S. D8 112
Garnett, Ks., U.S. M12 118
Garnish, Newf., Can. E18 106
Garonne, stm., Eur. H6 14
Garoua, Cam. G9 54
Garretson, S.D., U.S. H11 118
Garrett, In., U.S. A11 114
Garrett, Ky., U.S. B4 112
Garrison, Mt., U.S. D13 122
Garrison, N.D., U.S. D6 118
Garrison, Tx., U.S. K2 114
Garrovillas, Spain F5 16
Garry Bay, b., N.W. Ter., Can. C15 96
Garry Lake, l., N.W. Ter., Can. C12 96
Garson, Ont., Can. D15 110
Garson Lake, l., Can. B4 104
Garub, Nmb. F3 66
Garut, Indon. J13 39a
Garwin, Ia., U.S. H3 110
Garwolin, Pol. D21 10
Garwood, Tx., U.S. J10 116
Gary, In., U.S. A9 114
Gary, S.D., U.S. G11 118
Gary, Tx., U.S. J2 114
Gary, W.V., U.S. B5 112
Garyarsa, China E9 44
Garza, Arg. E7 80
Garzón, Col. F5 84
Garzón, Ur. H11 80
Gas City, In., U.S. B11 114
Gascogne, hist. reg., Fr. H6 14
Gasconade, stm., Mo., U.S. D5 114
Gascoyne, stm., Austl. E2 68
Gash (Nahr al-Qāsh), stm., Afr. F8 56
Gashaka, Nig. G9 54
Gaspar, Braz. D14 80
Gaspard Creek, stm., B.C., Can. F12 102
Gaspé, Que., Can. D9 106
Gaspé, Baie de, b., Que., Can. D9 106
Gaspé, Cap, c., Que., Can. D9 106
Gaspé Peninsula see Gaspésie, Péninsule de la, pen., Que., Can. D8 106
Gaspereau Lake, l., N.S., Can. H9 106
Gaspésie, Parc Provincial de la, Que., Can. D8 106
Gaspésie, Péninsule de la, pen., Que., Can. D8 106
Gassaway, W.V., U.S. I6 108
Gaston, N.C., U.S. C9 112
Gaston, Lake, res., U.S. C8 112
Gastonia, N.C., U.S. D5 112
Gastre, Arg. E3 78
Gata, Cabo de, c., Spain I9 16
Gátas, Akrotírion, c., Cyp. D2 48
Gatčina, Russia B13 22
Gate, Ok., U.S. C6 116
Gate City, Va., U.S. C4 112
Gateshead, Eng., U.K. G12 8
Gateshead Island, i., N.W. Ter., Can. B12 96
Gatesville, N.C., U.S. C10 112
Gatesville, Tx., U.S. H9 116
Gateway, Co., U.S. F8 120
Gatineau, Que., Can. B11 108
Gatineau, stm., Que., Can. G17 96
Gatineau, Parc de la, Que., Can. B10 108
Gatlinburg, Tn., U.S. D3 112
Gattinara, Italy D3 18
Gatton, Austl. F10 70
Gatún, Esclusas de, Pan. H15 92
Gatún, Lago, res., Pan. H15 92
Gauer Lake, l., Man., Can. A17 104
Gauley, stm., W.V., U.S. I5 108
Gauley Bridge, W.V., U.S. I5 108
Gaultois, Newf., Can. E18 106
Gaurīśaṅkar, mtn., Asia G12 44
Gause, Tx., U.S. I10 116
Gauting, Ger. G11 10
Gavà, Spain D14 16
Gávdhos, i., Grc. O8 20
Gavião, stm., Braz. C8 79
Gävle, Swe. K15 6
Gävleborgs Län, co., Swe. K15 6
Gavrilov-Jam, Russia D22 22
Gavrilov Posad, Russia E23 22
Gawler, Austl. J3 70
Gawler Ranges, mts., Austl. F7 68
Gaxun Nur, l., China C7 30
Gaya, India H11 44
Gaylord, Mi., U.S. E11 110
Gaylord, Mn., U.S. F1 110
Gayndah, Austl. E9 70
Gays Mills, Wi., U.S. G5 110
Gaza see Ghazzah, Isr. Occ. F3 48
Gaza Strip, hist. reg., Isr. Occ. F2 50
Gaziantep, Tur. C4 48
Gazimağusa (Famagusta), N. Cyp. D2 48
Gbangbatok, S.L. H3 64
Gbanhala, stm., Afr. G5 64
Gbarnga, Lib. H5 64
Gbongan, Nig. H12 64
Gcoverega, Bots. B7 66
Gdańsk (Danzig), Pol. A18 10
Gdansk, Gulf of, b., Eur. A19 10
Gdov, Russia C10 22
Gdyel, Alg. J11 16
Gdynia, Pol. A18 10
Gearhart Mountain, mtn., Or., U.S. H5 122
Geary, N.B., Can. G7 106
Geary, Ok., U.S. D8 116
Geba, stm., Afr. F4 54
Gebeit Mine, Sud. G9 60
Gebze, Tur. I13 20
Gecha, Eth. N8 60
Geddes, S.D., U.S. H9 118
Gedera, Isr. E3 50
Gediz, Tur. J13 20
Gedo, Eth. M9 60
Gedun, China H7 34
Geel, Bel. F7 12
Geelong, Austl. L6 70
Geesthacht, Ger. B10 10
Geeveston, Austl. N7 70
Gegong, China E6 34
Geiger, Al., U.S. J8 114
Geikie, stm., Sask., Can. E12 96
Geilo, Nor. K11 6
Geiranger, Nor. J10 6
Geislingen, Ger. G9 10
Geistown, Pa., U.S. G8 108
Geithain, Ger. D12 10
Gejiatun, China C7 32
Gejiu (Kokiu), China C7 40
Gela, Italy L9 18
Gelderland, prov., Neth. D8 12
Geldermalsen, Neth. E7 12
Geldrop, Neth. F8 12
Gelenbe, Tur. J11 20
Gelgaudiškis, Lith. F6 22
Gelibolu, Tur. I10 20
Gelibolu Yarımadası (Gallipoli Peninsula), pen., Tur. I10 20
Gelsenkirchen, Ger. D7 10
Geltsa, Eth. N9 60
Gemena, Zaire H4 56
Gemlik, Tur. I13 20
Gemsbok National Park, Bots. E5 66
Gemünden, Ger. E9 10
Gen, stm., China A11 30
Genale (Jubba), stm., Afr. G9 56
Gençay, Fr. F7 14
General, stm., C.R. H11 92
General Acha, Arg. I6 80
General Alvear, Arg. I8 80
General Alvear, Arg. H5 80
General Aquino, Para. C10 80
General Arenales, Arg. H8 80
General Belgrano, Arg. H9 80
General Bravo, Mex. E10 90
General Cabrera, Arg. G7 80
General Campos, Arg. F9 80
General Carneiro, Braz. C2 79
General Carrera, Lago (Lago Buenos Aires), l., S.A. F2 78
General Cepeda, Mex. E9 90
General Conesa, Arg. I10 80
General Daniel Cerri, Arg. J7 80
General Elizardo Aquino, Para. D10 80
General Enrique Martínez, Ur. G12 80
General Enrique Mosconi, Arg. B7 80
General Escobedo, Mex. E7 90
General Eugenio A. Garay, Para. C10 80
General Eugenio A. Garay, Para. I10 82
General Galarza, Arg. G9 80
General Güemes, Arg. C6 80
General Guido, Arg. I10 80
General José de San Martín, Arg. D9 80
General Juan José Ríos, Mex. E5 90
General Juan Madariaga, Arg. I10 80
General La Madrid, Arg. I8 80
General Lavalle, Arg. I10 80
General Leonidas Plaza Gutiérrez, Ec. I3 84
General Levalle, Arg. H7 80
General Manuel Belgrano, Cerro, mtn., Arg. E5 80
General O'Brien, Arg. H8 80
General Paz, Arg. H9 80
General Pico, Arg. H7 80
General Pinedo, Arg. D8 80
General Pinto, Arg. H8 80
General Pizarro, Arg. C6 80
General Roca, Arg. J5 80
General San Martín, Arg. H9 80
General San Martín, Arg. I7 80
General Santos, Phil. D8 38
General Terán, Mex. E10 90
General Viamonte (Los Toldos), Arg. H8 80
General Villegas, Arg. H7 80
Genesee, Id., U.S. D9 122
Genesee, stm., U.S. H18 110
Geneseo, Il., U.S. I5 110
Geneseo, Ks., U.S. M9 118
Geneseo, N.Y., U.S. E9 108
Geneva, Al., U.S. K11 114
Geneva, Il., U.S. I7 110
Geneva, In., U.S. B12 114
Geneva, Ne., U.S. K10 118
Geneva, N.Y., U.S. E9 108
Geneva, Oh., U.S. F6 108
Geneva, Lake, l., Eur. F13 14
Geneva see Genève, Switz. F13 14
Genève (Geneva), Switz. F5 13
Genève, state, Switz. F5 13
Genévriers, Île des, i., Que., Can. A15 106
Gengma, China C5 40
Genk, Bel. G8 12
Genlis, Fr. E12 14
Genoa, Il., U.S. H7 110
Genoa, Ne., U.S. J10 118
Genoa, Oh., U.S. F3 108
Genoa, Wi., U.S. G4 110
Genoa see Genova, Italy E3 18
Genova (Génova), Italy E3 18
Genova, Golfo di, b., Italy E3 18
Genrijetty, ostrov, i., Russia B23 28
Gent (Gand), Bel. F4 12
Genthin, Ger. C12 10
Gentry, Ar., U.S. F2 114
Geographe Bay, b., Austl. F3 68
Geographe Channel, strt., Austl. D2 68
Geokčaj, Azer. I7 26
Geok-Tepe, Turk. B14 48
George, S. Afr. I6 66
George, Ia., U.S. H11 118
George, stm., Que., Can. E19 96
George, Cape, c., N.S., Can. G12 106
George, Lake, l., Austl. J8 70
George, Lake, l., Ug. B6 58
George, Lake, l., Fl., U.S. J5 112
George, Lake, l., N.Y., U.S. D13 108
Georges Bank E13 86
George Town, Austl. M7 70
Georgetown, P.E.I., Can. F11 106
George Town, Cay. Is. E4 94
Georgetown, Gam. E2 64
Georgetown, Guy. D13 84
George Town (Pinang), Malay. L6 40
Georgetown, St. Vin. H14 94
Georgetown, Co., U.S. E11 120
Georgetown, De., U.S. I11 108
Georgetown, Fl., U.S. J5 112
Georgetown, Ga., U.S. H1 112
Georgetown, Id., U.S. H14 122
Georgetown, Il., U.S. C9 114
Georgetown, Ky., U.S. I2 108
Georgetown, Ms., U.S. K6 114
Georgetown, Oh., U.S. I3 108
Georgetown, S.C., U.S. F7 112
Georgetown, Tx., U.S. I9 116
George V Coast, Ant. B7 73
George VI Sound, strt., Ant. C12 73
George West, Tx., U.S. K8 116
Georgia, ctry., Asia I6 26
Georgia, state, U.S. E10 98
Georgia, Strait of, strt., N.A. H11 102
Georgiana, Al., U.S. K10 114
Georgian Bay, b., Ont., Can. E14 110
Georgian Bay Islands National Park, Ont., Can. F16 110
Georgijevsk, Russia I6 26
Georgina, stm., Austl. D3 70
Gera, Ger. E12 10
Geral, Serra, clf, Braz. D14 80
Gerald, Mo., U.S. D5 114
Geral de Goiás, Serra, clf, Braz. B5 79
Geraldine, Mt., U.S. C15 122
Geraldton, Austl. E2 68
Geraldton, Ont., Can. G15 96
Gérardmer, Fr. D13 14
Gerber, Ca., U.S. D3 124
Gerdine, Mount, mtn., Ak., U.S. F18 100
Gereshk, Afg. E1 44
Gering, Ne., U.S. J4 118
Gerlachovský štít, mtn., Czech. F20 10
Germain, Grand lac, l., Que., Can. A7 106
Germansen, Mount, mtn., B.C., Can. B10 102
Germansen Lake, l., B.C., Can. B10 102
Germansen Landing, B.C., Can. B10 102
Germantown, Il., U.S. D7 114
Germantown, Tn., U.S. G7 114
Germantown, Wi., U.S. G7 110
Germany, ctry., Eur. E9 4
Germfask, Mi., U.S. D10 110
Germiston, S. Afr. F9 66
Gernika-Lumo (Guernica y Luno), Spain B9 16
Geronimo, Ok., U.S. E8 116
Gers, dept., Fr. I7 14
Gerufa, Bots. B8 66
Gêrzê, China D11 44
Gesher HaZiw, Isr. B4 50
Getafe, Spain E8 16
Gettysburg, Pa., U.S. H9 108
Gettysburg, S.D., U.S. F8 118
Getulina, Braz. F4 79
Getúlio Vargas, Braz. D12 80
Gevgelija, Mac. H6 20
Gévora, stm., Eur. F4 16
Gex, Fr. F13 14
Geyikli, Tur. J10 20
Geyser, Mt., U.S. C15 122
Geyserville, Ca., U.S. F3 124
Ghaapplato, plat., Afr. F7 66
Ghadāmis, Libya E15 62
Ghāghara, stm., Asia G10 44
Ghana, ctry., Afr. G6 54
Ghanzi, Bots. C5 66
Ghanzi, dept., Bots. D6 66
Gharbi, Oued el, val., Alg. D11 62
Gharbīyah, Aṣ-Ṣaḥrā' al- (Western Desert), des., Egypt D4 60
Ghardaïa, Alg. D12 62
Ghardimaou, Tun. M3 18
Gharig, Sud. L4 60
Gharyān, Libya B3 56
Ghaṣm, Syria C6 50
Ghāt, Libya H16 62
Ghātāl, India I12 44
Għawdex (Gozo), i., Malta M9 18
Ghawr ash-Sharqīyah, Qanāt al- (East Ghor Canal), Jord. D5 50
Ghayth, Wādī, val., Jord. G5 50
Ghazāl, Baḥr al-, stm., Sud. M5 60
Ghazal, Bahr el, val., Chad F4 56
Ghāziābād, India F7 44
Ghāzīpur, India H10 44
Ghazlūna, Pak. E2 44
Ghaznī, Afg. D3 44
Ghazzah (Gaza), Isr. Occ. F3 48
Ghedi, Italy D5 18
Ghent see Gent, Bel. F4 12
Gheorghe Gheorghiu-Dej, Rom. C10 20
Gheorgheni, Rom. C9 20
Gherla, Rom. B7 20
Ghilizane, Alg. C11 62
Ghisonaccia, Fr. L24 15a
Ghudāf, Wādī al-, val., Iraq E7 48
Ghūrīān, Afg. D16 48
Giant's Castle, mtn., Afr. G9 66
Giarre, Italy L10 18
Gibara, Cuba D6 94
Gibbon, Mn., U.S. F1 110
Gibbon, Ne., U.S. K9 118
Gibbons, Alta., Can. D21 102
Gibbonsville, Id., U.S. E12 122
Gibeon, Nmb. E3 66
Gibraleón, Spain H5 16
Gibraltar, Gib. I6 16
Gibraltar, dep., Eur. H6 4
Gibraltar, Strait of (Estrecho de Gibraltar), strt. J6 16
Gibsland, La., U.S. J3 114
Gibson, Ga., U.S. F4 112
Gibson City, Il., U.S. J7 110
Gibson Desert, des., Austl. D5 68
Gibsons, B.C., Can. H11 102
Gidami, Eth. M8 60
Gidda, Eth. M8 60
Giddings, Tx., U.S. I10 116
Gideon, Mo., U.S. F7 114
Gidole, Eth. O9 60
Gidrotorf, Russia E26 22
Gien, Fr. E9 14
Giessen, Ger. E8 10
Gifford, Fl., U.S. L6 112
Gifford, stm., N.W. Ter., Can. B16 96
Gifhorn, Ger. C10 10
Gifu, Japan L11 36
Giganta, Sierra de la, mts., Mex. E4 90
Gigante, Col. F5 84
Gijón, Spain B6 16
Gila, stm., U.S. L2 120
Gila Bend, Az., U.S. L4 120
Gila Bend Mountains, mts., Az., U.S. K3 120
Gila Mountains, mts., Az., U.S. K7 120
Gilbert, La., U.S. J5 114
Gilbert, Mn., U.S. C3 110
Gilbert, stm., Austl. A4 70
Gilbert, Mount, mtn., B.C., Can. G10 102
Gilbertown, Al., U.S. K8 114
Gilbert Plains, Man., Can. G14 104
Gilboa', Haré, hills, Asia D4 50
Gilbués, Braz. E9 76
Gildford, Mt., U.S. B15 122
Gilford Island, i., B.C., Can. G8 102
Gilgandra, Austl. H8 70
Gilgit, Pak. C6 44
Gilgit, stm., Pak. B5 44
Gil Island, i., B.C., Can. D5 102
Gillam, Man., Can. B20 104
Gilles, Lake, l., Austl. I2 70
Gillespie, Il., U.S. C7 114
Gillett, Ar., U.S. H5 114
Gillett, Wi., U.S. F7 110
Gillette, Wy., U.S. G2 118
Gillian, Lake, l., N.W. Ter., Can. C17 96
Gills Rock, Wi., U.S. E8 110
Gilman, Il., U.S. J8 110
Gilman, Ia., U.S. I3 110
Gilman, Wi., U.S. E5 110
Gilmer, Tx., U.S. G12 116
Gilmore City, Ia., U.S. I13 118
Gilroy, Ca., U.S. G4 124
Giltner, Ne., U.S. K9 118
Giluwe, Mount, mtn., Pap. N. Gui. m15 68a
Gimbi, Eth. M8 60
Gimie, Mount, mtn., St. Luc. H14 94
Gimli, Man., Can. H18 104
Gimoly, Russia J23 6
Gimont, Fr. I7 14
Gin Gin, Austl. E9 70
Ginir, Eth. G9 56
Ginosa, Italy I11 18
Gioia del Colle, Italy I11 18
Gioia Tauro, Italy K10 18
Gipuzkoako, prov., Spain B9 16
Girard, Il., U.S. C7 114
Girard, Ks., U.S. N13 118
Girard, Oh., U.S. F6 108
Girard, Pa., U.S. E6 108
Girard, Tx., U.S. F6 116
Girardot, Col. E5 84
Girbovu, Rom. E7 20
Girgarre, Austl. K6 70
Girīdīh, India H12 44
Girne, N. Cyp. D2 48
Giromagny, Fr. E13 14
Girón, Ec. I3 84
Girona, Spain D14 16
Gironde, dept., Fr. G6 14
Gironde, est., Fr. G6 14
Girouxville, Alta., Can. B17 102
Giru, Austl. B7 70
Giruá, Braz. E11 80
Girvas, Russia J23 6
Gisborne, N.Z. C7 72
Gisborne Lake, l., Newf., Can. E19 106
Giscome, B.C., Can. C12 102
Gisenyi, Rw. B5 58
Gisors, Fr. C8 14
Giswil, Switz. E9 13
Gitega, Bdi. B5 58
Giugliano [in Campania], Italy I9 18
Giulianova, Italy G8 18
Giurgiu, Rom. F9 20
Giv'atayim, Isr. D3 50
Givet, Fr. B11 14
Givors, Fr. G11 14
Givry, Fr. F11 14
Giyon, Eth. M9 60
Giza see Al-Jīzah, Egypt B6 60
Gīzāb, Afg. D2 44
Gižduvan, Uzb. I10 26
Gizen, Sud. L8 60
Gižiginskaja guba, b., Russia E23 28
Giżycko, Pol. A21 10
Gjandža, Azer. I7 26
Gjirokastër, Alb. I4 20
Gjoa Haven, N.W. Ter., Can. C13 96
Gjøvik, Nor. K12 6
Gjuhëzës, Kep i, c., Alb. I3 20
Glace Bay, N.S., Can. F14 106
Glacier, B.C., Can. F17 102
Glacier Bay, b., Ak., U.S. G26 100
Glacier National Park, B.C., Can. F17 102
Glacier National Park, Mt., U.S. B12 122
Glacier Peak, mtn., Wa., U.S. B4 122
Gladbach see Mönchengladbach, Ger. D6 10
Gladbeck, Ger. D6 10
Gladbrook, Ia., U.S. H3 110
Glade Spring, Va., U.S. C5 112
Gladewater, Tx., U.S. G12 116
Gladstone, Austl. I3 70
Gladstone, Austl. D9 70
Gladstone, Man., Can. H16 104
Gladstone, Mi., U.S. E8 110
Gladstone, Mo., U.S. C2 114
Gladwin, Mi., U.S. G11 110
Gladys Lake, l., B.C., Can. G28 100
Glåma, stm., Nor. K12 6
Glarner Alpen, mts., Switz. E10 13
Glarus, Switz. D11 13
Glarus, state, Switz. E11 13
Glasco, Ks., U.S. L10 118
Glasgow, Scot., U.K. F9 8
Glasgow, Ky., U.S. F11 114
Glasgow, Mo., U.S. C4 114
Glasgow, Mt., U.S. B19 122
Glasgow, Va., U.S. B7 112
Glaslyn, Sask., Can. E6 104
Glassboro, N.J., U.S. H11 108
Glattfelden, Switz. C10 13
Glauchau, Ger. E12 10
Glaževo, Russia B15 22
Glazov, Russia F8 26
Glazunovka, Russia I19 22
Gleason, Tn., U.S. F8 114
Gleichen, Alta., Can. G21 102
Gleisdorf, Aus. H15 10
Glen Alpine, N.C., U.S. D5 112
Glenavon, Sask., Can. H11 104
Glenboro, Man., Can. I15 104
Glenburn, N.D., U.S. C6 118
Glen Burnie, Md., U.S. H10 108
Glen Canyon, val., U.S. G5 120
Glencoe, Austl. K4 70
Glencoe, Ont., Can. H14 110
Glencoe, Al., U.S. I11 114
Glencoe, Mn., U.S. F1 110
Glen Cove, N.Y., U.S. G13 108
Glendale, Az., U.S. K4 120
Glendale, Ca., U.S. J7 124
Glendale, Ms., U.S. K7 114
Glendale, Or., U.S. H2 122
Glendale, Ut., U.S. G4 120
Glendale, Wi., U.S. G8 110
Glendive, Mt., U.S. D3 118
Glendo, Wy., U.S. B11 120
Glendon, Alta., Can. C23 102
Gleneden Beach, Or., U.S. F1 122
Glen Elder, Ks., U.S. L9 118
Glen Flora, Tx., U.S. J10 116
Glen Innes, Austl. G9 70
Glen Lyon, Pa., U.S. F10 108
Glenmora, La., U.S. L4 114
Glenmorgan, Austl. F8 70
Glennallen, Ak., U.S. E22 100
Glenns Ferry, Id., U.S. H10 122
Glennville, Ga., U.S. H5 112
Glenoma, Wa., U.S. D3 122
Glenormiston, Austl. D3 70
Glenreagh, Austl. H10 70
Glen Robertson, Ont., Can. B12 108
Glen Rock, Pa., U.S. H10 108
Glenrock, Wy., U.S. B11 120
Glen Rose, Tx., U.S. G9 116
Glens Falls, N.Y., U.S. D13 108
Glenties, Ire. G5 8
Glen Ullin, N.D., U.S. E6 118
Glenville, Mn., U.S. G2 110
Glenville, W.V., U.S. I6 108
Glen White, W.V., U.S. B5 112
Glenwood, Alta., Can. H21 102
Glenwood, Newf., Can. D19 106
Glenwood, Al., U.S. K10 114
Glenwood, Ar., U.S. H3 114
Glenwood, Ga., U.S. G4 112
Glenwood, Ia., U.S. J12 118
Glenwood, Mn., U.S. F12 118
Glenwood, N.M., U.S. K8 120
Glenwood, Ut., U.S. F5 120
Glenwood, Va., U.S. C7 112
Glenwood City, Wi., U.S. E3 110
Glenwood Springs, Co., U.S. E9 120
Glidden, Ia., U.S. I13 118
Glidden, Wi., U.S. D5 110
Glide, Or., U.S. G2 122
Glinka, Russia G15 22
Gliwice (Gleiwitz), Pol. E18 10
Globe, Az., U.S. K6 120
Gloggnitz, Aus. H15 10
Głogów, Pol. D16 10
Glória de Dourados, Braz. G1 79

Name	Map Ref.	Page
Glorieta, N.M., U.S.	I11	120
Glorieuses, Îles, is., Reu.	D9	58
Gloster, Ms., U.S.	K5	114
Gloucester, Austl.	H9	70
Gloucester, Eng., U.K.	J11	8
Gloucester, Ma., U.S.	E16	108
Gloucester, Va., U.S.	B10	112
Gloucester Island, i., Austl.	C8	70
Gloucestershire, co., Eng., U.K.	J11	8
Glouster, Oh., U.S.	H4	108
Glover, stm., Ok., U.S.	E12	116
Glover Island, i., Newf., Can.	D16	106
Glovers Reef, rf., Belize	I16	90
Gloversville, N.Y., U.S.	D12	108
Glovertown, Newf., Can.	D19	106
Głowno, Pol.	D19	10
Głubczyce, Pol.	E17	10
Glubokoje, Bela.	F10	22
Głuchołazy, Pol.	E17	10
Glückstadt, Ger.	B9	10
Gluša, Bela.	H11	22
Glusk, Bela.	I11	22
Glybokaja, Ukr.	A9	20
Glyndon, Mn., U.S.	E11	118
Gmünd, Aus.	G15	10
Gmunden, Aus.	H13	10
Gnalta, Austl.	H5	70
Gnezdovo, Russia	G14	22
Gniew, Pol.	B18	10
Gniewkowo, Pol.	C18	10
Gniezno, Pol.	C17	10
Gnjilane, Yugo.	G5	20
Gnowangerup, Austl.	F3	68
Goa, state, India	E2	46
Goalen Head, c., Austl.	K9	70
Goālpāra, India	G14	44
Goan, Mali	E7	64
Goascorán, Hond.	D7	92
Goascorán, stm., N.A.	D7	92
Goat Mountain, mtn., Mt., U.S.	C12	122
Goba, Eth.	G9	56
Gobabis, Nmb.	D4	66
Gobabis, dept., Nmb.	D4	66
Gobernador Gregores, Arg.	F2	78
Gobernador Ingeniero Valentín Virasoro, Arg.	I10	80
Gobernador Juan E. Martínez, Arg.	E9	80
Gobernador Racedo, Arg.	F8	80
Gobi, des., Asia	C7	30
Gobles, Mi., U.S.	H10	110
Gobō, Japan	N10	36
Goce Delčev, Bul.	H7	20
Goch, Ger.	D6	10
Gochas, Nmb.	E4	66
Godāvari, stm., India	D6	46
Godbout, Que., Can.	C6	106
Godbout, stm., Que., Can.	C6	106
Goderich, Ont., Can.	G14	110
Goderville, Fr.	C7	14
Godfrey, Il., U.S.	D6	114
Godhavn, Grnld.	C14	86
Godhra, India	I5	44
Godinne, Bel.	H6	12
Godoy Cruz, Arg.	G4	80
Gods, stm., Man., Can.	B22	104
Gods Lake, Man., Can.	D20	104
Gods Lake, l., Man., Can.	D20	104
Gods Mercy, Bay of, b., N.W. Ter., Can.	D15	96
Godthåb, Grnld.	C14	86
Godwin Austen see K2, mtn., Asia	C7	44
Goéland, Lac au, l., Que., Can.	G17	96
Goélands, Lac aux, l., Que., Can.	E20	96
Goes, Neth.	E4	12
Goff, Ks., U.S.	L12	118
Goffstown, N.H., U.S.	D15	108
Gogama, Ont., Can.	C14	110
Gogebic, Lake, l., Mi., U.S.	D6	110
Gogland, ostrov, i., Russia	A10	22
Gogonou, Benin	F11	64
Gohad, India	G8	44
Gohitafla, I.C.	H7	64
Goiana, Braz.	E12	76
Goianápolis, Braz.	D4	79
Goiandira, Braz.	E4	79
Goianésia, Braz.	D4	79
Goiânia, Braz.	D4	79
Goiás, Braz.	C3	79
Goiás, state, Braz.	B4	79
Goiatuba, Braz.	E4	79
Goio-Erê, Braz.	C12	80
Gôio-Erê, stm., Braz.	B12	80
Goito, Italy	D5	18
Gojō, Japan	M10	36
Gokāk, India	D3	46
Gol, Nor.	K11	6
Golāghāt, India	G15	44
Golan Heights, clf, Isr. Occ.	C5	50
Golbāf, Iran	G14	48
Golconda, Il., U.S.	E8	114
Golconda, Nv., U.S.	D8	124
Gölcük, Tur.	J11	20
Gołdap, Pol.	A22	10
Gold Beach, Or., U.S.	H1	122
Goldboro, N.S., Can.	G12	106
Gold Bridge, B.C., Can.	G12	102
Gold Coast, Ghana	I9	64
Gold Creek, stm., B.C., Can.	H19	102
Golden, B.C., Can.	F18	102
Golden, Co., U.S.	E11	120
Golden, Il., U.S.	B5	114
Golden City, Mo., U.S.	E2	114
Goldendale, Wa., U.S.	E5	122
Golden Ears Provincial Park, B.C., Can.	H12	102
Golden Hinde, mtn., B.C., Can.	H9	102
Golden Meadow, La., U.S.	M6	114
Golden Prairie, Sask., Can.	H5	104
Goldfield, Ia., U.S.	H2	110
Goldfield, Nv., U.S.	G8	124
Goldonna, La., U.S.	J4	114
Gold River, B.C., Can.	H8	102
Gold Rock, Ont., Can.	I22	104
Goldsand Lake, l., Man., Can.	A13	104
Goldsboro, N.C., U.S.	D9	112
Goldsmith, Tx., U.S.	H4	116
Goldston, N.C., U.S.	D7	112
Goldsworthy, Austl.	D3	68
Goldthwaite, Tx., U.S.	H8	116
Golela, S. Afr.	F10	66
Goleniów, Pol.	B14	10
Goleta, Ca., U.S.	J6	124
Golfito, C.R.	I11	92
Golfo de Santa Clara, Mex.	B2	90
Goliad, Tx., U.S.	K9	116
Golicyno, Russia	F19	22
Golmud, China	D5	30
Golo, stm., Fr.	J16	14
Golovanevsk, Ukr.	A14	20
Golovin, Ak., U.S.	D13	100
Golpāyegān, Iran	E11	48
Golva, N.D., U.S.	E4	118
Golynki, Russia	G14	22
Golyšmanovo, Russia	F11	26
Goma, Zaire	B5	58
Gomel', Bela.	I14	22
Gomera, i., Spain	O23	17b
Gómez Farías, Mex.	C6	90
Gómez Palacio, Mex.	E8	90
Gómez Plata, Col.	D5	84
Gonābād, Iran	D15	48
Gonaïves, Haiti	E8	94
Gonâve, Golfe de la, b., Haiti	E8	94
Gonâve, Île de la, i., Haiti	E8	94
Gonbad-e Qābūs, Iran	C13	48
Gonda, India	G9	44
Gondal, India	J4	44
Gondarbal, India	C6	44
Gonder, Eth.	K9	60
Gondia, India	J9	44
Gondrecourt-le-Château, Fr.	D12	14
Gönen, Tur.	I11	20
Gongbo'gyamda, China	F5	30
Gongchenqiao, China	E9	34
Gongchuan, China	I6	34
Gongdian, China	G5	34
Gongga Shan, mtn., China	F7	30
Gongkou, China	H7	32
Gongola, stm., Nig.	F9	54
Gongpingxu, China	I1	34
Gongxian, China	E9	30
Gongyingzi, China	C7	32
Goñi, Ur.	G10	80
Goniądz, Pol.	B22	10
Gonzales, Ca., U.S.	H4	124
Gonzales, La., U.S.	L6	114
Gonzales, Tx., U.S.	J9	116
González, Mex.	F10	90
González, Riacho, stm., Para.	B9	80
González Chaves, Arg.	J8	80
González Moreno, Arg.	H7	80
Gonzanamá, Ec.	J3	84
Goochland, Va., U.S.	B9	112
Goodenough, Mount, mtn., N.W. Ter., Can.	C27	100
Gooderham, Ont., Can.	F17	110
Goodeve, Sask., Can.	G11	104
Good Hope, S. Afr.	H5	66
Good Hope, Cape of, c., S. Afr.	J4	66
Good Hope Mountain, mtn., B.C., Can.	F10	102
Goodhue, Mn., U.S.	F3	110
Gooding, Id., U.S.	H11	122
Goodland, Fl., U.S.	N5	112
Goodland, In., U.S.	B9	114
Goodland, Ks., U.S.	L6	118
Goodlands, Man., Can.	I14	104
Goodman, Ms., U.S.	J7	114
Goodman, Wi., U.S.	E7	110
Goodnews Bay, Ak., U.S.	G14	100
Goodnight, Co., U.S.	F12	120
Goodrich, N.D., U.S.	D7	118
Goodrich, Tx., U.S.	I12	116
Good Spirit Lake, l., Sask., Can.	G12	104
Good Spirit Lake Provincial Park, Sask., Can.	G12	104
Good Thunder, Mn., U.S.	F1	110
Goodview, Mn., U.S.	F4	110
Goodwater, Al., U.S.	I10	114
Goodwell, Ok., U.S.	C5	116
Goodyear, Az., U.S.	K4	120
Goolgowi, Austl.	I6	70
Goombalie, Austl.	G6	70
Goondiwindi, Austl.	G9	70
Goose, stm., Alta., Can.	C18	102
Goose, stm., N.D., U.S.	D10	118
Goose Bay see Happy Valley-Goose Bay, Newf., Can.	F20	96
Goose Creek, S.C., U.S.	G6	112
Goose Island, i., B.C., Can.	F6	102
Goose Lake, l., Man., Can.	D13	104
Goose Lake, l., Ont., Can.	G21	104
Goose Lake, l., Sask., Can.	G7	104
Goose Lake, l., U.S.	C5	124
Gooty, India	E4	46
Gopichettipālaiyam, India	G4	46
Goppenstein, Switz.	F8	13
Göppingen, Ger.	G9	10
Goqēn, China	F6	30
Góra, Pol.	D16	10
Goradit, Eth.	L10	60
Gorakhpur, India	G10	44
Gor'any, Bela.	F12	22
Goražde, Bos.	F2	20
Gorbatov, Russia	E26	22
Gorbatovka, Russia	E26	22
Gorboviči, Bela.	H13	22
Gorčucha, Russia	D26	22
Gorda, Punta, c., Chile	H6	82
Gorda, Punta, c., Cuba	C3	94
Gorda, Punta, c., Nic.	F11	92
Gorda, Punta, c., Nic.	C11	92
Gordo, Al., U.S.	I9	114
Gordon, Ga., U.S.	G3	112
Gordon, Ne., U.S.	I5	118
Gordon, Wi., U.S.	D4	110
Gordon, Lake, res., Austl.	N7	70
Gordon Horne Peak, mtn., B.C., Can.	F16	102
Gordon Indian Reserve, Sask., Can.	G10	104
Gordon Lake, l., Alta., Can.	B4	104
Gordon Lake, l., Sask., Can.	C8	104
Gordonsville, Va., U.S.	I8	108
Gordonvale, Austl.	A6	70
Gore, N.S., Can.	G10	106
Gore, Eth.	M8	60
Gore, N.Z.	G2	72
Gore Bay, Ont., Can.	E13	110
Goree, Tx., U.S.	F7	116
Gore Point, c., Austl.	A3	70
Goreville, Il., U.S.	E8	114
Gorgān, Iran	C13	48
Gorgona, Isla, i., Col.	F3	84
Gorgor, Peru	D3	82
Gorgora, Eth.	K9	60
Gorham, Me., U.S.	D16	108
Gorham, N.H., U.S.	C15	108
Gori, Geor.	I6	26
Goricy, Russia	D19	22
Gorinchem, Neth.	E7	12
Goris, Arm.	B9	48
Gorizia, Italy	D8	18
Gorj, co., Rom.	E7	20
Gorkhā, Nepal	F11	44
Gorki, Bela.	G13	22
Gor'kovskoje vodochranilišče, res., Russia	D26	22
Gorky see Nižnij Novgorod, Russia	E27	22
Gorlice, Pol.	F21	10
Görlitz, Ger.	D14	10
Gorlovka, Ukr.	H5	26
Gorlovo, Russia	H22	22
Gorman, Tx., U.S.	G8	116
Gorn'ackij, Russia	D10	26
Gorn'ak, Russia	H22	22
Gornji Milanovac, Yugo.	E4	20
Gorno-Altajsk, Russia	G9	28
Gornozavodsk, Russia	H20	28
Gorochovec, Russia	E25	22
Gorodec, Russia	E26	22
Gorodec, Russia	C12	22
Gorodeja, Bela.	H9	22
Gorodenka, Ukr.	A9	20
Gorodišče, Bela.	H9	22
Gorodišče, Bela.	H12	22
Gorodkovka, Ukr.	A12	20
Gorodok, Bela.	F12	22
Goroka, Pap. N. Gui.	G12	38
Gorontalo, Indon.	E7	38
Gorouol, stm., Afr.	D10	64
Gorutuba, stm., Braz.	C7	79
Gorzów Wielkopolski (Landsberg an der Warthe), Pol.	C15	10
Gosford, Austl.	I9	70
Goshabi, Sud.	I6	60
Goshen, N.S., Can.	G12	106
Goshen, Ca., U.S.	H6	124
Goshen, In., U.S.	A11	114
Goshen, N.Y., U.S.	F12	108
Goslar, Ger.	D10	10
Gosport, In., U.S.	C10	114
Gossas, Sen.	D1	64
Gossi, Mali	D9	64
Gostivar, Mac.	H4	20
Gostyń, Pol.	D17	10
Gostynin, Pol.	C19	10
Göta älv, stm., Swe.	M13	6
Gotebo, Ok., U.S.	D8	116
Göteborg (Gothenburg), Swe.	M12	6
Göteborgs Och Bohus län, co., Swe.	L12	6
Gotemba, Japan	L13	36
Gotešty, Mol.	C12	20
Gotha, Ger.	E10	10
Gothenburg, Ne., U.S.	K7	118
Gothenburg see Göteborg, Swe.	M12	6
Gothèye, Niger	E10	64
Gotland, i., Swe.	M16	6
Gotlands Län, co., Swe.	M16	6
Gotō-rettō, is., Japan	O3	36
Göttingen, Ger.	D9	10
Gouarec, Fr.	D3	14
Gouda, Neth.	D6	12
Goudge, Arg.	H4	80
Goudiry, Sen.	D3	64
Gough Island, i., St. Hel.	M6	52
Gough Lake, l., Alta., Can.	E22	102
Gouin, Réservoir, res., Que., Can.	G18	96
Goulburn, Austl.	J8	70
Goulburn Islands, is., Austl.	B6	68
Gould, Ar., U.S.	I5	114
Gould City, Mi., U.S.	D10	110
Goulds, Fl., U.S.	N6	112
Goulet Lake, l., Man., Can.	C18	104
Goulimime, Mor.	F5	62
Goundam, Mali	C8	64
Gourdon, Fr.	H8	14
Gouré, Niger	E15	64
Gourin, Fr.	D3	14
Gourma Rharous, Mali	C9	64
Gournay-en-Bray, Fr.	C8	14
Gouveia, Braz.	E7	79
Gouverneur, N.Y., U.S.	C11	108
Gouyadong, China	J1	34
Govan, Sask., Can.	G9	104
Gove, Ks., U.S.	M7	118
Govena, mys, c., Russia	F25	28
Govenlock, Sask., Can.	I5	104
Governador Valadares, Braz.	E8	79
Governor's Harbour, Bah.	B6	94
Govind Ballabh Pant Sāgar, res., India	H10	44
Govind Sāgar, res., India	E7	44
Gowan, stm., Man., Can.	C20	104
Gowanda, N.Y., U.S.	E8	108
Gowan Range, mts., Austl.	E6	70
Gower, Mo., U.S.	C2	114
Gowmal (Gumal), stm., Asia	D3	44
Gowrie, Ia., U.S.	I13	118
Goya, Arg.	E9	80
Goyelle, Lac, l., Que., Can.	B13	106
Gozo see Għawdex, i., Malta	M9	18
Graaff-Reinet, S. Afr.	I7	66
Grabo, I.C.	I6	64
Grabowiec, Pol.	E23	10
Gračanica, Bos.	E2	20
Grace, Id., U.S.	H14	122
Gracefield, Que., Can.	A10	108
Graceville, Fl., U.S.	I1	112
Graceville, Mn., U.S.	F11	118
Gracias, Hond.	C6	92
Gracias a Dios, dept., Hond.	B10	92
Gracias a Dios, Cabo, c., N.A.	B11	92
Gradačac, Bos.	E2	20
Gradaús, Braz.	E8	76
Grado, Italy	D8	18
Grady, Ar., U.S.	H5	114
Grady, N.M., U.S.	E3	116
Graettinger, Ia., U.S.	H13	118
Grafenau, Ger.	G13	10
Gräfenhainichen, Ger.	D12	10
Grafing [bei München], Ger.	G11	10
Graford, Tx., U.S.	G8	116
Grafton, Austl.	G10	70
Grafton, Il., U.S.	D6	114
Grafton, N.D., U.S.	C10	118
Grafton, W.V., U.S.	H6	108
Grafton, Wi., U.S.	G8	110
Grafton, Cape, c., Austl.	A6	70
Graham, N.C., U.S.	C7	112
Graham, Tx., U.S.	F8	116
Graham, Mount, mtn., Az., U.S.	L7	120
Graham Island, i., B.C., Can.	D2	102
Graham Land, reg., Ant.	B12	73
Graham Moore, Cape, c., N.W. Ter., Can.	B17	96
Graham Moore Bay, b., N.W. Ter., Can.	A12	96
Grahamstown, S. Afr.	I8	66
Grain Coast, Lib.	I5	64
Grainfield, Ks., U.S.	L7	118
Grajaú, Braz.	E9	76
Grajaú, stm., Braz.	D9	76
Grajewo, Pol.	B22	10
Gramada, Bul.	F6	20
Gramado, Braz.	E13	80
Gramalote, Col.	D6	84
Grambling, La., U.S.	J4	114
Gramilla, Arg.	D6	80
Grammichele, Italy	L9	18
Grampian, prov., Scot., U.K.	D11	8
Grampian Mountains, mts., Scot., U.K.	E9	8
Grampians National Park, Austl.	K5	70
Granada, Col.	F6	84
Granada, Nic.	F9	92
Granada, Spain	H8	16
Granada, Co., U.S.	M5	118
Granada, Mn., U.S.	G1	110
Granada, dept., Nic.	F8	92
Granadilla de Abona, Spain	O24	17b
Granbury, Tx., U.S.	G9	116
Granby, Que., Can.	B14	108
Granby, Co., U.S.	D11	120
Granby, Mo., U.S.	F2	114
Granby, stm., B.C., Can.	H16	102
Granby, Lake, res., Co., U.S.	D11	120
Gran Canaria, i., Spain	O25	17b
Gran Chaco, pl., S.A.	C8	80
Grand, stm., U.S.	C3	114
Grand, stm., Mi., U.S.	G9	110
Grand, stm., Oh., U.S.	F5	108
Grand, stm., S.D., U.S.	F7	118
Grand, stm., Wi., U.S.	G7	110
Grand Bahama, i., Bah.	A5	94
Grand Bank, Newf., Can.	E18	106
Grand Banks of Newfoundland	E14	86
Grand-Bassam, I.C.	I8	64
Grand Bay, N.B., Can.	G7	106
Grand Bay, Al., U.S.	L8	114
Grand Beach, Man., Can.	H18	104
Grand Bend, Ont., Can.	G14	110
Grand Blanc, Mi., U.S.	H12	110
Grand Bruit, Newf., Can.	E15	106
Grand Canal, Ire.	H6	8
Grand Canal see Da Yunhe, China	E10	30
Grand Cane, La., U.S.	J3	114
Grand Canyon, Az., U.S.	H4	120
Grand Canyon, val., Az., U.S.	H4	120
Grand Canyon National Park, Az., U.S.	H4	120
Grand Cayman, i., Cay. Is.	E4	94
Grand Centre, Alta., Can.	D4	104
Grand Cess, Lib.	I5	64
Grand Chenier, La., U.S.	M4	114
Grand Combin, mtn., Switz.	G7	13
Grand Coulee, Wa., U.S.	C6	122
Grand Coulee, val., Wa., U.S.	C6	122
Grand Coulee Dam, Wa., U.S.	C7	122
Grand-Couronne, Fr.	C8	14
Grande, stm., Arg.	I4	80
Grande, stm., Arg.	C6	80
Grande, stm., Bol.	G9	82
Grande, stm., Braz.	F10	76
Grande, stm., Braz.	E3	79
Grande, stm., Chile	F3	80
Grande, stm., Nic.	E8	92
Grande, stm., Pan.	I14	92
Grande, stm., Peru	F4	82
Grande, Arroyo, stm., Ur.	G10	80
Grande, Bahía, Arg.	G3	78
Grande, Boca, mth., Ven.	C12	84
Grande, Cerro, mtn., Mex.	G8	90
Grande, Cerro, mtn., Mex.	C6	90
Grande, Corixa, stm., S.A.	G7	76
Grande, Corixa (Curiche Grande), sw., S.A.	G12	82
Grande, Cuchilla, mtn., Ur.	G11	80
Grande, Ilha, i., Braz.	G6	79
Grande, Ilha, i., Braz.	B11	80
Grande, Ponta, c., Braz.	D9	79
Grande, Punta, c., Chile	A3	80
Grande, Rio (Bravo del Norte), stm., N.A.	F7	98
Grande-Anse, N.B., Can.	E8	106
Grande Cache, Alta., Can.	D15	102
Grande Cayemite, i., Haiti	E8	94
Grande de Lipez, stm., Bol.	I8	82
Grande de Manacapuru, Lago, l., Braz.	I12	84
Grande de Matagalpa, stm., Nic.	D11	92
Grande de Santiago, stm., Mex.	G7	90
Grande de Tarija, stm., S.A.	J9	82
Grande de Térraba, stm., C.R.	I11	92
Grande do Gurupá, Ilha, i., Braz.	D8	76
Grand-Entrée, Que., Can.	E12	106
Grande-Prairie, Alta., Can.	B16	102
Grand Erg de Bilma, des., Niger	E9	54
Grand Erg Occidental, des., Alg.	E11	62
Grand Erg Oriental, des., Alg.	E14	62
Grande-Rivière, Que., Can.	D9	106
Grande Rivière, La, stm., Que., Can.	F17	96
Grande Ronde, stm., U.S.	E8	122
Grandes, Salinas, pl., Arg.	F6	80
Grandes, Salinas, pl., Arg.	B6	80
Grand-Étang, N.S., Can.	F12	106
Grande-Terre, i., Guad.	F14	94
Grand Falls, N.B., Can.	E6	106
Grand Falls, Newf., Can.	D18	106
Grandfalls, Tx., U.S.	H4	116
Grandfield, Ok., U.S.	E8	116
Grand Forks, B.C., Can.	H16	102
Grand Forks, N.D., U.S.	D10	118
Grand Haven, Mi., U.S.	G9	110
Grand Hers, stm., Fr.	I8	14
Grandiči, Bela.	H6	22
Grandin, Lac, l., N.W. Ter., Can.	D9	96
Grand Island, Ne., U.S.	K9	118
Grand Island, i., Mi., U.S.	D9	110
Grand Isle, La., U.S.	M7	114
Grand Junction, Co., U.S.	E8	120
Grand Junction, Ia., U.S.	I13	118
Grand Junction, Tn., U.S.	G7	114
Grand-Lahou, I.C.	I7	64
Grand Lake, Co., U.S.	D11	120
Grand Lake, l., N.B., Can.	G7	106
Grand Lake, l., Newf., Can.	D16	106
Grand Lake, l., N.A.	G6	106
Grand Lake, l., La., U.S.	M5	114
Grand Lake, l., La., U.S.	M4	114
Grand Lake, l., Oh., U.S.	G2	108
Grand Ledge, Mi., U.S.	H11	110
Grand Manan Channel, strt., N.A.	H7	106
Grand Manan Island, i., N.B., Can.	H7	106
Grand Marais, Mi., U.S.	D10	110
Grand Marais, Mn., U.S.	C5	110
Grand Meadow, Mn., U.S.	G3	110
Grand-Mère, Que., Can.	G18	96
Grand Mesa, mtn., Co., U.S.	E8	120
Grandmesnil, Lac, l., Que., Can.	A6	106
Grand Pabos, Rivière du, stm., Que., Can.	D9	106
Grand-Popo, Benin	H10	64
Grand Portage, Mn., U.S.	C6	110
Grand Prairie, Tx., U.S.	G10	116
Grand Pré National Historic Park, N.S., Can.	G9	106
Grand Rapids, Man., Can.	E15	104
Grand Rapids, Mi., U.S.	H10	110
Grand Rapids, Mn., U.S.	C2	110
Grandrieu, Bel.	H5	12
Grand-Saint-Bernard, Col du, Eur.	G7	13
Grand-Saint-Bernard, Tunnel du, Eur.	G14	14
Grand Saline, Tx., U.S.	G11	116
Grand Teton, mtn., Wy., U.S.	A6	120
Grand Teton National Park, Wy., U.S.	G15	122
Grand Tower, Il., U.S.	E7	114
Grand Traverse Bay, b., Mi., U.S.	E10	110
Grand Turk, T./C. Is.	D9	94
Grandview, Man., Can.	G14	104
Grandview, Mo., U.S.	D2	114
Grandview, Tx., U.S.	G9	116
Grandview, Wa., U.S.	D6	122
Grand View, Wi., U.S.	D4	110
Graneros, Chile	H3	80
Granger, Tx., U.S.	I9	116
Granger, Wa., U.S.	D5	122
Granger, Wy., U.S.	C7	120
Grangeville, Id., U.S.	E9	122
Gran Guardia, Arg.	C9	80
Granite, Ok., U.S.	E7	116
Granite City, Il., U.S.	D6	114
Granite Falls, Mn., U.S.	G12	118
Granite Falls, N.C., U.S.	D5	112
Granite Falls, Wa., U.S.	B4	122
Granite Lake, res., Newf., Can.	D16	106
Granite Peak, mtn., Mt., U.S.	E16	122
Graniteville, S.C., U.S.	F5	112
Graniteville, Vt., U.S.	C14	108
Granollers, Spain	D14	16
Gran Pajonal, mts., Peru	D4	82
Gran Paradiso, mtn., Italy	D2	18
Gran Sasso d'Italia, mts., Italy	G8	18
Grant, Fl., U.S.	L6	112
Grant, Mi., U.S.	G10	110
Grant, Ne., U.S.	K6	118
Grant, stm., Wi., U.S.	H5	110
Grant, Mount, mtn., Nv., U.S.	F7	124
Gran Tarajal, Spain	O26	17b
Grant City, Mo., U.S.	B2	114
Grant Park, Il., U.S.	I8	110
Grant Point, c., N.W. Ter., Can.	C13	96
Grants, N.M., U.S.	I9	120
Grantsburg, Wi., U.S.	E3	110
Grants Pass, Or., U.S.	H2	122
Grant-Suttie Bay, b., N.W. Ter., Can.	C17	96
Grantsville, Ut., U.S.	D4	120
Grantsville, W.V., U.S.	I5	108
Grantville, Ga., U.S.	F2	112
Granum, Alta., Can.	H21	102
Granville, Fr.	D5	14
Granville, Il., U.S.	I6	110
Granville, N.Y., U.S.	D13	108
Granville, N.D., U.S.	C7	118
Granville, Oh., U.S.	G4	108
Granville, W.V., U.S.	H7	108
Granville Lake, l., Man., Can.	B14	104
Granvin, Nor.	K10	6
Grão Mogol, Braz.	D7	79
Grapeland, Tx., U.S.	H11	116
Grapevine Lake, res., Tx., U.S.	G9	116
Gras, Lac de, l., N.W. Ter., Can.	D10	96
Grasmere, S. Afr.	F8	66
Grasonville, Md., U.S.	I10	108
Grass, stm., Man., Can.	B18	104
Grass, stm., N.Y., U.S.	C11	108
Grass Creek, Wy., U.S.	G17	122
Grasse, Fr.	I13	14
Grassflat, Pa., U.S.	F8	108
Grass Lake, Mi., U.S.	H11	110
Grass Range, Mt., U.S.	C17	122
Grass River Provincial Park, Man., Can.	D14	104
Grass Valley, Ca., U.S.	E4	124
Grassy, Austl.	M6	70
Grassy Island Lake, l., Alta., Can.	G4	104
Grassy Lake, Alta., Can.	H23	102
Grassy Plains, B.C., Can.	D9	102
Grates Point, c., Newf., Can.	D21	106
Graubünden (Grischun), state, Switz.	E11	13
Gravatá, Braz.	E11	76
Gravatá, stm., Braz.	D7	79
Gravelbourg, Sask., Can.	I8	104
Gravelines, Fr.	B9	14
Gravell Point, c., N.W. Ter., Can.	C17	96
Gravenhurst, Ont., Can.	F16	110
Grave Peak, mtn., Id., U.S.	D11	122
Gravette, Ar., U.S.	F2	114
Gravina in Puglia, Italy	I11	18
Gray, Fr.	E12	14
Gray, Ga., U.S.	F3	112
Gray, Ky., U.S.	C2	112
Grayback Mountain, mtn., Or., U.S.	H2	122
Grayling, Ak., U.S.	E14	100
Grayling, Mi., U.S.	F11	110
Grays Harbor, b., Wa., U.S.	D1	122
Grayson, Sask., Can.	H12	104
Grayson, Al., U.S.	H9	114
Grayson, Ky., U.S.	I4	108
Grayson, La., U.S.	J4	114
Grays Peak, mtn., Co., U.S.	E11	120
Graysville, Tn., U.S.	G11	114
Grayville, Il., U.S.	E8	114
Graz, Aus.	H15	10
Grazalema, Spain	I6	16
Gr'azi, Russia	I22	22
Gr'aznoje, Russia	G22	22
Gr'azovec, Russia	C23	22
Great Artesian Basin, Austl.	E5	70
Great Australian Bight, Austl.	F5	68
Great Barrier Island, i., N.Z.	B5	72
Great Barrier Reef, rf., Austl.	C9	68
Great Barrier Reef Marine Park, Austl.	C9	68
Great Barrington, Ma., U.S.	E13	108
Great Basin, U.S.	C3	98
Great Bear, stm., N.W. Ter., Can.	D32	100
Great Bear Lake, l., N.W. Ter., Can.	C8	96
Great Beaver Lake, l., B.C., Can.	C11	102
Great Bend, Ks., U.S.	M9	118
Great Britain, i., U.K.	E7	4
Great Burnt Lake, l., Newf., Can.	D17	106
Great Central, B.C., Can.	H10	102
Great Central Lake, l., B.C., Can.	H9	102
Great Channel, strt., Asia	K3	40
Great Dismal Swamp, sw., U.S.	C10	112
Great Divide Basin, Wy., U.S.	H17	122
Great Dividing Range, mts., Austl.	E9	68
Greater Antilles, is., N.A.	D7	94
Greater Khingan Range see Da Hinggan Ling, mts., China	B11	30
Greater Sunda Islands, is., Asia	F5	38
Great Exuma, i., Bah.	C7	94
Great Falls, Man., Can.	H18	104
Great Falls, Mt., U.S.	C14	122
Great Falls, S.C., U.S.	E6	112
Great Guana Cay, i., Bah.	E6	94
Great Inagua, i., Bah.	D8	94
Great Indian Desert (Thar Desert), des., Asia	G4	44
Great Karroo, plat., S. Afr.	I6	66
Great Lake, l., Austl.	M7	70
Great Miami, stm., U.S.	H2	108
Great Namaqualand, hist. reg., Nmb.	E3	66
Great Nicobar, i., India	K2	40
Great Palm Island, i., Austl.	B7	70
Great Pee Dee, stm., S.C., U.S.	F7	112
Great Plain of the Koukdjuak, pl., N.W. Ter., Can.	C18	96
Great Plains, pl., N.A.	E9	86
Great Pubnico Lake, l., N.S., Can.	I8	106
Great Ruaha, stm., Tan.	C7	58
Great Sacandaga Lake, l., N.Y., U.S.	D12	108
Great Saint Bernard Pass see Grand-Saint-Bernard, Col du, Eur.	G7	13
Great Salt Lake, l., Ut., U.S.	C4	120
Great Salt Lake Desert, des., Ut., U.S.	D3	120
Great Sand Hills, hills, Sask., Can.	H5	104
Great Sandy Desert, des., Austl.	D4	68
Great Scarcies (Kolenté), stm., Afr.	G3	64
Great Slave Lake, l., N.W. Ter., Can.	D10	96
Great Smoky Mountains, mts., U.S.	D3	112
Great Smoky Mountains National Park, U.S.	D3	112
Great Victoria Desert, des., Austl.	E5	68
Great Wall, sci., B.A.T.	B1	73
Great Wall see Chang Cheng, hist., China	C4	32
Great Yarmouth, Eng., U.K.	I15	8
Great Zab (Büyükzap) (Az-Zāb al-Kabīr), stm., Asia	C7	48
Gréboun, mtn., Niger	A14	64
Grecia, C.R.	G10	92
Greco, Ur.	G10	80
Greece, N.Y., U.S.	D9	108
Greece (Ellás), ctry., Eur.	H12	4
Greeley, Co., U.S.	D12	120
Greeley, Ks., U.S.	M12	118
Greeley, Ne., U.S.	J9	118
Greeleyville, S.C., U.S.	F7	112
Green, stm., N.B., Can.	E5	106
Green, stm., U.S.	F7	120
Green, stm., Il., U.S.	I6	110
Green, stm., Ky., U.S.	E9	114
Green, stm., N.D., U.S.	D4	118
Green, stm., Wa., U.S.	C3	122
Greenacres, Wa., U.S.	C8	122
Green Bay, Wi., U.S.	F7	110
Green Bay, b., Newf., Can.	C18	106
Green Bay, b., U.S.	F8	110
Greenbrier, Ar., U.S.	G4	114
Green Brier, Tn., U.S.	F10	114
Greenbrier, stm., W.V., U.S.	J6	108
Greenburg, La., U.S.	L6	114
Greenbush, Mn., U.S.	C11	118
Greencastle, In., U.S.	C10	114
Greencastle, Pa., U.S.	H9	108
Green City, Mo., U.S.	B4	114
Green Cove Springs, Fl., U.S.	J5	112
Greendale, In., U.S.	C12	114
Greene, Ia., U.S.	H3	110
Greene, N.Y., U.S.	E11	108
Greeneville, Tn., U.S.	C4	112
Greenfield, Ca., U.S.	H4	124
Greenfield, Il., U.S.	C6	114
Greenfield, Ia., U.S.	J13	118
Greenfield, Ma., U.S.	E14	108
Greenfield, Mo., U.S.	E3	114
Greenfield, Oh., U.S.	H3	108
Greenfield, Tn., U.S.	F8	114
Green Forest, Ar., U.S.	F3	114
Green Head, c., Austl.	F2	68
Green Lake, Sask., Can.	D7	104
Green Lake, Wi., U.S.	G7	110
Green Lake, l., B.C., Can.	F13	102
Green Lake, l., Sask., Can.	D7	104
Greenland, Ar., U.S.	G2	114
Greenland, Mi., U.S.	D6	110
Greenland (Kalaallit Nunaat), dep., N.A.	B15	86
Greenland Sea	B20	86
Greenleaf, Ks., U.S.	L11	118
Green Mountains, mts., Vt., U.S.	D14	108
Green Peter Lake, res., Or., U.S.	F3	122
Green Pond, Al., U.S.	I9	114
Greenport, N.Y., U.S.	F14	108
Green River, Ut., U.S.	F6	120
Green River, Wy., U.S.	C7	120
Green River Lake, res., Ky., U.S.	E11	114
Greensboro, Al., U.S.	J9	114
Greensboro, Fl., U.S.	I2	112
Greensboro, Ga., U.S.	F3	112
Greensboro, Md., U.S.	I11	108
Greensboro, N.C., U.S.	C7	112
Greensburg, In., U.S.	C11	114
Greensburg, Ks., U.S.	N8	118
Greensburg, Ky., U.S.	E11	114
Greensburg, Pa., U.S.	G7	108
Greens Peak, mtn., Az., U.S.	J7	120
Greenspond, Newf., Can.	C20	106
Green Springs, Oh., U.S.	F3	108
Green Swamp, sw., N.C., U.S.	E8	112
Greentown, In., U.S.	B11	114
Greenup, Il., U.S.	C8	114
Greenup, Ky., U.S.	I4	108
Greenvale, Austl.	B6	70
Green Valley, Az., U.S.	M6	120
Green Valley, Il., U.S.	J6	110
Greenview, Il., U.S.	B7	114
Greenville, Lib.	I5	64
Greenville, Al., U.S.	K10	114
Greenville, Ca., U.S.	D5	124
Greenville, Fl., U.S.	I3	112
Greenville, Ga., U.S.	F2	112
Greenville, Il., U.S.	D7	114
Greenville, Ky., U.S.	E9	114
Greenville, Me., U.S.	B17	108
Greenville, Mi., U.S.	G10	110
Greenville, Ms., U.S.	I5	114
Greenville, Mo., U.S.	E6	114
Greenville, N.H., U.S.	E15	108
Greenville, N.C., U.S.	D9	112
Greenville, Oh., U.S.	G2	108
Greenville, Pa., U.S.	F6	108
Greenville, S.C., U.S.	E4	112
Greenville, Tx., U.S.	F10	116
Greenwater Lake Provincial Park, Sask., Can.	F11	104
Greenwich, Ct., U.S.	F13	108
Greenwich, N.Y., U.S.	D13	108
Greenwich, Oh., U.S.	F4	108
Greenwood, B.C., Can.	H16	102
Greenwood, Ar., U.S.	G2	114
Greenwood, In., U.S.	C10	114
Greenwood, Ms., U.S.	I6	114
Greenwood, Ne., U.S.	K11	118
Greenwood, S.C., U.S.	E4	112
Greenwood, Wi., U.S.	F5	110
Greenwood, Lake, res., S.C., U.S.	E4	112
Greer, S.C., U.S.	E4	112
Greers Ferry Lake, res., Ar., U.S.	G4	114

Name — Map Ref. — Page

Gregoire Lake Indian Reserve, Alta., Can. B3 104
Gregório, stm., Braz. B6 82
Gregory, Mi., U.S. H11 110
Gregory, S.D., U.S. H8 118
Gregory, Tx., U.S. L9 116
Gregory, stm., Austl. B3 70
Gregory, Lake, l., Austl. G3 70
Gregory Range, mts., Austl. B5 70
Greifswald, Ger. A13 10
Greiz, Ger. E12 10
Grem'ačinsk, Russia F9 26
Grenada, Ms., U.S. I7 114
Grenada, ctry., N.A. H14 94
Grenadines, is., N.A. H14 94
Grenchen, Switz. D7 13
Grenfell, Austl. I8 70
Grenfell, Sask., Can. H12 104
Grenoble, Fr. G12 14
Grenola, Ks., U.S. N11 118
Grenora, N.D., U.S. C4 118
Grenville, Cape, c., Austl. B8 68
Grenville Channel, strt., B.C., Can. D5 102
Gréoux-les-Bains, Fr. I12 14
Gresham, Or., U.S. E3 122
Gresham Park, Ga., U.S. F2 112
Gresik, Indon. J16 39a
Gresten, Aus. G15 10
Gretna, Man., Can. I17 104
Gretna, La., U.S. M6 114
Gretna, Va., U.S. C7 112
Greven, Ger. C7 10
Grevená, Grc. I5 20
Grevenbroich, Ger. D6 10
Greville Bay, b., N.S., Can. G9 106
Grey, stm., Newf., Can. E17 106
Greybull, Wy., U.S. F17 122
Greybull, stm., Wy., U.S. F17 122
Grey Eagle, Mn., U.S. E1 110
Grey Islands, is., Newf., Can. B18 106
Greylock, Mount, mtn., Ma., U.S. E13 108
Greymouth, N.Z. E3 72
Grey Range, mts., Austl. G5 70
Grey River, Newf., Can. E16 106
Greys, stm., Wy., U.S. G15 122
Greytown, S. Afr. G10 66
Gribanovskij, Russia G6 26
Gribbel Island, i., B.C., Can. D5 102
Gridley, Ca., U.S. E4 124
Gridley, Il., U.S. J7 110
Griesbach, Ger. G13 10
Griesheim, Ger. F8 10
Griffin, Sask., Can. I11 104
Griffin, Ga., U.S. F2 112
Griffith, Austl. J7 70
Griffith Island, i., N.W. Ter., Can. B13 96
Grifton, N.C., U.S. D9 112
Griggsville, Il., U.S. C6 114
Grignan, Fr. H11 14
Grigoriopol', Mol. B13 20
Grijalva, stm., Mex. I13 90
Grijalva (Cuilco), stm., N.A. B3 92
Grijpskerk, Neth. B9 12
Grim, Cape, c., Austl. M6 70
Grimma, Ger. D12 10
Grimsby, Ont., Can. G16 110
Grimsby, Eng., U.K. H13 8
Grimselpass, Switz. E9 13
Grimshaw, Alta., Can. A17 102
Grímsstaðir, Ice. B5 6a
Grimstad, Nor. L11 6
Grímsvötn, mtn., Ice. B5 6a
Grin'ava, Ukr. B8 20
Grindelwald, Switz. E9 13
Grindstone Island see Cap-aux-Meules, Que., Can. E12 106
Grinnell, Ia., U.S. I3 110
Grinnell Peninsula, pen., N.W. Ter., Can. A13 96
Gris-Nez, Cap, c., Fr. B8 14
Griswold, Man., Can. I14 104
Griswold, Ia., U.S. J12 118
Grizzly Bear Mountain, mtn., N.W. Ter., Can. C8 96
Grizzly Bear's Head and Lean Man Indian Reserve, Sask., Can. F6 104
Groais Island, i., Newf., Can. B18 106
Grobiņa, Lat. E4 22
Groblersdal, S. Afr. E9 66
Groblershoop, S. Afr. G5 66
Grodków, Pol. E17 10
Grodno, Bela. H6 22
Grodzisk Mazowiecki, Pol. C20 10
Groede, Neth. F4 12
Groenlo, Neth. D10 12
Groesbeck, Tx., U.S. H10 116
Groesbeek, Neth. E8 12
Groix, Fr. E3 14
Grójec, Pol. D20 10
Grombalia, Tun. M5 18
Gronau, Ger. C7 10
Groningen, Neth. B10 12
Groningen, prov., Neth. B10 12
Gronlid, Sask., Can. E10 104
Groom, Tx., U.S. D5 116
Groot-Brakrivier, S. Afr. J5 66
Groote Eylandt, i., Austl. B7 68
Grootfontein, Nmb. B4 66
Groot Karasberge, mts., Nmb. F4 66
Groot-Kei, stm., Afr. I9 66
Groot Laagte, stm., Afr. C5 66
Groot-Marico, S. Afr. E8 66
Groot-Vis, stm., Afr. I8 66
Gros Mécatina, Cap du, c., Que., Can. B14 106
Gros Morne, mtn., Newf., Can. C16 106
Gros Morne National Park, Newf., Can. C16 106
Grosse Île, La, i., Que., Can. E12 106
Grossenhain, Ger. D13 10
Grosse Pointe, Mi., U.S. H13 110
Grosseto, Italy G6 18
Gross-Gerau, Ger. F8 10
Grossglockner, mtn., Aus. H12 10
Grosshöchstetten, Switz. E8 13
Grossräschen, Ger. D14 10
Gros Ventre, stm., Wy., U.S. G15 122
Groswater Bay, b., Newf., Can. F21 96
Groton, Ct., U.S. F14 108
Groton, N.Y., U.S. E10 108
Groton, S.D., U.S. F9 118
Grottaglie, Italy I12 18
Grottoes, Va., U.S. I8 108
Grouard Mission, Alta., Can B18 102
Groundbirch, B.C., Can. B14 102
Groundhog, stm., Ont., Can. G16 96
Groundhog, stm., Ont., Can. B13 100
Grove, Ok., U.S. C12 116
Grove City, Mn., U.S. F13 118
Grove City, Oh., U.S. H3 108
Grove City, Pa., U.S. F6 108
Grove Hill, Al., U.S. K9 114
Groveland, Fl., U.S. K5 112
Grover City, Ca., U.S. I5 124
Groves, Tx., U.S. M3 114
Groveton, N.H., U.S. C15 108
Groveton, Tx., U.S. H11 116
Grovetown, Ga., U.S. F4 112
Groznyj, Russia I7 26
Grudziądz, Pol. B18 10
Gruetli-Laager, Tn., U.S. G11 114
Gruitrode, Bel. F8 12
Grulla, Tx., U.S. M8 116
Grünau, Nmb. F4 66
Grünau [im Almtal], Aus. H13 10
Grundy, Va., U.S. B4 112
Grundy Center, Ia., U.S. H3 110
Grunthal, Man., Can. I18 104
Gruver, Tx., U.S. C5 116
Gruziya see Georgia, ctry., Asia I6 26
Grybów, Pol. F20 10
Gryfice, Pol. B15 10
Gstaad, Switz. F7 13
Guabito, Pan. H12 92
Guacanayabo, Golfo de, b., Cuba D6 94
Guacara, Ven. B9 84
Guacarí, Col. F4 84
Gu Achi, Az., U.S. L4 120
Guachiría, stm., Col. E7 84
Guachochi, Mex. D6 90
Guaçuí, Braz. F8 79
Guadalajara, Mex. G8 90
Guadalajara, Spain E8 16
Guadalcanal, i., Sol.Is. I20 126
Guadalén, stm., Spain G8 16
Guadalén, Embalse de, res., Spain G8 16
Guadalmena, stm., Spain G9 16
Guadalquivir, stm., Spain H6 16
Guadalupe, Bol. H9 82
Guadalupe, Col. F5 84
Guadalupe, C.R. H10 92
Guadalupe, Mex. E9 90
Guadalupe, Mex. F8 90
Guadalupe, Peru B2 82
Guadalupe, Ca., U.S. J5 124
Guadalupe, stm., Tx., U.S. K9 116
Guadalupe [Bravos], Mex. B6 90
Guadalupe Mountains National Park, Tx., U.S. H2 116
Guadalupe Peak, mtn., Tx., U.S. H2 116
Guadalupe Victoria, Mex. E7 90
Guadalupita, N.M., U.S. H11 120
Guadarrama, Sierra de, mts., Spain E7 16
Guadeloupe, dep., N.A. F14 94
Guadeloupe Passage, strt., N.A. F14 94
Guadiana, stm., Eur. H4 16
Guadix, Spain H8 16
Guaíba, Braz. F13 80
Guaíba, est., Braz. F13 80
Guaihe, China B1 34
Guaimaca, Hond. C8 92
Guaimoreto, Laguna de, b., Hond. B9 92
Guainía, dept., Col. F8 84
Guainía, stm., S.A. F9 84
Guaiquinima, Cerro, mtn., Ven. E11 84
Guaíra, Braz. F4 79
Guaíra, Braz. C11 80
Guairá, dept., Para. C10 80
Guáitara, stm., Col. G4 84
Guajaba, Cayo, i., Cuba D6 94
Guajará-Mirim, Braz. D9 82
Gualaca, Pan. C1 84
Gualaceo, Ec. I3 84
Gualala, Ca., U.S. F2 124
Gualán, Guat. B5 92
Gualaquiza, Ec. I3 84
Gualdo Tadino, Italy F7 18
Gualeguay, Arg. G9 80
Gualeguay, stm., Arg. G9 80
Gualeguaychú, Arg. G9 80
Gualicho, Salina del, pl., Arg. E3 78
Guam, dep., Oc. F22 2
Guamal, Col. C5 84
Guamal, Col. F6 84
Guaminí, Arg. I7 80
Guamo, Col. E5 84
Guamote, Ec. H3 84
Guamúchil, Mex. E5 90
Guamués, stm., Col. G4 84
Guanacaste, prov., C.R. G9 92
Guanacaste, Cordillera de, mts., C.R. G9 92
Guanacaste, Parque Nacional, C.R. G9 92
Guanacaure, Cerro, mtn., Hond. D7 92
Guanaceví, Mex. E7 90
Guanache, stm., Peru B4 82
Guanahacabibes, Golfo de, b., Cuba C2 94
Guanaja, Hond. A9 92
Guanaja, Isla de, i., Hond. A9 92
Guanajay, Cuba C3 94
Guanajuato, Mex. G9 90
Guanajuato, state, Mex. G9 90
Guanambi, Braz. C7 79
Guanaparo, Caño, stm., Ven. C8 84
Guañape, Islas, is., Peru C2 82
Guanare, Ven. C8 84
Guanare, stm., Ven. C8 84
Guanarito, Ven. C8 84
Guanay, Bol. F8 82
Guanay, Cerro, mtn., Ven. E9 84
Guanbuqiao, China F3 34
Guandacol, Arg. E4 80
Guandanghu, China E2 34
Guandian, China C7 34
Guane, Cuba C2 94
Guang'an, China E8 30
Guangde, China E8 34
Guangdong (Kwangtung), prov., China G9 30
Guanghua, China E9 30
Guangnan, China G8 30
Guangrao, China F6 32
Guangxi Zhuangzu Zizhiqu (Kwangsi Chuang), prov., China G8 30
Guangyuan, China E8 30
Guangzhou (Canton), China L2 34
Guanhães, Braz. E7 79
Guanipa, stm., Ven. C11 84
Guankou, China E4 34
Guano, Ec. H3 84
Guanqian, China E6 34
Guanqiaopu, China D1 34
Guanta, Ven. B10 84
Guantánamo, Cuba D7 94
Guantao (Nanguantao), China G3 32
Guantou, China G9 34
Guanxian, China E7 30
Guanyintang, China D1 34
Guanzhuang, China F2 32
Guanzhuang, China C3 34
Guapi, Col. F4 84
Guapiara, Braz. H4 79
Guápiles, C.R. G11 92
Guaporé, Braz. E13 80
Guaporé (Itenes), stm., S.A. E10 82
Guaqui, Bol. G7 82
Guará, stm., Braz. B6 79
Guarabira, Braz. E11 76
Guaraçaí, Braz. F3 79
Guaraci, Braz. F4 79
Guaraciaba, Braz. D7 79
Guaramirim, Braz. D14 80
Guaranda, Ec. H3 84
Guaraniaçu, Braz. C12 80
Guarani das Missões, Braz. E11 80
Guarani de Goiás, Braz. B5 79
Guarapari, Braz. F8 79
Guarapuava, Braz. C13 80
Guaraqueçaba, Braz. C14 80
Guararé, Pan. D2 84
Guaratinguetá, Braz. G6 79
Guaratuba, Braz. C14 80
Guarda, Port. E4 16
Guardafui, Cape see Caseyr, c., Som. F11 56
Guardavalle, Italy K11 18
Guardia Escolta, Arg. E7 80
Guardiagrele, Italy G9 18
Guardo, Spain C7 16
Guareña, Spain G5 16
Guarenas, Ven. B9 84
Guariba, stm., Braz. C11 82
Guarico, Ven. C8 84
Guárico, state, Ven. C9 84
Guárico, stm., Ven. C9 84
Guárico, Embalse del, res., Ven. C9 84
Guariquito, stm., Ven. D9 84
Guarizama, Hond. C8 92
Guarulhos, Braz. G5 79
Guasare, stm., Ven. B6 84
Guasave, Mex. E5 90
Guasdualito, Ven. D7 84
Guasipati, Ven. D12 84
Guastalla, Italy E5 18
Guastatoya, Guat. C4 92
Guatajiagua, El Sal. D6 92
Guatemala, Guat. C4 92
Guatemala, dept., Guat. C4 92
Guatemala, ctry., N.A. E6 88
Guateque, Col. E6 84
Guatimozín, Arg. G7 80
Guatopo, Parque Nacional, Ven. C9 84
Guatraché, Arg. I7 80
Guaviare, ter., Col. F6 84
Guaviare, stm., Col. F8 84
Guaxupé, Braz. F5 79
Guayabal, Cuba D6 94
Guayabal, Ven. C9 84
Guayabero, stm., Col. F6 84
Guayacán, Chile E3 80
Guayama, P.R. F11 94
Guayambre, stm., Hond. C8 92
Guayape, Hond. C8 92
Guayape, stm., Hond. C9 92
Guayapo, stm., Ven. E9 84
Guayaquil, Ec. I32 126
Guayaquil, Golfo de, b., S.A. I2 84
Guayaramerín, Bol. D9 82
Guayas, prov., Ec. H2 84
Guayas, stm., Col. G5 84
Guayas, stm., Ec. I3 84
Guayatayoc, Laguna de, l., Arg. B6 80
Guaycora, Mex. C5 90
Guaymas, Mex. D4 90
Guayquiraró, stm., Arg. F9 80
Guayuriba, stm., Col. F6 84
Guazacapán, Guat. C4 92
Guazapares, Mex. D5 90
Guazárachi, Mex. D6 90
Guba, Eth. L8 60
Gubacha, Russia F9 26
Gubbio, Italy F7 18
Guben, Ger. D14 10
Gubin, Pol. D14 10
Gubkin, Russia G5 26
Gucheng, China G9 30
Gūdalūr, India G4 46
Gudermes, Russia I7 26
Gudianzi, China D5 34
Gudiyāttam, India F5 46
Gūdūr, India E5 46
Guebwiller, Fr. E14 14
Güéjar, stm., Col. F6 84
Guelma, Alg. B14 62
Guelph, Ont., Can. G15 110
Guémené-sur-Scorff, Fr. D3 14
Guené, Benin F11 64
Guérande, Fr. E4 14
Guercif, Mor. C9 62
Güere, stm., Ven. C10 84
Guéréda, Chad J2 60
Guéret, Fr. F8 14
Guerneville, Ca., U.S. F2 124
Guernsey, Wy., U.S. B12 120
Guernsey, dep., Eur. F7 4
Guerrero, Mex. C6 90
Guerrero, state, Mex. I9 90
Guerzim, Alg. F10 62
Guessou-Sud, Benin F11 64
Gueydan, La., U.S. L4 114
Gugang, China G2 34
Guge, mtn., Eth. N9 60
Guia, Braz. F13 82
Guía de Isora, Spain O24 17b
Guia Lopes da Laguna, Braz. I13 82
Guibes, Nmb. F3 66
Guicán, Col. D6 84
Guichen, Fr. E5 14
Guichón, Ur. G10 80
Guidan Roumji, Niger E13 64
Guide, China D7 30
Guide Rock, Ne., U.S. K9 118
Guidigri, Niger E14 64
Guidimouni, Niger E14 64
Guiding, China A9 40
Guifujie, China E8 30
Guiglo, I.C. H6 64
Güija, Lago de, l., N.A. C5 92
Guildford, Eng., U.K. J13 8
Guildhall, Vt., U.S. C15 108
Guilford, Me., U.S. B17 108
Guilin (Kweilin), China B11 40
Guillaume-Delisle, Lac, l., Que., Can. E17 96
Guillaumes, Fr. H13 14
Güimar, Spain O24 17b
Guimarães, Port. D3 16
Guin, Al., U.S. I9 114
Guinea (Guinée), ctry., Afr. F4 54
Guinea, Gulf of, b., Afr. H7 52
Guinea-Bissau (Guiné-Bissau), ctry., Afr. F3 54
Guinecourt, Lac, l., Que., Can. B4 106
Güines, Cuba C3 94
Guînes, Fr. B8 14
Guingamp, Fr. D3 14
Güinope, Hond. D8 92
Guiones, Punta, c., C.R. H9 92
Guiping, China C11 40
Guir, Hammada du, des., Afr. E9 62
Guir, Oued, val., Afr. E9 62
Güira de Melena, Cuba C3 94
Guiraí, stm., Braz. G2 79
Guiratinga, Braz. D2 79
Güiria, Ven. B11 84
Guiricema, Braz. F7 79
Guise, Fr. C10 14
Güisisil, mtn., Nic. E8 92
Guita Koulouba, Cen. Afr. Rep. O2 60
Guitou, China K2 34
Guîtres, Fr. G6 14
Guiuan, Phil. C8 38
Guixi, China G6 34
Guixian, China C10 40
Guiyang (Kweiyang), China A9 40
Güiza, stm., Col. G3 84
Guizhou (Kweichow), prov., China F8 30
Gujarāt, state, India I4 44
Gujrānwāla, Pak. D6 44
Gujrāt, Pak. D6 44
Gulbarga, India D4 46
Gulbene, Lat. D9 22
Guledagudda, India D3 46
Guleitou, China L6 34
Gulf Hammock, Fl., U.S. J4 112
Gulfport, Fl., U.S. L4 112
Gulfport, Ms., U.S. L7 114
Gulf Shores, Al., U.S. L9 114
Gulgong, Austl. I8 70
Gulistān, Pak. E2 44
Gulistan, Uzb. I11 26
Gull Lake, Sask., Can. H6 104
Gull Lake, l., Alta., Can. E21 102
Gull Lake, l., Ont., Can. G23 104
Gullrock Lake, l., Ont., Can. H21 104
Güllük, Tur. L11 20
Gulnam, Sud. N5 60
Gülpınar, Tur. J10 20
Guluy, Eth. J9 60
Gumal (Gowmal), stm., Asia D3 44
Gumare, Bots. B6 66
Gumiao, China C2 34
Gummersbach, Ger. D7 10
Gummi, Nig. E12 64
Gümüşhane, Tur. A5 48
Guna, India H7 44
Gundagai, Austl. J8 70
Gungu, Zaire C3 58
Gunisao, stm., Man., Can. E17 104
Gunisao Lake, l., Man., Can. E18 104
Gunnar, Sask., Can. E11 96
Gunnbjørn Fjeld, mtn., Grnld. C17 86
Gunnedah, Austl. H9 70
Gunnison, Co., U.S. F10 120
Gunnison, Ut., U.S. E5 120
Gunnison, stm., Co., U.S. F8 120
Guntakal, India E4 46
Guntersville, Al., U.S. H10 114
Guntersville Lake, res., Al., U.S. H10 114
Guntūr, India D6 46
Gunungsitoli, Indon. N4 40
Gunzenhausen, Ger. F10 10
Guolutan, China C4 34
Guozhuang, China H5 32
Gupei, China I5 32
Guraferda, Eth. N8 60
Gura-Galbena, Mol. C12 20
Gurara, stm., Nig. G13 64
Gurdāspur, India D6 44
Gurdon, Ar., U.S. I3 114
Güre, Tur. K13 20
Gurgueia, stm., Braz. E10 76
Guri, Embalse de, res., Ven. D11 84
Gurjev, Kaz. H8 26
Gurjevsk, Russia G3 22
Gurjevsk, Russia G15 26
Gurupá, Braz. D8 76
Gurupi, Braz. F9 76
Gurupi, stm., Braz. D9 76
Gusau, Nig. E13 64
Gus'-Chrustal'nyj, Russia F23 22
Gusev, Russia G5 22
Gusevskij, Russia F23 22
Gushanzi, China C8 32
Gushi, China C4 34
Gushikawa, Japan U2 37b
Gusino, Russia G14 22
Gusinoozersk, Russia G13 28
Guspini, Italy J3 18
Gustavus, Ak., U.S. G27 100
Gustine, Ca., U.S. G5 124
Gustine, Tx., U.S. H8 116
Güstrow, Ger. B12 10
Gus'-Železnyj, Russia F24 22
Gütersloh, Ger. D8 10
Guthrie, Ky., U.S. F9 114
Guthrie, Ok., U.S. D9 116
Guthrie, Tx., U.S. F6 116
Guthrie Center, Ia., U.S. J13 118
Guthrie Lake, l., Man., Can. C14 104
Gutian, China I7 34
Gutiérrez, Bol. H10 82
Gutiérrez Zamora, Mex. G11 90
Guttenberg, Ia., U.S. H5 110
Gutu, Zimb. B10 66
Guwāhāti, India G14 44
Guxian, China F9 32
Guxiansi, China C5 34
Guyana, ctry., S.A. B7 76
Guyandotte, stm., W.V., U.S. I4 108
Guyi, China J7 34
Guymon, Ok., U.S. C5 116
Guyot, Mount, mtn., U.S. D3 112
Guyra, Austl. H9 70
Guysborough, N.S., Can. G12 106
Guyton, Ga., U.S. G5 112
Guyuan, China D8 30
Guzar, Uzb. J11 26
Guzhu, China I5 34
Guzmán, Mex. B6 90
Guzmán, Laguna, l., Mex. B6 90
Gvardejsk, Russia G4 22
Gvozdec, Ukr. A9 20
Gwa, Burma F3 40
Gwadabawa, Nig. E12 64
Gwādar, Pak. I17 48
Gwai, Zimb. B8 66
Gwāl Haidarzai, Pak. E3 44
Gwalior, India G8 44
Gwanda, Zimb. C9 66
Gwātar Bay, b., Asia I16 48
Gwent, co., Wales, U.K. J11 8
Gweru, Zimb. B9 66
Gweta, Bots. C7 66
Gwinn, Mi., U.S. D8 110
Gwinner, N.D., U.S. E10 118
Gwynedd, co., Wales, U.K. H9 8
Gy, Fr. E12 14
Gyangzê, China F13 44
Gyaring Co, l., China E13 44
Gyaring Hu, l., China E6 30
Gydanskaja guba, b., Russia C13 26
Gydanskij poluostrov, pen., Russia C13 26
Gyirong, China F11 44
Gym Peak, mtn., N.M., U.S. L9 120
Gympie, Austl. F10 70
Gyobingauk, Burma E3 40
Gyoma, Hung. I20 10
Gyöngyös, Hung. H19 10
Győr, Hung. H17 10
Győr-Sopron, co., Hung. H17 10
Gypsum, Co., U.S. E10 120
Gypsum, Ks., U.S. M10 118
Gypsum Point, c., N.W. Ter., Can. D10 96
Gypsumville, Man., Can. G16 104
Gyula, Hung. I21 10

H

Haag in Oberbayern, Ger. G12 10
Haalenberg, Nmb. F2 66
Haaltert, Bel. G5 12
Haapajärvi, Fin. J19 6
Haapamäki, Fin. J19 6
Haapsalu, Est. C6 22
Ha'Arava (Wādī al-'Arabah), val., Asia G4 50
Ha'Arava (Wādī al-Jayb), val., Asia H4 50
Haarlem, Neth. D6 12
Habarūt, Yemen F8 47
Habbān, Yemen G5 47
Habbūsh, Leb. B4 50
Habermehl Peak, mtn., Ant. C3 73
Habiganj, Bngl. H14 44
Habomai-shotō see Malaja Kuril'skaja Gr'ada, is., Russia d21 36a
Hache, Lac la, l., B.C., Can. F13 102
Hachijō-jima, i., Japan E14 30
Hachinohe, Japan G16 36
Hachiōji, Japan L14 36
Hacienda Miravalles, C.R. G9 92
Hacienda Murciélago, C.R. G9 92
Hackberry, Az., U.S. I3 120
Hackberry, La., U.S. M3 114
Hackensack, N.J., U.S. G12 108
Hackett, Ar., U.S. G2 114
Hackettstown, N.J., U.S. G12 108
Hackleburg, Al., U.S. H9 114
Hadalīya, Sud. I9 60
Ḥadd, Ra's al-, c., Oman C11 47
Haddam, Ks., U.S. L10 118
Haddington, Scot., U.K. F11 8
Haddock, Ga., U.S. F3 112
Hadejia, Nig. E14 64
Hadejia, stm., Nig. E14 64
Hadera, Isr. D3 50
Hadera, stm., Asia D3 50
Hadley Bay, b., N.W. Ter., Can. B11 96
Hadlock, Wa., U.S. B3 122
Hadong, Viet. D8 40
Ḥaḍramawt, reg., Yemen G6 47
Haeju, N. Kor. E13 32
Haenam, S. Kor. I14 32
Hafford, Sask., Can. F7 104
Haffouz, Tun. N4 18
Hafīrat al-'Ayda, Sau. Ar. H5 48
Hafnarfjörður, Ice. B3 6a
Haft Gel, Iran F10 48
Hafun, Ras, c., Som. F11 56
Hagan, Ga., U.S. G5 112
Hagen, Ger. D7 10
Hagensborg, B.C., Can. E8 102
Hagere Hiywet, Eth. M9 60
Hagere Selam, Eth. N10 60
Hagerman, Id., U.S. H11 122
Hagerman, N.M., U.S. F2 116
Hagerstown, In., U.S. C11 114
Hagerstown, Md., U.S. H9 108
Hagersville, Ont., Can. H15 110
Hagetmau, Fr. I6 14
Haggin, Mount, mtn., Mt., U.S. D12 122
Ha Giang, Viet. C8 40
Hagondange, Fr. C13 14
Hague, Sask., Can. F8 104
Hague, N.D., U.S. E8 118
Hague, Cap de la, c., Fr. C5 14
Haguenau, Fr. D14 14
Hagues Peak, mtn., Co., U.S. D11 120
Hahaïa, Com. K15 67a
Hahira, Ga., U.S. I3 112
Haian Shanmo, mts., Tai. L10 34
Haicheng, China C10 32
Haïdra, Tun. N3 18
Hai Duong, Viet. D9 40
Haifa see Hefa, Isr. C4 50
Haifeng, China M4 34
Haig, Austl. F5 68
Haig, Mount, mtn., Can. H20 102
Haigler, Ne., U.S. K6 118
Haikang (Leizhou), China D11 40
Haikou, China D11 40
Ḥā'il, Sau. Ar. H6 48
Hailākāndi, India H15 44
Hailar, China B10 30
Hailar, stm., China B11 30
Hailey, Id., U.S. G11 122
Haileybury, Ont., Can. C16 110
Haileyville, Ok., U.S. E11 116
Hailong (Meihekou), China A13 32
Hailun, China B12 30
Haimen, China G10 34
Haimen, China L5 34
Hainan, prov., China H8 30
Hainan Dao, i., China E10 40
Hainaut, prov., Bel. G4 12
Hainaut, hist. reg., Eur. H4 12
Haines, Ak., U.S. G27 100
Haines, Or., U.S. F8 122
Haines City, Fl., U.S. K5 112
Haines Junction, Yukon, Can. F26 100
Hainfeld, Aus. G15 10
Hai Phong, Viet. D9 40
Haiti (Haïti), ctry., N.A. E8 94
Haitou, China I7 32
Haiyaopu, China A6 40
Haizhou, China A8 34
Hajdú-Bihar, co., Hung. H21 10
Hajdúböszörmény, Hung. H21 10
Hajdúnánás, Hung. H21 10
Hajeb el Ayoun, Tun. N4 18
Haji Langar, China C8 44
Hājīpur, India H11 44
Hajjah, Yemen G3 47
Hajnówka, Pol. C23 10
Ḥakīm, Abyār al-, well, Libya B2 60
Hakkâri, Tur. C7 48
Hakodate, Japan F15 36a
Hakui, Japan K11 36
Halab (Aleppo), Syria C4 48
Halabjah, Iraq D8 48
Halachó, Mex. G14 90
Halā'ib, Egypt F9 60
Halaula, Hi., U.S. q18 125a
Halawa, Cape, c., Hi., U.S. p17 125a
Halawotelake, China B14 44
Halberstadt, Ger. D11 10
Halbrite, Sask., Can. I11 104
Haldwāni, India F8 44
Hale, Mo., U.S. C3 114
Haleakala Crater, crat., Hi., U.S. q17 125a
Haleakala National Park, Hi., U.S. q17 125a
Hale Center, Tx., U.S. E5 116
Haleyville, Al., U.S. H9 114
Halfmoon Bay, B.C., Can. H11 102
Halfway, Md., U.S. H9 108
Halfway, Or., U.S. F8 122
Halfway, stm., B.C., Can. E8 96
Halfway Lake, l., Man., Can. C16 104
Haliburton, Ont., Can. E17 110
Halifax, Austl. B7 70
Halifax, N.S., Can. H10 106
Halifax, N.C., U.S. C9 112
Halifax, Va., U.S. C8 112
Halifax, Canadian Forces Base, mil., N.S., Can. H10 106
Halifax Bay, b., Austl. B7 70
Halifax Citadel National Historic Park, N.S., Can. H10 106
Halifax Harbour, b., N.S., Can. H10 106
Hallam Peak, mtn., B.C., Can. E16 102
Hallandale, Fl., U.S. N6 112
Hallands Län, co., Swe. M13 6
Halla-san, mtn., S. Kor. E12 30
Halle (Hal), Bel. G5 12
Halle, Ger. D11 10
Hallein, Aus. H13 10
Hallettsville, Tx., U.S. J10 116
Halliday, N.D., U.S. D5 118
Hall in Tirol, Aus. H11 10
Hall Lake, l., N.W. Ter., Can. C16 96
Hällnäs, Swe. I16 6
Hallock, Mn., U.S. C11 118
Hallowell, Me., U.S. C17 108
Hall Peninsula, pen., N.W. Ter., Can. D19 96
Halls, Tn., U.S. G7 114
Hallsberg, Swe. L14 6
Halls Creek, Austl. C5 68
Hallstavik, Swe. K16 6
Hallstead, Pa., U.S. F11 108
Hallsville, Mo., U.S. C4 114
Hallsville, Tx., U.S. J2 114
Halma, Bel. H7 12
Halmahera, i., Indon. E8 38
Halmahera, Laut (Halmahera Sea), Indon. F8 38
Halmstad, Swe. M13 6
Halsey, Ne., U.S. J7 118
Halsey, Or., U.S. F2 122
Hälsingborg see Helsingborg, Swe. M13 6
Halstad, Mn., U.S. D11 118
Halstead, Ks., U.S. M10 118
Haltern, Ger. D7 10
Haltiatunturi, mtn., Eur. G17 6
Haltom City, Tx., U.S. G9 116
Halton Hills, Ont., Can. G16 110
Halvorson, Mount, mtn., B.C., Can. D14 102
Hamad, Sud. J7 60
Hamada, Japan M7 36
Hamadān, Iran D10 48
Ḥamāh, Syria D4 48
Hamale, Ghana F8 64
Hamamatsu, Japan M12 36
Hamar, Nor. K12 6
Ḥamāṭah, Jabal, mtn., Egypt I3 48
Hamber Provincial Park, B.C., Can. E17 102
Hamburg, Ger. B9 10
Hamburg, Ar., U.S. I5 114
Hamburg, Ia., U.S. K12 118
Hamburg, N.J., U.S. F12 108
Hamburg, N.Y., U.S. E8 108
Hamburg, Pa., U.S. G11 108
Hamdānah, Sau. Ar. E2 47
Hamden, Ct., U.S. F14 108
Hamden, Oh., U.S. H4 108
Hämeen lääni, prov., Fin. K19 6
Hämeenlinna, Fin. K19 6
Hameln, Ger. C9 10
Hamersley Range, mts., Austl. D3 68
Hamersley Range National Park, Austl. D3 68
Hamhŭng, N. Kor. D15 32
Hami, China C5 30
Hamilton, Austl. K5 70
Hamilton, Ber. B12 88
Hamilton, Ont., Can. G16 110
Hamilton, N.Z. B5 72
Hamilton, Scot., U.K. F9 8
Hamilton, Al., U.S. H9 114
Hamilton, Ga., U.S. G2 112
Hamilton, Il., U.S. J4 110
Hamilton, Ks., U.S. N11 118
Hamilton, Mi., U.S. H9 110
Hamilton, Mo., U.S. C3 114
Hamilton, Mt., U.S. D11 122
Hamilton, N.Y., U.S. E11 108
Hamilton, N.C., U.S. D9 112
Hamilton, Oh., U.S. H2 108
Hamilton, Tx., U.S. H8 116
Hamilton, stm., Austl. D4 70
Hamilton, Mount, mtn., Nv., U.S. E10 124
Hamilton City, Ca., U.S. E3 124
Hamilton Creek Indian Reserve, B.C., Can. G14 102
Hamilton Dome, Wy., U.S. A8 120
Hamilton Hotel, Austl. D4 70
Hamilton Inlet, b., Newf., Can. F21 96
Hamilton Sound, strt., Newf., Can. C19 106
Hamina, Fin. K20 6
Hamiota, Man., Can. H14 104
Hāmir, Wādī, val., Asia F7 48
Hamīrpur, India H9 44
Hamlet, N.C., U.S. E7 112
Hamlin, Tx., U.S. G6 116
Hamlin, W.V., U.S. I4 108
Hamm, Ger. D7 10
Hammamet, Alg. N2 18
Hammamet, Tun. M5 18
Hammamet, Golfe de, b., Tun. M5 18
Hammam Lif, Tun. M5 18
Hammār, Hawr al-, l., Iraq F9 48
Hamme, Bel. F5 12
Hammerdal, Swe. J14 6
Hammerfest, Nor. F18 6
Hammon, Ok., U.S. D7 116
Hammond, In., U.S. A9 114
Hammond, La., U.S. L6 114
Hammond, Wi., U.S. F3 110
Hammondsport, N.Y., U.S. E9 108
Hammonton, N.J., U.S. H12 108
Hamoyet, Jabal, mtn., Afr. I10 60
Hampden, Newf., Can. C17 106
Hampden, Me., U.S. C18 108
Hampden, N.D., U.S. C9 118
Hampden Sydney, Va., U.S. B8 112
Hampshire, Il., U.S. H7 110
Hampshire, co., Eng., U.K. J12 8
Hampstead, N.C., U.S. E9 112
Hampton, N.B., Can. G8 106
Hampton, Ar., U.S. I4 114
Hampton, Fl., U.S. J4 112
Hampton, Ga., U.S. F2 112
Hampton, Ia., U.S. H2 110
Hampton, Ne., U.S. K10 118
Hampton, N.H., U.S. E16 108
Hampton, N.J., U.S. G12 108
Hampton, S.C., U.S. G5 112
Hampton, Tn., U.S. C4 112
Hampton, Va., U.S. B10 112
Hampton Bays, N.Y., U.S. G14 108
Hampton Butte, mtn., Or., U.S. G5 122

Name — Map Ref. — Page

Hamra, As Saquia al, val., W. Sah. G4 62
Hams Fork, stm., Wy., U.S. C6 120
Hamyang, S. Kor. H15 32
Han, stm., China E9 30
Hana, Hi., U.S. q18 125a
Hanahan, S.C., U.S. G6 112
Hanamaki, Japan H16 36
Hanapepe, Hi., U.S. p14 125a
Hanau, Ger. E8 10
Hanbury, stm., N.W. Ter., Can. D11 96
Hanceville, B.C., Can. F11 102
Hanceville, Al., U.S. H10 114
Hancheng, China D9 30
Hancock, Md., U.S. H8 108
Hancock, Mi., U.S. C7 110
Hancock, Mn., U.S. F12 118
Hancock, N.Y., U.S. F11 108
Hancock, Wi., U.S. F6 110
Handa, Japan M11 36
Handa, Som. F11 56
Handan, China G2 32
Handsworth, Sask., Can. I11 104
Handub, Sud. H9 60
HaNegev (Negev Desert), reg., Isr. G3 50
Haney, B.C., Can. H12 102
Hanford, Ca., U.S. H6 124
Han'gang, China I2 32
Han-gang, stm., Asia F14 32
Hangchow see Hangzhou, China E9 34
Hanggin Houqi, China C8 30
Hanggin Qi, China D8 30
Hangö (Hanko), Fin. L18 6
Hangu, China D5 32
Hangu, Pak. D4 44
Hangzhou (Hangchow), China E9 34
Hangzhou Wan (Hangchow Bay), b., China E10 34
Hani, Tur. B6 48
Hanīsh, is., Yemen H3 47
Hanita, Isr. B4 50
Hanjiang, China J8 34
Hankey, S. Afr. I7 66
Hankinson, N.D., U.S. E11 118
Hanko see Hangö, Fin. D12 4
Hankow see Wuhan, China E3 34
Hanley, Sask., Can. G8 104
Hanmer, Ont., Can. D15 110
Hanna, Alta., Can. F23 102
Hanna, Ok., U.S. D11 116
Hanna, Wy., U.S. C10 120
Hanna City, Il., U.S. J6 110
Hannaford, N.D., U.S. D9 118
Hannah, N.D., U.S. C9 118
Hannah Bay, b., Ont., Can. F17 96
Hannibal, Mo., U.S. C5 114
Hannover, Ger. C9 10
Ha Noi, Viet. D8 40
Hanover, Ont., Can. F14 110
Hanover, Il., U.S. H5 110
Hanover, In., U.S. D11 114
Hanover, Ks., U.S. L11 118
Hanover, N.H., U.S. D14 108
Hanover, N.M., U.S. L8 120
Hanover, Pa., U.S. H10 108
Hanover, Va., U.S. B9 112
Hanover see Hannover, Ger. C9 10
Hansard, B.C., Can. C13 102
Hānsi, India F6 44
Hanska, Mn., U.S. G13 118
Hanson Lake, l., Sask., Can. D12 104
Hant's Harbour, Newf., Can. D20 106
Hantsport, N.S., Can. G9 106
Hantzsch, stm., N.W. Ter., Can. C18 96
Hanumangarh, India F6 44
Hanušovice, Czech. E16 10
Hanwood, Austl. J7 70
Hanzhong, China E8 30
Hanzhuang, China I5 32
Haohekou, China G1 34
Hāora, India I13 44
Hapeville, Ga., U.S. F2 112
Happy, Tx., U.S. E5 116
Happy Camp, Ca., U.S. C2 124
Happy Jack, Az., U.S. J5 120
Happy Valley-Goose Bay, Newf., Can. F20 96
Hāpur, India F7 44
Haquira, Peru F5 82
Harad, Sau. Ar. B6 47
Harad, Jabal al-, mtn., Jord. I5 50
Harare (Salisbury), Zimb. A10 66
Harash, Bi'r al-, well, Libya E2 60
Harbin, China B12 30
Harbor, Or., U.S. H1 122
Harbor Beach, Mi., U.S. G13 110
Harbor Springs, Mi., U.S. E11 110
Harbour Breton, Newf., Can. E18 106
Harbour Buffett, Newf., Can. E19 106
Harbour Deep, Newf., Can. B17 106
Harbour Grace, Newf., Can. E20 106
Harbourville, N.S., Can. G9 106
Harcuvar Mountains, mts., Az., U.S. K3 120
Harda, India I7 44
Hardangerfjorden, Nor. K10 6
Hardeeville, S.C., U.S. G5 112
Harderwijk, Neth. D8 12
Hardesty, Ok., U.S. C5 116
Hardin, Il., U.S. C6 114
Hardin, Mt., U.S. E18 122
Harding, S. Afr. H9 66
Harding Lake, l., Man., Can. B16 104
Hardinsburg, Ky., U.S. E10 114
Hardisty, Alta., Can. E23 102
Hardisty Lake, l., N.W. Ter., Can. D9 96
Hardoi, India G9 44
Hardtner, Ks., U.S. N9 118
Hardwick, Ga., U.S. F3 112
Hardwick, Vt., U.S. C14 108
Hardwood, La., U.S. L5 114
Hardy, Ar., U.S. F5 114
Hardy, Ne., U.S. K10 118
Hardy Bay, b., N.W. Ter., Can. A9 96
Hare, Mount, mtn., Yukon, Can. C26 100
Hare Bay, Newf., Can. D19 106
Hare Bay, b., Newf., Can. A18 106
Hare Indian, stm., N.W. Ter., Can. C31 100
Harer, Eth. G9 56
Hareto, Eth. M9 60
Hargeysa, Som. G9 56
Harghita, co., Rom. C9 20
Hargrave, stm., Man., Can. D15 104
Hargrave Lake, l., Man., Can. D15 104
Har Hu, l., China D6 30
Hari, stm., Indon. F3 38
Haría, Spain N27 17b
Haridwār, India F8 44
Harihar, India E3 46
Haringvliet, strt., Neth. E5 12
Harīrūd (Tedžen), stm., Asia C16 48
Harkers Island, N.C., U.S. E10 112
Harlan, Ia., U.S. J12 118
Harlan, Ky., U.S. C3 112
Harlan County Lake, res., Ne., U.S. K8 118
Harlem, Fl., U.S. M6 112
Harlem, Ga., U.S. F4 112
Harlem, Mt., U.S. B17 122
Harlingen, Neth. B7 12
Harlingen, Tx., U.S. M9 116
Harlowton, Mt., U.S. D16 122
Harman, W.V., U.S. I7 108
Harmanli, Bul. H9 20
Harmony, In., U.S. C9 114
Harmony, Mn., U.S. G3 110
Harney Peak, mtn., S.D., U.S. H4 118
Härnösand, Swe. J15 6
Haro, Spain C9 16
Haro, Cabo, c., Mex. D4 90
Harper, Lib. I6 64
Harper, Ks., U.S. N9 118
Harper, Tx., U.S. I7 116
Harqin Qi (Jinshan), China B6 32
Harrān al-'Awāmīd, Syria B7 50
Harrell, Ar., U.S. I4 114
Harricana, stm., Can. F17 96
Harriman, Tn., U.S. D2 112
Harrington, De., U.S. I11 108
Harrington, Me., U.S. C19 108
Harrington, Wa., U.S. C7 122
Harris, Sask., Can. G7 104
Harris, Mn., U.S. E3 110
Harrisburg, Ar., U.S. G6 114
Harrisburg, Il., U.S. E8 114
Harrisburg, Ne., U.S. J4 118
Harrisburg, Or., U.S. F2 122
Harrisburg, Pa., U.S. G10 108
Harrismith, S. Afr. G9 66
Harrison, Ar., U.S. F3 114
Harrison, Id., U.S. C9 122
Harrison, Mi., U.S. F11 110
Harrison, Ne., U.S. I4 118
Harrison, Cape, c., Newf., Can. F21 96
Harrisonburg, La., U.S. K5 114
Harrisonburg, Va., U.S. I8 108
Harrison Islands, is., N.W. Ter., Can. C14 96
Harrison Lake, l., B.C., Can. H13 102
Harrisonville, Mo., U.S. D2 114
Harriston, Ont., Can. G15 110
Harriston, Ms., U.S. K5 114
Harrisville, Mi., U.S. F12 110
Harrisville, N.Y., U.S. C11 108
Harrisville, W.V., U.S. H5 108
Harrodsburg, Ky., U.S. E12 114
Harrogate, Eng., U.K. G12 8
Harrold, Tx., U.S. E7 116
Harrop Lake, l., Man., Can. F19 104
Harrow, Ont., Can. H13 110
Harrowsmith, Ont., Can. F19 110
Harry S. Truman Reservoir, res., Mo., U.S. D3 114
Harsīn, Iran D9 48
Hart, Mi., U.S. G9 110
Hart, Tx., U.S. E4 116
Hart, stm., Yukon, Can. D26 100
Hart, Lake, l., Austl. H2 70
Hartberg, Aus. H15 10
Hartford, Al., U.S. G11 116
Hartford, Ar., U.S. G2 114
Hartford, Ct., U.S. F14 108
Hartford, Ks., U.S. M12 118
Hartford, Ky., U.S. E10 114
Hartford, Mi., U.S. H9 110
Hartford, S.D., U.S. H11 118
Hartford, Wi., U.S. G7 110
Hartford City, In., U.S. B11 114
Hartington, Ne., U.S. I10 118
Hartland, N.B., Can. F6 106
Hartland, Me., U.S. C17 108
Hartlepool, Eng., U.K. G12 8
Hartley, Ia., U.S. H12 118
Hartley, Tx., U.S. D4 116
Hartley Bay, B.C., Can. D5 102
Hart Mountain, mtn., Man., Can. F13 104
Hartney, Man., Can. I14 104
Harts, stm., Afr. G7 66
Hartselle, Al., U.S. H10 114
Hartshorne, Ok., U.S. E11 116
Hartsville, S.C., U.S. E6 112
Hartsville, Tn., U.S. F10 114
Hartville, Mo., U.S. E4 114
Hartwell, Ga., U.S. E4 112
Hartwell Lake, res., U.S. E4 112
Harvard, Il., U.S. H7 110
Harvard, Ne., U.S. K9 118
Harvey, N.B., Can. G9 106
Harvey, Il., U.S. I8 110
Harvey, N.D., U.S. D8 118
Harwich, Eng., U.K. J15 8
Haryāna, state, India F7 44
Harz, mts., Ger. D10 10
Hasā, Bi'r al-, well, Egypt J3 48
Hasan Kīādeh, Iran C10 48
Hāsbānī, Nahr al-, stm., Asia B5 50
Hasenkamp, Arg. F9 80
Hashā', Jabal al-, mtn., Yemen H4 47
Hāsilpur, Pak. F5 44
Haskell, Ok., U.S. D11 116
Haskell, Tx., U.S. F7 116
Haskovo, Bul. H9 20
Hasperos Canyon, val., N.M., U.S. K11 120
Hassan, India F4 46
Hasselt, Bel. G7 12
Hassi Bel Guebbour, Alg. F14 62
Hassi el Ghella, Alg. J10 16
Hassi Mameche, Alg. J12 16
Hassi Messaoud, Alg. E13 62
Hassi Zehana, Alg. J11 16
Hässleholm, Swe. M13 6
Hastings, Ont., Can. F18 110
Hastings, N.Z. C6 72
Hastings, Eng., U.K. K14 8
Hastings, Fl., U.S. J5 112
Hastings, Mi., U.S. H10 110
Hastings, Mn., U.S. F3 110
Hastings, Ne., U.S. K9 118
Hasty, Co., U.S. M5 118
Haswell, Co., U.S. M4 118
Hatch, N.M., U.S. L9 120
Hatch, Ut., U.S. G4 120
Hatchet Lake, N.S., Can. H10 106
Hatchie, stm., U.S. G7 114
Hatfield, Ar., U.S. H2 114
Hatfield, Pa., U.S. G11 108
Hāthras, India G8 44
Ha Tien, Viet. I8 40
Ha Tinh, Viet. E8 40
Hato Mayor [del Rey], Dom. Rep. E10 94
Hatteras, N.C., U.S. D11 112
Hatteras, Cape, c., N.C., U.S. D11 112
Hatteras Island, i., N.C., U.S. D11 112
Hattiesburg, Ms., U.S. K7 114
Hatton, Al., U.S. H9 114
Hatton, N.D., U.S. D10 118
Hatvan, Hung. H19 10
Hat Yai, Thai. K6 40
Haubstadt, In., U.S. D9 114
Hauge, Nor. L10 6
Haugesund, Nor. L9 6
Haugsdorf, Aus. G16 10
Haultain, stm., Sask., Can. B8 104
Haunstetten, Ger. G10 10
Hauraki Gulf, b., N.Z. B5 72
Haut Atlas, mts., Mor. E7 62
Haute-Corse, dept., Fr. L24 15a
Haute-Garonne, dept., Fr. I8 14
Haute-Loire, dept., Fr. G10 14
Haute-Marne, dept., Fr. D12 14
Hauterive, Que., Can. C5 106
Hautes-Alpes, dept., Fr. H13 14
Haute-Saône, dept., Fr. E13 14
Haute-Savoie, dept., Fr. F13 14
Hautes Fagnes, mts., Eur. E6 10
Hautes-Pyrénées, dept., Fr. I7 14
Haute-Vienne, dept., Fr. G8 14
Haut-Folin, mtn., Fr. E11 14
Hautmont, Fr. B10 14
Haut-Rhin, dept., Fr. E14 14
Hauula, Hi., U.S. p16 125a
Havana, Ar., U.S. G3 114
Havana, Fl., U.S. I2 112
Havana, Il., U.S. B6 114
Havana, N.D., U.S. F10 118
Havana see La Habana, Cuba C3 94
Havasu, Lake, res., U.S. J2 120
Havelock, Ont., Can. F18 110
Havelock, N.C., U.S. E10 112
Haven, Ks., U.S. N10 118
Haverhill, Ma., U.S. E15 108
Hāveri, India E3 46
Haviland, Ks., U.S. N8 118
Havířov, Czech. F18 10
Havlíčkův Brod, Czech. F15 10
Havre, Mt., U.S. B16 122
Havre-Aubert, Que., Can. E12 106
Havre Aubert, Île du, i., Que., Can. E12 106
Havre aux Maisons, Île du, i., Que., Can. E12 106
Havre de Grace, Md., U.S. H10 108
Havre North, Mt., U.S. B16 122
Havre-Saint-Pierre, Que., Can. B10 106
Havsa, Tur. H10 20
Haw, stm., N.C., U.S. D7 112
Hawaii, state, U.S. q16 125a
Hawaii, i., Hi., U.S. r18 125a
Hawaiian Islands, is., Hi., U.S. q16 125a
Hawaiian Ridge F22 126
Hawaii Volcanoes National Park, Hi., U.S. r18 125a
Hawarden, Sask., Can. G8 104
Hawarden, Ia., U.S. I11 118
Hawea, Lake, l., N.Z. F2 72
Hawera, N.Z. C5 72
Hawesville, Ky., U.S. E10 114
Hawi, Hi., U.S. q18 125a
Hawick, Scot., U.K. F11 8
Hawke, Cape, c., Austl. I10 70
Hawke Bay, b., N.Z. C6 72
Hawker, Austl. H3 70
Hawkes, Mount, mtn., Ant. D1 73
Hawkesbury, Ont., Can. B12 108
Hawkesbury Island, i., B.C., Can. D5 102
Hawkins, Tx., U.S. G11 116
Hawkins, Wi., U.S. E5 110
Hawkinsville, Ga., U.S. G3 112
Hawk Junction, Ont., Can. B11 110
Hawk Lake, Ont., Can. I21 104
Hawksbill, mtn., Va., U.S. I8 108
Hawks Nest Point, c., Bah. B7 94
Hawley, Mn., U.S. E11 118
Hawley, Pa., U.S. F11 108
Hawthorne, Fl., U.S. J4 112
Hawthorne, Nv., U.S. F7 124
Hawwārah, Jord. C5 50
Hawza, W. Sah. G5 62
Hawzen, Eth. K10 60
Haxtun, Co., U.S. K5 118
Hay, Austl. J6 70
Hay, stm., Austl. D2 70
Hay, stm., Can. E9 96
Hay, stm., Wi., U.S. E4 110
Hay, Cape, c., N.W. Ter., Can. B10 96
Hay, Mount, mtn., N.A. G26 100
Hayange, Fr. C13 14
Haybān, Sud. L6 60
Hayden, Az., U.S. K6 120
Hayden, Co., U.S. D9 120
Haydenville, Oh., U.S. H4 108
Hayes, La., U.S. L4 114
Hayes, stm., Man., Can. B22 104
Hayes, stm., N.W. Ter., Can. C14 96
Hayes, Mount, mtn., Ak., U.S. E21 100
Hayes Center, Ne., U.S. K6 118
Hayesville, N.C., U.S. D3 112
Hayesville, Or., U.S. F3 122
Hayfield, Mn., U.S. G3 110
Hayfork, Ca., U.S. D2 124
Haykota, Eth. J9 60
Hay Lakes, Alta., Can. D21 102
Haymana, Tur. B2 48
Haynes, Ar., U.S. H6 114
Haynesville, La., U.S. J3 114
Hayneville, Al., U.S. J10 114
Hay River, N.W. Ter., Can. D9 96
Hays, Alta., Can. G23 102
Hays, Ks., U.S. M8 118
Hays, Mt., U.S. C17 122
Hay Springs, Ne., U.S. I5 118
Haystack Mountain, mtn., Nv., U.S. C10 124
Haysville, Ks., U.S. N10 118
Hayti, Mo., U.S. F7 114
Hayti, S.D., U.S. G10 118
Hayward, Ca., U.S. G3 124
Hayward, Wi., U.S. D4 110
Haywood, Man., Can. I16 104
Hazard, Ky., U.S. B3 112
Hazārībāg, India I11 44
Hazebrouck, Fr. B9 14
Hazel, stm., Va., U.S. I9 108
Hazel Green, Wi., U.S. H5 110
Hazelton, B.C., Can. B7 102
Hazelton, Id., U.S. H11 122
Hazelton, N.D., U.S. E7 118
Hazelton Mountains, mts., B.C., Can. C6 102
Hazelwood, N.C., U.S. D3 112
Hazen, Ar., U.S. H5 114
Hazen, N.D., U.S. D6 118
Hazlehurst, Ga., U.S. H4 112
Hazlehurst, Ms., U.S. K6 114
Hazlet, Sask., Can. H6 104
Hazleton, Ia., U.S. H4 110
Hazleton, Pa., U.S. G11 108
Hazor HaGelilit, Isr. C5 50
Head Bay d'Espoir, Newf., Can. E18 106
Headland, Al., U.S. K11 114
Headley, Mount, mtn., Mt., U.S. C10 122
Healdsburg, Ca., U.S. F3 124
Healdton, Ok., U.S. E9 116
Healesville, Austl. K6 70
Healy, Ak., U.S. E20 100
Healy, Ks., U.S. M7 118
Heany Junction, Zimb. C9 66
Heard Island, i., Austl. N11 126
Hearne, Tx., U.S. I10 116
Hearst, Ont., Can. G16 96
Hearst Island, i., Ant. B12 73
Heart, stm., Alta., Can. A17 102
Heart, stm., N.D., U.S. E6 118
Heart Lake, l., Alta., Can. B23 102
Heart Lake Indian Reserve, Alta., Can. B23 102
Heart's Content, Newf., Can. E20 106
Heath, stm., S.A. E7 82
Heath, Pointe, c., Que., Can. C12 106
Heathcote, Austl. K6 70
Heath Springs, S.C., U.S. E6 112
Heathsville, Va., U.S. B10 112
Heavener, Ok., U.S. H2 114
Hebbronville, Tx., U.S. L8 116
Hebei (Hopeh), prov., China D10 30
Heber, Az., U.S. J6 120
Heber, Ca., U.S. L10 124
Heber City, Ut., U.S. D5 120
Heber Springs, Ar., U.S. G4 114
Hebi, China H2 32
Hebrides, is., Scot., U.K. D6 4
Hebron, Newf., Can. E20 96
Hebron, Il., U.S. H7 110
Hebron, In., U.S. A9 114
Hebron, Md., U.S. I11 108
Hebron, Ne., U.S. K10 118
Hebron, N.D., U.S. E5 118
Hebron see Al-Khalīl, Isr. Occ. E4 50
Hebu, China H4 34
Hecate Strait, strt., B.C., Can. D3 102
Hecelchakán, Mex. G14 90
Hechi, China B10 40
Hechingen, Ger. G8 10
Hechuan, China E8 30
Hecla, Man., Can. G18 104
Hecla, S.D., U.S. F9 118
Hecla Island, i., Man., Can. G18 104
Hecla Provincial Park, Man., Can. G18 104
Hectanooga, N.S., Can. H7 106
Hector, Mn., U.S. G13 118
Hédé, Fr. D5 14
He Devil, mtn., Id., U.S. E9 122
Hedian, China C3 34
Hedley, B.C., Can. H14 102
Hedley, Tx., U.S. E6 116
Hedmark, co., Nor. K12 6
Hedrick, Ia., U.S. I3 110
Heerenveen, Neth. C8 12
Heerlen, Neth. G8 12
Hefa (Haifa), Isr. C4 50
Hefei, China D6 34
Heflin, Al., U.S. I11 114
Hegang, China B13 30
Heho, Burma D4 40
Heichengzi, China A9 32
Heide, Ger. A9 10
Heidelberg, Ger. F8 10
Heidelberg, S. Afr. J5 66
Heidelberg, S. Afr. F9 66
Heidelberg, Ms., U.S. K8 114
Heidenheim, Ger. F10 10
Heidenreichstein, Aus. G15 10
Heilbron, S. Afr. F8 66
Heilbronn, Ger. F9 10
Heiligenstadt, Ger. D10 10
Heilin, China H6 32
Heilong (Amur), stm., Asia A12 30
Heilongjiang (Heilungkiang), prov., China B12 30
Heimaey, i., Ice. C3 6a
Heirnkut, Burma H16 44
Heishan, China B10 32
Heishantou, China A13 32
Heisler, Alta., Can. E22 102
Hejian, China E4 32
Hekla, vol., Ice. C4 6a
Hekou, China C7 40
Hel, Pol. A18 10
Helen, Mount, mtn., Austl. C4 70
Helena, Ar., U.S. H6 114
Helena, Mt., U.S. D13 122
Helena, Ok., U.S. C8 116
Helensburgh, Scot., U.K. E9 8
Helenwood, Tn., U.S. C2 112
Helgoland, i., Ger. A7 10
Helgoländer Bucht, b., Ger. A8 10
Heliuji, China B5 34
Hellertown, Pa., U.S. G11 108
Hellín, Spain G10 16
Hell Point, c., N.S., Can. H9 106
Hells Canyon, val., U.S. E9 122
Hells Gate, val., B.C., Can. H13 102
Hell-Ville, Madag. N23 67b
Helmand, stm., Asia D1 44
Helmcken Falls, wtfl, B.C., Can. F14 102
Helmond, Neth. F8 12
Helmstedt, Ger. C11 10
Helper, Ut., U.S. E6 120
Helsingborg, Swe. M13 6
Helsingfors see Helsinki, Fin. K19 6
Helsingør (Elsinore), Den. M13 6
Helsinki (Helsingfors), Fin. K19 6
Helska, Mierzeja, spit, Pol. A18 10
Helvecia, Arg. F8 80
Hemau, Ger. F11 10
Hemel Hempstead, Eng., U.K. J13 8
Hemet, Ca., U.S. K9 124
Hemford, N.S., Can. H9 106
Hemingford, Ne., U.S. I4 118
Hemingway, S.C., U.S. F7 112
Hemphill, Tx., U.S. K3 114
Hempstead, Tx., U.S. I10 116
Hemujing, China F3 32
Henan (Honan), prov., China E9 30
Henderson, Arg. I8 80
Henderson, Ky., U.S. E9 114
Henderson, Mn., U.S. F2 110
Henderson, N.C., U.S. C8 112
Henderson, Ne., U.S. K10 118
Henderson, Nv., U.S. H11 124
Henderson, Tn., U.S. G8 114
Henderson, Tx., U.S. J2 114
Henderson Island, i., Pit. K27 126
Hendersonville, N.C., U.S. D4 112
Hendersonville, Tn., U.S. F10 114
Hendījān, Iran F10 48
Hendricks, Mn., U.S. G11 118
Hendricks, W.V., U.S. H7 108
Henefer, Ut., U.S. C5 120
Hengdaohe, China A11 32
Hengelo, Neth. D10 12
Henggang, China F4 34
Hengshan, China D8 30
Hengshan, China H1 34
Hengshui, China F3 32
Hengxian, China C10 40
Hengyang, China F9 30
Henlopen, Cape, c., De., U.S. I11 108
Hennaya, Alg. K10 16
Hennebont, Fr. E3 14
Hennef, Ger. E7 10
Hennenman, S. Afr. F8 66
Hennepin, Il., U.S. I6 110
Hennessey, Ok., U.S. C9 116
Hennigsdorf, Ger. C13 10
Henniker, N.H., U.S. D15 108
Henning, Mn., U.S. E12 118
Henning, Tn., U.S. G7 114
Henri, Cap, c., Que., Can. C9 106
Henri-Chapelle (Hendrik-Kapelle), Bel. G8 12
Henrietta, N.Y., U.S. D9 108
Henrietta, N.C., U.S. D5 112
Henrietta, Tx., U.S. F8 116
Henrietta Maria, Cape, c., Ont., Can. E16 96
Henri Pittier, Parque Nacional, Ven. B9 84
Henry, Il., U.S. I6 110
Henry, S.D., U.S. G10 118
Henry, Cape, c., Va., U.S. C10 112
Henry, Mount, mtn., Mt., U.S. B10 122
Henryetta, Ok., U.S. D11 116
Henry Kater, Cape, c., N.W. Ter., Can. C19 96
Henrys Fork, stm., U.S. C6 120
Hensall, Ont., Can. G14 110
Hensley, Ar., U.S. H4 114
Hentiesbaai, Nmb. D2 66
Henty, Austl. J7 70
Henzada, Burma F3 40
Hepburn, Sask., Can. F8 104
Hephzibah, Ga., U.S. F4 112
Heping, China K3 34
Heppenheim, Ger. F8 10
Heppner, Or., U.S. E6 122
Hepu (Lianzhou), China D10 40
Heqiao, China D8 34
Herāt, Afg. D17 48
Hérault, dept., Fr. I10 14
Herbert, Sask., Can. H7 104
Herbert, stm., Austl. B6 70
Herberton, Austl. A6 70
Herbignac, Fr. E4 14
Herb Lake, Man., Can. D15 104
Herblet Lake, l., Man., Can. D15 104
Herceg-Novi, Yugo. G2 20
Herculaneum, Mo., U.S. D6 114
Hércules, Mex. C8 90
Heredia, C.R. G10 92
Heredia, prov., C.R. G10 92
Hereford, Az., U.S. M6 120
Hereford, Tx., U.S. E4 116
Hereford and Worcester, co., Eng., U.K. I11 8
Herencia, Spain F8 16
Herentals, Bel. F6 12
Hereroland Oos, dept., Nmb. C5 66
Hereroland Wes, dept., Nmb. C4 66
Herford, Ger. C8 10
Hergla, Tun. M5 18
Herington, Ks., U.S. M11 118
Herisau, Switz. D11 13
Herkimer, N.Y., U.S. D12 108
Herleshausen, Ger. D10 10
Herlong, Ca., U.S. D5 124
Herman, Mn., U.S. F11 118
Herman, Ne., U.S. J11 118
Hermann, Mo., U.S. D5 114
Hermansville, Mi., U.S. E8 110
Hermanus, S. Afr. J4 66
Hermanville, Ms., U.S. K6 114
Hermiston, Or., U.S. E6 122
Hermitage, Newf., Can. E18 106
Hermitage, Ar., U.S. I4 114
Hermitage, Mo., U.S. E3 114
Hermitage Bay, b., Newf., Can. E17 106
Hermleigh, Tx., U.S. G6 116
Hermon, Mount see Shaykh, Jabal ash-, mtn., Asia B5 50
Hermosillo, Mex. C4 90
Hermoso, Cerro, mtn., Ec. H3 84
Hernád, stm., Eur. G21 10
Hernandarias, Para. C11 80
Hernando, Arg. G7 80
Hernando, Fl., U.S. K4 112
Hernando, Ms., U.S. H7 114
Herndon, Ks., U.S. L7 118
Herndon, Pa., U.S. G10 108
Herne, Ger. D7 10
Heroica Zitácuaro, Mex. H9 90
Heron Island, i., Austl. D9 70
Heron Lake, Mn., U.S. H12 118
Herradura, Arg. D9 80
Herreid, S.D., U.S. F7 118
Herrera, Arg. E7 80
Herrera, prov., Pan. I14 92
Herrick Creek, stm., B.C., Can. C13 102
Herrin, Il., U.S. E7 114
Herring Cove, N.S., Can. H10 106
Herring Cove, Ak., U.S. I29 100
Herschel, Sask., Can. G6 104
Herschel Island, i., Yukon, Can. B25 100
Herscher, Il., U.S. I7 110
Hershey, Ne., U.S. J6 118
Hershey, Pa., U.S. G10 108
Herstal, Bel. G8 12
Hertford, N.C., U.S. C10 112
Hertfordshire, co., Eng., U.K. J13 8
Hervey Bay, b., Austl. E10 70
Herzberg, Ger. D13 10
Herzberg [am Harz], Ger. D10 10
Herzliyya, Isr. D3 50
Herzogenburg, Aus. G15 10
Hesdin, Fr. B9 14
Heshangqiao, China A2 34
Heshi, China J7 34
Heshuijian, China E5 34
Hesperia, Mi., U.S. G9 110
Hesperus Mountain, mtn., Co., U.S. G8 120
Hess, stm., Yukon, Can. E28 100
Hessen, state, Ger. E9 10
Hesston, Ks., U.S. M10 118
Hetang, China I8 34
Hetch Hetchy Aqueduct, Ca., U.S. G4 124
Hetou, China K2 34
Hettinger, N.D., U.S. E5 118
Hettstedt, Ger. D11 10
Hetupu, China E5 34
Heuvelton, N.Y., U.S. C11 108
Heves, Hung. H20 10
Heves, co., Hung. H20 10
Hevron, Nahal, val., Asia F3 50
Hexi, China K6 34
Hexian, China G9 30
Heyburn, Id., U.S. H12 122
Heywood, Austl. L4 70
Heyworth, Il., U.S. B8 114
Heze (Caozhou), China H3 32
Hezhen, China F9 34
Hialeah, Fl., U.S. N6 112
Hiawassee, Ga., U.S. E3 112
Hiawatha, Ks., U.S. L12 118
Hiawatha, Ut., U.S. E5 120
Hibbing, Mn., U.S. C3 110
Hibbs, Point, c., Austl. N6 70
Hibernia Reef, rf., Austl. B4 68
Hickman, Ky., U.S. F7 114
Hickman, Ne., U.S. K11 118
Hickman's Harbour, Newf., Can. D20 106
Hickory, Ms., U.S. J7 114
Hickory, N.C., U.S. D5 112
Hickory Flat, Ms., U.S. H7 114
Hicks, Point, c., Austl. K8 70
Hickson Lake, l., Sask., Can. B10 104
Hicksville, Oh., U.S. F2 108
Hico, Tx., U.S. H8 116
Hidalgo, Mex. D10 90
Hidalgo, Mex. E9 90
Hidalgo, Mex. E10 90
Hidalgo, Mex. F8 90
Hidalgo, state, Mex. G10 90
Hidalgo del Parral, Mex. D7 90
Hida-sammyaku, mts., Japan K12 36
Hidrolândia, Braz. D4 79
Hidrolina, Braz. C4 79
Hieflau, Aus. H14 10
Hierro (Ferro), i., Spain P22 17b
Higashine, Japan I15 36
Higashiōsaka, Japan M10 36
Higbee, Mo., U.S. C4 114
Higgins, Tx., U.S. C6 116
Higginsville, Mo., U.S. C3 114
High Bar Indian Reserve, B.C., Can. F13 102
High Hill, stm., Can. B4 104
High Hill, stm., Man., Can. C20 104
High Hill Lake, l., Man., Can. C19 104
Highland, Ca., U.S. J8 124
Highland, Il., U.S. D7 114
Highland, In., U.S. A9 114
Highland, Ks., U.S. L12 118
Highland, prov., Scot., U.K. D8 8
Highland Home, Al., U.S. K10 114
Highland Park, Il., U.S. H8 110
Highland Park, Tx., U.S. G10 116
Highlands, N.J., U.S. G13 108
Highlands, N.C., U.S. D3 112
Highlands, Tx., U.S. J11 116
Highland Springs, Va., U.S. B9 112
Highmore, S.D., U.S. G8 118
High Point, N.C., U.S. D6 112
High Point, mtn., N.J., U.S. F12 108
High Prairie, Alta., Can. B18 102
High River, Alta., Can. G21 102
Highrock Indian Reserve, Man., Can. C14 104
Highrock Lake, l., Man., Can. C14 104
Highrock Lake, l., Sask., Can. A9 104
High Rock Lake, res., N.C., U.S. D6 112
High Springs, Fl., U.S. J4 112
Hightstown, N.J., U.S. G12 108
Highwood, Mt., U.S. C15 122
Highwood, stm., Alta., Can. G20 102
High Wycombe, Eng., U.K. J13 8
Higuera de Abuya, Mex. E6 90
Higuera de Zaragoza, Mex. E5 90
Higüero, Punta, c., P.R. E11 94
Higüey, Dom. Rep. E10 94
Higuito, stm., Hond. C6 92
Hiiumaa, i., Est. C5 22
Hikone, Japan L11 36
Hilbert, Wi., U.S. F7 110
Hilda, Alta., Can. H4 104
Hildburghausen, Ger. E10 10
Hildesheim, Ger. C9 10
Hildreth, Ne., U.S. K8 118
Hillaby, Mount, mtn., Barb. H15 94
Hill Bank, Belize I15 90
Hill City, Ks., U.S. L8 118
Hill City, Mn., U.S. D2 110
Hill City, S.D., U.S. H4 118
Hillcrest Center, Ca., U.S. I7 124
Hillcrest Mines, Alta., Can. H20 102
Hilli, Bngl. H13 44
Hilliard, Fl., U.S. I5 112
Hill Island Lake, l., N.W. Ter., Can. D11 96
Hillister, Tx., U.S. L2 114
Hillman, Mi., U.S. E12 110
Hills, Mn., U.S. H11 118
Hillsboro, Il., U.S. C7 114
Hillsboro, Ks., U.S. M10 118
Hillsboro, Mo., U.S. D6 114
Hillsboro, N.H., U.S. D15 108
Hillsboro, N.M., U.S. L9 120
Hillsboro, N.D., U.S. D10 118
Hillsboro, Oh., U.S. H3 108
Hillsboro, Or., U.S. E3 122
Hillsboro, Tx., U.S. G9 116
Hillsboro, Wi., U.S. G5 110
Hillsboro Canal, Fl., U.S. M6 112
Hillsborough, N.B., Can. G9 106
Hillsborough, N.C., U.S. C7 112
Hillsborough, stm., Fl., U.S. K4 112
Hillsborough, Cape, c., Austl. C8 70
Hillsborough Bay, b., P.E.I., Can. F10 106
Hillsdale, Mi., U.S. I11 110
Hillsdale Lake, res., Ks., U.S. M13 118
Hillston, Austl. I6 70
Hillsville, Va., U.S. C6 112
Hilo, Hi., U.S. r18 125a
Hilo Bay, b., Hi., U.S. r18 125a
Hilton, N.Y., U.S. D9 108
Hilton Head Island, i., S.C., U.S. G6 112
Hilversum, Neth. D7 12
Hima, Ky., U.S. B3 112
Himāchal Pradesh, state, India E7 44
Himalayas, mts., Asia F11 44
Himeji, Japan M9 36
Himi, Japan K11 36
Ḥimṣ (Homs), Syria D4 48
Hinche, Haiti E8 94
Hinchinbrook Entrance, strt., Ak., U.S. F21 100
Hinchinbrook Island, i., Austl. B7 70
Hinchinbrook Island, i., Ak., U.S. F21 100
Hinckley, Il., U.S. I7 110
Hinckley, Mn., U.S. D3 110
Hinckley, Ut., U.S. E4 120
Hindaun, India G7 44
Hindman, Ky., U.S. B4 112
Hindmarsh, Lake, l., Austl. K4 70
Hinds Lake, l., Newf., Can. D17 106
Hindu Kush, mts., Asia B4 44
Hindupur, India F4 46
Hines, Or., U.S. G6 122
Hines Creek, Alta., Can. A16 102
Hines Creek, stm., Alta., Can. A16 102
Hinesville, Ga., U.S. H5 112
Hinganghāt, India B5 46
Hingham, Ma., U.S. E16 108
Hingol, stm., Pak. H1 44
Hingoli, India C4 46
Hınıs, Tur. B6 48
Hinnøya, i., Nor. G14 6
Hinojosa del Duque, Spain G6 16
Hinsdale, Mt., U.S. B18 122
Hinsdale, N.H., U.S. E14 108
Hinterrhein, stm., Switz. E11 13
Hinton, Alta., Can. D17 102
Hinton, Ok., U.S. D8 116
Hinton, W.V., U.S. B6 112
Hipólito, Mex. E9 90

Name	Map Ref.	Page
Hipólito Yrigoyen, Arg.	G5	80
Hirado, Japan	N4	36
Hīrākud Reservoir, res., India	B7	46
Hiram, Me., U.S.	D16	108
Hirata, Japan	L7	36
Hiratsuka, Japan	L14	36
Hirhafok, Alg.	I13	62
Ḥirjillah, Syria	B6	50
Hirosaki, Japan	G15	36
Hiroshima, Japan	M7	36
Hirson, Fr.	C11	14
Hisār, India	F6	44
Ḥisbān, Jord.	E5	50
Ḥiṣn al-Qarn, Yemen	G6	47
Hispaniola, i., N.A.	E9	94
Hita, Japan	N5	36
Hitachi, Japan	K15	36
Hitchcock, Tx., U.S.	J11	116
Hitchins, Ky., U.S.	I4	108
Hitoyoshi, Japan	O5	36
Hitra, i., Nor.	J11	6
Hiva Oa, i., Fr. Poly.	I26	126
Hiwannee, Ms., U.S.	K8	114
Hiwassee, stm., U.S.	D2	112
Hixon, B.C., Can.	D12	102
Hixson, Tn., U.S.	G11	114
Hkakabo Razi, mtn., Burma	F6	30
Hkok (Kok), stm., Asia	D5	40
Hlatikulu, Swaz.	F10	66
Hlegu, Burma	F4	40
Hlinsko, Czech.	F15	10
Hlobane, S. Afr.	F10	66
Hlohovec, Czech.	G17	10
Hluboká nad Vltavou, Czech.	F14	10
Hlučín, Czech.	F18	10
Hmawbi, Burma	F4	40
Ho, Ghana	H10	64
Hoa Binh, Viet.	D8	40
Hoare Bay, b., N.W. Ter., Can.	C20	96
Hoback, stm., Wy., U.S.	G15	122
Hobart, Austl.	N7	70
Hobart, Ok., U.S.	D7	116
Hobbs, N.M., U.S.	G3	116
Hobe Sound, Fl., U.S.	L6	112
Hobgood, N.C., U.S.	C9	112
Hobo, Col.	F5	84
Hoboken, Bel.	F5	12
Hobson, Mt., U.S.	C16	122
Hobson Lake, l., B.C., Can.	E14	102
Hobyo, Som.	G10	56
Hochalmspitze, mtn., Aus.	H13	10
Hochkönig, mtn., Aus.	H13	10
Höchstadt an der Aisch, Ger.	F10	10
Hockenheim, Ger.	F8	10
Hocking, stm., Oh., U.S.	H5	108
Hodeida see Al-Ḥudaydah, Yemen	G3	47
Hodge, La., U.S.	J4	114
Hodgenville, Ky., U.S.	E11	114
Hodges Hill, hill, Newf., Can.	C18	106
Hodgeville, Sask., Can.	H8	104
Hodgson, Man., Can.	G17	104
Hódmezővásárhely, Hung.	I20	10
Hodna, Chott el, l., Alg.	C13	62
Hodonín, Czech.	G17	10
Hoehne, Co., U.S.	N3	118
Hoek van Holland, Neth.	E5	12
Hoeryŏng, N. Kor.	A17	32
Hoeyang, N. Kor.	E15	32
Hof, Ger.	E11	10
Hof, Ice.	B6	6a
Hoffman, Mn., U.S.	F12	118
Hofmeyr, S. Afr.	H7	66
Höfn, Ice.	B6	6a
Hofors, Swe.	K15	6
Hōfu, Japan	M6	36
Hofuf see Al-Hufūf, Sau. Ar.	I10	48
Hogansville, Ga., U.S.	F2	112
Hoggar see Ahaggar, mts., Alg.	I13	62
Högsby, Swe.	M15	6
Hoh, stm., Wa., U.S.	C1	122
Hohenau, Para.	D11	80
Hohenau an der March, Aus.	G16	10
Hohenlimburg, Ger.	D7	10
Hohenthurn, Aus.	I13	10
Hohenwald, Tn., U.S.	G9	114
Hoher Dachstein, mtn., Aus.	H13	10
Hohe Tauern, mts., Aus.	H12	10
Hohhot, China	C9	30
Hohoe, Ghana	H10	64
Hoh Xil Shan, mts., China	C13	44
Hoi An, Viet.	G10	40
Hoisington, Ks., U.S.	M9	118
Hojāi, India	G15	44
Hokah, Mn., U.S.	G4	110
Hokes Bluff, Al., U.S.	I11	114
Hokitika, N.Z.	E3	72
Hokkaidō, i., Japan	D17	36a
Holberg, B.C., Can.	G6	102
Holbrook, Austl.	J7	70
Holbrook, Az., U.S.	J6	120
Holbrook, Ne., U.S.	K7	118
Holden, Alta., Can.	D22	102
Holden, Mo., U.S.	D3	114
Holden, Ut., U.S.	E4	120
Holden, W.V., U.S.	J4	108
Holdenville, Ok., U.S.	D10	116
Holder, Fl., U.S.	K4	112
Holdfast, Sask., Can.	H9	104
Holdingford, Mn., U.S.	E1	110
Holdrege, Ne., U.S.	K8	118
Hole in the Mountain Peak, mtn., Nv., U.S.	D10	124
Holgate, Oh., U.S.	F2	108
Holguín, Cuba	D6	94
Holíč, Czech.	G17	10
Hollabrunn, Aus.	G16	10
Holladay, Ut., U.S.	D5	120
Holland, Man., Can.	I16	104
Holland, Mi., U.S.	H9	110
Holland, Tx., U.S.	I9	116
Hollandale, Ms., U.S.	I6	114
Holland see Netherlands, ctry., Eur.	E9	4
Hollandsbird Island, i., S. Afr.	E2	66
Hollandsch Diep, strt., Neth.	E5	12
Holley, N.Y., U.S.	D8	108
Holliday, Tx., U.S.	F8	116
Hollidaysburg, Pa., U.S.	G8	108
Hollins, Va., U.S.	B7	112
Hollis, Ok., U.S.	E7	116
Hollister, Ca., U.S.	H4	124
Hollow Rock, Tn., U.S.	F8	114
Holly, Co., U.S.	M5	118
Holly Grove, Ar., U.S.	H5	114
Holly Hill, Fl., U.S.	J5	112
Holly Hill, S.C., U.S.	F6	112
Holly Springs, Ms., U.S.	H7	114
Hollywood, Fl., U.S.	M6	112
Holman, N.W. Ter., Can.	B9	96
Holmen, Wi., U.S.	G4	110
Holmes, Mount, mtn., Wy., U.S.	F15	122
Holmes Lake, l., Man., Can.	A18	104
Holmestrand, Nor.	L12	6
Holmia, Guy.	E13	84
Holod, Rom.	C6	20
Holoit, Punta, c., Mex.	G15	90
Ḥolon, Isr.	D3	50
Holoog, Nmb.	F3	66
Holstebro, Den.	M11	6
Holstein, Ia., U.S.	I12	118
Holston, stm., Tn., U.S.	C3	112
Holston High Knob, mtn., Tn., U.S.	C4	112
Holt, Al., U.S.	I9	114
Holt, Fl., U.S.	L10	114
Holt, Mi., U.S.	H11	110
Holton, Ks., U.S.	L12	118
Holts Summit, Mo., U.S.	D4	114
Holtville, Ca., U.S.	L10	124
Holy Cross, Ak., U.S.	E15	100
Holy Cross Mountain, mtn., B.C., Can.	D14	102
Holyoke, Co., U.S.	K5	118
Holyoke, Ma., U.S.	E14	108
Holyrood, Ks., U.S.	M9	118
Holzkirchen, Ger.	H11	10
Holzminden, Ger.	D9	10
Homalin, Burma	B3	40
Homathko, stm., B.C., Can.	F10	102
Homathko Icefield, B.C., Can.	F10	102
Homberg, Ger.	D9	10
Hombori Tondo, mtn., Mali	D9	64
Hombre Muerto, Salar del, pl., Arg.	C5	80
Homburg, Ger.	F7	10
Homburg see Bad Homburg vor der Höhe, Ger.	E8	10
Home Bay, b., N.W. Ter., Can.	C19	96
Homedale, Id., U.S.	G9	122
Home Hill, Austl.	B7	70
Homeland Park, S.C., U.S.	E4	112
Homer, Ak., U.S.	G19	100
Homer, Ga., U.S.	E3	112
Homer, La., U.S.	J3	114
Homer, Mi., U.S.	H11	110
Homer, Ne., U.S.	I11	118
Homer, N.Y., U.S.	E10	108
Homer City, Pa., U.S.	G7	108
Homerville, Ga., U.S.	H4	112
Homestead, Fl., U.S.	N6	112
Homewood, Al., U.S.	I10	114
Hominy, Ok., U.S.	C10	116
Homochitto, stm., Ms., U.S.	K5	114
Homosassa, Fl., U.S.	K4	112
Homs see Al-Khums, Libya	B3	56
Homs see Ḥimṣ, Syria	D4	48
Honaker, Va., U.S.	B5	112
Honan see Henan, prov., China	E9	30
Honaz, Tur.	L13	20
Honda, Col.	E5	84
Honda, Bahía, b., Col.	A7	84
Hondeklipbaai, S. Afr.	H3	66
Hondo, Alta., Can.	B20	102
Hondo, N.M., U.S.	K11	120
Hondo, Tx., U.S.	J7	116
Hondo, stm., N.A.	H15	90
Hondo, Rio, stm., N.M., U.S.	F2	116
Hondsrug, hills, Neth.	C10	12
Honduras, ctry., N.A.	B8	92
Honduras, Cabo de, c., Hond.	A8	92
Honduras, Gulf of, b., N.A.	E7	88
Honduras, Port, b., Belize	A6	92
Honea Path, S.C., U.S.	E4	112
Hønefoss, Nor.	K12	6
Honesdale, Pa., U.S.	F11	108
Honey Grove, Tx., U.S.	F11	116
Honey Lake, l., Ca., U.S.	D5	124
Honeyville, Ut., U.S.	C4	120
Honfleur, Fr.	C7	14
Hon Gai, Viet.	D9	40
Hong'an, China	D3	34
Hongch'ŏn, S. Kor.	F15	32
Hongcun, China	H5	34
Honghu, China	F2	34
Hongjiang, China	F8	30
Hong Kong, dep., Asia	G9	30
Honglai, China	J7	34
Hongliuyuan, China	C6	30
Honglu, China	J8	34
Hongmendu, China	A7	40
Hong Ngu, Viet.	I8	40
Hong see Red, stm., Asia	C8	40
Hongshi, China	B7	32
Hongshui, stm., China	C10	40
Hongshuyangzi, China	C4	32
Hongsŏng, S. Kor.	G14	32
Hongtong, China	D9	30
Honguedo, Détroit d', strt., Que., Can.	C10	106
Hongwŏn, N. Kor.	C15	32
Hongxingqiao, China	E8	34
Hongyang, China	L5	34
Hongze Hu, l., China	B7	34
Honiara, Sol.Is.	I19	126
Honokaa, Hi., U.S.	q18	125a
Honolulu, Hi., U.S.	p16	125a
Honomu, Hi., U.S.	r18	125a
Hon Quan, Viet.	I9	40
Honshū, i., Japan	K13	36
Hood, stm., N.W. Ter., Can.	C10	96
Hood, Mount, mtn., Or., U.S.	E4	122
Hood Canal, b., Wa., U.S.	C2	122
Hoodoo Peak, mtn., Wa., U.S.	B5	122
Hood Point, c., Austl.	F3	68
Hood River, Or., U.S.	E4	122
Hoodsport, Wa., U.S.	C2	122
Hoods Range, mts., Austl.	G6	70
Hooker, Ok., U.S.	C5	116
Hookina, Austl.	H3	70
Hook Island, i., Austl.	C8	70
Hooks, Tx., U.S.	I2	114
Hoolehua, Hi., U.S.	p16	125a
Hoonah, Ak., U.S.	G27	100
Hoopa, Ca., U.S.	C2	124
Hooper, Ne., U.S.	J11	118
Hooper Bay, Ak., U.S.	F11	100
Hoopeston, Il., U.S.	J8	110
Hooping Harbour, Newf., Can.	B17	106
Hoople, N.D., U.S.	C10	118
Hoosick Falls, N.Y., U.S.	E13	108
Hoover Dam, U.S.	H2	120
Hooversville, Pa., U.S.	G8	108
Hopatcong, N.J., U.S.	G12	108
Hope, B.C., Can.	H13	102
Hope, Ar., U.S.	I3	114
Hope, In., U.S.	C11	114
Hope, N.D., U.S.	D10	118
Hope, Point, c., Ak., U.S.	B11	100
Hopedale, Newf., Can.	E20	96
Hopedale, Il., U.S.	B7	114
Hopedale, La., U.S.	M7	114
Hopefield, S. Afr.	I4	66
Hope Island, i., B.C., Can.	G7	102
Hopelchén, Mex.	H15	90
Hope Mills, N.C., U.S.	E8	112
Hopes Advance, Cap, c., Que., Can.	D19	96
Hopetoun, Austl.	F4	68
Hopetoun, Austl.	J5	70
Hopetown, S. Afr.	G7	66
Hope Valley, R.I., U.S.	F15	108
Hopewell, Va., U.S.	B9	112
Hopewell Islands, is., N.W. Ter., Can.	E17	96
Hopkins, Mi., U.S.	H10	110
Hopkins, Mo., U.S.	B2	114
Hopkinsville, Ky., U.S.	F9	114
Hopkinton, Ia., U.S.	H4	110
Hopland, Ca., U.S.	F2	124
Hopólito Bouchard, Arg.	H7	80
Hopwood, Mount, mtn., Austl.	C6	70
Hoquiam, Wa., U.S.	D2	122
Horancia, Eth.	N10	60
Horatio, Ar., U.S.	I2	114
Horconcitos, Pan.	I12	92
Hordaland, co., Nor.	K10	6
Horezu, Rom.	D7	20
Horgen, Switz.	D10	13
Horicon, Wi., U.S.	G7	110
Horizontina, Braz.	D11	80
Horlick Mountains, mts., Ant.	D10	73
Hormuz, Strait of, strt., Asia	H14	48
Horn, Aus.	G15	10
Horn, c., Ice.	A2	6a
Horn, stm., N.W. Ter., Can.	D9	96
Horn, Cape see Hornos, Cabo de, c., Chile	H3	78
Hornaday, stm., N.W. Ter., Can.	B33	100
Hornbeak, Tn., U.S.	F7	114
Hornbeck, La., U.S.	K3	114
Hornbrook, Ca., U.S.	C3	124
Hornby Bay, b., N.W. Ter., Can.	C9	96
Hornell, N.Y., U.S.	E9	108
Hornepayne, Ont., Can.	G16	96
Horn Island, i., Ms., U.S.	L8	114
Hornito, Cerro, mtn., Pan.	I12	92
Horn Lake, Ms., U.S.	H6	114
Hornos, Cabo de (Cape Horn), c., Chile	H3	78
Horn Plateau, plat., N.W. Ter., Can.	D9	96
Horqin Youyi Qianqi, China	B11	30
Horqueta, Para.	B10	80
Horse, stm., Alta., Can.	B3	104
Horse Cave, Ky., U.S.	E11	114
Horse Creek, Wy., U.S.	C11	120
Horsefly, B.C., Can.	E13	102
Horsefly Lake, l., B.C., Can.	E14	102
Horseheads, N.Y., U.S.	E10	108
Horse Islands, is., Newf., Can.	B18	106
Horsens, Den.	N11	6
Horseshoe Bend, Ar., U.S.	F5	114
Horseshoe Bend, Id., U.S.	G9	122
Horseshoe Lake, l., Man., Can.	F19	104
Horse Shoe Reef, rf., Br. Vir. Is.	E12	94
Horsham, Austl.	K5	70
Horsham, Eng., U.K.	J13	8
Horst, Neth.	F9	12
Horton, Ks., U.S.	L12	118
Horton, stm., N.W. Ter., Can.	B31	100
Horton Lake, l., N.W. Ter., Can.	C33	100
Hortonville, Wi., U.S.	F7	110
Hosaina, Eth.	N9	60
Hoséré Vokré, mtn., Cam.	G9	54
Hosford, Fl., U.S.	I2	112
Hoshangābād, India	I7	44
Hoshiārpur, India	E6	44
Hosmer, B.C., Can.	H20	102
Hosmer, S.D., U.S.	F8	118
Hospers, Ia., U.S.	H12	118
Hospet, India	E4	46
Hossegor, Fr.	I5	14
Hosston, La., U.S.	J3	114
Hosta Butte, mtn., N.M., U.S.	I8	120
Hoste, Isla, i., Chile	H3	78
Hot, Thai.	E5	40
Hotan, China	D2	30
Hotan, stm., China	D3	30
Hotazel, S. Afr.	F6	66
Hotchkiss, Co., U.S.	F9	120
Hotevilla, Az., U.S.	I6	120
Hotham Inlet, b., Ak., U.S.	C14	100
Hot Springs, Mt., U.S.	C11	122
Hot Springs, N.C., U.S.	D4	112
Hot Springs, S.D., U.S.	H4	118
Hot Springs, Va., U.S.	B7	112
Hot Springs National Park, Ar., U.S.	H3	114
Hot Springs see Truth or Consequences, N.M., U.S.	K9	120
Hot Sulphur Springs, Co., U.S.	D10	120
Hottah Lake, l., N.W. Ter., Can.	C9	96
Hottentotbaai, b., Nmb.	F2	66
Houbao, China	B13	32
Houdan, Fr.	D8	14
Houghton, Mi., U.S.	C7	110
Houghton, N.Y., U.S.	E8	108
Houghton Lake, Mi., U.S.	F11	110
Houghton Lake, l., Sask., Can.	F9	104
Houghton Lake, l., Mi., U.S.	F11	110
Houjie, China	M2	34
Houlka, Ms., U.S.	H7	114
Houlton, Me., U.S.	A19	108
Houma, China	D9	30
Houma, La., U.S.	M6	114
Houndé, Burkina	F8	64
Housatonic, Ma., U.S.	E13	108
House, N.M., U.S.	E3	116
House, stm., Alta., Can.	C2	104
Houston, B.C., Can.	C8	102
Houston, Mn., U.S.	G4	110
Houston, Ms., U.S.	I8	114
Houston, Mo., U.S.	E5	114
Houston, Tx., U.S.	J11	116
Houston, stm., La., U.S.	L3	114
Houston, Lake, res., Tx., U.S.	J11	116
Houtman Abrolhos, is., Austl.	E2	68
Houtzdale, Pa., U.S.	G8	108
Houxijie, China	G7	34
Houxinqiu, China	A10	32
Hoven, S.D., U.S.	F8	118
Howar, Wādī (Ouadi Howa), val., Afr.	I3	60
Howard, Austl.	E10	70
Howard, Ks., U.S.	N11	118
Howard, Pa., U.S.	F9	108
Howard, S.D., U.S.	G10	118
Howard, Wi., U.S.	F7	110
Howard City, Mi., U.S.	G10	110
Howard Lake, Mn., U.S.	E1	110
Howe, In., U.S.	A11	114
Howe, Tx., U.S.	F10	116
Howe, Cape, c., Austl.	K8	70
Howeke, Lib.	I6	64
Howell, Mi., U.S.	H12	110
Howells, Ne., U.S.	J10	118
Howe Sound, strt., B.C., Can.	H11	102
Howick, S. Afr.	G10	66
Howitt, Mount, mtn., Austl.	K7	70
Howland, Me., U.S.	B18	108
Howland Island, i., Oc.	H22	126
Howley, Newf., Can.	C16	106
Howley, Mount, mtn., Newf., Can.	D15	106
Howse Peak, mtn., Can.	F18	102
Howser, B.C., Can.	G18	102
Howson Peak, mtn., B.C., Can.	C7	102
Hoxie, Ar., U.S.	F6	114
Hoxie, Ks., U.S.	L7	118
Höxter, Ger.	D9	10
Høyanger, Nor.	K10	6
Hoyerswerda, Ger.	D14	10
Hoyleton, Il., U.S.	D7	114
Hoyt Lakes, Mn., U.S.	C3	110
Hradec Králové, Czech.	E15	10
Hranice, Czech.	F17	10
Hron, stm., Czech.	G18	10
Hronov, Czech.	E16	10
Hrubieszów, Pol.	E23	10
Hrvatska see Croatia, ctry., Eur.	D10	18
Hsihu, Tai.	L9	34
Hsilo, Tai.	L9	34
Hsinchu, Tai.	K9	34
Hsinchuang, Tai.	J10	34
Hsinhua, Tai.	L9	34
Hsintien, Tai.	K10	34
Hsipaw, Burma	C4	40
Hsüehchia, Tai.	L9	34
Hua'an, China	J6	34
Huacaña, Peru	F4	82
Huacaraje, Bol.	E10	82
Huachacalla, Bol.	H7	82
Huacheng, China	K4	34
Huachi, Laguna, l., Bol.	F10	82
Huacho, Peru	D3	82
Huachón, Peru	D4	82
Huachos, Peru	E4	82
Huachuca City, Az., U.S.	M6	120
Huaco, Arg.	F4	80
Huacrachuco, Peru	C3	82
Huadian, China	C12	30
Hua Hin, Thai.	H5	40
Huai, stm., China	C6	34
Huai'an, China	B8	34
Huaibin, China	C4	34
Huaide, China	C11	30
Huailai, China	C3	32
Huaillati, Peru	F5	82
Huainan, China	C6	34
Huaining, China	E5	34
Huaitunas, Lagunas, l., Bol.	E8	82
Huaiyang, China	B3	34
Huaiyuan, China	C6	34
Huajuapan de León, Mex.	I11	90
Huakou, China	J6	34
Hualahuises, Mex.	E10	90
Hualalai, vol., Hi., U.S.	r18	125a
Hualañé, Chile	H3	80
Hualapai Peak, mtn., Az., U.S.	I3	120
Hualfín, Arg.	D5	80
Hualgayoc, Peru	B2	82
Hualien, Tai.	L10	34
Huallaga, stm., Peru	A4	82
Huallanca, Peru	C3	82
Huallanca, Peru	C3	82
Huallayabamba, stm., Peru	B3	82
Huamanquiquia, Peru	E4	82
Huambo (Nova Lisboa), Ang.	D3	58
Huambos, Peru	B2	82
Huancabamba, Peru	D4	82
Huancabamba, Peru	A2	82
Huancané, Peru	F7	82
Huancapi, Peru	E4	82
Huancarama, Peru	E5	82
Huancarqui, Peru	G5	82
Huancavelica, Peru	E4	82
Huancavelica, dept., Peru	E4	82
Huancaybamba, Peru	C3	82
Huancayo, Peru	E4	82
Huanchaca, Bol.	I8	82
Huanchaca, Serranía de, mts., S.A.	F11	82
Huando, Peru	E4	82
Huang, stm., Asia	F6	40
Huang (Yellow), stm., China	D10	30
Huang'an, China	H3	32
Huangbai, China	B14	32
Huangchuan, China	C4	34
Huangdu, China	D10	34
Huanggang, China	E3	34
Huangguoshu, China	A8	40
Huanghua, China	E5	32
Huangkeng, China	H6	34
Huangling, China	D8	30
Huangmao, China	G3	34
Huangnihe, China	D6	34
Huangqi, China	I8	34
Huangqiao, China	C9	34
Huangshapu, China	J1	34
Huangshatuo, China	B10	32
Huangshi, China	E4	34
Huangshiguan, China	I4	34
Huangtankou, China	G7	34
Huangtianfan, China	F9	34
Huangtugang, China	D4	34
Huanguelén, Arg.	I8	80
Huangyan, China	G10	34
Huangyuan, China	D7	30
Huangzhuang, China	A1	34
Huanjiang, China	B10	40
Huanta, Peru	E4	82
Huántar, Peru	C3	82
Huánuco, Peru	C3	82
Huánuco, dept., Peru	C4	82
Huanuni, Bol.	H8	82
Huanxi, China	I2	34
Huanzo, Cordillera de, mts., Peru	F5	82
Huapí, Serranías, mts., Nic.	E10	92
Huara, Chile	H7	82
Huaral, Peru	D3	82
Huaráz, Peru	C3	82
Huari, Peru	C3	82
Huariaca, Peru	D3	82
Huaribamba, Peru	E4	82
Huarina, Bol.	G7	82
Huarmey, Peru	D2	82
Huarochirí, Peru	E3	82
Huarocondo, Peru	E5	82
Huasaga, stm., S.A.	I4	84
Huascarán, Nevado, mtn., Peru	C3	82
Huasco, Chile	E3	80
Huasco, stm., Chile	E3	80
Huashan, China	I4	32
Huashi, China	D9	34
Huatabampo, Mex.	D5	90
Huatong, China	C9	32
Huauchinango, Mex.	G10	90
Huaura, Peru	D3	82
Huaura, stm., Peru	D3	82
Huautla, Mex.	H11	90
Huaxian, China	L2	34
Huayllay, Peru	D3	82
Huayna Potosí, Nevado, mtn., Bol.	G7	82
Huaytará, Peru	E4	82
Huayuanzui, China	B7	34
Huayunca, Nevado, mtn., Peru	F5	82
Huayuri, Pampa de, pl., Peru	F4	82
Huazhou, China	D11	40
Hubbard, Ia., U.S.	H2	110
Hubbard, Tx., U.S.	H10	116
Hubbard Creek Reservoir, res., Tx., U.S.	G7	116
Hubbard Lake, l., Mi., U.S.	F12	110
Hubbards, N.S., Can.	H9	106
Hubbell, Mi., U.S.	C7	110
Hubei (Hupeh), prov., China	E9	30
Huberdeau, Que., Can.	B12	108
Hubli-Dhārwār, India	E3	46
Huch'ang, N. Kor.	B15	32
Huchi, China	D6	34
Huddersfield, Eng., U.K.	H12	8
Hūdī, Sud.	I8	60
Hudiksvall, Swe.	K15	6
Hudson, Ia., U.S.	H3	110
Hudson, Ma., U.S.	E15	108
Hudson, Mi., U.S.	I11	110
Hudson, N.H., U.S.	E15	108
Hudson, N.Y., U.S.	E13	108
Hudson, N.C., U.S.	D5	112
Hudson, Oh., U.S.	F5	108
Hudson, S.D., U.S.	H11	118
Hudson, Wi., U.S.	F3	110
Hudson, Wy., U.S.	B8	120
Hudson, stm., U.S.	F12	108
Hudson, Lake, res., Ok., U.S.	C11	116
Hudson Bay, Sask., Can.	F12	104
Hudson Bay, b., Can.	D15	96
Hudson-Bayonet Point, Fl., U.S.	K4	112
Hudson Falls, N.Y., U.S.	D13	108
Hudson Hope, B.C., Can.	A13	102
Hudson Strait, strt., Can.	D18	96
Hudsonville, Mi., U.S.	H10	110
Hudwin Lake, l., Man., Can.	E19	104
Hue, Viet.	F9	40
Huehuetán, Mex.	B2	92
Huehuetenango, Guat.	B3	92
Huehuetenango, dept., Guat.	B3	92
Huejutla de Reyes, Mex.	G10	90
Huelgoat, Fr.	D3	14
Huelva, Spain	H5	16
Huenque, stm., Peru	G7	82
Huentelauquén, Chile	F3	80
Huércal-Overa, Spain	H10	16
Huerfano, stm., Co., U.S.	M3	118
Huerfano Mountain, mtn., N.M., U.S.	H9	120
Huerva, stm., Spain	D10	16
Huesca, Spain	C11	16
Huéscar, Spain	H9	16
Huetamo de Núñez, Mex.	H9	90
Hueytown, Al., U.S.	I10	114
Huggins, Mount, mtn., Ant.	C8	73
Hugh Butler Lake, res., Ne., U.S.	K7	118
Hughenden, Austl.	C6	70
Hughes, Ak., U.S.	C17	100
Hughes, Ar., U.S.	H6	114
Hughes, stm., Man., Can.	B14	104
Hughes Springs, Tx., U.S.	I2	114
Hughesville, Pa., U.S.	F10	108
Hugh Keenleyside Dam, B.C., Can.	H17	102
Hughson, Ca., U.S.	G5	124
Hugh Town, Eng., U.K.	L7	8
Hugli, stm., India	J12	44
Hugo, Co., U.S.	L4	118
Hugo, Ok., U.S.	E11	116
Hugoton, Ks., U.S.	N6	118
Hugou, China	B6	34
Huichang, China	J4	34
Huichapan, Mex.	G10	90
Hŭich'ŏn, N. Kor.	C14	32
Huicungo, Peru	B3	82
Huidong, China	A7	40
Huila, dept., Col.	F5	84
Huila, Nevado del, mtn., Col.	F4	84
Huili, China	A7	40
Huillapima, Arg.	E6	80
Huilong, China	K2	34
Huimin, China	F5	32
Huinan (Chaoyang), China	A14	32
Huínaymarca, Lago, l., S.A.	G7	82
Huinca Renancó, Arg.	H6	80
Huisduinen, Neth.	C6	12
Huiting, China	I4	32
Huitzo, Mex.	I11	90
Huitzuco de los Figueroa, Mex.	H10	90
Huixtla, Mex.	J13	90
Huiyang, China	A5	38
Huize, China	A7	40
Huizen, Neth.	D7	12
Huizhou, China	L3	34
Hukeng, China	H3	34
Ḥukūmah, Sud.	K9	60
Hukuntsi, Bots.	E5	66
Hulan, China	B12	30
Hulan Ergi, China	B11	30
Hulbert, Mi., U.S.	D10	110
Hulbert, Ok., U.S.	G1	114
Hulett, Wy., U.S.	G3	118
Hulin, China	B13	30
Hull, Que., Can.	B11	108
Hull, Il., U.S.	C5	114
Hull, Ia., U.S.	H11	118
Hull, Tx., U.S.	I12	116
Hull see Kingston upon Hull, Eng., U.K.	H13	8
Hulun Nur, l., China	B10	30
Ḥulwān, Egypt	C6	60
Huma, China	A12	30
Huma, stm., China	A11	30
Humacao, P.R.	E12	94
Humahuaca, Arg.	B6	80
Humaitá, Braz.	B10	82
Humaitá, Para.	D9	80
Humaitá, stm., Braz.	C5	82
Humansdorp, S. Afr.	J7	66
Humansville, Mo., U.S.	E3	114
Humayingzi, China	B4	32
Humbe, Ang.	E2	58
Humber, stm., Eng., U.K.	H13	8
Humberside, co., Eng., U.K.	H13	8
Humbird, Wi., U.S.	F5	110
Humboldt, Sask., Can.	F9	104
Humboldt, Az., U.S.	J4	120
Humboldt, Il., U.S.	C8	114
Humboldt, Ia., U.S.	I13	118
Humboldt, Ks., U.S.	N12	118
Humboldt, Ne., U.S.	K12	118
Humboldt, S.D., U.S.	H10	118
Humboldt, Tn., U.S.	G8	114
Humboldt, stm., Nv., U.S.	D7	124
Hume, Ca., U.S.	H7	124
Hume, Lake, res., Austl.	K7	70
Humeburn, Austl.	F6	70
Humenné, Czech.	G21	10
Humeston, Ia., U.S.	J2	110
Humphrey, Ar., U.S.	H5	114
Humphrey, Ne., U.S.	J10	118
Humphreys, Mount, mtn., Ca., U.S.	G7	124
Humphreys Peak, mtn., Az., U.S.	I5	120
Humptulips, stm., Wa., U.S.	C2	122
Humpty Doo, Austl.	B6	68
Humuya, stm., Hond.	C7	92
Húnaflói, b., Ice.	B3	6a
Hunan, prov., China	F9	30
Hunchun, China	A18	32
Hundred, W.V., U.S.	H6	108
Hunedoara, Rom.	D6	20
Hunedoara, co., Rom.	D6	20
Hünfeld, Ger.	E9	10
Hungary (Magyarország), ctry., Eur.	F12	4
Hungerford, Tx., U.S.	J10	116
Hŭngnam, N. Kor.	D15	32
Hungry Horse, Mt., U.S.	B11	122
Hungry Horse Reservoir, res., Mt., U.S.	B12	122
Hung Yen, Viet.	D9	40
Huningue, Fr.	E14	14
Hunjiang (Badaojiang), China	B14	32
Ḥunkurāb, Ra's, c., Egypt	I3	48
Hunlen Falls, wtfl, B.C., Can.	E9	102
Hunsberge, mts., Nmb.	F3	66
Hunsrück, mts., Ger.	F6	10
Hunter, N.D., U.S.	D10	118
Hunter, Mount, mtn., Ak., U.S.	E19	100
Hunter Island, i., Austl.	M6	70
Hunter Island, i., B.C., Can.	F6	102
Hunter River, P.E.I., Can.	F10	106
Hunters Road, Zimb.	B9	66
Huntersville, N.C., U.S.	D6	112
Huntingburg, In., U.S.	D10	114
Huntingdon, Que., Can.	B12	108
Huntingdon, Pa., U.S.	G8	108
Huntingdon, Tn., U.S.	F8	114
Huntington, In., U.S.	B11	114
Huntington, N.Y., U.S.	G13	108
Huntington, Or., U.S.	F8	122
Huntington, Tx., U.S.	K2	114
Huntington, Ut., U.S.	E6	120
Huntington, W.V., U.S.	I4	108
Huntington Beach, Ca., U.S.	K8	124
Huntland, Tn., U.S.	G10	114
Huntley, Mt., U.S.	E17	122
Huntly, N.Z.	B5	72
Hunt Mountain, mtn., Wy., U.S.	F18	122
Huntsville, Ont., Can.	E16	110
Huntsville, Al., U.S.	H10	114
Huntsville, Ar., U.S.	F3	114
Huntsville, Mo., U.S.	C4	114
Huntsville, Tn., U.S.	C2	112
Huntsville, Tx., U.S.	I11	116
Huntsville, Ut., U.S.	C5	120
Hunucmá, Mex.	G15	90
Hunyani, stm., Afr.	E6	58
Hunyuan, China	D1	32
Huon Gulf, b., Pap. N. Gui.	m16	68a
Huonville, Austl.	N7	70
Huoqiu, China	C5	34
Huotong, China	I8	34
Hupeh see Hubei, prov., China	E9	30
Ḥuraymilā, Sau. Ar.	B5	47
Hurd, Cape, c., Ont., Can.	E14	110
Hure Qi, China	A9	32
Huriel, Fr.	F9	14
Hurley, Ms., U.S.	L8	114
Hurley, N.M., U.S.	L8	120
Hurley, S.D., U.S.	H10	118
Hurley, Wi., U.S.	D5	110
Hurlock, Md., U.S.	I11	108
Huron, Ca., U.S.	H5	124
Huron, Oh., U.S.	F4	108
Huron, S.D., U.S.	G9	118
Huron, stm., Mi., U.S.	H12	110
Huron, Lake, l., N.A.	F13	110
Hurricane, Ut., U.S.	G3	120
Hurricane, W.V., U.S.	I4	108
Hurricane Cliffs, clf, U.S.	H3	120
Hurstbridge, Austl.	K6	70
Hurt, Va., U.S.	B7	112
Hurtado, stm., Chile	F3	80
Hurtsboro, Al., U.S.	J11	114
Húsavik, Faer. Is.	E8	6b
Húsavík, Ice.	A5	6a
Husheib, Sud.	J8	60
Hushiha, China	C4	32
Huşi, Rom.	C12	20
Huslia, Ak., U.S.	D16	100
Hussar, Alta., Can.	F22	102
Hustisford, Wi., U.S.	G7	110
Husum, Ger.	A9	10
Husum, Swe.	J16	6
Hutanopan, Indon.	N5	40
Hutchinson, S. Afr.	H6	66
Hutchinson, Ks., U.S.	M10	118
Hutchinson, Mn., U.S.	F1	110
Hutouya, China	F7	32
Hutsonville, Il., U.S.	C9	114
Hutte Sauvage, Lac de la, l., Que., Can.	E20	96
Huttig, Ar., U.S.	I4	114
Hutto, Tx., U.S.	I9	116
Huttwil, Switz.	D8	13
Huwei, Tai.	L9	34
Ḥuwwārah, Isr. Occ.	D4	50
Huxford, Al., U.S.	K9	114
Huxley, Alta., Can.	F21	102
Huyangzhen, China	C1	34
Hūzgān, Iran	F10	48
Huzhou, China	E9	34
Hvannadalshnúkur, mtn., Ice.	B5	6a
Hvar, Cro.	F11	18
Hvar, Otok, i., Cro.	F11	18
Hveragerði, Ice.	B3	6a
Hvolsvöllur, Ice.	C3	6a
Hwange, Zimb.	B8	66
Hwang Ho see Huang, stm., China	D10	30
Hwangju, N. Kor.	E13	32
Hyannis, Ma., U.S.	F16	108
Hyannis, Ne., U.S.	I6	118
Hyattville, Wy., U.S.	F18	122
Hyco, stm., U.S.	C8	112
Hydaburg, Ak., U.S.	I28	100
Hyden, Austl.	F3	68
Hyden, Ky., U.S.	B3	112
Hyde Park, Guy.	D13	84
Hyde Park, N.Y., U.S.	F13	108
Hyde Park, Vt., U.S.	C14	108
Hyderābād, India	D5	46
Hyderābād, Pak.	H3	44
Hydra see Ídhra, i., Grc.	L7	20
Hydraulic, B.C., Can.	E13	102
Hydro, Ok., U.S.	D8	116
Hydrographers Passage, strt., Austl.	C8	70
Hyères, Fr.	I13	14
Hyères, Îles d', is., Fr.	B18	16
Hyesan, N. Kor.	B16	32
Hyland, stm., Can.	F30	100
Hymaya, stm., Mex.	E6	90
Hymera, In., U.S.	C9	114
Hyndman, Pa., U.S.	H8	108
Hyndman Peak, mtn., Id., U.S.	G11	122
Hyŏpch'ŏn, S. Kor.	H16	32
Hyrra Banda, Cen. Afr. Rep.	O2	60
Hyrum, Ut., U.S.	C5	120
Hysham, Mt., U.S.	D18	122
Hythe, Alta., Can.	B15	102
I		
Iacanga, Braz.	F4	79
Iaciara, Braz.	C5	79
Iaco (Yaco), stm., S.A.	C7	82
Iaçu, Braz.	B8	79
Iaeger, W.V., U.S.	B5	112
Ialomiţa, co., Rom.	E11	20
Ialomiţa, stm., Rom.	E11	20
Ianakafy, Madag.	S21	67b
Iapó, stm., Braz.	C13	80

Name	Map Ref.	Page
Iapu, Braz.	E7	79
Iași, Rom.	B11	20
Iași, co., Rom.	B11	20
Iauaretê, Braz.	G8	84
Ibadan, Nig.	H11	64
Ibagué, Col.	E5	84
Ibaiti, Braz.	G3	79
Ibans, Laguna de, b., Hond.	B10	92
Ibapah Peak, mtn., Ut., U.S.	E3	120
Ibarra, Ec.	G3	84
Ibarreta, Arg.	C9	80
Ibb, Yemen	G4	47
Ibbenbüren, Ger.	C7	10
Iberia, Mo., U.S.	D4	114
Ibérico, Sistema, mts., Spain	D9	16
Iberville, Mont d' (Mount Caubvick), mtn., Can.	E20	96
Ibeto, Nig.	F12	64
Ibiá, Braz.	E5	79
Ibicaraí, Braz.	C9	79
Ibicuí, Braz.	C9	79
Ibicuí, stm., Braz.	E10	80
Ibicuy, Arg.	G9	80
Ibiquera, Braz.	B8	79
Ibiraci, Braz.	F5	79
Ibiraçu, Braz.	E8	79
Ibirama, Braz.	D14	80
Ibirapuã, Braz.	D8	79
Ibirapuitã, stm., Braz.	F11	80
Ibirataia, Braz.	C9	79
Ibirubá, Braz.	E12	80
Ibitiara, Braz.	B7	79
Ibitinga, Braz.	F4	79
Ibo, Moz.	D8	58
Ibotirama, Braz.	B7	79
ʻIbrī, Oman	C10	47
Ibshawāy, Egypt	C6	60
Ibusuki, Japan	P5	36
Ica, Peru	F4	82
Ica, dept., Peru	F4	82
Ica, stm., Peru	F4	82
Içá (Putumayo), stm., S.A.	I8	84
Icabarú, stm., Ven.	E11	84
Icamaquã, stm., Braz.	E11	80
Içana, Braz.	G9	84
Içana (Isana), stm., S.A.	G9	84
Icaño, Arg.	E6	80
Icaño, Arg.	E7	80
Iceberg Pass, Co., U.S.	D11	120
İçel, Tur.	C3	48
Iceland (Ísland), ctry., Eur.	B4	4
Icém, Braz.	F4	79
Ice Mountain, mtn., B.C., Can.	C13	102
Ichaikaronji, India	D3	46
Ichikawa, Japan	L14	36
Ichilo, stm., Bol.	G9	82
Ichinomiya, Japan	L11	36
Ichinoseki, Japan	I16	36
Ichkeul, Lac, l., Tun.	L4	18
Ichoa, stm., Bol.	F9	82
Ichoca, Bol.	G8	82
Ich'on, N. Kor.	E14	32
Ich'ŏn, S. Kor.	F15	32
Ičinskaja Sopka, vulkan, vol., Russia	F23	28
Icó, Braz.	E11	76
Iconha, Braz.	F8	79
Icy Bay, b., Ak., U.S.	F24	100
Ida, Mi., U.S.	I12	110
Idabel, Ok., U.S.	I2	114
Ida Grove, Ia., U.S.	I12	118
Idah, Nig.	H13	64
Idaho, state, U.S.	C4	98
Idaho City, Id., U.S.	G10	122
Idaho Falls, Id., U.S.	G13	122
Idaho Springs, Co., U.S.	E11	120
Idalou, Tx., U.S.	F5	116
Idanre, Nig.	H12	64
Idāppādi, India	G4	46
Idar-Oberstein, Ger.	F7	10
Idelès, Alg.	I13	62
Idfū, Egypt	E7	60
Ídhi Óros, mtn., Grc.	N8	20
Ídhra, i., Grc.	L7	20
Idi, Indon.	L4	40
Idiofa, Zaire	C3	58
Idlib, Syria	D4	48
Idre, Swe.	K13	6
Idrica, Russia	E11	22
Idrija, Slo.	C9	18
Idutywa, Transkei	I9	66
Idyllwild, Ca., U.S.	K9	124
Iecava, Lat.	E7	22
Iepê, Braz.	G3	79
Ieper (Ypres), Bel.	G2	12
Ierisós, Grc.	I7	20
Ife, Nig.	H12	64
Iferouâne, Niger	B14	64
Ifni, hist. reg., Mor.	F5	62
Ifôghas, Adrar des, mts., Afr.	E7	54
Ifon-Oshogbo, Nig.	H12	64
Igal, Hung.	I17	10
Iganna, Nig.	H11	64
Igaporã, Braz.	B7	79
Igara Paraná, stm., Col.	H6	84
Igarka, Russia	D9	28
Igbasa-Odo, Nig.	H11	64
Iğdır, Tur.	B8	48
Igharghar, Oued, val., Afr.	J14	62
Igizyar, China	A7	44
Iglesia, Arg.	F4	80
Iglesias, Italy	J3	18
Igli, Alg.	E9	62
Igloolik, N.W. Ter., Can.	C16	96
Ignacej, Mol.	B12	20
Ignacio, Co., U.S.	G9	120
Ignacio Zaragoza, Mex.	C6	90
Ignalina, Lith.	F9	22
İğneada, Tur.	H11	20
Iguaçu, stm., S.A.	C12	80
Iguaçu, Cataratas do (Iguassu Falls), wtfl, S.A.	C11	80
Iguaí, Braz.	C8	79
Iguala, Mex.	H10	90
Igualada, Spain	D13	16
Iguana, stm., Ven.	C10	84
Iguape, Braz.	C15	80
Iguassu Falls see Iguaçu, Cataratas 99do, wtfl, S.A.	C11	80
Iguatemi, Braz.	G1	79
Iguatemi, stm., Braz.	G1	79
Iguatu, Braz.	E11	76
Iguazú, Parque Nacional, S.A.	C11	80
Iguéla, Gabon	B1	58
Iguîdi, 'Erg, dunes, Afr.	C5	54
Igžej, Russia	G12	28
Iheya-shima, i., Japan	T2	37b
Ihiala, Nig.	I13	64
Ihosy, Madag.	S22	67b
Ihtiman, Bul.	G7	20
Iida, Japan	L12	36
Iisaku, Est.	B10	22
Ii-shima, i., Japan	F12	30
Iiyama, Japan	K13	36
Iizuka, Japan	N5	36
Ijâfene, des., Afr.	D5	54
Ijaji, Eth.	M9	60
Ijebu-Igbo, Nig.	H12	64
IJmuiden, Neth.	D6	12
IJssel, stm., Neth.	C8	12
IJsselmeer (Zuiderzee), Neth.	C7	12
IJsselstein, Neth.	D7	12
Ijuí, Braz.	E12	80
Ijuí, stm., Braz.	E11	80
Ikalamavony, Madag.	R22	67b
Ikang, Nig.	I14	64
Ikaría, i., Grc.	L10	20
Ikeja, Nig.	H11	64
Ikela, Zaire	B4	58
Ikirun, Nig.	H12	64
Ikot Ekpene, Nig.	I13	64
Ikša, Russia	E20	22
Ilabaya, Peru	G6	82
Ilagan, Phil.	M19	39b
Ilaka, Madag.	Q23	67b
Īlām, Iran	E9	48
Ilām, Nepal	G12	44
Ilan, Tai.	K10	34
Ilanskij, Russia	F17	26
Ilanz, Switz.	E11	13
Ilaro, Nig.	H11	64
Iława, Pol.	B19	10
Ilbenge, Russia	E16	28
Île-à-la-Crosse, Sask., Can.	C7	104
Île-à-la-Crosse, Lac, l., Sask., Can.	C7	104
Ilebo, Zaire	B4	58
Île-de-France, hist. reg., Fr.	C9	14
Ilek, stm., Asia	G8	26
Îles, Lac des, l., Sask., Can.	D5	104
Ilesha, Nig.	H12	64
Ilesha Ibarida, Nig.	G11	64
Ilford, Man., Can.	B19	104
Ilfov, co., Rom.	E10	20
Ilfracombe, Austl.	D6	70
Ilhabela, Braz.	G6	79
Ilha Grande, Baía da, b., Braz.	G6	79
Ilhéus, Braz.	C9	79
Ili, stm., Asia	H12	26
Iliamna, Ak., U.S.	G17	100
Iliamna Lake, l., Ak., U.S.	G17	100
Ilicínia, Braz.	F6	79
Iliff, Co., U.S.	K4	118
Iligan, Phil.	D7	38
Ilimsk, Russia	F12	28
Ilinza, mtn., Ec.	H3	84
Ilion, N.Y., U.S.	D11	108
Ilizi, Alg.	G15	62
Iljinskij, Russia	K23	6
Iljinskij, Russia	H20	28
Iljinskoje, Russia	E20	22
Iljinskoje, Russia	D21	22
Iljinskoje-Chovanskoje, Russia	E22	22
Ilkal, India	E4	46
Il'kino, Russia	F24	22
Illampu, Nevado, mtn., Bol.	F7	82
Illapel, Chile	F3	80
Ille-et-Vilaine, dept., Fr.	D5	14
Illéla, Niger	D12	64
Iller, stm., Ger.	H10	10
Illescas, Mex.	F8	90
Illescas, Spain	E8	16
Illiers, Fr.	D8	14
Illimani, Nevado, mtn., Bol.	G8	82
Illimo, Peru	B2	82
Illinois, state, U.S.	D9	98
Illinois, stm., U.S.	F2	114
Illinois, stm., Il., U.S.	I6	110
Illinois, stm., Or., U.S.	H2	122
Illinois Peak, mtn., U.S.	C10	122
Illiopolis, Il., U.S.	C7	114
Il'men', ozero, l., Russia	C14	22
Ilmenau, Ger.	E10	10
Ilo, Peru	G6	82
Ilobasco, El Sal.	D6	92
Iloilo, Phil.	C7	38
Ilopango, Lago de, l., El Sal.	D5	92
Ilora, Nig.	H11	64
Ilorin, Nig.	G12	64
Ilūkste, Lat.	F9	22
Ilwaki, Indon.	G8	38
Imabari, Japan	M8	36
Imabu, stm., Braz.	H14	84
Imandra, ozero, l., Russia	H23	6
Imari, Japan	N4	36
Imaruí, Braz.	E14	80
Imaruí, Lagoa do, b., Braz.	E14	80
Imatra, Fin.	K21	6
Imbabura, prov., Ec.	G3	84
Imbituba, Braz.	E14	80
Imbituva, Braz.	C13	80
Imboden, Ar., U.S.	F5	114
Imeni Babuškina, Russia	B26	22
Imeni 0206 Bakinskich Komissarov, Azer.	B10	48
Imeni C'urupy, Russia	F21	22
Imeni Vorovskogo, Russia	F24	22
Imeni Žel'abova, Russia	C19	22
Imerimandroso, Madag.	P23	67b
Imi, Eth.	G9	56
Imías, Cuba	D7	94
Imilac, Chile	C4	80
Imi-n'Tanout, Mor.	E6	62
Imišli, Azer.	B10	48
Imjin-gang, stm., Asia	F14	32
Imlay, Nv., U.S.	D7	124
Imlay City, Mi., U.S.	G12	110
Immingham Dock, Eng., U.K.	H13	8
Immokalee, Fl., U.S.	M5	112
Imola, Italy	E6	18
Imotski, Cro.	F12	18
Imperatriz, Braz.	E9	76
Imperia, Italy	F3	18
Imperial, Sask., Can.	G9	104
Imperial, Peru	E3	82
Imperial, Ca., U.S.	L10	124
Imperial, Ne., U.S.	K6	118
Imperial, Tx., U.S.	H4	116
Imperial, stm., Chile	J2	80
Imperial Beach, Ca., U.S.	L8	124
Imperial Mills, Alta., Can.	B23	102
Imperial Valley, val., Ca., U.S.	L10	124
Impfondo, Congo	A3	58
Imphāl, India	H15	44
Impilachti, Russia	K22	6
Imsil, S. Kor.	H15	32
Imuris, Mex.	B4	90
Ina, Japan	L12	36
Ina, Il., U.S.	D8	114
Inambari, stm., Peru	E7	82
In Amguel, Alg.	I13	62
In Amnas, Alg.	F15	62
Iñapari, Peru	D7	82
In'aptuk, gora, mtn., Russia	F14	28
Inari, Fin.	G20	6
Inarijärvi, l., Fin.	G20	6
Inauini, stm., Braz.	C8	82
Inawashiro-ko, l., Japan	J15	36
In Belbel, Alg.	G11	62
Inca, Spain	F14	16
Inca de Oro, Chile	D4	80
Incaguasi, Chile	E3	80
İncesu, Tur.	B3	48
Inch'ŏn, S. Kor.	F14	32
Incline Village, Nv., U.S.	E6	124
Incomáti (Komati), stm., Afr.	E11	66
Indaiá, stm., Braz.	E6	79
Inda Silase, Eth.	J10	60
Indaw, Burma	C3	40
Indé, Mex.	E7	90
Independence, Ca., U.S.	H7	124
Independence, Ia., U.S.	H4	110
Independence, Ks., U.S.	N12	118
Independence, Ky., U.S.	I2	108
Independence, La., U.S.	L6	114
Independence, Mo., U.S.	C2	114
Independence, Or., U.S.	F2	122
Independence, Va., U.S.	C5	112
Independence, Wi., U.S.	F4	110
Independence, stm., N.Y., U.S.	D11	108
Independence Mountains, mts., Nv., U.S.	C9	124
Independencia, Bol.	G8	82
Independencia, Isla, i., Peru	F3	82
India (Bhārat), ctry., Asia	E10	42
Indialantic, Fl., U.S.	K6	112
Indian, stm., Mi., U.S.	D9	110
Indiana, Pa., U.S.	G7	108
Indiana, state, U.S.	C9	98
Indiana Dunes National Lakeshore, In., U.S.	A9	114
Indianapolis, In., U.S.	C10	114
Indian Brook, N.S., Can.	F13	106
Indian Church, Belize	I15	90
Indian Head, Sask., Can.	H11	104
Indian Lake, N.Y., U.S.	D12	108
Indian Ocean	J11	126
Indianola, Ia., U.S.	I2	110
Indianola, Ms., U.S.	I6	114
Indianola, Ne., U.S.	K7	118
Indianópolis, Braz.	E5	79
Indian Peak, mtn., Ut., U.S.	F3	120
Indian Peak, mtn., Wy., U.S.	F16	122
Indian River, Mi., U.S.	E11	110
Indian River, b., Fl., U.S.	K6	112
Indian Springs, Nv., U.S.	H10	124
Indiantown, Fl., U.S.	L6	112
Indiaporã, Braz.	E3	79
Indibir, Eth.	M9	60
Indigirka, stm., Russia	D21	28
Indio, Ca., U.S.	K9	124
Indio, stm., Nic.	F10	92
Indio, stm., Pan.	H14	92
Indira Gandhi Canal, India	F5	44
Indispensable Reefs, rf., Sol.Is.	B12	68
Indochina, reg., Asia	H11	24
Indonesia, ctry., Asia	G7	38
Indore, India	I6	44
Indragiri, stm., Indon.	O7	40
Indrāvati, stm., India	C6	46
Indre, dept., Fr.	F8	14
Indre-et-Loire, dept., Fr.	E7	14
Indura, Bela.	H6	22
Indus, stm., Asia	H2	44
Industry, Il., U.S.	B6	114
Industry, Tx., U.S.	J10	116
Indwe, S. Afr.	H8	66
İnece, Tur.	H11	20
In Ecker, Alg.	H13	62
İnegöl, Tur.	I13	20
Inez, Ky., U.S.	B4	112
Inez, Tx., U.S.	K10	116
Inferior, Laguna, b., Mex.	I12	90
Infiernillo, Presa del, res., Mex.	H9	90
Ingal, Niger	C13	64
Ingelheim, Ger.	F8	10
Ingelmunster, Bel.	G3	12
Ingende, Zaire	B3	58
Ingeniero Luiggi, Arg.	H6	80
Ingeniero Luis A. Huergo, Arg.	J5	80
Ingeniero White, Arg.	J7	80
Ingenio La Esperanza, Arg.	C6	80
Ingenio Santa Ana, Arg.	D6	80
Ingersoll, Ont., Can.	G15	110
Ingham, Austl.	B7	70
Ingleside, Tx., U.S.	L9	116
Inglewood, Austl.	G9	70
Inglewood, Ca., U.S.	K7	124
Inglis, Man., Can.	H13	104
Ingoda, stm., Russia	G14	28
Ingolstadt, Ger.	G11	10
Ingonish, N.S., Can.	F13	106
Ingornachoix Bay, b., Newf., Can.	B16	106
Ingrāj Bāzār, India	H13	44
Ingram, Tx., U.S.	I7	116
In Guezzam, Alg.	B12	64
Ingwiller, Fr.	D14	14
Inhaca, Ilha da, i., Moz.	F11	66
Inhafenga, Moz.	C11	66
Inhambane, Moz.	D12	66
Inhambupe, Braz.	A9	79
Inhaminga, Moz.	B12	66
Inhanduí, stm., Braz.	F1	79
Inhapim, Braz.	E7	79
Inharrime, Moz.	E12	66
Inhaúma, Braz.	E6	79
Inhumas, Braz.	D4	79
Inimutaba, Braz.	E6	79
Inírida, stm., Col.	F8	84
Inisa, Nig.	H12	64
Inishmore, i., Ire.	H4	8
Injibara, Eth.	L9	60
Injune, Austl.	E8	70
Inkom, Id., U.S.	H13	122
Inkster, N.D., U.S.	C10	118
Inland Lake, l., Man., Can.	F15	104
Inland Sea see Seto-naikai, Japan	M7	36
Inle Lake, l., Burma	D4	40
Inman, Ks., U.S.	M10	118
Inman, S.C., U.S.	D4	112
Inman Mills, S.C., U.S.	D4	112
Inn (En), stm., Eur.	D20	14
Innamincka, Austl.	F4	70
Inner Channel, strt., Belize	I15	90
Inner Hebrides, is., Scot., U.K.	E7	8
Inner Mongolia see Nei Monggol Zizhiqu, prov., China	C10	30
Innertkirchen, Switz.	E9	13
Innisfail, Austl.	A7	70
Innisfail, Alta., Can.	E21	102
Innisfree, Alta., Can.	D23	102
Innsbruck, Aus.	H11	10
Inocência, Braz.	E3	79
Inola, Ok., U.S.	C11	116
Inongo, Zaire	B3	58
Inowrocław, Pol.	C18	10
In Rhar, Alg.	G11	62
In Salah, Alg.	G12	62
Ińsko, Pol.	B15	10
Inspiration, Az., U.S.	K6	120
Instow, Sask., Can.	I6	104
Inta, Russia	D10	26
Intendente Alvear, Arg.	H7	80
İntepe, Tur.	I10	20
Interlaken, Switz.	E8	13
Interlândia, Braz.	D4	79
International Falls, Mn., U.S.	B2	110
Inthanon, Doi, mtn., Thai.	E5	40
Intibucá, Hond.	C6	92
Intibucá, dept., Hond.	C6	92
Intipucá, El Sal.	D6	92
Intiyaco, Arg.	E8	80
Intracoastal Waterway, U.S.	H5	112
Intracoastal Waterway, U.S.	K10	116
Intuto, Peru	I5	84
Inukjuak, Que., Can.	E17	96
Inuvik, N.W. Ter., Can.	B28	100
Inuya, stm., Peru	D5	82
Invercargill, N.Z.	G2	72
Inverell, Austl.	G9	70
Invergordon, Scot., U.K.	D9	8
Invermay, Sask., Can.	G11	104
Invermere, B.C., Can.	G18	102
Inverness, N.S., Can.	F12	106
Inverness, Scot., U.K.	D9	8
Inverness, Ca., U.S.	F3	124
Inverness, Fl., U.S.	K4	112
Inverness, Ms., U.S.	I6	114
Investigator Group, is., Austl.	F6	68
Investigator Strait, strt., Austl.	J2	70
Inwood, Man., Can.	H17	104
Inwood, Ia., U.S.	H11	118
Inyangani, mtn., Zimb.	B11	66
Inyantue, Zimb.	B8	66
Inyati, Zimb.	B9	66
Inyokern, Ca., U.S.	I8	124
Inywa, Burma	C4	40
Inza, Russia	G7	26
Inzana Lake, l., B.C., Can.	C10	102
Inžavino, Russia	I25	22
Ioánnina, Grc.	J4	20
Iō-jima (Iwo Jima), i., Japan	F18	126
Iola, Ks., U.S.	N12	118
Iola, Wi., U.S.	F6	110
Iolotan', Turk.	J10	26
Iona, N.S., Can.	G13	106
Iona, Id., U.S.	G14	122
Ione, Ca., U.S.	F5	124
Ione, Or., U.S.	E6	122
Ione, Wa., U.S.	B8	122
Ionia, Mi., U.S.	H10	110
Ionian Islands see Iónioi Nísoi, is., Grc.	K4	20
Ionian Sea, Eur.	H11	4
Iónioi Nísoi, is., Grc.	K4	20
Íos, i., Grc.	M9	20
Iosegun, stm., Alta., Can.	C18	102
Iosegun Lake, Alta., Can.	C18	102
Iota, La., U.S.	L4	114
Iowa, La., U.S.	L3	114
Iowa, state, U.S.	C8	98
Iowa, stm., Ia., U.S.	I4	110
Iowa City, Ia., U.S.	I4	110
Iowa Falls, Ia., U.S.	H2	110
Iowa Park, Tx., U.S.	F8	116
Ipameri, Braz.	D4	79
Ipatinga, Braz.	E7	79
Ipava, Il., U.S.	B6	114
Ípeiros, hist. reg., Grc.	J4	20
Ipel' (Ipoly), stm., Eur.	G19	10
Ipiales, Col.	G4	84
Ipiaú, Braz.	C9	79
Ipirá, Braz.	B9	79
Ipiranga, Braz.	C13	80
Ipita, Bol.	H10	82
Ipixuna, stm., Braz.	B5	82
Ipixuna, stm., Braz.	B10	82
Ipixuna, stm., Braz.	B10	82
Ipoh, Malay.	L6	40
Ipoly (Ipel'), stm., Eur.	G18	10
Iporá, Braz.	D3	79
Iporã, Braz.	G2	79
Ipoti-Ekiti, Nig.	H12	64
Ipswich, Austl.	F10	70
Ipswich, Eng., U.K.	I15	8
Ipswich, Ma., U.S.	E16	108
Ipswich, S.D., U.S.	F8	118
Ipu, Braz.	D10	76
Ipupiara, Braz.	A7	79
Iqaluit, N.W. Ter., Can.	D19	96
Iquique, Chile	G7	74
Iquique, Chile	I6	82
Iquitos, Peru	I6	84
Ira, Tx., U.S.	G5	116
Iraan, Tx., U.S.	I5	116
Iracajá, Cachoeira do, wtfl, Braz.	D9	82
Iraí, Braz.	D12	80
Iráklion, Grc.	N9	20
Iran (Īrān), ctry., Asia	C5	42
Iran, Pegunungan, mts., Asia	E5	38
Īrānshahr, Iran	H16	48
Irapa, Ven.	B11	84
Irapuato, Mex.	G9	90
Iraq (Al-ʻIrāq), ctry., Asia	C3	42
Irará, Braz.	B9	79
Irati, Braz.	C13	80
Irazú, Volcán, vol., C.R.	H11	92
Irbeni väin (Irves šaurums), strt., Eur.	D5	22
Irbid, Jord.	C5	50
Irbīl, Iraq	C8	48
Irbit, Russia	F10	26
Ireland (Eire), ctry., Eur.	E6	4
Irene, S. Afr.	E9	66
Irene, S.D., U.S.	H10	118
Ireng (Maú), stm., S.A.	E13	84
Ireton, Ia., U.S.	I11	118
Irgiz, Kaz.	H10	26
Iri, S. Kor.	H14	32
Iriba, Chad	J2	60
Irîgui, reg., Afr.	C7	64
Iringa, Tan.	C7	58
Iriona, Hond.	B9	92
Iriri, stm., Braz.	D8	76
Irish, Mount, mtn., Nv., U.S.	G10	124
Irish Sea, Eur.	H8	8
Irkutsk, Russia	G12	28
Irma, Alta., Can.	E23	102
Iron Belt, Wi., U.S.	D5	110
Iron Bridge, Ont., Can.	D12	110
Iron City, Tn., U.S.	G9	114
Iron Creek, stm., Alta., Can.	E23	102
Irondale, Al., U.S.	I10	114
Irondale, Mo., U.S.	E6	114
Irondequoit, N.Y., U.S.	D9	108
Iron Gate, val., Eur.	E6	20
Iron Gate Reservoir, res., Eur.	E6	20
Iron Knob, Austl.	I2	70
Iron Mountain, Mi., U.S.	E7	110
Iron Mountains, mts., U.S.	C5	112
Iron Range, Austl.	B8	68
Iron River, Mi., U.S.	D7	110
Iron River, Wi., U.S.	D4	110
Ironton, Mn., U.S.	D2	110
Ironton, Mo., U.S.	E6	114
Ironton, Oh., U.S.	I4	108
Ironwood, Mi., U.S.	D5	110
Iroquois, Ont., Can.	C11	108
Iroquois, S.D., U.S.	G10	118
Iroquois, stm., U.S.	J8	110
Iroquois Falls, Ont., Can.	B15	110
Irrawaddy see Ayeyarwady, stm., Burma	F3	40
Irricana, Alta., Can.	F21	102
Irrigon, Or., U.S.	E6	122
Iršava, Ukr.	A7	20
Irtyš (Ertix), stm., Asia	E11	26
Irtyš (Ertix), stm., Asia	A3	30
Irtyšsk, Kaz.	G13	26
Irumu, Zaire	A5	58
Irún, Spain	B10	16
Irupana, Bol.	G8	82
Irurzun, Spain	C10	16
Irú Tepuy, mtn., Ven.	E12	84
Irves šaurums (Irbeni väin), strt., Eur.	D5	22
Irvine, Alta., Can.	I4	104
Irvine, Scot., U.K.	F9	8
Irvine, Ky., U.S.	B3	112
Irvines Landing, B.C., Can.	H10	102
Irving, Il., U.S.	C7	114
Irving, Tx., U.S.	G10	116
Irvington, Ky., U.S.	E10	114
Irwinton, Ga., U.S.	G3	112
Isaac, stm., Austl.	D8	70
Isaac Lake, l., B.C., Can.	D14	102
Isabel, S.D., U.S.	F6	118
Isabela, Phil.	D7	38
Isabela, Cabo, c., Dom. Rep.	E9	94
Isabela, Isla, i., Ec.	J13	84a
Isabela, Isla, i., Mex.	G7	90
Isabelia, Cordillera, mts., Nic.	D9	92
Isabelle, stm., Mn., U.S.	C4	110
Isaccea, Rom.	D12	20
Ísafjörður, Ice.	A2	6a
Isahaya, Japan	O5	36
Īsa Khel, Pak.	D4	44
Ișalnița, Rom.	E7	20
Isana (Içana), stm., S.A.	G8	84
Isanti, Mn., U.S.	E2	110
Isar, stm., Eur.	G11	10
Isara, Nig.	H11	64
Ischia, Italy	I8	18
Ischia, Isola d', i., Italy	I8	18
Iscuandé, stm., Col.	F4	84
Ise (Uji-yamada), Japan	M11	36
Iseo, Lago d', l., Italy	D5	18
Isère, dept., Fr.	G12	14
Isère, stm., Fr.	G12	14
Iserlohn, Ger.	D7	10
Isernia, Italy	H9	18
Isesaki, Japan	K14	36
Iset', stm., Russia	F11	26
Iseyin, Nig.	H11	64
Isherton, Guy.	F13	84
Ishinomaki, Japan	I16	36
Ishioka, Japan	K15	36
Ishpeming, Mi., U.S.	D8	110
Isigny, Fr.	C5	14
Isil'kul', Russia	G12	26
Išim, Russia	F11	26
Išim, stm., Asia	F12	26
Išimbaj, Russia	G9	26
Isiolo, Kenya	A7	58
Isipingo, S. Afr.	G10	66
Isiro, Zaire	H6	56
Isisford, Austl.	E6	70
Iskâr, stm., Bul.	F8	20
Iskâr, jazovir, res., Bul.	G7	20
İskele, N. Cyp.	D2	48
İskenderun, Tur.	C4	48
İskenderun Körfezi, b., Tur.	H15	4
Iskitim, Russia	G8	28
Iskut, stm., B.C., Can.	H29	100
Isla, Mex.	H12	90
Isla, Salar de la, pl., Chile	C4	80
Isla Cristina, Spain	H4	16
Isla de Maipo, Chile	G3	80
Islāmābād, Pak.	D5	44
Islāmkot, Pak.	H4	44
Islāmpur, India	D3	46
Isla Mujeres, Mex.	G16	90
Island, Ky., U.S.	E9	114
Island Falls, Sask., Can.	C12	104
Island Falls, Me., U.S.	A18	108
Island Lagoon, l., Austl.	H2	70
Island Lake, Man., Can.	E20	104
Island Lake, l., Man., Can.	E20	104
Island Park, Id., U.S.	F14	122
Island Park Reservoir, res., Id., U.S.	F14	122
Island Pond, Vt., U.S.	C15	108
Island Pond, l., Newf., Can.	D17	106
Islands, Bay of, b., Newf., Can.	C15	106
Isla Patrulla, Ur.	G11	80
Islas de la Bahía, dept., Hond.	A8	92
Isla Verde, Arg.	G7	80
Isla Vista, Ca., U.S.	J6	124
Islay, i., Scot., U.K.	F7	8
Islay, Punta, c., Peru	G5	82
Isle, Mn., U.S.	D2	110
Isle-aux-Morts, Newf., Can.	E15	106
Isle of Hope, Ga., U.S.	H5	112
Isle of Man, dep., Eur.	E7	4
Isle of Palms, S.C., U.S.	G7	112
Isle of Wight, Va., U.S.	C10	112
Isle of Wight, co., Eng., U.K.	K12	8
Isle Royale National Park, Mi., U.S.	B7	110
Islesboro Island, i., Me., U.S.	C18	108
Isleta, N.M., U.S.	J10	120
Isleton, Ca., U.S.	F4	124
Islets-Caribou, Que., Can.	C6	106
Islón, Chile	E3	80
Ismael Cortinas, Ur.	G10	80
Ismailia see Al-Ismāʻīlīyah, Egypt	B7	60
İsmailli, Tur.	K11	20
Isnā, Egypt	E7	60
Isojoki, Fin.	J17	6
Isola, Ms., U.S.	I6	114
Isone, Switz.	F10	13
Isparta, Tur.	H14	4
İspir, Tur.	A6	48
Israel (Yisra'el), ctry., Asia	C2	42
Israel, stm., N.H., U.S.	C15	108
Issano, Guy.	E13	84
Issoire, Fr.	G10	14
Issoudun, Fr.	F9	14
Is-sur-Tille, Fr.	E12	14
Issyk-Kul' (Rybačje), Kyrg.	I13	26
Issyk-Kul', ozero, l., Kyrg.	I13	26
İstanbul, Tur.	H12	20
İstanbul Boğazı (Bosporus), strt., Tur.	H13	20
Istmina, Col.	E4	84
Isto, Mount, mtn., Ak., U.S.	B23	100
Istokpoga, Lake, l., Fl., U.S.	L5	112
Istra, Russia	F19	22
Istra, pen., Eur.	D8	18
Istria see Istra, pen., Eur.	D8	18
Itá, Para.	C10	80
Itabaiana, Braz.	E11	76
Itabaiana, Braz.	F11	76
Itabapoana, Braz.	F8	79
Itaberá, Braz.	G4	79
Itaberaba, Braz.	B8	79
Itaberaí, Braz.	D4	79
Itabira, Braz.	E7	79
Itabuna, Braz.	C9	79
Itacambiruçu, stm., Braz.	D7	79
Itacaré, Braz.	C9	79
Itacoatiara, Braz.	I13	84
Itacurubí del Rosario, Para.	C10	80
Itaeté, Braz.	B8	79
Itagi, Braz.	C8	79
Itaguaçu, Braz.	E8	79
Itaguajé, Braz.	G3	79
Itaguara, Braz.	F6	79
Itaguari, stm., Braz.	C6	79
Itaguaru, Braz.	C4	79
Itagüí, Col.	D5	84
Itaí, Braz.	G4	79
Itá-Ibaté, Arg.	D10	80
Itaiópolis, Braz.	D14	80
Itaituba, Braz.	D7	76
Itajá, Braz.	E3	79
Itajaí, Braz.	D14	80
Itajaí do Sul, stm., Braz.	D14	80
Itajubá, Braz.	G6	79
Itaju do Colônia, Braz.	C9	79
Itajuípe, Braz.	C9	79
Italy, Tx., U.S.	G10	116
Italy (Italia), ctry., Eur.	G10	4
Itamaraju, Braz.	D9	79
Itamarandiba, Braz.	D7	79
Itamarandiba, stm., Braz.	D7	79
Itamari, Braz.	B9	79
Itambacuri, Braz.	E8	79
Itambé, Braz.	C8	79
Itami, Japan	M10	36
Itanhaém, Braz.	H5	79
Itanhauã, stm., Braz.	A9	82
Itanhém, Braz.	D8	79
Itanhomi, Braz.	E8	79
Itaobim, Braz.	D8	79
Itapaci, Braz.	C4	79
Itapagipe, Braz.	E4	79
Itaparaná, stm., Braz.	B10	82
Itaparica, Ilha de, i., Braz.	B9	79
Itapaya, Bol.	G8	82
Itapé, Braz.	C9	79
Itapebi, Braz.	C9	79
Itapecerica, Braz.	F6	79
Itapecuru-Mirim, Braz.	D10	76
Itapemirim, Braz.	F8	79
Itaperuna, Braz.	F8	79
Itapetinga, Braz.	C8	79
Itapetininga, Braz.	G4	79
Itapetininga, stm., Braz.	G5	79
Itapeva, Braz.	G4	79
Itapicuru, stm., Braz.	D10	76
Itapicuru, stm., Braz.	F11	76
Itapira, Braz.	G5	79
Itapiranga, Braz.	D12	80
Itapiranga, Braz.	I13	84
Itapirapuã, Braz.	C3	79
Itapitanga, Braz.	C9	79
Itápolis, Braz.	F4	79
Itaporã, Braz.	G1	79
Itaporanga, Braz.	G4	79
Itapúa, dept., Para.	D11	80
Itapuranga, Braz.	C4	79
Itaquaí, stm., Braz.	J7	84
Itaquara, Braz.	B9	79
Itaquari, Braz.	F8	79
Itaqui, Braz.	E10	80
Itaquyry, Para.	C11	80
Itarantim, Braz.	C8	79
Itararé, Braz.	H4	79
Itārsi, India	I7	44
Itarumã, Braz.	E3	79
Itasca, Tx., U.S.	G9	116
Itasca, Lake, l., Mn., U.S.	D12	118
Itata, stm., Chile	I2	80
Itatí, Arg.	D9	80
Itatiaia, Parque Nacional do, Braz.	G6	79
Itatinga, Braz.	G4	79
Itaúna, Braz.	F6	79
Itenes (Guaporé), stm., S.A.	E10	82
Ithaca, Mi., U.S.	G11	110
Ithaca, N.Y., U.S.	E10	108
Itháki, Grc.	K4	20
Itháki, i., Grc.	K4	20
Itinga, Braz.	D8	79
Itinga, stm., Braz.	D8	79
Itiquira, Braz.	D1	79
Itirapina, Braz.	G5	79
Itiruçu, Braz.	B8	79
Itō, Japan	M14	36
Itoigawa, Japan	J12	36
Itomamo, Lac, l., Que., Can.	C3	106
Itonamas, stm., Bol.	E9	82
Itororó, Braz.	C8	79
Itsā, Egypt	C6	60
Itta Bena, Ms., U.S.	I6	114
Itú, Braz.	G5	79
Itu, stm., Braz.	E11	80
Ituaçu, Braz.	B8	79
Ituango, Col.	D5	84
Ituberá, Braz.	B9	79
Itucumã, stm., Braz.	B7	82
Itueta, Braz.	E8	79
Ituí, stm., Braz.	J7	84
Ituim, stm., Braz.	E13	80
Ituiutaba, Braz.	E4	79
Itumbiara, Braz.	E4	79
Ituna, Sask., Can.	G11	104
Ituni, Guy.	E13	84
Ituporanga, Braz.	D14	80
Iturama, Braz.	E3	79
Iturbe, Para.	D10	80
Iturbide, Mex.	H15	90
Iturup, ostrov (Etorofu-tō), i., Russia	C22	36a
Ituverava, Braz.	F5	79
Ituxi, stm., Braz.	B9	82
Ituzaingó, Arg.	D10	80
Itzehoe, Ger.	B9	10
Iuka, Ms., U.S.	H8	114
Iúna, Braz.	F8	79
Iva, S.C., U.S.	E4	112
Ivacevići, Bela.	I8	22
Ivahona, Madag.	S22	67b
Ivaí, stm., Braz.	G2	79
Ivaiporã, Braz.	C13	80
Ivane-Puste, Ukr.	A10	20
Ivangorod, Russia	B11	22
Ivangrad, Yugo.	G3	20
Ivanhoe, Austl.	I6	70
Ivanhoe, Ca., U.S.	H6	124
Ivanhoe, Mn., U.S.	G11	118
Ivanhoe, Va., U.S.	C6	112
Ivan'kovo, Russia	G20	22
Ivan'kovskij, Russia	E23	22
Ivan'kovskoje vodochranilišče, res., Russia	E19	22
Ivano-Frankovsk, Ukr.	H2	26
Ivanovo, Bela.	I8	22
Ivanovo, Russia	D23	22
Ivato, Madag.	R22	67b
Ivatuba, Braz.	G2	79
Ivdel', Russia	E10	26
Ivenec, Bela.	H9	22
Ivinheima, stm., Braz.	G2	79
Ivje, Bela.	H8	22
Ivón, stm., Bol.	D8	82
Ivorogbo, Nig.	I13	64
Ivory Coast (Côte d'Ivoire), ctry., Afr.	G5	54
Ivory Coast, I.C.	I7	64
Ivrea, Italy	D2	18
İvrindi, Tur.	J11	20
Ivujivik, Que., Can.	D17	96
Iwaki (Taira), Japan	J15	36
Iwakuni, Japan	M7	36
Iwamizawa, Japan	D16	36a
Iwanai, Japan	E15	36a
Iwo, Nig.	H12	64
Iwo Jima see Iō-jima, i., Japan	F18	126
Iwŏn, N. Kor.	C16	32
Ixcán, stm., N.A.	B3	92
Ixchiguán, Guat.	B3	92
Ixiamas, Bol.	E7	82
Iximché, hist., Guat.	C4	92
Ixmiquilpan, Mex.	G10	90
Ixopo, S. Afr.	H10	66
Ixtahuacán, Guat.	B3	92
Ixtapa, Mex.	I9	90
Ixtepec, Mex.	I12	90
Ixtlán de Juárez, Mex.	I11	90
Ixtlán del Río, Mex.	G7	90
ʻIyāl Bakhīt, Sud.	K5	60
Iyo-mishima, Japan	N8	36
Izabal, Guat.	B5	92
Izabal, dept., Guat.	B5	92
Izabal, Lago de, l., Guat.	B5	92
Īzad Khvāst, Iran	F12	48
Izalco, El Sal.	D5	92
Izamal, Mex.	G15	90
Izapa, hist., Mex.	J13	90

Name	Map Ref.	Page
ʻIzbat Abū Ṣuql, Egypt	F1	50
Izberbaš, Russia	I7	26
Izbica, Pol.	A17	10
Izd'oškovo, Russia	F16	22
Izegem, Bel.	G3	12
Īzeh, Iran	F10	48
Iževsk, Russia	F8	26
Izkī, Oman	C10	47
Ižma, stm., Russia	E8	26
Izmail, Ukr.	H3	26
Izmalkovo, Russia	I20	22
İzmir (Smyrna), Tur.	K11	20
İzmit, Tur.	G13	4
Iznajar, Embalse de, res., Spain	H7	16
Izoplit, Russia	E19	22
Izopo, Punta, c., Hond.	B7	92
Izozog, Bañados del, sw., Bol.	H10	82
Izraʻ, Syria	C6	50
Izsák, Hung.	I19	10
Iztaccíhuatl, Volcán, vol., Mex.	H10	90
Iztaccíhuatl y Popocatéptl, Parques Nacionales, Mex.	H10	90
Iztapa, Guat.	D4	92
Izucar de Matamoros, Mex.	H10	90
Izuhara, Japan	M4	36
Iz'um, Ukr.	H5	26
Izumi, Japan	C5	36
Izumi, Japan	M10	36
Izumi, Japan	I15	36
Izumo, Japan	L7	36
Izu-shotō, is., Japan	E15	30
Izvestij CIK, ostrova, is., Russia	B14	26
J		
Jaba, Eth.	N8	60
Jabal al-Awliyā', Sud.	J7	60
Jabalpur, India	I8	44
Jabālyah, Isr. Occ.	E2	50
Jabiru, Austl.	B6	68
Jabjabah, Wādī, val., Afr.	G7	60
Jablah, Syria	D3	48
Jablonec nad Nisou, Czech.	E15	10
Jabłonka, Pol.	F19	10
Jablonov, Ukr.	A8	20
Jablonovyj chrebet, mts., Russia	G14	28
Jaboatão, Braz.	E11	76
Jaborandi, Braz.	F4	79
Jaboticabal, Braz.	F4	79
Jabung, Tanjung, c., Indon.	O8	40
Jaca, Spain	C11	16
Jacala, Mex.	G10	90
Jacaleapa, Hond.	C8	92
Jacaltenango, Guat.	B3	92
Jacaraci, Braz.	C7	79
Jacaré, stm., Braz.	B8	79
Jacaré, stm., Braz.	B10	82
Jacareí, Braz.	G6	79
Jacarezinho, Braz.	G4	79
Jaceel, val., Som.	F11	56
Jáchal, stm., Arg.	F4	80
Jachroma, Russia	E20	22
Jaciara, Braz.	C1	79
Jacinto, Braz.	D8	79
Jacinto Aráuz, Arg.	J7	80
Jacinto City, Tx., U.S.	J11	116
Jacinto Machado, Braz.	E14	80
Jaciparaná, Braz.	C9	82
Jaciparaná, stm., Braz.	D9	82
Jackfish Lake, l., Sask., Can.	E6	104
Jackhead Harbour, Man., Can.	G17	104
Jackman, Me., U.S.	B16	108
Jack Mountain, mtn., Wa., U.S.	B5	122
Jackpot, Nv., U.S.	C11	124
Jacksboro, Tn., U.S.	C2	112
Jacksboro, Tx., U.S.	F8	116
Jacks Fork, stm., Mo., U.S.	E5	114
Jackson, Al., U.S.	K9	114
Jackson, Ca., U.S.	F5	124
Jackson, Ga., U.S.	F3	112
Jackson, Ky., U.S.	B3	112
Jackson, La., U.S.	L5	114
Jackson, Mi., U.S.	H11	110
Jackson, Mn., U.S.	H13	118
Jackson, Ms., U.S.	J6	114
Jackson, Mo., U.S.	E7	114
Jackson, N.C., U.S.	C9	112
Jackson, Oh., U.S.	H4	108
Jackson, S.C., U.S.	F5	112
Jackson, Tn., U.S.	G8	114
Jackson, Wy., U.S.	A6	120
Jackson, Mount, mtn., Ant.	C12	73
Jackson Center, Oh., U.S.	G2	108
Jackson Creek, stm., Can.	I13	104
Jackson Lake, l., Wy., U.S.	G15	122
Jackson's Arm, Newf., Can.	C17	106
Jacksonville, Al., U.S.	I11	114
Jacksonville, Ar., U.S.	H4	114
Jacksonville, Fl., U.S.	I5	112
Jacksonville, Il., U.S.	C6	114
Jacksonville, N.C., U.S.	E9	112
Jacksonville, Or., U.S.	H3	122
Jacksonville, Tx., U.S.	H11	116
Jacksonville Beach, Fl., U.S.	I5	112
Jacmel, Haiti	E8	94
Jaco, Mex.	D7	90
Jacobābād, Pak.	F3	44
Jacobina, Braz.	F10	76
Jacobsdal, S. Afr.	G7	66
Jacques, Lac à, l., N.W. Ter., Can.	C31	100
Jacques-Cartier, Détroit de, strt., Que., Can.	C10	106
Jacques-Cartier, Mont, mtn., Que., Can.	D8	106
Jacquet River, N.B., Can.	E7	106
Jacqueville, I.C.	I7	64
Jacuba, stm., Braz.	E2	79
Jacuí, stm., Braz.	F12	80
Jacuípe, stm., Braz.	B9	79
Jacumba, Ca., U.S.	L9	124
Jacupiranga, Braz.	C14	80
Jaén, Peru	A2	82
Jaén, Spain	H8	16
Jāfarābād, India	B1	46
Jaffa, Cape, c., Austl.	K3	70
Jaffa, Tel Aviv- see Tel Aviv-Yafo, Isr.	D3	50
Jaffna, Sri L.	H6	46
Jaffrey, N.H., U.S.	E14	108
Jafr, Qāʻal-, depr., Jord.	H6	50
Jagādhri, India	E7	44
Jagdalpur, India	C7	46
Jagersfontein, S. Afr.	G7	66
Jagodnoje, Russia	E21	28
Jagraon, India	E6	44
Jagtiāl, India	C5	46
Jaguaquara, Braz.	B9	79
Jaguarão, Braz.	G12	80
Jaguarão (Yaguarón), stm., S.A.	G12	80
Jaguari, Braz.	E11	80
Jaguariaíva, Braz.	C14	80
Jaguaribe, stm., Braz.	E11	76
Jaguaripe, Braz.	B9	79
Jaguaruna, Braz.	E14	80
Jagüé, Arg.	E4	80
Jagüey Grande, Cuba	C4	94
Jahānābād, India	H11	44
Jahrom, Iran	G12	48
Jailolo, Indon.	E8	38
Jaipur, India	G6	44
Jaisalmer, India	G4	44
Jaja, Russia	F15	26
Jājapur, India	J12	44
Jajce, Bos.	E12	18
Jakarta, Indon.	J13	39a
Jake Creek Mountain, mtn., Nv., U.S.	C9	124
Jakobstad (Pietarsaari), Fin.	J18	6
Jakša, Russia	E9	26
Jakutsk, Russia	E17	28
Jal, N.M., U.S.	G3	116
Jalālābād, Afg.	C4	44
Jalāmīd, Sau. Ar.	B10	60
Jalán, stm., Hond.	C8	92
Jalandhar, India	E6	44
Jalapa, Guat.	C5	92
Jalapa, Nic.	D8	92
Jalapa, dept., Guat.	C5	92
Jālgaon, India	J6	44
Jalisco, state, Mex.	G7	90
Jālna, India	C3	46
Jālor, India	H5	44
Jalostotitlán, Mex.	G8	90
Jalpa, Mex.	G8	90
Jalpāiguri, India	G13	44
Jalpan, Mex.	G10	90
Jalta, Ukr.	I4	26
Jaltepec, stm., Mex.	I12	90
Jalūlā', Iraq	D8	48
Jalutorovsk, Russia	F11	26
Jamaame, Som.	A8	58
Jamaica, ctry., N.A.	E6	94
Jamaica Channel, strt., N.A.	E7	94
Jamal, poluostrov, pen., Russia	C12	26
Jamālpur, Bngl.	H13	44
Jamālpur, India	H12	44
Jamantau, gora, mtn., Russia	G9	26
Jamanxim, stm., Braz.	A13	82
Jamari, stm., Braz.	C10	82
Jamarovka, Russia	G14	28
Jambelí, Canal de, strt., Ec.	I2	84
Jambi, Indon.	F3	38
Jambol, Bul.	G10	20
James, stm., Alta., Can.	F20	102
James, stm., U.S.	H10	118
James, stm., Mo., U.S.	E3	114
James, stm., Va., U.S.	B9	112
James Bay, b., Can.	F16	96
James City, N.C., U.S.	D9	112
James Craik, Arg.	G7	80
James Island, S.C., U.S.	G7	112
Jamesport, Mo., U.S.	C3	114
James Ross, Cape, c., N.W. Ter., Can.	B10	96
James Ross Strait, strt., N.W. Ter., Can.	C13	96
James Smith Indian Reserve, Sask., Can.	E10	104
Jamestown, Austl.	I3	70
Jamestown, S. Afr.	H8	66
Jamestown, Ca., U.S.	G5	124
Jamestown, Ks., U.S.	L10	118
Jamestown, Ky., U.S.	F11	114
Jamestown, N.Y., U.S.	E7	108
Jamestown, N.C., U.S.	D7	112
Jamestown, N.D., U.S.	E9	118
Jamestown, Oh., U.S.	H3	108
Jamestown, Tn., U.S.	F12	114
Jamestown Reservoir, res., N.D., U.S.	D9	118
Jaminauá, stm., Braz.	C6	82
Jamkhandi, India	D3	46
Jamm, Russia	C11	22
Jammu, India	D6	44
Jammu and Kashmīr, dep., Asia	C10	42
Jamnagar, India	I4	44
Jampol', Ukr.	A12	20
Jamsah, Egypt	D7	60
Jamshedpur, India	I12	44
Jamsk, Russia	F22	28
Jämtlands Län, co., Swe.	J13	6
Jamūi, India	H12	44
Jamuna, stm., Bngl.	H13	44
Jamundí, Col.	F4	84
Jana, stm., Russia	C19	28
Janauacá, Lago, l., Braz.	I12	84
Janaúba, Braz.	C7	79
Janaucu, Ilha, i., Braz.	C8	76
Jand, Pak.	D5	44
Jandaia, Braz.	D3	79
Jandaia do Sul, Braz.	G3	79
Jandaq, Iran	D13	48
Jandiāla, India	E6	44
Jandiatuba, stm., Braz.	J8	84
Janeiro, Rio de, stm., Braz.	A6	79
Janesville, Ca., U.S.	D5	124
Janesville, Mn., U.S.	F2	110
Janesville, Wi., U.S.	H6	110
Jangijul', Uzb.	I11	26
Jangīpur, India	H13	44
Janīn, Isr. Occ.	D4	50
Janjina, Madag.	R21	67b
Jan Kempdorp (Andalusia), S. Afr.	F7	66
Jan Lake, l., Sask., Can.	D12	104
Jan Mayen, i., Sval.	A6	52
Janos, Mex.	B5	90
Jánoshalma, Hung.	I19	10
Jánosháza, Hung.	H17	10
Janoviči, Bela.	F13	22
Jansen, Sask., Can.	G10	104
Janskij zaliv, b., Russia	C19	28
Jantarnyj, Russia	G2	22
Januária, Braz.	C6	79
Janzé, Fr.	E5	14
Jaora, India	I6	44
Japan (Nihon), ctry., Asia	D14	30
Japan, Sea of (Nihon-kai), Asia	K7	36
Japim, Braz.	B5	82
Japurá, Braz.	H9	84
Japurá (Caquetá), stm., S.A.	H8	84
Jaqué, Pan.	D3	84
Jaquí, Peru	F4	82
Jarābulus, Syria	C5	48
Jarad, Sau. Ar.	E2	47
Jaraguá, Braz.	C4	79
Jaraguá do Sul, Braz.	D14	80
Jaraiz de la Vera, Spain	E6	16
Jarales, N.M., U.S.	J10	120
Jarama, stm., Spain	E8	16
Jaramānah, Syria	B6	50
Jaransk, Russia	F7	26
Jarash, Jord.	D5	50
Jarbidge, stm., U.S.	H10	122
Jarcevo, Russia	F15	22
Jardim, Braz.	I13	82
Jardín América, Arg.	D11	80
Jardine River National Park, Austl.	B8	68
Jardines de la Reina, Archipiélago de los, is., Cuba	D5	94
Jardinópolis, Braz.	F5	79
Jaredi, Nig.	E12	64
Jaremča, Ukr.	A8	20
Jarensk, Russia	E7	26
Jargara, Mol.	C12	20
Jargeau, Fr.	E9	14
Jari, stm., Braz.	A10	82
Jari, Lago, l., Braz.	J11	84
Jaridih, India	I12	44
Jarmen, Ger.	B13	10
Jarnac, Fr.	G6	14
Jarocin, Pol.	D17	10
Jaroměř, Czech.	E15	10
Jaroslavl', Russia	D22	22
Jarosław, Pol.	E22	10
Jarratt, Va., U.S.	C9	112
Jarreau, La., U.S.	L5	114
Jaru, Braz.	D10	82
Jaru, stm., Braz.	D10	82
Järva-Jaani, Est.	B8	22
Järvenpää, Fin.	K19	6
Jarvie, Alta., Can.	C21	102
Jarvis, Ont., Can.	H15	110
Jarvisburg, N.C., U.S.	C11	112
Jarvis Island, i., Oc.	I23	126
Jaša Tomić, Yugo.	D4	20
Jasikan, Ghana	H10	64
Jasin'a, Ukr.	A8	20
Jāsk, Iran	I14	48
Jasło, Pol.	F21	10
Jasnogorsk, Russia	G20	22
Jason Islands, is., Falk. Is.	G4	78
Jasonville, In., U.S.	C9	114
Jasper, Alta., Can.	E16	102
Jasper, Al., U.S.	I9	114
Jasper, Ar., U.S.	F3	114
Jasper, Fl., U.S.	I4	112
Jasper, Ga., U.S.	E2	112
Jasper, In., U.S.	D10	114
Jasper, Mn., U.S.	H11	118
Jasper, Mo., U.S.	E2	114
Jasper, Tn., U.S.	G11	114
Jasper, Tx., U.S.	L3	114
Jasper Lake, l., Alta., Can.	D16	102
Jasper National Park, Alta., Can.	E17	102
Jászapáti, Hung.	H20	10
Jászberény, Hung.	H19	10
Jász-Nagykun-Szolnok, co., Hung.	H20	10
Jataí, Braz.	D3	79
Jatapu, stm., Braz.	H13	84
Jataté, stm., Mex.	I14	90
Jatni, India	J11	44
Jatobá, stm., Braz.	B1	79
Jaú, Braz.	G4	79
Jaú, stm., Braz.	H12	84
Jauaperi, stm., Braz.	H12	84
Jauja, Peru	D4	82
Jaungulbene, Lat.	D9	22
Jaunjelgava, Lat.	E8	22
Jaunpiebalga, Lat.	D9	22
Jaunpur, India	H10	44
Jaupaci, Braz.	D3	79
Jauquara, stm., Braz.	F13	82
Jauru, stm., Braz.	E1	79
Jauru, stm., Braz.	G13	82
Java, S.D., U.S.	F8	118
Java see Jawa, i., Indon.	J15	39a
Javari (Yavarí), stm., S.A.	D4	76
Javas, Russia	G25	22
Java Sea see Jawa, Laut, Indon.	G5	38
Java Trench	J11	24
Jawa (Java), i., Indon.	J15	39a
Jawa, Laut (Java Sea), Indon.	G5	38
Jawbar, Syria	A6	50
Jawor, Pol.	D16	10
Jaworzno, Pol.	E19	10
Jay, Fl., U.S.	L9	114
Jay, Ok., U.S.	C12	116
Jaya, Puncak, mtn., Indon.	F10	38
Jayanca, Peru	B2	82
Jayapura (Sukarnapura), Indon.	F11	38
Jayb, Wādī al- (Ha'Arava), val., Asia	H4	50
Jaynes, Az., U.S.	L5	120
Jaypur, India	C7	46
Jayton, Tx., U.S.	F6	116
Jaželbicy, Russia	C15	22
Jeanerette, La., U.S.	M5	114
Jebba, Nig.	G12	64
Jebeniana, Tun.	C16	62
Jeberos, Peru	A3	82
Jechegnadzor, Arm.	B8	48
Jeddore Lake, res., Newf., Can.	D18	106
Jędrzejów, Pol.	E20	10
Jefawa, Sud.	L2	60
Jeffara (Al-Jifārah), pl., Afr.	D16	62
Jeffers, Mn., U.S.	G12	118
Jefferson, Ga., U.S.	E3	112
Jefferson, Ia., U.S.	I13	118
Jefferson, N.C., U.S.	C5	112
Jefferson, Oh., U.S.	F6	108
Jefferson, Or., U.S.	F2	122
Jefferson, S.C., U.S.	E6	112
Jefferson, S.D., U.S.	I11	118
Jefferson, Tx., U.S.	J2	114
Jefferson, Wi., U.S.	G7	110
Jefferson, stm., Mt., U.S.	E13	122
Jefferson, Mount, mtn., U.S.	F14	122
Jefferson, Mount, mtn., Nv., U.S.	F9	124
Jefferson, Mount, mtn., Or., U.S.	F4	122
Jefferson City, Mo., U.S.	D4	114
Jefferson City, Tn., U.S.	C3	112
Jeffersonton, Va., U.S.	I9	108
Jeffersontown, Ky., U.S.	D11	114
Jeffersonville, Ga., U.S.	G3	112
Jeffersonville, In., U.S.	D11	114
Jeffersonville, Oh., U.S.	H3	108
Jeffrey City, Wy., U.S.	B9	120
Jefimovskij, Russia	L24	6
Jefremov, Russia	G5	26
Jega, Nig.	E12	64
Jegenstorf, Switz.	D8	13
Jegorjevsk, Russia	F22	22
Jejsk, Russia	H5	26
Jēkabpils, Lat.	E8	22
Jekaterinburg, Russia	F10	26
Jekateriny, proliv, strt., Russia	I21	28
Jekimoviči, Russia	G16	22
Jekyll Island, i., Ga., U.S.	H5	112
Jelabuga, Russia	F8	26
Jelancy, Russia	G13	28
Jel'cy, Russia	E16	22
Jelec, Russia	I21	22
Jelenia Góra (Hirschberg), Pol.	E15	10
Jelenskij, Russia	H18	22
Jelgava, Lat.	E6	22
Jelizarovo, Russia	C27	22
Jelizavety, mys, c., Russia	G20	28
Jelizovo, Bela.	H12	22
Jellico, Tn., U.S.	C2	112
Jelm Mountain, mtn., Wy., U.S.	C11	120
Jel'n'a, Russia	G16	22
Jelnat', Russia	D25	22
Jeloguj, stm., Russia	E15	26
Jelšava, Czech.	G20	10
Jemanželinsk, Russia	G10	26
Jember, Indon.	G5	38
Jemca, Russia	J27	6
Jemez, stm., N.M., U.S.	I10	120
Jemez Springs, N.M., U.S.	I10	120
Jemmal, Tun.	N5	18
Jena, Ger.	E11	10
Jena, La., U.S.	K4	114
Jenašimskij Polkan, gora, mtn., Russia	F16	26
Jenbach, Aus.	H11	10
Jendouba (Souk el Arba), Tun.	M3	18
Jenisej (Yenisey), stm., Russia	D15	26
Jenisejsk, Russia	F10	28
Jenisejskij kr'až, mts., Russia	F16	26
Jenisejskij zaliv, b., Russia	C8	28
Jenkins, Ky., U.S.	B4	112
Jenkinsville, S.C., U.S.	E5	112
Jenkintown, Pa., U.S.	G11	108
Jenks, Ok., U.S.	C11	116
Jennersdorf, Aus.	I16	10
Jennings, Fl., U.S.	I3	112
Jennings, La., U.S.	L4	114
Jenpeg Dam, Man., Can.	D16	104
Jensen, Ut., U.S.	D7	120
Jensen Beach, Fl., U.S.	L6	112
Jens Munk Island, i., N.W. Ter., Can.	C17	96
Jeparit, Austl.	K4	70
Jepelacio, Peru	B3	82
Jepifan', Russia	H21	22
Jequeri, Braz.	F7	79
Jequetepeque, stm., Peru	B2	82
Jequié, Braz.	B8	79
Jequitaí, Braz.	D6	79
Jequitinhonha, Braz.	D8	79
Jequitinhonha, stm., Braz.	D9	79
Jerada, Mor.	C9	62
Jeradou, Tun.	M5	18
Jerba, Île de, i., Tun.	D16	62
Jerécuaro, Mex.	G9	90
Jérémie, Haiti	E7	94
Jeremoabo, Braz.	F11	76
Jerevan, Arm.	I6	26
Jerez de García Salinas, Mex.	F8	90
Jerez de la Frontera, Spain	I5	16
Jerez de los Caballeros, Spain	G5	16
Jergeni, hills, Russia	H6	26
Jericho see Arīḥā, Isr. Occ.	E4	50
Jericó, Col.	E5	84
Jerid, Chott, sw., Tun.	D15	62
Jerilderie, Austl.	J6	70
Jerimoth Hill, hill, R.I., U.S.	F15	108
Jermiš', Russia	G25	22
Jermolajevo, Russia	E19	4
Jermolino, Russia	F19	22
Jeroaquara, Braz.	C3	79
Jerofej Pavlovič, Russia	G16	28
Jerome, Az., U.S.	J4	120
Jerome, Id., U.S.	H11	122
Jersey, dep., Eur.	F7	4
Jersey City, N.J., U.S.	G12	108
Jersey Mountain, mtn., Id., U.S.	E10	122
Jersey Shore, Pa., U.S.	F9	108
Jerseyville, Il., U.S.	C6	114
Jeršov, Russia	G7	26
Jerusalem see Yerushalayim, Isr.	E4	50
Jervis, Cape, c., Austl.	J3	70
Jervis Bay, b., Austl.	J9	70
Jervis Inlet, b., B.C., Can.	H10	102
Jesenice, Czech.	E13	10
Jesi, Italy	F8	18
Jesil', Kaz.	G11	26
Jessentuki, Russia	I6	26
Jessore, Bngl.	I13	44
Jessup, Pa., U.S.	F11	108
Jesup, Ga., U.S.	H5	112
Jesup, Ia., U.S.	H3	110
Jesús, Para.	D11	80
Jesús Carranza, Mex.	I12	90
Jesús de Otoro, Hond.	C7	92
Jesús María, Arg.	F6	80
Jesús María, Mex.	E6	90
Jesús María, stm., Mex.	F7	90
Jesús Menéndez, Cuba	D6	94
Jet, Ok., U.S.	C8	116
Jetmore, Ks., U.S.	M8	118
Jetpur, India	J4	44
Jette, Bel.	G5	12
Jeumont, Fr.	B11	14
Jeune Landing, B.C., Can.	G7	102
Jever, Ger.	B7	10
Jevlach, Azer.	I7	26
Jevpatorija, Ukr.	H4	26
Jewell, Ia., U.S.	H2	110
Jewell, Ks., U.S.	L9	118
Jewell Ridge, Va., U.S.	B5	112
Jewett, Il., U.S.	C8	114
Jewett, Tx., U.S.	H10	116
Jewett City, Ct., U.S.	F15	108
Jewett Lake, l., Sask., Can.	B10	104
Jezerce, mtn., Alb.	G3	20
Jezerišče, Bela.	F12	22
Jeziorany, Pol.	B20	10
Jhābua, India	I6	44
Jhālāwār, India	H7	44
Jhal Jhao, Pak.	G1	44
Jhang Sadar, Pak.	E5	44
Jhānsi, India	H8	44
Jharia, India	I12	44
Jhārsuguda, India	B8	46
Jhelum, Pak.	D5	44
Jhelum, stm., Asia	E5	44
Jhok Rind, Pak.	E4	44
Jhunjhunūn, India	F6	44
Jiaban, China	B9	40
Jiading, China	D10	34
Jiāganj, India	H13	44
Jiakou, China	E8	34
Jiali, China	E5	30
Jialing, stm., China	E8	30
Jialou, China	C2	34
Jiamusi, China	B13	30
Ji'an, China	H3	34
Jianchang, China	B12	32
Jianchuan, China	A5	40
Jiangbeixu, China	I4	34
Jiangbianzhai, China	C6	40
Jiangcun, China	G6	34
Jiangdihe, China	B6	40
Jiangduo, China	C9	34
Jianggezhuang, China	D7	32
Jiangji, China	C4	34
Jiangjin, China	F8	30
Jiangkou, China	G9	30
Jiangkou, China	H7	34
Jiangkouji, China	C5	34
Jiangliadian, China	A5	32
Jiangmen, China	M2	34
Jiangsu (Kiangsu), prov., China	E10	30
Jiangtun, China	B10	32
Jiangxi (Kiangsi), prov., China	F10	30
Jiangxiang, China	C6	34
Jiangyin, China	D9	34
Jiangzhasiji, China	E13	44
Jianli, China	F1	34
Jianning, China	I5	34
Jian'ou, China	H7	34
Jianshan, China	F9	34
Jianshui, China	C7	40
Jiantouji, China	I5	32
Jiaohe, China	C12	30
Jiaomei, China	K6	34
Jiaoshanhe, China	F1	34
Jiaoxian, China	G7	32
Jiaozuo, China	D9	30
Jiashan, China	C7	34
Jiashun Hu, l., China	C12	44
Jiawang, China	A6	34
Jiaxian, China	B2	34
Jiaxing, China	E9	34
Jiayu, China	F2	34
Jiazi, China	M5	34
Jibiya, Nig.	E13	64
Jiboa, stm., El Sal.	D5	92
Jicarón, Isla, i., Pan.	D2	84
Jicatuyo, stm., Hond.	C6	92
Jiddah (Jeddah), Sau. Ar.	D1	47
Jidingxilin, China	D15	44
Jiedong, China	I2	34
Jiehe, China	H5	32
Jieji, China	B7	34
Jiepai, China	E8	34
Jiesheng, China	M4	34
Jieshou, China	B4	34
Jieshou, China	B8	34
Jieyang, China	L5	34
Jieznas, Lith.	G7	22
Jigongzhen, China	A4	34
Jiguaní, Cuba	D6	94
Jiguanshan, China	A12	32
Jigüey, Bahía de, b., Cuba	C5	94
Jihlava, Czech.	F15	10
Jijel, Alg.	B13	62
Jijiadianzi, China	H6	32
Jikawo, Eth.	M7	60
Jikawo, stm., Afr.	M8	60
Jilib, Som.	A8	58
Jili Hu, l., China	B4	30
Jilin, China	C12	30
Jilin (Kirin), prov., China	C12	30
Jill, Kediet ej, mtn., Maur.	I4	62
Jima, Eth.	N9	60
Jimbolia, Rom.	D4	20
Jiménez, Mex.	C9	90
Jiménez, Mex.	D7	90
Jiménez del Téul, Mex.	F7	90
Jimo, China	G8	32
Jim Thorpe, Pa., U.S.	G11	108
Jin (Gam), stm., Asia	C8	40
Jināḥ, Egypt	E6	60
Jinan (Tsinan), China	G4	32
Jinbang, China	J7	34
Jincheng, China	D9	30
Jīnd, India	F7	44
Jindřichův Hradec, Czech.	F15	10
Jingangtou, China	H2	34
Jingcheng, China	K6	34
Jingdezhen (Kingtechen), China	F6	34
Jinggang, China	G1	34
Jinggangshan (Ciping), China	I3	34
Jinghai, China	E4	32
Jinghaiwei, China	G10	32
Jinghong, China	C6	40
Jingning, China	H8	34
Jingoutun, China	B5	32
Jingxi, China	C9	40
Jingxian, China	F4	32
Jingyu, China	A14	32
Jingzhi, China	G7	32
Jinhua, China	F8	34
Jining, China	C9	30
Jining, China	H4	32
Jinja, Ug.	A6	58
Jinjiang, China	A6	40
Jinjing, China	G2	34
Jinkeng, China	H6	34
Jinkou, China	G8	32
Jinlingzhen, China	G6	32
Jinning, China	B7	40
Jinotega, Nic.	D8	92
Jinotega, dept., Nic.	D9	92
Jinotepe, Nic.	F8	92
Jinping, China	A10	40
Jinrui, China	H3	34
Jinsha, stm., China	F6	30
Jinshan, China	E10	34
Jinshi, China	F9	30
Jintian, China	H3	34
Jinxi, China	C8	32
Jinxian, China	D9	32
Jinyun, China	G9	34
Jinzhaizhen, China	D4	34
Jinzhou (Chinchou), China	B9	32
Ji-Paraná, Braz.	D11	82
Jipijapa, Ec.	H2	84
Jiquilisco, El Sal.	D6	92
Jiquilisco, Bahía de, b., El Sal.	D6	92
Jiquiriçá, stm., Braz.	B8	79
Jirāfī, Wādī al- (Naḥal Paran), val.	I3	50
Jirbān, Sud.	L6	60
Jirjā, Egypt	D6	60
Jirkov, Czech.	E13	10
Jīroft, Iran	G14	48
Jisr ash-Shughūr, Syria	D4	48
Jitan, China	K4	34
Jitaúna, Braz.	C9	79
Jiu, stm., Rom.	F7	20
Jiubao, China	J4	34
Jiucheng, China	E5	32
Jiuguan, China	F9	32
Jiuhu, China	F5	32
Jiuhuaxian, China	L2	34
Jiujiang, China	F4	34
Jiukou, China	E1	34
Jiulian Shan, mts., China	K3	34
Jiuling Shan, mts., China	G3	34
Jiulong, China	K1	34
Jiumianyang, China	E2	34
Jiuningyang, China	J6	34
Jiuquan, China	D6	30
Jiushangshui, China	B3	34
Jiutai, China	C12	30
Jiuxian, China	B2	34
Jiuxiangcheng, China	B3	34
Jixi, China	B13	30
Jixian, China	H2	32
Jixian, China	C5	32
Jixingji, China	C5	34
Jiyang, China	G5	32
Jīzān, Sau. Ar.	F3	47
Joaçaba, Braz.	D13	80
Joaíma, Braz.	D8	79
Joanna, S.C., U.S.	E5	112
João Neiva, Braz.	E8	79
João Pessoa, Braz.	E12	76
João Pinheiro, Braz.	D5	79
Joaquim Távora, Braz.	G4	79
Joaquin, Tx., U.S.	K2	114
Joaquín V. González, Arg.	C6	80
Job Peak, mtn., Nv., U.S.	E7	124
Jocolí, Arg.	G4	80
Jocón, Hond.	B8	92
Jocoro, El Sal.	D6	92
Jocotán, Guat.	C5	92
Jódar, Spain	H8	16
Jodhpur, India	G5	44
Joe Batt's Arm, Newf., Can.	C19	106
Joensuu, Fin.	J21	6
Joetsu, Japan	J13	36
Joffre, Mount, mtn., Can.	G19	102
Jõgeva, Est.	C9	22
Jog Falls, wtfl, India	E3	46
Joggins, N.S., Can.	G9	106
Jogui, stm., Braz.	G1	79
Johannesburg, S. Afr.	F9	66
Johannesburg, Ca., U.S.	I8	124
John Day, Or., U.S.	F7	122
John Day, stm., Or., U.S.	E5	122
John H. Kerr Reservoir, res., U.S.	C8	112
John Martin Reservoir, res., Co., U.S.	M4	118
John O'Groats, Scot., U.K.	C10	8
John Redmond Reservoir, res., Ks., U.S.	M12	118
Johnson, Ar., U.S.	F2	114
Johnson, Ks., U.S.	N6	118
Johnson, Ne., U.S.	K12	118
Johnson, Vt., U.S.	C14	108
Johnsonburg, Pa., U.S.	F8	108
Johnson City, N.Y., U.S.	E11	108
Johnson City, Tn., U.S.	C4	112
Johnson City, Tx., U.S.	I8	116
Johnsondale, Ca., U.S.	I7	124
Johnsons Crossing, Yukon, Can.	F28	100
Johnsonville, S.C., U.S.	F7	112
Johnston, Ia., U.S.	I2	110
Johnston, S.C., U.S.	F5	112
Johnston Atoll, atoll, Oc.	G23	126
Johnston City, Il., U.S.	E8	114
Johnstone Strait, strt., B.C., Can.	G8	102
Johnstown, Co., U.S.	D12	120
Johnstown, N.Y., U.S.	D12	108
Johnstown, Oh., U.S.	G4	108
Johnstown, Pa., U.S.	G8	108
Johor Baharu, Malay.	N7	40
Joigny, Fr.	E10	14
Joiner, Ar., U.S.	G6	114
Joinvile, Braz.	D14	80
Joinville, Fr.	D12	14
Joinville Island, i., Ant.	B1	73
Jokkmokk, Swe.	H16	6
Jolārpettai, India	F5	46
Jolfā, Iran	B8	48
Joliet, Il., U.S.	I7	110
Joliet, Mt., U.S.	E17	122
Joliette, Que., Can.	A13	108
Jolo, Phil.	D7	38
Jomda, China	E6	30
Jonava, Lith.	F7	22
Jones, Ok., U.S.	D9	116
Jonesboro, Ar., U.S.	G6	114
Jonesboro, Ga., U.S.	F2	112
Jonesboro, Il., U.S.	E7	114
Jonesboro, In., U.S.	B11	114
Jonesboro, La., U.S.	J4	114
Jonesboro, Tn., U.S.	C4	112
Jonesburg, Mo., U.S.	D5	114
Jones Mill, Ar., U.S.	H4	114
Jonesport, Me., U.S.	C19	108
Jones Sound, strt., N.W. Ter., Can.	A15	96
Jonestown, Ms., U.S.	H6	114
Jonesville, La., U.S.	K5	114
Jonesville, Mi., U.S.	I11	110
Jonesville, N.C., U.S.	C6	112
Jonesville, S.C., U.S.	E5	112
Jonesville, Va., U.S.	C3	112
Jónicas, Islas see Iónioi Nísoi, is., Grc.	K4	20
Joniškėlis, Lith.	E7	22
Joniškis, Lith.	E6	22
Jönköping, Swe.	M14	6
Jonquière, Que., Can.	D2	106
Jonuta, Mex.	H13	90
Joplin, Mo., U.S.	E2	114
Joplin, Mt., U.S.	B15	122
Joppa, Il., U.S.	E8	114
Jordan, Mn., U.S.	F2	110
Jordan, Mt., U.S.	C19	122
Jordan, N.Y., U.S.	D10	108
Jordan (Al-Urdun), ctry., Asia	C2	42
Jordan (Nahr al-Urdunn) (HaYarden), stm., Asia	E5	50
Jordan, stm., Ut., U.S.	D5	120
Jordânia, Braz.	C8	79
Jordanów, Pol.	F19	10
Jordan Valley, Or., U.S.	H8	122
Jordão, stm., Braz.	C13	80
Jordet, Nor.	K13	6
Jorhāt, India	G16	44
Jornado del Muerto, des., N.M., U.S.	K10	120
Jos, Nig.	G14	64
José Batlle y Ordóñez, Ur.	G11	80
José Bonifácio, Braz.	F4	79
José Francisco Vergara, Chile	B4	80
Joselândia, Braz.	G13	82
José Pedro Varela, Ur.	G11	80
Joseph, Or., U.S.	E8	122
Joseph, Lac, l., Newf., Can.	F19	96
Joseph Bonaparte Gulf, b., Austl.	B5	68
Joseph City, Az., U.S.	J6	120
Joshua, Tx., U.S.	G9	116
Joshua Tree, Ca., U.S.	J9	124
Joškar-Ola, Russia	F7	26
Josselin, Fr.	E4	14
Joubertina, S. Afr.	I6	66
Jourdanton, Tx., U.S.	K8	116
Jovellanos, Cuba	C4	94
Joviânia, Braz.	D4	79
Jowhar, Som.	H10	56
Joy, Il., U.S.	I5	110
Joy, Mount, mtn., Yukon, Can.	E28	100
Joyce, La., U.S.	K4	114
Józefów, Pol.	C21	10
J. Percy Priest Lake, res., Tn., U.S.	F10	114
Juami, stm., Braz.	H9	84
Juan Aldama, Mex.	E8	90
Juan B. Arruabarrena, Arg.	F9	80
Juan Bautista Alberdi, Arg.	D6	80
Juan de Fuca, Strait of, strt., N.A.	I10	102
Juan de Mena, Para.	C10	80
Juan de Nova, Île, i., Reu.	E8	58
Juan E. Barra, Arg.	I8	80
Juan Eugenio, Mex.	E8	90
Juan Fernández, Archipiélago, is., Chile	C1	78
Juangriego, Ven.	B11	84
Juan Guerra, Peru	B3	82
Juan Jorba, Arg.	G6	80
Juan José Castelli, Arg.	C8	80
Juán José Perez, Bol.	F7	82
Juanjuí, Peru	B3	82
Juan L. Lacaze, Ur.	H10	80
Juan N. Fernández, Arg.	J9	80
Juan Perez Sound, strt., B.C., Can.	E3	102
Juan Viñas, C.R.	H11	92
Juárez, Mex.	D9	90
Juárez, Mex.	B5	90
Juárez, Sierra de, mts., Mex	B2	90
Juárez see Ciudad Juárez, Mex.	B6	90
Juatinga, Ponta de, c., Braz.	G6	79
Juàzeiro, Braz.	E10	76
Juazeiro do Norte, Braz.	E11	76
Jūbā, Sud.	H7	56
Juba, stm., Braz.	F12	82
Jūbāl, Maḍīq, strt., Egypt	D7	60
Jubal, Strait of see Jūbāl, Maḍīq, strt., Egypt	D7	60

Name	Map Ref.	Page
Jubaysho, Eth.	O9	60
Jubayt, Sud.	H9	60
Jubba (Genale), stm., Afr.	H9	56
Jubbah, Sau. Ar.	G6	48
Jubilee Lake, l., Newf., Can.	D18	106
Jubones, stm., Ec.	I3	84
Juby, Cap, c., Mor.	G4	62
Júcar (Xúquer), stm., Spain	F10	16
Juçara, Braz.	C3	79
Júcaro, Cuba	D5	94
Juchipila, Mex.	G8	90
Juchitán de Zaragoza, Mex.	I12	90
Juchnov, Russia	G18	22
Juchoviči, Bela.	E11	22
Jucuapa, El Sal.	D6	92
Jucurucu, stm., Braz.	D9	79
Judaea, hist. reg., Asia	E4	50
Judas, Punta, c., C.R.	H10	92
Jude Island, i., Newf., Can.	E19	106
Judenburg, Aus.	H14	10
Judique, N.S., Can.	G12	106
Judith, stm., Mt., U.S.	C16	122
Judith Gap, Mt., U.S.	D16	122
Judith Mountains, mts., Mt., U.S.	C16	122
Judson, S.C., U.S.	E4	112
Judsonia, Ar., U.S.	G5	114
Juexi, China	F10	34
Jufari, stm., Braz.	H11	84
Jugon, Fr.	D4	14
Juḥā, Sau. Ar.	F3	47
Juidongshan, China	L6	34
Juigalpa, Nic.	E9	92
Juína, stm., Braz.	E12	82
Juiz de Fora, Braz.	F7	79
Jujuy, prov., Arg.	B5	80
Jukagirskoje ploskogorje, plat., Russia	D23	28
Julesburg, Co., U.S.	K5	118
Juli, Peru	G7	82
Juliaca, Peru	F6	82
Julia Creek, Austl.	C4	70
Julianakanaal, Neth.	F8	12
Julian Alps, mts., Eur.	C8	18
Juliana Top, mtn., Sur.	F14	84
Julianehåb, Grnld.	C15	86
Jülich, Ger.	E6	10
Julimes, Mex.	C7	90
Júlio de Castilhos, Braz.	E12	80
Julu, China	F3	32
Juma, Russia	I23	6
Jumay, Volcán, vol., Guat.	C5	92
Jumbilla, Peru	A3	82
Jumboo, Som.	B8	58
Jumentos Cays, is., Bah.	C7	94
Jumet, Bel.	H5	12
Jumilla, Spain	G10	16
Jump, stm., Wi., U.S.	E5	110
Jūnāgadh, India	J4	44
Junaynah, Ra's al-, mtn., Egypt	G2	48
Junction, Tx., U.S.	I7	116
Junction, Ut., U.S.	F4	120
Junction City, Ar., U.S.	I4	114
Junction City, Ks., U.S.	L11	118
Junction City, Ky., U.S.	E12	114
Junction City, Or., U.S.	F2	122
Jundiaí, Braz.	G5	79
Jundiaí do Sul, Braz.	G3	79
Juneau, Ak., U.S.	G27	100
Juneau, Wi., U.S.	G7	110
Junee, Austl.	J7	70
June Lake, Ca., U.S.	G6	124
Jungar Qi, China	D9	30
Jungfrau, mtn., Switz.	E8	13
Junggar Pendi, China	B4	30
Jungshāhi, Pak.	H2	44
Juniata, Ne., U.S.	K9	118
Juniata, stm., Pa., U.S.	G9	108
Junín, Arg.	H8	80
Junín, Ec.	H2	84
Junín, Peru	D3	82
Junín, dept., Peru	D4	82
Junín, Lago de, l., Peru	D3	82
Junior, W.V., U.S.	I7	108
Juniper, N.B., Can.	F6	106
Juniville, Fr.	C11	14
Junqueirópolis, Braz.	F3	79
Juntas, C.R.	G9	92
Junxian, China	E9	30
Juparanã, Lagoa, l., Braz.	E8	79
Jupilingo, stm., Guat.	C5	92
Jupiter, Fl., U.S.	M6	112
Jupiter, stm., Que., Can.	C10	106
Juquiá, Braz.	C15	80
Juquiá, Ponta do, c., Braz.	C15	80
Jur, Czech.	G17	10
Jur, stm., Sud.	M5	60
Jura, state, Switz.	D7	13
Jura, dept., Fr.	F12	14
Jura, mts., Eur.	F13	14
Jura, i., Scot., U.K.	E8	8
Juramento, Braz.	D7	79
Juratiški, Bela.	G8	22
Jurbarkas, Lith.	F5	22
Jurf ad-Darāwīsh, Jord.	G5	50
Jurga, Russia	F8	28
Jurjevec, Russia	D26	22
Jurjev-Pol'skij, Russia	E22	22
Jūrmala, Lat.	E6	22
Jurty, Russia	F17	26
Juruá, Braz.	I9	84
Juruá, stm., S.A.	D5	76
Juruá-mirim, stm., Braz.	C5	82
Juruena, stm., Braz.	B12	82
Jurupari, stm., Braz.	C7	82
Jur'uzan', Russia	G9	26
Juscelândia, Braz.	C3	79
Jusepín, Ven.	C11	84
Juskatla, B.C., Can.	D2	102
Jussey, Fr.	E12	14
Justiniano Posse, Arg.	G7	80
Justo Daract, Arg.	G6	80
Jutaí, Braz.	A7	82
Jutaí, stm., Braz.	D5	76
Jüterbog, Ger.	D13	10
Juti, Braz.	G1	79
Jutiapa, Guat.	C5	92
Jutiapa, dept., Guat.	C5	92
Juticalpa, Hond.	C8	92
Jutiquile, Hond.	C8	92
Jutland see Jylland, pen., Den.	M11	6
Juva, Fin.	K20	6
Juventud, Isla de la (Isla de Pinos), i., Cuba	D3	94
Juxi, China	H8	34
Juža, Russia	E25	22
Južno-Sachalinsk, Russia	H20	28
Južno-Ural'sk, Russia	G10	26
Južnyj, mys, c., Russia	F23	28
Južnyj Bug, stm., Ukr.	H4	26
Jwayyā, Leb.	B4	50
Jylland, pen., Den.	M11	6
Jyväskylä, Fin.	J19	6

K

Name	Map Ref.	Page
K2 (Qogir Feng), mtn., Asia	C7	44
Kaachka, Turk.	J9	26
Kaachka, Turk.	C15	48
Kaala, mtn., Hi., U.S.	p15	125a
Kaapstad see Cape Town, S. Afr.	I4	66
Kabah, hist., Mex.	G15	90
Kabale, Ug.	B5	58
Kabalega Falls, wtfl, Ug.	H7	56
Kabalo, Zaire	C5	58
Kabambare, Zaire	B5	58
Kabba, Nig.	H13	64
Kabetogama Lake, l., Mn., U.S.	B3	110
Kabinda, Zaire	C4	58
Kabīr Kūh, mts., Iran	E9	48
Kabkābīyah, Sud.	K3	60
Kabna, Sud.	H7	60
Kābol, Afg.	C3	44
Kābol, stm., Asia	C4	44
Kabompo, stm., Zam.	D4	58
Kabongo, Zaire	C5	58
Kabot, Gui.	F2	64
Kabou, Togo	G10	64
Kabr, Sud.	L4	60
Kābul see Kābol, Afg.	C3	44
Kaburuang, Pulau, i., Indon.	E8	38
Kabwe (Broken Hill), Zam.	D5	58
Kačanik, Yugo.	G5	20
Kačerginė, Lith.	G6	22
Kachchh, Gulf of, b., India	I3	44
Kachemak Bay, b., Ak., U.S.	G19	100
Kachisi, Eth.	M9	60
Kachovskoje vodochranilišče, res., Ukr.	H4	26
K'achta, Russia	G13	28
Kachul (Kagul), Mol.	H3	26
Kačug, Russia	G13	28
Kadaiyanallūr, India	H4	46
Kadanai (Kadaney), stm., Asia	E2	44
Kadaney (Kadanai), stm., Asia	E2	44
Kadan Kyun, i., Burma	H5	40
Kade, Ghana	H9	64
Kadéï, stm., Afr.	H4	56
Kadi, India	I5	44
Kadiana, Mali	F6	64
Kadina, Austl.	I2	70
Kadiri, India	E5	46
Kadirli, Tur.	C4	48
Kadja, Ouadi (Wādī Kaja), val., Afr.	L3	60
Kadnikov, Russia	B23	22
Kadnikovskij, Russia	A23	22
Kado, Nig.	H14	64
Kadodo, Sud.	L5	60
Kadoka, S.D., U.S.	H6	118
Kadom, Russia	G25	22
Kadoma, Zimb.	B9	66
Kaduj, Russia	B20	22
Kaduna, Nig.	F13	64
Kaduna, stm., Nig.	G12	64
Kāduqlī, Sud.	L5	60
Kadyj, Russia	D26	22
Kadykčan, Russia	E21	28
Kadžerom, Russia	E9	26
Kaech'ŏn, N. Kor.	D13	32
Kaédi, Maur.	C3	64
Kaegudeck Lake, l., Newf., Can.	D18	106
Kaena Point, c., Hi., U.S.	p15	125a
Kaesŏng, N. Kor.	F14	32
Kāf, Sau. Ar.	F4	48
Kafan, Arm.	B9	48
Kafanchan, Nig.	G14	64
Kaffraria, hist. reg., Transkei	H9	66
Kaffrine, Sen.	D2	64
Kafia Kingi, Sud.	M3	60
Kafin Madaki, Nig.	F14	64
Kafirévs, Ákra, c., Grc.	K8	20
Kafr ad-Dawwār, Egypt	B6	60
Kafr ash-Shaykh, Egypt	B6	60
Kafue, stm., Zam.	E5	58
Kagan, Uzb.	J10	26
Kagaznagar, India	C5	46
Kagelike, China	B12	44
Kagera, stm., Afr.	B6	58
Kağızman, Tur.	A7	48
Kagmar, Sud.	J6	60
Kagoshima, Japan	P5	36
Kagoshima-wan, b., Japan	P5	36
Kahayan, stm., Indon.	F5	38
Kahemba, Zaire	C3	58
Kahnūj, Iran	H14	48
Kahoka, Mo., U.S.	B5	114
Kahoolawe, i., Hi., U.S.	q17	125a
Kahramanmaraş, Tur.	C4	48
Kahuku, Hi., U.S.	p16	125a
Kahuku Point, c., Hi., U.S.	p16	125a
Kahului, Hi., U.S.	q17	125a
Kahului Bay, b., Hi., U.S.	q17	125a
Kai, Kepulauan, is., Indon.	G9	38
Kaiama, Nig.	G11	64
Kaiapoi, N.Z.	E4	72
Kaibab Plateau, plat., Az., U.S.	H4	120
Kaibito Plateau, plat., Az., U.S.	H5	120
Kaidu, stm., China	C4	30
Kaieteur Fall, wtfl, Guy.	E13	84
Kaifeng, China	I2	32
Kaikoura, N.Z.	E4	72
Kailahun, S.L.	G4	64
Kaili, China	A9	40
Kailu, China	C11	30
Kailua, Hi., U.S.	p16	125a
Kailua Kona, Hi., U.S.	r18	125a
Kaimanawa Mountains, mts., N.Z.	C5	72
Kainan, Japan	M10	36
Kaipara Harbour, b., N.Z.	B5	72
Kaiping, China	G9	30
Kairāna, India	F7	44
Kairouan, Tun.	N5	18
Kaiserslautern, Ger.	F7	10
Kaishantun, China	A17	32
Kaišiadorys, Lith.	G7	22
Kaitangata, N.Z.	G2	72
Kaithal, India	F7	44
Kaituma, stm., Guy.	D13	84
Kaiwi Channel, strt., Hi., U.S.	p16	125a
Kaiyuan, China	A12	32
Kaja, Wādī (Ouadi Kadja), val., Afr.	L3	60
Kajaani, Fin.	I20	6
Kajang, Malay.	M6	40
Kajnar, Kaz.	H13	26
Kaka, Cen. Afr. Rep.	N4	60
Kākā, Sud.	L7	60
Kakadu National Park, Austl.	B6	68
Kakagi Lake, l., Ont., Can.	I21	104
Kakamas, S. Afr.	G5	66
Kake, Ak., U.S.	H28	100
Kakegawa, Japan	M13	36
Kākināda, India	D7	46
Kakisa Lake, l., N.W. Ter., Can.	D9	96
Kako, stm., Guy.	E12	84
Kakoaka, Bots.	B7	66
Kakogawa, Japan	M9	36
Kaktovik, Ak., U.S.	A23	100
Kakwa, stm., Alta., Can.	C15	102
Kalaa Kebira, Tun.	N5	18
Kalaallit Nunaat see Greenland, dep., N.A.	B15	86
Kalaa Sghira, Tun.	N5	18
Kālābagh, Pak.	D4	44
Kalabo, Zam.	D4	58
Kalač, Russia	G6	26
Kalačinsk, Russia	F12	26
Kalač-na-Donu, Russia	H6	26
Kaladan, stm., Asia	D2	40
Ka Lae, c., Hi., U.S.	s18	125a
Kalagwe, Burma	C4	40
Kalahari Desert, des., Afr.	E5	66
Kalai-Chumb, Taj.	A4	44
Kalai-Mor, Turk.	D17	48
Kalajoki, Fin.	I18	6
Kalakamate, Bots.	C8	66
Kalām, Pak.	C5	44
Kalama, Wa., U.S.	D3	122
Kalámai, Grc.	L6	20
Kalamalka Lake, l., B.C., Can.	G15	102
Kalamariá, Grc.	I6	20
Kalamazoo, Mi., U.S.	H10	110
Kalamazoo, stm., Mi., U.S.	H9	110
Kalampáka, Grc.	J5	20
Kalapana, Hi., U.S.	r19	125a
Kalaraš, Mol.	B12	20
Kalasin, Thai.	F7	40
Kalašnikovo, Russia	D18	22
Kalāt, Pak.	F2	44
Kalaw, Burma	D4	40
Kal'azin, Russia	D20	22
Kalb, Ra's al-, c., Yemen	G6	47
Kalbā', U.A.E.	B10	47
Kalbarri, Austl.	E2	68
Kale, Tur.	L12	20
Kaleden, B.C., Can.	H15	102
Kalemie (Albertville), Zaire	C5	58
Kalemyo, Burma	C3	40
Kaletwa, Burma	D2	40
Kalevala, Russia	D4	26
Kalewa, Burma	C3	40
Kálfafell, Ice.	C5	6a
Kalgan see Zhangjiakou, China	C2	32
Kalgoorlie, Austl.	F4	68
Kali, Mali	E4	64
Kaliakra, nos, c., Bul.	F12	20
Kalibo, Phil.	C7	38
Kalima, Zaire	B5	58
Kalimantan see Borneo, i., Asia	E5	38
Kálimnos, Grc.	M10	20
Kālimpang, India	G13	44
Kaliningrad (Königsberg), Russia	G3	22
Kalinin see Tver', Russia	E18	22
Kalinkoviči, Bela.	I12	22
Kalinovik, Bos.	F2	20
Kalispell, Mt., U.S.	B11	122
Kalisz, Pol.	D18	10
Kalkaska, Mi., U.S.	F10	110
Kalkfontein, Bots.	D5	66
Kallaste, Est.	C10	22
Kallavesi, l., Fin.	J20	6
Kalliecahoolie Lake, l., Man., Can.	D19	104
Kallnach, Switz.	D7	13
Kalmar, Swe.	M15	6
Kālna, India	I13	44
Kalnciems, Lat.	E6	22
Kālol, India	I5	44
Kalomo, Zam.	E5	58
Kalona, Ia., U.S.	I4	110
Kalone Peak, mtn., B.C., Can.	E8	102
Kalpeni Island, i., India	G2	46
Kalskag, Ak., U.S.	F14	100
Kaltag, Ak., U.S.	D15	100
Kaltan, Russia	G15	26
Kaluga, Russia	G19	22
Kalundborg, Den.	N12	6
Kałuszyn, Pol.	C21	10
Kalutara, Sri L.	I5	46
Kalvarija, Lith.	G6	22
Kalyān, India	C2	46
Kama, stm., Russia	F8	26
Kamaishi, Japan	H16	36
Kamakou, mtn., Hi., U.S.	p17	125a
Kamakura, Japan	L14	36
Kamamaung, Burma	F4	40
Kamanjab, Nmb.	B2	66
Kamarān, i., Yemen	G3	47
Kamarang, stm., S.A.	E12	84
Kamas, Ut., U.S.	D5	120
Kamatsi Lake, l., Sask., Can.	B12	104
Kamay, Tx., U.S.	F8	116
Kamba, Nig.	F11	64
Kambam, India	H4	46
Kambar, Pak.	G3	44
Kambarka, Russia	F8	26
Kambia, S.L.	G3	64
Kamčatka, poluostrov (Kamchatka), pen., Russia	F24	28
Kamčatskij zaliv, b., Russia	F24	28
Kamchatka see Kamčatka, poluostrov, pen., Russia	F24	28
Kâmchay Méa, Camb.	I8	40
Kamčija, stm., Bul.	F11	20
Kamen', Bela.	F11	22
Kamen', gora, mtn., Russia	D16	26
Kamenec, Bela.	I6	22
Kamenec-Podol'skij, Ukr.	H3	26
Kamenjak, Rt, c., Cro.	E8	18
Kamenka, Mol.	A12	20
Kamenka, Russia	G6	26
Kamen'-na-Obi, Russia	G8	28
Kamennogorsk, Russia	K21	6
Kamensk-Ural'skij, Russia	F10	26
Kameškovo, Russia	E24	22
Kāmet, mtn., Asia	E8	44
Kamiah, Id., U.S.	D9	122
Kamienna Góra, Pol.	E16	10
Kamieńsk, Pol.	D19	10
Kamilukuak Lake, l., N.W. Ter., Can.	D12	96
Kamina, Zaire	C5	58
Kaminak Lake, l., N.W. Ter., Can.	D13	96
Kaminaljuyú, hist., Guat.	J14	90
Kaminaljuyú, hist., Guat.	C4	92
Kaminoyama, Japan	I15	36
Kaminskij, Russia	D24	22
Kaminuriak Lake, l., N.W. Ter., Can.	D13	96
Kamishak Bay, b., Ak., U.S.	G18	100
Kamisunagawa, Japan	D17	36a
Kamloops, B.C., Can.	G14	102
Kamloops Indian Reserve, B.C., Can.	G14	102
Kamloops Lake, l., B.C., Can.	G14	102
Kamo, Arm.	A8	48
Kamoa Mountains, mts., Guy.	G13	84
Kampala, Ug.	A6	58
Kampar, Malay.	L6	40
Kampar, stm., Indon.	N7	40
Kampen, Neth.	C8	12
Kamphaeng Phet, Thai.	F5	40
Kamp'o, S. Kor.	H17	32
Kâmpóng Cham, Camb.	H8	40
Kâmpóng Chhnăng, Camb.	H8	40
Kâmpóng Saôm, Camb.	I7	40
Kâmpóng Saôm, Chhâk, b., Camb.	I7	40
Kâmpóng Thum, Camb.	H8	40
Kâmpôt, Camb.	I8	40
Kampsville, Il., U.S.	C6	114
Kâmpŭchéa see Cambodia, ctry., Asia	C4	38
Kamsack, Sask., Can.	G13	104
Kamskoje vodochranilišče, res., Russia	F9	26
Kāmthi, India	B5	46
Kamuchawie Lake, l., Can.	B12	104
Kamuela (Waimea), Hi., U.S.	q18	125a
Kámuk, Cerro, mtn., C.R.	H11	92
Kamyšin, Russia	G7	26
Kamyšlov, Russia	F10	26
Kanaaupscow, stm., Que., Can.	F17	96
Kanab, Ut., U.S.	G4	120
Kanab Plateau, plat., U.S.	H4	120
Kanafis, Sud.	M3	60
Kanaga Volcano, vol., Ak., U.S.	K6	100
Kanairiktok, stm., Newf., Can.	F20	96
Kananaskis, stm., Alta., Can.	G19	102
Kananga (Luluabourg), Zaire	C4	58
Kanarraville, Ut., U.S.	G3	120
Kanaš, Russia	F7	26
Kanawha, Ia., U.S.	H2	110
Kanawha, stm., W.V., U.S.	I4	108
Kanazawa, Japan	K11	36
Kanchanaburi, Thai.	G5	40
Kānchenjunga, mtn., Asia	G13	44
Kānchipuram, India	F5	46
Kandahar, Sask., Can.	G10	104
Kandalakša, Russia	D4	26
Kandalakšskaja guba, b., Russia	H23	6
Kandangan, Indon.	F6	38
Kandava, Lat.	D5	22
Kandersteg, Switz.	E8	13
Kandi, Benin	F11	64
Kandi, India	I13	44
Kandiāro, Pak.	G3	44
Kandik, stm., N.A.	D24	100
Kandos, Austl.	I8	70
Kandrāch, Pak.	H1	44
Kandy, Sri L.	I6	46
Kane, Il., U.S.	C6	114
Kane, Pa., U.S.	F8	108
Kaneohe, Hi., U.S.	p16	125a
Kaneohe Bay, b., Hi., U.S.	p16	125a
Kang, Bots.	D6	66
Kangal, Tur.	B4	48
Kangalassy, Russia	E17	28
Kangar, Malay.	K6	40
Kangaroo Island, i., Austl.	J2	70
Kangāvar, Iran	D9	48
Kangaz, Mol.	C12	20
Kangding, China	E7	30
Kangdong, N. Kor.	D14	32
Kangean, Kepulauan, is., Indon.	G6	38
Kanggye, N. Kor.	C14	32
Kanghwa, S. Kor.	F14	32
Kanghwa-man, b., S. Kor.	F14	32
Kangiqsualujjuaq, Que., Can.	E19	96
Kangiqsujuaq, Que., Can.	D18	96
Kangirsuk, Que., Can.	D18	96
Kangjin, S. Kor.	I14	32
Kangnichumike, China	D9	44
Kangnŭng, S. Kor.	F16	32
Kango, Gabon	A2	58
Kangping, China	A11	32
Kangrinboqê Feng, mtn., China	E9	44
Kangshan, Tai.	M9	34
Kangsŏ, N. Kor.	E13	32
Kangto, mtn., Asia	G15	44
Kangyidaung, Burma	F3	40
Kani, Burma	C3	40
Kaniama, Zaire	C4	58
Kanin, poluostrov, pen., Russia	D7	26
Kanin Nos, mys, c., Russia	D6	26
Kaniva, Austl.	K4	70
Kanjiža, Yugo.	C4	20
Kankakee, Il., U.S.	I8	110
Kankakee, stm., U.S.	A8	114
Kankan, Gui.	F5	64
Kankéla, Mali	F6	64
Kankossa, Maur.	D4	64
Kanmaw Kyun, i., Burma	I5	40
Kannapolis, N.C., U.S.	D6	112
Kannauj, India	G8	44
Kano, Nig.	E14	64
Kanonji, Japan	M8	36
Kanopolis, Ks., U.S.	M9	118
Kanorado, Ks., U.S.	L5	118
Kanosh, Ut., U.S.	F4	120
Kanoya, Japan	P5	36
Kānpur, India	G9	44
Kansas, Il., U.S.	C9	114
Kansas, state, U.S.	D7	98
Kansas, stm., Ks., U.S.	L11	118
Kansas City, Ks., U.S.	L13	118
Kansas City, Mo., U.S.	C2	114
Kansau, Burma	C2	40
Kanshan, China	E9	34
Kansk, Russia	F11	28
Kansu see Gansu, prov., China	D7	30
Kant, Kyrg.	I12	26
Kantang, Thai.	K5	40
Kantché, Niger	E14	64
Kantishna, stm., Ak., U.S.	D19	100
Kantō-sanchi, mts., Japan	K13	36
Kantunilkin, Mex.	G16	90
Kanuku Mountains, mts., Guy.	F13	84
Kanuma, Japan	K14	36
Kanus, Nmb.	F4	66
Kan'utino, Russia	F16	22
Kanye, Bots.	E7	66
Kanyu, Bots.	C7	66
Kaohsiung, Tai.	M9	34
Kaohsiunghsien, Tai.	M9	34
Kaokoland, dept., Nmb.	A1	66
Kaoko Veld, plat., Nmb.	B1	66
Kaolack, Sen.	D1	64
Kaoma, Zam.	D4	58
Kaoshanpu, China	E3	34
Kapaa, Hi., U.S.	o14	125a
Kapadvanj, India	I5	44
Kapanga, Zaire	C4	58
Kapčagaj, Kaz.	I13	26
Kapčagajskoje vodochranilišče, res., Kaz.	I13	26
Kapfenberg, Aus.	H15	10
Kapikik Lake, l., Ont., Can.	G23	104
Kapiskau, stm., Ont., Can.	F16	96
Kaplan, La., U.S.	M4	114
Kapoe, Thai.	J5	40
Kaposvár, Hung.	I17	10
Kaposvar Creek, stm., Sask., Can.	H12	104
Kappeln, Ger.	A9	10
Kapps, Nmb.	D3	66
Kaprun, Aus.	H12	10
Kapsan, N. Kor.	B16	32
Kapuas, stm., Indon.	F4	38
Kapuas Hulu, Pegunungan, mts., Asia	E5	38
Kapunda, Austl.	J3	70
Kapūrthala, India	E6	44
Kapuskasing, Ont., Can.	G16	96
Kapuskasing, stm., Ont., Can.	G16	96
Kapuvár, Hung.	H17	10
Kara, stm., Afr.	G10	64
Kara-Balta, Kyrg.	I12	26
Karabanovo, Russia	E21	22
Karabaš, Russia	F10	26
Karabekaul, Turk.	B18	48
Kara-Bogaz-Gol, zaliv, b., Turk.	I8	26
Karabük, Tur.	G14	4
Karacabey, Tur.	I12	20
Karacadağ, Tur.	H11	20
Karačev, Russia	H18	22
Karāchi, Pak.	H2	44
Karād, India	D3	46
Karaganda, Kaz.	H12	26
Karaginskij, ostrov, i., Russia	F24	28
Karaginskij zaliv, b., Russia	F24	28
Karagoš, gora, mtn., Russia	G15	26
Kāraikāl, India	G5	46
Kāraikkudi, India	G5	46
Karaj, Iran	D11	48
Karakax, stm., China	B8	44
Karakelong, Pulau, i., Indon.	E8	38
Karakol (Prževal'sk), Kyrg.	I13	26
Karakoram Pass, Asia	C7	44
Karakoram Range, mts., Asia	C7	44
Karakoro, stm., Afr.	D4	64
Karakumskij kanal, Turk.	C16	48
Karakumy, des., Turk.	J9	26
Karaman, Tur.	L13	20
Karaman, Tur.	C2	48
Karamay, China	B3	30
Karamea Bight, N.Z.	D3	72
Karamürsel, Tur.	I13	20
Karamyševo, Russia	D11	22
Kāranja, India	B4	46
Karapınar, Tur.	C2	48
Karasburg, Nmb.	G4	66
Karasburg, dept., Nmb.	G4	66
Kara Sea see Karskoje more, Russia	C11	26
Karasjok, Nor.	G19	6
Karasu, stm., Tur.	B5	48
Karasuk, Russia	G7	28
Karatau, Kaz.	I12	26
Karatau, chrebet, mts., Kaz.	I12	26
Karaton, Kaz.	H8	26
Karatsu, Japan	N4	36
Karauli, India	G7	44
Karawang, Indon.	J13	39a
Karawang, Tanjung, c., Indon.	I13	39a
Karawanken, mts., Eur.	C9	18
Karaye, Nig.	F14	64
Karažal, Kaz.	H12	26
Karbalā', Iraq	E8	48
Karcag, Hung.	H20	10
Kardhítsa, Grc.	J5	20
Kärdla, Est.	B5	22
Kardymovo, Russia	G15	22
Kârdžali, Bul.	H9	20
Karelia, hist. reg., Eur.	J22	6
Karesuando, Swe.	G18	6
Kargopol', Russia	E5	26
Karia-Ba-Mohammed, Mor.	C8	62
Kariba, Zimb.	E5	58
Kariba, Lake, res., Afr.	E5	58
Karibib, Nmb.	C2	66
Karigasniemi, Fin.	G19	6
Karimata, Kepulauan, is., Indon.	F4	38
Karimata, Selat (Karimata Strait), strt., Indon.	F4	38
Karīmnagar, India	C5	46
Karimunjawa, Kepulauan, is., Indon.	G5	38
Karin, Som.	F10	56
Karis (Karjaa), Fin.	K18	6
Karisimbi, Volcan, vol., Afr.	B5	58
Kariya, Japan	M11	36
Kārīz, Iran	D16	48
Karkaralinsk, Kaz.	H13	26
Karl-Marx-Stadt see Chemnitz, Ger.	E12	10
Karloske, stm., Man., Can.	C20	104
Karlovac, Cro.	D10	18
Karlovo, Bul.	G8	20
Karlovy Vary, Czech.	E12	10
Karlsborg, Swe.	I18	6
Karlskoga, Swe.	L14	6
Karlskrona, Swe.	M14	6
Karlsruhe, Ger.	F8	10
Karlstad, Mn., U.S.	C11	118
Karlstadt, Ger.	F9	10
Karma, Niger	E10	64
Karmah, Sud.	H6	60
Karmel, Har (Mount Carmel), mtn., Isr.	C4	50
Karmiyya, Isr.	E3	50
Karnack, Tx., U.S.	J2	114
Karnak, Il., U.S.	E8	114
Karnak see Al-Karnak, Egypt	E7	60
Karnāl, India	F7	44
Karṇālī, stm., Asia	F9	44
Karnātaka, state, India	E3	46
Karnes City, Tx., U.S.	K9	116
Karnobat, Bul.	G10	20
Kärnten, state, Aus.	I13	10
Karonga, Mwi.	C6	58
Karora, Sud.	I10	60
Kárpathos, i., Grc.	N11	20
Karpenísion, Grc.	K5	20
Karpinsk, Russia	F10	26
Karpogory, Russia	E6	26
Karratha, Austl.	D3	68
Kars, Tur.	A7	48
Karsakpaj, Kaz.	H11	26
Karsakuwigamak Lake, l., Man., Can.	B15	104
Kärsämäki, Fin.	J19	6
Kārsava, Lat.	E10	22
Karši, Uzb.	J11	26
Karsin, Pol.	B17	10
Karskije Vorota, proliv, strt., Russia	C9	26
Karskoje more (Kara Sea), Russia	C11	26
Kartaly, Russia	G10	26
Karthaus, Pa., U.S.	F8	108
Kartuzy, Pol.	A18	10
Karukuwisa, Nmb.	B4	66
Karūr, India	G5	46
Karviná, Czech.	F18	10
Kārwār, India	E3	46
Karymskoje, Russia	G14	28
Kas, Sud.	K3	60
Kasaan, Ak., U.S.	I28	100
Kasai (Cassai), stm., Afr.	B3	58
Kasaji, Zaire	D4	58
Kasama, Zam.	D6	58
Kasan, Uzb.	B18	48
Kasane, Bots.	A7	66
Kasanga, Tan.	C6	58
Kasaoka, Japan	M8	36
Kāsaragod, India	F3	46
Kasba Lake, l., N.W. Ter., Can.	D12	96
Kasba-Tadla, Mor.	D7	62
Kaseda, Japan	P5	36
Kasempa, Zam.	D5	58
Kasenga, Zaire	D5	58
Kasese, Zaire	B5	58
Kāsganj, India	G8	44
Kāshān, Iran	K8	26
Kashgar see Kashi, China	D2	30
Kashi, China	F8	24
Kashi, China	D2	30
Kashihara, Japan	M10	36
Kashima, Japan	N5	36
Kāshīpur, India	F8	44
Kashiwazaki, Japan	J13	36
Kāshmar, Iran	D15	48
Kashmor, Pak.	F3	44
Kashunuk, stm., Ak., U.S.	F12	100
Kasigluk, Ak., U.S.	F13	100
Kasimov, Russia	G24	22
Kašin, Russia	D20	22
Kasinka, Bots.	B7	66
Kašira, Russia	G21	22
Kasiruta, Pulau, i., Indon.	F8	38
Kaskaskia, stm., Il., U.S.	D7	114
Kaskattama, stm., Man., Can.	E14	96
Kaskö (Kaskinen), Fin.	J17	6
Kasli, Russia	F10	26
Kaslo, B.C., Can.	H18	102
Kasn'a, Russia	F17	22
Kasongo, Zaire	B5	58
Kasongo-Lunda, Zaire	C3	58
Kásos, i., Grc.	N10	20
Kasota, Mn., U.S.	F2	110
Kaspijsk, Russia	I7	26
Kaspijskij, Russia	H7	26
Kasr, Ra's, c., Afr.	H10	60
Kassalā, Sud.	J9	60
Kassándra, pen., Grc.	I7	20
Kassándras, Kólpos, b., Grc.	I7	20
Kassel, Ger.	D9	10
Kasserine, Tun.	C15	62
Kassikaityu, stm., Guy.	G13	84
Kassinger, Sud.	H6	60
Kasson, Mn., U.S.	F3	110
Kastamonu, Tur.	G14	4
Kastoría, Grc.	I5	20
Kastrávion, Tekhnití Límni, res., Grc.	K5	20
Kasūr, Pak.	E6	44
Kataeregi, Nig.	G13	64
Katahdin, Mount, mtn., Me., U.S.	B18	108
Katanga, hist. reg., Zaire	D5	58
Katanga, stm., Russia	F12	28
Katanning, Austl.	F3	68
Katchall Island, i., India	K2	40
Katélé, Mali	F7	64
Katepwa Beach, Sask., Can.	H11	104
Kateríni, Grc.	I6	20
Kates Needle, mtn., N.A.	H28	100
Katha, Burma	B4	40
Katherine, Austl.	B6	68
Kāthiāwār Peninsula, pen., India	I4	44
Kāṭhmāṇḍau, Nepal	G11	44
Kathrabbā, Jord.	F5	50
Katihār, India	F4	30
Katimik Lake, l., Man., Can.	F15	104
Katiola, I.C.	G7	64
Kātmāndu see Kāṭhmāṇḍau, Nepal	G11	44
Katoomba, Austl.	I9	70
Katoúna, Grc.	K5	20
Katowice, Pol.	E19	10
Kātrīnā, Jabal, mtn., Egypt	C7	60
Katsepe, Madag.	O22	67b
Katsina, Nig.	E13	64
Katsina Ala, Nig.	H14	64
Katsina Ala, stm., Afr.	G8	54
Katsuta, Japan	K15	36
Katsuura, Japan	L15	36
Katsuyama, Japan	K11	36
Kattakurgan, Uzb.	J11	26
Kattaviá, Grc.	N11	20
Kattegat, strt., Eur.	M12	6
Katun', stm., Russia	G9	28
Katunki, Russia	E26	22
Kātwa, India	I13	44
Katwijk aan Zee, Neth.	D5	12
Katyn, Russia	G14	22
Kauai, i., Hi., U.S.	o14	125a
Kauai Channel, strt., Hi., U.S.	p15	125a
Kau Desert, des., Hi., U.S.	r18	125a
Kaufbeuren, Ger.	H10	10
Kaufman, Tx., U.S.	G10	116
Kaukauna, Wi., U.S.	F7	110
Kaukau Veld, plat., Afr.	B5	66
Kauliranta, Fin.	H18	6
Kaumalapau, Hi., U.S.	q17	125a
Kaunakakai, Hi., U.S.	p16	125a
Kaunas, Lith.	G6	22
Kaura Namoda, Nig.	E13	64
Kauru, Nig.	F14	64
Kaušany, Mol.	C13	20
Kaustinen, Fin.	J18	6
Kautokeino, Nor.	G18	6
Kavacık, Tur.	J12	20
Kavajë, Alb.	H3	20
Kavála, Grc.	I8	20
Kavalerovo, Russia	I19	28
Kāvali, India	E5	46
Kavaratti Island, i., India	G2	46
Kāveri, stm., India	G5	46
Kāveri Falls, wtfl, India	F4	46
Kaverino, Russia	G24	22
Kavieng, Pap. N. Gui.	k17	68a
Kavimba, Bots.	B7	66
Kavīr, Dasht-e, des., Iran	D13	48
Kaw, Ok., U.S.	C10	116
Kawagoe, Japan	L14	36
Kawaguchi, Japan	L14	36
Kawaihae Bay, b., Hi., U.S.	q18	125a
Kawaikini, mtn., Hi., U.S.	o14	125a
Kawambwa, Zam.	C5	58
Kawara Débé, Niger	E11	64
Kawasaki, Japan	L14	36
Kawdut, Burma	G4	40
Kaweenakumik Lake, l., Man., Can.	F15	104
Kawich Peak, mtn., Nv., U.S.	G9	124
Kaw Lake, res., Ok., U.S.	C10	116
Kawludo, Burma	E4	40
Kawm Umbū, Egypt	E7	60
Kawthaung, Burma	J5	40
Kaxgar, stm., China	D2	30
Kaya, Burkina	E9	64
Kayak Island, i., Ak., U.S.	G22	100
Kayan, Burma	F4	40
Kayan, stm., Indon.	E6	38
Kāyankulam, India	H4	46
Kaycee, Wy., U.S.	A10	120
Kayenta, Az., U.S.	H6	120
Kayes, Congo	B2	58
Kayes, Mali	D4	64
Kay Point, c., Yukon, Can.	B25	100
Kayser Gebergte, mts., Sur.	F14	84
Kayseri, Tur.	B3	48
Kaysville, Ut., U.S.	C5	120
Kazachskij melkosopočnik, hills, Kaz.	H12	26
Kazačinskoje, Russia	F16	26
Kazakhstan, ctry., Asia	H11	26
Kazaki, Russia	I21	22
Kazaklija, Mol.	C12	20
Kazakstan see Kazakhstan, ctry., Asia	H11	26
Kazalinsk, Kaz.	H10	26
Kazan', Russia	F7	26
Kazan, stm., N.W. Ter., Can.	D13	96
Kazandžik, Turk.	J9	26
Kazanlâk, Bul.	G9	20
Kazan Lake, l., Sask., Can.	C6	104

Name	Map Ref.	Page
Kazanovka, Russia	H21	22
Kazbek, gora, mtn.	I6	26
Kāzerūn, Iran	G11	48
Kazi-Magomed, Azer.	I7	26
Kazimierza Wielka, Pol.	E20	10
Kazincbarcika, Hung.	G20	10
Kazinka, Russia	I22	22
Kazlų Rūda, Lith.	G6	22
Kazungula, Zam.	A7	66
Kazym, stm., Russia	E5	28
Kazyr, stm., Russia	G17	26
Kcynia, Pol.	B17	10
Kdyně, Czech.	F13	10
Kéa, i., Grc.	L8	20
Keaau, Hi., U.S.	r18	125a
Keahole Point, c., Hi., U.S.	r17	125a
Kealakekua Bay, b., Hi., U.S.	r18	125a
Keams Canyon, Az., U.S.	I6	120
Kearney, Mo., U.S.	C2	114
Kearney, Ne., U.S.	K8	118
Kearns, Ut., U.S.	D5	120
Kearny, Az., U.S.	K6	120
Kebeiti, China	B8	44
Kébémer, Sen.	D1	64
Kebili, Tun.	D15	62
Kebnekaise, mtn., Swe.	H16	6
Kebri Dehar, Eth.	G9	56
Kecel, Hung.	I19	10
Kech, stm., Pak.	H17	48
Kechika, stm., B.C., Can.	E7	96
Kecskemét, Hung.	I19	10
Kėdainiai, Lith.	F7	22
Kedgwick, N.B., Can.	E6	106
Kedgwick, stm., Can.	E6	106
Kediri, Indon.	J16	39a
Kédougou, Sen.	E3	64
Kędzierzyn Kozle, Pol.	E18	10
Keefers, B.C., Can.	G13	102
Keele, stm., N.W. Ter., Can.	D31	100
Keele Peak, mtn., Yukon, Can.	D6	96
Keele Peak, mtn., Yukon, Can.	E29	100
Keeley Lake, l., Sask., Can.	D6	104
Keeling Islands see Cocos Islands, dep., Oc.	K10	24
Keels, Newf., Can.	D20	106
Keene, Ky., U.S.	B2	112
Keene, N.H., U.S.	E14	108
Keene, Tx., U.S.	G9	116
Keenesburg, Co., U.S.	D12	120
Keerbergen, Bel.	F6	12
Keeseville, N.Y., U.S.	C13	108
Keetmanshoop, Nmb.	F4	66
Keewatin, Ont., Can.	I20	104
Keewatin, Mn., U.S.	C2	110
Kefallinía, i., Grc.	K4	20
Kefar Blum, Isr.	B5	50
Kefar 'Eẕyon, Isr. Occ.	E4	50
Kefar Naḥum (Capernaum), hist., Isr.	C5	50
Kefar Sava, Isr.	D3	50
Keffi, Nig.	G13	64
Keffin Hausa, Nig.	E14	64
Keflavík, Ice.	B2	6a
Keftya, Eth.	K9	60
Ke Ga, Mui, c., Viet.	H10	40
Kégashka, Que., Can.	B12	106
Kégashka, Lac, l., Que., Can.	B12	106
Keg River, Alta., Can.	E9	96
Kegums, Lat.	E7	22
Kehiwin Indian Reserve, Alta., Can.	C24	102
Kehra, Est.	B8	22
Ke-hsi Mānsām, Burma	D4	40
Keila, Est.	B7	22
Keimoes, S. Afr.	G5	66
Keiser, Ar., U.S.	G6	114
Keith, Scot., U.K.	D11	8
Keith Arm, b., N.W. Ter., Can.	C8	96
Keithley Creek, B.C., Can.	E13	102
Keithsburg, Il., U.S.	I5	110
Keizer, Or., U.S.	F2	122
Kejimkujik National Park, N.S., Can.	H8	106
Kekaha, Hi., U.S.	p14	125a
Kékes, mtn., Hung.	H20	10
Kekexili, China	D5	30
Kelafo, Eth.	G9	56
Kelang, Malay.	M6	40
Kelantan, stm., Malay.	L7	40
Kelegou, China	B6	32
Kelibia, Tun.	M6	18
Kellerberrin, Austl.	F3	68
Keller Lake, l., N.W. Ter., Can.	D8	96
Keller Lake, l., Sask., Can.	B8	104
Kellett, Cape, c., N.W. Ter., Can.	B7	96
Kelleys Island, i., Oh., U.S.	F4	108
Kelliher, Sask., Can.	G11	104
Kellogg, Id., U.S.	C9	122
Kellogg, Ia., U.S.	I3	110
Kellogg, Mn., U.S.	F4	110
Kelly Lake, l., N.W. Ter., Can.	D31	100
Kellyville, Ok., U.S.	D10	116
Kelmė, Lith.	F5	22
Kel'mency, Ukr.	A10	20
Kelmet, Eth.	I10	60
Kelo, Chad	G4	56
Kelolokan, Indon.	E6	38
Kelowna, B.C., Can.	H15	102
Kelsey Bay, B.C., Can.	G9	102
Kelsey Lake, l., Man., Can.	E13	104
Kelseyville, Ca., U.S.	F3	124
Kelso, Wa., U.S.	D3	122
Keluang, Malay.	M7	40
Kelvington, Sask., Can.	F11	104
Kem', Russia	E4	26
Kemah, Tx., U.S.	J11	116
Kemalpaşa, Tur.	K11	20
Kemano, B.C., Can.	D7	102
Kemer Barajı, res., Tur.	L12	20
Kemerovo, Russia	F9	28
Kemi, Fin.	I19	6
Kemijärvi, Fin.	H20	6
Kemijoki, stm., Fin.	H19	6
Kemmerer, Wy., U.S.	C6	120
Kemnath, Ger.	F11	10
Kemp, Tx., U.S.	G10	116
Kemp, Lake, res., Tx., U.S.	F7	116
Kemparana, Mali	E7	64
Kempele, Fin.	I19	6
Kempen, Ger.	D6	10
Kempner, Tx., U.S.	H8	116
Kemps Bay, Bah.	B6	94
Kempsey, Austl.	H10	70
Kempt, Lac, l., Que., Can.	G18	96
Kempten [Allgäu], Ger.	H10	10
Kemptville, Ont., Can.	B11	108
Kenai, Ak., U.S.	F19	100
Kenai Peninsula, pen., Ak., U.S.	G19	100
Kenansville, Fl., U.S.	L6	112
Kenansville, N.C., U.S.	E9	112
Kenaston, Sask., Can.	G8	104
Kenbridge, Va., U.S.	C8	112
Kendal, Sask., Can.	H11	104
Kendal, S. Afr.	F9	66
Kendall, Fl., U.S.	N6	112
Kendall, Wi., U.S.	G5	110
Kendall, Cape, c., N.W. Ter., Can.	D15	96
Kendallville, In., U.S.	A11	114
Kendari, Indon.	F7	38
Kendrāparha, India	J12	44
Kendrick, Fl., U.S.	J4	112
Kendrick, Id., U.S.	D9	122
Kenedy, Tx., U.S.	K9	116
Kenema, S.L.	H4	64
Kenesaw, Ne., U.S.	K9	118
Kenge, Zaire	B3	58
Kengtian, China	J8	34
Kēng Tung, Burma	D5	40
Kenhardt, S. Afr.	G5	66
Kenilworth, Ut., U.S.	E6	120
Kenitra, Mor.	C7	62
Kenly, N.C., U.S.	D8	112
Kenmare, N.D., U.S.	C5	118
Kennard, Tx., U.S.	H11	116
Kennebec, S.D., U.S.	H8	118
Kennebec, stm., Me., U.S.	C17	108
Kennebecasis Bay, b., N.B., Can.	G8	106
Kennebunk, Me., U.S.	D16	108
Kennedy, Al., U.S.	I9	114
Kennedy, Zimb.	B8	66
Kennedy, Cape see Canaveral, Cape, c., Fl., U.S.	K6	112
Kennedy, Mount, mtn., B.C., Can.	G9	102
Kennedy, Mount, mtn., Yukon, Can.	F25	100
Kennedy Entrance, strt., Ak., U.S.	G18	100
Kennedy Lake, l., B.C., Can.	H9	102
Kenner, La., U.S.	M6	114
Kennetcook, N.S., Can.	G10	106
Kennett, Mo., U.S.	F6	114
Kennett Square, Pa., U.S.	H11	108
Kennewick, Wa., U.S.	D6	122
Kenney Dam, B.C., Can.	D10	102
Kenn Reef, rf., Austl.	D11	68
Kénogami, Que., Can.	D2	106
Kenogami, stm., Ont., Can.	G15	96
Kénogami, Lac, l., Que., Can.	D2	106
Keno Hill, Yukon, Can.	E27	100
Kenora, Ont., Can.	I20	104
Kenosha, Wi., U.S.	H8	110
Kenova, W.V., U.S.	I4	108
Kensal, N.D., U.S.	D9	118
Kensett, Ar., U.S.	G5	114
Kensington, P.E.I., Can.	F10	106
Kensington, Ks., U.S.	L8	118
Kensington Park, Fl., U.S.	L4	112
Kent, S.L.	G3	64
Kent, Oh., U.S.	F5	108
Kent, Wa., U.S.	C3	122
Kent, co., Eng., U.K.	J14	8
Kentau, Kaz.	I11	26
Kent Group, is., Austl.	L7	70
Kentland, In., U.S.	B9	114
Kenton, Mi., U.S.	D7	110
Kenton, Oh., U.S.	G3	108
Kenton, Tn., U.S.	F7	114
Kent Peninsula, pen., N.W. Ter., Can.	C11	96
Kentucky, state, U.S.	D9	98
Kentucky, stm., Ky., U.S.	D11	114
Kentucky Lake, res., U.S.	F8	114
Kentville, N.S., Can.	G9	106
Kentwood, La., U.S.	L6	114
Kenya, ctry., Afr.	B7	58
Kenya, Mount see Kirinyaga, mtn., Kenya	B7	58
Kenyon, Mn., U.S.	F3	110
Keokea, Hi., U.S.	q17	125a
Keokuk, Ia., U.S.	J4	110
Keo Neua, Col de, Asia	E8	40
Keosauqua, Ia., U.S.	J4	110
Keota, Ia., U.S.	I4	110
Keota, Ok., U.S.	D12	116
Kępice, Pol.	A16	10
Kępno, Pol.	D17	10
Keppel Bay, b., Austl.	D9	70
Kequan, China	G2	32
Kerala, state, India	G4	46
Kerang, Austl.	J5	70
Kerby, Or., U.S.	H2	122
Kerč', Ukr.	H5	26
Keremeos, B.C., Can.	H15	102
Keren, Eth.	J10	60
Kerend, Iran	D9	48
Kerens, Tx., U.S.	G10	116
Keret', ozero, l., Russia	I23	6
Kerewan, Gam.	E1	64
Kerguélen, Îles, is., F.S.A.T.	M10	126
Kericho, Kenya	B7	58
Keri Kera, Sud.	K7	60
Kerinci, Gunung, mtn., Indon.	F3	38
Keriya, stm., China	B9	44
Kerkebet, Eth.	I9	60
Kerkenna, Îles, is., Tun.	C16	62
Kerkhoven, Mn., U.S.	F12	118
Kerki, Turk.	J11	26
Kérkira (Corfu), Grc.	J3	20
Kérkira, i., Grc.	J3	20
Kerkrade, Neth.	G9	12
Kermadec Islands, is., N.Z.	K22	126
Kermān, Iran	F14	48
Kerman, Ca., U.S.	H5	124
Kermit, Tx., U.S.	H3	116
Kermode, Mount, mtn., B.C., Can.	E3	102
Kern, stm., Ca., U.S.	I7	124
Kernersville, N.C., U.S.	C6	112
Kernville, Ca., U.S.	I7	124
Kérou, Benin	F11	64
Kerpinen', Mol.	C12	20
Kerrobert, Sask., Can.	G5	104
Kerrville, Tx., U.S.	I7	116
Kerry, co., Ire.	I4	8
Kershaw, S.C., U.S.	E6	112
Kersley, B.C., Can.	E12	102
Kerulen (Cherlen) (Herlen), stm., Asia	B10	30
Kerzaz, Alg.	F10	62
Kerzers, Switz.	E7	13
Kesagami Lake, l., Ont., Can.	F16	96
Keşan, Tur.	I10	20
Kesennuma, Japan	I16	36
Keshena, Wi., U.S.	F7	110
Keshendeh, Afg.	B2	44
Keshod, India	J4	44
Keskin, Tur.	B2	48
Keski-Suomen lääni, prov., Fin.	J19	6
Keskozero, Russia	K23	6
Kes'ma, Russia	C20	22
Kesova Gora, Russia	D20	22
Kesra, Tun.	N4	18
Kesten'ga, Russia	I22	6
Keszthely, Hung.	I17	10
Ket', stm., Russia	F8	28
Keta, Ghana	I10	64
Keta, ozero, l., Russia	D10	28
Ketama, Mor.	K7	16
Ketang, China	M4	34
Ketchikan, Ak., U.S.	I29	100
Ketchum, Id., U.S.	G11	122
Kete Krachi, Ghana	H9	64
Kétou, Benin	H11	64
Kętrzyn (Rastenburg), Pol.	A21	10
Kettering, Eng., U.K.	I13	8
Kettering, Oh., U.S.	H2	108
Kettle, stm., Man., Can.	B20	104
Kettle, stm., N.A.	I16	102
Kettle, stm., Mn., U.S.	D3	110
Kettle Falls, Wa., U.S.	B7	122
Kettle Rapids Dam, Man., Can.	B20	104
Keuka Lake, l., N.Y., U.S.	E9	108
Kevin, Mt., U.S.	B14	122
Kew, T./C. Is.	D8	94
Kewanee, Il., U.S.	I6	110
Kewanna, In., U.S.	A10	114
Kewaunee, Wi., U.S.	F8	110
Keweenaw Bay, b., Mi., U.S.	C7	110
Keweenaw Peninsula, pen., Mi., U.S.	C7	110
Keweenaw Point, c., Mi., U.S.	C8	110
Keya Paha, stm., U.S.	I8	118
Keyes, Ok., U.S.	C4	116
Key Largo, Fl., U.S.	N6	112
Key Largo, i., Fl., U.S.	N6	112
Keyser, W.V., U.S.	H8	108
Keystone, Ia., U.S.	I3	110
Keystone, S.D., U.S.	H4	118
Keystone, W.V., U.S.	B5	112
Keystone Lake, res., Ok., U.S.	C10	116
Keysville, Va., U.S.	B8	112
Keytesville, Mo., U.S.	C4	114
Key West, Fl., U.S.	O5	112
Kežmarok, Czech.	F20	10
Kgalagadi, dept., Bots.	E5	66
Kgatleng, dept., Bots.	E8	66
Khābūr, Nahr al-, stm., Asia	D6	48
Khadki (Kirkee), India	C2	46
Khairpur, Pak.	G3	44
Khajrāho, India	H8	44
Khakhea, Bots.	E6	66
Khalkhalah, Syria	B7	50
Khalkidhikí, hist. reg., Grc.	I7	20
Khalkís, Grc.	K7	20
Khalūf, Oman	D11	47
Khambhāliya, India	I3	44
Khambhāt, India	I5	44
Khambhāt, Gulf of, b., India	J5	44
Khāmgaon, India	B4	46
Khamir, Yemen	F3	47
Khamīs Mushayṭ, Sau. Ar.	E3	47
Khamkeut, Laos	E8	40
Khammam, India	D6	46
Khānābād, Afg.	B3	44
Khān al-Baghdādī, Iraq	E7	48
Khānaqīn, Iraq	D8	48
Khancoban, Austl.	K8	70
Khandwa, India	J7	44
Khānewāl, Pak.	E4	44
Khāngarh, Pak.	F4	44
Khaniá, Grc.	N8	20
Khānpur, Pak.	F4	44
Khān Yūnus, Isr. Occ.	F2	50
Kharagpur, India	I12	44
Kharānoq, Iran	E13	48
Kharg Island see Khārk, Jazīreh-ye, i., Iran	G11	48
Khargon, India	J6	44
Khāriān Cantonment, Pak.	D5	44
Kharkov see Char'kov, Ukr.	E15	4
Khartoum see Al-Kharṭūm, Sud.	J7	60
Khartoum North see Al-Kharṭūm Baḥrī, Sud.	J7	60
Khartum see Al-Kharṭūm, Sud.	J7	60
Khasebake, Bots.	C7	66
Khāsh, Afg.	F17	48
Khāsh, Iran	G16	48
Khashm al-Qirbah, Sud.	J8	60
Khatt, Oued al, val., W. Sah.	G4	62
Khawsa, Burma	G4	40
Khemis, Alg.	B12	62
Khemmarat, Thai.	F8	40
Khenchla, Alg.	C14	62
Khenifra, Mor.	D8	62
Kherrata, Alg.	B13	62
Khíos, Grc.	K10	20
Khíos, i., Grc.	K10	20
Khirbat 'Awwād, Syria	D7	50
Khlong Thom, Thai.	K5	40
Kholm, Afg.	B2	44
Khomeyn, Iran	E11	48
Khomeynīshahr, Iran	E11	48
Khomodimo, Bots.	D6	66
Khon Kaen, Thai.	F7	40
Khóra, Grc.	L5	20
Khorramābād, Iran	E10	48
Khorramshahr, Iran	F10	48
Khossanto, Sen.	E4	64
Khouribga, Mor.	D7	62
Khowst, Afg.	D3	44
Khuff, Sau. Ar.	B4	47
Khugaung, Burma	A5	40
Khuis, Bots.	F5	66
Khu Khan, Thai.	G8	40
Khulna, Bngl.	I13	44
Khūnjerāb Pass, Asia	B6	44
Khurai, India	H8	44
Khurīyā Murīyā, Jazā'ir, is., Oman	F10	47
Khurja, India	F7	44
Khuzdār, Pak.	G2	44
Khvāf, Iran	D16	48
Khvor, Iran	E13	48
Khvormūj, Iran	G11	48
Khvoy, Iran	B8	48
Khwae Noi, stm., Thai.	G5	40
Khyber Pass, Asia	C4	44
Kiama, Austl.	J9	70
Kiamichi, stm., Ok., U.S.	E11	116
Kiana, Ak., U.S.	C14	100
Kiangarow, Mount, mtn., Austl.	F9	70
Kiangsi see Jiangxi, prov., China	F10	30
Kiangsu see Jiangsu, prov., China	E10	30
Kibangou, Congo	B2	58
Kibombo, Zaire	B5	58
Kibre Mengist, Eth.	O10	60
Kičevo, Mac.	H4	20
Kickany, Mol.	C13	20
Kickapoo, stm., Wi., U.S.	G5	110
Kicking Horse Pass, Can.	F18	102
Kicman', Ukr.	A9	20
Kidal, Mali	B10	64
Kidira, Sen.	D3	64
Kiel, Ger.	A10	10
Kiel, Wi., U.S.	G7	110
Kiel Canal see Nord-Ostsee-Kanal, Ger.	A9	10
Kielce, Pol.	E20	10
Kieler Bucht, b., Ger.	A10	10
Kiester, Mn., U.S.	G2	110
Kiev see Kijev, Ukr.	G4	26
Kiffa, Maur.	C4	64
Kifisiá, Grc.	K7	20
Kifrī, Iraq	D8	48
Kigali, Rw.	B6	58
Kigille, Sud.	M8	60
Kigoma, Tan.	B5	58
Kihei, Hi., U.S.	q17	125a
Kihniö, Fin.	J18	6
Kihnu, i., Est.	C7	22
Kii-suidō, strt., Japan	N9	36
Kijev (Kiev), Ukr.	G4	26
Kijevskoje vodochranilišče, res., Ukr.	G4	26
Kikerino, Russia	B12	22
Kikerk Lake, l., N.W. Ter., Can.	C10	96
Kikinda, Yugo.	D4	20
Kikládhes (Cyclades), is., Grc.	L9	20
Kikori, Pap. N. Gui.	G11	38
Kikwit, Zaire	C3	58
Kilambé, Cerro, mtn., Nic.	D9	92
Kilauea, Hi., U.S.	o14	125a
Kilauea Crater, crat., Hi., U.S.	r18	125a
Kilchu, N. Kor.	C17	32
Kilcoy, Austl.	F10	70
Kildare, Ire.	H7	8
Kildare, co., Ire.	H7	8
Kildare, Cape, c., P.E.I., Can.	F10	106
Kil'din, ostrov, i., Russia	G24	6
Kil'dinstroj, Russia	G23	6
Kildonan, B.C., Can.	H9	102
Kilgore, Tx., U.S.	J2	114
Kilian Island, i., N.W. Ter., Can.	B11	96
Kilibo, Benin	G11	64
Kilija, Ukr.	D13	20
Kilikollūr, India	H4	46
Kilimanjaro, mtn., Tan.	B7	58
Kilimavony, Madag.	S20	67b
Kilingi-Nõmme, Est.	C7	22
Kilis, Tur.	C4	48
Kilkenny, Ire.	I6	8
Kilkenny, co., Ire.	I6	8
Kilkís, Grc.	H6	20
Killaloe, Ire.	I5	8
Killaloe Station, Ont., Can.	E18	110
Killam, Alta., Can.	E23	102
Killarney, Man., Can.	I15	104
Killarney, Ont., Can.	E14	110
Killarney, Ire.	I4	8
Killbuck, Oh., U.S.	G5	108
Killdeer, N.D., U.S.	D5	118
Killeen, Tx., U.S.	H9	116
Killen, Al., U.S.	H9	114
Killington Peak, mtn., Vt., U.S.	D14	108
Killiniq Island, i., Can.	D20	96
Killinkoski, Fin.	J18	6
Kilmarnock, Scot., U.K.	F9	8
Kilmarnock, Va., U.S.	B10	112
Kilmichael, Ms., U.S.	I7	114
Kilomines, Zaire	A6	58
Kilosa, Tan.	C7	58
Kilpisjärvi, Fin.	G17	6
Kilrush, Ire.	I4	8
Kilttān Island, i., India	G2	46
Kilwa, Zaire	C5	58
Kim, Co., U.S.	N4	118
Kim, stm., Cam.	G9	54
Kimba, Austl.	I2	70
Kimball, Mn., U.S.	E1	110
Kimball, Ne., U.S.	J4	118
Kimball, S.D., U.S.	H9	118
Kimberley, B.C., Can.	H19	102
Kimberley, S. Afr.	G7	66
Kimberley Plateau, plat., Austl.	C5	68
Kimberling City, Mo., U.S.	F3	114
Kimberly, Id., U.S.	H11	122
Kimberly, Wi., U.S.	F7	110
Kimch'aek (Sŏngjin), N. Kor.	C17	32
Kimch'ŏn, S. Kor.	G16	32
Kimito (Kemiö), Fin.	K18	6
Kimiwan Lake, l., Alta., Can.	B18	102
Kimje, S. Kor.	H14	32
Kimovsk, Russia	H21	22
Kimry, Russia	E20	22
Kimsquit, B.C., Can.	E8	102
Kinabalu, Gunong, mtn., Malay.	D6	38
Kinbasket Lake, res., B.C., Can.	F17	102
Kincaid, Sask., Can.	I7	104
Kincaid, Il., U.S.	C7	114
Kincardine, Ont., Can.	F14	110
Kincolith, B.C., Can.	B5	102
Kindberg, Aus.	H15	10
Kinde, Mi., U.S.	G13	110
Kinder, La., U.S.	L4	114
Kindersley, Sask., Can.	G5	104
Kindia, Gui.	F3	64
Kindred, N.D., U.S.	E10	118
Kindu, Zaire	B5	58
Kinel', Russia	G8	26
Kinešma, Russia	D25	22
King, N.C., U.S.	C6	112
King and Queen Court House, Va., U.S.	B10	112
Kingaroy, Austl.	F9	70
King City, Ont., Can.	G16	110
King City, Ca., U.S.	H4	124
King City, Mo., U.S.	B2	114
King Cove, Ak., U.S.	I13	100
Kingfield, Me., U.S.	C16	108
Kingfisher, Ok., U.S.	D9	116
King George, Va., U.S.	I9	108
King George, Mount, mtn., B.C., Can.	G19	102
King George Island, i., B.A.T.	B1	73
King George Islands, is., N.W. Ter., Can.	E17	96
King Hill, Id., U.S.	G10	122
Kingisepp, Russia	B11	22
King Island, i., Austl.	L6	70
King Island, i., B.C., Can.	E7	102
King Lear Peak, mtn., Nv., U.S.	C7	124
King Leopold Ranges, mts., Austl.	C5	68
Kingman, Az., U.S.	I2	120
Kingman, Ks., U.S.	N9	118
Kingman Reef, rf., Oc.	H23	126
King Mountain, mtn., B.C., Can.	G30	100
King Mountain, mtn., Or., U.S.	G7	122
Kings, Ms., U.S.	J6	114
Kings, stm., Ar., U.S.	F3	114
Kings, stm., Ca., U.S.	H6	124
Kings, stm., Nv., U.S.	C7	124
King Salmon, Ak., U.S.	G16	100
Kings Beach, Ca., U.S.	E5	124
Kingsburg, Ca., U.S.	H6	124
Kings Canyon National Park, Ca., U.S.	H7	124
Kingscote, Austl.	J2	70
Kingsford, Mi., U.S.	E7	110
Kingsgate, B.C., Can.	H18	102
Kingsland, Ar., U.S.	I4	114
Kingsland, Ga., U.S.	I5	112
Kingsland, Tx., U.S.	I8	116
Kingsley, Ia., U.S.	I12	118
Kingsley, Mi., U.S.	F10	110
King's Lynn, Eng., U.K.	I14	8
Kingsmere Lake, l., Sask., Can.	D8	104
Kings Mountain, N.C., U.S.	D5	112
King Solomon's Mines see Mikhrot Shelomo Hamelekh, hist., Isr.	I3	50
King Sound, strt., Austl.	C4	68
Kings Peak, mtn., Ut., U.S.	D6	120
King's Point, Newf., Can.	C17	106
Kingsport, Tn., U.S.	C4	112
Kingston, N.S., Can.	H9	106
Kingston, Ont., Can.	F19	110
Kingston, Jam.	E6	94
Kingston, N.Z.	F2	72
Kingston, Ga., U.S.	E2	112
Kingston, Ma., U.S.	F16	108
Kingston, Mo., U.S.	C2	114
Kingston, N.Y., U.S.	F13	108
Kingston, Oh., U.S.	H4	108
Kingston, Ok., U.S.	F10	116
Kingston, Pa., U.S.	F11	108
Kingston, Tn., U.S.	D2	112
Kingston Southeast, Austl.	K3	70
Kingston upon Hull, Eng., U.K.	H13	8
Kingstown, St. Vin.	H14	94
Kingstree, S.C., U.S.	F7	112
Kingsville, Ont., Can.	H13	110
Kingsville, Tx., U.S.	L9	116
King William, Va., U.S.	B9	112
King William Island, i., N.W. Ter., Can.	C13	96
King William's Town, S. Afr.	I8	66
Kingwood, W.V., U.S.	H7	108
Kinistino, Sask., Can.	F9	104
Kinkony, Lac, l., Madag.	P21	67b
Kinmundy, Il., U.S.	D8	114
Kinnaird, B.C., Can.	H17	102
Kinnaird Head, c., Scot., U.K.	D11	8
Kinneret, Yam (Sea of Galilee), l., Isr.	C5	50
Kinsale, Old Head of, c., Ire.	J5	8
Kinshasa (Léopoldville), Zaire	B3	58
Kinsley, Ks., U.S.	N8	118
Kinsman, Oh., U.S.	F6	108
Kinston, Al., U.S.	K10	114
Kinston, N.C., U.S.	D9	112
Kintampo, Ghana	G9	64
Kintyre, pen., Scot., U.K.	F8	8
Kintyre, Mull of, c., Scot., U.K.	F8	8
Kinuseo Falls, wtfl, B.C., Can.	C13	102
Kinuso, Alta., Can.	B19	102
Kinyeti, mtn., Sud.	H7	56
Kinzua, Or., U.S.	F5	122
Kiowa, Co., U.S.	L3	118
Kiowa, Ks., U.S.	N9	118
Kiowa, Ok., U.S.	E11	116
Kipahigan Lake, l., Can.	C12	104
Kipengere Range, mts., Tan.	C6	58
Kiperčeny, Mol.	B12	20
Kipling, Sask., Can.	H12	104
Kipnuk, Ak., U.S.	G12	100
Kipushi, Zaire	D5	58
Kirane, Mali	D4	64
Kirazlı, Tur.	I10	20
Kirbyville, Tx., U.S.	L3	114
Kirchberg, Ger.	F9	10
Kirchheim, Ger.	G10	10
Kirchheimbolanden, Ger.	F8	10
Kirchmöser, Ger.	C12	10
Kirchschlag in der Buckligen Welt, Aus.	H16	10
Kirejevsk, Russia	H20	22
Kirenga, stm., Russia	F13	28
Kirensk, Russia	F13	28
Kirghizia see Kyrgyzstan, ctry., Asia	I13	26
Kirgizskij chrebet, mts., Asia	I12	26
Kiri, Zaire	B3	58
Kiribati, ctry., Oc.	F24	2
Kırıkhan, Tur.	C4	48
Kırıkkale, Tur.	B2	48
Kirillov, Russia	B21	22
Kirillovskoje, Russia	A12	22
Kirin see Jilin, China	C12	30
Kirin see Jilin, prov., China	C12	30
Kirinyaga, mtn., Kenya	B7	58
Kiriši, Russia	B15	22
Kiriwina Islands, is., Pap. N. Gui.	A10	68
Kırkağaç, Tur.	J11	20
Kirkcaldy, Scot., U.K.	E10	8
Kirkcudbright, Scot., U.K.	G9	8
Kirkenes, Nor.	G22	6
Kirkjubæjarklaustur, Ice.	C4	6a
Kirkland, Il., U.S.	H7	110
Kirkland, Tx., U.S.	E6	116
Kirkland, Wa., U.S.	C3	122
Kirkland Lake, Ont., Can.	B15	110
Kırklareli, Tur.	H11	20
Kirklin, In., U.S.	B10	114
Kirkness Lake, l., Ont., Can.	G21	104
Kirkpatrick, Mount, mtn., Ant.	D8	73
Kirkpatrick Lake, l., Alta., Can.	F23	102
Kirksville, Mo., U.S.	B4	114
Kirkūk, Iraq	D8	48
Kirkwall, Scot., U.K.	C11	8
Kirkwood, S. Afr.	I7	66
Kirkwood, Il., U.S.	J5	110
Kirkwood, Mo., U.S.	D6	114
Kirov, Russia	G17	22
Kirov, Russia	F7	26
Kirovakan, Arm.	I6	26
Kirovgrad, Russia	F10	26
Kirovograd, Ukr.	H4	26
Kirovsk, Bela.	H12	22
Kirovsk, Russia	B14	22
Kirovsk, Russia	D4	26
Kirovskij, Azer.	I7	26
Kirovskij, Kaz.	I13	26
Kirs, Russia	F8	26
Kirsanov, Russia	I25	22
Kırşehir, Tur.	B3	48
Kīrthar Range, mts., Pak.	G2	44
Kirtland, N.M., U.S.	H8	120
Kiruna, Swe.	H17	6
Kirwin, Ks., U.S.	L8	118
Kiryū, Japan	K14	36
Kiržač, Russia	E21	22
Kisa, Swe.	M14	6
Kisangani (Stanleyville), Zaire	A5	58
Kisarazu, Japan	L14	36
Kisbey, Sask., Can.	I12	104
Kisel'ovsk, Russia	G9	28
Kishanganj, India	G12	44
Kishangarh Bās, India	G6	44
Kishi, Nig.	G11	64
Kishikas, stm., Ont., Can.	F23	104
Kishiwada, Japan	M10	36
Kishorganj, Bngl.	H14	44
Kisii, Kenya	B6	58
Kišin'ov, Mol.	H3	26
Kiska Island, i., Ak., U.S.	J3	101a
Kiskatinaw, stm., B.C., Can.	B14	102
Kiski Lake, l., Man., Can.	D16	104
Kiskittogisu Lake, l., Man., Can.	D16	104
Kiskitto Lake, l., Man., Can.	D16	104
Kiskunfélegyháza, Hung.	I19	10
Kiskunhalas, Hung.	I19	10
Kiskunmajsa, Hung.	I19	10
Kislovodsk, Russia	I6	26
Kismaayo, Som.	B8	58
Kiso-sammyaku, mts., Japan	L12	36
Kispiox, B.C., Can.	B7	102
Kispiox, stm., B.C., Can.	B7	102
Kispiox Mountain, mtn., B.C., Can.	B7	102
Kisseynew Lake, l., Can.	D13	104
Kissidougou, Gui.	G4	64
Kissimmee, Fl., U.S.	K5	112
Kissimmee, stm., Fl., U.S.	L6	112
Kissimmee, Lake, l., Fl., U.S.	L5	112
Kississing, Man., Can.	C13	104
Kississing Lake, l., Man., Can.	C13	104
Kistigan Lake, l., Man., Can.	D22	104
Kisújszállás, Hung.	H20	10
Kisumu, Kenya	B6	58
Kisvárda, Hung.	G22	10
Kita, Mali	E5	64
Kita-Daitō-jima, i., Japan	F13	30
Kitaibaraki, Japan	K15	36
Kitakata, Japan	J14	36
Kitakyūshū, Japan	N5	36
Kitale, Kenya	A7	58
Kitami, Japan	D18	36a
Kitami-sanchi, mts., Japan	C17	36a
Kit Carson, Co., U.S.	M5	118
Kitchener, Ont., Can.	G15	110
Kiteiyab, Sud.	I7	60
Kíthira, Grc.	M7	20
Kíthira, i., Grc.	M6	20
Kíthnos, i., Grc.	L8	20
Kitimat, B.C., Can.	C6	102
Kitimat, stm., B.C., Can.	C6	102
Kitimat Ranges, mts., B.C., Can.	D5	102
Kitlope, stm., B.C., Can.	D7	102
Kitlope Lake, l., B.C., Can.	D7	102
Kitscoty, Alta., Can.	E4	104
Kittanning, Pa., U.S.	G7	108
Kittery, Me., U.S.	D16	108
Kittilä, Fin.	H19	6
Kittitas, Wa., U.S.	D5	122
Kitui, Kenya	B7	58
Kitwanga, B.C., Can.	B6	102
Kitwangar Indian Reserve, B.C., Can.	B6	102
Kitwe, Zam.	D5	58
Kitwitwi, Nmb.	A4	66
Kitzbühel, Aus.	H12	10
Kitzingen, Ger.	F10	10
Kiukiang see Jiujiang, China	F4	34
Kiviõli, Est.	B9	22
Kivu, Lac, l., Afr.	B5	58
Kıyıköy, Tur.	H12	20
Kiyiu Lake, l., Sask., Can.	G6	104
Kizel, Russia	F9	26
Kızıl, stm., Tur.	A2	48
Kızıltepe, Tur.	C6	48
Kizl'ar, Russia	I7	26
Kizyl-Arvat, Turk.	J9	26
Kizyl-Atrek, Turk.	J8	26
Kizyl-Su, Turk.	B12	48
Kjustendil, Bul.	G6	20
Kladanj, Bos.	E2	20
Kladno, Czech.	E14	10
Klagenfurt, Aus.	I14	10
Klahoose Indian Reserve, B.C., Can.	G10	102
Klaipėda (Memel), Lith.	F4	22
Klaksvík, Faer. Is.	D8	6b
Klamath, Ca., U.S.	C1	124
Klamath, stm., U.S.	C1	124
Klamath Falls, Or., U.S.	H4	122
Klamath Mountains, mts., U.S.	B2	124
Klangpi, Burma	C2	40
Klarälven, stm., Eur.	K13	6
Kl'asticy, Bela.	F11	22
Klatovy, Czech.	F13	10
Klawer, S. Afr.	H4	66
Klawock, Ak., U.S.	I28	100
Kl'az'ma, stm., Russia	E25	22
Kleck, Bela.	H9	22
Kleena Kleene, B.C., Can.	F10	102
Klemme, Ia., U.S.	G2	110
Klemtu, B.C., Can.	E6	102
Klerksdorp, S. Afr.	F8	66
Klet', mtn., Czech.	G14	10
Kletn'a, Russia	H16	22
Kleve, Ger.	D6	10
Kličev, Bela.	H12	22
Klickitat, Wa., U.S.	E4	122
Klickitat, stm., Wa., U.S.	E4	122
Klimoviči, Bela.	H14	22
Klimovo, Russia	I15	22
Klimovsk, Russia	F20	22
Klin, Russia	E19	22
Klinaklini, stm., B.C., Can.	F9	102
Klincy, Russia	I15	22
Klipplaat, S. Afr.	I7	66
Kliškovcy, Ukr.	A10	20
Kłobuck, Pol.	E18	10
Kłodzko, Pol.	E16	10
Klondike, hist. reg., Yukon, Can.	E25	100
Klondike, stm., Yukon, Can.	D26	100
Klosterneuburg, Aus.	G16	10
Klosters, Switz.	E12	13
Kloten, Switz.	D10	13
Klotz, Lac, l., Que., Can.	D18	96
Klötze, Ger.	C11	10
Klouto, Togo	H10	64
Kluane, stm., Yukon, Can.	F25	100
Kluane Lake, l., Yukon, Can.	F25	100
Kluane National Park, Yukon, Can.	F25	100
Kl'učevskaja Sopka, vulkan, vol., Russia	F24	28
Kl'uči, Russia	F24	28
Kluczbork, Pol.	E18	10
Klukwan, Ak., U.S.	G27	100
Knapp, Wi., U.S.	F3	110
Knäred, Swe.	M13	6
Kn'ažji Gory, Russia	E18	22
Kneehills Creek, stm., Alta., Can.	F21	102
Knee Lake, l., Man., Can.	C20	104
Knee Lake, l., Sask., Can.	C7	104
Knevicy, Russia	D15	22
Kneža, Bul.	F8	20
Knić, Yugo.	F4	20
Knickerbocker, Tx., U.S.	H6	116
Knife, stm., N.D., U.S.	D6	118
Knife Lake, l., Ont., Can.	E23	104
Knight Inlet, b., B.C., Can.	G9	102
Knights Landing, Ca., U.S.	F4	124
Knightstown, In., U.S.	C11	114
Knik Arm, b., Ak., U.S.	F20	100
Knin, Cro.	E11	18
Knippa, Tx., U.S.	J7	116
Knittelfeld, Aus.	H14	10
Knob Noster, Mo., U.S.	D3	114
Knokke-Heist, Bel.	F3	12
Knox, In., U.S.	A10	114
Knox, Pa., U.S.	F7	108
Knox, Cape, c., B.C., Can.	C1	102
Knox City, Tx., U.S.	F7	116
Knox Coast, Ant.	B6	73
Knoxville, Ga., U.S.	G3	112
Knoxville, Il., U.S.	J5	110
Knoxville, Ia., U.S.	I2	110
Knoxville, Tn., U.S.	D3	112
Knysna, S. Afr.	J6	66
Knyszyn, Pol.	B22	10
Kobar Sink, depr., Eth.	F9	56
Kobayashi, Japan	P5	36
Kōbe, Japan	M10	36

Name	Map Ref.	Page
København (Copenhagen), Den.	N13	6
Koblenz, Ger.	E7	10
Koboža, Russia	C18	22
Kobrin, Bela.	I7	22
Kobrinskoje, Russia	B13	22
Kobuk, Ak., U.S.	C16	100
Kobylin, Pol.	D17	10
Kočani, Mac.	H6	20
Kočečum, stm., Russia	D12	28
Kočetovka, Russia	I23	22
Kočevje, Slo.	D9	18
Kŏch'ang, S. Kor.	H14	32
Kochanovo, Bela.	G13	22
Koch Bihār, India	G13	44
Kōchi, Japan	N8	36
Koch Island, i., N.W. Ter., Can.	C17	96
Kochma, Russia	E24	22
Kodaikānal, India	G4	46
Kodāri, Nepal	G11	44
Kodiak, Ak., U.S.	H18	100
Kodiak Island, i., Ak., U.S.	H18	100
Kodino, Russia	J26	6
Kodok, Sud.	M7	60
Kodyma, Ukr.	A13	20
Koekelare, Bel.	F2	12
Koersel, Bel.	F7	12
Koes, Nmb.	E4	66
Köflach, Aus.	H15	10
Koforidua, Ghana	H9	64
Kōfu, Japan	L13	36
Koga, Japan	K14	36
Kogaluc, stm., Que., Can.	E17	96
Kogaluc, Baie, b., Que., Can.	E17	96
Kogaluk, stm., Newf., Can.	E20	96
Kogan, Austl.	F9	70
Køge, Den.	N13	6
Kogoni, Mali	D6	64
Kohāt, Pak.	D4	44
Kohila, Est.	B7	22
Kohīma, India	H16	44
Kohler, Wi., U.S.	G8	110
Kohtla-Järve, Est.	B10	22
Kohŭng, S. Kor.	I15	32
Kohunlich, hist., Mex.	H15	90
Koidern, Yukon, Can.	F24	100
Koidu, S.L.	G4	64
Koigi, Est.	C8	22
Koimbani, Com.	K15	67a
Kojgorodok, Russia	E8	26
Kojŏ, N. Kor.	E15	32
Kok (Hkok), stm., Asia	D5	40
Kokand, Uzb.	I12	26
Kokanee Glacier Provincial Park, B.C., Can.	H17	102
Kokčetav, Kaz.	G11	26
Koki, Sen.	D2	64
Kokka, Sud.	G6	60
Kokkola (Karleby), Fin.	J18	6
Koknese, Lat.	E8	22
Koko, Nig.	F12	64
Kokoda, Pap. N. Gui.	A9	68
Kokomo, In., U.S.	B10	114
Kokomo, Ms., U.S.	K6	114
Kokong, Bots.	E6	66
Koko Nor see Qinghai Hu, l., China	D7	30
Kokopo, Pap. N. Gui.	k17	68a
Kokorevka, Russia	I17	22
Kokšaalatau, chrebet, mts., Asia	I13	26
Koksan, N. Kor.	E14	32
Koksoak, stm., Que., Can.	E19	96
Koksŏng, S. Kor.	H15	32
Kokstad, S. Afr.	H9	66
Kola, Russia	G23	6
Kolahun, Lib.	G4	64
Kola Peninsula see Kol'skij poluostrov, pen., Russia	D5	26
Kolār, India	F5	46
Kolār Gold Fields, India	F5	46
Kolárovo, Czech.	H18	10
Kolbasna, Mol.	B13	20
Kolbio, Kenya	B8	58
Kolchozabad, Taj.	B3	44
Kol'čugino, Russia	E22	22
Kolda, Sen.	E2	64
Kolenté (Great Scarcies), stm., Afr.	G3	64
Kolgujev, ostrov, i., Russia	D7	26
Kolhāpur, India	D3	46
Kolia, I.C.	G6	64
Koliba (Corubal), stm., Afr.	E3	64
Koliganek, Ak., U.S.	G16	100
Kolimbine, stm., Afr.	D4	64
Kolín, Czech.	E15	10
Kolka, Lat.	D5	22
Kolkasrags, c., Lat.	D5	22
Kollegāl, India	F4	46
Köln (Cologne), Ger.	E6	10
Kolno, Pol.	B21	10
Kolo, Niger	E11	64
Koło, Pol.	C18	10
Koloa, Hi., U.S.	p14	125a
Kolobovo, Russia	E24	22
Kołobrzeg, Pol.	A15	10
Kolodn'a, Russia	G15	22
Kologriv, Russia	C27	22
Koloko, Burkina	F7	64
Kolomna, Russia	F21	22
Kolomyja, Ukr.	H3	26
Kol'osnoje, Ukr.	C13	20
Kolpaševo, Russia	F8	28
Kolpino, Russia	B13	22
Kolpny, Russia	I20	22
Kol'skij poluostrov (Kola Peninsula), pen., Russia	D5	26
Kol'ubakino, Russia	F19	22
Kolwezi, Zaire	D5	58
Kolyma, stm., Russia	D23	28
Kolymskaja nizmennost', pl., Russia	D22	28
Koma, Eth.	M9	60
Komadugu Gana, stm., Nig.	F9	54
Komadugu Yobe, stm., Afr.	F9	54
Komandorskije ostrova, is., Russia	F25	28
Komariči, Russia	I17	22
Komarniki, Ukr.	F23	10
Komárno, Czech.	H18	10
Komárom, Hung.	H18	10
Komárom-Esztergom, co., Hung.	H18	10
Komarovo, Russia	C16	22
Komati (Incomáti), stm., Afr.	E10	66
Komatipoort, S. Afr.	E10	66
Komatsu, Japan	K11	36
Komatsushima, Japan	M9	36
Kombone, Cam.	I14	64
Komin Yanga, Burkina	F10	64
Komló, Hung.	I18	10
Kommunarsk, Ukr.	H5	26
Kommunizma, pik, mtn., Taj.	J12	26
Komodo, Pulau, i., Indon.	G6	38
Komoé, stm., Afr.	G6	54
Komotiní, Grc.	H9	20
Komrat, Mol.	C12	20
Komsomolec, Kaz.	G10	26
Komsomolec, ostrov, i., Russia	A17	26
Komsomolec, zaliv, b., Kaz.	H8	26
Komsomol'sk, Russia	D23	22
Komsomol'sk, Turk.	B17	48
Komsomol'sk-na-Amure, Russia	G19	28
Komsomol'skoj Pravdy, ostrova, is., Russia	B13	28
Kona, Mali	D8	64
Kona Coast, Hi., U.S.	r18	125a
Konakovo, Russia	E19	22
Konakpınar, Tur.	J11	20
Konar, stm., Asia	C4	44
Konārak, India	K12	44
Konawa, Ok., U.S.	E10	116
Konceba, Ukr.	A13	20
Konch, India	H8	44
Konda, stm., Russia	E5	28
Kondoa, Tan.	B7	58
Kondopoga, Russia	E4	26
Kondratjevo, Russia	A11	22
Kondrovo, Russia	G18	22
Kondūz, Afg.	B3	44
Konfara, Gui.	F5	64
Kông, stm., Asia	H9	40
Kongcheng, China	D6	34
Kongfang, China	H5	34
Kongju, S. Kor.	G15	32
Konglong, China	F4	34
Kongolo, Zaire	C5	58
Kongor, Sud.	N6	60
Kongsvinger, Nor.	K13	6
Kongur Shan, mtn., China	D2	30
Kongzhen, China	D8	34
Konice, Czech.	F16	10
Königswinter, Ger.	E7	10
Konin, Pol.	C18	10
Köniz, Switz.	E7	13
Konjic, Bos.	F1	20
Könkämäälven, stm., Eur.	G17	6
Kon'-Kolodez', Russia	I22	22
Konkouré, stm., Gui.	F3	64
Konnur, India	D3	46
Konoša, Russia	E6	26
Konotop, Ukr.	G4	26
Kon'ovo, Russia	J26	6
Konqi, stm., China	C4	30
Końskie, Pol.	D20	10
Konstantinovka, Ukr.	H5	26
Konstantinovskij, Russia	D22	22
Konstanz, Ger.	H9	10
Kontagora, Nig.	F12	64
Kontejevo, Russia	C24	22
Kontich, Bel.	F5	12
Kontiomäki, Fin.	I21	6
Kon Tum, Viet.	G10	40
Kontum, Plateau du, plat., Viet.	H10	40
Konya, Tur.	C2	48
Konza, Kenya	B7	58
Konžakovskij Kamen', gora, mtn., Russia	F9	26
Koocanusa, Lake, res., N.A.	B10	122
Koolamarra, Austl.	C4	70
Koolau Range, mts., Hi., U.S.	p15	125a
Kooloonong, Austl.	J5	70
Koondrook, Austl.	J6	70
Koontz Lake, In., U.S.	A10	114
Koosharem, Ut., U.S.	F5	120
Kooskia, Id., U.S.	D10	122
Koossa, Gui.	G5	64
Kootenai (Kootenay), stm., N.A.	I18	102
Kootenay (Kootenai), stm., N.A.	H17	102
Kootenay Indian Reserve, B.C., Can.	H19	102
Kootenay Lake, l., B.C., Can.	H18	102
Kootenay National Park, B.C., Can.	F18	102
Kootjieskolk, S. Afr.	H5	66
Kopargaon, India	C3	46
Kópasker, Ice.	A5	6a
Kopcevіči, Bela.	I11	22
Kopejsk, Russia	F10	26
Koper, Slo.	D8	18
Kopetdag, chrebet, mts., Asia	C15	48
Koppal, India	E4	46
Kopparbergs Län, co., Swe.	K14	6
Koprivnica, Cro.	C11	18
Kopt'ovo, Russia	E23	22
Kopyl', Bela.	H10	22
Kopys', Bela.	G13	22
Korab, mts., Eur.	H4	20
Korablino, Russia	H23	22
Kor'akskaja Sopka, vulkan, vol., Russia	G23	28
Korāput, India	C7	46
Korba, Tun.	M5	18
Korbach, Ger.	D8	10
Korbous, Tun.	M5	18
Korçë, Alb.	I4	20
Korčula, Otok, i., Cro.	G11	18
Kord Kūy, Iran	C13	48
Korea, North, ctry., Asia	C12	30
Korea, South, ctry., Asia	D12	30
Korea Bay, b., Asia	E11	32
Korea Strait, strt., Asia	I16	32
Korekozevo, Russia	G19	22
Koreliči, Bela.	H9	22
Korfovskij, Russia	H19	28
Korgus, Sud.	H7	60
Korhogo, I.C.	G7	64
Korinthiakós Kólpos, b., Grc.	K6	20
Kórinthos (Corinth), Grc.	L6	20
Korínthou, Dhiórix, Grc.	L6	20
Kōriyama, Japan	J15	36
Korkino, Russia	G10	26
Korla, China	C4	30
Kornešty, Mol.	B11	20
Korneuburg, Aus.	G16	10
Koro, Mali	D8	64
Korogwe, Tan.	C7	58
Koroit, Austl.	L5	70
Korol'ovo, Ukr.	A7	20
Koróni, Grc.	M5	20
Koronowo, Pol.	B17	10
Körös, stm., Hung.	I21	10
Korosten', Ukr.	G3	26
Korotovo, Russia	C20	22
Korpilahti, Fin.	J19	6
Korpo (Korppoo), Fin.	K17	6
Korsakov, Russia	H20	28
Korsør, Den.	N12	6
Korsze, Pol.	A21	10
Kortrijk (Courtrai), Bel.	G3	12
Koruçam Burnu, c., N. Cyp.	D2	48
Korumburra, Austl.	L6	70
Koryŏng, S. Kor.	H16	32
Kos, Grc.	M11	20
Kos, i., Grc.	M11	20
Kosa, Eth.	N9	60
Kosa, Russia	F8	26
Koš-Agač, Russia	G15	26
Kosaja Gora, Russia	G20	22
Koščagyl, Kaz.	H8	26
Kościan, Pol.	C16	10
Kościerzyna, Pol.	A18	10
Kosciusko, Ms., U.S.	I7	114
Kosciusko, Mount, mtn., Austl.	K8	70
Kosciusko National Park, Austl.	K8	70
Koshikijima-rettō, is., Japan	P4	36
Koshkonong, Mo., U.S.	F5	114
Košice, Czech.	G21	10
Köşk, Tur.	L12	20
Koskaecodde Lake, l., Newf., Can.	D18	106
Koski, Fin.	K18	6
Koslan, Russia	E7	26
Kosmynino, Russia	D23	22
Kosŏng, N. Kor.	E16	32
Kosov, Ukr.	A9	20
Kosse, Tx., U.S.	H10	116
Koster, S. Afr.	E8	66
Kosterevo, Russia	F22	22
Kostešty, Mol.	C12	20
Kostešty-Stynka, vodochranilišče (Lacul Stînca-Costeşti), res., Eur.	B11	20
Kostriževka, Ukr.	A9	20
Kostroma, Russia	D23	22
Kostroma, stm., Russia	C23	22
Kostrzyn, Pol.	C14	10
Kost'ukoviči, Bela.	H15	22
Kost'ukovka, Bela.	I13	22
Koszalin (Köslin), Pol.	A16	10
Kőszeg, Hung.	H16	10
Kota, India	H6	44
Kota Baharu, Malay.	K7	40
Kotabaru, Indon.	F6	38
Kotabumi, Indon.	F3	38
Kotadabok, Indon.	O8	40
Kotcho Lake, l., B.C., Can.	E8	96
Kotel'nič, Russia	F7	26
Kotel'nikovo, Russia	H6	26
Kotel'nyj, ostrov, i., Russia	B19	28
Köthen, Ger.	D11	10
Kotka, Fin.	K20	6
Kot Kapūra, India	E6	44
Kotlas, Russia	E7	26
Kotli, Pak.	D5	44
Kotlin, ostrov, i., Russia	A12	22
Kotly, Russia	B11	22
Koton-Karifi, Nig.	G13	64
Kotonkoro, Nig.	F12	64
Kotor, Yugo.	G2	20
Kotoriba, Cro.	C11	18
Kotorovo, Russia	G24	22
Kotouba, I.C.	G8	64
Kotovsk, Russia	I24	22
Kotovsk, Ukr.	H3	26
Kottagūdem, India	D6	46
Kottayam, India	H4	46
Kotto, stm., Cen. Afr. Rep.	G5	56
Kotuj, stm., Russia	C12	28
Kot'užen', Mol.	B12	20
Kotzebue, Ak., U.S.	C13	100
Kotzebue Sound, strt., Ak., U.S.	C13	100
Kötzting, Ger.	F12	10
Kou'an, China	C8	34
Kouandé, Benin	F10	64
Kouchibouguac National Park, N.B., Can.	F8	106
Koudougou, Burkina	E8	64
Kouéré, Burkina	F8	64
Koukdjuak, stm., N.W. Ter., Can.	C18	96
Koulamoutou, Gabon	B2	58
Koulikoro, Mali	E6	64
Koulouguidi, Mali	E4	64
Koulountou, stm., Afr.	E3	64
Koumbakara, Sen.	E2	64
Koumbal, Cen. Afr. Rep.	M2	60
Koumpentoum, Sen.	E2	64
Koumra, Chad	G4	56
Koundara, Gui.	E3	64
Koungheul, Sen.	E2	64
Kounradskij, Kaz.	H13	26
Kountze, Tx., U.S.	L2	114
Koupéla, Burkina	E9	64
Kouroukoto, Mali	E4	64
Kouroussa, Gui.	F5	54
Koussanar, Sen.	E2	64
Koussané, Mali	D4	64
Koussane, Sen.	D3	64
Koussi, Emi, mtn., Chad	E4	56
Koussili, Mali	E4	64
Koutia Ba, Sen.	D2	64
Koutiala, Mali	E7	64
Kouto, I.C.	G6	64
Koutou, China	E2	32
Kouts, In., U.S.	A9	114
Kovarskas, Lith.	F7	22
Kovdor, Russia	H22	6
Kovel', Ukr.	G2	26
Kovernino, Russia	D26	22
Kovilpatti, India	H4	46
Kovrov, Russia	F6	26
Kovvur, India	D6	46
Kowalewo Pomorskie, Pol.	B18	10
Kowloon (Jiulong), H.K.	M3	34
Kowŏn, N. Kor.	D15	32
Koyna Reservoir, res., India	D2	46
Koyuk, Ak., U.S.	D14	100
Koyukuk, Ak., U.S.	D16	100
Koyukuk, stm., Ak., U.S.	D17	100
Kozan, Tur.	C3	48
Kozáni, Grc.	I5	20
Kozel'sk, Russia	G18	22
Kozlov Bereg, Russia	C10	22
Kozlovo, Russia	E19	22
Kozlovščina, Bela.	H8	22
Kpandae, Ghana	G9	64
Kpandu, Ghana	H10	64
Kra, Isthmus of, Asia	I5	40
Krabi, Thai.	J5	40
Krâchéh, Camb.	H9	40
Kragerø, Nor.	L11	6
Kragujevac, Yugo.	E4	20
Krajenka, Pol.	B17	10
Krakatoa see Rakata, Pulau, i., Indon.	J12	39a
Krâkôr, Camb.	H8	40
Kraków, Pol.	E19	10
Kralendijk, Neth. Ant.	H10	94
Kraljevo, Yugo.	F4	20
Kralovice, Czech.	F13	10
Kramatorsk, Ukr.	H5	26
Kranj, Slo.	C9	18
Kranzberg, Nmb.	C2	66
Kraskino, Russia	A18	32
Krāslava, Lat.	F10	22
Krasnaja Gorbatka, Russia	F24	22
Krasnaja Gorka, Russia	E26	22
Krasnaja Zar'a, Russia	I20	22
Kraśnik, Pol.	E22	10
Krasnoarmejsk, Russia	E21	22
Krasnodar, Russia	H5	26
Krasnofarfornyj, Russia	B14	22
Krasnogorsk, Russia	F20	22
Krasnogorsk, Russia	H20	28
Krasnoil'sk, Ukr.	A9	20
Krasnojarsk, Russia	F10	28
Krasnojarskoje vodochranilišče, res., Russia	F16	26
Krasnoje, Bela.	G10	22
Krasnoje, Mol.	C13	20
Krasnoje Echo, Russia	F23	22
Krasnoje-na-Volge, Russia	D24	22
Krasnoje Selo, Russia	B13	22
Krasnoje Znam'a, Turk.	C17	48
Krasnokamsk, Russia	F9	26
Krasnolesje, Russia	G5	22
Krasnoslobodsk, Russia	H6	26
Krasnoturjinsk, Russia	F10	26
Krasnoufimsk, Russia	D19	4
Krasnoural'sk, Russia	F10	26
Krasnovišersk, Russia	E9	26
Krasnovodskij poluostrov, pen., Turk.	A12	48
Krasnovodskij zaliv, b., Turk.	B12	48
Krasnozavodsk, Russia	E21	22
Krasnoznamenskij, Kaz.	G11	26
Krasnoz'orskoje, Russia	G13	26
Krasnyj Bogatyr', Russia	E24	22
Krasnyj Cholm, Russia	C20	22
Krasnyje Okny, Ukr.	B13	20
Krasnyje Tkači, Russia	D22	22
Krasnyj Kut, Russia	G7	26
Krasnyj Luč, Russia	D13	22
Krasnyj Luč, Ukr.	H5	26
Krasnyj Okt'abr', Russia	E21	22
Krasnyj Profintern, Russia	D23	22
Krasnyj Rog, Russia	I16	22
Krasnyj Tkač, Russia	F22	22
Krasnystaw, Pol.	E23	10
Kraszna (Crasna), stm., Eur.	A6	20
Krebs, Ok., U.S.	E11	116
Krečetovo, Russia	K26	6
Krečevicy, Russia	C14	22
Krefeld, Ger.	D6	10
Kremastón, Tekhnití Límni, res., Grc.	K5	20
Kremenčug, Ukr.	H4	26
Kremenčugskoje vodochranilišče, res., Ukr.	H4	26
Kremmling, Co., U.S.	D10	120
Krems an der Donau, Aus.	G15	10
Kress, Tx., U.S.	E5	116
Kresta, zaliv, b., Russia	D28	28
Krestcy, Russia	C15	22
Kretinga, Lith.	F4	22
Kribi, Cam.	H8	54
Kričov, Bela.	H14	22
Kriens, Switz.	D9	13
Kriljon, mys, c., Russia	B17	36a
Křimice, Czech.	F13	10
Kriničnoje, Ukr.	D12	20
Krishna, stm., India	D5	46
Krishnagiri, India	F5	46
Krishnanagar, India	I13	44
Krishnarāja Sāgara, res., India	F4	46
Kristdala, Swe.	M15	6
Kristiansand, Nor.	L11	6
Kristianstad, Swe.	M14	6
Kristiansund, Nor.	J10	6
Kristineberg, Swe.	I16	6
Kríti (Crete), i., Grc.	N8	20
Kritikón Pélagos (Sea of Crete), Grc.	N8	20
Kriva Palanka, Mac.	G6	20
Kriviči, Bela.	G10	22
Krivodol, Bul.	F7	20
Krivoje Ozero, Ukr.	B14	20
Krivoj Rog, Ukr.	H4	26
Križevci, Cro.	C11	18
Krk, Otok, i., Cro.	D9	18
Krnov, Czech.	E17	10
Krobia, Pol.	D16	10
Krokek, Swe.	L15	6
Kroken, Nor.	I14	6
Krokowa, Pol.	A18	10
Krombi Pits, Bots.	B7	66
Kroměříž, Czech.	F17	10
Kromy, Russia	I18	22
Krŏng Kaôh Kŏng, Camb.	I7	40
Krŏng Kêb, Camb.	I8	40
Kronobergs Län, co., Swe.	M14	6
Kronoby (Kruunupyy), Fin.	J18	6
Kronockaja Sopka, vulkan, vol., Russia	G24	28
Kronockij zaliv, b., Russia	G24	28
Kronštadt, Russia	B12	22
Kroonstad, S. Afr.	F8	66
Kropotkin, Russia	H6	26
Krosno, Pol.	F21	10
Krotoszyn, Pol.	D17	10
Krotz Springs, La., U.S.	L5	114
Kr'učkovo, Russia	D18	22
Krugersdorp, S. Afr.	F8	66
Kruidfontein, S. Afr.	I5	66
Kruisfontein, S. Afr.	J7	66
Krukira, Laguna de, b., Nic.	D11	92
Kr'ukovo, Russia	F20	22
Krulevščina, Bela.	F10	22
Krumbach [Schwaben], Ger.	G10	10
Krung Thep (Bangkok), Thai.	H6	40
Krupka, Czech.	E13	10
Krupki, Bela.	G12	22
Kruševac, Yugo.	F5	20
Kruševo, Mac.	H5	20
Krušné hory (Erzgebirge), mts., Eur.	B19	14
Kruszwica, Pol.	C18	10
Krutoje, Russia	I20	22
Kruzenšterna, proliv, strt., Russia	H22	28
Kruzof Island, i., Ak., U.S.	H27	100
Krydor, Sask., Can.	F7	104
Krymskij poluostrov (Crimea), pen., Ukr.	H4	26
Krynica, Pol.	F20	10
Kryžopol', Ukr.	A12	20
Ksar Chellala, Alg.	C12	62
Ksar el Barka, Maur.	B3	64
Ksar-el-Kebir, Mor.	J6	16
Ksar-el-Seghir, Mor.	J6	16
Ksar Hellal, Tun.	N5	18
Ksenjevka, Russia	G15	28
Ksour, Monts des, mts., Alg.	D10	62
Ksour Essaf, Tun.	N6	18
Kuala Kangsar, Malay.	L6	40
Kualakapuas, Indon.	F5	38
Kuala Lipis, Malay.	L7	40
Kuala Lumpur, Malay.	M6	40
Kuala Pilah, Malay.	M7	40
Kuala Terengganu, Malay.	L7	40
Kuancheng, China	C6	32
Kuantan, Malay.	M7	40
Kuba, Azer.	I7	26
Kuban', stm., Russia	H5	26
Kubbum, Sud.	L2	60
Kubenskoje, Russia	B22	22
Kubenskoje, ozero, l., Russia	B22	22
Kučevo, Yugo.	E5	20
Kuchāman, India	G6	44
Kuching, Malay.	N11	40
Kuçovë, Alb.	I3	20
Kudirkos Naumiestis, Lith.	G5	22
Kudus, Indon.	J15	39a
Kudymkar, Russia	F8	26
Kuee Ruins, hist., Hi., U.S.	r18	125a
Kufstein, Aus.	H12	10
Kuga, China	C3	30
Kugaluk, stm., N.W. Ter., Can.	B29	100
Kugmallit Bay, b., N.W. Ter., Can.	B28	100
Kūhdasht, Iran	E9	48
Kūhpāyeh, Iran	E12	48
Kuidesu, China	B7	32
Kuidou, China	J7	34
Kuiseb, stm., Afr.	D2	66
Kuito, Ang.	D3	58
Kuiu Island, i., Ak., U.S.	H27	100
Kujang, N. Kor.	D14	32
Kujbyšev, Russia	F13	26
Kujbyšev see Samara, Russia	G8	26
Kujbyševskij, Uzb.	J11	26
Kujbyševskoje vodochranilišče, res., Russia	G7	26
Kujman', Russia	I22	22
Kukalaya, stm., Nic.	D11	92
Kukawa, Nig.	F9	54
Kukawa, Nig.	F3	56
Kukkola, Fin.	I19	6
Kula, Yugo.	D3	20
Kul'ab, Taj.	J11	26
Kula Kangri, mtn., Bhu.	F14	44
Kulākh, Sau. Ar.	D2	47
Kulautuva, Lith.	G6	22
Kulaykilī, Sud.	L3	60
Kuldīga, Lat.	E4	22
Kule, Bots.	D5	66
Kulebaki, Russia	F25	22
Kulikovo, Russia	I22	22
Kulim, Malay.	L6	40
Kulm, N.D., U.S.	E9	118
Kulmbach, Ger.	E11	10
Kuloj, Russia	E6	26
Kulongshan, China	B4	32
Kulotino, Russia	C16	22
Kul'sary, Kaz.	H8	26
Kulti, India	I12	44
Kulumadau, Pap. N. Gui.	A10	68
Kulundinskaja step', pl., Asia	G7	28
Kuma, stm., Russia	I7	26
Kumagaya, Japan	K14	36
Kumajri, Arm.	I6	26
Kumamoto, Japan	O5	36
Kumanovo, Mac.	G5	20
Kumārapālaiyam, India	G4	46
Kumasi, Ghana	H9	64
Kumba, Cam.	I14	64
Kumbakonam, India	G5	46
Kumba Pits, Bots.	B7	66
Kŭmch'ŏn, N. Kor.	E14	32
Kum-Dag, Turk.	J8	26
Kume-jima, i., Japan	U1	37b
Kŭmhwa, S. Kor.	E15	32
Kumla, Swe.	L14	6
Kumo, Nig.	F9	54
Kumukahi, Cape, c., Hi., U.S.	r19	125a
Kumukuli, China	B13	44
Kumzār, Oman	A10	47
Kuna, Id., U.S.	G9	122
Kunašir, ostrov (Kunashiri-tō), i., Russia	C21	36a
Kunchhā, Nepal	F11	44
Kunda, Est.	B9	22
Kundar, stm., Asia	E3	44
Kunene (Cunene), stm., Afr.	E2	58
Kunghit Island, i., B.C., Can.	E3	102
Kungrad, Uzb.	I9	26
Kungsbacka, Swe.	M13	6
Kungur, Russia	F9	26
Kunhegyes, Hung.	H20	10
Kunja, Russia	E13	22
Kunjāh, Pak.	D5	44
Kunlong, Burma	C5	40
Kunlun Shan, mts., China	B12	44
Kunming, China	B7	40
Kunsan, S. Kor.	H14	32
Kunshan, China	D9	34
Kunszentmárton, Hung.	I20	10
Kuntair, Gam.	E1	64
Kuntaur, Gam.	E2	64
Kunting, China	F10	34
Kununurra, Austl.	C5	68
Kunwi, S. Kor.	G16	32
Kuokegan, China	B13	44
Kuopio, Fin.	J20	6
Kuopion lääni, prov., Fin.	J20	6
Kupang, Indon.	H7	38
Kup'ansk, Ukr.	H5	26
Kupanskoje, Russia	E21	22
Kupino, Russia	G7	28
Kupiškis, Lith.	F7	22
Küplü, Tur.	H10	20
Kupreanof Island, i., Ak., U.S.	H28	100
Kura, stm., Asia	B10	48
Kurashiki, Japan	M8	36
Kuraymah, Sud.	H6	60
Kurayyimah, Jord.	D5	50
Kurba, Russia	D22	22
K'urdamir, Azer.	A10	48
Kurdistan, hist. reg., Asia	B4	42
Kure, Japan	M7	36
Kurejka, stm., Russia	D9	28
Kuresaare, Est.	C5	22
Kurgan, Russia	F11	26
Kurgan-T'ube, Taj.	J11	26
Kuria Muria Islands see Khurīyā Murīyā, is., Oman	F10	47
Kuridala, Austl.	C4	70
Kurīgrām, Bngl.	H13	44
Kuril Islands see Kuril'skije ostrova, is., Russia	H22	28
Kuril'skije ostrova (Kuril Islands), is., Russia	H22	28
Kuril Strait see Pervyj Kuril'skij proliv, strt., Russia	G23	28
Kuril Trench	D19	126
Kurinskaja kosa, spit, Azer.	B10	48
Kurinwás, stm., Nic.	E11	92
Kurkino, Russia	H21	22
Kurlovskij, Russia	F23	22
Kurmuk, Sud.	L8	60
Kurnool, India	E5	46
Kurovskoje, Russia	F21	22
Kurow, N.Z.	F3	72
Kuršėnai, Lith.	E5	22
Kursk, Russia	G5	26
Kurskaja kosa, spit, Eur.	F4	22
Kurskij zaliv, b., Eur.	F3	22
Kūrtī, Sud.	H6	60
Kurtistown, Hi., U.S.	r18	125a
Kuru, Sud.	N4	60
Kuruman, S. Afr.	F6	66
Kuruman, stm., Afr.	F5	66
Kurumanheuwels, hills, Afr.	F6	66
Kurume, Japan	N5	36
Kurumkan, Russia	G14	28
Kurun, stm., Afr.	O8	60
Kurunegala, Sri L.	I6	46
Kurzeme, hist. reg., Lat.	E5	22
Kusa, Russia	F9	26
Kušalino, Russia	D19	22
Kusawa Lake, l., Yukon, Can.	F26	100
Kusel, Ger.	F7	10
Kushaka, Nig.	F13	64
Kushiro, Japan	E19	36a
Kushtia, Bngl.	I13	44
Kushui, China	C5	30
Kuška, Turk.	J10	26
Kuška, stm., Asia	C17	48
Kuskokwim, stm., Ak., U.S.	F14	100
Kuskokwim Mountains, mts., Ak., U.S.	E16	100
Kušmurun, Kaz.	G10	26
Küsnacht, Switz.	D10	13
Kušnica, Ukr.	A7	20
Kusŏng, N. Kor.	D13	32
Kussharo-ko, l., Japan	D19	36a
Küssnacht am Rigi, Switz.	D9	13
Kustanaj, Kaz.	G10	26
Kustar'ovka, Russia	G25	22
Kūstī, Sud.	K7	60
Kušva, Russia	F9	26
Kut, Ko, i., Thai.	I7	40
Kuta, Nig.	G13	64
Kütahya, Tur.	H13	4
Kutaisi, Geor.	I6	26
Kutch, Rann of (Rann of Kachchh), reg., Asia	H4	44
Kutina, Cro.	D11	18
Kutná Hora, Czech.	F15	10
Kutno, Pol.	C19	10
Kutse Game Reserve, Bots.	D7	66
Kuttura, Fin.	G20	6
Kuttusoja, Fin.	H21	6
Kutu, Zaire	B3	58
Kutum, Sud.	J3	60
Kuty, Ukr.	A9	20
Kutztown, Pa., U.S.	G11	108
Kuujjuaq, Que., Can.	E19	96
Kuusamo, Fin.	I21	6
Kuusankoski, Fin.	K20	6
Kuvandyk, Russia	G9	26
Kuvango, Ang.	D3	58
Kuvšinovo, Russia	D17	22
Kuwait (Al-Kuwayt), ctry., Asia	D4	42
Kuwait see Al-Kuwayt, Kuw.	G9	48
Kuwana, Japan	L11	36
Kuwayt, Jūn al- (Kuwait Bay), b., Kuw.	G10	48
Kuybyshev see Samara, Russia	G8	26
Kūysanjaq, Iraq	C8	48
Kuyuwini, stm., Guy.	F13	84
Kuženkino, Russia	D16	22
Kuzneck, Russia	G7	26
Kuzneckij Alatau, mts., Russia	G9	28
Kvaløy, i., Nor.	G16	6
Kwai see Khwae Noi, stm., Thai.	G5	40
Kwajok, Sud.	M4	60
Kwakoegron, Sur.	B7	76
Kwando (Cuando), stm., Afr.	E4	58
Kwangchow see Guangzhou, China	L2	34
Kwangju, S. Kor.	H14	32
Kwango (Cuango), stm., Afr.	B3	58
Kwangtung see Guangdong, prov., China	G9	30
Kwangyang, S. Kor.	I15	32
Kweisui see Hohhot, China	C9	30
Kwekwe, Zimb.	B9	66
Kweneng, dept., Bots.	E7	66
Kwenge, stm., Afr.	C3	58
Kwethluk, Ak., U.S.	F14	100
Kwidzyn, Pol.	B18	10
Kwigillingok, Ak., U.S.	G13	100
Kwilu (Cuilo), stm., Afr.	B3	58
Kwitaro, stm., Guy.	F13	84
Kwolla, Nig.	G14	64
Kyabra, Austl.	F5	70
Kyabram, Austl.	K6	70
Kyaiklat, Burma	F3	40
Kyaikto, Burma	F4	40
Kyaukhnyat, Burma	E4	40
Kyaukpyu, Burma	E2	40
Kyaukse, Burma	D4	40
Kyauktaw, Burma	D2	40
Kyaunggon, Burma	F3	40
Kybartai, Lith.	G5	22
Kyeikdon, Burma	F5	40
Kyindwe, Burma	D2	40
Kykotsmovi Village, Az., U.S.	I6	120
Kyle, Sask., Can.	H6	104
Kyle, S.D., U.S.	H5	118
Kyle, Tx., U.S.	J9	116
Kyle of Lochalsh, Scot., U.K.	D8	8
Kymen lääni, prov., Fin.	K20	6
Kyneton, Austl.	K6	70
Kyoga, Lake, l., Ug.	A6	58
Kyogle, Austl.	G10	70
Kyŏnggi-man, b., Asia	F13	32
Kyŏngju, S. Kor.	H17	32
Kyŏngsan, S. Kor.	H16	32
Kyŏngsŏng, N. Kor.	B17	32
Kyŏngwŏn, N. Kor.	A18	32
Kyōto, Japan	L10	36
Kyren, Russia	G12	28
Kyrgyzstan, ctry., Asia	I13	26
Kyritz, Ger.	C12	10
Kyštovka, Russia	F13	26
Kyštym, Russia	F10	26
Kyunhla, Burma	C3	40
Kyuquot, B.C., Can.	G7	102
Kyuquot Sound, strt., B.C., Can.	G7	102
Kyūshū, i., Japan	O5	36
Kywebwe, Burma	E4	40
Kywong, Austl.	J7	70
Kyyjärvi, Fin.	J19	6
Kyzyl, Russia	G10	28
Kyzyl-Kija, Kyrg.	I12	26
Kyzylkum, des., Asia	I10	26
Kzyl-Orda, Kaz.	I11	26
Kzyltu, Kaz.	G12	26

L

Name	Map Ref.	Page
Laa an der Thaya, Aus.	G16	10
La Aguja, Cabo de, c., Col.	B5	84
La Alcarria, reg., Spain	E9	16
La Algaba, Spain	H5	16
La Antigua, Salina, pl., Arg.	E5	80
La Araucanía, prov., Chile	J2	80
La Arena, Pan.	J14	92
Laas Caanood, Som.	G10	56
La Ascención, Mex.	E10	90
La Asunción, Ven.	B11	84
La Atravesada, Loma, hill, Mex.	C3	90
Laau Point, c., Hi., U.S.	p16	125a
La Babia, Mex.	C8	90
Labadieville, La., U.S.	M6	114
La Baie, Que., Can.	D3	106
La Banda, Arg.	D6	80
La Bandera, Cerro, mtn., Mex.	E7	90
La Bañeza, Spain	C6	16
La Barca, Mex.	G8	90
La Barge, Wy., U.S.	B6	120
La Barra, Nic.	E11	92
La Barrita, Guat.	C3	92
La Bassée, Fr.	B9	14
La Baule-Escoublac, Fr.	E4	14
Labé, Gui.	F3	64
Labe (Elbe), stm., Eur.	B9	10
Labelle, Que., Can.	A12	108
La Belle, Fl., U.S.	M5	112
La Belle, Mo., U.S.	B5	114
Laberge, Lake, l., Yukon, Can.	F27	100
La Biche, stm., Alta., Can.	B22	102
Labin, Cro.	D9	18
Labinsk, Russia	I6	26
La Bisbal, Spain	D15	16
La Blanca Grande, Laguna, l., Arg.	J7	80
Labná, hist., Mex.	G15	90
Laboe, Ger.	A10	10
Laborde, Arg.	G7	80
Labouheyre, Fr.	H6	14
Laboulaye, Arg.	H7	80

Name	Map Ref.	Page
Labrador, reg., Newf., Can.	F20	96
Labrador City, Newf., Can.	F19	96
Labrador Sea, N.A.	E22	96
Lábrea, Braz.	E6	76
Lábrea, Braz.	B9	82
Labrieville, Réserve, Que., Can.	C4	106
Labrit, Fr.	H6	14
La Broquerie, Man., Can.	I18	104
Labutta, Burma	F3	40
Labytnangi, Russia	D11	26
Lača, ozero, l., Russia	K26	6
Laca Jahuira, stm., Bol.	H8	82
La Cal, stm., Bol.	G12	82
La Calera, Chile	G3	80
Lac-Allard, Que., Can.	B10	106
La Campana, Spain	H6	16
La Canada, Ca., U.S.	J7	124
La Candelaria, Arg.	D6	80
Lacantún, stm., Mex.	I14	90
La Capelle [-en-Thierache], Fr.	C10	14
Lacapelle-Marival, Fr.	H8	14
La Carlota, Arg.	G7	80
La Carolina, Spain	G8	16
Lacaune, Fr.	I9	14
Laccadive Islands see Lakshadweep, is., India	G2	46
Lac du Flambeau, Wi., U.S.	E6	110
La Ceiba, Hond.	B8	92
La Ceiba, Ven.	C7	84
La Center, Ky., U.S.	E8	114
Lac-Etchemin, Que., Can.	F3	106
Lacey, Wa., U.S.	C3	122
Lac-Frontière, Que., Can.	F3	106
La Chambre, Fr.	G13	14
La Chapelle-d'Angillon, Fr.	E9	14
La Chartre-sur-le-Loir, Fr.	E7	14
La Châtaigneraie, Fr.	F6	14
La Chaux-de-Fonds, Switz.	D6	13
Lachay, Punta, c., Peru	D3	82
Lachdenpochja, Russia	K22	6
Lachen, Switz.	D10	13
Lachhmangarh Sīkar, India	G6	44
Lachine, Que., Can.	B13	108
Lachkaltsap Indian Reserve, B.C., Can.	B5	102
Lachlan, stm., Austl.	J6	70
La Chorrera, Col.	H6	84
La Chorrera, Pan.	C3	84
L'achovići, Bela.	H9	22
L'achovskije ostrova, is., Russia	C20	28
Lachute, Que., Can.	B12	108
Lachva, Bela.	I10	22
La Ciénaga, Arg.	D5	80
La Ciotat, Fr.	I12	14
La Citadelle, hist., Haiti	E8	94
La Ciudad, Mex.	F7	90
Lackawanna, N.Y., U.S.	E8	108
Lac la Biche, Alta., Can.	C23	102
Lac la Hache, B.C., Can.	F13	102
Lac la Ronge Provincial Park, Sask., Can.	C10	104
Laclede, Id., U.S.	I18	102
Laclede, Mo., U.S.	C3	114
La Clotilde, Arg.	D8	80
Lac-Mégantic, Que., Can.	B16	108
La Cocha, Arg.	D6	80
La Colorada, Mex.	C4	90
La Coma, Mex.	E10	90
Lacombe, Alta., Can.	E21	102
Lacombe, La., U.S.	L7	114
Lacon, Il., U.S.	I6	110
Lacona, Ia., U.S.	I2	110
La Concepción, Pan.	C1	84
La Concepción, Ven.	B7	84
Laconia, N.H., U.S.	D15	108
La Conner, Wa., U.S.	B3	122
La Consulta, Arg.	G4	80
Lacoochee, Fl., U.S.	K4	112
La Coruña, Spain	B3	16
La Coste, Tx., U.S.	J8	116
Lac qui Parle, stm., Mn., U.S.	G11	118
La Crescent, Mn., U.S.	G4	110
La Crosse, In., U.S.	A10	114
La Crosse, Ks., U.S.	M8	118
La Crosse, Va., U.S.	C8	112
Lacrosse, Wa., U.S.	D8	122
La Crosse, Wi., U.S.	G4	110
La Crosse, stm., Wi., U.S.	G4	110
La Cruz, Arg.	E10	80
La Cruz, Col.	G4	84
La Cruz, C.R.	F9	92
La Cruz, Ur.	G10	80
La Cruz, Cerro, mtn., Mex.	I9	90
La Cruz de Río Grande, Nic.	D10	92
Lac Seul, Ont., Can.	H22	104
Lac Seul Indian Reserve, Ont., Can.	H22	104
La Cuesta, C.R.	I12	92
La Cumbre, Arg.	F6	80
La Cygne, Ks., U.S.	M13	118
Ladainha, Braz.	D8	79
Ladākh Range, mts., Asia	C7	44
Ladário, Braz.	H13	82
Ladd, Il., U.S.	I6	110
Laddonia, Mo., U.S.	C5	114
La Désirade, i., Guad.	F14	94
La Digue, i., Sey.	B11	58
Ladismith, S. Afr.	I5	66
Lādīz, Iran	G16	48
Lādnūn, India	G6	44
Ladoga, In., U.S.	C10	114
Ladoga, Lake see Ladožskoje ozero, l., Russia	E4	26
Ladonia, Tx., U.S.	F11	116
La Dorada, Col.	E5	84
La Dormida, Arg.	G5	80
Ladožskoje Ozero, Russia	A14	22
Ladožskoje ozero (Lake Ladoga), l., Russia	E4	26
Ladson, S.C., U.S.	G6	112
Ladue, stm., N.A.	E24	100
Laduškin, Russia	G3	22
Ladva-Vetka, Russia	K24	6
L'ady, Russia	C11	22
Lady Ann Strait, strt., N.W. Ter., Can.	A16	96
Ladybrand, S. Afr.	G8	66
Lady Elliot Island, i., Austl.	E10	70
Ladysmith, B.C., Can.	I11	102
Ladysmith, S. Afr.	G9	66
Ladysmith, Wi., U.S.	E4	110
Lae, Pap. N. Gui.	m16	68a
La Encantada, Mex.	E9	90
La Esmeralda, Mex.	D8	90
La Esmeralda, Para.	B7	80
La Esmeralda, Ven.	F10	84
La Esperanza, Cuba	C3	94
La Esperanza, Hond.	C6	92
La Estrella, Bol.	G10	82
La Falda, Arg.	F6	80
La Farge, Wi., U.S.	G5	110
Lafayette, Al., U.S.	J11	114
Lafayette, Ca., U.S.	G3	124
Lafayette, Co., U.S.	L2	118
Lafayette, Ga., U.S.	E1	112
Lafayette, In., U.S.	B10	114
Lafayette, La., U.S.	L4	114
Lafayette, Mn., U.S.	F1	110
Lafayette, Tn., U.S.	F10	114
La Fé, Cuba	D3	94
La Fère, Fr.	C10	14
La Feria, Tx., U.S.	M9	116
La Ferté-Bernard, Fr.	D7	14
La Ferté-Gaucher, Fr.	D10	14
La Ferté-Macé, Fr.	D6	14
La Ferté-Saint-Aubin, Fr.	E8	14
Lafia, Nig.	G14	64
Lafleche, Sask., Can.	I8	104
La Flèche, Fr.	E6	14
La Florida, Guat.	I14	90
Lafnitz, stm., Eur.	H16	10
La Follette, Tn., U.S.	C2	112
La Fontaine, In., U.S.	B11	114
Lafourche, Bayou, stm., La., U.S.	M6	114
La Fragua, Arg.	D6	80
La Francia, Arg.	F7	80
La Fría, Ven.	C6	84
La Galite, i., Tun.	L3	18
La Gallareta, Arg.	E8	80
Lagangzong, China	F14	44
Lagarto, C.R.	G10	92
Lagawe, Phil.	M19	39b
Lage, China	F11	44
Lågen, stm., Nor.	K11	6
Lågen, stm., Nor.	K12	6
Lages, Braz.	D13	80
Lage Zwaluwe, Neth.	E6	12
Laghouat, Alg.	D12	62
La Gleize, Bel.	H8	12
La Gloria, Col.	C6	84
Lagoa da Prata, Braz.	F6	79
Lagoa Formosa, Braz.	E5	79
Lagoa Santa, Braz.	E7	79
Lagoa Vermelha, Braz.	E13	80
Lagolândia, Braz.	C4	79
Lagos, Nig.	H11	64
Lagos, Port.	H3	16
Lagos de Moreno, Mex.	G9	90
La Gouèra, W. Sah.	J2	62
La Goulette, Tun.	M5	18
La Grand'Combe, Fr.	H11	14
La Grande, Or., U.S.	E7	122
La Grande Deux, Réservoir, res., Que., Can.	F17	96
La Grande Quatre, Réservoir, res., Que., Can.	F18	96
La Grange, Austl.	C4	68
La Grange, Ga., U.S.	F1	112
Lagrange, In., U.S.	A11	114
La Grange, Ky., U.S.	D11	114
La Grange, Mo., U.S.	B5	114
La Grange, N.C., U.S.	D9	112
La Grange, Tx., U.S.	J10	116
Lagrange, Wy., U.S.	J3	118
La Gran Sabana, pl., Ven.	E12	84
La Grita, Ven.	C7	84
Lagu, China	A6	40
La Guadeloupe (Saint-Évariste), Que., Can.	B16	108
La Guajira, dept., Col.	B6	84
La Guajira, Península de, pen., S.A.	A7	84
La Guardia, Arg.	E6	80
La Guardia, Bol.	G10	82
La Guardia, Spain	D3	16
La Guerche-de-Bretagne, Fr.	E5	14
La Guerche-sur-l'Aubois, Fr.	F9	14
Laguna, Braz.	E14	80
Laguna, N.M., U.S.	I9	120
Laguna, Ilha da, i., Braz.	D8	76
Laguna Beach, Ca., U.S.	K8	124
Laguna Larga, Arg.	F7	80
Laguna Limpia, Arg.	D9	80
Laguna Paiva, Arg.	F8	80
Lagunas, Peru	A4	82
Lagunas de Chacagua, Parque Nacional, Mex.	I11	90
Lagunas de Montebello, Parque Nacional, Mex.	A3	92
Lagunillas, Bol.	H10	82
Lagunillas, Ven.	C7	84
Lagunillas, Laguna, l., Peru	F6	82
Laguntara, p., Hond.	C8	92
La Habana (Havana), Cuba	C3	94
Lahaina, Hi., U.S.	q17	125a
La Harpe, Il., U.S.	J5	110
La Harpe, Ks., U.S.	N12	118
Lahat, Indon.	F3	38
LaHave, stm., N.S., Can.	H9	106
La Haye-du-Puits, Fr.	C5	14
La Higuera, Chile	E3	80
Lahij, Yemen	H4	47
Lāhījān, Iran	C11	48
Lahnstein, Ger.	E7	10
Lahontan Reservoir, res., Nv., U.S.	E6	124
Lahore, Pak.	E6	44
La Horqueta, Col.	F6	84
Lahr, Ger.	G7	10
Lahri, Pak.	F3	44
Lahti, Fin.	K19	6
La Huaca, Peru	A1	82
La Huacana, Mex.	H9	90
La Huerta, N.M., U.S.	G2	116
Laibin, China	C10	40
Lai Chau, Viet.	C7	40
Laifang, China	J5	34
L'Aigle, Fr.	D7	14
Laignes, Fr.	E11	14
La Independencia, Bahía de, b., Peru	F3	82
Laingsburg, S. Afr.	I5	66
Laingsburg, Mi., U.S.	H11	110
La Inmaculada, Mex.	C4	90
Laird Hill, Tx., U.S.	J2	114
Laishan, China	F9	32
Laishui, China	D3	32
Laiwu, China	G5	32
Laiyang, China	G8	32
Laizhou Wan (Laichow Bay), b., China	F7	32
Laja, stm., Chile	I3	80
Laja, Laguna de la, l., Chile	I3	80
Laja, Salto del, wtfl, Chile	I3	80
La Jalca, Peru	B3	82
La Jara, Co., U.S.	G11	120
La Jara Canyon, val., N.M., U.S.	H9	120
Lajas, Cuba	C4	94
Laje, Braz.	B9	79
Lajeado, Braz.	E13	80
Lajes, Braz.	E11	76
Lajinha, Braz.	F8	79
La Jolla, Ca., U.S.	L8	124
Lajord, Sask., Can.	H10	104
Lajosmizse, Hung.	H19	10
La Joya, Peru	G6	82
La Junta, Co., U.S.	N4	118
Lakamané, Mali	D5	64
Lake, Ms., U.S.	J7	114
Lake Alfred, Fl., U.S.	K5	112
Lake Andes, S.D., U.S.	H9	118
Lake Arthur, La., U.S.	L4	114
Lake Arthur, N.M., U.S.	G2	116
Lake Benton, Mn., U.S.	G11	118
Lake Brownwood, Tx., U.S.	H7	116
Lake Butler, Fl., U.S.	I4	112
Lake Cargelligo, Austl.	I7	70
Lake Carmel, N.Y., U.S.	F13	108
Lake Charles, La., U.S.	L3	114
Lake City, Ar., U.S.	G6	114
Lake City, Co., U.S.	F9	120
Lake City, Fl., U.S.	I4	112
Lake City, Ia., U.S.	I13	118
Lake City, Mi., U.S.	F10	110
Lake City, Mn., U.S.	F3	110
Lake City, Pa., U.S.	E6	108
Lake City, S.C., U.S.	F7	112
Lake City, Tn., U.S.	C2	112
Lake Cowichan, B.C., Can.	I10	102
Lake Crystal, Mn., U.S.	F1	110
Lake Dallas, Tx., U.S.	F9	116
Lake Delton, Wi., U.S.	G6	110
Lake Elsinore, Ca., U.S.	K8	124
Lakefield, Ont., Can.	F17	110
Lakefield, Mn., U.S.	H12	118
Lakefield National Park, Austl.	C8	68
Lake Forest, Fl., U.S.	N6	112
Lake Forest, Il., U.S.	H8	110
Lake Fork, stm., Ut., U.S.	D6	120
Lake Geneva, Wi., U.S.	H7	110
Lake George, N.Y., U.S.	D13	108
Lake Harbor, Fl., U.S.	M6	112
Lake Harbour, N.W. Ter., Can.	D19	96
Lake Havasu City, Az., U.S.	J2	120
Lake Helen, Fl., U.S.	K5	112
Lakehurst, N.J., U.S.	G12	108
Lake Isabella, Ca., U.S.	I7	124
Lake Jackson, Tx., U.S.	J11	116
Lakeland, Fl., U.S.	K5	112
Lakeland, Ga., U.S.	H3	112
Lake Linden, Mi., U.S.	C7	110
Lake Louise, Alta., Can.	F18	102
Lake Mills, Ia., U.S.	G2	110
Lake Mills, Wi., U.S.	G7	110
Lakemont, Pa., U.S.	G8	108
Lake Nash, Austl.	C2	70
Lake Norden, S.D., U.S.	G10	118
Lake Odessa, Mi., U.S.	H10	110
Lake Oswego, Or., U.S.	E3	122
Lake Ozark, Mo., U.S.	D4	114
Lake Park, Fl., U.S.	M6	112
Lake Park, Ia., U.S.	H12	118
Lake Park, Mn., U.S.	E11	118
Lake Placid, Fl., U.S.	L5	112
Lake Placid, N.Y., U.S.	C13	108
Lake Pleasant, N.Y., U.S.	D12	108
Lakeport, Ca., U.S.	E3	124
Lakeport, Mi., U.S.	G13	110
Lake Preston, S.D., U.S.	G10	118
Lake Providence, La., U.S.	J5	114
Lakes District, Wa., U.S.	C3	122
Lakeshore, Ms., U.S.	L7	114
Lakeside, N.S., Can.	H10	106
Lakeside, Az., U.S.	J7	120
Lakeside, Ca., U.S.	L9	124
Lakeside, Mt., U.S.	B11	122
Lakeside, Or., U.S.	G1	122
Lake Stevens, Wa., U.S.	B3	122
Laketown, Ut., U.S.	C5	120
Lake View, Ar., U.S.	H6	114
Lakeview, Ga., U.S.	E1	112
Lake View, Ia., U.S.	I12	118
Lakeview, Mi., U.S.	H10	110
Lakeview, Mi., U.S.	G10	110
Lake View, N.Y., U.S.	E8	108
Lakeview, Oh., U.S.	G3	108
Lakeview, Or., U.S.	H5	122
Lake View, S.C., U.S.	E7	112
Lakeview, Tx., U.S.	M3	114
Lakeview, Tx., U.S.	E6	116
Lakeview Mountain, mtn., B.C., Can.	H14	102
Lake Village, Ar., U.S.	I5	114
Lakeville, Mn., U.S.	F2	110
Lake Wales, Fl., U.S.	L5	112
Lake Wilson, Mn., U.S.	H12	118
Lakewood, Co., U.S.	E11	120
Lakewood, N.J., U.S.	G12	108
Lakewood, N.Y., U.S.	E7	108
Lakewood, Oh., U.S.	F5	108
Lakewood, Wi., U.S.	E7	110
Lakewood Park, N.D., U.S.	C9	118
Lake Worth, Fl., U.S.	M6	112
Lakhīmpur, India	G9	44
Lakhish, val., Asia	E3	50
Lakin, Ks., U.S.	N6	118
Lakinsk, Russia	E22	22
Lakonikós Kólpos, b., Grc.	M6	20
Lakota, Ia., U.S.	H13	118
Lakota, N.D., U.S.	C9	118
Lakshadweep, ter., India	H2	46
Lakshadweep, is., India	G2	46
Lakshadweep Sea, Asia	H3	46
La Lajilla, Mex.	D10	90
L'Albufera, l., Spain	F11	16
La Leonesa, Arg.	D9	80
Lalibela, Eth.	K10	60
La Libertad, El Sal.	D5	92
La Libertad, Guat.	I14	90
La Libertad, Hond.	C7	92
La Libertad, Nic.	E9	92
La Libertad, dept., Peru	B2	82
La Ligua, Chile	G3	80
La Lima, Hond.	B7	92
La Línea, Spain	I6	16
Lalitpur, India	H8	44
Lālmanir Hāt, Bngl.	H13	44
La Loche, Sask., Can.	B5	104
La Loche, stm., Sask., Can.	B5	104
La Loche, Lac, l., Sask., Can.	B5	104
La Loupe, Fr.	D8	14
Lalupon, Nig.	H12	64
La Luz, Mex.	E11	90
La Luz, Nic.	C10	92
La Luz, N.M., U.S.	L11	120
Lama, ozero, l., Russia	D16	26
La Macarena, Serranía de, mts., Col.	F6	84
La Maddalena, Italy	H4	18
Lamadong, China	C7	32
La Madrid, Arg.	D6	80
La Malbaie, Que., Can.	E3	106
Lamaline, Newf., Can.	F18	106
La Mancha, reg., Spain	G8	16
Lamar, Co., U.S.	M5	118
Lamar, Mo., U.S.	E2	114
Lamar, S.C., U.S.	E6	112
Lamar, stm., Wy., U.S.	F16	122
Lamarche, Fr.	D12	14
La Mariscala, Ur.	H11	80
Lamarque, Arg.	J6	80
La Marque, Tx., U.S.	J12	116
La Marsa, Tun.	M5	18
Lamas, Peru	B3	82
La Masica, Hond.	B7	92
Lamastre, Fr.	H11	14
Lamballe, Fr.	D4	14
Lambaréné, Gabon	B2	58
Lambari, stm., Braz.	F6	79
Lambayeque, Peru	B2	82
Lambayeque, dept., Peru	B1	82
Lambayeque, stm., Peru	B2	82
Lambert, Ms., U.S.	H6	114
Lambert, Mt., U.S.	D3	118
Lambert Glacier, Ant.	C5	73
Lamberton, Mn., U.S.	G12	118
Lambert's Bay, S. Afr.	I4	66
Lambertville, N.J., U.S.	G12	108
Lambeth, Ont., Can.	H14	110
Lambomakondro, Madag.	S21	67b
Lambrama, Peru	E5	82
Lambton, Cape, c., N.W. Ter., Can.	B8	96
Lame Deer, Mt., U.S.	E19	122
La Media Luna, Arrecifes de, rf., Hond.	B12	92
La Mendieta, Arg.	C6	80
Lamèque, N.B., Can.	E9	106
Lamèque, Île, i., N.B., Can.	E9	106
La Merced, Arg.	E6	80
La Merced, Arg.	C6	80
La Merced, Peru	D4	82
La Mesa, Pan.	I13	92
La Mesa, Ca., U.S.	L8	124
La Mesa, N.M., U.S.	L10	120
Lamesa, Tx., U.S.	G5	116
Lamía, Grc.	K6	20
L'amin, stm., Russia	E12	26
Lamine, stm., Mo., U.S.	D4	114
Lamming Mills, B.C., Can.	D14	102
La Moille, Il., U.S.	I6	110
Lamoille, Nv., U.S.	D10	124
Lamoille, stm., Vt., U.S.	C14	108
La Moine, stm., Il., U.S.	B6	114
Lamon Bay, b., Phil.	N19	39b
Lamoni, Ia., U.S.	J2	110
Lamont, Alta., Can.	D22	102
Lamont, Ca., U.S.	I7	124
Lamont, Ia., U.S.	H4	110
Lamont, Ok., U.S.	C9	116
La Monte, Mo., U.S.	D3	114
La Mosquitia, hist. reg., Hond.	B11	92
La Mothe, Lac, res., Que., Can.	D2	106
La Mothe-Achard, Fr.	F5	14
Lamotte-Beuvron, Fr.	E9	14
La Moure, N.D., U.S.	E9	118
Lampa, Peru	F6	82
Lampang, Thai.	E5	40
Lampasas, Tx., U.S.	H8	116
Lampasas, stm., Tx., U.S.	H8	116
Lampazos de Naranjo, Mex.	D9	90
Lampedusa, Isola di, i., Italy	N7	18
Lamphun, Thai.	E5	40
Lampman, Sask., Can.	I12	104
Lamud, Peru	B3	82
La Muerte, Cerro, mtn., C.R.	H11	92
Lana, Italy	C6	18
Lanai, i., Hi., U.S.	q17	125a
Lanai City, Hi., U.S.	q17	125a
Lanalhue, Lago, l., Chile	I2	80
Lanark, Ont., Can.	E19	110
Lanark, Il., U.S.	H6	110
Lanbi Kyun, i., Burma	I5	40
Lancashire, co., Eng., U.K.	H11	8
Lancaster, Ont., Can.	B12	108
Lancaster, Eng., U.K.	G11	8
Lancaster, Ca., U.S.	J7	124
Lancaster, Ky., U.S.	B2	112
Lancaster, Mn., U.S.	C11	118
Lancaster, Mo., U.S.	B4	114
Lancaster, N.H., U.S.	C15	108
Lancaster, N.Y., U.S.	E8	108
Lancaster, Oh., U.S.	H4	108
Lancaster, Pa., U.S.	G10	108
Lancaster, S.C., U.S.	E6	112
Lancaster, Tx., U.S.	G10	116
Lancaster, Va., U.S.	B10	112
Lancaster, Wi., U.S.	H5	110
Lancaster Sound, strt., N.W. Ter., Can.	B16	96
Lance Creek, Wy., U.S.	A12	120
Lanciano, Italy	G9	18
Lančin, Ukr.	A8	20
Lancones, Peru	J2	84
Lancun, China	G8	32
Łańcut, Pol.	E22	10
Lancy, Switz.	F5	13
Landau, Ger.	F8	10
Landau an der Isar, Ger.	G12	10
Landeck, Aus.	H10	10
Landen, Bel.	G7	12
Lander, Wy., U.S.	B8	120
Landerneau, Fr.	D2	14
Landes, dept., Fr.	H6	14
Landete, Spain	F10	16
Landing Lake, l., Man., Can.	C17	104
Landis, Sask., Can.	F6	104
Landis, N.C., U.S.	D6	112
Landivisiau, Fr.	D2	14
Lando, S.C., U.S.	E5	112
Land O'Lakes, Wi., U.S.	D6	110
Landquart, Switz.	E12	13
Landrum, S.C., U.S.	D4	112
Landsberg [am Lech], Ger.	G10	10
Land's End, c., Eng., U.K.	K8	8
Landshut, Ger.	G12	10
Landskrona, Swe.	N13	6
La Negra, Chile	B3	80
Lanesboro, Mn., U.S.	G4	110
Lanett, Al., U.S.	J11	114
Lanezi Lake, l., B.C., Can.	D14	102
Lang, Sask., Can.	I10	104
Langano, Lake, l., Eth.	N10	60
Langara Island, i., B.C., Can.	C1	102
Langarūd, Iran	C11	48
Langbank, Sask., Can.	H12	104
Lang Bay, B.C., Can.	H10	102
Langdale, Al., U.S.	G1	112
Langdon, N.D., U.S.	C9	118
Langeac, Fr.	G10	14
Langeais, Fr.	E7	14
Langenburg, Sask., Can.	H13	104
Langenhagen, Ger.	C9	10
Langenthal, Switz.	D8	13
Langford, S.D., U.S.	F10	118
Langham, Sask., Can.	F7	104
Langholm, Scot., U.K.	F10	8
Langley, B.C., Can.	H12	102
Langley, Ok., U.S.	C11	116
Langley, S.C., U.S.	F5	112
Langlo, stm., Austl.	E6	70
Langlois, Or., U.S.	H1	122
Langnau, Switz.	E8	13
Langogne, Fr.	H10	14
Langon, Fr.	H6	14
Langøya, i., Nor.	G14	6
Langqiao, China	E7	34
Langres, Fr.	E12	14
Langruth, Man., Can.	H16	104
Langsa, Indon.	L4	40
Lang Son, Viet.	D9	40
Langtian, China	J2	34
Langtue, Hond.	D7	92
Languedoc, hist. reg., Fr.	I9	14
Langui Layo, Laguna de, l., Peru	F6	82
L'Anguille, stm., Ar., U.S.	G6	114
Langxi, China	D8	34
Langzhong, China	E8	30
Lanigan, Sask., Can.	G9	104
Lanigan Creek, stm., Sask., Can.	G9	104
Lankou, China	L4	34
Lannemezan, Fr.	I7	14
Lannilis, Fr.	D2	14
Lannion, Fr.	D3	14
L'Annonciation, Que., Can.	A12	108
Lanquín, Guat.	B5	92
L'Anse, Mi., U.S.	D7	110
L'Anse-aux-Meadows National Historic Park, Newf., Can.	A18	106
Lansford, N.D., U.S.	C6	118
Lansing, Ia., U.S.	G4	110
Lansing, Ks., U.S.	L13	118
Lansing, Mi., U.S.	E2	108
Lanslebourg, Fr.	G13	14
Lantana, Fl., U.S.	M6	112
Lantang, China	L3	34
Lantau Island, i., H.K.	M2	34
Lantsch, Switz.	E12	13
Lanusei, Italy	J4	18
Lanxi, China	F8	34
Lanzarote, i., Spain	N27	17b
Lanzhou, China	D7	30
Laoag, Phil.	L19	39b
Lao Cai, Viet.	C7	40
Laochang, China	B8	40
Laoge, China	C8	34
Laoha, stm., China	A7	32
Laois, co., Ire.	I6	8
Laojie, China	B5	40
La Oliva, Spain	O27	17b
Laon, Fr.	C10	14
Laona, Wi., U.S.	E7	110
La Orchila, Isla, i., Ven.	B10	84
La Orchila, Isla, i., Ven.	I11	94
La Orotava, Spain	O24	17b
La Oroya, Peru	D4	82
Laos (Lao), ctry., Asia	B3	38
Laoxinkou, China	E1	34
Laoyingpan, China	I4	34
Laozishan, China	B7	34
Lapa, Braz.	C14	80
Lapalisse, Fr.	F10	14
La Palma, Col.	E5	84
La Palma, El Sal.	C5	92
La Palma, Pan.	D2	84
La Palma, Pan.	C3	84
La Palma, i., Spain	O23	17b
La Palma del Condado, Spain	H5	16
La Paloma, Ur.	H11	80
La Pampa, prov., Arg.	I5	80
La Paragua, Ven.	D11	84
La Pasión, Río de, stm., Guat.	I14	90
La Paz, Arg.	F9	80
La Paz, Arg.	G5	80
La Paz, Bol.	G7	82
La Paz, Col.	B6	84
La Paz, Hond.	C7	92
La Paz, Mex.	E4	90
La Paz, Mex.	F9	90
La Paz, Ur.	H10	80
La Paz, dept., Bol.	F7	82
La Paz, dept., Hond.	C7	92
La Paz, Bahía de, b., Mex.	E4	90
La Paz, Río de, stm., Bol.	G8	82
La Paz Centro, Nic.	E8	92
La Pedrera, Col.	H8	84
Lapeer, Mi., U.S.	G12	110
La Perla, Mex.	C7	90
La Perouse Strait (Sōya-kaikyō), strt., Asia	B17	36a
La Pesca, Mex.	F11	90
La Piedad de Cabadas, Mex.	G8	90
La Pine, Or., U.S.	G4	122
Lapin lääni, prov., Fin.	H20	6
Lapinlahti, Fin.	J20	6
La Pintada, Pan.	I14	92
Lapland, hist. reg., Eur.	H18	6
La Plata, Arg.	H10	80
La Plata, Col.	F5	84
La Plata, Md., U.S.	I10	108
La Plata, Mo., U.S.	B4	114
La Plata, stm., U.S.	H8	120
La Plata Peak, mtn., Co., U.S.	E10	120
La Plonge Indian Reserve, Sask., Can.	C7	104
La Pobla de Segur, Spain	C12	16
La Pocatière, Que., Can.	E3	106
La Poile, Newf., Can.	E15	106
La Poile Bay, b., Newf., Can.	E15	106
Laporte, Co., U.S.	D11	120
La Porte, In., U.S.	A10	114
Laporte, Pa., U.S.	F10	108
La Porte City, Ia., U.S.	H3	110
La Potherie, Lac, l., Que., Can.	E18	96
La Poza Grande, Mex.	E3	90
Lappeenranta, Fin.	K21	6
Lappfjärd (Lapväärtti), Fin.	J17	6
La Presa, stm., Mex.	E4	90
Laprida, Arg.	E6	80
Laprida, Arg.	I8	80
La Pryor, Tx., U.S.	K7	116
Lâpseki, Tur.	I10	20
Laptev Sea see Laptevych, more, Russia	B17	28
Laptevych, more (Laptev Sea), Russia	B17	28
La Puebla de Cazalla, Spain	H6	16
La Puebla de Montalbán, Spain	F7	16
La Puerta, Arg.	E6	80
La Purísima, Mex.	D3	90
Lăpuş, Rom.	B8	20
Lapwai, Id., U.S.	D9	122
La Quiaca, Arg.	B6	80
La Quiaca, Arg.	J9	82
L'Aquila, Italy	G8	18
Lār, Iran	H13	48
Lara, state, Ven.	B8	84
Larache, Mor.	J5	16
Laragne-Montéglin, Fr.	H12	14
Laramate, Peru	F4	82
Laramie, Wy., U.S.	C11	120
Laramie, stm., U.S.	B12	120
Laramie Mountains, mts., Wy., U.S.	B11	120
Laranjaí, stm., Braz.	G1	79
Laranjal, Braz.	F7	79
Laranjeiras do Sul, Braz.	C12	80
Laraos, Peru	E4	82
Larap, Phil.	N20	39b
La Raya, Abra, Peru	F6	82
L'Arbresle, Fr.	G11	14
Larche, Col de, Eur.	H13	14
Larchwood, Ia., U.S.	H11	118
Lardeau, B.C., Can.	G18	102
L'Ardoise, N.S., Can.	G13	106
Laredo, Spain	B8	16
Laredo, Tx., U.S.	L7	116
Laredo Sound, strt., B.C., Can.	E6	102
La Reforma, Mex.	E5	90
La Réole, Fr.	H6	14
Lares, Peru	E5	82
La Restinga, Spain	P23	17b
Largo, Fl., U.S.	L4	112
Largo, Cañon, val., N.M., U.S.	H9	120
Largo, Cayo, i., Cuba	D4	94
Largs, Scot., U.K.	F9	8
Lari, Peru	F6	82
Larimore, N.D., U.S.	D10	118
Larino, Italy	H9	18
La Rioja, Arg.	E5	80
La Rioja, prov., Arg.	E5	80
La Rioja, prov., Spain	C9	16
Lárisa, Grc.	J6	20
Lārkāna, Pak.	G3	44
Lark Harbour, Newf., Can.	C15	106
Lárnax (Larnaca), Cyp.	D2	48
Larned, Ks., U.S.	M8	118
La Rochefoucauld, Fr.	G7	14
La Rochelle, Fr.	F5	14
La Roche-sur-Yon, Fr.	F5	14
La Roda, Spain	F9	16
La Romaine, Que., Can.	B13	106
La Romana, Dom. Rep.	E10	94
La Ronge, Sask., Can.	C9	104
Larose, La., U.S.	M6	114
La Rosita, Nic.	D10	92
Larreynaga, Nic.	E8	92
Larroque, Arg.	G9	80
Larrys River, N.S., Can.	G12	106
Larsen Bay, Ak., U.S.	H17	100
Larsen Ice Shelf, Ant.	B12	73
Larteh Aheneasi, Ghana	I10	64
La Rubia, Arg.	F8	80
La Rue, Oh., U.S.	G3	108
Laruns, Fr.	J6	14
Larus Lake, l., Ont., Can.	G20	104
Larvik, Nor.	L12	6
La Sabana, Arg.	D9	80
La Sal, Ut., U.S.	F7	120
La Salle, Co., U.S.	D12	120
La Salle, Il., U.S.	I6	110
La Salle, stm., Man., Can.	I17	104
Las Almejas, Bahía, b., Mex.	E4	90
Las Animas, Co., U.S.	M4	118
La Sarraz, Switz.	E6	13
Las Arrias, Arg.	F7	80
Las Aves, Islas, is., Ven.	A9	84
Las Ballenas, Canal de, strt., Mex.	C3	90
Las Bonitas, Ven.	D10	84
Las Breñas, Arg.	D8	80
Las Cabezas de San Juan, Spain	I6	16
Las Cabras, Chile	H3	80
Lascano, Ur.	G11	80
Lascar, Volcán, vol., Chile	B5	80
Las Catitas, Arg.	G4	80
Lascaux, Grotte de, Fr.	G8	14
Las Cejas, Arg.	D6	80
Las Choapas, Mex.	I12	90
La Scie, Newf., Can.	C18	106
Las Cruces, N.M., U.S.	L10	120
Las Cuevas, Mex.	C9	90
Las Delicias, Mex.	J14	90
La Selle, Morne, mtn., Haiti	E9	94
La Serena, Chile	E3	80
La Seyne, Fr.	I12	14
Las Flores, Arg.	I9	80
Las Flores, Arg.	F4	80
Las Flores, Arroyo, stm., Arg.	H9	80
Las Flores, Cerro, mtn., Mex.	I12	90
Las Garcitas, Arg.	D9	80
Las Guayabas, Mex.	E11	90
Lashburn, Sask., Can.	E5	104
Lāsh-e Joveyn, Afg.	F16	48
Las Heras, Arg.	G4	80
Lashio, Burma	C4	40
Las Hormigas, Mex.	E10	90
La Sierra, Montaña, mts., Hond.	C7	92
Las Iglesias, Cerro, mtn., Mex.	D6	90
Łasin, Pol.	B19	10
Łask, Pol.	D19	10
L'askel'a, Russia	K22	6
Las Lajas, Arg.	J3	80
Las Lajas, Pan.	C2	84
Las Lajitas, Arg.	C6	80
Las Lomas, Peru	J2	84
Las Lomitas, Arg.	C8	80
Lašma, Russia	G24	22
Las Malvinas, Arg.	H4	80
Las Margaritas, Mex.	I14	90
Las Marianas, Arg.	H9	80
Las Mercedes, Ven.	C9	84
Las Minas, Cerro, mtn., Hond.	C6	92
Las Nieves, Mex.	D7	90
Las Nopaleras, Cerro, mtn., Mex.	E8	90
La Solana, Spain	G8	16
La Soledad, Cerro, mtn., Mex.	D6	90
Las Ovejas, Arg.	I3	80
Las Palmas, Arg.	D9	80
Las Palmas, Pan.	C2	84
Las Palmas, prov., Spain	O26	17b
Las Palmas de Gran Canaria, Spain	O25	17b
La Spezia, Italy	E4	18
Las Piedras, Ur.	H10	80
Las Piedras, Río de, stm., Peru	E7	82
Las Plumas, Arg.	E3	78
Lasqueti Island, i., B.C., Can.	H10	102
Las Rosas, Arg.	G8	80
Las Rosas, Mex.	I13	90
Lassance, Braz.	D6	79
Lassay, Fr.	D6	14
Lassen Peak, vol., Ca., U.S.	D4	124
Lassen Volcanic National Park, Ca., U.S.	D4	124
Las Tablas, Pan.	D2	84
Las Tinajas, Arg.	D7	80
Last Mountain, mtn., Sask., Can.	G10	104
Last Mountain Lake, l., Sask., Can.	G9	104
Las Toscas, Arg.	E9	80
Lastoursville, Gabon	B2	58
Las Tunas, Cuba	D6	94
Las Tunas Grandes, Laguna, l., Arg.	I7	80
La Suze, Fr.	E7	14
Las Varas, Mex.	C5	90
Las Varas, Mex.	G7	90
Las Varillas, Arg.	F7	80
Las Vegas, Nv., U.S.	H10	124
Las Vegas, N.M., U.S.	I11	120
Las Vegas, Ven.	C8	84
La Tabatière, Que., Can.	B15	106
Latacunga, Ec.	H3	84
Latady Island, i., Ant.	C12	73
La Tagua, Col.	H5	84
Latakia see Al-Lādhiqīyah, Syria	D3	48
Laterrière, Que., Can.	D2	106
La Teste-de-Buch, Fr.	H5	14
La Tetilla, Cerro, mtn., Mex.	G7	90
Lathrop, Mo., U.S.	C2	114
Latimer, Ia., U.S.	H2	110
Latina, Italy	H7	18
Latisana, Italy	D8	18
La Toma, Arg.	G6	80
Latorica, stm., Eur.	G22	10
Latornell, stm., Alta., Can.	C16	102
La Tortuga, Isla, i., Ven.	B10	84
Latouche Treville, Cape, c., Austl.	C4	68
La Tour-du-Pin, Fr.	G12	14
Latowicz, Pol.	C21	10
La Tremblade, Fr.	G5	14
La Trimouille, Fr.	F8	14
La Trinidad, Arg.	D6	80
La Trinidad, Nic.	E8	92
La Trinidad de Orichuna, Ven.	D8	84
La Trinitaria, Mex.	I13	90
La Trinité, Mart.	G14	94
Latrobe, Austl.	M7	70
Latrobe, Pa., U.S.	G7	108
Latta, S.C., U.S.	E7	112
La Tuque, Que., Can.	G18	96
Lātūr, India	C4	46
Latvia (Latvija), ctry., Eur.	E8	22
Lauca, stm., Bol.	H7	82
Lauchhammer, Ger.	D13	10
Lauder, Scot., U.K.	F11	8
Lauderdale, Ms., U.S.	J8	114

Name	Map Ref.	Page
Lucas, Ia., U.S.	I2	110
Lucas, Ks., U.S.	L9	118
Lucas González, Arg.	G9	80
Lucasville, Oh., U.S.	I4	108
Lucca, Italy	F5	18
Lucedale, Ms., U.S.	L8	114
Lucena, Phil.	O19	39b
Lucena, Spain	H7	16
Lučenec, Czech.	G19	10
Lucera, Italy	H10	18
Lucerne, Ca., U.S.	E3	124
Lucerne, Lake see Vierwaldstätter See, l., Switz.	D9	13
Lucerne see Luzern, Switz.	D9	13
Luch, stm., Russia	E25	22
Lucheng, China	B9	40
Luchovicy, Russia	G22	22
Lüchow, Ger.	C11	10
Luchow see Luzhou, China	F8	30
Luchuan, China	C11	40
Luci, China	F8	34
Lucie, stm., Sur.	F14	84
Lucindale, Austl.	K4	70
Lucira, Ang.	D2	58
Luck, Ukr.	G3	26
Luck, Wi., U.S.	E3	110
Luckau, Ger.	D13	10
Luckenwalde, Ger.	C13	10
Luckhoff, S. Afr.	G7	66
Luckiamute, stm., Or., U.S.	F2	122
Luck Lake, l., Sask., Can.	G7	104
Lucknow, Ont., Can.	G14	110
Lucknow, India	G9	44
Lucky Lake, Sask., Can.	G7	104
Luçon, Fr.	F5	14
Lucun, China	G6	32
Lüda see Dalian, China	E9	32
Lüdenscheid, Ger.	D7	10
Lüderitz, Nmb.	F2	66
Ludhiāna, India	E6	44
Lüdinghausen, Ger.	D7	10
Ludington, Mi., U.S.	G9	110
L'udinovo, Russia	H17	22
L'udkovo, Russia	G17	22
Ludlow, Ma., U.S.	E14	108
Ludlow, Vt., U.S.	D14	108
Ludowici, Ga., U.S.	H5	112
Ludvika, Swe.	K14	6
Ludwigsburg, Ger.	G9	10
Ludwigsfelde, Ger.	C13	10
Ludwigshafen, Ger.	F8	10
Ludwigslust, Ger.	B11	10
Ludza, Lat.	E10	22
Luebo, Zaire	C4	58
Lueders, Tx., U.S.	G7	116
Luena, Ang.	D3	58
Luena, Zaire	C5	58
Luena, stm., Ang.	D4	58
Luepa, Ven.	E12	84
Lufeng, China	M4	34
Lufeng, China	B7	40
Lufkin, Tx., U.S.	K2	114
Luga, Russia	C12	22
Lugano, Switz.	F10	13
Lugano, Lago di, l., Eur.	C4	18
Lugansk (Vorošilovgrad), Ukr.	H5	26
Lugenda, stm., Moz.	D7	58
Lugnaquillia Mountain, mtn., Ire.	I7	8
Lugo, Italy	E6	18
Lugo, Spain	B4	16
Lugoj, Rom.	D5	20
Lühedian, China	C3	34
Luik (Liège), Bel.	G8	12
Luino, Italy	C3	18
Luishia, Zaire	D5	58
Luiza, Zaire	C4	58
Luiziânia, Braz.	F3	79
Luján, Arg.	G4	80
Luján, Arg.	G6	80
Lujiao, China	F1	34
Lukang, Tai.	K9	34
Lukanga Swamp, sw., Zam.	D5	58
Lukeville, Az., U.S.	M4	120
Luknovo, Russia	E25	22
Lukolela, Zaire	B3	58
Lukou, China	H3	34
Lukoupu, China	F2	34
Łuków, Pol.	D22	10
Lukulu, Zam.	D4	58
Lula, Ms., U.S.	H6	114
Luleå, Swe.	I18	6
Lüleburgaz, Tur.	H11	20
Lules, Arg.	D6	80
Luliang, China	B7	40
Lüliang Shan, mts., China	D9	30
Luling, Tx., U.S.	J9	116
Lumaling, China	F15	44
Lumbala N'guimbo, Ang.	D4	58
Lumber, stm., U.S.	E7	112
Lumber City, Ga., U.S.	H4	112
Lumberport, W.V., U.S.	H6	108
Lumberton, Ms., U.S.	K7	114
Lumberton, N.C., U.S.	E7	112
Lumberton, Tx., U.S.	L2	114
Lumbres, Fr.	B9	14
Lumby, B.C., Can.	G16	102
Lumding, India	H15	44
Lumpkin, Ga., U.S.	G2	112
Lumsden, Newf., Can.	C20	106
Lumsden, Sask., Can.	H10	104
Lumut, Malay.	L6	40
Luna, stm., Braz.	J12	84
Luna Pier, Mi., U.S.	I12	110
Lūnāvāda, India	I5	44
Lund, B.C., Can.	H10	102
Lund, Swe.	N13	6
Lund, Nv., U.S.	F10	124
Lundale, W.V., U.S.	J5	108
Lundar, Man., Can.	H16	104
Lundazi, Zam.	D6	58
Lundi, stm., Zimb.	C10	66
Lüneburg, Ger.	B10	10
Lüneburger Heide, reg., Ger.	B10	10
Lunel, Fr.	I11	14
Lünen, Ger.	D7	10
Lunenburg, N.S., Can.	H9	106
Lunenburg, Va., U.S.	C8	112
Lunéville, Fr.	D13	14
Lunga, stm., Zam.	D5	58
Lunge'nake, China	E11	44
Lungi, S.L.	G3	64
Lungué-Bungo, stm., Afr.	D4	58
Lunin, Bela.	I9	22
Luninec, Bela.	I9	22
Lunjiao, China	M2	34
Lunno, Bela.	H7	22
Luo, stm., China	E9	30
Luochanghe, China	D6	34
Luoci, China	B7	40
Luofang, China	H4	34
Luogang, China	K4	34
Luohe, China	B3	34
Luoheya, China	H6	32
Luoji, China	C6	34
Luokeng, China	K2	34
Luoqiao, China	I8	34
Luoshuihe, China	D2	32
Luotuodian, China	C2	34
Luoyang, China	E9	30
Lupala, Nmb.	A4	66
Lupani, Zimb.	B8	66
Lupeni, Rom.	D7	20
Luqu, China	E7	30
Luray, Va., U.S.	I8	108
Lure, Fr.	E13	14
Luremo, Ang.	C3	58
Luribay, Bol.	G8	82
Lurín, Peru	E3	82
Lúrio, Moz.	D8	58
Lúrio, stm., Moz.	D7	58
Lusaka, Zam.	E5	58
Lusambo, Zaire	B4	58
Lusanga, Zaire	B3	58
Luscar, Alta., Can.	D17	102
Luseland, Sask., Can.	F5	104
Lushan, China	E7	30
Lu Shan, mtn., China	F10	30
Lushanguanliju, China	F4	34
Lushnje, Alb.	I3	20
Lushoto, Tan.	B7	58
Lushui, China	A5	40
Lüshun (Port Arthur), China	E9	32
Lüsi, China	C10	34
Lusignan, Fr.	F7	14
L'usino, Bela.	I9	22
Lusk, Wy., U.S.	B12	120
Lustenau, Aus.	H9	10
Lūt, Dasht-e, des., Iran	E15	48
Lutai, China	B4	34
Lutang, China	J1	34
Lutcher, La., U.S.	L6	114
Lutesville, Mo., U.S.	E7	114
Luther, Mi., U.S.	F10	110
Luther, Ok., U.S.	D9	116
Lutian, China	I3	34
Luton, Eng., U.K.	J13	8
Lutong, Malay.	E5	38
Lutou, China	C1	34
Luttrell, Tn., U.S.	C3	112
Lutz, Fl., U.S.	K4	112
Lützow-Holm Bay, b., Ant.	B4	73
Lutzputs, S. Afr.	G5	66
Lutzville, S. Afr.	H4	66
Luuq, Som.	H9	56
Luverne, Al., U.S.	K10	114
Lu Verne, Ia., U.S.	H1	110
Luverne, Mn., U.S.	H11	118
Luvuvhu, stm., Afr.	D10	66
Luxana Bay, b., B.C., Can.	E3	102
Luxembourg (Luxemburg), Lux.	I9	12
Luxembourg, prov., Bel.	I7	12
Luxembourg, ctry., Eur.	F9	4
Luxemburg, Wi., U.S.	F8	110
Luxeuil-les-Bains, Fr.	E13	14
Luxi (Mangshi), China	B5	40
Lüxia, China	I9	34
Luxora, Ar., U.S.	G7	114
Luxor see Al-Uqṣur, Egypt	E7	60
Lüyang, China	B9	32
Luz, Braz.	E6	79
Luza, Russia	E7	26
Luzarches, Fr.	C9	14
Luzern, Switz.	D9	13
Luzern, state, Switz.	D9	13
Luzhou, China	F8	30
Luziânia, Braz.	D5	79
Lužnice, stm., Eur.	G14	10
Luzon, i., Phil.	N19	39b
Luzon Strait, strt., Asia	N9	34
Luzy, Fr.	F10	14
L'vov, Ukr.	H2	26
L'vovskij, Russia	F20	22
Lwówek, Pol.	C16	10
Lybster, Scot., U.K.	C10	8
Lyčkovo, Russia	D15	22
Lycksele, Swe.	I16	6
Lycoming Creek, stm., Pa., U.S.	F9	108
Lydenburg, S. Afr.	E10	66
Lydia Mills, S.C., U.S.	E5	112
Lyell, Mount, mtn., Can.	F17	102
Lyell Island, i., B.C., Can.	E3	102
Lyerly, Ga., U.S.	E1	112
Lyford, Tx., U.S.	M9	116
Lykens, Pa., U.S.	G10	108
Lykošino, Russia	C16	22
Lyle, Mn., U.S.	G3	110
Lyles, Tn., U.S.	G9	114
Lyman, Ne., U.S.	J3	118
Lyman, S.C., U.S.	E4	112
Lyman, Wy., U.S.	C6	120
Lyme Regis, Eng., U.K.	K11	8
Łyna (Lava), stm., Eur.	G3	22
Lynch, Ky., U.S.	C4	112
Lynch, Ne., U.S.	I9	118
Lynchburg, Oh., U.S.	H3	108
Lynchburg, S.C., U.S.	E6	112
Lynchburg, Tn., U.S.	G10	114
Lynchburg, Va., U.S.	B7	112
Lynches, stm., U.S.	F7	112
Lynden, Wa., U.S.	B3	122
Lyndhurst, Austl.	H3	70
Lyndon, Ks., U.S.	M12	118
Lyndon, Ky., U.S.	D11	114
Lyndonville, Vt., U.S.	C14	108
Lyndora, Pa., U.S.	G7	108
Lyngdal, Nor.	L10	6
Lyngen, Nor.	G17	6
Lyngør, Nor.	L11	6
Lynn, Al., U.S.	H9	114
Lynn, In., U.S.	B12	114
Lynn, Ma., U.S.	E16	108
Lynn Canal, b., Ak., U.S.	G27	100
Lynndyl, Ut., U.S.	E4	120
Lynn Garden, Tn., U.S.	C4	112
Lynn Haven, Fl., U.S.	L11	114
Lynn Lake, Man., Can.	B13	104
Lynnville, Ia., U.S.	I3	110
Lyntupy, Bela.	F9	22
Lynx Lake, l., N.W. Ter., Can.	D11	96
Lyon, Fr.	G11	14
Lyon Inlet, b., N.W. Ter., Can.	C16	96
Lyon Mountain, N.Y., U.S.	C13	108
Lyonnais, Monts du, mts., Fr.	G11	14
Lyons, Co., U.S.	D11	120
Lyons, Ga., U.S.	G4	112
Lyons, In., U.S.	D9	114
Lyons, Ks., U.S.	M9	118
Lyons, Mi., U.S.	H11	110
Lyons, Ne., U.S.	J11	118
Lyons, N.Y., U.S.	D10	108
Lyons, stm., Austl.	D3	68
Lys (Leie), stm., Eur.	B9	14
Lys'va, Russia	F9	26
Lytle, Tx., U.S.	J8	116
Lytton, B.C., Can.	G13	102

M

Name	Map Ref.	Page
Ma, stm., Asia	D8	40
Maalaea Bay, b., Hi., U.S.	q17	125a
Ma'alot-Tarshiḥa, Isr.	B4	50
Ma'ān, Jord.	H5	50
Ma'anshan, China	D7	34
Maardu, Est.	B8	22
Ma'arrat an-Nu'mān, Syria	D4	48
Maas (Meuse), stm., Eur.	D5	10
Maaseik, Bel.	F8	12
Maasmechelen, Bel.	G8	12
Maastricht, Neth.	G8	12
Maave, Moz.	C12	66
Maba, China	C7	34
Mababe Depression, depr., Bots.	B7	66
Mabank, Tx., U.S.	G10	116
Mabaruma, Guy.	C13	84
Mabeleapodi, Bots.	C6	66
Mabel Lake, l., B.C., Can.	G16	102
Maben, Ms., U.S.	I7	114
Mabeul, Tun.	M5	18
Mableton, Ga., U.S.	F2	112
Mabou, N.S., Can.	F12	106
Mabrūk, Sud.	M5	60
Mabton, Wa., U.S.	D6	122
Mabuasehube Game Reserve, Bots.	E6	66
Mabuguai, China	F1	34
Macachín, Arg.	I7	80
Macaé, Braz.	G8	79
Macajuba, Braz.	B8	79
Macalister, B.C., Can.	E12	102
Macalister, stm., Austl.	K6	70
Macalister, Mount, mtn., Austl.	J8	70
Macallum Lake, l., Sask., Can.	C6	104
MacAlpine Lake, l., N.W. Ter., Can.	C12	96
Macão, Port.	F3	16
Macapá, Braz.	C8	76
Macará, Ec.	J3	84
Macarani, Braz.	C8	79
Macareo, Caño, mth., Ven.	C12	84
Macas, Ec.	I3	84
Macau, Braz.	E11	76
Macau (Aomen), Macao	M2	34
Macau, dep., Asia	G9	30
Macauã, stm., Braz.	C7	82
Macaúbas, Braz.	B7	79
Macaya, Pic, mtn., Haiti	E7	94
MacClenny, Fl., U.S.	I4	112
Macclesfield, Eng., U.K.	H11	8
Macdhui, Ben, mtn., Afr.	H8	66
Macdonald Range, mts., B.C., Can.	H20	102
MacDonnell Ranges, mts., Austl.	D6	68
MacDowell Lake, l., Ont., Can.	F22	104
Macduff, Scot., U.K.	D11	8
Macdui, Ben, mtn., Scot., U.K.	D10	8
Macedonia, hist. reg., Eur.	H6	20
Macedonia (Makedonija), ctry., Eur.	H5	20
Maceió, Braz.	E11	76
Macenta, Gui.	G5	64
Maceo, Col.	D5	84
Macerata, Italy	F8	18
MacFarlane, stm., Sask., Can.	E11	96
Macfarlane, Lake, l., Austl.	H2	70
MacGregor, Man., Can.	I16	104
Machacamarca, Bol.	H8	82
Machachi, Ec.	H3	84
Machačkala, Russia	I7	26
Machadinho, stm., Braz.	C10	82
Machado, Braz.	F6	79
Machado, stm., Braz.	C10	82
Machagai, Arg.	D8	80
Machakos, Kenya	B7	58
Machala, Ec.	I3	84
Machalí, Chile	H3	80
Machaneng, Bots.	D8	66
Machang, China	A7	32
Machangfu, China	B7	40
Machaquilá, stm., Guat.	A5	92
Machattie, Lake, l., Austl.	E3	70
Machecoul, Fr.	E5	14
Machias, Me., U.S.	C19	108
Machias, stm., Me., U.S.	C19	108
Machichi, stm., Man., Can.	B23	104
Machico, Port.	M21	17a
Machilīpatnam (Bandar), India	D6	46
Machiques, Ven.	B6	84
Machupicchu, Peru	E5	82
Machupicchu, hist., Peru	E5	82
Machupo, stm., Bol.	E9	82
Machynlleth, Wales, U.K.	I10	8
Maciá, Arg.	G9	80
Macintyre, stm., Austl.	G8	70
Macintyre, stm., Austl.	G9	70
Mackay, Austl.	C8	70
Mackay, Id., U.S.	G12	122
MacKay, stm., Alta., Can.	B2	104
Mackay, Lake, l., Austl.	D5	68
MacKay Lake, l., N.W. Ter., Can.	D10	96
Mackenzie, Guy.	D13	84
Mackenzie, stm., N.W. Ter., Can.	C6	96
Mackenzie Bay, b., Can.	B26	100
Mackenzie Delta, N.W. Ter., Can.	B27	100
Mackenzie Mountains, mts., Can.	D29	100
Mackinac, Straits of, strt., Mi., U.S.	E11	110
Mackinac Island, Mi., U.S.	E11	110
Mackinac Island, i., Mi., U.S.	E11	110
Mackinaw, Il., U.S.	J6	110
Mackinaw, stm., Il., U.S.	J6	110
Mackinaw City, Mi., U.S.	E11	110
Mackinnon Road, Kenya	B7	58
Macklin, Sask., Can.	F5	104
Macksville, Austl.	H10	70
Macksville, Ks., U.S.	M9	118
Maclean, Austl.	G10	70
Macleod, Lake, l., Austl.	D2	68
Maclovia Herrera, Mex.	C7	90
Macmillan, stm., Yukon, Can.	E27	100
Macomb, Il., U.S.	J5	110
Macomer, Italy	I3	18
Mâcon, Fr.	F11	14
Macon, Ga., U.S.	G3	112
Macon, Il., U.S.	C8	114
Macon, Ms., U.S.	I8	114
Macon, Mo., U.S.	C4	114
Macon, Bayou, stm., U.S.	J5	114
Macorís, Cabo, c., Dom. Rep.	E9	94
Macoun Lake, l., Sask., Can.	B11	104
Macquarie, stm., Austl.	M7	70
Macquarie, stm., Austl.	H7	70
Macquarie Harbour, b., Austl.	N6	70
Macquarie Island, i., Austl.	A8	73
Mac. Robertson Land, reg., Ant.	B5	73
Macroom, Ire.	J5	8
MacTier, Ont., Can.	E16	110
Macucuau, stm., Braz.	H12	84
Macuelizo, Hond.	B6	92
Macujer, Col.	G6	84
Macunqiao, China	B5	34
Macuro, Ven.	B12	84
Macusani, Peru	F6	82
Macuspana, Mex.	I13	90
Macusse, Ang.	A5	66
Mad, stm., Ca., U.S.	D2	124
Mad, stm., Oh., U.S.	H2	108
Mad, stm., Vt., U.S.	C14	108
Ma'dabā, Jord.	E5	50
Madagascar (Madagasikara), ctry., Afr.	E9	58
Madā'in Ṣāliḥ, Sau. Ar.	H4	48
Madame, Isle, i., N.S., Can.	G12	106
Madanapalle, India	F5	46
Madang, Pap. N. Gui.	m16	68a
Mādārīpur, Bngl.	I14	44
Madawaska, stm., Ont., Can.	E18	110
Maddaloni, Italy	H9	18
Maddock, N.D., U.S.	D8	118
Madeira, i., Port.	M21	17a
Madeira, stm., S.A.	E6	76
Madeira, Arquipélago da, is., Port.	M21	17a
Madeirinha, stm., Braz.	C11	82
Madeirinha, Paraná, mth., Braz.	I13	84
M'adel', Bela.	G9	22
Mädelegabel, mtn., Eur.	E17	14
Madeleine, Îles de la, is., Que., Can.	E12	106
Madeleine-Centre, Que., Can.	C8	106
Madelia, Mn., U.S.	F1	110
Madeline Island, i., Wi., U.S.	D5	110
Maden, Tur.	B5	48
Madera, Mex.	C5	90
Madera, Ca., U.S.	H5	124
Maderas, Volcán, vol., Nic.	F9	92
Madhubani, India	G12	44
Madhya Pradesh, state, India	I8	44
Madibogo, S. Afr.	F7	66
Madidi, stm., Bol.	E8	82
Madill, Ok., U.S.	E10	116
Madimba, Zaire	B3	58
Madina do Boé, Gui.-B.	F2	64
Madinani, I.C.	G6	64
Madīnat ash-Sha'b (Al-Ittihad), Yemen	H4	47
Madingou, Congo	B2	58
Madirobe, Madag.	P22	67b
Madison, Al., U.S.	H10	114
Madison, Fl., U.S.	I3	112
Madison, Ga., U.S.	F3	112
Madison, In., U.S.	D11	114
Madison, Ks., U.S.	M11	118
Madison, Me., U.S.	C17	108
Madison, Mn., U.S.	F11	118
Madison, Mo., U.S.	C4	114
Madison, Ne., U.S.	J10	118
Madison, N.C., U.S.	C7	112
Madison, Oh., U.S.	F5	108
Madison, S.D., U.S.	G10	118
Madison, Va., U.S.	I8	108
Madison, W.V., U.S.	I5	108
Madison, Wi., U.S.	G6	110
Madison, stm., U.S.	E14	122
Madison Heights, Va., U.S.	B7	112
Madison Range, mts., Mt., U.S.	E14	122
Madisonville, Ky., U.S.	E9	114
Madisonville, La., U.S.	L6	114
Madisonville, Tn., U.S.	D2	112
Madisonville, Tx., U.S.	I11	116
Madiun, Indon.	J15	39a
Madoc, Ont., Can.	F18	110
Madoi, China	E6	30
Madol, Sud.	M4	60
Madona, Lat.	E9	22
Madougou, Mali	D8	64
Madrakah, Sau. Ar.	D1	47
Madrakah, Ra's al-, c., Oman	E10	47
Madras, India	G11	42
Madras, Or., U.S.	F4	122
Madras see Tamil Nādu, state, India	G5	46
Madre, Laguna, b., Mex.	E11	90
Madre, Laguna, b., Tx., U.S.	M9	116
Madre, Sierra, mts., Phil.	M20	39b
Madre de Chiapas, Sierra, mts., N.A.	B2	92
Madre de Dios, dept., Peru	D6	82
Madre de Dios, stm., S.A.	D8	82
Madre de Dios, Isla, i., Chile	A12	73
Madre de Dios, Isla, i., Chile	J7	74
Madre del Sur, Sierra, mts., Mex.	I10	90
Madre Occidental, Sierra, mts., Mex.	E6	90
Madre Oriental, Sierra, mts., Mex.	F9	90
Madre Vieja, stm., Guat.	C3	92
Madrid, Col.	E5	84
Madrid, Spain	E8	16
Madrid, Al., U.S.	K11	114
Madrid, Ia., U.S.	I2	110
Madrid, Ne., U.S.	K6	118
Madrid, prov., Spain	E8	16
Madridejos, Spain	F8	16
Madriz, dept., Nic.	D8	92
Madsen, Ont., Can.	H21	104
Madura, i., Indon.	J16	39a
Madurai, India	H5	46
Maebashi, Japan	K14	36
Mae Hong Son, Thai.	E4	40
Mae Klong, stm., Thai.	G5	40
Maengsan, N. Kor.	D14	32
Mae Sariang, Thai.	E4	40
Maeser, Ut., U.S.	D7	120
Mae Sot, Thai.	F5	40
Maesteg, Wales, U.K.	J10	8
Maestra, Sierra, mts., Cuba	D6	94
Maevatanana, Madag.	P22	67b
Mafeking, Man., Can.	F13	104
Mafeteng, Leso.	G8	66
Maffra, Austl.	K7	70
Mafia Island, i., Tan.	C7	58
Mafikeng, Boph.	G5	58
Mafikeng, S. Afr.	E7	66
Mafra, Braz.	D14	80
Magadan, Russia	F22	28
Magadi, Kenya	B7	58
Magaguadavic Lake, l., N.B., Can.	G6	106
Magallanes, Phil.	O20	39b
Magallanes, Estrecho de (Strait of Magellan), strt., S.A.	G3	78
Magangué, Col.	C5	84
Magazine Mountain, mtn., Ar., U.S.	G3	114
Magburaka, S.L.	G4	64
Magdagači, Russia	G17	28
Magdalena, Arg.	H10	80
Magdalena, Bol.	E9	82
Magdalena, Mex.	G8	90
Magdalena, Peru	B3	82
Magdalena, N.M., U.S.	J9	120
Magdalena, dept., Col.	B5	84
Magdalena, stm., Col.	C5	84
Magdalena, stm., Mex.	B4	90
Magdalena, Bahía, b., Mex.	E3	90
Magdalena, Isla, i., Chile	E2	78
Magdalena, Isla, i., Mex.	E3	90
Magdalena, Punta, c., Col.	F4	84
Magdalena de Kino, Mex.	B4	90
Magdeburg, Ger.	C11	10
Magee, Ms., U.S.	K7	114
Magelang, Indon.	J15	39a
Magellan, Strait of see Magallanes, Estrecho de, strt., S.A.	G3	78
Magenta, Italy	D3	18
Maggia, Switz.	F10	13
Maggiore, Lago, l., Eur.	C3	18
Maghāghah, Egypt	C6	60
Maghama, Maur.	D3	64
Maghniyya, Alg.	C10	62
Magill Lake, l., Man., Can.	D20	104
Magione, Italy	F7	18
Magiss Lake, l., Ont., Can.	F23	104
Maglaj, Bos.	E2	20
Magnet, Man., Can.	G15	104
Magnitogorsk, Russia	G9	26
Magnolia, Ar., U.S.	I3	114
Magnolia, Mn., U.S.	H11	118
Magnolia, Ms., U.S.	K6	114
Magog, Que., Can.	B14	108
Magozal, Mex.	G11	90
Magpie, Que., Can.	B9	106
Magpie, stm., Que., Can.	B9	106
Magpie, Lac, l., Que., Can.	A9	106
Magpie Ouest, stm., Que., Can.	A8	106
Magrath, Alta., Can.	H22	102
Maguari, Cabo, c., Braz.	D9	76
Maguse Lake, l., N.W. Ter., Can.	D13	96
Maguzhan, China	E13	44
Magway, Burma	D3	40
Mahābād, Iran	C8	48
Mahābaleshwar, India	F9	42
Mahabe, Madag.	P21	67b
Mahābhārat Lek, mts., Nepal	F10	44
Mahabo, Madag.	S22	67b
Mahabo, Madag.	R21	67b
Mahaicony Village, Guy.	D14	84
Mahajamba, Helodranon' i, b., Madag.	O22	67b
Mahajanga, Madag.	O22	67b
Mahākālī (Sārda), stm., Asia	F9	44
Mahakam, stm., Indon.	E6	38
Mahalatswe, Bots.	D8	66
Maḥallāt, Iran	E11	48
Mahanoro, Madag.	Q23	67b
Mahanoy City, Pa., U.S.	G10	108
Mahārāshtra, state, India	C3	46
Maha Sarakham, Thai.	F7	40
Mahasoa, Madag.	S22	67b
Mahasolo, Madag.	Q22	67b
Mahates, Col.	B5	84
Mahatsinjo, Madag.	R21	67b
Maḥaṭṭat al-Ḥafīf, Jord.	D8	50
Mahbūbnagar, India	D4	46
Mahd adh-Dhahab, Sau. Ar.	C2	47
Mahdia, Tun.	N6	18
Mahe, India	G3	46
Mahébourg, Mrts.	V18	67c
Mahé Island, i., Sey.	B11	58
Mahendra Giri, mtn., India	C8	46
Mahesāna, India	I5	44
Mahia Peninsula, pen., N.Z.	C7	72
Mahnomen, Mn., U.S.	D12	118
Mahoba, India	H8	44
Mahomet, Il., U.S.	B8	114
Mahone Bay, N.S., Can.	H9	106
Mahone Bay, b., N.S., Can.	H9	106
Mahony Lake, l., N.W. Ter., Can.	D32	100
Mahood Falls, B.C., Can.	F14	102
Mahood Lake, l., B.C., Can.	F14	102
Mahres, Tun.	C16	62
Mahuva, India	B1	46
Mai Aini, Eth.	J10	60
Maicao, Col.	B6	84
Maîche, Fr.	E13	14
Maici, stm., Braz.	B11	82
Maicuru, stm., Braz.	D8	76
Maiden, N.C., U.S.	D5	112
Maidenhead, Eng., U.K.	J13	8
Maidstone, Sask., Can.	E5	104
Maidstone, Eng., U.K.	J14	8
Maiduguri, Nig.	F9	54
Maienfeld, Switz.	D12	13
Maigatari, Nig.	E14	64
Maignelay, Fr.	C9	14
Maillezais, Fr.	F6	14
Mai Mefales, Eth.	J10	60
Main, stm., Ger.	F9	10
Main Channel, strt., Ont., Can.	E14	110
Mai-Ndombe, Lac, l., Zaire	B3	58
Maine, hist. reg., Fr.	D6	14
Maine, state, U.S.	B13	98
Maine, Gulf of, b., N.A.	C13	98
Maine-et-Loire, dept., Fr.	E6	14
Mainhardt, Ger.	F9	10
Mainland, i., Scot., U.K.	B10	8
Mainland, i., Scot., U.K.	A12	8
Mainpuri, India	G8	44
Maintenon, Fr.	D8	14
Maintirano, Madag.	Q21	67b
Main Topsail, mtn., Newf., Can.	C17	106
Mainz, Ger.	E8	10
Maio, i., C.V.	m17	64a
Maipo, stm., Chile	G3	80
Maipo, Volcán, vol., S.A.	H4	80
Maipú, Arg.	I10	80
Maipú, Arg.	G4	80
Maipú, Chile	G3	80
Maiquetía, Ven.	B9	84
Mairipotaba, Braz.	D4	79
Maitengwe, Bots.	C8	66
Maitengwe, stm., Afr.	C8	66
Maitland, Austl.	J2	70
Maitland, Austl.	I9	70
Maitland, N.S., Can.	G10	106
Maíz, stm., Nic.	F10	92
Maíz, Islas del, is., Nic.	E11	92
Maizuru, Japan	L10	36
Maja, stm., Russia	F18	28
Majagual, Col.	C5	84
Majaki, Ukr.	C14	20
Majari, stm., Braz.	F12	84
Majé, Braz.	G7	79
Maji, Eth.	N8	60
Majia, China	C7	34
Majie, China	B7	40
Majja, Russia	E18	28
Majkain, Kaz.	G13	26
Majkop, Russia	I6	26
Majorca see Mallorca, i., Spain	F15	16
Maka, Sen.	E2	64
Makabana, Congo	B2	58
Makalamabedi, Bots.	C6	66
Makallé, Arg.	D9	80
Makālu, mtn., Asia	G12	44
Makanza, Zaire	A3	58
Makaoo Indian Reserve, Alta., Can.	E4	104
Makarjev, Russia	D26	22
Makarov, Russia	H20	28
Makarska, Cro.	F12	18
Makasar, Selat (Makassar Strait), strt., Indon.	F6	38
Makassar Strait see Makasar, Selat, strt., Indon.	F6	38
Makat, Kaz.	H8	26
Makawao, Hi., U.S.	q17	125a
Makedonija see Macedonia, ctry., Eur.	H5	20
Makejevka, Ukr.	H5	26
Makeni, S.L.	G3	64
Makgadikgadi, pl., Bots.	C7	66
Makgadikgadi Pans Game Reserve, Bots.	C7	66
Makhfar al-Quwayrah, Jord.	I4	50
Makhfar Ramn, Jord.	I4	50
Makhrūq, Wādī al-, val., Asia	F7	50
Makindu, Kenya	B7	58
Makinsk, Kaz.	G12	26
M'akiševo, Russia	E11	22
M'akit, Russia	E22	28
Makkah (Mecca), Sau. Ar.	D1	47
Makó, Hung.	I20	10
Makokou, Gabon	A2	58
Makoua, Congo	A3	58
Makrāna, India	G6	44
Makran Coast, Asia	I16	48
M'aksa, Russia	C21	22
Maksaticha, Russia	D18	22
Makthar, Tun.	N4	18
Mākū, Iran	B8	48
Makumbi, Zaire	C4	58
Makung (P'enghu), Tai.	L8	34
Makurdi, Nig.	H14	64
Makwa Lake, l., Sask., Can.	D5	104
Makwassie, S. Afr.	F8	66
Mal, Maur.	C3	64
Mala, Peru	E3	82
Mala, stm., Peru	E3	82
Mala, Punta, c., Pan.	D3	84
Malabang, Phil.	D7	38
Malabar Coast, India	F3	46
Malabo, Eq. Gui.	J14	64
Malacacheta, Braz.	D7	79
Malacca, Strait of, strt., Asia	M6	40
Malacky, Czech.	G17	10
Malad, stm., U.S.	C4	120
Malad City, Id., U.S.	H13	122
Málaga, Col.	D6	84
Málaga, Spain	I7	16
Malaga, N.M., U.S.	G2	116
Malagash, N.S., Can.	G10	106
Malagasy Republic see Madagascar, ctry., Afr.	E9	58
Malagón, Spain	F8	16
Malaimbandy, Madag.	R21	67b
Malaja Kuril'skaja Gr'ada (Habomai-Shotō), is., Russia	D21	36a
Malaja Višera, Russia	C15	22
Malakāl, Sud.	M6	60
Malakoff, Tx., U.S.	G10	116
Malān, Burma	B4	40
Malang, Indon.	J16	39a
Malanggwā, Nepal	G11	44
Malanje, Ang.	C3	58
Malanville, Benin	F11	64
Malanzán, Arg.	F5	80
Mälaren, l., Swe.	L15	6
Malargüe, Arg.	H4	80
Malaspina Glacier, Ak., U.S.	G24	100
Malaspina Strait, strt., B.C., Can.	H10	102
Malatya, Tur.	B5	48
Malaut, India	E6	44
Malawi, ctry., Afr.	D6	58
Malawi, Lake see Nyasa, Lake, l., Afr.	D6	58
Malaybalay, Phil.	D8	38
Malāyer, Iran	D10	48
Malay Peninsula, pen., Asia	K6	40
Malay Reef, rf., Austl.	A8	70
Malaysia, ctry., Asia	E3	38
Malazgirt, Tur.	B7	48
Malbaie, stm., Que., Can.	E3	106
Malbaie, La, b., Que., Can.	D9	106
Malbork, Pol.	A19	10
Malbrán, Arg.	E7	80
Malcolm, Austl.	E4	68
Malcolm Island, i., B.C., Can.	G7	102
Malcom, Ia., U.S.	I3	110
Maldegem, Bel.	F3	12
Malden, Mo., U.S.	F7	114
Maldive Islands, is., Mald.	I2	46
Maldives, ctry., Asia	I8	24
Maldonado, Ur.	H11	80
Malé, Italy	C5	18
Male, Mald.	I8	24
Maléa, Ákra, c., Grc.	M7	20
Mālegaon, India	B3	46
Malek, Sud.	N6	60
Malek Sīāh, Kūh-e, mtn., Asia	G16	48
Malema, Moz.	D7	58
Malen'ga, Russia	J25	6
Māler Kotla, India	E6	44
Malesherbes, Fr.	D9	14
Malestroit, Fr.	E4	14
Malha Wells, Sud.	J4	60
Malheur, stm., Or., U.S.	G8	122
Malheur Lake, l., Or., U.S.	G7	122
Mali, ctry., Afr.	E6	54
Mali, stm., Burma	A4	40
Maligne, stm., Alta., Can.	E17	102
Maligne Lake, l., Alta., Can.	E17	102
Malik, Wādī al-, val., Sud.	I6	60
Mali Kyun, i., Burma	H5	40
Malin, Or., U.S.	H4	122
Malinalco, hist., Mex.	H10	90
Malinaltepec, Mex.	I10	90
Malines (Mechelen), Bel.	F5	12
Malin Head, c., Ire.	F6	8
Maliwun, Burma	I5	40
Maljamar, N.M., U.S.	G3	116
Malka, Russia	G23	28
Malkāpur, India	B4	46
Malkara, Tur.	I10	20
Mallāḥ, Syria	C7	50
Mallaig, Alta., Can.	C23	102
Mallaig, Scot., U.K.	D8	8
Mallala, Austl.	J3	70
Mallaoua, Niger	E14	64
Mallawī, Egypt	D6	60
Mallery Lake, l., N.W. Ter., Can.	D13	96
Mallet, Braz.	C13	80
Malligasta, Arg.	E5	80
Mallnitz, Aus.	I13	10
Mallorca, i., Spain	F15	16
Mallow, Ire.	I5	8
Malmédy, Bel.	H9	12
Malmesbury, S. Afr.	I4	66
Malmö, Swe.	N13	6
Malmöhus Län, co., Swe.	N13	6
Maloarchangel'sk, Russia	I19	22
Maloja, Switz.	F12	13
Malojaroslavec, Russia	F19	22
Maloje Kozino, Russia	E26	22
Maloje Skuratovo, Russia	H20	22
Malolos, Phil.	N19	39b
Malone, Fl., U.S.	I1	112
Malone, N.Y., U.S.	C12	108
Malonga, Zaire	D4	58
Małopolska, reg., Pol.	E21	10
Malošujka, Russia	E5	26
Måløy, Nor.	K9	6
Malpaisillo, Nic.	E8	92
Malpas, Austl.	J4	70
Malpelo, Isla de, i., Col.	C2	76
Malpeque Bay, b., P.E.I., Can.	F10	106
Malta, Lat.	E10	22
Malta, Mt., U.S.	B18	122
Malta, Oh., U.S.	H5	108
Malta, ctry., Eur.	H10	4
Malta, i., Malta	N9	18
Malta Channel, strt., Eur.	M9	18
Maltahöhe, Nmb.	E3	66
Maltepe, Tur.	I11	20
Maluku (Moluccas), is., Indon.	F8	38
Maluku, Laut (Molucca Sea), Indon.	F7	38

Name	Map Ref.	Page
Lipki, Russia	H20	22
Lipno, Pol.	C19	10
Lipno, údolní nádrž, res., Czech.	G14	10
Lipova, Rom.	C5	20
Lippe, stm., Ger.	D8	10
Lippstadt, Ger.	D8	10
Lipscomb, Tx., U.S.	C6	116
Lipton, Sask., Can.	H11	104
Liptovský Mikuláš, Czech.	F19	10
Liptrap, Cape, c., Austl.	L6	70
Lira, Ug.	H7	56
Lircay, Peru	E4	82
Liren, China	B7	34
Lisala, Zaire	A4	58
Lisboa (Lisbon), Port.	G2	16
Lisbon, N.H., U.S.	C15	108
Lisbon, N.D., U.S.	E10	118
Lisbon, Oh., U.S.	G6	108
Lisbon Falls, Me., U.S.	D16	108
Lisbon see Lisboa, Port.	G2	16
Lisburn, N. Ire., U.K.	G7	8
Lisburne, Cape, c., Ak., U.S.	B11	100
Lishe, China	F10	34
Lishui, China	G8	34
Lisičansk, Ukr.	H5	26
Lisieux, Sask., Can.	I9	104
Lisieux, Fr.	C7	14
Liski (Georgiu-Dež), Russia	G5	26
L'Isle Jourdain, Fr.	F7	14
L'Isle-sur-le-Doubs, Fr.	E13	14
Lisman, Al., U.S.	J8	114
Lismore, Austl.	G10	70
Lismore, N.S., Can.	G11	106
Lišov, Czech.	F14	10
Listowel, Ont., Can.	G15	110
Lita, China	H5	34
Litang, China	E7	30
Litang, China	G8	30
Litang, stm., China	F7	30
Litchfield, Il., U.S.	C7	114
Litchfield, Mi., U.S.	H11	110
Litchfield, Mn., U.S.	E1	110
Litchfield, Ne., U.S.	J8	118
Litchfield Park, Az., U.S.	K4	120
Litchville, N.D., U.S.	E9	118
Lithgow, Austl.	I9	70
Líthinon, Ákra, c., Grc.	O8	20
Lithonia, Ga., U.S.	F2	112
Lithuania (Lietuva), ctry., Eur.	F6	22
Litian, China	I3	34
Lititz, Pa., U.S.	G10	108
Litoměřice, Czech.	E14	10
Litomyšl, Czech.	F16	10
Litovko, Russia	H19	28
Little, stm., U.S.	I2	114
Little, stm., Al., U.S.	H11	114
Little, stm., Ga., U.S.	F4	112
Little, stm., Ky., U.S.	F9	114
Little, stm., La., U.S.	K4	114
Little, stm., Ok., U.S.	D10	116
Little, stm., S.C., U.S.	E5	112
Little, stm., Tn., U.S.	D3	112
Little Abaco, i., Bah.	A6	94
Little Andaman, i., India	I2	40
Little Arkansas, stm., Ks., U.S.	M9	118
Little Bay, Newf., Can.	E15	106
Little Bay Islands, Newf., Can.	C18	106
Little Bear, stm., Ut., U.S.	C5	120
Little Belt Mountains, mts., Mt., U.S.	D15	122
Little Bighorn, stm., U.S.	E18	122
Little Bitterroot, stm., Mt., U.S.	C11	122
Little Black Bear Indian Reserve, Sask., Can.	G11	104
Little Blackfoot, stm., Mt., U.S.	D13	122
Little Blue, stm., U.S.	L11	118
Little Bow, stm., Alta., Can.	G21	102
Little Buffalo, stm., Can.	D10	96
Little Bullhead, Man., Can.	G18	104
Little Catalina, Newf., Can.	D20	106
Little Cayman, i., Cay. Is.	E4	94
Little Cedar, stm., U.S.	G3	110
Little Churchill, stm., Man., Can.	A19	104
Little Chute, Wi., U.S.	F7	110
Little Colorado, stm., Az., U.S.	I5	120
Little Cottonwood, stm., Mn., U.S.	G13	118
Little Current, Ont., Can.	F14	110
Little Current, stm., Ont., Can.	F15	96
Little Deschutes, stm., Or., U.S.	G4	122
Little Desert, des., Austl.	K4	70
Little Diomede Island, i., Ak., U.S.	D10	100
Little Eau Pleine, stm., Wi., U.S.	F5	110
Little Exuma, i., Bah.	C7	94
Little Falls, Mn., U.S.	E1	110
Little Falls, N.Y., U.S.	D12	108
Littlefield, Tx., U.S.	F4	116
Littlefork, Mn., U.S.	B2	110
Little Fork, stm., Mn., U.S.	B2	110
Little Fort, B.C., Can.	F14	102
Little Harbour Deep, Newf., Can.	B17	106
Little Humboldt, stm., Nv., U.S.	C8	124
Little Inagua, i., Bah.	D8	94
Little Juniata, stm., Pa., U.S.	G8	108
Little Kanawha, stm., W.V., U.S.	H5	108
Little Lake, l., La., U.S.	M6	114
Little Limestone Lake, l., Man., Can.	E15	104
Little Manitou Lake, l., Sask., Can.	G9	104
Little Mecatina, stm., Can.	F20	96
Little Mexico, Tx., U.S.	I4	116
Little Missouri, stm., U.S.	D4	118
Little Missouri, stm., Ar., U.S.	I3	114
Little Muddy, stm., Il., U.S.	E7	114
Little Muddy, stm., N.D., U.S.	C4	118
Little Nemaha, stm., Ne., U.S.	K11	118
Little Nicobar, i., India	K2	40
Little Osage, stm., U.S.	D2	114
Little Pee Dee, stm., S.C., U.S.	F7	112
Little Pine and Lucky Man Indian Reserve, Sask., Can.	F5	104
Little Platte, stm., Mo., U.S.	C2	114
Little Powder, stm., U.S.	G2	118
Little Quill Lake, l., Sask., Can.	G10	104
Little Rann of Kachchh, pl., India	I4	44
Little Red, stm., Ar., U.S.	G5	114
Little Red Deer, stm., Alta., Can.	F20	102
Little Red River Indian Reserve, Sask., Can.	E9	104
Little River, Ks., U.S.	M9	118
Little Rock, Ar., U.S.	H4	114
Little Rock, Ia., U.S.	H12	118
Little Sable Point, c., Mi., U.S.	G9	110
Little Sac, stm., Mo., U.S.	E3	114
Little Sachigo Lake, l., Ont., Can.	D22	104
Little Saint Bernard Pass see Petit-Saint-Bernard, Col du, Eur.	G13	14
Little Salkehatchie, stm., S.C., U.S.	F6	112
Little Salmon Lake, l., Yukon, Can.	E27	100
Little Sandy, stm., Ky., U.S.	I3	108
Little Saskatchewan, stm., Man., Can.	H14	104
Little Scarcies, stm., Afr.	G4	54
Little Sioux, stm., U.S.	I12	118
Little Smoky, stm., Alta., Can.	B17	102
Little Snake, stm., U.S.	D8	120
Little Southwest Miramichi, stm., N.B., Can.	F7	106
Littlestown, Pa., U.S.	H9	108
Little Tallapoosa, stm., U.S.	F1	112
Little Tennessee, stm., U.S.	D2	112
Littleton, Co., U.S.	E11	120
Littleton, N.H., U.S.	C15	108
Littleton, N.C., U.S.	C9	112
Littleton, W.V., U.S.	H6	108
Little Traverse Bay, b., Mi., U.S.	E10	110
Little Turtle, stm., Ont., Can.	J22	104
Little Valley, N.Y., U.S.	E8	108
Little Vermilion Lake, l., Ont., Can.	G21	104
Little Wabash, stm., Il., U.S.	D8	114
Little Washita, stm., Ok., U.S.	E8	116
Little White, stm., S.D., U.S.	H6	118
Little White Mountain, mtn., B.C., Can.	H15	102
Little Wolf, stm., Wi., U.S.	F6	110
Little Wood, stm., Id., U.S.	G11	122
Little Zab (Zāb-e Kūchek) (Az-Zāb aṣ-Ṣaghīr), stm., Asia	D7	48
Litvínov, Czech.	E13	10
Liuchen, China	C11	40
Liucheng, China	B10	40
Liucura, Chile	J3	80
Liudaogou, China	B15	32
Liufangling, China	E3	34
Liuguan, China	F2	34
Liuhe, China	A13	32
Liuhe, China	C7	34
Liujia, China	B9	40
Liujiadu, China	C9	34
Liujiahe, China	C2	34
Liuku, China	B5	40
Liulongtai, China	B8	32
Liuquan, China	I5	32
Liurenba, China	F3	34
Liushilipu, China	C4	34
Liushuigou, China	D1	34
Liutai, China	B1	32
Liuwanglou, China	I4	32
Liuyang, China	G2	34
Liuyuan, China	G2	32
Liuzhou, China	B10	40
Liuzhuang, China	B9	34
Līvāni, Lat.	E9	22
Lively, Ont., Can.	D14	110
Live Oak, Ca., U.S.	E4	124
Live Oak, Fl., U.S.	I4	112
Livermore, Ca., U.S.	G4	124
Livermore, Ia., U.S.	H1	110
Livermore, Ky., U.S.	E9	114
Livermore Falls, Me., U.S.	C16	108
Liverpool, N.S., Can.	H9	106
Liverpool, Eng., U.K.	H11	8
Liverpool, Pa., U.S.	G10	108
Liverpool, Cape, c., N.W. Ter., Can.	B17	96
Liverpool Bay, b., N.W. Ter., Can.	B29	100
Liverpool Bay, b., N.S., Can.	H9	106
Lívingston, Guat.	B6	92
Livingston, Al., U.S.	J8	114
Livingston, Ca., U.S.	G5	124
Livingston, Il., U.S.	D7	114
Livingston, Ky., U.S.	B2	112
Livingston, La., U.S.	L6	114
Livingston, Mt., U.S.	E15	122
Livingston, Tn., U.S.	F11	114
Livingston, Tx., U.S.	I12	116
Livingston, Wi., U.S.	H5	110
Livingstone, Zam.	A7	66
Livingstone, Chutes de, wtfl, Afr.	B2	58
Livingstone, Lake, res., Tx., U.S.	I11	116
Livingstone Falls see Livingstone, Chutes de, wtfl, Afr.	B2	58
Livingstone Mountains, mts., N.Z.	F2	72
Livingstonia, Mwi.	D6	58
Livingston Island, i., B.A.T.	B12	73
Livingston Manor, N.Y., U.S.	F12	108
Livno, Bos.	F12	18
Livny, Russia	I20	22
Livonia, La., U.S.	L5	114
Livonia, Mi., U.S.	H12	110
Livonia, N.Y., U.S.	E9	108
Livorno (Leghorn), Italy	F5	18
Livramento do Brumado, Braz.	B8	79
Lixi, China	F3	34
Lixian, China	E3	32
Lixing, China	B4	34
Liyang, China	D8	34
Liyuanbao, China	J1	34
Liyujiang, China	J2	34
Lizard Head Peak, mtn., Wy., U.S.	H16	122
Lizard Point, c., Eng., U.K.	L8	8
Lizard Point Indian Reserve, Man., Can.	H14	104
Lizhu, China	F9	34
Ljubija, Bos.	E11	18
Ljubljana, Slo.	C9	18
Ljubuški, Bos.	F12	18
Ljungby, Swe.	M13	6
Ljusdal, Swe.	K15	6
Llaima, Volcán, vol., Chile	J3	80
Llamara, Salar de, pl., Chile	I7	82
Llancanelo, Laguna, l., Arg.	H4	80
Llandrindod Wells, Wales, U.K.	I10	8
Llangefni, Wales, U.K.	H9	8
Llangollen, Wales, U.K.	I10	8
Llanidloes, Wales, U.K.	I10	8
Llano, Tx., U.S.	I8	116
Llano, stm., Tx., U.S.	I8	116
Llanos, pl., S.A.	E7	84
Llanwrtyd Wells, Wales, U.K.	I10	8
Llata, Peru	C3	82
Lleida, Spain	D12	16
Llera de Canales, Mex.	F10	90
Lleulleu, Lago, l., Chile	J2	80
Llica, Bol.	H7	82
Llico, Chile	H2	80
Lliria, Spain	F11	16
Llorona, Punta, c., C.R.	I11	92
Lloydminster, Sask., Can.	E4	104
Lloyds, stm., Newf., Can.	D16	106
Llucmajor, Spain	F14	16
Llullaillaco, Volcán, vol., S.A.	C4	80
Llusco, Peru	F5	82
Lluta, stm., Chile	H7	82
Lo (Panlong), stm., Asia	C8	40
Loa, Ut., U.S.	F5	120
Loa, stm., Chile	I7	82
Loami, Il., U.S.	C7	114
Loanda, Braz.	G2	79
Loange (Luangue), stm., Afr.	C3	58
Lobanovo, Russia	H21	22
Lobatse, Bots.	E7	66
Lobaye, stm., Cen. Afr. Rep.	H4	56
Lobelville, Tn., U.S.	G9	114
Lobería, Arg.	J9	80
Lobito, Ang.	D2	58
Lobitos, Peru	J2	84
Lobn'a, Russia	E20	22
Lobos, Arg.	H9	80
Lobos, Cay, i., Bah.	C6	94
Lobos, Isla, i., Mex.	D4	90
Lobos, Punta, c., Chile	I6	82
Lobos de Afuera, Islas, is., Peru	B1	82
Lobos de Tierra, Isla, i., Peru	B1	82
Locarno, Switz.	F10	13
Loches, Fr.	E8	14
Lochmaben, Scot., U.K.	F10	8
Lock, Austl.	I1	70
Lockeport, N.S., Can.	I8	106
Lockerbie, Scot., U.K.	F10	8
Lockesburg, Ar., U.S.	I2	114
Lockhart, Austl.	J7	70
Lockhart, Tx., U.S.	J9	116
Lock Haven, Pa., U.S.	F9	108
Lockney, Tx., U.S.	E5	116
Löcknitz, Ger.	B14	10
Lockport, Man., Can.	H18	104
Lockport, Il., U.S.	I7	110
Lockport, La., U.S.	M6	114
Lockport, N.Y., U.S.	D8	108
Lockwood, Mo., U.S.	E3	114
Loc Ninh, Viet.	I9	40
Locri, Italy	K11	18
Locroja, Peru	E4	82
Locumba, Peru	G6	82
Locumba, stm., Peru	G6	82
Locust Fork, stm., Al., U.S.	H10	114
Locust Grove, Ok., U.S.	C11	116
Lod (Lydda), Isr.	E3	50
Lodejnoje Pole, Russia	A16	22
Lodève, Fr.	I10	14
Lodge Grass, Mt., U.S.	E18	122
Lodgepole, Alta., Can.	D19	102
Lodgepole, Ne., U.S.	J5	118
Lodi, Italy	D4	18
Lodi, Ca., U.S.	F4	124
Lodi, Oh., U.S.	F4	108
Lodi, Wi., U.S.	G6	110
Lodja, Zaire	B4	58
Lodwar, Kenya	H8	56
Łódź, Pol.	D19	10
Loei, Thai.	F6	40
Loeriesfontein, S. Afr.	H4	66
Lofa, stm., Afr.	G4	54
Lofoten, is., Nor.	G13	6
Loga, Niger	E11	64
Logan, Ia., U.S.	J12	118
Logan, Ks., U.S.	L8	118
Logan, N.M., U.S.	D3	116
Logan, Oh., U.S.	H4	108
Logan, Ut., U.S.	C5	120
Logan, W.V., U.S.	J5	108
Logan, stm., Alta., Can.	B23	102
Logan, stm., Ut., U.S.	C5	120
Logan, Mount, mtn., Yukon, Can.	F24	100
Logandale, Nv., U.S.	H11	124
Logan Martin Lake, res., Al., U.S.	I10	114
Logan Mountains, mts., Yukon, Can.	E30	100
Logan Pass, Mt., U.S.	B12	122
Logansport, In., U.S.	B10	114
Logansport, La., U.S.	K3	114
Loganville, Ga., U.S.	F3	112
Logojsk, Bela.	G10	22
Logone, stm., Afr.	F4	56
Logroño, Spain	C9	16
Løgstør, Den.	M11	6
Lohiniva, Fin.	H19	6
Lohit, stm., Asia	G16	44
Lohja, Fin.	K19	6
Lohne, Ger.	C8	10
Lohr, Ger.	E9	10
Lohrville, Ia., U.S.	I13	118
Loi, stm., Asia	D6	40
Loi-kaw, Burma	E4	40
Loimaa, Fin.	K18	6
Loire, dept., Fr.	G11	14
Loire, stm., Fr.	E5	14
Loire-Atlantique, dept., Fr.	E5	14
Loiret, dept., Fr.	D9	14
Loir-et-Cher, dept., Fr.	E8	14
Loitz, Ger.	B13	10
Loja, Ec.	E7	74
Loja, Ec.	I3	84
Loja, Ec.	J12	86
Loja, Spain	H7	16
Loja, prov., Ec.	J3	84
Lokandu, Zaire	B5	58
Lokan tekojärvi, res., Fin.	H20	6
Lokbatan, Azer.	A10	48
Lokka, Fin.	H20	6
Løkken, Den.	M11	6
Lokn'a, Russia	E13	22
Loko, Nig.	G13	64
Lokoja, Nig.	H13	64
Lokolama, Zaire	B3	58
Lokossa, Benin	H10	64
Lokot', Russia	I17	22
Loks Land, i., N.W. Ter., Can.	D20	96
Lol, Sud.	N5	60
Lol, stm., Sud.	M4	60
Lola, Gui.	H5	64
Loleta, Ca., U.S.	D1	124
Lolita, Tx., U.S.	K10	116
Lolo, Mt., U.S.	D11	122
Lolo Pass, U.S.	D11	122
Lolotique, El Sal.	D6	92
Lom, Bul.	F7	20
Lom, Russia	D22	22
Lom, stm., Afr.	G9	54
Loma, Eth.	N9	60
Lomas de Zamora, Arg.	H9	80
Lomax, Il., U.S.	J4	110
Lombardia, prov., Italy	D4	18
Lomblen, Pulau, i., Indon.	G7	38
Lombok, i., Indon.	G6	38
Lomé, Togo	H10	64
Lomela, Zaire	B4	58
Lometa, Tx., U.S.	H8	116
Lomira, Wi., U.S.	G7	110
Lo Miranda, Chile	H3	80
Lommel, Bel.	F7	12
Lomond, Alta., Can.	G22	102
Lomond, Loch, l., N.S., Can.	G13	106
Lomond, Loch, l., Scot., U.K.	E9	8
Lomonosov, Russia	B12	22
Lomonosovskij, Kaz.	G11	26
Lompoc, Ca., U.S.	J5	124
Lom Sak, Thai.	F6	40
Łomża, Pol.	B22	10
Lonaconing, Md., U.S.	H8	108
Loncoche, Chile	D2	78
Loncopué, Arg.	J3	80
Londinières, Fr.	C8	14
London, Ont., Can.	H14	110
London, Eng., U.K.	J13	8
London, Ky., U.S.	B2	112
London, Oh., U.S.	H3	108
London, Tx., U.S.	I7	116
Londonderry, N.S., Can.	G10	106
Londonderry, N. Ire., U.K.	F6	8
Londonderry, Cape, c., Austl.	B5	68
Londres, Arg.	D5	80
Londrina, Braz.	G3	79
Lone Grove, Ok., U.S.	E9	116
Lonely Lake, l., Man., Can.	G15	104
Lone Mountain, mtn., Nv., U.S.	F8	124
Lone Oak, Ky., U.S.	E8	114
Lone Oak, Tx., U.S.	F11	116
Lone Pine, Ca., U.S.	H7	124
Lone Rock, Wi., U.S.	G5	110
Lone Star, Tx., U.S.	J2	114
Lone Tree, Ia., U.S.	I4	110
Lone Wolf, Ok., U.S.	E7	116
Longa, stm., Ang.	D2	58
Longa, proliv, strt., Russia	C27	28
Long'an, China	B10	40
Longaví, Chile	H3	80
Long Bay, b., U.S.	F8	112
Long Beach, Ca., U.S.	K7	124
Long Beach, Ms., U.S.	L7	114
Long Beach, N.Y., U.S.	G13	108
Long Beach, Wa., U.S.	D1	122
Longboat Key, Fl., U.S.	L4	112
Long Branch, N.J., U.S.	G13	108
Long Branch, stm., Mo., U.S.	C4	114
Long Cay, i., Bah.	C7	94
Longchang, China	F8	30
Longchuan, China	K4	34
Longchuan (Shweli), stm., Asia	B4	40
Long Creek, Or., U.S.	F6	122
Long Creek, stm., N.A.	I11	104
Longcun, China	L4	34
Longdou, China	H6	34
Longeau, Fr.	E12	14
Longford, Austl.	L7	70
Longford, co., Ire.	H6	8
Long Harbour, Newf., Can.	E20	106
Long Harbour, b., Newf., Can.	E18	106
Longhua, China	B5	32
Long Island, i., Austl.	D8	70
Long Island, i., Bah.	C7	94
Long Island, i., Newf., Can.	E19	106
Long Island, i., N.W. Ter., Can.	F17	96
Long Island, i., N.S., Can.	H7	106
Long Island, i., N.Y., U.S.	G14	108
Long Island Sound, strt., U.S.	F14	108
Longitudinal, Valle, val., Chile	H3	80
Longjiang, China	B11	30
Longjin, China	G5	34
Longka, China	D8	44
Longkangji, China	B5	34
Longkou, China	D11	30
Longkou, China	I4	34
Long Lake, N.Y., U.S.	D12	108
Long Lake, l., N.D., U.S.	E7	118
Longleaf, La., U.S.	K4	114
Long Leaf Park, N.C., U.S.	E9	112
Longlegged Lake, l., Ont., Can.	H20	104
Longli, China	F8	30
Longling, China	B5	40
Longmeadow, Ma., U.S.	E14	108
Longmensuo, China	C3	32
Longming, China	C9	40
Longmont, Co., U.S.	D11	120
Longnan, China	K3	34
Longnawan, Indon.	E5	38
Longny, Fr.	M14	8
Long Pine, Ne., U.S.	I8	118
Long Point, c., Newf., Can.	D15	106
Long Point, c., N.S., Can.	F13	106
Long Point, pen., Man., Can.	E16	104
Long Point, pen., Ont., Can.	H15	110
Long Prairie, Mn., U.S.	F13	118
Long Prairie, stm., Mn., U.S.	E13	118
Longquan, China	G8	34
Longquanguan, China	E1	32
Long Range Mountains, mts., Newf., Can.	D16	106
Longreach, Austl.	D6	70
Long Reach, b., N.B., Can.	G7	106
Long-Sault, Ont., Can.	B12	108
Longshansuo, China	E10	34
Longsheng, China	B11	40
Longs Peak, mtn., Co., U.S.	D11	120
Longtian, China	J8	34
Long Tom, stm., Or., U.S.	F2	122
Longton, Ks., U.S.	N11	118
Longtoupu, China	H2	34
Longueuil, Que., Can.	B13	108
Longuyon, Fr.	C12	14
Longview, Alta., Can.	G20	102
Longview, N.C., U.S.	D5	112
Longview, Tx., U.S.	J2	114
Longview, Wa., U.S.	D3	122
Longwangmiao, China	G3	32
Longwood Park, N.C., U.S.	E7	112
Longworth, B.C., Can.	D13	102
Longwy, Fr.	C12	14
Longxi, China	E7	30
Long Xuyen, Viet.	I8	40
Longyan, China	J6	34
Longyuanba, China	K3	34
Longzhou, China	C9	40
Lonigo, Italy	D6	18
Löningen, Ger.	C7	10
Lonoke, Ar., U.S.	H5	114
Lonsdale, Mn., U.S.	F2	110
Lons-le-Saunier, Fr.	F12	14
Lonton, Burma	B4	40
Lontra, Ribeirão da, stm., Braz.	F2	79
Loogootee, In., U.S.	D10	114
Looking Glass, stm., Mi., U.S.	H11	110
Lookout, Cape, c., N.C., U.S.	E10	112
Lookout Mountain, mtn., U.S.	H11	114
Lookout Mountain, mtn., Or., U.S.	F5	122
Lookout Pass, U.S.	C10	122
Lookout Ridge, mts., Ak., U.S.	B15	100
Loomis, Ne., U.S.	K8	118
Loon, stm., Man., Can.	B13	104
Loon Lake, l., Can.	C12	104
Loon op Zand, Neth.	E7	12
Loop, Tx., U.S.	G4	116
Lop, China	B9	44
Lopar'ovo, Russia	C25	22
Lopatina, gora, mtn., Russia	G20	28
Lopatka, mys, c., Russia	G23	28
Lop Buri, Thai.	G6	40
López, Mex.	D7	90
Lopez, Cap, c., Gabon	B1	58
Lop Nur (Lop Nor), l., China	C5	30
Łopuszno, Pol.	E20	10
Lora, stm., Ven.	C6	84
Lora, Hāmūn-i-, l., Asia	F1	44
Lora del Río, Spain	H6	16
Lorain, Oh., U.S.	F4	108
Loraine, Tx., U.S.	G6	116
Lorca, Spain	H10	16
Lord Howe Island, i., Austl.	F11	68
Lord Mayor Bay, b., N.W. Ter., Can.	C14	96
Lordsburg, N.M., U.S.	L8	120
Loreauville, La., U.S.	L5	114
Loreley, Ger.	E7	10
Lorena, Braz.	G6	79
Lorenzo, Tx., U.S.	F5	116
Lorenzo Geyres (Queguay), Ur.	G10	80
Loreto, Arg.	D10	80
Loreto, Bol.	F9	82
Loreto, Braz.	E9	76
Loreto, Mex.	F9	90
Loreto, Mex.	D4	90
Loreto, Para.	B10	80
Loreto, dept., Peru	I5	84
Loreto Mocagua, Col.	I7	84
Lorette, Man., Can.	I18	104
Loretto, Ky., U.S.	E11	114
Loretto, Tn., U.S.	G9	114
Lorica, Col.	C5	84
Lorient, Fr.	E3	14
L'Orignal, Ont., Can.	B12	108
Lorimor, Ia., U.S.	A2	114
Loriol, Fr.	H11	14
Loris, S.C., U.S.	E8	112
Lorman, Ms., U.S.	K5	114
Lorne, Austl.	L5	70
Lorne, N.B., Can.	E7	106
Lörrach, Ger.	H7	10
Lorraine, hist. reg., Fr.	D13	14
Lorris, Fr.	E9	14
Losada, stm., Col.	F5	84
Los Alamos, Ca., U.S.	J5	124
Los Alamos, N.M., U.S.	I10	120
Los Aldamas, Mex.	D10	90
Los Amates, Guat.	B5	92
Los Americanos, Barra, i., Mex.	E11	90
Los Andes, Chile	G3	80
Los Ángeles, Chile	I2	80
Los Angeles, Ca., U.S.	J7	124
Los Angeles Aqueduct, Ca., U.S.	I7	124
Los Banos, Ca., U.S.	G5	124
Los Berros, Arg.	F4	80
Los Blancos, Arg.	B7	80
Los Bolones, Cerro, mtn., Mex.	I13	90
Los Cerrillos, Arg.	F6	80
Los Chacos, Bol.	F10	82
Los Chiles, C.R.	F10	92
Los Conquistadores, Arg.	F9	80
Los Cristianos, Spain	O24	17b
Los Ebanos, Tx., U.S.	M8	116
Los Esclavos, stm., Guat.	D4	92
Los Frentones, Arg.	D8	80
Los Fresnos, Tx., U.S.	M9	116
Los Gatos, Ca., U.S.	G4	124
Los Hermanos, Islas, is., Ven.	B10	84
Łosice, Pol.	C22	10
Los Juríes, Arg.	E7	80
Los Lagos, Chile	D2	78
Los Llanos de Aridane, Spain	O23	17b
Los Lunas, N.M., U.S.	J10	120
Los Maribios, Cordillera, mts., Nic.	E8	92
Los Micos, Laguna de, b., Hond.	B7	92
Los Mochis, Mex.	E5	90
Los Molinos, Ca., U.S.	D3	124
Lošnica, Bela.	G11	22
Los Padillas, N.M., U.S.	J10	120
Los Palacios, Arg.	E4	80
Los Palacios, Cuba	C3	94
Los Palacios y Villafranca, Spain	H6	16
Los Pinos, stm., U.S.	G9	120
Los Quirquinchos, Arg.	G8	80
Los Ríos, prov., Ec.	H3	84
Los Rodríguez, Mex.	D9	90
Los Roques, Islas, is., Ven.	B9	84
Los Santos, prov., Pan.	J14	92
Los Santos de Maimona, Spain	G5	16
Los Sauces, Chile	I2	80
Los Sauces, Spain	O23	17b
Lossiemouth, Scot., U.K.	D10	8
Lost, stm., U.S.	H4	122
Lost, stm., In., U.S.	D10	114
Lost, stm., Mn., U.S.	D12	118
Lost, stm., W.V., U.S.	I8	108
Los Taques, Ven.	B7	84
Los Telares, Arg.	E7	80
Los Teques, Ven.	B9	84
Los Testigos, Islas, is., Ven.	B11	84
Lost Hills, Ca., U.S.	I6	124
Lostine, stm., Or., U.S.	E8	122
Lost Nation, Ia., U.S.	I5	110
Lost River Range, mts., Id., U.S.	F12	122
Lost Trail Pass, U.S.	E12	122
Losuia, Pap. N. Gui.	A10	68
Los Vidrios, Mex.	B3	90
Los Vilos, Chile	F3	80
Lot, dept., Fr.	H8	14
Lot, stm., Fr.	H7	14
Lota, Chile	I2	80
Lot-et-Garonne, dept., Fr.	H7	14
Lothair, S. Afr.	F10	66
Lothair, Ky., U.S.	B3	112
Lothian, prov., Scot., U.K.	F10	8
Lotsane, stm., Bots.	D8	66
Lott, Tx., U.S.	H9	116
Lotung, Tai.	K10	34
Louang Namtha, Laos	D6	40
Louangphrabang, Laos	E7	40
Louchi, Russia	D4	26
Loudéac, Fr.	D4	14
Loudon, Tn., U.S.	D2	112
Loudonville, Oh., U.S.	G4	108
Loudun, Fr.	E7	14
Loué, Fr.	D6	14
Louga, Sen.	D1	64
Louge, Arg.	I8	80
Louhans, Fr.	F12	14
Louin, Ms., U.S.	J7	114
Louisa, Ky., U.S.	A4	112
Louisa, Va., U.S.	A8	112
Louisbourg, N.S., Can.	G14	106
Louis Bull Indian Reserve, Alta., Can.	E21	102
Louisburg, Ks., U.S.	M13	118
Louisburg, N.C., U.S.	C8	112
Louisdale, N.S., Can.	G12	106
Louise, Ms., U.S.	J6	114
Louise, Tx., U.S.	J10	116
Louise, Lake, l., Ak., U.S.	E21	100
Louise Island, i., B.C., Can.	E3	102
Louiseville, Que., Can.	A14	108
Louisiade Archipelago, is., Pap. N. Gui.	B10	68
Louisiana, Mo., U.S.	C5	114
Louisiana, state, U.S.	E8	98
Louis Trichardt, S. Afr.	D9	66
Louisville, Al., U.S.	K11	114
Louisville, Ga., U.S.	F4	112
Louisville, Il., U.S.	D8	114
Louisville, Ky., U.S.	D11	114
Louisville, Ms., U.S.	I7	114
Louisville, Ne., U.S.	K11	118
Louisville, Oh., U.S.	G5	108
Louis-XIV, Pointe, c., Que., Can.	F17	96
Loujiaying, China	A4	32
Lount Lake, l., Ont., Can.	H20	104
Loup, stm., Ne., U.S.	J10	118
Loup City, Ne., U.S.	J9	118
Loups Marins, Lacs des, l., Que., Can.	E18	96
Lourdes, Newf., Can.	D14	106
Lourdes, Fr.	I6	14
Lourenço Marques see Maputo, Moz.	E11	66
Louta, Burkina	E8	64
Louth, co., Ire.	H7	8
Loutre, stm., Mo., U.S.	D5	114
Louvain (Leuven), Bel.	G6	12
Louviers, Fr.	C8	14
Louviers, Co., U.S.	E11	120
Lovat', stm., Russia	D14	22
Love, Sask., Can.	E10	104
Loveč, Bul.	F8	20
Lovelady, Tx., U.S.	H11	116
Loveland, Co., U.S.	D11	120
Lovell, Wy., U.S.	F17	122
Lovelock, Nv., U.S.	D7	124
Lovely, Ky., U.S.	B4	112
Lovere, Italy	D5	18
Loves Park, Il., U.S.	H6	110
Lovilia, Ia., U.S.	I3	110
Loving, N.M., U.S.	G2	116
Loving, Tx., U.S.	F8	116
Lovingston, Va., U.S.	B8	112
Lovington, Il., U.S.	C8	114
Lovington, N.M., U.S.	G3	116
Lovosice, Czech.	E14	10
Lovozero, Russia	G24	6
Lovozero, ozero, l., Russia	H24	6
Lövstabruk, Swe.	K15	6
Low, Que., Can.	B11	108
Low, Cape, c., N.W. Ter., Can.	D15	96
Lowden, Ia., U.S.	I5	110
Lowell, Ar., U.S.	F2	114
Lowell, In., U.S.	A9	114
Lowell, Ma., U.S.	E15	108
Lowell, Mi., U.S.	H10	110
Lowell, Or., U.S.	G3	122
Lowelli, Sud.	O7	60
Löwenberg, Ger.	C13	10
Lower Arrow Lake, l., B.C., Can.	H16	102
Lower California see Baja California, pen., Mex.	C3	90
Lower Fort Garry National Historic Park, Man., Can.	H18	104
Lower Hutt, N.Z.	D5	72
Lower Kalskag, Ak., U.S.	F14	100
Lower Klamath Lake, l., Ca., U.S.	C4	124
Lower Manitou Lake, l., Ont., Can.	I21	104
Lower Post, B.C., Can.	E7	96
Lower Red Lake, l., Mn., U.S.	D12	118
Lower Saxony see Niedersachsen, state, Ger.	C8	10
Lower West Pubnico, N.S., Can.	I8	106
Lower Wood's Harbour, N.S., Can.	I8	106
Lowestoft, Eng., U.K.	I15	8
Łowicz, Pol.	C19	10
Lowmoor, Va., U.S.	B7	112
Lowrah (Pishīn Lora), stm., Asia	G18	48
Low Rocky Point, c., Austl.	N6	70
Lowry City, Mo., U.S.	D3	114
Lowville, N.Y., U.S.	D11	108
Loxley, Al., U.S.	L9	114
Loxton, Austl.	J4	70
Loxton, S. Afr.	H6	66
Loyal, Wi., U.S.	F5	110
Loyalton, Ca., U.S.	E5	124
Lozère, dept., Fr.	H10	14
Loznica, Yugo.	E3	20
Lualaba, stm., Zaire	B5	58
Lu'an, China	D5	34
Luan, stm., China	C10	30
Luanda, Ang.	C2	58
Luando, stm., Ang.	D3	58
Luang, Thale, b., Thai.	K6	40
Luang Prabang Range, mts., Asia	E6	40
Luangue (Loange), stm., Afr.	C3	58
Luanguinga, stm., Afr.	D4	58
Luangwa, stm., Afr.	D6	58
Luanhaizi, China	C15	44
Luanshishan, China	A11	32
Luanshya, Zam.	D5	58
Luán Toro, Arg.	I6	80
Luapula, stm., Afr.	D5	58
Luau, Ang.	D4	58
Luba, Eq. Gui.	H8	54
Lubaantun, hist., Belize	I15	90
L'uban', Bela.	I10	22
Lubań, Pol.	D15	10
L'uban', Russia	B14	22
Lubāna, Lat.	E9	22
Lubango, Ang.	D2	58
Lubao, China	L1	34
L'ubašovka, Ukr.	B14	20
Lubawa, Pol.	B19	10
Lübbenau, Ger.	D13	10
Lubbock, Tx., U.S.	F5	116
L'ubča, Bela.	H9	22
Lubec, Me., U.S.	C20	108
Lübeck, Ger.	B10	10
Lubefu, Zaire	B4	58
L'ubercy, Russia	F20	22
L'ubim, Russia	C23	22
Lubin, Pol.	D16	10
Lublin, Pol.	D22	10
Lubliniec, Pol.	E18	10
Lubnān, Jabal (Lebanon Mountains), mts., Leb.	A5	50
L'ubnica, Russia	D15	22
Lubny, Ukr.	G4	26
L'ubochna, Russia	H17	22
Luboń, Pol.	C16	10
L'ubotin, Ukr.	H5	26
Lubraniec, Pol.	C18	10
Lubsko, Pol.	D14	10
Lubudi, Zaire	C5	58
Lubumbashi (Élisabethville), Zaire	D5	58
Lubutu, Zaire	B5	58
L'ubytino, Russia	C16	22
Lübz, Ger.	B12	10
Lucan, Ont., Can.	G14	110
Lucanas, Peru	F4	82
Lucania, Mount, mtn., Yukon, Can.	F24	100

Name	Map Ref.	Page
Lucas, Ia., U.S.	I2	110
Lucas, Ks., U.S.	L9	118
Lucas González, Arg.	G9	80
Lucasville, Oh., U.S.	I4	108
Lucca, Italy	F5	18
Lucedale, Ms., U.S.	L8	114
Lucena, Phil.	O19	39b
Lucena, Spain	H7	16
Lučenec, Czech.	G19	10
Lucera, Italy	H10	18
Lucerne, Ca., U.S.	E3	124
Lucerne, Lake see Vierwaldstätter See, l., Switz.	D9	13
Lucerne see Luzern, Switz.	D9	13
Luch, stm., Russia	E25	22
Lucheng, China	B9	40
Luchovicy, Russia	G22	22
Lüchow, Ger.	C11	10
Luchow see Luzhou, China	F8	30
Luchuan, China	C11	40
Luci, China	F8	34
Lucie, stm., Sur.	F14	84
Lucindale, Austl.	K4	70
Lucira, Ang.	D2	58
Luck, Ukr.	G3	26
Luck, Wi., U.S.	E3	110
Luckau, Ger.	D13	10
Luckenwalde, Ger.	C13	10
Luckhoff, S. Afr.	G7	66
Luckiamute, stm., Or., U.S.	F2	122
Luck Lake, l., Sask., Can.	G7	104
Lucknow, Ont., Can.	G14	110
Lucknow, India	G9	44
Lucky Lake, Sask., Can.	G7	104
Luçon, Fr.	F5	14
Lucun, China	G6	32
Lüda see Dalian, China	E9	32
Lüdenscheid, Ger.	D7	10
Lüderitz, Nmb.	F2	66
Ludhiāna, India	E6	44
Lüdinghausen, Ger.	D7	10
Ludington, Mi., U.S.	G9	110
L'udinovo, Russia	H17	22
L'udkovo, Russia	G17	22
Ludlow, Ma., U.S.	E14	108
Ludlow, Vt., U.S.	D14	108
Ludowici, Ga., U.S.	H5	112
Ludvika, Swe.	K14	6
Ludwigsburg, Ger.	G9	10
Ludwigsfelde, Ger.	C13	10
Ludwigshafen, Ger.	F8	10
Ludwigslust, Ger.	B11	10
Ludza, Lat.	E10	22
Luebo, Zaire	C4	58
Lueders, Tx., U.S.	G7	116
Luena, Ang.	D3	58
Luena, Zaire	C5	58
Luena, stm., Ang.	D4	58
Luepa, Ven.	E12	84
Lufeng, China	M4	34
Lufeng, China	B7	40
Lufkin, Tx., U.S.	K2	114
Luga, Russia	C12	22
Lugano, Switz.	F10	13
Lugano, Lago di, l., Eur.	C4	18
Lugansk (Vorošilovgrad), Ukr.	H5	26
Lugenda, stm., Moz.	D7	58
Lugnaquillia Mountain, mtn., Ire.	I7	8
Lugo, Italy	E6	18
Lugo, Spain	B4	16
Lugoj, Rom.	D5	20
Lühedian, China	C3	34
Luik (Liège), Bel.	G8	12
Luino, Italy	C3	18
Luishia, Zaire	D5	58
Luiza, Zaire	C4	58
Luiziânia, Braz.	F3	79
Luján, Arg.	G4	80
Luján, Arg.	G6	80
Lujiao, China	F1	34
Lukang, Tai.	K9	34
Lukanga Swamp, sw., Zam.	D5	58
Lukeville, Az., U.S.	M4	120
Luknovo, Russia	E25	22
Lukolela, Zaire	B3	58
Lukou, China	H3	34
Lukoupu, China	F2	34
Łuków, Pol.	D22	10
Lukulu, Zam.	D4	58
Lula, Ms., U.S.	H6	114
Luleå, Swe.	I18	6
Lüleburgaz, Tur.	H11	20
Lules, Arg.	D6	80
Luliang, China	B7	40
Lüliang Shan, mts., China	D9	30
Luling, Tx., U.S.	J9	116
Lumaling, China	F15	44
Lumbala N'guimbo, Ang.	D4	58
Lumber, stm., U.S.	E7	112
Lumber City, Ga., U.S.	H4	112
Lumberport, W.V., U.S.	H6	108
Lumberton, Ms., U.S.	K7	114
Lumberton, N.C., U.S.	E7	112
Lumberton, Tx., U.S.	L2	114
Lumbres, Fr.	B9	14
Lumby, B.C., Can.	G16	102
Lumding, India	H15	44
Lumpkin, Ga., U.S.	G2	112
Lumsden, Newf., Can.	C20	106
Lumsden, Sask., Can.	H10	104
Lumut, Malay.	L6	40
Luna, stm., Braz.	J12	84
Luna Pier, Mi., U.S.	I12	110
Lūnāvāda, India	I5	44
Lund, B.C., Can.	H10	102
Lund, Swe.	N13	6
Lund, Nv., U.S.	F10	124
Lundale, W.V., U.S.	J5	108
Lundar, Man., Can.	H16	104
Lundazi, Zam.	D6	58
Lundi, stm., Zimb.	C10	66
Lüneburg, Ger.	B10	10
Lüneburger Heide, reg., Ger.	B10	10
Lunel, Fr.	I11	14
Lünen, Ger.	D7	10
Lunenburg, N.S., Can.	H9	106
Lunenburg, Va., U.S.	C8	112
Lunéville, Fr.	D13	14
Lunga, stm., Zam.	D5	58
Lunge'nake, China	E11	44
Lungi, S.L.	G3	64
Lungué-Bungo, stm., Afr.	D4	58
Lunin, Bela.	I9	22
Luninec, Bela.	I9	22
Lunjiao, China	M2	34
Lunno, Bela.	H7	22
Luo, stm., China	E9	30
Luochanghe, China	D6	34
Luoci, China	B7	40
Luofang, China	H4	34
Luogang, China	K4	34
Luohe, China	B3	34
Luoheya, China	H6	32
Luoji, China	C6	34
Luokeng, China	K2	34
Luoqiao, China	I8	34
Luoshuihe, China	D2	32
Luotuodian, China	C2	34
Luoyang, China	E9	30
Lupala, Nmb.	A4	66
Lupani, Zimb.	B8	66
Lupeni, Rom.	D7	20
Luqu, China	E7	30
Luray, Va., U.S.	I8	108
Lure, Fr.	E13	14
Luremo, Ang.	C3	58
Luribay, Bol.	G8	82
Lurín, Peru	E3	82
Lúrio, Moz.	D8	58
Lúrio, stm., Moz.	D7	58
Lusaka, Zam.	E5	58
Lusambo, Zaire	B4	58
Lusanga, Zaire	B3	58
Luscar, Alta., Can.	D17	102
Luseland, Sask., Can.	F5	104
Lushan, China	E7	30
Lu Shan, mtn., China	F10	30
Lushanguanliju, China	F4	34
Lushnje, Alb.	I3	20
Lushoto, Tan.	B7	58
Lushui, China	A5	40
Lüshun (Port Arthur), China	E9	32
Lüsi, China	C10	34
Lusignan, Fr.	F7	14
L'usino, Bela.	I9	22
Lusk, Wy., U.S.	B12	120
Lustenau, Aus.	H9	10
Lūt, Dasht-e, des., Iran	E15	48
Lutai, China	B4	34
Lutang, China	J1	34
Lutcher, La., U.S.	L6	114
Lutesville, Mo., U.S.	E7	114
Luther, Mi., U.S.	F10	110
Luther, Ok., U.S.	D9	116
Lutian, China	I3	34
Luton, Eng., U.K.	J13	8
Lutong, Malay.	E5	38
Lutou, China	C1	34
Luttrell, Tn., U.S.	C3	112
Lutz, Fl., U.S.	K4	112
Lützow-Holm Bay, b., Ant.	B4	73
Lutzputs, S. Afr.	G5	66
Lutzville, S. Afr.	H4	66
Luuq, Som.	H9	56
Luverne, Al., U.S.	K10	114
Lu Verne, Ia., U.S.	H1	110
Luverne, Mn., U.S.	H11	118
Luvuvhu, stm., Afr.	D10	66
Luxana Bay, b., B.C., Can.	E3	102
Luxembourg (Luxemburg), Lux.	I9	12
Luxembourg, prov., Bel.	I7	12
Luxembourg, ctry., Eur.	F9	4
Luxemburg, Wi., U.S.	F8	110
Luxeuil-les-Bains, Fr.	E13	14
Luxi (Mangshi), China	B5	40
Lüxia, China	I9	34
Luxora, Ar., U.S.	G7	114
Luxor see Al-Uqṣur, Egypt	E7	60
Lüyang, China	B9	32
Luz, Braz.	E6	79
Luza, Russia	E7	26
Luzarches, Fr.	C9	14
Luzern, Switz.	D9	13
Luzern, state, Switz.	D9	13
Luzhou, China	F8	30
Luziânia, Braz.	D5	79
Lužnice, stm., Eur.	G14	10
Luzon, i., Phil.	N19	39b
Luzon Strait, strt., Asia	N9	34
Luzy, Fr.	F10	14
L'vov, Ukr.	H2	26
L'vovskij, Russia	F20	22
Lwówek, Pol.	C16	10
Lybster, Scot., U.K.	C10	8
Lyčkovo, Russia	D15	22
Lycksele, Swe.	I16	6
Lycoming Creek, stm., Pa., U.S.	F9	108
Lydenburg, S. Afr.	E10	66
Lydia Mills, S.C., U.S.	E5	112
Lyell, Mount, mtn., Can.	F17	102
Lyell Island, i., B.C., Can.	E3	102
Lyerly, Ga., U.S.	E1	112
Lyford, Tx., U.S.	M9	116
Lykens, Pa., U.S.	G10	108
Lykošino, Russia	C16	22
Lyle, Mn., U.S.	G3	110
Lyles, Tn., U.S.	G9	114
Lyman, Ne., U.S.	J3	118
Lyman, S.C., U.S.	E4	112
Lyman, Wy., U.S.	C6	120
Lyme Regis, Eng., U.K.	K11	8
Łyna (Lava), stm., Eur.	G3	22
Lynch, Ky., U.S.	C4	112
Lynch, Ne., U.S.	I9	118
Lynchburg, Oh., U.S.	H3	108
Lynchburg, S.C., U.S.	E6	112
Lynchburg, Tn., U.S.	G10	114
Lynchburg, Va., U.S.	B7	112
Lynches, stm., U.S.	F7	112
Lynden, Wa., U.S.	B3	122
Lyndhurst, Austl.	H3	70
Lyndon, Ks., U.S.	M12	118
Lyndon, Ky., U.S.	D11	114
Lyndonville, Vt., U.S.	C14	108
Lyndora, Pa., U.S.	G7	108
Lyngdal, Nor.	L10	6
Lyngen, Nor.	G17	6
Lyngør, Nor.	L11	6
Lynn, Al., U.S.	H9	114
Lynn, In., U.S.	B12	114
Lynn, Ma., U.S.	E16	108
Lynn Canal, b., Ak., U.S.	G27	100
Lynndyl, Ut., U.S.	E4	120
Lynn Garden, Tn., U.S.	C4	112
Lynn Haven, Fl., U.S.	L11	114
Lynn Lake, Man., Can.	B13	104
Lynnville, Ia., U.S.	I3	110
Lyntupy, Bela.	F9	22
Lynx Lake, l., N.W. Ter., Can.	D11	96
Lyon, Fr.	G11	14
Lyon Inlet, b., N.W. Ter., Can.	C16	96
Lyon Mountain, N.Y., U.S.	C13	108
Lyonnais, Monts du, mts., Fr.	G11	14
Lyons, Co., U.S.	D11	120
Lyons, Ga., U.S.	G4	112
Lyons, In., U.S.	D9	114
Lyons, Ks., U.S.	M9	118
Lyons, Mi., U.S.	H11	110
Lyons, Ne., U.S.	J11	118
Lyons, N.Y., U.S.	D10	108
Lyons, stm., Austl.	D3	68
Lys (Leie), stm., Eur.	B9	14
Lys'va, Russia	F9	26
Lytle, Tx., U.S.	J8	116
Lytton, B.C., Can.	G13	102

M

Name	Map Ref.	Page
Ma, stm., Asia	D8	40
Maalaea Bay, b., Hi., U.S.	q17	125a
Ma'alot-Tarshiḥa, Isr.	B4	50
Ma'ān, Jord.	H5	50
Ma'anshan, China	D7	34
Maardu, Est.	B8	22
Ma'arrat an-Nu'mān, Syria	D4	48
Maas (Meuse), stm., Eur.	D5	10
Maaseik, Bel.	F8	12
Maasmechelen, Bel.	G8	12
Maastricht, Neth.	G8	12
Maave, Moz.	C12	66
Maba, China	C7	34
Mababe Depression, depr., Bots.	B7	66
Mabank, Tx., U.S.	G10	116
Mabaruma, Guy.	C13	84
Mabeleapodi, Bots.	C6	66
Mabel Lake, l., B.C., Can.	G16	102
Maben, Ms., U.S.	I7	114
Mabeul, Tun.	M5	18
Mableton, Ga., U.S.	F2	112
Mabou, N.S., Can.	F12	106
Mabrūk, Sud.	M5	60
Mabton, Wa., U.S.	D6	122
Mabuasehube Game Reserve, Bots.	E6	66
Mabuguai, China	F1	34
Macachín, Arg.	I7	80
Macaé, Braz.	G8	79
Macajuba, Braz.	B8	79
Macalister, B.C., Can.	E12	102
Macalister, stm., Austl.	K6	70
Macalister, Mount, mtn., Austl.	J8	70
Macallum Lake, l., Sask., Can.	C6	104
MacAlpine Lake, l., N.W. Ter., Can.	C12	96
Macão, Port.	F3	16
Macapá, Braz.	C8	76
Macará, Ec.	J3	84
Macarani, Braz.	C8	79
Macareo, Caño, mth., Ven.	C12	84
Macas, Ec.	I3	84
Macau, Braz.	E11	76
Macau (Aomen), Macao	M2	34
Macau, dep., Asia	G9	30
Macauã, stm., Braz.	C7	82
Macaúbas, Braz.	B7	79
Macaya, Pic, mtn., Haiti	E7	94
MacClenny, Fl., U.S.	I4	112
Macclesfield, Eng., U.K.	H11	8
Macdhui, Ben, mtn., Afr.	H8	66
Macdonald Range, mts., B.C., Can.	H20	102
MacDonnell Ranges, mts., Austl.	D6	68
MacDowell Lake, l., Ont., Can.	F22	104
Macduff, Scot., U.K.	D11	8
Macdui, Ben, mtn., Scot., U.K.	D10	8
Macedonia, hist. reg., Eur.	H6	20
Macedonia (Makedonija), ctry., Eur.	H5	20
Maceió, Braz.	E11	76
Macenta, Gui.	G5	64
Maceo, Col.	D5	84
Macerata, Italy	F8	18
MacFarlane, stm., Sask., Can.	E11	96
Macfarlane, Lake, l., Austl.	H2	70
MacGregor, Man., Can.	I16	104
Machacamarca, Bol.	H8	82
Machachi, Ec.	H3	84
Machačkala, Russia	I7	26
Machadinho, stm., Braz.	C10	82
Machado, Braz.	F6	79
Machado, stm., Braz.	C10	82
Machagai, Arg.	D8	80
Machakos, Kenya	B7	58
Machala, Ec.	I3	84
Machalí, Chile	H3	80
Machaneng, Bots.	D8	66
Machang, China	A7	32
Machangfu, China	B7	40
Machaquilá, stm., Guat.	A5	92
Machattie, Lake, l., Austl.	E3	70
Machecoul, Fr.	E5	14
Machias, Me., U.S.	C19	108
Machias, stm., Me., U.S.	C19	108
Machichi, stm., Man., Can.	B23	104
Machico, Port.	M21	17a
Machilīpatnam (Bandar), India	D6	46
Machiques, Ven.	B6	84
Machupicchu, Peru	E5	82
Machupicchu, hist., Peru	E5	82
Machupo, stm., Bol.	E9	82
Machynlleth, Wales, U.K.	I10	8
Maciá, Arg.	G9	80
Macintyre, stm., Austl.	G8	70
Macintyre, stm., Austl.	G9	70
Mackay, Austl.	C8	70
Mackay, Id., U.S.	G12	122
MacKay, stm., Alta., Can.	B2	104
Mackay, Lake, l., Austl.	D5	68
MacKay Lake, l., N.W. Ter., Can.	D10	96
Mackenzie, Guy.	D13	84
Mackenzie, stm., N.W. Ter., Can.	C6	96
Mackenzie Bay, b., Can.	B26	100
Mackenzie Delta, N.W. Ter., Can.	B27	100
Mackenzie Mountains, mts., Can.	D29	100
Mackinac, Straits of, strt., Mi., U.S.	E11	110
Mackinac Island, Mi., U.S.	E11	110
Mackinac Island, i., Mi., U.S.	E11	110
Mackinaw, Il., U.S.	J6	110
Mackinaw, stm., Il., U.S.	J6	110
Mackinaw City, Mi., U.S.	E11	110
Mackinnon Road, Kenya	B7	58
Macklin, Sask., Can.	F5	104
Macksville, Austl.	H10	70
Macksville, Ks., U.S.	M9	118
Maclean, Austl.	G10	70
Macleod, Lake, l., Austl.	D2	68
Maclovia Herrera, Mex.	C7	90
Macmillan, stm., Yukon, Can.	E27	100
Macomb, Il., U.S.	J5	110
Macomer, Italy	I3	18
Mâcon, Fr.	F11	14
Macon, Ga., U.S.	G3	112
Macon, Il., U.S.	C8	114
Macon, Ms., U.S.	I8	114
Macon, Mo., U.S.	C4	114
Macon, Bayou, stm., U.S.	J5	114
Macorís, Cabo, c., Dom. Rep.	E9	94
Macoun Lake, l., Sask., Can.	B11	104
Macquarie, stm., Austl.	M7	70
Macquarie, stm., Austl.	H7	70
Macquarie Harbour, b., Austl.	N6	70
Macquarie Island, i., Austl.	A8	73
Mac. Robertson Land, reg., Ant.	B5	73
Macroom, Ire.	J5	8
MacTier, Ont., Can.	E16	110
Macucuau, stm., Braz.	H12	84
Macuelizo, Hond.	B6	92
Macujer, Col.	G6	84
Macunqiao, China	B5	34
Macuro, Ven.	B12	84
Macusani, Peru	F6	82
Macuspana, Mex.	I13	90
Macusse, Ang.	A5	66
Mad, stm., Ca., U.S.	D2	124
Mad, stm., Oh., U.S.	H2	108
Mad, stm., Vt., U.S.	C14	108
Ma'dabā, Jord.	E5	50
Madagascar (Madagasikara), ctry., Afr.	E9	58
Madā'in Ṣāliḥ, Sau. Ar.	H4	48
Madame, Isle, i., N.S., Can.	G12	106
Madanapalle, India	F5	46
Madang, Pap. N. Gui.	m16	68a
Mādārīpur, Bngl.	I14	44
Madawaska, stm., Ont., Can.	E18	110
Maddaloni, Italy	H9	18
Maddock, N.D., U.S.	D8	118
Madeira, i., Port.	M21	17a
Madeira, stm., S.A.	E6	76
Madeira, Arquipélago da, is., Port.	M21	17a
Madeirinha, stm., Braz.	C11	82
Madeirinha, Paraná, mth., Braz.	I13	84
M'adel', Bela.	G9	22
Mädelegabel, mtn., Eur.	E17	14
Madeleine, Îles de la, is., Que., Can.	E12	106
Madeleine-Centre, Que., Can.	C8	106
Madelia, Mn., U.S.	F1	110
Madeline Island, i., Wi., U.S.	D5	110
Maden, Tur.	B5	48
Madera, Mex.	C5	90
Madera, Ca., U.S.	H5	124
Maderas, Volcán, vol., Nic.	F9	92
Madhubani, India	G12	44
Madhya Pradesh, state, India	I8	44
Madibogo, S. Afr.	F7	66
Madidi, stm., Bol.	E8	82
Madill, Ok., U.S.	E10	116
Madimba, Zaire	B3	58
Madina do Boé, Gui.-B.	F2	64
Madinani, I.C.	G6	64
Madīnat ash-Sha'b (Al-Ittihad), Yemen	H4	47
Madingou, Congo	B2	58
Madirobe, Madag.	P22	67b
Madison, Al., U.S.	H10	114
Madison, Fl., U.S.	I3	112
Madison, Ga., U.S.	F3	112
Madison, In., U.S.	D11	114
Madison, Ks., U.S.	M11	118
Madison, Me., U.S.	C17	108
Madison, Mn., U.S.	F11	118
Madison, Mo., U.S.	C4	114
Madison, Ne., U.S.	J10	118
Madison, N.C., U.S.	C7	112
Madison, Oh., U.S.	F5	108
Madison, S.D., U.S.	G10	118
Madison, Va., U.S.	I8	108
Madison, W.V., U.S.	I5	108
Madison, Wi., U.S.	G6	110
Madison, stm., U.S.	E14	122
Madison Heights, Va., U.S.	B7	112
Madison Range, mts., Mt., U.S.	E14	122
Madisonville, Ky., U.S.	E9	114
Madisonville, La., U.S.	L6	114
Madisonville, Tn., U.S.	D2	112
Madisonville, Tx., U.S.	I11	116
Madiun, Indon.	J15	39a
Madoc, Ont., Can.	F18	110
Madoi, China	E6	30
Madol, Sud.	M4	60
Madona, Lat.	E9	22
Madougou, Mali	D8	64
Madrakah, Sau. Ar.	D1	47
Madrakah, Ra's al-, c., Oman	E10	47
Madras, India	G11	42
Madras, Or., U.S.	F4	122
Madras see Tamil Nādu, state, India	G5	46
Madre, Laguna, b., Mex.	E11	90
Madre, Laguna, b., Tx., U.S.	M9	116
Madre, Sierra, mts., Phil.	M20	39b
Madre de Chiapas, Sierra, mts., N.A.	B2	92
Madre de Dios, dept., Peru	D6	82
Madre de Dios, stm., S.A.	D8	82
Madre de Dios, Isla, i., Chile	A12	73
Madre de Dios, Isla, i., Chile	J7	74
Madre del Sur, Sierra, mts., Mex.	I10	90
Madre Occidental, Sierra, mts., Mex.	E6	90
Madre Oriental, Sierra, mts., Mex.	F9	90
Madre Vieja, stm., Guat.	C3	92
Madrid, Col.	E5	84
Madrid, Spain	E8	16
Madrid, Al., U.S.	K11	114
Madrid, Ia., U.S.	I2	110
Madrid, Ne., U.S.	K6	118
Madrid, prov., Spain	E8	16
Madridejos, Spain	F8	16
Madriz, dept., Nic.	D8	92
Madsen, Ont., Can.	H21	104
Madura, i., Indon.	J16	39a
Madurai, India	H5	46
Maebashi, Japan	K14	36
Mae Hong Son, Thai.	E4	40
Mae Klong, stm., Thai.	G5	40
Maengsan, N. Kor.	D14	32
Mae Sariang, Thai.	E4	40
Maeser, Ut., U.S.	D7	120
Mae Sot, Thai.	F5	40
Maesteg, Wales, U.K.	J10	8
Maestra, Sierra, mts., Cuba	D6	94
Maevatanana, Madag.	P22	67b
Mafeking, Man., Can.	F13	104
Mafeteng, Leso.	G8	66
Maffra, Austl.	K7	70
Mafia Island, i., Tan.	C7	58
Mafikeng, Boph.	G5	58
Mafikeng, S. Afr.	E7	66
Mafra, Braz.	D14	80
Magadan, Russia	F22	28
Magadi, Kenya	B7	58
Magaguadavic Lake, l., N.B., Can.	G6	106
Magallanes, Phil.	O20	39b
Magallanes, Estrecho de (Strait of Magellan), strt., S.A.	G3	78
Magangué, Col.	C5	84
Magazine Mountain, mtn., Ar., U.S.	G3	114
Magburaka, S.L.	G4	64
Magdagači, Russia	G17	28
Magdalena, Arg.	H10	80
Magdalena, Bol.	E9	82
Magdalena, Mex.	G8	90
Magdalena, Peru	B3	82
Magdalena, N.M., U.S.	J9	120
Magdalena, dept., Col.	B5	84
Magdalena, stm., Col.	C5	84
Magdalena, stm., Mex.	B4	90
Magdalena, Bahía, b., Mex.	E3	90
Magdalena, Isla, i., Chile	E2	78
Magdalena, Isla, i., Mex.	E3	90
Magdalena, Punta, c., Col.	F4	84
Magdalena de Kino, Mex.	B4	90
Magdeburg, Ger.	C11	10
Magee, Ms., U.S.	K7	114
Magelang, Indon.	J15	39a
Magellan, Strait of see Magallanes, Estrecho de, strt., S.A.	G3	78
Magenta, Italy	D3	18
Maggia, Switz.	F10	13
Maggiore, Lago, l., Eur.	C3	18
Maghāghah, Egypt	C6	60
Maghama, Maur.	D3	64
Maghniyya, Alg.	C10	62
Magill Lake, l., Man., Can.	D20	104
Magione, Italy	F7	18
Magiss Lake, l., Ont., Can.	F23	104
Maglaj, Bos.	E2	20
Magnet, Man., Can.	G15	104
Magnitogorsk, Russia	G9	26
Magnolia, Ar., U.S.	I3	114
Magnolia, Mn., U.S.	H11	118
Magnolia, Ms., U.S.	K6	114
Magog, Que., Can.	B14	108
Magozal, Mex.	G11	90
Magpie, Que., Can.	B9	106
Magpie, stm., Que., Can.	B9	106
Magpie, Lac, l., Que., Can.	A9	106
Magpie Ouest, stm., Que., Can.	A8	106
Magrath, Alta., Can.	H22	102
Maguari, Cabo, c., Braz.	D9	76
Maguse Lake, l., N.W. Ter., Can.	D13	96
Maguzhan, China	E13	44
Magway, Burma	D3	40
Mahābād, Iran	C8	48
Mahābaleshwar, India	F9	42
Mahabe, Madag.	P21	67b
Mahābhārat Lek, mts., Nepal	F10	44
Mahabo, Madag.	S22	67b
Mahabo, Madag.	R21	67b
Mahaicony Village, Guy.	D14	84
Mahajamba, Helodranon' i, b., Madag.	O22	67b
Mahajanga, Madag.	O22	67b
Mahākālī (Sārda), stm., Asia	F9	44
Mahakam, stm., Indon.	E6	38
Mahalatswe, Bots.	D8	66
Maḥallāt, Iran	E11	48
Mahanoro, Madag.	Q23	67b
Mahanoy City, Pa., U.S.	G10	108
Mahārāshtra, state, India	C3	46
Maha Sarakham, Thai.	F7	40
Mahasoa, Madag.	S22	67b
Mahasolo, Madag.	Q22	67b
Mahates, Col.	B5	84
Mahatsinjo, Madag.	R21	67b
Maḥaṭṭat al-Ḥafīf, Jord.	D8	50
Mahbūbnagar, India	D4	46
Mahd adh-Dhahab, Sau. Ar.	C2	47
Mahdia, Tun.	N6	18
Mahe, India	G3	46
Mahébourg, Mrts.	V18	67c
Mahé Island, i., Sey.	B11	58
Mahendra Giri, mtn., India	C8	46
Mahesāna, India	I5	44
Mahia Peninsula, pen., N.Z.	C7	72
Mahnomen, Mn., U.S.	D12	118
Mahoba, India	H8	44
Mahomet, Il., U.S.	B8	114
Mahone Bay, N.S., Can.	H9	106
Mahone Bay, b., N.S., Can.	H9	106
Mahony Lake, l., N.W. Ter., Can.	D32	100
Mahood Falls, B.C., Can.	F14	102
Mahood Lake, l., B.C., Can.	F14	102
Mahres, Tun.	C16	62
Mahuva, India	B1	46
Mai Aini, Eth.	J10	60
Maicao, Col.	B6	84
Maîche, Fr.	E13	14
Maici, stm., Braz.	B11	82
Maicuru, stm., Braz.	D8	76
Maiden, N.C., U.S.	D5	112
Maidenhead, Eng., U.K.	J13	8
Maidstone, Sask., Can.	E5	104
Maidstone, Eng., U.K.	J14	8
Maiduguri, Nig.	F9	54
Maienfeld, Switz.	D12	13
Maigatari, Nig.	E14	64
Maignelay, Fr.	C9	14
Maillezais, Fr.	F6	14
Mai Mefales, Eth.	J10	60
Main, stm., Ger.	F9	10
Main Channel, strt., Ont., Can.	E14	110
Mai-Ndombe, Lac, l., Zaire	B3	58
Maine, hist. reg., Fr.	D6	14
Maine, state, U.S.	B13	98
Maine, Gulf of, b., N.A.	C13	98
Maine-et-Loire, dept., Fr.	E6	14
Mainhardt, Ger.	F9	10
Mainland, i., Scot., U.K.	B10	8
Mainland, i., Scot., U.K.	A12	8
Mainpuri, India	G8	44
Maintenon, Fr.	D8	14
Maintirano, Madag.	Q21	67b
Main Topsail, mtn., Newf., Can.	C17	106
Mainz, Ger.	E8	10
Maio, i., C.V.	m17	64a
Maipo, stm., Chile	G3	80
Maipo, Volcán, vol., S.A.	H4	80
Maipú, Arg.	I10	80
Maipú, Arg.	G4	80
Maipú, Chile	G3	80
Maiquetía, Ven.	B9	84
Mairipotaba, Braz.	D4	79
Maitengwe, Bots.	C8	66
Maitengwe, stm., Afr.	C8	66
Maitland, Austl.	J2	70
Maitland, Austl.	I9	70
Maitland, N.S., Can.	G10	106
Maíz, stm., Nic.	F10	92
Maíz, Islas del, is., Nic.	E11	92
Maizuru, Japan	L10	36
Maja, stm., Russia	F18	28
Majagual, Col.	C5	84
Majaki, Ukr.	C14	20
Majari, stm., Braz.	F12	84
Majé, Braz.	G7	79
Maji, Eth.	N8	60
Majia, China	C7	34
Majie, China	B7	40
Majja, Russia	E18	28
Majkain, Kaz.	G13	26
Majkop, Russia	I6	26
Majorca see Mallorca, i., Spain	F15	16
Maka, Sen.	E2	64
Makabana, Congo	B2	58
Makalamabedi, Bots.	C6	66
Makallé, Arg.	D9	80
Makālu, mtn., Asia	G12	44
Makanza, Zaire	A3	58
Makaoo Indian Reserve, Alta., Can.	E4	104
Makarjev, Russia	D26	22
Makarov, Russia	H20	28
Makarska, Cro.	F12	18
Makasar, Selat (Makassar Strait), strt., Indon.	F6	38
Makassar Strait see Makasar, Selat, strt., Indon.	F6	38
Makat, Kaz.	H8	26
Makawao, Hi., U.S.	q17	125a
Makedonija see Macedonia, ctry., Eur.	H5	20
Makejevka, Ukr.	H5	26
Makeni, S.L.	G3	64
Makgadikgadi, pl., Bots.	C7	66
Makgadikgadi Pans Game Reserve, Bots.	C7	66
Makhfar al-Quwayrah, Jord.	I4	50
Makhfar Ramn, Jord.	I4	50
Makhrūq, Wādī al-, val., Asia	F7	50
Makindu, Kenya	B7	58
Makinsk, Kaz.	G12	26
M'akiševo, Russia	E11	22
M'akit, Russia	E22	28
Makkah (Mecca), Sau. Ar.	D1	47
Makó, Hung.	I20	10
Makokou, Gabon	A2	58
Makoua, Congo	A3	58
Makrāna, India	G6	44
Makran Coast, Asia	I16	48
M'aksa, Russia	C21	22
Maksaticha, Russia	D18	22
Makthar, Tun.	N4	18
Mākū, Iran	B8	48
Makumbi, Zaire	C4	58
Makung (P'enghu), Tai.	L8	34
Makurdi, Nig.	H14	64
Makwa Lake, l., Sask., Can.	D5	104
Makwassie, S. Afr.	F8	66
Mal, Maur.	C3	64
Mala, Peru	E3	82
Mala, stm., Peru	E3	82
Mala, Punta, c., Pan.	D3	84
Malabang, Phil.	D7	38
Malabar Coast, India	F3	46
Malabo, Eq. Gui.	J14	64
Malacacheta, Braz.	D7	79
Malacca, Strait of, strt., Asia	M6	40
Malacky, Czech.	G17	10
Malad, stm., U.S.	C4	120
Malad City, Id., U.S.	H13	122
Málaga, Col.	D6	84
Málaga, Spain	I7	16
Malaga, N.M., U.S.	G2	116
Malagash, N.S., Can.	G10	106
Malagasy Republic see Madagascar, ctry., Afr.	E9	58
Malagón, Spain	F8	16
Malaimbandy, Madag.	R21	67b
Malaja Kuril'skaja Gr'ada (Habomai-Shotō), is., Russia	D21	36a
Malaja Višera, Russia	C15	22
Malakāl, Sud.	M6	60
Malakoff, Tx., U.S.	G10	116
Malān, Burma	B4	40
Malang, Indon.	J16	39a
Malanggwā, Nepal	G11	44
Malanje, Ang.	C3	58
Malanville, Benin	F11	64
Malanzán, Arg.	F5	80
Mälaren, l., Swe.	L15	6
Malargüe, Arg.	H4	80
Malaspina Glacier, Ak., U.S.	G24	100
Malaspina Strait, strt., B.C., Can.	H10	102
Malatya, Tur.	B5	48
Malaut, India	E6	44
Malawi, ctry., Afr.	D6	58
Malawi, Lake see Nyasa, Lake, l., Afr.	D6	58
Malaybalay, Phil.	D8	38
Malāyer, Iran	D10	48
Malay Peninsula, pen., Asia	K6	40
Malay Reef, rf., Austl.	A8	70
Malaysia, ctry., Asia	E3	38
Malazgirt, Tur.	B7	48
Malbaie, stm., Que., Can.	E3	106
Malbaie, La, b., Que., Can.	D9	106
Malbork, Pol.	A19	10
Malbrán, Arg.	E7	80
Malcolm, Austl.	E4	68
Malcolm Island, i., B.C., Can.	G7	102
Malcom, Ia., U.S.	I3	110
Maldegem, Bel.	F3	12
Malden, Mo., U.S.	F7	114
Maldive Islands, is., Mald.	I2	46
Maldives, ctry., Asia	I8	24
Maldonado, Ur.	H11	80
Malé, Italy	C5	18
Male, Mald.	I8	24
Maléa, Ákra, c., Grc.	M7	20
Mālegaon, India	B3	46
Malek, Sud.	N6	60
Malek Sīāh, Kūh-e, mtn., Asia	G16	48
Malema, Moz.	D7	58
Malen'ga, Russia	J25	6
Māler Kotla, India	E6	44
Malesherbes, Fr.	D9	14
Malestroit, Fr.	E4	14
Malha Wells, Sud.	J4	60
Malheur, stm., Or., U.S.	G8	122
Malheur Lake, l., Or., U.S.	G7	122
Mali, ctry., Afr.	E6	54
Mali, stm., Burma	A4	40
Maligne, stm., Alta., Can.	E17	102
Maligne Lake, l., Alta., Can.	E17	102
Malik, Wādī al-, val., Sud.	I6	60
Mali Kyun, i., Burma	H5	40
Malin, Or., U.S.	H4	122
Malinalco, hist., Mex.	H10	90
Malinaltepec, Mex.	I10	90
Malines (Mechelen), Bel.	F5	12
Malin Head, c., Ire.	F6	8
Maliwun, Burma	I5	40
Maljamar, N.M., U.S.	G3	116
Malka, Russia	G23	28
Malkāpur, India	B4	46
Malkara, Tur.	I10	20
Mallāḥ, Syria	C7	50
Mallaig, Alta., Can.	C23	102
Mallaig, Scot., U.K.	D8	8
Mallala, Austl.	J3	70
Mallaoua, Niger	E14	64
Mallawī, Egypt	D6	60
Mallery Lake, l., N.W. Ter., Can.	D13	96
Mallet, Braz.	C13	80
Malligasta, Arg.	E5	80
Mallnitz, Aus.	I13	10
Mallorca, i., Spain	F15	16
Mallow, Ire.	I5	8
Malmédy, Bel.	H9	12
Malmesbury, S. Afr.	I4	66
Malmö, Swe.	N13	6
Malmöhus Län, co., Swe.	N13	6
Maloarchangel'sk, Russia	I19	22
Maloja, Switz.	F12	13
Malojaroslavec, Russia	F19	22
Maloje Kozino, Russia	E26	22
Maloje Skuratovo, Russia	H20	22
Malolos, Phil.	N19	39b
Malone, Fl., U.S.	I1	112
Malone, N.Y., U.S.	C12	108
Malonga, Zaire	D4	58
Małopolska, reg., Pol.	E21	10
Malošujka, Russia	E5	26
Måløy, Nor.	K9	6
Malpaisillo, Nic.	E8	92
Malpas, Austl.	J4	70
Malpelo, Isla de, i., Col.	C2	76
Malpeque Bay, b., P.E.I., Can.	F10	106
Malta, Lat.	E10	22
Malta, Mt., U.S.	B18	122
Malta, Oh., U.S.	H5	108
Malta, ctry., Eur.	H10	4
Malta, i., Malta	N9	18
Malta Channel, strt., Eur.	M9	18
Maltahöhe, Nmb.	E3	66
Maltepe, Tur.	I11	20
Maluku (Moluccas), is., Indon.	F8	38
Maluku, Laut (Molucca Sea), Indon.	F7	38

Name	Map Ref.	Page
Labrador, reg., Newf., Can.	F20	96
Labrador City, Newf., Can.	F19	96
Labrador Sea, N.A.	E22	96
Lábrea, Braz.	E6	76
Lábrea, Braz.	B9	82
Labrieville, Réserve, Que., Can.	C4	106
Labrit, Fr.	H6	14
La Broquerie, Man., Can.	I18	104
Labutta, Burma	F3	40
Labytnangi, Russia	D11	26
Lača, ozero, l., Russia	K26	6
Laca Jahuira, stm., Bol.	H8	82
La Cal, stm., Bol.	G12	82
La Calera, Chile	G3	80
Lac-Allard, Que., Can.	B10	106
La Campana, Spain	H6	16
La Canada, Ca., U.S.	J7	124
La Candelaria, Arg.	D6	80
Lacantún, stm., Mex.	I14	90
La Capelle [-en-Thierache], Fr.	C10	14
Lacapelle-Marival, Fr.	H8	14
La Carlota, Arg.	G7	80
La Carolina, Spain	G8	16
Lacaune, Fr.	I9	14
Laccadive Islands see Lakshadweep, is., India	G2	46
Lac du Flambeau, Wi., U.S.	E6	110
La Ceiba, Hond.	B8	92
La Ceiba, Ven.	C7	84
La Center, Ky., U.S.	E8	114
Lac-Etchemin, Que., Can.	F3	106
Lacey, Wa., U.S.	C3	122
Lac-Frontière, Que., Can.	F3	106
La Chambre, Fr.	G13	14
La Chapelle-d'Angillon, Fr.	E9	14
La Chartre-sur-le-Loir, Fr.	E7	14
La Châtaigneraie, Fr.	F6	14
La Chaux-de-Fonds, Switz.	D6	13
Lachay, Punta, c., Peru	D3	82
Lachdenpochja, Russia	K22	6
Lachen, Switz.	D10	13
Lachhmangarh Sīkar, India	G6	44
Lachine, Que., Can.	B13	108
Lachkaltsap Indian Reserve, B.C., Can.	B5	102
Lachlan, stm., Austl.	J6	70
La Chorrera, Col.	H6	84
La Chorrera, Pan.	C3	84
L'achoviči, Bela.	H9	22
L'achovskije ostrova, is., Russia	C20	28
Lachute, Que., Can.	B12	108
Lachva, Bela.	I10	22
La Ciénaga, Arg.	D5	80
La Ciotat, Fr.	I12	14
La Citadelle, hist., Haiti	E8	94
La Ciudad, Mex.	F7	90
Lackawanna, N.Y., U.S.	E8	108
Lac la Biche, Alta., Can.	C23	102
Lac la Hache, B.C., Can.	F13	102
Lac la Ronge Provincial Park, Sask., Can.	C10	104
Laclede, Id., U.S.	I18	102
Laclede, Mo., U.S.	C3	114
La Clotilde, Arg.	D8	80
Lac-Mégantic, Que., Can.	B16	108
La Cocha, Arg.	D6	80
La Colorada, Mex.	C4	90
La Coma, Mex.	E10	90
Lacombe, Alta., Can.	E21	102
Lacombe, La., U.S.	L7	114
Lacon, Il., U.S.	I6	110
Lacona, Ia., U.S.	I2	110
La Concepción, Pan.	C1	84
La Concepción, Ven.	B7	84
Laconia, N.H., U.S.	D15	108
La Conner, Wa., U.S.	B3	122
La Consulta, Arg.	G4	80
Lacoochee, Fl., U.S.	K4	112
La Coruña, Spain	B3	16
La Coste, Tx., U.S.	J8	116
Lac qui Parle, stm., Mn., U.S.	G11	118
La Crescent, Mn., U.S.	G4	110
La Crosse, In., U.S.	A10	114
La Crosse, Ks., U.S.	M8	118
La Crosse, Va., U.S.	C8	112
Lacrosse, Wa., U.S.	D8	122
La Crosse, Wi., U.S.	G4	110
La Crosse, stm., Wi., U.S.	G4	110
La Cruz, Arg.	E10	80
La Cruz, Col.	G4	84
La Cruz, C.R.	F9	92
La Cruz, Ur.	G10	80
La Cruz, Cerro, mtn., Mex.	I9	90
La Cruz de Río Grande, Nic.	D10	92
Lac Seul, Ont., Can.	H22	104
Lac Seul Indian Reserve, Ont., Can.	H22	104
La Cuesta, C.R.	I12	92
La Cumbre, Arg.	F6	80
La Cygne, Ks., U.S.	M13	118
Ladainha, Braz.	D8	79
Ladākh Range, mts., Asia	C7	44
Ladário, Braz.	H13	82
Ladd, Il., U.S.	I6	110
Laddonia, Mo., U.S.	C5	114
La Désirade, i., Guad.	F14	94
La Digue, i., Sey.	B11	58
Ladismith, S. Afr.	I5	66
Lādīz, Iran	G16	48
Lādnūn, India	G6	44
Ladoga, In., U.S.	C10	114
Ladoga, Lake see Ladožskoje ozero, l., Russia	E4	26
Ladonia, Tx., U.S.	F11	116
La Dorada, Col.	E5	84
La Dormida, Arg.	G5	80
Ladožskoje Ozero, Russia	A14	22
Ladožskoje ozero (Lake Ladoga), l., Russia	E4	26
Ladson, S.C., U.S.	G6	112
Ladue, stm., N.A.	E24	100
Laduškin, Russia	G3	22
Ladva-Vetka, Russia	K24	6
L'ady, Russia	C11	22
Lady Ann Strait, strt., N.W. Ter., Can.	A16	96
Ladybrand, S. Afr.	G8	66
Lady Elliot Island, i., Austl.	E10	70
Ladysmith, B.C., Can.	I11	102
Ladysmith, S. Afr.	G9	66
Ladysmith, Wi., U.S.	E4	110
Lae, Pap. N. Gui.	m16	68a
La Encantada, Mex.	E9	90
La Esmeralda, Mex.	D8	90
La Esmeralda, Para.	B7	80
La Esmeralda, Ven.	F10	84
La Esperanza, Cuba	C3	94
La Esperanza, Hond.	C6	92
La Estrella, Bol.	G10	82
La Falda, Arg.	F6	80
La Farge, Wi., U.S.	G5	110
Lafayette, Al., U.S.	J11	114
Lafayette, Ca., U.S.	G3	124
Lafayette, Co., U.S.	L2	118
Lafayette, Ga., U.S.	E1	112
Lafayette, In., U.S.	B10	114
Lafayette, La., U.S.	L4	114
Lafayette, Mn., U.S.	F1	110
Lafayette, Tn., U.S.	F10	114
La Fé, Cuba	D3	94
La Fère, Fr.	C10	14
La Feria, Tx., U.S.	M9	116
La Ferté-Bernard, Fr.	D7	14
La Ferté-Gaucher, Fr.	D10	14
La Ferté-Macé, Fr.	D6	14
La Ferté-Saint-Aubin, Fr.	E8	14
Lafia, Nig.	G14	64
Lafleche, Sask., Can.	I8	104
La Flèche, Fr.	E6	14
La Florida, Guat.	I14	90
Lafnitz, stm., Eur.	H16	10
La Follette, Tn., U.S.	C2	112
La Fontaine, In., U.S.	B11	114
Lafourche, Bayou, stm., La., U.S.	M6	114
La Fragua, Arg.	D6	80
La Francia, Arg.	F7	80
La Fría, Ven.	C6	84
La Galite, i., Tun.	L3	18
La Gallareta, Arg.	E8	80
Lagangzong, China	F14	44
Lagarto, C.R.	G10	92
Lagawe, Phil.	M19	39b
Lage, China	F11	44
Lågen, stm., Nor.	K11	6
Lågen, stm., Nor.	K12	6
Lages, Braz.	D13	80
Lage Zwaluwe, Neth.	E6	12
Laghouat, Alg.	D12	62
La Gleize, Bel.	H8	12
La Gloria, Col.	C6	84
Lagoa da Prata, Braz.	F6	79
Lagoa Formosa, Braz.	E5	79
Lagoa Santa, Braz.	E7	79
Lagoa Vermelha, Braz.	E13	80
Lagolândia, Braz.	C4	79
Lagos, Nig.	H11	64
Lagos, Port.	H3	16
Lagos de Moreno, Mex.	G9	90
La Gouèra, W. Sah.	J2	62
La Goulette, Tun.	M5	18
La Grand'Combe, Fr.	H11	14
La Grande, Or., U.S.	E7	122
La Grande Deux, Réservoir, res., Que., Can.	F17	96
La Grande Quatre, Réservoir, res., Que., Can.	F18	96
La Grange, Austl.	C4	68
La Grange, Ga., U.S.	F1	112
Lagrange, In., U.S.	A11	114
La Grange, Ky., U.S.	D11	114
La Grange, Mo., U.S.	B5	114
La Grange, N.C., U.S.	D9	112
La Grange, Tx., U.S.	J10	116
Lagrange, Wy., U.S.	J3	118
La Gran Sabana, pl., Ven.	E12	84
La Grita, Ven.	C7	84
Lagu, China	A6	40
La Guadeloupe (Saint-Évariste), Que., Can.	B16	108
La Guajira, dept., Col.	B6	84
La Guajira, Península de, pen., S.A.	A7	84
La Guardia, Arg.	E6	80
La Guardia, Bol.	G10	82
La Guardia, Spain	D3	16
La Guerche-de-Bretagne, Fr.	E5	14
La Guerche-sur-l'Aubois, Fr.	F9	14
Laguna, Braz.	E14	80
Laguna, N.M., U.S.	I9	120
Laguna, Ilha da, i., Braz.	D8	76
Laguna Beach, Ca., U.S.	K8	124
Laguna Larga, Arg.	F7	80
Laguna Limpia, Arg.	D9	80
Laguna Paiva, Arg.	F8	80
Lagunas, Peru	A4	82
Lagunas de Chacagua, Parque Nacional, Mex.	I11	90
Lagunas de Montebello, Parque Nacional, Mex.	A3	92
Lagunillas, Bol.	H10	82
Lagunillas, Ven.	C7	84
Lagunillás, Laguna, l., Peru	F6	82
Laguntara, b., Hond.	B10	92
La Habana (Havana), Cuba	C3	94
Lahaina, Hi., U.S.	q17	125a
La Harpe, Il., U.S.	J5	110
La Harpe, Ks., U.S.	N12	118
Lahat, Indon.	F3	38
LaHave, stm., N.S., Can.	H9	106
La Haye-du-Puits, Fr.	C5	14
La Higuera, Chile	E3	80
Lahij, Yemen	H4	47
Lāhījān, Iran	C11	48
Lahnstein, Ger.	E7	10
Lahontan Reservoir, res., Nv., U.S.	E6	124
Lahore, Pak.	E6	44
La Horqueta, Col.	F6	84
Lahr, Ger.	G7	10
Lahri, Pak.	F3	44
Lahti, Fin.	K19	6
La Huaca, Peru	A1	82
La Huacana, Mex.	H9	90
La Huerta, N.M., U.S.	G2	116
Laibin, China	C10	40
Lai Chau, Viet.	C7	40
Laifang, China	J5	34
L'Aigle, Fr.	D7	14
Laignes, Fr.	E11	14
La Independencia, Bahía de, b., Peru	F3	82
Laingsburg, S. Afr.	I5	66
Laingsburg, Mi., U.S.	H11	110
La Inmaculada, Mex.	C4	90
Laird Hill, Tx., U.S.	J2	114
Laishan, China	F9	32
Laishui, China	D3	32
Laiwu, China	G5	32
Laiyang, China	G8	32
Laizhou Wan (Laichow Bay), b., China	F7	32
Laja, stm., Chile	I3	80
Laja, Laguna de la, l., Chile	I3	80
Laja, Salto del, wtfl, Chile	I3	80
La Jalca, Peru	B3	82
La Jara, Co., U.S.	G11	120
La Jara Canyon, val., N.M., U.S.	H9	120
Lajas, Cuba	C4	94
Laje, Braz.	B9	79
Lajeado, Braz.	E13	80
Lajes, Braz.	E11	76
Lajinha, Braz.	F8	79
La Jolla, Ca., U.S.	L8	124
Lajord, Sask., Can.	H10	104
Lajosmizse, Hung.	H19	10
La Joya, Peru	G6	82
La Junta, Co., U.S.	N4	118
Lakamané, Mali	D5	64
Lake, Ms., U.S.	J7	114
Lake Alfred, Fl., U.S.	K5	112
Lake Andes, S.D., U.S.	H9	118
Lake Arthur, La., U.S.	L4	114
Lake Arthur, N.M., U.S.	G2	116
Lake Benton, Mn., U.S.	G11	118
Lake Brownwood, Tx., U.S.	H7	116
Lake Butler, Fl., U.S.	I4	112
Lake Cargelligo, Austl.	I7	70
Lake Carmel, N.Y., U.S.	F13	108
Lake Charles, La., U.S.	L3	114
Lake City, Ar., U.S.	G6	114
Lake City, Co., U.S.	F9	120
Lake City, Fl., U.S.	I4	112
Lake City, Ia., U.S.	I13	118
Lake City, Mi., U.S.	F10	110
Lake City, Mn., U.S.	F3	110
Lake City, Pa., U.S.	E6	108
Lake City, S.C., U.S.	F7	112
Lake City, Tn., U.S.	C2	112
Lake Cowichan, B.C., Can.	I10	102
Lake Crystal, Mn., U.S.	F1	110
Lake Dallas, Tx., U.S.	F9	116
Lake Delton, Wi., U.S.	G6	110
Lake Elsinore, Ca., U.S.	K8	124
Lakefield, Ont., Can.	F17	110
Lakefield, Mn., U.S.	H12	118
Lakefield National Park, Austl.	C8	68
Lake Forest, Fl., U.S.	N6	112
Lake Forest, Il., U.S.	H8	110
Lake Fork, stm., Ut., U.S.	D6	120
Lake Geneva, Wi., U.S.	H7	110
Lake George, N.Y., U.S.	D13	108
Lake Harbor, Fl., U.S.	M6	112
Lake Harbour, N.W. Ter., Can.	D19	96
Lake Havasu City, Az., U.S.	J2	120
Lake Helen, Fl., U.S.	K5	112
Lakehurst, N.J., U.S.	G12	108
Lake Isabella, Ca., U.S.	I7	124
Lake Jackson, Tx., U.S.	J11	116
Lakeland, Fl., U.S.	K5	112
Lakeland, Ga., U.S.	H3	112
Lake Linden, Mi., U.S.	C7	110
Lake Louise, Alta., Can.	F18	102
Lake Mills, Ia., U.S.	G2	110
Lake Mills, Wi., U.S.	G7	110
Lakemont, Pa., U.S.	G8	108
Lake Nash, Austl.	C2	70
Lake Norden, S.D., U.S.	G10	118
Lake Odessa, Mi., U.S.	H10	110
Lake Oswego, Or., U.S.	E3	122
Lake Ozark, Mo., U.S.	D4	114
Lake Park, Fl., U.S.	M6	112
Lake Park, Ia., U.S.	H12	118
Lake Park, Mn., U.S.	E11	118
Lake Placid, Fl., U.S.	L5	112
Lake Placid, N.Y., U.S.	C13	108
Lake Pleasant, N.Y., U.S.	D12	108
Lakeport, Ca., U.S.	E3	124
Lakeport, Mi., U.S.	G13	110
Lake Preston, S.D., U.S.	G10	118
Lake Providence, La., U.S.	J5	114
Lakes District, Wa., U.S.	C3	122
Lakeshore, Ms., U.S.	L7	114
Lakeside, N.S., Can.	H10	106
Lakeside, Az., U.S.	J7	120
Lakeside, Ca., U.S.	L9	124
Lakeside, Mt., U.S.	B11	122
Lakeside, Or., U.S.	G1	122
Lake Stevens, Wa., U.S.	B3	122
Laketown, Ut., U.S.	C5	120
Lake View, Ar., U.S.	H6	114
Lakeview, Ga., U.S.	E1	112
Lake View, Ia., U.S.	I12	118
Lakeview, Mi., U.S.	H10	110
Lakeview, Mi., U.S.	G10	110
Lake View, N.Y., U.S.	E8	108
Lakeview, Oh., U.S.	G3	108
Lakeview, Or., U.S.	H5	122
Lake View, S.C., U.S.	E7	112
Lakeview, Tx., U.S.	M3	114
Lakeview, Tx., U.S.	E6	116
Lakeview Mountain, mtn., B.C., Can.	H14	102
Lake Village, Ar., U.S.	I5	114
Lakeville, Mn., U.S.	F2	110
Lake Wales, Fl., U.S.	L5	112
Lake Wilson, Mn., U.S.	H12	118
Lakewood, Co., U.S.	E11	120
Lakewood, N.J., U.S.	G12	108
Lakewood, N.Y., U.S.	E7	108
Lakewood, Oh., U.S.	F5	108
Lakewood, Wi., U.S.	E7	110
Lakewood Park, N.D., U.S.	C9	118
Lake Worth, Fl., U.S.	M6	112
Lakhīmpur, India	G9	44
Lakhish, val., Asia	E3	50
Lakin, Ks., U.S.	N6	118
Lakinsk, Russia	E22	22
Lakonikós Kólpos, b., Grc.	M6	20
Lakota, Ia., U.S.	H13	118
Lakota, N.D., U.S.	C9	118
Lakshadweep, ter., India	H2	46
Lakshadweep, is., India	G2	46
Lakshadweep Sea, Asia	H3	46
La Lajilla, Mex.	D10	90
L'Albufera, l., Spain	F11	16
La Leonesa, Arg.	D9	80
Lalibela, Eth.	K10	60
La Libertad, El Sal.	D5	92
La Libertad, Guat.	I14	90
La Libertad, Hond.	C7	92
La Libertad, Nic.	E9	92
La Libertad, dept., Peru	B2	82
La Ligua, Chile	G3	80
La Lima, Hond.	B7	92
La Línea, Spain	I6	16
Lalitpur, India	H8	44
Lālmanir Hāt, Bngl.	H13	44
La Loche, Sask., Can.	B5	104
La Loche, stm., Sask., Can.	B5	104
La Loche, Lac, l., Sask., Can.	B5	104
La Loupe, Fr.	D8	14
Lalupon, Nig.	H12	64
La Luz, Mex.	E11	90
La Luz, Nic.	D10	92
La Luz, N.M., U.S.	L11	120
Lama, ozero, l., Russia	D16	26
La Macarena, Serranía de, mts., Col.	F6	84
La Maddalena, Italy	H4	18
Lamadong, China	C7	32
La Madrid, Arg.	D6	80
La Malbaie, Que., Can.	E3	106
Lamaline, Newf., Can.	F18	106
La Mancha, reg., Spain	G8	16
Lamar, Co., U.S.	M5	118
Lamar, Mo., U.S.	E2	114
Lamar, S.C., U.S.	E6	112
Lamar, stm., Wy., U.S.	F16	122
Lamarche, Fr.	D12	14
La Mariscala, Ur.	H11	80
Lamarque, Arg.	J6	80
La Marque, Tx., U.S.	J12	116
La Marsa, Tun.	M5	18
Lamas, Peru	B3	82
La Masica, Hond.	B7	92
Lamastre, Fr.	H11	14
Lamballe, Fr.	D4	14
Lambaréné, Gabon	B2	58
Lambari, stm., Braz.	F6	79
Lambayeque, Peru	B2	82
Lambayeque, dept., Peru	B1	82
Lambayeque, stm., Peru	B2	82
Lambert, Ms., U.S.	H6	114
Lambert, Mt., U.S.	D3	118
Lambert Glacier, Ant.	C5	73
Lambert's Bay, S. Afr.	I4	66
Lambertville, N.J., U.S.	G12	108
Lambeth, Ont., Can.	H14	110
Lambomakondro, Madag.	S21	67b
Lambrama, Peru	E5	82
Lambton, Cape, c., N.W. Ter., Can.	B8	96
Lame Deer, Mt., U.S.	E19	122
La Media Luna, Arrecifes de, rf., Hond.	B12	92
La Mendieta, Arg.	C6	80
Lamèque, N.B., Can.	E9	106
Lamèque, Île, i., N.B., Can.	E9	106
La Merced, Arg.	E6	80
La Merced, Arg.	C6	80
La Merced, Peru	D4	82
La Mesa, Pan.	I13	92
La Mesa, Ca., U.S.	L8	124
La Mesa, N.M., U.S.	L10	120
Lamesa, Tx., U.S.	G5	116
Lamía, Grc.	K6	20
L'amin, stm., Russia	E12	26
Lamine, stm., Mo., U.S.	D4	114
Lamming Mills, B.C., Can.	D14	102
La Moille, Il., U.S.	I6	110
Lamoille, Nv., U.S.	D10	124
Lamoille, stm., Vt., U.S.	C14	108
La Moine, stm., Il., U.S.	B6	114
Lamon Bay, b., Phil.	N19	39b
Lamoni, Ia., U.S.	J2	110
Lamont, Alta., Can.	D22	102
Lamont, Ca., U.S.	I7	124
Lamont, Ia., U.S.	H4	110
Lamont, Ok., U.S.	C9	116
La Monte, Mo., U.S.	D3	114
La Mosquitia, hist. reg., Hond.	B11	92
La Mothe, Lac, res., Que., Can.	D2	106
La Mothe-Achard, Fr.	F5	14
Lamotte-Beuvron, Fr.	E9	14
La Moure, N.D., U.S.	E9	118
Lampa, Peru	F6	82
Lampang, Thai.	E5	40
Lampasas, Tx., U.S.	H8	116
Lampasas, stm., Tx., U.S.	H8	116
Lampazos de Naranjo, Mex.	D9	90
Lampedusa, Isola di, i., Italy	N7	18
Lamphun, Thai.	E5	40
Lampman, Sask., Can.	I12	104
Lamud, Peru	B3	82
La Muerte, Cerro, mtn., C.R.	H11	92
Lana, Italy	C6	18
Lanai, i., Hi., U.S.	q17	125a
Lanai City, Hi., U.S.	q17	125a
Lanalhue, Lago, l., Chile	I2	80
Lanark, Ont., Can.	E19	110
Lanark, Il., U.S.	H6	110
Lanbi Kyun, i., Burma	I5	40
Lancashire, co., Eng., U.K.	H11	8
Lancaster, Ont., Can.	B12	108
Lancaster, Eng., U.K.	G11	8
Lancaster, Ca., U.S.	J7	124
Lancaster, Ky., U.S.	B2	112
Lancaster, Mn., U.S.	C11	118
Lancaster, Mo., U.S.	B4	114
Lancaster, N.H., U.S.	C15	108
Lancaster, N.Y., U.S.	E8	108
Lancaster, Oh., U.S.	H4	108
Lancaster, Pa., U.S.	G10	108
Lancaster, S.C., U.S.	E6	112
Lancaster, Tx., U.S.	G10	116
Lancaster, Va., U.S.	B10	112
Lancaster, Wi., U.S.	H5	110
Lancaster Sound, strt., N.W. Ter., Can.	B16	96
Lance Creek, Wy., U.S.	A12	120
Lanciano, Italy	G9	18
Lančin, Ukr.	A8	20
Lancones, Peru	J2	84
Lancun, China	G8	32
Łańcut, Pol.	E22	10
Lancy, Switz.	F5	13
Landau, Ger.	F8	10
Landau an der Isar, Ger.	G12	10
Landeck, Aus.	H10	10
Landen, Bel.	G7	12
Lander, Wy., U.S.	B8	120
Landerneau, Fr.	D2	14
Landes, dept., Fr.	H6	14
Landete, Spain	F10	16
Landing Lake, l., Man., Can.	C17	104
Landis, Sask., Can.	F6	104
Landis, N.C., U.S.	D6	112
Landivisiau, Fr.	D2	14
Lando, S.C., U.S.	E5	112
Land O'Lakes, Wi., U.S.	D6	110
Landquart, Switz.	E12	13
Landrum, S.C., U.S.	D4	112
Landsberg [am Lech], Ger.	G10	10
Land's End, c., Eng., U.K.	K8	8
Landshut, Ger.	G12	10
Landskrona, Swe.	N13	6
La Negra, Chile	B3	80
Lanesboro, Mn., U.S.	G4	110
Lanett, Al., U.S.	J11	114
Lanezi Lake, l., B.C., Can.	D14	102
Lang, Sask., Can.	I10	104
Langano, Lake, l., Eth.	N10	60
Langara Island, i., B.C., Can.	C1	102
Langarūd, Iran	C11	48
Langbank, Sask., Can.	H12	104
Lang Bay, B.C., Can.	H10	102
Langdale, Al., U.S.	G1	112
Langdon, N.D., U.S.	C9	118
Langeac, Fr.	G10	14
Langeais, Fr.	E7	14
Langenburg, Sask., Can.	H13	104
Langenhagen, Ger.	C9	10
Langenthal, Switz.	D8	13
Langford, S.D., U.S.	F10	118
Langham, Sask., Can.	F8	104
Langholm, Scot., U.K.	F10	8
Langley, B.C., Can.	H12	102
Langley, Ok., U.S.	C11	116
Langley, S.C., U.S.	F5	112
Langlo, stm., Austl.	E6	70
Langlois, Or., U.S.	H1	122
Langnau, Switz.	E8	13
Langogne, Fr.	H10	14
Langon, Fr.	H6	14
Langøya, i., Nor.	G14	6
Langqiao, China	E7	34
Langres, Fr.	E12	14
Langruth, Man., Can.	H16	104
Langsa, Indon.	L4	40
Lang Son, Viet.	D9	40
Langtian, China	J2	34
Langue, Hond.	D7	92
Languedoc, hist. reg., Fr.	I9	14
Langui Layo, Laguna de, l., Peru	F6	82
L'Anguille, stm., Ar., U.S.	G6	114
Langxi, China	D8	34
Langzhong, China	E8	30
Lanigan, Sask., Can.	G9	104
Lanigan Creek, stm., Sask., Can.	G9	104
Lankou, China	L4	34
Lannemezan, Fr.	I7	14
Lannilis, Fr.	D2	14
Lannion, Fr.	D3	14
L'Annonciation, Que., Can.	A12	108
Lanquín, Guat.	B5	92
L'Anse, Mi., U.S.	D7	110
L'Anse-aux-Meadows National Historic Park, Newf., Can.	A18	106
Lansford, N.D., U.S.	C6	118
Lansing, Ia., U.S.	G4	110
Lansing, Ks., U.S.	L13	118
Lansing, Mi., U.S.	E2	108
Lanslebourg, Fr.	G13	14
Lantana, Fl., U.S.	M6	112
Lantang, China	L3	34
Lantau Island, i., H.K.	M2	34
Lantsch, Switz.	E12	13
Lanusei, Italy	J4	18
Lanxi, China	F8	34
Lanzarote, i., Spain	N27	17b
Lanzhou, China	D7	30
Laoag, Phil.	L19	39b
Lao Cai, Viet.	C7	40
Laochang, China	B8	40
Laoge, China	C8	34
Laoha, stm., China	A7	32
Laois, co., Ire.	I6	8
Laojie, China	B5	40
La Oliva, Spain	O27	17b
Laon, Fr.	C10	14
Laona, Wi., U.S.	E7	110
La Orchila, Isla, i., Ven.	B10	84
La Orchila, Isla, i., Ven.	I11	94
La Orotava, Spain	O24	17b
La Oroya, Peru	D4	82
Laos (Lao), ctry., Asia	B3	38
Laoxinkou, China	E1	34
Laoyingpan, China	I4	34
Laozishan, China	B7	34
Lapa, Braz.	C14	80
Lapalisse, Fr.	F10	14
La Palma, Col.	E5	84
La Palma, El Sal.	C5	92
La Palma, Pan.	D2	84
La Palma, Pan.	C3	84
La Palma, i., Spain	O23	17b
La Palma del Condado, Spain	H5	16
La Paloma, Ur.	H11	80
La Pampa, prov., Arg.	I5	80
La Paragua, Ven.	D11	84
La Pasión, Río de, stm., Guat.	I14	90
La Paz, Arg.	F9	80
La Paz, Arg.	G5	80
La Paz, Bol.	G7	82
La Paz, Col.	B6	84
La Paz, Hond.	C7	92
La Paz, Mex.	E4	90
La Paz, Mex.	F9	90
La Paz, Ur.	H10	80
La Paz, dept., Bol.	F7	82
La Paz, dept., Hond.	C7	92
La Paz, Bahía de, b., Mex.	E4	90
La Paz, Río de, stm., Bol.	G8	82
La Paz Centro, Nic.	E8	92
La Pedrera, Col.	H8	84
Lapeer, Mi., U.S.	G12	110
La Perla, Mex.	C7	90
La Perouse Strait (Sōya-kaikyō), strt., Asia	B17	36a
La Pesca, Mex.	F11	90
La Piedad de Cabadas, Mex.	G8	90
La Pine, Or., U.S.	G4	122
Lapin lääni, prov., Fin.	H20	6
Lapinlahti, Fin.	J20	6
La Pintada, Pan.	I14	92
Lapland, hist. reg., Eur.	H18	6
La Plata, Arg.	H10	80
La Plata, Col.	F5	84
La Plata, Md., U.S.	I10	108
La Plata, Mo., U.S.	B4	114
La Plata, stm., U.S.	H8	120
La Plata Peak, mtn., Co., U.S.	E10	120
La Plonge Indian Reserve, Sask., Can.	C7	104
La Pobla de Segur, Spain	C12	16
La Pocatière, Que., Can.	E3	106
La Poile, Newf., Can.	E15	106
La Poile Bay, b., Newf., Can.	E15	106
Laporte, Co., U.S.	D11	120
La Porte, In., U.S.	A10	114
Laporte, Pa., U.S.	F10	108
La Porte City, Ia., U.S.	H3	110
La Potherie, Lac, l., Que., Can.	E18	96
La Poza Grande, Mex.	E3	90
Lappeenranta, Fin.	K21	6
Lappfjärd (Lapväärtti), Fin.	J17	6
La Presa, stm., Mex.	E4	90
Laprida, Arg.	E6	80
Laprida, Arg.	I8	80
La Pryor, Tx., U.S.	K7	116
Lâpseki, Tur.	I10	20
Laptev Sea see Laptevych, more, Russia	B17	28
Laptevych, more (Laptev Sea), Russia	B17	28
La Puebla de Cazalla, Spain	H6	16
La Puebla de Montalbán, Spain	F7	16
La Puerta, Arg.	E6	80
La Purísima, Mex.	D3	90
Lăpuș, Rom.	B8	20
Lapwai, Id., U.S.	D9	122
La Quiaca, Arg.	B6	80
La Quiaca, Arg.	J9	82
L'Aquila, Italy	G8	18
Lār, Iran	H13	48
Lara, state, Ven.	B8	84
Larache, Mor.	J5	16
Laragne-Montéglin, Fr.	H12	14
Laramate, Peru	F4	82
Laramie, Wy., U.S.	C11	120
Laramie, stm., U.S.	B12	120
Laramie Mountains, mts., Wy., U.S.	B11	120
Laranjal, stm., Braz.	G1	79
Laranjal, Braz.	F7	79
Laranjeiras do Sul, Braz.	C12	80
Laraos, Peru	E4	82
Larap, Phil.	N20	39b
La Raya, Abra, Peru	F6	82
L'Arbresle, Fr.	G11	14
Larche, Col de, Eur.	H13	14
Larchwood, Ia., U.S.	H11	118
Lardeau, B.C., Can.	G18	102
L'Ardoise, N.S., Can.	G13	106
Laredo, Spain	B8	16
Laredo, Tx., U.S.	L7	116
Laredo Sound, strt., B.C., Can.	E6	102
La Reforma, Mex.	E5	90
La Réole, Fr.	H6	14
Lares, Peru	E5	82
La Restinga, Spain	P23	17b
Largo, Fl., U.S.	L4	112
Largo, Cañon, val., N.M., U.S.	H9	120
Largo, Cayo, i., Cuba	D4	94
Largs, Scot., U.K.	F9	8
Lari, Peru	F6	82
Larimore, N.D., U.S.	D10	118
Larino, Italy	H9	18
La Rioja, Arg.	E5	80
La Rioja, prov., Arg.	E5	80
La Rioja, prov., Spain	C9	16
Lárisa, Grc.	J6	20
Lārkāna, Pak.	G3	44
Lark Harbour, Newf., Can.	C15	106
Lárnax (Larnaca), Cyp.	D2	48
Larned, Ks., U.S.	M8	118
La Rochefoucauld, Fr.	G7	14
La Rochelle, Fr.	F5	14
La Roche-sur-Yon, Fr.	F5	14
La Roda, Spain	F9	16
La Romaine, Que., Can.	B13	106
La Romana, Dom. Rep.	E10	94
La Ronge, Sask., Can.	C9	104
Larose, La., U.S.	M6	114
La Rosita, Nic.	D10	92
Larreynaga, Nic.	E8	92
Larroque, Arg.	G9	80
Larrys River, N.S., Can.	G12	106
Larsen Bay, Ak., U.S.	H17	100
Larsen Ice Shelf, Ant.	B12	73
Larteh Aheneasi, Ghana	I10	64
La Rubia, Arg.	F8	80
La Rue, Oh., U.S.	G3	108
Laruns, Fr.	J6	14
Larus Lake, l., Ont., Can.	G20	104
Larvik, Nor.	L12	6
La Sabana, Arg.	D9	80
La Sal, Ut., U.S.	F7	120
La Salle, Co., U.S.	D12	120
La Salle, Il., U.S.	I6	110
La Salle, stm., Man., Can.	I17	104
Las Almejas, Bahía, b., Mex.	E4	90
Las Animas, Co., U.S.	M4	118
La Sarraz, Switz.	E6	13
Las Arrias, Arg.	F7	80
Las Aves, Islas, is., Ven.	A9	84
Las Ballenas, Canal de, strt., Mex.	C3	90
Las Bonitas, Ven.	D10	84
Las Breñas, Arg.	D8	80
Las Cabezas de San Juan, Spain	I6	16
Las Cabras, Chile	H3	80
Lascano, Ur.	G11	80
Lascar, Volcán, vol., Chile	B5	80
Las Catitas, Arg.	G4	80
Lascaux, Grotte de, Fr.	G8	14
Las Cejas, Arg.	D6	80
Las Choapas, Mex.	I12	90
La Scie, Newf., Can.	C18	106
Las Cruces, N.M., U.S.	L10	120
Las Cuevas, Mex.	C9	90
Las Delicias, Mex.	J14	90
La Selle, Morne, mtn., Haiti	E9	94
La Serena, Chile	E3	80
La Seyne, Fr.	I12	14
Las Flores, Arg.	I9	80
Las Flores, Arg.	F4	80
Las Flores, Arroyo, stm., Arg.	H9	80
Las Flores, Cerro, mtn., Mex.	I12	90
Las Garcitas, Arg.	D9	80
Las Guayabas, Mex.	E11	90
Lashburn, Sask., Can.	E5	104
Lāsh-e Joveyn, Afg.	F16	48
Las Heras, Arg.	G4	80
Lashio, Burma	C4	40
Las Hormigas, Mex.	E10	90
La Sierra, Montaña, mts., Hond.	C7	92
Las Iglesias, Cerro, mtn., Mex.	D6	90
Łasin, Pol.	B19	10
Łask, Pol.	D19	10
L'askel'a, Russia	K22	6
Las Lajas, Arg.	J3	80
Las Lajas, Pan.	C2	84
Las Lajitas, Arg.	C6	80
Las Lomas, Peru	J2	84
Las Lomitas, Arg.	C8	80
Lašma, Russia	G24	22
Las Malvinas, Arg.	H4	80
Las Margaritas, Mex.	I14	90
Las Marianas, Arg.	H9	80
Las Mercedes, Ven.	C9	84
Las Minas, Cerro, mtn., Hond.	C6	92
Las Nieves, Mex.	D7	90
Las Nopaleras, Cerro, mtn., Mex.	E8	90
La Solana, Spain	G8	16
La Soledad, Cerro, mtn., Mex.	D6	90
Las Ovejas, Arg.	I3	80
Las Palmas, Arg.	D9	80
Las Palmas, Pan.	C2	84
Las Palmas, prov., Spain	O26	17b
Las Palmas de Gran Canaria, Spain	O25	17b
La Spezia, Italy	E4	18
Las Piedras, Ur.	H10	80
Las Piedras, Río de, stm., Peru	E7	82
Las Plumas, Arg.	E3	78
Lasqueti Island, i., B.C., Can.	H10	102
Las Rosas, Arg.	G8	80
Las Rosas, Mex.	I13	90
Lassance, Braz.	D6	79
Lassay, Fr.	D6	14
Lassen Peak, vol., Ca., U.S.	D4	124
Lassen Volcanic National Park, Ca., U.S.	D4	124
Las Tablas, Pan.	D2	84
Las Tinajas, Arg.	D7	80
Last Mountain, mtn., Sask., Can.	G10	104
Last Mountain Lake, l., Sask., Can.	G9	104
Las Toscas, Arg.	E9	80
Lastoursville, Gabon	B2	58
Las Tunas, Cuba	D6	94
Las Tunas Grandes, Laguna, l., Arg.	I7	80
La Suze, Fr.	E7	14
Las Varas, Mex.	C5	90
Las Varas, Mex.	G7	90
Las Varillas, Arg.	F7	80
Las Vegas, Nv., U.S.	H10	124
Las Vegas, N.M., U.S.	I11	120
Las Vegas, Ven.	C8	84
La Tabatière, Que., Can.	B15	106
Latacunga, Ec.	H3	84
Latady Island, i., Ant.	C12	73
La Tagua, Col.	H5	84
Latakia see Al-Lādhiqīyah, Syria	D3	48
Laterrière, Que., Can.	D2	106
La Teste-de-Buch, Fr.	H5	14
La Tetilla, Cerro, mtn., Mex.	G7	90
Lathrop, Mo., U.S.	C2	114
Latimer, Ia., U.S.	H2	110
Latina, Italy	H7	18
Latisana, Italy	D8	18
La Toma, Arg.	G6	80
Latorica, stm., Eur.	G22	10
Latornell, stm., Alta., Can.	C16	102
La Tortuga, Isla, i., Ven.	B10	84
Latouche Treville, Cape, c., Austl.	C4	68
La Tour-du-Pin, Fr.	G12	14
Latowicz, Pol.	C21	10
La Tremblade, Fr.	G5	14
La Trimouille, Fr.	F8	14
La Trinidad, Arg.	D6	80
La Trinidad, Nic.	E8	92
La Trinidad de Orichuna, Ven.	D8	84
La Trinitaria, Mex.	I13	90
La Trinité, Mart.	G14	94
Latrobe, Austl.	M7	70
Latrobe, Pa., U.S.	G7	108
Latta, S.C., U.S.	E7	112
Lātūr, India	C4	46
La Tuque, Que., Can.	G18	96
Latvia (Latvija), ctry., Eur.	D8	22
Lauca, stm., Bol.	H7	82
Lauchhammer, Ger.	D13	10
Lauder, Scot., U.K.	F11	8
Lauderdale, Ms., U.S.	J8	114

Name	Map Ref.	Page
Lauf an der Pegnitz, Ger.	F11	10
Läufelfingen, Switz.	D8	13
Laufen, Switz.	D8	13
Laukuva, Lith.	F5	22
Launceston, Austl.	M7	70
Launceston, Eng., U.K.	K9	8
La Unión, Chile	E2	78
La Unión, Col.	G4	84
La Unión, El Sal.	D7	92
La Unión, Mex.	I9	90
La Unión, Peru	C3	82
La Unión, Peru	A1	82
La Unión, Spain	H11	16
La Union, N.M., U.S.	M10	120
La Unión, Ven.	C9	84
Laura, Austl.	C8	68
La Urbana, Ven.	D9	84
Laurel, De., U.S.	I11	108
Laurel, Fl., U.S.	L4	112
Laurel, In., U.S.	C11	114
Laurel, Md., U.S.	H10	108
Laurel, Ms., U.S.	K7	114
Laurel, Mt., U.S.	E17	122
Laurel, Ne., U.S.	I10	118
Laurel, stm., Ky., U.S.	B2	112
Laurel Bay, S.C., U.S.	G6	112
Laureldale, Pa., U.S.	G11	108
Laureles, Ur.	F11	80
Laurel Hill, N.C., U.S.	E7	112
Laurelville, Oh., U.S.	H4	108
Laurens, Ia., U.S.	I13	118
Laurens, S.C., U.S.	E4	112
Laurentides, Les, plat., Que., Can.	G18	96
Laurentides, Parc Provincial des, Que., Can.	E2	106
Lauria, Italy	I10	18
Laurie Island, i., B.A.T.	B1	73
Laurie Island, i., B.A.T.	K10	74
Laurie Lake, l., Can.	B12	104
Laurier, Man., Can.	H15	104
Laurière, Fr.	F8	14
Laurinburg, N.C., U.S.	E7	112
Laurium, Mi., U.S.	C7	110
Lausanne, Switz.	E6	13
Laut, Pulau, i., Indon.	F6	38
Lauta, Ger.	D14	10
Lautaro, Chile	J2	80
Lauterbach, Ger.	E9	10
Lauterbrunnen, Switz.	E8	13
Lauter [Sachsen], Ger.	E12	10
Laut Kecil, Kepulauan, is., Indon.	F6	38
Lauzon, Que., Can.	F2	106
Lava (Łyna), stm., Eur.	G4	22
Lava, Nosy, i., Madag.	O22	67b
Lavaca, stm., Tx., U.S.	J10	116
Lava Hot Springs, Id., U.S.	H13	122
Lavaisse, Arg.	G6	80
Laval, Que., Can.	B13	108
Laval, Fr.	D6	14
La Vall d'Uixo, Spain	F11	16
Lavalle, Arg.	E9	80
Lavalle, Arg.	E6	80
La Valley, Co., U.S.	G11	120
Lavapié, Punta, c., Chile	I2	80
Lávara, Grc.	H10	20
Lavardac, Fr.	H7	14
Lava-Tudo, stm., Braz.	E13	80
La Vega, Dom. Rep.	E9	94
La Vela, Cabo de, c., Col.	A6	84
La Vela de Coro, Ven.	B8	84
Lavelanet, Fr.	J8	14
Lavello, Italy	H10	18
La Venta, hist., Mex.	H12	90
La Ventura, Mex.	E9	90
La Verde, Arg.	D9	80
La Vergne, Tn., U.S.	F10	114
Laverne, Ok., U.S.	C7	116
La Vernia, Tx., U.S.	J8	116
Laverton, Austl.	E4	68
La Veta, Co., U.S.	G11	120
La Victoria, Ven.	B9	84
La Vila Joiosa, Spain	G11	16
La Villa, stm., Pan.	J14	92
Lavillette, N.B., Can.	E8	106
La Viña, Arg.	C6	80
Lavina, Mt., U.S.	D17	122
La Virginia, Col.	E5	84
La Vista, Ne., U.S.	J11	118
Lavonia, Ga., U.S.	E3	112
La Voulte-sur-Rhône, Fr.	H11	14
Lavras, Braz.	F6	79
Lavras do Sul, Braz.	F12	80
Lavumisa, Swaz.	F10	66
Lawdar, Yemen	H4	47
Lawford Lake, l., Man., Can.	D18	104
Lawksawk, Burma	D4	40
Lawler, Ia., U.S.	G3	110
Lawn, Newf., Can.	F18	106
Lawn, Tx., U.S.	G7	116
Lawn Bay, b., Newf., Can.	F18	106
Lawndale, N.C., U.S.	D5	112
Lawn Hill, Austl.	B3	70
Lawrence, In., U.S.	C10	114
Lawrence, Ks., U.S.	M12	118
Lawrence, Ma., U.S.	E15	108
Lawrence, Ne., U.S.	K9	118
Lawrenceburg, In., U.S.	C12	114
Lawrenceburg, Ky., U.S.	D12	114
Lawrenceburg, Tn., U.S.	G9	114
Lawrenceville, Il., U.S.	D9	114
Lawrenceville, N.J., U.S.	G12	108
Lawrenceville, Va., U.S.	C9	112
Lawson, Mo., U.S.	C2	114
Lawtey, Fl., U.S.	I4	112
Lawton, Mi., U.S.	H10	110
Lawton, N.D., U.S.	C9	118
Lawton, Ok., U.S.	E8	116
Lawz, Jabal al-, mtn., Sau. Ar.	G3	48
Laxå, Swe.	L14	6
Lax Kw'alaams, B.C., Can.	C4	102
Laylā, Sau. Ar.	C5	47
Layton, Ut., U.S.	C5	120
Laytonville, Ca., U.S.	E2	124
La Zarca, Mex.	E7	90
Lázaro Cárdenas, Mex.	B2	90
Lázaro Cárdenas, Mex.	I8	90
Lázaro Cárdenas, Presa, res., Mex.	E7	90
Lazdijai, Lith.	G6	22
Lazhulong, China	C9	44
Lazio, prov., Italy	G7	18
Léach, Camb.	H7	40
Leachville, Ar., U.S.	G6	114
Lead, S.D., U.S.	G4	118
Leader, Sask., Can.	H5	104
Leadore, Id., U.S.	F12	122
Leadville, Co., U.S.	E10	120
Leaf, stm., Mn., U.S.	E12	118
Leaf, stm., Ms., U.S.	K8	114
Leaf Lake, l., Sask., Can.	E12	104
League City, Tx., U.S.	J11	116
Leakesville, Ms., U.S.	K8	114
Leakey, Tx., U.S.	J7	116
Leaksville, N.C., U.S.	C7	112
Lealman, Fl., U.S.	L4	112
Leamington, Ont., Can.	H13	110
Leán, stm., Hond.	B7	92
Leandro N. Alem, Arg.	D11	80
Leary, Ga., U.S.	H2	112
Leask, Sask., Can.	E8	104
Leatherman Peak, mtn., Id., U.S.	F12	122
Leavenworth, Ks., U.S.	L13	118
Leavenworth, Wa., U.S.	C5	122
Leawood, Mo., U.S.	E2	114
Lebak, Phil.	D7	38
Lebam, Wa., U.S.	D2	122
Lebanon, In., U.S.	B10	114
Lebanon, Ks., U.S.	L9	118
Lebanon, Ky., U.S.	E11	114
Lebanon, Mo., U.S.	E4	114
Lebanon, N.H., U.S.	D14	108
Lebanon, Oh., U.S.	H2	108
Lebanon, Or., U.S.	F3	122
Lebanon, Pa., U.S.	G10	108
Lebanon, S.D., U.S.	F8	118
Lebanon, Tn., U.S.	F10	114
Lebanon, Va., U.S.	C4	112
Lebanon (Lubnān), ctry., Asia	C2	42
Lebanon Junction, Ky., U.S.	E11	114
Leb'ažje, Kaz.	G13	26
Lebec, Ca., U.S.	J7	124
Lebed'an', Russia	H22	22
Le Blanc, Fr.	F8	14
Lebo, Ks., U.S.	M12	118
Lebombo Mountains, hills, Afr.	E10	66
Lębork, Pol.	A17	10
Lebrija, Spain	I5	16
Lebrija, stm., Col.	D6	84
Lebu, Chile	I2	80
Le Cannet, Fr.	I14	14
Le Cateau, Fr.	B10	14
Lecce, Italy	I13	18
Lecco, Italy	D4	18
Le Center, Mn., U.S.	F2	110
Lech, stm., Eur.	G10	10
Le Châble, Switz.	F7	13
Le Chesne, Fr.	C11	14
Le Cheylard, Fr.	H11	14
Lechiguanas, Islas de las, is., Arg.	G9	80
Lechtaler Alpen, mts., Aus.	H10	10
Lechuguilla, Cerro, mtn., Mex.	F7	90
Le Claire, Ia., U.S.	I5	110
Lecompte, La., U.S.	K4	114
Le Creusot, Fr.	F11	14
Łęczyca, Pol.	C19	10
Led'anaja, gora, mtn., Russia	E26	28
Lede, Bel.	G4	12
Ledo, India	D14	42
Ledong, China	E10	40
Le Doré, Lac, l., Que., Can.	A12	106
Ledu, China	D7	30
Leduc, Alta., Can.	D21	102
Lee, Ma., U.S.	E13	108
Leechburg, Pa., U.S.	G7	108
Leech Lake, l., Sask., Can.	G12	104
Leech Lake, l., Mn., U.S.	C1	110
Leedey, Ok., U.S.	D7	116
Leeds, Eng., U.K.	H12	8
Leeds, Al., U.S.	I10	114
Leeds, N.D., U.S.	C8	118
Leek, Neth.	B9	12
Leelanau Peninsula, pen., Mi., U.S.	E10	110
Leende, Neth.	F8	12
Leer, Ger.	B7	10
Leesburg, Fl., U.S.	K5	112
Leesburg, Ga., U.S.	H2	112
Leesburg, Va., U.S.	H9	108
Lees Summit, Mo., U.S.	D2	114
Leesville, La., U.S.	K3	114
Leesville, S.C., U.S.	F5	112
Leesville, Tx., U.S.	J9	116
Leeton, Austl.	J7	70
Leeuwarden, Neth.	B8	12
Leeuwin, Cape, c., Austl.	F3	68
Lee Vining, Ca., U.S.	G6	124
Lefors, Tx., U.S.	D6	116
Leftrook Lake, l., Man., Can.	B16	104
Legal, Alta., Can.	D21	102
Leganés, Spain	E8	16
Legaspi, Phil.	O20	39b
Leggett, Ca., U.S.	E2	124
Leghorn see Livorno, Italy	F5	18
Legion Mine, Zimb.	C9	66
Legionowo, Pol.	C20	10
Legnago, Italy	D6	18
Legnano, Italy	D3	18
Legnica (Liegnitz), Pol.	D16	10
Le Grand, Ca., U.S.	G5	124
Le Grand-Lucé, Fr.	E7	14
Le Grau-du-Roi, Fr.	I11	14
Leh, India	C7	44
Le Havre, Fr.	C7	14
Lehi, Ut., U.S.	D5	120
Lehigh, Ia., U.S.	H1	110
Lehigh, Ok., U.S.	E10	116
Lehigh Acres, Fl., U.S.	M5	112
Lehighton, Pa., U.S.	G11	108
Leho, Sud.	N7	60
Lehr, N.D., U.S.	F8	118
Lehrte, Ger.	C9	10
Lehtse, Est.	B8	22
Lehututu, Bots.	D5	66
Leiah, Pak.	E4	44
Leibnitz, Aus.	I15	10
Leicester, Eng., U.K.	I12	8
Leicestershire, co., Eng., U.K.	I12	8
Leichhardt, stm., Austl.	A3	70
Leichhardt Range, mts., Austl.	C7	70
Leiden, Neth.	D6	12
Leie (Lys), stm., Eur.	B10	14
Leigh Creek, Austl.	H3	70
Leighton, Al., U.S.	H9	114
Leikanger, Nor.	K10	6
Leinan, Sask., Can.	H7	104
Leinster, hist. reg., Ire.	H6	8
Leipsic, Oh., U.S.	F3	108
Leipzig, Ger.	D12	10
Leitchfield, Ky., U.S.	E10	114
Leitha, stm., Eur.	H16	10
Leitrim, co., Ire.	H6	8
Leiyang, China	I1	34
Leizhou Bandao, pen., China	D11	40
Leizhuang, China	D6	32
Lek, stm., Neth.	E6	12
Le Kreïder, Alg.	C11	62
Leksand, Swe.	K14	6
Leksozero, ozero, l., Russia	J22	6
Le Lamentin, Mart.	G14	94
Leland, Il., U.S.	I7	110
Leland, Mi., U.S.	E10	110
Leland, Ms., U.S.	I6	114
Leleiwi Point, c., Hi., U.S.	r18	125a
Leleque, Arg.	E2	78
Le Limbé, Haiti	E8	94
Leli Shan, mtn., China	D9	44
Le Locle, Switz.	D6	13
Le Lude, Fr.	E7	14
Lelystad, Neth.	C7	12
Lema, Nig.	E12	64
Le Maire, Estrecho de, strt., Arg.	G4	78
Le Mans, Fr.	D7	14
Le Mars, Ia., U.S.	I11	118
Lemay, Mo., U.S.	D6	114
Lemay, Lac, l., Que., Can.	B5	106
Lemberg, Sask., Can.	H11	104
Lemdiyya, Alg.	B12	62
Leme, Braz.	G5	79
Lemesós (Limassol), Cyp.	D2	48
Lemeta, Ak., U.S.	D21	100
Lemgo, Ger.	C8	10
Lemhi Pass, U.S.	F12	122
Lemhi Range, mts., Id., U.S.	F12	122
Lemieux Islands, is., N.W. Ter., Can.	D20	96
Lemin, China	D10	40
Leming, Tx., U.S.	J8	116
Lemitar, N.M., U.S.	J10	120
Lemmon, S.D., U.S.	F5	118
Lemnos see Límnos, i., Grc.	J9	20
Lemoncove, Ca., U.S.	H6	124
Lemon Grove, Ca., U.S.	L8	124
Lemont, Pa., U.S.	G9	108
Le Mont-Saint-Michel, Fr.	D5	14
Lemoore, Ca., U.S.	H6	124
Le Moule, Guad.	F14	94
Lempa, stm., N.A.	D6	92
Lempira, dept., Hond.	C6	92
Lemsid, W. Sah.	G4	62
Lena, Il., U.S.	H6	110
Lena, Wi., U.S.	F7	110
Lena, stm., Russia	C17	28
Lençóis, Braz.	B8	79
Lendery, Russia	J22	6
Lenghu, China	D5	30
Lenhovda, Swe.	M14	6
Lenina, pik, mtn., Asia	J12	26
Leningrad see Sankt-Peterburg, Russia	B13	22
Leningradskaja, sci., Ant.	B8	73
Leninogorsk, Kaz.	G8	28
Leninogorsk, Russia	G8	26
Leninsk, Kaz.	H10	26
Leninsk, Uzb.	I12	26
Leninsk-Kuzneckij, Russia	G9	28
Lenk, Switz.	F7	13
Lenkoran', Azer.	J7	26
Lennox, S.D., U.S.	H11	118
Lennox, Isla, i., Chile	H3	78
Lennoxville, Que., Can.	B15	108
Lenoir, N.C., U.S.	D5	112
Lenoir City, Tn., U.S.	D2	112
Lenore Lake, l., Sask., Can.	F9	104
Lenox, Ga., U.S.	H3	112
Lenox, Ia., U.S.	K13	118
Lenox, Ma., U.S.	E13	108
Lenox, Tn., U.S.	F7	114
Lens, Fr.	B9	14
Lensk, Russia	E14	28
Lenti, Hung.	I16	10
Lentini, Italy	L10	18
Lentvaris, Lith.	G8	22
Lenzburg, Switz.	D9	13
Léo, Burkina	F8	64
Leoben, Aus.	H15	10
Léogâne, Haiti	E8	94
Leola, Ar., U.S.	H4	114
Leola, S.D., U.S.	F9	118
Leominster, Ma., U.S.	E15	108
Léon, Fr.	I5	14
León, Nic.	E8	92
León, Spain	C6	16
Leon, Ia., U.S.	J2	110
Leon, Ks., U.S.	N11	118
León, dept., Nic.	E8	92
León, hist. reg., Spain	D6	16
Leon, stm., Tx., U.S.	H9	116
Leona, Punta, c., C.R.	H10	92
Leonard, N.D., U.S.	E10	118
Leonard, Tx., U.S.	F10	116
Leonardtown, Md., U.S.	I10	108
Leonardville, Ks., U.S.	L11	118
León [de los Aldamas], Mex.	G9	90
Leones, Arg.	G7	80
Leonforte, Italy	L9	18
Leongatha, Austl.	L6	70
Leonora, Austl.	E4	68
Leonville, La., U.S.	L5	114
Leopold and Astrid Coast, Ant.	B5	73
Leopoldina, Braz.	F7	79
Leopoldo de Bulhões, Braz.	D4	79
Léopoldville see Kinshasa, Zaire	B3	58
Leoti, Ks., U.S.	M6	118
Leoville, Sask., Can.	E7	104
Leovo, Mol.	C12	20
Le Palais, Fr.	E3	14
Lepanto, C.R.	H9	92
Lepanto, Ar., U.S.	G6	114
Lepe, Spain	H4	16
Lepel', Bela.	G11	22
Le Pellerin, Fr.	E5	14
Lephepe, Bots.	D7	66
Leping, China	G6	34
L'Épiphanie, Que., Can.	B13	108
Le Pont-de-Beauvoisin, Fr.	G12	14
Lepontine, Alpi, mts., Eur.	F15	14
Le Port, Reu.	V17	67c
Lepreau, Point, c., N.B., Can.	G7	106
Lepsy, Kaz.	H13	26
Le Puy, Fr.	G10	14
Lequeitio, Spain	I4	14
Léraba, stm., Afr.	G7	64
Lere, Nig.	F14	64
Lerici, Italy	E4	18
Lérida, Col.	G7	84
Lerma, stm., Mex.	G9	90
Léros, i., Grc.	L10	20
Le Roy, Il., U.S.	B8	114
Le Roy, Ks., U.S.	M12	118
Le Roy, Mn., U.S.	G3	110
Le Roy, N.Y., U.S.	E9	108
Lerwick, Scot., U.K.	A12	8
Les Andelys, Fr.	C8	14
Les Borges Blanques, Spain	D12	16
Lesbos see Lésvos, i., Grc.	J10	20
Les Cayes, Haiti	E8	94
Leshan, China	F7	30
Les Haudères, Switz.	F8	13
Lesjaskog, Nor.	J11	6
Lesko, Pol.	F22	10
Leskovac, Yugo.	G5	20
Leskov Island, i., S. Geor.	A2	73
Leskov Island, i., S. Geor.	J12	74
Leslie, S. Afr.	F9	66
Leslie, Ar., U.S.	G4	114
Leslie, Ga., U.S.	H2	112
Leslie, Mi., U.S.	H11	110
Leslie, W.V., U.S.	I6	108
Les Mosses, Switz.	F7	13
Lesnaja, Bela.	I8	22
Lesnoj, Russia	G23	22
Lesogorskij, Russia	K21	6
Lesosibirsk, Russia	F10	28
Lesotho, ctry., Afr.	G5	58
Lesozavodsk, Russia	H18	28
Les Pieux, Fr.	C5	14
Les Riceys, Fr.	E11	14
Les Sables-d'Olonne, Fr.	F5	14
Les Saintes, is., Guad.	G14	94
Lessay, Fr.	C5	14
Lessen (Lessines), Bel.	G4	12
Lesser Antilles, is.	H14	94
Lesser Khingan Range see Xiao Hinggan Ling, mts., China	B12	30
Lesser Slave, stm., Alta., Can.	B20	102
Lesser Slave Lake, l., Alta., Can.	B19	102
Lesser Sunda Islands see Tenggara, Nusa, is., Indon.	G7	38
Lessines (Lessen), Bel.	G4	12
Lestock, Sask., Can.	G10	104
Le Sueur, Mn., U.S.	F2	110
Le Sueur, stm., Mn., U.S.	F2	110
Lešukonskoje, Russia	E7	26
Les Vans, Fr.	H11	14
Lésvos, i., Grc.	J10	20
Leszno, Pol.	D16	10
Letcher, S.D., U.S.	H9	118
Letenye, Hung.	I16	10
Lethbridge, Alta., Can.	H22	102
Lethbridge, Newf., Can.	D20	106
Lethem, Guy.	F13	84
Le Thillot, Fr.	E13	14
Leti, Kepulauan, is., Indon.	G8	38
Leticia, Col.	J8	84
Leting, China	D6	32
Letjiesbos, S. Afr.	I6	66
Letlhakane, Bots.	C7	66
Letlhakeng, Bots.	E7	66
Letnerečenskij, Russia	I24	6
Letpadan, Burma	F3	40
Le Trayas, Fr.	I13	14
Le Tréport, Fr.	B8	14
Letsôk-aw Kyun, i., Burma	I5	40
Letterkenny, Ire.	G6	8
Leu, Rom.	E8	20
Leucadia, Ca., U.S.	K8	124
Leuk, Switz.	F8	13
Leuna, Ger.	D12	10
Leuser, Gunung, mtn., Indon.	M4	40
Leutkirch, Ger.	H10	10
Leuven (Louvain), Bel.	G6	12
Leuze, Bel.	G4	12
Levack, Ont., Can.	D14	110
Levádhia, Grc.	K6	20
Levan, Ut., U.S.	E5	120
Levanto, Italy	E4	18
Levelland, Tx., U.S.	F4	116
Levelock, Ak., U.S.	G16	100
Leveque, Cape, c., Austl.	C4	68
Levering, Mi., U.S.	E11	110
Leverkusen, Ger.	D6	10
Levice, Czech.	G18	10
Levie, Fr.	H4	18
Levier, Fr.	F13	14
Le Vigan, Fr.	I10	14
Levin, N.Z.	D5	72
Lévis, Que., Can.	F2	106
Levisa Fork, stm., U.S.	B4	112
Levittown, N.Y., U.S.	G13	108
Levittown, Pa., U.S.	G12	108
Levkás, Grc.	K4	20
Levkás, i., Grc.	K4	20
Levkímmi, Grc.	J4	20
Levroux, Fr.	F8	14
Lev Tolstoj, Russia	H22	22
Lewe, Burma	E4	40
Lewellen, Ne., U.S.	J5	118
Lewes, Eng., U.K.	K14	8
Lewes, De., U.S.	I11	108
Lewis, Ia., U.S.	J12	118
Lewis, Ks., U.S.	N8	118
Lewis, stm., Wa., U.S.	E3	122
Lewis, Butt of, c., Scot., U.K.	C7	8
Lewis, Isle of, i., Scot., U.K.	C7	8
Lewis, Mount, mtn., Nv., U.S.	D9	124
Lewis and Clark Lake, res., U.S.	I10	118
Lewis and Clark Range, mts., Mt., U.S.	C13	122
Lewisburg, Ky., U.S.	F10	114
Lewisburg, Pa., U.S.	G10	108
Lewisburg, Tn., U.S.	G10	114
Lewisburg, W.V., U.S.	J6	108
Lewisport, Ky., U.S.	E10	114
Lewisporte, Newf., Can.	C18	106
Lewis Range, mts., Mt., U.S.	B12	122
Lewis Run, Pa., U.S.	F8	108
Lewis Smith Lake, res., Al., U.S.	H9	114
Lewiston, Ca., U.S.	D3	124
Lewiston, Id., U.S.	D8	122
Lewiston, Me., U.S.	C16	108
Lewiston, Mi., U.S.	F11	110
Lewiston, Mn., U.S.	G4	110
Lewiston, N.Y., U.S.	D7	108
Lewiston, Ut., U.S.	C5	120
Lewiston Orchards, Id., U.S.	D9	122
Lewistown, Il., U.S.	B6	114
Lewistown, Mo., U.S.	B5	114
Lewistown, Mt., U.S.	C16	122
Lewistown, Pa., U.S.	G9	108
Lewisville, N.B., Can.	F9	106
Lewisville, Ar., U.S.	I3	114
Lewisville, Tx., U.S.	F10	116
Lewisville Lake, res., Tx., U.S.	F9	116
Lewvan, Sask., Can.	H10	104
Lexa, Ar., U.S.	H6	114
Lexington, Ga., U.S.	F3	112
Lexington, Il., U.S.	J7	110
Lexington, Ky., U.S.	A2	112
Lexington, Ma., U.S.	E15	108
Lexington, Mi., U.S.	G13	110
Lexington, Ms., U.S.	I6	114
Lexington, Mo., U.S.	C3	114
Lexington, Ne., U.S.	K8	118
Lexington, N.C., U.S.	D6	112
Lexington, Ok., U.S.	D9	116
Lexington, Or., U.S.	E6	122
Lexington, S.C., U.S.	F5	112
Lexington, Tn., U.S.	G8	114
Lexington, Tx., U.S.	I9	116
Lexington, Va., U.S.	B7	112
Lexington Park, Md., U.S.	I10	108
Leyond, stm., Man., Can.	G19	104
Leyte, i., Phil.	C7	38
Leyte Gulf, b., Phil.	C8	38
Leža, Russia	C23	22
Leżajsk, Pol.	E22	10
Lezama, Ven.	C9	84
Ležn'ovo, Russia	E23	22
L'gov, Russia	G5	26
Lhasa, China	F14	44
Lhazê, China	F12	44
Lhokseumawe, Indon.	L4	40
Lhorong, China	E6	30
L'Hospitalet de Llobregat, Spain	D14	16
Lhozhag, China	F14	44
Lhuntsi Dzong, Bhu.	G14	44
Li, stm., China	F9	30
Liangcheng, China	H7	32
Lianghe, China	B5	40
Liangjiadian, China	D9	32
Liangjiang, China	C10	40
Liangkou, China	L2	34
Liangmentou, China	G10	34
Liangtian, China	J2	34
Liangying, China	L5	34
Lianhe, China	A13	32
Lianjiang, China	I8	34
Lianpu, China	I7	34
Lianshui, China	B8	34
Lianxian, China	G9	30
Lianyungang, China	I7	32
Lianyungang (Xinpu), China	I7	32
Liao, stm., China	C11	30
Liaocheng, China	G3	32
Liaodong Bandao (Liaotung Peninsula), pen., China	D10	32
Liaodong Wan, b., China	C11	30
Liaojiangshi, China	I2	34
Liaoning, prov., China	C11	30
Liaoyang, China	B11	32
Liaoyuan, China	C12	30
Liaozhong, China	B10	32
Liard, stm., Can.	D8	96
Líbano, Col.	E5	84
Libby, Mt., U.S.	B10	122
Libenge, Zaire	H4	56
Liberal, Ks., U.S.	N7	118
Liberal, Mo., U.S.	E2	114
Liberdade, Braz.	G6	79
Liberdade, stm., Braz.	B6	82
Liberec, Czech.	E15	10
Liberia, C.R.	G9	92
Liberia, ctry., Afr.	G5	54
Libertad, Ur.	H10	80
Libertad, Ven.	C8	84
Libertad, Ven.	C8	84
Libertador General Bernardo O'Higgins, prov., Chile	H3	80
Libertador General San Martín, Arg.	B6	80
Liberty, In., U.S.	C12	114
Liberty, Ky., U.S.	E12	114
Liberty, Ms., U.S.	K6	114
Liberty, Mo., U.S.	C2	114
Liberty, Ne., U.S.	K11	118
Liberty, N.Y., U.S.	F12	108
Liberty, N.C., U.S.	D7	112
Liberty, S.C., U.S.	E4	112
Liberty, Tx., U.S.	I12	116
Liberty Center, Oh., U.S.	F2	108
Liberty Hill, Tx., U.S.	I9	116
Libertyville, Il., U.S.	H8	110
Lībīyah, Aṣ-Ṣaḥrā' al- (Libyan Desert), des., Afr.	D6	56
Libourne, Fr.	H6	14
Libramont, Bel.	I7	12
Libres, Mex.	H11	90
Libreville, Gabon	A1	58
Libu, China	C11	40
Libya (Lībiyā), ctry., Afr.	C4	56
Libyan Desert see Lībīyah, Aṣ-Ṣaḥrā' al-, des., Afr.	D6	56
Libyan Plateau see Aḍ-Ḍiffah, plat., Afr.	B3	60
Licancábur, Volcán, vol., S.A.	J8	82
Licantén, Chile	H2	80
Licata, Italy	L8	18
Lice, Tur.	B6	48
Lichinga, Moz.	D7	58
Lichoslavl', Russia	D18	22
Lichtenfels, Ger.	E11	10
Lichuan, China	H5	34
Lickershamn, Swe.	M16	6
Licking, Mo., U.S.	E5	114
Licking, stm., Ky., U.S.	I2	108
Lida, Bela.	H8	22
Lidao, China	F10	32
Liddon Gulf, b., N.W. Ter., Can.	A10	96
Liden, Swe.	J15	6
Lidesi, China	B4	34
Lidgerwood, N.D., U.S.	E10	118
Lídice, Pan.	C3	84
Lidköping, Swe.	L13	6
Lidzbark, Pol.	B19	10
Lidzbark Warmiński, Pol.	A20	10
Liechtenstein, ctry., Eur.	F9	4
Liège (Luik), Bel.	G8	12
Liège, prov., Bel.	G8	12
Liegnitz see Legnica, Pol.	D16	10
Lielvārde, Lat.	E7	22
Lienz, Aus.	I12	10
Liepāja, Lat.	E4	22
Lier (Lierre), Bel.	F6	12
Lierre (Lier), Bel.	F6	12
Lieshout, Neth.	E8	12
Liestal, Switz.	D8	13
Liévin, Fr.	B9	14
Lièvre, Rivière du, stm., Que., Can.	B11	108
Lièvres, Île aux, i., Que., Can.	E4	106
Liezen, Aus.	H14	10
Liffré, Fr.	D5	14
Līgatne, Lat.	D8	22
Lighthouse Point, Fl., U.S.	M6	112
Lighthouse Point, c., Mi., U.S.	E10	110
Lighthouse Reef, rf., Belize	I16	90
Lightning Creek, stm., Sask., Can.	I13	104
Lignières, Fr.	F9	14
Lignite, N.D., U.S.	C5	118
Ligny-en-Barrois, Fr.	D12	14
Ligonha, stm., Moz.	E7	58
Ligonier, In., U.S.	A11	114
Ligonier, Pa., U.S.	G7	108
Ligui, Mex.	E4	90
Liguria, prov., Italy	E3	18
Ligurian Sea, Eur.	F4	18
Lihue, Hi., U.S.	p14	125a
Lihula, Est.	C6	22
Lijia, China	F6	32
Lijiang, China	F7	30
Lijiawobao, China	B10	32
Likasi (Jadotville), Zaire	D5	58
Likely, B.C., Can.	E13	102
Likino-Dulevo, Russia	F21	22
Liknes, Nor.	L10	6
Likoma Island, i., Mwi.	D6	58
Likou, China	F6	34
Likus, stm., Nic.	C11	92
Lilbourn, Mo., U.S.	F7	114
L'Île-Rousse, Fr.	J15	14
Lilienfeld, Aus.	G15	10
Liling, China	H2	34
Lille, Fr.	B10	14
Lillebonne, Fr.	C7	14
Lillehammer, Nor.	K12	6
Lillers, Fr.	B9	14
Lillesand, Nor.	L11	6
Lillestrøm, Nor.	L12	6
Lillington, N.C., U.S.	D8	112
Lillooet, B.C., Can.	G13	102
Lillooet, stm., B.C., Can.	H12	102
Lillooet Lake, l., B.C., Can.	G12	102
Lilongwe, Mwi.	D6	58
Lilo Viejo, Arg.	D7	80
Liloy, Phil.	D7	38
Lily, Ky., U.S.	B2	112
Lilydale, Austl.	M7	70
Lima, Para.	B10	80
Lima, Peru	E3	82
Lima, Mt., U.S.	F13	122
Lima, N.Y., U.S.	E9	108
Lima, Oh., U.S.	G2	108
Lima, dept., Peru	D3	82
Lima (Limia), stm., Eur.	D3	16
Limache, Chile	G3	80
Liman, Ukr.	D13	20
Limanowa, Pol.	F20	10
Limanskoje, Ukr.	C14	20
Limarí, stm., Chile	F3	80
Limay, stm., Arg.	J4	80
Limay Mahuida, Arg.	I5	80
Limbani, Peru	F7	82
Limbaži, Lat.	D7	22
Līmbdi, India	I4	44
Limburg, prov., Bel.	G7	12
Limburg, prov., Neth.	F8	12
Limburg an der Lahn, Ger.	E8	10
Limeira, Braz.	G5	79
Limen, China	H8	34
Limerick, Sask., Can.	I8	104
Limerick, Ire.	I5	8
Limerick, co., Ire.	I5	8
Lime Springs, Ia., U.S.	G3	110
Limestone, stm., Man., Can.	B20	104
Limestone Bay, b., Man., Can.	E16	104
Limestone Lake, l., Man., Can.	B18	104
Limestone Lake, l., Sask., Can.	D11	104
Limestone Point, pen., Man., Can.	E16	104
Limestone Point Lake, l., Man., Can.	C14	104
Limfjorden, strt., Den.	M11	6
Limia (Lima), stm., Eur.	D3	16
Liminka, Fin.	I19	6
Limmen Bight, Austl.	B7	68
Límnos, i., Grc.	J9	20
Limoges, Fr.	G8	14
Limogne, Fr.	H8	14
Limón, Hond.	B9	92
Limon, Co., U.S.	L4	118
Limón, prov., C.R.	H11	92
Limoux, Fr.	I9	14
Limpopo, stm., Afr.	E11	66
Limu, China	B11	40
Linachamari, Russia	G22	6
Līnah, Sau. Ar.	G7	48
Lin'an, China	E8	34
Linares, Chile	H3	80
Linares, Col.	G4	84
Linares, Mex.	E10	90
Linares, Spain	G8	16
Lincang, China	C7	40
Linch, Wy., U.S.	A10	120
Lincoln, Arg.	H8	80
Lincoln, Eng., U.K.	H13	8
Lincoln, Ar., U.S.	G2	114
Lincoln, Ca., U.S.	F4	124
Lincoln, Il., U.S.	B7	114
Lincoln, Ks., U.S.	L9	118
Lincoln, Me., U.S.	B18	108
Lincoln, Mi., U.S.	F12	110
Lincoln, Mo., U.S.	D3	114
Lincoln, Mt., U.S.	D13	122
Lincoln, Ne., U.S.	K11	118
Lincoln, N.H., U.S.	C15	108
Lincoln, Mount, mtn., Co., U.S.	E10	120
Lincoln City, Or., U.S.	F1	122
Lincoln Park, Co., U.S.	F11	120
Lincoln Park, Ga., U.S.	G2	112
Lincoln Park, Mi., U.S.	H12	110
Lincoln Sea, N.A.	A14	86
Lincolnshire, co., Eng., U.K.	H13	8
Lincolnton, Ga., U.S.	F4	112
Lincolnton, N.C., U.S.	D5	112
Lincoln Village, Ca., U.S.	F4	124
Lind, Wa., U.S.	D7	122
Linda, Russia	E27	22
Linda, Ca., U.S.	E4	124
Lindale, Ga., U.S.	E1	112
Lindale, Tx., U.S.	G11	116
Lindau, Ger.	H9	10
Linde, stm., Russia	D16	28
Linden, Guy.	D13	84
Linden, Al., U.S.	J9	114
Linden, In., U.S.	B10	114
Linden, Mi., U.S.	H12	110
Linden, Tn., U.S.	G9	114
Linden, Tx., U.S.	I2	114
Lindi, Tan.	D7	58
Lindley, S. Afr.	G8	66
Lindon, Co., U.S.	L4	118
Lindong, China	I7	34
Lindsay, Ont., Can.	F17	110
Lindsay, Ca., U.S.	H6	124
Lindsay, Ne., U.S.	J10	118
Lindsay, Ok., U.S.	E9	116
Lindsborg, Ks., U.S.	M10	118
Line Islands, is., Oc.	H24	126
Linesville, Pa., U.S.	F6	108
Lineville, Al., U.S.	I11	114
Lineville, Ia., U.S.	J2	110
Linfen, China	D9	30
Linganamakki Reservoir, res., India	F3	46
Lingao, China	E10	40
Lingayen, Phil.	M19	39b
Lingbi, China	B6	34
Lingen, Ger.	C7	10
Lingfengwei, China	K4	34
Lingga, Kepulauan, is., Indon.	O8	40
Lingga, Pulau, i., Indon.	O8	40
Linghu, China	E9	34
Lingle, Wy., U.S.	B12	120
Lingling, China	A11	40
Linglongta, China	C7	32
Lingqiu, China	D2	32
Lingshan, China	G8	32
Lingshui, China	E11	40
Linguère, Sen.	D2	64
Lingxiazhu, China	F8	34
Lingyuan, China	B7	32
Linh, Ngoc, mtn., Viet.	G9	40
Linhai, China	G10	34
Linhares, Braz.	E8	79
Linhe, China	C8	30
Linhuaiguan, China	C6	34
Linjiang, China	B14	32
Linjianghu, China	G6	34
Linköping, Swe.	L14	6
Linkou, China	B13	30
Linksmakalnis, Lith.	G6	22
Linkuva, Lith.	E6	22
Linn, Ks., U.S.	L10	118
Linn, Mo., U.S.	D5	114
Linnancang, China	D5	32
Linqing, China	G3	32
Linqu, China	G6	32
Linquan, China	B4	34
Linru, China	A1	34
Linruzhen, China	A1	34
Lins, Braz.	F4	79
Linshanhe, China	E3	34
Lintao, China	D7	30
Linthal, Switz.	E11	13
Linton, In., U.S.	C9	114
Linton, N.D., U.S.	E7	118
Linville, N.C., U.S.	C5	112
Linxi, China	C10	30
Linxia, China	D7	30
Linxiang, China	F2	34
Linyanti, Nmb.	B7	66
Linyanti, stm., Afr.	B7	66
Linyi, China	H6	32
Linying, China	B2	34
Linz, Aus.	G14	10
Linzhai, China	K4	34
Linzikou, China	G1	34
Lion, Golfe du, b., Fr.	I11	14
Liozno, Bela.	F13	22
Lipan, Tx., U.S.	G8	116
Lipari, Isola, i., Italy	K9	18
Lipeck, Russia	I22	22
Lipeckoje Vtoroje, Ukr.	B13	20
Lipetsk see Lipeck, Russia	I22	22
Lipez, Cerro, mtn., Bol.	I8	82
Lipin Bor, Russia	A20	22
Lipkany, Mol.	A10	20

Name — Map Ref. — Page

Malumfashi, Nig. F13 64
Malvern, Ar., U.S. H4 114
Malvern, Ia., U.S. J12 118
Malvern, Oh., U.S. G5 108
Malvinas, Arg. E9 80
Malwal, Sud. M6 60
Malý Dunaj, stm., Czech. H17 10
Malyj, ostrov, i., Russia A11 22
Malyj An'uj, stm., Russia D24 28
Malyj Jenisej, stm., Russia G11 28
Malyj Kavkaz, mts., Asia I6 26
Malyj Tajmyr, ostrov, i., Russia B13 28
Malyj T'uters, ostrov, i., Russia B9 22
Malyj Uzen', stm., Asia H7 26
Malyševo, Russia D18 22
Mamakwash Lake, l., Ont., Can. G22 104
Mamara, Peru F5 82
Mambaí, Braz. C5 79
Mamberamo, stm., Indon. F10 38
Mambéré, stm., Cen. Afr. Rep. H4 56
Ma-Me-O Beach, Alta., Can. E21 102
Mamers, Fr. D7 14
Mamfe, Cam. G8 54
Mamiá, Lago, l., Braz. J11 84
Mamie, N.C., U.S. C11 112
Mamiña, Chile I7 82
Mammoth, Az., U.S. L6 120
Mammoth, W.V., U.S. I5 108
Mammoth Cave National Park, Ky., U.S. E10 114
Mammoth Lakes, Ca., U.S. G7 124
Mammoth Spring, Ar., U.S. F5 114
Mamonovo, Russia G2 22
Mamoré, stm., S.A. D9 82
Mamori, Lago, l., Braz. I12 84
Mamoriá, stm., Braz. B8 82
Mamou, Gui. F3 64
Mamou, La., U.S. L4 114
Mamoutzou, May. L16 67a
Mampikony, Madag. P22 67b
Mamry, Jezioro, l., Pol. A21 10
Mamuchi, China H6 32
Ma'mūn, Sud. K2 60
Mamuno, Bots. D5 66
Mamuru, stm., Braz. I14 84
Man, I.C. H6 64
Man, W.V., U.S. B5 112
Mana, Hi., U.S. o14 125a
Mana, stm., Fr. Gu. B8 76
Manabí, prov., Ec. H2 84
Manacacías, stm., Col. F6 84
Manacapuru, Braz. I12 84
Manacor, Spain F15 16
Manado, Indon. E7 38
Managua, Nic. E8 92
Managua, dept., Nic. E8 92
Managua, Lago de, l., Nic. E8 92
Manakara, Madag. S23 67b
Manāli, India C10 42
Manama see Al-Manāmah, Bahr. H11 48
Manambato, Madag. N23 67b
Manambolosy, Madag. P23 67b
Mánamo, Caño, mth., Ven. C11 84
Mananara, Madag. P23 67b
Mananjary, Madag. R23 67b
Manantenina, Madag. T22 67b
Manapiare, stm., Ven. E9 84
Manapire, stm., Ven. C9 84
Manaquiri, Lago, l., Braz. I12 84
Manaravolo, Madag. S21 67b
Manas, China C4 30
Manās, stm., Asia G14 44
Manas Hu, l., China B4 30
Manāslu, mtn., Nepal F11 44
Manasquan, N.J., U.S. G12 108
Manassa, Co., U.S. G11 120
Manassas, Va., U.S. I9 108
Manatí, Col. B5 84
Manatí, P.R. E11 94
Manaung, Burma E2 40
Manaus, Braz. I12 84
Manawa, Wi., U.S. F7 110
Manawan Lake, l., Sask., Can. C11 104
Manbij, Syria C4 48
Mancelona, Mi., U.S. F10 110
Mancha Real, Spain H8 16
Manche, dept., Fr. C5 14
Manchester, Eng., U.K. H11 8
Manchester, Ct., U.S. F14 108
Manchester, Ga., U.S. G2 112
Manchester, Ia., U.S. H4 110
Manchester, Ky., U.S. B3 112
Manchester, Ma., U.S. E16 108
Manchester, Mi., U.S. H11 110
Manchester, N.H., U.S. E15 108
Manchester, Oh., U.S. I3 108
Manchester, Tn., U.S. G10 114
Manchester, Vt., U.S. D13 108
Manchón, Guat. C2 92
Manchuria, hist. reg., China B12 30
Máncora, Peru J2 84
Mancos, Co., U.S. G8 120
Mancos, stm., U.S. G8 120
Mandabe, Madag. R21 67b
Mandaguari, Braz. G3 79
Mandal, Nor. L10 6
Mandala, Puncak, mtn., Indon. F11 38
Mandalay, Burma C4 40
Mandalgov', Mong. B8 30
Mandalī, Iraq E8 48
Mandan, N.D., U.S. E7 118
Mandara Mountains, mts., Afr. F9 54
Mandas, Italy J4 18
Mandeb, Bab el, strt. H3 47
Mandel, Afg. E16 48
Manderson, Wy., U.S. F18 122
Mandeville, Jam. E6 94
Mandeville, La., U.S. L6 114
Mandi, India E7 44
Mandiana, Gui. F5 64
Mandimba, Moz. D7 58
Mandioli, Pulau, i., Indon. F8 38
Mandioré, Lagoa, l., S.A. H13 82
Mandla, India A6 46
Mandoto, Madag. Q22 67b
Mandouri, Togo F10 64
Mandra, Pak. D5 44
Mandritsara, Madag. O23 67b
Mandronarivo, Madag. R21 67b
Mandsaur, India H6 44
Manduria, Italy I12 18
Māndvi, India I3 44
Mandya, India F4 46
Manfalūṭ, Egypt D6 60
Manfredonia, Italy H10 18
Manfredonia, Golfo di, b., Italy H11 18
Manga, Braz. C7 79
Manga, Burkina F9 64
Mangabeiras, Chapada das, hills, Braz. F9 76
Mangalagiri, India D6 46
Mangalore, India F3 46
Mangaoka, Madag. N23 67b
Mangchang, China F8 30
Mange, China D10 44
Mange, S.L. G3 64
Mangham, La., U.S. J5 114
Manglares, Cabo, c., Col. G3 84
Mangochi, Mwi. D7 58
Mangoky, stm., Madag. R21 67b
Mangole, Pulau, i., Indon. F8 38
Mangoupa, Cen. Afr. Rep. O3 60
Mangrol, India J4 44
Mangrove Cay, i., Bah. B6 94
Mangueira, Lagoa, b., Braz. G12 80
Mangueirinha, Braz. C12 80
Mangulile, Hond. B8 92
Mangum, Ok., U.S. E7 116
Mangya, China D5 30
Manhattan, Ks., U.S. L11 118
Manhattan, Mt., U.S. E14 122
Manhuaçu, Braz. F7 79
Manhuaçu, stm., Braz. E8 79
Manhumirim, Braz. F8 79
Maniago, Italy C7 18
Maniamba, Moz. D7 58
Manic Deux, Réservoir, res., Que., Can. C5 106
Manicoré, Braz. A11 82
Manicoré, stm., Braz. B11 82
Manicouagan, stm., Que., Can. C5 106
Manicouagan, Réservoir, res., Que., Can. A5 106
Manic Trois, Réservoir, res., Que., Can. B5 106
Manignan, I.C. F6 64
Manigotagan, Man., Can. G18 104
Manigotagan, stm., Can. H19 104
Manila, Phil. N19 39b
Manila, Ar., U.S. G6 114
Manila, Ut., U.S. D7 120
Manila Bay, b., Phil. N19 39b
Manilla, Austl. H9 70
Manilla, Ia., U.S. J12 118
Manily, Russia E25 28
Manimpé, Mali D7 64
Manino, Russia H17 22
Manipur, state, India H15 44
Manipur, stm., Asia C2 40
Manisa, Tur. K11 20
Manissauá-Miçu, stm., Braz. A1 79
Manistee, Mi., U.S. F9 110
Manistee, stm., Mi., U.S. F9 110
Manistique, Mi., U.S. E9 110
Manistique, stm., Mi., U.S. D9 110
Manito, Il., U.S. B7 114
Manitoba, prov., Can. D17 104
Manitoba, Lake, l., Man., Can. H16 104
Manitou, Man., Can. I16 104
Manitou, stm., Ont., Can. I21 104
Manitou, stm., Que., Can. B8 106
Manitou, Lac, l., Que., Can. B10 106
Manitou, Lac, l., Que., Can. B8 106
Manitou Beach, Sask., Can. G9 104
Manitou Lake, l., Sask., Can. F5 104
Manitoulin Island, i., Ont., Can. E13 110
Manitou Springs, Co., U.S. F12 120
Manitowaning, Ont., Can. E14 110
Manitowish Waters, Wi., U.S. D6 110
Manitowoc, Wi., U.S. F8 110
Manitowoc, stm., Wi., U.S. F7 110
Maniwaki, Que., Can. A11 108
Manizales, Col. E5 84
Manja, Madag. R21 67b
Manjacaze, Moz. E11 66
Manjakandriana, Madag. Q22 67b
Manjimup, Austl. F3 68
Mankato, Ks., U.S. L9 118
Mankato, Mn., U.S. F2 110
Mankayane, Swaz. F10 66
Mankota, Sask., Can. I7 104
Manlleu, Spain C14 16
Manly, Ia., U.S. G2 110
Manmād, India B3 46
Mannahill, Austl. I3 70
Mannar, Gulf of, b., Asia H5 46
Mannārgudi, India G5 46
Männedorf, Switz. D10 13
Mannford, Ok., U.S. C10 116
Mannheim, Ger. F8 10
Manni, China C12 44
Manning, Ia., U.S. J12 118
Manning, N.D., U.S. D5 118
Manning, S.C., U.S. F6 112
Mannington, W.V., U.S. H6 108
Mannum, Austl. J3 70
Mannville, Alta., Can. D23 102
Mano, stm., Afr. H4 64
Manoa, Bol. C9 82
Manoel Ribas, Braz. C13 80
Manokotak, Ak., U.S. G15 100
Manombo, Madag. S20 67b
Manono, Zaire C5 58
Manor, Sask., Can. I12 104
Manor, Tx., U.S. I9 116
Manosque, Fr. I12 14
Manouane, stm., Que., Can. B3 106
Manouane, Lac, l., Que., Can. B3 106
Manouanis, stm., Que., Can. A3 106
Manouanis, Lac, l., Que., Can. B3 106
Manp'o, N. Kor. B14 32
Manresa, Spain D13 16
Mānsa, India F6 44
Mansa, Zam. D5 58
Mansel Island, i., N.W. Ter., Can. D17 96
Mansfield, Austl. K7 70
Mansfield, Ar., U.S. G2 114
Mansfield, Ga., U.S. F3 112
Mansfield, Il., U.S. B8 114
Mansfield, La., U.S. J3 114
Mansfield, Ma., U.S. E15 108
Mansfield, Mo., U.S. E4 114
Mansfield, Oh., U.S. G4 108
Mansfield, Pa., U.S. F9 108
Mansfield, Tx., U.S. G9 116
Mansfield, Mount, mtn., Vt., U.S. C14 108
Mansión, C.R. G9 92
Mansle, Fr. G7 14
Manso, stm., Braz. F13 82
Manson, Ia., U.S. I13 118
Manson, stm., B.C., Can. B11 102
Manson Creek, B.C., Can. B10 102
Mansura, La., U.S. K4 114
Mansura see Al-Manṣūrah, Egypt B6 60
Manta, Ec. H2 84
Manta, Bahía de, b., Ec. H2 84
Mantagao, stm., Man., Can. G17 104
Mantaro, stm., Peru E4 82
Manteca, Ca., U.S. G4 124
Mantecal, Ven. D8 84
Manteno, Il., U.S. I8 110
Manteo, N.C., U.S. D11 112
Mantes-la-Jolie, Fr. D8 14
Manti, Ut., U.S. E5 120
Mantiqueira, Serra da, mts., Braz. G6 79
Manton, Mi., U.S. F10 110
Mantorville, Mn., U.S. F3 110
Mantos Blancos, Chile B3 80
Mantova, Italy D5 18
Mantua, Cuba C2 94
Mantua, Oh., U.S. F5 108
Mantua see Mantova, Italy D5 18
Manturovo, Russia C27 22
Mäntyharju, Fin. K20 6
Manu, Peru E6 82
Manú, stm., Peru E6 82
Manua Islands, is., Am. Sam. J23 126
Manuel, Mex. F10 90
Manuel Antonio, Parque Nacional, C.R. H10 92
Manuel Benavides, Mex. C8 90
Manuel Derqui, Arg. D9 80
Manuel Urbano, Braz. C7 82
Manuripe (Mamuripi), stm., S.A. D8 82
Manuripi, stm., Bol. E8 82
Manus Island, i., Pap. N. Gui. k16 68a
Manvel, N.D., U.S. C10 118
Many, La., U.S. K3 114
Manyana, Bots. D5 66
Manyara, Lake, l., Tan. B7 58
Manyberries, Alta., Can. I4 104
Manyč, stm., Russia H6 26
Many Island Lake, l., Can. H4 104
Manzanares, Spain F8 16
Manzanillo, Cuba D6 94
Manzanillo, Mex. H7 90
Manzanillo, Punta, c., Pan. H15 92
Manzanillo Bay, b., N.A. E9 94
Manzano, N.M., U.S. J10 120
Manzanola, Co., U.S. M4 118
Manzano Peak, mtn., N.M., U.S. J10 120
Manzhouli, China B10 30
Manzini, Swaz. F10 66
Mao, Chad F4 56
Mao, Dom. Rep. E9 94
Maó, Spain F16 16
Maoke, Pegunungan, mts., Indon. F10 38
Maoming, China G9 30
Maouri, Dallol, val., Niger E11 64
Mapari, stm., Braz. I9 84
Mapastepec, Mex. J13 90
Mapia, Kepulauan, is., Indon. E9 38
Mapimí, Mex. E8 90
Mapimí, Bolsón de, des., Mex. D8 90
Maping, China D2 34
Mapinhane, Moz. D12 66
Mapire, Ven. D10 84
Mapiri, Bol. F7 82
Mapiri, stm., Bol. D8 82
Mapixari, Ilha, i., Braz. I10 84
Maple, stm., U.S. F9 118
Maple, stm., Ia., U.S. I12 118
Maple, stm., Mi., U.S. G11 110
Maple, stm., Mn., U.S. G1 110
Maple, stm., N.D., U.S. E10 118
Maple Creek, Sask., Can. I5 104
Maple Lake, Mn., U.S. E1 110
Maple Mount, Ky., U.S. E9 114
Maplesville, Al., U.S. J10 114
Mapleton, Ia., U.S. I12 118
Mapleton, Mn., U.S. G2 110
Mapleton, Or., U.S. F2 122
Mapleton, Ut., U.S. D5 120
Mapuera, stm., Braz. H14 84
Mapulanguene, Moz. E11 66
Maputo, Moz. E11 66
Maputo, stm., Afr. F11 66
Maqna, Sau. Ar. G3 48
Maquela do Zombo, Ang. C3 58
Maquereau, Pointe au, c., Que., Can. D9 106
Maquilaú, stm., Braz. G11 84
Maquinchao, Arg. E3 78
Maquoketa, Ia., U.S. H5 110
Maquoketa, stm., Ia., U.S. H5 110
Mar, Serra do, clf, Braz. C14 80
Mara, Peru F5 82
Mara, stm., Afr. B6 58
Maraã, Braz. H10 84
Marabá, Braz. E9 76
Maracá, Ilha de, i., Braz. F12 84
Maracaí, Braz. G3 79
Maracaibo, Ven. B7 84
Maracaibo, Lago de, l., Ven. C7 84
Maracaju, Braz. F1 79
Maracaju, Serra de, hills, S.A. F1 79
Maracanã, stm., Braz. C12 82
Maracás, Braz. B8 79
Maracay, Ven. B9 84
Marādah, Libya C4 56
Maradi, Niger E13 64
Maradi, Goulbin, stm., Afr. E13 64
Marāgheh, Iran C9 48
Maragogipe, Braz. F11 76
Maragogipe, Braz. B9 79
Marahuaca, Cerro, mtn., Ven. F10 84
Maraiche Lake, l., Sask., Can. D12 104
Marais des Cygnes, stm., U.S. D1 114
Marajó, Baía de, b., Braz. D9 76
Marajó, Ilha de, i., Braz. D9 76
Marakabei, Leso. G9 66
Maralal, Kenya A7 58
Maralaleng, Bots. E6 66
Marampa, S.L. G3 64
Maramureș, co., Rom. B8 20
Maran, Malay. M7 40
Marana, Az., U.S. L5 120
Marand, Iran B8 48
Marangani, Peru F6 82
Maranguape, Braz. D11 76
Maranhão, stm., Braz. C4 79
Maranoa, stm., Austl. E9 68
Marañón, stm., Peru D3 76
Marapanim, Braz. D9 76
Marapi, stm., Braz. G14 84
Maras, Peru E5 82
Marathon, Austl. C5 70
Marathon, Ont., Can. B9 110
Marathón, Grc. K7 20
Marathon, N.Y., U.S. E10 108
Marathon, Tx., U.S. I3 116
Marathon, Wi., U.S. F6 110
Maraú, Braz. C9 79
Marau, Braz. E12 80
Marauiá, stm., Braz. H10 84
Maravilha, Braz. D12 80
Maravillas, Mex. D7 90
Marawī, Sud. H6 60
Marayes, Arg. F5 80
Marbach, Switz. E8 13
Marbella, Spain I7 16
Marble, Mn., U.S. C2 110
Marble, N.C., U.S. D3 112
Marble Bar, Austl. D3 68
Marble Canyon, val., Az., U.S. H5 120
Marble Falls, Tx., U.S. I8 116
Marble Hall, S. Afr. E9 66
Marblehead, Oh., U.S. F4 108
Marble Hill, Mo., U.S. E7 114
Marble Rock, Ia., U.S. H3 110
Marburg, Ger. E8 10
Marcala, Hond. C6 92
Marcali, Hung. I17 10
Marcaria, Italy D5 18
Marceau, Lac, l., Que., Can. A7 106
Marcelin, Sask., Can. F8 104
Marceline, Mo., U.S. C4 114
Marcelino Ramos, Braz. D13 80
Marcellus, Mi., U.S. H10 110
March (Morava), stm., Eur. G16 10
Marcha, stm., Russia E15 28
Marche, prov., Italy F8 18
Marche, hist. reg., Fr. F8 14
Marche-en-Famenne, Bel. H7 12
Marchegg, Aus. G16 10
Marchena, Spain H6 16
Mar Chiquita, Laguna, b., Arg. I10 80
Mar Chiquita, Laguna, l., Arg. F7 80
Marcigny, Fr. F11 14
Marcola, Or., U.S. F3 122
Marcona, Peru F4 82
Marcos Juárez, Arg. G7 80
Marcos Paz, Arg. H9 80
Marcus, Ia., U.S. I12 118
Marcus Baker, Mount, mtn., Ak., U.S. F21 100
Marcy, Mount, mtn., N.Y., U.S. C13 108
Mardān, Pak. C5 44
Mardarovka, Ukr. B13 20
Mar del Plata, Arg. J10 80
Mardin, Tur. C6 48
Marea de Portillo, Cuba E6 94
Marechal Cândido Rondon, Braz. C11 80
Marechal Taumaturgo, Braz. C5 82
Mareeba, Austl. A6 70
Marengo, Il., U.S. H7 110
Marengo, In., U.S. D10 114
Marengo, Ia., U.S. I3 110
Marenisco, Mi., U.S. D6 110
Marfa, Tx., U.S. I2 116
Marganec, Ukr. H4 26
Margaree, N.S., Can. F12 106
Margaree Harbour, N.S., Can. F12 106
Margaret Bay, B.C., Can. F7 102
Margaretville, N.Y., U.S. E12 108
Margarita, Isla, i., Col. C5 84
Margarita, Isla de, i., Ven. B10 84
Margarita Belén, Arg. D9 80
Margate, S. Afr. H10 66
Margate, Eng., U.K. J15 8
Margate, Fl., U.S. M6 112
Margate City, N.J., U.S. H12 108
Margecany, Czech. G21 10
Margherita Peak, mtn., Afr. A5 58
Marghī, Afg. C2 44
Margilan, Uzb. I12 26
Margos, Peru D3 82
Margot Lake, l., Ont., Can. F21 104
Māršgow, Dasht-e, des., Afg. F17 48
Marguerite Bay, b., Ant. B12 73
María Cleofas, Isla, i., Mex. G6 90
María Elena, Chile B4 80
Maria Gail, Aus. I13 10
María Ignacia (Vela), Arg. I9 80
Maria Island, i., Austl. N8 70
María la Baja, Col. C5 84
María Madre, Isla, i., Mex. G6 90
María Magdalena, Isla, i., Mex. G6 90
Mariana, Braz. F7 79
Mariana Islands, is., Oc. G18 126
Mariana Trench G18 126
Mariāni, India G16 44
Marian Lake, l., N.W. Ter., Can. D9 96
Marianna, Ar., U.S. H6 114
Marianna, Fl., U.S. I1 112
Mariano I. Loza, Arg. E9 80
Mariano Moreno, Arg. J3 80
Mariánské Lázně, Czech. F12 10
Marias, stm., Mt., U.S. B15 122
Marías, Islas, is., Mex. G6 90
Marias Pass, Mt., U.S. B12 122
María Teresa, Arg. H8 80
Mariato, Punta, c., Pan. D2 84
Mā'rib, Yemen G4 47
Maribor, Slo. C10 18
Marica (Évros) (Meriç), stm., Eur. H10 20
Marico, stm., Afr. E8 66
Maricopa, Az., U.S. K4 120
Maricopa, Ca., U.S. I6 124
Maricunga, Salar de, pl., Chile D4 80
Marié, stm., Braz. H9 84
Marie Byrd Land, reg., Ant. C10 73
Marie-Galante, i., Guad. G14 94
Mariehamn, Fin. K16 6
Marie Lake, l., Alta., Can. D4 104
Marienbad see Mariánské Lázně, Czech. F12 10
Marienburg see Malbork, Pol. A19 10
Mariental, Nmb. E3 66
Marienville, Pa., U.S. F7 108
Maries, stm., Mo., U.S. D4 114
Mariestad, Swe. L13 6
Marieta, stm., Ven. E9 84
Marietta, Ga., U.S. F2 112
Marietta, Mn., U.S. F11 118
Marietta, Oh., U.S. H5 108
Marietta, Ok., U.S. F9 116
Marieville, Que., Can. B13 108
Mariga, stm., Nig. F13 64
Marignane, Fr. I12 14
Marigot, Dom. G14 94
Marigot, Guad. E13 94
Mariinsk, Russia F9 28
Marijampole, Lith. G6 22
Marikana, S. Afr. E8 66
Marília, Braz. G4 79
Marimari, stm., Braz. J13 84
Marimba, Ang. C3 58
Marín, Spain C3 16
Marina di Ravenna, Italy E7 18
Marina Fall, wtfl, Guy. E13 84
Marine City, Mi., U.S. H13 110
Marinette, Wi., U.S. E8 110
Maringá, Braz. G3 79
Maringouin, La., U.S. L5 114
Marínguè, Moz. A12 66
Marino, Italy H7 18
Marion, Al., U.S. J9 114
Marion, Ar., U.S. G6 114
Marion, Il., U.S. E8 114
Marion, In., U.S. B11 114
Marion, Ia., U.S. H4 110
Marion, Ks., U.S. M10 118
Marion, Ky., U.S. E8 114
Marion, La., U.S. J4 114
Marion, Mi., U.S. F10 110
Marion, Ms., U.S. J8 114
Marion, N.C., U.S. D4 112
Marion, N.D., U.S. E9 118
Marion, Oh., U.S. G3 108
Marion, S.C., U.S. E7 112
Marion, S.D., U.S. H10 118
Marion, Va., U.S. C5 112
Marion, Wi., U.S. F7 110
Marion, Lake, res., S.C., U.S. F6 112
Marion Junction, Al., U.S. J9 114
Marion Lake, res., Ks., U.S. M10 118
Marion Reef, rf., Austl. B10 70
Marionville, Mo., U.S. E3 114
Marióра, Braz. D12 80
Maripa, Ven. D10 84
Mariposa, Ca., U.S. G6 124
Mariquita, Col. E5 84
Mariscal Estigarribia, Para. B8 80
Marissa, Il., U.S. D7 114
Maritime Alps, mts., Eur. H14 14
Mariupol' (Ždanov), Ukr. H5 26
Mariusa, Caño, mth., Ven. C12 84
Marīvān, Iran D9 48
Märjamaa, Est. C7 22
Marjina Gorka, Bela. H11 22
Marjinsko, Russia C11 22
Marka, Som. H9 56
Markala, Mali E6 64
Markdale, Ont., Can. F15 110
Marked Tree, Ar., U.S. G6 114
Markesan, Wi., U.S. G7 110
Markham, Ont., Can. G16 110
Markham, Tx., U.S. K10 116
Markham, Mount, mtn., Ant. D8 73
Markham Bay, b., N.W. Ter., Can. D18 96
Markle, In., U.S. B11 114
Markleeville, Ca., U.S. F6 124
Markovo, Russia D23 22
Markovo, Russia E26 28
Marks, Russia G7 26
Marks, Ms., U.S. H6 114
Marksville, La., U.S. K4 114
Marktheidenfeld, Ger. F9 10
Marktoberdorf, Ger. H10 10
Marktredwitz, Ger. E12 10
Mark Twain Lake, res., Mo., U.S. C5 114
Markundi, Sud. L2 60
Marlboro, Alta., Can. D18 102
Marlboro, N.Y., U.S. F13 108
Marlborough, Austl. D8 70
Marlborough, Guy. D13 84
Marlborough, Eng., U.K. J12 8
Marlborough, Ma., U.S. E15 108
Marle, Fr. C10 14
Marlette, Mi., U.S. G12 110
Marlin, Tx., U.S. H10 116
Marlinton, W.V., U.S. I6 108
Marlow, Ok., U.S. E9 116
Marmaduke, Ar., U.S. F6 114
Marmande, Fr. H7 14
Marmara Denizi (Sea of Marmara), Tur. I12 20
Marmara Ereğlisi, Tur. I11 20
Marmaris, Tur. M12 20
Marmarth, N.D., U.S. E4 118
Marmaton, stm., U.S. E2 114
Marmelos, Braz. B11 82
Marmelos, Rio dos, stm., Braz. B11 82
Marmet, W.V., U.S. I5 108
Marmora, Ont., Can. F18 110
Mar Muerto, Laguna, b., Mex. I12 90
Marnay, Fr. E12 14
Marne, Mi., U.S. G10 110
Marne, dept., Fr. D11 14
Marne, stm., Fr. C10 14
Marne au Rhin, Canal de la, Fr. D13 14
Maroa, Il., U.S. B8 114
Maroa, Ven. F9 84
Maroala, Madag. O22 67b
Maroantsetra, Madag. O23 67b
Maroelaboom, Nmb. B4 66
Marolambo, Madag. R23 67b
Maromme, Fr. C8 14
Maromokotro, mtn., Madag. O23 67b
Marondera, Zimb. B10 66
Maroni, stm., S.A. C8 76
Maros (Mureș), stm., Eur. C4 20
Maroseranana, Madag. Q23 67b
Maroua, Cam. F9 54
Marovato, Madag. O23 67b
Marovoay, Madag. P22 67b
Marquand, Mo., U.S. E6 114
Marquesas Islands see Marquises, Îles, is., Fr. Poly. I26 126
Marquesas Keys, is., Fl., U.S. O4 112
Marquette, Ks., U.S. M10 118
Marquette, Mi., U.S. D8 110
Marquise, Fr. B8 14
Marquises, Îles (Marquesas Islands), is., Fr. Poly. I26 126
Marrah, Jabal, mtn., Sud. K3 60
Marrakech, Mor. E6 62
Marrawah, Austl. M6 70
Marree, Austl. G3 70
Marrero, La., U.S. M6 114
Marromeu, Moz. B12 66
Mars, Pa., U.S. G6 108
Marsā al-Burayqah, Libya B4 56
Marsabit, Kenya H8 56
Marsala, Italy L7 18
Marsā Maṭrūḥ, Egypt B4 60
Marsden, Austl. I7 70
Marseille, Fr. I12 14
Marseille-en-Beauvaisis, Fr. C8 14
Marseilles, Il., U.S. I7 110
Marshall, Lib. G4 54
Marshall, Lib. H4 64
Marshall, Ar., U.S. G4 114
Marshall, Il., U.S. C9 114
Marshall, Mi., U.S. H11 110
Marshall, Mn., U.S. G12 118
Marshall, Mo., U.S. C3 114
Marshall, N.C., U.S. D4 112
Marshall, Tx., U.S. J2 114
Marshall, Va., U.S. I9 108
Marshallberg, N.C., U.S. E10 112
Marshall Islands, ctry., Oc. H20 126
Marshalltown, Ia., U.S. H3 110
Marshallville, Ga., U.S. G3 112
Marshfield, Mo., U.S. E4 114
Marshfield, Wi., U.S. F5 110
Marsh Harbour, Bah. A6 94
Mars Hill, N.C., U.S. D4 112
Marsh Island, i., La., U.S. M5 114
Marsh Lake, l., Yukon, Can. F27 100
Marsh Peak, mtn., Ut., U.S. D7 120
Marshville, N.C., U.S. E6 112
Marsing, Id., U.S. G9 122
Mart, Tx., U.S. H10 116
Martaban, Burma F4 40
Martaban, Gulf of, b., Burma F4 40
Martapura, Indon. F5 38
Marten Mountain, mtn., Alta., Can. B20 102
Marte R. Gómez, Presa, res., Mex. D10 90
Martha's Vineyard, i., Ma., U.S. F16 108
Martí, Cuba D6 94
Martigny, Switz. F7 13
Martigues, Fr. I12 14
Martil, Mor. J6 16
Martin, Czech. F18 10
Martin, Ky., U.S. B4 112
Martin, Mi., U.S. H10 110
Martin, N.D., U.S. D7 118
Martin, S.D., U.S. H6 118
Martin, Tn., U.S. F8 114
Martina Franca, Italy I12 18
Martindale, Tx., U.S. J9 116
Martinez, Ca., U.S. F3 124
Martinez, Ga., U.S. F4 112
Martínez de la Torre, Mex. G11 90
Martinho Campos, Braz. E6 79
Martinique, dep., N.A. G14 94
Martinique Passage, strt., N.A. G14 94
Martin Lake, res., Al., U.S. J11 114
Martinniemi, Fin. I19 6
Martinsberg, Aus. G15 10
Martinsburg, Pa., U.S. G8 108
Martinsburg, W.V., U.S. H9 108
Martins Ferry, Oh., U.S. G6 108
Martinsville, Il., U.S. C9 114
Martinsville, In., U.S. C10 114
Martinsville, Va., U.S. C7 112
Martin Vaz, Ilhas, is., Braz. G12 74
Martisovo, Russia E14 22
Martos, Spain H8 16
Martre, Lac la, l., N.W. Ter., Can. D9 96
Martti, Fin. H21 6
Maru, Nig. E13 64
Marugame, Japan M8 36
Marula, Zimb. C9 66
Marunga, Ang. A5 66
Marungu, mts., Zaire C5 58
Ma'rūt, Afg. E2 44
Marv Dasht, Iran G12 48
Marvejols, Fr. H10 14
Marvell, Ar., U.S. H6 114
Marvine, Mount, mtn., Ut., U.S. F5 120
Marwayne, Alta., Can. E4 104
Mary, Turk. J10 26
Maryborough, Austl. E10 70
Maryborough, Austl. K5 70
Marydale, S. Afr. G6 66
Maryfield, Sask., Can. I13 104
Mary Kathleen, Austl. C3 70
Maryland, state, U.S. D11 98
Maryneal, Tx., U.S. G6 116
Marys, stm., Nv., U.S. C10 124
Marystown, Newf., Can. E18 106
Marysvale, Ut., U.S. F4 120
Marysville, B.C., Can. H19 102
Marysville, N.B., Can. G7 106
Marysville, Ca., U.S. E4 124
Marysville, Ks., U.S. L11 118
Marysville, Mi., U.S. H13 110
Marysville, Oh., U.S. G3 108
Marysville, Pa., U.S. G10 108
Marysville, Wa., U.S. B3 122
Maryville, Mo., U.S. B2 114
Maryville, Tn., U.S. D3 112
Marzagão, Braz. D4 79
Marzo, Punta, c., Col. D4 84
Marzūq, Libya C3 56
Marzūq, Ṣaḥrā', des., Libya D3 56
Masachapa, Nic. F8 92
Masada see Meẓada, Ḥorvot, hist., Isr. F4 50
Masagua, Guat. C4 92
Masai Steppe, plat., Tan. B7 58
Masaka, Ug. B6 58
Masally, Azer. B10 48
Masan, S. Kor. H16 32
Masasi, Tan. D7 58
Masatepe, Nic. F8 92
Masaya, Nic. F8 92
Masaya, dept., Nic. E8 92
Masbate, Phil. C7 38
Mascarene Islands, is., Afr. F11 58
Mascasín, Arg. F5 80
Mascot, Tn., U.S. C3 112
Mascota, Mex. G7 90
Mascoutah, Il., U.S. D7 114
Masefield, Sask., Can. I7 104
Maseru, Leso. G8 66
Mashaba Mountains, mts., Zimb. B10 66
Mashābih, i., Sau. Ar. I4 48
Mashar, Sud. M4 60
Mashhad, Iran C15 48
Mashīz, Iran G14 48
Māshkel, Hāmūn-i-, l., Pak. G17 48
Māshkel, Rūd-i- (Māshkīd), stm., Asia G17 48
Mashra'ur-Raqq, Sud. M5 60
Masi Manimba, Zaire B3 58
Maṣīrah, Khalīj, b., Oman E11 47
Masisea, Peru C4 82
Masjed-e Soleymān, Iran F10 48
Mask, Lough, l., Ire. H4 8
Maska, Nig. F13 64
Maskanah, Syria C5 48
Maskin, Oman C10 47
Maskwa, stm., Man., Can. H19 104
Masoala, Madag. O24 67b
Masoala, Cap, c., Madag. O24 67b
Masoala, Presqu'île de, pen., Madag. O24 67b
Masoarivo, Madag. Q21 67b
Masomeloka, Madag. R23 67b
Mason, Mi., U.S. H11 110
Mason, Oh., U.S. H2 108
Mason, Tn., U.S. G7 114
Mason, Tx., U.S. I7 116
Mason, W.V., U.S. H4 108
Mason City, Il., U.S. B7 114
Mason City, Ia., U.S. G2 110
Mason City, Ne., U.S. J8 118
Masqaṭ (Muscat), Oman C11 47
Massa, Italy E5 18
Massachusetts, state, U.S. C12 98
Massachusetts Bay, b., Ma., U.S. E16 108
Massafra, Italy I12 18
Massa Marittima, Italy F5 18
Massangena, Moz. C11 66
Massarosa, Italy F5 18
Massena, Ia., U.S. J13 118
Massena, N.Y., U.S. C12 108
Massenya, Chad F4 56
Masset, B.C., Can. C2 102
Masset Inlet, b., B.C., Can. D2 102
Masseube, Fr. I7 14
Massey, Ont., Can. D13 110
Massillon, Oh., U.S. G5 108
Massina, reg., Mali D7 64
Massinga, Moz. D12 66
Massive, Mount, mtn., Co., U.S. E10 120
Mastābah, Sau. Ar. D1 47
Maštaga, Azer. I8 26
Masterson, Tx., U.S. D5 116
Masterton, N.Z. D5 72
Mastung, Pak. F2 44
Mastūrah, Sau. Ar. C1 47
Masuda, Japan M6 36
Masvingo, Zimb. C10 66
Matachewan, Ont., Can. C15 110
Matacuni, stm., Ven. F10 84
Mata de São João, Braz. B9 79
Matadi, Zaire C2 58
Matador, Tx., U.S. E6 116
Matagalpa, Nic. E9 92
Matagalpa, dept., Nic. E9 92
Matagami, Que., Can. G17 96
Matagorda, Tx., U.S. K11 116
Matagorda Bay, b., Tx., U.S. K10 116
Matagorda Island, i., Tx., U.S. K10 116
Matale, Sri L. I6 46
Matam, Sen. D3 64
Matama, Cerro, mtn., C.R. H11 92
Matamoras, Pa., U.S. F12 108
Matamoros, Mex. E11 90
Matamoros, Mex. E8 90
Matane, Que., Can. D6 106
Matanuska, stm., Ak., U.S. F20 100

Name | Map Ref. | Page

Matanzas, Cuba C4 94
Matanzas, Mex. G9 90
Matapalo, Cabo, c., C.R. I11 92
Matape, stm., Mex. C4 90
Matapédia, Que., Can. E7 106
Matapédia, Lac, l., Que., Can. D6 106
Mataquito, stm., Chile H3 80
Matará, Peru B2 82
Matara, Sri L. J6 46
Mataram, Indon. G6 38
Matarani, Peru G5 82
Mataró, Spain D14 16
Matatiele, S. Afr. H9 66
Mataurá, stm., Braz. B11 82
Mateare, Nic. E8 92
Matehuala, Mex. F9 90
Matera, Italy I11 18
Mátészalka, Hung. H22 10
Mateur, Tun. L4 18
Matewan, W.V., U.S. B4 112
Mather, Man., Can. I15 104
Mather, Pa., U.S. H6 108
Matheson, Ont., Can. B15 110
Matheson Island, Man., Can. G18 104
Mathews, Va., U.S. B10 112
Mathis, Tx., U.S. K9 116
Mathura, India G7 44
Matiacoali, Burkina E10 64
Matias Barbosa, Braz. F7 79
Matías Romero, Mex. I12 90
Maticora, stm., Ven. B7 84
Matignon, Fr. D4 14
Matiguás, Nic. E9 92
Matipó, Braz. F7 79
Matiyure, stm., Ven. D8 84
Matlamanyane, Bots. B7 66
M'atlevo, Russia G18 22
Matmata, Tun. D15 62
Mato, stm., Ven. D10 84
Mato, Cerro, mtn., Ven. D10 84
Matočkin Šar, proliv, strt., Russia C8 26
Mato Grosso, state, Braz. D13 82
Mato Grosso, Planalto do, plat., Braz. G7 76
Matonipi, stm., Que., Can. A4 106
Matopo Hills, hills, Zimb. C9 66
Matos, stm., Bol. F9 82
Matosinhos, Port. D3 16
Matou, Tai. L9 34
Matoury, Fr. Gu. C8 76
Matouying, China D6 32
Mato Verde, Braz. C7 79
Matozinhos, Braz. E6 79
Maṭraḥ, Oman C11 47
Matrei in Osttirol, Aus. H12 10
Matru, S.L. H3 64
Matsapha, Swaz. F10 66
Matsudo, Japan L14 36
Matsue, Japan L8 36
Matsumae, Japan F15 36
Matsumoto, Japan K12 36
Matsu Tao, i., Tai. I8 34
Matsuyama, Japan N7 36
Mattagami, stm., Ont., Can. F16 96
Mattagami, stm., Ont., Can. B14 110
Mattagami Heights, Ont., Can. B14 110
Mattawa, Ont., Can. D17 110
Mattawa, Wa., U.S. D6 122
Mattawamkeag, Me., U.S. B18 108
Mattawamkeag, stm., Me., U.S. B18 108
Matterhorn, mtn., Eur. G14 14
Matterhorn, mtn., Nv., U.S. C10 124
Mattersburg, Aus. H16 10
Matthews Ridge, Guy. D12 84
Matthew Town, Bah. D8 94
Mattī, Sabkhat, l., Asia J12 48
Mattighofen, Aus. G13 10
Mattoon, Il., U.S. C8 114
Mattoon, Wi., U.S. E6 110
Mattydale, N.Y., U.S. D10 108
Matuba, Moz. E11 66
Matucana, Peru D3 82
Maturín, Ven. C11 84
Maturino, Russia B20 22
Matutina, Braz. E6 79
Maú (Ireng), stm., S.A. E13 84
Maúa, Moz. D7 58
Maubeuge, Fr. B10 14
Maud, Ok., U.S. D10 116
Maud, Tx., U.S. I2 114
Maude, Austl. J6 70
Maués, Braz. I14 84
Maués, stm., Braz. I14 84
Maui, i., Hi., U.S. q17 125a
Mauldin, S.C., U.S. E4 112
Maule, prov., Chile H2 80
Maule, stm., Chile H2 80
Maule, Laguna del, l., Chile I3 80
Mauléon, Fr. F6 14
Maumee, Oh., U.S. F3 108
Maumee, stm., U.S. F2 108
Maun, Bots. C6 66
Mauna Kea, vol., Hi., U.S. r18 125a
Maunaloa, Hi., U.S. p16 125a
Mauna Loa, vol., Hi., U.S. r18 125a
Maunath Bhanjan, India H10 44
Maunatlala, Bots. D8 66
Maungdaw, Burma D2 40
Maunoir, Lac, l., N.W. Ter., Can. C32 100
Maupin, Or., U.S. E4 122
Mau Rānīpur, India H8 44
Maure-de-Bretagne, Fr. E5 14
Maurepas, Lake, l., La., U.S. L6 114
Mauri, stm., Bol. G7 82
Mauriac, Fr. G9 14
Mauritania (Mauritanie), ctry., Afr. D4 54
Mauritius, ctry., Afr. F11 58
Mauritius, i., Mrts. V18 67c
Mauron, Fr. D4 14
Maury Channel, strt., N.W. Ter., Can. A13 96
Mauston, Wi., U.S. G5 110
Mauterndorf, Aus. H13 10
Mauthausen, Aus. G14 10
Mauvezin, Fr. I7 14
Mavaca, stm., Ven. F10 84
Maverick, Az., U.S. K7 120
Mavinga, Ang. E4 58
Mawchi, Burma E4 40
Maw-daung Pass, Asia I5 40
Mawdesley Lake, l., Man., Can. D14 104
Mawkhi, Burma F5 40
Mawlaik, Burma C3 40
Mawlamyine (Moulmein), Burma F4 40
Maw Taung, mtn., Asia I5 40
Max, N.D., U.S. D6 118
Maxcanú, Mex. G15 90
Maxixe, Moz. D12 66
Maxton, N.C., U.S. E7 112
Maxville, Ont., Can. B12 108
Maxwell, Ca., U.S. E3 124
Maxwell, Ia., U.S. I2 110
Maxwell, Ne., U.S. J7 118
Maxwell, N.M., U.S. C2 116
Maxwell Bay, b., N.W. Ter., Can. B15 96
May, Tx., U.S. H8 116
May, stm., Alta., Can. B23 102
May, Cape, pen., N.J., U.S. I12 108
May, Mount, mtn., Alta., Can. C15 102
Mayaguana, i., Bah. C8 94
Mayaguana Passage, strt., Bah. C8 94
Mayagüez, P.R. E11 94
Mayales, Punta, c., Nic. F9 92
Maya Mountains, mts., N.A. I15 90
Mayapan, hist., Mex. G15 90
Mayarí, Cuba D7 94
Maybeury, W.V., U.S. B5 112
Maybole, Scot., U.K. F9 8
Mayenne, Fr. M13 8
Mayenne, dept., Fr. D6 14
Mayer, Az., U.S. J4 120
Mayersville, Ms., U.S. J5 114
Mayerthorpe, Alta., Can. D19 102
Mayfield, Ky., U.S. F8 114
Mayfield, Ut., U.S. E5 120
Mayflower, Ar., U.S. H4 114
May Inlet, b., N.W. Ter., Can. A12 96
May Jirgui, Niger E14 64
Maymont, Sask., Can. F7 104
Maymyo, Burma C4 40
Maynard, Ia., U.S. H4 110
Maynardville, Tn., U.S. C3 112
Mayne, stm., Austl. D4 70
Mayo, Yukon, Can. E27 100
Mayo, Fl., U.S. I3 112
Mayo, co., Ire. H4 8
Mayo, stm., Col. G4 84
Mayo, stm., Mex. D5 90
Mayo, stm., Peru B3 82
Mayodan, N.C., U.S. C7 112
Mayo Lake, l., Yukon, Can. E27 100
Mayon Volcano, vol., Phil. o20 39b
Mayor Buratovich, Arg. J7 80
Mayor Pablo Lagerenza, Para. H11 82
Mayotte, dep., Afr. D9 58
May Pen, Jam. F6 94
Mayrhofen, Aus. H11 10
Mays Landing, N.J., U.S. H12 108
Maysville, Ky., U.S. I3 108
Maysville, Mo., U.S. C2 114
Maysville, N.C., U.S. E9 112
Maysville, Ok., U.S. E9 116
Mayumba, Gabon B2 58
Māyūram, India G5 46
Mayville, Mi., U.S. G12 110
Mayville, N.Y., U.S. E7 108
Mayville, N.D., U.S. D10 118
Mayville, Wi., U.S. G7 110
Maywood, Ne., U.S. K7 118
Maza, Arg. I7 80
Mazabuka, Zam. E5 58
Mazagan see El-Jadida, Mor. D6 62
Mazagão, Braz. D8 76
Mazamet, Fr. I9 14
Mazán, stm., Peru I6 84
Mazār, Jabal, mtn., Asia A6 50
Mazara del Vallo, Italy L7 18
Mazār-e Sharīf, Afg. B2 44
Mazaruni, stm., Guy. E13 84
Mazatenango, Guat. C3 92
Mazatlán, Mex. F6 90
Mazatzal Peak, mtn., Az., U.S. J5 120
Mažeikiai, Lith. E5 22
Mazenod, Sask., Can. I8 104
Mazeppa, Mn., U.S. F3 110
Mazhuang, China C3 34
Mazirbe, Lat. D5 22
Mazoe, stm., Afr. E6 58
Mazomanie, Wi., U.S. G6 110
Mazon, Il., U.S. I7 110
Mazsalaca, Lat. D8 22
Mazunga, Zimb. C9 66
Mazury, reg., Pol. B20 10
Mbabane, Swaz. F10 66
Mbacké, Sen. D2 64
Mbage, Cen. Afr. Rep. O3 60
Mbaïki, Cen. Afr. Rep. H4 56
Mbala, Zam. C6 58
Mbale, Ug. A6 58
Mbalmayo, Cam. H9 54
Mbamba Bay, Tan. D6 58
Mbandaka (Coquilhatville), Zaire A3 58
Mbanga, Cam. I14 64
M'banza Congo, Ang. C2 58
Mbanza-Ngungu, Zaire C2 58
Mbarara, Ug. B6 58
Mbari, stm., Cen. Afr. Rep. G5 56
Mbashe, stm., Afr. I9 66
M'bengué, I.C. F7 64
Mbeya, Tan. C6 58
Mbinda, Congo B2 58
Mbini, Eq. Gui. H8 54
Mbomou (Bomu), stm., Afr. H5 56
Mbonge, Cam. I14 64
Mboro, Sud. N5 60
Mbour, Sen. D1 64
Mbout, Maur. C3 64
Mbuji-Mayi (Bakwanga), Zaire C4 58
Mburucuyá, Arg. E9 80
McAdam, N.B., Can. G6 106
McAdoo, Pa., U.S. G11 108
McAlester, Ok., U.S. E11 116
McAllen, Tx., U.S. M8 116
McArthur, Oh., U.S. H4 108
McAuley, Man., Can. H13 104
McBain, Mi., U.S. F10 110
McBee, S.C., U.S. E6 112
McBeth Fjord, N.W. Ter., Can. C19 96
McBride, B.C., Can. D14 102
McCall, Id., U.S. F9 122
McCall Creek, Ms., U.S. K6 114
McCallum, Newf., Can. E17 106
McCamey, Tx., U.S. H4 116
McCammon, Id., U.S. H13 122
McCauley Island, i., B.C., Can. D4 102
McCaysville, Ga., U.S. E2 112
McClarty Lake, l., Man., Can. D14 104
McCleary, Wa., U.S. C2 122
McClellanville, S.C., U.S. F7 112
McClintock, Mount, mtn., Ant. D8 73
McCloud, Ca., U.S. C3 124
McClure, Il., U.S. E7 114
McClure, Pa., U.S. G9 108
McClusky, N.D., U.S. D7 118
McColl, S.C., U.S. E7 112
McComas, W.V., U.S. B5 112
McComb, Ms., U.S. K6 114
McComb, Oh., U.S. F3 108
McConaughy, Lake, res., Ne., U.S. J6 118
McConnell Range, mts., N.W. Ter., Can. E33 100
McConnellsburg, Pa., U.S. H9 108
McConnelsville, Oh., U.S. H5 108
McCook, Ne., U.S. K7 118
McCormick, S.C., U.S. F4 112
McCoy Lake, l., Ont., Can. F22 104
McCreary, Man., Can. H15 104
McCrory, Ar., U.S. G5 114
McCune, Ks., U.S. N12 118
McCurtain, Ok., U.S. D12 116
McCusker, stm., Sask., Can. C5 104
McDade, Tx., U.S. I9 116
McDavid, Fl., U.S. L9 114
McDermitt, Nv., U.S. C8 124
McDermott, Oh., U.S. I3 108
McDonald, Ks., U.S. L6 118
McDonough, Ga., U.S. F2 112
Mcensk, Russia H19 22
McEwen, Tn., U.S. F9 114
McFadden, Wy., U.S. C10 120
McFarland, Ca., U.S. I6 124
McFarland, Wi., U.S. G6 110
McGavock Lake, l., Man., Can. B13 104
McGehee, Ar., U.S. I5 114
McGill, Nv., U.S. E11 124
McGrath, Ak., U.S. E17 100
McGraw, N.Y., U.S. E10 108
McGregor, Ia., U.S. G4 110
McGregor, Tx., U.S. H9 116
McGregor, stm., B.C., Can. C13 102
McGregor Lake, l., Alta., Can. G22 102
McGregor Range, mts., Austl. F5 70
McHenry, Il., U.S. H7 110
McHenry, Ms., U.S. L7 114
Mchinji, Mwi. D6 58
McInnes Lake, l., Ont., Can. F21 104
McIntosh, Al., U.S. K8 114
McIntosh, Mn., U.S. D12 118
McIntosh, S.D., U.S. F6 118
McIntosh Lake, l., Sask., Can. C9 104
McIntyre Bay, b., B.C., Can. C3 102
McKeand, stm., N.W. Ter., Can. D19 96
McKee, Ky., U.S. B3 112
McKeesport, Pa., U.S. G7 108
McKenzie, Al., U.S. K10 114
McKenzie, Tn., U.S. F8 114
McKenzie Bridge, Or., U.S. F3 122
McKenzie Island, Ont., Can. G21 104
McKenzie Lake, l., Sask., Can. D12 104
McKinley, Mount, mtn., Ak., U.S. E19 100
McKinleyville, Ca., U.S. D1 124
McKinney, Tx., U.S. F10 116
McKnight Lake, l., Man., Can. B13 104
McLain, Ms., U.S. K8 114
McLaughlin, S.D., U.S. F7 118
McLaughlin, stm., Man., Can. E18 104
McLaurin, Ms., U.S. K7 114
McLean, Sask., Can. H10 104
McLean, Il., U.S. B7 114
McLean, Tx., U.S. D6 116
McLean Lake, l., Sask., Can. B5 104
McLeansboro, Il., U.S. D8 114
McLennan, Alta., Can. B18 102
McLeod, stm., Alta., Can. D19 102
McLeod Bay, b., N.W. Ter., Can. D10 96
McLeod Lake, B.C., Can. C11 102
M'Clintock Channel, strt., N.W. Ter., Can. B12 96
McLoughlin, Mount, mtn., Or., U.S. H3 122
McLoughlin Bay, b., N.W. Ter., Can. C13 96
McLouth, Ks., U.S. L12 118
McLure, B.C., Can. F14 102
M'Clure Strait, strt., N.W. Ter., Can. B9 96
McMahon, Sask., Can. H7 104
McMillan, Lake, res., N.M., U.S. G2 116
McMinnville, Or., U.S. E2 122
McMinnville, Tn., U.S. G11 114
McMurdo, sci., Ant. C8 73
McMurdo Sound, strt., Ant. C8 73
McNary, Az., U.S. J7 120
McNeil, Ar., U.S. I3 114
McNeil, Mount, mtn., B.C., Can. C4 102
McNeill, Ms., U.S. L7 114
McPhail, stm., Man., Can. F19 104
McPherson, Ks., U.S. M10 118
McPherson Range, mts., Austl. G10 70
McQueeney, Tx., U.S. J8 116
McRae, Ar., U.S. G5 114
McRae, Ga., U.S. G4 112
McRoberts, Ky., U.S. B4 112
McVeigh, Ky., U.S. B4 112
McVille, N.D., U.S. D9 118
McWilliams, Al., U.S. K9 114
M'Daourouch, Alg. M2 18
Meacham, Sask., Can. F9 104
Mead, Ne., U.S. J11 118
Mead, Lake, res., U.S. H2 120
Meade, Ks., U.S. N7 118
Meaden Peak, mtn., Co., U.S. D9 120
Meadow, Tx., U.S. F4 116
Meadow, Ut., U.S. F4 120
Meadow Lake, Sask., Can. D6 104
Meadow Lake, l., Sask., Can. D6 104
Meadow Lake Provincial Park, Sask., Can. D5 104
Meadowview, Va., U.S. C5 112
Meadville, Ms., U.S. K6 114
Meadville, Mo., U.S. C3 114
Meadville, Pa., U.S. F6 108
Meaford, Ont., Can. F15 110
Meaghers Grant, N.S., Can. H10 106
Méan, Bel. H7 12
Meana, Turk. C16 48
Meandarra, Austl. F8 70
Meander River, Alta., Can. E9 96
Meath, co., Ire. H7 8
Meath, hist. reg., Ire. H6 8
Meaux, Fr. D9 14
Mebane, N.C., U.S. C7 112
Mecaya, stm., Col. G5 84
Mecca see Makkah, Sau. Ar. D1 47
Mechanic Falls, Me., U.S. C16 108
Mechanicsburg, Oh., U.S. G3 108
Mechanicsville, Ia., U.S. I4 110
Mechanicsville, Va., U.S. B9 112
Mechanicville, N.Y., U.S. E13 108
Mechelen (Malines), Bel. F5 12
Mechita, Arg. H8 80
Mechra Safsaf, Mor. K9 16
Mechriyya, Alg. D10 62
Mechroha, Alg. M2 18
Mecklenburg, hist. reg., Ger. B12 10
Mecklenburger Bucht, b., Ger. A11 10
Mecklenburg-Vorpommern, state, Ger. B12 10
Meda, Port. E4 16
Medan, Indon. M5 40
Médanos, Arg. J7 80
Medanosa, Punta, c., Arg. F3 78
Medaryville, In., U.S. A10 114
Mede, Italy D3 18
Medeiros Neto, Braz. D8 79
Medellín, Col. D5 84
Médenine, Tun. D16 62
Mederdra, Maur. C2 64
Medford, Ok., U.S. C9 116
Medford, Or., U.S. H3 122
Medford, Wi., U.S. E5 110
Medgidia, Rom. E12 20
Mediapolis, Ia., U.S. I4 110
Mediaș, Rom. C8 20
Medical Lake, Wa., U.S. C8 122
Medicina, Italy E6 18
Medicine Bow, Wy., U.S. C10 120
Medicine Bow, stm., Wy., U.S. B10 120
Medicine Bow Mountains, mts., U.S. C10 120
Medicine Bow Peak, mtn., Wy., U.S. C10 120
Medicine Hat, Alta., Can. F10 96
Medicine Hat, Alta., Can. H4 104
Medicine Lake, Mt., U.S. C3 118
Medicine Lodge, Ks., U.S. N9 118
Medicine Lodge, stm., U.S. B8 116
Medina, Braz. D8 79
Medina, N.Y., U.S. D8 108
Medina, N.D., U.S. E8 118
Medina, Oh., U.S. F5 108
Medina, Tx., U.S. J7 116
Medina, stm., Tx., U.S. J8 116
Medina see Al-Madīnah, Sau. Ar. B1 47
Medina del Campo, Spain D7 16
Medininkai, Lith. G8 22
Medinīpur, India I12 44
Medio, Punta, c., Chile D3 80
Mediterranean Sea E9 52
Medjerda, Monts de la, mts., Afr. M3 18
Mednogorsk, Russia G9 26
Mednoje, Russia E18 22
Mednyj, ostrov, i., Russia G25 28
Médoc, reg., Fr. G6 14
Medora, In., U.S. D10 114
Medora, N.D., U.S. E4 118
Medouneu, Gabon A2 58
Medstead, Sask., Can. E6 104
Meductic, N.B., Can. F6 106
Medveđa, Yugo. G5 20
Medvedevskoje, Russia C18 22
Medvedica, stm., Russia G6 26
Medvežjegorsk, Russia E4 26
Medvežji ostrova, is., Russia C24 28
Medway, stm., N.S., Can. H9 106
Medyn', Russia G18 22
Meekatharra, Austl. E3 68
Meeker, Co., U.S. D9 120
Meeks Bay, Ca., U.S. E5 124
Meelpaeg Lake, res., Newf., Can. D17 106
Meer, Bel. F6 12
Meerane, Ger. E12 10
Meerut, India F7 44
Meeteetse, Wy., U.S. F17 122
Mega, Eth. H8 56
Mégantic, Lac, l., Que., Can. B16 108
Mégara, Grc. K7 20
Megargel, Tx., U.S. F8 116
Meghālaya, state, India H14 44
Meghna, stm., Bngl. H14 44
Mehadia, Rom. E6 20
Mehar, Pak. G2 44
Mehdia, Alg. C11 62
Mehedinți, co., Rom. E6 20
Meherrin, stm., U.S. C9 112
Mehrān, Iran E9 48
Meia Ponte, Rio da, stm., Braz. D4 79
Meigs, Ga., U.S. H2 112
Meiktila, Burma D3 40
Meilie, China I6 34
Meiners Oaks, Ca., U.S. J6 124
Meiningen, Ger. E10 10
Meiringen, Switz. E9 13
Meissen, Ger. D13 10
Meixian, China K5 34
Meiyino, Sud. N8 60
Meizhai, China B10 40
Mejerda, Oued (Oued Medjerda), stm., Afr. M4 18
Mejez el Bab, Tun. M4 18
Mejicanos, El Sal. D5 92
Mejillones, Chile B3 80
Mejillones, Peninsula, pen., Chile B3 80
Mejillones del Sur, Bahía de, b., Chile B3 80
Mékambo, Gabon A2 58
Mekele, Eth. K10 60
Meknès, Mor. D8 62
Mekong, stm., Asia H8 40
Mekoryuk, Ak., U.S. F11 100
Mékrou, stm., Afr. F7 54
Melado, stm., Chile H3 80
Melaka, Malay. M7 40
Melanesia, is., Oc. I19 126
Melbourne, Austl. K6 70
Melbourne, Ar., U.S. F5 114
Melbourne, Fl., U.S. K5 112
Melbourne, Ia., U.S. I2 110
Melbourne Island, i., N.W. Ter., Can. C12 96
Melby House, Scot., U.K. A12 8
Melcher, Ia., U.S. I2 110
Melchor Múzquiz, Mex. D9 90
Meldorf, Ger. A9 10
Meldrum Bay, Ont., Can. E12 110
Meldrum Creek, B.C., Can. E12 102
Melechovo, Russia E24 22
Melegnano, Italy D4 18
Melenki, Russia F24 22
Meleuz, Russia G9 26
Mélèzes, Rivière aux, stm., Que., Can. E18 96
Melfi, Chad F4 56
Melfi, Italy H10 18
Melfort, Sask., Can. F10 104
Melgaço, Port. C3 16
Melgar, Col. E5 84
Melghir, Chott, l., Alg. C14 62
Melhus, Nor. J12 6
Meli, stm., Afr. G4 64
Meliane, Oued, stm., Tun. M5 18
Melide, Switz. G10 13
Melilla, Sp. N. Afr. C9 62
Melincué, Arg. G8 80
Melipilla, Chile G3 80
Melita, Man., Can. I13 104
Melitopol', Ukr. F15 4
Mellègue, Oued, stm., Afr. M3 18
Mellen, Wi., U.S. D5 110
Mellette, S.D., U.S. F9 118
Mel'nica-Podol'skaja, Ukr. A10 20
Mělník, Czech. E14 10
Melo, Ur. G11 80
Melo, stm., Para. I12 82
Melong, Cam. I14 64
Melos see Mílos, i., Grc. M8 20
Melrose, Mn., U.S. F13 118
Melrose, N.M., U.S. E3 116
Melrose, Wi., U.S. F5 110
Melstone, Mt., U.S. D18 122
Melton Mowbray, Eng., U.K. I13 8
Melúa, Col. F6 84
Melun, Burma D2 40
Melun, Fr. D9 14
Melvern, Ks., U.S. M12 118
Melville, Sask., Can. H12 104
Melville, La., U.S. L5 114
Melville, Détroit de see Viscount Melville Sound, strt., N.W. Ter., Can. B11 96
Melville, Lake, l., Newf., Can. F21 96
Melville Bugt, b., Grnld. B13 86
Melville Hills, hills, N.W. Ter., Can. B33 100
Melville Island, i., Austl. B6 68
Melville Island, i., N.W. Ter., Can. B8 86
Melville Peninsula, pen., N.W. Ter., Can. C16 96
Melville Sound, strt., N.W. Ter., Can. C11 96
Melvin, Il., U.S. J7 110
Melvin, Ky., U.S. B4 112
Melvin, Tx., U.S. H7 116
Melvin, Lough, l., Eur. G5 8
Melvin Lake, l., Man., Can. A14 104
Melyana, Alg. B12 62
Melzo, Italy D4 18
Memel, S. Afr. F9 66
Memel see Nemunas, stm., Eur. F6 22
Memmingen, Ger. H10 10
Memo, stm., Ven. C9 84
Mémót, Camb. I9 40
Mempawah, Indon. N10 40
Memphis, Fl., U.S. L4 112
Memphis, Mi., U.S. H13 110
Memphis, Mo., U.S. B4 114
Memphis, Tn., U.S. G6 114
Memphis, Tx., U.S. E6 116
Memphremagog, Lake, l., N.A. B14 108
Mena, Ar., U.S. H2 114
Menahga, Mn., U.S. E12 118
Ménaka, Mali D11 64
Menaldum, Neth. B8 12
Menan, Id., U.S. G14 122
Menard, Tx., U.S. I7 116
Menasha, Wi., U.S. F7 110
Menawashei, Sud. K3 60
Mendawai, stm., Indon. F5 38
Mende, Fr. H10 14
Menden, Ger. D7 10
Mendenhall, Ms., U.S. K7 114
Méndez, Mex. E10 90
Mendī, Eth. M8 60
Mendi, Pap. N. Gui. G11 38
Mendocino, Ca., U.S. E2 124
Mendocino, Cape, c., Ca., U.S. D1 124
Mendon, Il., U.S. B5 114
Mendon, Mi., U.S. H10 110
Mendota, Ca., U.S. H5 124
Mendota, Il., U.S. I6 110
Mendoza, Arg. G4 80
Mendoza, Peru B3 82
Mendoza, prov., Arg. H4 80
Mendoza, stm., Arg. G4 80
Ménéac, Fr. D4 14
Mene de Mauroa, Ven. B7 84
Mene Grande, Ven. C7 84
Menemen, Tur. K11 20
Menen (Menin), Bel. G3 12
Menfi, Italy L7 18
Mengcheng, China E10 30
Menggala, Indon. F4 38
Menggu, China A7 40
Menghai, China C6 40
Mengla, China D6 40
Mengzhi, China B5 40
Mengzi, China C7 40
Menihek Lakes, l., Newf., Can. F19 96
Menindee, Austl. I5 70
Menindee Lake, l., Austl. I5 70
Menlo Park, Ca., U.S. G3 124
Menno, S.D., U.S. H10 118
Meno, Ok., U.S. C8 116
Menominee, Mi., U.S. E8 110
Menominee, stm., U.S. E8 110
Menomonee Falls, Wi., U.S. G7 110
Menomonie, Wi., U.S. F4 110
Menongue, Ang. D3 58
Menorca, i., Spain F16 16
Mens, Fr. H12 14
Mentasta Mountains, mts., Ak., U.S. E23 100
Mentawai, Kepulauan, is., Indon. F2 38
Mentawai, Selat, strt., Indon. F3 38
Menton, Fr. I14 14
Mentone, Tx., U.S. H3 116
Mentor, Oh., U.S. F5 108
Menzel Bourguiba, Tun. L4 18
Menzel Bou Zelfa, Tun. M5 18
Menzel Djemil, Tun. L4 18
Menzel Temime, Tun. M5 18
Menzies, Austl. E4 68
Menzies, Mount, mtn., Ant. C5 73
Meoqui, Mex. C7 90
Meota, Sask., Can. E6 104
Meppel, Neth. C9 12
Meppen, Ger. C7 10
Meqerghane, Sebkha, pl., Alg. G11 62
Mequon, Wi., U.S. G8 110
Mer, Fr. E8 14
Meramec, stm., Mo., U.S. D5 114
Merano (Meran), Italy C6 18
Merasheen, Newf., Can. E19 106
Merasheen Island, i., Newf., Can. E19 106
Merate, Italy D4 18
Merauke, Indon. G11 38
Mercaderes, Col. G4 84
Mercara, India F3 46
Merced, Ca., U.S. G5 124
Merced, stm., Ca., U.S. G5 124
Mercedario, Cerro, mtn., Arg. F3 80
Mercedes, Arg. E9 80
Mercedes, Arg. G6 80
Mercedes, Arg. H9 80
Mercedes, Tx., U.S. M9 116
Mercedes, Ur. G9 80
Mercer, Mo., U.S. B3 114
Mercer, Pa., U.S. F6 108
Mercer, Wi., U.S. D5 110
Mercersburg, Pa., U.S. H9 108
Merchants Bay, b., N.W. Ter., Can. C20 96
Merchtem, Bel. G5 12
Mercoal, Alta., Can. D17 102
Mercury, Nv., U.S. H10 124
Mercy, Cape, c., N.W. Ter., Can. D20 96
Mercy Bay, b., N.W. Ter., Can. B9 96
Meredith, N.H., U.S. D15 108
Meredith, Lake, res., Tx., U.S. D5 116
Meredosia, Il., U.S. C6 114
Mereeg, Som. H10 56
Merenkurkku (Norra Kvarken), strt., Eur. J17 6
Merevari, stm., Ven. E10 84
Merewa, Eth. N9 60
Mergui (Myeik), Burma H5 40
Mergui Archipelago, is., Burma H5 40
Meriç (Marica) (Évros), stm., Eur. H10 20
Mérida, Mex. G15 90
Mérida, Spain G5 16
Mérida, Ven. C7 84
Mérida, state, Ven. C7 84
Mérida, Cordillera de, mts., Ven. C7 84
Meriden, Ct., U.S. F14 108
Meridian, Ga., U.S. H5 112
Meridian, Id., U.S. G9 122
Meridian, Ms., U.S. J8 114
Meridian, Tx., U.S. H9 116
Meridianville, Al., U.S. H10 114
Mérignac, Fr. H6 14
Merigold, Ms., U.S. I6 114
Merimbula, Austl. K8 70
Merín, Laguna (Lagoa Mirim), b., S.A. G12 80
Merino, Co., U.S. K4 118
Merinos, Ur. G10 80
Merkel, Tx., U.S. G6 116
Merkendorf, Ger. F10 10
Merkinė, Lith. G7 22
Merkulovići, Bela. I13 22
Merlin, Ont., Can. H13 110
Merlin, Or., U.S. H2 122
Merlo, Arg. G6 80
Merna, Ne., U.S. J8 118
Mernye, Hung. I17 10
Meron, Hare, mtn., Isr. C4 50
Merredin, Austl. F3 68
Merrickville, Ont., Can. C11 108
Merrill, Ia., U.S. I11 118
Merrill, Mi., U.S. G11 110
Merrill, Or., U.S. H4 122
Merrill, Wi., U.S. E6 110
Merrillan, Wi., U.S. F5 110
Merrillville, In., U.S. A9 114
Merrimack, stm., U.S. D15 108
Merriman, Ne., U.S. I6 118
Merritt, B.C., Can. G14 102
Merritt Island, Fl., U.S. K6 112
Merriwa, Austl. I9 70
Mer Rouge, La., U.S. J5 114
Merryville, La., U.S. L3 114
Mersch, Lux. I9 12
Merseburg, Ger. D11 10
Mersey, stm., Austl. M7 70
Mersey, stm., N.S., Can. H9 106
Mersing, Malay. M7 40
Mērsrags, Lat. D6 22
Merthyr Tydfil, Wales, U.K. J10 8
Mértola, Port. H4 16
Mertzon, Tx., U.S. H6 116
Méru, Fr. C9 14
Meru, Kenya A7 58
Meru, Mount, mtn., Tan. B7 58
Mervin, Sask., Can. E6 104
Méry, Fr. D10 14
Merzig, Ger. F6 10
Mesa, Az., U.S. K5 120
Mesa, stm., Spain D10 16
Mesabi Range, hills, Mn., U.S. C3 110
Mesagne, Italy I12 18
Mesa Mountain, mtn., Co., U.S. G10 120
Mesa Verde National Park, Co., U.S. G8 120
Mescalero, N.M., U.S. K11 120
Meschede, Ger. D8 10
Meščovsk, Russia G18 22
Mesfinto, Eth. K9 60
Mesgouez, Lac, l., Que., Can. F17 96
Meshgīn Shahr, Iran B9 48
Mesick, Mi., U.S. F10 110
Mesilinka, stm., B.C., Can. A10 102
Mesilla, N.M., U.S. L10 120
Meskiana, Alg. C14 62
Meslay-du-Maine, Fr. E6 14
Mesocco, Switz. F11 13
Mesolóngion, Grc. K5 20
Mesopotamia, hist. reg., Asia D8 48
Mesquita, Braz. E7 79
Mesquite, Nv., U.S. H11 124
Mesquite, Tx., U.S. G10 116
Messalo, stm., Moz. D7 58
Messina, Italy K10 18
Messina, S. Afr. D10 66
Messina, Stretto di, strt., Italy K10 18
Messíni, Grc. L6 20
Messiniakós Kólpos, b., Grc. M6 20
Messix Peak, mtn., Ut., U.S. C4 120
Messojacha, stm., Russia D13 26
Mestá, Grc. K9 20
Mesta (Néstos), stm., Eur. H7 20
Mestassa, Mor. C8 62
Mestghanem, Alg. C11 62
Mestre, Italy D7 18
Meszah Peak, mtn., B.C., Can. G29 100
Meta, dept., Col. F6 84
Meta, stm., S.A. D9 84
Meta Incognita Peninsula, pen., N.W. Ter., Can. D19 96
Metairie, La., U.S. M6 114
Metaline Falls, Wa., U.S. B8 122
Metamora, Il., U.S. J6 110
Metán, Arg. C6 80
Metapán, El Sal. C5 92
Meteghan, N.S., Can. H7 106
Metema, Eth. K9 60
Meteor Crater, crat., Az., U.S. I5 120
Methóni, Grc. M5 20
Methow, stm., Wa., U.S. B5 122
Metiskow, Alta., Can. F4 104
Metković, Cro. F12 18
Metlakatla, B.C., Can. C4 102
Metlakatla, Ak., U.S. I29 100
Metlaoui, Tun. C15 62
Metlatonoc, Mex. I10 90
Meto, Bayou, stm., Ar., U.S. H5 114
Metolius, stm., Or., U.S. F4 122
Metropolis, Il., U.S. E8 114
Metropolitan, Mi., U.S. D8 110
Metsematluku, Bots. E7 66
Metter, Ga., U.S. G4 112
Mettmann, Ger. D6 10
Mettuppālaiyam, India G4 46
Mettūr, India G4 46
Metu, Eth. M8 60
Metulla, Isr. B5 50
Metz, Fr. C13 14
Meulan, Fr. C8 14
Meureudu, Indon. L4 40
Meurthe, stm., Fr. D13 14
Meurthe-et-Moselle, dept., Fr. D13 14
Meuse, dept., Fr. D12 14
Meuse (Maas), stm., Eur. E5 10
Meuselwitz, Ger. D12 10
Mexia, Tx., U.S. H10 116
Mexiana, Ilha, i., Braz. D9 76
Mexicali, Mex. A2 90
Mexican Hat, Ut., U.S. G7 120
Mexico, Me., U.S. C16 108
Mexico, Mo., U.S. C5 114
Mexico, N.Y., U.S. D10 108
México, state, Mex. H10 90

Name	Map Ref.	Page
Mexico (México), ctry., N.A.	F9	90
Mexico, Gulf of, b., N.A.	C6	88
Mexico Beach, Fl., U.S.	J1	112
Mexico City see Ciudad de México, Mex.	H10	90
Meximieux, Fr.	G12	14
Meycauayan, Phil.	N19	39b
Meyers Chuck, Ak., U.S.	I28	100
Meyersdale, Pa., U.S.	H7	108
Meyísti, i., Grc.	H13	4
Meymac, Fr.	G9	14
Meymaneh, Afg.	C1	44
Meymeh, stm., Asia	E9	48
Meyrargues, Fr.	I12	14
Meyronne, Sask., Can.	I8	104
Meẕada, Ḥorvot (Masada), hist., Isr.	F4	50
Mezapa, Hond.	B7	92
Mezcala, Mex.	I10	90
Mezcalapa, stm., Mex.	I13	90
Meždurečensk, Russia	G9	28
Mèze, Fr.	I10	14
Mezen', Russia	D6	26
Mezen', stm., Russia	D6	26
Mežgorje, Ukr.	A7	20
Meziadin Lake, l., B.C., Can.	A5	102
Mézin, Fr.	H7	14
Mezinovskij, Russia	F23	22
Mezőberény, Hung.	I21	10
Mezőcsát, Hung.	H20	10
Mezőkovácsháza, Hung.	I20	10
Mezőkövesd, Hung.	H20	10
Mezőtúr, Hung.	H20	10
Mezquital, Mex.	F7	90
Mezquital, stm., Mex.	F7	90
Mglin, Russia	H15	22
M'goun, Irhil, mtn., Mor.	E7	62
Mhow, India	I6	44
Miahuatlán de Porfirio Díaz, Mex.	I11	90
Miajadas, Spain	F6	16
Miami, Man., Can.	I16	104
Miami, Az., U.S.	K6	120
Miami, Fl., U.S.	N6	112
Miami, Ok., U.S.	C12	116
Miami, Tx., U.S.	D6	116
Miami Beach, Fl., U.S.	N6	112
Miami Canal, Fl., U.S.	M6	112
Miamisburg, Oh., U.S.	H2	108
Miami Springs, Fl., U.S.	N6	112
Mīāndoāb, Iran	C9	48
Miandrivazo, Madag.	Q21	67b
Mīāneh, Iran	C9	48
Miangas, Pulau, i., Indon.	D8	38
Mianhu, China	L5	34
Miānwāli, Pak.	D4	44
Mianyang, China	E7	30
Mianyang, China	E2	34
Miaoli, Tai.	K9	34
Miarinavaratra, Madag.	R22	67b
Miass, Russia	G10	26
Miastko, Pol.	A17	10
Micanopy, Fl., U.S.	J4	112
Micaúne, Moz.	B13	66
Michajlov, Russia	G22	22
Michajlovka, Russia	G6	26
Michanoviči, Bela.	H10	22
Michaud, Point, c., N.S., Can.	G13	106
Micheal Peak, mtn., B.C., Can.	D8	102
Michel, B.C., Can.	H20	102
Miches, Dom. Rep.	E10	94
Michigamme, stm., Mi., U.S.	D7	110
Michigan, N.D., U.S.	C9	118
Michigan, state, U.S.	C9	98
Michigan, Lake, l., U.S.	F8	110
Michigan Center, Mi., U.S.	H11	110
Michigan City, In., U.S.	A10	114
Michipicoten Island, i., Ont., Can.	C10	110
Michnevo, Russia	F20	22
Michoacán, state, Mex.	H9	90
Mico, stm., Nic.	E10	92
Mico, Montañas del, mts., Guat.	B6	92
Micronesia, is., Oc.	G19	126
Micronesia, Federated States of, ctry., Oc.	H19	126
Mičurinsk, Russia	I23	22
Midale, Sask., Can.	I11	104
Midar, Mor.	C9	62
Mid-Atlantic Ridge	F9	128
Middelburg, Neth.	E4	12
Middelburg, S. Afr.	H7	66
Middelburg, S. Afr.	E9	66
Middelfart, Den.	N11	6
Middelharnis, Neth.	E5	12
Middelpos, S. Afr.	H5	66
Middelwater, S. Afr.	D10	66
Middenmeer, Neth.	C7	12
Middle, stm., B.C., Can.	B9	102
Middle, stm., Ia., U.S.	A2	114
Middle America Trench	H10	86
Middle Andaman, i., India	H2	40
Middle-Bay, Que., Can.	A16	106
Middleboro, Ma., U.S.	F16	108
Middlebourne, W.V., U.S.	H6	108
Middlebro, Man., Can.	I19	104
Middle Brook, Newf., Can.	D19	106
Middleburg, N.Y., U.S.	E12	108
Middleburg, Pa., U.S.	G9	108
Middlebury, Vt., U.S.	C13	108
Middle Caicos, i., T./C. Is.	D9	94
Middle Channel, mth., N.W. Ter., Can.	B27	100
Middle Fabius, stm., Mo., U.S.	C4	114
Middlefield, Oh., U.S.	F5	108
Middle Loup, stm., Ne., U.S.	J8	118
Middle Musquodoboit, N.S., Can.	G10	106
Middle Point, Oh., U.S.	G2	108
Middleport, Oh., U.S.	H4	108
Middlesboro, Ky., U.S.	C3	112
Middlesbrough, Eng., U.K.	G12	8
Middlesex, Belize	I15	90
Middlesex, N.C., U.S.	D8	112
Middle Stewiacke, N.S., Can.	G10	106
Middleton, N.S., Can.	H8	106
Middleton, Mi., U.S.	G11	110
Middleton, Tn., U.S.	G8	114
Middleton, Wi., U.S.	G6	110
Middleton Island, i., Ak., U.S.	G21	100
Middletown, Ca., U.S.	F3	124
Middletown, Ct., U.S.	F14	108
Middletown, De., U.S.	H11	108
Middletown, Il., U.S.	B7	114
Middletown, In., U.S.	B11	114
Middletown, Ky., U.S.	D11	114
Middletown, Md., U.S.	H9	108
Middletown, N.Y., U.S.	F12	108
Middletown, Oh., U.S.	H2	108
Middletown, Pa., U.S.	G10	108
Middletown, R.I., U.S.	F15	108
Middletown, Va., U.S.	H8	108
Middleville, Mi., U.S.	H10	110
Midelt, Mor.	D8	62
Midgic, N.B., Can.	G9	106
Mid Glamorgan, co., Wales, U.K.	J10	8
Midi, Canal du, Fr.	I9	14
Midi de Bigorre, Pic du, mtn., Fr.	J7	14
Midland, Ont., Can.	F16	110
Midland, Ca., U.S.	K11	124
Midland, Mi., U.S.	G11	110
Midland, N.C., U.S.	D6	112
Midland, S.D., U.S.	G6	118
Midland, Tx., U.S.	H4	116
Midlothian, Tx., U.S.	G10	116
Midnapore, Alta., Can.	G20	102
Midongy Sud, Madag.	S22	67b
Miduzhen, China	B6	40
Midvale, Id., U.S.	F9	122
Midville, Ga., U.S.	G4	112
Midway, B.C., Can.	H16	102
Midway, Al., U.S.	J11	114
Midway, Ky., U.S.	I2	108
Midway, Tx., U.S.	H11	116
Midway, Ut., U.S.	D5	120
Midway Islands, dep., Oc.	E1	2
Midway Park, N.C., U.S.	E9	112
Midwest, Wy., U.S.	A10	120
Midwest City, Ok., U.S.	D9	116
Midyat, Tur.	C6	48
Midžor (Midžur), mtn., Eur.	F6	20
Miechów, Pol.	E20	10
Międzychód, Pol.	C15	10
Międzyrzec Podlaski, Pol.	C22	10
Międzyrzecz, Pol.	C15	10
Miélan, Fr.	I7	14
Mielec, Pol.	E21	10
Mier, Mex.	D10	90
Miercurea-Ciuc, Rom.	C9	20
Mieres, Spain	B6	16
Mier y Noriega, Mex.	F9	90
Miesbach, Ger.	H11	10
Mifflinburg, Pa., U.S.	G9	108
Migdal, Isr.	C5	50
Migennes, Fr.	E10	14
Miguel Alemán, Presa, res., Mex.	H11	90
Miguel Auza, Mex.	E8	90
Miguel de la Borda, Pan.	H14	92
Miguel Hidalgo, Presa, res., Mex.	D5	90
Miguelópolis, Braz.	F4	79
Miguel Riglos, Arg.	I7	80
Mihajlovgrad, Bul.	F7	20
Mihara, Japan	M8	36
Mijdaḥah, Yemen	G6	47
Mikaševiči, Bela.	I10	22
Mikhrot Shelomo Hamelekh (Timna') (King Solomon's Mines), hist., Isr.	I3	50
Mikkeli, Fin.	K20	6
Mikkelin lääni, prov., Fin.	J20	6
Mikkwa, stm., Alta., Can.	E10	96
Mikołajki, Pol.	B21	10
Mikołów, Pol.	E18	10
Míkonos, Grc.	L9	20
Mikun', Russia	E8	26
Milaca, Mn., U.S.	E2	110
Milagro, Ec.	I3	84
Milan, Ga., U.S.	G3	112
Milan, In., U.S.	C11	114
Milan, Mi., U.S.	H12	110
Milan, Mn., U.S.	F12	118
Milan, Mo., U.S.	B3	114
Milan, N.M., U.S.	I9	120
Milan, Tn., U.S.	G8	114
Milan see Milano, Italy	D4	18
Milano (Milan), Italy	D4	18
Milano, Tx., U.S.	I10	116
Milanoa, Madag.	N23	67b
Milazzo, Italy	K10	18
Milbank, S.D., U.S.	F11	118
Milbanke Sound, strt., B.C., Can.	E6	102
Milburn, Ok., U.S.	E10	116
Milden, Sask., Can.	G7	104
Mildmay, Ont., Can.	F14	110
Mildred, Pa., U.S.	F10	108
Mildura, Austl.	J5	70
Mile, China	B7	40
Miles, Austl.	F9	70
Miles, Tx., U.S.	H6	116
Miles City, Mt., U.S.	D20	122
Mile Seven Hundred Thirty Three, Yukon, Can.	F29	100
Milestone, Sask., Can.	H10	104
Milevsko, Czech.	F14	10
Milford, Ct., U.S.	F13	108
Milford, De., U.S.	I11	108
Milford, Il., U.S.	J8	110
Milford, In., U.S.	A11	114
Milford, Ia., U.S.	H12	118
Milford, Me., U.S.	C18	108
Milford, Ma., U.S.	E15	108
Milford, Mi., U.S.	H12	110
Milford, N.H., U.S.	E15	108
Milford, N.J., U.S.	G11	108
Milford, Pa., U.S.	F12	108
Milford, Ut., U.S.	F3	120
Milford Center, Oh., U.S.	G3	108
Milford Haven, Wales, U.K.	J8	8
Milford Station, N.S., Can.	G10	106
Milḥ, Baḥr al-, l., Iraq	E7	48
Milicz, Pol.	D17	10
Milk, stm., N.A.	B19	122
Mil'kovo, Russia	G23	28
Milk River, Alta., Can.	H22	102
Milk River Ridge Reservoir, res., Alta., Can.	H22	102
Millard, Ne., U.S.	J11	118
Millau, Fr.	H10	14
Millboro, Va., U.S.	B7	112
Millbrook, Ont., Can.	F17	110
Millbrook, N.Y., U.S.	F13	108
Mill City, Or., U.S.	F3	122
Millcreek, Pa., U.S.	E6	108
Millcreek, Ut., U.S.	D5	120
Mill Creek, W.V., U.S.	I7	108
Milledgeville, Ga., U.S.	F3	112
Milledgeville, Il., U.S.	I6	110
Mille Lacs, Lac des, l., Ont., Can.	B5	110
Mille Lacs Lake, l., Mn., U.S.	D2	110
Millen, Ga., U.S.	G5	112
Miller, Mo., U.S.	E3	114
Miller, S.D., U.S.	G9	118
Miller Mountain, mtn., Nv., U.S.	F7	124
Millerovo, Russia	H6	26
Miller Peak, mtn., Az., U.S.	M6	120
Millersburg, Ky., U.S.	I2	108
Millersburg, Mi., U.S.	E11	110
Millersburg, Oh., U.S.	G5	108
Millersburg, Pa., U.S.	G10	108
Millers Ferry, Al., U.S.	J9	114
Millersport, Oh., U.S.	H4	108
Millersville, Pa., U.S.	H10	108
Millerton, N.Y., U.S.	F13	108
Millertown, Newf., Can.	D17	106
Millertown Junction, Newf., Can.	C17	106
Millet, Alta., Can.	D21	102
Millett, Tx., U.S.	K7	116
Millevaches, Plateau de, plat., Fr.	G9	14
Mill Hall, Pa., U.S.	F9	108
Millicent, Austl.	K4	70
Milligan, Fl., U.S.	L10	114
Milligan, Ne., U.S.	K10	118
Millington, Mi., U.S.	G12	110
Millington, Tn., U.S.	G7	114
Millinocket, Me., U.S.	B18	108
Mill Island, i., N.W. Ter., Can.	D17	96
Millmerran, Austl.	F9	70
Millport, Al., U.S.	I8	114
Millry, Al., U.S.	K8	114
Mills, Wy., U.S.	B10	120
Mills Lake, l., N.W. Ter., Can.	D9	96
Millstatt, Aus.	I13	10
Millstream Chichester Range National Park, Austl.	D3	68
Milltown, In., U.S.	D10	114
Milltown, Mt., U.S.	D12	122
Milltown, Wi., U.S.	E3	110
Mill Valley, Ca., U.S.	G3	124
Millville, N.J., U.S.	H11	108
Millwood, Va., U.S.	H8	108
Millwood Lake, res., Ar., U.S.	I2	114
Milne Bay, b., Pap. N. Gui.	B10	68
Milnor, N.D., U.S.	E10	118
Milo, Alta., Can.	G22	102
Milo, Ia., U.S.	I2	110
Milo, Me., U.S.	B18	108
Mílos, Grc.	M8	20
Mílos, i., Grc.	M8	20
Miloslavskoje, Russia	H22	22
Milparinka, Austl.	G4	70
Milpitas, Ca., U.S.	G4	124
Milroy, In., U.S.	C11	114
Milroy, Pa., U.S.	G9	108
Miltenberg, Ger.	F9	10
Milton, Ont., Can.	G16	110
Milton, N.Z.	G2	72
Milton, De., U.S.	I11	108
Milton, Fl., U.S.	L9	114
Milton, Ia., U.S.	J3	110
Milton, N.D., U.S.	C9	118
Milton, Pa., U.S.	F10	108
Milton, Vt., U.S.	C13	108
Milton, W.V., U.S.	I4	108
Milton, Wi., U.S.	H7	110
Milton-Freewater, Or., U.S.	E7	122
Miltonvale, Ks., U.S.	L10	118
Milverton, Ont., Can.	G15	110
Milwaukee, Wi., U.S.	G8	110
Milwaukee, stm., Wi., U.S.	G7	110
Milwaukie, Or., U.S.	E3	122
Mim, Ghana	H8	64
Mimbres, stm., N.M., U.S.	L9	120
Mimoso, Braz.	C4	79
Mimoso, Braz.	G14	82
Mimoso do Sul, Braz.	F8	79
Mims, Fl., U.S.	K6	112
Min, stm., China	E7	30
Min, stm., China	I7	34
Mina, Nv., U.S.	F7	124
Mīnāb, Iran	H14	48
Mina El Limón, Nic.	E8	92
Minago, stm., Man., Can.	D16	104
Minahasa, pen., Indon.	E7	38
Minamata, Japan	O5	36
Minami-Daitō-jima, i., Japan	F13	30
Mina Pirquitas, Arg.	B5	80
Minas, Cuba	D6	94
Minas, Ur.	H11	80
Minas, Sierra de las, mts., Guat.	B5	92
Minas Basin, b., N.S., Can.	G9	106
Minas Channel, strt., N.S., Can.	G9	106
Minas de Barroterán, Mex.	D9	90
Minas de Corrales, Ur.	F11	80
Minas de Matahambre, Cuba	C3	94
Minas de Oro, Hond.	C7	92
Minas Gerais, state, Braz.	E6	79
Minas Novas, Braz.	D7	79
Minatare, Ne., U.S.	J4	118
Minatitlán, Mex.	I12	90
Minbu, Burma	D3	40
Minco, Ok., U.S.	D9	116
Mindanao, i., Phil.	D8	38
Mindelo, C.V.	k16	64a
Mindemoya, Ont., Can.	E13	110
Minden, Ont., Can.	F17	110
Minden, Ger.	C8	10
Minden, La., U.S.	J3	114
Minden, Ne., U.S.	K9	118
Minden, Nv., U.S.	F6	124
Minden, W.V., U.S.	J5	108
Minden City, Mi., U.S.	G13	110
Mindenmines, Mo., U.S.	E2	114
Mindon, Burma	E3	40
Mindoro, i., Phil.	C7	38
Mindoro Strait, strt., Phil.	C7	38
Mine Centre, Ont., Can.	B3	110
Mineiros, Braz.	D2	79
Mineola, Tx., U.S.	G11	116
Miner, stm., Yukon, Can.	C25	100
Mineral, Wa., U.S.	D3	122
Mineral de Cucharas, Mex.	F7	90
Mineral'nyje Vody, Russia	I6	26
Mineral Point, Wi., U.S.	H5	110
Mineral Springs, Ar., U.S.	I3	114
Mineral Wells, Tx., U.S.	G8	116
Minersville, Pa., U.S.	G10	108
Minersville, Ut., U.S.	F4	120
Minerva, Oh., U.S.	G5	108
Minervino Murge, Italy	H11	18
Mineville, N.Y., U.S.	C13	108
Minfeng, China	D3	30
Mingan, Que., Can.	B9	106
Mingan, stm., Que., Can.	B10	106
Mingan, Îles de, is., Que., Can.	B10	106
Mingan Archipelago National Park, Que., Can.	B10	106
Mingečaur, Azer.	I7	26
Mingela, Austl.	B7	70
Minggang, China	C3	34
Mingo Junction, Oh., U.S.	G6	108
Minhang, China	D10	34
Minhla, Burma	F3	40
Minho, hist. reg., Port.	D3	16
Minho (Miño), stm., Eur.	D3	16
Minhou, China	I8	34
Minicoy Island, i., India	H2	46
Minier, Il., U.S.	B7	114
Minīn, Syria	A6	50
Miniota, Man., Can.	H13	104
Ministikwan Lake, l., Sask., Can.	D5	104
Minitonas, Man., Can.	F13	104
Minjar, Russia	F9	26
Min'kovo, Russia	B26	22
Minlaton, Austl.	J2	70
Minle, China	D7	30
Minna, Nig.	G13	64
Minneapolis, Ks., U.S.	L10	118
Minneapolis, Mn., U.S.	F2	110
Minnedosa, Man., Can.	H15	104
Minnehaha, Wa., U.S.	E3	122
Minneola, Ks., U.S.	N7	118
Minneota, Mn., U.S.	G12	118
Minnesota, state, U.S.	B8	98
Minnesota, stm., Mn., U.S.	F2	110
Minnesota Lake, Mn., U.S.	G2	110
Minnewanka, Lake, l., Alta., Can.	F19	102
Minnewaukan, N.D., U.S.	C8	118
Minnitaki Lake, l., Ont., Can.	I22	104
Mino, Japan	L11	36
Miño (Minho), stm., Eur.	D3	16
Minocqua, Wi., U.S.	E6	110
Minong, Wi., U.S.	D4	110
Minonk, Il., U.S.	J6	110
Minot, N.D., U.S.	C6	118
Minsk, Bela.	H10	22
Mińsk Mazowiecki, Pol.	C21	10
Minster, Oh., U.S.	G2	108
Mintaka Pass, Asia	B6	44
Minto, Man., Can.	I14	104
Minto, N.B., Can.	F7	106
Minto, Yukon, Can.	E26	100
Minto, Ak., U.S.	D20	100
Minto, N.D., U.S.	C10	118
Minto, Lac, l., Que., Can.	E17	96
Minto, Mount, mtn., Ant.	C8	73
Minto Inlet, b., N.W. Ter., Can.	B9	96
Minton, Sask., Can.	I10	104
Minturn, Co., U.S.	E10	120
Minturno, Italy	H8	18
Minusinsk, Russia	G10	28
Minxian, China	E7	30
Minya see Al-Minyā, Egypt	C6	60
Minya Konka see Gongga Shan, mtn., China	F7	30
Mio, Mi., U.S.	F11	110
Miory, Bela.	F10	22
Mir, Bela.	H9	22
Mira, Port.	E3	16
Mira, stm., N.S., Can.	G13	106
Mira, stm., Col.	G3	84
Mira Bay, b., N.S., Can.	F14	106
Miracema do Tocantins, Braz.	E9	76
Mirador, Braz.	E10	76
Miradouro, Braz.	F7	79
Miraflores, Arg.	E6	80
Miraflores, Col.	E6	84
Miraflores, Col.	G6	84
Miraflores, Esclusas de, Pan.	I15	92
Mīrah, Wādī al-, val., Asia	B11	60
Miraj, India	D3	46
Miramar, Arg.	J10	80
Miramar, Arg.	F7	80
Miramar, C.R.	G10	92
Miramas, Fr.	I12	14
Miramichi Bay, b., N.B., Can.	E9	106
Miranda, Braz.	I13	82
Miranda, Col.	F4	84
Miranda, Ca., U.S.	D2	124
Miranda, state, Ven.	B9	84
Miranda, stm., Braz.	H13	82
Miranda de Ebro, Spain	C9	16
Miranda do Douro, Port.	D5	16
Mirande, Fr.	I7	14
Mirandela, Port.	D4	16
Mirando City, Tx., U.S.	L7	116
Mirandola, Italy	E6	18
Mirante do Paranapanema, Braz.	G3	79
Mirapuxi, stm., Braz.	B3	79
Mira Taglio, Italy	D7	18
Miravalles, Volcán, vol., C.R.	G9	92
Mirbāṭ, Oman	F9	47
Mirebeau-sur-Bèze, Fr.	E12	14
Mirecourt, Fr.	D13	14
Miri, Malay.	E5	38
Miriam Vale, Austl.	E9	70
Mirim, Lagoa, b., S.A.	H9	74
Mirim, Lagoa (Laguna Merín), b., S.A.	G12	80
Miriñay, stm., Arg.	E10	80
Miritiparaná, stm., Col.	H7	84
Mīrjāveh, Iran	G16	48
Mirnyj, Russia	E14	28
Mirnyy, sci., Ant.	B6	73
Mirond Lake, l., Sask., Can.	C12	104
Mirow, Ger.	B12	10
Mīrpur, Pak.	D5	44
Mīrpur Khās, Pak.	H3	44
Mirria, Niger	E14	64
Mirror, Alta., Can.	E21	102
Mirzāpur, India	H10	44
Misāḥah, Bi'r, well, Egypt	F4	60
Misantla, Mex.	H11	90
Miscou Centre, N.B., Can.	E9	106
Miscou Island, i., N.B., Can.	E9	106
Miscou Point, c., N.B., Can.	D9	106
Misenheimer, N.C., U.S.	D6	112
Mishagua, stm., Peru	D5	82
Mishan, China	B13	30
Mishawaka, In., U.S.	A10	114
Mishbiḥ, Jabal, mtn., Egypt	J3	48
Mishicot, Wi., U.S.	F8	110
Misikan, China	C13	44
Misilmeri, Italy	K8	18
Misiones, prov., Arg.	D11	80
Misiones, dept., Para.	D10	80
Misión San Francisco de Laishí, Arg.	D9	80
Misión San Vicente, Mex.	B1	90
Miskī, Sud.	J3	60
Miskito Channel, strt., Nic.	C11	92
Miskitos, Cayos, is., Nic.	C12	92
Miskitos Reef, rf., Nic.	C12	92
Miskolc, Hung.	G20	10
Mislata, Spain	A10	62
Misool, Pulau, i., Indon.	F9	38
Misquamaebin Lake, l., Ont., Can.	E23	104
Misrātah, Libya	B4	56
Missinaibi, stm., Ont., Can.	F16	96
Missinaibi Lake, l., Ont., Can.	B12	110
Mission, S.D., U.S.	H7	118
Mission, Tx., U.S.	M8	116
Mission City, B.C., Can.	H12	102
Mississauga, Ont., Can.	G16	110
Mississinewa, stm., U.S.	B11	114
Mississippi, state, U.S.	E9	98
Mississippi, stm., U.S.	E8	98
Mississippi Delta, La., U.S.	M7	114
Mississippi Sound, strt., U.S.	L8	114
Mississippi State, Ms., U.S.	I8	114
Missoula, Mt., U.S.	D12	122
Missouri, state, U.S.	D8	98
Missouri, stm., U.S.	C7	98
Missouri Valley, Ia., U.S.	J12	118
Mistaken Point, c., Newf., Can.	F20	106
Mistanipisipou, stm., Que., Can.	A11	106
Mistassibi, stm., Que., Can.	G18	96
Mistassibi Nord-Est, stm., Que., Can.	B2	106
Mistassini, Que., Can.	F18	96
Mistassini, Lac, l., Que., Can.	F18	96
Mistatim, Sask., Can.	F11	104
Mistawasis Indian Reserve, Sask., Can.	E8	104
Mistelbach, Aus.	G16	10
Misterbianco, Italy	L10	18
Misterei, Sud.	K2	60
Misti, Volcán, vol., Peru	G6	82
Mistikokan, stm., Man., Can.	B23	104
Mistretta, Italy	L9	18
Mita, Punta, c., Mex.	G7	90
Mitchell, Austl.	F7	70
Mitchell, Ont., Can.	G14	110
Mitchell, In., U.S.	D10	114
Mitchell, Ne., U.S.	J4	118
Mitchell, Or., U.S.	F5	122
Mitchell, S.D., U.S.	H9	118
Mitchell, stm., Austl.	K7	70
Mitchell, Lake, res., Al., U.S.	J10	114
Mitchell, Mount, mtn., N.C., U.S.	D4	112
Mitchell Lake, l., B.C., Can.	E14	102
Mitchellville, Ia., U.S.	I2	110
Mitilíni, Grc.	J10	20
Mitis, Lac, l., Que., Can.	D6	106
Mitishto, stm., Man., Can.	D15	104
Mitla, hist., Mex.	I11	90
Mito, Japan	K15	36
Mitsamiouli, Com.	K15	67a
Mitsinjo, Madag.	P21	67b
Mitsio, Nosy, i., Madag.	N23	67b
Mitsiwa (Massawa), Eth.	J10	60
Mittellandkanal, Ger.	C9	10
Mittenwald, Ger.	H11	10
Mittersill, Aus.	H12	10
Mitú, Col.	G7	84
Mitumba, Monts, mts., Zaire	B5	58
Mitwaba, Zaire	C5	58
Mitzic, Gabon	A2	58
Miura, Japan	L14	36
Mixco Viejo, hist., Guat.	C4	92
Miyake-jima, i., Japan	M14	36
Miyako, Japan	H16	36
Miyakonojō, Japan	P6	36
Miyazaki, Japan	P6	36
Miyazu, Japan	L10	36
Miyun, China	C4	32
Mizan Teferi, Eth.	N8	60
Mizdah, Libya	B3	56
Mize, Ms., U.S.	K7	114
Mizen Head, c., Ire.	J4	8
Mizoram, state, India	I15	44
Miẕpé Ramon, Isr.	G3	50
Mizque, Bol.	G9	82
Mizque, stm., Bol.	H9	82
Mjøsa, l., Nor.	K12	6
Mladá Boleslav, Czech.	E14	10
Mladenovac, Yugo.	E4	20
Mlanje Peak see Sapitwa, mtn., Mwi.	E7	58
Mława, Pol.	B20	10
Mmabatho, Boph.	E7	66
Mmadinare, Bots.	C8	66
Mo, Nor.	H14	6
Mo, stm., Afr.	G10	64
Moa, stm., Afr.	G4	54
Moa, stm., Braz.	B5	82
Moab, Ut., U.S.	F7	120
Moaco, stm., Braz.	C7	82
Moa Island, i., Austl.	B8	68
Moama, Austl.	K6	70
Moanda, Gabon	B2	58
Moar Lake, l., Can.	F19	104
Mobara, Japan	L15	36
Mobaye, Cen. Afr. Rep.	H5	56
Mobeetie, Tx., U.S.	D6	116
Moberly, Mo., U.S.	C4	114
Moberly, stm., B.C., Can.	A13	102
Moberly Lake, B.C., Can.	B13	102
Moberly Lake, l., B.C., Can.	B13	102
Mobile, Al., U.S.	L8	114
Mobile, Az., U.S.	K4	120
Mobile, stm., Al., U.S.	L8	114
Mobile Bay, b., Al., U.S.	L8	114
Mobridge, S.D., U.S.	F7	118
Moca, Dom. Rep.	E9	94
Mocal, stm., N.A.	C6	92
Moçambique, Moz.	E8	58
Mocanal, Spain	P23	17b
Mocha, Isla, i., Chile	J2	80
Mocha see Al-Makhā', Yemen	H3	47
Moche, stm., Peru	C2	82
Moche, hist., Peru	C2	82
Mochudi, Bots.	E8	66
Mocímboa da Praia, Moz.	D8	58
Mocksville, N.C., U.S.	D6	112
Moclips, Wa., U.S.	C1	122
Môco, Serra, mtn., Ang.	D3	58
Mocoa, Col.	G4	84
Mococa, Braz.	F5	79
Mocoduene, Moz.	D12	66
Mocoretá, Arg.	F10	80
Mocorito, Mex.	E6	90
Moctezuma, Mex.	C5	90
Moctezuma, stm., Mex.	G10	90
Moctezuma, stm., Mex.	C5	90
Mocuba, Moz.	E7	58
Modane, Fr.	G13	14
Modderrivier, S. Afr.	G7	66
Modena, Italy	E5	18
Modesto, Ca., U.S.	G5	124
Modica, Italy	M9	18
Mödling, Aus.	G16	10
Moe, Austl.	L7	70
Moeda, Braz.	F6	79
Moema, Braz.	E6	79
Moengo, Sur.	B8	76
Moenkopi, Az., U.S.	H5	120
Moers, Ger.	D6	10
Moffit, N.D., U.S.	E7	118
Moga, India	E6	44
Mogadiscio see Muqdisho, Som.	H10	56
Mogadishu see Muqdisho, Som.	H10	56
Mogán, Spain	P25	17b
Mogapinyana, Bots.	D8	66
Mogaung, Burma	B4	40
Mogil'ov, Bela.	H13	22
Mogil'ov-Podol'skij, Ukr.	H3	26
Mogincual, Moz.	E8	58
Mogliano Veneto, Italy	D7	18
Mogoča, Russia	G15	28
Mogogh, Sud.	M6	60
Mogok, Burma	C4	40
Mogollon Rim, clf, Az., U.S.	J6	120
Mogotes, Col.	D6	84
Mogotón, mtn., N.A.	D8	92
Moguer, Spain	H5	16
Mogzon, Russia	G14	28
Mohács, Hung.	J18	10
Mohall, N.D., U.S.	C6	118
Mohammedia (Fedala), Mor.	D7	62
Mohave, Lake, res., U.S.	I11	124
Mohawk, Mi., U.S.	C7	110
Mohawk, stm., N.Y., U.S.	E12	108
Mohe, China	A11	30
Moho, stm., Belize	A6	92
Moinești, Rom.	C10	20
Mointy, Kaz.	H12	26
Moiporá, Braz.	D3	79
Mõisaküla, Est.	C8	22
Moisés Ville, Arg.	F8	80
Moisie, Que., Can.	B7	106
Moisie, stm., Que., Can.	F19	96
Moisie, stm., Que., Can.	B7	106
Moisie, Baie de, b., Que., Can.	B8	106
Moissac, Fr.	H8	14
Moitaco, Ven.	C10	84
Mojana, Brazo, mth., Col.	C5	84
Mojave, Ca., U.S.	I7	124
Mojave Desert, des., Ca., U.S.	J8	124
Mojicuaçu, stm., Braz.	F5	79
Mojimirim, Braz.	G5	79
Mojjero, stm., Russia	D12	28
Mojo, Eth.	M10	60
Mokāma, India	H11	44
Mokelumne, stm., Ca., U.S.	F4	124
Moknine, Tun.	N5	18
Mokp'o, S. Kor.	I14	32
Mokrisset, Mor.	K6	16
Mokša, stm., Russia	G24	22
Mokwa, Nig.	G12	64
Mol, Bel.	F7	12
Mola di Bari, Italy	H12	18
Molalla, Or., U.S.	E3	122
Molanosa, Sask., Can.	D9	104
Moldau see Vltava, stm., Czech.	F14	10
Moldavia, hist. reg., Rom.	B11	20
Moldavia see Moldova, ctry., Eur.	H3	26
Molde, Nor.	J10	6
Moldova, ctry., Eur.	F13	4
Moldoveanu, Vîrful, mtn., Rom.	D8	20
Môle, Cap du, c., Haiti	E8	94
Molega Lake, l., N.S., Can.	H9	106
Molepolole, Bots.	E7	66
Molėtai, Lith.	F8	22
Molfetta, Italy	H11	18
Molina, Chile	H3	80
Molina de Segura, Spain	G10	16
Moline, Il., U.S.	I5	110
Moline, Ks., U.S.	N11	118
Molino, Fl., U.S.	L9	114
Molinos, Arg.	C5	80
Molins de Rei, Spain	D14	16
Molise, prov., Italy	H9	18
Mollendo, Peru	G5	82
Mollepata, Peru	E5	82
Mölln, Ger.	B10	10
Mölndal, Swe.	M13	6
Moločnoje, Russia	B22	22
Molodečno, Bela.	G9	22
Mologa, stm., Russia	C19	22
Molokai, i., Hi., U.S.	p16	125a
Molong, Austl.	I8	70
Molopo, stm., Afr.	F5	66
Molotov see Perm', Russia	F9	26
Molou, Chad	K1	60
Molsheim, Fr.	D14	14
Molson Lake, l., Man., Can.	D18	104
Molteno, S. Afr.	H8	66
Molucca Sea see Maluku, Laut, Indon.	F7	38
Moluccas see Maluku, is., Indon.	F8	38
Moma, Moz.	E7	58
Moma, stm., Russia	D20	28
Momanga, Nmb.	B5	66
Mombachito, Cerro, mtn., Nic.	E9	92
Mombacho, Volcán, vol., Nic.	F9	92
Mombasa, Kenya	B7	58
Mombetsu, Japan	C18	36a
Momence, Il., U.S.	I8	110
Momotombo, Volcán, vol., Nic.	E8	92
Mompós, Col.	C5	84
Mona, Ut., U.S.	E5	120
Mona, Canal de la, strt., N.A.	E11	94
Mona, Isla de, i., P.R.	E11	94
Mona, Punta, c., C.R.	H12	92
Monaca, Pa., U.S.	G6	108
Monaco, Mon.	I14	14
Monaco, ctry., Eur.	G9	4
Monadnock Mountain, mtn., N.H., U.S.	E14	108
Monagas, state, Ven.	C11	84
Monaghan, co., Ire.	G6	8
Monagrillo, Pan.	D2	84
Monahans, Tx., U.S.	H4	116
Monango, N.D., U.S.	E9	118
Monarch, S.C., U.S.	E5	112
Monarch Mountain, mtn., B.C., Can.	F9	102
Monarch Pass, Co., U.S.	F10	120
Monashee Mountains, mts., B.C., Can.	F16	102
Monashee Provincial Park, B.C., Can.	G16	102
Monastir, Tun.	N5	18
Monastir see Bitola, Mac.	H5	20
Monastyrščina, Russia	G14	22
Moncalieri, Italy	D2	18
Monção, Braz.	D9	76
Mončegorsk, Russia	D4	26
Mönchengladbach, Ger.	D6	10
Moncks Corner, S.C., U.S.	F6	112
Monclova, Mex.	D9	90
Moncontour, Fr.	D4	14
Moncoutant, Fr.	F6	14
Moncton, N.B., Can.	F9	106
Mondaí, Braz.	D12	80
Monday, stm., Para.	C11	80
Mondoro, Mali	D9	64
Mondoubleau, Fr.	E7	14
Mondovi, Wi., U.S.	F4	110
Mondragone, Italy	H8	18
Monero, N.M., U.S.	H10	120
Moneron, ostrov, i., Russia	A16	36a
Monessen, Pa., U.S.	G7	108
Monesterio, Spain	G5	16
Monett, Mo., U.S.	F3	114
Monette, Ar., U.S.	G6	114
Monfalcone, Italy	D8	18
Monflanquin, Fr.	H7	14
Monforte, Port.	F4	16
Monforte de Lemos, Spain	C4	16
Mongaguá, Braz.	H5	79
Mongalla, Sud.	G7	56
Mong Cai, Viet.	D9	40
Monger, Îles, is., Que., Can.	A15	106
Mongers Lake, l., Austl.	E3	68
Möng Hsat, Burma	D5	40
Möng Mit, Burma	C4	40
Mongo, Chad	F4	56
Mongo, stm., Afr.	G4	64
Mongol Altajn nuruu, mts., Asia	H16	26
Mongolia (Mongol Ard Uls), ctry., Asia	B8	30
Mongororo, Chad	K2	60
Möng Pai, Burma	E4	40
Mongu, Zam.	E4	58
Möng Yawng, Burma	D6	40
Monheim, Ger.	G10	10
Monico, Wi., U.S.	E6	110
Monida Pass, U.S.	F13	122
Monino, Russia	F21	22
Moniquirá, Col.	E6	84
Monistrol-sur-Loire, Fr.	G11	14
Monitor Range, mts., Nv., U.S.	F9	124
Monitor Valley, val., Nv., U.S.	F9	124
Monkey River, Belize	A6	92
Mońki, Pol.	B22	10
Monkira, Austl.	E4	70
Monmouth, Il., U.S.	J5	110
Monmouth, Or., U.S.	F2	122
Monmouth Mountain, mtn., B.C., Can.	F11	102
Mono, stm., Afr.	G7	54
Mono, Caño, stm., Col.	E8	84
Mono, Punta, c., Nic.	F11	92
Mono Lake, l., Ca., U.S.	F7	124
Monon, In., U.S.	B10	114
Monona, Ia., U.S.	G4	110
Monona, Wi., U.S.	G6	110
Monongahela, stm., U.S.	H7	108
Monopoli, Italy	I12	18
Monòver, Spain	G11	16

Name	Map Ref.	Page
Monreale, Italy	K8	18
Monroe, Ga., U.S.	F3	112
Monroe, Ia., U.S.	I2	110
Monroe, La., U.S.	J4	114
Monroe, Mi., U.S.	I12	110
Monroe, Ne., U.S.	J10	118
Monroe, N.Y., U.S.	F12	108
Monroe, N.C., U.S.	E6	112
Monroe, Or., U.S.	F2	122
Monroe, Ut., U.S.	F4	120
Monroe, Va., U.S.	B7	112
Monroe, Wa., U.S.	C4	122
Monroe, Wi., U.S.	H6	110
Monroe City, In., U.S.	D9	114
Monroe City, Mo., U.S.	C5	114
Monroe Lake, res., In., U.S.	C10	114
Monroeville, Al., U.S.	K9	114
Monroeville, In., U.S.	B12	114
Monroeville, Oh., U.S.	F4	108
Monroeville, Pa., U.S.	G7	108
Monrovia, Lib.	H4	64
Mons (Bergen), Bel.	H4	12
Monsefú, Peru	B2	82
Monselice, Italy	D6	18
Monson, Me., U.S.	B17	108
Montabaur, Ger.	E7	10
Montagnana, Italy	D6	18
Montagu, S. Afr.	I5	66
Montague, P.E.I., Can.	F11	106
Montague, Ca., U.S.	C3	124
Montague, Mi., U.S.	G9	110
Montague, Tx., U.S.	F9	116
Montague, Isla, i., Mex.	B2	90
Montague Island, i., Ak., U.S.	F21	100
Montagu Island, i., S. Geor.	A2	73
Montaigu, Fr.	F5	14
Montalcino, Italy	F6	18
Montalegre, Port.	D4	16
Montana, Switz.	F7	13
Montana, state, U.S.	B4	98
Montana Indian Reserve, Alta., Can.	E21	102
Montargis, Fr.	D9	14
Montauban, Fr.	H8	14
Montauk, N.Y., U.S.	F15	108
Montauk Point, c., N.Y., U.S.	F15	108
Montbard, Fr.	E11	14
Montbarrey, Fr.	E12	14
Montbéliard, Fr.	E13	14
Mont Belvieu, Tx., U.S.	J12	116
Mont Blanc, Tunnel du, Eur.	G6	13
Montbrison, Fr.	G11	14
Montbron, Fr.	G7	14
Montceau [-les-Mines], Fr.	F11	14
Montcevelles, Lac, l., Que., Can.	A13	106
Montchanin, Fr.	F11	14
Montclair, Ca., U.S.	J8	124
Montclair, N.J., U.S.	G12	108
Mont-de-Marsan, Fr.	I6	14
Montdidier, Fr.	C9	14
Monte, Laguna del, l., Arg.	I7	80
Monteagle, Tn., U.S.	G11	114
Monteagudo, Bol.	H10	82
Monte Albán, hist., Mex.	I11	90
Monte Alegre, Braz.	D8	76
Monte Alegre de Goiás, Braz.	B5	79
Monte Alegre de Minas, Braz.	E4	79
Monte Azul, Braz.	C7	79
Monte Azul Paulista, Braz.	F4	79
Montebello, Que., Can.	B12	108
Monte Bello Islands, is., Austl.	D3	68
Monte Buey, Arg.	G7	80
Montecarlo, Arg.	D11	80
Monte Caseros, Arg.	F10	80
Montecassino, Abbazia di, Italy	H8	18
Montecatini-Terme, Italy	F5	18
Montecillos, Cordillera de, mts., Hond.	C7	92
Montecito, Ca., U.S.	J6	124
Monte Comán, Arg.	H5	80
Monte Creek, B.C., Can.	G15	102
Monte Cristi, Dom. Rep.	E9	94
Montecristi, Ec.	H2	84
Monte Cristo, Bol.	F11	82
Monte Escobedo, Mex.	F8	90
Montego Bay, Jam.	E6	94
Monte Grande, Chile	F3	80
Montegut, La., U.S.	M6	114
Monteith, Mount, mtn., B.C., Can.	B12	102
Montelíbano, Col.	C5	84
Montélimar, Fr.	H11	14
Montelindo, stm., Para.	B9	80
Montellano, Spain	H6	16
Montello, Nv., U.S.	C11	124
Montello, Wi., U.S.	G6	110
Monte Maíz, Arg.	G7	80
Montemorelos, Mex.	E10	90
Montemor-o-Novo, Port.	G3	16
Montemor-o-Vehlo, Port.	E3	16
Montendre, Fr.	G6	14
Montenegro, Braz.	E13	80
Montenegro see Crna Gora, state, Yugo.	G2	20
Monte Pascoal, Parque Nacional de, Braz.	D9	79
Monte Patria, Chile	F3	80
Montepuez, Moz.	D7	58
Montepulciano, Italy	F6	18
Monte Quemado, Arg.	C7	80
Montereau-Faut-Yonne, Fr.	D9	14
Monterey, Ca., U.S.	H4	124
Monterey, Tn., U.S.	F11	114
Monterey, Va., U.S.	I7	108
Monterey Bay, b., Ca., U.S.	H4	124
Montería, Col.	C5	84
Montero, Bol.	G10	82
Monteros, Arg.	D6	80
Monterotondo, Italy	G7	18
Monterrey, Mex.	E9	90
Montesano, Italy	I10	18
Montesano, Wa., U.S.	D2	122
Monte Sant'Angelo, Italy	H10	18
Montesarchio, Italy	H9	18
Montes Claros, Braz.	F10	74
Montes Claros, Braz.	D7	79
Montevallo, Al., U.S.	I10	114
Montevarchi, Italy	F6	18
Montevideo, Mn., U.S.	G12	118
Montevideo, Ur.	H10	80
Monte Vista, Co., U.S.	G10	120
Montezuma, Ga., U.S.	G2	112
Montezuma, In., U.S.	C9	114
Montezuma, Ia., U.S.	I3	110
Montezuma, Ks., U.S.	N7	118
Montfort, Fr.	D5	14
Montfort, Wi., U.S.	H5	110
Montgomery, Al., U.S.	J10	114
Montgomery, La., U.S.	K4	114
Montgomery, Mn., U.S.	F2	110
Montgomery, Pa., U.S.	F10	108
Montgomery, Tx., U.S.	I11	116
Montgomery, W.V., U.S.	I5	108
Montgomery City, Mo., U.S.	D5	114
Monthermé, Fr.	C11	14
Monthey, Switz.	F6	13
Monthois, Fr.	C11	14
Monticello, Ar., U.S.	I5	114
Monticello, Fl., U.S.	I3	112
Monticello, Ga., U.S.	F3	112
Monticello, Il., U.S.	B8	114
Monticello, In., U.S.	B10	114
Monticello, Ia., U.S.	H4	110
Monticello, Ky., U.S.	F12	114
Monticello, Mn., U.S.	E2	110
Monticello, Ms., U.S.	K6	114
Monticello, Mo., U.S.	B5	114
Monticello, N.Y., U.S.	F12	108
Monticello, Ut., U.S.	G7	120
Monticello, Wi., U.S.	H6	110
Montichiari, Italy	D5	18
Montignac, Fr.	G8	14
Montigny-le-Roi, Fr.	D12	14
Montigny-sur-Aube, Fr.	E11	14
Montijo, Pan.	D2	84
Montijo, Port.	G3	16
Montijo, Spain	G5	16
Montijo, Golfo de, b., Pan.	D2	84
Montilla, Spain	H7	16
Montividiu, Braz.	D3	79
Montivilliers, Fr.	C7	14
Mont-Joli, Que., Can.	D5	106
Mont-Laurier, Que., Can.	G17	96
Mont-Louis, Fr.	J9	14
Montluçon, Fr.	F9	14
Montluel, Fr.	G12	14
Montmagny, Que., Can.	F3	106
Montmédy, Fr.	C12	14
Montmirail, Fr.	D10	14
Montmorency, stm., Que., Can.	E2	106
Montmorency see Beauport, Que., Can.	F2	106
Montmorillon, Fr.	F7	14
Monto, Austl.	E9	70
Montoro, Spain	G7	16
Montour Falls, N.Y., U.S.	E10	108
Montoursville, Pa., U.S.	F10	108
Montpelier, Id., U.S.	H14	122
Montpelier, In., U.S.	G1	108
Montpelier, Ms., U.S.	I8	114
Montpelier, Oh., U.S.	F2	108
Montpelier, Vt., U.S.	C14	108
Montpellier, Fr.	I10	14
Montpon-Ménesterol, Fr.	G7	14
Montréal, Que., Can.	B13	108
Montreal, Wi., U.S.	D5	110
Montreal, stm., Sask., Can.	D9	104
Montreal Lake, Sask., Can.	D9	104
Montreal Lake, l., Sask., Can.	D9	104
Montreal Lake Indian Reserve, Sask., Can.	D9	104
Montreuil, Fr.	B8	14
Montreux, Switz.	F6	13
Montrevel [-en-Bresse], Fr.	F12	14
Montrose, Scot., U.K.	E11	8
Montrose, Co., U.S.	F9	120
Montrose, Ia., U.S.	J4	110
Montrose, Mi., U.S.	G12	110
Montrose, Pa., U.S.	F11	108
Montrose, S.D., U.S.	H10	118
Montross, Va., U.S.	I10	108
Monts, Pointe des, c., Que., Can.	C6	106
Mont-Sainte-Anne, Parc du, Que., Can.	E3	106
Mont-Saint-Michel see Le Mont-Saint-Michel, Fr.	D5	14
Montserrat, dep., N.A.	F13	94
Montvale, Va., U.S.	B7	112
Monument, Or., U.S.	F6	122
Monument Peak, mtn., Id., U.S.	H11	122
Monument Valley, val., U.S.	G6	120
Monywa, Burma	C3	40
Monza, Italy	D4	18
Monzón, Peru	C3	82
Monzón, Spain	D12	16
Moodie Island, i., N.W. Ter., Can.	D19	96
Moody, Tx., U.S.	H9	116
Mooirivier, S. Afr.	G9	66
Mookane, Bots.	E7	66
Moolawatana, Austl.	G3	70
Moonie, stm., Austl.	F8	70
Moonta, Austl.	J2	70
Moora, Austl.	F3	68
Moorcroft, Wy., U.S.	G3	118
Moore, Id., U.S.	G12	122
Moore, Mt., U.S.	D16	122
Moore, Ok., U.S.	D9	116
Moore, Tx., U.S.	J7	116
Moore, Lake, l., Austl.	E3	68
Moorefield, W.V., U.S.	H8	108
Moore Haven, Fl., U.S.	M5	112
Mooreland, Ok., U.S.	C7	116
Mooresville, In., U.S.	C10	114
Mooresville, N.C., U.S.	D6	112
Moorhead, Mn., U.S.	E11	118
Moorhead, Ms., U.S.	I6	114
Mooringsport, La., U.S.	J3	114
Moornanyah Lake, l., Austl.	I5	70
Moorreesburg, S. Afr.	I4	66
Moosburg, Ger.	G11	10
Moosehead Lake, l., Me., U.S.	B17	108
Moose Heights, B.C., Can.	D12	102
Moose Island, i., Man., Can.	G17	104
Moose Jaw, Sask., Can.	H9	104
Moose Jaw, stm., Sask., Can.	H9	104
Moose Lake, Man., Can.	E14	104
Moose Lake, Mn., U.S.	D3	110
Moose Lake, l., Alta., Can.	C24	102
Moose Lake, l., Man., Can.	E15	104
Mooselookmeguntic Lake, l., Me., U.S.	C16	108
Moose Mountain, mtn., Sask., Can.	I12	104
Moose Mountain Creek, stm., Sask., Can.	H11	104
Moose Mountain Provincial Park, Sask., Can.	I12	104
Moose Pass, Ak., U.S.	F20	100
Moosomin, Sask., Can.	H13	104
Moosomin Indian Reserve, Sask., Can.	E6	104
Moosonee, Ont., Can.	F16	96
Mopane, S. Afr.	D9	66
Mopipi, Bots.	C7	66
Mopti, Mali	D7	64
Moquegua, Peru	G6	82
Moquegua, dept., Peru	G6	82
Mór, Hung.	H18	10
Mora, Spain	F8	16
Mora, Swe.	K14	6
Mora, Mn., U.S.	E2	110
Mora, N.M., U.S.	I11	120
Mora, stm., N.M., U.S.	H11	120
Morādābād, India	F8	44
Morada Nova de Minas, Braz.	E6	79
Moradel, Montaña de, mtn., Hond.	B8	92
Mora de Rubielos, Spain	E11	16
Morafenobe, Madag.	P21	67b
Mórahalom, Hung.	I19	10
Mor'akovskij Zaton, Russia	F14	26
Moraleda, Canal, strt., Chile	E2	78
Morales, Guat.	B6	92
Morales, Peru	B3	82
Morales, Laguna, b., Mex.	F11	90
Moran, Ks., U.S.	N12	118
Moran, Mi., U.S.	E11	110
Moran, Tx., U.S.	G7	116
Morant Bay, Jam.	F6	94
Morant Cays, is., Jam.	F7	94
Morant Point, c., Jam.	F6	94
Moratalla, Spain	G10	16
Moratuwa, Sri L.	I5	46
Morava, hist. reg., Czech.	F17	10
Morava (March), stm., Eur.	G16	10
Moravia, C.R.	H11	92
Moravia, Ia., U.S.	J3	110
Moravia, N.Y., U.S.	E10	108
Moravia see Morava, hist. reg., Czech.	F17	10
Morawhanna, Guy.	C13	84
Moraya, Bol.	I9	82
Moray Firth, est., Scot., U.K.	D10	8
Morazán, Guat.	C4	92
Morazán, Hond.	B7	92
Morbegno, Italy	C4	18
Morbi, India	I4	44
Morbihan, dept., Fr.	E4	14
Morcenx, Fr.	H6	14
Morden, Man., Can.	I16	104
Mordovo, Russia	I23	22
Mordves, Russia	G21	22
Moreau, stm., S.D., U.S.	F6	118
Moreauville, La., U.S.	K5	114
Moree, Austl.	G8	70
Morée, Fr.	E8	14
Morehead, Ky., U.S.	I3	108
Morehead City, N.C., U.S.	E10	112
Morehouse, Mo., U.S.	F7	114
Moreland, Ga., U.S.	F2	112
Moreland, Ky., U.S.	E12	114
Morelia, Mex.	H9	90
Morell, P.E.I., Can.	F11	106
Morelos, Mex.	D6	90
Morelos, state, Mex.	H10	90
Moremi Wildlife Reserve, Bots.	B6	66
Morena, India	G8	44
Morena, Sierra, mts., Spain	G6	16
Morenci, Az., U.S.	K7	120
Morenci, Mi., U.S.	I11	110
Moreno, Bahía, b., Chile	B3	80
Møre og Romsdal, co., Nor.	J10	6
Moresby Island, i., B.C., Can.	E3	102
Mores Island, i., Bah.	A6	94
Moresnet, Bel.	G8	12
Moreton Island, i., Austl.	F10	70
Moreuil, Fr.	C9	14
Morez, Fr.	F13	14
Morgan, Ga., U.S.	H2	112
Morgan, Mn., U.S.	G13	118
Morgan, Tx., U.S.	G9	116
Morgan, Ut., U.S.	C5	120
Morgan City, Al., U.S.	H10	114
Morgan City, La., U.S.	M5	114
Morganfield, Ky., U.S.	E9	114
Morgan Hill, Ca., U.S.	G4	124
Morganito, Ven.	E9	84
Morganton, N.C., U.S.	D5	112
Morgantown, In., U.S.	C10	114
Morgantown, Ky., U.S.	E10	114
Morgantown, Ms., U.S.	K5	114
Morgantown, Ms., U.S.	K7	114
Morgantown, W.V., U.S.	H7	108
Morganza, La., U.S.	L5	114
Morgenzon, S. Afr.	F9	66
Morghāb (Murgab), stm., Asia	B16	48
Moriah, Mount, mtn., Nv., U.S.	E11	124
Moriarty, N.M., U.S.	J10	120
Moribaya, Gui.	G5	64
Morice, stm., B.C., Can.	C7	102
Morice Lake, l., B.C., Can.	C7	102
Morichal Largo, stm., Ven.	C11	84
Moriki, Nig.	E13	64
Moringen, Ger.	D9	10
Morino, Russia	D13	22
Morinville, Alta., Can.	D21	102
Morioka, Japan	H16	36
Morisset, Austl.	I9	70
Morkill, stm., B.C., Can.	D14	102
Morkiny Gory, Russia	D19	22
Morkoka, stm., Russia	D14	28
Morlaix, Fr.	D3	14
Morley, Mi., U.S.	G10	110
Mormal', Bela.	I12	22
Morney, Austl.	E4	70
Morning Sun, Ia., U.S.	I4	110
Mornington, Austl.	L6	70
Mornington, Isla, i., Chile	F1	78
Mornington Island, i., Austl.	A3	70
Moro, Or., U.S.	E5	122
Moro, stm., Afr.	H4	64
Morobe, Pap. N. Gui.	m16	68a
Morocco, In., U.S.	B9	114
Morocco (Al-Magreb), ctry., Afr.	B5	54
Morococala, Bol.	H8	82
Morococha, Peru	D3	82
Morogoro, Tan.	C7	58
Moro Gulf, b., Phil.	D7	38
Moroleón, Mex.	G9	90
Morombe, Madag.	R20	67b
Morón, Arg.	H9	80
Morón, Cuba	C5	94
Mörön, Mong.	B7	30
Morón, Ven.	B8	84
Morona, stm., Peru	I4	84
Morona-Santiago, prov., Ec.	I3	84
Morondava, Madag.	R21	67b
Morón de la Frontera, Spain	H6	16
Moroni, Com.	K15	67a
Moroni, Ut., U.S.	E5	120
Morotai, i., Indon.	E8	38
Morozovsk, Russia	H6	26
Morrill, Ne., U.S.	J4	118
Morrilton, Ar., U.S.	G4	114
Morrin, Alta., Can.	F22	102
Morrinhos, Braz.	D4	79
Morrinsville, N.Z.	B5	72
Morris, Man., Can.	I17	104
Morris, Il., U.S.	I7	110
Morris, Mn., U.S.	F12	118
Morris, Ok., U.S.	D11	116
Morris, stm., Man., Can.	I17	104
Morrisburg, Ont., Can.	C11	108
Morris Jesup, Kap, c., Grnld.	A16	86
Morrison, Arg.	G7	80
Morrison, Il., U.S.	I6	110
Morrisonville, Il., U.S.	C7	114
Morristown, Az., U.S.	K4	120
Morristown, In., U.S.	C11	114
Morristown, Mn., U.S.	F2	110
Morristown, S.D., U.S.	F6	118
Morristown, Tn., U.S.	C3	112
Morrisville, N.Y., U.S.	E11	108
Morrisville, Pa., U.S.	G12	108
Morrisville, Vt., U.S.	C14	108
Morrito, Nic.	F9	92
Morro, Ec.	I2	84
Morro, Punta, c., Mex.	H14	90
Morro Bay, Ca., U.S.	I5	124
Morro del Jable, Spain	O26	17b
Morro do Chapéu, Braz.	F10	76
Morropón, Peru	A1	82
Morrosquillo, Golfo de, b., Col.	C5	84
Morrow, La., U.S.	L4	114
Morrumbene, Moz.	D12	66
Moršansk, Russia	H24	22
Morse, Sask., Can.	H7	104
Morse, La., U.S.	L4	114
Morse, Tx., U.S.	C5	116
Morson, Ont., Can.	I20	104
Mortagne, Fr.	D7	14
Mortagne-sur-Sèvre, Fr.	E6	14
Mortain, Fr.	D6	14
Mortara, Italy	D3	18
Morteau, Fr.	E13	14
Morteros, Arg.	F7	80
Mortes, Rio das, stm., Braz.	B3	79
Mortesoro, Sud.	L8	60
Mortlach, Sask., Can.	H8	104
Mortlake, Austl.	L5	70
Morton, Il., U.S.	J6	110
Morton, Mn., U.S.	G13	118
Morton, Ms., U.S.	J7	114
Morton, Tx., U.S.	F4	116
Morton, Wa., U.S.	D3	122
Mortons Gap, Ky., U.S.	E9	114
Moruya, Austl.	J9	70
Morven, Austl.	F7	70
Morven, Ga., U.S.	I3	112
Morven, N.C., U.S.	E6	112
Morwell, Austl.	L7	70
Morženga, Russia	B23	22
Mosal'sk, Russia	G17	22
Moščnyj, ostrov, i., Russia	A10	22
Moscow, Id., U.S.	D9	122
Moscow see Moskva, Russia	F20	22
Mosel (Moselle), stm., Eur.	C13	14
Moselle, Ms., U.S.	K7	114
Moselle, dept., Fr.	D13	14
Moselle (Mosel), stm., Eur.	D13	14
Mosers River, N.S., Can.	H11	106
Moses Lake, Wa., U.S.	C6	122
Moses Point, Ak., U.S.	D13	100
Mosetse, Bots.	C8	66
Moshanpu, China	F1	34
Moshaweng, stm., Afr.	F6	66
Mosheim, Tn., U.S.	C4	112
Moshi, Tan.	B7	58
Mosina, Pol.	C16	10
Mosinee, Wi., U.S.	F6	110
Mosjøen, Nor.	I13	6
Moskva (Moscow), Russia	F20	22
Moskva, stm., Russia	F21	22
Moskvy, kanal imeni, Russia	E20	22
Mošok, Russia	F24	22
Mosolovo, Russia	G23	22
Mosomane, Bots.	E8	66
Mosonmagyaróvár, Hung.	H17	10
Mosopa, Bots.	E7	66
Mosquera, Col.	F3	84
Mosquero, N.M., U.S.	D3	116
Mosquito, Punta, c., Pan.	C4	84
Mosquito, Riacho, stm., Para.	B9	80
Mosquito Creek Lake, res., Oh., U.S.	F6	108
Mosquito Indian Reserve, Sask., Can.	F6	104
Mosquitos, Costa de, hist. reg., Nic.	D11	92
Mosquitos, Golfo de los, b., Pan.	H13	92
Moss, Nor.	L12	6
Mossaka, Congo	B3	58
Mossâmedes, Braz.	D3	79
Mossbank, Sask., Can.	I9	104
Mosselbaai, S. Afr.	J6	66
Mossendjo, Congo	B2	58
Mossleigh, Alta., Can.	G21	102
Mossoró, Braz.	E11	76
Moss Point, Ms., U.S.	L8	114
Moss Vale, Austl.	J9	70
Mossy, stm., Man., Can.	G15	104
Mossy, stm., Sask., Can.	D11	104
Most, Czech.	E13	10
Mosta, Russia	E25	22
Mostar, Bos.	F12	18
Mostardas, Braz.	F13	80
Mostiska, Ukr.	F23	10
Mostok, Bela.	H13	22
Mostoos Hills, hills, Sask., Can.	C5	104
Mosty, Bela.	H7	22
Mosul see Al-Mawṣil, Iraq	C7	48
Mota, Eth.	L9	60
Motagua, stm., N.A.	B6	92
Motala, Swe.	L14	6
Motatán, Ven.	C7	84
Motherwell, Scot., U.K.	F9	8
Motihāri, India	G11	44
Motloutse, Bots.	C8	66
Motozintla de Mendoza, Mex.	J13	90
Motril, Spain	I8	16
Motru, Rom.	E7	20
Mott, N.D., U.S.	E5	118
Mottola, Italy	I12	18
Motueka, N.Z.	D4	72
Motul [de Felipe Carrillo Puerto], Mex.	G15	90
Motupe, Peru	B2	82
Mouaskar, Alg.	C11	62
Mouchoir Passage, strt., N.A.	D9	94
Moudjéria, Maur.	C3	64
Moudon, Switz.	E6	13
Mouila, Gabon	B2	58
Mouit, Maur.	C3	64
Mouka, Cen. Afr. Rep.	N1	60
Moulamein, Austl.	J6	70
Moulay-Idriss, Mor.	C8	62
Moulins, Fr.	F10	14
Moulins-la-Marche, Fr.	D7	14
Moulmeingyun, Burma	F3	40
Moulmein see Mawlamyine, Burma	F4	40
Moulouya, Oued, stm., Mor.	C9	62
Moulton, Al., U.S.	H9	114
Moulton, Ia., U.S.	J3	110
Moulton, Tx., U.S.	J9	116
Moultrie, Ga., U.S.	H3	112
Moultrie, Lake, res., S.C., U.S.	F6	112
Mound Bayou, Ms., U.S.	I6	114
Mound City, Il., U.S.	E7	114
Mound City, Ks., U.S.	M13	118
Mound City, Mo., U.S.	B1	114
Mound City, S.D., U.S.	F7	118
Moundou, Chad	G4	56
Moundridge, Ks., U.S.	M10	118
Mounds, Il., U.S.	E7	114
Mounds, Ok., U.S.	D10	116
Moundsville, W.V., U.S.	H6	108
Moundville, Al., U.S.	J9	114
Mounlapamôk, Laos	G8	40
Mountain, Wi., U.S.	E7	110
Mountain, stm., N.W. Ter., Can.	D30	100
Mountainair, N.M., U.S.	J10	120
Mountainaire, Az., U.S.	I5	120
Mountain Brook, Al., U.S.	I10	114
Mountain City, Ga., U.S.	E3	112
Mountain City, Nv., U.S.	C10	124
Mountain City, Tn., U.S.	C5	112
Mountain Creek, Al., U.S.	J10	114
Mountain Grove, Mo., U.S.	E4	114
Mountain Home, Ar., U.S.	F4	114
Mountain Home, Id., U.S.	G10	122
Mountain Iron, Mn., U.S.	C3	110
Mountain Lake, Mn., U.S.	H13	118
Mountain Nile (Baḥr al-Jabal), stm., Sud.	M6	60
Mountain Park, Alta., Can.	E17	102
Mountain Pine, Ar., U.S.	H3	114
Mountain Point, Ak., U.S.	I29	100
Mountain View, Ar., U.S.	G4	114
Mountain View, Ca., U.S.	G3	124
Mountain View, Mo., U.S.	F5	114
Mountain View, Ok., U.S.	D8	116
Mountain View, Wy., U.S.	C6	120
Mountain View, Wy., U.S.	B10	120
Mountain Village, Ak., U.S.	E13	100
Mount Airy, Md., U.S.	H9	108
Mount Airy, N.C., U.S.	C6	112
Mount Alida, S. Afr.	G10	66
Mount Angel, Or., U.S.	E3	122
Mount Assiniboine Provincial Park, B.C., Can.	G19	102
Mount Ayr, Ia., U.S.	K13	118
Mount Barker, Austl.	F3	68
Mount Barker, Austl.	J3	70
Mount Brydges, Ont., Can.	H14	110
Mount Calm, Tx., U.S.	H10	116
Mount Carleton Provincial Park, N.B., Can.	E7	106
Mount Carmel, Newf., Can.	E20	106
Mount Carmel, Il., U.S.	D9	114
Mount Carmel, Pa., U.S.	G10	108
Mount Carroll, Il., U.S.	H6	110
Mount Clare, W.V., U.S.	H6	108
Mount Clemens, Mi., U.S.	H13	110
Mount Currie Indian Reserve, B.C., Can.	G12	102
Mount Desert Island, i., Me., U.S.	C18	108
Mount Dora, Fl., U.S.	K5	112
Mount Edgecumbe, Ak., U.S.	H27	100
Mount Enterprise, Tx., U.S.	K2	114
Mount Forest, Ont., Can.	G15	110
Mount Gambier, Austl.	K4	70
Mount Garnet, Austl.	A6	70
Mount Gay, W.V., U.S.	J4	108
Mount Gilead, N.C., U.S.	D6	112
Mount Gilead, Oh., U.S.	G4	108
Mount Hagen, Pap. N. Gui.	G11	38
Mount Holly, N.C., U.S.	D5	112
Mount Holly Springs, Pa., U.S.	G9	108
Mount Hope, Austl.	J1	70
Mount Hope, Ks., U.S.	N10	118
Mount Hope, W.V., U.S.	J5	108
Mount Horeb, Wi., U.S.	G6	110
Mount Ida, Ar., U.S.	H3	114
Mount Isa, Austl.	C3	70
Mount Jackson, Va., U.S.	I8	108
Mount Jewett, Pa., U.S.	F8	108
Mount Juliet, Tn., U.S.	F10	114
Mount Kisco, N.Y., U.S.	F13	108
Mount Lebanon, Pa., U.S.	G6	108
Mount Magnet, Austl.	E3	68
Mount Manara, Austl.	I5	70
Mount Morgan, Austl.	D9	70
Mount Morris, Il., U.S.	H6	110
Mount Morris, Mi., U.S.	G12	110
Mount Morris, N.Y., U.S.	E9	108
Mount Mulligan, Austl.	A6	70
Mount Olive, Il., U.S.	C7	114
Mount Olive, Ms., U.S.	K7	114
Mount Olive, N.C., U.S.	D8	112
Mount Olivet, Ky., U.S.	I2	108
Mount Orab, Oh., U.S.	H3	108
Mount Perry, Austl.	E9	70
Mount Pleasant, Ont., Can.	G15	110
Mount Pleasant, Ia., U.S.	J4	110
Mount Pleasant, Mi., U.S.	G11	110
Mount Pleasant, N.C., U.S.	D6	112
Mount Pleasant, Pa., U.S.	G7	108
Mount Pleasant, S.C., U.S.	G7	112
Mount Pleasant, Tn., U.S.	G9	114
Mount Pleasant, Tx., U.S.	F12	116
Mount Pleasant, Ut., U.S.	E5	120
Mount Pulaski, Il., U.S.	B7	114
Mount Rainier National Park, Wa., U.S.	D4	122
Mount Revelstoke National Park, B.C., Can.	F16	102
Mount Robson Provincial Park, B.C., Can.	E15	102
Mount Savage, Md., U.S.	H8	108
Mount Seymour Provincial Park, B.C., Can.	H12	102
Mount Shasta, Ca., U.S.	C3	124
Mount Sterling, Il., U.S.	C6	114
Mount Sterling, Ky., U.S.	A3	112
Mount Sterling, Oh., U.S.	H3	108
Mount Stewart, P.E.I., Can.	F11	106
Mount Stewart, S. Afr.	I7	66
Mount Surprise, Austl.	B6	70
Mount Uniacke, N.S., Can.	H10	106
Mount Union, Pa., U.S.	G9	108
Mount Vernon, Al., U.S.	K8	114
Mount Vernon, Ga., U.S.	G4	112
Mount Vernon, Il., U.S.	D8	114
Mount Vernon, In., U.S.	E9	114
Mount Vernon, Ia., U.S.	I4	110
Mount Vernon, Ky., U.S.	B2	112
Mount Vernon, Mo., U.S.	E3	114
Mount Vernon, Oh., U.S.	G4	108
Mount Vernon, Or., U.S.	F6	122
Mount Vernon, S.D., U.S.	H9	118
Mount Vernon, Tx., U.S.	F11	116
Mount Vernon, Wa., U.S.	B3	122
Mount Victory, Oh., U.S.	G3	108
Mount Wolf, Pa., U.S.	G10	108
Moura, Austl.	E8	70
Moura, Braz.	H12	84
Moura, Port.	G4	16
Mourdi, Dépression du, depr., Chad	E5	56
Mourdiah, Mali	D6	64
Mourne Mountains, mts., N. Ire., U.K.	G7	8
Moussoro, Chad	F4	56
Moutier, Switz.	D7	13
Moûtiers, Fr.	G13	14
Mouzon, Fr.	C12	14
Moville, Ire.	F6	8
Moville, Ia., U.S.	I11	118
Moweaqua, Il., U.S.	C7	114
Moya, Com.	L16	67a
Moya, Peru	E4	82
Moyahua, Mex.	G8	90
Moyamba, S.L.	G3	64
Moyen Atlas, mts., Mor.	D8	62
Moyeuvre-Grande, Fr.	C13	14
Moyie, B.C., Can.	H19	102
Moyie Springs, Id., U.S.	B9	122
Moyobamba, Peru	B3	82
Moyogalpa, Nic.	F9	92
Moyuta, Volcán, vol., Guat.	C4	92
Možajsk, Russia	F19	22
Mozambique (Moçambique), ctry., Afr.	E7	58
Mozambique Channel, strt., Afr.	E8	58
Mozarlândia, Braz.	C3	79
Mozdok, Russia	I6	26
Možga, Russia	F8	26
Mozyr', Bela.	G3	26
Mphoengs, Zimb.	C8	66
Mpika, Zam.	D6	58
Mpraeso, Ghana	H9	64
Mpwapwa, Tan.	C7	58
Mqanduli, Transkei	H9	66
Mrągowo, Pol.	B21	10
M'Ramani, Com.	L16	67a
Mrkopalj, Cro.	D9	18
M'Saken, Tun.	N5	18
M'Sila, Alg.	C13	62
Mšinskaja, Russia	B12	22
Msta, Russia	D17	22
Msta, stm., Russia	C14	22
Mstera, Russia	E24	22
Mstislavl', Bela.	G14	22
Mszczonów, Pol.	D20	10
Mtamvuna, stm., Afr.	H9	66
Mtwara, Tan.	D8	58
Mu, Cerro, mtn., S.A.	C6	84
Muanda, Zaire	C2	58
Muang Hôngsa, Laos	E6	40
Muang Huang, Laos	E7	40
Muang Khammouan, Laos	F8	40
Muang Khi, Laos	E6	40
Muang Không, Laos	G8	40
Muang Khôngxédôn, Laos	G8	40
Muang Long, Laos	D6	40
Muang Ngoy, Laos	D7	40
Muang Ou Nua, Laos	C6	40
Muang Ou Tai, Laos	C6	40
Muang Pak-Lay, Laos	E6	40
Muang Pakxan, Laos	E7	40
Muang Phiang, Laos	E6	40
Muang Phoun, Laos	E7	40
Muang Sing, Laos	D6	40
Muang Souy, Laos	E7	40
Muang Thadua, Laos	E6	40
Muang Vangviang, Laos	E7	40
Muang Vapi, Laos	G8	40
Muang Xaignabouri, Laos	E6	40
Muang Xay, Laos	D6	40
Muang Xépôn, Laos	F9	40
Muang Xon, Laos	D7	40
Muang You, Laos	E7	40
Muar (Bandar Maharani), Malay.	M7	40
Muarasiberut, Indon.	F2	38
Mucajaí, stm., Braz.	F12	84
Muchanovo, Russia	E21	22
Muchinga Mountains, mts., Zam.	D6	58
Muchtolovo, Russia	F26	22
Muckadilla, Austl.	F8	70
Mučkapskij, Russia	J25	22
Muconda, Ang.	D4	58
Mucuchíes, Ven.	C7	84
Mucugê, Braz.	B8	79
Mucuim, stm., Braz.	B9	82
Muçum, Braz.	E13	80
Mucupia, Moz.	B13	66
Mucupina, Monte, mtn., Hond.	B8	92
Mucur, Tur.	B3	48
Mucuri, Braz.	E9	79
Mucuri, stm., Braz.	E9	79
Mucusso, Ang.	B5	66
Mud, stm., Ky., U.S.	E10	114
Mud, stm., W.V., U.S.	I4	108
Mudan, stm., China	B12	30
Mudanjiang, China	C12	30
Muddy, stm., Nv., U.S.	H11	124
Mudgee, Austl.	I8	70
Mudjatik, stm., Sask., Can.	B7	104
Mudjuga, Russia	J26	6
Mudon, Burma	F4	40
Mudu, China	D9	34
Muelle de los Bueyes, Nic.	E10	92
Muenster, Tx., U.S.	F9	116
Muerto, stm., Arg.	B7	80
Mufulira, Zam.	D5	58
Mu Gia, Deo, Asia	F8	40
Muğla, Tur.	L12	20
Mugron, Fr.	I6	14
Muḥammad, Ra's, c., Egypt	D8	60
Muḥammad Qawl, Sud.	G9	60
Mühlacker, Ger.	G8	10
Mühldorf, Ger.	G12	10
Mühlhausen, Ger.	D10	10
Mühlig-Hofmann Mountains, mts., Ant.	C3	73
Muhu, i., Est.	C6	22
Muhu väin, strt., Est.	C6	22
Muiron Islands, is., Austl.	D2	68
Muisne, Ec.	G2	84
Mujang-ni, S. Kor.	H14	32
Mujezerskij, Russia	J22	6
Mujnak, Uzb.	I9	26
Muju, S. Kor.	G15	32
Mukačevo, Ukr.	H2	26
Mukah, Malay.	E5	38
Mukdahan, Thai.	F8	40
Mukden see Shenyang, China	B11	32
Mukilteo, Wa., U.S.	C3	122
Mukry, Turk.	J11	26
Muktsar, India	E6	44
Mukutawa, stm., Man., Can.	E18	104
Mukwonago, Wi., U.S.	H7	110
Mula, Spain	G10	16
Mulanje, Mwi.	E7	58
Mulas, Punta de, c., Cuba	D7	94
Mulatos, Mex.	C5	90
Mulberry, Ar., U.S.	G2	114
Mulberry, Fl., U.S.	L5	112
Mulberry, In., U.S.	B10	114
Mulberry, stm., Ar., U.S.	G3	114
Mulberry Fork, stm., Al., U.S.	I9	114
Mulchatna, stm., Ak., U.S.	F17	100
Mulchén, Chile	I2	80
Mulde, stm., Ger.	D12	10
Muldoon, Tx., U.S.	J9	116
Muldraugh, Ky., U.S.	E11	114
Muldrow, Ok., U.S.	G2	114
Mule, Lac la, l., Que., Can.	A8	106
Mulegé, Mex.	D3	90
Mulegns, Switz.	E12	13
Muleshoe, Tx., U.S.	E4	116
Mulgowie, Austl.	F10	70
Mulgrave, N.S., Can.	G12	106
Mulhacén, mtn., Spain	H8	16
Mulhall, Ok., U.S.	C9	116
Mulhouse, Fr.	E14	14
Mull, Island of, i., Scot., U.K.	E7	8
Mullan, Id., U.S.	C10	122
Mullen, Ne., U.S.	I6	118
Mullengudgery, Austl.	H7	70
Mullens, W.V., U.S.	B5	112
Muller, Pegunungan, mts., Indon.	E5	38
Mullett Lake, l., Mi., U.S.	E11	110
Mullewa, Austl.	E3	68
Mullica, stm., N.J., U.S.	H12	108
Mulligan, stm., Austl.	D3	70
Mullin, Tx., U.S.	H8	116
Mullingar, Ire.	H6	8
Mullins, S.C., U.S.	E7	112
Mullinville, Ks., U.S.	N8	118
Mullumbimby, Austl.	G10	70
Multān, Pak.	E4	44
Mulvane, Ks., U.S.	N10	118
Mulyah Mountain, mtn., Austl.	H6	70
Mumbwa, Zam.	D5	58
Mumford, Tx., U.S.	I10	116
Mumu, Sud.	K2	60
Mumungwe, Bots.	C8	66
Mun, stm., Thai.	G8	40
Muna, Mex.	G15	90
Munā, Sau. Ar.	D1	47
Muna, stm., Russia	D15	28
Münchberg, Ger.	E11	10
München (Munich), Ger.	G11	10
München-Gladbach see Mönchengladbach, Ger.	D6	10

Name	Map Ref.	Page
Münchenstein, Switz.	C8	13
Munchique, Cerro, mtn., Col.	F4	84
Munch'ŏn, N. Kor.	D15	32
Muncie, In., U.S.	B11	114
Muncy, Pa., U.S.	F10	108
Mundare, Alta., Can.	D22	102
Munday, Tx., U.S.	F7	116
Mundelein, Il., U.S.	H7	110
Münden, Ger.	D9	10
Mundo Novo, Braz.	A8	79
Mundubbera, Austl.	E9	70
Munene, Zimb.	C10	66
Munford, Tn., U.S.	G7	114
Munfordville, Ky., U.S.	E11	114
Mungallala, Austl.	F7	70
Mungbere, Zaire	H6	56
Munger, India	H12	44
Mungindi, Austl.	G8	70
Munhango, Ang.	D3	58
Munich see München, Ger.	G11	10
Munising, Mi., U.S.	D9	110
Muniz Freire, Braz.	F8	79
Munku-Sardyk, gora, mtn., Asia	G12	28
Munro Lake, l., Man., Can.	D19	104
Munsan, S. Kor.	F14	32
Münsingen, Switz.	E8	13
Munson, Alta., Can.	F22	102
Munsons Corners, N.Y., U.S.	E10	108
Munster, Fr.	D14	14
Munster, Ger.	C10	10
Münster, Ger.	D7	10
Munster, hist. reg., Ire.	I5	8
Munuscong Lake, l., N.A.	D11	110
Muong Saiapoun, Laos	E6	40
Muonio, Fin.	H18	6
Muoro, Italy	I4	18
Muqayshiṭ, i., U.A.E.	B8	47
Muqdisho (Mogadishu), Som.	H10	56
Muqi, China	B12	32
Muqui, Braz.	F8	79
Mur (Mura), stm., Eur.	I15	10
Mura (Mur), stm., Eur.	I16	10
Muradiye, Tur.	B7	48
Murakami, Japan	I14	36
Muraši, Russia	F7	26
Murat, stm., Tur.	B5	48
Muravjovo, Russia	E17	22
Murča, Port.	D4	16
Mūrcheh Khvort, Iran	E11	48
Murchison, Austl.	K6	70
Murchison, Tx., U.S.	G11	116
Murchison, stm., Austl.	E3	68
Murchison, Mount, mtn., N.Z.	E3	72
Murchison Falls see Kabalega Falls, wtfl, Ug.	H7	56
Murcia, Spain	H10	16
Murcia, prov., Spain	G10	16
Murciélago, Islas, is., C.R.	G9	92
Murdo, S.D., U.S.	H7	118
Mureck, Aus.	I15	10
Mureș, co., Rom.	C8	20
Mureș (Maros), stm., Eur.	C5	20
Muret, Fr.	I8	14
Murfreesboro, Ar., U.S.	H3	114
Murfreesboro, N.C., U.S.	C9	112
Murfreesboro, Tn., U.S.	G10	114
Murgab, Taj.	J12	26
Murgab (Morghāb), stm., Asia	B16	48
Murgha Kibzai, Pak.	E3	44
Murgon, Austl.	F9	70
Muri, Switz.	E7	13
Muriaé, Braz.	F7	79
Muriaé, stm., Braz.	F8	79
Muriel Lake, l., Alta., Can.	C24	102
Müritz, l., Ger.	B12	10
Murmansk, Russia	D4	26
Murmino, Russia	G23	22
Murnei, Sud.	K2	60
Murom, Russia	F25	22
Muroran, Japan	E15	36a
Muroto, Japan	N9	36
Murphy, Id., U.S.	G9	122
Murphy, N.C., U.S.	D2	112
Murphy Lake, l., B.C., Can.	E13	102
Murphys, Ca., U.S.	F5	124
Murphysboro, Il., U.S.	E7	114
Murray, Ia., U.S.	I2	110
Murray, Ky., U.S.	F8	114
Murray, Ut., U.S.	D5	120
Murray, stm., Austl.	J3	70
Murray, stm., B.C., Can.	B13	102
Murray, Lake, l., Pap. N. Gui.	G11	38
Murray, Lake, res., S.C., U.S.	E5	112
Murray, Mount, mtn., Yukon, Can.	F30	100
Murray Bay see La Malbaie, Que., Can.	E3	106
Murray Bridge, Austl.	J3	70
Murray City, Oh., U.S.	H4	108
Murray Harbour, P.E.I., Can.	F11	106
Murray Head, c., P.E.I., Can.	F11	106
Murray Maxwell Bay, b., N.W. Ter., Can.	B16	96
Murray River, P.E.I., Can.	F11	106
Murraysburg, S. Afr.	H6	66
Murrayville, Il., U.S.	C6	114
Murree, Pak.	D5	44
Murrhardt, Ger.	G9	10
Murrí, stm., Col.	D4	84
Murrumbidgee, stm., Austl.	J6	70
Murrumburrah, Austl.	J8	70
Murrurundi, Austl.	H9	70
Murska Sobota, Slo.	C11	18
Murtajāpur, India	B4	46
Murten, Switz.	E7	13
Murtle Lake, l., B.C., Can.	E15	102
Murtoa, Austl.	K5	70
Murtosa, Port.	E3	16
Muru, stm., Braz.	C6	82
Murud, Gunong, mtn., Malay.	E6	38
Murupara, N.Z.	C6	72
Murutinga, Braz.	I13	84
Murwāra, India	I9	44
Murwillumbah, Austl.	G10	70
Mürzzuschlag, Aus.	H15	10
Muş, Tur.	B6	48
Mūsā, Jabal (Mount Sinai), mtn., Egypt	C7	60
Musaid, Libya	B3	60
Musala, mtn., Bul.	G7	20
Musan, N. Kor.	A17	32
Musandam Peninsula, pen., Oman	A10	47
Mūsā Qal'eh, Afg.	D1	44
Musay'īd, Qatar	D11	56
Muscatatuck, stm., In., U.S.	D10	114
Muscatine, Ia., U.S.	I4	110
Muscat see Masqaṭ, Oman	C11	47
Mus-Chaja, gora, mtn., Russia	E20	28
Muscle Shoals, Al., U.S.	H9	114
Musclow, Mount, mtn., B.C., Can.	D7	102
Musclow Lake, l., Ont., Can.	G20	104
Muscoda, Wi., U.S.	G5	110
Muscowpetung Indian Reserve, Sask., Can.	H10	104
Müsgebi, Tur.	L11	20
Musgrave, Austl.	B8	68
Musgravetown, Newf., Can.	D20	106
Mushandike Sanctuary, Zimb.	C10	66
Mushie, Zaire	B3	58
Mushin, Nig.	H11	64
Muskeg, stm., Alta., Can.	D16	102
Muskeg Lake Indian Reserve, Sask., Can.	F8	104
Muskegon, Mi., U.S.	G9	110
Muskegon, stm., Mi., U.S.	D1	108
Muskegon Heights, Mi., U.S.	G9	110
Muskingum, stm., Oh., U.S.	H5	108
Muskoday Indian Reserve, Sask., Can.	E9	104
Muskogee, Ok., U.S.	D11	116
Muskowekwan Indian Reserve, Sask., Can.	G10	104
Muskrat Dam Lake, l., Ont., Can.	E23	104
Muskwa, stm., B.C., Can.	E8	96
Muskwa Lake, l., Alta., Can.	A20	102
Muslimbāgh, Pak.	E2	44
Musoma, Tan.	B6	58
Musquanousse, Lac, l., Que., Can.	B12	106
Musquaro, Lac, l., Que., Can.	B12	106
Musquodoboit Harbour, N.S., Can.	H10	106
Musselshell, stm., Mt., U.S.	C18	122
Mussomeli, Italy	L8	18
Mussuma, Ang.	D4	58
Mustafakemalpaşa, Tur.	I12	20
Mustang Island, i., Tx., U.S.	L10	116
Mustinka, stm., Mn., U.S.	F11	118
Mustla, Est.	C8	22
Mustvee, Est.	C9	22
Muswellbrook, Austl.	I9	70
Mūt, Egypt	E5	60
Mut, Tur.	C2	48
Mutá, Ponta do, c., Braz.	B9	79
Mutambara, Zimb.	B11	66
Mutare, Zimb.	B11	66
Mutlu (Rezovska), stm., Eur.	H11	20
Mutsamudu, Com.	L16	67a
Mutsu, Japan	F16	36
Mutsu-wan, b., Japan	F15	36
Muttaburra, Austl.	D6	70
Muttenz, Switz.	C8	13
Mutuípe, Braz.	B9	79
Mutum, Braz.	E8	79
Mutum, stm., Braz.	J8	84
Mutunópolis, Braz.	B4	79
Muxima, Ang.	C2	58
Muymano, stm., S.A.	D7	82
Muy Muy, Nic.	E9	92
Muyua Island, i., Pap. N. Gui.	A10	68
Muyua Island, i., Pap. N. Gui.	m17	68a
Muyumba, Zaire	C5	58
Muzaffarābād, Pak.	C5	44
Muzaffarnagar, India	F7	44
Muzaffarpur, India	G11	44
Muzat, stm., China	C3	30
Muztag, mtn., China	B9	44
Muztag, mtn., China	B12	44
Mvolo, Sud.	N5	60
Mvuma, Zimb.	B10	66
Mwali (Mohéli), i., Com.	L15	67a
Mwanza, Tan.	B6	58
Mweka, Zaire	B4	58
Mwenezi, Zimb.	C10	66
Mweru, Lake, l., Afr.	C5	58
Mwinilunga, Zam.	D4	58
Myaing, Burma	D3	40
Myanaung, Burma	E3	40
Myanmar see Burma, ctry., Asia	A2	38
Myaungmya, Burma	F3	40
Myebon, Burma	D2	40
Myerstown, Pa., U.S.	G10	108
Myingyan, Burma	D3	40
Myitkyinā, Burma	B4	40
Myittha, Burma	D4	40
Myjava, Czech.	G17	10
Myllymäki, Fin.	J19	6
Mymensingh, Bngl.	H14	44
Mynämäki, Fin.	K18	6
Mynfontein, S. Afr.	H6	66
Myrnam, Alta., Can.	D23	102
Myrskylä (Mörskom), Fin.	K19	6
Myrtle Beach, S.C., U.S.	F8	112
Myrtle Creek, Or., U.S.	G2	122
Myrtle Grove, Fl., U.S.	L9	114
Myrtle Point, Or., U.S.	G1	122
Myrtletowne, Ca., U.S.	D1	124
Myski, Russia	G9	28
Myškino, Russia	D21	22
Myślenice, Pol.	F19	10
Mysłowice, Pol.	E19	10
Mysore, India	F4	46
Mystic, Ct., U.S.	F15	108
Mystic, Ia., U.S.	J3	110
Myszków, Pol.	E19	10
Myt, Russia	E25	22
My Tho, Viet.	I9	40
Mytišči, Russia	F20	22
Myton, Ut., U.S.	D6	120
Mzimba, Mwi.	D6	58
Mzimvubu, stm., Afr.	H9	66
Mzuzu, Mwi.	D6	58
N		
Na (Tengtiao), stm., Asia	C7	40
Naalehu, Hi., U.S.	r18	125a
Naas, Ire.	H7	8
Nabā, Jabal an- (Mount Nebo), mtn., Jord.	E5	50
Nabalat Al-Ḥajanah, Sud.	K5	60
Nabburg, Ger.	F12	10
Naberežnyje Čelny, Russia	F8	26
Nabesna, Ak., U.S.	E23	100
Nabeul, Tun.	M5	18
Nābha, India	E7	44
Nabileque, stm., Braz.	I13	82
Nabī Shu'ayb, Jabal an-, mtn., Yemen	G3	47
Nabisipi, stm., Que., Can.	B11	106
Nabogame, Mex.	D6	90
Naboomspruit, S. Afr.	E9	66
Nabq, Egypt	C8	60
Nābulus, Isr. Occ.	D4	50
Nacala-Velha, Moz.	D8	58
Nacaome, Hond.	D7	92
Naches, stm., Wa., U.S.	D4	122
Nachičevan', Azer.	J7	26
Náchod, Czech.	E16	10
Nachodka, Russia	I18	28
Nachvak Fiord, Newf., Can.	E20	96
Nacimiento, Chile	I2	80
Naco, Mex.	B5	90
Naco, Az., U.S.	M7	120
Nacogdoches, Tx., U.S.	K2	114
Nácori Chico, Mex.	C5	90
Nacozari de García, Mex.	B5	90
Ñacunday, Para.	D11	80
Nadaleen Mountain, mtn., Yukon, Can.	D28	100
Naden Harbour, b., B.C., Can.	C2	102
Nadiād, India	I5	44
Nădlac, Rom.	C4	20
Nador, Mor.	C9	62
Nadvoicy, Russia	J24	6
Nadvornaja, Ukr.	A8	20
Nadym, Russia	D12	26
Nadym, stm., Russia	D12	26
Nafadji, Sen.	E4	64
Näfels, Switz.	D11	13
Nafī, Sau. Ar.	I7	48
Naga, Phil.	O20	39b
Nâga, Kreb en, clf, Afr.	I7	62
Naga Hills, mts., Asia	B3	40
Nāgāland, state, India	H16	44
Nagano, Japan	K13	36
Nagaoka, Japan	J13	36
Nagaon, India	G15	44
Nāgappattinam, India	G5	46
Nāgārjuna Sāgar, res., India	D5	46
Nagarote, Nic.	E8	92
Nagar Pārkar, Pak.	H4	44
Nagasaki, Japan	O4	36
Nāgaur, India	G5	44
Nagda, India	I6	44
Nāgercoil, India	H4	46
Nagīna, India	F8	44
Nagold, Ger.	G8	10
Nagornoje, Ukr.	D12	20
Nagornyj, Russia	F16	28
Nagoya, Japan	L11	36
Nāgpur, India	J8	44
Nagqu, China	E5	30
Nagua, Dom. Rep.	E10	94
Nagyatád, Hung.	I17	10
Nagybajom, Hung.	I17	10
Nagyecsed, Hung.	H22	10
Nagykálló, Hung.	H21	10
Nagykanizsa, Hung.	I17	10
Nagykőrös, Hung.	H19	10
Naha, Japan	U2	37b
Nāhan, India	E7	44
Nahang (Nihing), stm., Asia	H17	48
Nahanni National Park, N.W. Ter., Can.	F31	100
Nahariyya, Isr.	B4	50
Nahāvand, Iran	D10	48
Nahe, China	B11	30
Nahma, Mi., U.S.	E9	110
Nahualate, stm., Guat.	C3	92
Nahuel Huapí, Lago, l., Arg.	E2	78
Nahunta, Ga., U.S.	H5	112
Naica, Mex.	D7	90
Naicam, Sask., Can.	F10	104
Naikoon Provincial Park, B.C., Can.	D3	102
Nailin, China	B7	32
Nain, Newf., Can.	E20	96
Nā'īn, Iran	E12	48
Naini Tāl, India	F8	44
Nairn, La., U.S.	M7	114
Nairobi, Kenya	B7	58
Naissaar, i., Est.	B7	22
Naivasha, Kenya	B7	58
Najafābād, Iran	E11	48
Najasa, stm., Cuba	D6	94
Nájera, Spain	C9	16
Naj'Ḥammādī, Egypt	D7	60
Najībābād, India	F8	44
Najin, N. Kor.	A18	32
Najstenjarvi, Russia	J23	6
Naju, S. Kor.	H14	32
Nakadōri-shima, i., Japan	O4	36
Nakaminato, Japan	K15	36
Nakano-shima, i., Japan	R4	37b
Nakape, Sud.	O5	60
Nakatsu, Japan	N6	36
Nakfa, Eth.	I10	60
Nakhon Nayok, Thai.	G6	40
Nakhon Pathom, Thai.	H6	40
Nakhon Phanom, Thai.	F8	40
Nakhon Ratchasima, Thai.	G7	40
Nakhon Sawan, Thai.	G6	40
Nakhon Si Thammarat, Thai.	J5	40
Nakina, Ont., Can.	F15	96
Nakło nad Notecią, Pol.	B17	10
Naknek, Ak., U.S.	G16	100
Nakskov, Den.	N12	6
Nakuru, Kenya	B7	58
Nakusp, B.C., Can.	G17	102
Nalajch, Mong.	B8	30
Nālanda, India	D12	42
Nal'čik, Russia	I6	26
Nalgonda, India	D5	46
Nālūt, Libya	E16	62
Nam, stm., Asia	D5	40
Namaacha, Moz.	E11	66
Namak, Daryācheh-ye, l., Iran	D11	48
Namakan Lake, l., N.A.	B3	110
Namaksār, Kowl-e, l., Asia	D18	48
Namangan, Uzb.	I12	26
Namapa, Moz.	D7	58
Namatanai, Pap. N. Gui.	k17	68a
Nambour, Austl.	F10	70
Nambucca Heads, Austl.	H10	70
Nam Can, Viet.	J8	40
Nam Co, l., China	E14	44
Nam Dinh, Viet.	D9	40
Namekagon, stm., Wi., U.S.	D3	110
Namen (Namur), Bel.	H6	12
Namew Lake, l., Can.	D13	104
Namhkam, Burma	C4	40
Namib Desert, des., Afr.	D2	66
Namibe, Ang.	E2	58
Namibia, ctry., Afr.	F3	58
Namjagbarwa Feng, mtn., China	F16	44
Namoi, stm., Austl.	H8	70
Namounou, Burkina	F10	64
Nampa, Alta., Can.	A17	102
Nampa, Id., U.S.	G9	122
Nampawng, Burma	C4	40
Namp'o, N. Kor.	E13	32
Nampula, Moz.	E7	58
Namsang, Burma	D4	40
Namsos, Nor.	I12	6
Namtu, Burma	A2	38
Namu, B.C., Can.	F7	102
Namur (Namen), Bel.	H6	12
Namur, prov., Bel.	H6	12
Namutoni, Nmb.	B3	66
Namwŏn, S. Kor.	H15	32
Namyang, N. Kor.	A17	32
Namyit Island, i., Asia	C5	38
Namysłów, Pol.	D17	10
Nan, Thai.	E6	40
Nan, stm., Thai.	F6	40
Nanaimo, B.C., Can.	H11	102
Nanam, N. Kor.	B17	32
Nanango, Austl.	F10	70
Nanao, Japan	J11	36
Nanay, stm., Peru	I6	84
Nanchang, China	G4	34
Nancheng, China	H5	34
Nanchong, China	E8	30
Nancowry Island, i., India	K2	40
Nancun, China	G8	32
Nancy, Fr.	D13	14
Nanda Devi, mtn., India	E8	44
Nandaime, Nic.	F8	92
Nānded, India	C4	46
Nanding, stm., Asia	C5	40
N'andoma, Russia	E6	26
Nandu, stm., China	E11	40
Nandurbār, India	J6	44
Nandyāl, India	E5	46
Nanga Parbat, mtn., Pak.	C6	44
Nangin, Burma	I5	40
Nangnim, N. Kor.	C15	32
Nangola, Mali	E6	64
Nang Rong, Thai.	G7	40
Nanika Lake, l., B.C., Can.	D7	102
Nanjangūd, India	F4	46
Nanjiang, China	C9	34
Nanjing (Nanking), China	C7	34
Nankang, China	J3	34
Nanking see Nanjing, China	C7	34
Nankou, China	I6	34
Nan Ling, mts., China	J2	34
Nanlinqiao, China	F3	34
Nannine, Austl.	E3	68
Nanning, China	C10	40
Nanowin, stm., Man., Can.	E18	104
Nanpi, China	E4	32
Nanping, China	I7	34
Nanpu, China	D6	32
Nansa, stm., Spain	B7	16
Nansei-shotō (Ryukyu Islands), is., Japan	S4	37b
Nanshan Island, i., Asia	C6	38
Nanshan see Qilian Shan, mts., China	D6	30
Nant, Fr.	H10	14
Nantais, Lac, l., Que., Can.	D18	96
Nantang, China	I4	34
Nantes, Fr.	E5	14
Nanticoke, Pa., U.S.	F10	108
Nanticoke, stm., U.S.	I11	108
Nanton, Alta., Can.	G21	102
Nantong, China	C9	34
Nant'ou, Tai.	L9	34
Nantua, Fr.	F12	14
Nantucket, Ma., U.S.	F16	108
Nantucket Island, i., Ma., U.S.	F16	108
Nantucket Sound, strt., Ma., U.S.	F16	108
Nanty Glo, Pa., U.S.	G8	108
Nanuque, Braz.	D8	79
Nanwan, China	C2	34
Nanxiang, China	D10	34
Nanxiong, China	J3	34
Nanyang, China	B1	34
Nanzhao, China	B1	34
Naococane, Lac, l., Que., Can.	F18	96
Não-me-Toque, Braz.	E12	80
Naosap Lake, l., Man., Can.	D13	104
Náousa, Grc.	I6	20
Napa, Ca., U.S.	F3	124
Napakiak, Ak., U.S.	F14	100
Napanee, Ont., Can.	F19	110
Napaskiak, Ak., U.S.	F14	100
Napè, Laos	E8	40
Napenay, Arg.	D8	80
Naperville, Il., U.S.	I7	110
Napetipi, stm., Can.	A15	106
Napier, N.Z.	C6	72
Napier, S. Afr.	J4	66
Napier Mountains, mts., Ant.	B4	73
Napinka, Man., Can.	I14	104
Naples, Fl., U.S.	M5	112
Naples, Id., U.S.	B9	122
Naples, N.Y., U.S.	E9	108
Naples, Tx., U.S.	I2	114
Naples see Napoli, Italy	I9	18
Napo, prov., Ec.	H4	84
Napo, stm., S.A.	I6	84
Napoleon, N.D., U.S.	E8	118
Napoleon, Oh., U.S.	F2	108
Napoleonville, La., U.S.	M5	114
Napoli (Naples), Italy	I9	18
Nappanee, In., U.S.	A10	114
Naqādah, Egypt	E7	60
Naqadeh, Iran	C8	48
Nara, Japan	M10	36
Nara, Mali	D6	64
Naracoorte, Austl.	K4	70
Naradhan, Austl.	I7	70
Naramata, B.C., Can.	H15	102
Naranjal, Ec.	I3	84
Naranjito, Hond.	C6	92
Naranjo, C.R.	G10	92
Naranjo, stm., Guat.	C3	92
Narasapur, India	D6	46
Narasaraopet, India	D6	46
Narathiwat, Thai.	K6	40
Nara Visa, N.M., U.S.	D3	116
Nārāyanganj, Bngl.	I14	44
Nārāyaṇi (Gandak), stm., Asia	G11	44
Nārāyanpet, India	D4	46
Narbonne, Fr.	I10	14
Narcosli Creek, stm., B.C., Can.	E12	102
Nardò, Italy	I13	18
Nare, stm., Col.	D5	84
Nares Strait, strt., N.A.	A13	86
Narew, stm., Eur.	C21	10
Narinda, Baie de, b., Madag.	O22	67b
Nariño, dept., Col.	G3	84
Narita, Japan	L15	36
Nar'jan-Mar, Russia	D8	26
Narmada, stm., India	J5	44
Nārnaul, India	F7	44
Narni, Italy	G7	18
Naro, Italy	L8	18
Narodnaja, gora, mtn., Russia	D10	26
Naro-Fominsk, Russia	F19	22
Narol, Pol.	E23	10
Narooma, Austl.	K9	70
Narrabri, Austl.	H8	70
Narran, stm., Austl.	G7	70
Narrandera, Austl.	J7	70
Narraway, stm., Can.	C14	102
Narrogin, Austl.	F3	68
Narromine, Austl.	I8	70
Narrows, Va., U.S.	B6	112
Narsimhapur, India	I8	44
Narsīpatnam, India	D7	46
Narva, Est.	B11	22
Narva, stm., Eur.	B10	22
Narvik, Nor.	G15	6
Narvskij zaliv (Narva laht), b., Eur.	B10	22
Narvskoje vodochranilišče, res., Eur.	B11	22
Naryn, Kyrg.	I13	26
Naryn, stm., Asia	I12	26
Naryškino, Russia	I18	22
Na San, Thai.	J5	40
Nasarawa, Nig.	G13	64
Naschel, Arg.	G6	80
Nash, Tx., U.S.	I2	114
Nāshik, India	C2	46
Nashua, Ia., U.S.	H3	110
Nashua, Mt., U.S.	B19	122
Nashua, N.H., U.S.	E15	108
Nashville, Ar., U.S.	I3	114
Nashville, Ga., U.S.	H3	112
Nashville, Il., U.S.	D7	114
Nashville, In., U.S.	C10	114
Nashville, Mi., U.S.	H10	110
Nashville, N.C., U.S.	D9	112
Nashville, Tn., U.S.	F10	114
Nashwaak, stm., N.B., Can.	F7	106
Nashwaaksis, N.B., Can.	G7	106
Nashwauk, Mn., U.S.	C2	110
Nasielsk, Pol.	C20	10
Näsijärvi, l., Fin.	K18	6
Nāṣir, Sud.	M7	60
Nāṣir, Buḥayrat, res., Afr.	D7	56
Nasīrābād, India	G6	44
Nasīrābād, Pak.	F3	44
Naskaupi, stm., Newf., Can.	F20	96
Nass, stm., B.C., Can.	B5	102
Nassau, Bah.	B6	94
Nassau, N.Y., U.S.	E13	108
Nassawadox, Va., U.S.	B11	112
Nasser, Lake see Nāṣir, Buḥayrat, res., Afr.	D7	56
Nassereith, Aus.	H10	10
Nässjö, Swe.	M14	6
Nastapoca, stm., Que., Can.	E17	96
Nastapoka Islands, is., N.W. Ter., Can.	E17	96
Nasva, Russia	E13	22
Nata, Bots.	C8	66
Natá, Pan.	C2	84
Nata, stm., Afr.	B8	66
Natagaima, Col.	F5	84
Natal, Braz.	E11	76
Natal, B.C., Can.	H20	102
Natal, Indon.	E2	38
Natalia, Tx., U.S.	J8	116
Natalkuz Lake, l., B.C., Can.	D9	102
Natash, Wādī, val., Egypt	I2	48
Natashquan, Que., Can.	B12	106
Natashquan, stm., Can.	F20	96
Natashquan, Pointe de, c., Que., Can.	B12	106
Natashquan Est, stm., Que., Can.	A12	106
Natchez, Ms., U.S.	K5	114
Natchitoches, La., U.S.	K3	114
Natimuk, Austl.	K4	70
Nation, stm., B.C., Can.	B11	102
National City, Ca., U.S.	L8	124
Natipi, Lac, l., Que., Can.	A2	106
Natitingou, Benin	F10	64
Native Bay, b., N.W. Ter., Can.	D16	96
Nativity, Church of the, Isr. Occ.	E4	50
Natl, Jord.	E5	50
Natoma, Ks., U.S.	L8	118
Natong, China	C9	40
Natron, Lake, l., Afr.	B7	58
Natuna Besar, i., Indon.	L10	40
Natuna Besar, Kepulauan, is., Indon.	L10	40
Naturaliste, Cape, c., Austl.	F3	68
Naturaliste Channel, strt., Austl.	E2	68
Naturita, Co., U.S.	F8	120
Nau, Cap de la, c., Spain	G12	16
Nauders, Aus.	I10	10
Nauen, Ger.	C12	10
Naugatuck, Ct., U.S.	F13	108
Naughton, Ont., Can.	D14	110
Naujamiestis, Lith.	F7	22
Naujoji Akmenė, Lith.	E5	22
Naumburg, Ger.	D11	10
Naungpale, Burma	E4	40
Nauroz Kalāt, Pak.	F1	44
Nauru, ctry., Oc.	G24	2
Nauta, Peru	J6	84
Nautla, Mex.	G11	90
Nauvoo, Il., U.S.	J4	110
Nava, Mex.	C9	90
Navadwip, India	I13	44
Navahermosa, Spain	F7	16
Navajo, N.M., U.S.	I7	120
Navajo, stm., U.S.	G10	120
Navajo Mountain, mtn., Ut., U.S.	G6	120
Navajo Reservoir, res., U.S.	H9	120
Navalmoral de la Mata, Spain	F6	16
Navarin, mys, c., Russia	E27	28
Navarino, Isla, i., Chile	H3	78
Navarra, prov., Spain	C10	16
Navarre, Oh., U.S.	G5	108
Navarro, Arg.	H9	80
Navašino, Russia	F25	22
Navasota, Tx., U.S.	I10	116
Navasota, stm., Tx., U.S.	H10	116
Navassa, N.C., U.S.	E8	112
Navassa Island, i., N.A.	E7	94
Navia, Arg.	H5	80
Navidad, Chile	G3	80
Navidad, stm., Tx., U.S.	J10	116
Naviraí, Braz.	G1	79
Navl'a, Russia	I17	22
Năvodari, Rom.	E12	20
Navoi, Uzb.	I11	26
Navojoa, Mex.	D5	90
Navolato, Mex.	E6	90
Navoloki, Russia	D24	22
Návpaktos, Grc.	K5	20
Návplion, Grc.	L6	20
Navsāri, India	J5	44
Nawābganj, Bngl.	H13	44
Nawābshāh, Pak.	G3	44
Nāwah, Afg.	D2	44
Nawalgarh, India	G6	44
Náxos, Grc.	L9	20
Náxos, i., Grc.	L9	20
Nayarit, state, Mex.	F7	90
Nāy Band, Iran	E14	48
Naylor, Mo., U.S.	F6	114
Nayoro, Japan	C17	36a
Nazaré, Braz.	B9	79
Nazaré, Port.	F2	16
Nazaré da Mata, Braz.	E11	76
Nazareth, Pa., U.S.	G11	108
Nazareth see Naẕerat, Isr.	C4	50
Nazário, Braz.	D4	79
Nazarovo, Russia	F10	28
Nazas, Mex.	E7	90
Nazas, stm., Mex.	E7	90
Nazca, Peru	F4	82
Naze, Japan	S4	37b
N'azepetrovsk, Russia	F9	26
Naẕerat (Nazareth), Isr.	C4	50
Naẕerat 'Illit, Isr.	C4	50
Nazija, Russia	B14	22
Nazilli, Tur.	L12	20
Nazko, stm., B.C., Can.	E11	102
Nazret, Eth.	M10	60
Nazyvajevsk, Russia	F12	26
N'dalatando, Ang.	C2	58
Ndali, Benin	G11	64
Ndélé, Cen. Afr. Rep.	G5	56
Ndendé, Gabon	B2	58
N'Djamena, Chad	F4	56
Ndjolé, Gabon	B2	58
Ndola, Zam.	D5	58
Neagh, Lough, l., N. Ire., U.K.	G7	8
Neah Bay, Wa., U.S.	B1	122
Neamț, co., Rom.	C10	20
Néa Páfos (Paphos), Cyp.	D2	48
Near Islands, is., Ak., U.S.	J1	101a
Nebaj, Guat.	B3	92
Nebit-Dag, Turk.	J8	26
Nebit-Dag (Krasnovodsk), Turk.	I8	26
Neblina, Pico da, mtn., S.A.	G9	84
Nebo, Il., U.S.	C6	114
Nebo, Mount, mtn., Ut., U.S.	E5	120
Nebolči, Russia	B16	22
Nebraska, state, U.S.	C6	98
Nebraska City, Ne., U.S.	K12	118
Necedah, Wi., U.S.	F5	110
Nechako, stm., B.C., Can.	C11	102
Nechako Plateau, plat., B.C., Can.	C10	102
Nechako Range, mts., B.C., Can.	D10	102
Nechako Reservoir, res., B.C., Can.	D9	102
Neche, N.D., U.S.	C10	118
Neches, Tx., U.S.	H11	116
Neches, stm., Tx., U.S.	L2	114
Nechí, Col.	C5	84
Nechí, stm., Col.	D5	84
Nechmeya, Alg.	M2	18
Neckar, stm., Ger.	F9	10
Neckarsulm, Ger.	F9	10
Necochea, Arg.	J9	80
Nederland, Tx., U.S.	M3	114
Neder Rijn, mth., Neth.	E8	12
Nêdong, China	F5	30
Nédroma, Alg.	C10	62
Neebish Island, i., Mi., U.S.	D11	110
Needle Mountain, mtn., Wy., U.S.	F16	122
Needles, Ca., U.S.	J11	124
Needville, Tx., U.S.	J11	116
Ñeembucú, dept., Para.	D9	80
Neenah, Wi., U.S.	F7	110
Neepawa, Man., Can.	H15	104
Nefta, Tun.	D14	62
Nefza, Tun.	M4	18
Negage, Ang.	C3	58
Négala, Mali	E5	64
Negaunee, Mi., U.S.	D8	110
Negele, Eth.	G8	56
Negev Desert see HaNegev, reg., Isr.	G3	50
Negombo, Sri L.	I5	46
Negoreloje, Bela.	H10	22
Negotin, Yugo.	E6	20
Negra, Laguna, l., Ur.	H12	80
Negra, Punta, c., Belize	A6	92
Negra, Punta, c., Peru	B1	82
Negreira, Spain	C3	16
Negrești, Rom.	C11	20
Negrine, Alg.	C14	62
Negritos, Peru	J2	84
Negro, stm., Arg.	E4	78
Negro, stm., Bol.	D9	82
Negro, stm., Bol.	F10	82
Negro, stm., Braz.	C13	80
Negro, stm., Braz.	A6	82
Negro, stm., Braz.	H13	82
Negro, stm., Col.	E5	84
Negro, stm., N.A.	E7	92
Negro, stm., Para.	C10	80
Negro, stm., S.A.	G10	80
Negro, stm., S.A.	H13	84
Negros, i., Phil.	C7	38
Neguac, N.B., Can.	E8	106
Nehalem, stm., Or., U.S.	E2	122
Nehawka, Ne., U.S.	K12	118
Nehbandān, Iran	F16	48
Neiba, Dom. Rep.	E9	94
Neidpath, Sask., Can.	H7	104
Neiges, Piton des, mtn., Reu.	V17	67c
Neihart, Mt., U.S.	D15	122
Neihuang, China	H2	32
Neijiang, China	F8	30
Neilburg, Sask., Can.	F5	104
Neillsville, Wi., U.S.	F5	110
Nei Monggol Zizhiqu (Inner Mongolia), prov., China	C10	30
Neira, Col.	E5	84
Neisse (Nysa Łużycka) (Nisa), stm., Eur.	D14	10
Neiva, Col.	F5	84
Neixpa, stm., Mex.	H8	90
Neja, Russia	C26	22
Nejapa de Madero, Mex.	I12	90
Nejdek, Czech.	E12	10
Nejo, Eth.	M8	60
Nekemte, Eth.	M9	60
Nekoosa, Wi., U.S.	F6	110
Nekrasovskoje, Russia	D23	22
Neksø, Den.	N14	6
Nelidovo, Russia	E15	22
Neligh, Ne., U.S.	I9	118
Nellikuppam, India	G5	46
Nellore, India	E5	46
Nel'ma, Russia	H19	28
Nelson, B.C., Can.	H17	102
Nelson, N.Z.	D4	72
Nelson, Ne., U.S.	K9	118
Nelson, stm., Man., Can.	B21	104
Nelson, Cape, c., Austl.	L4	70
Nelson House, Man., Can.	C16	104
Nelson Lake, l., Man., Can.	C14	104
Nelsonville, Oh., U.S.	H4	108
Nelspoort, S. Afr.	I6	66
Nelspruit, S. Afr.	E10	66
Néma, Maur.	C6	64
Nemadji, stm., U.S.	D3	110
Nemaha, Ne., U.S.	K12	118
Neman, Russia	F5	22
Neman (Nemunas), stm., Eur.	F5	22
Nemeiben Lake, l., Sask., Can.	C9	104
Nemenčinė, Lith.	G8	22
Nemours, Fr.	D9	14
Nemuna, Bjeshkët e, mts., Eur.	G3	20
Nemunas (Neman), stm., Eur.	F6	22
Nemuro, Japan	D20	36a
Nemuro Strait, strt., Asia	C20	36a
Nen, stm., China	B11	30
Nenagh, Ire.	I5	8
Nenana, Ak., U.S.	D20	100
Nenana, stm., Ak., U.S.	D20	100
Nenaševo, Russia	G20	22
Nentón, stm., N.A.	B3	92
Neodesha, Ks., U.S.	N12	118
Neoga, Il., U.S.	C8	114
Neola, Ia., U.S.	J12	118
Neola, Ut., U.S.	D6	120
Neopit, Wi., U.S.	F7	110
Neosho, Mo., U.S.	F2	114
Neosho, stm., U.S.	F1	114
Nepa, stm., Russia	F13	28
Nepal (Nepāl), ctry., Asia	D11	42
Nepālgañj, Nepal	F9	44
Nepeña, Peru	C2	82
Nephi, Ut., U.S.	E5	120
Nepisiguit, stm., N.B., Can.	E8	106
Nepisiguit Bay, b., N.B., Can.	E8	106
Neptune, N.J., U.S.	G12	108
Neptune Beach, Fl., U.S.	I5	112
Nera, stm., Eur.	E5	20
Nerča, stm., Russia	G15	28
Nerčinsk, Russia	G15	28
Nerčinskij Zavod, Russia	G15	28
Nerechta, Russia	D23	22
Nereta, Lat.	E8	22
Neringa, Russia	F4	22
Neriquinha, Ang.	E4	58
Nerja, Spain	I8	16
Nerl', Russia	E23	22
Nerl', stm., Russia	E23	22

Name	Map Ref.	Page
Nerópolis, Braz.	D4	79
Nerussa, stm., Russia	I17	22
Nerva, Spain	H5	16
Nesher, Isr.	C4	50
Nesle, Fr.	C9	14
Ness, Loch, l., Scot., U.K.	D9	8
Ness City, Ks., U.S.	M8	118
Nesselrode, Mount, mtn., N.A.	G27	100
Nesselwang, Ger.	H10	10
Nesslau, Switz.	D11	13
Nesterov, Russia	G5	22
Nestoita, Ukr.	B13	20
Néstos (Mesta), stm., Eur.	H8	20
Nesviž, Bela.	H9	22
Nes Ẕiyyona, Isr.	E3	50
Netanya, Isr.	D3	50
Netherdale, Austl.	C8	70
Netherlands (Nederland), ctry., Eur.	E9	4
Netherlands Antilles (Nederlandse Antillen), dep., N.A.	H10	94
Netrakona, Bngl.	H14	44
Nettilling Fiord, N.W. Ter., Can.	C19	96
Nettilling Lake, l., N.W. Ter., Can.	C18	96
Nettleton, Ms., U.S.	H8	114
Nettuno, Italy	H7	18
Neubrandenburg, Ger.	B13	10
Neuburg an der Donau, Ger.	G11	10
Neuchâtel, Switz.	E6	13
Neuchâtel, state, Switz.	D6	13
Neuchâtel, Lac de, l., Switz.	E6	13
Neudorf, Sask., Can.	H12	104
Neuenhagen, Ger.	C13	10
Neuf-Brisach, Fr.	D14	14
Neufchâteau, Bel.	I7	12
Neufchâteau, Fr.	D12	14
Neufchâtel-en-Bray, Fr.	C8	14
Neuhausen, Switz.	C10	13
Neu-Isenburg, Ger.	E8	10
Neumarkt [im Hausruckkreis], Aus.	G13	10
Neumarkt in der Oberpfalz, Ger.	F11	10
Neumarkt in Steiermark, Aus.	H14	10
Neumarkt-Sankt Veit, Ger.	G12	10
Neumünster, Ger.	A9	10
Neunburg vorm Wald, Ger.	F12	10
Neunkirchen/Saar, Ger.	F7	10
Neuquén, Arg.	J4	80
Neuquén, prov., Arg.	J4	80
Neuquén, stm., Arg.	J4	80
Neurara, Chile	C4	80
Neuruppin, Ger.	C12	10
Neuschwanstein, Schloss, Ger.	C14	13
Neuse, stm., N.C., U.S.	E10	112
Neusiedl am See, Aus.	H16	10
Neusiedler See, l., Eur.	H16	10
Neustadt [an der Aisch], Ger.	F10	10
Neustadt an der Waldnaab, Ger.	F12	10
Neustadt an der Weinstrasse, Ger.	F8	10
Neustadt bei Coburg, Ger.	E11	10
Neustadt in Holstein, Ger.	A10	10
Neustrelitz, Ger.	B13	10
Neutral Hills, hills, Alta., Can.	F4	104
Neu-Ulm, Ger.	G10	10
Neuville-sur-Saône, Fr.	G11	14
Neuwied, Ger.	E7	10
Neva, stm., Russia	B13	22
Nevada, Ia., U.S.	H2	110
Nevada, Mo., U.S.	E2	114
Nevada, Oh., U.S.	G3	108
Nevada, state, U.S.	D3	98
Nevada, Sierra, mts., Spain	H8	16
Nevada, Sierra, mts., Ca., U.S.	F6	124
Nevada City, Ca., U.S.	E4	124
Nevado, Cerro, mtn., Arg.	H4	80
Nevado, Cerro, mtn., Col.	C4	76
Nevado, Cerro, mtn., Col.	F5	84
Nevado de Colima, Parque Nacional del, Mex.	H8	90
Nevado de Toluca, Parque Nacional, Mex.	H9	90
Nevel', Russia	E12	22
Nevel'sk, Russia	H20	28
Never, Russia	G16	28
Nevers, Fr.	E10	14
Nevertire, Austl.	H7	70
Nevesinje, Bos.	F2	20
Nevinnomyssk, Russia	I6	26
Nevis, i., St. K./N.	F13	94
Nevis, Ben, mtn., Scot., U.K.	E9	8
Nevjansk, Russia	F10	26
Nevşehir, Tur.	B3	48
New, stm., Belize	H15	90
New, stm., Guy.	F14	84
New, stm., N.A.	L10	124
New, stm., U.S.	B6	112
New, stm., S.C., U.S.	G6	112
New, stm., Tn., U.S.	C2	112
New Albany, In., U.S.	D11	114
New Albany, Ms., U.S.	H7	114
New Albin, Ia., U.S.	G4	110
New Alfa, Sud.	J8	60
New Amsterdam, Guy.	D14	84
Newark, Ar., U.S.	G5	114
Newark, De., U.S.	H11	108
Newark, N.J., U.S.	G12	108
Newark, N.Y., U.S.	D9	108
Newark, Oh., U.S.	G4	108
Newark-on-Trent, Eng., U.K.	H13	8
Newark Valley, N.Y., U.S.	E10	108
New Athens, Il., U.S.	D7	114
New Augusta, Ms., U.S.	K7	114
Newaygo, Mi., U.S.	G10	110
New Baden, Il., U.S.	D7	114
New Baltimore, Mi., U.S.	H13	110
New Bedford, Ma., U.S.	F16	108
Newberg, Or., U.S.	E3	122
New Berlin, Il., U.S.	C7	114
New Berlin, N.Y., U.S.	E11	108
New Berlin, Wi., U.S.	H7	110
Newbern, Al., U.S.	J9	114
New Bern, N.C., U.S.	D9	112
Newbern, Tn., U.S.	F7	114
Newberry, Fl., U.S.	J4	112
Newberry, Mi., U.S.	D10	110
Newberry, S.C., U.S.	E5	112
New Bethlehem, Pa., U.S.	F7	108
New Bight, Bah.	B7	94
New Bloomfield, Pa., U.S.	G9	108
New Boston, Il., U.S.	I5	110
New Boston, Oh., U.S.	I4	108
New Boston, Tx., U.S.	I2	114
New Braunfels, Tx., U.S.	J8	116
New Bremen, Oh., U.S.	G2	108
New Britain, Ct., U.S.	F14	108
New Britain, i., Pap. N. Gui.	m17	68a
New Brockton, Al., U.S.	K11	114
Newbrook, Alta., Can.	C22	102
New Brunswick, N.J., U.S.	G12	108
New Brunswick, prov., Can.	G19	96
New Buffalo, Mi., U.S.	I9	110
Newburg, Mo., U.S.	E5	114
Newburgh, Ont., Can.	F19	110
Newburgh, In., U.S.	E9	114
Newburgh, N.Y., U.S.	F12	108
Newbury, Eng., U.K.	J12	8
Newburyport, Ma., U.S.	E16	108
New Caledonia, dep., Oc.	H24	2
New-Carlisle, Que., Can.	D8	106
New Carlisle, Oh., U.S.	H2	108
Newcastle, Austl.	I9	70
Newcastle, N.B., Can.	E8	106
Newcastle, Ont., Can.	G17	110
Newcastle, S. Afr.	F9	66
Newcastle, Ca., U.S.	F4	124
New Castle, Co., U.S.	E9	120
New Castle, De., U.S.	H11	108
New Castle, In., U.S.	C11	114
New Castle, Ky., U.S.	D11	114
Newcastle, Ne., U.S.	I11	118
Newcastle, Ok., U.S.	D9	116
New Castle, Pa., U.S.	F6	108
Newcastle, Tx., U.S.	F8	116
New Castle, Va., U.S.	B6	112
Newcastle, Wy., U.S.	H3	118
Newcastle Mine, Alta., Can.	F22	102
Newcastle-under-Lyme, Eng., U.K.	H11	8
Newcastle upon Tyne, Eng., U.K.	G12	8
Newcastle Waters, Austl.	C6	68
New City, N.Y., U.S.	F13	108
Newcomerstown, Oh., U.S.	G5	108
New Concord, Oh., U.S.	H5	108
New Cumberland, W.V., U.S.	G6	108
New Dayton, Alta., Can.	H22	102
Newdegate, Austl.	F3	68
New Delhi, India	F7	44
New Denver, B.C., Can.	H17	102
New Edinburg, Ar., U.S.	I4	114
New Effington, S.D., U.S.	F11	118
New Egypt, N.J., U.S.	G12	108
Newell, Ia., U.S.	I12	118
Newell, S.D., U.S.	G4	118
Newell, W.V., U.S.	G6	108
Newell, Lake, l., Alta., Can.	G23	102
New Ellenton, S.C., U.S.	F5	112
Newellton, La., U.S.	J5	114
New England, N.D., U.S.	E5	118
New England Range, mts., Austl.	H9	70
Newfane, N.Y., U.S.	D8	108
Newfane, Vt., U.S.	E14	108
New Florence, Mo., U.S.	D5	114
New Florence, Pa., U.S.	G7	108
Newfound Gap, U.S.	D3	112
Newfoundland, prov., Can.	F21	96
Newfoundland, i., Newf., Can.	D17	106
New Franklin, Mo., U.S.	C4	114
New Freedom, Pa., U.S.	H10	108
New Galloway, Scot., U.K.	F9	8
Newgate, B.C., Can.	H19	102
New Georgia, i., Sol.Is.	A11	68
New Germany, N.S., Can.	H9	106
New Glarus, Wi., U.S.	H6	110
New Glasgow, N.S., Can.	G11	106
New Guinea, i.	m15	68a
Newgulf, Tx., U.S.	J11	116
Newhalem, Wa., U.S.	B4	122
Newhalen, Ak., U.S.	G17	100
Newhall, Ca., U.S.	J7	124
New Hamburg, Ont., Can.	G15	110
New Hampshire, state, U.S.	C12	98
New Hampton, Ia., U.S.	G3	110
New Hanover, i., Pap. N. Gui.	k17	68a
New Harmony, In., U.S.	D9	114
New Hartford, Ct., U.S.	F14	108
New Hartford, Ia., U.S.	H3	110
Newhaven, Eng., U.K.	K14	8
New Haven, Ct., U.S.	F14	108
New Haven, Il., U.S.	E8	114
New Haven, In., U.S.	A11	114
New Haven, Ky., U.S.	E11	114
New Haven, Mo., U.S.	D5	114
New Haven, W.V., U.S.	I5	108
New Hazelton, B.C., Can.	B7	102
New Hebrides Trench	K21	126
New Hebrides see Vanuatu, ctry., Oc.	H24	2
Newhebron, Ms., U.S.	K7	114
New Holland, Oh., U.S.	H3	108
New Holland, Pa., U.S.	G10	108
New Holstein, Wi., U.S.	G7	110
New Hope, Al., U.S.	H10	114
New Iberia, La., U.S.	L5	114
New Ireland, i., Pap. N. Gui.	k17	68a
New Jersey, state, U.S.	C12	98
New Johnsonville, Tn., U.S.	F9	114
New Kensington, Pa., U.S.	G7	108
New Kent, Va., U.S.	B10	112
Newkirk, Ok., U.S.	C9	116
Newland, N.C., U.S.	C5	112
Newlands, Austl.	C7	70
New Leipzig, N.D., U.S.	E6	118
New Lexington, Oh., U.S.	H4	108
New Lisbon, Wi., U.S.	G5	110
New Liskeard, Ont., Can.	C16	110
Newllano, La., U.S.	K3	114
New London, Ct., U.S.	F14	108
New London, Ia., U.S.	J4	110
New London, Mn., U.S.	F13	118
New London, Mo., U.S.	C5	114
New London, N.H., U.S.	D15	108
New London, Oh., U.S.	F4	108
New London, Tx., U.S.	J2	114
New London, Wi., U.S.	F7	110
New Madrid, Mo., U.S.	F7	114
Newman, Austl.	D3	68
Newman, Ca., U.S.	G4	124
Newman, Il., U.S.	C9	114
Newman Grove, Ne., U.S.	J10	118
Newmarket, Ont., Can.	F16	110
Newmarket, Ire.	I4	8
Newmarket, Eng., U.K.	I14	8
New Market, Al., U.S.	H10	114
New Market, Ia., U.S.	K13	118
Newmarket, N.H., U.S.	D16	108
New Market, Va., U.S.	I8	108
New Martinsville, W.V., U.S.	H6	108
New Meadows, Id., U.S.	F9	122
New Mexico, state, U.S.	E5	98
New Milford, Ct., U.S.	F13	108
New Milford, Pa., U.S.	F11	108
Newnan, Ga., U.S.	F2	112
New Norfolk, Austl.	N7	70
New Norway, Alta., Can.	E22	102
New Orleans, La., U.S.	M6	114
New Oxford, Pa., U.S.	H9	108
New Paltz, N.Y., U.S.	F12	108
New Paris, Oh., U.S.	H2	108
New Philadelphia, Oh., U.S.	G5	108
New Pine Creek, Or., U.S.	I5	122
New Plymouth, N.Z.	C5	72
New Plymouth, Id., U.S.	G9	122
Newport, Que., Can.	D9	106
Newport, Scot., U.K.	E11	8
Newport, Wales, U.K.	I9	8
Newport, Ar., U.S.	G5	114
Newport, In., U.S.	C9	114
Newport, Ky., U.S.	H2	108
Newport, Me., U.S.	C17	108
Newport, N.H., U.S.	D14	108
Newport, N.C., U.S.	E10	112
Newport, Or., U.S.	F1	122
Newport, Pa., U.S.	G9	108
Newport, R.I., U.S.	F15	108
Newport, Tn., U.S.	D3	112
Newport, Vt., U.S.	C14	108
Newport, Wa., U.S.	B8	122
Newport Beach, Ca., U.S.	K8	124
Newport News, Va., U.S.	C10	112
New Port Richey, Fl., U.S.	K4	112
New Prague, Mn., U.S.	F2	110
New Providence, Tn., U.S.	F9	114
New Providence, i., Bah.	B6	94
New Richland, Mn., U.S.	G2	110
New-Richmond, Que., Can.	D8	106
New Richmond, Oh., U.S.	I2	108
New Richmond, Wi., U.S.	E3	110
New Road, N.S., Can.	H10	106
New Roads, La., U.S.	L5	114
New Rochelle, N.Y., U.S.	G13	108
New Rockford, N.D., U.S.	D8	118
New Ross, N.S., Can.	H9	106
New Ross, Ire.	I7	8
Newry, N. Ire., U.K.	G7	8
Newry, S.C., U.S.	E4	112
New Salem, N.D., U.S.	E6	118
New Schwabenland, reg., Ant.	C2	73
New Sharon, Ia., U.S.	I3	110
New Siberian Islands see Novosibirskoje ostrova, is., Russia	B20	28
New Smyrna Beach, Fl., U.S.	J6	112
New South Wales, state, Austl.	F9	68
New Stuyahok, Ak., U.S.	G16	100
New Tazewell, Tn., U.S.	C3	112
New Thunderchild Indian Reserve, Sask., Can.	E6	104
Newtok, Ak., U.S.	F12	100
Newton, Ga., U.S.	H2	112
Newton, Il., U.S.	D8	114
Newton, Ia., U.S.	I2	110
Newton, Ks., U.S.	M10	118
Newton, Ma., U.S.	E15	108
Newton, Ms., U.S.	J7	114
Newton, N.J., U.S.	F12	108
Newton, N.C., U.S.	D5	112
Newton, Tx., U.S.	L3	114
Newton Abbot, Eng., U.K.	K10	8
Newton Falls, N.Y., U.S.	C12	108
Newton Stewart, Scot., U.K.	G9	8
Newtown, Newf., Can.	C20	106
New Town, N.D., U.S.	D5	118
Newtownabbey, N. Ire., U.K.	G8	8
New Ulm, Mn., U.S.	G13	118
New Ulm, Tx., U.S.	J10	116
New Vienna, Oh., U.S.	H3	108
Newville, Pa., U.S.	G9	108
New Vineyard, Me., U.S.	C16	108
New Washington, Oh., U.S.	G4	108
New Waterford, N.S., Can.	F13	106
New Waverly, Tx., U.S.	I11	116
New Westminster, B.C., Can.	H12	102
New Whiteland, In., U.S.	C10	114
New Wilmington, Pa., U.S.	F6	108
New World Island, i., Newf., Can.	C19	106
New York, N.Y., U.S.	G12	108
New York, state, U.S.	C11	98
New York Mills, Mn., U.S.	E12	118
New York State Barge Canal, N.Y., U.S.	D8	108
New Zealand, ctry., Oc.	D4	72
Ney Lake, l., Can.	D22	104
Neyrīz, Iran	G13	48
Neyshābūr, Iran	C15	48
Nezahualcóyotl, Mex.	H10	90
Nezahualcóyotl, Presa, res., Mex.	I13	90
Nežin, Ukr.	G4	26
Neznanovo, Russia	G23	22
Nezperce, Id., U.S.	D9	122
Ngami, Lake, l., Bots.	C6	66
Ngamiland, dept., Bots.	B6	66
Ngamo, Zimb.	B8	66
Ngangla Ringco, l., China	E10	44
Nganglong Kangri, mts., China	D10	44
Ngaoundéré, Cam.	G9	54
Ngezi Recreational Park, Zimb.	B10	66
Ngoko, stm., Afr.	A3	58
Ngolo, Cen. Afr. Rep.	M2	60
Ngoring Hu, l., China	E6	30
Ngotwane, stm., Afr.	E8	66
Nguigmi, Niger	F9	54
Nguiroungou, Cen. Afr. Rep.	N2	60
Nguru, Nig.	F9	54
Nhamundá, Braz.	I14	84
Nhamundá, stm., Braz.	H14	84
Nhandeara, Braz.	F3	79
Nha Trang, Viet.	H10	40
Nhill, Austl.	K4	70
Niafounké, Mali	D7	64
Niagara, Wi., U.S.	E8	110
Niagara Falls, Ont., Can.	G16	110
Niagara Falls, N.Y., U.S.	D7	108
Niagara-on-the-Lake, Ont., Can.	G16	110
Niamey, Niger	E11	64
Niangara, Zaire	H6	56
Niangoloko, Burkina	F7	64
Niangua, stm., Mo., U.S.	E4	114
Niantic, Il., U.S.	C7	114
Niaro, Sud.	L6	60
Nias, Pulau, i., Indon.	N4	40
Nica, stm., Russia	F10	26
Nicaragua, ctry., N.A.	E9	92
Nicaragua, Lago de, l., Nic.	F9	92
Nicastro, Italy	K11	18
Nice, Fr.	I14	14
Niceville, Fl., U.S.	L10	114
Nichinan, Japan	P6	36
Nicholas Channel, strt., N.A.	C4	94
Nicholasville, Ky., U.S.	B2	112
Nicholls, Ga., U.S.	H4	112
Nicholl's Town, Bah.	B5	94
Nicholson, Ms., U.S.	L7	114
Nicholson, Pa., U.S.	F11	108
Nicholson, stm., Austl.	A2	70
Nickerie, dept., Sur.	E14	84
Nickerie, stm., Sur.	E14	84
Nickerson, Ks., U.S.	M9	118
Nicobar Islands, is., India	J2	40
Nicola, B.C., Can.	G14	102
Nicola, stm., B.C., Can.	G14	102
Nicola Lake, l., B.C., Can.	G14	102
Nicola Mameet Indian Reserve, B.C., Can.	G14	102
Nicolet, Que., Can.	A14	108
Nicolet, Lake, l., Mi., U.S.	D11	110
Nicollet, Mn., U.S.	F1	110
Nicosia, Cyp.-N. Cyp.	D2	48
Nicosia, Italy	L9	18
Nicotera, Italy	K10	18
Nicoya, C.R.	G9	92
Nicoya, Golfo de, b., C.R.	H10	92
Nicoya, Península de, pen., C.R.	H9	92
Nictheroy see Niterói, Braz.	H10	76
Nidzica, Pol.	B20	10
Niederbronn-les-Bains, Fr.	D14	14
Niedermarsberg, Ger.	D8	10
Niederösterreich, state, Aus.	G15	10
Niedersachsen, state, Ger.	C8	10
Niedu, China	J3	34
Niekerkshoop, S. Afr.	G6	66
Niellé, I.C.	F7	64
Niemodlin, Pol.	E17	10
Niéna, Mali	F6	64
Nienburg, Ger.	C9	10
Niers, stm., Eur.	E9	12
Niesky, Ger.	D14	10
Nieszawa, Pol.	C18	10
Nieu Bethesda, S. Afr.	H7	66
Nieuw Amsterdam, Sur.	B7	76
Nieuwegein, Neth.	D7	12
Nieuweschans, Neth.	B11	12
Nieuwe Tonge, Neth.	E5	12
Nieuw Nickerie, Sur.	E14	84
Nieuwolda, Neth.	B10	12
Nieuwoudtville, S. Afr.	H4	66
Nieuwpoort (Nieuport), Bel.	F2	12
Nieuw-Schoonebeek, Neth.	C10	12
Nieva, stm., Peru	J4	84
Nièvre, dept., Fr.	E10	14
Niga, Mali	E7	64
Niğde, Tur.	C3	48
Nigei Island, i., B.C., Can.	G7	102
Niger, ctry., Afr.	E8	54
Niger, stm., Afr.	G8	54
Nigeria, ctry., Afr.	F8	54
Nigríta, Grc.	I7	20
Nihing (Nahang), stm., Asia	H17	48
Nihuil, Embalse del, res., Arg.	H4	80
Niigata, Japan	J14	36
Niihama, Japan	N8	36
Niihau, i., Hi., U.S.	p13	125a
Nii-jima, i., Japan	M14	36
Nijil, Jord.	G5	50
Nijkerk, Neth.	D8	12
Nijmegen, Neth.	E8	12
Nijvel (Nivelles), Bel.	G5	12
Nijverdal, Neth.	D9	12
Nikel', Russia	G22	6
Nikip Lake, l., Ont., Can.	F23	104
Nikki, Benin	G11	64
Nikkō, Japan	K14	36
Nikolajev, Ukr.	H4	26
Nikolajevka, Ukr.	C13	20
Nikolajevo, Russia	C12	22
Nikolajevsk-na-Amure, Russia	G20	28
Nikol'sk, Russia	F7	26
Nikol'sk, Russia	G7	26
Nikolski, Ak., U.S.	J10	100
Nikol'skij, Russia	K24	6
Nikopol', Ukr.	H4	26
Nīkshahr, Iran	H16	48
Nikšić, Yugo.	G2	20
Nikulino, Russia	C27	22
Niland, Ca., U.S.	K10	124
Nile (Nahr an-Nīl), stm., Afr.	C7	56
Niles, Il., U.S.	H8	110
Niles, Mi., U.S.	I9	110
Niles, Oh., U.S.	F6	108
Nilkitkwa, stm., B.C., Can.	B8	102
Nīmach, India	H6	44
Nimba, Mont, mtn., Afr.	G5	54
Nimba Range, mts., Afr.	G5	54
Nîmes, Fr.	I11	14
Nimmitabel, Austl.	K8	70
Nimpkish Lake, l., B.C., Can.	G8	102
Nimule, Sud.	H7	56
Nindigully, Austl.	G8	70
Nindirí, Nic.	E8	92
Nine Degree Channel, strt., India	H2	46
Ninette, Man., Can.	I15	104
Ninety Mile Beach, Austl.	L7	70
Ninety Six, S.C., U.S.	E4	112
Ninga, Man., Can.	I15	104
Ningari, Mali	D8	64
Ningbo, China	F10	34
Ningcheng (Tianyi), China	B7	32
Ningdu, China	I4	34
Ninghai, China	F10	34
Ningi, Nig.	F14	64
Ningming, China	C9	40
Ningshan, China	E8	30
Ningsia see Yinchuan, China	D8	30
Ningwu, China	D9	30
Ningxia Huizu Zizhiqu (Ningsia Hui), prov., China	D8	30
Ningxiang, China	G1	34
Ninh Binh, Viet.	D8	40
Ninhue, Chile	I2	80
Ninilchik, Ak., U.S.	F19	100
Ninnescah, stm., Ks., U.S.	N10	118
Nioaque, Braz.	I14	82
Nioaque, stm., Braz.	I14	82
Niobrara, Ne., U.S.	I9	118
Niobrara, stm., U.S.	I9	118
Nioki, Zaire	B3	58
Niono, Mali	D6	64
Nioro du Sahel, Mali	D5	64
Niort, Fr.	F6	14
Niota, Tn., U.S.	D2	112
Nipan, Austl.	E9	70
Nipāni, India	D3	46
Nipawin, Sask., Can.	E10	104
Nipawin Provincial Park, Sask., Can.	D10	104
Nipe, Bahía de, b., Cuba	D7	94
Nipekamew, stm., Sask., Can.	D9	104
Nipekamew Lake, l., Sask., Can.	D10	104
Nipigon, Ont., Can.	A7	110
Nipigon, Lake, l., Ont., Can.	G15	96
Nipin, stm., Sask., Can.	C6	104
Nipisi Lake, l., Alta., Can.	B20	102
Nipissing, Lake, l., Ont., Can.	D16	110
Nipissis, Lac, l., Que., Can.	A7	106
Nipisso, Lac, l., Que., Can.	B8	106
Nipomo, Ca., U.S.	I5	124
Nippers Harbour, Newf., Can.	C18	106
Niquelândia, Braz.	C4	79
Niquero, Cuba	D6	94
Niquivil, Arg.	F4	80
Nirgua, Ven.	B8	84
Nirmal, India	C5	46
Niš, Yugo.	F5	20
Nisa (Neisse) (Nysa Łużycka), stm., Eur.	E15	10
Nişāb, Sau. Ar.	G8	48
Niscemi, Italy	L9	18
Nishio, Japan	M12	36
Niska Lake, l., Sask., Can.	C6	104
Nisling, stm., Yukon, Can.	E25	100
Nisqually, stm., Wa., U.S.	D3	122
Nisswa, Mn., U.S.	D1	110
Nisutlin, stm., Yukon, Can.	F28	100
Niterói, Braz.	G7	79
Nithi River, B.C., Can.	C9	102
Nitinat Lake, l., B.C., Can.	I10	102
Nitra, Czech.	G18	10
Nitro, W.V., U.S.	I5	108
Niubu, China	D6	34
Niue, dep., Oc.	H1	2
Niut, Gunung, mtn., Indon.	N10	40
Niutuo, China	D4	32
Niuzhuang, China	C10	32
Nive, stm., Austl.	E7	70
Nivelles (Nijvel), Bel.	G5	12
Nivernais, hist. reg., Fr.	E10	14
Niverville, Man., Can.	I17	104
Nivskij, Russia	H23	6
Nixa, Mo., U.S.	E3	114
Nixon, Nv., U.S.	E6	124
Nixon, Tx., U.S.	J9	116
Nizāmābād, India	C5	46
Nizām Sāgar, res., India	C4	46
Nižankoviči, Ukr.	F22	10
Nizip, Tur.	C4	48
Nízke Tatry, mts., Czech.	G19	10
Nižn'aja Pojma, Russia	F11	28
Nižn'aja Tunguska, stm., Russia	E10	28
Nižn'aja Tura, Russia	F9	26
Nižneudinsk, Russia	G11	28
Nižnevartovsk, Russia	E13	26
Nižnij Novgorod (Gor'kij), Russia	E27	22
Nižnij P'andž, Taj.	J11	26
Nižnij Tagil, Russia	F9	26
Nizwā, Oman	C10	47
Niẓẓana, Isr.	G2	50
Njazidja (Grande Comore), i., Com.	K15	67a
Njombe, Tan.	C6	58
Nkhata Bay, Mwi.	D6	58
Nkhotakota, Mwi.	D6	58
Nkongsamba, Cam.	H8	54
Nkurenkuru, Nmb.	A4	66
Nmai, stm., Burma	B4	40
Noākhāli, Bngl.	I14	44
Noatak, Ak., U.S.	C13	100
Nobeoka, Japan	O6	36
Noble, Il., U.S.	D8	114
Noble, Ok., U.S.	D9	116
Noblesville, In., U.S.	B10	114
Noboribetsu, Japan	E16	36a
Nobres, Braz.	F13	82
Nobsa, Col.	E6	84
Nocatee, Fl., U.S.	L5	112
Nocera [Inferiore], Italy	I9	18
Noci, Italy	I12	18
Nockatunga, Austl.	F5	70
Nocona, Tx., U.S.	F9	116
Nocupétaro, Mex.	H9	90
Nodaway, stm., U.S.	B1	114
Noel, Mo., U.S.	F2	114
Noetinger, Arg.	G7	80
Nogales, Chile	G3	80
Nogales, Mex.	B4	90
Nogales, Az., U.S.	M6	120
Nogara, Eth.	K9	60
Nogaro, Fr.	I6	14
Nōgata, Japan	N5	36
Nogent-le-Rotrou, Fr.	D7	14
Noginsk, Russia	F21	22
Nogoa, stm., Austl.	D7	70
Nogoyá, Arg.	G9	80
Nógrád, co., Hung.	H19	10
Noirmoutier, Île de, i., Fr.	E4	14
Nokaneng, Bots.	B6	66
Nokomis, Sask., Can.	G9	104
Nokomis, Fl., U.S.	L4	112
Nokomis, Il., U.S.	C7	114
Nokomis Lake, l., Sask., Can.	B11	104
Nola, Italy	I9	18
Nolichucky, stm., U.S.	C3	112
Nolin, stm., Ky., U.S.	E10	114
Nolin Lake, res., Ky., U.S.	E10	114
Nolinsk, Russia	F7	26
Nombre de Dios, Mex.	F7	90
Nombre de Dios, Pan.	C3	84
Nombre de Dios, Cordillera, mts., Hond.	B8	92
Nome, Ak., U.S.	D12	100
Nomgon, Mong.	C8	30
Nominingue, Que., Can.	A11	108
Nonacho Lake, l., N.W. Ter., Can.	D11	96
Nondalton, Ak., U.S.	F17	100
Nondweni, S. Afr.	G10	66
Nong'an, China	C12	30
Nong Khai, Thai.	F7	40
Nongoma, S. Afr.	F10	66
Nono, Eth.	M9	60
Nonoai, Braz.	D12	80
Nonoava, Mex.	D6	90
Nonogasta, Arg.	E5	80
Nonsan, S. Kor.	G15	32
Nonthaburi, Thai.	H6	40
Nontron, Fr.	G7	14
Nooksack, stm., Wa., U.S.	B3	122
Noonan, N.D., U.S.	C4	118
Noord-Brabant, prov., Neth.	E6	12
Noord-Holland, prov., Neth.	C6	12
Noordoewer, Nmb.	G3	66
Noordoostpolder, reg., Neth.	C8	12
Noordwijk aan Zee, Neth.	D5	12
Noordzeekanaal, Neth.	D5	12
Noorvik, Ak., U.S.	C14	100
Nootka Island, i., B.C., Can.	H8	102
Nootka Sound, strt., B.C., Can.	H8	102
Nóqui, Ang.	C2	58
Nora Islands, is., Eth.	E9	56
Noralee, B.C., Can.	D8	102
Nora Springs, Ia., U.S.	G2	110
Norberto de la Riestra, Arg.	H9	80
Norborne, Mo., U.S.	C3	114
Norcatur, Ks., U.S.	L7	118
Norcia, Italy	G8	18
Norcross, Ga., U.S.	F2	112
Nord, dept., Fr.	B10	14
Nord, Grand lac du, l., Que., Can.	B6	106
Nord, Petit lac du, l., Que., Can.	B6	106
Nordaustlandet, i., Sval.	B3	24
Nordegg, Alta., Can.	E18	102
Nordegg, stm., Alta., Can.	E19	102
Norden, Ger.	B7	10
Nordenham, Ger.	B8	10
Nordenšel'da, archipelag, is., Russia	B11	28
Nordenskiold, stm., Yukon, Can.	F26	100
Norderstedt, Ger.	B10	10
Nordhausen, Ger.	D10	10
Nordheim, Tx., U.S.	K9	116
Nordhorn, Ger.	C7	10
Nordkapp, c., Nor.	F19	6
Nordland, co., Nor.	H14	6
Nördlingen, Ger.	G10	10
Nordostrundingen, c., Grnld.	A18	86
Nord-Ostsee-Kanal, Ger.	A9	10
Nordreisa, Nor.	G17	6
Nordrhein-Westfalen, state, Ger.	D7	10
Nord-Trøndelag, co., Nor.	I12	6
Nore, Nor.	K11	6
Norfolk, Ne., U.S.	I10	118
Norfolk, Va., U.S.	C10	112
Norfolk, co., Eng., U.K.	I15	8
Norfolk Island, dep., Oc.	K20	126
Norfork Lake, res., U.S.	F4	114
Noril'sk, Russia	D9	28
Norlina, N.C., U.S.	C8	112
Normal, Al., U.S.	H10	114
Normal, Il., U.S.	J7	110
Norman, Ar., U.S.	H3	114
Norman, Ok., U.S.	D9	116
Norman, stm., Austl.	B4	70
Norman, Lake, res., N.C., U.S.	D6	112
Normandie, hist. reg., Fr.	D6	14
Normandie, Collines de, hills, Fr.	D6	14
Normandy see Normandie, hist. reg., Fr.	D6	14
Normangee, Tx., U.S.	H10	116
Norman Park, Ga., U.S.	H3	112
Normanton, Austl.	A4	70
Norman Wells, N.W. Ter., Can.	D31	100
Norogachi, Mex.	D6	90
Norphlet, Ar., U.S.	I4	114
Norquay, Sask., Can.	G12	104
Norra Kvarken (Merenkurkku), strt., Eur.	J17	6
Norrbottens Län, co., Swe.	H16	6
Norridgewock, Me., U.S.	C17	108
Norris, Tn., U.S.	C2	112
Norris Arm, Newf., Can.	C18	106
Norris City, Il., U.S.	E8	114
Norris Lake, res., Tn., U.S.	C3	112
Norris Point, Newf., Can.	C16	106
Norristown, Pa., U.S.	G11	108
Norrköping, Swe.	L15	6
Norrtälje, Swe.	L16	6
Norseman, Austl.	F4	68
Norsk, Russia	G17	28
Norte, Canal do, strt., Braz.	C8	76
Norte, Serra do, plat., Braz.	D12	82
Norte de Santander, state, Col.	J8	94
Norte de Santander, dept., Col.	C6	84
Nortelândia, Braz.	F13	82
North, S.C., U.S.	F5	112
North, stm., Newf., Can.	E20	96
North, stm., Al., U.S.	I9	114
North, stm., Ia., U.S.	I2	110
North, Cape, c., N.S., Can.	E13	106
North Adams, Ma., U.S.	E13	108
North Adams, Mi., U.S.	I11	110
North Albany, Or., U.S.	F2	122
Northam, Austl.	F3	68
North America	E9	86
Northampton, Austl.	E2	68
Northampton, Eng., U.K.	I13	8
Northampton, Ma., U.S.	E14	108
Northampton, Pa., U.S.	G11	108
Northamptonshire, co., Eng., U.K.	I13	8
North Andaman, i., India	H2	40
North Anna, stm., Va., U.S.	B9	112
North Anson, Me., U.S.	C17	108
North Asheboro, N.C., U.S.	D7	112
North Atlanta, Ga., U.S.	F2	112
North Augusta, S.C., U.S.	F5	112
North Aulatsivik Island, i., Newf., Can.	E20	96
North Baltimore, Oh., U.S.	F3	108
North Battleford, Sask., Can.	F6	104
North Bay, Ont., Can.	D16	110
North Bend, B.C., Can.	H13	102
North Bend, Ne., U.S.	J11	118
North Bend, Or., U.S.	G1	122
North Bennington, Vt., U.S.	E13	108
North Berwick, Scot., U.K.	E11	8
North Berwick, Me., U.S.	D16	108
North Bourke, Austl.	H6	70
North Branch, Mi., U.S.	G12	110
North Branch, Mn., U.S.	E3	110
North Caicos, i., T./C. Is.	D9	94
North Canadian, stm., Ok., U.S.	D10	116
North Canton, Ga., U.S.	E2	112
North Canton, Oh., U.S.	G5	108
North Cape, c., P.E.I., Can.	E9	106
North Cape, c., N.Z.	A4	72
North Cape see Nordkapp, c., Nor.	F19	6
North Caribou Lake, l., Ont., Can.	F14	96
North Carolina, state, U.S.	D11	98
North Cascades National Park, Wa., U.S.	B4	122
North Channel, strt., Ont., Can.	D12	110
North Channel, strt., U.K.	F8	8
North Charleston, S.C., U.S.	G7	112
North Chicago, Il., U.S.	H8	110
North College Hill, Oh., U.S.	H2	108
North Collins, N.Y., U.S.	E8	108
North Conway, N.H., U.S.	C15	108
North Creek, N.Y., U.S.	D13	108
North Crossett, Ar., U.S.	I5	114
North Dakota, state, U.S.	B6	98
North East, Md., U.S.	H11	108
North East, Pa., U.S.	E7	108
North-East, dept., Bots.	C8	66
North East Point, c., Bah.	D8	94
North East Point, c., Bah.	C8	94
Northeast Providence Channel, strt., Bah.	B6	94
Northeim, Ger.	D10	10
North English, Ia., U.S.	I3	110
Northern Arm, Newf., Can.	C18	106
Northern Dvina see Severnaja Dvina, stm., Russia	E6	26
Northern Indian Lake, l., Man., Can.	E13	96
Northern Ireland, ter., U.K.	G7	8
Northern Mariana Islands, dep., Oc.	G19	126
Northern Territory, ter., Austl.	C6	68
North Fabius, stm., U.S.	B4	114
Northfield, Ma., U.S.	E14	108
Northfield, Mn., U.S.	F2	110
Northfield, Vt., U.S.	C14	108
North Flinders Range, mts., Austl.	H3	70
North Fond du Lac, Wi., U.S.	G7	110
North Foreland, c., Eng., U.K.	J15	8
North Fork, Ca., U.S.	G6	124
North Fork, stm., U.S.	F4	114
North Fort Myers, Fl., U.S.	M5	112
North Freedom, Wi., U.S.	G6	110
North Frisian Islands, is., Eur.	A8	10
Northglenn, Co., U.S.	E12	120
North Gulfport, Ms., U.S.	L7	114
North Henderson, N.C., U.S.	C8	112
North Henik Lake, l., N.W. Ter., Can.	D13	96
North Hero, Vt., U.S.	C13	108
North Highlands, Ca., U.S.	F4	124
North Island, i., N.Z.	B4	72
North Judson, In., U.S.	A10	114
North Kenai, Ak., U.S.	F19	100
North Kingsville, Oh., U.S.	F6	108
North Knife Lake, l., Man., Can.	E13	96
North La Junta, Co., U.S.	N4	118
North Lakhimpur, India	G16	44
North Las Vegas, Nv., U.S.	H10	124
North La Veta Pass, Co., U.S.	G11	120
North Liberty, In., U.S.	A10	114
North Little Rock, Ar., U.S.	H4	114
North Logan, Ut., U.S.	C5	120
North Loon Mountain, mtn., Id., U.S.	E10	122
North Loup, Ne., U.S.	J9	118
North Loup, stm., Ne., U.S.	J9	118

Name	Map Ref.	Page
North Macmillan, stm., Yukon, Can.	E28	100
North Magnetic Pole	B9	86
North Mamm Peak, mtn., Co., U.S.	E9	120
North Manchester, In., U.S.	A11	114
North Manitou Island, i., Mi., U.S.	E9	110
North Mankato, Mn., U.S.	F1	110
North Miami, Fl., U.S.	N6	112
North Miami Beach, Fl., U.S.	N6	112
North Moose Lake, l., Man., Can.	D14	104
North Muskegon, Mi., U.S.	G9	110
North Myrtle Beach, S.C., U.S.	F8	112
North Nahanni, stm., N.W. Ter., Can.	E32	100
North New River Canal, Fl., U.S.	M6	112
North Newton, Ks., U.S.	M10	118
North Ogden, Ut., U.S.	C5	120
Northome, Mn., U.S.	C1	110
North Palisade, mtn., Ca., U.S.	G7	124
North Palm Beach, Fl., U.S.	M6	112
North Park, Il., U.S.	H6	110
North Platte, Ne., U.S.	J7	118
North Platte, stm., U.S.	C6	98
North Pole, Ak., U.S.	D21	100
North Pole	A4	86
Northport, Al., U.S.	I9	114
Northport, Mi., U.S.	E10	110
Northport, Wa., U.S.	B8	122
North Portal, Sask., Can.	I12	104
North Powder, Or., U.S.	E8	122
North Ram, stm., Alta., Can.	E18	102
North Rhine-Westphalia see Nordrhein-Westfalen, state, Ger.	D7	10
North Richland Hills, Tx., U.S.	G9	116
North Rim, Az., U.S.	H4	120
North Rustico, P.E.I., Can.	F10	106
North Salt Lake, Ut., U.S.	D5	120
North Santiam, stm., Or., U.S.	F3	122
North Saskatchewan, stm., Can.	F10	96
North Sea, Eur.	D8	4
North Shoal Lake, l., Man., Can.	H17	104
North Siberian Lowland see Severo-Sibirskaja nizmennost', pl., Russia	C18	26
North Solitary Island, i., Austl.	G10	70
North Spicer Island, i., N.W. Ter., Can.	C17	96
North Spirit Lake, l., Ont., Can.	F22	104
North Spot, i., Belize	A6	92
North Stradbroke Island, i., Austl.	F10	70
North Sydney, N.S., Can.	F13	106
North Taranaki Bight, N.Z.	C5	72
North Terre Haute, In., U.S.	C9	114
North Thompson, stm., B.C., Can.	G14	102
North Troy, Vt., U.S.	C14	108
North Tunica, Ms., U.S.	H6	114
North Twin Lake, l., Newf., Can.	C18	106
North Uist, i., Scot., U.K.	D6	8
Northumberland, co., Eng., U.K.	F11	8
Northumberland Isles, is., Austl.	C9	70
Northumberland Strait, strt., Can.	F9	106
North Vancouver, B.C., Can.	H11	102
North Vernon, In., U.S.	C11	114
Northville, N.Y., U.S.	D12	108
North Wabasca Lake, l., Alta., Can.	A21	102
North West Cape, c., Austl.	D2	68
Northwest Gander, stm., Newf., Can.	D18	106
Northwest Miramichi, stm., N.B., Can.	E7	106
Northwest Providence Channel, strt., Bah.	A5	94
North West River, Newf., Can.	F20	96
Northwest Territories, prov., Can.	C12	96
North Wilkesboro, N.C., U.S.	C5	112
North Windham, Me., U.S.	D16	108
Northwood, Ia., U.S.	G2	110
Northwood, N.D., U.S.	D10	118
North Yamhill, stm., Or., U.S.	E2	122
North York, Ont., Can.	G16	110
North Yorkshire, co., Eng., U.K.	G12	8
North Zulch, Tx., U.S.	I10	116
Norton, N.B., Can.	G8	106
Norton, Ks., U.S.	L8	118
Norton, Va., U.S.	C4	112
Norton Shores, Mi., U.S.	G9	110
Norton Sound, strt., Ak., U.S.	E12	100
Nortonville, Ks., U.S.	L12	118
Nortorf, Ger.	A9	10
Norvegia, Cape, c., Ant.	C2	73
Norwalk, Ct., U.S.	F13	108
Norwalk, Ia., U.S.	I2	110
Norwalk, Oh., U.S.	F4	108
Norway, Ia., U.S.	I4	110
Norway, Me., U.S.	C16	108
Norway, Mi., U.S.	E8	110
Norway (Norge), ctry., Eur.	C10	4
Norway Bay, b., N.W. Ter., Can.	B12	96
Norway House, Man., Can.	E17	104
Norwegian Sea, Eur.	C1	24
Norwich, Ont., Can.	H15	110
Norwich, Eng., U.K.	I15	8
Norwich, Ct., U.S.	F14	108
Norwich, Ks., U.S.	N10	118
Norwich, N.Y., U.S.	E11	108
Norwood, Ont., Can.	F18	110
Norwood, Co., U.S.	F8	120
Norwood, Ma., U.S.	E15	108
Norwood, Mn., U.S.	F2	110
Norwood, N.Y., U.S.	C12	108
Norwood, N.C., U.S.	D6	112
Norwood, Oh., U.S.	H2	108
Norwoodville, Ia., U.S.	I2	110
Nose Creek, stm., Alta., Can.	C15	102
Noshiro, Japan	G15	36
Nosop (Nossob), stm., Afr.	E5	66
Nossa Senhora do Livramento, Braz.	F13	82
Nossob (Nosop), stm., Afr.	E5	66
Nosy Varika, Madag.	R23	67b
Notasulga, Al., U.S.	J11	114
Notch Hill, B.C., Can.	G15	102
Notch Peak, mtn., Ut., U.S.	E3	120
Noteć, stm., Pol.	C15	10
Notigi Lake, l., Man., Can.	C15	104
Notikewin, stm., Alta., Can.	E9	96
Noto, Italy	M10	18
Notodden, Nor.	L11	6
Noto-hantō, pen., Japan	J11	36
Notozero, ozero, l., Russia	H23	6
Notre-Dame, N.B., Can.	F9	106
Notre-Dame, Monts, mts., Que., Can.	D5	106
Notre Dame Bay, b., Newf., Can.	C18	106
Notre-Dame-de-Lourdes, Man., Can.	I16	104
Notre-Dame-du-Laus, Que., Can.	A11	108
Notrees, Tx., U.S.	H4	116
Nottawasaga Bay, b., Ont., Can.	F15	110
Nottaway, stm., Que., Can.	F17	96
Nottingham, Eng., U.K.	I12	8
Nottingham Island, i., N.W. Ter., Can.	D17	96
Nottinghamshire, co., Eng., U.K.	H12	8
Nottoway, Va., U.S.	B8	112
Nottoway, stm., Va., U.S.	C10	112
Notukeu Creek, stm., Sask., Can.	I7	104
Nouâdhibou, Maur.	J2	62
Nouâdhibou, Râs, c., Afr.	J2	62
Nouakchott, Maur.	B2	64
Nouâmghâr, Maur.	B1	64
Nouméa, N. Cal.	H24	2
Nouna, Burkina	E8	64
Noupoort, S. Afr.	H7	66
Nouveau-Québec, Cratère du, crat., Que., Can.	D18	96
Nouvelle, Que., Can.	D7	106
Nouvelle, stm., Que., Can.	D7	106
Nouvelle-France, Cap de, c., Que., Can.	D18	96
Nova América, Braz.	C4	79
Nova Andradina, Braz.	G2	79
Nova Caipemba, Ang.	C2	58
Nova Era, Braz.	E7	79
Nova Esperança, Braz.	G2	79
Nova Friburgo, Braz.	G7	79
Nova Gradiška, Cro.	D12	18
Nova Granada, Braz.	F4	79
Nova Iguaçu, Braz.	G7	79
Novaja Ivanovka, Ukr.	D13	20
Novaja Kachovka, Ukr.	H4	26
Novaja Kazanka, Kaz.	H7	26
Novaja Ladoga, Russia	A15	22
Novaja Sibir', ostrov, i., Russia	B21	28
Novaja Zeml'a, is., Russia	C9	26
Nova Lamego, Gui.-B.	E2	64
Nova Lima, Braz.	E7	79
Nova Mambone, Moz.	C12	66
Nova Olinda do Norte, Braz.	I13	84
Nova Ponte, Braz.	E5	79
Nova Prata, Braz.	E13	80
Novara, Italy	D3	18
Nova Roma, Braz.	B5	79
Nova Scotia, prov., Can.	G20	96
Nova Sofala, Moz.	C12	66
Novato, Ca., U.S.	F3	124
Nova Varoš, Yugo.	F3	20
Nova Venécia, Braz.	E8	79
Nova Vida, Braz.	D10	82
Nova Vida, Cachoeira, wtfl, Braz.	C10	82
Nova Zagora, Bul.	G10	20
Novelda, Spain	G11	16
Nové Zámky, Czech.	H18	10
Novgorod, Russia	C14	22
Novi Bečej, Yugo.	D4	20
Novice, Tx., U.S.	H7	116
Novigrad, Cro.	E10	18
Novi Ligure, Italy	E3	18
Novinger, Mo., U.S.	B4	114
Novi Pazar, Bul.	F11	20
Novi Pazar, Yugo.	F4	20
Novi Sad, Yugo.	D3	20
Novki, Russia	E24	22
Novl'anka, Russia	F24	22
Novlenskoje, Russia	B22	22
Novo, stm., Braz.	A6	82
Nôvo Acôrdo, Braz.	B5	79
Novoaltajsk, Russia	G8	28
Novoanninskij, Russia	G6	26
Novo Aripuanã, Braz.	J12	84
Novo Brasil, Braz.	D3	79
Novočerkassk, Russia	H6	26
Novo Cruzeiro, Braz.	D8	79
Novodugino, Russia	F17	22
Novodvinsk, Russia	E6	26
Novograd-Volynskij, Ukr.	G3	26
Novogrudok, Bela.	H8	22
Novo Hamburgo, Braz.	E13	80
Novo Horizonte, Braz.	F4	79
Novoizborsk, Russia	D10	22
Novoje Leušino, Russia	E23	22
Novojel'n'a, Bela.	H8	22
Novokaširsk, Russia	G21	22
Novokazalinsk, Kaz.	H10	26
Novokujbyševsk, Russia	G7	26
Novokuzneck, Russia	G9	28
Novol'vovsk, Russia	H21	22
Novo Mesto, Slo.	D10	18
Novomoskovsk, Russia	G21	22
Novomoskovsk, Ukr.	H5	26
Novopetrovskoje, Russia	F19	22
Novopiscovo, Russia	D24	22
Novopolock, Bela.	F11	22
Novorossijsk, Russia	I5	26
Novorybnoje, Russia	C13	28
Novoržev, Russia	D12	22
Novošachtinsk, Russia	H5	26
Novoselica, Ukr.	A10	20
Novosel'skoje, Ukr.	D12	20
Novosibirsk, Russia	F8	28
Novosibirskije ostrova, is., Russia	B20	28
Novosibirskoje vodochranilišče, res., Russia	G14	26
Novosil', Russia	I20	22
Novosokol'niki, Russia	E13	22
Novos'olki, Russia	G22	22
Novotroick, Russia	G9	26
Novouzensk, Russia	G7	26
Novov'atsk, Russia	F7	26
Novov'azniki, Russia	E25	22
Novovolynsk, Ukr.	G2	26
Novozavidovskij, Russia	E19	22
Novozybkov, Russia	I14	22
Novska, Cro.	D11	18
Nový Bohumín, Czech.	F18	10
Nový Jičín, Czech.	F18	10
Novyj Nekouz, Russia	D21	22
Novyj Ropsk, Russia	I15	22
Nowa Ruda, Pol.	E16	10
Nowa Sól (Neusalz), Pol.	D15	10
Nowata, Ok., U.S.	C11	116
Nowitna, stm., Ak., U.S.	D17	100
Nowogród, Pol.	H4	22
Nowogrodziec, Pol.	D15	10
Nowood, stm., Wy., U.S.	F18	122
Nowra, Austl.	J9	70
Nowshāk, mtn., Asia	B4	44
Nowshera, Pak.	C4	44
Nowy Dwór Mazowiecki, Pol.	C20	10
Nowy Sącz, Pol.	F20	10
Nowy Targ, Pol.	F20	10
Noxapater, Ms., U.S.	J7	114
Noxen, Pa., U.S.	F10	108
Noxon, Mt., U.S.	B10	122
Noxubee, stm., U.S.	I8	114
Noyon, Fr.	C10	14
Nsanje, Mwi.	E7	58
Nsawam, Ghana	I9	64
Nsukka, Nig.	H13	64
Ntakat, Maur.	C4	64
Ntem, stm., Afr.	H9	54
N'Tsaoueni, Com.	K15	67a
Ntwetwe Pan, pl., Bots.	C7	66
Nuanetsi, stm., Afr.	C10	66
Nuanli, China	C6	40
Nūbah, Jibāl an-, mts., Sud.	L6	60
Nubian Desert, des., Sud.	G8	60
Ñuble, stm., Chile	I3	80
Nucet, Rom.	C6	20
Nuchatlitz Inlet, b., B.C., Can.	H8	102
N'uchča, Russia	E7	26
Nucla, Co., U.S.	F8	120
Nucuray, stm., Peru	J5	84
Nueces, stm., Tx., U.S.	L9	116
Nueltin Lake, l., Can.	D13	96
Nuestra Señora de Talavera, Arg.	C7	80
Nueva, Isla, i., Chile	H3	78
Nueva Antioquia, Col.	D8	84
Nueva Asunción, dept., Para.	I11	82
Nueva Ciudad Guerrero, Mex.	D10	90
Nueva Concepción, El Sal.	C5	92
Nueva Esparta, state, Ven.	B10	84
Nueva Francia, Arg.	E6	80
Nueva Galia, Arg.	H6	80
Nueva Germania, Para.	B10	80
Nueva Gerona, Cuba	D3	94
Nueva Helvecia, Ur.	H10	80
Nueva Imperial, Chile	J2	80
Nueva Italia de Ruiz, Mex.	H8	90
Nueva Ocotepeque, Hond.	C5	92
Nueva Palmira, Ur.	G9	80
Nueva Rosita, Mex.	D9	90
Nueva San Salvador, El Sal.	D5	92
Nueva Segovia, dept., Nic.	D8	92
Nueva Venecia, Guat.	C3	92
Nueve, Canal Numero, Arg.	I9	80
Nueve de Julio, Arg.	H8	80
Nuevitas, Cuba	D6	94
Nuevo, Bajo, Col.	G5	94
Nuevo, Cayo, i., Mex.	G13	90
Nuevo Berlín, Ur.	G9	80
Nuevo Casas Grandes, Mex.	B6	90
Nuevo Chagres, Pan.	H14	92
Nuevo Delicias, Mex.	D8	90
Nuevo Laredo, Mex.	D10	90
Nuevo León, state, Mex.	D9	90
Nuevo Progreso, Mex.	H13	90
Nuevo Rocafuerte, Ec.	H5	84
Nuia, Est.	C8	22
Nuits-Saint-Georges, Fr.	E11	14
N'uja, stm., Russia	E14	28
N'uk, ozero, l., Russia	I22	6
Nukey Bluff, clf, Austl.	I1	70
Nukus, Uzb.	I9	26
Nulato, Ak., U.S.	D15	100
Nullagine, Austl.	D4	68
Nullarbor National Park, Austl.	F6	68
Nullarbor Plain, pl., Austl.	F5	68
Numabin Bay, b., Sask., Can.	B11	104
Numazu, Japan	L13	36
Numurkah, Austl.	K6	70
Nunapitchuk, Ak., U.S.	F13	100
Nunda, N.Y., U.S.	E9	108
Nungesser Lake, l., Ont., Can.	G21	104
Nunivak Island, i., Ak., U.S.	F11	100
Nunjiang, China	B12	30
Nunkini, Mex.	G14	90
Nunnelly, Tn., U.S.	G9	114
Nuomin, stm., China	B11	30
Nuon, stm., Afr.	H5	64
Nuoro, Italy	I4	18
Nuquí, Col.	E4	84
Nura, stm., Kaz.	G12	26
N'urba, Russia	E15	28
Nürburgring, Ger.	H10	12
Nurek, Taj.	A3	44
Nuremberg see Nürnberg, Ger.	F11	10
Nürnberg (Nuremberg), Ger.	F11	10
Nurri, Italy	J4	18
Nurri, Mount, hill, Austl.	H7	70
Nursery, Tx., U.S.	K9	116
Nürtingen, Ger.	G9	10
Nūsah, Yemen	G5	47
Nusaybin, Tur.	C6	48
Nu Shan, mts., China	F6	30
Nushki, Pak.	F2	44
Nut Lake Indian Reserve, Sask., Can.	F11	104
Nutrioso, Az., U.S.	K7	120
Nuttby Mountain, hill, N.S., Can.	G10	106
Nutter Fort, W.V., U.S.	H6	108
Nuwaybiʿ al-Muzayyinah, Egypt	C8	60
Nuwerus, S. Afr.	H4	66
Nxainxai, Bots.	B5	66
Nxai Pan National Park, Bots.	B7	66
Nxaunxau, Bots.	B5	66
Nyaake, Lib.	I6	64
Nyabing, Austl.	F3	68
Nyack, N.Y., U.S.	F13	108
Nyah West, Austl.	J5	70
Nyainqêntanglha Shan, mts., China	E13	44
Nyakrom, Ghana	I9	64
Nyala, Sud.	K3	60
Nyamandhlovu, Zimb.	B9	66
Nyamina, Mali	E6	64
Nyamlell, Sud.	M4	60
Nyanza, Rw.	B5	58
Nyasa, Lake (Lake Malawi), l., Afr.	D6	58
Nyasaland see Malawi, ctry., Afr.	D6	58
Nyaunglebin, Burma	F4	40
Nybergsund, Nor.	K13	6
Nyiel, Sud.	N6	60
Nyíradony, Hung.	H21	10
Nyírbátor, Hung.	H22	10
Nyíregyháza, Hung.	H21	10
Nykøbing, Den.	N12	6
Nykøbing, Den.	M11	6
Nyköping, Swe.	L15	6
Nylstroom, S. Afr.	E9	66
Nymburk, Czech.	E15	10
Nynäshamn, Swe.	L15	6
Nyngan, Austl.	H7	70
Nyon, Switz.	F5	13
Nyong, stm., Cam.	H9	54
Nýrsko, Czech.	F13	10
Nysa, Pol.	E17	10
Nysa Łużycka (Neisse) (Nisa), stm., Eur.	D14	10
Nyssa, Or., U.S.	G9	122
Nytva, Russia	F9	26
Nzébéla, Gui.	G5	64
Nzérékoré, Gui.	H5	64
N'zeto, Ang.	C2	58
Nzi, stm., I.C.	H7	64
Nzwani (Anjouan), i., Com.	L16	67a

O

Name	Map Ref.	Page
Oacoma, S.D., U.S.	H8	118
Oahe, Lake, res., U.S.	F7	118
Oahu, i., Hi., U.S.	p15	125a
Oak, stm., Man., Can.	I14	104
Oakbank, Austl.	I4	70
Oak Bay, B.C., Can.	I11	102
Oak Bluffs, Ma., U.S.	F16	108
Oakboro, N.C., U.S.	D6	112
Oakburn, Man., Can.	H14	104
Oak City, N.C., U.S.	D9	112
Oak City, Ut., U.S.	E4	120
Oak Creek, Co., U.S.	D10	120
Oak Creek, stm., Az., U.S.	J5	120
Oakdale, Ca., U.S.	G5	124
Oakdale, La., U.S.	L4	114
Oakdale, Ne., U.S.	I10	118
Oakdale, Tn., U.S.	D2	112
Oakes, N.D., U.S.	E9	118
Oakesdale, Wa., U.S.	C8	122
Oakey, Austl.	F9	70
Oakfield, Me., U.S.	A18	108
Oakfield, N.Y., U.S.	D8	108
Oakfield, Wi., U.S.	G7	110
Oak Grove, La., U.S.	J5	114
Oak Harbor, Wa., U.S.	B3	122
Oak Hill, Fl., U.S.	K6	112
Oak Hill, Mi., U.S.	F9	110
Oak Hill, Oh., U.S.	I4	108
Oak Hill, W.V., U.S.	J5	108
Oakhurst, Ca., U.S.	G6	124
Oakhurst, Tx., U.S.	I11	116
Oak Island, i., N.S., Can.	H9	106
Oak Knolls, Ca., U.S.	J5	124
Oak Lake, Man., Can.	I14	104
Oak Lake, l., Man., Can.	I14	104
Oak Lake, l., Ont., Can.	H21	104
Oakland, Ca., U.S.	G3	124
Oakland, Il., U.S.	C8	114
Oakland, Ia., U.S.	J12	118
Oakland, Me., U.S.	C17	108
Oakland, Md., U.S.	H7	108
Oakland, Ms., U.S.	H7	114
Oakland, Ne., U.S.	J11	118
Oakland, Or., U.S.	G2	122
Oakland City, In., U.S.	D9	114
Oakland Park, Fl., U.S.	M6	112
Oak Lawn, Il., U.S.	I8	110
Oaklawn, Ks., U.S.	N10	118
Oakley, Id., U.S.	H12	122
Oakley, Ks., U.S.	L7	118
Oakman, Al., U.S.	I9	114
Oak Park, Il., U.S.	I8	110
Oak Point, Man., Can.	H16	104
Oakridge, Or., U.S.	G3	122
Oak Ridge, Tn., U.S.	C2	112
Oaktown, In., U.S.	D9	114
Oak View, Ca., U.S.	J6	124
Oakville, Man., Can.	I17	104
Oakville, Ont., Can.	G16	110
Oakwood, Oh., U.S.	F2	108
Oakwood, Tx., U.S.	H11	116
Oamaru, N.Z.	F3	72
Oancea, Rom.	D12	20
Oatlands, Austl.	N7	70
Oatman, Az., U.S.	I2	120
Oaxaca, state, Mex.	I11	90
Oaxaca [de Juárez], Mex.	I11	90
Ob', stm., Russia	D11	26
Obama, Japan	L10	36
Oban, Austl.	C3	70
Oban, Nig.	I14	64
Oban, Scot., U.K.	E8	8
Obed, Alta., Can.	D17	102
Obed, stm., Tn., U.S.	C2	112
Obeliai, Lith.	F8	22
Oberá, Arg.	D11	80
Oberdrauburg, Aus.	I12	10
Obergurgl, Aus.	I11	10
Oberhausen, Ger.	D6	10
Oberlin, Ks., U.S.	L7	118
Oberlin, La., U.S.	L4	114
Oberlin, Oh., U.S.	F4	108
Obernai, Fr.	D14	14
Obernburg am Main, Ger.	F9	10
Oberon, Austl.	I8	70
Oberösterreich, state, Aus.	G13	10
Oberpullendorf, Aus.	H16	10
Obertin, Ukr.	A9	20
Oberursel, Ger.	E8	10
Obervellach, Aus.	I13	10
Oberwart, Aus.	H16	10
Obi, Nig.	G14	64
Obi, Kepulauan, is., Indon.	F8	38
Obiaruku, Nig.	I13	64
Óbidos, Braz.	D7	76
Obihiro, Japan	E18	36a
Obilatu, Pulau, i., Indon.	F8	38
Obing, Ger.	G12	10
Obion, Tn., U.S.	F7	114
Obion, stm., Tn., U.S.	F7	114
Oblong, Il., U.S.	C9	114
Oblučje, Russia	H18	28
Obninsk, Russia	F19	22
Obock, Dji.	F9	56
Obol', Bela.	F12	22
Oborniki, Pol.	C16	10
Oboz'orskij, Russia	J27	6
O'Brien, Or., U.S.	H2	122
Obščij Syrt, mtn., Asia	G8	26
Observatory Inlet, b., B.C., Can.	B5	102
Obskaja guba, b., Russia	D12	26
Obuasi, Ghana	H9	64
Obuchova, Russia	E15	22
Obžericha, Russia	D25	22
Ocala, Fl., U.S.	J4	112
Ocallí, Peru	B2	82
Ocamo, stm., Ven.	F10	84
Ocampo, Mex.	C5	90
Ocampo, Mex.	D8	90
Ocaña, Col.	C6	84
Occidental, Cordillera, mts., Col.	E4	84
Occidental, Cordillera, mts., Peru	C3	82
Oceana, W.V., U.S.	B5	112
Ocean Cape, c., Ak., U.S.	G25	100
Ocean City, Md., U.S.	I11	108
Ocean City, N.J., U.S.	H12	108
Ocean Falls, B.C., Can.	E7	102
Oceano, Ca., U.S.	I5	124
Ocean Park, Wa., U.S.	D1	122
Oceanside, Ca., U.S.	K8	124
Ocean Springs, Ms., U.S.	L8	114
Ocha, Russia	G20	28
Ochapowace Indian Reserve, Sask., Can.	H12	104
Ocheyedan, Ia., U.S.	H12	118
O'Chiese Indian Reserve, Alta., Can.	E19	102
Ochlocknee, Ga., U.S.	I2	112
Ochlockonee, stm., U.S.	I2	112
Ocho Rios, Jam.	E6	94
Ochota, stm., Russia	F20	28
Ochotsk, Russia	F20	28
Ochre River, Man., Can.	G15	104
Ochsenfurt, Ger.	F10	10
Ochvat, Russia	E15	22
Ocilla, Ga., U.S.	H3	112
Ocmulgee, stm., Ga., U.S.	H3	112
Ocoa, Bahía de, b., Dom. Rep.	E9	94
Ocoee, Fl., U.S.	K5	112
Ocoee (Toccoa), stm., U.S.	D2	112
Ocoña, Peru	G5	82
Ocoña, stm., Peru	G5	82
Oconee, stm., Ga., U.S.	G4	112
Ocongate, Peru	E6	82
Oconomowoc, Wi., U.S.	G7	110
Oconto, Wi., U.S.	F8	110
Oconto, stm., Wi., U.S.	F7	110
Oconto Falls, Wi., U.S.	F7	110
Ocós, Guat.	C2	92
Ocosingo, Mex.	I13	90
Ocotal, Nic.	D8	92
Ocotepeque, dept., Hond.	C5	92
Ocotlán, Mex.	G8	90
Ocotlán de Morelos, Mex.	I11	90
Ocozocoautla [de Espinosa], Mex.	I13	90
Ocracoke, N.C., U.S.	D11	112
Ocracoke Island, i., N.C., U.S.	D11	112
Ocros, Peru	D3	82
Ocú, Pan.	J14	92
Ocumare del Tuy, Ven.	B9	84
Ocuri, Bol.	H9	82
Ocussi, Indon.	A4	68
Oda, Ghana	I9	64
Oda, Jabal, mtn., Sud.	G9	60
Odanakumadona, Bots.	C7	66
Ōdate, Japan	G15	36
Odawara, Japan	L14	36
Odda, Nor.	K10	6
Odebolt, Ia., U.S.	I12	118
Odei, stm., Man., Can.	B17	104
Odell, Il., U.S.	I7	110
Odell, Ne., U.S.	K11	118
Odell, Tx., U.S.	E7	116
Odem, Tx., U.S.	L9	116
Ödemiş, Tur.	K11	20
Odendaalsrus, S. Afr.	F8	66
Odense, Den.	N12	6
Oder (Odra), stm., Eur.	C14	10
Oderberg, Ger.	C14	10
Oderhaff (Zalew Szczeciński), b., Eur.	B14	10
Oderzo, Italy	D7	18
Odessa, Ont., Can.	F19	110
Odessa, Ukr.	H4	26
Odessa, Mo., U.S.	D3	114
Odessa, Tx., U.S.	H4	116
Odessa, Wa., U.S.	C7	122
Odesskoje, Russia	G12	26
Odiakwe, Bots.	C7	66
Odib, Wādī, val., Afr.	F9	60
Odienné, I.C.	G6	64
Odin, Mount, mtn., B.C., Can.	G16	102
Odincovo, Russia	F20	22
Odojev, Russia	H19	22
Odon, In., U.S.	D10	114
O'Donnell, Tx., U.S.	G5	116
Odorheiu Secuiesc, Rom.	C9	20
Odum, Ga., U.S.	H4	112
Odzi, Zimb.	B11	66
Oebisfelde, Ger.	C10	10
Oeiras, Braz.	E10	76
Oelde, Ger.	D8	10
Oelsnitz, Ger.	E12	10
Oelwein, Ia., U.S.	H4	110
Oesterdam, Neth.	F5	12
Oettingen in Bayern, Ger.	G10	10
Oetz, Aus.	H10	10
O'Fallon, Mo., U.S.	D6	114
Ofaqim, Isr.	F3	50
Offa, Nig.	G12	64
Offaly, co., Ire.	H6	8
Offenbach, Ger.	E8	10
Offenburg, Ger.	G7	10
Oficina Alemania, Chile	C4	80
Oficina Alianza, Chile	I7	82
Oficina Chile, Chile	C4	80
Oficina Pedro de Valdivia, Chile	B4	80
Oficina Victoria, Chile	I7	82
Ōfunato, Japan	H16	36
Oga, Japan	H14	36
Ogaden, reg., Afr.	G9	56
Ōgaki, Japan	L11	36
Ogallala, Ne., U.S.	J6	118
Ogbomosho, Nig.	G12	64
Ogden, Ia., U.S.	H1	110
Ogden, Ks., U.S.	L11	118
Ogden, Ut., U.S.	C5	120
Ogden, Mount, mtn., N.A.	G28	100
Ogdensburg, N.Y., U.S.	C11	108
Ogeechee, stm., Ga., U.S.	G5	112
Ogema, Sask., Can.	I10	104
Ogilvie, Mn., U.S.	E2	110
Ogilvie, stm., Yukon, Can.	D25	100
Ogilvie Mountains, mts., Yukon, Can.	D25	100
Oglesby, Il., U.S.	I6	110
Oglesby, Tx., U.S.	H9	116
Oglethorpe, Ga., U.S.	G2	112
Oglio, stm., Italy	D5	18
Ogmore, Austl.	D8	70
Ognon, stm., Fr.	E12	14
Ogoja, Nig.	H14	64
Ogoki, stm., Ont., Can.	F15	96
Ogooué, stm., Afr.	B1	58
Ogorodnoje, Ukr.	D12	20
Ogr, Sud.	K4	60
Ogre, Lat.	E7	22
Ogulin, Cro.	D10	18
Ogunquit, Me., U.S.	D16	108
Ogurčinskij, ostrov, i., Turk.	B12	48
Oğuzeli, Tur.	C4	48
Ogwashi-Uku, Nig.	H13	64
Ohanet, Alg.	F15	62
Ōhara, Japan	L15	36
O'Higgins, Lago (Lago San Martín), l., S.A.	F2	78
Ohio, Il., U.S.	I6	110
Ohio, state, U.S.	C10	98
Ohio, stm., U.S.	D9	98
Ohio City, Oh., U.S.	G2	108
Ohře, stm., Eur.	E13	10
Ohrid, Mac.	H4	20
Ohrid, Lake, l., Eur.	H4	20
Öhringen, Ger.	F9	10
Ohuira, Bahía, b., Mex.	E5	90
Oiapoque, Braz.	C8	76
Oiapoque (Oyapock), stm., S.A.	C8	76
Oies, Île aux, i., Que., Can.	E3	106
Oil Center, N.M., U.S.	G3	116
Oil City, La., U.S.	J3	114
Oil City, Pa., U.S.	F7	108
Oil Creek, stm., Pa., U.S.	F7	108
Oildale, Ca., U.S.	I6	124
Oilton, Ok., U.S.	C10	116
Oilton, Tx., U.S.	L8	116
Oil Trough, Ar., U.S.	G5	114
Oise, dept., Fr.	C9	14
Oise, stm., Eur.	C9	14
Oisemont, Fr.	C8	14
Ōita, Japan	N6	36
Ojai, Ca., U.S.	J6	124
Ojat', stm., Russia	A16	22
Ojinaga, Mex.	C7	90
Ojocaliente, Mex.	F8	90
Ojo del Carrizo, Mex.	C7	90
Ojo de Liebre, Laguna, b., Mex.	D2	90
Ojos del Salado, Nevado, mtn., S.A.	D4	80
Ojos Negros, Mex.	B1	90
Oju, Nig.	H14	64
Oka, stm., Russia	E26	22
Oka, stm., Russia	G12	28
Okahandja, Nmb.	C3	66
Okanagan (Okanogan), stm., N.A.	H15	102
Okanagan Centre, B.C., Can.	G15	102
Okanagan Falls, B.C., Can.	H15	102
Okanagan Indian Reserve, B.C., Can.	G15	102
Okanagan Lake, l., B.C., Can.	G15	102
Okanagan Landing, B.C., Can.	G15	102
Okanagan Mountain Provincial Park, B.C., Can.	H15	102
Okanagan Range (Okanogan Range), mts., N.A.	H14	102
Okanogan, Wa., U.S.	B6	122
Okanogan (Okanagan), stm., N.A.	I15	102
Okanogan, stm., N.A.	B6	122
Okaputa, Nmb.	C3	66
Okāra, Pak.	E5	44
Okarche, Ok., U.S.	D9	116
Okaukuejo, Nmb.	B2	66
Okavango (Cubango), stm., Afr.	E3	58
Okavango Delta, Bots.	B6	66
Okawville, Il., U.S.	D7	114
Okaya, Japan	K13	36
Okayama, Japan	M8	36
Okazaki, Japan	M12	36
Okeechobee, Fl., U.S.	L6	112
Okeechobee, Lake, l., Fl., U.S.	M6	112
Okeene, Ok., U.S.	C8	116
Okefenokee Swamp, sw., U.S.	I4	112
Okeigbo, Nig.	H12	64
Okemah, Ok., U.S.	D10	116
Okemos, Mi., U.S.	H11	110
Okene, Nig.	H13	64
Oke-Ode, Nig.	G12	64
Okhotsk, Sea of, Asia	C19	36a
Okiep, S. Afr.	G3	66
Okinawa, Japan	U2	37b
Okinawa-jima, i., Japan	U2	37b
Okinawa-shotō, is., Japan	U2	37b
Okino-Daitō-jima, i., Japan	G13	30
Okino-Erabu-shima, i., Japan	T3	37b
Okino-Tori-shima (Parece Vela), i., Japan	G14	30
Oki-shotō, is., Japan	K8	36
Okladnevo, Russia	C16	22
Oklahoma, state, U.S.	D7	98
Oklahoma City, Ok., U.S.	D9	116
Oklawaha, Fl., U.S.	J5	112
Oklee, Mn., U.S.	D12	118
Okmulgee, Ok., U.S.	D11	116
Oknica, Mol.	A11	20
Okno, Ukr.	A9	20
Okolona, Ar., U.S.	I3	114
Okolona, Ky., U.S.	D11	114
Okolona, Ms., U.S.	H8	114
Okombahe, Nmb.	C2	66
Okotoks, Alta., Can.	G21	102
Okpara, stm., Afr.	H11	64
Okrika, Nig.	I13	64
Okt'abr', Russia	D20	22
Okt'abr'skij, Bela.	I11	22
Okt'abr'skij, Russia	D23	22
Okt'abr'skij, Russia	C27	22
Okt'abr'skij, Russia	G21	22
Okt'abr'skij, Russia	G8	26
Okt'abr'skoje, Russia	I22	22
Okt'abr'skoj Revol'ucii, ostrov, i., Russia	B17	26
Okulovka, Russia	C16	22
Okushiri-tō, i., Japan	E14	36a
Okuta, Nig.	G11	64
Okwa (Chapman's), stm., Afr.	D5	66
Okwoga, Nig.	H13	64
Olá, Pan.	I14	92
Ola, Ar., U.S.	G3	114
Ólafsfjörður, Ice.	A4	6a
Olancha, Ca., U.S.	H7	124
Olancha Peak, mtn., Ca., U.S.	H7	124
Olanchito, Hond.	B8	92
Olancho, dept., Hond.	C9	92
Öland, i., Swe.	M15	6
Olanta, S.C., U.S.	F7	112
Olar, S.C., U.S.	F5	112
Olary, Austl.	I4	70
Olascoaga, Arg.	H8	80
Olathe, Co., U.S.	F9	120
Olathe, Ks., U.S.	M13	118
Olavarría, Arg.	I8	80
Oława, Pol.	E17	10
Olbia, Italy	I4	18
Olca, Volcán, vol., S.A.	I7	82
Olcott, N.Y., U.S.	D8	108
Old Bahama Channel, strt., N.A.	C5	94
Old Crow, Yukon, Can.	C25	100
Old Crow, stm., N.A.	B24	100
Olden, Tx., U.S.	G8	116
Oldenburg, hist. reg., Ger.	B8	10
Oldenburg [in Holstein], Ger.	A10	10
Oldenzaal, Neth.	D10	12
Old Faithful Geyser, well, Wy., U.S.	F15	122
Old Forge, N.Y., U.S.	D12	108
Old Forge, Pa., U.S.	F11	108
Old Fort Mountain, mtn., B.C., Can.	B8	102
Oldham, S.D., U.S.	G10	118
Old Harbor, Ak., U.S.	H18	100
Old Hickory Lake, res., Tn., U.S.	F10	114
Oldman, stm., Alta., Can.	H23	102
Old Man Mountain, mtn., Newf., Can.	C16	106
Oldmeldrum, Scot., U.K.	D11	8
Old Orchard Beach, Me., U.S.	D16	108
Old Perlican, Newf., Can.	D20	106
Olds, Alta., Can.	F20	102
Old Saybrook, Ct., U.S.	F14	108
Old Tate, Bots.	C8	66
Old Town, Me., U.S.	C18	108
Old Trap, N.C., U.S.	C10	112
Olduvai Gorge, val., Tan.	B7	58
Old Wives Lake, l., Sask., Can.	H8	104
Olean, N.Y., U.S.	E8	108
O'Leary, P.E.I., Can.	F9	106
Olecko, Pol.	A22	10
Olen, Bel.	F6	12
Ølen, Nor.	L9	6
Olenegorsk, Russia	D4	26
Olenij, ostrov, i., Russia	C13	26
Olenino, Russia	E16	22
Olen'ok, stm., Russia	C16	28
Olen'okskij zaliv, b., Russia	C16	28
Oléron, Île d', i., Fr.	G5	14
Oleśnica, Pol.	D17	10
Olesno, Pol.	E18	10
Ol'ga, Russia	I19	28
Ölgij, Mong.	B4	30

Name	Map Ref.	Page
Ol'gopol', Ukr.	A13	20
Olhão, Port.	H4	16
Oli, stm., Afr.	G12	64
Olifants (Rio dos Elefantes), stm., Afr.	E10	66
Ólimbos, mtn., Cyp.	D2	48
Ólimbos, mtn., Grc.	I6	20
Olímpia, Braz.	F4	79
Olin, Ia., U.S.	I4	110
Olinalá, Mex.	I10	90
Olinda, Braz.	E12	76
Olio, Austl.	C5	70
Oliva, Arg.	G7	80
Oliva, Spain	G11	16
Oliva de la Frontera, Spain	G5	16
Olivares, Cerro de, mtn., S.A.	F4	80
Olive Branch, Ms., U.S.	H7	114
Olive Hill, Ky., U.S.	I3	108
Olivehurst, Ca., U.S.	E4	124
Oliveira, Braz.	F6	79
Oliveira dos Brejinhos, Braz.	B7	79
Olivenza, Spain	G4	16
Oliver, B.C., Can.	H15	102
Oliver Lake, l., Sask., Can.	B11	104
Oliver Springs, Tn., U.S.	C2	112
Olivet, Mi., U.S.	H11	110
Olivet, S.D., U.S.	H10	118
Olivia, Mn., U.S.	G13	118
Olla, La., U.S.	K4	114
Ollagüe, Chile	I7	82
Ollagüe, Volcán, vol., S.A.	I7	82
Ollantaitambo, Peru	E5	82
Olmos, Peru	A2	82
Olney, Il., U.S.	D8	114
Olney, Tx., U.S.	F8	116
Ol'okma, stm., Russia	F16	28
Ol'okminsk, Russia	E16	28
Olomane, stm., Que., Can.	A13	106
Olomega, Laguna, l., El Sal.	D6	92
Olomouc, Czech.	F17	10
Olonec, Russia	E4	26
Olongapo, Phil.	N19	39b
Oloron-Sainte-Marie, Fr.	I6	14
Olot, Spain	C14	16
Olov'annaja, Russia	G15	28
Olpe, Ger.	D7	10
Olpe, Ks., U.S.	M11	118
Olsztyn (Allenstein), Pol.	B20	10
Olsztynek, Pol.	B20	10
Olt, co., Rom.	E8	20
Olt, stm., Rom.	F8	20
Olta, Arg.	F5	80
Olten, Switz.	D8	13
Olteniţa, Rom.	E10	20
Olton, Tx., U.S.	E4	116
Oltu, Tur.	A6	48
Oluan Pi, c., Tai.	N9	34
Olukonda, Nmb.	B3	66
Olustee, Fl., U.S.	I4	112
Olustee, Ok., U.S.	E7	116
Ol'utorskij, mys, c., Russia	F26	28
Ol'utorskij zaliv, b., Russia	E25	28
Olvera, Spain	I6	16
Olympia, Wa., U.S.	C3	122
Olympic Mountains, mts., Wa., U.S.	C2	122
Olympic National Park, Wa., U.S.	C2	122
Olympus, Mount, mtn., Wa., U.S.	C2	122
Olympus, Mount see Ólimbos, mtn., Grc.	I6	20
Om', stm., Russia	F7	28
Omagh, N. Ire., U.K.	G6	8
Omaguas, Peru	J6	84
Omaha, Ne., U.S.	J12	118
Omaha, Tx., U.S.	I2	114
Omak, Wa., U.S.	B6	122
Oman ('Umān), ctry., Asia	E6	42
Oman, Gulf of, b., Asia	B10	47
Omar, W.V., U.S.	B5	112
Omarama, N.Z.	F2	72
Omaruru, Nmb.	C2	66
Omas, Peru	E3	82
Omatako, stm., Nmb.	B5	66
Omate, Peru	G6	82
Ombombo, Nmb.	B1	66
Omboué, Gabon	B1	58
Omčak, Russia	E21	28
Omdurman see Umm Durmān, Sud.	J7	60
Omega, Ga., U.S.	H3	112
Omegna, Italy	D3	18
Omemee, Ont., Can.	F17	110
Omeo, Austl.	K7	70
Ometepe, Isla de, i., Nic.	F9	92
Ometepec, Mex.	I10	90
Om Hajer, Eth.	J9	60
Omineca, stm., B.C., Can.	B10	102
Omineca Mountains, mts., B.C., Can.	B9	102
Ōmiya, Japan	L14	36
Ommaney, Cape, c., Ak., U.S.	H27	100
Ommanney Bay, b., N.W. Ter., Can.	B12	96
Omo, stm., Afr.	G8	56
Omoa, Bahía de, b., N.A.	B6	92
Omoloj, stm., Russia	C18	28
Omolon, stm., Russia	D23	28
Omro, Wi., U.S.	F7	110
Omsk, Russia	F6	28
Omsukčan, Russia	E23	28
Omu-Aran, Nig.	G12	64
Ōmuta, Japan	N5	36
Omutninsk, Russia	F8	26
On, Viet.	D9	40
Onabas, Mex.	C5	90
Onaga, Ks., U.S.	L11	118
Onamia, Mn., U.S.	D2	110
Onancock, Va., U.S.	B11	112
Onarga, Il., U.S.	J7	110
Onatchiway, Lac, l., Que., Can.	C2	106
Onawa, Ia., U.S.	I11	118
Onaway, Mi., U.S.	E11	110
Oncativo, Arg.	F7	80
Once, Canal Numero, Arg.	I9	80
Onda, Spain	F11	16
Ondangwa, Nmb.	A3	66
Ondas, Rio de, stm., Braz.	B6	79
Onderdijk, Neth.	C7	12
Ondjiva, Ang.	E3	58
Ondo, Nig.	H12	64
Öndörchaan, Mong.	B9	30
Ondozero, ozero, l., Russia	J23	6
One Arrow Indian Reserve, Sask., Can.	F8	104
Oneco, Fl., U.S.	L4	112
Onega, Russia	E5	26
Onega, stm., Russia	J26	6
Onega, Lake see Onežskoje ozero, l., Russia	E5	26
One Hundred and Two, stm., Mo., U.S.	C2	114
One Hundred Fifty Mile House, B.C., Can.	E13	102
One Hundred Mile House, B.C., Can.	F13	102
Oneida, Il., U.S.	I5	110
Oneida, Ky., U.S.	B3	112
Oneida, N.Y., U.S.	D11	108
Oneida, Tn., U.S.	C2	112
Oneida Lake, l., N.Y., U.S.	D11	108
O'Neill, Ne., U.S.	I9	118
Onekama, Mi., U.S.	F9	110
Onekotan, ostrov, i., Russia	H22	28
Oneonta, Al., U.S.	I10	114
Oneonta, N.Y., U.S.	E11	108
Onežskaja guba, b., Russia	I25	6
Onežskij poluostrov, pen., Russia	I25	6
Onežskoje ozero, l., Russia	E5	26
Ongjin, N. Kor.	F13	32
Ongole, India	E6	46
Onida, S.D., U.S.	G7	118
Onistagane, Lac, l., Que., Can.	B2	106
Onitsha, Nig.	H13	64
Ōno, Japan	L11	36
Onoda, Japan	N6	36
Onomichi, Japan	M8	36
Onon, stm., Asia	A9	30
Onoto, Ven.	C10	84
Onoway, Alta., Can.	D20	102
Onseepkans, S. Afr.	G4	66
Onset, Ma., U.S.	F16	108
Onslow, Austl.	D3	68
Onslow Bay, b., N.C., U.S.	E9	112
Ontario, Ca., U.S.	J8	124
Ontario, Oh., U.S.	G4	108
Ontario, Or., U.S.	F9	122
Ontario, prov., Can.	F15	96
Ontario, Lake, l., N.A.	G18	110
Ontinyent (Onteniente), Spain	G11	16
Ontonagon, Mi., U.S.	D6	110
Ontonagon, stm., Mi., U.S.	D6	110
Onverwacht, Sur.	B7	76
Ŏnyang, S. Kor.	G15	32
Oodnadatta, Austl.	E7	68
Ooldea, Austl.	F6	68
Oolitic, In., U.S.	D10	114
Oologah, Ok., U.S.	C11	116
Oologah Lake, res., Ok., U.S.	C11	116
Oona River, B.C., Can.	D4	102
Oostburg, Wi., U.S.	G8	110
Oostelijk Flevoland, reg., Neth.	C8	12
Oostende (Ostende), Bel.	F2	12
Oosterend, Neth.	B6	12
Oosterhout, Neth.	E6	12
Oosterschelde, b., Neth.	E4	12
Oosterscheldedam, Neth.	E4	12
Oosterwolde, Neth.	C9	12
Oostflakkee, Neth.	E5	12
Oost-Vlaanderen, prov., Bel.	G4	12
Oostvleteren, Bel.	G2	12
Ootsa Lake, B.C., Can.	D8	102
Ootsa Lake, l., B.C., Can.	D8	102
Ootsi, Bots.	E7	66
Opala, Zaire	B4	58
Opalaca, Cordillera, mts., Hond.	C6	92
Oparino, Russia	F7	26
Opasquia, Ont., Can.	E21	104
Opasquia Lake, l., Ont., Can.	E21	104
Opatów, Pol.	E21	10
Opava, Czech.	F17	10
Opava, stm., Eur.	E17	10
Opelika, Al., U.S.	J11	114
Opelousas, La., U.S.	L4	114
Opheim, Mt., U.S.	B19	122
Ophir, Or., U.S.	H1	122
Opihikao, Hi., U.S.	r19	125a
Opinaca, stm., Que., Can.	F17	96
Opiscotéo, Lac, l., Que., Can.	F19	96
Opobo, Nig.	I13	64
Opočka, Russia	E11	22
Opoczno, Pol.	D20	10
Opole (Oppeln), Pol.	E17	10
Oponono, Lake, l., Nmb.	B2	66
Oporto see Porto, Port.	D3	16
Opotiki, N.Z.	B6	72
Opp, Al., U.S.	K10	114
Oppland, co., Nor.	K11	6
Opportunity, Mt., U.S.	D13	122
Opportunity, Wa., U.S.	C8	122
Opsa, Bela.	F9	22
Optic Lake, Man., Can.	D13	104
Opuwo, Nmb.	B1	66
Oquawka, Il., U.S.	J5	110
Ora, Italy	C6	18
Oracle, Az., U.S.	L6	120
Oradea, Rom.	B5	20
Orai, India	H8	44
Oran, Mo., U.S.	E7	114
Orange, Austl.	I8	70
Orange, Fr.	H11	14
Orange, Ma., U.S.	E14	108
Orange, Tx., U.S.	L3	114
Orange, Va., U.S.	I8	108
Orange (Oranje), stm., Afr.	G4	66
Orange, Cabo, c., Braz.	D9	74
Orange, Cabo, c., Braz.	C8	76
Orangeburg, S.C., U.S.	F6	112
Orange City, Fl., U.S.	K5	112
Orange City, Ia., U.S.	H11	118
Orange Cove, Ca., U.S.	H6	124
Orange Grove, Tx., U.S.	L9	116
Orange Lake, Fl., U.S.	J4	112
Orange Park, Fl., U.S.	I5	112
Orangeville, Ont., Can.	G15	110
Orangeville, Ut., U.S.	E5	120
Orange Walk, Belize	H15	90
Oranienburg, Ger.	C13	10
Oranjefontein, S. Afr.	D8	66
Oranjemund, Nmb.	G3	66
Oranjerivier, S. Afr.	G7	66
Oranjestad, Aruba	H9	94
Oran see Wahran, Alg.	A6	54
Or 'Aqiva, Isr.	C3	50
Orarak, Sud.	N7	60
Orăştie, Rom.	D7	20
Oravais (Oravainen), Fin.	J18	6
Orbe, Switz.	E6	13
Orbetello, Italy	G6	18
Orbisonia, Pa., U.S.	G9	108
Orbost, Austl.	K8	70
Orcadas, sci., B.A.T.	B1	73
Orcera, Spain	G9	16
Orchard, Ne., U.S.	I9	118
Orchard City, Co., U.S.	F9	120
Orchard Homes, Mt., U.S.	D11	122
Orchard Mesa, Co., U.S.	E8	120
Orchard Park, N.Y., U.S.	E8	108
Orchard Valley, Wy., U.S.	C12	120
Orchej (Orgejev), Mol.	B12	20
Orchies, Fr.	B10	14
Orchon, stm., Mong.	B7	30
Ord, Ne., U.S.	J9	118
Ord, stm., Austl.	C5	68
Ord, Mount, mtn., Austl.	C5	68
Orderville, Ut., U.S.	G4	120
Ordoqui, Arg.	H8	80
Ordu, Tur.	G15	4
Ordway, Co., U.S.	M4	118
Ore, Nig.	H12	64
Örebro, Swe.	L14	6
Orechovo-Zujevo, Russia	F21	22
Orechovsk, Bela.	G13	22
Ore City, Tx., U.S.	J2	114
Oredež, Russia	C13	22
Oregon, Il., U.S.	H6	110
Oregon, Mo., U.S.	C1	114
Oregon, Oh., U.S.	F3	108
Oregon, state, U.S.	C2	98
Oregon City, Or., U.S.	E3	122
Orellana, Peru	B4	82
Orel see Or'ol, Russia	I19	22
Orem, Ut., U.S.	D5	120
Orenburg, Russia	G9	26
Örencik, Tur.	J13	20
Orense, Arg.	J9	80
Orense, Spain	C4	16
Orestes Pereyra, Mex.	D7	90
Orestiás, Grc.	H10	20
Orfanoú, Kólpos, b., Grc.	I7	20
Orfordville, Wi., U.S.	H6	110
Organ Needle, mtn., N.M., U.S.	L10	120
Orgelet, Fr.	F12	14
Orgtrud, Russia	E23	22
Orgūn, Afg.	D3	44
Orhanlar, Tur.	J11	20
Orica, Hond.	C8	92
Orichuna, stm., Ven.	D8	84
Orick, Ca., U.S.	C1	124
Orient, Ia., U.S.	J13	118
Oriental, N.C., U.S.	D10	112
Oriental, Cordillera, mts., Col.	E6	84
Oriental, Cordillera, mts., Peru	C4	82
Oriente, Arg.	J8	80
Orillia, Ont., Can.	F16	110
Orinduik, Guy.	E12	84
Orinoco, stm., S.A.	C11	84
Orinoco, Delta del, Ven.	C12	84
Oriola (Orihuela), Spain	G11	16
Orion, Il., U.S.	I5	110
Oripää, Fin.	K18	6
Oriskany, N.Y., U.S.	D11	108
Orissa, state, India	B7	46
Orissaare, Est.	C6	22
Oristano, Italy	J3	18
Orituco, stm., Ven.	C9	84
Oriximiná, Braz.	D7	76
Orizaba, Mex.	H11	90
Orizaba, Pico de (Volcán Citlaltépetl), vol., Mex.	H11	90
Orizona, Braz.	D4	79
Orkney, Sask., Can.	I7	104
Orkney, S. Afr.	F8	66
Orkney, prov., Scot., U.K.	B10	8
Orkney Islands, is., Scot., U.K.	B10	8
Orland, Ca., U.S.	E3	124
Orlândia, Braz.	F5	79
Orlando, Fl., U.S.	K5	112
Orléanais, hist. reg., Fr.	E8	14
Orléans, Ont., Can.	B11	108
Orléans, Fr.	E8	14
Orleans, Ca., U.S.	C2	124
Orleans, In., U.S.	D10	114
Orleans, Ma., U.S.	F17	108
Orleans, Ne., U.S.	K8	118
Orleans, Vt., U.S.	C14	108
Orléans, Île d', i., Que., Can.	F3	106
Orlová, Czech.	F18	10
Ormāra, Pak.	I18	48
Ormiston, Sask., Can.	I9	104
Ormoc, Phil.	C7	38
Ormond Beach, Fl., U.S.	J5	112
Ornans, Fr.	E13	14
Orne, dept., Fr.	D7	14
Orne, stm., Fr.	D6	14
Örnsköldsvik, Swe.	J16	6
Oro, N. Kor.	C15	32
Orocué, Col.	E7	84
Orocuina, Hond.	D7	92
Orodara, Burkina	F7	64
Orofino, Id., U.S.	D9	122
Oro Grande, Ca., U.S.	J8	124
Or'ol, Russia	I19	22
Oromocto, N.B., Can.	G7	106
Oromocto Lake, l., N.B., Can.	G7	106
Oron, Nig.	I14	64
Orono, Ont., Can.	G17	110
Orono, Me., U.S.	C18	108
Oronoque, stm., Guy.	F14	84
Orosháza, Hung.	I20	10
Orosí, Volcán, vol., C.R.	G9	92
Oroville, Ca., U.S.	E4	124
Oroville, Wa., U.S.	B6	122
Oroville, Lake, res., Ca., U.S.	E4	124
Orrick, Mo., U.S.	C2	114
Orrin, N.D., U.S.	C7	118
Orr Lake, l., Man., Can.	B17	104
Orroroo, Austl.	I3	70
Orrs Island, Me., U.S.	D17	108
Orrville, Al., U.S.	J9	114
Orrville, Oh., U.S.	G5	108
Orša, Bela.	G13	22
Orsières, Switz.	F7	13
Orsk, Russia	G9	26
Orta Nova, Italy	H10	18
Ortega, Col.	F5	84
Ortegal, Cabo, c., Spain	B4	16
Orteguaza, stm., Col.	G5	84
Orthez, Fr.	I6	14
Orthon, stm., Bol.	D8	82
Orting, Wa., U.S.	C3	122
Ortisei, Italy	C6	18
Ortiz, Mex.	C4	90
Ortiz, Ven.	C9	84
Ortles (Otler), mtn., Italy	E14	13
Ortona, Italy	G9	18
Ortonville, Mn., U.S.	F11	118
Orūmīyeh (Reẕā'īyeh), Iran	C8	48
Oruro, Bol.	G8	82
Oruro, dept., Bol.	H8	82
Orvieto, Italy	G7	18
Orwell, Oh., U.S.	F6	108
Orxon, stm., China	B10	30
Or Yehuda, Isr.	D3	50
Orzinuovi, Italy	D4	18
Orzola, Spain	N27	17b
Orzysz, Pol.	B21	10
Oš, Kyrg.	I12	26
Osa, Península de, pen., C.R.	I11	92
Osage, Ia., U.S.	G3	110
Osage, Wy., U.S.	H3	118
Osage, stm., Mo., U.S.	D4	114
Osage Beach, Mo., U.S.	D4	114
Osage City, Ks., U.S.	M12	118
Ōsaka, Japan	M10	36
Ōsaka-wan, b., Japan	M10	36
Osakis, Mn., U.S.	F12	118
Osan, S. Kor.	F15	32
Osawatomie, Ks., U.S.	M13	118
Osborne, Ks., U.S.	L9	118
Osburn, Id., U.S.	C10	122
Oscar Peak, mtn., B.C., Can.	C5	102
Osceola, Ar., U.S.	G7	114
Osceola, Ia., U.S.	I2	110
Osceola, Mo., U.S.	D3	114
Osceola, Ne., U.S.	J10	118
Osceola, Wi., U.S.	E3	110
Osceola Mills, Pa., U.S.	G8	108
Oschatz, Ger.	D13	10
Oschersleben, Ger.	C11	10
Oscoda, Mi., U.S.	F12	110
Osgood, In., U.S.	C11	114
O'Shanassy, stm., Austl.	B3	70
Oshawa, Ont., Can.	G17	110
Oshigambo, Nmb.	A3	66
Ō-shima, i., Japan	M14	36
Ō-shima, i., Japan	F14	36a
Oshkosh, Ne., U.S.	J5	118
Oshkosh, Wi., U.S.	F7	110
Oshnovīyeh, Iran	C8	48
Oshogbo, Nig.	H12	64
Oshwe, Zaire	B3	58
Osi, Nig.	G12	64
Osich'ŏn-ni, N. Kor.	B16	32
Osijek, Cro.	D2	20
Osilinka, stm., B.C., Can.	A10	102
Osimo, Italy	F8	18
Osinniki, Russia	G9	28
Osipoviči, Bela.	H11	22
Osire, Nmb.	C3	66
Oskaloosa, Ia., U.S.	I3	110
Oskaloosa, Ks., U.S.	L12	118
Oskarshamn, Swe.	M15	6
Oskū, Iran	C9	48
Oslo, Nor.	L12	6
Osmānābād, India	C4	46
Osmaniye, Tur.	C4	48
Ošm'any, Bela.	G8	22
Osmond, Ne., U.S.	I10	118
Osmore, stm., Peru	G6	82
Osnabrück, Ger.	C8	10
Osório Fonseca, Braz.	I13	84
Osorno, Chile	E2	78
Osoyoos, B.C., Can.	H15	102
Osoyoos Indian Reserve, B.C., Can.	H15	102
Osoyoos Lake, l., N.A.	H15	102
Ospino, Ven.	C8	84
Ospwagan Lake, l., Man., Can.	C16	104
Ossa, Mount, mtn., Austl.	M7	70
Ossabaw Island, i., Ga., U.S.	H5	112
Osse, stm., Nig.	H12	64
Osseo, Wi., U.S.	F4	110
Ossian, In., U.S.	B11	114
Ossian, Ia., U.S.	G4	110
Ossining, N.Y., U.S.	F13	108
Ossipee, N.H., U.S.	D15	108
Ossora, Russia	F24	28
Ošta, Russia	K24	6
Ostaškov, Russia	D16	22
Ostende (Oostende), Bel.	F2	12
Osterburg, Ger.	C11	10
Östergötlands Län, co., Swe.	L14	6
Osterholz-Scharmbeck, Ger.	B8	10
Osterode, Ger.	D10	10
Östersund, Swe.	J14	6
Osterwieck, Ger.	D10	10
Østfold, co., Nor.	L12	6
Ostfriesische Inseln, is., Ger.	B7	10
Ostfriesland, hist. reg., Ger.	B7	10
Ost'or, Russia	G15	22
Ostrava, Czech.	F18	10
Ostróda, Pol.	B19	10
Ostrogožsk, Russia	G5	26
Ostrołęka, Pol.	B21	10
Ostrošickij Gorodok, Bela.	G10	22
Ostrov, Czech.	E12	10
Ostrov, Russia	D11	22
Ostrov, i., Czech.	H17	10
Ostrovno, Bela.	F12	22
Ostrovskoje, Russia	D25	22
Ostrowiec Świętokrzyski, Pol.	E21	10
Ostrów Mazowiecka, Pol.	C21	10
Ostrów Wielkopolski, Pol.	D17	10
Ostrzeszów, Pol.	D17	10
Ostúa, stm., N.A.	C5	92
Ostuni, Italy	I12	18
Ōsumi-kaikyō, strt., Japan	Q5	36
Ōsumi-shotō, is., Japan	Q5	37b
Osuna, Spain	H6	16
Osvaldo Cruz, Braz.	F3	79
Osveja, Bela.	E11	22
Oswego, Il., U.S.	I7	110
Oswego, Ks., U.S.	N12	118
Oswego, N.Y., U.S.	D10	108
Oswego, stm., N.Y., U.S.	D10	108
Oświęcim, Pol.	E19	10
Osyka, Ms., U.S.	K6	114
Otaki, N.Z.	D5	72
Otanmäki, Fin.	I20	6
Otaru, Japan	D16	36a
Otava, Fin.	K20	6
Otava, stm., Czech.	F13	10
Otavalo, Ec.	G3	84
Otavi, Nmb.	B3	66
Otepää, Est.	C9	22
Oteros, stm., Mex.	D5	90
Othello, Wa., U.S.	D6	122
Óthiris, Óros, mts., Grc.	J6	20
Oti, stm., Afr.	G7	54
Otinapa, Mex.	E7	90
Otis, Co., U.S.	K5	118
Otis, Ks., U.S.	M8	118
Otish, Monts, mts., Que., Can.	F18	96
Otjimbingue, Nmb.	D3	66
Otjiwarongo, Nmb.	C3	66
Otočac, Cro.	E10	18
Otoque, Isla, i., Pan.	I15	92
Otoro, stm., Hond.	C6	92
Otoskwin, stm., Ont., Can.	F14	96
Otra, stm., Nor.	L10	6
Otradnyj, Russia	G8	26
Otranto, Italy	I13	18
Otranto, Strait of, strt., Eur.	I2	20
Otsego, Mi., U.S.	H10	110
Otselic, stm., N.Y., U.S.	E11	108
Ōtsu, Japan	L10	36
Otta, Nor.	K11	6
Ottawa, Ont., Can.	B11	108
Ottawa, Il., U.S.	I7	110
Ottawa, Ks., U.S.	M12	118
Ottawa, Oh., U.S.	F2	108
Ottawa, stm., Can.	G17	96
Ottawa Islands, is., N.W. Ter., Can.	E16	96
Otterburne, Man., Can.	I17	104
Otter Creek, Fl., U.S.	J4	112
Otter-Lake, Que., Can.	B10	108
Otter Lake, Mi., U.S.	G12	110
Otter Lake, l., Sask., Can.	C10	104
Otter Tail, stm., Mn., U.S.	E11	118
Otterville, Mo., U.S.	D3	114
Ottoville, Oh., U.S.	G2	108
Ottumwa, Ia., U.S.	I3	110
Ottweiler, Ger.	F7	10
Otu, Nig.	G11	64
Otumpa, Arg.	D7	80
Otuquis, Bañados de, sw., Bol.	H12	82
Oturkpo, Nig.	H14	64
Otway, Cape, c., Austl.	L5	70
Otwock, Pol.	C21	10
Otyn'a, Ukr.	A8	20
Ötztaler Alpen, mts., Eur.	C5	18
Ou, stm., China	J2	34
Ou, stm., Laos	D7	40
Ouachita, stm., U.S.	K5	114
Ouachita, Lake, res., Ar., U.S.	H3	114
Ouachita Mountains, mts., U.S.	H2	114
Ouadâne, Maur.	J5	62
Ouadda, Cen. Afr. Rep.	M2	60
Ouagadougou, Burkina	E9	64
Ouahigouya, Burkina	F6	54
Ouahigouya, Burkina	E8	64
Ouaka, stm., Cen. Afr. Rep.	G5	56
Oualâta, Maur.	C6	64
Oualé, stm., Afr.	F10	64
Oualidia, Mor.	D6	62
Ouallam, Niger	D11	64
Ouallene, Alg.	H11	62
Ouanda Djallé, Cen. Afr. Rep.	M2	60
Ouaninou, I.C.	G6	64
Ouan Taredert, Alg.	G15	62
Ouarâne, reg., Maur.	A4	64
Ouarkziz, Jbel, mts., Afr.	F6	62
Ouarzazate, Mor.	E7	62
Ouassoulou, stm., Afr.	F5	64
Ouatcha, Niger	E14	64
Oubangui (Ubangi), stm., Afr.	H8	52
Oud-Beijerland, Neth.	E5	12
Ouddorp, Neth.	F4	12
Oudenaarde (Audenarde), Bel.	G4	12
Oude Pekela, Neth.	B10	12
Oudtshoorn, S. Afr.	I6	66
Oudyoumoudi, Burkina	D9	64
Oued Cheham, Alg.	M2	18
Oued Meliz, Tun.	M3	18
Oued Tlelat, Alg.	J11	16
Oued Zarga, Tun.	M4	18
Oued-Zem, Mor.	D7	62
Ouémé, stm., Benin	H11	64
Ouenza, Alg.	N3	18
Ouessant, Île d' (Ushant), i., Fr.	D1	14
Ouesso, Congo	A3	58
Ouest, Pointe de l', c., Que., Can.	C9	106
Ouezzane, Mor.	C8	62
Ouham, stm., Afr.	G4	56
Ouidah, Benin	H11	64
Ouistreham, Fr.	C6	14
Oujda, Mor.	C10	62
Oulainen, Fin.	I19	6
Oulu, Fin.	I19	6
Oulujärvi, l., Fin.	I20	6
Oulujoki, stm., Fin.	I20	6
Oulun lääni, prov., Fin.	I20	6
Oum-Chalouba, Chad	E5	56
Oum El Bouagui, Alg.	C14	62
Oum er Rbia, Oued, stm., Mor.	D7	62
Ounara, Mor.	E6	62
Ounianga Kébir, Chad	E5	56
Ouray, Co., U.S.	F9	120
Ouray, Mount, mtn., Co., U.S.	F10	120
Ourinhos, Braz.	G4	79
Ouro, Paraná do, stm., Braz.	C6	82
Ouro Fino, Braz.	G5	79
Ouro Preto, Braz.	F7	79
Ouro Preto, stm., Braz.	D9	82
Oursi, Burkina	D9	64
Ourthe, stm., Bel.	H8	12
Ōu-sammyaku, mts., Japan	I15	36
Ouse, stm., Eng., U.K.	H12	8
Outaouais, Rivière des see Ottawa, stm., Can.	G17	96
Outardes, Baie aux, b., Que., Can.	C5	106
Outardes, Rivière aux, stm., Que., Can.	C5	106
Outardes Quatre, Réservoir, res., Que., Can.	C4	106
Outardes Trois, Barrage, Que., Can.	C5	106
Outer Hebrides, is., Scot., U.K.	D6	8
Outer Island, i., Wi., U.S.	C5	110
Outjo, Nmb.	C3	66
Outlook, Sask., Can.	G7	104
Outlook, Mt., U.S.	C3	118
Ouvidor, Braz.	E5	79
Ouyen, Austl.	J5	70
Ouzouer-le-Marché, Fr.	E8	14
Ouzzal, Oued i-n-, val., Alg.	J12	62
Ovalle, Chile	F3	80
Ovamboland, hist. reg., Nmb.	A3	66
Ovana, Cerro, mtn., Ven.	E9	84
Ovejas, Col.	C5	84
Overbrook, Ks., U.S.	M12	118
Overflakkee, i., Neth.	E5	12
Overflowing, stm., Can.	E13	104
Overhalla, Nor.	I12	6
Overijssel, prov., Neth.	D9	12
Overland Park, Ks., U.S.	M13	118
Overpelt, Bel.	F7	12
Overton, Ne., U.S.	K8	118
Overton, Nv., U.S.	H11	124
Overton, Tx., U.S.	G12	116
Övertorneå, Swe.	H18	6
Ovett, Ms., U.S.	K7	114
Ovid, Mi., U.S.	G11	110
Ovid, N.Y., U.S.	E10	108
Oviedo, Spain	B6	16
Ovino, Russia	B16	22
Ovstug, Russia	H16	22
Owando, Congo	B3	58
Owasso, Ok., U.S.	C11	116
Owatonna, Mn., U.S.	F2	110
Owbeh, Afg.	D17	48
Owego, N.Y., U.S.	E10	108
Owen, Wi., U.S.	F5	110
Owensboro, Ky., U.S.	E9	114
Owens Lake, l., Ca., U.S.	H8	124
Owen Sound, Ont., Can.	F15	110
Owen Stanley Range, mts., Pap. N. Gui.	m16	68a
Owensville, In., U.S.	D9	114
Owensville, Mo., U.S.	D5	114
Owenton, Ky., U.S.	D12	114
Owerri, Nig.	I13	64
Owikeno Lake, l., B.C., Can.	F7	102
Owingsville, Ky., U.S.	I3	108
Owl, stm., Alta., Can.	B23	102
Owl, stm., Man., Can.	E14	96
Owl Creek Mountains, mts., Wy., U.S.	G17	122
Owo, Nig.	H12	64
Owosso, Mi., U.S.	H11	110
Owyhee, Nv., U.S.	C9	124
Owyhee, stm., U.S.	G8	122
Owyhee, Lake, res., Or., U.S.	G8	122
Oxapampa, Peru	D4	82
Oxbow, Sask., Can.	I12	104
Oxford, N.S., Can.	G10	106
Oxford, Eng., U.K.	J12	8
Oxford, Al., U.S.	I11	114
Oxford, In., U.S.	B9	114
Oxford, Ia., U.S.	I4	110
Oxford, Ks., U.S.	N10	118
Oxford, Me., U.S.	C16	108
Oxford, Md., U.S.	I10	108
Oxford, Mi., U.S.	H12	110
Oxford, Ms., U.S.	H7	114
Oxford, Ne., U.S.	K8	118
Oxford, N.Y., U.S.	E11	108
Oxford, N.C., U.S.	C8	112
Oxford, Oh., U.S.	H2	108
Oxford, Pa., U.S.	H11	108
Oxford, Wi., U.S.	G6	110
Oxford House, Man., Can.	D19	104
Oxford House Indian Reserve, Man., Can.	D19	104
Oxford Junction, Ia., U.S.	I5	110
Oxford Lake, l., Man., Can.	D19	104
Oxfordshire, co., Eng., U.K.	J12	8
Oxkutzcab, Mex.	G15	90
Oxley, Austl.	J6	70
Oxnard, Ca., U.S.	J6	124
Oyama, B.C., Can.	G15	102
Oyama, Japan	K14	36
Oyem, Gabon	A2	58
Oyen, Alta., Can.	G4	104
Oyo, Nig.	H11	64
Oyón, Peru	D3	82
Oyonnax, Fr.	F12	14
Oyotún, Peru	B2	82
Ozamiz, Phil.	D7	38
Ozariči, Bela.	I12	22
Ozark, Al., U.S.	K11	114
Ozark, Ar., U.S.	G3	114
Ozark, Mo., U.S.	E3	114
Ozark Plateau, plat., U.S.	F3	114
Ozark Reservoir, res., Ar., U.S.	G2	114
Ozarks, Lake of the, res., Mo., U.S.	D4	114
Ózd, Hung.	G20	10
Oželje, Russia	G21	22
Ozernovskij, Russia	G23	28
Ozery, Russia	G21	22
Ozieri, Italy	I4	18
Ozimek, Pol.	E18	10
Ozona, Tx., U.S.	I5	116
Ozorków, Pol.	D19	10
Oz'ornyj, Russia	D23	22
Oz'ory, Bela.	H7	22
Ozubulu, Nig.	I13	64
Ozuluama, Mex.	G11	90

P

Name	Map Ref.	Page
Paarl, S. Afr.	I4	66
Paauilo, Hi., U.S.	q18	125a
Pabellones, Ensenada, b., Mex.	E6	90
Pabianice, Pol.	D19	10
Pablo, Mt., U.S.	C11	122
Pābna, Bngl.	H13	44
Pabradė, Lith.	G8	22
Pacaás Novos, stm., Braz.	D9	82
Pacaás Novos, Serra dos, mts., Braz.	D10	82
Pacaembu, Braz.	F3	79
Pacaltsdorp, S. Afr.	J6	66
Pacarán, Peru	E3	82
Pacaraos, Peru	D3	82
Pacasmayo, Peru	B2	82
Pace, Fl., U.S.	L9	114
Pace, Ms., U.S.	I6	114
Pachacamac, hist., Peru	E3	82
Pachino, Italy	M10	18
Pachitea, stm., Peru	C4	82
Pachiza, Peru	B3	82
Pachmarhi, India	I8	44
Pacho, Col.	E5	84
Pachuca [de Soto], Mex.	G10	90
Pacific, B.C., Can.	C6	102
Pacific, Mo., U.S.	D6	114
Pacifica, Ca., U.S.	G3	124
Pacific Grove, Ca., U.S.	H4	124
Pacific Ocean	F2	98
Pacific Ocean	J24	126
Pacific Ranges, mts., B.C., Can.	F8	102
Pacific Rim National Park, B.C., Can.	I9	102
Pacllón, Peru	D3	82
Pacohuaras, stm., Bol.	D8	82
Pacolet, stm., S.C., U.S.	E5	112
Pacolet Mills, S.C., U.S.	E5	112
Pacora, Pan.	C3	84
Pacquet, Newf., Can.	C18	106
Pacuare, stm., C.R.	G11	92
Pacuí, stm., Braz.	D6	79
Pacuneiro, stm., Braz.	B2	79
Padamo, stm., Ven.	F10	84
Padang, Indon.	O6	40
Padang Endau, Malay.	M7	40
Padangpanjang, Indon.	O6	40
Padangsidempuan, Indon.	N5	40
Padauari, stm., Braz.	G10	84
Padcaya, Bol.	I9	82
Paddle, stm., Alta., Can.	C20	102
Paddle Prairie, Alta., Can.	E9	96
Paden City, W.V., U.S.	H6	108
Paderborn, Ger.	D8	10
Padilla, Bol.	H9	82
Padloping Island, i., N.W. Ter., Can.	C20	96
Padova, Italy	D6	18
Padre Bernardo, Braz.	C4	79
Padre Island, i., Tx., U.S.	L9	116
Padre Paraíso, Braz.	D8	79
Padua see Padova, Italy	D6	18
Paducah, Ky., U.S.	E8	114
Paducah, Tx., U.S.	E6	116
Paektu-san, mtn., Asia	A16	32
Páez, stm., Col.	F4	84
Pafúri, Moz.	D10	66
Pag, Cro.	E10	18
Pag, Otok, i., Cro.	E10	18
Pagadian, Phil.	D7	38
Pagai Selatan, Pulau, i., Indon.	F3	38
Pagai Utara, Pulau, i., Indon.	F3	38
Pagan, Burma	D3	40
Pagancillo, Arg.	E4	80
Pagasitikós Kólpos, b., Grc.	J6	20
Pagato, stm., Sask., Can.	B12	104
Pagato Lake, l., Sask., Can.	B12	104
Page, Az., U.S.	H5	120
Page, N.D., U.S.	D10	118
Pagėgiai, Lith.	F4	22
Pageland, S.C., U.S.	E6	112
Pagoda Peak, mtn., Co., U.S.	D9	120
Pagoda Point, c., Burma	G3	40
Pagon, Bukit, mtn., Asia	E6	38
Pagosa Springs, Co., U.S.	G9	120
Pagouda, Togo	G10	64
Paguate, N.M., U.S.	I9	120
Pahala, Hi., U.S.	r18	125a
Pahang, stm., Malay.	M7	40
Páhara, Laguna, b., Nic.	C11	92
Pahoa, Hi., U.S.	r19	125a
Pahokee, Fl., U.S.	M6	112
Pahrump, Nv., U.S.	H10	124
Pahvant Range, mts., Ut., U.S.	F4	120
Pai, stm., Asia	E5	40
Paico, Peru	F5	82
Paide, Est.	C8	22
Paige, Tx., U.S.	I9	116
Paignton, Eng., U.K.	K10	8
Paiguano, Chile	F3	80
Paiján, Peru	B2	82
Päijänne, l., Fin.	K19	6
Paila, stm., Bol.	G10	82
Pailīn, Camb.	H7	40
Pailitas, Col.	C6	84
Paimpol, Fr.	D3	14
Painesdale, Mi., U.S.	C7	110
Painesville, Oh., U.S.	F5	108
Paint, stm., Mi., U.S.	D7	110
Painted Desert, des., Az., U.S.	I5	120
Painted Rock Reservoir, res., Az., U.S.	K4	120
Paint Lake, l., Man., Can.	C17	104
Paint Rock, Tx., U.S.	H7	116
Paint Rock, stm., Al., U.S.	H10	114
Paintsville, Ky., U.S.	B4	112
Paisley, Scot., U.K.	F9	8

Name — Map Ref. — Page

Paisley, Or., U.S. H5 122
Paita, Peru A1 82
Paita, Bahía de, b., Peru A1 82
Paizhou, China E2 34
Pajala, Swe. H18 6
Pajan, Ec. H2 84
Pájara, Spain O26 17b
Pajjer, gora, mtn., Russia D10 26
Pakaraima Mountains, mts., S.A. D8 74
Pakaraima Mountains, mts., S.A. E12 84
Pak Ban, Laos D7 40
Pakch'ŏn, N. Kor. D13 32
Pakeng, Sud. N6 60
Pakhoi see Beihai, China G8 30
Pakistan (Pākistān), ctry., Asia C9 42
Pakokku, Burma D3 40
Pakouabo, I.C. H7 64
Pakowki Lake, l., Alta., Can. I4 104
Pākpattan, Pak. E5 44
Pak Phanang, Thai. J6 40
Pak Phraek, Thai. J6 40
Pakrac, Cro. D12 18
Pakruojis, Lith. F6 22
Paks, Hung. I18 10
P'akupur, stm., Russia E7 28
Pakwash Lake, l., Ont., Can. H21 104
Pakxé, Laos G8 40
Pala, Chad G3 56
Palacca Point, c., Bah. D8 94
Palacios, Tx., U.S. K10 116
Palacios, stm., Bol. G10 82
Palagonia, Italy L9 18
Palagruža, Otoci, is., Cro. G11 18
Pālakodu, India D6 46
Palamós, Spain D15 16
Palana, Russia F23 28
Palanga, Lith. F4 22
Palangkaraya, Indon. F5 38
Palani, India G4 46
Pālanpur, India H5 44
Palapye, Bots. D8 66
Palatka, Russia E22 28
Palatka, Fl., U.S. J5 112
Palau (Belau), dep., Oc. D9 38
Palau, dep., Oc. H17 126
Palauk, Burma H5 40
Palawan, i., Phil. D6 38
Pālayankottai, India H4 46
Palca, Bol. G8 82
Palca, Peru D4 82
Palcamayo, Peru D4 82
Pal'co, Russia H17 22
Paldiski, Est. B7 22
Palech, Russia E24 22
Palembang, Indon. F3 38
Palena, Italy H9 18
Palencia, Spain C7 16
Palenque, Mex. I14 90
Palenque, hist., Mex. I13 90
Palenque, Punta, c., Dom. Rep. E9 94
Palermo, Col. F5 84
Palermo, Italy K8 18
Palermo, Ur. G11 80
Palestina, Braz. F4 79
Palestine, Ar., U.S. H6 114
Palestine, Il., U.S. C9 114
Palestine, Tx., U.S. H11 116
Palestine, hist. reg., Asia D4 50
Palestine, Lake, res., Tx., U.S. G11 116
Palestrina, Italy H7 18
Paletwa, Burma D2 40
Pālghāt, India G4 46
Pāli, India H5 44
Palín, Guat. C4 92
Palisade, Co., U.S. E8 120
Palisade, Ne., U.S. K6 118
Palisades, Id., U.S. G14 122
Palisades Reservoir, res., U.S. G14 122
Paliseul, Bel. I7 12
Pālitāna, India B1 46
Palivere, Est. C6 22
Palizada, Mex. H13 90
Palk Bay, b., Asia H5 46
Palk Strait, strt., Asia H5 46
Palla Bianca (Weisskugel), mtn., Eur. E14 13
Pallasca, Peru C2 82
Palling, B.C., Can. C9 102
Palliser, Cape, c., N.Z. D5 72
Palma, Braz. F7 79
Palma, Moz. D8 58
P'al'ma, Russia J24 6
Palma, stm., Braz. B5 79
Palma del Río, Spain H6 16
Palma [de Mallorca], Spain F14 16
Palma di Montechiaro, Italy L8 18
Palmar, stm., Ven. B6 84
Palmar Camp, Belize I15 90
Palmar de los Sepúlveda, Mex. E6 90
Palmar de Varela, Col. B5 84
Palmares, Braz. E11 76
Palmares, C.R. G10 92
Palmares, C.R. H11 92
Palmares do Sul, Braz. F13 80
Palmarito, Ven. D7 84
Palmar Sur, C.R. I11 92
Palmas, Braz. D12 80
Palmas Bellas, Pan. C2 84
Palmas de Monte Alto, Braz. C7 79
Palma Soriano, Cuba D6 94
Palm Bay, Fl., U.S. K6 112
Palm Beach, Fl., U.S. M6 112
Palmdale, Ca., U.S. J7 124
Palm Desert, Ca., U.S. K9 124
Palmeira, Braz. C13 80
Palmeira, C.V. k17 64a
Palmeira das Missões, Braz. D12 80
Palmeira d'Oeste, Braz. F3 79
Palmeiras, Braz. B8 79
Palmeiras, stm., Braz. C3 79
Palmelo, Braz. D4 79
Palmer, Ak., U.S. F20 100
Palmer, Ma., U.S. E14 108
Palmer, Ms., U.S. K7 114
Palmer, Ne., U.S. J9 118
Palmer, Tn., U.S. G11 114
Palmer, Tx., U.S. G10 116
Palmer, sci., B.A.T. B12 73
Palmer Lake, Co., U.S. F12 120
Palmer Land, reg., Ant. C12 73
Palmerston, Ont., Can. G15 110
Palmerston, N.Z. F3 72
Palmerston, Cape, c., Austl. C8 70
Palmerston North, N.Z. D5 72
Palmerton, Pa., U.S. G11 108
Palmetto, Fl., U.S. L4 112
Palmetto, Ga., U.S. F2 112
Palmetto, La., U.S. L5 114
Palmi, Italy K10 18
Palminópolis, Braz. D3 79
Palmira, Arg. G4 80
Palmira, Col. F4 84
Palmira, Cuba C4 94
Palmira, Ec. I3 84
Palmitas, Ur. G10 80
Palmitos, Braz. D12 80
Palm Springs, Ca., U.S. K9 124
Palmyra, Il., U.S. C7 114
Palmyra, Mo., U.S. C5 114
Palmyra, N.Y., U.S. D9 108
Palmyra, Pa., U.S. G10 108
Palmyra, Va., U.S. B8 112
Palmyra, hist., Syria D5 48
Palmyra Atoll, atoll, Oc. H23 126
Palmyra see Tudmur, Syria D5 48
Palo Alto, Ca., U.S. G3 124
Palo Flechado Pass, N.M., U.S. H11 120
Paloich, Sud. L7 60
Palomar Mountain, mtn., Ca., U.S. K9 124
Palomas Viejo, Mex. B6 90
Palo Negro, Ven. B9 84
Palo Pinto, Tx., U.S. G8 116
Palopo, Indon. F7 38
Palora, stm., Ec. H3 84
Palos, Cabo de, c., Spain H11 16
Palo Santo, Arg. C9 80
Palos de la Frontera, Spain H5 16
Palos see Palos de la Frontera, Spain H5 16
Palouse, Wa., U.S. D8 122
Palouse, stm., U.S. D7 122
Palo Verde, Ca., U.S. K11 124
Palo Verde, Parque Nacional, C.R. G9 92
Palpa, Peru F4 82
Palpalá, Arg. C6 80
Palu, Indon. F6 38
Palwal, India F7 44
Pama, Burkina F10 64
Pāmban Island, i., India H5 46
Pambeguwa, Nig. F14 64
Pamekasan, Indon. J16 39a
Pamiers, Fr. I8 14
Pamir, mts., Asia B5 44
Pamlico, stm., N.C., U.S. D10 112
Pamlico Sound, strt., N.C., U.S. D11 112
Pampa, Tx., U.S. D6 116
Pampã, stm., Braz. D8 79
Pampa, reg., Arg. I6 80
Pampa Almirón, Arg. D9 80
Pampacolca, Peru F5 82
Pampa del Chañar, Arg. F4 80
Pampa del Indio, Arg. D9 80
Pampa del Infierno, Arg. D8 80
Pampa de los Guanacos, Arg. D8 80
Pampa Grande, Bol. H9 82
Pampas, Peru E4 82
Pampas, stm., Peru E5 82
Pamplico, S.C., U.S. F7 112
Pamplona, Col. D6 84
Pamplona, Spain C10 16
Pampoenpoort, S. Afr. H6 66
Pamunkey, stm., Va., U.S. B9 112
Pana, Il., U.S. C7 114
Panabá, Mex. G15 90
Panaca, Nv., U.S. G11 124
Panacea, Fl., U.S. I2 112
Panaji (Panjim), India E2 46
Panamá, Braz. E4 79
Panamá, Pan. C3 84
Panama, Il., U.S. C7 114
Panama, Ok., U.S. G2 114
Panamá, prov., Pan. I15 92
Panama (Panamá), ctry., N.A. G8 88
Panamá, Bahía de, b., Pan. C3 84
Panamá, Canal de, Pan. H15 92
Panamá, Golfo de, b., Pan. C3 84
Panamá, Istmo de, Pan. C2 84
Panama City, Fl., U.S. L11 114
Panamá Vieja, hist., Pan. H15 92
Panambi, Braz. E12 80
Panamint Range, mts., Ca., U.S. H8 124
Panao, Peru C3 82
Pančevo, Yugo. E4 20
Pandamatenga, Bots. B7 66
Pan de Azúcar, Ur. H11 80
Pandėlys, Lith. E8 22
Pandharpur, India D3 46
Pāndhurna, India B5 46
Pando, dept., Bol. D8 82
P'andž (Panj), stm., Asia A4 44
Panevėžys, Lith. F7 22
Panfang, China H4 34
Panfilov, Kaz. I14 26
Pangala, Congo B2 58
Pangalanes, Canal des, Madag. Q23 67b
Pangani, Tan. C7 58
Pangburn, Ar., U.S. G5 114
Pangfou see Bengbu, China E10 30
Pangi, Zaire B5 58
Pangkalanbuun, Indon. F5 38
Pangkalpinang, Indon. F4 38
Pangman, Sask., Can. I10 104
Pangnirtung, N.W. Ter., Can. C19 96
Pangong Tso, l., Asia D8 44
Panguitch, Ut., U.S. G4 120
Panhandle, Tx., U.S. D5 116
Panino, Russia E17 22
Pānīpat, India F7 44
Panj (P'andž), stm., Asia B4 44
Panjāb, Afg. C2 44
Panjgūr, Pak. H18 48
Panjim see Panaji, India E2 46
Pankshin, Nig. G14 64
Panlong (Lo), stm., Asia C8 40
P'anmunjŏm, N. Kor. F14 32
Panna, India H9 44
Pannawonica, Austl. D3 68
Panola, Al., U.S. K10 114
Panora, Ia., U.S. J13 118
Panorama, Braz. F3 79
Pansik, Rápido, wtfl, N.A. C9 92
Pantelleria, Isola di, i., Italy M7 18
Pantha, Burma C3 40
Pánuco, Mex. F10 90
Pánuco, stm., Mex. G10 90
Panuke Lake, l., N.S., Can. H9 106
Panxian, China B8 40
Panxidu, China H3 32
Panyam, Nig. G14 64
Panyang, Sud. L5 60
Panyu, China M2 34
Panzós, Guat. B5 92
Pao, stm., Ven. C8 84
Pao, stm., Ven. C10 84
Paola, Italy J11 18
Paola, Ks., U.S. M13 118
Paoli, In., U.S. D10 114
Paonia, Co., U.S. F9 120
Paotow see Baotou, China C8 30
P'aozero, ozero, l., Russia H22 6
Paozi, China A10 32
Pápa, Hung. H17 10
Papagaio, stm., Braz. I11 84
Papagayo, Golfo de, b., C.R. G9 92
Papaikou, Hi., U.S. r18 125a
Papantla [de Olarte], Mex. G11 90
Papenburg, Ger. B7 10
Papilė, Lith. E5 22
Papillion, Ne., U.S. J11 118
Papineau-Labelle, Réserve, Que., Can. B11 108
Paposo, Chile C3 80
Papua, Gulf of, b., Pap. N. Gui. m15 68a
Papua New Guinea, ctry., Oc. m15 68a
Papudo, Chile G3 80
Papun, Burma E4 40
Papunáua, stm., Col. G7 84
Papurí, stm., S.A. G7 84
Paquera, C.R. H10 92
Pará, state, Braz. B13 82
Pará, stm., Braz. E9 74
Pará, stm., Braz. E6 79
Paraburdoo, Austl. D3 68
Paracari, stm., Braz. A13 82
Paracas, Bahía de, b., Peru E3 82
Paracas, Península de, pen., Peru E3 82
Paracatu, Braz. D5 79
Paracatu, stm., Braz. D6 79
Paracatu, stm., Braz. D6 79
Paracel Islands see Xisha Qundao, is., China B5 38
Parachilna, Austl. H3 70
Paracho de Verduzco, Mex. H8 90
Parachute, Co., U.S. E8 120
Paraćin, Yugo. F5 20
Parád, Hung. H20 10
Parada, Punta, c., Peru F4 82
Paradas, Spain H6 16
Paradise, Guy. D14 84
Paradise, Ca., U.S. E4 124
Paradise, Mt., U.S. C11 122
Paradise, Nv., U.S. H10 124
Paradise, Tx., U.S. F9 116
Paradise Hill, Sask., Can. E5 104
Paradise Valley, Az., U.S. K5 120
Paradise Valley, Nv., U.S. C8 124
Parado, stm., Braz. D14 82
Paragonah, Ut., U.S. G4 120
Paragould, Ar., U.S. F6 114
Paraguá, stm., Bol. E11 82
Paragua, stm., Ven. D11 84
Paraguaçu, stm., Braz. F10 74
Paraguaçu, stm., Braz. B9 79
Paraguaçu Paulista, Braz. G3 79
Paraguaipoa, Ven. B7 84
Paraguaná, Península de, pen., Ven. B8 84
Paraguarí, Para. C10 80
Paraguarí, dept., Para. D10 80
Paraguay, ctry., S.A. A5 78
Paraguay (Paraguai), stm., S.A. G9 74
Paraíba do Sul, stm., Braz. F7 79
Paraíso, Braz. E2 79
Paraíso, C.R. H11 92
Paraíso, Mex. H13 90
Paraiso, Pan. C3 84
Paraíso do Norte, Braz. G2 79
Paraisópolis, Braz. G6 79
Paraitinga, stm., Braz. G6 79
Parakou, Benin G11 64
Paramakkudi, India H5 46
Paramaribo, Sur. B7 76
Paramirim, Braz. B7 79
Paramirim, stm., Braz. B7 79
Paramonga, Peru D3 82
Paramušir, ostrov, i., Russia G23 28
Paran, Naḥal (Wādī al-Jirāfī), val. H3 50
Paraná, Arg. F8 80
Paranã, Braz. B5 79
Paraná, state, Braz. C13 80
Paranã, stm., Braz. B5 79
Paraná, stm., S.A. H9 74
Paranaguá, Braz. C14 80
Paranaguá, Baía de, b., Braz. C14 80
Paranaíba, Braz. E3 79
Paranaíba, stm., Braz. E3 79
Paranaíta, stm., Braz. C13 82
Paranam, Sur. B7 76
Paranapanema, stm., Braz. G3 79
Paranapiacaba, Serra do, mts., Braz. C14 80
Paranavaí, Braz. G2 79
Paranhos, Braz. G1 79
Paranoá, Lago do, l., Braz. C5 79
Paraopeba, Braz. E6 79
Parapara, Ven. C9 84
Parapetí, stm., Bol. H10 82
Paras, Peru E4 82
Paratinga, Braz. B7 79
Parauari, stm., Braz. J13 84
Paraúna, Braz. D3 79
Paray-le-Monial, Fr. F11 14
Pārbati, stm., India H7 44
Pārbatipur, Bngl. H13 44
Parbhani, India C4 46
Parchment, Mi., U.S. H10 110
Parczew, Pol. D22 10
Pardeeville, Wi., U.S. G6 110
Pardes Hanna-Karkur, Isr. D3 50
Pardo, stm., Braz. C6 79
Pardo, stm., Braz. F2 79
Pardo, stm., Braz. F4 79
Pardo, stm., Braz. G4 79
Pardo, stm., Braz. C9 79
Pardo, stm., Braz. E12 80
Pardubice, Czech. E15 10
Parecis, Braz. F13 82
Parecis, stm., Braz. E13 82
Parecis, Chapada dos, mts., Braz. F12 82
Paredón, Mex. E9 90
Paren', stm., Russia E24 28
Parent, Que., Can. G18 96
Parepare, Indon. F6 38
Parera, Arg. H6 80
Parfino, Russia D14 22
Paria, stm., U.S. H5 120
Paria, Gulf of, b. B11 84
Paria, Península de, pen., Ven. B11 84
Pariaguán, Ven. C10 84
Pariaman, Indon. O6 40
Pariamanu, stm., Peru E6 82
Pariči, Bela. I12 22
Paricutín, vol., Mex. H8 90
Parida, Isla, i., Pan. I12 92
Parika, Guy. D13 84
Parima, stm., Braz. F11 84
Parima, Sierra, mts., S.A. F10 84
Pariñas, Punta, c., Peru J2 84
Parîngu Mare, Vîrful, mtn., Rom. D7 20
Parintins, Braz. I14 84
Pariquera-Açu, Braz. C15 80
Paris, Ont., Can. G15 110
Paris, Fr. D9 14
Paris, Ar., U.S. G3 114
Paris, Id., U.S. H14 122
Paris, Il., U.S. C9 114
Paris, Ky., U.S. I2 108
Paris, Me., U.S. C16 108
Paris, Mo., U.S. C4 114
Paris, Tn., U.S. F8 114
Paris, Tx., U.S. F11 116
Parismina, C.R. G11 92
Parismina, stm., C.R. G11 92
Parita, Bahía de, b., Pan. I14 92
Parit Buntar, Malay. L6 40
Park, stm., N.D., U.S. C10 118
Parkano, Fin. J18 6
Park City, Ks., U.S. N10 118
Park City, Mt., U.S. E17 122
Park City, Ut., U.S. D5 120
Parkdale, P.E.I., Can. F10 106
Parkdale, Or., U.S. E4 122
Parker, Az., U.S. J2 120
Parker, Co., U.S. L3 118
Parker, Fl., U.S. L11 114
Parker, S.D., U.S. H10 118
Parker, Cape, c., N.W. Ter., Can. A17 96
Parker City, In., U.S. B11 114
Parker Dam, Ca., U.S. J11 124
Parkersburg, Il., U.S. D8 114
Parkersburg, Ia., U.S. H3 110
Parkersburg, W.V., U.S. H5 108
Parkers Prairie, Mn., U.S. E12 118
Parkes, Austl. I8 70
Park Falls, Wi., U.S. E5 110
Park Forest, Il., U.S. I8 110
Parkhill, Ont., Can. G14 110
Parkin, Ar., U.S. G6 114
Parkland, Wa., U.S. C3 122
Park Range, mts., Co., U.S. D10 120
Park Rapids, Mn., U.S. E12 118
Park River, N.D., U.S. C10 118
Parkrose, Or., U.S. E3 122
Parksley, Va., U.S. B11 112
Parkston, S.D., U.S. H10 118
Parksville, B.C., Can. H10 102
Parkville, Md., U.S. H10 108
Parkville, Mo., U.S. C2 114
Parkwater, Wa., U.S. C8 122
Parla, Spain E8 16
Parlākimidi, India C8 46
Parle, Lac qui, l., Mn., U.S. F11 118
Parli, India C4 46
Parma, Italy E5 18
Parma, Id., U.S. G9 122
Parma, Mo., U.S. F7 114
Parma, Oh., U.S. F5 108
Parnaguá, Braz. F10 76
Parnaíba, Braz. D10 76
Parnaíba, stm., Braz. D10 76
Parnassós, mtn., Grc. K6 20
Pärnu, Est. C7 22
Pärnu-Jaagupi, Est. C7 22
Paro, Bhu. G13 44
Paromaj, Russia G20 28
Paroo, stm., Austl. H5 70
Páros, i., Grc. L9 20
Parowan, Ut., U.S. G4 120
Parpaillon, mts., Fr. H13 14
Parpan, Switz. E12 13
Parral, Chile I3 80
Parral, stm., Mex. D7 90
Parral see Hidalgo del Parral, Mex. D7 90
Parramatta, Austl. I9 70
Parras de la Fuente, Mex. E8 90
Parrish, Al., U.S. I9 114
Parrish, Fl., U.S. L4 112
Parrita, C.R. H10 92
Parrita, stm., C.R. H10 92
Parrsboro, N.S., Can. G9 106
Parry, Cape, c., N.W. Ter., Can. B8 96
Parry, Mount, mtn., B.C., Can. E6 102
Parry Bay, b., N.W. Ter., Can. C16 96
Parry Channel, strt., N.W. Ter., Can. B9 86
Parry Peninsula, pen., N.W. Ter., Can. B32 100
Parry Sound, Ont., Can. E15 110
Parsberg, Ger. F11 10
Parseier Spitze, mtn., Aus. D13 13
Parshall, N.D., U.S. D5 118
Parsnip, stm., B.C., Can. C12 102
Parsons, Ks., U.S. N12 118
Parsons, Tn., U.S. G8 114
Parsons, W.V., U.S. H7 108
Parson's Pond, Newf., Can. B16 106
Parsons Pond, l., Newf., Can. B16 106
Pärsti, Est. C8 22
Partanna, Italy L7 18
Parthenay, Fr. F6 14
Partinico, Italy K8 18
Partizansk, Russia I18 28
Partridge Crop Lake, l., Man., Can. C17 104
Partridge Point, c., Newf., Can. B17 106
Paru, stm., Braz. D8 76
Parú, stm., Ven. E10 84
Paru de Oeste, stm., Braz. D7 76
Paruro, Peru E6 82
Pārvatīpuram, India C7 46
Paryang, China E10 44
Pasaco, Guat. D4 92
Pasadena, Newf., Can. C16 106
Pasadena, Ca., U.S. J7 124
Pasadena, Tx., U.S. J11 116
Pasado, Cabo, c., Ec. H2 84
Pasaje, Ec. I3 84
Pasaje, stm., Arg. C6 80
Pa Sak, stm., Thai. G6 40
Pasawng, Burma E4 40
Pascagoula, Ms., U.S. L8 114
Pascagoula, stm., Ms., U.S. L8 114
Paşcani, Rom. B10 20
Pasco, Wa., U.S. D6 122
Pasco, dept., Peru D4 82
Pascoag, R.I., U.S. F15 108
Pascua, Isla de (Easter Island), i., Chile G4 74
Pas-de-Calais, dept., Fr. B9 14
Pasewalk, Ger. B14 10
Pasig, Phil. N19 39b
P'asina, stm., Russia C9 28
Pasinler, Tur. B6 48
P'asino, ozero, l., Russia D9 28
P'asinskij zaliv, b., Russia C14 26
Pasir Puteh, Malay. L7 40
Pasley Bay, b., N.W. Ter., Can. B13 96
Pasmore, stm., Austl. H3 70
Pasni, Pak. I17 48
Paso del Cerro, Ur. F11 80
Paso de los Libres, Arg. E10 80
Paso de los Toros, Ur. G10 80
Paso de Patria, Para. D9 80
Paso Hondo, Mex. J13 90
Pasorapa, Bol. H9 82
Paso Robles, Ca., U.S. I5 124
Pasqua Indian Reserve, Sask., Can. H10 104
Pasquel, Punta, c., Mex. E4 90
Pasquia Hills, hills, Sask., Can. E12 104
Pasquotank, stm., N.C., U.S. C10 112
Pasrūr, Pak. D6 44
Passadumkeag, Me., U.S. B18 108
Passage Point, c., N.W. Ter., Can. B9 96
Passaic, N.J., U.S. G12 108
Passamaquoddy Bay, b., N.A. G7 106
Passau, Ger. G13 10
Passero, Capo, c., Italy M10 18
Pass Island, Newf., Can. E17 106
Paššskij Perevoz, Russia A15 22
Passo Fundo, Braz. E12 80
Passos, Braz. F5 79
Pastaza, prov., Ec. H4 84
Pastaza, stm., S.A. J4 84
Pastecho, stm., Alta., Can. B20 102
Pasteur, Lac, l., Que., Can. B7 106
Pasto, Col. G4 84
Pastora Peak, mtn., Az., U.S. H7 120
Pasuruan, Indon. J16 39a
Pasvalys, Lith. E7 22
Pásztó, Hung. H19 10
Patacamaya, Bol. G8 82
Patagonia, Az., U.S. M6 120
Patagonia, reg., Arg. F3 78
Pātan, India I5 44
Patargān, Daqq-e, sw., Asia E16 48
Pataz, Peru B3 82
Patchewollock, Austl. J5 70
Patchogue, N.Y., U.S. G13 108
Patea, N.Z. C5 72
Pategi, Nig. G12 64
Pate Island, i., Kenya B8 58
Patensie, S. Afr. I7 66
Paterna, Spain F11 16
Paternion, Aus. I13 10
Paternò, Italy L9 18
Pateros, Wa., U.S. B6 122
Paterson, S. Afr. I7 66
Paterson, N.J., U.S. G12 108
Pathānkot, India D6 44
Pathein (Bassein), Burma F3 40
Pathfinder Reservoir, res., Wy., U.S. B10 120
Pathiong, Sud. N6 60
Patía, Col. F4 84
Patía, stm., Col. F3 84
Patiāla, India E7 44
P'atigorsk, Russia I6 26
Pătîrlagele, Rom. D10 20
Pativilca, Peru D3 82
Pativilca, stm., Peru D3 82
Pātkai Range, mts., Asia G16 44
Patna, India H11 44
Pato Branco, Braz. D12 80
Patoka, Il., U.S. D7 114
Patoka, stm., In., U.S. D9 114
Patos, Braz. E11 76
Patos, Lagoa dos, b., Braz. F13 80
Patos, Río de los, stm., Arg. F4 80
Patos, Rio dos, stm., Braz. E13 82
Patos de Minas, Braz. E5 79
P'atovskij, Russia G19 22
Patquía, Arg. F5 80
Pátrai, Grc. K5 20
Patraïkós Kólpos, b., Grc. K5 20
Patras see Pátrai, Grc. K5 20
Patrocínio, Braz. E5 79
Patrocínio Paulista, Braz. F5 79
Pattada, Italy I4 18
Pattani, Thai. K6 40
Patten, Me., U.S. B18 108
Patterson, Ca., U.S. G4 124
Patterson, Ga., U.S. H4 112
Patterson, La., U.S. M5 114
Patterson, Mount, mtn., Yukon, Can. D27 100
Patti, Italy K9 18
Pattison, Ms., U.S. K6 114
Patton, Pa., U.S. G8 108
Pattonsburg, Mo., U.S. B2 114
Pattullo, Mount, mtn., B.C., Can. H30 100
Patuca, stm., Hond. B10 92
Patuca, Punta, c., Hond. B10 92
Patul, Cerro, mtn., Ec. I3 84
Patulul, Guat. C3 92
Patuxent, stm., Md., U.S. I10 108
Pátzcuaro, Mex. H9 90
Patzicía, Guat. C4 92
Patzún, Guat. C3 92
Pau, Fr. I6 14
Pau Brasil, Braz. C9 79
Paucarbamba, Peru E4 82
Paucarpata, Peru G6 82
Paucartambo, Peru E6 82
Pauini, Braz. B8 82
Pauini, stm., Braz. B8 82
Pauini, stm., Braz. H11 84
Pauk, Burma D3 40
Paul, Id., U.S. H12 122
Paul, Lac à, l., Que., Can. C3 106
Paulaya, stm., Hond. B9 92
Paulding, Ms., U.S. J7 114
Paulding, Oh., U.S. F2 108
Paulhan, Fr. I10 14
Paulicéia, Braz. F3 79
Paulina Peak, mtn., Or., U.S. G4 122
Pauline, Mount, mtn., Can. D15 102
Paulistana, Braz. E10 76
Paulistas, Braz. E7 79
Paullina, Ia., U.S. I12 118
Paull Lake, l., Sask., Can. B10 104
Paulo Afonso, Braz. E11 76
Paulo de Faria, Braz. F4 79
Pauloff Harbor (Pavlof Harbor), Ak., U.S. I13 100
Paulpietersburg, S. Afr. F10 66
Pauls Valley, Ok., U.S. E9 116
Paungbyin, Burma B3 40
Paungde, Burma E3 40
Pausa, Peru F5 82
Pausania, Italy I4 18
Paute, Ec. I3 84
Paute, stm., Ec. I3 84
Pauto, stm., Col. E7 84
Pāveh, Iran D9 48
Pavelec, Russia H22 22
Pavia, Italy D4 18
Pavilion, B.C., Can. G13 102
Pavillion, Wy., U.S. A8 120
Pavilly, Fr. C7 14
Pāvilosta, Lat. E4 22
Pavlikeni, Bul. F9 20
Pavlodar, Kaz. G7 28
Pavlovo, Russia F26 22
Pavlovsk, Russia B13 22
Pavlovskij Posad, Russia F21 22
Pavo, Ga., U.S. H2 112
Pavón, Col. F6 84
Paw Creek, N.C., U.S. D6 112
Pawhuska, Ok., U.S. C10 116
Pawnee, Il., U.S. C7 114
Pawnee, Ok., U.S. C10 116
Pawnee, stm., Ks., U.S. M8 118
Pawnee City, Ne., U.S. K11 118
Pawnee Rock, Ks., U.S. M9 118
Paw Paw, Il., U.S. I7 110
Paw Paw, Mi., U.S. H10 110
Paw Paw, W.V., U.S. H8 108
Paw Paw Lake, Mi., U.S. H9 110
Pawtucket, R.I., U.S. F15 108
Paxton, Il., U.S. J7 110
Paxton, Ne., U.S. J6 118
Paya, Hond. B9 92
Payakumbuh, Indon. O6 40
Payas, Cerro, mtn., Hond. B9 92
Payerne, Switz. E6 13
Payette, Id., U.S. F9 122
Payette, stm., Id., U.S. G9 122
Payne, Oh., U.S. F2 108
Payne, Lac, l., Que., Can. E18 96
Payne Bay, b., Can. D19 96
Paynesville, Mn., U.S. F13 118
Paynton, Sask., Can. E6 104
Paysandú, Ur. H9 74
Paysandú, Ur. G9 80
Payson, Az., U.S. J5 120
Payson, Il., U.S. C5 114
Payson, Ut., U.S. D5 120
Payún, Cerro, mtn., Arg. I4 80
Paz, stm., N.A. D4 92
Pazardžik, Bul. G8 20
Pazarköy, Tur. J11 20
Paz de Ariporo, Col. E7 84
Paz de Río, Col. E6 84
P'ažijeva Sel'ga, Russia K24 6
Pazin, Cro. D8 18
Pazña, Bol. H8 82
Pea, stm., U.S. K10 114
Peabody, Ks., U.S. M10 118
Peabody, Ma., U.S. E16 108
Peace, stm., Can. E10 96
Peace, stm., Fl., U.S. L5 112
Peace Canyon Dam, B.C., Can. B13 102
Peace River, Alta., Can. A17 102
Peach Creek, W.V., U.S. J5 108
Peachland, B.C., Can. H15 102
Peach Orchard, Ga., U.S. F4 112
Peach Springs, Az., U.S. I3 120
Peacock Hills, hills, N.W. Ter., Can. C11 96
Peak Hill, Austl. E3 68
Peak Hill, Austl. I8 70
Peale, Mount, mtn., Ut., U.S. F7 120
Pearce, Az., U.S. M7 120
Pearisburg, Va., U.S. B6 112
Pearl, Il., U.S. C6 114
Pearl, Ms., U.S. J6 114
Pearl, stm., U.S. L7 114
Pearland, Tx., U.S. J11 116
Pearl Harbor, b., Hi., U.S. p16 125a
Pearl Peak, mtn., Nv., U.S. D10 124
Pearl River, La., U.S. L7 114
Pearl River, N.Y., U.S. F12 108
Pearsall, Tx., U.S. K7 116
Pearse Island, i., B.C., Can. C4 102
Pearsoll Peak, mtn., Or., U.S. H2 122
Pearson, Ga., U.S. H4 112
Pearson Lake, l., Man., Can. B17 104
Pearston, S. Afr. I7 66
Peary Land, reg., Grnld. A16 86
Pebane, Moz. E7 58
Pebas, Peru I7 84
Peć, Yugo. G4 20
Pecan Bayou, stm., Tx., U.S. H7 116
Pecan Gap, Tx., U.S. F11 116
Peçanha, Braz. E7 79
Peças, Ilha das, i., Braz. C14 80
Pecatonica, Il., U.S. H6 110
Pecatonica, stm., U.S. H6 110
Pečenežin, Ukr. A8 20
Pečenga, Russia D4 26
Pechora see Pečora, stm., Russia D8 26
Pecica, Rom. C5 20
Peck, Mi., U.S. G13 110
Pečora, Russia D9 26
Pečora, stm., Russia D8 26
Pečorskaja guba, b., Russia D8 26
Pečorskoje more, Russia D8 26
Pečory, Russia D10 22
Pecos, N.M., U.S. I11 120
Pecos, Tx., U.S. H3 116
Pecos, stm., U.S. J5 116
Pécs, Hung. I18 10
Pedasí, Pan. D2 84
Peddāpuram, India D7 46
Pedder, Lake, res., Austl. N7 70
Pedernales, Arg. H9 80
Pedernales, Dom. Rep. E9 94
Pedernales, Ven. C11 84
Pedernales, stm., Tx., U.S. I7 116
Pedernales, Salar de, pl., Chile D4 80
Pedra Azul, Braz. D8 79
Pedra Grande, Recifes da, rf., Braz. D9 79
Pedra Lume, C.V. k17 64a
Pedras, Braz. I14 84
Pedras Negras, Braz. E10 82
Pedraza, Col. B5 84
Pedregal, Pan. C1 84
Pedregal, Ven. B7 84
Pedregulho, Braz. F5 79
Pedreiras, Braz. D10 76
Pedriceña, Mex. E8 90
Pedro Afonso, Braz. E9 76
Pedro Cays, is., Jam. F6 94
Pedrógão Grande, Port. F3 16
Pedro Gomes, Braz. E1 79
Pedro II, Braz. D10 76
Pedro II, Ilha, i., S.A. G9 84
Pedro Juan Caballero, Para. B11 80
Pedro Leopoldo, Braz. E6 79
Pedro Luro, Arg. J7 80
Pedro Muñoz, Spain F9 16
Pedro Osório, Braz. F12 80
Pedro R. Fernández, Arg. E9 80
Peebinga, Austl. J4 70
Peebles, Oh., U.S. I3 108
Pee Dee, stm., U.S. D6 112
Peekskill, N.Y., U.S. F13 108
Peel, I. of Man G9 8
Peel, stm., Can. C27 100
Peel Channel, mth., N.W. Ter., Can. C27 100
Pe Ell, Wa., U.S. D2 122
Peel Point, c., N.W. Ter., Can. B10 96
Peel Sound, strt., N.W. Ter., Can. B13 96
Peene, stm., Ger. B13 10
Peepeekisis Indian Reserve, Sask., Can. H11 104
Peerless, Mt., U.S. B20 122
Peers, Alta., Can. D18 102
Peesane, Sask., Can. F11 104
Peetz, Co., U.S. K4 118
Pegasus Bay, b., N.Z. E4 72
Pegnitz, Ger. F11 10
Pegnitz, stm., Ger. F11 10
Pego, Spain G11 16
Pegu see Bago, Burma F4 40
Peguis Indian Reserve, Man., Can. G17 104
Pegu Yoma, mts., Burma E3 40
Pehčevo, Mac. H6 20
Pehuajó, Arg. H8 80
Peigan Indian Reserve, Alta., Can. H21 102
Peikang, Tai. L9 34
Peine, Ger. C10 10
Peipus, Lake see Čudskoje ozero, l., Eur. C10 22
Peissenberg, Ger. H11 10
Peixe, Braz. B4 79
Peixe, Rio do, stm., Braz. C3 79
Peixe, Rio do, stm., Braz. G3 79
Peixian, China E10 30
Peiziyan, China H3 32
Pekalongan, Indon. J14 39a
Pekanbaru, Indon. N6 40
Pekin, Il., U.S. J6 110
Pekin, In., U.S. D10 114
Peking see Beijing, China D4 32
Peklino, Russia H16 22
Pelabuhan Kelang, Malay. M6 40
Pelagie, Isole, is., Italy N7 18
Pelahatchie, Ms., U.S. J7 114
Pełczyce, Pol. B15 10
Peleaga, Vîrful, mtn., Rom. D6 20

Name	Map Ref.	Page
Pelechuco, Bol.	F7	82
Pelée, Montagne, mtn., Mart.	G14	94
Pelee, Point, c., Ont., Can.	I13	110
Pelham, Al., U.S.	I10	114
Pelham, Ga., U.S.	H2	112
Pelhřimov, Czech.	F15	10
Pelican, stm., Mn., U.S.	E11	118
Pelican Bay, b., Man., Can.	F14	104
Pelican Lake, Wi., U.S.	E6	110
Pelican Lake, l., Alta., Can.	B21	102
Pelican Lake, l., Man., Can.	E18	104
Pelican Lake, l., Man., Can.	I15	104
Pelican Lake, l., Man., Can.	F14	104
Pelican Lake, l., Sask., Can.	H8	104
Pelican Lake, l., Sask., Can.	C11	104
Pelican Mountain, mtn., Alta., Can.	B21	102
Pelican Narrows, Sask., Can.	C12	104
Pelican Rapids, Man., Can.	F14	104
Pelican Rapids, Mn., U.S.	E11	118
Pelileo, Ec.	H3	84
Pelister, mtn., Mac.	H5	20
Pelkosenniemi, Fin.	H20	6
Pella, Ia., U.S.	I3	110
Pell City, Al., U.S.	I10	114
Pellegrini, Arg.	I7	80
Pellegrini, Lago, l., Arg.	J4	80
Pelletier Lake, l., Man., Can.	B17	104
Pello, Fin.	H19	6
Pellston, Mi., U.S.	E11	110
Pelly, Sask., Can.	G13	104
Pelly, stm., Yukon, Can.	E26	100
Pelly Bay, b., N.W. Ter., Can.	C14	96
Pelly Crossing, Yukon, Can.	E26	100
Pelly Lake, l., N.W. Ter., Can.	C12	96
Pelly Mountains, mts., Yukon, Can.	F28	100
Pelón, Cerro, mtn., Mex.	G10	90
Peloncillo Mountains, mts., U.S.	L7	120
Peloponnesos see Pelopónnisos, pen., Grc.	L6	20
Pelopónnisos, pen., Grc.	L6	20
Pelotas, Braz.	F12	80
Pelotas, stm., Braz.	D13	80
Pel'ušn'a, Russia	C15	22
Pemadumcook Lake, l., Me., U.S.	B18	108
Pemalang, Indon.	J14	39a
Pematangsiantar, Indon.	M5	40
Pemba, Moz.	D8	58
Pemba, i., Tan.	C7	58
Pemberton, Austl.	F3	68
Pemberton, B.C., Can.	G12	102
Pembina, N.D., U.S.	C10	118
Pembina, stm., Alta., Can.	C20	102
Pembina, stm., N.A.	I16	104
Pembine, Wi., U.S.	E8	110
Pembroke, Ont., Can.	E18	110
Pembroke, Wales, U.K.	J9	8
Pembroke, Ga., U.S.	G5	112
Pembroke, Ky., U.S.	F9	114
Pembroke, Me., U.S.	C19	108
Pembroke, N.C., U.S.	E7	112
Pembroke, Va., U.S.	B5	112
Pembroke, Cape, c., N.W. Ter., Can.	D16	96
Pembroke Pines, Fl., U.S.	M6	112
Pemichigamau Lake, l., Man., Can.	B15	104
Pemigewasset, stm., N.H., U.S.	D15	108
Pemmican Portage, Sask., Can.	E12	104
Pemuco, Chile	I2	80
Pemynoos Indian Reserve, B.C., Can.	G13	102
Peña Barroza, Bol.	J8	82
Peña Blanca, Pan.	I13	92
Penafiel, Port.	D3	16
Peña Gorda, Cerro, mtn., Mex.	G7	90
Penápolis, Braz.	F3	79
Peñaranda de Bracamonte, Spain	E6	16
Pen Argyl, Pa., U.S.	G11	108
Peñarroya-Pueblonuevo, Spain	G6	16
Penas, Golfo de, b., Chile	F2	78
Penasco, N.M., U.S.	H11	120
Peñasco, Rio, stm., N.M., U.S.	L11	120
Pencahue, Chile	H3	80
Pence, Wi., U.S.	D5	110
Pendembu, S.L.	G3	64
Pender, Ne., U.S.	I11	118
Pendjari, stm., Afr.	F7	54
Pendleton, In., U.S.	C11	114
Pendleton, Or., U.S.	E7	122
Pendleton, S.C., U.S.	E4	112
Pend Oreille, stm., N.A.	B8	122
Pend Oreille, Lake, l., Id., U.S.	B9	122
Penedo, Braz.	F11	76
Penedono, Port.	E4	16
Penetanguishene, Ont., Can.	F16	110
Penfield, Pa., U.S.	F8	108
Penganga, stm., India	C5	46
Penge, S. Afr.	E10	66
P'enghu Ch'üntao (Pescadores), is., Tai.	L8	34
P'enghu Shuitao, strt., Tai.	L8	34
Pengkou, China	J5	34
Penglai (Dengzhou), China	F8	32
Pengshui, China	F8	30
Penguin, Austl.	M7	70
Pengxian, China	E7	30
Penha, Braz.	D14	80
Penhold, Alta., Can.	E21	102
Penhold, Canadian Forces Base, mil., Alta., Can.	E21	102
Peniche, Port.	F2	16
Penitas, Tx., U.S.	M8	116
Penjamillo [de Degollado], Mex.	G9	90
Pennant Point, c., N.S., Can.	H10	106
Pennant Station, Sask., Can.	H6	104
Pennask Lake, l., B.C., Can.	G14	102
Pennask Mountain, mtn., B.C., Can.	H14	102
Penne, Italy	G8	18
Penn Hills, Pa., U.S.	G7	108
Pennines, mts., Eng., U.K.	G11	8
Pennines, Alpes, mts., Eur.	C2	18
Pennington Gap, Va., U.S.	C3	112
Pennsboro, W.V., U.S.	H6	108
Penns Grove, N.J., U.S.	H11	108
Pennsylvania, state, U.S.	C11	98
Penny, B.C., Can.	D13	102
Penn Yan, N.Y., U.S.	E9	108
Pennycutaway, stm., Man., Can.	B21	104
Penny Ice Cap, N.W. Ter., Can.	C19	96
Penny Strait, strt., N.W. Ter., Can.	A13	96
Peno, Russia	E15	22
Penobscot, stm., Me., U.S.	B18	108
Penobscot Bay, b., Me., U.S.	C18	108
Penola, Austl.	K4	70
Peñón Blanco, Mex.	E7	90
Penong, Austl.	F6	68
Penonomé, Pan.	C2	84
Penrith, Austl.	I9	70
Pensacola, Fl., U.S.	L9	114
Pensacola Bay, b., Fl., U.S.	L9	114
Pensacola Mountains, mts., Ant.	D1	73
Pensaukee, stm., Wi., U.S.	F7	110
Pense, Sask., Can.	H9	104
Pensilvania, Col.	E5	84
Pentagon Mountain, mtn., Mt., U.S.	C12	122
Pentecôte, stm., Que., Can.	B6	106
Pentecôte, Lac, l., Que., Can.	C6	106
Penticton, B.C., Can.	H15	102
Penticton Indian Reserve, B.C., Can.	H15	102
Pentland, Austl.	C6	70
Pentland Firth, strt., Scot., U.K.	C10	8
Pentwater, Mi., U.S.	G9	110
Pènwègon, Burma	E4	40
Penwell, Tx., U.S.	H4	116
Penza, Russia	G7	26
Penzance, Eng., U.K.	K8	8
Penzberg, Ger.	H11	10
Penžina, stm., Russia	E25	28
Penžinskaja guba, b., Russia	E24	28
Peoria, Az., U.S.	K4	120
Peoria, Il., U.S.	J6	110
Peoria Heights, Il., U.S.	J6	110
Peotone, Il., U.S.	I8	110
Pepaw, stm., Sask., Can.	F12	104
Pepel, S.L.	G3	64
Peper, Sud.	N7	60
Pepin, Wi., U.S.	F3	110
Pepin, Lake, l., U.S.	F3	110
Pequot Lakes, Mn., U.S.	D1	110
Perabumulih, Indon.	F3	38
Perak, stm., Malay.	L6	40
Peralillo, Chile	H3	80
Peralta, N.M., U.S.	J10	120
Perämeri (Bottenviken), b., Eur.	I18	6
Percé, Que., Can.	D9	106
Perchtoldsdorf, Aus.	G16	10
Percy Isles, is., Austl.	C9	70
Perdeberg, S. Afr.	G7	66
Perdido, Al., U.S.	K9	114
Perdido, stm., Braz.	I13	82
Perdido, stm., U.S.	L9	114
Perdido, Monte, mtn., Spain	C12	16
Perdido Bay, b., U.S.	L9	114
Perdizes, Braz.	E5	79
Perdu, Lac, l., Que., Can.	B3	106
Perdue, Sask., Can.	F7	104
Perečin, Ukr.	G22	10
Peregonovka, Ukr.	A14	20
Pereira, Col.	E5	84
Pereira Barreto, Braz.	F3	79
Pere Marquette, stm., Mi., U.S.	G10	110
Peremyšl', Russia	G19	22
Perené, stm., Peru	D4	82
Pereslavl'-Zalesskij, Russia	E21	22
Peresypkino Pervoje, Russia	I25	22
Pérez, Arg.	G8	80
Perg, Aus.	G14	10
Pergamino, Arg.	G8	80
Pergine Valsugana, Italy	C6	18
Pergola, Italy	F7	18
Perham, Mn., U.S.	E12	118
Péribonca, stm., Que., Can.	C2	106
Péribonca, Lac, l., Que., Can.	B2	106
Perico, Arg.	C6	80
Pericos, Mex.	E6	90
Peridot, Az., U.S.	K6	120
Périers, Fr.	C5	14
Périgord, hist. reg., Fr.	G7	14
Périgueux, Fr.	G7	14
Perijá, Serranía De, mts., S.A.	B6	84
Periyakulam, India	G4	46
Perkasie, Pa., U.S.	G11	108
Perkins, Ok., U.S.	D9	116
Perkinston, Ms., U.S.	L7	114
Perlas, Archipiélago de las, is., Pan.	C3	84
Perlas, Laguna de, b., Nic.	E11	92
Perlas, Punta de, c., Nic.	E11	92
Perleberg, Ger.	B11	10
Perm', Russia	F9	26
Pernatty Lagoon, l., Austl.	H2	70
Pernik, Bul.	G7	20
Péronne, Fr.	C9	14
Perote, Mex.	H11	90
Peroto, Bol.	F9	82
Perow, B.C., Can.	C8	102
Perpignan, Fr.	J9	14
Perrault Falls, Ont., Can.	H21	104
Perrin, Tx., U.S.	F8	116
Perrine, Fl., U.S.	N6	112
Perris, Ca., U.S.	K8	124
Perro, Laguna del, l., N.M., U.S.	J11	120
Perros, Bahía de, b., Cuba	C5	94
Perry, Fl., U.S.	I3	112
Perry, Ga., U.S.	G3	112
Perry, Ia., U.S.	I1	110
Perry, Ks., U.S.	L12	118
Perry, Mi., U.S.	H11	110
Perry, Mo., U.S.	C5	114
Perry, N.Y., U.S.	E8	108
Perry, Ok., U.S.	C9	116
Perry, Ut., U.S.	C4	120
Perry Lake, res., Ks., U.S.	L12	118
Perrysburg, Oh., U.S.	F3	108
Perrysville, Oh., U.S.	G4	108
Perryton, Tx., U.S.	C6	116
Perryville, Ak., U.S.	I15	100
Perryville, Ar., U.S.	G4	114
Perryville, Ky., U.S.	B2	112
Perryville, Mo., U.S.	E7	114
Peršaj, Bela.	G9	22
Perseverancia, Bol.	F10	82
Persia, Ia., U.S.	J12	118
Persia see Iran, ctry., Asia	C5	42
Persian Gulf (Arabian Gulf), b., Asia	H11	48
Pertek, Tur.	B5	48
Perth, Austl.	F3	68
Perth, Ont., Can.	F19	110
Perth, Scot., U.K.	E10	8
Perth Amboy, N.J., U.S.	G12	108
Perth-Andover, N.B., Can.	F6	106
Pertokar, Eth.	I9	60
Peru, Il., U.S.	I6	110
Peru, In., U.S.	B10	114
Peru, Ne., U.S.	K12	118
Peru, N.Y., U.S.	C13	108
Peru (Perú), ctry., S.A.	E3	76
Peruaçu, stm., Braz.	C6	79
Peru-Chile Trench	G7	74
Perugia, Italy	F7	18
Peruíbe, Braz.	C15	80
Peruípe, stm., Braz.	D9	79
Pervoavgustovskij, Russia	I18	22
Pervomajsk, Ukr.	H4	26
Pervomajskij, Bela.	H8	22
Pervomajskij, Russia	H23	22
Pervoural'sk, Russia	F9	26
Pervyj Kuril'skij proliv, strt., Russia	G23	28
Pes', Russia	C17	22
Pesaro, Italy	F7	18
Pesca, Col.	E6	84
Pescadores, Punta, c., Mex.	F5	90
Pescadores, Punta, c., Peru	G5	82
Pescadores see P'enghu Ch'üntao, is., Tai.	L8	34
Pesčanaja, Ukr.	A13	20
Pesčanka, Ukr.	A12	20
Pesčanoje, Russia	J24	6
Pescara, Italy	G9	18
Pescia, Italy	F5	18
Pesé, Pan.	D2	84
Peseux, Switz.	E6	13
Peshāwar, Pak.	C4	44
Peshtigo, Wi., U.S.	E8	110
Peshtigo, stm., Wi., U.S.	E7	110
Peski, Russia	F21	22
Pesmes, Fr.	E12	14
Pesočenskij, Russia	G19	22
Pesočnoje, Russia	C22	22
Pesočnyj, Russia	A13	22
Peso da Régua, Port.	D4	16
Pespire, Hond.	D7	92
Pesqueira, Braz.	E11	76
Pessac, Fr.	H6	14
Pest, co., Hung.	H19	10
Pest'aki, Russia	E25	22
Peštera, Bul.	G8	20
Pestovo, Russia	C18	22
Petacalco, Bahía, b., Mex.	I8	90
Petaḥ Tiqwa, Isr.	D3	50
Petal, Ms., U.S.	K7	114
Petalcingo, Mex.	I13	90
Petalión, Kólpos, b., Grc.	L8	20
Petaluma, Ca., U.S.	F3	124
Pétange, Lux.	I8	12
Petare, Ven.	B9	84
Petatlán, Mex.	I9	90
Petawawa, Ont., Can.	E18	110
Petén, dept., Guat.	A5	92
Petén Itzá, Lago, l., Guat.	I15	90
Petenwell Lake, res., Wi., U.S.	F6	110
Peterborough, Austl.	I3	70
Peterborough, Ont., Can.	F17	110
Peterborough, Eng., U.K.	I13	8
Peterborough, N.H., U.S.	E15	108
Peterculter, Scot., U.K.	D11	8
Peterhead, Scot., U.K.	D12	8
Peter I Island, i., Ant.	B11	73
Peter Lake, l., N.W. Ter., Can.	D14	96
Peter Lake, l., Sask., Can.	A11	104
Peter Lougheed Provincial Park, Alta., Can.	G19	102
Peterman, Al., U.S.	K9	114
Peter Pond Lake, l., Sask., Can.	C6	104
Peter Pond Lake Indian Reserve, Sask., Can.	C5	104
Petersburg, Ak., U.S.	H28	100
Petersburg, Il., U.S.	B7	114
Petersburg, In., U.S.	D9	114
Petersburg, Mi., U.S.	I12	110
Petersburg, Ne., U.S.	J9	118
Petersburg, Tn., U.S.	G10	114
Petersburg, Tx., U.S.	F5	116
Petersburg, Va., U.S.	B9	112
Petersburg, W.V., U.S.	I7	108
Peterson, Ia., U.S.	I12	118
Pétervására, Hung.	G20	10
Petilia Policastro, Italy	J11	18
Pétionville, Haiti	E8	94
Petit Bois Island, i., U.S.	L8	114
Petitcodiac, N.B., Can.	G8	106
Petitcodiac, stm., N.B., Can.	F9	106
Petite Rivière Noire, Piton de la, mtn., Mrts.	V18	67c
Petit Forte, Newf., Can.	E19	106
Petit-Goâve, Haiti	E8	94
Petit Jean, stm., Ar., U.S.	G3	114
Petit Mécatina, Île du, i., Que., Can.	B14	106
Petitot, stm., Can.	E8	96
Petit-Saint-Bernard, Col du, Eur.	G13	14
Petitsikapau Lake, l., Newf., Can.	F19	96
Petlād, India	I5	44
Petlalcingo, Mex.	H11	90
Peto, Mex.	G15	90
Petorca, Chile	G3	80
Petoskey, Mi., U.S.	E11	110
Petownikip Lake, l., Ont., Can.	F22	104
Petra see Batrā, hist., Jord.	H4	50
Petra Velikogo, zaliv, b., Russia	I18	28
Petre, Point, c., Ont., Can.	G18	110
Petrified Forest National Park, Az., U.S.	J7	120
Petrikov, Bela.	I11	22
Petrila, Rom.	D7	20
Petrinja, Cro.	D11	18
Petrodvorec, Russia	B12	22
Petrokrepost', Russia	B14	22
Petrólea, Col.	C6	84
Petrolia, Ont., Can.	H13	110
Petrolia, Tx., U.S.	E8	116
Petrolina, Braz.	E10	76
Petrolina de Goiás, Braz.	D4	79
Petropavlovsk, Kaz.	G11	26
Petropavlovsk-Kamčatskij, Russia	G23	28
Petrópolis, Braz.	G7	79
Petros, Tn., U.S.	C2	112
Petroşani, Rom.	D7	20
Petrovsk, Russia	G7	26
Petrovskoje, Russia	I23	22
Petrovskoje, Russia	D22	22
Petrovsk-Zabajkal'skij, Russia	G13	28
Petrozavodsk, Russia	E4	26
Petrusburg, S. Afr.	G7	66
Petrus Steyn, S. Afr.	F9	66
Petrusville, S. Afr.	H7	66
Petten, Neth.	C6	12
Pettus, Tx., U.S.	K9	116
Petty Harbour, Newf., Can.	E21	106
Petuchovo, Russia	F11	26
Petuški, Russia	F22	22
Peuerbach, Aus.	G13	10
Pevek, Russia	D26	28
Peykjahlið, Ice.	B5	6a
Pézenas, Fr.	I10	14
Pezinok, Czech.	G17	10
Pfäffikon, Switz.	D10	13
Pfarrkirchen, Ger.	G12	10
Pforzheim, Ger.	G8	10
Pfronten, Ger.	H10	10
Pfungstadt, Ger.	F8	10
Pha-an, Burma	F4	40
Phagwāra, India	E6	44
Phala, Bots.	D8	66
Phalaborwa, S. Afr.	D10	66
Phalodi, India	G5	44
Phalsbourg, Fr.	D14	14
Phaltan, India	D3	46
Phan, Thai.	E5	40
Phangan, Ko, i., Thai.	J6	40
Phangnga, Thai.	J5	40
Phanom Dongrak, Thiu Khao, mts., Asia	G7	40
Phan Rang, Viet.	I10	40
Phan Thiet, Viet.	I10	40
Phariāro, Pak.	G3	44
Pharr, Tx., U.S.	M8	116
Phatthalung, Thai.	K6	40
Phayao, Thai.	E5	40
Pheasant Creek, stm., Sask., Can.	G11	104
Pheba, Ms., U.S.	I8	114
Phelps, N.Y., U.S.	E9	108
Phelps, Wi., U.S.	D6	110
Phenix City, Al., U.S.	G1	112
Phepane, stm., Afr.	E6	66
Phetchabun, Thai.	F6	40
Phetchabun, Thiu Khao, mts., Thai.	F6	40
Phetchaburi, Thai.	H5	40
Phichit, Thai.	F6	40
Philadelphia, Ms., U.S.	J7	114
Philadelphia, N.Y., U.S.	C11	108
Philadelphia, Pa., U.S.	H11	108
Philadelphia, Tn., U.S.	D2	112
Phil Campbell, Al., U.S.	H9	114
Philip, S.D., U.S.	G6	118
Philipp, Ms., U.S.	I6	114
Philippeville, Bel.	H6	12
Philippi, W.V., U.S.	H6	108
Philippi, Lake, l., Austl.	E3	70
Philippines (Pilipinas), ctry., Asia	C7	38
Philippine Sea	G17	126
Philippine Trench	H16	126
Philippolis, S. Afr.	H7	66
Philipsburg, Neth. Ant.	F13	94
Philipsburg, Mt., U.S.	D12	122
Philipsburg, Pa., U.S.	G8	108
Philipstown, S. Afr.	H7	66
Phillip Island, i., Austl.	L6	70
Phillips, Me., U.S.	C16	108
Phillips, Tx., U.S.	D5	116
Phillips, Wi., U.S.	E5	110
Phillipsburg, Ga., U.S.	H3	112
Phillipsburg, Ks., U.S.	L8	118
Phillipsburg, N.J., U.S.	G11	108
Philmont, N.Y., U.S.	E13	108
Philo, Il., U.S.	B8	114
Philo, Oh., U.S.	H5	108
Philomath, Or., U.S.	F2	122
Philpots Island, i., N.W. Ter., Can.	B17	96
Phimai, Thai.	G7	40
Phitsanulok, Thai.	F6	40
Phnom Penh see Phnum Pénh, Camb.	I8	40
Phnum Pénh, Camb.	I8	40
Phoenix, Az., U.S.	K4	120
Phoenix, N.Y., U.S.	D10	108
Phoenix Islands, is., Kir.	I22	126
Phoenixville, Pa., U.S.	G11	108
Phon, Thai.	G7	40
Phôngsali, Laos	D7	40
Phrae, Thai.	E6	40
Phra Nakhon Si Ayutthaya, Thai.	G6	40
Phuket, Thai.	K5	40
Phuket, Ko, i., Thai.	J5	40
Phu Ly, Viet.	D8	40
Phumī Bēng, Camb.	H8	40
Phumi Chhuk, Camb.	I8	40
Phumi Kâmpóng Trâbêk, Camb.	H8	40
Phumi Kaôh Kŏng, Camb.	I7	40
Phumi Sâmraông, Camb.	G7	40
Phumi Srê Rôneām, Camb.	H9	40
Phuoc Binh, Viet.	I9	40
Phu Quoc, Dao, i., Viet.	I8	40
Phu Tho, Viet.	D8	40
Phutthaisong, Thai.	G7	40
Phu Yen, Viet.	D8	40
Piacenza, Italy	D4	18
Piacouadie, Lac, l., Que., Can.	A3	106
Pialba, Austl.	E10	70
Piana, Fr.	L23	15a
Pianoro, Italy	E6	18
Piapot, Sask., Can.	I5	104
Piapot Indian Reserve, Sask., Can.	H10	104
Piaseczno, Pol.	C21	10
Piashti, Lac, l., Que., Can.	B11	106
Piatã, Braz.	B8	79
Piatra-Neamţ, Rom.	C10	20
Piauí, stm., Braz.	D8	79
Piaus, stm., Braz.	B4	79
Piave, stm., Italy	D7	18
Piaxtla, stm., Mex.	E7	90
Piazza Armerina, Italy	L9	18
Pibor, stm., Afr.	G7	56
Pibor Post, Sud.	N7	60
Pibroch, Alta., Can.	C21	102
Pica, Chile	I7	82
Picacho, Az., U.S.	L5	120
Picardie, hist. reg., Fr.	C9	14
Picayune, Ms., U.S.	L7	114
Piccadilly, Newf., Can.	D15	106
Pichana, stm., Peru	I7	84
Pichanal, Arg.	B6	80
Picher, Ok., U.S.	C12	116
Pichilemu, Chile	H2	80
Pichimá, Col.	E4	84
Pichi-Mahuida, Arg.	J6	80
Pichincha, prov., Ec.	H3	84
Pichis, stm., Peru	D4	82
Pichucalco, Mex.	I13	90
Pickardville, Alta., Can.	C21	102
Pickens, Ms., U.S.	J7	114
Pickens, S.C., U.S.	E4	112
Pickens, W.V., U.S.	I6	108
Pickensville, Al., U.S.	I8	114
Pickerel Lake, l., Man., Can.	F15	104
Pickering, Ont., Can.	G16	110
Pickford, Mi., U.S.	D11	110
Pickle Crow, Ont., Can.	F14	96
Pickstown, S.D., U.S.	H9	118
Pickton, Tx., U.S.	F11	116
Pickwick Lake, res., U.S.	H8	114
Pico, i., Port.	k19	62a
Pico, Ponta do, mtn., Port.	k19	62a
Pico de Orizaba, Parque Nacional, Mex.	H11	90
Picos, Braz.	E10	76
Picota, Peru	B3	82
Picton, Austl.	J9	70
Picton, Ont., Can.	F18	110
Picton, N.Z.	D5	72
Picton, Isla, i., Chile	H3	78
Pictou, N.S., Can.	G11	106
Pictou Island, i., N.S., Can.	G11	106
Picture Butte, Alta., Can.	H22	102
Pidálion, Akrotírion, c., Cyp.	D3	48
Pidurutalagala, mtn., Sri L.	I6	46
Piedecuesta, Col.	D6	84
Piedicroce, Fr.	L24	15a
Piedmont, Al., U.S.	I11	114
Piedmont, Mo., U.S.	E6	114
Piedmont, S.C., U.S.	E4	112
Piedra, C.R.	H11	92
Piedra Roja, Pan.	I13	92
Piedras, Punta, c., Arg.	H10	80
Piedras, Punta, c., Ven.	B12	84
Piedras Blancas, Arg.	F9	80
Piedras Coloradas, Ur.	G10	80
Piedras Negras, Guat.	I14	90
Piedras Negras, Mex.	C9	90
Piedras Negras, hist., Guat.	I14	90
Piedra Sola, Ur.	G10	80
Pieksämäki, Fin.	J20	6
Pielavesi, Fin.	J20	6
Pielinen, l., Fin.	J21	6
Piemonte, prov., Italy	E2	18
Piendamó, Col.	F4	84
Pienza, Italy	F6	18
Pierce, Co., U.S.	D12	120
Pierce, Id., U.S.	D10	122
Pierce, Ne., U.S.	I10	118
Pierce City, Mo., U.S.	F2	114
Pierce Lake, l., Can.	D22	104
Pierce Lake, l., Sask., Can.	D5	104
Pierceton, In., U.S.	A11	114
Pierpont, S.D., U.S.	F10	118
Pierre, S.D., U.S.	G7	118
Pierre, Bayou, stm., La., U.S.	K3	114
Pierre Part, La., U.S.	M5	114
Pierson, Fl., U.S.	J5	112
Pierz, Mn., U.S.	E1	110
Piešťany, Czech.	G17	10
Pietermaritzburg, S. Afr.	G10	66
Pietersburg, S. Afr.	D9	66
Pietrasanta, Italy	F5	18
Piet Retief, S. Afr.	F10	66
Pigeon, Mi., U.S.	G12	110
Pigeon, stm., Man., Can.	F18	104
Pigeon, stm., U.S.	I10	110
Pigeon, stm., U.S.	D3	112
Pigeon, stm., Mi., U.S.	E11	110
Pigeon Forge, Tn., U.S.	D3	112
Pigeon Lake, l., Alta., Can.	D20	102
Pigg, stm., Va., U.S.	C7	112
Piggott, Ar., U.S.	F6	114
Piggs Peak, Swaz.	E10	66
Pigna, Italy	F2	18
Pigüé, Arg.	I7	80
Pihtipudas, Fin.	J19	6
P'ihyŏn, N. Kor.	C12	32
Pijijiapan, Mex.	J13	90
Pijol, Pico, mtn., Hond.	B7	92
Pikal'ovo, Russia	B17	22
Pikangikum, Ont., Can.	G20	104
Pikangikum Lake, l., Ont., Can.	G20	104
Pike, stm., Wi., U.S.	E8	110
Pikes Peak, mtn., Co., U.S.	F11	120
Pikesville, Md., U.S.	H10	108
Piketberg, S. Afr.	I4	66
Piketon, Oh., U.S.	H3	108
Pikeville, Ky., U.S.	B4	112
Pikeville, Tn., U.S.	G11	114
Pikwitonei, Man., Can.	C17	104
Pila, Arg.	I9	80
Piła (Schneidemühl), Pol.	B16	10
Pilar, Arg.	F7	80
Pilar, Arg.	F8	80
Pilar, Para.	D9	80
Pilar de Goiás, Braz.	C4	79
Pilar do Sul, Braz.	G5	79
Pilawa, Pol.	D21	10
Pilaya, stm., Bol.	I9	82
Pilcomayo, stm., S.A.	G8	74
Pilcomayo, Brazo Norte, stm., Para.	C9	80
Pilcomayo, Brazo Sur, stm., S.A.	C9	80
Pilger, Ne., U.S.	I10	118
Pīlībhīt, India	F8	44
Pilica, stm., Pol.	D21	10
Pillaro, Ec.	H3	84
Pilley's Island, Newf., Can.	C18	106
Pilot, mtn., Austl.	K8	70
Pilot Butte, Sask., Can.	H10	104
Pilot Grove, Mo., U.S.	D4	114
Pilot Knob, Mo., U.S.	E6	114
Pilot Mound, Man., Can.	I16	104
Pilot Mountain, N.C., U.S.	C6	112
Pilot Peak, mtn., Nv., U.S.	F8	124
Pilot Point, Tx., U.S.	F10	116
Pilot Rock, Or., U.S.	E7	122
Pilot Station, Ak., U.S.	F13	100
Pilottown, La., U.S.	M7	114
Pilpah Range, mts., Austl.	C3	70
Pilsen see Plzeň, Czech.	F13	10
Piltene, Lat.	D4	22
Pim, stm., Russia	E6	28
Pima, Az., U.S.	L7	120
Pimba, Austl.	H2	70
Pimenta Bueno, stm., Braz.	E8	82
Pimentel, Peru	B2	82
Pina, Spain	D11	16
Pinalón, Cerro, mtn., Guat.	B5	92
Pinang, Pulau, i., Malay.	L6	40
Pinang see George Town, Malay.	L6	40
Pınarbaşı, Tur.	B4	48
Pinar del Río, Cuba	C3	94
Pinardville, N.H., U.S.	E15	108
Pinarhisar, Tur.	H11	20
Pinas, Arg.	F6	80
Piñas, Ec.	I3	84
Piñas, Cerro, mtn., Hond.	B9	92
Pincher Creek, Alta., Can.	H21	102
Pinchi Lake, l., B.C., Can.	C10	102
Pinckney, Mi., U.S.	H12	110
Pinckneyville, Il., U.S.	D7	114
Pinconning, Mi., U.S.	G12	110
Pińczów, Pol.	E20	10
Pindaíba, Ribeirão, stm., Braz.	C3	79
Pindamonhangaba, Braz.	G6	79
Píndhos Óros, mts., Grc.	J5	20
Pinduši, Russia	J24	6
Pindus Mountains see Píndhos Óros, mts., Grc.	J5	20
Pine, stm., B.C., Can.	A13	102
Pine, stm., Man., Can.	G14	104
Pine, stm., Mi., U.S.	F12	110
Pine, stm., Wi., U.S.	E7	110
Pine Apple, Al., U.S.	K10	114
Pine Barrens, reg., N.J., U.S.	H12	108
Pine Bluff, Ar., U.S.	H4	114
Pine Bluffs, Wy., U.S.	J3	118
Pine Bush, N.Y., U.S.	F12	108
Pine Castle, Fl., U.S.	K5	112
Pine City, Mn., U.S.	E3	110
Pine Creek, Austl.	B6	68
Pine Creek, stm., Alta., Can.	C22	102
Pine Creek Indian Reserve, Man., Can.	F14	104
Pine Creek Lake, res., Ok., U.S.	E11	116
Pinedale, Ca., U.S.	H6	124
Pinedale, Wy., U.S.	A8	120
Pine Falls, Man., Can.	H18	104
Pinega, stm., Russia	E7	26
Pine Grove, Pa., U.S.	G10	108
Pine Grove, W.V., U.S.	H6	108
Pine Hill, Al., U.S.	K9	114
Pine Hills, Fl., U.S.	K5	112
Pinehouse Lake, Sask., Can.	C8	104
Pinehouse Lake, l., Sask., Can.	C8	104
Pinehurst, Ga., U.S.	G3	112
Pinehurst, Id., U.S.	E9	122
Pinehurst, N.C., U.S.	D7	112
Pinehurst Lake, l., Alta., Can.	C23	102
Pine Island, Mn., U.S.	F3	110
Pine Island, i., Fl., U.S.	M4	112
Pine Island Bay, b., Ant.	C11	73
Pineland, Tx., U.S.	K3	114
Pinellas Park, Fl., U.S.	L4	112
Pine Mountain, mtn., Wy., U.S.	I16	122
Pine Pass, B.C., Can.	B12	102
Pine Point, N.W. Ter., Can.	D10	96
Pine Portage Dam, Ont., Can.	G15	96
Pine Prairie, La., U.S.	L4	114
Pine Ridge, S.D., U.S.	H5	118
Pine River, Man., Can.	G14	104
Pine River, Mn., U.S.	D1	110
Pinerolo, Italy	E2	18
Pinetop, Az., U.S.	J7	120
Pinetops, N.C., U.S.	D9	112
Pinetown, S. Afr.	G10	66
Pine Valley, val., Ut., U.S.	F3	120
Pineville, Ky., U.S.	C3	112
Pineville, La., U.S.	K4	114
Pineville, Mo., U.S.	F2	114
Pineville, N.C., U.S.	D6	112
Pineville, W.V., U.S.	B5	112
Pinewood, S.C., U.S.	F6	112
Piney, Fr.	D11	14
Piney, stm., Tn., U.S.	G9	114
Piney Woods, Ms., U.S.	J7	114
Ping, stm., Thai.	F5	40
Ping'anbu, China	B4	32
Pingdingshan, China	B2	34
Pingdu, China	G7	32
Pinghe, China	K6	34
Pinghu, China	E10	34
Pingjiang, China	G2	34
Pingliang, China	D8	30
Pingquan, China	C6	32
Pingshui, China	F9	34
P'ingtung, Tai.	M9	34
Pingwu, China	E7	30
Pingxiang, China	H2	34
Pingxiang, China	C9	40
Pingyao, China	D9	30
Pingyi, China	H5	32
Pinhal Novo, Port.	G3	16
Pinheiro, Braz.	D9	76
Pinheiro Machado, Braz.	F12	80
Pinhel, Port.	E4	16
Pinhuã, stm., Braz.	B9	82
Pini, Pulau, i., Indon.	N5	40
Pinillos, Col.	C5	84
Piniós, stm., Grc.	J6	20
Pinjarra, Austl.	F3	68
Pinlebu, Burma	B3	40
Pinnacle Buttes, mtn., Wy., U.S.	G16	122
Pinnaroo, Austl.	J4	70
Pinneberg, Ger.	B9	10
Pinos, Mex.	F9	90
Pinos-Puente, Spain	H8	16
Pinrang, Indon.	F6	38
Pinsk, Bela.	I9	22
Pinson, Al., U.S.	I10	114
Pintado, stm., Braz.	B4	79
Pintados, Chile	I7	82
Pintados, Salar de, pl., Chile	I7	82
Pinto Butte, mtn., Sask., Can.	I7	104
Pinto Creek, stm., Alta., Can.	D17	102
Pinto Creek, stm., Sask., Can.	I7	104
Pintoyacu, stm., Ec.	H4	84
Pintoyacu, stm., Peru	I5	84
Pin'ug, Russia	E7	26
Pioche, Nv., U.S.	G11	124
Piombino, Italy	G5	18
Pioneer, Oh., U.S.	F2	108
Pioneer Mine, B.C., Can.	G12	102
Pioner, ostrov, i., Russia	B16	26
Pionerskij, Russia	G3	22
Pionki, Pol.	D21	10
Piorini, stm., Braz.	I11	84
Piorini, Lago, l., Braz.	I11	84
Piotrków Trybunalski, Pol.	D19	10
Pipanaco, Salar de, pl., Arg.	D5	80
Pipestone, Mn., U.S.	G11	118
Pipestone, stm., Ont., Can.	F14	96
Pipestone Creek, stm., Can.	I13	104
Pipinas, Arg.	H10	80
Pipmuacan, Réservoir, res., Que., Can.	C3	106
Piqua, Oh., U.S.	G2	108
Piquiri, stm., Braz.	C12	80
Piquiri, stm., Braz.	G14	82
Piquiri, stm., Braz.	G14	82
Pira, Benin	G10	64
Piracanjuba, Braz.	D4	79
Piracanjuba, stm., Braz.	D4	79
Piracicaba, Braz.	G5	79
Piracicaba, stm., Braz.	G5	79
Piraçununga, Braz.	F5	79
Piraeus see Piraiévs, Grc.	L7	20
Piraí do Sul, Braz.	C14	80
Piraiévs (Piraeus), Grc.	L7	20
Piraju, Braz.	G4	79
Pirajuba, Braz.	E4	79
Pirajuí, Braz.	F4	79
Piran, Slo.	D8	18
Piranè, Arg.	C9	80
Piranga, Braz.	F7	79
Piranhas, Braz.	D3	79
Pīrān Shahr, Iran	C8	48
Pirapó, stm., Braz.	G2	79
Pirapora, Braz.	D6	79
Piraputanga, Braz.	F1	79
Piraquara, Braz.	C14	80
Pirarajá, Ur.	G11	80
Piratinga, stm., Braz.	C5	79
Piratini, Braz.	F12	80
Piratini, stm., Braz.	E11	80
Piratuba, Braz.	D13	80
Piratucu, stm., Braz.	I14	84
Piraube, Lac, l., Que., Can.	B2	106
Piray, stm., Bol.	G10	82
Pirenópolis, Braz.	C4	79
Pires do Rio, Braz.	D4	79
Pírgos, Grc.	L5	20
Piriápolis, Ur.	H11	80
Piribebuy, Para.	C10	80
Píritu, Ven.	B8	84
Píritu, Ven.	C8	84
Pirmasens, Ger.	F7	10
Pirna, Ger.	E13	10
Pirot, Yugo.	F6	20
Pirovano, Arg.	I8	80
Pīr Panjāl Range, mts., Asia	D6	44
Pirtleville, Az., U.S.	M7	120
Pisa, Italy	F5	18
Pisagua, Chile	H6	82
Pisco, Peru	E3	82
Pisco, stm., Peru	E4	82
Piscovo, Russia	D23	22
Písek, Czech.	F14	10
Pisgah Forest, N.C., U.S.	D4	112
Pishan, China	B8	44
Pishīn, Pak.	E2	44
Pishīn Lora (Lowrah), stm., Asia	G18	48
Pisinemo, Az., U.S.	L4	120
Pismo Beach, Ca., U.S.	I5	124
Pisqui, stm., Peru	B4	82
Pisticci, Italy	I11	18
Pistoia, Italy	F5	18
Pistolet Bay, b., Newf., Can.	A18	106
Pisz, Pol.	B21	10
Pit, stm., Ca., U.S.	D3	124
Pital, Col.	F5	84
Pitalito, Col.	G4	84

Name	Map Ref.	Page
Pitanga, Braz.	C13	80
Pitangueiras, Braz.	F4	79
Pitangui, Braz.	E6	79
Pitcairn, dep., Oc.	K27	126
Piteå, Swe.	I17	6
Pitelino, Russia	G24	22
Pitești, Rom.	E8	20
Pithapuram, India	D7	46
Pithiviers, Fr.	D9	14
Pitigliano, Italy	G6	18
Pitiquito, Mex.	B3	90
Pitk'aranta, Russia	K22	6
Pitt Island, i., B.C., Can.	D5	102
Pitt Lake, l., B.C., Can.	H12	102
Pittsboro, Ms., U.S.	I7	114
Pittsboro, N.C., U.S.	D7	112
Pittsburg, Ks., U.S.	N13	118
Pittsburg, Tx., U.S.	G12	116
Pittsburgh, Pa., U.S.	G7	108
Pittsfield, Il., U.S.	C6	114
Pittsfield, Me., U.S.	C17	108
Pittsfield, Ma., U.S.	E13	108
Pittsfield, N.H., U.S.	D15	108
Pittsford, Mi., U.S.	I11	110
Pittston, Pa., U.S.	F11	108
Pittsview, Al., U.S.	J11	114
Pittsworth, Austl.	F9	70
Pituil, Arg.	E5	80
Pitumarca, Peru	E6	82
Pium, Braz.	F9	76
Piura, Peru	A1	82
Piura, dept., Peru	A1	82
Piura, stm., Peru	A1	82
Pivan', Russia	G19	28
Pivijay, Col.	B5	84
Pixley, Ca., U.S.	I6	124
Pizzo, Italy	K11	18
Placentia, Newf., Can.	E20	106
Placentia Bay, b., Newf., Can.	E19	106
Placerville, Ca., U.S.	F5	124
Placetas, Cuba	C5	94
Plachtejevka, Ukr.	C13	20
Plácido de Castro, Braz.	D8	82
Plácido Rosas, Ur.	G12	80
Plain City, Oh., U.S.	G3	108
Plain City, Ut., U.S.	C4	120
Plain Dealing, La., U.S.	J3	114
Plainfield, Ct., U.S.	F15	108
Plainfield, In., U.S.	C10	114
Plainfield, N.J., U.S.	G12	108
Plainfield, Wi., U.S.	F6	110
Plains, Ga., U.S.	G2	112
Plains, Ks., U.S.	N7	118
Plains, Mt., U.S.	C11	122
Plains, Tx., U.S.	F4	116
Plainview, Mn., U.S.	F3	110
Plainview, Ne., U.S.	I10	118
Plainview, Tx., U.S.	E5	116
Plainville, In., U.S.	D9	114
Plainville, Ks., U.S.	L8	118
Plainwell, Mi., U.S.	H10	110
Plaisance, Baie de, b., Que., Can.	E12	106
Plaistow, N.H., U.S.	E15	108
Plamondon, Alta., Can.	C22	102
Planada, Ca., U.S.	G5	124
Planalto, Braz.	C8	79
Planalto, Braz.	D12	80
Planeta Rica, Col.	C5	84
Plankinton, S.D., U.S.	H9	118
Plano, Il., U.S.	I7	110
Plano, Tx., U.S.	F10	116
Plantagenet, Ont., Can.	B11	108
Plantation, Fl., U.S.	M6	112
Plant City, Fl., U.S.	K4	112
Plantersville, Al., U.S.	J10	114
Plantersville, Ms., U.S.	H8	114
Plantsite, Az., U.S.	K7	120
Plaquemine, La., U.S.	L5	114
Plasencia, Spain	E5	16
Plast, Russia	G10	26
Plaster Rock, N.B., Can.	F6	106
Plata, Isla de la, i., Ec.	H2	84
Plata, Río de la, est., S.A.	H10	80
Plato, Col.	C5	84
Platonovka, Russia	I24	22
Platta, Switz.	E10	13
Platte, S.D., U.S.	H9	118
Platte, stm., Mn., U.S.	D1	110
Platte, stm., Ne., U.S.	J11	118
Platte, stm., Wi., U.S.	H5	110
Platte Center, Ne., U.S.	J10	118
Platte City, Mo., U.S.	C2	114
Platteville, Co., U.S.	D12	120
Platteville, Wi., U.S.	H5	110
Plattsburg, Mo., U.S.	C2	114
Plattsburgh, N.Y., U.S.	C13	108
Plattsmouth, Ne., U.S.	J12	118
Platveld, Nmb.	B3	66
Plau, Ger.	B12	10
Plauen, Ger.	E12	10
Plav, Yugo.	G3	20
Pļaviņas, Lat.	E8	22
Plavsk, Russia	H20	22
Playa Azul, Mex.	I8	90
Playa Bonita, C.R.	H10	92
Playa del Carmen, Mex.	G16	90
Playa Noriega, Laguna, l., Mex.	C4	90
Playas Lake, l., N.M., U.S.	M8	120
Playa Vicente, Mex.	I12	90
Play Cu, Viet.	H10	40
Playgreen Lake, l., Man., Can.	D16	104
Plaza, N.D., U.S.	C6	118
Plaza de Caisán, Pan.	I12	92
Plaza Huincul, Arg.	J4	80
Pleasant, Lake, res., Az., U.S.	K4	120
Pleasant, Mount, hill, N.B., Can.	G7	106
Pleasant Bay, N.S., Can.	F13	106
Pleasantdale, Sask., Can.	F10	104
Pleasant Gap, Pa., U.S.	G9	108
Pleasant Garden, N.C., U.S.	D7	112
Pleasant Grove, Ut., U.S.	D5	120
Pleasant Hill, Il., U.S.	C6	114
Pleasant Hill, La., U.S.	K3	114
Pleasant Hill, Mo., U.S.	D2	114
Pleasanton, Ks., U.S.	M13	118
Pleasanton, Tx., U.S.	K8	116
Pleasant Plains, Il., U.S.	C7	114
Pleasantville, Ia., U.S.	I2	110
Pleasantville, N.J., U.S.	H12	108
Pleasantville, Pa., U.S.	F7	108
Plechanovo, Russia	G20	22
Pléneuf, Fr.	D4	14
Plenty, Sask., Can.	G6	104
Plenty, Bay of, b., N.Z.	B6	72
Plentywood, Mt., U.S.	C3	118
Pleščenicy, Bela.	G10	22
Pleseck, Russia	E6	26
Plessisville, Que., Can.	A15	108
Pleszew, Pol.	D17	10
Plétipi, Lac, l., Que., Can.	F18	96
Pleven, Bul.	F8	20
Plevna, Mt., U.S.	E3	118
Pljevlja, Yugo.	F3	20
Ploaghe, Italy	I3	18
Płock, Pol.	C19	10
Plöckenpass, Eur.	I12	10
Ploërmel, Fr.	E4	14
Ploești see Ploiești, Rom.	E10	20
Ploiești, Rom.	E10	20
Plomárion, Grc.	K10	20
Plön, Ger.	A10	10
Plonge, Lac la, l., Sask., Can.	C7	104
Płońsk, Pol.	C20	10
Pl'os, Russia	D24	22
Ploskoje, Russia	I21	22
Plottier, Arg.	J4	80
Plouay, Fr.	E3	14
Ploudalmézeau, Fr.	D2	14
Plouguenast, Fr.	D4	14
Plouha, Fr.	D4	14
Plovdiv, Bul.	G8	20
Plover, stm., Wi., U.S.	F6	110
Plumas, Man., Can.	H15	104
Plumerville, Ar., U.S.	G4	114
Plummer, Id., U.S.	C9	122
Plumtree, Zimb.	C8	66
Plungė, Lith.	F4	22
Pl'ussa, Russia	C12	22
Pl'ussa, stm., Russia	C11	22
Plutarco Elías Calles, Presa, res., Mex.	C5	90
Plymouth, Monts.	F13	94
Plymouth, Eng., U.K.	K9	8
Plymouth, Ca., U.S.	F5	124
Plymouth, Il., U.S.	B6	114
Plymouth, In., U.S.	A10	114
Plymouth, Ma., U.S.	F16	108
Plymouth, Ne., U.S.	K11	118
Plymouth, N.H., U.S.	D15	108
Plymouth, N.C., U.S.	D10	112
Plymouth, Oh., U.S.	F4	108
Plymouth, Pa., U.S.	F11	108
Plymouth, Wi., U.S.	G8	110
Plzeň, Czech.	F13	10
Pô, Burkina	F9	64
Po, stm., Italy	E7	18
Poana, stm., Braz.	G14	84
Poás, Volcán, vol., C.R.	G10	92
Pobé, Benin	H11	64
Pobeda, gora, mtn., Russia	D21	28
Pobeda Ice Island, i., Ant.	B6	73
Pobedino, Russia	H20	28
Pobedy, pik, mtn., Asia	I14	26
Pocahontas, Ar., U.S.	F6	114
Pocahontas, Il., U.S.	D7	114
Pocahontas, Ia., U.S.	I13	118
Pocatalico, stm., W.V., U.S.	I5	108
Pocatello, Id., U.S.	H13	122
Počep, Russia	I16	22
Pöchlarn, Aus.	G15	10
Pochvistnevo, Russia	G8	26
Počinok, Russia	G15	22
Pocitos, Salar, pl., Arg.	C5	80
Pocoata, Bol.	H8	82
Poções, Braz.	C8	79
Pocola, Ok., U.S.	G2	114
Pocomoke, stm., U.S.	J11	108
Pocomoke City, Md., U.S.	I11	108
Pocona, Bol.	G9	82
Poconé, Braz.	G13	82
Pocono Mountains, hills, Pa., U.S.	F11	108
Pocono Summit, Pa., U.S.	F11	108
Poços de Caldas, Braz.	F5	79
Pocrane, Braz.	E8	79
Pocrí, Pan.	I14	92
Podberezje, Russia	E13	22
Podborovje, Russia	B18	22
Poddorje, Russia	D14	22
Poděbrady, Czech.	E15	10
Podkamennaja Tunguska, stm., Russia	E11	28
Podol'sk, Russia	F20	22
Podor, Maur.	C2	64
Podoz'orskij, Russia	D23	22
Podporožje, Russia	E4	26
Podravska Slatina, Cro.	D1	20
Podsvilje, Bela.	F10	22
Podujevo, Yugo.	G5	20
Podu Turcului, Rom.	C11	20
Pofadder, S. Afr.	G4	66
Pogan, China	G5	34
Pogar, Russia	I16	22
Poggibonsi, Italy	F6	18
Pogoanele, Rom.	E11	20
Pogoreloje Gorodišče, Russia	E17	22
Pogost, Bela.	H12	22
Pograničnyj, Russia	I18	28
P'ohang, S. Kor.	G17	32
Pohénégamook, Que., Can.	E4	106
Pohjois-Karjalan lääni, prov., Fin.	J21	6
Poinsett, Cape, c., Ant.	B6	73
Point, Tx., U.S.	G11	116
Point Arena, Ca., U.S.	F2	124
Point Au Fer Island, i., La., U.S.	M5	114
Point Comfort, Tx., U.S.	K10	116
Pointe-à-la-Frégate, Que., Can.	C9	106
Pointe-à-la-Garde, Que., Can.	D7	106
Pointe a la Hache, La., U.S.	M7	114
Pointe-à-Maurier, Que., Can.	B14	106
Pointe-à-Pitre, Guad.	F14	94
Point Edward, Ont., Can.	G13	110
Pointe-Noire, Congo	B2	58
Point Fortin, Trin.	I14	94
Point Hope, Ak., U.S.	B11	100
Point Imperial, mtn., Az., U.S.	H5	120
Point Lake, l., N.W. Ter., Can.	C10	96
Point Leamington, Newf., Can.	C18	106
Point Marion, Pa., U.S.	H7	108
Point Pelee National Park, Ont., Can.	I13	110
Point Pleasant, N.J., U.S.	G12	108
Point Pleasant, W.V., U.S.	I4	108
Point Sapin, N.B., Can.	F9	106
Poisson Blanc, Réservoir du, res., Que., Can.	A11	108
Poissy, Fr.	D9	14
Poitiers, Fr.	F7	14
Poix, Fr.	C8	14
Pojarkovo, Russia	H17	28
Pojo, Bol.	G9	82
Pojoaque Valley, N.M., U.S.	I10	120
Pojuca, Braz.	B9	79
Pojuca, stm., Braz.	B9	79
Pokharā, Nepal	F10	44
Pokrov, Russia	F22	22
Pokrovsk, Russia	E17	28
Pokrovskoje, Russia	I19	22
Pola, Russia	D14	22
Polacca, Az., U.S.	I6	120
Pola de Lena, Spain	B6	16
Polān, Iran	I16	48
Polanco, Ur.	G11	80
Poland (Polska), ctry., Eur.	E11	4
Polanów, Pol.	A16	10
Pol'arnyj, Russia	D4	26
Polatlı, Tur.	B2	48
Polcura, Chile	I3	80
Pol-e Khomrī, Afg.	C3	44
Polesje, reg., Eur.	G3	26
Polessk [Labiau], Russia	G4	22
Polevskoj, Russia	F10	26
Polgár, Hung.	H21	10
Pŏlgyo, S. Kor.	I15	32
Police, Pol.	B14	10
Poligny, Fr.	F12	14
Pólis, Cyp.	D2	48
Polistena, Italy	K11	18
Políyiros, Grc.	I7	20
Polk, Ne., U.S.	J10	118
Polk, Pa., U.S.	F7	108
Polkton, N.C., U.S.	D6	112
Polla, Italy	I10	18
Pollāchi, India	G4	46
Pöllau, Aus.	H15	10
Pollock, La., U.S.	K4	114
Pollock, S.D., U.S.	F7	118
Pol'noje-Jaltunovo, Russia	H24	22
Polo, Il., U.S.	I6	110
Polo, Mo., U.S.	C2	114
Polochic, stm., Guat.	B5	92
Polock, Bela.	F11	22
Polonio, Cabo, c., Ur.	H12	80
Polonnaruwa, Sri L.	I6	46
Polotn'anyj, Russia	G19	22
Polson, Mt., U.S.	C11	122
Poltava, Ukr.	H4	26
Poltimore, Que., Can.	B11	108
Põltsamaa, Est.	C8	22
Poluj, stm., Russia	D11	26
Polunočnoje, Russia	E10	26
Polynesia, is., Oc.	I24	126
Polysajevo, Russia	G15	26
Pomabamba, Peru	C3	82
Pomacanchi, Peru	F6	82
Pomata, Peru	G7	82
Pombal, Port.	F3	16
Pomene, Moz.	D12	66
Pomerania, hist. reg., Pol.	A16	10
Pomeranian Bay, b., Eur.	A14	10
Pomerene, Az., U.S.	M6	120
Pomerode, Braz.	D14	80
Pomeroon, stm., Guy.	D13	84
Pomeroy, Ia., U.S.	I13	118
Pomeroy, Oh., U.S.	H4	108
Pomeroy, Wa., U.S.	D8	122
Pomme de Terre, stm., Mn., U.S.	F11	118
Pomme de Terre, stm., Mo., U.S.	E3	114
Pomona, Ca., U.S.	J8	124
Pomona, Ks., U.S.	M12	118
Pomona Park, Fl., U.S.	J5	112
Pompano Beach, Fl., U.S.	M6	112
Pompei, Italy	I9	18
Pompei, hist., Italy	I9	18
Pompéia, Braz.	G3	79
Pompéu, Braz.	E6	79
Pompton Lakes, N.J., U.S.	F12	108
Pomquet, N.S., Can.	G12	106
Ponask Lake, l., Ont., Can.	D22	104
Ponass Lakes, l., Sask., Can.	F11	104
Ponca, Ne., U.S.	I11	118
Ponca City, Ok., U.S.	C9	116
Ponce, P.R.	E11	94
Ponce de Leon, Fl., U.S.	L11	114
Ponchatoula, La., U.S.	L6	114
Pond, stm., Ky., U.S.	E9	114
Pondcreek, Ok., U.S.	C9	116
Pondicherry, India	G5	46
Pondicherry, ter., India	G5	46
Pond Inlet, N.W. Ter., Can.	B17	96
Pond Inlet, b., N.W. Ter., Can.	B17	96
Pondoland, hist. reg., Transkei	H9	66
Pondosa, Ca., U.S.	C4	124
Ponferrada, Spain	C5	16
Ponhook Lake, l., N.S., Can.	H9	106
Ponnūru Nidubrolu, India	D6	46
Ponoj, stm., Russia	D5	26
Ponoka, Alta., Can.	E21	102
Ponorogo, Indon.	J15	39a
Pons, Fr.	G6	14
Ponta do Sol, Port.	M20	17a
Ponta Grossa, Braz.	C13	80
Pontalina, Braz.	D4	79
Ponta Porã, Braz.	G1	79
Pontarlier, Fr.	F13	14
Pontassieve, Italy	F6	18
Pont-Audemer, Fr.	C7	14
Pont-Aven, Fr.	E3	14
Pont Canavese, Italy	D2	18
Pontchartrain, Lake, l., La., U.S.	L6	114
Pont-d'Ain, Fr.	F12	14
Pont-de-Vaux, Fr.	F11	14
Ponte Alta do Bom Jesus, Braz.	B5	79
Ponte Branca, Braz.	D2	79
Pontedera, Italy	F5	18
Ponteix, Sask., Can.	I7	104
Ponte Nova, Braz.	F7	79
Ponte Serrada, Braz.	D13	80
Pontevedra, Spain	C3	16
Ponte Vedra Beach, Fl., U.S.	I5	112
Pontiac, Il., U.S.	J7	110
Pontiac, Mi., U.S.	H12	110
Pontianak, Indon.	F4	38
Pontivy, Fr.	D4	14
Pont-l'Abbé, Fr.	E2	14
Pont-l'Évêque, Fr.	C7	14
Pontoise, Fr.	C9	14
Pontorson, Fr.	D5	14
Pontotoc, Ms., U.S.	H8	114
Pontotoc, Tx., U.S.	I8	116
Pontremoli, Italy	E4	18
Pontresina, Switz.	F12	13
Ponts, Spain	D13	16
Pont-sur-Yonne, Fr.	D10	14
Pontypridd, Wales, U.K.	J10	8
Pony, Mt., U.S.	E14	122
Ponyri, Russia	I19	22
Ponziane, Isole, is., Italy	I7	18
Poole, Eng., U.K.	K12	8
Pooler, Ga., U.S.	G5	112
Pooley Island, i., B.C., Can.	E6	102
Pool's Cove, Newf., Can.	E18	106
Poolville, Tx., U.S.	G9	116
Poona see Pune, India	C2	46
Poopo, Bol.	H8	82
Poopó, Lago, l., Bol.	H8	82
Poor Man Indian Reserve, Sask., Can.	G10	104
Popa, Isla, i., Pan.	H12	92
Popayán, Col.	F4	84
Pope, Ms., U.S.	H7	114
Poperinge, Bel.	G2	12
Popham Bay, b., N.W. Ter., Can.	D19	96
Popigaj, stm., Russia	C14	28
Popiltah Lake, l., Austl.	I4	70
Poplar, Mt., U.S.	C2	118
Poplar, Wi., U.S.	D4	110
Poplar, stm., Can.	F18	104
Poplar, stm., Mn., U.S.	D11	118
Poplar Bluff, Mo., U.S.	F6	114
Poplar Hill, Ont., Can.	F20	104
Poplar Point, Man., Can.	H17	104
Poplarville, Ms., U.S.	L7	114
Poplevinskij, Russia	H22	22
Popocatépetl, Volcán, vol., Mex.	H10	90
Popokabaka, Zaire	C3	58
Popoli, Italy	G8	18
Popondetta, Pap. N. Gui.	m16	68a
Popovo, Bul.	F10	20
Poppel, Bel.	F7	12
Poppi, Italy	F6	18
Popple, stm., Wi., U.S.	E7	110
Poprad, Czech.	F20	10
Poprad, stm., Eur.	F20	10
Pŏptong, N. Kor.	E15	32
Poptún, Guat.	A5	92
Poquoson, Va., U.S.	B10	112
Porangatu, Braz.	B4	79
Porbandar, India	J3	44
Porce, stm., Col.	D5	84
Porcher Island, i., B.C., Can.	D4	102
Porchov, Russia	D12	22
Porciúncula, Braz.	F7	79
Porco, Bol.	H9	82
Porcos, Rio dos, stm., Braz.	B6	79
Porcuna, Spain	H7	16
Porcupine, stm., N.A.	C23	100
Porcupine Hills, hills, Can.	F13	104
Pordenone, Italy	D7	18
Porecatu, Braz.	G3	79
Porečje, Bela.	H7	22
Porečje Rybnoje, Russia	D22	22
Pori, Fin.	K17	6
Porlamar, Ven.	B11	84
Poroma, Bol.	H9	82
Poronajsk, Russia	H20	28
Poroškovo, Ukr.	G22	10
Porosozero, Russia	J23	6
Porozovo, Bela.	I7	22
Porpoise Bay, b., Ant.	B7	73
Porrentruy, Switz.	D7	13
Portachuelo, Bol.	G10	82
Port Adelaide, Austl.	J3	70
Portadown, N. Ire., U.K.	G7	8
Portage, Mi., U.S.	H10	110
Portage, Ut., U.S.	C4	120
Portage, Wi., U.S.	G6	110
Portage, stm., Oh., U.S.	F3	108
Portage Bay, b., Man., Can.	G16	104
Portage-la-Prairie, Man., Can.	I16	104
Portageville, Mo., U.S.	F7	114
Portal, Ga., U.S.	G5	112
Portal, N.D., U.S.	C5	118
Port Alberni, B.C., Can.	H10	102
Portal del Infierno, wtfl, Hond.	C9	92
Portales, N.M., U.S.	E3	116
Port Alfred (Kowie), S. Afr.	I8	66
Port Alice, B.C., Can.	G7	102
Port Allegany, Pa., U.S.	F8	108
Port Allen, La., U.S.	L5	114
Port Angeles, Wa., U.S.	B2	122
Port Anson, Newf., Can.	C18	106
Port Antonio, Jam.	E6	94
Port Aransas, Tx., U.S.	L9	116
Port Arthur, Austl.	N7	70
Port Arthur, Tx., U.S.	M3	114
Port Arthur see Lüshun, China	E9	32
Port Arthur see Thunder Bay, Ont., Can.	B6	110
Port Augusta, Austl.	I2	70
Port au Port, Newf., Can.	D15	106
Port au Port Bay, b., Newf., Can.	D15	106
Port au Port Peninsula, pen., Newf., Can.	D14	106
Port-au-Prince, Haiti	E8	94
Port-au-Prince, Baie de, b., Haiti	E8	94
Port Austin, Mi., U.S.	F13	110
Port-aux-Basques see Channel-Port-aux-Basques, Newf., Can.	E14	106
Port Barre, La., U.S.	L5	114
Port-Bergé, Madag.	O22	67b
Port Blair, India	I2	40
Port Blandford, Newf., Can.	D19	106
Port Borden, P.E.I., Can.	F10	106
Port-Bouët, I.C.	I8	64
Port Broughton, Austl.	I2	70
Port Byron, Il., U.S.	I5	110
Port Canning, India	I13	44
Port-Cartier, Que., Can.	B7	106
Port-Cartier Sept-Îles, Réserve, Que., Can.	B6	106
Port Chalmers, N.Z.	F3	72
Port Charlotte, Fl., U.S.	M4	112
Port Chester, N.Y., U.S.	F13	108
Port Clements, B.C., Can.	D2	102
Port Clinton, Oh., U.S.	F4	108
Port Clyde, Me., U.S.	D17	108
Port Colborne, Ont., Can.	H16	110
Port Coquitlam, B.C., Can.	H12	102
Port Credit, Ont., Can.	G16	110
Port-Daniel, Réserve, Que., Can.	D9	106
Port-de-Paix, Haiti	E8	94
Port Dickson, Malay.	M6	40
Port Dover, Ont., Can.	H15	110
Porte Crayon, Mount, mtn., W.V., U.S.	I7	108
Port Edward, B.C., Can.	C4	102
Port Edward, S. Afr.	H10	66
Port Edwards, Wi., U.S.	F6	110
Portegolpe, C.R.	G9	92
Porteirinha, Braz.	C7	79
Portel, Braz.	D8	76
Port Elgin, N.B., Can.	F9	106
Port Elgin, Ont., Can.	F14	110
Port Elizabeth, S. Afr.	I7	66
Port-en-Bessin, Fr.	C6	14
Porter, Ok., U.S.	D11	116
Porter, Tx., U.S.	I11	116
Porter Lake, l., Sask., Can.	B7	104
Porterville, Ca., U.S.	H6	124
Porterville, Ms., U.S.	J8	114
Port Essington, B.C., Can.	C5	102
Portete, Bahía, b., Col.	A6	84
Port Fairy, Austl.	L5	70
Port Gamble, Wa., U.S.	C3	122
Port Gentil, Gabon	B1	58
Port Germein, Austl.	I3	70
Port Gibson, Ms., U.S.	K6	114
Port Graham, Ak., U.S.	G19	100
Port Greville, N.S., Can.	G9	106
Port Harcourt, Nig.	I13	64
Port Hardy, B.C., Can.	G7	102
Port Hawkesbury, N.S., Can.	G12	106
Port Hedland, Austl.	D3	68
Port Henry, N.Y., U.S.	C13	108
Port Hill, P.E.I., Can.	F10	106
Port Hood, N.S., Can.	F12	106
Port Hope, Ont., Can.	G17	110
Port Hope, Mi., U.S.	G13	110
Port Howe, Bah.	B7	94
Port Huron, Mi., U.S.	H13	110
Port-Iljič, Azer.	B10	48
Portimão, Port.	H3	16
Port Isabel, Tx., U.S.	M9	116
Port Jervis, N.Y., U.S.	F12	108
Port Kembla, Austl.	J9	70
Portland, Austl.	I9	70
Portland, Austl.	L4	70
Portland, Ar., U.S.	I5	114
Portland, In., U.S.	B12	114
Portland, Me., U.S.	D16	108
Portland, Mi., U.S.	H11	110
Portland, N.D., U.S.	D10	118
Portland, Or., U.S.	E3	122
Portland, Tn., U.S.	F10	114
Portland, Tx., U.S.	L9	116
Portland, Bill of, c., Eng., U.K.	K11	8
Portland, Cape, c., Austl.	M7	70
Portland Bay, b., Austl.	L4	70
Portland Bight, Jam.	F6	94
Portland Canal, b., N.A.	B4	102
Portland Creek Pond, l., Newf., Can.	B16	106
Portland Inlet, b., B.C., Can.	C4	102
Portland Point, c., Jam.	F6	94
Port Laoise, Ire.	H6	8
Port Lavaca, Tx., U.S.	K10	116
Port Leyden, N.Y., U.S.	D11	108
Port Lincoln, Austl.	J1	70
Port Lions, Ak., U.S.	H18	100
Port Loko, S.L.	G3	64
Port-Louis, Fr.	E3	14
Port Louis, Mrts.	V18	67c
Port Macquarie, Austl.	H10	70
Port Maitland, N.S., Can.	I7	106
Port Maria, Jam.	E6	94
Port McNeill, B.C., Can.	G7	102
Port McNicoll, Ont., Can.	F16	110
Port Mellon, B.C., Can.	H11	102
Port-Menier, Que., Can.	C9	106
Port Moody, B.C., Can.	H12	102
Port Moresby, Pap. N. Gui.	m16	68a
Port Morien, N.S., Can.	F14	106
Port Mouton, N.S., Can.	I9	106
Port Neches, Tx., U.S.	M3	114
Port Nelson, Man., Can.	A22	104
Portneuf, stm., Que., Can.	D4	106
Portneuf, stm., Id., U.S.	H13	122
Portneuf, Lac, l., Que., Can.	C3	106
Portneuf-sur-Mer, Que., Can.	D4	106
Port Neville, B.C., Can.	G8	102
Port Nolloth, S. Afr.	G3	66
Port Norris, N.J., U.S.	H11	108
Porto, Port.	D3	16
Porto Acre, Braz.	C8	82
Porto Alegre, Braz.	F13	80
Porto Amboim, Ang.	D2	58
Porto Belo, Braz.	D14	80
Portobelo, Pan.	C3	84
Port O'Connor, Tx., U.S.	K10	116
Porto de Moz, Braz.	D8	76
Porto de Pedras, Braz.	E11	76
Porto Empedocle, Italy	L8	18
Porto Esperança, Braz.	H13	82
Porto Esperidião, Braz.	F12	82
Porto Farina, Tun.	L5	18
Porto Feliz, Braz.	G5	79
Porto Ferreira, Braz.	F5	79
Port of Spain, Trin.	I14	94
Portogruaro, Italy	D7	18
Porto Inglês, C.V.	m17	64a
Portola, Ca., U.S.	E5	124
Porto Lucena, Braz.	D11	80
Pörtom (Pirttikylä), Fin.	J17	6
Porto Mendes, Braz.	C11	80
Porto Murtinho, Braz.	I13	82
Porto Nacional, Braz.	F9	76
Porto-Novo, Benin	H11	64
Port Orange, Fl., U.S.	J6	112
Port Orchard, Wa., U.S.	C3	122
Porto Recanati, Italy	F8	18
Port Orford, Or., U.S.	H1	122
Porto San Giorgio, Italy	F8	18
Porto Sant'Elpidio, Italy	F8	18
Porto Santo, i., Port.	L21	17a
Porto São José, Braz.	G2	79
Porto Seguro, Braz.	D9	79
Porto-Séguro, Togo	H10	64
Porto Torres, Italy	I3	18
Porto União, Braz.	D13	80
Porto Válter, Braz.	C5	82
Porto-Vecchio, Fr.	M24	15a
Porto Velho, Braz.	C10	82
Portoviejo, Ec.	H2	84
Port Perry, Ont., Can.	F17	110
Port Phillip Bay, b., Austl.	L6	70
Port Pirie, Austl.	I3	70
Port Rexton, Newf., Can.	D20	106
Port Richey, Fl., U.S.	K4	112
Port Rowan, Ont., Can.	H15	110
Port Royal, Pa., U.S.	G9	108
Port Royal, S.C., U.S.	G6	112
Port Royal National Historic Park, N.S., Can.	H8	106
Port Said see Būr Saʽīd, Egypt	B7	60
Port Saint Joe, Fl., U.S.	J1	112
Port Saint Johns, Transkei	H9	66
Port Saint Lucie, Fl., U.S.	L6	112
Port-Saint-Servan, Que., Can.	A15	106
Port Sanilac, Mi., U.S.	G13	110
Port Saunders, Newf., Can.	B16	106
Portsea, Austl.	L6	70
Port Shepstone, S. Afr.	H10	66
Portsmouth, Eng., U.K.	K12	8
Portsmouth, N.H., U.S.	D16	108
Portsmouth, Oh., U.S.	I4	108
Portsmouth, Va., U.S.	C10	112
Portsoy, Scot., U.K.	D11	8
Port Stanley, Ont., Can.	H14	110
Port Sudan see Būr Sūdān, Sud.	H9	60
Port Sulphur, La., U.S.	M7	114
Port Talbot, Wales, U.K.	J10	8
Port Taufiq see Būr Tawfīq, Egypt	G2	48
Porttipahdan tekojärvi, res., Fin.	G20	6
Port Townsend, Wa., U.S.	B3	122
Portugal, ctry., Eur.	H6	4
Portugal, Cachoeira, wtfl, Braz.	C9	82
Portugal Cove South, Newf., Can.	F20	106
Portugalete, Spain	B8	16
Portuguesa, state, Ven.	C8	84
Portuguesa, stm., Ven.	C9	84
Portuguese Guinea see Guinea-Bissau, ctry., Afr.	F3	54
Port Union, Newf., Can.	D20	106
Port-Vendres, Fr.	J10	14
Portville, N.Y., U.S.	E8	108
Port Wakefield, Austl.	J3	70
Port Wakefield, Ak., U.S.	G18	100
Port Washington, Wi., U.S.	G8	110
Port Wentworth, Ga., U.S.	G5	112
Port Wing, Wi., U.S.	D4	110
Porum, Ok., U.S.	D11	116
Porvenir, Chile	G2	78
Porvenir, Mex.	B7	90
Porz, Ger.	E7	10
Porzuna, Spain	F7	16
Posada, Italy	I4	18
Posadas, Arg.	D11	80
Posadas, Spain	H6	16
Poschiavo, Switz.	F13	13
Pošechonje-Volodarsk, Russia	C22	22
Posen, Mi., U.S.	E12	110
Posen see Poznań, Pol.	C16	10
Positano, Italy	I9	18
Posjet, Russia	I18	28
Posse, Braz.	C5	79
Possession Islands, is., Ant.	C8	73
Pössneck, Ger.	E11	10
Possum Kingdom Lake, res., Tx., U.S.	G8	116
Post, Tx., U.S.	F5	116
Postavy, Bela.	F9	22
Poste-de-la-Baleine, Que., Can.	E17	96
Postelle, Tn., U.S.	D2	112
Poste Ramartina, Madag.	Q21	67b
Post Falls, Id., U.S.	C9	122
Postojna, Slo.	D9	18
P'ostraja Dresva, Russia	E23	28
Postrevalle, Bol.	H10	82
Postville, Ia., U.S.	G4	110
Pótam, Mex.	D4	90
Potaro, stm., Guy.	E13	84
Potaro Landing, Guy.	E13	84
Poté, Braz.	D8	79
Poteau, Ok., U.S.	G2	114
Poteau, stm., U.S.	G2	114
Poteet, Tx., U.S.	J8	116
Potenza, Italy	I10	18
Potes, Spain	B7	16
Potgietersrus, S. Afr.	E9	66
Poth, Tx., U.S.	J8	116
Potholes Reservoir, res., Wa., U.S.	C6	122
Poti, Geor.	I6	26
Poti, stm., Braz.	E10	76
Potiraguá, Braz.	C9	79
Potirendaba, Braz.	F4	79
Potiskum, Nig.	F9	54
Potlatch, Id., U.S.	D9	122
Potomac, Il., U.S.	B9	114
Potomac, stm., U.S.	I10	108
Potomac Heights, Md., U.S.	I9	108
Potosí, Bol.	F8	74
Potosí, Bol.	H9	82
Potosi, Mo., U.S.	E6	114
Potosí, dept., Bol.	I8	82
Potrerillos, Chile	D4	80
Potrerillos, Hond.	B7	92
Potrerillos Arriba, Pan.	I12	92
Potrero, C.R.	G9	92
Potrero Grande, C.R.	H11	92
Potro, Cerro del, mtn., S.A.	E4	80
Potsdam, Ger.	C13	10
Potsdam, N.Y., U.S.	C12	108
Potter, Ne., U.S.	J4	118
Potterville, Mi., U.S.	H11	110
Potts Camp, Ms., U.S.	H7	114
Pottstown, Pa., U.S.	G11	108
Pottsville, Pa., U.S.	G10	108
Potwin, Ks., U.S.	N10	118
P'otzu, Tai.	L9	34
Pouancé, Fr.	E5	14
Pouce-Coupe, B.C., Can.	B14	102
Pouce Coupé, stm., Can.	A15	102
Pouch Cove, Newf., Can.	E21	106
Poughkeepsie, N.Y., U.S.	F13	108
Poulan, Ga., U.S.	H3	112
Poulin-de-Courval, Lac, l., Que., Can.	D3	106
Poulsbo, Wa., U.S.	C3	122
Poultney, Vt., U.S.	D13	108
Poŭn, S. Kor.	G15	32
Pound, Va., U.S.	B4	112
Poundmaker Indian Reserve, Sask., Can.	F5	104
Pouso Alegre, Braz.	G6	79
Pouso Redondo, Braz.	D14	80
Poŭthĭsăt, Camb.	H7	40
Považská Bystrica, Czech.	F18	10
Povenec, Russia	J24	6
Póvoa de Varzim, Port.	D3	16
Povorino, Russia	G6	26
Povungnituk, Que., Can.	D17	96
Povungnituk, Rivière de, stm., Que., Can.	D18	96
Powassan, Ont., Can.	D16	110
Poway, Ca., U.S.	L8	124
Powder, stm., U.S.	B5	98
Powder, stm., Or., U.S.	F8	122
Powderly, Ky., U.S.	E9	114
Powderly, Tx., U.S.	F11	116
Powell, Wy., U.S.	F17	122
Powell, stm., U.S.	C3	112
Powell, Lake, res., U.S.	G6	120
Powell, Mount, mtn., Co., U.S.	E10	120
Powellhurst, Or., U.S.	E3	122
Powell Lake, l., B.C., Can.	G10	102
Powell River, B.C., Can.	H10	102
Powellton, W.V., U.S.	I5	108
Powers, Mi., U.S.	E8	110
Powers, Or., U.S.	H1	122
Powers Lake, N.D., U.S.	C5	118
Powhatan, La., U.S.	K3	114
Powhatan, Va., U.S.	B9	112
Powhatan Point, Oh., U.S.	H6	108
Powys, co., Wales, U.K.	I10	8
Poxoréo, Braz.	C1	79
Poyang Hu, l., China	F5	34
Poyen, Ar., U.S.	H4	114
Poygan, Lake, l., Wi., U.S.	F7	110
Poynette, Wi., U.S.	G6	110
Požarevac, Yugo.	E5	20
Poza Rica, Mex.	G11	90
Poznań, Pol.	C16	10
Pozo Almonte, Chile	I7	82
Pozoblanco, Spain	G7	16
Pozo Colorado, Para.	B9	80
Pozo del Molle, Arg.	G7	80
Pozo del Tigre, Arg.	C8	80
Pozo Hondo, Arg.	D6	80
Pozo Negro, Spain	O27	17b
Pozuelo de Alarcón, Spain	E8	16
Pozuelos, Ven.	B10	84
Pozuelos, Laguna, l., Arg.	B6	80
Pozuzo, Peru	D4	82
Pozuzo, stm., Peru	C4	82
Pozzallo, Italy	M9	18
Pozzuoli, Italy	I9	18
Prachin Buri, Thai.	G6	40
Prachuap Khiri Khan, Thai.	I5	40
Pradera, Col.	F4	84
Prades, Fr.	J9	14
Prado, Braz.	D9	79
Prados, Braz.	F6	79
Prague, Ne., U.S.	J11	118
Prague, Ok., U.S.	D10	116
Prague see Praha, Czech.	E14	10
Praha (Prague), Czech.	E14	10
Prahova, co., Rom.	D10	20
Praia, C.V.	m17	64a
Praia Grande, Braz.	E14	80
Prainha Nova, Braz.	B11	82
Prairie, stm., Mn., U.S.	C2	110
Prairie, stm., Wi., U.S.	E6	110
Prairie City, Il., U.S.	J5	110
Prairie City, Ia., U.S.	I2	110
Prairie City, Or., U.S.	F7	122
Prairie du Chien, Wi., U.S.	G4	110
Prairie du Sac, Wi., U.S.	G6	110
Prairie Grove, Ar., U.S.	G2	114
Prairie River, Sask., Can.	F11	104
Prairies, Lake of the, res., Can.	G13	104
Prairie View, Tx., U.S.	I11	116
Prairie Village, Ks., U.S.	M13	118
Prampram, Ghana	I10	64
Pran Buri, Thai.	H5	40
Praslin, Lac, l., Que., Can.	B4	106
Praslin Island, i., Sey.	B11	58
Prata, Braz.	E4	79
Prata, Rio da, stm., Braz.	D5	79
Prata, Rio da, stm., Braz.	E4	79
Pratāpgarh, India	H6	44
Pratápolis, Braz.	F5	79
Pratas Island see Tungsha Tao, i., Tai.	G10	30
Pratinha, Braz.	E5	79
Prato, Italy	F6	18
Pratt, Ks., U.S.	N9	118
Prattsburg, N.Y., U.S.	E9	108
Prattville, Al., U.S.	J10	114
Pratudão, stm., Braz.	B6	79
Pravdinsk, Russia	G4	22

Name — Map Ref. — Page

Pravdinsk, Russia E26 22
Pravdinskij, Russia E20 22
Praya, Indon. G6 38
Pr'aža, Russia K23 6
Prečistoje, Russia F15 22
Prečistoje, Russia C23 22
Preda, Switz. E12 13
Predazzo, Italy C6 18
Predeal, Rom. D9 20
Predeşti, Rom. E7 20
Predlitz [-Turrach], Aus. H13 10
Preeceville, Sask., Can. G12 104
Pré-en-Pail, Fr. D6 14
Preetz, Ger. A10 10
Pregarten, Aus. G14 10
Pregol'a, stm., Russia G4 22
Pregonero, Ven. C7 84
Preila, Lith. F4 22
Preiļi, Lat. E9 22
Prelate, Sask., Can. H5 104
Premnitz, Ger. C12 10
Premont, Tx., U.S. L8 116
Prentice, Wi., U.S. E5 110
Prentiss, Ms., U.S. K7 114
Prenzlau, Ger. B13 10
Preparis Island, i., Burma G2 40
Preparis North Channel, strt., Burma G3 40
Preparis South Channel, strt., Burma G3 40
Přerov, Czech. F17 10
Prescott, Ont., Can. C11 108
Prescott, Az., U.S. J4 120
Prescott, Ar., U.S. I3 114
Prescott, Wi., U.S. F3 110
Prescott Island, i., N.W. Ter., Can. B13 96
Preševo, Yugo. G5 20
Presho, S.D., U.S. H7 118
Presidencia de la Plaza, Arg. D9 80
Presidencia Roca, Arg. D9 80
Presidencia Roque Sáenz Peña, Arg. D8 80
Presidente Epitácio, Braz. F2 79
Presidente Getúlio, Braz. D14 80
Presidente Hayes, dept., Para. C9 80
Presidente Olegário, Braz. E5 79
Presidente Prudente, Braz. G3 79
Presidente Venceslau, Braz. F3 79
Presidio, Tx., U.S. J2 116
Presidio, stm., Mex. F7 90
Prešov, Czech. F21 10
Prespa, Lake, l., Eur. I5 20
Presque Isle, pen., Pa., U.S. E6 108
Preston, Eng., U.K. H11 8
Preston, Ga., U.S. G2 112
Preston, Id., U.S. H14 122
Preston, Ia., U.S. H5 110
Preston, Ks., U.S. N9 118
Preston, Mn., U.S. G3 110
Prestonsburg, Ky., U.S. B4 112
Prestville, Alta., Can. B16 102
Prestwick, Scot., U.K. F9 8
Preto, stm., Braz. B4 79
Preto, stm., Braz. D5 79
Preto, stm., Braz. E3 79
Preto, stm., Braz. F4 79
Preto, stm., Braz. C10 82
Preto, stm., Braz. H10 84
Preto do Igapó-açu, stm., Braz. J12 84
Pretoria, S. Afr. E9 66
Pretty Prairie, Ks., U.S. N9 118
Préveza, Grc. K4 20
Prey Vêng, Camb. I8 40
Pribilof Islands, is., Ak., U.S. H9 100
Priboj, Yugo. F3 20
Příbram, Czech. F14 10
Price, Tx., U.S. J2 114
Price, Ut., U.S. E6 120
Price, stm., Ut., U.S. E6 120
Price Island, i., B.C., Can. E6 102
Prichard, Al., U.S. L8 114
Priddy, Tx., U.S. H8 116
Priego de Córdoba, Spain H7 16
Priekule, Lat. E4 22
Priekule, Lith. F4 22
Prienai, Lith. G6 22
Prieska, S. Afr. G6 66
Priest, stm., Id., U.S. B9 122
Priest Lake, l., Id., U.S. B9 122
Priestley, Mount, mtn., B.C., Can. B6 102
Priest River, Id., U.S. B9 122
Prievidza, Czech. G18 10
Prijedor, Bos. E11 18
Prijutovo, Russia G8 26
Prikaspijskaja nizmennost', pl., Asia H7 26
Prilep, Mac. H5 20
Priluki, Ukr. G4 26
Primeiro de Maio, Braz. G3 79
Primera, Tx., U.S. M9 116
Primero, stm., Arg. F7 80
Primghar, Ia., U.S. H12 118
Primorje [Warnicken], Russia G3 22
Primorsk, Azer. A10 48
Primorsk, Russia G3 22
Primorsk, Russia A11 22
Primorsko, Bul. G11 20
Primrose Lake, l., Can. D5 104
Prince Albert, Sask., Can. E9 104
Prince Albert, S. Afr. I6 66
Prince Albert Mountains, mts., Ant. C8 73
Prince Albert National Park, Sask., Can. D8 104
Prince Albert Sound, strt., N.W. Ter., Can. B9 96
Prince Charles Island, i., N.W. Ter., Can. C17 96
Prince Charles Mountains, mts., Ant. C5 73
Prince Edward Island, prov., Can. G20 96
Prince Edward Island National Park, P.E.I., Can. F10 106
Prince Edward Islands, is., S. Afr. M7 126
Prince Frederick, Md., U.S. I10 108
Prince George, B.C., Can. D12 102
Prince George, Va., U.S. B9 112
Prince Leopold Island, i., N.W. Ter., Can. B15 96
Prince of Wales, Cape, c., Ak., U.S. D10 100
Prince of Wales Island, i., Austl. B8 68
Prince of Wales Island, i., N.W. Ter., Can. B13 96
Prince of Wales Island, i., Ak., U.S. I28 100
Prince of Wales Strait, strt., N.W. Ter., Can. B9 96
Prince Olav Coast, Ant. B4 73
Prince Patrick Island, i., N.W. Ter., Can. B8 86
Prince Regent Inlet, b., N.W. Ter., Can. B14 96
Prince Rupert, B.C., Can. C4 102
Princess Anne, Md., U.S. I11 108
Princess Astrid Coast, Ant. C3 73
Princess Martha Coast, Ant. C2 73
Princess Ragnhild Coast, Ant. C3 73
Princess Royal Channel, strt., B.C., Can. D6 102
Princess Royal Island, i., B.C., Can. E6 102
Princes Town, Trin. I14 94
Princeton, B.C., Can. H14 102
Princeton, Newf., Can. D20 106
Princeton, Ca., U.S. E3 124
Princeton, Il., U.S. I6 110
Princeton, In., U.S. D9 114
Princeton, Ky., U.S. E9 114
Princeton, Me., U.S. B19 108
Princeton, Mi., U.S. D8 110
Princeton, Mn., U.S. E2 110
Princeton, Mo., U.S. B3 114
Princeton, N.J., U.S. G12 108
Princeton, N.C., U.S. D8 112
Princeton, W.V., U.S. B5 112
Princeton, Wi., U.S. G6 110
Princeville, Que., Can. A15 108
Princeville, Il., U.S. J6 110
Princeville, N.C., U.S. D9 112
Prince William Sound, strt., Ak., U.S. F21 100
Príncipe, i., S. Tom./P. A1 58
Principe Channel, strt., B.C., Can. D4 102
Príncipe da Beira, Braz. E9 82
Prineville, Or., U.S. F5 122
Prinzapolka, Nic. D11 92
Prinzapolka, stm., Nic. D11 92
Prior, Cabo, c., Spain B3 16
Prioz'orsk, Russia K22 6
Prip'at', stm., Eur. G3 26
Pripet Marshes see Polesje, reg., Eur. G3 26
Prišib, Azer. B10 48
Priština, Yugo. G5 20
Pritchett, Co., U.S. N5 118
Pritzwalk, Ger. B12 10
Privas, Fr. H11 14
Priverno, Italy H8 18
Privolžsk, Russia D24 22
Privolžskaja vozvyšennost', plat., Russia G7 26
Privolžskij, Russia G7 26
Prizren, Yugo. G4 20
Prizzi, Italy L8 18
Prnjavor, Bos. E12 18
Probolinggo, Indon. J16 39a
Probstzella, Ger. E11 10
Prochladnyj, Russia I6 26
Procter, B.C., Can. H18 102
Proctor, Mn., U.S. D3 110
Proctor, Vt., U.S. D13 108
Proddatūr, India E5 46
Progreso, Mex. G15 90
Progreso, Ur. H10 80
Project City, Ca., U.S. D3 124
Prokopjevsk, Russia G9 28
Prokuplje, Yugo. F5 20
Proletarij, Russia C14 22
Proletarskij, Russia F20 22
Prome (Pyè), Burma E3 40
Promissão, Braz. F4 79
Promontogno, Switz. F12 13
Pronsk, Russia G22 22
Prophet, stm., B.C., Can. E8 96
Prophetstown, Il., U.S. I6 110
Propriá, Braz. F11 76
Propriano, Fr. M23 15a
Proserpine, Austl. C8 70
Prospect, Oh., U.S. G3 108
Prosser, Wa., U.S. D6 122
Prostějov, Czech. F17 10
Proston, Austl. F9 70
Protection, Ks., U.S. N8 118
Protem, S. Afr. J5 66
Protville, Tun. M5 18
Provadija, Bul. F11 20
Provencal, La., U.S. K3 114
Provence, hist. reg., Fr. I13 14
Providence, Ky., U.S. E9 114
Providence, R.I., U.S. F15 108
Providence, Ut., U.S. C5 120
Providence, Cape, c., N.Z. F1 72
Providence Island, i., Sey. C10 58
Providencia, Isla de, i., Col. H4 94
Providenciales, i., T./C. Is. D8 94
Providenija, Russia E29 28
Provincetown, Ma., U.S. E16 108
Provins, Fr. D10 14
Provo, Ut., U.S. D5 120
Provo, stm., Ut., U.S. D5 120
Provost, Alta., Can. F4 104
Prudentópolis, Braz. C13 80
Prudhoe Bay, b., Ak., U.S. A20 100
Prudhoe Island, i., Austl. C8 70
Prudnik, Pol. E17 10
Prudy, Bela. H9 22
Prüm, Ger. E6 10
Pruszków, Pol. C20 10
Prut, stm., Eur. D12 20
Prutz, Aus. H10 10
Pružany, Bela. I7 22
Prydz Bay, b., Ant. B5 73
Pryor, Ok., U.S. C11 116
Przasnysz, Pol. B20 10
Przedbórz, Pol. D19 10
Przemyśl, Pol. F22 10
Przeworsk, Pol. E22 10
Pskov, Russia D11 22
Pskovskoje ozero, l., Eur. C11 22
Pszczyna, Pol. F18 10
Ptarmigan, Cape, c., N.W. Ter., Can. B9 96
Ptolemaís, Grc. I5 20
Ptuj, Slo. C10 18
Puán, Arg. I7 80
Puan, S. Kor. H14 32
Pubnico, N.S., Can. I8 106
Pucallpa, Peru C4 82
Pucara, Bol. H9 82
Pucarani, Bol. G7 82
Puccha, stm., Peru C3 82
Pučež, Russia E26 22
Pucheng, China H7 34
Pucheta, Arg. E10 80
Puchoviči, Bela. H11 22
Puck, Pol. A18 10
Pudding, stm., Or., U.S. E3 122
Pudops Dam, Newf., Can. D17 106
Pudož, Russia E5 26
Puduari, stm., Braz. I12 84
Puduhe, China B7 40
Pudukkottai, India G5 46
Puebla, state, Mex. H10 90
Puebla [de Zaragoza], Mex. H10 90
Pueblo, Co., U.S. F12 120
Pueblo Libertador, Arg. F9 80
Pueblo Nuevo, Col. C5 84
Pueblo Nuevo, Nic. D8 92
Pueblo Nuevo, Ven. B8 84
Pueblo Nuevo Tiquisate, Guat. C3 92
Pueblo of Acoma, N.M., U.S. I9 120
Puebloviejo, Ec. H3 84
Pueblo Viejo, Laguna, b., Mex. F11 90
Pueblo Yaqui, Mex. D4 90
Puelches, Arg. J6 80
Puente Alto, Chile G3 80
Puente-Genil, Spain H7 16
Puerco, stm., U.S. I7 120
Puerco, Rio, stm., N.M., U.S. J10 120
Puerto Acosta, Bol. F7 82
Puerto Adela, Para. C11 80
Puerto Aisén, Chile F2 78
Puerto Alegre, Bol. E11 82
Puerto Ángel, Mex. J11 90
Puerto Arista, Mex. J13 90
Puerto Armuelles, Pan. C1 84
Puerto Asís, Col. G4 84
Puerto Ayacucho, Ven. E9 84
Puerto Bahía Negra, Para. I12 82
Puerto Baquerizo Moreno, Ec. J14 84a
Puerto Barrios, Guat. B6 92
Puerto Bermejo, Arg. D9 80
Puerto Bermúdez, Peru D4 82
Puerto Berrío, Col. D5 84
Puerto Bolívar, Ec. I3 84
Puerto Boyacá, Col. E5 84
Puerto Busch, Bol. I13 82
Puerto Cabello, Ven. B8 84
Puerto Cabezas, Nic. C11 92
Puerto Carreño, Col. D9 84
Puerto Casado, Para. B10 80
Puerto Castilla, Hond. A8 92
Puerto Chicama, Peru B2 82
Puerto Colombia, Col. B5 84
Puerto Cortés, Hond. B7 92
Puerto Cumarebo, Ven. B8 84
Puerto de Eten, Peru B2 82
Puerto de la Cruz, Spain O24 17b
Puerto Delicia, Arg. D11 80
Puerto de Lomas, Peru F4 82
Puerto Delón, Hond. C9 92
Puerto del Rosario, Spain O27 17b
Puerto El Triunfo, El Sal. D6 92
Puerto Escondido, Mex. J11 90
Puerto Esperanza, Arg. D11 80
Puerto Fonciere, Para. B10 80
Puerto Francisco de Orellana, Ec. H4 84
Puerto Guaraní, Para. I13 82
Puerto Heath, Bol. E7 82
Puerto Iguazú, Arg. C11 80
Puerto Inírida, Col. F9 84
Puerto Jiménez, C.R. I11 92
Puerto Juárez, Mex. G16 90
Puerto la Cruz, Ven. B10 84
Puerto Leda, Para. I12 82
Puerto Leguízamo, Col. H5 84
Puerto Lempira, Hond. B11 92
Puerto Libertad, Arg. C11 80
Puerto Libertad, Mex. C3 90
Puerto Limón, Col. F6 84
Puerto Limon, C.R. A2 76
Puerto Limón, C.R. G11 92
Puertollano, Spain G7 16
Puerto López, Col. E6 84
Puerto Madero, Mex. C2 92
Puerto Maldonado, Peru E7 82
Puerto Manatí, Cuba D6 94
Puerto Mihanovich, Para. I13 82
Puerto Montt, Chile E2 78
Puerto Morazán, Nic. E7 92
Puerto Morelos, Mex. G16 90
Puerto Nariño, Col. E9 84
Puerto Natales, Chile G2 78
Puerto Padre, Cuba D6 94
Puerto Páez, Ven. D9 84
Puerto Peñasco, Mex. B3 90
Puerto Pilón, Pan. H15 92
Puerto Pinasco, Para. B10 80
Puerto Piray, Arg. D11 80
Puerto Píritu, Ven. B10 84
Puerto Plata, Dom. Rep. E9 94
Puerto Portillo, Peru C5 82
Puerto Princesa, Phil. D6 38
Puerto Real, Spain I5 16
Puerto Rico, Arg. D11 80
Puerto Rico, Bol. D8 82
Puerto Rico, Col. G5 84
Puerto Rico, dep., N.A. E11 94
Puerto Rico Trench G13 86
Puerto Rondón, Col. D7 84
Puerto Saavedra, Chile J2 80
Puerto Salgar, Col. E5 84
Puerto Sandino, Nic. E8 92
Puerto San José, Guat. D4 92
Puerto San Julián, Arg. F3 78
Puerto Santa Cruz, Arg. G3 78
Puerto Sastre, Para. B10 80
Puerto Siles, Bol. E9 82
Puerto Suarez, Bol. H13 82
Puerto Supe, Peru D3 82
Puerto Tejada, Col. F4 84
Puerto Tolosa, Col. H5 84
Puerto Umbría, Col. G4 84
Puerto Vallarta, Mex. G7 90
Puerto Varas, Chile E2 78
Puerto Victoria, Arg. D11 80
Puerto Victoria, Peru C4 82
Puerto Viejo, C.R. H12 92
Puerto Viejo, C.R. G11 92
Puerto Villamil, Ec. J13 84a
Puerto Villamizar, Col. C6 84
Puerto Villarroel, Bol. G9 82
Puerto Wilches, Col. D6 84
Puerto Ybapobó, Para. B10 80
Pueyrredón, Lago (Lago Cochrane), l., S.A. F2 78
Pugačov, Russia G7 26
Puget Sound, strt., Wa., U.S. C3 122
Puget-Théniers, Fr. I13 14
Puglia, prov., Italy I11 18
Pugwash, N.S., Can. G10 106
Puica, Peru F5 82
Puigcerdá, Spain C13 16
Puigmal, mtn., Eur. C14 16
Puinahua, Canal de, mth., Peru A4 82
Pujehun, S.L. H4 64
Pujiang, China F8 34
Pujilí, Ec. H3 84
Pukch'ang, N. Kor. D14 32
Pukch'ŏng, N. Kor. C16 32
Pukeashun Mountain, mtn., B.C., Can. F15 102
Pukekohe, N.Z. B5 72
Pukhan-gang, stm., Asia F15 32
Pukou, China C7 34
Puksoozero, Russia J27 6
Pula, Cro. E8 18
Pulacayo, Bol. I8 82
Púlar, Cerro, mtn., Chile C4 80
Pulaski, N.Y., U.S. D10 108
Pulaski, Tn., U.S. G9 114
Pulaski, Va., U.S. B6 112
Pulaski, Wi., U.S. F7 110
Puławy, Pol. D21 10
Pulgaon, India B5 46
Puli, Tai. L9 34
Puliyangudi, India H4 46
Pullman, Wa., U.S. D8 122
Púllo, Peru F5 82
Pully, Switz. E6 13
Pulog, Mount, mtn., Phil. M19 39b
Pulsano, Italy I12 18
Pułtusk, Pol. C21 10
Puná, Isla, i., Ec. I2 84
Punakha, Bhu. G13 44
Punata, Bol. G9 82
Pūnch, India D6 44
Punchaw, B.C., Can. D11 102
Punduga, Russia A23 22
Pune (Poona), India C2 46
Púngoè, stm., Afr. B11 66
P'ungsan, N. Kor. C16 32
Punia, Zaire B5 58
Punilla, Sierra de la, mts., Arg. E4 80
Puning, China L5 34
Punitaqui, Chile C2 78
Punitaqui, Chile F3 80
Punjab, state, India E6 44
Punnichy, Sask., Can. G10 104
Puno, Peru F6 82
Puno, dept., Peru F6 82
Punta, Cerro de, mtn., P.R. E11 94
Punta Alta, Arg. J7 80
Punta Arenas, Chile G2 78
Punta Banda, Cabo, c., Mex. B1 90
Punta Cardón, Ven. B7 84
Punta Colnett, Mex. B1 90
Punta de Bombón, Peru G6 82
Punta de Díaz, Chile E3 80
Punta del Cobre, Chile D3 80
Punta del Este, Ur. H11 80
Punta de los Llanos, Arg. F5 80
Punta de Mata, Ven. C11 84
Punta de Piedras, Ven. B10 84
Punta Gorda, Belize I15 90
Punta Gorda, Nic. F11 92
Punta Gorda, Fl., U.S. M4 112
Punta Gorda, stm., Nic. F11 92
Punta Gorda, Bahía de, b., Nic. F11 92
Punta Negra, Salar de, pl., Chile C4 80
Punta Prieta, Mex. C2 90
Puntarenas, C.R. H10 92
Puntarenas, prov., C.R. I11 92
Puntas del Sauce, Ur. G10 80
Punto Fijo, Ven. B7 84
Puntzi Lake, l., B.C., Can. E10 102
Punxsutawney, Pa., U.S. G8 108
Puolanka, Fin. I20 6
Puqi, China F9 30
Puquio, Peru F4 82
Pur, stm., Russia D7 28
Puracé, Volcán, vol., Col. F4 84
Purcell, Ok., U.S. D9 116
Purcell Mountains, mts., N.A. G18 102
Purcellville, Va., U.S. H9 108
Purdy, Mo., U.S. F3 114
Purgatoire, stm., Co., U.S. N4 118
Puri, India K11 44
Purificación, Col. F5 84
Purificación, Mex. H7 90
Purificación, stm., Mex. E10 90
Purikari neem, c., Est. B8 22
Purmerend, Neth. C6 12
Pūrnia, India H12 44
Purros, Nmb. B1 66
Puruí, stm., Braz. H8 84
Puruliya, India I12 44
Puruni, stm., Guy. D13 84
Purus (Purús), stm., S.A. D6 76
Purvis, Ms., U.S. K7 114
Purwakarta, Indon. J13 39a
Purwokerto, Indon. J14 39a
Pusan, S. Kor. H17 32
Pushkar, India G6 44
Pushthrough, Newf., Can. E17 106
Puskiakiwenin Indian Reserve, Alta., Can. E4 104
Puškin, Russia B13 22
Puškino, Russia E20 22
Puškinskije Gory, Russia D11 22
Puskwaskau, stm., Alta., Can. B17 102
Püspökladány, Hung. H21 10
Püssi, Est. B10 22
Pustoška, Russia E12 22
Putaendo, Chile G3 80
Putao, Burma G17 44
Put'atino, Russia G24 22
Putian, China J8 34
Putila, Ukr. A9 20
Putina, Peru F7 82
Puting, Tanjung, c., Indon. F5 38
Putnam, Ct., U.S. F15 108
Putnam, Tx., U.S. G7 116
Putney, Ga., U.S. H2 112
Putney, Vt., U.S. E14 108
Putorana, plato, plat., Russia D17 26
Putre, Chile H7 82
Puttalam, Sri L. H5 46
Puttgarden, Ger. A11 10
Putú, Chile H2 80
Putumayo, ter., Col. G4 84
Putumayo (Içá), stm., S.A. I7 84
Putuo, China F11 34
Pu'uhonua o Honaunau National Historical Park, Hi., U.S. r18 125a
Puukohola National Historic Site, hist., Hi., U.S. q18 125a
Puula, l., Fin. K20 6
Puumala, Fin. K21 6
Puurmani, Est. C9 22
Puxi, China J8 34
Puxico, Mo., U.S. F6 114
Puyallup, Wa., U.S. C3 122
Puyallup, stm., Wa., U.S. D3 122
Puyang, China H2 32
Puyango (Tumbes), stm., S.A. I3 84
Puy-de-Dôme, dept., Fr. G10 14
Puylaurens, Fr. I9 14
Puyo, Ec. H4 84
Puyŏ, S. Kor. G14 32
Pweto, Zaire C5 58
Pyapon, Burma F3 40
Pyaye, Burma E3 40
Pye Islands, is., Ak., U.S. G19 100
Pyhäjoki, Fin. I19 6
Pyhäselkä, l., Fin. J21 6
Pyinmana, Burma E4 40
Pymatuning Reservoir, res., U.S. F6 108
Pyŏktong, N. Kor. C13 32
Pyŏlch'ang-ni, N. Kor. D14 32
P'yŏngch'ang, S. Kor. F16 32
P'yŏngsan, N. Kor. E14 32
P'yŏngt'aek, S. Kor. F15 32
P'yŏngyang, N. Kor. D13 32
Pyote, Tx., U.S. H3 116
Pyramid Lake, l., Nv., U.S. D6 124
Pyrenees, mts., Eur. C13 16
Pyrénées-Atlantiques, dept., Fr. I6 14
Pyrénées-Orientales, dept., Fr. J9 14
Pyrzyce, Pol. B14 10
Pytalovo, Russia D10 22
Pyu, Burma E4 40
Pyuntaza, Burma F4 40

Q

Qacentina (Constantine), Alg. B14 62
Qā'emshahr, Iran C12 48
Qā'en, Iran E15 48
Qaidam Pendi, China B16 44
Qalāt, Afg. D2 44
Qal'at ash-Shaqīf (Beaufort Castle), hist., Leb. B5 50
Qal'at Bīshah, Sau. Ar. D3 47
Qal'at Ṣāliḥ, Iraq F9 48
Qal'at Sukkar, Iraq F9 48
Qal'eh-ye Now, Afg. C2 44
Qallābāt, Sud. K9 60
Qalqilīya, Isr. Occ. D3 50
Qamar, Ghubbat al-, b., Yemen F8 47
Qamdo, China E6 30
Qānā, Leb. B4 50
Qanā, Sau. Ar. H6 48
Qandahār, Afg. E1 44
Qandala, Som. F10 56
Qantur, Sud. M3 60
Qārah, Sau. Ar. G6 48
Qardho, Som. G10 56
Qarqan, stm., China D4 30
Qārūn, Birkat, l., Egypt C6 60
Qāsh, Nahr al- (Gash), stm., Afr. E8 56
Qaṣr al-Farāfirah, Egypt D4 60
Qasr el-Boukhari, Alg. C12 62
Qaṣr-e Shīrīn, Iran D8 48
Qa'ṭabah, Yemen H4 47
Qaṭanā, Syria B6 50
Qatar (Qaṭar), ctry., Asia D5 42
Qattara Depression see Qaṭṭārah, Munkhafaḍ al-, depr., Egypt B4 60
Qaṭṭārah, Munkhafaḍ al- (Qattara Depression), depr., Egypt B4 60
Qazvīn, Iran C11 48
Qesari, Ḥorbat (Cæsarea), hist., Isr. C3 50
Qeshm, Iran H14 48
Qeshm, Jazīreh-ye, i., Iran H13 48
Qetura, Isr. I4 50
Qezel Owzan, stm., Iran C10 48
Qianfang, China G5 34
Qianqi, China H9 34
Qianyang, China F9 30
Qiaogou, China C4 34
Qiddīsah Kātrīnā, Dayr al- (Monastery of Saint Catherine), Egypt G3 48
Qidong, China D10 34
Qidu, China E6 34
Qiemo, China A11 44
Qifṭ (Coptos), Egypt D7 60
Qijiang, China F8 30
Qijiawan, China E3 34
Qila Lādgasht, Pak. H17 48
Qilian Shan, mtn., China D6 30
Qilian Shan, mts., China D6 30
Qimen, China J2 34
Qinā, Egypt D7 60
Qinā, Wādī, val., Egypt H2 48
Qingchengzi, China C11 32
Qingdao (Tsingtao), China G8 32
Qinghai (Tsinghai), prov., China D6 30
Qinghai Hu, l., China D7 30
Qinghezhen, China F5 32
Qingjiang, China G4 34
Qingjiang, China B8 34
Qinglian, China K1 34
Qinglong, China B8 40
Qingpu, China D10 34
Qingshan, China E3 34
Qingshui, stm., China D8 30
Qingshui, stm., China F8 30
Qingtang, China K2 34
Qingyang, China D8 30
Qingyangzhen, China D9 34
Qingyuan, China G8 30
Qingyuan, China L2 34
Qingzhou, China L5 34
Qinhuangdao (Chinwangtao), China D7 32
Qin Ling, mts., China E8 30
Qinzhou, China D10 40
Qionglai, China E7 30
Qiongzhong, China E10 40
Qiongzhou Haixia, strt., China D11 40
Qipanshan, China A5 32
Qiqian, China A11 30
Qiqihar (Tsitsihar), China B11 30
Qiryat Ata, Isr. C4 50
Qiryat Bialik, Isr. C4 50
Qiryat Gat, Isr. E3 50
Qiryat Mal'akhi, Isr. E3 50
Qiryat Motzkin, Isr. C4 50
Qiryat Ono, Isr. D3 50
Qiryat Shemona, Isr. B5 50
Qiryat Yam, Isr. C4 50
Qishn, Yemen G7 47
Qishon, stm., Asia C4 50
Qishuyan, China D9 34
Qitai, China C4 30
Qiyang, China A11 40
Qnadsa, Alg. E9 62
Qogir Feng (K2), mtn., Asia C7 44
Qom, Iran D11 48
Qomsheh, Iran E11 48
Qondūz, Afg. J11 26
Qondūz, stm., Afg. B3 44
Qonggyai, China F5 30
Qorveh, Iran D9 48
Quabbin Reservoir, res., Ma., U.S. E14 108
Quadra Island, i., B.C., Can. G9 102
Quadros, Lagoa dos, b., Braz. E13 80
Quakenbrück, Ger. C7 10
Quakertown, Pa., U.S. G11 108
Qualicum Beach, B.C., Can. H10 102
Quanah, Tx., U.S. E7 116
Quangang, China G4 34
Quang Ngai, Viet. G10 40
Quang Trach, Viet. F9 40
Quantico, Va., U.S. I9 108
Quanzhou (Chuanchou), China K7 34
Qu'Appelle, Sask., Can. H11 104
Qu'Appelle, stm., Can. H13 104
Qu'Appelle Dam, Sask., Can. G8 104
Quaraí, Braz. F10 80
Quaraí, stm., S.A. F10 80
Quarryville, Pa., U.S. H10 108
Quartu Sant'Elena, Italy J4 18
Quartz Hill, Ca., U.S. J7 124
Quartz Lake, l., N.W. Ter., Can. B16 96
Quartz Mountain, mtn., Or., U.S. G3 122
Quartzsite, Az., U.S. K2 120
Quatsino Sound, strt., B.C., Can. G7 102
Qūchān, Iran C15 48
Queanbeyan, Austl. J8 70
Québec, Que., Can. F2 106
Québec, prov., Can. F18 96
Quebeck, Tn., U.S. G11 114
Quebra-Anzol, stm., Braz. E5 79
Quebracho, Ur. F10 80
Quedas, Moz. B11 66
Quedlinburg, Ger. D11 10
Queen Alexandra Range, mts., Ant. D8 73
Queen Bess, Mount, mtn., B.C., Can. F10 102
Queen Charlotte, B.C., Can. D2 102
Queen Charlotte Islands, is., B.C., Can. D2 102
Queen Charlotte Mountains, mts., B.C., Can. D2 102
Queen Charlotte Sound, strt., B.C., Can. F5 102
Queen Charlotte Strait, strt., B.C., Can. G7 102
Queen City, Mo., U.S. B4 114
Queen City, Tx., U.S. I2 114
Queen Elizabeth Islands, is., N.W. Ter., Can. B9 86
Queen Mary Coast, Ant. B6 73
Queen Maud Gulf, b., N.W. Ter., Can. C12 96
Queen Maud Land, reg., Ant. C3 73
Queen Maud Mountains, mts., Ant. D9 73
Queens Channel, strt., N.W. Ter., Can. A13 96
Queenscliff, Austl. L6 70
Queensland, state, Austl. D9 68
Queensport, N.S., Can. G12 106
Queens Sound, strt., B.C., Can. F6 102
Queenstown, Austl. N6 70
Queenstown, Guy. D13 84
Queenstown, N.Z. F2 72
Queenstown, S. Afr. H8 66
Queguay Grande, stm., Ur. G10 80
Queimados, Braz. G7 79
Quelimane, Moz. A13 66
Quemado, N.M., U.S. J8 120
Quemado, Tx., U.S. K6 116
Quemado, Punta de, c., Cuba D7 94
Quemado de Güines, Cuba C4 94
Quemoy see Chinmen Tao, i., Tai. K7 34
Quemú Quemú, Arg. I7 80
Quepos, C.R. H10 92
Quequén, Arg. J9 80
Querary, stm., Col. G7 84
Quercy, hist. reg., Fr. H8 14
Querecotillo, Peru A1 82
Querétaro, Mex. G9 90
Querétaro, state, Mex. G10 90
Querobabi, Mex. B4 90
Quesada, C.R. G10 92
Quesada, Spain H8 16
Queshan, China C3 34
Quesnel, B.C., Can. E12 102
Quesnel, stm., B.C., Can. E12 102
Quesnel Lake, l., B.C., Can. E13 102
Questa, N.M., U.S. H11 120
Quetta, Pak. E2 44
Quettehou, Fr. C5 14
Quetzaltenango, Guat. C3 92
Quetzaltenango, dept., Guat. C3 92
Quevedo, Ec. H3 84
Quezaltepeque, El Sal. D5 92
Quezaltepeque, Guat. C5 92
Quezon City, Phil. N19 39b
Qufu, China H5 32
Quibdó, Col. E4 84
Quiberon, Fr. E3 14
Quíbor, Ven. C8 84
Quiches, Peru C3 82
Quiindy, Para. C10 80
Quila, Mex. E6 90
Quilalí, Nic. D8 92
Quilcene, Wa., U.S. C3 122
Quilimarí, Chile G3 80
Quilino, Arg. F6 80
Quillabamba, Peru E5 82
Quillacollo, Bol. G8 82
Quillagua, Chile I7 82
Quillan, Fr. J9 14
Quill Lake, Sask., Can. F10 104
Quillota, Chile G3 80
Quilon, India H4 46
Quilpie, Austl. F6 70
Quilpué, Chile G3 80
Quimarí, Alto de, mtn., Col. C4 84
Quimbaya, Col. E5 84
Quimby, Ia., U.S. I12 118
Quime, Bol. G8 82
Quimilí, Arg. D7 80
Quimper, Fr. D2 14
Quimperlé, Fr. E3 14
Quinault, stm., Wa., U.S. C2 122
Quince Mil, Peru E6 82
Quinches, Peru E3 82
Quincy, Ca., U.S. E5 124
Quincy, Fl., U.S. I2 112
Quincy, Il., U.S. C5 114
Quincy, Ma., U.S. E15 108
Quincy, Mi., U.S. I11 110
Quincy, Wa., U.S. C6 122
Quindío, dept., Col. E5 84
Quines, Arg. G6 80
Quinga, Moz. E8 58
Quinhagak, Ak., U.S. G14 100
Qui Nhon, Viet. H10 40
Quinlan, Tx., U.S. G10 116
Quinn, stm., Nv., U.S. C7 124
Quintanar de la Orden, Spain F8 16
Quintana Roo, state, Mex. H15 90
Quinte, Bay of, b., Ont., Can. F18 110
Quinter, Ks., U.S. L7 118
Quintero, Chile G3 80
Quintette Mountain, mtn., B.C., Can. C14 102
Quintin, Fr. D4 14
Quinto, stm., Arg. H6 80
Quinto de Noviembre, Presa, El Sal. D6 92
Quinton, Sask., Can. G10 104
Quinton, Ok., U.S. D11 116
Quiriguá, hist., Guat. B5 92
Quirihue, Chile I2 80
Quirindi, Austl. H9 70
Quirinópolis, Braz. E3 79
Quiriquire, Ven. C11 84
Quiroga, Mex. H9 90
Quiroga, Spain C4 16
Quirós, Arg. E6 80
Quirpon Island, i., Newf., Can. A18 106
Quissanga, Moz. D8 58
Quitaque, Tx., U.S. E5 116
Quitilipi, Arg. D8 80
Quitman, Ga., U.S. I3 112
Quitman, Ms., U.S. J8 114
Quitman, Tx., U.S. G11 116
Quito, Ec. I32 126
Quivilla, Peru C3 82
Quixadá, Braz. D11 76
Quixito, stm., Braz. J7 84
Qujiang, China K2 34
Qujing, China B7 40
Qulin, Mo., U.S. F6 114
Qumar, stm., China D5 30
Qumarlêb, China E6 30
Quoich, stm., N.W. Ter., Can. D14 96
Quorn, Austl. I3 70
Qurayyāt, Oman C11 47
Qurdūd, Sud. L5 60
Qūṣ, Egypt E7 60
Quthing, Leso. H8 66
Quxi, China L5 34
Quxian, China G7 34
Quyon, Que., Can. B10 108
Quyquyó, Para. D10 80

Name	Map Ref.	Page
Quzhou, China	G2	32

R

Name	Map Ref.	Page
Raab (Rába), stm., Eur.	H15	10
Raahe, Fin.	I19	6
Raalte, Neth.	D9	12
Ra'ananna, Isr.	D3	50
Raasiku, Est.	B8	22
Raba, Indon.	G6	38
Rába (Raab), stm., Eur.	H17	10
Rabak, Sud.	K7	60
Rabat (Victoria), Malta	M9	18
Rabat, Mor.	C7	62
Rabaul, Pap. N. Gui.	k17	68a
Rabbit Ears Pass, Co., U.S.	D10	120
Rābigh, Sau. Ar.	C1	47
Rābigh, Sau. Ar.	J5	48
Rabinal, Guat.	B4	92
Rabka, Pol.	F19	10
Rabkavi Banhatti, India	D3	46
Rabočeostrovsk, Russia	I24	6
Rabyānah, Ṣaḥrā', des., Libya	D5	56
Raccoon, stm., Ia., U.S.	A3	114
Race, Cape, c., Newf., Can.	F20	106
Raceland, La., U.S.	M6	114
Race Point, c., Ma., U.S.	E16	108
Rach'a, Russia	A13	22
Rach Gia, Viet.	I8	40
Rachov, Ukr.	A8	20
Racibórz (Ratibor), Pol.	E18	10
Racine, Wi., U.S.	H8	110
Ráckeve, Hung.	H18	10
Rădăuți, Rom.	B9	20
Radcliff, Ky., U.S.	E11	114
Radeberg, Ger.	D13	10
Radebeul, Ger.	D13	10
Rades, Tun.	B16	62
Radford, Va., U.S.	B6	112
Rādhanpur, India	I4	44
Radisson, Sask., Can.	F7	104
Radium Hot Springs, B.C., Can.	G18	102
Radofinnikovo, Russia	B13	22
Radolfzell, Ger.	H8	10
Radom, Pol.	D21	10
Radomsko, Pol.	D19	10
Radoškoviči, Bela.	G10	22
Radoviš, Mac.	H6	20
Radun', Bela.	G8	22
Radviliškis, Lith.	F6	22
Radville, Sask., Can.	I10	104
Radwā, Jabal, mtn., Sau. Ar.	E10	60
Radway, Alta., Can.	C22	102
Rae, N.W. Ter., Can.	D9	96
Rae, stm., N.W. Ter., Can.	C9	96
Rāe Bareli, India	G9	44
Raeford, N.C., U.S.	E7	112
Rae Isthmus, N.W. Ter., Can.	C15	96
Rae Strait, strt., N.W. Ter., Can.	C13	96
Raetihi, N.Z.	C5	72
Rafaela, Arg.	F8	80
Rafaḥ, Isr. Occ.	F2	50
Raffadali, Italy	L8	18
Rafḥā', Sau. Ar.	G7	48
Rafsanjān, Iran	F14	48
Raft, stm., U.S.	H12	122
Raft River Mountains, mts., Ut., U.S.	C3	120
Rafz, Switz.	C10	13
Raga, Sud.	M3	60
Ragged Island, i., Bah.	C7	94
Ragged Island Range, is., Bah.	C7	94
Ragland, Al., U.S.	I10	114
Ragusa, Italy	M9	18
Raguva, Lith.	F7	22
Rahad, Nahr ar-, stm., Afr.	F8	56
Rahad al-Bardī, Sud.	L2	60
Rahīmyār Khān, Pak.	F4	44
Rahway, N.J., U.S.	G12	108
Rāichūr, India	D4	46
Raiford, Fl., U.S.	I4	112
Raiganj, India	H13	44
Raigarh, India	J10	44
Railton, Austl.	M7	70
Rainbow Falls, wtfl, B.C., Can.	E15	102
Rainelle, W.V., U.S.	J6	108
Rainier, Mount, mtn., Wa., U.S.	D4	122
Rainy, stm., N.A.	J20	104
Rainy, stm., Mi., U.S.	E11	110
Rainy Lake, l., N.A.	B2	110
Rainy River, Ont., Can.	B1	110
Raipur, India	J9	44
Ra'īs, Sau. Ar.	C1	47
Raisin, stm., Mi., U.S.	I12	110
Raití, Nic.	C9	92
Rājahmundry, India	D6	46
Rajāj, Sud.	L3	60
Rajang, stm., Malay.	E5	38
Rājapālaiyam, India	H4	46
Rājasthān, state, India	G5	44
Rajčichinsk, Russia	H17	28
Rajka, Hung.	G17	10
Rājkot, India	I4	44
Rāj Nāndgaon, India	J9	44
Rājpipla, India	B2	46
Rājshāhi, Bngl.	H13	44
Rakamaz, Hung.	G21	10
Rakaposhi, mtn., Pak.	B6	44
Rakata, Pulau, i., Indon.	J12	39a
Rakops, Bots.	C7	66
Rakovník, Czech.	E13	10
Rakvere, Est.	B9	22
Raleigh, Newf., Can.	A18	106
Raleigh, Ms., U.S.	J7	114
Raleigh, N.C., U.S.	D8	112
Ralls, Tx., U.S.	F5	116
Ralston, Ne., U.S.	J11	118
Ralston, Pa., U.S.	F10	108
Ram, stm., Alta., Can.	E19	102
Rama, Isr.	C4	50
Rama, Nic.	E10	92
Rama, stm., Nic.	F10	92
Ramacca, Italy	L9	18
Ramah, N.M., U.S.	I8	120
Rām Allāh, Isr. Occ.	E4	50
Rāmanāthapuram, India	H5	46
Ramasucha, Russia	I16	22
Ramat Gan, Isr.	D3	50
Ramat HaSharon, Isr.	D3	50
Ramathlabama, Bots.	E7	66
Rambervillers, Fr.	D13	14
Rambouillet, Fr.	D8	14
Ramea, Newf., Can.	E16	106
Ramea Islands, is., Newf., Can.	E16	106
Ramenskoje, Russia	F21	22
Ramer, Al., U.S.	J10	114
Rameški, Russia	D19	22
Rāmeswaram, India	H10	42
Rāmhormoz, Iran	F10	48
Ramingstein, Aus.	H13	10
Ramiriquí, Col.	E6	84
Ramla, Isr.	E3	50
Ramlu, mtn., Eth.	F9	56
Ramm, Jabal, mtn., Jord.	I4	50
Ramona, Ca., U.S.	K9	124
Ramona, Ok., U.S.	C11	116
Ramona, S.D., U.S.	G10	118
Ramos, Mex.	F9	90
Ramos, stm., Mex.	E7	90
Ramot, Isr. Occ.	C5	50
Ramotswa, Bots.	E7	66
Rampart, Ak., U.S.	D19	100
Ramparts, stm., N.W. Ter., Can.	D29	100
Rāmpur, India	F8	44
Rāmpur Hāt, India	H12	44
Ramree Island, i., Burma	E2	40
Ramseur, N.C., U.S.	D7	112
Ramsey, I. of Man	G9	8
Ramsey, Il., U.S.	C7	114
Rāmshīr, Iran	F10	48
Ramu, stm., Pap. N. Gui.	m16	68a
Ramygala, Lith.	F7	22
Rānāghāt, India	I13	44
Ranburne, Al., U.S.	I11	114
Rancagua, Chile	H3	80
Rance, stm., Fr.	D4	14
Rancevo, Russia	E17	22
Rancharia, Braz.	G3	79
Rancheria, Yukon, Can.	F29	100
Ranchería, stm., Col.	B6	84
Ranches of Taos, N.M., U.S.	H11	120
Ranchester, Wy., U.S.	F18	122
Rānchi, India	I11	44
Ranchillos, Arg.	D6	80
Ranch Lake, l., Sask., Can.	F10	104
Rancho Cordova, Ca., U.S.	F4	124
Rancul, Arg.	H6	80
Randers, Den.	M12	6
Randleman, N.C., U.S.	D7	112
Randlett, Ok., U.S.	E8	116
Randolph, Az., U.S.	L5	120
Randolph, Me., U.S.	C17	108
Randolph, Ne., U.S.	I10	118
Randolph, N.Y., U.S.	E8	108
Randolph, Ut., U.S.	C5	120
Randolph, Vt., U.S.	D14	108
Randolph, Wi., U.S.	G6	110
Random Island, i., Newf., Can.	D20	106
Random Lake, Wi., U.S.	G8	110
Råneå, Swe.	I18	6
Rāngāmāti, Bngl.	I15	44
Range Indian Reserve, B.C., Can.	H15	102
Rangeley, Me., U.S.	C16	108
Rangely, Co., U.S.	D8	120
Ranger, Tx., U.S.	G8	116
Rangoon see Yangon, Burma	F4	40
Rangpur, Bngl.	H13	44
Ranguana Cay, i., Belize	A6	92
Ranguana Entrance, strt., Belize	A6	92
Rānībennur, India	E3	46
Rānīganj, India	I12	44
Rānikhet, India	F8	44
Ranken, stm., Austl.	C2	70
Ranken Store, Austl.	B2	70
Rankin, Il., U.S.	B9	114
Rankin, Tx., U.S.	H5	116
Rankin Inlet, N.W. Ter., Can.	D14	96
Ranlo, N.C., U.S.	D5	112
Ranohira, Madag.	S21	67b
Ranomafana, Madag.	T22	67b
Ranong, Thai.	J5	40
Ranopiso, Madag.	T22	67b
Ranotsara Nord, Madag.	S22	67b
Ransom, Ks., U.S.	M8	118
Ranson, W.V., U.S.	H9	108
Rantauprapat, Indon.	M5	40
Rantekombola, Bulu, mtn., Indon.	F7	38
Rantoul, Il., U.S.	B8	114
Ranua, Fin.	I20	6
Ranwanalenaus, Bots.	B6	66
Raoping, China	L6	34
Raoul, Ga., U.S.	E3	112
Rapa, Ponta do, c., Braz.	D14	80
Rapallo, Italy	E4	18
Rapel, stm., Chile	G3	80
Rapelli, Arg.	D6	80
Rapid, stm., Mi., U.S.	D8	110
Rapid, stm., Mn., U.S.	B1	110
Rapidan, stm., Va., U.S.	I9	108
Rapid City, Man., Can.	H14	104
Rapid City, Mi., U.S.	F10	110
Rapid City, S.D., U.S.	G4	118
Rapid River, Mi., U.S.	E9	110
Räpina, Est.	C10	22
Rapla, Est.	B7	22
Rappahannock, stm., Va., U.S.	B10	112
Rapperswil, Switz.	D10	13
Rāpti, stm., Asia	G10	44
Rapulo, stm., Bol.	F8	82
Raron, Switz.	F8	13
Rasa, Punta, c., Arg.	I10	80
Ra's al-ʿAyn, Syria	C6	48
Ra's al-Khaymah, U.A.E.	B9	47
Ra's an-Naqb, Egypt	I3	50
Ra's an-Naqb, Jord.	H4	50
Ras Dashen Terara, mtn., Eth.	K10	60
Raseiniai, Lith.	F6	22
Râs el Aïoun, Alg.	N3	18
Ras el Ma, Alg.	C10	62
Rashād, Sud.	L6	60
Rashīd, Egypt	B6	60
Rasht, Iran	C10	48
Rāsipuram, India	G5	46
Raška, Yugo.	F4	20
Raškov, Mol.	B12	20
Rass Jebel, Tun.	L5	18
Rasskazovo, Russia	I24	22
Rasšua, ostrov, i., Russia	H22	28
Ra's Tannūrah, Sau. Ar.	H11	48
Rastatt, Ger.	G8	10
Rastede, Ger.	B8	10
Rasūl, Pak.	D5	44
Rat, stm., Man., Can.	I18	104
Rat, stm., Man., Can.	B15	104
Ratangarh, India	F6	44
Rätansbyn, Swe.	J14	6
Rāth, India	H8	44
Rathbun Lake, res., Ia., U.S.	J2	110
Rathdrum, Id., U.S.	C9	122
Rathenow, Ger.	C12	10
Rathwell, Man., Can.	I16	104
Ratingen, Ger.	D6	10
Rat Islands, is., Ak., U.S.	K4	101a
Rat Lake, l., Man., Can.	B15	104
Ratlām, India	I6	44
Ratnāgiri, India	D2	46
Ratnapura, Sri L.	I6	46
Ratomka, Bela.	H10	22
Raton, N.M., U.S.	C2	116
Raton Pass, N.M., U.S.	O3	118
Rattlesnake, Mt., U.S.	D12	122
Rattling Brook, Newf., Can.	C17	106
Ratz, Mount, mtn., B.C., Can.	H28	100
Ratzeburg, Ger.	B10	10
Raub, Malay.	M6	40
Rauch, Arg.	I9	80
Raul Soares, Braz.	F7	79
Rauma, Fin.	K17	6
Raurkela, India	I11	44
Ravanusa, Italy	L8	18
Rāvar, Iran	F14	48
Ravelo, Bol.	H9	82
Raven, Va., U.S.	B5	112
Ravena, N.Y., U.S.	E13	108
Ravenna, Italy	E7	18
Ravenna, Ky., U.S.	B3	112
Ravenna, Mi., U.S.	G10	110
Ravenna, Ne., U.S.	J9	118
Ravenna, Oh., U.S.	F5	108
Ravensburg, Ger.	H9	10
Ravenscrag, Sask., Can.	I5	104
Ravenshoe, Austl.	A6	70
Ravensthorpe, Austl.	F4	68
Ravenswood, W.V., U.S.	I5	108
Rāvi, stm., Asia	E5	44
Ravnina, Turk.	C17	48
Rāwalpindi, Pak.	D5	44
Rawa Mazowiecka, Pol.	D20	10
Rāwāndūz, Iraq	C8	48
Rawdon, Que., Can.	A13	108
Rawicz, Pol.	D16	10
Rawlinna, Austl.	F5	68
Rawlins, Wy., U.S.	C9	120
Rawson, Arg.	E3	78
Rawson, Arg.	H8	80
Raxāul, India	D11	42
Ray, N.D., U.S.	C4	118
Ray, Cape, c., Newf., Can.	E14	106
Raya, Bukit, mtn., Indon.	F5	38
Rāyadurg, India	E4	46
Raymond, Alta., Can.	H22	102
Raymond, Il., U.S.	C7	114
Raymond, Mn., U.S.	F12	118
Raymond, Ms., U.S.	J6	114
Raymond, Wa., U.S.	D2	122
Raymond Terrace, Austl.	I9	70
Raymondville, Tx., U.S.	M9	116
Raymore, Sask., Can.	G10	104
Rayne, La., U.S.	L4	114
Rayón, Mex.	C4	90
Rayones, Mex.	E9	90
Rayong, Thai.	H6	40
Raytown, Mo., U.S.	C2	114
Rayville, La., U.S.	J5	114
Razan, Iran	D10	48
R'azan', Russia	G22	22
R'azancevo, Russia	E22	22
Ražanj, Yugo.	F5	20
Razdan, Arm.	A8	48
Razdel'naja, Ukr.	C14	20
Razgrad, Bul.	F10	20
Razorback Mountain, mtn., B.C., Can.	F10	102
R'ažsk, Russia	H23	22
Ré, Île de, i., Fr.	F5	14
Reading, Eng., U.K.	J13	8
Reading, Ks., U.S.	M12	118
Reading, Mi., U.S.	I11	110
Reading, Oh., U.S.	H2	108
Reading, Pa., U.S.	G11	108
Readlyn, Ia., U.S.	H3	110
Readstown, Wi., U.S.	G5	110
Real, Cordillera, mts., S.A.	H9	82
Real, Estero, stm., Nic.	E7	92
Real del Padre, Arg.	H5	80
Realicó, Arg.	H6	80
Realitos, Tx., U.S.	L8	116
Reardan, Wa., U.S.	C8	122
Reata, Mex.	D9	90
Reay, Scot., U.K.	C10	8
Reboly, Russia	J22	6
Rebouças, Braz.	C13	80
Rebun-tō, i., Japan	B16	36a
Recalde, Arg.	I8	80
Recanati, Italy	F8	18
Rečane, Russia	E14	22
Recherche, Archipelago of the, is., Austl.	F4	68
Rečica, Bela.	I13	22
Recife, Braz.	E12	76
Recinto, Chile	I3	80
Recklinghausen, Ger.	D7	10
Reconquista, Arg.	E9	80
Recreio, Braz.	F7	79
Recreo, Arg.	E6	80
Rector, Ar., U.S.	F6	114
Recuay, Peru	C3	82
Red (Hong) (Yuan), stm., Asia	C8	40
Red, stm., N.A.	B7	98
Red, stm., U.S.	E8	98
Red, stm., Ky., U.S.	B3	112
Red, stm., N.M., U.S.	H11	120
Red, stm., Wi., U.S.	E7	110
Redange, Lux.	I8	12
Red Bank, N.J., U.S.	G12	108
Red Bank, Tn., U.S.	G11	114
Red Banks, Ms., U.S.	H7	114
Red Bay, Newf., Can.	A17	106
Red Bay, Al., U.S.	H8	114
Redbay, Fl., U.S.	L11	114
Redberry Lake, l., Sask., Can.	F7	104
Red Bluff, Ca., U.S.	D3	124
Red Bluff Reservoir, res., U.S.	B8	90
Red Boiling Springs, Tn., U.S.	F11	114
Red Bud, Il., U.S.	D7	114
Red Cedar, stm., Mi., U.S.	H11	110
Red Cedar, stm., Wi., U.S.	E4	110
Redcliff, Alta., Can.	H4	104
Red Cliff, Co., U.S.	E10	120
Redcliff, Zimb.	B9	66
Redcliffe, Austl.	F10	70
Red Cliffs, Austl.	J5	70
Red Cloud, Ne., U.S.	K9	118
Red Cross Lake, l., Man., Can.	C22	104
Red Deer, Alta., Can.	E21	102
Red Deer, stm., Can.	F10	96
Red Deer, stm., Can.	F12	104
Red Deer Lake, l., Alta., Can.	E21	102
Red Deer Lake, l., Man., Can.	F13	104
Red Devil, Ak., U.S.	F16	100
Redding, Ca., U.S.	D3	124
Redeye, stm., Mn., U.S.	E12	118
Redfield, Ia., U.S.	J13	118
Redfield, S.D., U.S.	G9	118
Redford, Tx., U.S.	J2	116
Red Hook, N.Y., U.S.	F13	108
Red Indian Lake, l., Newf., Can.	D17	106
Red Island, i., Newf., Can.	E19	106
Redkey, In., U.S.	B11	114
Redkino, Russia	E19	22
Red Lake, Ont., Can.	G21	104
Redlake, Mn., U.S.	D12	118
Red Lake, l., Ont., Can.	F14	96
Red Lake, l., Ont., Can.	G20	104
Red Lake, stm., Mn., U.S.	D11	118
Red Lake Falls, Mn., U.S.	D11	118
Red Lake Road, Ont., Can.	I21	104
Redlands, S. Afr.	G6	66
Redlands, Ca., U.S.	J8	124
Redlands, Co., U.S.	E8	120
Red Level, Al., U.S.	K10	114
Red Lick, Ms., U.S.	K6	114
Red Lion, Pa., U.S.	H10	108
Red Lodge, Mt., U.S.	E16	122
Redmond, Or., U.S.	F4	122
Redmond, Ut., U.S.	E5	120
Redmond, Wa., U.S.	C3	122
Red Mountain, mtn., Ca., U.S.	C2	124
Red Mountain Pass, Co., U.S.	G9	120
Red Oak, Ia., U.S.	J12	118
Red Oak, Ok., U.S.	E11	116
Redon, Fr.	E4	14
Redonda, i., Antig.	F13	94
Redonda Islands, is., B.C., Can.	G10	102
Redondo, Port.	G4	16
Redondo Beach, Ca., U.S.	K7	124
Red Pass, B.C., Can.	E16	102
Red Pheasant Indian Reserve, Sask., Can.	F6	104
Red Rock, B.C., Can.	D12	102
Red Rock, Ont., Can.	B7	110
Red Rock, stm., Mt., U.S.	F13	122
Red Rock, Lake, res., Ia., U.S.	I2	110
Red Sea	D8	56
Red Springs, N.C., U.S.	E7	112
Redstone, B.C., Can.	E11	102
Redstone, stm., N.W. Ter., Can.	E32	100
Red Sucker, stm., Man., Can.	C22	104
Red Sucker Lake, l., Man., Can.	D21	104
Redvers, Sask., Can.	I13	104
Redwater, Alta., Can.	D21	102
Redwater, stm., Mt., U.S.	D2	118
Redwillow, stm., Can.	B15	102
Red Wing, Mn., U.S.	F3	110
Redwood, stm., Mn., U.S.	G12	118
Redwood City, Ca., U.S.	G3	124
Redwood Falls, Mn., U.S.	G12	118
Redwood National Park, Ca., U.S.	C1	124
Redwood Valley, Ca., U.S.	E2	124
Ree, Lough, l., Ire.	H5	8
Reed City, Mi., U.S.	G10	110
Reeder, N.D., U.S.	E5	118
Reed Lake, l., Man., Can.	D14	104
Reed Lake, l., Sask., Can.	H7	104
Reedley, Ca., U.S.	H6	124
Reedsburg, Wi., U.S.	G5	110
Reeds Peak, mtn., N.M., U.S.	K9	120
Reedsport, Or., U.S.	G1	122
Reedsville, Wi., U.S.	F8	110
Reefton, N.Z.	E3	72
Reelfoot Lake, l., Tn., U.S.	F7	114
Reese, Mi., U.S.	G12	110
Reese, stm., Nv., U.S.	D8	124
Reeseville, Wi., U.S.	G7	110
Reform, Al., U.S.	I8	114
Refuge Cove, B.C., Can.	G10	102
Refugio, Tx., U.S.	K9	116
Regaïa, Mor.	J6	16
Regência, Braz.	E9	79
Regensburg, Ger.	F12	10
Regent, N.D., U.S.	E5	118
Reggâne, Alg.	G11	62
Reggello, Italy	F6	18
Reggio di Calabria, Italy	K10	18
Reggio nell'Emilia, Italy	E5	18
Reghin, Rom.	C8	20
Regina, Sask., Can.	H10	104
Régina, Fr. Gu.	C8	76
Regina Beach, Sask., Can.	H9	104
Región Metropolitana, prov., Chile	G3	80
Registro, Braz.	C15	80
Registro do Araguaia, Braz.	C3	79
Regnéville, Fr.	C5	14
Reguengos de Monsaraz, Port.	G4	16
Rehau, Ger.	E12	10
Rehoboth, Nmb.	D3	66
Rehoboth Beach, De., U.S.	I11	108
Reḥovot, Isr.	E3	50
Reichenau, Switz.	E11	13
Reichenbach, Ger.	E12	10
Reid Lake, res., Sask., Can.	H6	104
Reidsville, Ga., U.S.	G4	112
Reidsville, N.C., U.S.	C7	112
Reigate, Eng., U.K.	J13	8
Reigoldswil, Switz.	D8	13
Reims, Fr.	C11	14
Reinach, Switz.	C8	13
Reinach, Switz.	D9	13
Reinbeck, Ia., U.S.	H3	110
Reindeer, stm., Sask., Can.	C11	104
Reindeer Island, i., Man., Can.	F17	104
Reindeer Lake, l., Can.	E12	96
Reindeer Station, N.W. Ter., Can.	B27	100
Reinga, Cape, c., N.Z.	A4	72
Reinosa, Spain	B7	16
Reisdorf, Lux.	I9	12
Reisterstown, Md., U.S.	H10	108
Reitz, S. Afr.	F9	66
Reliance, N.W. Ter., Can.	D11	96
Reliance, Wy., U.S.	C7	120
Remada, Tun.	D16	62
Remagen, Ger.	B14	14
Remanso, Braz.	E10	76
Rembang, Indon.	J15	39a
Remecó, Arg.	I7	80
Remedios, Col.	D5	84
Remedios, Pan.	C2	84
Remedios, Punta, c., El Sal.	D5	92
Remer, Mn., U.S.	C2	110
Remeshk, Iran	H15	48
Remington, In., U.S.	B9	114
Remington, Va., U.S.	I9	108
Remiremont, Fr.	D13	14
Remoulins, Fr.	I11	14
Remscheid, Ger.	D7	10
Remsen, Ia., U.S.	I12	118
Remus, Mi., U.S.	G10	110
Renaix (Ronse), Bel.	G4	12
Renata, B.C., Can.	H16	102
Rencēni, Lat.	D8	22
Rencontre East, Newf., Can.	E18	106
Rende, Italy	J11	18
Rend Lake, res., Il., U.S.	D8	114
Rendsburg, Ger.	A9	10
Renens, Switz.	E6	13
Renews, Newf., Can.	F21	106
Renfrew, Ont., Can.	E19	110
Rengat, Indon.	O7	40
Rengo, Chile	H3	80
Reng Tlāng, mtn., Asia	J15	44
Renhua, China	J2	34
Reni, Ukr.	D12	20
Renick, W.V., U.S.	J6	108
Renmark, Austl.	J4	70
Rennell, i., Sol.Is.	B12	68
Rennell Sound, strt., B.C., Can.	D2	102
Rennes, Fr.	D5	14
Rennick Glacier, Ant.	C8	73
Rennie, Man., Can.	I19	104
Reno, Nv., U.S.	E6	124
Reno, stm., Italy	E6	18
Renous, N.B., Can.	F8	106
Renous, stm., N.B., Can.	F7	106
Renovo, Pa., U.S.	F9	108
Renshou, China	H6	34
Rensselaer, In., U.S.	B9	114
Rensselaer, N.Y., U.S.	E13	108
Rentería, Spain	B10	16
Renton, Wa., U.S.	C3	122
Renville, Mn., U.S.	G12	118
Renwick, Ia., U.S.	H2	110
Répce, stm., Eur.	H16	10
Repetek, Turk.	J10	26
Repino, Russia	A12	22
Repton, Al., U.S.	K9	114
Republic, Ks., U.S.	L10	118
Republic, Mi., U.S.	D8	110
Republic, Mo., U.S.	E3	114
Republic, Wa., U.S.	B7	122
Republican, stm., U.S.	L10	118
Repulse Bay, N.W. Ter., Can.	C15	96
Repulse Bay, b., Austl.	C8	70
Requena, Peru	A5	82
Requena, Spain	F10	16
Réquista, Fr.	H9	14
Reschenpass, Eur.	F17	14
Resen, Mac.	H5	20
Reserva, Braz.	C13	80
Reserve, La., U.S.	L6	114
Reserve, N.M., U.S.	K8	120
Rešetnikovo, Russia	E19	22
Resistencia, Arg.	D9	80
Reșița, Rom.	D5	20
Rešma, Russia	D25	22
Resolute, N.W. Ter., Can.	B14	96
Resolution Island, i., N.W. Ter., Can.	D19	96
Resolution Island, i., N.Z.	F1	72
Resplendor, Braz.	E8	79
Restigouche (Ristigouche), stm., Can.	E6	106
Restín, Punta, c., Peru	J2	84
Restinga, Mor.	J6	16
Restinga Seca, Braz.	E12	80
Reston, Man., Can.	I13	104
Restrepo, Col.	E6	84
Restrepo, Col.	F4	84
Retalhuleu, Guat.	C3	92
Retalhuleu, dept., Guat.	C3	92
Retamosa, Ur.	G11	80
Rethel, Fr.	C11	14
Réthimnon, Grc.	N8	20
Reunion (Réunion), dep., Afr.	F11	58
Reus, Spain	D13	16
Reuss, stm., Switz.	D9	13
Reuterstadt Stavenhagen, Ger.	B12	10
Reutlingen, Ger.	G9	10
Rev'akino, Russia	G20	22
Revda, Russia	F9	26
Revelstoke, B.C., Can.	G16	102
Reventazón, Peru	B1	82
Reventazón, stm., C.R.	G11	92
Revigny-sur-Ornain, Fr.	D11	14
Revillagigedo, Islas, is., Mex.	H4	90
Revillagigedo Island, i., Ak., U.S.	I29	100
Revillo, S.D., U.S.	F11	118
Revin, Fr.	C11	14
Revol'ucii, pik, mtn., Taj.	A5	44
Revolución Mexicana, Mex.	A1	92
Revuè, stm., Afr.	B11	66
Rewa, India	H9	44
Rewa, stm., Guy.	F13	84
Rewāri, India	F7	44
Rexburg, Id., U.S.	G14	122
Rexford, Ks., U.S.	L7	118
Rexford, Mt., U.S.	B10	122
Rexton, N.B., Can.	F9	106
Rey, Isla del, i., Pan.	C3	84
Rey, Laguna del, l., Mex.	D8	90
Reyes, Bol.	F8	82
Reyes, Point, c., Ca., U.S.	F2	124
Reyhanlı, Tur.	C4	48
Reykjanes, pen., Ice.	C2	6a
Reykjavík, Ice.	B3	6a
Reyno, Ar., U.S.	F6	114
Reynolds, Ga., U.S.	G2	112
Reynolds, N.D., U.S.	D10	118
Reynoldsville, Pa., U.S.	F8	108
Reynosa, Mex.	D10	90
Rež, Russia	F10	26
Reza, gora (Kūh-e Rīzeh), mtn., Asia	C15	48
Rezé, Fr.	E5	14
Rēzekne, Lat.	E10	22
Rezeny, Mol.	C12	20
Rezina, Mol.	B12	20
Rezovska (Mutlu), stm., Eur.	G11	20
Rhaetian Alps, mts., Eur.	F16	14
Rhame, N.D., U.S.	E4	118
Rheda-Wiedenbrück, Ger.	D8	10
Rheims see Reims, Fr.	C11	14
Rhein, Sask., Can.	G12	104
Rheine, Ger.	C7	10
Rheinfelden, Ger.	H7	10
Rheinland-Pfalz, state, Ger.	E6	10
Rhein see Rhine, stm., Eur.	D6	10
Rhine, Ga., U.S.	H3	112
Rhine (Rhein) (Rhin), stm., Eur.	D6	10
Rhinebeck, N.Y., U.S.	F13	108
Rhinelander, Wi., U.S.	E6	110
Rhir, Cap, c., Mor.	E6	62
Rho, Italy	D4	18
Rhode Island, state, U.S.	C12	98
Rhode Island Sound, strt., U.S.	F15	108
Rhodesia see Zimbabwe, ctry., Afr.	E5	58
Rhodes see Ródhos, i., Grc.	M12	20
Rhodope Mountains, mts., Eur.	H8	20
Rhön, mts., Ger.	E9	10
Rhône, dept., Fr.	G11	14
Rhône, stm., Eur.	H11	14
Rhône au Rhin, Canal du, Fr.	H7	10
Rhourde-El-Baguel, Alg.	E14	62
Riaba, Eq. Gui.	J14	64
Riachão, Braz.	E9	76
Riacho de Santana, Braz.	B7	79
Rialma, Braz.	C4	79
Rianápolis, Braz.	C4	79
Riangnom, Sud.	M6	60
Riaño, Spain	C6	16
Riau, Kepulauan, is., Indon.	N8	40
Ribas do Rio Pardo, Braz.	F2	79
Ribeauvillé, Fr.	D14	14
Ribeira, Braz.	C14	80
Ribeira do Iguape, stm., Braz.	C14	80
Ribeira Grande, C.V.	k16	64a
Ribeirão do Pinhal, Braz.	G3	79
Ribeirão Preto, Braz.	F5	79
Ribeirão Vermelho, Braz.	F6	79
Ribeirãozinho, Braz.	D2	79
Ribemont, Fr.	C10	14
Ribera, Italy	L8	18
Riberalta, Bol.	D8	82
Rib Lake, Wi., U.S.	E5	110
Ribnica, Slo.	D9	18
Ribnitz-Damgarten, Ger.	A12	10
Ribstone Creek, stm., Alta., Can.	F3	104
Ricardo Flores Magón, Mex.	C6	90
Ricaurte, Col.	G4	84
Riccia, Italy	H9	18
Riccione, Italy	F7	18
Rice, Tx., U.S.	G10	116
Rice Lake, Wi., U.S.	E4	110
Riceville, Ia., U.S.	G3	110
Riceville, Tn., U.S.	D2	112
Richan, Ont., Can.	I22	104
Richard Collinson Inlet, b., N.W. Ter., Can.	B10	96
Richards, Tx., U.S.	I11	116
Richard's Bay, S. Afr.	G11	66
Richard's Bay, b., S. Afr.	G11	66
Richard's Harbour, Newf., Can.	E17	106
Richards Island, i., N.W. Ter., Can.	C6	96
Richards Island, i., N.W. Ter., Can.	B27	100
Richardson, Tx., U.S.	G10	116
Richardson, stm., Can.	E10	96
Richardson Mountains, mts., Can.	C26	100
Richardton, N.D., U.S.	E5	118
Riche, Pointe, c., Newf., Can.	B16	106
Richelieu, Fr.	E7	14
Richer, Man., Can.	I18	104
Richey, Mt., U.S.	D2	118
Richfield, Id., U.S.	G11	122
Richfield, Mn., U.S.	F2	110
Richfield, Pa., U.S.	G9	108
Richfield, Ut., U.S.	F4	120
Richfield Springs, N.Y., U.S.	E12	108
Richford, Vt., U.S.	C14	108
Rich Hill, Mo., U.S.	D2	114
Richibucto, N.B., Can.	F9	106
Richisau, Switz.	D10	13
Richland, Ga., U.S.	G2	112
Richland, Mi., U.S.	H10	110
Richland, Mo., U.S.	E4	114
Richland, Tx., U.S.	H10	116
Richland, Wa., U.S.	D6	122
Richland Center, Wi., U.S.	G5	110
Richlands, N.C., U.S.	E9	112
Richlands, Va., U.S.	B5	112
Richland Springs, Tx., U.S.	H8	116
Richmond, Austl.	I9	70
Richmond, Austl.	C5	70
Richmond, B.C., Can.	H11	102
Richmond, Ont., Can.	B11	108
Richmond, Que., Can.	B14	108
Richmond, N.Z.	D4	72
Richmond, S. Afr.	H6	66
Richmond, S. Afr.	G10	66
Richmond, Ca., U.S.	G3	124
Richmond, In., U.S.	C12	114
Richmond, Ks., U.S.	M12	118
Richmond, Ky., U.S.	B2	112
Richmond, Me., U.S.	C17	108
Richmond, Mi., U.S.	H13	110
Richmond, Mn., U.S.	F13	118
Richmond, Mo., U.S.	C3	114
Richmond, Tx., U.S.	J11	116
Richmond, Ut., U.S.	C5	120
Richmond, Vt., U.S.	C14	108
Richmond, Va., U.S.	B9	112
Richmond Heights, Fl., U.S.	N6	112
Richmond Highlands, Wa., U.S.	C3	122
Richmond Hill, Ont., Can.	G16	110
Richmond Hill, Ga., U.S.	H5	112
Richmondville, N.Y., U.S.	E12	108
Rich Square, N.C., U.S.	C9	112
Richton, Ms., U.S.	K8	114
Richwood, Oh., U.S.	G3	108
Richwood, W.V., U.S.	I6	108
Rico, Co., U.S.	G8	120
Riddle, Or., U.S.	H2	122
Riddle Mountain, mtn., Or., U.S.	G7	122
Ridgecrest, Ca., U.S.	I8	124
Ridgedale, Sask., Can.	E10	104
Ridge Farm, Il., U.S.	C9	114
Ridgefield, Ct., U.S.	F13	108
Ridgeland, Ms., U.S.	J6	114
Ridgeland, S.C., U.S.	G6	112
Ridgely, Tn., U.S.	F7	114
Ridgetown, Ont., Can.	H14	110
Ridgeville, Man., Can.	I17	104
Ridgeville, S.C., U.S.	F6	112
Ridgeway, Mo., U.S.	B3	114
Ridgeway, Wi., U.S.	G6	110
Ridgway, Co., U.S.	F9	120
Ridgway, Il., U.S.	E8	114
Ridgway, Pa., U.S.	F8	108
Riding Mountain, mtn., Man., Can.	H15	104
Riding Mountain National Park, Man., Can.	H14	104
Ried im Innkreis, Aus.	G13	10
Riegelwood, N.C., U.S.	E8	112
Rienzi, Ms., U.S.	H8	114
Riesa, Ger.	D13	10
Riesco, Isla, i., Chile	G2	78
Riesi, Italy	L9	18
Rietavas, Lith.	F4	22
Rietfontein, Nmb.	C5	66
Rieti, Italy	G7	18
Rif, mts., Mor.	C8	62
Riffe Lake, res., Wa., U.S.	D3	122
Rifle, Co., U.S.	E9	120
Rifle, stm., Mi., U.S.	F11	110
Rift Valley, val., Afr.	I9	52
Rīga, Lat.	E7	22
Riga, Gulf of (Rīgas jūras līcis) (Riia laht), b., Eur.	D6	22
Rigacikun, Nig.	F13	64
Rīgān, Iran	G15	48
Rigby, Id., U.S.	G14	122
Rīgestān, reg., Afg.	E1	44
Riggins, Id., U.S.	E9	122
Rigi, mtn., Switz.	D10	13
Rigo, Pap. N. Gui.	A9	68
Rigolet, Newf., Can.	F21	96
Riiser-Larsen Peninsula, pen., Ant.	B4	73
Rijeka, Cro.	D9	18
Rijswijk, Neth.	D5	12
Riley, Ks., U.S.	L11	118
Rillito, Az., U.S.	L5	120
Rima, stm., Nig.	E12	64
Rímac, stm., Peru	D3	82
Rimachi, Laguna, l., Peru	J4	84
Rimavská Sobota, Czech.	G20	10
Rimbey, Alta., Can.	E20	102
Rimersburg, Pa., U.S.	F7	108
Rimi, Nig.	E13	64
Rimini, Italy	E7	18
Rîmnicu Sărat, Rom.	D11	20
Rîmnicu Vîlcea, Rom.	D8	20
Rimouski, Que., Can.	D5	106
Rimouski, stm., Que., Can.	D5	106
Rimouski, Réserve, Que., Can.	D5	106
Rincón, C.R.	I11	92
Rincon, Ga., U.S.	G5	112
Rincon, N.M., U.S.	L9	120
Rinconada, Arg.	B5	80
Rincón de la Vieja, Parque Nacional, C.R.	G9	92
Rincón del Bonete, Lago Artificial de, res., Ur.	G11	80
Rincón del Ocote, Cerro, mtn., Hond.	D7	92
Rincón de Romos, Mex.	F8	90
Rindal, Nor.	J11	6
Ringebu, Nor.	K12	6
Ringgold, Ga., U.S.	E1	112
Ringgold, La., U.S.	J3	114
Ringim, Nig.	E14	64
Ringling, Ok., U.S.	E9	116
Ringsted, Ia., U.S.	H13	118
Rinjani, Gunung, mtn., Indon.	G6	38

Name	Map Ref.	Page
Salton City, Ca., U.S.	K10	124
Salton Sea, l., Ca., U.S.	K10	124
Saltville, Va., U.S.	C5	112
Saluda, S.C., U.S.	E5	112
Saluda, Va., U.S.	B10	112
Saluda, stm., S.C., U.S.	E5	112
Sālūr, India	C7	46
Saluzzo, Italy	E2	18
Salvador, Braz.	B9	79
Salvador, El see El Salvador, ctry., N.A.	D6	92
Salvador, Lake, l., La., U.S.	M6	114
Salvador Mazza, Arg.	B7	80
Salvage, Newf., Can.	D20	106
Salvaterra de Magos, Port.	F3	16
Salvatierra, Mex.	G9	90
Salwā, Dawḩat, b., Asia	I11	48
Salwā Baḩrī, Egypt	E7	60
Salween (Nu) (Thanlwin), stm., Asia	D5	40
Salyān, Nepal	F10	44
Salyer, Ca., U.S.	D2	124
Salyersville, Ky., U.S.	B3	112
Salzach, stm., Eur.	G12	10
Salzburg, Aus.	H13	10
Salzburg, state, Aus.	H13	10
Salzgitter, Ger.	C10	10
Salzkammergut, reg., Aus.	H13	10
Salzwedel, Ger.	C11	10
Samā, Jord.	D6	50
Sama, stm., Peru	G6	82
Samacá, Col.	E6	84
Sama [de Langreo], Spain	B6	16
Samaipata, Bol.	H10	82
Samalá, stm., Guat.	C3	92
Sāmalkot, India	D7	46
Samālūt, Egypt	C6	60
Samambaia, stm., Braz.	G2	79
Samaná, Dom. Rep.	E10	94
Samaná, Bahía de, b., Dom. Rep.	E10	94
Samaná, Cabo, c., Dom. Rep.	E10	94
Samana Cay, i., Bah.	C8	94
Samandağı, Tur.	C3	48
Samaniego, Col.	G4	84
Samar, Isr.	I4	50
Samara (Kujbyšev), Russia	G8	26
Samara, stm., Russia	G8	26
Samarai, Pap. N. Gui.	n17	68a
Samaria, Id., U.S.	H13	122
Samariapo, Ven.	E9	84
Samarinda, Indon.	F6	38
Samarkand, Uzb.	J11	26
Sāmarrā', Iraq	D7	48
Samastīpur, India	H11	44
Samaúna, Braz.	B11	82
Sambalpur, India	J10	44
Sambas, Indon.	N10	40
Sambava, Madag.	O24	67b
Sambawizi, Zimb.	B8	66
Sambhal, India	F8	44
Sāmbhar, India	G6	44
Sâmbor, Camb.	H8	40
Sambor, Ukr.	F23	10
Samborombón, stm., Arg.	H10	80
Samborombón, Bahía, b., Arg.	I10	80
Samborondón, Ec.	H3	84
Sambre, stm., Eur.	B11	14
Sambú, stm., Pan.	C3	84
Sambusu, Nmb.	A4	66
Samch'ŏk, S. Kor.	F17	32
Samch'ŏnp'o, S. Kor.	I16	32
Samedan, Switz.	E12	13
Samho, N. Kor.	D15	32
Samiria, stm., Peru	J5	84
Samnaungruppe, mts., Eur.	D13	13
Samnye, S. Kor.	H15	32
Samoa Islands, is., Oc.	J22	126
Samo Alto, Chile	F3	80
Samoded, Russia	E6	26
Sámos, Grc.	L11	20
Sámos, i., Grc.	L10	20
Samoset, Fl., U.S.	L4	112
Samosir, Pulau, i., Indon.	M5	40
Samothrace see Samothráki, i., Grc.	I9	20
Samothráki, i., Grc.	I9	20
S'amozero, Russia	K23	6
Sampacho, Arg.	G6	80
Sampit, Indon.	F5	38
Sampués, Col.	C5	84
Sampur, Russia	I24	22
Sam Rayburn Reservoir, res., Tx., U.S.	K2	114
Samre, Eth.	K10	60
Samreboi, Ghana	I8	64
Samson, Al., U.S.	K10	114
Samson Indian Reserve, Alta., Can.	E21	102
Samsun, Tur.	G15	4
Samtown, La., U.S.	K4	114
Samuhú, Arg.	D8	80
Samui, Ko, i., Thai.	J6	40
Samut Prakan, Thai.	H6	40
Samut Sakhon, Thai.	H6	40
Samut Songkhram, Thai.	H6	40
S'amža, Russia	A24	22
San, Mali	E7	64
San (Xan), stm., Asia	H9	40
San, stm., Eur.	E22	10
Saña, Peru	B2	82
Şan'ā', Yemen	G4	47
Sanaba, stm., Afr.	D4	64
Sanaga, stm., Cam.	J14	64
San Agustín, Arg.	J9	80
San Agustín, Arg.	F6	80
San Agustín, Col.	G4	84
San Agustín de Valle Fértil, Arg.	F5	80
San Alejo, El Sal.	D7	92
Sanalona, Presa, res., Mex.	E6	90
San Ambrosio, Isla, i., Chile	B1	78
Sanana, Pulau, i., Indon.	F8	38
Sanandaj, Iran	D9	48
Sanandita, Bol.	I10	82
San Andreas, Ca., U.S.	F5	124
San Andrés, Col.	H4	94
San Andrés, Mex.	D2	90
San Andrés, Pan.	I12	92
San Andrés, Isla de, i., Col.	H4	94
San Andrés de Giles, Arg.	H9	80
San Andres Mountains, mts., N.M., U.S.	L10	120
San Andrés Sajcabajá, Guat.	B4	92
San Andrés Tuxtla, Mex.	H12	90
San Andrés y Providencia, ter., Col.	H4	94
Sananduva, Braz.	D13	80
San Angelo, Tx., U.S.	H6	116
San Anselmo, Ca., U.S.	G3	124
San Antero, Col.	C5	84
San Antonio, Arg.	C6	80
San Antonio, Arg.	E6	80
San Antonio, Belize	A5	92
San Antonio, Chile	D3	80
San Antonio, Chile	G3	80
San Antonio, Col.	F5	84
San Antonio, C.R.	G9	92
San Antonio, Peru	B3	82
San Antonio, N.M., U.S.	I10	120
San Antonio, Tx., U.S.	J8	116
San Antonio, Ur.	F10	80
San Antonio, stm., Mex.	B2	90
San Antonio, stm., Tx., U.S.	K9	116
San Antonio, Cabo, c., Arg.	I10	80
San Antonio, Cabo de, c., Cuba	D2	94
San Antonio, Mount, mtn., Ca., U.S.	J8	124
San Antonio, Punta, c., Mex.	C2	90
San Antonio, Punta, c., Mex.	D4	90
San Antonio, Rio, stm., U.S.	H10	120
San Antonio Bay, b., Tx., U.S.	K10	116
San Antonio de Areco, Arg.	H9	80
San Antonio de los Baños, Cuba	C3	94
San Antonio de los Cobres, Arg.	C5	80
San Antonio del Táchira, Ven.	D6	84
San Antonio de Tamanaco, Ven.	C9	84
San Antonio El Bravo, Mex.	B7	90
San Antonio Mountain, mtn., N.M., U.S.	H10	120
San Antonio Suchitepéquez, Guat.	C3	92
Sanatorium, Ms., U.S.	K7	114
San Augustine, Tx., U.S.	K2	114
San Augustin Pass, N.M., U.S.	L10	120
San Bartolomé, Spain	N27	17b
San Benedetto del Tronto, Italy	G8	18
San Benedicto, Isla, i., Mex.	H4	90
San Benito, Bol.	G9	82
San Benito, Guat.	I15	90
San Benito, Peru	B2	82
San Benito, Tx., U.S.	M9	116
San Benito, stm., Ca., U.S.	H4	124
San Bernardino, Switz.	F11	13
San Bernardino, Ca., U.S.	J8	124
San Bernardino Mountains, mts., Ca., U.S.	J9	124
San Bernardo, Arg.	D8	80
San Bernardo, Chile	G3	80
San Bernardo, Mex.	E7	90
San Bernardo, Isla, i., Nic.	F9	92
San Bernardo, Islas de, is., Col.	C4	84
San Bernardo del Viento, Col.	C5	84
San Blas, Mex.	G7	90
San Blas, Mex.	D5	90
San Blas, Cape, c., Fl., U.S.	J1	112
San Blas, Golfo de, b., Pan.	C3	84
San Blas, Serranía De, mts., Pan.	C3	84
San Blas de los Sauces, Arg.	E5	80
San Borja, Bol.	F8	82
Sanborn, Ia., U.S.	H12	118
Sanborn, Mn., U.S.	G12	118
Sanborn, N.D., U.S.	E9	118
San Bruno, Ca., U.S.	G3	124
San Buenaventura, Bol.	F8	82
San Buenaventura, Mex.	D9	90
Sancang, China	C9	34
San Carlos, Arg.	D11	80
San Carlos, Arg.	G4	80
San Carlos, Arg.	C6	80
San Carlos, Chile	I3	80
San Carlos, Mex.	C9	90
San Carlos, Mex.	E10	90
San Carlos, Nic.	F10	92
San Carlos, Pan.	C3	84
San Carlos, Para.	B10	80
San Carlos, Phil.	C7	38
San Carlos, Phil.	N19	39b
San Carlos, Az., U.S.	K6	120
San Carlos, Ca., U.S.	G3	124
San Carlos, Ur.	H11	80
San Carlos, Ven.	C8	84
San Carlos, stm., C.R.	G10	92
San Carlos, stm., Ven.	C8	84
San Carlos, Riacho, stm., Para.	B9	80
San Carlos Centro, Arg.	F8	80
San Carlos de Bariloche, Arg.	E2	78
San Carlos de Bolívar, Arg.	I8	80
San Carlos de Guaroa, Col.	F6	84
San Carlos del Zulia, Ven.	C7	84
San Carlos de Río Negro, Ven.	G9	84
San Cataldo, Italy	L8	18
San Cayetano, Arg.	J9	80
Sancerre, Fr.	E9	14
Sánchez, Dom. Rep.	E10	94
Sanch'ŏng, S. Kor.	H15	32
San Ciro de Acosta, Mex.	G10	90
San Clemente, Spain	F9	16
San Clemente, Ca., U.S.	K8	124
San Clemente, Cerro, mtn., Chile	F2	78
San Clemente Island, i., Ca., U.S.	L7	124
San Cosme, Arg.	D9	80
San Cristóbal, Arg.	F8	80
San Cristóbal, Dom. Rep.	E9	94
San Cristóbal, Ven.	D6	84
San Cristóbal, Bahía, b., Mex.	D2	90
San Cristóbal, Isla, i., Ec.	J14	84a
San Cristóbal, Volcán, vol., Nic.	E7	92
San Cristóbal de la Laguna, Spain	O24	17b
San Cristóbal de las Casas, Mex.	I13	90
San Cristóbal Totonicapán, Guat.	C3	92
San Cristóbal Verapaz, Guat.	B4	92
Sancti Spíritus, Cuba	D5	94
Sancy, Puy de, mtn., Fr.	G9	14
Sand, stm., Alta., Can.	D3	104
San Damián, Peru	E3	82
Sandaré, Mali	D4	64
Sand Coulee, Mt., U.S.	C14	122
Sanders, Az., U.S.	I7	120
Sanderson, Tx., U.S.	I4	116
Sandersville, Ga., U.S.	G4	112
Sandersville, Ms., U.S.	K7	114
Sandfly Lake, l., Sask., Can.	C8	104
Sand Fork, W.V., U.S.	I6	108
Sandgate, Austl.	F10	70
Sand Hill, stm., Mn., U.S.	D11	118
Sand Hills, hills, Ne., U.S.	J6	118
Sandia, Peru	F7	82
Sandia Crest, mtn., N.M., U.S.	I10	120
San Diego, Ca., U.S.	L8	124
San Diego, Tx., U.S.	L8	116
San Diego, stm., Ca., U.S.	L9	124
San Diego, Cabo, c., Arg.	G3	78
San Diego Aqueduct, Ca., U.S.	K8	124
San Diego de la Unión, Mex.	G9	90
San Dionisio, Nic.	E9	92
Sand Lake, l., Ont., Can.	H20	104
Sandoa, Zaire	C4	58
Sandomierz, Pol.	E21	10
Sandoná, Col.	G4	84
San Donà di Piave, Italy	D7	18
Sandoval, Il., U.S.	D7	114
Sandovalina, Braz.	G3	79
Sandovo, Russia	C19	22
Sandoway, Burma	E3	40
Sandpoint, Id., U.S.	B9	122
Sandringham, Eng., U.K.	I13	8
Sandspit, B.C., Can.	D3	102
Sand Springs, Ok., U.S.	C10	116
Sand Springs, Tx., U.S.	G5	116
Sandston, Va., U.S.	B9	112
Sandstone, Austl.	E3	68
Sandstone, Mn., U.S.	D3	110
Sandu Ao, b., China	I8	34
Sandusky, Mi., U.S.	G13	110
Sandusky, Oh., U.S.	F4	108
Sandusky, stm., Oh., U.S.	F3	108
Sandvika, Nor.	L12	6
Sandviken, Swe.	K15	6
Sandwich, Il., U.S.	I7	110
Sandwich, Ma., U.S.	F16	108
Sandwich Bay, b., Newf., Can.	F21	96
Sandwick, B.C., Can.	H10	102
Sandwīp Island, i., Bngl.	I14	44
Sandy, Or., U.S.	E3	122
Sandy, Ut., U.S.	D5	120
Sandy, stm., Me., U.S.	C17	108
Sandy Bay, b., Nic.	C11	92
Sandy Bay Indian Reserve, Man., Can.	H16	104
Sandy Cape, c., Austl.	E10	70
Sandy Hook, Ky., U.S.	A3	112
Sandy Hook, Ms., U.S.	K7	114
Sandy Hook, spit, N.J., U.S.	G12	108
Sandykači, Turk.	J10	26
Sandy Lake, l., Newf., Can.	C17	106
Sandy Lake, l., Ont., Can.	E22	104
Sandy Point Town, St. K./N.	F13	94
Sandy Springs, Ga., U.S.	F2	112
San Elizario, Tx., U.S.	M10	120
San Enrique, Arg.	H8	80
San Estanislao, Para.	C10	80
San Esteban, Hond.	B9	92
San Esteban, Isla, i., Mex.	C3	90
San Felipe, Chile	G3	80
San Felipe, Col.	G9	84
San Felipe, Mex.	B2	90
San Felipe, Mex.	G9	90
San Felipe, Phil.	N19	39b
San Felipe, Ven.	B8	84
San Felipe, Castillo de, hist., Guat.	B5	92
San Felipe, Cayos de, is., Cuba	D3	94
San Felipe de Vichayal, Peru	A1	82
San Felipe Nuevo Mercurio, Mex.	E8	90
San Felipe Pueblo, N.M., U.S.	I10	120
San Félix, stm., Pan.	I13	92
San Félix, Isla, i., Chile	K31	126
San Fernando, Chile	H3	80
San Fernando, Mex.	E10	90
San Fernando, Phil.	M19	39b
San Fernando, Phil.	N19	39b
San Fernando, Spain	I5	16
San Fernando, Trin.	I14	94
San Fernando, Ca., U.S.	J7	124
San Fernando, Ven.	D9	84
San Fernando de Atabapo, Ven.	E9	84
San Fernando del Valle de Catamarca, Arg.	E6	80
Sanford, Co., U.S.	G11	120
Sanford, Fl., U.S.	K5	112
Sanford, Me., U.S.	D16	108
Sanford, Mi., U.S.	G11	110
Sanford, N.C., U.S.	D7	112
Sanford, Tx., U.S.	D5	116
Sanford, Mount, mtn., Ak., U.S.	E22	100
San Francisco, Arg.	F7	80
San Francisco, Col.	G4	84
San Francisco, C.R.	H9	92
San Francisco, El Sal.	D6	92
San Francisco, Pan.	I14	92
San Francisco, Ca., U.S.	G3	124
San Francisco, stm., Arg.	B6	80
San Francisco, stm., U.S.	K8	120
San Francisco, Paso de, S.A.	D4	80
San Francisco Bay, b., Ca., U.S.	G3	124
San Francisco de Borja, Mex.	D6	90
San Francisco de la Paz, Hond.	C8	92
San Francisco del Chañar, Arg.	E7	80
San Francisco del Monte de Oro, Arg.	G5	80
San Francisco del Oro, Mex.	D7	90
San Francisco del Rincón, Mex.	G9	90
San Francisco de Macoris, Dom. Rep.	E9	94
San Francisco de Mostazal, Chile	G3	80
San Francisco Libre, Nic.	E8	92
San Franco, Cerro, mtn., Hond.	B7	92
San Gabriel, Ec.	G4	84
San Gabriel, stm., Tx., U.S.	I9	116
San Gabriel Chilac, Mex.	H11	90
San Gabriel Mountains, mts., Ca., U.S.	J7	124
Sangamner, India	C3	46
Sangamon, stm., Il., U.S.	B6	114
Sanga Puitã, Braz.	G1	79
Sangay, vol., Ec.	H3	84
Sangayán, Isla, i., Peru	E3	82
Sangchungshih, Tai.	J10	34
Sang-e Māsheh, Afg.	D2	44
Sanger, Ca., U.S.	H6	124
Sanger, Tx., U.S.	F9	116
Sangerhausen, Ger.	D11	10
San Germán, Cuba	D6	94
San Germán, P.R.	E11	94
Sangerville, Me., U.S.	B17	108
Sanggan, stm., China	C9	30
Sangha, stm., Afr.	A3	58
Sangihe, Kepulauan, is., Indon.	E8	38
Sangihe, Pulau, i., Indon.	E8	38
San Gil, Col.	D6	84
San Gimignano, Italy	F6	18
San Giovanni in Fiore, Italy	J11	18
San Giovanni in Persiceto, Italy	E6	18
San Giovanni Rotondo, Italy	H10	18
San Giovanni Valdarno, Italy	F6	18
Sangju, S. Kor.	G16	32
Sāngli, India	D3	46
Sangolquí, Ec.	H3	84
San Gorgonio Mountain, mtn., Ca., U.S.	J9	124
San Gottardo, Passo del, Switz.	E10	13
Sangre de Cristo Mountains, mts., U.S.	G11	120
San Gregorio, Arg.	H7	80
San Gregorio, Ur.	G11	80
Sangre Grande, Trin.	I14	94
Sangrūr, India	E6	44
Sanguandian, China	D7	34
Sangudo, Alta., Can.	D20	102
Sangue, Rio do, stm., Braz.	D12	82
Sanhecun, China	A17	32
San Hipólito, Punta, c., Mex.	D3	90
Sanibel Island, i., Fl., U.S.	M4	112
San Ignacio, Arg.	D11	80
San Ignacio, C.R.	H10	92
San Ignacio, Hond.	C7	92
San Ignacio, Mex.	D3	90
San Ignacio, Mex.	F9	90
San Ignacio, Para.	D10	80
San Ignacio, Isla, i., Mex.	E5	90
San Ignacio, Laguna, l., Mex.	D3	90
San Ignacio de Moxo, Bol.	F9	82
San Ignacio de Velasco, Bol.	G11	82
San Ildefonso, Cerro, mtn., Hond.	B6	92
San Isidro, Arg.	H9	80
San Isidro, Arg.	E6	80
San Isidro, C.R.	H11	92
San Isidro, Nic.	E8	92
San Isidro, Tx., U.S.	M8	116
San Jacinto, Col.	C5	84
San Jacinto, Ca., U.S.	K9	124
San Jacinto, West Fork, stm., Tx., U.S.	I11	116
San Javier, Arg.	D11	80
San Javier, Arg.	F9	80
San Javier, Bol.	F9	82
San Javier, Bol.	G10	82
San Javier, Ur.	G9	80
San Javier, stm., Arg.	E9	80
San Javier de Loncomilla, Chile	H3	80
Sanjāwi, Pak.	E3	44
San Jerónimo, Guat.	B4	92
San Jerónimo Norte, Arg.	F8	80
Sanjō, Japan	J13	36
San Joaquín, Bol.	E9	82
San Joaquín, Para.	C10	80
San Joaquín, stm., Bol.	E10	82
San Joaquin, stm., Ca., U.S.	G4	124
San Joaquin Valley, val., Ca., U.S.	H5	124
San Jon, N.M., U.S.	D3	116
San Jorge, Arg.	F8	80
San Jorge, El Sal.	D6	92
San Jorge, Nic.	F9	92
San Jorge, stm., Col.	C5	84
San Jorge, Bahía, b., Mex.	B3	90
San Jorge, Golfo, b., Arg.	F3	78
San José, Arg.	D11	80
San José, C.R.	H10	92
San José, Para.	C10	80
San Jose, Phil.	N19	39b
San Jose, Ca., U.S.	G4	124
San Jose, Il., U.S.	B7	114
San Jose, N.M., U.S.	I11	120
San José, prov., C.R.	H11	92
San Jose, stm., B.C., Can.	F13	102
San José, Isla, i., Mex.	E4	90
San José, Isla, i., Pan.	C3	84
San Jose, Rio, stm., N.M., U.S.	J9	120
San José Batuc, Mex.	C5	90
San José Buena Vista, Guat.	D4	92
San José de Bácum, Mex.	D4	90
San José de Chiquitos, Bol.	G11	82
San José de Copán, Hond.	C6	92
San José de Feliciano, Arg.	F9	80
San José de Guanipa, Ven.	C10	84
San José de Guaribe, Ven.	C10	84
San José de Jáchal, Arg.	F4	80
San José de la Esquina, Arg.	G8	80
San José de las Lajas, Cuba	C3	94
San José de las Raíces, Mex.	E9	90
San José del Cabo, Mex.	F5	90
San José del Guaviare, Col.	F6	84
San José de los Molinos, Peru	E4	82
San José de Mayo, Ur.	H10	80
San José de Ocuné, Col.	E7	84
San José de Sisa, Peru	B3	82
San José de Tiznados, Ven.	C9	84
San Jose Island, i., Tx., U.S.	K10	116
San Juan, Arg.	F4	80
San Juan, Guat.	B6	92
San Juan, Peru	F4	82
San Juan, P.R.	E11	94
San Juan, prov., Arg.	F4	80
San Juan, stm., Arg.	G5	80
San Juan, stm., Col.	E4	84
San Juan, stm., Mex.	E10	90
San Juan, stm., N.A.	G10	92
San Juan, stm., Peru	E4	82
San Juan, stm., S.A.	G3	84
San Juan, stm., U.S.	G6	120
San Juan, stm., Ven.	B11	84
San Juan, Pico, mtn., Cuba	D4	94
San Juan Bautista, Para.	D10	80
San Juan Bautista, Ca., U.S.	H4	124
San Juan Cotzal, Guat.	B3	92
San Juan de Abajo, Mex.	G7	90
San Juan de Colón, Ven.	C6	84
San Juan de Guadalupe, Mex.	E8	90
San Juan [de la Maguana], Dom. Rep.	E9	94
San Juan del César, Col.	B6	84
San Juan del Norte, Nic.	G11	92
San Juan del Oro, stm., Bol.	I9	82
San Juan de los Cayos, Ven.	B8	84
San Juan de los Morros, Ven.	C9	84
San Juan del Río, Mex.	E7	90
San Juan del Río, Mex.	G9	90
San Juan del Sur, Nic.	F9	92
San Juan de Micay, stm., Col.	F4	84
San Juan de Payara, Ven.	D9	84
San Juan Evangelista, Mex.	I12	90
San Juanico, Mex.	D3	90
San Juanillo, C.R.	G9	92
San Juan Islands, is., Wa., U.S.	B3	122
San Juanito, Isla, i., Mex.	G6	90
San Juan Mountains, mts., Co., U.S.	G9	120
San Juan Nepomuceno, Col.	C5	84
San Juan Nepomuceno, Para.	D11	80
San Juan Sacatepéquez, Guat.	C4	92
San Juan Teotihuacán, Mex.	H10	90
San Justo, Arg.	F8	80
Sankarani, stm., Afr.	F5	64
Sankosh, stm., Asia	G14	44
Sankt Aegyd am Neuwalde, Aus.	H15	10
Sankt Anton [am Arlberg], Aus.	H10	10
Sankt Gallen, Aus.	H14	10
Sankt Gallen, Switz.	D11	13
Sankt Gallen, state, Switz.	D11	13
Sankt Gilgen, Aus.	H13	10
Sankt Goar, Ger.	E7	10
Sankt Goarshausen, Ger.	E7	10
Sankt Ingbert, Ger.	F7	10
Sankt Johann im Pongau, Aus.	H13	10
Sankt Johann in Tirol, Aus.	H12	10
Sankt Moritz, Switz.	E12	13
Sankt Niklaus, Switz.	F8	13
Sankt Paul [im Lavanttal], Aus.	I14	10
Sankt Peter, Ger.	A8	10
Sankt-Peterburg (Saint Petersburg), Russia	B13	22
Sankt Pölten, Aus.	G15	10
Sankt Valentin, Aus.	G14	10
Sankt Veit an der Glan, Aus.	I14	10
Sankt Vith (Saint-Vith), Bel.	H9	12
Sankt Wendel, Ger.	F7	10
San Lázaro, Para.	B10	80
San Lázaro, Cabo, c., Mex.	E3	90
San Leandro, Ca., U.S.	G3	124
Sanlicheng, China	D3	34
San Lope, Col.	D7	84
San Lorenzo, Arg.	E9	80
San Lorenzo, Arg.	G8	80
San Lorenzo, Bol.	I9	82
San Lorenzo, Ec.	G3	84
San Lorenzo, Hond.	D7	92
San Lorenzo, Mex.	E8	90
San Lorenzo, Nic.	E9	92
San Lorenzo, Ven.	C7	84
San Lorenzo, stm., Mex.	E6	90
San Lorenzo, Bahía de, b., Hond.	D7	92
San Lorenzo, Cabo, c., Ec.	H2	84
San Lorenzo, Isla, i., Mex.	C3	90
San Lorenzo, Isla, i., Peru	E3	82
San Lorenzo de El Escorial, Spain	E7	16
Sanlúcar de Barrameda, Spain	I5	16
Sanlúcar la Mayor, Spain	H5	16
San Lucas, Bol.	I9	82
San Lucas, Ec.	I3	84
San Lucas, Mex.	F5	90
San Lucas, Cabo, c., Mex.	F5	90
San Luis, Arg.	G5	80
San Luis, Cuba	D7	94
San Luis, Guat.	A5	92
San Luis, Az., U.S.	L5	120
San Luis, Co., U.S.	G11	120
San Luis, Ven.	B8	84
San Luis, prov., Arg.	H5	80
San Luís, Laguna, l., Bol.	E9	82
San Luis, Sierra de, mts., Arg.	G6	80
San Luis de la Paz, Mex.	G9	90
San Luis del Cordero, Mex.	E7	90
San Luis del Palmar, Arg.	D9	80
San Luis Gonzaga, Mex.	E4	90
San Luis Gonzaga, Bahía, b., Mex.	C2	90
San Luis Jilotepeque, Guat.	C5	92
San Luis Obispo, Ca., U.S.	I5	124
San Luis Peak, mtn., Co., U.S.	G10	120
San Luis Potosí, Mex.	F9	90
San Luis Potosí, state, Mex.	F9	90
San Luis Reservoir, res., Ca., U.S.	G4	124
San Luis Río Colorado, Mex.	A2	90
San Luis Valley, val., Co., U.S.	G10	120
Sanluri, Italy	J3	18
San Manuel, Arg.	I9	80
San Manuel, Az., U.S.	L6	120
San Marcial, stm., Mex.	C4	90
San Marcos, Chile	F3	80
San Marcos, Col.	C5	84
San Marcos, C.R.	H10	92
San Marcos, El Sal.	D5	92
San Marcos, Guat.	C3	92
San Marcos, Hond.	C6	92
San Marcos, Hond.	B6	92
San Marcos, Mex.	I10	90
San Marcos, Tx., U.S.	J9	116
San Marcos, dept., Guat.	B3	92
San Marcos, stm., Tx., U.S.	J9	116
San Marcos, Isla, i., Mex.	D3	90
San Marcos de Colón, Hond.	D8	92
San Marino, S. Mar.	F7	18
San Marino, ctry., Eur.	G10	4
San Martín, Arg.	E6	80
San Martín, Arg.	G4	80
San Martín, Col.	F6	84
San Martín, dept., Peru	B3	82
San Martín, stm., Bol.	D8	82
San Martín, stm., Bol.	E10	82
San Martín, Lago (Lago O'Higgins), l., S.A.	F2	78
San Martín de los Andes, Arg.	E2	78
San Martín Texmelucan, Mex.	H10	90
San Mateo, Ca., U.S.	G3	124
San Mateo, Fl., U.S.	J5	112
San Mateo, N.M., U.S.	I9	120
San Mateo, Ven.	C10	84
San Mateo Ixtatán, Guat.	B3	92
San Matías, Bol.	G12	82
San Matías, Golfo, b., Arg.	E4	78
Sanmenxia, China	E9	30
San Miguel, Arg.	E10	80
San Miguel, Bol.	G11	82
San Miguel, Ec.	H3	84
San Miguel, El Sal.	D6	92
San Miguel, Mex.	C9	90
San Miguel, Pan.	C3	84
San Miguel, Peru	E5	82
San Miguel, Spain	O24	17b
San Miguel, Ca., U.S.	I5	124
San Miguel, stm., Bol.	F10	82
San Miguel (Cuilco), stm., N.A.	B2	92
San Miguel, stm., S.A.	H11	82
San Miguel, stm., Co., U.S.	F8	120
San Miguel, Cerro, hill, Bol.	H11	82
San Miguel, Golfo de, b., Pan.	C3	84
San Miguel, Volcán de, vol., El Sal.	D6	92
San Miguel de Allende, Mex.	G9	90
San Miguel de Cruces, Mex.	E7	90
San Miguel del Monte, Arg.	H9	80
San Miguel de Pallaques, Peru	B2	82
San Miguel de Salcedo, Ec.	H3	84
San Miguel de Tucumán, Arg.	D6	80
San Miguel el Alto, Mex.	G8	90
San Miguelito, Nic.	F10	92
San Miguel Ixtahuacán, Guat.	B3	92
San Miniato, Italy	F5	18
Sannār, Sud.	K7	60
Sannicandro Garganico, Italy	H10	18
San Nicolás, Hond.	B6	92
San Nicolás, Peru	F4	82
San Nicolás, Spain	P25	17b
San Nicolás, stm., Mex.	H7	90
San Nicolás de los Arroyos, Arg.	G8	80
San Nicolás de los Garza, Mex.	E9	90
San Nicolas Island, i., Ca., U.S.	K6	124
Sannikova, proliv, strt., Russia	C20	28
Sanniquellie, Lib.	H5	64
Sano, Japan	K14	36
Sañogasta, Arg.	E5	80
Sanok, Pol.	F22	10
San Onofre, Col.	C5	84
San Pablo, Col.	G4	84
San Pablo, Phil.	N19	39b
San Pablo, stm., Bol.	F10	82
San Pablo, stm., Pan.	I13	92
San Pablo Bay, b., Ca., U.S.	F3	124
San Pedro, Arg.	G9	80
San Pedro, Arg.	C6	80
San Pedro, Arg.	D6	80
San Pedro, Chile	A4	80
San Pedro, Chile	G3	80
San Pedro, Col.	C5	84
San Pedro, C.R.	H10	92
San Pédro, I.C.	I6	64
San Pedro, Para.	C10	80
San Pedro, Tx., U.S.	L9	116
San Pedro, Ven.	C7	84
San Pedro, dept., Para.	C10	80
San Pedro, stm., Mex.	B5	90
San Pedro, stm., N.A.	I14	90
San Pedro, stm., N.A.	L6	120
San Pedro, Punta, c., Chile	C3	80
San Pedro, Volcán, vol., Chile	A4	80
San Pedro Ayampuc, Guat.	C4	92
San Pedro Carchá, Guat.	B4	92
San Pedro Channel, strt., Ca., U.S.	K7	124
San Pedro de Atacama, Chile	B4	80
San Pedro de Buena Vista, Bol.	H9	82
San Pedro de Curahuara, Bol.	G7	82
San Pedro de la Cueva, Mex.	C5	90
San Pedro de las Colonias, Mex.	E8	90
San Pedro del Gallo, Mex.	E7	90
San Pedro de Lloc, Peru	B2	82
San Pedro del Norte, Nic.	D10	92
San Pedro del Paraná, Para.	D10	80
San Pedro de Macorís, Dom. Rep.	E10	94
San Pedro Peaks, mts., N.M., U.S.	H10	120
San Pedro Pinula, Guat.	C5	92
San Pedro Pochutla, Mex.	J11	90
San Pedro Sacatepéquez, Guat.	C3	92
San Pedro Sula, Hond.	B6	92
San Pedro Tabasco, Mex.	I14	90
San Pelayo, Col.	C5	84
San Pitch, stm., Ut., U.S.	E5	120
Sanpoil, stm., Wa., U.S.	B7	122
San Quintín, Cabo, c., Mex.	B1	90
San Rafael, Arg.	H4	80
San Rafael, Chile	H3	80
San Rafael, Mex.	E9	90
San Rafael, Ca., U.S.	G3	124
San Rafael, N.M., U.S.	I9	120
San Rafael, Ven.	B7	84
San Rafael, stm., Bol.	H12	82
San Rafael, stm., Ut., U.S.	F6	120
San Rafael del Norte, Nic.	D8	92
San Rafael del Sur, Nic.	F8	92
San Rafael Desert, des., Ut., U.S.	F6	120
San Rafael Oriente, El Sal.	D6	92
San Rafael Swell, plat., Ut., U.S.	F6	120
San Rafael Tasajera, El Sal.	D6	92
San Ramón, Arg.	D6	80
San Ramón, Bol.	E9	82
San Ramón, C.R.	G10	92
San Ramón, Hond.	C10	92
San Ramón, Peru	D4	82
San Ramón, Ur.	H11	80
San Ramón de la Nueva Orán, Arg.	B6	80
Sanrao, China	L5	34
San Remo, Italy	F2	18
San Román, stm., Guat.	A4	92
San Román, Cabo, c., Ven.	A7	84
San Roque, Arg.	E9	80
San Roque, Arg.	F4	80
San Roque, Spain	I6	16
San Roque, Punta, c., Mex.	D2	90
San Rosendo, Chile	I2	80
San Saba, Tx., U.S.	H8	116
San Saba, stm., Tx., U.S.	I7	116
San Salvador, Arg.	E10	80
San Salvador, Arg.	F9	80
San Salvador, El Sal.	D5	92
San Salvador (Watling Island), i., Bah.	B7	94
San Salvador, Volcán de, vol., El Sal.	D5	92
San Salvador de Jujuy, Arg.	C6	80
Sansanné-Mango, Togo	F10	64
San Sebastián, El Sal.	D6	92
San Sebastián, Guat.	C3	92
San Sebastián, Hond.	C6	92
San Sebastián de la Gomera, Spain	O23	17b
San Sebastián de Yalí, Nic.	D8	92
Sansepolcro, Italy	F7	18
San Severo, Italy	H10	18
Sanshui, China	L1	34
San Simon, Az., U.S.	L7	120
San Simón, stm., Bol.	E10	82
San Simon, stm., Az., U.S.	L7	120
Sanso, Mali	F6	64
San Solano, Arg.	F6	80
Sans-Souci, hist., Haiti	E8	94
Santa, Peru	C2	82
Santa, stm., Peru	C2	82
Santa, Isla del, i., Peru	C2	82
Santa Adélia, Braz.	F4	79
Santa Albertina, Braz.	F3	79
Santa Ana, Arg.	D11	80
Santa Ana, Bol.	E9	82
Santa Ana, Bol.	H12	82
Santa Ana, Col.	C5	84
Santa Ana, Ec.	H2	84
Santa Ana, El Sal.	D5	92
Santa Ana, Mex.	E9	90
Santa Ana, Mex.	B4	90
Santa Ana, Ca., U.S.	K8	124
Santa Ana, Ven.	C10	84
Santa Ana, Volcán de, vol., El Sal.	D5	92
Santa Ana del Alto Beni, Bol.	F8	82
Santa Anna, Tx., U.S.	H7	116
Santa Bárbara, Chile	I2	80
Santa Barbara, Col.	E5	84
Santa Bárbara, Hond.	C6	92
Santa Bárbara, Mex.	D7	90
Santa Barbara, Ca., U.S.	J6	124
Santa Bárbara, Ven.	F9	84
Santa Bárbara, Ven.	D7	84

Name — Map Ref. — Page

Ryukyu Islands see Nansei-shotō, is., Japan F12 30
Ryukyu Trench F16 126
Rżaksa, Russia I25 22
Ržanica, Russia H16 22
Rzeszów, Pol. E22 10
Ržev, Russia E17 22

S

Saale, stm., Ger. D11 10
Saales, Fr. D14 14
Saalfeld, Ger. E11 10
Saar, stm., Eur. J10 12
Saarbrücken, Ger. F6 10
Saarburg, Ger. F6 10
Sääre, Est. D5 22
Saaremaa, i., Est. C5 22
Saarland, state, Ger. F6 10
Saarlouis, Ger. F6 10
Saar see Saarland, state, Ger. F6 10
Saas Grund, Switz. F8 13
Saatly, Azer. B10 48
Saavedra, Arg. I7 80
Saba, i., Neth. Ant. F13 94
Šabac, Yugo. E3 20
Sabadell, Spain D14 16
Sabae, Japan L11 36
Sabana, Archipiélago de, is., Cuba C4 94
Sabana de La Mar, Dom. Rep. E10 94
Sabana de Mendoza, Ven. C7 84
Sabanagrande, Hond. D7 92
Sabanalarga, Col. B5 84
Sabancuy, Mex. H14 90
Sabaneta, Dom. Rep. E9 94
Sabaneta, Ven. C8 84
Sabang, Indon. E6 38
Sabang, Indon. L3 40
Sabanillas, Mex. E9 90
Sabará, Braz. E7 79
Sabastīyah (Samaria), Isr. Occ. D4 50
Sabaudia, Italy H8 18
Sabaya, Bol. H7 82
Sabāyā, Jabal, i., Sau. Ar. E2 47
Şāberī, Hāmūn-e, l., Asia F16 48
Sabetha, Ks., U.S. L12 118
Sabhā, Libya C3 56
Sabi (Save), stm., Afr. C11 66
Sábiè, stm., Afr. E11 66
Sabile, Lat. D5 22
Sabina, Oh., U.S. H3 108
Sabinal, Tx., U.S. J7 116
Sabinal, Cayo, i., Cuba D6 94
Sabiñánigo, Spain C11 16
Sabinas, Mex. D9 90
Sabinas, stm., Mex. D9 90
Sabinas, stm., Mex. D10 90
Sabinas Hidalgo, Mex. D9 90
Sabine, stm., U.S. E8 98
Sabine Bay, b., N.W. Ter., Can. A11 96
Sabine Lake, l., U.S. M3 114
Sabine Pass, b., U.S. M3 114
Sabine Peninsula, pen., N.W. Ter., Can. A11 96
Sabinópolis, Braz. E7 79
Sabinosa, Spain P22 17b
Sabirabad, Azer. A10 48
Sable, Cape, c., N.S., Can. I8 106
Sable, Cape, pen., Fl., U.S. N5 112
Sable, Île de, i., N. Cal. C11 68
Sable, Rivière du, stm., Que., Can. E19 96
Sable Island, i., N.S., Can. I14 106
Sablé-sur-Sarthe, Fr. E6 14
Sabogal, stm., C.R. G10 92
Sabonkafi, Niger D14 64
Sabou, Burkina E8 64
Sabres, Fr. H6 14
Sabrina Coast, Ant. B7 73
Sabula, Ia., U.S. H5 110
Şabyā, Sau. Ar. F3 47
Sabzevār, Iran C14 48
Sac, stm., Mo., U.S. E3 114
Sacaba, Bol. G8 82
Sacaca, Bol. H8 82
Sacajawea Peak, mtn., Or., U.S. E8 122
Sacanche, Peru B3 82
Sacariúna, stm., Braz. E13 82
Sacaton, Az., U.S. K5 120
Sac City, Ia., U.S. I13 118
Săcele, Rom. D9 20
Sachalin, ostrov (Sakhalin), i., Russia G20 28
Sachalinskij zaliv, b., Russia G20 28
Şachayoj, Arg. D8 80
Sachbuz, Azer. B8 48
Sachigo, stm., Ont., Can. F14 96
Sachigo Lake, l., Ont., Can. E22 104
Šachovskaja, Russia E18 22
Šachrisabz, Uzb. J11 26
Sachsen, state, Ger. D13 10
Sachsen-Anhalt, state, Ger. C11 10
Sachs Harbour, N.W. Ter., Can. B7 96
Šachty, Russia H6 26
Šachunja, Russia F7 26
Sack, Russia G24 22
Sackets Harbor, N.Y., U.S. D10 108
Sackville, N.B., Can. G9 106
Saco, Me., U.S. D16 108
Saco, Mt., U.S. B18 122
Saco, stm., U.S. D16 108
Sacramento, Braz. E5 79
Sacramento, Ca., U.S. F4 124
Sacramento, stm., Ca., U.S. F4 124
Sacramento, stm., N.M., U.S. L11 120
Sacramento, Pampa del, pl., Peru C4 82
Sacramento Mountains, mts., N.M., U.S. L11 120
Sacramento Valley, val., Ca., U.S. D3 124
Sacre, stm., Braz. E12 82
Sacred Heart, Mn., U.S. G12 118
Sacupana, Ven. C12 84
Sada, Spain B3 16
Sa'dah, Yemen F3 47
Saddle Lake Indian Reserve, Alta., Can. D23 102
Saddle Mountain, mtn., Co., U.S. F11 120
Sa Dec, Viet. I8 40
Sadêng, China E16 44
Sadiola, Mali E4 64
Sadiya, India D14 42
Sadler Lake, l., Sask., Can. C11 104
Sado, i., Japan I13 36
Šadrinsk, Russia F10 26
Sädvaluspen, Swe. H15 6
Saegertown, Pa., U.S. F6 108
Safad see Zefat, Isr. C5 50
Safājah, Jazīrat, i., Egypt H2 48
Safford, Az., U.S. L7 120
Safi, Mor. D6 62
Safonovo, Russia F4 26
Saga, China F4 30
Saga, Japan N5 36
Sagaing, Burma D3 40
Sagamihara, Japan L14 36
Sagami-nada, b., Japan L14 36
Saganthit Kyun, i., Burma I5 40
Šagany, ozero, l., Ukr. D13 20
Sāgar, India I8 44
Sagavanirktok, stm., Ak., U.S. B20 100
Sagemace Bay, b., Man., Can. G14 104
Sagerton, Tx., U.S. F7 116
Saginaw, Mi., U.S. G12 110
Saginaw, stm., Mi., U.S. G12 110
Saginaw Bay, b., Mi., U.S. G12 110
Sagleipie, Lib. H5 64
Saglek Bay, b., Newf., Can. E20 96
Sagonar, Russia G16 26
Saguache, Co., U.S. F10 120
Sagua de Tánamo, Cuba D7 94
Sagua la Grande, Cuba C4 94
Saguenay, stm., Que., Can. D3 106
Sagunt, Spain F11 16
Sa'gya, China F13 44
Sahāb, Jord. E6 50
Sahaba, Sud. H6 60
Sahagún, Col. C5 84
Sahara, des., Afr. F7 52
Sahāranpur, India F7 44
Sahaswān, India F8 44
Sahel see Sudan, reg., Afr. F11 54
Sāhibganj, India H12 44
Şahin, Tur. H10 20
Sāhīwal, Pak. E5 44
Sahuaripa, Mex. C5 90
Sahuarita, Az., U.S. M6 120
Sahuayo de José María Morelos, Mex. G8 90
Sai Buri, Thai. K6 40
Saïda, Alg. C11 62
Saïdia, Mor. C9 62
Saidpur, Bngl. H13 44
Saidu, Pak. C5 44
Saignelégier, Switz. D7 13
Saigon see Thanh Pho Ho Chi Minh, Viet. I9 40
Saijō, Japan N8 36
Saiki, Japan O6 36
Saimaa, l., Fin. K20 6
Saín Alto, Mex. F8 90
Saint-Affrique, Fr. I9 14
Sainte-Agathe, Man., Can. I17 104
Sainte-Agathe-des-Monts, Que., Can. A12 108
Saint Alban's, Newf., Can. E18 106
Saint Albans, Eng., U.K. J13 8
Saint Albans, Vt., U.S. C13 108
Saint Albans, W.V., U.S. I5 108
Saint Albert, Alta., Can. D21 102
Saint-Alexandre-de-Kamouraska, Que., Can. E4 106
Saint-Amand-Montrond, Fr. F9 14
Sainte-Amélie, Man., Can. H15 104
Saint-Amour, Fr. F12 14
Saint-André, Reu. V17 67c
Saint-André, Cap, c., Madag. P21 67b
Saint-André-Avellin, Que., Can. B11 108
Saint Andrews, N.B., Can. G6 106
Saint Andrews, Scot., U.K. E11 8
Saint Andrews, S.C., U.S. G7 112
Saint Andrews Channel, strt., N.S., Can. F13 106
Saint Anne, Il., U.S. I8 110
Sainte Anne, Lac, l., Alta., Can. D20 102
Sainte-Anne, Lac, l., Que., Can. B6 106
Sainte-Anne-de-Beaupré, Que., Can. E3 106
Sainte-Anne-de-Madawaska, N.B., Can. E5 106
Sainte-Anne-des-Chênes, Man., Can. I18 104
Sainte-Anne-des-Monts, Que., Can. C7 106
Saint Anne's, Eng., U.K. H10 8
Saint Ann's Bay, Jam. E6 94
Saint Anns Bay, b., N.S., Can. F13 106
Saint-Anselme, Que., Can. F3 106
Saint Ansgar, Ia., U.S. G3 110
Saint Anthony, N.B., Can. F9 106
Saint Anthony, Newf., Can. A18 106
Saint Anthony, Id., U.S. G14 122
Saint Arnaud, Austl. K5 70
Saint-Augustin, stm., Can. F21 96
Saint Augustine, Fl., U.S. J5 112
Saint-Augustin Nord-Ouest, stm., Que., Can. A14 106
Saint-Augustin-Saguenay, Que., Can. A15 106
Saint-Avold, Fr. C13 14
Saint Barbe, Newf., Can. A17 106
Saint-Barthélemy, i., Guad. F13 94
Saint-Basile, N.B., Can. E5 106
Saint-Béat, Fr. J7 14
Saint-Blaise, Switz. D6 13
Saint-Bonnet, Fr. H13 14
Saint-Bonnet-de-Joux, Fr. F11 14
Saint Brendan's, Newf., Can. D20 106
Saint Bride, Mount, mtn., Alta., Can. F19 102
Saint Bride's, Newf., Can. F19 106
Saint-Brieuc, Fr. D4 14
Saint-Brieux, Sask., Can. F10 104
Saint-Calais, Fr. E7 14
Saint Catharines, Ont., Can. G16 110
Saint Catherines Island, i., Ga., U.S. H5 112
Saint-Cergue, Switz. F5 13
Saint-Chamond, Fr. G11 14
Saint Charles, Ar., U.S. H5 114
Saint Charles, Id., U.S. H14 122
Saint Charles, Il., U.S. I7 110
Saint Charles, Mi., U.S. G11 110
Saint Charles, Mn., U.S. G3 110
Saint Charles, Mo., U.S. D6 114
Saint Charles Mesa, Co., U.S. M3 118
Saint Christopher (Saint Kitts), i., St. K./N. F13 94
Saint Christopher-Nevis see Saint Kitts and Nevis, ctry., N.A. F13 94
Saint Clair, Mi., U.S. H13 110
Saint Clair, Mo., U.S. D6 114
Saint Clair, stm., N.A. H13 110
Saint Clair, Lake, l., N.A. H13 110
Saint Clair Shores, Mi., U.S. H13 110
Saint Clairsville, Oh., U.S. G6 108
Saint-Claude, Man., Can. I16 104
Saint-Claude, Fr. F12 14
Saint Cloud, Fl., U.S. K5 112
Saint Cloud, Mn., U.S. E1 110
Sainte-Croix, Switz. E6 13
Saint Croix, i., V.I.U.S. F12 94
Saint Croix, stm., N.A. G6 106
Saint Croix, stm., U.S. E3 110
Saint Croix Falls, Wi., U.S. E3 110
Saint Cyr Range, mts., Yukon, Can. F28 100
Saint David, Az., U.S. M6 120
Saint David, Il., U.S. J5 110
Saint David's, Newf., Can. D15 106
Saint David's Head, c., Wales, U.K. J8 8
Saint-Denis, Fr. D9 14
Saint-Denis, Reu. V17 67c
Saint-Dié, Fr. D13 14
Saint-Dizier, Fr. D11 14
Saint Edward, Ne., U.S. J10 118
Saint Eleanor's, P.E.I., Can. F10 106
Saint Elias, Cape, c., Ak., U.S. G22 100
Saint Elias, Mount, mtn., N.A. F24 100
Saint Elias Mountains, mts., N.A. F24 100
Saint-Élie, Fr. Gu. C8 76
Saint Elmo, Il., U.S. C8 114
Saint-Éloi, Que., Can. D4 106
Saint-Étienne, Fr. G11 14
Saint-Eustache, Que., Can. B13 108
Saint-Fabien, Que., Can. D5 106
Saint-Félicien, Que., Can. G18 96
Sainte-Félicité, Que., Can. D6 106
Saint-Félix-de-Valois, Que., Can. A13 108
Saint-Florent, Fr. L24 15a
Saint-Flour, Fr. G10 14
Sainte-Foy, Que., Can. F2 106
Sainte-Foy-la-Grande, Fr. H7 14
Saint Francis, Ks., U.S. L6 118
Saint Francis, S.D., U.S. H7 118
Saint Francis, Wi., U.S. H8 110
Saint Francis, stm., N.A. E4 106
Saint Francis, stm., U.S. H6 114
Saint Francis, Cape, c., Newf., Can. E21 106
Saint Francis, Lake, l., Can. B12 108
Saint Francisville, La., U.S. L5 114
Saint-François, Lac, l., Que., Can. B15 108
Saint-Gabriel, Que., Can. A13 108
Saint-Gabriel-de-Gaspé, Que., Can. D9 106
Saint-Gabriel-de-Rimouski, Que., Can. D5 106
Saint-Gaudens, Fr. I7 14
Sainte Genevieve, Mo., U.S. E6 114
Saint George, Austl. E8 70
Saint George, N.B., Can. G7 106
Saint George, Ont., Can. G15 110
Saint George, S.C., U.S. F6 112
Saint George, Ut., U.S. G3 120
Saint George, Cape, c., Newf., Can. D14 106
Saint George Island, Ak., U.S. H10 100
Saint George Island, i., Fl., U.S. J2 112
Saint George's, Newf., Can. D15 106
Saint-Georges, Que., Can. A16 108
Saint-Georges, Fr. Gu. C8 76
Saint George's, Gren. H14 94
Saint George's Bay, b., Newf., Can. D14 106
Saint Georges Bay, b., N.S., Can. G12 106
Saint George's Channel, strt., Eur. J7 8
Saint Georges Head, c., Austl. J9 70
Saint-Germain, Fr. D9 14
Saint-Germain-du-Bois, Fr. F12 14
Saint-Gervais-les-Bains, Fr. G13 14
Saint-Géry, Fr. H8 14
Saint-Gilles (Sint-Gillis), Bel. G5 12
Saint-Gingolph, Switz. F6 13
Saint-Girons, Fr. J8 14
Saint Gregory, Mount, mtn., Newf., Can. C15 106
Saint-Guénolé, Fr. E2 14
Saint Helena, Ca., U.S. F3 124
Saint Helena, dep., Afr. J6 52
Saint Helena Sound, strt., S.C., U.S. G6 112
Saint Helens, Austl. M8 70
Saint Helens, Or., U.S. E3 122
Saint Helens, Mount, vol., Wa., U.S. D3 122
Saint Helier, Jersey L11 8
Saint-Hilaire-du-Harcouët, Fr. D5 14
Saint-Hippolyte, Fr. E13 14
Saint-Hippolyte-du-Fort, Fr. I10 14
Saint-Hyacinthe, Que., Can. B14 108
Saint-Ignace, N.B., Can. F8 106
Saint Ignace, Mi., U.S. E11 110
Saint Ignace Island, i., Ont., Can. B10 110
Saint Ignatius, Guy. F13 84
Saint Ignatius, Mt., U.S. C11 122
Saint-Imier, Switz. D7 13
Saint-Isidore, N.B., Can. E8 106
Saint James, Mi., U.S. E10 110
Saint James, Mn., U.S. H13 118
Saint James, Mo., U.S. E5 114
Saint James, N.Y., U.S. G13 108
Saint James, Cape, c., B.C., Can. F3 102
Saint-Jean, stm., Que., Can. D8 106
Saint-Jean, stm., Que., Can. B9 106
Saint-Jean, Lac, l., Que., Can. G18 96
Saint-Jean-Baptiste, Man., Can. I17 104
Saint-Jean-d'Angély, Fr. G6 14
Saint-Jean-de-Losne, Fr. E12 14
Saint-Jean-de-Luz, Fr. I5 14
Saint-Jean-Pied-de-Port, Fr. I5 14
Saint-Jean-Port-Joli, Que., Can. E3 106
Saint-Jean-sur-Richelieu, Que., Can. B13 108
Saint-Jérôme, Que., Can. B12 108
Saint Jo, Tx., U.S. F9 116
Saint John, N.B., Can. G7 106
Saint John, Ks., U.S. M9 118
Saint John, N.D., U.S. C8 118
Saint John, Wa., U.S. C8 122
Saint John, i., V.I.U.S. E12 94
Saint John, stm., N.A. G7 106
Saint John, Cape, c., Newf., Can. B18 106
Saint John, Lake, l., Newf., Can. D19 106
Saint John Bay, b., Newf., Can. B16 106
Saint John Island, i., Newf., Can. B16 106
Saint John's, Antig. F14 94
Saint John's, Newf., Can. E21 106
Saint Johns, Az., U.S. J7 120
Saint Johns, Mi., U.S. G11 110
Saint Johns, stm., Fl., U.S. I5 112
Saint Johnsbury, Vt., U.S. C14 108
Saint Joseph, N.B., Can. G9 106
Saint Joseph, Il., U.S. B8 114
Saint Joseph, La., U.S. K5 114
Saint Joseph, Mi., U.S. H9 110
Saint Joseph, Mn., U.S. E1 110
Saint Joseph, Mo., U.S. C2 114
Saint Joseph, Tn., U.S. G9 114
Saint Joseph, stm., U.S. I11 110
Saint Joseph, stm., U.S. I9 110
Saint Joseph, Lake, l., Ont., Can. F14 96
Saint-Joseph-d'Alma see Alma, Que., Can. D2 106
Saint-Joseph-de-Beauce, Que., Can. F3 106
Saint Joseph Island, i., Ont., Can. D12 110
Saint-Jovite, Que., Can. A12 108
Saint-Julien-en-Born, Fr. H5 14
Saint-Julien-en-Genevois, Fr. F13 14
Sainte-Julienne, Que., Can. B13 108
Saint-Junien, Fr. G7 14
Saint-Just-en-Chaussée, Fr. C9 14
Saint Kilda, i., Scot., U.K. D5 8
Saint Kitts and Nevis, ctry., N.A. F13 94
Saint Kitts see Saint Christopher, i., St. K./N. F13 94
Saint-Lambert, Que., Can. B13 108
Saint Landry, La., U.S. L4 114
Saint-Laurent, Man., Can. H17 104
Saint-Laurent-du-Maroni, Fr. Gu. B8 76
Saint Lawrence, Austl. D8 70
Saint Lawrence, Newf., Can. F18 106
Saint Lawrence, stm., N.A. G19 96
Saint Lawrence, Cape, c., N.S., Can. E13 106
Saint Lawrence, Gulf of, b., Can. D11 106
Saint Lawrence Island, i., Ak., U.S. E9 100
Saint-Lazare, Man., Can. H13 104
Saint-Léandre, Que., Can. D6 106
Saint-Léonard, N.B., Can. E6 106
Saint-Léonard-d'Aston, Que., Can. A14 108
Saint-Lô, Fr. C5 14
Saint-Louis, Sask., Can. F9 104
Saint-Louis, Reu. V17 67c
Saint-Louis, Sen. C1 64
Saint Louis, Mi., U.S. G11 110
Saint Louis, Mo., U.S. D6 114
Saint Louis, stm., U.S. D3 110
Saint-Louis, Lac, l., Que., Can. B13 108
Saint-Louis-de-Kent, N.B., Can. F9 106
Saint Louis Park, Mn., U.S. F2 110
Saint-Loup-sur-Semouse, Fr. E13 14
Saint Lucia, ctry., N.A. H14 94
Saint Lucia Channel, strt., N.A. G14 94
Sainte-Lucie, Fr. M24 15a
Saint Lucie Canal, Fl., U.S. L6 112
Saint-Malo, Fr. D4 14
Saint-Malo, Golfe de, b., Fr. D4 14
Saint-Marc, Haiti E8 94
Saint-Marc, Canal de, strt., Haiti E8 94
Saint Margaret Bay, b., Newf., Can. A17 106
Saint Margarets Bay, b., N.S., Can. H9 106
Sainte-Marguerite, stm., Que., Can. B7 106
Sainte-Marguerite, Baie, b., Que., Can. B7 106
Sainte-Marie, Cap, c., Madag. T21 67b
Sainte-Marie-aux-Mines, Fr. D14 14
Saint Maries, Id., U.S. C9 122
Saint Marks, Fl., U.S. I2 112
Sainte-Marthe-de-Gaspé, Que., Can. C7 106
Saint-Martin (Sint Maarten), i., N.A. E13 94
Saint Martin, Lake, l., Man., Can. G16 104
Saint Martins, N.B., Can. G8 106
Saint Martinville, La., U.S. L5 114
Saint Mary, Mo., U.S. E7 114
Saint Mary, stm., B.C., Can. H18 102
Saint Mary, stm., N.A. H21 102
Saint Mary Peak, mtn., Austl. H3 70
Saint Mary Reservoir, res., Alta., Can. H21 102
Saint Marys, Austl. M8 70
Saint Mary's, Newf., Can. F20 106
Saint Mary's, Ont., Can. G14 110
Saint Marys, Ak., U.S. E13 100
Saint Marys, Ga., U.S. I5 112
Saint Marys, Ks., U.S. L11 118
Saint Marys, Oh., U.S. G2 108
Saint Marys, Pa., U.S. F8 108
Saint Marys, W.V., U.S. H5 108
Saint Marys, stm., N.S., Can. G11 106
Saint Marys, stm., N.A. D11 110
Saint Marys, stm., U.S. G2 108
Saint Marys, stm., U.S. I5 112
Saint Mary's, Cape, c., Newf., Can. F19 106
Saint Marys, Cape, c., N.S., Can. H7 106
Saint Mary's Bay, b., Newf., Can. F20 106
Saint Marys Bay, b., N.S., Can. H7 106
Saint-Mathieu, Fr. G7 14
Saint Matthew Island, i., Ak., U.S. F8 100
Saint Matthews, Ky., U.S. D11 114
Saint Matthews, S.C., U.S. F6 112
Saint-Maur [-des-Fossés], Fr. D9 14
Saint-Maurice, stm., Que., Can. G18 96
Sainte-Maxime, Fr. I13 14
Saint-Méen-le-Grand, Fr. D4 14
Saint Meinrad, In., U.S. D10 114
Sainte-Menehould, Fr. C11 14
Sainte-Mère-Église, Fr. C5 14
Saint Michael, Ak., U.S. E13 100
Saint Michaels, Md., U.S. I10 108
Saint-Mihiel, Fr. D12 14
Saint-Moritz see Sankt Moritz, Switz. F16 14
Saint-Nazaire, Fr. E4 14
Saint Nazianz, Wi., U.S. F8 110
Saint-Nicolas see Sint-Niklaas, Bel. F5 12
Saint-Omer, Fr. B9 14
Saintonge, hist. reg., Fr. G6 14
Saint-Pacôme, Que., Can. E4 106
Saint-Pamphile, Que., Can. F4 106
Saint Paris, Oh., U.S. G3 108
Saint-Pascal, Que., Can. E4 106
Saint Paul, Alta., Can. D23 102
Saint-Paul, Fr. I14 14
Saint-Paul, Reu. V17 67c
Saint Paul, In., U.S. C11 114
Saint Paul, Ks., U.S. N12 118
Saint Paul, Mn., U.S. F2 110
Saint Paul, Ne., U.S. J9 118
Saint Paul, Va., U.S. C4 112
Saint-Paul, stm., Can. F21 96
Saint Paul, stm., Lib. H4 64
Saint-Paul, Île, i., F.S.A.T. L11 126
Saint Paul Island, Ak., U.S. H9 100
Saint Paul Island, i., N.S., Can. E13 106
Saint Pauls, N.C., U.S. E8 112
Saint Pauls Inlet, b., Newf., Can. C16 106
Saint Peter, Mn., U.S. F2 110
Saint Peter Island, i., Austl. F6 68
Saint Peter Port, Guernsey C4 14
Saint Peters, N.S., Can. G13 106
Saint Peters Bay, P.E.I., Can. F11 106
Saint Petersburg, Fl., U.S. L4 112
Saint Petersburg see Sankt-Peterburg, Russia B13 22
Saint-Pierre, Mart. G14 94
Saint-Pierre, Reu. V17 67c
Saint-Pierre, Lac, l., Que., Can. B5 106
Saint Pierre and Miquelon (Saint-Pierre-et-Miquelon), dep., N.A. F17 106
Saint-Pierre-Église, Fr. C5 14
Saint Pierre Island, i., Sey. C10 58
Saint Pierre-Jolys, Man., Can. I18 104
Saint-Pol-de-Léon, Fr. D3 14
Saint-Pol-sur-Ternoise, Fr. B9 14
Saint-Pons, Fr. I9 14
Saint-Prosper-de-Dorchester, Que., Can. F3 106
Saint-Quentin, N.B., Can. E6 106
Saint-Quentin, Fr. C10 14
Saint-Raphaël, Fr. I13 14
Saint Regis, Mt., U.S. C10 122
Saint Regis, stm., N.A. C12 108
Saint Regis Falls, N.Y., U.S. C12 108
Saint-Rémi-d'Amherst, Que., Can. A12 108
Saint-Rémy-de-Provence, Fr. I11 14
Saint Robert, Mo., U.S. E4 114
Saint-Romuald, Que., Can. F2 106
Sainte-Rose-du-Lac, Man., Can. G15 104
Saintes, Fr. G6 14
Saint-Seine-l'Abbaye, Fr. E11 14
Saint Shotts, Newf., Can. F20 106
Saint-Siméon, Que., Can. E4 106
Saint Simons Island, Ga., U.S. H5 112
Saint Simons Island, i., Ga., U.S. H5 112
Saintes-Maries-de-la-Mer, Fr. I11 14
Saint Stephen, N.B., Can. G6 106
Saint Stephen, S.C., U.S. F7 112
Sainte-Thérèse, Que., Can. B13 108
Saint Thomas, Ont., Can. H14 110
Saint Thomas, N.D., U.S. C10 118
Saint Thomas, i., V.I.U.S. E12 94
Saint-Tite-des-Caps, Que., Can. E3 106
Saint-Trond see Sint-Truiden, Bel. G7 12
Saint-Tropez, Fr. I13 14
Saint-Urbain-de-Charlevoix, Que., Can. E3 106
Saint-Valéry-en-Caux, Fr. C7 14
Saint-Valéry-sur-Somme, Fr. B8 14
Saint-Vallier-de-Thiey, Fr. I13 14
Saint Vincent, Mn., U.S. C10 118
Saint Vincent, i., St. Vin. H14 94
Saint Vincent, Cape see São Vicente, Cabo de, c., Port. H2 16
Saint Vincent, Gulf, b., Austl. J3 70
Saint Vincent and the Grenadines, ctry., N.A. H14 94
Saint-Vincent-de-Tyrosse, Fr. I5 14
Saint Vincent Passage, strt., N.A. H14 94
Saint Vincent's, Newf., Can. F20 106
Saint-Vith (Sankt Vith), Bel. H9 12
Saint Walburg, Sask., Can. E5 104
Saint-Yvon, Que., Can. C9 106
Saitula, China D2 30
Sai Yok, Thai. G5 40
Sajama, Bol. H7 82
Sajama, Nevado, mtn., Bol. H7 82
Sajano-Šušenskoje vodochranilišče, res., Russia G16 26
Şajat, Turk. B17 48
Šajmak', Taj. B6 44
Sajnšand, Mong. C9 30
Sajó, stm., Eur. G20 10
Sajószentpéter, Hung. G20 10
Sa Kaeo, Thai. H7 40
Sakai, Japan M10 36
Sakaiminato, Japan L8 36
Sakākah, Sau. Ar. G6 48
Sakakawea, Lake, res., N.D., U.S. D5 118
Sakami, stm., Que., Can. F17 96
Sakami, Lac, l., Que., Can. F17 96
Sakania, Zaire D5 58
Sakaraha, Madag. S21 67b
Sakarya, stm., Tur. G14 4
Sakata, Japan I14 36
Sakchu, N. Kor. C13 32
Saketé, Benin H11 64
Sakhalin see Sachalin, ostrov, i., Russia G20 28
Sakhrīyāt, Jabal as-, mtn., Jord. F6 50
Sakht Sar, Iran C11 48
Šakiai, Lith. G6 22
Sakiet Sidi Youssef, Tun. M3 18
Sakon Nakhon, Thai. F8 40
Sakrand, Pak. G3 44
Sakrivier, S. Afr. H5 66
Saks, Al., U.S. I11 114
Sakwaso Lake, l., Ont., Can. E23 104
Sal, i., C.V. k17 64a
Sal, stm., Russia H6 26
Sal, Cay, i., Bah. C4 94
Sal, Punta, c., Hond. B7 92
Sala, Swe. L15 6
Salaberry-de-Valleyfield, Que., Can. B12 108
Salacgrīva, Lat. D7 22
Salada, Laguna, l., Mex. A2 90
Saladas, Arg. E9 80
Saladillo, Arg. H9 80
Saladillo, stm., Arg. E7 80
Saladillo, stm., Arg. G7 80
Saladillo Dulce, Arroyo, stm., Arg. F8 80
Salado, Arg. E5 80
Salado, stm., Arg. H5 80
Salado, stm., Arg. E5 80
Salado, stm., Arg. F8 80
Salado, stm., Arg. H9 80
Salado, stm., Cuba D6 94
Salado, stm., Mex. D10 90
Salado, Rio, stm., N.M., U.S. J9 120
Şălaj, co., Rom. B7 20
Šalakuša, Russia J27 6
Salala, Chile F3 80
Salala, Lib. H4 64
Şalālah, Oman F9 47
Salamá, Guat. B4 92
Salamá, Hond. C8 92
Salamanca, Chile F3 80
Salamanca, Mex. G9 90
Salamanca, Peru F5 82
Salamanca, Spain E6 16
Salamanca, N.Y., U.S. E8 108
Salamat, Bahr, stm., Chad F4 56
Salamina, Col. E5 84
Salamís, Grc. L7 20
Salamís, i., Grc. L7 20
Salamonie, stm., In., U.S. B11 114
Salantai, Lith. E4 22
Salaquí, Col. D4 84
Salaquí, stm., Col. D4 84
Salas, Peru B2 82
Salatiga, Indon. J15 39a
Salavat, Russia G9 26
Salaverry, Peru C2 82
Salavina, Arg. E7 80
Sala y Gómez, Isla, i., Chile K29 126
Salcajá, Guat. C3 92
Salccantay, Nevado, mtn., Peru E5 82
Şalcedo, Dom. Rep. E9 94
Šalčininkai, Lith. G8 22
Saldaña, stm., Col. F5 84
Saldanha, S. Afr. I3 66
Saldungaray, Arg. J8 80
Saldus, Lat. E5 22
Sale, Austl. L7 70
Salé, Mor. C7 62
Salebabu, Pulau, i., Indon. E8 38
Salechard, Russia D5 28
Sale Creek, Tn., U.S. G11 114
Salem, India G5 46
Salem, Ar., U.S. F5 114
Salem, Il., U.S. D8 114
Salem, In., U.S. D10 114
Salem, Ia., U.S. J4 110
Salem, Ky., U.S. E8 114
Salem, Ma., U.S. E16 108
Salem, Mo., U.S. E5 114
Salem, N.H., U.S. E15 108
Salem, N.J., U.S. H11 108
Salem, N.Y., U.S. D13 108
Salem, Oh., U.S. G6 108
Salem, Or., U.S. F2 122
Salem, S.D., U.S. H10 118
Salem, Ut., U.S. D5 120
Salem, Va., U.S. B6 112
Salem, W.V., U.S. H6 108
Salemi, Italy L7 18
Salentina, Penisola, pen., Italy I13 18
Salerno, Italy I9 18
Salerno, Golfo di, b., Italy I9 18
Salgar, Col. E5 84
Salgótarján, Hung. G19 10
Sali, Alg. G10 62
Salí, stm., Arg. D6 80
Salida, Co., U.S. F11 120
Salies-de-Béarn, Fr. I6 14
Salihli, Tur. K12 20
Salim, Sud. K5 60
Salima, Mwi. D6 58
Salimani, Com. K15 67a
Salina, Ks., U.S. M10 118
Salina, Ok., U.S. C11 116
Salina, Ut., U.S. F5 120
Salina Cruz, Mex. I12 90
Salina Point, c., Bah. C7 94
Salinas, Braz. D7 79
Salinas, Ec. I2 84
Salinas, Ca., U.S. H4 124
Salinas, stm., Braz. D7 79
Salinas, stm., Ca., U.S. H4 124
Salinas, Pampa de las, pl., Arg. G5 80
Salinas de Garci Mendoza, Bol. H8 82
Salinas de Hidalgo, Mex. F9 90
Saline, La., U.S. J4 114
Saline, Mi., U.S. H12 110
Saline, stm., Ar., U.S. I4 114
Saline, stm., Il., U.S. E8 114
Saline, stm., Ks., U.S. M10 118
Saline Bayou, stm., La., U.S. J3 114
Salingyi, Burma D3 40
Salisbury, Austl. J3 70
Salisbury, Eng., U.K. J12 8
Salisbury, Md., U.S. I11 108
Salisbury, Mo., U.S. C4 114
Salisbury, N.C., U.S. D6 112
Salisbury, Pa., U.S. H7 108
Salisbury see Harare, Zimb. A10 66
Salisbury Island, i., N.W. Ter., Can. D17 96
Salisbury Plain, pl., Eng., U.K. J12 8
Salish Mountains, mts., Mt., U.S. B11 122
Salitpa, Al., U.S. K8 114
Saljany, Azer. J7 26
Salkehatchie, stm., S.C., U.S. F5 112
Salkhad, Syria D7 50
Sallanches, Fr. G13 14
Salliqueló, Arg. I7 80
Sallisaw, Ok., U.S. D12 116
Salluit, Que., Can. D17 96
Sallūm, Khalīj as-, b., Afr. B3 60
Salmās, Iran B8 48
Salmi, Russia K22 6
Salmo, B.C., Can. H17 102
Salmon, Id., U.S. E12 122
Salmon, stm., B.C., Can. C11 102
Salmon, stm., N.B., Can. F8 106
Salmon, stm., N.A. C12 108
Salmon, stm., Id., U.S. E9 122
Salmon, stm., N.Y., U.S. D11 108
Salmon, stm., Or., U.S. E4 122
Salmon Arm, B.C., Can. G15 102
Salmon-Bay, Que., Can. A16 106
Salmon Mountain, mtn., N.A. B15 108
Salmon Mountains, mts., Ca., U.S. C2 124
Salmon River Mountains, mts., Id., U.S. E10 122
Salmon Valley, B.C., Can. C12 102
Salo, Fin. K18 6
Salò, Italy D5 18
Salobra, stm., Braz. I13 82
Salome, Az., U.S. K3 120
Salon-de-Provence, Fr. I12 14
Salonika see Thessaloníki, Grc. I6 20
Salonta, Rom. C5 20
Saloum, stm., Sen. D2 64
Sal Rei, C.V. k17 64a
Salsacate, Arg. F6 80
Salsilgo, Qawz, dunes, Afr. L2 60
Salsipuedes, Canal, strt., Mex. C3 90
Salsipuedes, Punta, c., C.R. I11 92
Salsipuedes, Punta, c., Mex. A1 90
Sal'sk, Russia H6 26
Salsomaggiore Terme, Italy E4 18
Salt, stm., U.S. G14 122
Salt, stm., Az., U.S. K5 120
Salt, stm., Ky., U.S. D11 114
Salt, stm., Mo., U.S. C5 114
Salta, Arg. C6 80
Salta, prov., Arg. C5 80
Saltcoats, Sask., Can. G12 104
Saltillo, Mex. E9 90
Saltillo, Ms., U.S. H8 114
Saltillo, Tn., U.S. G8 114
Salt Lake City, Ut., U.S. D5 120
Salto, Arg. H8 80
Salto, Ur. F10 80
Salto da Divisa, Braz. D9 79
Salto de las Rosas, Arg. H4 80
Salto del Guairá, Para. C11 80
Salto Grande, Braz. G4 79

Name	Map Ref.	Page
Salton City, Ca., U.S.	K10	124
Salton Sea, l., Ca., U.S.	K10	124
Saltville, Va., U.S.	C5	112
Saluda, S.C., U.S.	E5	112
Saluda, Va., U.S.	B10	112
Saluda, stm., S.C., U.S.	E5	112
Sālūr, India	C7	46
Saluzzo, Italy	E2	18
Salvador, Braz.	B9	79
Salvador, El see El Salvador, ctry., N.A.	D6	92
Salvador, Lake, l., La., U.S.	M6	114
Salvador Mazza, Arg.	B7	80
Salvage, Newf., Can.	D20	106
Salvaterra de Magos, Port.	F3	16
Salvatierra, Mex.	G9	90
Salwā, Dawhat, b., Asia	I11	48
Salwā Baḥrī, Egypt	E7	60
Salween (Nu) (Thanlwin), stm., Asia	D5	40
Salyān, Nepal	F10	44
Salyer, Ca., U.S.	D2	124
Salyersville, Ky., U.S.	B3	112
Salzach, stm., Eur.	G12	10
Salzburg, Aus.	H13	10
Salzburg, state, Aus.	H13	10
Salzgitter, Ger.	C10	10
Salzkammergut, reg., Aus.	H13	10
Salzwedel, Ger.	C11	10
Samā, Jord.	D6	50
Sama, stm., Peru	G6	82
Samacá, Col.	E6	84
Sama [de Langreo], Spain	B6	16
Samaipata, Bol.	H10	82
Samalá, stm., Guat.	C3	92
Sāmalkot, India	D7	46
Samālūt, Egypt	C6	60
Samambaia, stm., Braz.	G2	79
Samaná, Dom. Rep.	E10	94
Samaná, Bahía de, b., Dom. Rep.	E10	94
Samaná, Cabo, c., Dom. Rep.	E10	94
Samana Cay, i., Bah.	C8	94
Samandağı, Tur.	C3	48
Samaniego, Col.	G4	84
Samar, Isr.	I4	50
Samara (Kujbyšev), Russia	G8	26
Samara, stm., Russia	G8	26
Samarai, Pap. N. Gui.	n17	68a
Samaria, Id., U.S.	H13	122
Samariapo, Ven.	E9	84
Samarinda, Indon.	F6	38
Samarkand, Uzb.	J11	26
Sāmarrā', Iraq	D7	48
Samastīpur, India	H11	44
Samaúna, Braz.	B11	82
Sambalpur, India	J10	44
Sambas, Indon.	N10	40
Sambava, Madag.	O24	67b
Sambawizi, Zimb.	B8	66
Sambhal, India	F8	44
Sāmbhar, India	G6	44
Sambor, Camb.	H8	40
Sambor, Ukr.	F23	10
Samborombón, stm., Arg.	H10	80
Samborombón, Bahía, b., Arg.	I10	80
Samborondón, Ec.	H3	84
Sambre, stm., Eur.	B11	14
Sambú, stm., Pan.	C3	84
Sambusu, Nmb.	A4	66
Samch'ŏk, S. Kor.	F17	32
Samch'ŏnp'o, S. Kor.	I16	32
Samedan, Switz.	E12	13
Samho, N. Kor.	D15	32
Samiria, stm., Peru	J5	84
Samnaungruppe, mts., Eur.	D13	13
Samnye, S. Kor.	H15	32
Samoa Islands, is., Oc.	J22	126
Samo Alto, Chile	F3	80
Samoded, Russia	E6	26
Sámos, Grc.	L11	20
Sámos, i., Grc.	L10	20
Samoset, Fl., U.S.	L4	112
Samosir, Pulau, i., Indon.	M5	40
Samothrace see Samothráki, i., Grc.	I9	20
Samothráki, i., Grc.	I9	20
S'amozero, Russia	K23	6
Sampacho, Arg.	G6	80
Sampit, Indon.	F5	38
Sampués, Col.	C5	84
Sampur, Russia	I24	22
Sam Rayburn Reservoir, res., Tx., U.S.	K2	114
Samre, Eth.	K10	60
Samreboi, Ghana	I8	64
Samson, Al., U.S.	K10	114
Samson Indian Reserve, Alta., Can.	E21	102
Samsun, Tur.	G15	4
Samtown, La., U.S.	K4	114
Samuhú, Arg.	D8	80
Samui, Ko, i., Thai.	J6	40
Samut Prakan, Thai.	H6	40
Samut Sakhon, Thai.	H6	40
Samut Songkhram, Thai.	H6	40
S'amža, Russia	A24	22
San, Mali	E7	64
San (Xan), stm., Asia	H9	40
San, stm., Eur.	E22	10
Saña, Peru	B2	82
Şan'ā', Yemen	G4	47
Sanaba, stm., Afr.	D4	64
Sanaga, stm., Cam.	J14	64
San Agustín, Arg.	J9	80
San Agustín, Arg.	F6	80
San Agustín, Col.	G4	84
San Agustín de Valle Fértil, Arg.	F5	80
San Alejo, El Sal.	D7	92
Sanalona, Presa, res., Mex.	E6	90
San Ambrosio, Isla, i., Chile	B1	78
Sanana, Pulau, i., Indon.	F8	38
Sanandaj, Iran	D9	48
Sanandita, Bol.	I10	82
San Andreas, Ca., U.S.	F5	124
San Andrés, Col.	H4	94
San Andrés, Mex.	D2	90
San Andrés, Pan.	I12	92
San Andrés, Isla de, i., Col.	H4	94
San Andrés de Giles, Arg.	H9	80
San Andres Mountains, mts., N.M., U.S.	L10	120
San Andrés Sajcabajá, Guat.	B4	92
San Andrés Tuxtla, Mex.	H12	90
San Andrés y Providencia, ter., Col.	H4	94
Sananduva, Braz.	D13	80
San Angelo, Tx., U.S.	H6	116
San Anselmo, Ca., U.S.	G3	124
San Antero, Col.	C5	84
San Antonio, Arg.	C6	80
San Antonio, Arg.	E8	80
San Antonio, Belize	A5	92
San Antonio, Chile	D3	80
San Antonio, Chile	G3	80
San Antonio, Col.	F5	84
San Antonio, C.R.	G9	92
San Antonio, Peru	B3	82
San Antonio, N.M., U.S.	I10	120
San Antonio, Tx., U.S.	J8	116
San Antonio, Ur.	F10	80
San Antonio, stm., Mex.	B2	90
San Antonio, stm., Tx., U.S.	K9	116
San Antonio, Cabo, c., Arg.	I10	80
San Antonio, Cabo de, c., Cuba	D2	94
San Antonio, Mount, mtn., Ca., U.S.	J8	124
San Antonio, Punta, c., Mex.	C2	90
San Antonio, Punta, c., Mex.	D4	90
San Antonio, Rio, stm., U.S.	H10	120
San Antonio Bay, b., Tx., U.S.	K10	116
San Antonio de Areco, Arg.	H9	80
San Antonio de los Baños, Cuba	C3	94
San Antonio de los Cobres, Arg.	C5	80
San Antonio del Táchira, Ven.	D6	84
San Antonio de Tamanaco, Ven.	C9	84
San Antonio El Bravo, Mex.	B7	90
San Antonio Mountain, mtn., N.M., U.S.	H10	120
San Antonio Suchitepéquez, Guat.	C3	92
Sanatorium, Ms., U.S.	K7	114
San Augustine, Tx., U.S.	K2	114
San Augustin Pass, N.M., U.S.	L10	120
San Bartolomé, Spain	N27	17b
San Benedetto del Tronto, Italy	G8	18
San Benedicto, Isla, i., Mex.	H4	90
San Benito, Bol.	G9	82
San Benito, Guat.	I15	90
San Benito, Peru	B2	82
San Benito, Tx., U.S.	M9	116
San Benito, stm., Ca., U.S.	H4	124
San Bernardino, Switz.	F11	13
San Bernardino, Ca., U.S.	J8	124
San Bernardino Mountains, mts., Ca., U.S.	J9	124
San Bernardo, Arg.	D8	80
San Bernardo, Chile	G3	80
San Bernardo, Mex.	D5	90
San Bernardo, Isla de, i., Nic.	F9	92
San Bernardo, Islas de, is., Col.	C4	84
San Bernardo del Viento, Col.	C5	84
San Blas, Mex.	G7	90
San Blas, Mex.	D5	90
San Blas, Cape, c., Fl., U.S.	J1	112
San Blas, Golfo de, b., Pan.	C3	84
San Blas, Serranía De, mts., Pan.	C3	84
San Blas de los Sauces, Arg.	E5	80
San Borja, Bol.	F8	82
Sanborn, Ia., U.S.	H12	118
Sanborn, Mn., U.S.	G12	118
Sanborn, N.D., U.S.	E9	118
San Bruno, Ca., U.S.	G3	124
San Buenaventura, Bol.	F8	82
San Buenaventura, Mex.	D9	90
Sancang, China	C9	34
San Carlos, Arg.	D11	80
San Carlos, Arg.	G4	80
San Carlos, Arg.	C6	80
San Carlos, Chile	I3	80
San Carlos, Mex.	C9	90
San Carlos, Mex.	E10	90
San Carlos, Nic.	F10	92
San Carlos, Pan.	C3	84
San Carlos, Para.	B10	80
San Carlos, Phil.	C7	38
San Carlos, Phil.	N19	39b
San Carlos, Az., U.S.	K6	120
San Carlos, Ca., U.S.	G3	124
San Carlos, Ur.	H11	80
San Carlos, Ven.	C8	84
San Carlos, stm., C.R.	G10	92
San Carlos, stm., Ven.	C8	84
San Carlos, Riacho, stm., Para.	B9	80
San Carlos Centro, Arg.	F8	80
San Carlos de Bariloche, Arg.	E2	78
San Carlos de Bolívar, Arg.	I8	80
San Carlos de Guaroa, Col.	F6	84
San Carlos del Zulia, Ven.	C7	84
San Carlos de Río Negro, Ven.	G9	84
San Cataldo, Italy	L8	18
San Cayetano, Arg.	J9	80
Sancerre, Fr.	E9	14
Sánchez, Dom. Rep.	E10	94
Sanch'ŏng, S. Kor.	H15	32
San Ciro de Acosta, Mex.	G10	90
San Clemente, Spain	F9	16
San Clemente, Ca., U.S.	K8	124
San Clemente, Cerro, mtn., Chile	F2	78
San Clemente Island, i., Ca., U.S.	L7	124
San Cosme, Arg.	D9	80
San Cristóbal, Arg.	F8	80
San Cristóbal, Dom. Rep.	E9	94
San Cristóbal, Ven.	D6	84
San Cristóbal, Bahía, b., Mex.	D2	90
San Cristóbal, Isla, i., Ec.	J14	84a
San Cristóbal, Volcán, vol., Nic.	E7	92
San Cristóbal de la Laguna, Spain	O24	17b
San Cristóbal de las Casas, Mex.	I13	90
San Cristóbal Totonicapán, Guat.	C3	92
San Cristóbal Verapaz, Guat.	B4	92
Sancti Spíritus, Cuba	D5	94
Sancy, Puy de, mtn., Fr.	G9	14
Sand, stm., Alta., Can.	D3	104
San Damián, Peru	E3	82
Sandaré, Mali	D4	64
Sand Coulee, Mt., U.S.	C14	122
Sanders, Az., U.S.	I7	120
Sanderson, Tx., U.S.	I4	116
Sandersville, Ga., U.S.	G4	112
Sandersville, Ms., U.S.	K7	114
Sandfly Lake, l., Sask., Can.	C8	104
Sand Fork, W.V., U.S.	I6	108
Sandgate, Austl.	F10	70
Sand Hill, stm., Mn., U.S.	D11	118
Sand Hills, hills, Ne., U.S.	J6	118
Sandia, Peru	F7	82
Sandia Crest, mtn., N.M., U.S.	I10	120
San Diego, Ca., U.S.	L8	124
San Diego, Tx., U.S.	L8	116
San Diego, stm., Ca., U.S.	L9	124
San Diego, Cabo, c., Arg.	G3	78
San Diego Aqueduct, Ca., U.S.	K8	124
San Diego de la Unión, Mex.	G9	90
San Dionisio, Nic.	E9	92
Sand Lake, l., Ont., Can.	H20	104
Sandoa, Zaire	C4	58
Sandomierz, Pol.	E21	10
Sandoná, Col.	G4	84
San Donà di Piave, Italy	D7	18
Sandoval, Il., U.S.	D7	114
Sandovalina, Braz.	G3	79
Sandovo, Russia	C19	22
Sandoway, Burma	E3	40
Sandpoint, Id., U.S.	B9	122
Sandringham, Eng., U.K.	I13	8
Sandspit, B.C., Can.	D3	102
Sand Springs, Ok., U.S.	C10	116
Sand Springs, Tx., U.S.	G5	116
Sandston, Va., U.S.	B9	112
Sandstone, Austl.	E3	68
Sandstone, Mn., U.S.	D3	110
Sandu Ao, b., China	I8	34
Sandusky, Mi., U.S.	G13	110
Sandusky, Oh., U.S.	F4	108
Sandusky, stm., Oh., U.S.	F3	108
Sandvika, Nor.	L12	6
Sandviken, Swe.	K15	6
Sandwich, Il., U.S.	I7	110
Sandwich, Ma., U.S.	F16	108
Sandwich Bay, b., Newf., Can.	F21	96
Sandwick, B.C., Can.	H10	102
Sandwīp Island, i., Bngl.	I14	44
Sandy, Or., U.S.	E3	122
Sandy, Ut., U.S.	D5	120
Sandy, stm., Me., U.S.	C17	108
Sandy Bay, b., Nic.	C11	92
Sandy Bay Indian Reserve, Man., Can.	H16	104
Sandy Cape, c., Austl.	E10	70
Sandy Hook, Ky., U.S.	A3	112
Sandy Hook, Ms., U.S.	K7	114
Sandy Hook, spit, N.J., U.S.	G12	108
Sandykači, Turk.	J10	26
Sandy Lake, l., Newf., Can.	C17	106
Sandy Lake, l., Ont., Can.	E22	104
Sandy Point Town, St. K./N.	F13	94
Sandy Springs, Ga., U.S.	F2	112
San Elizario, Tx., U.S.	M10	120
San Enrique, Arg.	H8	80
San Estanislao, Para.	C10	80
San Esteban, Hond.	B9	92
San Esteban, Isla, i., Mex.	C3	90
San Felipe, Chile	G3	80
San Felipe, Col.	G9	84
San Felipe, Mex.	B2	90
San Felipe, Mex.	G9	90
San Felipe, Phil.	N19	39b
San Felipe, Ven.	B8	84
San Felipe, Castillo de, hist., Guat.	B5	92
San Felipe, Cayos de, is., Cuba	D3	94
San Felipe de Vichayal, Peru	A1	82
San Felipe Nuevo Mercurio, Mex.	E8	90
San Felipe Pueblo, N.M., U.S.	I10	120
San Félix, stm., Pan.	I13	92
San Félix, Isla, i., Chile	K31	126
San Fernando, Chile	H3	80
San Fernando, Mex.	E10	90
San Fernando, Phil.	M19	39b
San Fernando, Phil.	N19	39b
San Fernando, Spain	I5	16
San Fernando, Trin.	I14	94
San Fernando, Ca., U.S.	J7	124
San Fernando, Ven.	D9	84
San Fernando de Atabapo, Ven.	E9	84
San Fernando del Valle de Catamarca, Arg.	E6	80
Sanford, Co., U.S.	G11	120
Sanford, Fl., U.S.	K5	112
Sanford, Me., U.S.	D16	108
Sanford, Mi., U.S.	G11	110
Sanford, N.C., U.S.	D7	112
Sanford, Tx., U.S.	D5	116
Sanford, Mount, mtn., Ak., U.S.	E22	100
San Francisco, Arg.	F7	80
San Francisco, Col.	G4	84
San Francisco, C.R.	H9	92
San Francisco, El Sal.	D6	92
San Francisco, Pan.	I14	92
San Francisco, Ca., U.S.	G3	124
San Francisco, stm., Arg.	B6	80
San Francisco, stm., U.S.	K8	120
San Francisco, Paso de, S.A.	E4	80
San Francisco Bay, b., Ca., U.S.	G3	124
San Francisco de Borja, Mex.	D6	90
San Francisco de la Paz, Hond.	C8	92
San Francisco del Chañar, Arg.	E7	80
San Francisco del Monte de Oro, Arg.	G5	80
San Francisco del Oro, Mex.	D7	90
San Francisco del Rincón, Mex.	G9	90
San Francisco de Macorís, Dom. Rep.	E9	94
San Francisco de Mostazal, Chile	G3	80
San Francisco Libre, Nic.	E8	92
San Franco, Cerro, mtn., Hond.	B7	92
San Gabriel, Ec.	G4	84
San Gabriel, stm., Tx., U.S.	I9	116
San Gabriel Chilac, Mex.	H11	90
San Gabriel Mountains, mts., Ca., U.S.	J7	124
Sangamner, India	C3	46
Sangamon, stm., Il., U.S.	B6	114
Sanga Puitã, Braz.	G1	79
Sangay, vol., Ec.	I3	84
Sangayán, Isla, i., Peru	E3	82
Sangchungshih, Tai.	J10	34
Sang-e Māsheh, Afg.	D2	44
Sanger, Ca., U.S.	H6	124
Sanger, Tx., U.S.	F9	116
Sangerhausen, Ger.	D11	10
San Germán, Cuba	D6	94
San Germán, P.R.	E11	94
Sangerville, Me., U.S.	B17	108
Sanggan, stm., China	C9	30
Sangha, stm., Afr.	A3	58
Sangihe, Kepulauan, is., Indon.	E8	38
Sangihe, Pulau, i., Indon.	E8	38
San Gil, Col.	D6	84
San Gimignano, Italy	F6	18
San Giovanni in Fiore, Italy	J11	18
San Giovanni in Persiceto, Italy	E6	18
San Giovanni Rotondo, Italy	H10	18
San Giovanni Valdarno, Italy	F6	18
Sangju, S. Kor.	G16	32
Sāngli, India	D3	46
Sangolquí, Ec.	H3	84
San Gorgonio Mountain, mtn., Ca., U.S.	J9	124
San Gottardo, Passo del, Switz.	E10	13
Sangre de Cristo Mountains, mts., U.S.	G11	120
San Gregorio, Arg.	H7	80
San Gregorio, Ur.	G11	80
Sangre Grande, Trin.	I14	94
Sangrūr, India	E6	44
Sanguandian, China	D7	34
Sangudo, Alta., Can.	D20	102
Sangue, Rio do, stm., Braz.	D12	82
Sanhecun, China	A17	32
San Hipólito, Punta, c., Mex.	D3	90
Sanibel Island, i., Fl., U.S.	M4	112
San Ignacio, Arg.	D11	80
San Ignacio, C.R.	H10	92
San Ignacio, Hond.	C7	92
San Ignacio, Mex.	D3	90
San Ignacio, Mex.	F9	90
San Ignacio, Para.	D10	80
San Ignacio, Isla, i., Mex.	E5	90
San Ignacio, Laguna, l., Mex.	D3	90
San Ignacio de Moxo, Bol.	F9	82
San Ignacio de Velasco, Bol.	G11	82
San Ildefonso, Cerro, mtn., Hond.	B6	92
San Isidro, Arg.	H9	80
San Isidro, Arg.	E6	80
San Isidro, C.R.	H11	92
San Isidro, Nic.	E8	92
San Isidro, Tx., U.S.	M8	116
San Jacinto, Col.	C5	84
San Jacinto, Ca., U.S.	K9	124
San Jacinto, West Fork, stm., Tx., U.S.	I11	116
San Javier, Arg.	D11	80
San Javier, Arg.	F9	80
San Javier, Bol.	F9	82
San Javier, Bol.	G10	82
San Javier, Ur.	G9	80
San Javier, stm., Arg.	E9	80
San Javier de Loncomilla, Chile	H3	80
Sanjāwi, Pak.	E3	44
San Jerónimo, Guat.	B4	92
San Jerónimo Norte, Arg.	F8	80
Sanjō, Japan	J13	36
San Joaquín, Bol.	E9	82
San Joaquín, Para.	C10	80
San Joaquín, stm., Bol.	E10	82
San Joaquin, stm., Ca., U.S.	G4	124
San Joaquin Valley, val., Ca., U.S.	H5	124
San Jon, N.M., U.S.	D3	116
San Jorge, Arg.	F8	80
San Jorge, El Sal.	D6	92
San Jorge, Nic.	F9	92
San Jorge, stm., Col.	C5	84
San Jorge, Bahía, b., Mex.	B3	90
San Jorge, Golfo, b., Arg.	F3	78
San José, Arg.	D11	80
San José, C.R.	H10	92
San José, Para.	C10	80
San Jose, Phil.	N19	39b
San Jose, Ca., U.S.	G4	124
San Jose, Il., U.S.	B7	114
San Jose, N.M., U.S.	I11	120
San José, prov., C.R.	H11	92
San Jose, stm., B.C., Can.	F13	102
San José, Isla, i., Mex.	E4	90
San José, Isla, i., Pan.	C3	84
San Jose, Rio, stm., N.M., U.S.	J9	120
San José Batuc, Mex.	C5	90
San José Buena Vista, Guat.	D4	92
San José de Bácum, Mex.	D4	90
San José de Chiquitos, Bol.	G11	82
San José de Copán, Hond.	C6	92
San José de Feliciano, Arg.	F9	80
San José de Guanipa, Ven.	C10	84
San José de Guaribe, Ven.	C10	84
San José de Jáchal, Arg.	F4	80
San José de la Esquina, Arg.	G8	80
San José de las Lajas, Cuba	C3	94
San José de las Raíces, Mex.	E9	90
San José del Cabo, Mex.	F5	90
San José del Guaviare, Col.	F6	84
San José de los Molinos, Peru	E4	82
San José de Mayo, Ur.	H10	80
San José de Ocuné, Col.	E7	84
San José de Sisa, Peru	B3	82
San José de Tiznados, Ven.	C9	84
San Jose Island, i., Tx., U.S.	K10	116
San Juan, Arg.	F4	80
San Juan, Guat.	B6	92
San Juan, Peru	F4	82
San Juan, P.R.	E11	94
San Juan, prov., Arg.	F4	80
San Juan, stm., Arg.	G5	80
San Juan, stm., Col.	E4	84
San Juan, stm., Mex.	E10	90
San Juan, stm., N.A.	G10	92
San Juan, stm., Peru	E4	82
San Juan, stm., S.A.	G3	84
San Juan, stm., U.S.	G6	120
San Juan, stm., Ven.	B11	84
San Juan, Pico, mtn., Cuba	D4	94
San Juan Bautista, Para.	D10	80
San Juan Bautista, Ca., U.S.	H4	124
San Juan Cotzal, Guat.	B3	92
San Juan de Abajo, Mex.	G7	90
San Juan de Colón, Ven.	C6	84
San Juan de Guadalupe, Mex.	E8	90
San Juan [de la Maguana], Dom. Rep.	E9	94
San Juan del César, Col.	B6	84
San Juan del Norte, Nic.	G11	92
San Juan del Oro, stm., Bol.	I9	82
San Juan de los Cayos, Ven.	B8	84
San Juan de los Morros, Ven.	C9	84
San Juan del Río, Mex.	E7	90
San Juan del Río, Mex.	G9	90
San Juan del Sur, Nic.	F9	92
San Juan de Micay, stm., Col.	F4	84
San Juan de Payara, Ven.	D9	84
San Juan Evangelista, Mex.	I12	90
San Juanico, Mex.	D3	90
San Juanillo, C.R.	G9	92
San Juan Islands, is., Wa., U.S.	B3	122
San Juanito, Isla, i., Mex.	G6	90
San Juan Mountains, mts., Co., U.S.	G9	120
San Juan Nepomuceno, Col.	C5	84
San Juan Nepomuceno, Para.	D11	80
San Juan Sacatepéquez, Guat.	C4	92
San Juan Teotihuacán, Mex.	H10	90
San Justo, Arg.	F8	80
Sankarani, stm., Afr.	F5	64
Sankosh, stm., Asia	G14	44
Sankt Aegyd am Neuwalde, Aus.	H15	10
Sankt Anton [am Arlberg], Aus.	H10	10
Sankt Gallen, Aus.	H14	10
Sankt Gallen, Switz.	D11	13
Sankt Gallen, state, Switz.	D11	13
Sankt Gilgen, Aus.	H13	10
Sankt Goar, Ger.	E7	10
Sankt Goarshausen, Ger.	E7	10
Sankt Ingbert, Ger.	F7	10
Sankt Johann im Pongau, Aus.	H13	10
Sankt Johann in Tirol, Aus.	H12	10
Sankt Moritz, Switz.	E12	13
Sankt Niklaus, Switz.	F8	13
Sankt Paul [im Lavanttal], Aus.	I14	10
Sankt Peter, Ger.	A8	10
Sankt-Peterburg (Saint Petersburg), Russia	B13	22
Sankt Pölten, Aus.	G15	10
Sankt Valentin, Aus.	G14	10
Sankt Veit an der Glan, Aus.	I14	10
Sankt Vith (Saint-Vith), Bel.	H9	12
Sankt Wendel, Ger.	F7	10
San Lázaro, Para.	B10	80
San Lázaro, Cabo, c., Mex.	E3	90
San Leandro, Ca., U.S.	G3	124
Sanlicheng, China	D3	34
San Lope, Col.	D7	84
San Lorenzo, Arg.	E9	80
San Lorenzo, Arg.	G8	80
San Lorenzo, Bol.	I9	82
San Lorenzo, Ec.	G3	84
San Lorenzo, Hond.	D7	92
San Lorenzo, Mex.	E8	90
San Lorenzo, Nic.	E9	92
San Lorenzo, Ven.	C7	84
San Lorenzo, stm., Mex.	E6	90
San Lorenzo, Bahía de, b., Hond.	D7	92
San Lorenzo, Cabo, c., Ec.	H2	84
San Lorenzo, Isla, i., Mex.	C3	90
San Lorenzo, Isla, i., Peru	E3	82
San Lorenzo de El Escorial, Spain	E7	16
Sanlúcar de Barrameda, Spain	I5	16
Sanlúcar la Mayor, Spain	H5	16
San Lucas, Bol.	I9	82
San Lucas, Ec.	I3	84
San Lucas, Mex.	F5	90
San Lucas, Cabo, c., Mex.	F5	90
San Luis, Arg.	G5	80
San Luis, Cuba	D7	94
San Luis, Guat.	A5	92
San Luis, Az., U.S.	L5	120
San Luis, Co., U.S.	G11	120
San Luis, Ven.	B8	84
San Luis, prov., Arg.	H5	80
San Luis, Laguna, l., Bol.	E9	82
San Luis, Sierra de, mts., Arg.	G6	80
San Luis de la Paz, Mex.	G9	90
San Luis del Cordero, Mex.	E7	90
San Luis del Palmar, Arg.	D9	80
San Luis Gonzaga, Mex.	E4	90
San Luis Gonzaga, Bahía, b., Mex.	C2	90
San Luis Jilotepeque, Guat.	C5	92
San Luis Obispo, Ca., U.S.	I5	124
San Luis Peak, mtn., Co., U.S.	G10	120
San Luis Potosí, Mex.	F9	90
San Luis Potosí, state, Mex.	F9	90
San Luis Reservoir, res., Ca., U.S.	G4	124
San Luis Río Colorado, Mex.	A2	90
San Luis Valley, val., Co., U.S.	G10	120
Sanluri, Italy	J3	18
San Manuel, Arg.	I9	80
San Manuel, Az., U.S.	L6	120
San Marcial, stm., Mex.	C4	90
San Marcos, Chile	F3	80
San Marcos, Col.	C5	84
San Marcos, C.R.	H10	92
San Marcos, El Sal.	D5	92
San Marcos, Guat.	C3	92
San Marcos, Hond.	C6	92
San Marcos, Hond.	B6	92
San Marcos, Mex.	I10	90
San Marcos, Tx., U.S.	J9	116
San Marcos, dept., Guat.	B3	92
San Marcos, stm., Tx., U.S.	J9	116
San Marcos, Isla, i., Mex.	D3	90
San Marcos de Colón, Hond.	D8	92
San Marino, S. Mar.	F7	18
San Marino, ctry., Eur.	G10	4
San Martín, Arg.	E6	80
San Martín, Arg.	G4	80
San Martín, Col.	F6	84
San Martín, dept., Peru	B3	82
San Martín, stm., Bol.	D8	82
San Martín, stm., Bol.	E10	82
San Martín, Lago (Lago O'Higgins), l., S.A.	F2	78
San Martín de los Andes, Arg.	E2	78
San Martín Texmelucan, Mex.	H10	90
San Mateo, Ca., U.S.	G3	124
San Mateo, Fl., U.S.	J5	112
San Mateo, N.M., U.S.	I9	120
San Mateo, Ven.	C10	84
San Mateo Ixtatán, Guat.	B3	92
San Matías, Bol.	G12	82
San Matías, Golfo, b., Arg.	E4	78
Sanmenxia, China	E9	30
San Miguel, Arg.	E10	80
San Miguel, Bol.	G11	82
San Miguel, Col.	H3	84
San Miguel, Ec.	H3	84
San Miguel, El Sal.	D6	92
San Miguel, Mex.	C9	90
San Miguel, Pan.	C3	84
San Miguel, Peru	E5	82
San Miguel, Spain	O24	17b
San Miguel, Ca., U.S.	I5	124
San Miguel, stm., Bol.	F10	82
San Miguel (Cuilco), stm., N.A.	B2	92
San Miguel, stm., S.A.	H11	82
San Miguel, stm., Co., U.S.	F8	120
San Miguel, Cerro, hill, Bol.	H11	82
San Miguel, Golfo de, b., Pan.	C3	84
San Miguel, Volcán de, vol., El Sal.	D6	92
San Miguel de Allende, Mex.	G9	90
San Miguel de Cruces, Mex.	E7	90
San Miguel del Monte, Arg.	H9	80
San Miguel de Pallaques, Peru	B2	82
San Miguel de Salcedo, Ec.	H3	84
San Miguel de Tucumán, Arg.	D6	80
San Miguel el Alto, Mex.	G8	90
San Miguelito, Nic.	F10	92
San Miguel Ixtahuacán, Guat.	B3	92
San Miniato, Italy	F5	18
Sannār, Sud.	K7	60
Sannicandro Garganico, Italy	H10	18
San Nicolás, Hond.	B6	92
San Nicolás, Peru	F4	82
San Nicolás, Spain	P25	17b
San Nicolás, stm., Mex.	H7	90
San Nicolás de los Arroyos, Arg.	G8	80
San Nicolás de los Garza, Mex.	E9	90
San Nicolas Island, i., Ca., U.S.	K6	124
Sannikova, proliv, strt., Russia	C20	28
Sanniquellie, Lib.	H5	64
Sano, Japan	K14	36
Sañogasta, Arg.	E5	80
Sanok, Pol.	F22	10
San Onofre, Col.	C5	84
San Pablo, Col.	G4	84
San Pablo, Phil.	N19	39b
San Pablo, stm., Bol.	F10	82
San Pablo, stm., Pan.	I13	92
San Pablo Bay, b., Ca., U.S.	F3	124
San Pedro, Arg.	G9	80
San Pedro, Arg.	C6	80
San Pedro, Arg.	D6	80
San Pedro, Chile	A4	80
San Pedro, Chile	G3	80
San Pedro, Col.	C5	84
San Pedro, C.R.	H10	92
San Pédro, I.C.	I6	64
San Pedro, Para.	C10	80
San Pedro, Tx., U.S.	L9	116
San Pedro, Ven.	C7	84
San Pedro, dept., Para.	C10	80
San Pedro, stm., Mex.	B5	90
San Pedro, stm., N.A.	I14	90
San Pedro, stm., N.A.	L6	120
San Pedro, Punta, c., Chile	C3	80
San Pedro, Volcán, vol., Chile	A4	80
San Pedro Ayampuc, Guat.	C4	92
San Pedro Carchá, Guat.	B4	92
San Pedro Channel, strt., Ca., U.S.	K7	124
San Pedro de Atacama, Chile	B4	80
San Pedro de Buena Vista, Bol.	H9	82
San Pedro de Curahuara, Bol.	G7	82
San Pedro de la Cueva, Mex.	C5	90
San Pedro de las Colonias, Mex.	E8	90
San Pedro del Gallo, Mex.	E7	90
San Pedro de Lloc, Peru	B2	82
San Pedro del Norte, Nic.	D10	92
San Pedro del Paraná, Para.	D10	80
San Pedro de Macorís, Dom. Rep.	E10	94
San Pedro Peaks, mts., N.M., U.S.	H10	120
San Pedro Pinula, Guat.	C5	92
San Pedro Pochutla, Mex.	J11	90
San Pedro Sacatepéquez, Guat.	C3	92
San Pedro Sula, Hond.	B6	92
San Pedro Tabasco, Mex.	I14	90
San Pelayo, Col.	C5	84
San Pitch, stm., Ut., U.S.	E5	120
Sanpoil, stm., Wa., U.S.	B7	122
San Quintín, Cabo, c., Mex.	B1	90
San Rafael, Arg.	H4	80
San Rafael, Chile	H3	80
San Rafael, Mex.	E9	90
San Rafael, Ca., U.S.	G3	124
San Rafael, N.M., U.S.	I9	120
San Rafael, Ven.	B7	84
San Rafael, stm., Bol.	H12	82
San Rafael, stm., Ut., U.S.	F6	120
San Rafael del Norte, Nic.	D8	92
San Rafael del Sur, Nic.	F8	92
San Rafael Desert, des., Ut., U.S.	F6	120
San Rafael Oriente, El Sal.	D6	92
San Rafael Swell, plat., Ut., U.S.	F6	120
San Rafael Tasajera, El Sal.	D6	92
San Ramón, Arg.	D6	80
San Ramón, Bol.	E9	82
San Ramón, C.R.	G10	92
San Ramón, Hond.	C10	92
San Ramón, Peru	D4	82
San Ramón, Ur.	H11	80
San Ramón de la Nueva Orán, Arg.	B6	80
Sanrao, China	L5	34
San Remo, Italy	F2	18
San Román, stm., Guat.	A4	92
San Román, Cabo, c., Ven.	A7	84
San Roque, Arg.	E9	80
San Roque, Arg.	F4	80
San Roque, Spain	I6	16
San Roque, Punta, c., Mex.	D2	90
San Rosendo, Chile	I2	80
San Saba, Tx., U.S.	H8	116
San Saba, stm., Tx., U.S.	I7	116
San Salvador, Arg.	E10	80
San Salvador, Arg.	F9	80
San Salvador, El Sal.	D5	92
San Salvador (Watling Island), i., Bah.	B7	94
San Salvador, Volcán de, vol., El Sal.	D5	92
San Salvador de Jujuy, Arg.	C6	80
Sansanné-Mango, Togo	F10	64
San Sebastián, El Sal.	D6	92
San Sebastián, Guat.	C3	92
San Sebastián, Hond.	C6	92
San Sebastián de la Gomera, Spain	O23	17b
San Sebastián de Yalí, Nic.	D8	92
Sansepolcro, Italy	F7	18
San Severo, Italy	H10	18
Sanshui, China	L1	34
San Simon, Az., U.S.	L7	120
San Simón, stm., Bol.	E10	82
San Simon, stm., Az., U.S.	L7	120
Sanso, Mali	F6	64
San Solano, Arg.	F6	80
Sans-Souci, hist., Haiti	E8	94
Santa, Peru	C2	82
Santa, stm., Peru	C2	82
Santa, Isla del, i., Peru	C2	82
Santa Adélia, Braz.	F4	79
Santa Albertina, Braz.	F3	79
Santa Ana, Arg.	D11	80
Santa Ana, Bol.	E9	82
Santa Ana, Bol.	H12	82
Santa Ana, Col.	C5	84
Santa Ana, Ec.	H2	84
Santa Ana, El Sal.	D5	92
Santa Ana, Mex.	E9	90
Santa Ana, Mex.	B4	90
Santa Ana, Ca., U.S.	K8	124
Santa Ana, Ven.	C10	84
Santa Ana, Volcán de, vol., El Sal.	D5	92
Santa Ana del Alto Beni, Bol.	F8	82
Santa Anna, Tx., U.S.	H7	116
Santa Bárbara, Chile	I2	80
Santa Bárbara, Col.	E5	84
Santa Bárbara, Hond.	C6	92
Santa Bárbara, Mex.	D7	90
Santa Barbara, Ca., U.S.	J6	124
Santa Bárbara, Ven.	F9	84
Santa Bárbara, Ven.	D7	84

Name | Map Ref. | Page

Quzhou, China G2 32

R

Raab (Rába), stm., Eur. H15 10
Raahe, Fin. I19 6
Raalte, Neth. D9 12
Ra'anana, Isr. D3 50
Raasiku, Est. B8 22
Raba, Indon. G6 38
Rába (Raab), stm., Eur. H17 10
Rabak, Sud. K7 60
Rabat (Victoria), Malta M9 18
Rabat, Mor. C7 62
Rabaul, Pap. N. Gui. k17 68a
Rabbit Ears Pass, Co., U.S. D10 120
Rābigh, Sau. Ar. C1 47
Rābigh, Sau. Ar. J5 48
Rabinal, Guat. B4 92
Rabka, Pol. F19 10
Rabkavi Banhatti, India D3 46
Rabočeostrovsk, Russia I24 6
Rabyānah, Ṣaḥrā', des., Libya D5 56
Raccoon, stm., Ia., U.S. A3 114
Race, Cape, c., Newf., Can. F20 106
Raceland, La., U.S. M6 114
Race Point, c., Ma., U.S. E16 108
Rach'a, Russia A13 22
Rach Gia, Viet. I8 40
Rachov, Ukr. A8 20
Racibórz (Ratibor), Pol. E18 10
Racine, Wi., U.S. H8 110
Ráckeve, Hung. H18 10
Rădăuţi, Rom. B9 20
Radcliff, Ky., U.S. E11 114
Radeberg, Ger. D13 10
Radebeul, Ger. D13 10
Rades, Tun. B16 62
Radford, Va., U.S. B6 112
Rādhanpur, India I4 44
Radisson, Sask., Can. F7 104
Radium Hot Springs, B.C., Can. G18 102
Radofinnikovo, Russia B13 22
Radolfzell, Ger. H8 10
Radom, Pol. D21 10
Radomsko, Pol. D19 10
Radoškoviči, Bela. G10 22
Radoviš, Mac. H6 20
Radun', Bela. G8 22
Radviliškis, Lith. F6 22
Radville, Sask., Can. I10 104
Radwā, Jabal, mtn., Sau. Ar. E10 60
Radway, Alta., Can. C22 102
Rae, N.W. Ter., Can. D9 96
Rae, stm., N.W. Ter., Can. C9 96
Rāe Bareli, India G9 44
Raeford, N.C., U.S. E7 112
Rae Isthmus, N.W. Ter., Can. C15 96
Rae Strait, strt., N.W. Ter., Can. C13 96
Raetihi, N.Z. C5 72
Rafaela, Arg. F8 80
Rafah, Isr. Occ. F2 50
Raffadali, Italy L8 18
Rafhā', Sau. Ar. G7 48
Rafsanjān, Iran F14 48
Raft, stm., U.S. H12 122
Raft River Mountains, mts., Ut., U.S. C3 120
Rafz, Switz. C10 13
Raga, Sud. M3 60
Ragged Island, i., Bah. C7 94
Ragged Island Range, is., Bah. C7 94
Ragland, Al., U.S. I10 114
Ragusa, Italy M9 18
Raguva, Lith. F7 22
Rahad, Nahr ar-, stm., Afr. F8 56
Rahad al-Bardī, Sud. L2 60
Rahīmyār Khān, Pak. F4 44
Rahway, N.J., U.S. G12 108
Rāichūr, India D4 46
Raiford, Fl., U.S. I4 112
Raiganj, India H13 44
Raigarh, India J10 44
Railton, Austl. M7 70
Rainbow Falls, wtfl, B.C., Can. E15 102
Rainelle, W.V., U.S. J6 108
Rainier, Mount, mtn., Wa., U.S. D4 122
Rainy, stm., N.A. J20 104
Rainy, stm., Mi., U.S. E11 110
Rainy Lake, l., N.A. B2 110
Rainy River, Ont., Can. B1 110
Raipur, India J9 44
Ra'īs, Sau. Ar. C1 47
Raisin, stm., Mi., U.S. I12 110
Raiti, Nic. C9 92
Rājahmundry, India D6 46
Rajaj, Sud. L3 60
Rajang, stm., Malay. E5 38
Rājapālaiyam, India H4 46
Rājasthān, state, India G5 44
Rajčichinsk, Russia H17 28
Rajka, Hung. G17 10
Rājkot, India I4 44
Rāj Nāndgaon, India J9 44
Rājpipla, India B2 46
Rājshāhi, Bngl. H13 44
Rakamaz, Hung. G21 10
Rakaposhi, mtn., Pak. B6 44
Rakata, Pulau, i., Indon. J12 39a
Rakops, Bots. C7 66
Rakovník, Czech. E13 10
Rakvere, Est. B9 22
Raleigh, Newf., Can. A18 106
Raleigh, Ms., U.S. J7 114
Raleigh, N.C., U.S. D8 112
Ralls, Tx., U.S. F5 116
Ralston, Ne., U.S. J11 118
Ralston, Pa., U.S. F10 108
Ram, stm., Alta., Can. E19 102
Rama, Isr. C4 50
Rama, Nic. E10 92
Rama, stm., Nic. F10 92
Ramacca, Italy L9 18
Ramah, N.M., U.S. I8 120
Rām Allāh, Isr. Occ. E4 50
Rāmanāthapuram, India H5 46
Ramasucha, Russia I16 22
Ramat Gan, Isr. D3 50
Ramat HaSharon, Isr. D3 50
Ramathlabama, Bots. E7 66
Rambervillers, Fr. D13 14
Rambouillet, Fr. D8 14
Ramea, Newf., Can. E16 106
Ramea Islands, is., Newf., Can. E16 106
Ramenskoje, Russia F21 22
Ramer, Al., U.S. J10 114
Rameški, Russia D19 22
Rāmeswaram, India H10 42
Rāmhormoz, Iran F10 48
Ramingstein, Aus. H13 10
Ramiriquí, Col. E6 84
Ramla, Isr. E3 50
Ramlu, mtn., Eth. F9 56
Ramm, Jabal, mtn., Jord. I4 50
Ramona, Ca., U.S. K9 124
Ramona, Ok., U.S. C11 116
Ramona, S.D., U.S. G10 118
Ramos, Mex. F9 90
Ramos, stm., Mex. E7 90
Ramot, Isr. Occ. C5 50
Ramotswa, Bots. E7 66
Rampart, Ak., U.S. D19 100
Ramparts, stm., N.W. Ter., Can. D29 100
Rāmpur, India F8 44
Rāmpur Hāt, India H12 44
Ramree Island, i., Burma E2 40
Ramseur, N.C., U.S. D7 112
Ramsey, I. of Man G9 8
Ramsey, Il., U.S. C7 114
Rāmshīr, Iran F10 48
Ramu, stm., Pap. N. Gui. m16 68a
Rāmygala, Lith. F7 22
Rānāghāt, India I13 44
Ranburne, Al., U.S. I11 114
Rancagua, Chile H3 80
Rance, stm., Fr. D4 14
Rancevo, Russia E17 22
Rancharia, Braz. G3 79
Rancheria, Yukon, Can. F29 100
Rancheria, stm., Col. B6 84
Ranches of Taos, N.M., U.S. H11 120
Ranchester, Wy., U.S. F18 122
Rānchi, India I11 44
Ranchillos, Arg. D6 80
Ranch Lake, l., Sask., Can. F10 104
Rancho Cordova, Ca., U.S. F4 124
Rancul, Arg. H6 80
Randers, Den. M12 6
Randleman, N.C., U.S. D7 112
Randlett, Ok., U.S. E8 116
Randolph, Az., U.S. L5 120
Randolph, Me., U.S. C17 108
Randolph, Ne., U.S. I10 118
Randolph, N.Y., U.S. E8 108
Randolph, Ut., U.S. C5 120
Randolph, Vt., U.S. D14 108
Randolph, Wi., U.S. G6 110
Random Island, i., Newf., Can. D20 106
Random Lake, Wi., U.S. G8 110
Råneå, Swe. I18 6
Rāngāmāti, Bngl. I15 44
Range Indian Reserve, B.C., Can. H15 102
Rangeley, Me., U.S. C16 108
Rangely, Co., U.S. D8 120
Ranger, Tx., U.S. G8 116
Rangoon see Yangon, Burma F4 40
Rangpur, Bngl. H13 44
Ranguana Cay, i., Belize A6 92
Ranguana Entrance, strt., Belize A6 92
Rānībennur, India E3 46
Rānīganj, India I12 44
Rānikhet, India F8 44
Ranken, stm., Austl. C2 70
Ranken Store, Austl. B2 70
Rankin, Il., U.S. B9 114
Rankin, Tx., U.S. H5 116
Rankin Inlet, N.W. Ter., Can. D14 96
Ranlo, N.C., U.S. D5 112
Ranohira, Madag. S21 67b
Ranomafana, Madag. T22 67b
Ranong, Thai. J5 40
Ranopiso, Madag. T22 67b
Ranotsara Nord, Madag. S22 67b
Ransom, Ks., U.S. M8 118
Ranson, W.V., U.S. H9 108
Rantauprapat, Indon. M5 40
Rantekombola, Bulu, mtn., Indon. F7 38
Rantoul, Il., U.S. B8 114
Ranua, Fin. I20 6
Ranwanalenaus, Bots. B6 66
Raoping, China L6 34
Raoul, Ga., U.S. E3 112
Rapa, Ponta do, c., Braz. D14 80
Rapallo, Italy E4 18
Rapel, stm., Chile G3 80
Rapelli, Arg. D6 80
Rapid, stm., Mi., U.S. D8 110
Rapid, stm., Mn., U.S. B1 110
Rapidan, stm., Va., U.S. I9 108
Rapid City, Man., Can. H14 104
Rapid City, Mi., U.S. F10 110
Rapid City, S.D., U.S. G4 118
Rapid River, Mi., U.S. E9 110
Rāpina, Est. C10 22
Rapla, Est. B7 22
Rappahannock, stm., Va., U.S. B10 112
Rapperswil, Switz. D10 13
Rāpti, stm., Asia G10 44
Rapulo, stm., Bol. F8 82
Raron, Switz. F8 13
Rasa, Punta, c., Arg. I10 80
Ra's al-'Ayn, Syria C6 48
Ra's al-Khaymah, U.A.E. B9 47
Ra's an-Naqb, Egypt I3 50
Ra's an-Naqb, Jord. H4 50
Ras Dashen Terara, mtn., Eth. K10 60
Raseiniai, Lith. F6 22
Râs el Aîoun, Alg. N3 18
Ras el Ma, Alg. C10 62
Rashād, Sud. L6 60
Rashīd, Egypt B6 60
Rasht, Iran C10 48
Rāsipuram, India G5 46
Raška, Yugo. F4 20
Raškov, Mol. B12 20
Rass Jebel, Tun. L5 18
Rasskazovo, Russia I24 22
Rassua, ostrov, i., Russia H22 28
Ra's Tannūrah, Sau. Ar. H11 48
Rastatt, Ger. G8 10
Rastede, Ger. B8 10
Rasūl, Pak. D5 44
Rat, stm., Man., Can. I18 104
Rat, stm., Man., Can. B15 104
Ratangarh, India F6 44
Rätansbyn, Swe. J14 6
Rāth, India H8 44
Rathbun Lake, res., Ia., U.S. J2 110
Rathdrum, Id., U.S. C9 122
Rathenow, Ger. C12 10
Rathwell, Man., Can. I16 104
Ratingen, Ger. D6 10
Rat Islands, is., Ak., U.S. K4 101a
Rat Lake, l., Man., Can. B15 104
Ratlām, India I6 44
Ratnāgiri, India D2 46
Ratnapura, Sri L. I6 46
Ratomka, Bela. H10 22
Raton, N.M., U.S. C2 116
Raton Pass, N.M., U.S. O3 118
Rattlesnake, Mt., U.S. D12 122
Rattling Brook, Newf., Can. C17 106
Ratz, Mount, mtn., B.C., Can. H28 100
Ratzeburg, Ger. B10 10
Raub, Malay. M6 40
Rauch, Arg. I9 80
Raul Soares, Braz. F7 79
Rauma, Fin. K17 6
Raurkela, India I11 44
Ravanusa, Italy L8 18
Rāvar, Iran F14 48
Ravelo, Bol. H9 82
Raven, Va., U.S. B5 112
Ravena, N.Y., U.S. E13 108
Ravenna, Italy E7 18
Ravenna, Ky., U.S. B3 112
Ravenna, Mi., U.S. G10 110
Ravenna, Ne., U.S. J9 118
Ravenna, Oh., U.S. F5 108
Ravensburg, Ger. H9 10
Ravenscrag, Sask., Can. I5 104
Ravenshoe, Austl. A6 70
Ravensthorpe, Austl. F4 68
Ravenswood, W.V., U.S. I5 108
Rāvi, stm., Asia E5 44
Ravnina, Turk. C17 48
Rāwalpindi, Pak. D5 44
Rawa Mazowiecka, Pol. D20 10
Rawāndūz, Iraq C8 48
Rawdon, Que., Can. A13 108
Rawicz, Pol. D16 10
Rawlinna, Austl. F5 68
Rawlins, Wy., U.S. C9 120
Rawson, Arg. E3 78
Rawson, Arg. H8 80
Raxāul, India G11 44
Ray, N.D., U.S. C4 118
Ray, Cape, c., Newf., Can. E14 106
Raya, Bukit, mtn., Indon. F5 38
Rāyadurg, India E4 46
Raymond, Alta., Can. H22 102
Raymond, Il., U.S. C7 114
Raymond, Mn., U.S. F12 118
Raymond, Ms., U.S. J6 114
Raymond, Wa., U.S. D2 122
Raymond Terrace, Austl. I9 70
Raymondville, Tx., U.S. M9 116
Raymore, Sask., Can. G10 104
Rayne, La., U.S. L4 114
Rayón, Mex. C4 90
Rayones, Mex. E9 90
Rayong, Thai. H6 40
Raytown, Mo., U.S. C2 114
Rayville, La., U.S. J5 114
Razan, Iran D10 48
R'azan', Russia G22 22
R'azancevo, Russia E22 22
Ražanj, Yugo. F5 20
Razdan, Arm. A8 48
Razdel'naja, Ukr. C14 20
Razgrad, Bul. F10 20
Razorback Mountain, mtn., B.C., Can. F10 102
R'ažsk, Russia H23 22
Ré, Île de, i., Fr. F5 14
Reading, Eng., U.K. J13 8
Reading, Ks., U.S. M12 118
Reading, Mi., U.S. I11 110
Reading, Oh., U.S. H2 108
Reading, Pa., U.S. G11 108
Readlyn, Ia., U.S. H3 110
Readstown, Wi., U.S. G5 110
Real, Cordillera, mts., S.A. H9 82
Real, Estero, stm., Nic. E7 92
Real del Padre, Arg. H5 80
Realicó, Arg. H6 80
Realitos, Tx., U.S. L8 116
Reardan, Wa., U.S. C8 122
Reata, Mex. D9 90
Reay, Scot., U.K. C10 8
Rebolly, Russia J22 6
Rebouças, Braz. C13 80
Rebun-tō, i., Japan B16 36a
Recalde, Arg. I8 80
Recanati, Italy F8 18
Rečane, Russia E14 22
Recherche, Archipelago of the, is., Austl. F4 68
Rečica, Bela. I13 22
Recife, Braz. E12 76
Recinto, Chile I3 80
Recklinghausen, Ger. D7 10
Reconquista, Arg. E9 80
Recreio, Braz. F7 79
Recreo, Arg. E6 80
Rector, Ar., U.S. F6 114
Recuay, Peru C3 82
Red (Hong) (Yuan), stm., Asia C8 40
Red, stm., N.A. B7 98
Red, stm., U.S. E8 98
Red, stm., Ky., U.S. B3 112
Red, stm., N.M., U.S. H11 120
Red, stm., Wi., U.S. F7 110
Redange, Lux. I8 12
Red Bank, N.J., U.S. G12 108
Red Bank, Tn., U.S. G11 114
Red Banks, Ms., U.S. H7 114
Red Bay, Newf., Can. A17 106
Red Bay, Al., U.S. H8 114
Redbay, Fl., U.S. L11 114
Redberry Lake, l., Sask., Can. F7 104
Red Bluff, Ca., U.S. D3 124
Red Bluff Reservoir, res., U.S. B8 90
Red Boiling Springs, Tn., U.S. F11 114
Red Bud, Il., U.S. D7 114
Red Cedar, stm., Mi., U.S. H11 110
Red Cedar, stm., Wi., U.S. E4 110
Redcliff, Alta., Can. H4 104
Red Cliff, Co., U.S. E10 120
Redcliff, Zimb. B9 66
Redcliffe, Austl. F10 70
Red Cliffs, Austl. J5 70
Red Cloud, Ne., U.S. K9 118
Red Cross Lake, l., Man., Can. C22 104
Red Deer, Alta., Can. E21 102
Red Deer, stm., Can. F10 96
Red Deer, stm., Can. F12 104
Red Deer Lake, l., Alta., Can. E21 102
Red Deer Lake, l., Man., Can. F13 104
Red Devil, Ak., U.S. F16 100
Redding, Ca., U.S. D3 124
Redeye, stm., Mn., U.S. E12 118
Redfield, Ia., U.S. J13 118
Redfield, S.D., U.S. G9 118
Redford, Tx., U.S. J2 116
Red Hook, N.Y., U.S. F13 108
Red Indian Lake, l., Newf., Can. D17 106
Red Island, i., Newf., Can. E19 106
Redkey, In., U.S. B11 114
Redkino, Russia E19 22
Red Lake, Ont., Can. G21 104
Redlake, Mn., U.S. D12 118
Red Lake, l., Ont., Can. F14 96
Red Lake, l., Ont., Can. G20 104
Red Lake, stm., Mn., U.S. D11 118
Red Lake Falls, Mn., U.S. D11 118
Red Lake Road, Ont., Can. I21 104
Redlands, S. Afr. G6 66
Redlands, Ca., U.S. J8 124
Redlands, Co., U.S. E8 120
Red Level, Al., U.S. K10 114
Red Lick, Ms., U.S. K6 114
Red Lion, Pa., U.S. H10 108
Red Lodge, Mt., U.S. E16 122
Redmond, Or., U.S. F4 122
Redmond, Ut., U.S. E5 120
Redmond, Wa., U.S. C3 122
Red Mountain, mtn., Ca., U.S. C2 124
Red Mountain Pass, Co., U.S. G9 120
Red Oak, Ia., U.S. J12 118
Red Oak, Ok., U.S. E11 116
Redon, Fr. E4 14
Redonda, i., Antig. F13 94
Redonda Islands, is., B.C., Can. G10 102
Redondo, Port. G4 16
Redondo Beach, Ca., U.S. K7 124
Red Pass, B.C., Can. E16 102
Red Pheasant Indian Reserve, Sask., Can. F6 104
Red Rock, B.C., Can. D12 102
Red Rock, Ont., Can. B7 110
Red Rock, stm., Mt., U.S. F13 122
Red Rock, Lake, res., Ia., U.S. I2 110
Red Sea D8 56
Red Springs, N.C., U.S. E7 112
Redstone, B.C., Can. E11 102
Redstone, stm., N.W. Ter., Can. E32 100
Red Sucker, stm., Man., Can. C22 104
Red Sucker Lake, l., Man., Can. D21 104
Redvers, Sask., Can. I13 104
Redwater, Alta., Can. D21 102
Redwater, stm., Mt., U.S. D2 118
Redwillow, stm., Can. B15 102
Red Wing, Mn., U.S. F3 110
Redwood, stm., Mn., U.S. G12 118
Redwood City, Ca., U.S. G3 124
Redwood Falls, Mn., U.S. G12 118
Redwood National Park, Ca., U.S. C1 124
Redwood Valley, Ca., U.S. E2 124
Ree, Lough, l., Ire. H5 8
Reed City, Mi., U.S. G10 110
Reeder, N.D., U.S. E5 118
Reed Lake, l., Man., Can. D14 104
Reed Lake, l., Sask., Can. H7 104
Reedley, Ca., U.S. H6 124
Reedsburg, Wi., U.S. G5 110
Reeds Peak, mtn., N.M., U.S. K9 120
Reedsport, Or., U.S. G1 122
Reedsville, Wi., U.S. F8 110
Reefton, N.Z. E3 72
Reelfoot Lake, l., Tn., U.S. F7 114
Reese, Mi., U.S. G12 110
Reese, stm., Nv., U.S. D8 124
Reeseville, Wi., U.S. G7 110
Reform, Al., U.S. I8 114
Refuge Cove, B.C., Can. G10 102
Refugio, Tx., U.S. K9 116
Regaïa, Mor. J6 16
Regência, Braz. E9 79
Regensburg, Ger. F12 10
Regent, N.D., U.S. E5 118
Reggâne, Alg. G11 62
Reggello, Italy F6 18
Reggio di Calabria, Italy K10 18
Reggio nell'Emilia, Italy E5 18
Reghin, Rom. C8 20
Regina, Sask., Can. H10 104
Regina, Fr. Gu. C8 76
Regina Beach, Sask., Can. H9 104
Región Metropolitana, prov., Chile G3 80
Registro, Braz. C15 80
Registro do Araguaia, Braz. C3 79
Regnéville, Fr. C5 14
Reguengos de Monsaraz, Port. G4 16
Rehau, Ger. E12 10
Rehoboth, Nmb. D3 66
Rehoboth Beach, De., U.S. I11 108
Rehovot, Isr. E3 50
Reichenau, Switz. E11 13
Reichenbach, Ger. E12 10
Reid Lake, res., Sask., Can. H6 104
Reidsville, Ga., U.S. G4 112
Reidsville, N.C., U.S. C7 112
Reigate, Eng., U.K. J13 8
Reigoldswil, Switz. D8 13
Reims, Fr. C11 14
Reinach, Switz. C8 13
Reinach, Switz. D9 13
Reinbeck, Ia., U.S. H3 110
Reindeer, stm., Sask., Can. C11 104
Reindeer Island, i., Man., Can. F17 104
Reindeer Lake, l., Can. E12 96
Reindeer Station, N.W. Ter., Can. B27 100
Reinga, Cape, c., N.Z. A4 72
Reinosa, Spain B7 16
Reisdorf, Lux. I9 12
Reisterstown, Md., U.S. H10 108
Reitz, S. Afr. F9 66
Reliance, N.W. Ter., Can. D11 96
Reliance, Wy., U.S. C7 120
Remada, Tun. D16 62
Remagen, Ger. B14 14
Remanso, Braz. E10 76
Rembang, Indon. J15 39a
Remecó, Arg. I7 80
Remedios, Col. D5 84
Remedios, Pan. C2 84
Remedios, Punta, c., El Sal. D5 92
Remer, Mn., U.S. C2 110
Remeshk, Iran H15 48
Remington, In., U.S. B9 114
Remington, Va., U.S. I9 108
Remiremont, Fr. D13 14
Remoulins, Fr. I11 14
Remscheid, Ger. D7 10
Remsen, Ia., U.S. I12 118
Remus, Mi., U.S. G10 110
Renaix (Ronse), Bel. G4 12
Renata, B.C., Can. H16 102
Rencēni, Lat. D8 22
Rencontre East, Newf., Can. E18 106
Rende, Italy J11 18
Rend Lake, res., Il., U.S. D8 114
Rendsburg, Ger. A9 10
Renens, Switz. E6 13
Renews, Newf., Can. F21 106
Renfrew, Ont., Can. E19 110
Rengat, Indon. O7 40
Rengo, Chile H3 80
Reng Tlāng, mtn., Asia J15 44
Renhua, China J2 34
Reni, Ukr. D12 20
Renick, W.V., U.S. J6 108
Renmark, Austl. J4 70
Rennell, i., Sol.Is. B12 68
Rennell Sound, strt., B.C., Can. D2 102
Rennes, Fr. D5 14
Rennick Glacier, Ant. C8 73
Rennie, Man., Can. I19 104
Reno, Nv., U.S. E6 124
Reno, stm., Italy E6 18
Renous, N.B., Can. F8 106
Renous, stm., N.B., Can. F7 106
Renovo, Pa., U.S. F9 108
Renshou, China H6 34
Rensselaer, In., U.S. B9 114
Rensselaer, N.Y., U.S. E13 108
Rentería, Spain B10 16
Renton, Wa., U.S. C3 122
Renville, Mn., U.S. G12 118
Renwick, Ia., U.S. H2 110
Répce, stm., Eur. H16 10
Repetek, Turk. J10 26
Repino, Russia A12 22
Repton, Al., U.S. K9 114
Republic, Ks., U.S. L10 118
Republic, Mi., U.S. D8 110
Republic, Mo., U.S. E3 114
Republic, Wa., U.S. B7 122
Republican, stm., U.S. L10 118
Repulse Bay, N.W. Ter., Can. C15 96
Repulse Bay, b., Austl. C8 70
Requena, Peru A5 82
Requena, Spain F10 16
Réquista, Fr. H9 14
Reschenpass, Eur. F17 14
Resen, Mac. H5 20
Reserva, Braz. C13 80
Reserve, La., U.S. L6 114
Reserve, N.M., U.S. K8 120
Rešetnikovo, Russia E19 22
Resistencia, Arg. D9 80
Reşiţa, Rom. D5 20
Rešma, Russia D25 22
Resolute, N.W. Ter., Can. B14 96
Resolution Island, i., N.W. Ter., Can. D19 96
Resolution Island, i., N.Z. F1 72
Resplendor, Braz. E8 79
Restigouche (Ristigouche), stm., Can. E6 106
Restín, Punta, c., Peru J2 84
Restinga, Mor. J6 16
Restinga Seca, Braz. E12 80
Reston, Man., Can. I13 104
Restrepo, Col. E6 84
Restrepo, Col. F4 84
Retalhuleu, Guat. C3 92
Retalhuleu, dept., Guat. C3 92
Retamosa, Ur. G11 80
Rethel, Fr. C11 14
Réthimnon, Grc. N8 20
Reunion (Réunion), dep., Afr. F11 58
Reus, Spain D13 16
Reuss, stm., Switz. D9 13
Reuterstadt Stavenhagen, Ger. B12 10
Reutlingen, Ger. G9 10
Rev'akino, Russia G20 22
Revda, Russia F9 26
Revelstoke, B.C., Can. G16 102
Reventazón, Peru B1 82
Reventazón, stm., C.R. G11 92
Revigny-sur-Ornain, Fr. D11 14
Revillagigedo, Islas, is., Mex. H4 90
Revillagigedo Island, i., Ak., U.S. I29 100
Revillo, S.D., U.S. F11 118
Revin, Fr. C11 14
Revol'ucii, pik, mtn., Taj. A5 44
Revolución Mexicana, Mex. A1 92
Revué, stm., Afr. B11 66
Rewa, India H9 44
Rewa, stm., Guy. F13 84
Rewāri, India F7 44
Rexburg, Id., U.S. G14 122
Rexford, Ks., U.S. L7 118
Rexford, Mt., U.S. B10 122
Rexton, N.B., Can. F9 106
Rey, Isla del, i., Pan. C3 84
Rey, Laguna del, l., Mex. D8 90
Reyes, Bol. F8 82
Reyes, Point, c., Ca., U.S. F2 124
Reyhanlı, Tur. C4 48
Reykjanes, pen., Ice. C2 6a
Reykjavík, Ice. B3 6a
Reyno, Ar., U.S. F6 114
Reynolds, Ga., U.S. G2 112
Reynolds, N.D., U.S. D10 118
Reynoldsville, Pa., U.S. F8 108
Reynosa, Mex. D10 90
Rež, Russia F10 26
Reza, gora (Kūh-e Rīzeh), mtn., Asia C15 48
Rezé, Fr. E5 14
Rēzekne, Lat. E10 22
Rezeny, Mol. C12 20
Rezina, Mol. B12 20
Rezovska (Mutlu), stm., Eur. G11 20
Rhaetian Alps, mts., Eur. F16 14
Rhame, N.D., U.S. E4 118
Rheda-Wiedenbrück, Ger. D8 10
Rheims see Reims, Fr. C11 14
Rhein, Sask., Can. G12 104
Rheine, Ger. C7 10
Rheinfelden, Ger. H7 10
Rheinland-Pfalz, state, Ger. E6 10
Rhein see Rhine, stm., Eur. D6 10
Rhine, Ga., U.S. H3 112
Rhine (Rhein) (Rhin), stm., Eur. D6 10
Rhinebeck, N.Y., U.S. F13 108
Rhinelander, Wi., U.S. E6 110
Rhir, Cap, c., Mor. E6 62
Rho, Italy D4 18
Rhode Island, state, U.S. C12 98
Rhode Island Sound, strt., U.S. F15 108
Rhodesia see Zimbabwe, ctry., Afr. E5 58
Rhodes see Ródhos, i., Grc. M12 20
Rhodope Mountains, mts., Eur. H8 20
Rhön, mts., Ger. E9 10
Rhône, dept., Fr. G11 14
Rhône, stm., Eur. H11 14
Rhône au Rhin, Canal du, Fr. H7 10
Rhourde-El-Baguel, Alg. E14 62
Riaba, Eq. Gui. J14 64
Riacho de Santana, Braz. B7 79
Rialma, Braz. C4 79
Rianápolis, Braz. C4 79
Riangnom, Sud. M6 60
Riaño, Spain C6 16
Riau, Kepulauan, is., Indon. N8 40
Ribas do Rio Pardo, Braz. F2 79
Ribeauvillé, Fr. D14 14
Ribeira, Braz. C14 80
Ribeira do Iguape, stm., Braz. C14 80
Ribeira Grande, C.V. k16 64a
Ribeirão do Pinhal, Braz. G3 79
Ribeirão Preto, Braz. F5 79
Ribeirão Vermelho, Braz. F6 79
Ribeirãozinho, Braz. D2 79
Ribemont, Fr. C10 14
Ribera, Italy L8 18
Riberalta, Bol. D8 82
Rib Lake, Wi., U.S. E5 110
Ribnica, Slo. D9 18
Ribnitz-Damgarten, Ger. A12 10
Ribstone Creek, stm., Alta., Can. F3 104
Ricardo Flores Magón, Mex. C6 90
Ricaurte, Col. G4 84
Riccia, Italy H9 18
Riccione, Italy F7 18
Rice, Tx., U.S. G10 116
Rice Lake, Wi., U.S. E4 110
Riceville, Ia., U.S. G3 110
Riceville, Tn., U.S. D2 112
Richan, Ont., Can. I22 104
Richard Collinson Inlet, b., N.W. Ter., Can. B10 96
Richards, Tx., U.S. I11 116
Richard's Bay, S. Afr. G11 66
Richard's Bay, b., S. Afr. G11 66
Richard's Harbour, Newf., Can. E17 106
Richards Island, i., N.W. Ter., Can. C6 96
Richards Island, i., N.W. Ter., Can. B27 100
Richardson, Tx., U.S. G10 116
Richardson, stm., Can. E10 96
Richardson Mountains, mts., Can. C26 100
Richardton, N.D., U.S. E5 118
Riche, Pointe, c., Newf., Can. B16 106
Richelieu, Fr. E7 14
Richer, Man., Can. I18 104
Richey, Mt., U.S. D2 118
Richfield, Id., U.S. G11 122
Richfield, Mn., U.S. F2 110
Richfield, Pa., U.S. G9 108
Richfield, Ut., U.S. F4 120
Richfield Springs, N.Y., U.S. E12 108
Richford, Vt., U.S. C14 108
Rich Hill, Mo., U.S. D2 114
Richibucto, N.B., Can. F9 106
Richisau, Switz. D10 13
Richland, Ga., U.S. G2 112
Richland, Mi., U.S. H10 110
Richland, Mo., U.S. E4 114
Richland, Tx., U.S. H10 116
Richland, Wa., U.S. D6 122
Richland Center, Wi., U.S. G5 110
Richlands, N.C., U.S. E9 112
Richlands, Va., U.S. B5 112
Richland Springs, Tx., U.S. H8 116
Richmond, Austl. I9 70
Richmond, Austl. C5 70
Richmond, B.C., Can. H11 102
Richmond, Ont., Can. B11 108
Richmond, Que., Can. B14 108
Richmond, N.Z. D4 72
Richmond, S. Afr. H6 66
Richmond, S. Afr. G10 66
Richmond, Ca., U.S. G3 124
Richmond, In., U.S. C12 114
Richmond, Ks., U.S. M12 118
Richmond, Ky., U.S. B2 112
Richmond, Me., U.S. C17 108
Richmond, Mi., U.S. H13 110
Richmond, Mn., U.S. F13 118
Richmond, Mo., U.S. C3 114
Richmond, Tx., U.S. J11 116
Richmond, Ut., U.S. C5 120
Richmond, Vt., U.S. C14 108
Richmond, Va., U.S. B9 112
Richmond Heights, Fl., U.S. N6 112
Richmond Highlands, Wa., U.S. C3 122
Richmond Hill, Ont., Can. G16 110
Richmond Hill, Ga., U.S. H5 112
Richmondville, N.Y., U.S. E12 108
Rich Square, N.C., U.S. C9 112
Richton, Ms., U.S. K8 114
Richwood, Oh., U.S. G3 108
Richwood, W.V., U.S. I6 108
Rico, Co., U.S. G8 120
Riddle, Or., U.S. H2 122
Riddle Mountain, mtn., Or., U.S. G7 122
Ridgecrest, Ca., U.S. I8 124
Ridgedale, Sask., Can. E10 104
Ridge Farm, Il., U.S. C9 114
Ridgefield, Ct., U.S. F13 108
Ridgeland, Ms., U.S. J6 114
Ridgeland, S.C., U.S. G6 112
Ridgely, Tn., U.S. F7 114
Ridgetown, Ont., Can. H14 110
Ridgeville, Man., Can. I17 104
Ridgeville, S.C., U.S. F6 112
Ridgeway, Mo., U.S. B3 114
Ridgeway, Wi., U.S. G6 110
Ridgway, Co., U.S. F9 120
Ridgway, Il., U.S. E8 114
Ridgway, Pa., U.S. F8 108
Riding Mountain, mtn., Man., Can. H15 104
Riding Mountain National Park, Man., Can. H14 104
Ried im Innkreis, Aus. G13 10
Riegelwood, N.C., U.S. E8 112
Rienzi, Ms., U.S. H8 114
Riesa, Ger. D13 10
Riesco, Isla, i., Chile G2 78
Riesi, Italy L9 18
Rietavas, Lith. F4 22
Rietfontein, Nmb. C5 66
Rieti, Italy G7 18
Rif, mts., Mor. C8 62
Riffe Lake, res., Wa., U.S. D3 122
Rifle, Co., U.S. E9 120
Rifle, stm., Mi., U.S. F11 110
Rift Valley, val., Afr. I9 52
Rīga, Lat. E7 22
Riga, Gulf of (Rīgas jūras līcis) (Riia laht), b., Eur. D6 22
Rigacikun, Nig. F13 64
Rīgān, Iran G15 48
Rigby, Id., U.S. G14 122
Rīgestān, reg., Afg. E1 44
Riggins, Id., U.S. E9 122
Rigi, mtn., Switz. D10 13
Rigo, Pap. N. Gui. A9 68
Rigolet, Newf., Can. F21 96
Riiser-Larsen Peninsula, pen., Ant. B4 73
Rijeka, Cro. D9 18
Rijswijk, Neth. D5 12
Riley, Ks., U.S. L11 118
Rillito, Az., U.S. L5 120
Rima, stm., Nig. E12 64
Rímac, stm., Peru D3 82
Rimachi, Laguna, l., Peru J4 84
Rimavská Sobota, Czech. G20 10
Rimbey, Alta., Can. E20 102
Rimersburg, Pa., U.S. F7 108
Rimi, Nig. E13 64
Rimini, Italy E7 18
Rîmnicu Sărat, Rom. D11 20
Rîmnicu Vîlcea, Rom. D8 20
Rimouski, Que., Can. D5 106
Rimouski, stm., Que., Can. D5 106
Rimouski, Réserve, Que., Can. D5 106
Rincón, C.R. I11 92
Rincon, Ga., U.S. G5 112
Rincon, N.M., U.S. L9 120
Rinconada, Arg. B5 80
Rincón de la Vieja, Parque Nacional, C.R. G9 92
Rincón del Bonete, Lago Artificial de, res., Ur. G11 80
Rincón del Ocote, Cerro, mtn., Hond. D7 92
Rincón de Romos, Mex. F8 90
Rindal, Nor. J11 6
Ringebu, Nor. K12 6
Ringgold, Ga., U.S. E1 112
Ringgold, La., U.S. J3 114
Ringim, Nig. E14 64
Ringling, Ok., U.S. E9 116
Ringsted, Ia., U.S. H13 118
Rinjani, Gunung, mtn., Indon. G6 38

Name — Map Ref. — Page

Rinteln, Ger. C9 10
Rio, Wi., U.S. G6 110
Rio Azul, Braz. C13 80
Riobamba, Ec. H3 84
Río Blanco, Chile G3 80
Rio Branco, Braz. C8 82
Río Branco, Ur. G12 80
Río Bravo, Mex. E10 90
Rio Brilhante, Braz. F1 79
Río Caribe, Ven. B11 84
Rio Casca, Braz. F7 79
Río Ceballos, Arg. F6 80
Río Chico, Ven. B10 84
Rio Claro, Braz. G5 79
Rio Claro, Trin. I14 94
Río Colorado, Arg. J6 80
Río Cuarto, Arg. G6 80
Rio de Contas, Braz. B8 79
Rio de Janeiro, Braz. G7 79
Rio de Janeiro, state, Braz. G7 79
Río de Jesús, Pan. J13 92
Rio Dell, Ca., U.S. D1 124
Río de Oro, Col. C6 84
Rio do Prado, Braz. D8 79
Rio do Sul, Braz. D14 80
Rio Espera, Braz. F7 79
Río Gallegos, Arg. G3 78
Rio Grande, Braz. G12 80
Río Grande, Mex. F8 90
Río Grande, Nic. E8 92
Rio Grande City, Tx., U.S. M8 116
Rio Grande do Sul, state, Braz. E11 80
Rio Grande see Grande, Rio, stm., N.A. F7 98
Ríohacha, Col. B6 84
Río Hato, Pan. C2 84
Rio Hondo, Tx., U.S. M9 116
Rioja, Peru B3 82
Río Lagartos, Mex. G15 90
Riolândia, Braz. E4 79
Rio Largo, Braz. E11 76
Riom, Fr. G10 14
Río Mulatos, Bol. H8 82
Riondel, B.C., Can. H18 102
Rio Negro, Braz. E1 79
Rio Negro, Braz. D14 80
Rionegro, Col. D5 84
Rionegro, Col. D6 84
Río Negro, prov., Arg. J6 80
Rio Negro, Pantanal do, sw., Braz. H13 82
Rionero in Vulture, Italy I10 18
Rio Novo do Sul, Braz. F8 79
Rio Pardo, Braz. E12 80
Rio Pardo de Minas, Braz. C7 79
Río Piedras, Arg. C6 80
Río Pilcomayo, Parque Nacional, Arg. C9 80
Rio Piracicaba, Braz. E7 79
Rio Pomba, Braz. F7 79
Rio Preto, Braz. G7 79
Río Rancho, N.M., U.S. I10 120
Río San Juan, dept., Nic. F10 92
Río Segundo, Arg. F7 80
Ríosucio, Col. E5 84
Ríosucio, Col. D4 84
Río Tercero, Arg. G6 80
Rio Tinto, Braz. E11 76
Rio Verde, Braz. D3 79
Ríoverde, Mex. G10 90
Rio Verde de Mato Grosso, Braz. E1 79
Rio Vermelho, Braz. E7 79
Rio Vista, Ca., U.S. F4 124
Rioz, Fr. E13 14
Riozinho, stm., Braz. I9 84
Ripley, Ms., U.S. H8 114
Ripley, N.Y., U.S. E7 108
Ripley, Oh., U.S. I3 108
Ripley, Tn., U.S. G7 114
Ripley, W.V., U.S. I5 108
Ripoll, Spain C14 16
Ripon, Que., Can. B11 108
Ripon, Eng., U.K. G12 8
Ripon, Ca., U.S. G4 124
Ripon, Wi., U.S. G7 110
Riposto, Italy L10 18
Ririe, Id., U.S. G14 122
Risaralda, dept., Col. E4 84
Riscle, Fr. I6 14
Risco, Ilha do, i., Braz. I13 84
Rishiri-tō, i., Japan B16 36a
Rishmayyā, Leb. A5 50
Rishon LeZiyyon, Isr. E3 50
Rising Star, Tx., U.S. G8 116
Rising Sun, In., U.S. D12 114
Rising Sun, Md., U.S. H10 108
Risingsun, Oh., U.S. F3 108
Rison, Ar., U.S. I4 114
Risør, Nor. L11 6
Rissani, Mor. E8 62
Risti, Est. C7 22
Ristigouche (Restigouche), stm., Can. E6 106
Ritter, Mount, mtn., Ca., U.S. G6 124
Rittman, Oh., U.S. G5 108
Ritzville, Wa., U.S. C7 122
Riva, Italy D5 18
Rivadavia, Arg. H7 80
Rivadavia, Arg. G4 80
Rivadavia, Arg. C7 80
Rivadavia, Arg. F4 80
Rivadavia, Chile E3 80
Rivanna, stm., Va., U.S. B8 112
Rivas, Nic. F9 92
Rivas, dept., Nic. F8 92
Rive-de-Gier, Fr. G11 14
Rivera, Arg. I7 80
Rivera, Col. F5 84
Rivera, Ur. F11 80
Riverbank, Ca., U.S. G5 124
River Cess, Lib. I5 64
Riverdale, Ca., U.S. H6 124
Riverdale, N.D., U.S. D6 118
River Falls, Al., U.S. K10 114
River Falls, Wi., U.S. F3 110
Rivergaro, Italy E4 18
Riverhead, N.Y., U.S. G14 108
River Hébert, N.S., Can. G9 106
Riverhurst, Sask., Can. H8 104
Riverina, reg., Austl. J6 70
River John, N.S., Can. G10 106
Rivermont, N.C., U.S. D9 112
River of Ponds, Newf., Can. B16 106
River Road, Or., U.S. F2 122
Rivers, Man., Can. H14 104
Rivers, Lake of the, l., Sask., Can. I9 104
Riversdale, S. Afr. J5 66
Riverside, Ca., U.S. K8 124
Riverside, Ia., U.S. I4 110
Riverside, Tx., U.S. I11 116
Rivers Inlet, B.C., Can. F7 102
Rivers Inlet, b., B.C., Can. F7 102
Riverton, Man., Can. H18 104
Riverton, N.Z. G2 72
Riverton, Il., U.S. C7 114
Riverton, Ne., U.S. K9 118
Riverton, Ut., U.S. D5 120
Riverton, Va., U.S. I8 108
Riverton, Wy., U.S. A8 120
Riverton Heights, Wa., U.S. C3 122
River View, Al., U.S. J11 114
Riverview, Fl., U.S. L4 112
Riverview, Ks., U.S. N10 118
Rives, Tn., U.S. F7 114
Rivesaltes, Fr. J9 14
Rivesville, W.V., U.S. H6 108
Riviera, Az., U.S. I2 120
Riviera, Tx., U.S. L9 116
Riviera Beach, Fl., U.S. M6 112
Rivière-à-Claude, Que., Can. C8 106
Rivière-au-Tonnerre, Que., Can. B9 106
Rivière-Bleue, Que., Can. E4 106
Rivière-de-la-Chaloupe, Que., Can. C11 106
Rivière-du-Loup, Que., Can. E4 106
Rivière-Matane, Que., Can. D6 106
Rivière-Pentecôte, Que., Can. C6 106
Rivière-Verte, N.B., Can. E5 106
Riviersonderend, S. Afr. J4 66
Rivoli, Italy D2 18
Riyadh see Ar-Riyāḍ, Sau. Ar. B5 47
Rize, Tur. G16 4
Rizhao, China H7 32
Roa, Nor. K12 6
Roachdale, In., U.S. C10 114
Road Town, Br. Vir. Is. E12 94
Roan Cliffs, clf, U.S. E7 120
Roan Mountain, Tn., U.S. C4 112
Roanne, Fr. F11 14
Roanoke, Al., U.S. I11 114
Roanoke, Il., U.S. J6 110
Roanoke, In., U.S. B11 114
Roanoke, Va., U.S. B7 112
Roanoke (Staunton), stm., U.S. C9 112
Roanoke Island, i., N.C., U.S. D11 112
Roanoke Rapids, N.C., U.S. C9 112
Roan Plateau, plat., U.S. E6 120
Roaring Spring, Pa., U.S. G8 108
Roaring Springs, Tx., U.S. F6 116
Roatán, Hond. A8 92
Roatán, Isla de, i., Hond. A8 92
Robāa Oued Yahia, Tun. M4 18
Robāt Karīm, Iran D11 48
Robbins, N.C., U.S. D7 112
Robbins, Tn., U.S. C2 112
Robbins Island, i., Austl. M6 70
Robbinsville, N.C., U.S. D3 112
Röbel, Ger. B12 10
Robeline, La., U.S. K3 114
Robersonville, N.C., U.S. D9 112
Roberta, Ga., U.S. G2 112
Roberta Mills, N.C., U.S. D6 112
Robert Lee, Tx., U.S. H6 116
Roberts, Id., U.S. G13 122
Roberts, Mt., U.S. E16 122
Robert's Arm, Newf., Can. C18 106
Roberts Creek Mountain, mtn., Nv., U.S. E9 124
Robertsdale, Al., U.S. L9 114
Robertsdale, Pa., U.S. G8 108
Robertsfield, Lib. H4 64
Robert S. Kerr Lake, res., Ok., U.S. D11 116
Robertson, S. Afr. I4 66
Robertson, Lac, l., Que., Can. A14 106
Roberts Peak, mtn., B.C., Can. E14 102
Robertsport, Lib. H4 64
Roberval, Que., Can. G18 96
Robinson, Il., U.S. C9 114
Robinson, Tx., U.S. H9 116
Róbinson Crusoe, Isla, i., Chile H7 74
Robinson Range, mts., Austl. E3 68
Robinsons, Newf., Can. D15 106
Robinvale, Austl. J5 70
Roblin, Man., Can. G13 104
Roboré, Bol. H12 82
Robson, Mount, mtn., B.C., Can. D15 102
Robstown, Tx., U.S. L9 116
Roby, Tx., U.S. G6 116
Roca, Cabo da, c., Port. G2 16
Rocafuerte, Ec. H2 84
Rocanville, Sask., Can. H13 104
Roca Partida, Isla, i., Mex. H3 90
Roca Partida, Punta, c., Mex. H12 90
Rocas, Atol das, atoll, Braz. D12 76
Roccastrada, Italy F6 18
Rocciamelone, mtn., Italy D2 18
Rocha, Ur. H9 74
Rocha, Ur. H11 80
Rochedinho, Braz. F1 79
Rochedinho, Braz. I14 82
Rochedo, Braz. E1 79
Rochefort, Bel. H7 12
Rochefort, Fr. G6 14
Rochelle, Ga., U.S. H3 112
Rochelle, Il., U.S. I6 110
Rochelle, Tx., U.S. H7 116
Roche-Percée, Sask., Can. I12 104
Rochester, Austl. K6 70
Rochester, In., U.S. A10 114
Rochester, Mi., U.S. H12 110
Rochester, Mn., U.S. F3 110
Rochester, N.H., U.S. D16 108
Rochester, N.Y., U.S. D9 108
Rochester, Tx., U.S. F7 116
Rochlitz, Ger. D12 10
Rock, Mi., U.S. D8 110
Rock, stm., U.S. I6 110
Rock, stm., U.S. H11 118
Rockall, i., Scot., U.K. D5 4
Rock Bay, B.C., Can. G9 102
Rockcastle, stm., Ky., U.S. B2 112
Rock Creek Butte, mtn., Or., U.S. F7 122
Rockdale, Il., U.S. I7 110
Rockdale, Tx., U.S. I9 116
Rockefeller Plateau, plat., Ant. D10 73
Rockenhausen, Ger. F7 10
Rock Falls, Il., U.S. I6 110
Rockford, Al., U.S. J10 114
Rockford, Il., U.S. H6 110
Rockford, Ia., U.S. G3 110
Rockford, Mi., U.S. G10 110
Rockford, Oh., U.S. G2 108
Rockford, Tn., U.S. D3 112
Rockglen, Sask., Can. I9 104
Rock Hall, Md., U.S. H10 108
Rockhampton, Austl. D9 70
Rock Hill, S.C., U.S. E5 112
Rockingham, N.C., U.S. E7 112
Rockingham Bay, b., Austl. B7 70
Rock Island, Il., U.S. I5 110
Rocklake, N.D., U.S. C8 118
Rock Lake, l., Man., Can. I15 104
Rockland, Ont., Can. B11 108
Rockland, Id., U.S. H13 122
Rockland, Me., U.S. C17 108
Rockland, Ma., U.S. E16 108
Rockland, Mi., U.S. D6 110
Rocklands Reservoir, res., Austl. K5 70
Rockledge, Fl., U.S. K6 112
Rocklin, Ca., U.S. F4 124
Rockmart, Ga., U.S. E1 112
Rockport, Ky., U.S. E10 114
Rockport, Me., U.S. C17 108
Rockport, Ma., U.S. E16 108
Rock Port, Mo., U.S. B1 114
Rockport, Tx., U.S. K9 116
Rock Rapids, Ia., U.S. H11 118
Rock River, Wy., U.S. C11 120
Rock Sound, Bah. B6 94
Rocksprings, Tx., U.S. I6 116
Rock Springs, Wy., U.S. C7 120
Rockstone, Guy. E13 84
Rockton, Il., U.S. H6 110
Rock Valley, Ia., U.S. H11 118
Rockville, In., U.S. C9 114
Rockville, Md., U.S. H9 108
Rockwall, Tx., U.S. G10 116
Rockwell, Ia., U.S. H2 110
Rockwell, N.C., U.S. D6 112
Rockwell City, Ia., U.S. I13 118
Rockwood, Me., U.S. B17 108
Rockwood, Pa., U.S. H7 108
Rockwood, Tn., U.S. D2 112
Rocky, Ok., U.S. D7 116
Rocky, stm., Alta., Can. D17 102
Rocky, stm., N.C., U.S. D7 112
Rockyford, Alta., Can. F21 102
Rocky Ford, Co., U.S. M4 118
Rocky Harbour, Newf., Can. C16 106
Rocky Lake, l., Man., Can. D13 104
Rocky Mount, N.C., U.S. D9 112
Rocky Mount, Va., U.S. C7 112
Rocky Mountain, mtn., Mt., U.S. C13 122
Rocky Mountain House, Alta., Can. E20 102
Rocky Mountain National Park, Co., U.S. K2 118
Rocky Mountains, mts., N.A. E8 86
Roda, Va., U.S. C4 112
Rodalben, Ger. F7 10
Rødbyhavn, Den. N12 6
Roddickton, Newf., Can. B17 106
Rodeo, Arg. F4 80
Rodeo, Mex. E7 90
Rodeo, N.M., U.S. M7 120
Roderick Island, i., B.C., Can. E6 102
Rodewisch, Ger. E12 10
Rodez, Fr. H9 14
Ródhos (Rhodes), Grc. M12 20
Ródhos (Rhodes), i., Grc. M12 20
Rodi Garganico, Italy H10 18
Roding, Ger. F12 10
Rodney, Ont., Can. H14 110
Rodney, Ms., U.S. K5 114
Rodniki, Russia D24 22
Rodrigues, i., Mrts. K7 24
Roebourne, Austl. D3 68
Roeland Park, Ks., U.S. L13 118
Roelofarendsveen, Neth. D6 12
Roer (Rur), stm., Eur. F9 12
Roermond, Neth. F8 12
Roes Welcome Sound, strt., N.W. Ter., Can. D15 96
Roff, Ok., U.S. E10 116
Rogačevo, Russia E20 22
Rogačov, Bela. H13 22
Rogagua, Laguna, l., Bol. E8 82
Rogaguado, Laguna, l., Bol. E9 82
Rogaland, co., Nor. L10 6
Rogatica, Bos. F3 20
Rogers, Ar., U.S. F2 114
Rogers, Tx., U.S. I9 116
Rogers, Mount, mtn., Va., U.S. C5 112
Rogers City, Mi., U.S. E12 110
Rogers Lake, l., Ca., U.S. J8 124
Rogers Pass, B.C., Can. F17 102
Rogersville, N.B., Can. F8 106
Rogersville, Al., U.S. H9 114
Rogersville, Tn., U.S. C3 112
Rogliano, Fr. J16 14
Rogoźno, Pol. C17 10
Rogue, stm., Mi., U.S. G10 110
Rogue, stm., Or., U.S. H1 122
Rogue River, Or., U.S. H2 122
Rohtak, India F7 44
Rohunta, Laguna, b., Hond. B11 92
Roi Et, Thai. F7 40
Roisel, Fr. C10 14
Roja, Lat. D5 22
Rojas, Arg. H8 80
Roji'anka, Ukr. C13 20
Rojo, Cabo, c., Mex. G11 90
Rojo, Cabo, c., P.R. F11 94
Rokeby National Park, Austl. B8 68
Rokiškis, Lith. F8 22
Rokycany, Czech. F13 10
Roland, Man., Can. I17 104
Roland, Ar., U.S. H4 114
Roland, Ia., U.S. H2 110
Rolândia, Braz. G3 79
Røldal, Nor. L10 6
Roldán, Arg. G8 80
Roldanillo, Col. E4 84
Rolette, N.D., U.S. C8 118
Rolfe, Ia., U.S. I13 118
Roll, Az., U.S. L3 120
Rolla, B.C., Can. B14 102
Rolla, Ks., U.S. N6 118
Rolla, Mo., U.S. E5 114
Rolla, N.D., U.S. C8 118
Rolle, Switz. F5 13
Rolleston, Austl. E8 70
Rolling Fork, Ms., U.S. J6 114
Rolling Fork, stm., Ky., U.S. E11 114
Rolling River Indian Reserve, Man., Can. H15 104
Rollingstone, Austl. B7 70
Roma, Austl. F8 70
Roma (Rome), Italy H7 18
Roma, Tx., U.S. M7 116
Romagna, hist. reg., Italy H18 14
Romaine, stm., Can. F20 96
Roman, Rom. C10 20
Romania (România), ctry., Eur. F13 4
Roman-Koš, gora, mtn., Ukr. I4 26
Romankovcy, Ukr. A11 20
Romano, Cayo, i., Cuba C6 94
Romanshorn, Switz. C11 13
Romans [-sur-Isère], Fr. G12 14
Rome, Ga., U.S. E1 112
Rome, Il., U.S. J6 110
Rome, Ms., U.S. I6 114
Rome, N.Y., U.S. D11 108
Romeo, Mi., U.S. H12 110
Rome see Roma, Italy H7 18
Rometan, Uzb. B18 48
Romilly-sur-Seine, Fr. D10 14
Rommani, Mor. C7 62
Romney, W.V., U.S. H8 108
Romny, Ukr. G4 26
Romont, Switz. E6 13
Romorantin-Lanthenay, Fr. E8 14
Ron, Mui, c., Viet. E9 40
Ronan, Mt., U.S. C11 122
Roncador, Serra do, plat., Braz. F8 76
Ronceverte, W.V., U.S. B6 112
Ronchamp, Fr. E13 14
Ronda, Spain I6 16
Rønde, Den. M12 6
Rondon, Braz. G2 79
Rondônia, state, Braz. D10 82
Rondonópolis, Braz. D1 79
Ronge, Lac la, l., Sask., Can. C9 104
Rongshui, China B10 40
Rõngu, Est. C9 22
Rønne, Den. N14 6
Ronneby, Swe. M14 6
Ronne Entrance, b., Ant. C12 73
Ronne Ice Shelf, Ant. C12 73
Ronse (Renaix), Bel. G4 12
Ronuro, stm., Braz. B1 79
Roodhouse, Il., U.S. C6 114
Rooiboklaagte, stm., Nmb. C5 66
Roorkee, India F7 44
Roosendaal, Neth. E5 12
Roosevelt, Az., U.S. K5 120
Roosevelt, Mn., U.S. C12 118
Roosevelt, Ok., U.S. E7 116
Roosevelt, Ut., U.S. D7 120
Roosevelt, stm., Braz. B11 82
Roosevelt Campobello International Park, N.B., Can. H7 106
Roosevelt Island, i., Ant. C9 73
Root, stm., N.W. Ter., Can. E32 100
Root, stm., Mn., U.S. G4 110
Root, stm., Wi., U.S. H8 110
Root Lake, l., Man., Can. D13 104
Roper, N.C., U.S. D10 112
Roper, stm., Austl. B6 68
Ropesville, Tx., U.S. F4 116
Roquefort, Fr. H6 14
Roque Pérez, Arg. H9 80
Roraima, state, Braz. G12 84
Roraima, Mount, mtn., S.A. E12 84
Rorey Lake, l., N.W. Ter., Can. C30 100
Rorke Lake, l., Can. D22 104
Rorketon, Man., Can. G15 104
Røros, Nor. J12 6
Rorschach, Switz. D12 13
Rørvik, Nor. I12 6
Rosa, Lake, l., Bah. D8 94
Rosa, Monte, mtn., Eur. G8 13
Rošal', Russia F22 22
Rosales, Mex. C7 90
Rosalia, Wa., U.S. C8 122
Rosamond, Ca., U.S. J7 124
Rosamorada, Mex. F7 90
Rosana, Braz. B12 80
Rosario, Arg. G8 80
Rosário, Braz. D10 76
Rosario, Mex. F7 90
Rosario, Mex. D5 90
Rosario, Para. C10 80
Rosario, Ur. H10 80
Rosario, Ven. B6 84
Rosario, stm., Arg. C6 80
Rosario, Bahía, b., Mex. C2 90
Rosario, Islas del, is., Col. B5 84
Rosario de Arriba, Mex. B2 90
Rosario de la Frontera, Arg. C6 80
Rosario de Lerma, Arg. C6 80
Rosario del Tala, Arg. G9 80
Rosário do Sul, Braz. F11 80
Rosário Oeste, Braz. F13 82
Rosarito, Mex. D4 90
Rosarno, Italy K10 18
Roščino, Russia A12 22
Roscoe, S.D., U.S. F8 118
Roscoe, Tx., U.S. G6 116
Roscoe, stm., N.W. Ter., Can. B34 100
Roscommon, Ire. H5 8
Roscommon, Mi., U.S. F11 110
Roscommon, co., Ire. H5 8
Roscrea, Ire. I6 8
Rose, Mount, mtn., Nv., U.S. E6 124
Roseau, Dom. G14 94
Roseau, Mn., U.S. C12 118
Roseau, stm., N.A. B11 118
Roseberry Lakes, l., Ont., Can. F22 104
Rosebery, Austl. M6 70
Rose-Blanche, Newf., Can. E15 106
Roseboro, N.C., U.S. E8 112
Rosebud, Mt., U.S. D19 122
Rosebud, S.D., U.S. H7 118
Rosebud, Tx., U.S. H10 116
Rosebud, stm., Alta., Can. F21 102
Roseburg, Or., U.S. G2 122
Rosebush, Mi., U.S. G11 110
Rose City, Mi., U.S. F11 110
Rosedale, Austl. E9 70
Rosedale, Alta., Can. F22 102
Rosedale, In., U.S. C9 114
Rosedale, La., U.S. L5 114
Rosedale, Ms., U.S. I5 114
Rosehall, Guy. D14 84
Rosehearty, Scot., U.K. D11 8
Rose-Hill, Mrts. V18 67c
Rose Hill, N.C., U.S. E8 112
Rose Hill, Va., U.S. C3 112
Rose Lake, B.C., Can. C8 102
Roseland, La., U.S. L6 114
Rosemary, Alta., Can. G22 102
Rosenberg, Tx., U.S. J11 116
Rosendal, Nor. L10 6
Rosenheim, Ger. H12 10
Rosepine, La., U.S. L3 114
Rose Point, c., B.C., Can. C3 102
Rosetown, Sask., Can. G6 104
Rosetta see Rashīd, Egypt B6 60
Rose Valley, Sask., Can. F11 104
Roseville, Ca., U.S. F4 124
Roseville, Il., U.S. J5 110
Roseville, Mi., U.S. H13 110
Roseville, Mn., U.S. E2 110
Roseville, Oh., U.S. H4 108
Rosewood, Austl. F10 70
Rosh Ha'Ayin, Isr. D3 50
Rosholt, S.D., U.S. F11 118
Rosholt, Wi., U.S. F6 110
Rosh Pinna, Isr. C5 50
Rosiclare, Il., U.S. E8 114
Rosignano Marittimo, Italy F5 18
Rosignol, Guy. D14 84
Roșiori de Vede, Rom. E9 20
Roskilde, Den. N13 6
Rosl'akovo, Russia G23 6
Rosl'atino, Russia B27 22
Roslavl', Russia H15 22
Roslyn, Wa., U.S. C5 122
Rosman, N.C., U.S. D4 112
Rosporden, Fr. E3 14
Ross, Austl. N7 70
Ross, N.Z. E3 72
Ross, stm., Yukon, Can. E29 100
Rossano, Italy J11 18
Rossburn, Man., Can. H14 104
Rossel y Rius, Ur. G11 80
Rossford, Oh., U.S. F3 108
Ross Ice Shelf, Ant. D9 73
Rossignol, Lake, l., N.S., Can. H8 106
Ross Island, i., Ant. C8 73
Ross Island, i., Man., Can. D17 104
Rossiter, Pa., U.S. G8 108
Rossija see Russia, ctry., Eur. E14 26
Ross Lake, res., N.A. B4 122
Rossland, B.C., Can. H17 102
Rosslare, Ire. I7 8
Rosslau, Ger. D12 10
Rosso, Maur. C2 64
Ross-on-Wye, Eng., U.K. J11 8
Rossony, Bela. F11 22
Rossoš', Russia G5 26
Ross R. Barnett Reservoir, res., Ms., U.S. J6 114
Ross River, Yukon, Can. F28 100
Ross Sea, Ant. C9 73
Rossville, Ga., U.S. E1 112
Rossville, Il., U.S. B9 114
Rossville, In., U.S. B10 114
Rossville, Ks., U.S. L12 118
Rosthern, Sask., Can. F8 104
Rostock, Ger. A12 10
Rostov, Russia D22 22
Rostov-na-Donu, Russia H5 26
Roswell, Ga., U.S. E2 112
Roswell, N.M., U.S. F2 116
Rota, Spain I5 16
Rotan, Tx., U.S. G6 116
Rotenburg, Ger. D9 10
Rotenburg, Ger. B9 10
Roth, Ger. F11 10
Rothaargebirge, mts., Ger. D8 10
Rothenburg ob der Tauber, Ger. F10 10
Rothesay, N.B., Can. G7 106
Rothsay, Mn., U.S. E11 118
Rothschild, Wi., U.S. F6 110
Rothwell, N.B., Can. F7 106
Roti, Pulau, i., Indon. H7 38
Roto, Austl. I6 70
Rotondella, Italy I11 18
Rotorua, N.Z. C6 72
Rott am Inn, Ger. H12 10
Rottenburg, Ger. G8 10
Rottenmann, Aus. H14 10
Rotterdam, Neth. E5 12
Rotterdam, N.Y., U.S. E13 108
Rottweil, Ger. G8 10
Roubaix, Fr. B10 14
Roudnice, Czech. E14 10
Rouen, Fr. C8 14
Rougé, Fr. E5 14
Rougemont, Fr. E13 14
Rough, stm., Ky., U.S. E10 114
Rough River Lake, res., Ky., U.S. E10 114
Rouillac, Fr. G6 14
Rouleau, Sask., Can. H10 104
Roulette, Pa., U.S. F8 108
Round Harbour, Newf., Can. C18 106
Round Hill Head, c., Austl. E9 70
Round Lake, Mn., U.S. H12 118
Round Lake, l., Newf., Can. A17 106
Round Lake, l., Sask., Can. H12 104
Round Mountain, Nv., U.S. F8 124
Round Mountain, mtn., Austl. H10 70
Round Pond, l., Newf., Can. D17 106
Round Rock, Tx., U.S. I9 116
Roundup, Mt., U.S. D17 122
Rouses Point, N.Y., U.S. B13 108
Roussillon, hist. reg., Fr. J9 14
Routhierville, Que., Can. D6 106
Rouvray, Lac, l., Que., Can. C3 106
Rouxville, S. Afr. H8 66
Rovaniemi, Fin. H19 6
Rovato, Italy D5 18
Rovereto, Italy D6 18
Roversi, Arg. D8 80
Rovigo, Italy D6 18
Rovira, Col. E5 84
Rovno, Ukr. G3 26
Rovuma (Ruvuma), stm., Afr. D7 58
Rowan Lake, l., Ont., Can. I21 104
Rowena, Tx., U.S. H6 116
Rowland, N.C., U.S. E7 112
Rowlesburg, W.V., U.S. H7 108
Rowley, stm., N.W. Ter., Can. B17 96
Rowley Island, i., N.W. Ter., Can. C17 96
Rowley Shoals, rf., Austl. C3 68
Roxas, Phil. C7 38
Roxboro, N.C., U.S. C8 112
Roxburgh, N.Z. F2 72
Roxie, Ms., U.S. K5 114
Roxo, Cap, c., Afr. E1 64
Roxton, Tx., U.S. F11 116
Roy, N.M., U.S. D2 116
Roy, Ut., U.S. C4 120
Roy, Wa., U.S. C3 122
Royal, Ia., U.S. H12 118
Royal Canal, Ire. H6 8
Royal Center, In., U.S. B10 114
Royal City, Wa., U.S. D6 122
Royale, Isle, i., Mi., U.S. B7 110
Royal Gorge, val., Co., U.S. F11 120
Royal Leamington Spa, Eng., U.K. I12 8
Royal Oak, Mi., U.S. H12 110
Royalton, Mn., U.S. E1 110
Royal Tunbridge Wells, Eng., U.K. J14 8
Royan, Fr. G5 14
Roye, Fr. C9 14
Royse City, Tx., U.S. G10 116
Royston, Ga., U.S. E3 112
Rožaj, Yugo. G4 20
Roždestvo, Russia D16 22
Rožňava, Czech. G20 10
Roznov, Rom. C10 20
Roztocze, hills, Eur. E22 10
Rtiščevo, Russia G6 26
Ruacaná, Nmb. A2 66
Ruacana Falls, wtfl, Afr. A2 66
Ruapehu, mtn., N.Z. C5 72
Ruapehu, Mount, mtn., N.Z. L21 126
Rub' al Khālī see Ar-Rub' al-Khālī, des., Asia D7 47
Rubcovsk, Russia G8 28
Rubežnoje, Ukr. H5 26
Rubiataba, Braz. C4 79
Rubim, Braz. D8 79
Rubino, I.C. H7 64
Rubio, Ven. D6 84
Ruboani, Sud. M6 60
Ruby, Ak., U.S. D17 100
Ruby, stm., Mt., U.S. E13 122
Ruby Dome, mtn., Nv., U.S. D10 124
Ruby Mountains, mts., Nv., U.S. D10 124
Ruby Valley, val., Nv., U.S. D10 124
Rucava, Lat. E4 22
Rudall, Austl. I2 70
Rudall River National Park, Austl. D4 68
Ruda Śląska, Pol. E18 10
Rūdbār, Afg. F17 48
Rudensk, Bela. H10 22
Rüdersdorf, Ger. C13 10
Rüdesheim, Ger. F7 10
Rūdiškės, Lith. G7 22
Rudn'a, Russia G14 22
Rudnica, Ukr. A12 20
Rudnyj, Kaz. G10 26
Rudo, Bos. F3 20
Rudolf, Lake (Lake Turkana), l., Afr. H8 56
Rudolstadt, Ger. E11 10
Rudong, China C10 34
Rūdsar, Iran C11 48
Rudyard, Mi., U.S. D11 110
Rudyard, Mt., U.S. B15 122
Rue, Fr. B8 14
Ruen, mtn., Eur. G6 20
Rufā'ah, Sud. J7 60
Ruffieux, Fr. G12 14
Ruffin, S.C., U.S. F6 112
Rufino, Arg. H7 80
Rufisque, Sen. D1 64
Rufus, Or., U.S. E5 122
Rugao, China C9 34
Rugby, Eng., U.K. I12 8
Rugby, N.D., U.S. C8 118
Rügen, i., Ger. A13 10
Rugged Mountain, mtn., B.C., Can. G8 102
Ruhr, stm., Ger. F10 12
Rui'an, China H9 34
Ruidoso, N.M., U.S. K11 120
Ruidoso, Río, stm., N.M., U.S. K11 120
Ruidoso Downs, N.M., U.S. K11 120
Ruijin, China J5 34
Ruivo, Pico, mtn., Port. M21 17a
Ruiz, Mex. G7 90
Ruiz de Montoya, Arg. D11 80
Rūjiena, Lat. D8 22
Rukwa, Lake, l., Tan. C6 58
Rule, Tx., U.S. F7 116
Ruleville, Ms., U.S. I6 114
Rulo, Ne., U.S. K12 118
Rum, stm., Mn., U.S. E2 110
Ruma, Yugo. D3 20
Rumbek, Sud. N5 60
Rumbeke, Bel. G3 12
Rum Cay, i., Bah. C7 94
Rumford, Me., U.S. C16 108
Rumia, Pol. A18 10
Rumigny, Fr. C11 14
Rum Jungle, Austl. B6 68
Rummānah, Egypt B7 60
Rumoi, Japan D16 36a
Runan, China B3 34
Runanga, N.Z. E3 72
Rundu, Nmb. A4 66
Runge, Tx., U.S. K9 116
Rungwa, Tan. C6 58
Rungwa, stm., Tan. C6 58
Ruo, stm., China C6 30
Ruoqiang, China D4 30
Ruoxi, China F4 34
Rupea, Rom. C9 20
Rupert, Id., U.S. H12 122
Rupert, W.V., U.S. J6 108
Rupert, Rivière de, stm., Que., Can. F17 96
Rupununi, stm., Guy. F13 84
Ruqqād, Wādī ar-, val., Asia C5 50
Rur (Roer), stm., Eur. F9 12
Rural Hall, N.C., U.S. C6 112
Rural Retreat, Va., U.S. C5 112
Rurrenabaque, Bol. F8 82
Rurstausee, res., Ger. G9 12
Rušan, Taj. B4 44
Rusape, Zimb. B11 66
Ruṣayriṣ, Khazzān ar-, res., Afr. L8 60
Ruse, Bul. F9 20
Rush, stm., N.D., U.S. D10 118
Rush, stm., Wi., U.S. F3 110
Rush Center, Ks., U.S. M8 118
Rush City, Mn., U.S. E3 110
Rushford, Mn., U.S. G4 110
Rushmore, Mn., U.S. H12 118
Rush Springs, Ok., U.S. E9 116
Rushville, Il., U.S. B6 114
Rushville, In., U.S. C11 114
Rushville, Ne., U.S. I5 118
Rusk, Tx., U.S. H11 116
Ruskin, Fl., U.S. L4 112
Russas, Braz. D11 76
Russell, Man., Can. H13 104
Russell, Ont., Can. B11 108
Russell, Ia., U.S. J2 110
Russell, Ks., U.S. M9 118
Russell, Ky., U.S. I4 108
Russell, Mn., U.S. G12 118
Russell, Pa., U.S. F7 108
Russell, Cape, c., N.W. Ter., Can. A9 96
Russell Island, i., N.W. Ter., Can. B13 96
Russell Lake, l., Man., Can. B13 104
Russells Point, Oh., U.S. G3 108
Russell Springs, Ky., U.S. E11 114
Russellville, Al., U.S. H9 114
Russellville, Ar., U.S. G3 114
Russellville, Ky., U.S. F10 114
Russellville, Mo., U.S. D4 114
Rüsselsheim, Ger. E8 10
Russia, ctry., Eur. E14 26
Russian, stm., Ca., U.S. F2 124
Russiaville, In., U.S. B10 114
Russkij, ostrov, i., Russia B17 26
Rust, Aus. H16 10
Rustavi, Geor. I7 26
Rustburg, Va., U.S. B7 112
Rustenburg, S. Afr. E8 66
Ruston, La., U.S. J4 114
Rute, Spain H7 16
Ruteng, Indon. G7 38
Rutenga, Zimb. C10 66
Ruth, Ms., U.S. K6 114
Ruth, Nv., U.S. E11 124
Rutherford, Tn., U.S. F8 114
Rutherfordton, N.C., U.S. D5 112
Ruthton, Mn., U.S. G11 118
Ruthven, Ia., U.S. H13 118
Rüti, Switz. D10 13
Rutland, B.C., Can. H15 102
Rutland, N.D., U.S. E10 118
Rutland, Vt., U.S. D14 108
Rutledge, Ga., U.S. F3 112
Rutledge, Tn., U.S. C3 112
Rutog, China D8 44
Rutshuru, Zaire B5 58
Rutter, Ont., Can. D15 110
Ruvuma (Rovuma), stm., Afr. D7 58
Ruy Barbosa, Braz. B8 79
Ruza, Russia F19 22
Ruzajevka, Russia G6 26
Ružany, Bela. I7 22
Ružomberok, Czech. F19 10
Rwanda, ctry., Afr. B6 58
Ryan, Ok., U.S. E9 116
Ryan, stm., B.C., Can. G11 102
Rybačij, poluostrov, pen., Russia G23 6
Rybačje, Kaz. H8 28
Rybinsk, Russia C21 22
Rybinskoje vodochranilišče, res., Russia C21 22
Rybnica, Mol. B13 20
Rybnik, Pol. E18 10
Rybnoje, Russia G22 22
Rycroft, Alta., Can. B16 102
Ryd, Swe. M14 6
Ryde, Eng., U.K. K12 8
Ryder, N.D., U.S. D6 118
Ryderwood, Wa., U.S. D2 122
Ryegate, Mt., U.S. D16 122
Rye Patch Reservoir, res., Nv., U.S. D7 124
Ryes, Fr. C6 14
Rykerts, B.C., Can. H18 102
Ryley, Alta., Can. D22 102
Rymanów, Pol. F21 10
Rypin, Pol. B19 10
Ryškany, Mol. B11 20
Rysy, mtn., Eur. F20 10

Name	Map Ref.	Page
Santa Bárbara, dept., Hond.	B6	92
Santa Bárbara, stm., Bol.	G11	82
Santa Barbara Channel, strt., Ca., U.S.	J5	124
Santa Bárbara do Sul, Braz.	E12	80
Santa Catalina, Arg.	A5	80
Santa Catalina, Gulf of, b., Ca., U.S.	L7	124
Santa Catalina, Isla, i., Mex.	E4	90
Santa Catalina Island, i., Ca., U.S.	K7	124
Santa Catalina o Calovébora, Pan.	I13	92
Santa Catarina, Mex.	E9	90
Santa Catarina, state, Braz.	D13	80
Santa Catarina, Ilha de, i., Braz.	D14	80
Santa Cecília, Braz.	D13	80
Santa Clara, Col.	I8	84
Santa Clara, Cuba	C5	94
Santa Clara, Mex.	C6	90
Santa Clara, Ca., U.S.	G4	124
Santa Clara, Ut., U.S.	G3	120
Santa Clara, stm., Ut., U.S.	G3	120
Santa Clara de Olimar, Ur.	G11	80
Santa Clotilde, Peru	I6	84
Santa Coloma de Farners, Spain	D14	16
Santa Comba Dão, Port.	E3	16
Santa Cruz, Braz.	E8	79
Santa Cruz, Chile	H3	80
Santa Cruz, C.R.	G9	92
Santa Cruz, Peru	B2	82
Santa Cruz, Phil.	N19	39b
Santa Cruz, Phil.	O20	39b
Santa Cruz, Port.	M21	17a
Santa Cruz, Ca., U.S.	H3	124
Santa Cruz, Ven.	C7	84
Santa Cruz, dept., Bol.	G11	82
Santa Cruz, stm., Arg.	G2	78
Santa Cruz, stm., N.A.	L5	120
Santa Cruz, Isla, i., Ec.	J13	84a
Santa Cruz, Sierra de, mts., Guat.	B5	92
Santa Cruz Cabrália, Braz.	D9	79
Santa Cruz de Goiás, Braz.	D4	79
Santa Cruz de la Palma, Spain	O23	17b
Santa Cruz de la Sierra, Bol.	G10	82
Santa Cruz del Quiché, Guat.	B3	92
Santa Cruz del Sur, Cuba	D5	94
Santa Cruz de Tenerife, Spain	O24	17b
Santa Cruz de Tenerife, prov., Spain	O23	17b
Santa Cruz do Rio Pardo, Braz.	G4	79
Santa Cruz do Sul, Braz.	E12	80
Santa Cruz Island, i., Ca., U.S.	J6	124
Santa Cruz Islands, is., Sol.Is.	J20	126
Santa Elena, Arg.	F9	80
Santa Elena, Ec.	I2	84
Santa Elena, El Sal.	D6	92
Santa Elena, Mex.	D8	90
Santa Elena, stm., Bol.	G8	82
Santa Elena, Bahía de, b., Ec.	I2	84
Santa Elena, Golfo de, b., C.R.	G9	92
Santa Elena, Punta, c., C.R.	G9	92
Santa Elena, Punta, c., Ec.	I2	84
Santa Elena de Uairén, Ven.	E12	84
Santa Eugenia, Spain	C2	16
Santa Eulalia, Guat.	B3	92
Santa Eulària del Riu, Spain	G13	16
Santa Fe, Arg.	F8	80
Santa Fé, Braz.	C3	79
Santa Fé, Braz.	G3	79
Santa Fe, Hond.	B8	92
Santa Fé, Pan.	I13	92
Santa Fe, Spain	H8	16
Santa Fe, N.M., U.S.	I11	120
Santa Fe, prov., Arg.	F8	80
Santa Fe, stm., N.M., U.S.	I10	120
Santa Fe Baldy, mtn., N.M., U.S.	I11	120
Santa Fe de Bogotá, Col.	E5	84
Santa Fé do Sul, Braz.	F3	79
Santa Filomena, Braz.	E9	76
Santa Helena de Goiás, Braz.	D3	79
Santai, China	E8	30
Santa Inês, Braz.	B9	79
Santa Inés, Bahía, b., Mex.	D4	90
Santa Inés, Isla, i., Chile	G2	78
Santa Isabel, Arg.	I5	80
Santa Isabel, Arg.	G8	80
Santa Isabel, Ec.	I3	84
Santa Isabel, i., Sol.Is.	I19	126
Santa Isabel, stm., Guat.	B5	92
Santa Isabel de Sihuas, Peru	G5	82
Santa Juliana, Braz.	E5	79
Santa Lucía, Arg.	F4	80
Santa Lucía, Arg.	E9	80
Santa Lucía, Cuba	D6	94
Santa Lucía, Ur.	H10	80
Santa Lucía, Ven.	C8	84
Santa Lucía Cotzumalguapa, Guat.	C3	92
Santa Lucia Range, mts., Ca., U.S.	H4	124
Santa Luzia, i., C.V.	E2	54
Santa Magdalena, Arg.	H7	80
Santa Margarita, Ca., U.S.	I5	124
Santa Margarita, Isla, i., Mex.	E4	90
Santa Margherita Ligure, Italy	E4	18
Santa María, Arg.	D5	80
Santa Maria, Braz.	E12	80
Santa Maria, C.V.	k17	64a
Santa María, C.R.	H11	92
Santa María, Pan.	I14	92
Santa Maria, Switz.	F11	13
Santa Maria, Switz.	E13	13
Santa Maria, Ca., U.S.	J5	124
Santa Maria, stm., Braz.	F11	80
Santa Maria, stm., Braz.	A11	80
Santa María, stm., Mex.	B6	90
Santa María, stm., Mex.	G10	90
Santa María, stm., Pan.	I14	92
Santa María, Bahía, b., Mex.	E5	90
Santa María, Cabo, c., Ur.	H11	80
Santa Maria, Cabo de, c., Ang.	D2	58
Santa Maria, Cape, c., Bah.	C7	94
Santa María, Isla, i., Chile	I2	80
Santa María, Isla, i., Ec.	J13	84a
Santa María, Laguna, l., Mex.	B6	90
Santa María, Volcán, vol., Guat.	C3	92
Santa Maria Asunción Tlaxiaco, Mex.	I11	90
Santa Maria Capua Vetere, Italy	H9	18
Santa María Colotepec, Mex.	J11	90
Santa Maria da Vitória, Braz.	B6	79
Santa María de Huazamota, Mex.	F7	90
Santa María de Ipire, Ven.	C10	84
Santa Maria de Itabira, Braz.	E7	79
Santa María del Oro, Mex.	E7	90
Santa María del Río, Mex.	G9	90
Santa Mariá de Mohovano, Mex.	D8	90
Santa Maria di Leuca, Capo, c., Italy	J13	18
Santa Maria do Suaçuí, Braz.	E7	79
Santa Maria Madalena, Braz.	F7	79
Santa-Maria-Siché, Fr.	M23	15a
Santa Marinella, Italy	G6	18
Santa Marta, Col.	B5	84
Santa Marta, Guat.	D3	92
Santa Marta, Cerro, mtn., Mex.	H12	90
Santa Marta, Ciénaga Grande, b., Col.	B5	84
Santa Marta Grande, Cabo de, c., Braz.	E14	80
Santa Monica, Ca., U.S.	J7	124
Santa Monica Bay, b., Ca., U.S.	K7	124
Santana, Braz.	B6	79
Santana, Port.	M21	17a
Santana, stm., Braz.	E3	79
Santana, Coxilha de, hills, S.A.	F11	80
Santana da Boa Vista, Braz.	F12	80
Santana do Livramento, Braz.	F11	80
Santander, Col.	F4	84
Santander, Spain	B8	16
Santander, dept., Col.	D6	84
Santander Jiménez, Mex.	E10	90
Santanilla, Islas, is., Hond.	F3	94
Sant Antoni de Portmany, Spain	G13	16
Santa Paula, Ca., U.S.	J6	124
Santaquin, Ut., U.S.	E5	120
Santarém, Braz.	D8	76
Santarém, Port.	F3	16
Santaren Channel, strt., Bah.	C5	94
Santa Rita, Col.	G6	84
Santa Rita, Hond.	B7	92
Santa Rita, Mex.	C4	90
Santa Rita, Ven.	B7	84
Santa Rita de Catuna, Arg.	F5	80
Santa Rita do Araguaia, Braz.	D2	79
Santa Rita do Weil, Braz.	I8	84
Santa Rosa, Arg.	I6	80
Santa Rosa, Arg.	B6	80
Santa Rosa, Bol.	F8	82
Santa Rosa, Bol.	D8	82
Santa Rosa, Bol.	G10	82
Santa Rosa, Braz.	B6	78
Santa Rosa, Braz.	C5	79
Santa Rosa, Braz.	D11	80
Santa Rosa, Col.	F8	84
Santa Rosa, C.R.	G9	92
Santa Rosa, Ec.	I3	84
Santa Rosa, Para.	D10	80
Santa Rosa, Para.	I11	82
Santa Rosa, Ca., U.S.	F3	124
Santa Rosa, N.M., U.S.	E2	116
Santa Rosa, Tx., U.S.	M9	116
Santa Rosa, Ven.	C8	84
Santa Rosa, dept., Guat.	C4	92
Santa Rosa, Parque Nacional, C.R.	G9	92
Santa Rosa Beach, Fl., U.S.	L10	114
Santa Rosa de Aguán, Hond.	B9	92
Santa Rosa de Amanadona, Ven.	G9	84
Santa Rosa de Cabal, Col.	E5	84
Santa Rosa [de Copán], Hond.	C6	92
Santa Rosa del Conlara, Arg.	G6	80
Santa Rosa de Leales, Arg.	D6	80
Santa Rosa de Lima, El Sal.	D7	92
Santa Rosa del Palmar, Bol.	G10	82
Santa Rosa de Osos, Col.	D5	84
Santa Rosa de Río Primero, Arg.	F7	80
Santa Rosa de Sucumbíos, Ec.	G4	84
Santa Rosa de Viterbo, Col.	E6	84
Santa Rosa Island, i., Ca., U.S.	K5	124
Santa Rosa Island, i., Fl., U.S.	L10	114
Santa Rosalía, Mex.	D3	90
Santa Rosalía, Ven.	C8	84
Santa Rosa Range, mts., Nv., U.S.	C8	124
Šantarskije ostrova, is., Russia	F19	28
Santa Sylvina, Arg.	D8	80
Santa Teresa, Braz.	E8	79
Santa Teresa, Mex.	E11	90
Santa Teresa, stm., Braz.	B4	79
Santa Teresa, Embalse de, res., Spain	E6	16
Santa Tereza de Goiás, Braz.	B4	79
Santa Vitória, Braz.	E3	79
Santa Vitória do Palmar, Braz.	G12	80
Santa Ynez, stm., Ca., U.S.	J5	124
Sant Carles de la Ràpita, Spain	E12	16
Santee, Ca., U.S.	L9	124
Santee, stm., S.C., U.S.	F7	112
Sant Feliu de Guíxols, Spain	D15	16
Santhià, Italy	D3	18
Santiago, Bol.	H12	82
Santiago, Braz.	E11	80
Santiago, Chile	G3	80
Santiago, Mex.	F5	90
Santiago, Pan.	C2	84
Santiago, Para.	D10	80
Santiago, Peru	F4	82
Santiago, i., C.V.	G4	52
Santiago, i., C.V.	m17	64a
Santiago, stm., Mex.	E7	90
Santiago, stm., S.A.	I4	84
Santiago, Cerro, mtn., Pan.	I13	92
Santiago, Isla, i., Ec.	J13	84a
Santiago, Serranía de, mts., Bol.	H12	82
Santiago Atitlán, Guat.	C3	92
Santiago Choapan, Mex.	I12	90
Santiago de Cao, Peru	B2	82
Santiago de Chocorvos, Peru	E4	82
Santiago de Chuco, Peru	C2	82
Santiago de Compostela, Spain	C3	16
Santiago de Cuba, Cuba	D7	94
Santiago de Huari, Bol.	H8	82
Santiago de Huata, Bol.	G7	82
Santiago del Estero, Arg.	D6	80
Santiago del Estero, prov., Arg.	E7	80
Santiago [de los Caballeros], Dom. Rep.	E9	94
Santiago de Machaca, Bol.	G7	82
Santiago de Méndez, Ec.	I3	84
Santiago Ixcuintla, Mex.	G7	90
Santiago Jamiltepec, Mex.	I11	90
Santiago Larre, Arg.	H9	80
Santiago Papasquiaro, Mex.	E7	90
Santiaguillo, Laguna, l., Mex.	E7	90
Santiam Pass, Or., U.S.	F4	122
San Timoteo, Ven.	C7	84
Säntis, mtn., Switz.	D11	13
Sant Jordi, Golf de, b., Spain	E13	16
Santo, Tx., U.S.	G8	116
Santo Amaro, Braz.	B9	79
Santo Anastácio, Braz.	F3	79
Santo André, Braz.	G5	79
Santo Ângelo, Braz.	E11	80
Santo Antão, i., C.V.	k16	64a
Santo António, S. Tom./P.	A1	58
Santo Antônio, stm., Braz.	E6	79
Santo Antônio da Patrulha, Braz.	E13	80
Santo Antônio de Jesus, Braz.	B9	79
Santo Antônio de Pádua, Braz.	F7	79
Santo Antônio do Amparo, Braz.	F6	79
Santo Antônio do Içá, Braz.	I9	84
Santo Antônio do Leverger, Braz.	F13	82
Santo Antônio do Rio Verde, Braz.	D5	79
Santo Antônio do Sudoeste, Braz.	D12	80
Santo Augusto, Braz.	D12	80
Santo Corazón, Bol.	G12	82
Santo Domingo, Dom. Rep.	E10	94
Santo Domingo, Mex.	E3	90
Santo Domingo, Nic.	E9	92
Santo Domingo, stm., Mex.	A3	92
Santo Domingo de los Colorados, Ec.	H3	84
Santo Domingo Pueblo, N.M., U.S.	I10	120
Santo Domingo Tehuantepec, Mex.	I12	90
Santo Domingo Zanatepec, Mex.	I12	90
Santo Estêvão, Braz.	B9	79
San Tomé, Ven.	C10	84
Santoña, Spain	B8	16
Santo Onofre, stm., Braz.	B7	79
Santorini see Thíra, i., Grc.	M9	20
Santos, Braz.	G5	79
Santos Dumont, Braz.	F7	79
Santos Tomás del Norte, Nic.	D8	92
Santo Tomás, Col.	B5	84
Santo Tomás, Mex.	B1	90
Santo Tomás, Nic.	E9	92
Santo Tomás, Peru	B3	82
Santo Tomás, Peru	F5	82
Santo Tomás, stm., Peru	F5	82
Santo Tomás, Punta, c., Mex.	B1	90
Santo Tomé, Arg.	E10	80
Santo Tomé, Arg.	F8	80
Santuario de Quillacas, Bol.	H8	82
Santunying, China	C6	32
San Ubaldo, Nic.	F9	92
San Vicente, Arg.	E6	80
San Vicente, El Sal.	D6	92
San Vicente, Volcán de, vol., El Sal.	D6	92
San Vicente de Cañete, Peru	E3	82
San Vicente de Chucurí, Col.	D6	84
San Vicente del Caguán, Col.	F5	84
San Vicente de Tagua-Tagua, Chile	H3	80
San Vincenzo, Italy	F5	18
San Vito, C.R.	I12	92
San Vito, Italy	J4	18
San Vito dei Normanni, Italy	I12	18
San Ygnacio, Tx., U.S.	L7	116
Sanyuan, China	E8	30
Sanza Pombo, Ang.	C3	58
Sanzha, China	B2	32
São Benedito, stm., Braz.	C13	82
São Bento, Braz.	D10	76
São Bento do Sul, Braz.	D14	80
São Borja, Braz.	E10	80
São Caetano do Sul, Braz.	G5	79
São Carlos, Braz.	G5	79
São Cristóvão, Braz.	F11	76
São Domingos, Braz.	B5	79
São Domingos, Braz.	D12	80
São Domingos, Gui.-B.	E1	64
São Domingos, stm., Braz.	B5	79
São Domingos, stm., Braz.	E3	79
São Domingos, stm., Braz.	E2	79
São Domingos, stm., Braz.	E9	82
São Felipe, Braz.	C8	79
São Filipe, C.V.	m16	64a
São Francisco, Braz.	C6	79
São Francisco, stm., Braz.	E11	76
São Francisco, stm., Braz.	C8	79
São Francisco, stm., Braz.	B7	79
São Francisco, Baía de, b., Braz.	D14	80
São Francisco, Ilha de, i., Braz.	D14	80
São Francisco de Assis, Braz.	E11	80
São Francisco de Goiás, Braz.	C4	79
São Francisco de Paula, Braz.	E13	80
São Francisco do Sul, Braz.	D14	80
São Gabriel, Braz.	F11	80
São Gabriel da Palha, Braz.	E8	79
São Gabriel de Goiás, Braz.	C5	79
São Gonçalo do Abaeté, Braz.	E6	79
São Gonçalo do Sapucaí, Braz.	F6	79
São Gonçalo dos Campos, Braz.	B9	79
Sao Hill, Tan.	C7	58
São Jerônimo, Braz.	E13	80
São Jerônimo, Serra de, plat., Braz.	D1	79
São Jerônimo da Serra, Braz.	G3	79
São João, stm., Braz.	B3	79
São João da Barra, Braz.	F8	79
São João da Boa Vista, Braz.	F5	79
São João D'Aliança, Braz.	C5	79
São João da Madeira, Port.	E3	16
São João da Ponte, Braz.	C6	79
São João del-Rei, Braz.	F6	79
São João do Araguaia, Braz.	E9	76
São João do Paraíso, Braz.	C7	79
São João Evangelista, Braz.	E7	79
São Joaquim, Braz.	E14	80
São Joaquim, Parque Nacional de, Braz.	E14	80
São Joaquim da Barra, Braz.	F5	79
São José, Braz.	D14	80
São José, stm., Braz.	E8	79
São José de Anauá, Braz.	G12	84
São José do Cedro, Braz.	D12	80
São José do Norte, Braz.	G12	80
São José do Rio Preto, Braz.	F4	79
São José dos Campos, Braz.	G6	79
São José dos Pinhais, Braz.	C14	80
São Leopoldo, Braz.	E13	80
São Lourenço, Braz.	G6	79
São Lourenço, Pantanal de, sw., Braz.	G13	82
São Lourenço do Oeste, Braz.	D12	80
São Lourenço do Sul, Braz.	F13	80
São Luís, Braz.	D10	76
São Luís de Montes Belos, Braz.	D3	79
São Luís Gonzaga, Braz.	E11	80
São Manuel, Braz.	G4	79
São Manuel, stm., Braz.	C13	82
São Marcos, stm., Braz.	D5	79
São Mateus, Braz.	E9	79
São Mateus, Braço Norte, stm., Braz.	E8	79
São Mateus do Sul, Braz.	C13	80
São Miguel, i., Port.	m21	62a
São Miguel, stm., Braz.	D8	79
São Miguel do Araguaia, Braz.	B3	79
São Miguel d'Oeste, Braz.	D12	80
Saona, Isla, i., Dom. Rep.	E10	94
Saône, stm., Fr.	F11	14
Saône-et-Loire, dept., Fr.	F11	14
São Nicolau, i., C.V.	k16	64a
São Paulo, Braz.	G5	79
São Paulo, state, Braz.	G4	79
São Paulo de Olivença, Braz.	I8	84
São Pedro, Braz.	E3	79
São Pedro, stm., Braz.	D8	79
São Pedro do Sul, Braz.	E11	80
São Pedro do Sul, Port.	E3	16
São Raimundo Nonato, Braz.	E10	76
São Romão, Braz.	D6	79
São Roque, Braz.	G5	79
São Roque, Cabo de, c., Braz.	E11	76
São Sebastião, Braz.	G6	79
São Sebastião, Ilha de, i., Braz.	G6	79
São Sebastião, Ponta, c., Moz.	D12	66
São Sebastião do Maranhão, Braz.	E7	79
São Sebastião do Paraíso, Braz.	F5	79
São Sebastião do Rio Claro, Braz.	C3	79
São Sepé, Braz.	F12	80
São Simão, Braz.	F5	79
São Simão, Braz.	E3	79
São Tiago, Braz.	F6	79
São Timóteo, Braz.	B7	79
São Tomé, S. Tom./P.	A1	58
São Tomé, i., S. Tom./P.	A1	58
São Tomé, stm., Braz.	C13	82
São Tomé, Cabo de, c., Braz.	F8	79
Sao Tome and Principe (São Tomé e Principe), ctry., Afr.	A1	58
Saoura, Oued, val., Alg.	F10	62
São Vicente, Braz.	G5	79
São Vicente, i., C.V.	k16	64a
São Vicente, Cabo de (Cape Saint Vincent), c., Port.	H2	16
São Vicente de Minas, Braz.	F6	79
Sapé, Braz.	E11	76
Sapele, Nig.	I12	64
Sapello, stm., N.M., U.S.	I11	120
Sapelo Island, i., Ga., U.S.	H5	112
Şaphane, Tur.	J13	20
Şapitwa, mtn., Mwi.	E7	58
Šapki, Russia	B14	22
Sa Pobla, Spain	F15	16
Sapodilla Cays, i., Belize	A6	92
Saponé, Burkina	E9	64
Saposoa, Peru	B3	82
Sapožok, Russia	H23	22
Sapporo, Japan	D16	36a
Sapri, Italy	I10	18
Saptakośī, stm., Nepal	G12	44
Sapulpa, Ok., U.S.	D10	116
Sāqiat al-'Abd, Sud.	G6	60
Saqqez, Iran	C9	48
Saquena, Peru	A5	82
Saquisilí, Ec.	H3	84
Sarāb, Iran	C9	48
Saraburi, Thai.	G6	40
Saracura, stm., Braz.	B8	79
Saragosa, Tx., U.S.	H3	116
Saragossa see Zaragoza, Spain	D11	16
Saraguro, Ec.	I3	84
Sarai, Russia	H24	22
Sarajevo, Bos.	F2	20
Sarakhs, Iran	C16	48
Saraland, Al., U.S.	L8	114
Saran', Kaz.	H12	26
Saranac, Mi., U.S.	H10	110
Saranac, stm., N.Y., U.S.	C13	108
Saranac Lake, N.Y., U.S.	C12	108
Sarandi, Braz.	D12	80
Sarandí del Yi, Ur.	G11	80
Sarandí Grande, Ur.	G10	80
Saransk, Russia	G7	26
Sarapiquí, stm., C.R.	G11	92
Sarapul, Russia	F8	26
Sarare, Ven.	C8	84
Sara Sara, Nevado, mtn., Peru	F5	82
Sarasota, Fl., U.S.	L4	112
Sarata, Ukr.	C13	20
Saratoga, Ca., U.S.	G3	124
Saratoga, Tx., U.S.	I12	116
Saratoga, Wy., U.S.	C10	120
Saratoga Springs, N.Y., U.S.	D13	108
Saratov, Russia	G7	26
Saratovskoje vodochranilišče, res., Russia	G7	26
Saraurcu, mtn., Ec.	H4	84
Saravan, Laos	G9	40
Saraya, Gui.	F4	64
Sarayköy, Tur.	L12	20
Sarbāz, Iran	H16	48
Sárbogárd, Hung.	I18	10
Sarcee Indian Reserve, Alta., Can.	G20	102
Sarcoxie, Mo., U.S.	E2	114
Sārda (Mahākālī), stm., Asia	F9	44
Sardārshahr, India	F6	44
Sardegna, prov., Italy	I4	18
Sardegna (Sardinia), i., Italy	I4	18
Sardinal, C.R.	G9	92
Sardinata, Col.	C6	84
Sardinia see Sardegna, i., Italy	I4	18
Sardis, Al., U.S.	J10	114
Sardis, Ga., U.S.	G5	112
Sardis, Ms., U.S.	H7	114
Sardis, Tn., U.S.	G8	114
Sardis Lake, res., Ms., U.S.	H7	114
Sar-e Pol, Afg.	B1	44
Sarepta, La., U.S.	J3	114
Sargans, Switz.	D11	13
Sargasso Sea	B8	74
Sargent, Ga., U.S.	F2	112
Sargent, Ne., U.S.	J8	118
Sargodha, Pak.	D5	44
Sarh, Chad	G4	56
Sārī, Iran	C12	48
Saric, Mex.	B4	90
Şarif, Yemen	F7	47
Sarıkamış, Tur.	A7	48
Sarina, Austl.	C8	70
Sariñena, Spain	D11	16
Sarīr, Libya	D2	60
Sarita, Tx., U.S.	B9	116
Şariwŏn, N. Kor.	E13	32
Šarja, Russia	F7	26
Sark, i., Guernsey	L11	8
Sarkad, Hung.	I21	10
Şarkışla, Tur.	B4	48
Šarkovščina, Bela.	F10	22
Şarköy, Tur.	I11	20
Šarlauk, Turk.	B13	48
Sarles, N.D., U.S.	C9	118
Sármellék, Hung.	I17	10
Sarmiento de Gamboa, Cerro, mtn., Chile	G2	78
Särna, Swe.	K13	6
Sarnen, Switz.	E9	13
Sarnia, Ont., Can.	H13	110
Sarno, Italy	I9	18
Saron, S. Afr.	I4	66
Saronikós Kólpos, b., Grc.	L7	20
Saronno, Italy	D4	18
Sárospatak, Hung.	G21	10
Sarpsborg, Nor.	L12	6
Sarralbe, Fr.	C14	14
Sarrebourg, Fr.	D14	14
Sarreguemines, Fr.	C14	14
Sarre-Union, Fr.	D14	14
Sarro, Mali	E7	64
Sarstoon (Sarstún), stm., N.A.	B5	92
Sarstún (Sarstoon), stm., N.A.	B5	92
Sartang, stm., Russia	D18	28
Sartell, Mn., U.S.	E1	110
Sartène, Fr.	H3	18
Sarthe, dept., Fr.	D7	14
Sartilly, Fr.	D5	14
Saruhanlı, Tur.	K11	20
Sarūr, Oman	C11	47
Sárvár, Hung.	H16	10
Sarvestān, Iran	G12	48
Saryg-Sep, Russia	G17	26
Sarykol'skij chrebet, mts., Asia	A6	44
Saryozek, Kaz.	I13	26
Sarysu, stm., Kaz.	H11	26
Sary-Taš, Kyrg.	J12	26
Sarzana, Italy	E4	18
Sasaginnigak Lake, l., Man., Can.	G19	104
Sasakwa, Ok., U.S.	E10	116
Sāsarām, India	H11	44
Sásd, Hung.	I18	10
Sasebo, Japan	N4	36
Saskatchewan, prov., Can.	F11	96
Saskatchewan, stm., Can.	E13	104
Saskatoon, Sask., Can.	F8	104
Saslaya, Cerro, mtn., Nic.	H2	94
Sasolburg, S. Afr.	F8	66
Sasovo, Russia	G24	22
Saspamco, Tx., U.S.	J8	116
Sassafras, Ky., U.S.	B3	112
Sassafras Mountain, mtn., U.S.	D4	112
Sassandra, I.C.	I6	64
Sassandra, stm., I.C.	I6	64
Sassari, Italy	I3	18
Sassoferrato, Italy	F7	18
Sasso Marconi, Italy	E6	18
S'as'stroj, Russia	A15	22
Sassuolo, Italy	E5	18
Sastown, Lib.	I5	64
Sastre, Arg.	F8	80
Sasyk, ozero, l., Ukr.	D13	20
Satah Mountain, mtn., B.C., Can.	E10	102
Šatalovo, Russia	G15	22
Sata-misaki, c., Japan	Q5	36
Satanta, Ks., U.S.	N7	118
Sātāra, India	D2	46
Satara, S. Afr.	E10	66
Satélite, Mex.	B6	90
Satellite Beach, Fl., U.S.	K6	112
Satipo, Peru	D4	82
Satīt (Tekeze), stm., Afr.	J9	60
Satka, Russia	F9	26
Satna, India	H9	44
Sátoraljaújhely, Hung.	G21	10
Sātpura Range, mts., India	J7	44
Satsuma, Al., U.S.	L8	114
Satsunan-shotō, is., Japan	R4	37b
Sattahip, Thai.	H6	40
Satthwa, Burma	F3	40
Satu Mare, Rom.	B6	20
Satu Mare, co., Rom.	B6	20
Şatun, Thai.	K6	40
Šatura, Russia	F22	22
Şaturnino M. Laspiur, Arg.	F7	80
Šaturtorf, Russia	F22	22
Sauce, Arg.	F9	80
Sauce, Peru	B3	82
Sauce, Ur.	H10	80
Sauce Corto, Arroyo, stm., Arg.	I8	80
Saucier, Ms., U.S.	L7	114
Saucillo, Mex.	C7	90
Sauda, Nor.	L10	6
Saudi Arabia (Al-'Arabīyah as-Su'ūdīyah), ctry., Asia	D4	42
Sauer (Sûre), stm., Eur.	I10	12
Saueruiná, stm., Braz.	E12	82
Sauê-Uiná, stm., Braz.	E12	82
Saugatuck, Mi., U.S.	H9	110
Saugerties, N.Y., U.S.	E13	108
Saugstad, Mount, mtn., B.C., Can.	E8	102
Saujil, Arg.	E5	80
Sauk, stm., Mn., U.S.	E1	110
Sauk Centre, Mn., U.S.	F13	118
Sauk City, Wi., U.S.	G6	110
Sauk Rapids, Mn., U.S.	E1	110
Saukville, Wi., U.S.	G8	110
Saül, Fr. Gu.	C8	76
Saulgau, Ger.	G9	10
Saulieu, Fr.	E11	14
Saulkrasti, Lat.	D7	22
Sault-au-Mouton, Que., Can.	D4	106
Sault aux Cochons, Rivière du, stm., Que., Can.	D4	106
Saulteaux, stm., Alta., Can.	C20	102
Saulteaux Indian Reserve, Sask., Can.	E6	104
Sault Sainte Marie, Ont., Can.	D11	110
Sault Sainte Marie, Mi., U.S.	D11	110
Saumarez Reef, rf., Austl.	C10	70
Saumons, Rivíere aux, stm., Que., Can.	C11	106
Saumur, Fr.	E6	14
Saunders Island, i., S. Geor.	A2	73
Saunders Island, i., S. Geor.	J12	74
Sauquoit, N.Y., U.S.	D11	108
Saurimo, Ang.	C4	58
Sausalito, Ca., U.S.	G3	124
Sauveterre-de-Béarn, Fr.	I6	14
Sauvo, Fin.	K18	6
Sava, Italy	I12	18
Sava, stm., Eur.	F11	4
Savage, Md., U.S.	H10	108
Savage, Mt., U.S.	D3	118
Savai'i, i., W. Sam.	J22	126
Savalou, Benin	H10	64
Savane, stm., Que., Can.	A2	106
Savanna, Il., U.S.	H5	110
Savanna, Ok., U.S.	E11	116
Savannah, Ga., U.S.	G5	112
Savannah, Mo., U.S.	C2	114
Savannah, Tn., U.S.	G8	114
Savannah, stm., U.S.	G5	112
Savannakhét, Laos	F8	40
Savanna-la-Mar, Jam.	E5	94
Savé, Benin	G11	64
Save (Sabi), stm., Afr.	C12	66
Sāveh, Iran	D11	48
Savelli, Italy	J11	18
Saverdun, Fr.	I8	14
Saverne, Fr.	D14	14
Savigliano, Italy	E2	18
Savino, Russia	E24	22
Şavinskij, Russia	J27	6
Šavnik, Yugo.	G3	20
Savognin, Switz.	E12	13
Savoie, dept., Fr.	G13	14
Savona, B.C., Can.	G14	102
Savona, Italy	E3	18
Savoonga, Ak., U.S.	E9	100
Savoy, Tx., U.S.	F10	116
Savran', Ukr.	A14	20
Savu Sea see Sawu, Laut, Indon.	G7	38
Sawahlunto, Indon.	O6	40
Sawāi Mādhopur, India	H7	44
Sawākin, Sud.	H9	60
Sawankhalok, Thai.	F5	40
Sawatch Range, mts., Co., U.S.	E10	120
Sawdā', Jabal, mtn., Sau. Ar.	E3	47
Sawdā', Jabal as-, hills, Libya	C4	56
Sawdā', Qurnat as-, mtn., Leb.	D4	48
Sawdirī, Sud.	J5	60
Sawhāj, Egypt	D6	60
Sawknah, Libya	C4	56
Şawqirah, Ghubbat, b., Oman	E10	47
Sawu, Laut (Savu Sea), Indon.	G7	38
Sawu, Pulau, i., Indon.	H7	38
Sawyer, Mi., U.S.	I9	110
Sawyer, N.D., U.S.	C6	118
Sawyers Hill, hill, Newf., Can.	E20	106
Saxby, stm., Austl.	B4	70
Saxis, Va., U.S.	B11	112
Saxon, Switz.	F7	13
Saxon, Wi., U.S.	D5	110
Saxony see Sachsen, state, Ger.	C9	10
Saxton, Pa., U.S.	G8	108
Say, Niger	E11	64
Sayán, Peru	D3	82
Sayan Mountains (Sajany), mts., Asia	G11	28
Sayaxché, Guat.	I14	90
Saybrook, Il., U.S.	B8	114
Şaydā (Sidon), Leb.	A4	50
Şayḩūt, Yemen	G7	47
Sayil, hist., Mex.	G15	90
Saylorville Lake, res., Ia., U.S.	I2	110
Saylūn, Khirbat (Shiloh), hist., Isr. Occ.	D4	50
Sayre, Ok., U.S.	D7	116
Sayre, Pa., U.S.	F10	108
Sayreville, N.J., U.S.	G12	108
Sayula, Mex.	H8	90
Sayward, B.C., Can.	G9	102
Saywūn, Yemen	G6	47
Şazonovo, Russia	B18	22
Šazud, Taj.	B5	44
Sba, Alg.	F10	62
Sbeïtla, Tun.	N4	18
Sbiba, Tun.	N4	18
Scafell Pikes, mtn., Eng., U.K.	G10	8
Scalea, Italy	J10	18
Scammon, Ks., U.S.	N13	118
Scandia, Ks., U.S.	L10	118
Scanlon, Mn., U.S.	D3	110
Scapa, Alta., Can.	F23	102
Scapa Flow, b., Scot., U.K.	C10	8
Scapegoat Mountain, mtn., Mt., U.S.	C13	122
Ščapino, Russia	F23	28
Scappoose, Or., U.S.	E3	122
Scarborough, Ont., Can.	G16	110
Scarborough, Trin.	I14	94
Scarborough, Eng., U.K.	G13	8
Scatarie Island, i., N.S., Can.	G14	106
Şcawfell Island, i., Austl.	C8	70
Ščelkovo, Russia	F21	22
Şceptre, Sask., Can.	H5	104
Ščerbinka, Russia	F20	22
Schaerbeek (Schaarbeek), Bel.	G5	12
Schaffhausen, Switz.	C10	13
Schaffhausen, state, Switz.	C10	13
Schaller, Ia., U.S.	I12	118
Schärding, Aus.	G13	10
Schefferville, Que., Can.	F19	96
Scheibbs, Aus.	G15	10
Scheinfeld, Ger.	F10	10
Schelde (Escaut), stm., Eur.	D4	10
Schenectady, N.Y., U.S.	E13	108
Schertz, Tx., U.S.	J8	116
Schesslitz, Ger.	F11	10
Scheveningen, Neth.	D5	12
Schiedam, Neth.	E5	12
Schiermonnikoog, Neth.	B9	12
Schiermonnikoog, i., Neth.	B9	12
Schiltigheim, Fr.	D14	14
Schio, Italy	D6	18
Schipbeek, stm., Eur.	D9	12
Schkeuditz, Ger.	D12	10
Schladming, Aus.	H13	10
Schlater, Ms., U.S.	I6	114
Schleswig, Ger.	A9	10
Schleswig, Ia., U.S.	I12	118
Schleswig-Holstein, state, Ger.	A9	10
Schleusingen, Ger.	E10	10
Schlieren, Switz.	D9	13
Schlitz, Ger.	E9	10
Schlüchtern, Ger.	E9	10
Schmalkalden, Ger.	E10	10
Schmidmühlen, Ger.	F11	10
Schmölln, Ger.	E12	10
Schneverdingen, Ger.	B9	10
Schodn'a, Russia	F20	22
Schofield, Wi., U.S.	F6	110
Schoharie, N.Y., U.S.	E12	108
Schönebeck, Ger.	C11	10
Schongau, Ger.	H10	10
Schoolcraft, Mi., U.S.	H10	110
Schopfheim, Ger.	H7	10
Schorndorf, Ger.	G9	10

Name — Map Ref. — Page

Schouten Island, i., Austl. N8 70
Schouwen, i., Neth. E4 12
Schramberg, Ger. G8 10
Schreiber, Ont., Can. B8 110
Schriever, La., U.S. M6 114
Schroffenstein, mtn., Nmb. F4 66
Schruns, Aus. H9 10
Schulenburg, Tx., U.S. J10 116
Schultz Lake, l., N.W. Ter., Can. D13 96
Schumacher, Ont., Can. B14 110
Schüpfheim, Switz. E9 13
Schuyler, Ne., U.S. J10 118
Schuyler, Va., U.S. B8 112
Schuylkill, stm., Pa., U.S. G11 108
Schuylkill Haven, Pa., U.S. G10 108
Schwabach, Ger. F11 10
Schwaben, hist. reg., Ger. G10 10
Schwäbische Alb, mts., Ger. G9 10
Schwäbisch Gmünd, Ger. G9 10
Schwäbisch Hall, Ger. F9 10
Schwabmünchen, Ger. G10 10
Schwanden, Switz. D11 13
Schwandorf, Ger. F12 10
Schwaner, Pegunungan, mts., Indon. F5 38
Schwarza, Ger. E11 10
Schwarzach im Pongau, Aus. H13 10
Schwarzenburg, Switz. E7 13
Schwarzwald (Black Forest), mts., Ger. G8 10
Schwaz, Aus. H11 10
Schwedt, Ger. B14 10
Schweinfurt, Ger. E10 10
Schweizer Nationalpark, Switz. E13 13
Schwerin, Ger. B11 10
Schwyz, Switz. D10 13
Schwyz, state, Switz. D10 13
Sciacca, Italy L8 18
Scicli, Italy M9 18
Scilla, Italy K10 18
Scilly, Isles of, is., Eng., U.K. L7 8
Scio, Oh., U.S. G5 108
Scio, Or., U.S. F3 122
Scioto, stm., Oh., U.S. I3 108
Scipio, Ut., U.S. E4 120
Scobey, Mt., U.S. B20 122
Ščokino, Russia G20 22
Scone, Austl. I9 70
Scooba, Ms., U.S. J8 114
Scordia, Italy L9 18
Scotia, Ne., U.S. J9 118
Scotia, N.Y., U.S. E13 108
Scotia Sea, S.A. A1 73
Scotland, Ont., Can. G15 110
Scotland, S.D., U.S. H10 118
Scotland, Tx., U.S. F8 116
Scotland, ter., U.K. D9 8
Scotland Neck, N.C., U.S. C9 112
Scotlandville, La., U.S. L5 114
Scotsburn, N.S., Can. G11 106
Scott, Sask., Can. F6 104
Scott, Ms., U.S. I5 114
Scott, stm., Ca., U.S. C3 124
Scott, Cape, c., B.C., Can. G6 102
Scott, Mount, mtn., Or., U.S. H3 122
Scott Base, sci., Ant. C8 73
Scottburgh, S. Afr. H10 66
Scott City, Ks., U.S. M7 118
Scott City, Mo., U.S. E7 114
Scottdale, Pa., U.S. G7 108
Scott Islands, is., B.C., Can. G6 102
Scott Mountain, mtn., Id., U.S. F10 122
Scott Reef, rf., Austl. B4 68
Scottsbluff, Ne., U.S. J4 118
Scottsboro, Al., U.S. H10 114
Scottsburg, In., U.S. D11 114
Scottsdale, Austl. M7 70
Scottsdale, Az., U.S. K5 120
Scotts Hill, Tn., U.S. G8 114
Scottsville, Ky., U.S. F10 114
Scottville, Mi., U.S. G9 110
Scout Lake, Sask., Can. I8 104
Scranton, Ia., U.S. I13 118
Scranton, N.D., U.S. E4 118
Scranton, Pa., U.S. F11 108
Screven, Ga., U.S. H4 112
Scribner, Ne., U.S. J11 118
Ščučin, Bela. H7 22
Ščučinsk, Kaz. G12 26
Scuol (Schuls), Switz. E13 13
Scurry, Tx., U.S. G10 116
Scutari, Lake, l., Eur. G3 20
Seabird Island Indian Reserve, B.C., Can. H13 102
Seaboard, N.C., U.S. C9 112
Seadrift, Tx., U.S. K10 116
Seaford, De., U.S. I11 108
Seaforth, Ont., Can. G14 110
Seager Wheeler Lake, l., Sask., Can. D11 104
Seagraves, Tx., U.S. G4 116
Seahorse Point, c., N.W. Ter., Can. D16 96
Sea Islands, is., U.S. I5 112
Sea Isle City, N.J., U.S. H12 108
Seal, stm., Man., Can. E13 96
Sea Lake, Austl. J5 70
Seal Cays, is., T./C. Is. D9 94
Seal Cove, N.B., Can. H7 106
Seal Cove, Newf., Can. C17 106
Seale, Al., U.S. J11 114
Sealevel, N.C., U.S. E10 112
Seal Island, i., N.S., Can. I7 106
Seal Lake, l., Newf., Can. F20 96
Sealy, Tx., U.S. J10 116
Seara, Braz. D12 80
Searchlight, Nv., U.S. I11 124
Searcy, Ar., U.S. G5 114
Searsport, Me., U.S. C18 108
Seaside, Ca., U.S. H4 124
Seaside, Or., U.S. E2 122
Seaside Park, N.J., U.S. H12 108
Seattle, Wa., U.S. C3 122
Seattle, Mount, mtn., N.A. F25 100
Sébaco, Nic. E8 92
Sebago Lake, l., Me., U.S. D16 108
Sebakwe Recreational Area, Zimb. B10 66
Šebalino, Russia G15 26
Sebastian, Tx., U.S. M9 116
Sebastián Vizcaíno, Bahía, b., Mex. C2 90
Sebastopol, Ca., U.S. F3 124
Sebastopol, Ms., U.S. J7 114
Sebderat, Eth. J9 60
Sebeka, Mn., U.S. E12 118
Seberi, Braz. D12 80
Sebeș, Rom. D7 20
Sebes Körös (Crișul Repede), stm., Eur. B5 20
Sebewaing, Mi., U.S. G12 110
Sebež, Russia E11 22
Şebinkarahisar, Tur. A5 48
Šebiș, Rom. C6 20
Sebnitz, Ger. E14 10
Sebree, Ky., U.S. E9 114
Sebring, Fl., U.S. L5 112
Secas, Islas, is., Pan. J12 92
Sechelt, B.C., Can. H11 102
Sechura, Peru A1 82
Sechura, Bahía de, b., Peru A1 82
Sechura, Desierto de, des., Peru A1 82
Seclantas, Arg. C5 80
Seco, stm., Arg. B7 80
Sečovce, Czech. G21 10
Section, Al., U.S. H11 114
Sécure, stm., Bol. F9 82
Security, Co., U.S. M3 118
Seda, China E7 30
Seda, Lat. D8 22
Seda, Lith. E5 22
Sedalia, Alta., Can. G4 104
Sedalia, Mo., U.S. D3 114
Sedan, Fr. C11 14
Sedan, Ks., U.S. N11 118
Sedano, Spain C8 16
Sedel'nikovo, Russia F13 26
Sederot, Isr. E3 50
Sedgefield, N.C., U.S. D6 112
Sedgewick, Alta., Can. E23 102
Sedgwick, Co., U.S. K5 118
Sedgwick, Ks., U.S. N10 118
Sedgwick, Mount, mtn., N.M., U.S. I8 120
Sedini, Italy I3 18
Sedlčany, Czech. F14 10
Sedom (Sodom), hist., Isr. F4 50
Sedona, Az., U.S. J5 120
Sedot Yam, Isr. D3 50
Sedova, pik, mtn., Russia C8 26
Sedrata, Alg. M2 18
Sedro Woolley, Wa., U.S. B3 122
Šeduva, Lith. F6 22
Seeberg, Switz. D8 13
Seeber Lake, l., Ont., Can. E21 104
Seefeld in Tirol, Aus. H11 10
Seehausen, Ger. C11 10
Seeheim, Nmb. F3 66
Seeis, Nmb. D3 66
Seekaskootch Indian Reserve, Sask., Can. E5 104
Seeley Lake, Mt., U.S. C12 122
Seelow, Ger. C14 10
Seelyville, In., U.S. C9 114
Seengen, Switz. D9 13
Sées, Fr. D7 14
Seesen, Ger. D10 10
Sefadu, S.L. G4 64
Sefar, hist., Alg. H15 62
Sefare, Bots. D8 66
Sefīd Ābeh, Iran F16 48
Sefrou, Mor. D8 62
Segamat, Malay. M7 40
Şegarcea, Rom. E7 20
Šegbana, Benin F11 64
Segbwema, S.L. G4 64
Segeža, Russia E4 26
Segni, Italy H8 18
Segorbe, Spain F11 16
Ségou, Mali E6 64
Segovia, Col. D5 84
Segovia, Spain E7 16
Segozero, ozero, l., Russia J23 6
Segre, stm., Eur. D12 16
Séguédine, Niger D9 54
Séguéla, I.C. H6 64
Séguéla, Mali D6 64
Seguí, Arg. F8 80
Seguin, Tx., U.S. J9 116
Segundo, Co., U.S. N3 118
Segundo, stm., Arg. F7 80
Segura, Port. F5 16
Segura, stm., Spain G11 16
Sehithwa, Bots. C6 66
Seia, Port. E4 16
Seibert, Co., U.S. L5 118
Seiling, Ok., U.S. C8 116
Seilo, Sud. K2 60
Sein, Île de, i., Fr. D2 14
Seinäjoki, Fin. J18 6
Seine, stm., Man., Can. I18 104
Seine, stm., Ont., Can. B3 110
Seine, stm., Fr. C7 14
Seine, Baie de la, b., Fr. C6 14
Seine-et-Marne, dept., Fr. D10 14
Seine-Maritime, dept., Fr. C8 14
Seixal, Port. G2 16
Sejm, stm., Eur. G4 26
Sejmčan, Russia E22 28
Šeke, Eth. M10 60
Šeki (Nucha), Azer. I7 26
Seki, Japan L11 36
Seki, Tur. M13 20
Sekoma, Bots. E6 66
Sekondi-Takoradi, Ghana I9 64
Şekota, Eth. K10 60
Šeksna, Russia B21 22
Šelagskij, mys, c., Russia C26 28
Selah, Wa., U.S. D5 122
Selaru, Pulau, i., Indon. G9 38
Selatan, Tanjung, c., Indon. F5 38
Selawik, Ak., U.S. C14 100
Selayar, Pulau, i., Indon. G7 38
Selb, Ger. E12 10
Selbu, Nor. J12 6
Selby, S.D., U.S. F7 118
Selbyville, De., U.S. I11 108
Sel'co, Russia H17 22
Selden, Ks., U.S. L7 118
Seldovia, Ak., U.S. G19 100
Selebi Phikwe, Bots. D8 66
Selenga (Selenge), stm., Asia G19 26
Selenge (Selenga), stm., Asia B7 30
Selenn'ach, stm., Russia D20 28
Sélestat, Fr. D14 14
Selezn'ovo, Russia A11 22
Selfridge, N.D., U.S. E7 118
Şélibaby, Maur. D3 64
Šelichova, zaliv, b., Russia F23 28
Seliger, ozero, l., Russia D16 22
Seligman, Az., U.S. I4 120
Seligman, Mo., U.S. F3 114
Selinsgrove, Pa., U.S. G10 108
Seliščе, Russia E16 22
Seližarovo, Russia E16 22
Selje, Nor. J9 6
Seljord, Nor. L11 6
Selkirk, Man., Can. H18 104
Selkirk, Scot., U.K. F11 8
Selkirk Mountains, mts., N.A. F16 102
Seller Lake, l., Man., Can. C20 104
Sellers, S.C., U.S. E7 112
Sellersburg, In., U.S. D11 114
Sells, Az., U.S. M5 120
Selm, Ger. D7 10
Selma, Al., U.S. J9 114
Selma, Ca., U.S. H6 124
Selma, N.C., U.S. D8 112
Selmer, Tn., U.S. G8 114
Selmont, Al., U.S. J9 114
Selous, Mount, mtn., Yukon, Can. E28 100
Seltz, Fr. D15 14
Selva, Arg. E7 80
Selvas, for., Braz. E6 76
Selwyn, Austl. C4 70
Selwyn, Mount, mtn., B.C., Can. B11 102
Selwyn Lake, l., Can. E12 96
Selwyn Mountains, mts., Can. D28 100
Şelwyn Range, mts., Austl. C4 70
Šemacha, Azer. A10 48
Seman, stm., Alb. I3 20
Semans, Sask., Can. G10 104
Semarang, Indon. J15 39a
Semeru, Gunung, mtn., Indon. K16 39a
Semeževo, Bela. I10 22
Semibratovo, Russia D22 22
Seminary, Ms., U.S. K7 114
Seminoe Reservoir, res., Wy., U.S. B10 120
Seminole, Ok., U.S. D10 116
Seminole, Tx., U.S. G4 116
Seminole, Lake, res., U.S. I2 112
Semipalatinsk, Kaz. G8 28
Semmens Lake, l., Man., Can. C20 104
Semnān, Iran D12 48
Şemois, stm., Eur. I7 12
Šemonaicha, Kaz. G14 26
Sem'onov, Russia F6 26
Sem'onovka, Ukr. I15 22
Semple Lake, l., Man., Can. C19 104
Semporna, Malay. E6 38
Semuliki, stm., Afr. A5 58
Semur-en-Auxois, Fr. E11 14
Sena, Bol. D8 82
Sena, Moz. E7 58
Senador Canedo, Braz. D4 79
Senador Firmino, Braz. F7 79
Senador Pompeu, Braz. E11 76
Senahú, Guat. B5 92
Sena Madureira, Braz. C7 82
Senanga, Zam. E4 58
Senate, Sask., Can. I5 104
Senath, Mo., U.S. F6 114
Senatobia, Ms., U.S. H7 114
Sendafa, Eth. M10 60
Sendai, Japan I15 36
Sêndo, China E15 44
Seneca, Il., U.S. I7 110
Seneca, Ks., U.S. L11 118
Seneca, Mo., U.S. F2 114
Seneca, Or., U.S. F7 122
Seneca, S.C., U.S. E4 112
Seneca Falls, N.Y., U.S. E10 108
Seneca Lake, l., N.Y., U.S. E10 108
Senegal (Sénégal), ctry., Afr. F4 54
Sénégal, stm., Afr. E4 54
Senekal, S. Afr. G8 66
Senftenberg, Ger. D14 10
Sengés, Braz. H4 79
Senhor do Bonfim, Braz. F10 76
Senica, Czech. G17 10
Senigallia, Italy F8 18
Senise, Italy I11 18
Senj, Cro. E9 18
Şenja, i., Nor. G15 6
Šenkursk, Russia E6 26
Senlac, Sask., Can. F5 104
Senlis, Fr. C9 14
Senmonorom, Camb. H9 40
Sennori, Italy I3 18
Senoia, Ga., U.S. F2 112
Senqu see Orange, stm., Afr. G4 66
Sens, Fr. D10 14
Sensuntepeque, El Sal. D6 92
Senta, Yugo. D4 20
Sentinel, Ok., U.S. D7 116
Sentinel Peak, mtn., B.C., Can. C13 102
Seo de Urgel, Spain C13 16
Seoni, India I8 44
Seoul see Sŏul, S. Kor. F14 32
Sepatini, stm., Braz. B9 82
Şepetiba, Baía de, b., Braz. G7 79
Šepetovka, Ukr. G3 26
Sepik, stm., Pap. N. Gui. k15 68a
Sępólno Krajeńskie, Pol. B17 10
Sepopa, Bots. B6 66
Sepoti, stm., Braz. B11 82
Sepotuba, stm., Braz. F13 82
Sept-Îles (Seven Islands), Que., Can. B7 106
Sepulga, stm., Al., U.S. K10 114
Sequatchie, stm., Tn., U.S. D1 112
Sequeros, Spain E5 16
Sequim, Wa., U.S. B2 122
Sequoia National Park, Ca., U.S. H7 124
Šerabad, Uzb. B2 44
Serachs, Turk. C16 48
Serafimovič, Russia H6 26
Seraidi, Alg. M2 18
Seraing, Bel. G7 12
Seram (Ceram), i., Indon. F8 38
Seram, Laut (Ceram Sea), Indon. F8 38
Serang, Indon. J13 39a
Serbia see Srbija, state, Yugo. F4 20
Serdobsk, Russia G6 26
Serebr'anyje Prudy, Russia G21 22
Sered', Czech. G17 10
Seredejskij, Russia G18 22
Seredina-Buda, Ukr. I17 22
Seredžius, Lith. F6 22
Seremban, Malay. M6 40
Serengeti Plain, pl., Tan. B6 58
Şerenje, Zam. D6 58
Šereševo, Bela. I7 22
Sergeant Bluff, Ia., U.S. I11 118
Sergeja Kirova, ostrova, is., Russia B15 26
Sergejevka, Russia I18 28
Sergijev Posad, Russia E21 22
Seria, Bru. E5 38
Serian, Malay. N11 40
Sérifos, i., Grc. L8 20
Sérigny, stm., Que., Can. E19 96
Şerkhe, Cerro, mtn., Bol. G7 82
Šerlovaja Gora, Russia G15 28
Sermata, Pulau, i., Indon. G8 38
Serodino, Arg. G8 80
Serov, Russia F10 26
Serowe, Bots. D8 66
Serpa, Port. H4 16
Serpent, Rivière au, stm., Que., Can. C2 106
Serpents Mouth, strt. C12 84
Serpuchov, Russia G20 22
Serra, Braz. F8 79
Serra do Navio, Braz. C8 76
Serra do Salitre, Braz. E5 79
Sérrai, Grc. H7 20
Serrana, Braz. F5 79
Serrânia, Braz. F5 79
Serranópolis, Braz. E2 79
Serra Talhada, Braz. E11 76
Serrezuela, Arg. F6 80
Serrinha, Braz. F11 76
Serro, Braz. E7 79
Sersale, Italy J11 18
Sertânia, Braz. E11 76
Seruini, stm., Braz. C8 82
Serule, Bots. C8 66
Sêrxu, China E6 30
Sesfontein, Nmb. B1 66
Sesheke, Zam. E4 58
Seskar, ostrov, i., Russia A11 22
Sessa Aurunca, Italy H8 18
Sestao, Spain B8 16
Sestri Levante, Italy E4 18
Şestroreck, Russia A12 22
Šešupe, stm., Eur. G5 22
Setana, Japan E14 36a
Sète, Fr. I10 14
Sete Barras, Braz. C15 80
Sete de Setembro, stm., Braz. B2 79
Sete Lagoas, Braz. E6 79
Sete Quedas, Parque Nacional de, Braz. C11 80
Seth Ward, Tx., U.S. E5 116
Set Net, Punta, c., Nic. E11 92
Seto, Japan L12 36
Seto-naikai, Japan M7 36
Seton Lake, l., B.C., Can. G12 102
Seton Portage, B.C., Can. G12 102
Settat, Mor. D7 62
Setté Cama, Gabon B1 58
Sette-Daban, chrebet, mts., Russia E19 28
Settee Lake, l., Man., Can. A18 104
Setting Lake, l., Man., Can. C16 104
Setúbal, Port. G3 16
Setúbal, Baía de, b., Port. G3 16
Seui, Italy J4 18
Seul, Lac, l., Ont., Can. H22 104
Seurre, Fr. E12 14
Sevan, Arm. A8 48
Sevan, ozero, l., Arm. I7 26
Sévaré, Mali D7 64
Şevastopol', Ukr. I4 26
Ševčenko, Kaz. I8 26
Ševčenkovo, Ukr. D13 20
Seven Islands see Sept-Îles, Que., Can. B7 106
Seven Persons, Alta., Can. I4 104
Seven Sisters Peaks, mts., B.C., Can. C6 102
Seventy Mile House, B.C., Can. F13 102
Severn, stm., Ont., Can. E15 96
Severn, stm., U.K. J11 8
Severnaja Dvina, stm., Russia E6 26
Severnaja Sos'va, stm., Russia E4 28
Severnaja Zeml'a, is., Russia B17 26
Severna Park, Md., U.S. H10 108
Severn Lake, l., Ont., Can. E24 104
Severnyje uvaly, hills, Russia B27 22
Severodvinsk, Russia E5 26
Severo-Dvinskij kanal, Russia B21 22
Severomorsk, Russia D4 26
Severo-Sibirskaja nizmennost', pl., Russia C18 26
Severoural'sk, Russia E9 26
Severo-Zadonsk, Russia G21 22
Severskij Donec, stm., Eur. H5 26
Severy, Ks., U.S. N11 118
Sevier, stm., Ut., U.S. E4 120
Sevier Desert, des., Ut., U.S. E4 120
Sevier Lake, l., Ut., U.S. F3 120
Sevierville, Tn., U.S. D3 112
Sevilla, Col. E5 84
Sevilla (Seville), Spain H6 16
Sevilla, Isla, i., Pan. I12 92
Seville, Fl., U.S. J5 112
Seville, Oh., U.S. F5 108
Seville see Sevilla, Spain H6 16
Şevketiye, Tur. I11 20
Ševsk, Russia I17 22
Sewanee, Tn., U.S. G11 114
Seward, Ak., U.S. F20 100
Seward, Ne., U.S. K10 118
Seward, Pa., U.S. G7 108
Seward Glacier, N.A. F24 100
Seward Peninsula, pen., Ak., U.S. D13 100
Sewell, Chile H3 80
Sexsmith, Alta., Can. B16 102
Sextin, stm., Mex. E7 90
Seybaplaya, Mex. H14 90
Seychelles, ctry., Afr. B11 58
Seyđisfjörđur, Ice. B6 6a
Seylac, Som. F9 56
Seymour, Austl. K6 70
Seymour, Ciskei I8 66
Seymour, Ct., U.S. F13 108
Seymour, In., U.S. D11 114
Seymour, Ia., U.S. J2 110
Seymour, Mo., U.S. E4 114
Seymour, Tx., U.S. F7 116
Seymour, Wi., U.S. F7 110
Seymour, stm., B.C., Can. F8 102
Seymour Inlet, b., B.C., Can. F7 102
Seymourville, La., U.S. L5 114
Seyssel, Fr. G12 14
Sezela, S. Afr. H10 66
Sfax, Tun. C16 62
Sfîntu-Gheorghe, Rom. D9 20
Sfizef, Alg. C10 62
's-Gravenbrakel see Braine-le-Comte, Bel. G5 12
's-Gravenhage (The Hague), Neth. D5 12
Shaanxi (Shensi), prov., China D8 30
Shabeelle (Shebele), stm., Afr. H9 56
Shabwah, Yemen G5 47
Shache (Yarkand), China A7 44
Shackan Indian Reserve, B.C., Can. G13 102
Shackleton Ice Shelf, Ant. B6 73
Shādegān, Iran F10 48
Shady Cove, Or., U.S. H3 122
Shady Grove, Fl., U.S. I3 112
Shadyside, Oh., U.S. H6 108
Shafer Butte, mtn., Id., U.S. G9 122
Shafter, Ca., U.S. I6 124
Shagamu, Nig. H11 64
Shageluk, Ak., U.S. E15 100
Shag Rocks, S. Geor. G8 78
Shāhābād, India E7 44
Shāhābād, India D4 46
Shah Alam, Malay. M6 40
Shahdād, Namakzār-e, pl., Iran F15 48
Shahdol, India I9 44
Shahe, China I6 32
Shāhjahānpur, India G8 44
Shāh Jūy, Afg. D2 44
Shāhpur, Pak. F3 44
Shāhpura, India H6 44
Shahrak, Afg. C1 44
Shahr-e Bābak, Iran F13 48
Shahr-e Kord, Iran E11 48
Shā'ib al-Banāt, Jabal, mtn., Egypt H2 48
Shaikou, China H6 34
Shakawe, Bots. B5 66
Shaker Heights, Oh., U.S. F5 108
Shaki, Nig. G11 64
Shākir, Jazīrat, i., Egypt H2 48
Shakopee, Mn., U.S. F2 110
Shaktoolik, Ak., U.S. D14 100
Shala, Lake, l., Eth. N10 60
Shalalth, B.C., Can. G12 102
Shalatayn, Bi'r, well, Egypt J3 48
Shaler Mountains, mts., N.W. Ter., Can. B10 96
Shaleshanto, Bots. B6 66
Shallotte, N.C., U.S. F8 112
Shallowater, Tx., U.S. F5 116
Shām, Bādiyat ash- (Syrian Desert), des., Asia E6 48
Shām, Jabal ash-, mtn., Oman C10 47
Shamattawa, Man., Can. C22 104
Shambe, Sud. N6 60
Shambu, Eth. M9 60
Shamīl, Iran H14 48
Shāmli, India F7 44
Shamokin, Pa., U.S. G10 108
Shamrock, Fl., U.S. J3 112
Shamrock, Tx., U.S. D6 116
Shamva, Zimb. E6 58
Shanbiao, China H1 32
Shandī, Sud. I7 60
Shandong (Shantung), prov., China D10 30
Shandong Bandao (Shantung Peninsula), pen., China F8 32
Shangani, Zimb. B9 66
Shangani, stm., Zimb. B9 66
Shangcheng, China D4 34
Shangfu, China G3 34
Shanggu, China C6 32
Shanghai, China D10 34
Shanghai Shi, China E11 30
Shangjiaodao, China F8 34
Shangping, China K3 34
Shangqing, China G6 34
Shangqiu (Zhuji), China A4 34
Shangrao, China G6 34
Shangshui, China B3 34
Shangxian, China E8 30
Shangxingzhen, China D8 34
Shangyuan, China B8 32
Shangzhi, China B12 30
Shanhaiguan, China C7 32
Shankou, China G3 34
Shannon, S. Afr. G8 66
Shannon, Ga., U.S. E1 112
Shannon, Il., U.S. H6 110
Shannon, Ms., U.S. H8 114
Shannon, stm., Ire. I4 8
Shannontown, S.C., U.S. F6 112
Shanpo, China E3 34
Shansi see Shanxi, prov., China D9 30
Shāntipur, India I13 44
Shantou (Swatow), China L5 34
Shanxi (Shansi), prov., China D9 30
Shanxian, China I4 32
Shanxu, China C9 40
Shanyin, China D9 30
Shaodian, China B3 34
Shaoguan, China K2 34
Shaowu, China H6 34
Shaoxing, China E9 34
Shaoyang, China F9 30
Shaqqā, Syria C7 50
Shaqrā', Sau. Ar. I8 48
Shaqrā', Yemen H4 47
Sharafkhāneh, Iran B8 48
Sharbatāt, Ra's ash-, c., Oman F10 47
Sharbot Lake, Ont., Can. F19 110
Share, Nig. G12 64
Shark Bay, b., Austl. E2 68
Sharktooth Mountain, mtn., B.C., Can. E7 96
Sharktooth Mountain, mtn., B.C., Can. G31 100
Sharm ash-Shaykh, Egypt D8 60
Sharon, N.D., U.S. D10 118
Sharon, Pa., U.S. F6 108
Sharon, Tn., U.S. F8 114
Sharon, Wi., U.S. H7 110
Sharon Springs, Ks., U.S. M6 118
Sharpe, Lake, res., S.D., U.S. G8 118
Sharpe Lake, l., Man., Can. D21 104
Sharqī, Al-Jabal ash- (Anti-Lebanon), mts., Asia A6 50
Sharqīyah, Aṣ-Ṣaḥrā' ash- (Arabian Desert), des., Egypt D7 60
Shasha, Eth. N8 60
Shashe, stm., Afr. C9 66
Shashemene, Eth. N10 60
Shashi, China E9 30
Shasta, Ca., U.S. D3 124
Shasta, stm., Ca., U.S. C3 124
Shasta, Mount, vol., Ca., U.S. C3 124
Shasta Lake, res., Ca., U.S. D3 124
Shatawī, Sud. J7 60
Shattuck, Ok., U.S. C7 116
Shatuji, China H3 32
Shaunavon, Sask., Can. I6 104
Shaw, Ms., U.S. I6 114
Shawano, Wi., U.S. F7 110
Shawinigan, Que., Can. G18 96
Shawnee, Ks., U.S. L13 118
Shawnee, Oh., U.S. H4 108
Shawnee, Ok., U.S. D10 116
Shawneetown, Il., U.S. E8 114
Shawo, China G3 34
Shawville, Que., Can. B10 108
Shaybārā, i., Sau. Ar. I4 48
Shay Gap, Austl. D4 68
Shaykh, Jabal ash- (Mount Hermon), mtn., Asia B5 50
Shaykh 'Uthmān, Yemen H4 47
Shayuan, China H9 34
Shebele (Shabeelle), stm., Afr. G9 56
Shebelē Wenz, stm., Afr. H3 42
Sheberghān, Afg. B1 44
Sheboygan, Wi., U.S. G8 110
Sheboygan, stm., Wi., U.S. G8 110
Sheboygan Falls, Wi., U.S. G8 110
Shechem see Nābulus, Isr. Occ. D4 50
Shediac, N.B., Can. F9 106
Shedin Peak, mtn., B.C., Can. B7 102
Sheenjek, stm., Ak., U.S. C23 100
Sheep, stm., Alta., Can. G20 102
Sheep Creek, stm., Alta., Can. D15 102
Sheep Mountain, mtn., Wy., U.S. G15 122
Sheet Harbour, N.S., Can. H11 106
Shefar'am, Isr. C4 50
Sheffield, N.Z. E4 72
Sheffield, Eng., U.K. H12 8
Sheffield, Al., U.S. H9 114
Sheffield, Il., U.S. I6 110
Sheffield, Ia., U.S. H2 110
Sheffield, Pa., U.S. F7 108
Sheffield, Tx., U.S. I5 116
Sheffield Lake, l., Newf., Can. C17 106
Shegaon, India B4 46
Sheho, Sask., Can. G11 104
Sheikh Hasan, Eth. K8 60
Shekatika, Que., Can. A15 106
Shekhūpura, Pak. E5 44
Shelagyote Peak, mtn., B.C., Can. B7 102
Shelbina, Mo., U.S. C4 114
Shelburn, In., U.S. C9 114
Shelburne, N.S., Can. I8 106
Shelburne, Ont., Can. F15 110
Shelburne Falls, Ma., U.S. E14 108
Shelby, Ia., U.S. J12 118
Shelby, Mi., U.S. G9 110
Shelby, Ms., U.S. I6 114
Shelby, Mt., U.S. B14 122
Shelby, Ne., U.S. J10 118
Shelby, N.C., U.S. D5 112
Shelby, Oh., U.S. G4 108
Shelbyville, Il., U.S. C8 114
Shelbyville, In., U.S. C11 114
Shelbyville, Ky., U.S. D11 114
Shelbyville, Mo., U.S. C4 114
Shelbyville, Tn., U.S. G10 114
Shelbyville, Lake, res., Il., U.S. C8 114
Sheldon, Ia., U.S. H12 118
Sheldon, Mo., U.S. E2 114
Shelikof Strait, strt., Ak., U.S. H17 100
Shell, stm., Man., Can. G13 104
Shellbrook, Sask., Can. E8 104
Shell Brook, stm., Sask., Can. E8 104
Shelley, B.C., Can. C12 102
Shelley, Id., U.S. G13 122
Shellharbour, Austl. J9 70
Shell Lake, Sask., Can. E7 104
Shell Lake, Wi., U.S. E4 110
Shellman, Ga., U.S. H2 112
Shellmouth Dam, Man., Can. H13 104
Shell Rock, Ia., U.S. H3 110
Shell Rock, stm., U.S. G2 110
Shellsburg, Ia., U.S. H4 110
Shelton, Ct., U.S. F13 108
Shelton, Ne., U.S. K9 118
Shelton, Wa., U.S. C2 122
Shemogue, N.B., Can. F9 106
Shemya Station, Ak., U.S. J2 101a
Shenandoah, Ia., U.S. K12 118
Shenandoah, Pa., U.S. G10 108
Shenandoah, Va., U.S. I8 108
Shenandoah, stm., U.S. H9 108
Shenandoah National Park, Va., U.S. I8 108
Shendam, Nig. G14 64
Shengang, China H5 34
Shengtian, China H2 34
Shengze, China E9 34
Shenqiu, China B4 34
Shensi see Shaanxi, prov., China D8 30
Shenyang (Mukden), China B11 32
Sheopur, India H7 44
Shepard, Alta., Can. G21 102
Shepherd, Mi., U.S. G11 110
Shepherd, Tx., U.S. L1 114
Shepherdstown, W.V., U.S. H9 108
Shepherdsville, Ky., U.S. E11 114
Sheppard Peak, mtn., B.C., Can. H28 100
Shepparton, Austl. K6 70
Sheqi, China B1 34
Sherab, Sud. L3 60
Sherada, Eth. N9 60
Sherard, Cape, c., N.W. Ter., Can. B16 96
Sherbro Island, i., S.L. H3 64
Sherbrooke, N.S., Can. G12 106
Sherbrooke, Que., Can. B15 108
Sherbrooke Lake, l., N.S., Can. H9 106
Sherburn, Mn., U.S. H13 118
Sherburne, N.Y., U.S. E11 108
Sheridan, Ar., U.S. H4 114
Sheridan, In., U.S. B10 114
Sheridan, Mt., U.S. E13 122
Sheridan, Or., U.S. E2 122
Sheridan, Tx., U.S. J10 116
Sheridan, Wy., U.S. F19 122
Sherman, Ms., U.S. H8 114
Sherman, N.Y., U.S. E7 108
Sherman, Tx., U.S. F10 116
Sherman Mills, Me., U.S. B18 108
Sherman Station, Me., U.S. B18 108
Sherpur, Bngl. H14 44
Sherrard, Il., U.S. I5 110
Sherridon, Man., Can. C13 104
Sherrill, N.Y., U.S. D11 108
Shertallai, India H4 46
's-Hertogenbosch, Neth. E7 12
Sherwood, P.E.I., Can. F10 106
Sherwood, Ar., U.S. H4 114
Sherwood, N.D., U.S. C6 118
Sherwood, Oh., U.S. F2 108
Sherwood, Tn., U.S. G11 114
Sherwood Park, Alta., Can. D21 102
Sherwood Shores, Tx., U.S. I8 116
Sheshea, stm., Peru C5 82
Shetland, prov., Scot., U.K. A12 8
Shetland Islands, is., Scot., U.K. A12 8
Shewa Gimira, Eth. N8 60
Shexian, China F7 34
Sheyenne, N.D., U.S. D8 118
Sheyenne, stm., N.D., U.S. E10 118
Sheykhābād, Afg. C3 44
Shḥīm, Leb. A4 50
Shiba, China C7 34
Shibām, Yemen G6 47
Shibarni, Sud. J3 60
Shibata, Japan J14 36
Shibetsu, Japan C17 36a
Shibīn al-Kawm, Egypt B6 60
Shicheng, China I5 34
Shickley, Ne., U.S. K10 118
Shickshinny, Pa., U.S. F10 108
Shidao, China G10 32
Shidler, Ok., U.S. C10 116
Shields, stm., Mt., U.S. E15 122
Shifodian, China C4 34
Shigaib, Sud. J2 60
Shigezhuang, China E4 32
Shiḥan, Wādī, val., Asia E8 47
Shihe, China D9 32
Shijiazhuang, China E2 32
Shijing, China K7 34
Shikārpur, Pak. G3 44
Shikohābād, India G8 44
Shikoku, i., Japan N8 36
Shiliguri, India G13 44
Shillelagh, Ire. I7 8
Shillington, Pa., U.S. G11 108
Shillong, India H14 44
Shilo, Canadian Forces Base, mil., Man., Can. I15 104
Shiloh, Oh., U.S. H2 108
Shiloh see Saylūn, Khirbat, hist., Isr. Occ. D4 50
Shilong, China L2 34
Shimabara, Japan O5 36
Shimada, Japan M13 36
Shimber Berris, mtn., Som. F10 56
Shimen, China D6 32
Shimian, China F7 30
Shimiaozi, China C11 32
Shimizu, Japan L13 36
Shimla, India E7 44
Shimodate, Japan K14 36
Shimoga, India F3 46
Shimokita-hantō, pen., Japan F16 36
Shimonoseki, Japan N5 36
Shināṣ, Oman B10 47
Shīndand, Afg. E17 48
Shiner, Tx., U.S. J9 116
Shingbwiyang, Burma A4 40
Shinglehouse, Pa., U.S. F8 108
Shingū, Japan M9 36

Name — Map Ref. — Page

Shingū, Japan N10 36
Shingwidzi (Singuédeze), stm., Afr. C10 66
Shinjō, Japan I15 36
Shinkolobwe, Zaire D5 58
Shinnston, W.V., U.S. H6 108
Shinyanga, Tan. B6 58
Shiocton, Wi., U.S. F7 110
Shiogama, Japan I16 36
Shiojiri, Japan K12 36
Shiono-misaki, c., Japan N10 36
Ship Cove, Newf., Can. E19 106
Shiping, China C7 40
Shipman, Va., U.S. B8 112
Shippegan, N.B., Can. E9 106
Shippensburg, Pa., U.S. G9 108
Shiprock, N.M., U.S. H8 120
Ship Rock, mtn., N.M., U.S. H8 120
Shipshaw, stm., Que., Can. D2 106
Shipu, China F10 34
Shirakami-misaki, c., Japan F15 36a
Shiraoi, Japan E16 36a
Shīrāz, Iran G12 48
Shire, stm., Afr. E6 58
Shiretoko-misaki, c., Japan C20 36a
Shirley, In., U.S. C11 114
Shiroishi, Japan I15 36
Shirpur, India B3 46
Shīrvān, Iran C14 48
Shishmaref, Ak., U.S. C11 100
Shitan, China L2 34
Shively, Ky., U.S. D11 114
Shivpuri, India H7 44
Shivwits Plateau, plat., Az., U.S. H3 120
Shixia, China C2 32
Shizheng, China K4 34
Shizuoka, Japan M13 36
Shkodër, Alb. G3 20
Shoal Harbour, Newf., Can. D20 106
Shoal Lake, Man., Can. H14 104
Shoal Lake, l., Can. I19 104
Shoals, In., U.S. D10 114
Shoalwater Bay, b., Austl. D9 70
Shōdo-shima, i., Japan M9 36
Shoe Cove, Newf., Can. C18 106
Shoreacres, B.C., Can. H17 102
Shorewood, Wi., U.S. G8 110
Shortsville, N.Y., U.S. E9 108
Shoshone, Id., U.S. H11 122
Shoshone, stm., Wy., U.S. F17 122
Shoshone Basin, Wy., U.S. H17 122
Shoshone Mountains, mts., Nv., U.S. F8 124
Shoshong, Bots. D8 66
Shoshoni, Wy., U.S. A8 120
Shouning, China H8 34
Shouxian, China C5 34
Show Low, Az., U.S. J6 120
Shreve, Oh., U.S. G4 108
Shreveport, La., U.S. J3 114
Shrewsbury, Eng., U.K. I11 8
Shrewsbury, Ma., U.S. E15 108
Shri Dūngargarh, India F6 44
Shrīrangapattana, India F4 46
Shropshire, co., Eng., U.K. I11 8
Shuajingsi, China E7 30
Shuangcheng, China B12 30
Shuanghe, China D5 34
Shuangjiangqiao, China B5 40
Shuangliao, China C11 30
Shuangmiaozi, China A10 32
Shuangyashan, China B13 30
Shubenacadie, stm., N.S., Can. G10 106
Shubrā al-Khaymah, Egypt B6 60
Shubuta, Ms., U.S. K8 114
Shuhong, China G9 34
Shuijing, China A5 40
Shuikouguan, China C9 40
Shuitouwei, China I4 34
Shuksan, Mount, mtn., Wa., U.S. B4 122
Shulaps Peak, mtn., B.C., Can. G12 102
Shule, stm., China C6 30
Shullsburg, Wi., U.S. H5 110
Shunchang, China I6 34
Shunde, China M2 34
Shungnak, Ak., U.S. C16 100
Shuqualak, Ms., U.S. J8 114
Shurugwi, Zimb. B10 66
Shūsh, Iran E10 48
Shūshtar, Iran E10 48
Shuswap, stm., B.C., Can. G16 102
Shuswap Lake, l., B.C., Can. G15 102
Shuwak, Sud. J8 60
Shwebo, Burma C3 40
Shweli (Longchuan), stm., Asia C4 40
Shyok, stm., Asia C7 44
Siālkot, Pak. D6 44
Siam, Gulf of see Thailand, Gulf of, b., Asia I6 40
Siam see Thailand, ctry., Asia B3 38
Si'an, China E8 34
Sian see Xi'an, China E8 30
Siapa, stm., Ven. G10 84
Siasconset, Ma., U.S. F17 108
Šiaškotan, ostrov, i., Russia H22 28
Šiauliai, Lith. F6 22
Sibā'ī, Jabal as-, mtn., Egypt I3 48
Sibaj, Russia E19 4
Sibasa, Venda D10 66
Sibbald, Alta., Can. G4 104
Šibenik, Cro. F10 18
Siberia see Sibir', reg., Russia D14 28
Siberut, Pulau, i., Indon. F2 38
Sibi, Pak. F2 44
Sibir' (Siberia), reg., Russia D14 28
Sibir'akova, ostrov, i., Russia C13 26
Sibiti, Congo B2 58
Sibiu, Rom. D8 20
Sibiu, co., Rom. D8 20
Sibley, Ia., U.S. H12 118
Sibley, La., U.S. J3 114
Sibley, Ms., U.S. K5 114
Sibley Peninsula, pen., Ont., Can. B7 110
Sibolga, Indon. N5 40
Sibsāgar, India G16 44
Sibuyan Island, i., Phil. C7 38
Sibuyan Sea, Phil. C7 38
Sicamous, B.C., Can. G15 102
Siccus, stm., Austl. H3 70
Sichote-Alin', mts., Russia H19 28
Sichuan (Szechwan), prov., China E7 30
Sichuanzhai, China C6 40
Sicilia, prov., Italy L9 18
Sicilia (Sicily), i., Italy L9 18
Sicily, Strait of, strt. L6 18
Sicily Island, La., U.S. K5 114
Sicily see Sicilia, i., Italy L9 18
Sico Tinto, stm., Hond. B9 92
Sicuani, Peru F6 82
Šid, Yugo. D3 20
Siddhapur, India I5 44
Siddipet, India C5 46
Sidéradougou, Burkina F7 64
Siderópolis, Braz. E14 80
Sidheros, Ákra, c., Grc. N10 20

Sidhi, India H9 44
Sīdī 'Abd ar-Raḥmān, Egypt B5 60
Sidi Aïssa, Alg. C12 62
Sidi Ali Ben Nasrallah, Tun. N4 18
Sīdī Barrānī, Egypt B3 60
Sidi bel Abbès, Alg. C11 62
Sidi Bennour, Mor. D6 62
Sidi Bou Zid, Tun. C15 62
Sidi Daoud, Tun. L5 18
Sīdī Hunaysh, Egypt B4 60
Sidi Ifni, Mor. F5 62
Sidi Kacem, Mor. C8 62
Sidikalang, Indon. M5 40
Sidi Moussa, Oued, val., Alg. G13 62
Sidi Okba, Alg. C13 62
Sidi Slimane, Mor. C8 62
Sidi Smaïl, Mor. D6 62
Sidley, Mount, mtn., Ant. C10 73
Sidmouth, Eng., U.K. K10 8
Sidnaw, Mi., U.S. D7 110
Sidney, B.C., Can. I11 102
Sidney, Il., U.S. B8 114
Sidney, Ia., U.S. K12 118
Sidney, Mt., U.S. D3 118
Sidney, Ne., U.S. J5 118
Sidney, N.Y., U.S. E11 108
Sidney, Oh., U.S. G2 108
Sidney Lanier, Lake, res., Ga., U.S. E3 112
Sido, Mali F6 64
Sidon, Ms., U.S. I6 114
Sidon see Ṣaydā, Leb. A4 50
Sidra, Gulf of see Surt, Khalīj, b., Libya B4 56
Sidrolândia, Braz. F1 79
Siedlce, Pol. C22 10
Siegburg, Ger. E7 10
Siegen, Ger. E8 10
Siemianowice Śląskie, Pol. E19 10
Siemiatycze, Pol. C22 10
Siĕmréab, Camb. H7 40
Siena, Italy F6 18
Sieradz, Pol. D18 10
Sierck-les-Bains, Fr. C13 14
Sierpc, Pol. C19 10
Sierra Blanca, Tx., U.S. M11 120
Sierra Blanca Peak, mtn., N.M., U.S. K11 120
Sierra Chica, Arg. I8 80
Sierra Colorada, Arg. E3 78
Sierra de Agua, Belize I15 90
Sierra de Outes, Spain C3 16
Sierra Gorda, Chile B4 80
Sierra Leone, ctry., Afr. G4 54
Sierra Nevada, Parque Nacional, Ven. C7 84
Sierras Bayas, Arg. I8 80
Sierra Vista, Az., U.S. M6 120
Sierre, Switz. F8 13
Siesta Key, Fl., U.S. L4 112
Siete Puntas, stm., Para. B9 80
Sífnos, i., Grc. M8 20
Sifton, Man., Can. G14 104
Sig, Alg. J11 16
Sig, Russia I24 6
Sigean, Fr. I9 14
Sighetu Marmației, Rom. B7 20
Sighișoara, Rom. C8 20
Sigli, Indon. L3 40
Siglufjörður, Ice. A4 6a
Sigmaringen, Ger. G9 10
Signal Hill National Historic Park, Newf., Can. E21 106
Signal Mountain, Tn., U.S. G11 114
Signal Peak, mtn., Ut., U.S. G3 120
Signy, sci., B.A.T. B1 73
Signy-l'Abbaye, Fr. C11 14
Sigourney, Ia., U.S. I3 110
Sigre, stm., Hond. B10 92
Sigsig, Ec. I3 84
Siguanea, Ensenada de la, b., Cuba D3 94
Siguatepeque, Hond. C7 92
Sigüenza, Spain D9 16
Siguiri, Gui. F5 64
Sigulda, Lat. D7 22
Sigurd, Ut., U.S. F5 120
Sihanoukville see Kâmpóng Saôm, Camb. I7 40
Sihu, China I5 32
Sihuas, Peru C3 82
Sihuas, stm., Peru G5 82
Siirt, Tur. G6 48
Sijiazi, China B8 32
Sikandarābād, India F7 44
Sikanni Chief, stm., B.C., Can. E8 96
Sīkar, India G6 44
Sikasso, Mali F7 64
Sikéai, Grc. M6 20
Sikensi, I.C. I7 64
Sikeston, Mo., U.S. F7 114
Sikkim, state, India G13 44
Šikosi, Nmb. A6 66
Šikotan, ostrov (Shikotan-tō), i., Russia D21 36a
Silacayoapan, Mex. I10 90
Šilalė, Lith. F5 22
Silandro, Italy C5 18
Silao, Mex. G9 90
Silas, Al., U.S. K8 114
Silat az-Zahr, Isr. Occ. D4 50
Silay, Phil. C7 38
Silchar, India H15 44
Şile, Tur. H13 20
Siler City, N.C., U.S. D7 112
Silesia, hist. reg., Pol. D16 10
Silet, Alg. I13 62
Siletz, Or., U.S. F2 122
Siletz, stm., Or., U.S. F2 122
Silgadhī, Nepal F9 44
Silifke, Tur. C2 48
Siling Co, l., China E13 44
Silistra, Bul. E11 20
Şilivri, Tur. H12 20
Siljan, l., Swe. K14 6
Šilka, stm., Russia G15 28
Šilka, Russia G15 28
Sillamäe, Est. B10 22
Sillem Island, i., N.W. Ter., Can. B18 96
Sillian, Aus. I12 10
Sillustani, hist., Peru F6 82
Siloam Springs, Ar., U.S. F2 114
Šilovo, Russia G23 22
Silsbee, Tx., U.S. L2 114
Silsby Lake, l., Man., Can. C19 104
Silton, Sask., Can. H10 104
Šiluas, Lith. H12 64
Šilutė, Lith. F4 22
Silvan (Miyafarkin), Tur. B6 48
Silvânia, Braz. D4 79
Silvaplana, Switz. F12 13
Silver, Tx., U.S. G6 116
Silver Bank Passage, strt., N.A. D9 94
Silver Bay, Mn., U.S. C4 110
Silver Bell, Az., U.S. L5 120
Silver City, N.M., U.S. L8 120
Silver City, N.C., U.S. D7 112
Silver Creek, Ms., U.S. K7 114
Silver Creek, Ne., U.S. J10 118
Silver Creek, N.Y., U.S. E7 108
Silverdale, Wa., U.S. C3 122
Silver Lake, Ma., U.S. L12 118

Silver Lake, Mn., U.S. F1 110
Silver Lake, Or., U.S. G4 122
Silver Lake, Wi., U.S. H7 110
Silver Spring, Md., U.S. I9 108
Silver Star Mountain, mtn., Wa., U.S. B5 122
Silver Star Provincial Park, B.C., Can. G15 102
Silverthrone Mountain, mtn., B.C., Can. F8 102
Silvertip Mountain, mtn., Mt., U.S. C12 122
Silverton, B.C., Can. H17 102
Silverton, Co., U.S. G9 120
Silverton, Or., U.S. E3 122
Silverton, Tx., U.S. E5 116
Silvi, Italy G9 18
Silvia, Col. F4 84
Silvretta Gruppe, mts., Eur. E13 13
Sima, Com. L16 67a
Sima, Russia E22 22
Simanovsk, Russia G17 28
Simao, China G7 30
Simav, Tur. J12 20
Simcoe, Ont., Can. H15 110
Simcoe, Lake, l., Ont., Can. F16 110
Simeria, Rom. D7 20
Simeulue, Pulau, i., Indon. M4 40
Simferopol', Ukr. I4 26
Sími, i., Grc. M11 20
Simikot, Nepal F9 44
Similkameen, stm., N.A. H14 102
Simiri, Niger D11 64
Simití, Col. D6 84
Simi Valley, Ca., U.S. J7 124
Simla, Co., U.S. L3 118
Simmern, Ger. F7 10
Simmesport, La., U.S. L5 114
Simmie, Sask., Can. I6 104
Simms, Mt., U.S. C14 122
Simnas, Lith. G6 22
Simoca, Arg. D6 80
Simojovel, Mex. I13 90
Simonette, stm., Alta., Can. C17 102
Simonhouse Lake, l., Man., Can. D13 104
Simon's Town, S. Afr. J4 66
Simoom Sound, B.C., Can. G8 102
Šimorskoje, Russia F25 22
Simpang-kiri, stm., Indon. M4 40
Simplon Pass, Switz. F9 13
Simplon Tunnel, Eur. F9 13
Simpson, La., U.S. K3 114
Simpson Desert, des., Austl. D7 68
Simpson Desert National Park, Austl. E3 70
Simpson Lake, l., N.W. Ter., Can. B31 100
Simpson Peak, mtn., B.C., Can. G29 100
Simpson Peninsula, pen., N.W. Ter., Can. C15 96
Simpson Strait, strt., N.W. Ter., Can. C13 96
Simpsonville, S.C., U.S. E4 112
Simsbury, Ct., U.S. F14 108
Šimsk, Russia C13 22
Simušir, ostrov, i., Russia H22 28
Sīnā', Shibh Jazīrat (Sinai Peninsula), pen., Egypt C7 60
Sinai, Mount see Mūsā, Jabal, mtn., Egypt E7 60
Sinaia, Rom. D9 20
Sinai Peninsula see Sīnā', Shibh Jazīrat, pen., Egypt C7 60
Sin'aja, stm., Russia E16 28
Sinaloa, state, Mex. E6 90
Sinaloa, stm., Mex. F6 90
Sinalunga, Italy F6 18
Sinamaica, Ven. B7 84
Sinan, China F8 30
Sinanju, N. Kor. D13 32
Sin'avka, Bela. I9 22
Sīnāwin, Libya E16 62
Sinbo, Burma B4 40
Sincé, Col. C5 84
Sincelejo, Col. C5 84
Sinch'ang, N. Kor. C16 32
Sinch'ŏn, N. Kor. E13 32
Sinclair, Wy., U.S. C9 120
Sinclair, Lake, res., Ga., U.S. F3 112
Sinclair Mills, B.C., Can. C13 102
Sindara, Gabon B2 58
Sindelfingen, Ger. G9 10
Sindi, Est. C7 22
Sındırgı, Tur. J12 20
Sindri, India I12 44
Sine, val., Sen. D2 64
Sinekçi, Tur. I11 20
Sinendé, Benin F11 64
Sinevir, Ukr. A7 20
Sinez'orki, Russia H17 22
Singapore, Sing. N7 40
Singapore, ctry., Asia N7 40
Singapore Strait, strt., Asia N8 40
Singaraja, Indon. G6 38
Sing Buri, Thai. G6 40
Singen [Hohentwiel], Ger. H8 10
Singer, La., U.S. L3 114
Singida, Tan. B6 58
Singkaling Hkāmti, Burma A3 40
Singkang, Indon. F7 38
Singkawang, Indon. N10 40
Singkep, Pulau, i., Indon. O8 40
Singleton, Austl. I9 70
Singuédeze (Shingwidzi), stm., Afr. D10 66
Sinhŭng, N. Kor. C15 32
Sinj, Cro. F11 18
Sinjah, Sud. K7 60
Sinjai, Indon. G7 38
Sinkāt, Sud. H9 60
Sinkiang see Xinjiang Uygur Zizhiqu, prov., China C3 30
Sinmak, N. Kor. E14 32
Sinnai, Italy J4 18
Sinnamahoning, Pa., U.S. F8 108
Sinnamary, Fr. Gu. B8 76
Sinnar, India C3 46
Sinnes, Nor. L10 6
Sînnicolau Mare, Rom. C4 20
Sinnūris, Egypt C6 60
Sinop, Tur. G15 4
Sinp'o, N. Kor. C16 32
Sinsheim, Ger. F8 10
Sint-Amandsberg, Bel. F4 12
Sintang, Indon. E5 38
Sint Annaland, Neth. E5 12
Sint Annaparochie, Neth. B8 12
Sint Eustatius, i., Neth. Ant. F13 94
Sint Maarten (Saint-Martin), i., N.A. E13 94
Sint-Michiels, Bel. F3 12
Sint-Niklaas (Saint-Nicolas), Bel. F5 12
Sinton, Tx., U.S. K9 116
Sintra, Port. G2 16
Sint-Truiden (Saint-Trond), Bel. G7 12
Sinú, stm., Col. C5 84
Sinŭiju, N. Kor. C12 32
Siocon, Phil. D7 38
Siófok, Hung. I18 10
Sion (Sitten), Switz. F7 13
Sioux Center, Ia., U.S. H11 118

Sioux City, Ia., U.S. I11 118
Sioux Falls, S.D., U.S. H11 118
Sioux Lookout, Ont., Can. H23 104
Sioux Narrows, Ont., Can. I20 104
Sioux Rapids, Ia., U.S. I12 118
Sipaliwini, stm., Sur. F14 84
Sipapo, stm., Ven. E9 84
Siparia, Trin. I14 94
Siping, China C11 30
Sipiwesk, Man., Can. C17 104
Sipiwesk Lake, l., Man., Can. C17 104
Siple, sci., Ant. C12 73
Siple, Mount, mtn., Ant. C10 73
Sipsey, stm., Al., U.S. I9 114
Šipu, China C1 32
Šipunskij, mys, c., Russia G24 28
Siqueira Campos, Braz. G4 79
Siquia, stm., Nic. E10 92
Siquirres, C.R. G11 92
Siquisique, Ven. B8 84
Si Racha, Thai. H6 40
Siracusa, Italy I11 82
Siracusa, Italy L10 18
Sirājganj, Bngl. H13 44
Sir Alexander, Mount, mtn., B.C., Can. D14 102
Sirasso, I.C. G6 64
Sirba, stm., Afr. E11 64
Sirdar, B.C., Can. H18 102
Sir Douglas, Mount, mtn., Can. G19 102
Sire, Eth. M9 60
Sir Edward Pellew Group, is., Austl. C7 68
Sirega, Russia A24 22
Siret, stm., Eur. D11 20
Sirevåg, Nor. L9 6
Sir Francis Drake, Mount, mtn., B.C., Can. G10 102
Sirḥān, Wādī as-, val., Sau. Ar. F5 48
Siriya-zaki, c., Japan F16 36
Sir James MacBrien, Mount, mtn., N.W. Ter., Can. E31 100
Sīrjān, Iran G13 48
Sir Joseph Banks Group, is., Austl. J2 70
Sirohi, India H5 44
Sironj, India H7 44
Síros, i., Grc. L8 20
Sirotino, Bela. F12 22
Sir Sandford, Mount, mtn., B.C., Can. F17 102
Sirsi, India E3 46
Sirte, Gulf of see Surt, Khalīj, b., Libya B4 56
Sirupa, stm., Mex. C5 90
Şirvān (Diyālā), stm., Asia E8 48
Širvintos, Lith. F7 22
Sir Wilfrid Laurier, Mount, mtn., B.C., Can. E15 102
Sis, stm., Guat. C3 92
Sisak, Cro. D11 18
Si Sa Ket, Thai. G8 40
Sishen, S. Afr. F6 66
Sishui, China H5 32
Šišicy, Bela. H10 22
Sisib Lake, l., Man., Can. F15 104
Sisipuk Lake, l., Can. C13 104
Siskiyou Mountains, mts., U.S. C2 124
Siskiyou Pass, Or., U.S. H3 122
Sisquoc, stm., Ca., U.S. J6 124
Sissach, Switz. D8 13
Sisseton, S.D., U.S. F10 118
Sissili, stm., Afr. F9 64
Sisson Branch Reservoir, res., N.B., Can. E6 106
Sissonne, Fr. C10 14
Sistersville, W.V., U.S. I5 108
Sīstān, reg., Asia F17 48
Sister Bay, Wi., U.S. E8 110
Sisters, Or., U.S. F4 122
Sistersville, W.V., U.S. H6 108
Sitabamba, Peru C3 82
Sitakili, Mali E4 64
Sītāmarhi, India G11 44
Sitampiky, Madag. P22 67b
Sītāpur, India G9 44
Siteki, Swaz. F10 66
Sitidgi Lake, l., N.W. Ter., Can. B28 100
Sitio D'Abadia, Braz. C5 79
Sitka, Ak., U.S. H27 100
Sitona, Eth. J9 60
Sitrah, Bahr. H11 48
Sittard, Neth. F8 12
Sittoung, stm., Burma F4 40
Sittwe (Akyab), Burma D2 40
Siuna, Nic. D10 92
Siuri, India I12 44
Sivakāsi, India H4 46
Sivas, Tur. B4 48
Šivė, Maur. D3 64
Ševeluč, vulkan, vol., Russia F24 28
Siverek, Tur. C5 48
Siverskij, Russia B13 22
Sīwah, Egypt C3 60
Siwān, India G11 44
Sixaola, stm., N.A. H12 92
Sixtou, China H8 34
Siyāl, Jazā'ir, is., Egypt J4 48
Siyeteb, Sud. H8 60
Sizun, Fr. D2 14
Sjælland, i., Den. N12 6
Sjenica, Yugo. F4 20
Skærbæk, Den. N11 6
Skaftung, Fin. J17 6
Skagen, Den. M12 6
Skagerrak, strt., Eur. M11 6
Skagit, stm., N.A. B4 122
Skagway, Ak., U.S. G27 100
Skaidi, Nor. F19 6
Skaistkalne, Lat. E7 22
Skalino, Russia C23 22
Skalistyj Golec, gora, mtn., Russia F15 28
Skanderborg, Den. M11 6
Skaraborgs Län, co., Swe. L13 6
Skard, Ice. B4 6a
Skārdu, Pak. C6 44
Skarżysko-Kamienna, Pol. D20 10
Skaudvilė, Lith. F5 22
Skawina, Pol. F19 10
Skeena, stm., B.C., Can. C5 102
Skeena Crossing, B.C., Can. B7 102
Skeena Mountains, mts., B.C., Can. A7 102
Skei, Nor. K10 6
Skeleton Coast, Nmb. B1 66
Skellefteå, Swe. I17 6
Skellytown, Tx., U.S. D5 116
Skene, Swe. M13 6
Skiatook, Ok., U.S. C10 116
Skidegate, B.C., Can. D2 102
Skidegate Inlet, b., B.C., Can. D3 102
Skidel', Bela. H7 22
Skidmore, Tx., U.S. K9 116
Skien, Nor. L11 6
Skierniewice, Pol. D20 10
Skihist Mountain, mtn., B.C., Can. G13 102

Skikda (Philippeville), Alg. B14 62
Skilak Lake, l., Ak., U.S. F19 100
Skillet Fork, stm., Il., U.S. D8 114
Skipton, Austl. K5 70
Skiros, Grc. K8 20
Škive, Den. M11 6
Šklov, Bela. G13 22
Škofja Loka, Slo. C9 18
Skokie, Il., U.S. H8 110
Skopin, Russia H22 22
Skopje, Mac. H5 20
Skövde, Swe. L13 6
Skovorodino, Russia G16 28
Skowhegan, Me., U.S. C17 108
Skownan, Man., Can. G15 104
Skrīveri, Lat. E8 22
Skrudaļiena, Lat. F9 22
Skuodas, Lith. E4 22
Skukuza, S. Afr. E10 66
Skull Valley, Az., U.S. J4 120
Skuna, stm., Ms., U.S. I7 114
Skunk, stm., Ia., U.S. J4 110
Skuodas, Lith. E4 22
Skuratovskij, Russia G20 22
Skye, Island of, i., Scot., U.K. D7 8
Skykomish, stm., Wa., U.S. C4 122
Skyland, N.C., U.S. D4 112
Skyring, Seno, strt., Chile G2 78
Slagoviŝči, Russia H18 22
Slamet, Gunung, mtn., Indon. J14 39a
Slancy, Russia B11 22
Slaný, Czech. E14 10
Slater, Ia., U.S. I2 110
Slater, Mo., U.S. C3 114
Slatina, Rom. E8 20
Slaton, Tx., U.S. F5 116
Slaughter, La., U.S. L5 114
Slav'ansk, Ukr. H5 26
Slav'ansk-na-Kubani, Russia H5 26
Slave, stm., Can. D10 96
Slave Coast, Afr. I11 64
Slave Lake, Alta., Can. B20 102
Slavgorod, Bela. H13 22
Slavgorod, Russia G7 28
Slavkov u Brna, Czech. F16 10
Slavonija, hist. reg., Cro. D12 18
Slavonska Požega, Cro. D12 18
Slavonski Brod, Cro. D13 18
Slavsk, Russia F4 22
Sławno, Pol. A16 10
Slayton, Mn., U.S. H12 118
Sledge, Ms., U.S. H6 114
Sled Lake, l., Sask., Can. D7 104
Sled'uki, Bela. H13 22
Sleepy Eye, Mn., U.S. G13 118
Slidell, La., U.S. L7 114
Sliedrecht, Neth. E6 12
Sligo, Ire. G5 8
Sligo, Pa., U.S. F7 108
Sligo, co., Ire. G5 8
Slinger, Wi., U.S. G7 110
Slippery Rock, Pa., U.S. F6 108
Sliven, Bul. G10 20
Slivnica, Bul. G7 20
Sloan, Ia., U.S. I11 118
Sloan, Nv., U.S. I10 124
Slobodka, Ukr. B13 20
Slobodskoj, Russia F8 26
Slobodzeja, Mol. C13 20
Slobozia, Rom. E11 20
Slobozia, Rom. F9 20
Slocan, B.C., Can. H17 102
Slocan Lake, l., B.C., Can. H17 102
Slocomb, Al., U.S. K11 114
Slonim, Bela. H8 22
Slosh Indian Reserve, B.C., Can. G12 102
Slovakia see Slovensko, hist. reg., Czech. G19 10
Slovenia (Slovenija), ctry., Eur. C9 18
Slovenija see Slovenia, ctry., Eur. C9 18
Slovenska Bistrica, Slo. C10 18
Slovenská Republika, state, Czech. G20 10
Slovensko, hist. reg., Czech. G19 10
Sluck, Bela. H10 22
Sl'ud'anka, Russia G12 28
Slunj, Cro. D10 18
Słupca, Pol. C17 10
Słupsk (Stolp), Pol. A17 10
Slurry, S. Afr. E7 66
Smackover, Ar., U.S. I4 114
Smalininkai, Lith. F5 22
Smallwood Reservoir, res., Newf., Can. F20 96
Smara, W. Sah. G5 62
Smeaton, Sask., Can. E10 104
Smederevo, Yugo. E4 20
Smela, Ukr. H4 26
Smethport, Pa., U.S. F8 108
Smidovič, Russia H18 28
Šmidta, ostrov, i., Russia A16 26
Smiley, Sask., Can. G5 104
Smiley, Tx., U.S. J9 116
Smilovići, Bela. H11 22
Smiltene, Lat. D8 22
Smirnovskij, Kaz. G11 26
Smith, Alta., Can. B20 102
Smith, stm., U.S. C6 112
Smith, stm., Ca., U.S. C1 124
Smith, stm., Mt., U.S. C14 122
Smith, stm., Or., U.S. G2 122
Smith Arm, b., N.W. Ter., Can. C33 100
Smith Center, Ks., U.S. L9 118
Smithers, B.C., Can. C7 102
Smithers, W.V., U.S. I5 108
Smithfield, S. Afr. H8 66
Smithfield, N.C., U.S. D8 112
Smithfield, Ut., U.S. C5 120
Smithfield, Va., U.S. C10 112
Smith Island, i., B.A.T. B12 73
Smithland, Ky., U.S. E8 114
Smith Mountain Lake, res., Va., U.S. B7 112
Smith Point, c., N.S., Can. G10 106
Smith River, Ca., U.S. C1 124
Smiths, Al., U.S. J11 114
Smiths Falls, Ont., Can. E19 110
Smiths Grove, Ky., U.S. E10 114
Smith Sound, strt., B.C., Can. F7 102
Smithton, Austl. M6 70
Smithton, Mo., U.S. D3 114
Smithville, Ga., U.S. H2 112
Smithville, Ms., U.S. H8 114
Smithville, Mo., U.S. C2 114
Smithville, Tn., U.S. G11 114
Smithville, Tx., U.S. I9 116
Smokey, Cape, c., N.S., Can. F13 106
Smokey Dome, mtn., Id., U.S. G11 122
Smoky, stm., Alta., Can. B17 102
Smoky Cape, c., Austl. H10 70
Smoky Hill, stm., U.S. M10 118
Smoky Lake, Alta., Can. C22 102
Smol'anica, Bela. I7 22
Smolensk, Russia G15 22
Smolevići, Bela. G11 22
Smoljan, Bul. H8 20
Smoot, Wy., U.S. B6 120

Smoothstone, stm., Sask., Can. C8 104
Smoothstone Lake, l., Sask., Can. D8 104
Smorgon', Bela. G9 22
Smyrna, De., U.S. H11 108
Smyrna, Ga., U.S. F2 112
Smyrna, Tn., U.S. G10 114
Smyrna see İzmir, Tur. K11 20
Smythe, Mount, mtn., B.C., Can. E8 96
Snag, Yukon, Can. E24 100
Snake, stm., Yukon, Can. D28 100
Snake, stm., U.S. B3 98
Snake, stm., U.S. D7 122
Snake, stm., Mn., U.S. E2 110
Snake, stm., Ne., U.S. I6 118
Snake Indian, stm., Alta., Can. D16 102
Snake River Plain, pl., Id., U.S. G12 122
Snake Valley, val., U.S. E12 124
Snares Islands, is., N.Z. M20 126
Sn'atyn, Ukr. A9 20
Sneads, Fl., U.S. I2 112
Sneedville, Tn., U.S. C3 112
Sneek, Neth. B8 12
Snelling, Ca., U.S. G5 124
Sniardwy, Jezioro, l., Pol. B21 10
Snina, Czech. G22 10
Snipe Lake, l., Alta., Can. B18 102
Snohomish, Wa., U.S. C3 122
Snoqualmie Pass, Wa., U.S. C4 122
Snøtinden, mtn., Nor. H14 6
Snover, Mi., U.S. G13 110
Snowbird Lake, l., N.W. Ter., Can. D12 96
Snowden, Sask., Can. E10 104
Snowdon, mtn., Wales, U.K. H9 8
Snowdoun, Al., U.S. J10 114
Snowdrift, N.W. Ter., Can. D10 96
Snowflake, Az., U.S. J6 120
Snow Hill, Md., U.S. I11 108
Snow Hill, N.C., U.S. D9 112
Snow Lake, Man., Can. D14 104
Snowmass Mountain, mtn., Co., U.S. E9 120
Snow Peak, mtn., Wa., U.S. B7 122
Snowy, stm., Austl. K8 70
Snowy Mountains, mts., Austl. K8 70
Snowyside Peak, mtn., Id., U.S. G11 122
Snyder, Ok., U.S. E8 116
Snyder, Tx., U.S. G6 116
Soacha, Col. E5 84
Soahany, Madag. Q21 67b
Soalala, Madag. P21 67b
Soamanonga, Madag. S21 67b
Soanindrariny, Madag. Q22 67b
Soap Lake, Wa., U.S. C6 122
Soatá, Col. D6 84
Soavinandriana, Madag. Q22 67b
Sobaek-sanmaek, mts., S. Kor. G15 32
Sobat, stm., Sud. M7 60
Sobernheim, Ger. F7 10
Sobinka, Russia F23 22
Soboko, Cen. Afr. Rep. N3 60
Sobolevka, Ukr. A13 20
Sobradinho, Braz. E12 80
Sobrado, Port. D3 16
Sobral, Braz. D10 76
Socaire, Chile B5 80
Soc Giang, Viet. C9 40
Sochaczew, Pol. C20 10
Sochi see Soči, Russia G15 4
Sŏch'ŏn, S. Kor. G14 32
Soči, Russia I5 26
Social Circle, Ga., U.S. F3 112
Société, Îles de la (Society Islands), is., Fr. Poly. J24 126
Society Hill, S.C., U.S. E7 112
Soco, stm., Dom. Rep. E10 94
Socoltenango, Mex. I13 90
Socompa, Paso, S.A. C4 80
Socorro, Col. D6 84
Socorro, N.M., U.S. J10 120
Socorro, Tx., U.S. M10 120
Socorro, Isla, i., Mex. H4 90
Socota, Peru B2 82
Socotra see Suquṭrā, i., Yemen G5 42
Soc Trang, Viet. J8 40
Socuéllamos, Spain F9 16
Soda Creek, B.C., Can. E12 102
Soda Lake, l., Ca., U.S. I9 124
Soda Springs, Id., U.S. H14 122
Soddy-Daisy, Tn., U.S. G11 114
Söderhamn, Swe. K15 6
Södermanlands Län, co., Swe. L15 6
Södertälje, Swe. L15 6
Sodo, Eth. N9 60
Södra Kvarken, strt., Eur. A2 22
Sodus, N.Y., U.S. D9 108
Soe, Indon. G7 38
Soekmekaar, S. Afr. D9 66
Soela väin, strt., Est. C5 22
Soest, Ger. D8 10
Sofia, stm., Madag. O22 67b
Sofia see Sofija, Bul. G7 20
Sofija (Sofia), Bul. G7 20
Sofrino, Russia E20 22
Sogakofe, Ghana H10 64
Sogamoso, Col. E6 84
Sogamoso, stm., Col. D6 84
Sognafjorden, Nor. K9 6
Søgne, Nor. L10 6
Sogn og Fjordane, co., Nor. K10 6
Sogo Nur, l., China C7 30
Söğütalan, Tur. I12 20
Sogxian, China E5 30
Soin, Burkina E8 64
Sointula, B.C., Can. G7 102
Soissons, Fr. C10 14
Sojat, India H5 44
Sokal'skogo, proliv, strt., Russia B12 28
Sokch'o, S. Kor. E16 32
Söke, Tur. L11 20
Sokir'any, Ukr. A11 20
Sokodé, Togo G10 64
Sokol, Russia C23 22
Sokółka, Pol. B23 10
Sokolov, Czech. E12 10
Sokolovo, Russia I17 22
Sokołów, Pol. E22 10
Sokołów Podlaski, Pol. C22 10
Sokoto, Nig. E12 64
Solacolu, Rom. E10 20
Solana, Fl., U.S. L5 112
Solano, Phil. M19 39b
Solāpur, India D3 46
Solca, Arg. F5 80
Sol'cy, Russia C13 22
Sol de Julio, Arg. E7 80
Soldiers Grove, Wi., U.S. G5 110
Soldotna, Ak., U.S. F19 100
Soledad, Col. B5 84
Soledad, Ca., U.S. H4 124
Soledad, Ven. C11 84
Soledad Díez Gutiérrez, Mex. F9 90
Soledade, Braz. E12 80
Soleduck, stm., Wa., U.S. B1 122

Name	Map Ref.	Page
Solen, N.D., U.S.	E7	118
Solentiname, Archipiélago de, is., Nic.	F9	92
Solenzara, Fr.	M24	15a
Soligalič, Russia	B25	22
Soligorsk, Bela.	I10	22
Solikamsk, Russia	F9	26
Solila, Madag.	R22	67b
Sol'-Ileck, Russia	G8	26
Soliman, Tun.	M5	18
Solimões see Amazon, stm., S.A.	D7	76
Solingen, Ger.	D7	10
Solís, Ur.	H11	80
Sollefteå, Swe.	J15	6
Sóller, Spain	F14	16
Solnečnogorsk, Russia	E19	22
Sologne, reg., Fr.	E9	14
Solok, Indon.	O6	40
Sololá, Guat.	C3	92
Sololá, dept., Guat.	C3	92
Solomon, Az., U.S.	L7	120
Solomon, Ks., U.S.	M10	118
Solomon, stm., Ks., U.S.	L10	118
Solomon Islands, ctry., Oc.	G23	2
Solomon Sea, Oc.	I19	126
Solomon's Pools see Sulaymān, Birak, hist., Isr. Occ.	E4	50
Solon, China	B11	30
Solon, Ia., U.S.	I4	110
Solon, Me., U.S.	C17	108
Solon Springs, Wi., U.S.	D4	110
Solopaca, Italy	H9	18
Solotča, Russia	G22	22
Solothurn, Switz.	D8	13
Solothurn, state, Switz.	D7	13
Solotvin, Ukr.	A8	20
Solotvina, Ukr.	B7	20
Soloveckije ostrova, is., Russia	I24	6
Solovjevsk, Russia	H15	28
Solovjovka, Russia	A13	22
Solovjovsk, Russia	H21	26
Solsona, Spain	D13	16
Solt, Hung.	I19	10
Solvang, Ca., U.S.	J5	124
Solvay, N.Y., U.S.	D10	108
Sol'vyčegodsk, Russia	E7	26
Solway Firth, est., U.K.	G10	8
Solwezi, Zam.	D5	58
Soly, Bela.	G9	22
Sōma, Japan	J15	36
Soma, Tur.	J11	20
Somalia (Somaliya), ctry., Afr.	G10	56
Somali Republic see Somalia, ctry., Afr.	G10	56
Sombor, Yugo.	D3	20
Sombrerete, Mex.	F8	90
Sombrero, i., St. K./N.	E13	94
Sombrero Channel, strt., India	K2	40
Sombrio, Braz.	E14	80
Sombrio, Lagoa do, b., Braz.	E14	80
Sõmerpalu, Est.	D9	22
Somers, Mt., U.S.	B11	122
Somerset, Austl.	M6	70
Somerset, Man., Can.	I16	104
Somerset, Co., U.S.	F9	120
Somerset, Ky., U.S.	B2	112
Somerset, Ma., U.S.	F15	108
Somerset, Oh., U.S.	H4	108
Somerset, Pa., U.S.	G7	108
Somerset, Tx., U.S.	J8	116
Somerset, Wi., U.S.	E3	110
Somerset, co., Eng., U.K.	J11	8
Somerset East, S. Afr.	I7	66
Somerset Island, i., N.W. Ter., Can.	B14	96
Somerset West, S. Afr.	J4	66
Somers Point, N.J., U.S.	H12	108
Somersworth, N.H., U.S.	D16	108
Somerton, Az., U.S.	L2	120
Somerville, N.J., U.S.	G12	108
Somerville, Tn., U.S.	G7	114
Somerville, Tx., U.S.	I10	116
Somerville Lake, res., Tx., U.S.	I10	116
Someș (Szamos), stm., Eur.	B7	20
Somino, Russia	B17	22
Somme, dept., Fr.	C9	14
Somme, stm., Fr.	C9	14
Sömmerda, Ger.	D11	10
Somo, stm., Wi., U.S.	E6	110
Somogy, co., Hung.	I17	10
Somotillo, Nic.	D8	92
Somoto, Nic.	D8	92
Somport, Puerto de, Eur.	C11	16
Sompuis, Fr.	D11	14
Son, stm., India	H10	44
Soná, Pan.	C2	84
Sonaguera, Hond.	B8	92
Sonceboz, Switz.	D7	13
Sŏnch'ŏn, N. Kor.	D12	32
Sønderborg, Den.	N11	6
Sondershausen, Ger.	D10	10
Sondrio, Italy	C4	18
Sonepur, India	B7	46
Songbu, China	D3	34
Sŏngbyŏn-ni, N. Kor.	E13	32
Song Cau, Viet.	H10	40
Songea, Tan.	D7	58
Songhua, stm., China	B13	30
Songhua Hu, res., China	C12	30
Songhwa, N. Kor.	E13	32
Songjiang, China	D10	34
Songjiangzhen, China	A14	32
Songjŏng, S. Kor.	H14	32
Sŏngju, S. Kor.	H16	32
Songkhla, Thai.	K6	40
Songlinba, China	K4	34
Sŏngnam, S. Kor.	F15	32
Songnim, N. Kor.	E13	32
Şongshu, China	D10	32
Songuj, Russia	G23	6
Sonid Youqi, China	C9	30
Sonīpat, India	F7	44
Sonkovo, Russia	D20	22
Son La, Viet.	D7	40
Sonmiāni, Pak.	H2	44
Sonneberg, Ger.	E11	10
Sonningdale, Sask., Can.	F7	104
Sono, Rio do, stm., Braz.	D6	79
Sonoma, Ca., U.S.	F3	124
Sonora, Ca., U.S.	G5	124
Sonora, Tx., U.S.	I6	116
Sonora, state, Mex.	C4	90
Sonora, stm., Mex.	C4	90
Sonoran Desert, des., N.A.	F8	86
Sonoyta, Mex.	B3	90
Sonqor, Iran	D9	48
Sŏnsan, S. Kor.	G16	32
Sonseca, Spain	F8	16
Sonskyn, S. Afr.	H8	66
Sonsón, Col.	E5	84
Sonsonate, El Sal.	D5	92
Sontag, Ms., U.S.	K6	114
Son Tay, Viet.	D8	40
Sonthofen, Ger.	H10	10
Soochow see Suzhou, China	D9	34
Sooke, B.C., Can.	I11	102
Soo see Sault Sainte Marie, Mi., U.S.	D11	110
Sopchoppy, Fl., U.S.	I2	112
Soperton, Ga., U.S.	G4	112
Sop Hao, Laos	D8	40
Sophia, W.V., U.S.	B5	112
Sopot, Pol.	A18	10
Sopron, Hung.	H16	10
Sopur, India	C6	44
Sora, Italy	H8	18
Soras, Peru	F5	82
Sorata, Bol.	F7	82
Soraya, Peru	F5	82
Sorel, Que., Can.	A13	108
Sorell, Austl.	N7	70
Sorell, Cape, c., Austl.	N6	70
Sørfold, Nor.	H14	6
Sorgono, Italy	I4	18
Soria, Spain	D9	16
Soriano, Ur.	G9	80
Sørli, Nor.	I13	6
Sorocaba, Braz.	G5	79
Soročinsk, Russia	G8	26
Soroka (Soroki), Mol.	A12	20
Sorong, Indon.	F9	38
Soroti, Ug.	H7	56
Sørøya, i., Nor.	F18	6
Sorrento, Italy	I9	18
Sorrento, La., U.S.	L6	114
Sorris Sorris, Nmb.	C2	66
Sør Rondane Mountains, mts., Ant.	C3	73
Sorsele, Swe.	I15	6
Sorsogon, Phil.	O21	39b
Sortavala, Russia	E4	26
Sortland, Nor.	G14	6
Sør-Trøndelag, co., Nor.	J12	6
Sõrve neem, c., Est.	D5	22
Sŏsan, S. Kor.	G14	32
Sosneado, Cerro, mtn., Arg.	H4	80
Sosnogorsk, Russia	E8	26
Sosnovec, Russia	I24	6
Sosnovo, Russia	A13	22
Sosnovo-Oz'orskoje, Russia	G14	28
Sosnovskoje, Russia	F26	22
Sosnovyj Bor, Bela.	I12	22
Sosnovyj Bor, Russia	B12	22
Sosnowiec, Pol.	E19	10
Şoso, Ms., U.S.	K7	114
Šostka, Ukr.	G4	26
Sos'va, Russia	F10	26
Sotkamo, Fin.	I21	6
Soto la Marina, Mex.	F10	90
Soto la Marina, Barra, i., Mex.	E11	90
Sotomayor, Bol.	H9	82
Sotteville, Fr.	C8	14
Souderton, Pa., U.S.	G11	108
Soufrière, mtn., Guad.	F14	94
Soufrière, mtn., St. Vin.	H14	94
Souguer, Alg.	C11	62
Souhegan, stm., N.H., U.S.	E15	108
Souilly, Fr.	C12	14
Souk-el-Arba-des-Beni-Hassan, Mor.	J6	16
Souk-Khemis-du-Sahel, Mor.	J5	16
Sŏul (Seoul), S. Kor.	F14	32
Soulougou, Burkina	E10	64
Sounding Creek, stm., Alta., Can.	G4	104
Sounding Lake, l., Alta., Can.	F4	104
Soúnion, Ákra, c., Grc.	L8	20
Souq Ahras, Alg.	B14	62
Sources, Mont aux, mtn., Afr.	G9	66
Soure, Port.	E3	16
Sour el Ghozlane, Alg.	B12	62
Souris, Man., Can.	I14	104
Souris, P.E.I., Can.	F11	106
Souris, stm., N.A.	B7	118
Sourlake, Tx., U.S.	L2	114
Sourou, stm., Afr.	E8	64
Sousa, Braz.	E11	76
Sousânia, Braz.	D4	79
Sousel, Port.	G4	16
Sousse, Tun.	N5	18
South, stm., Ia., U.S.	A3	114
South Africa (Suid-Afrika), ctry., Afr.	H4	58
South America	F8	74
Southampton, N.S., Can.	G9	106
Southampton, Ont., Can.	F14	110
Southampton, Eng., U.K.	K12	8
Southampton, N.Y., U.S.	G14	108
Southampton, Cape, c., N.W. Ter., Can.	D16	96
Southampton Island, i., N.W. Ter., Can.	D16	96
South Andaman, i., India	I2	40
South Anna, stm., Va., U.S.	B9	112
South Aulatsivik Island, i., Newf., Can.	E20	96
South Australia, state, Austl.	F7	68
Southaven, Ms., U.S.	H6	114
South Bald Mountain, mtn., Co., U.S.	D11	120
South Baldy, mtn., N.M., U.S.	K9	120
Southbank, B.C., Can.	C9	102
South Bay, Fl., U.S.	M6	112
South Bay, b., Man., Can.	B15	104
South Bay, b., N.W. Ter., Can.	D16	96
South Baymouth, Ont., Can.	E13	110
South Beloit, Il., U.S.	H6	110
South Bend, In., U.S.	A10	114
South Bend, Wa., U.S.	D2	122
South Bentinck Arm, b., B.C., Can.	E8	102
South Boston, Va., U.S.	C8	112
South Branch, Newf., Can.	E14	106
Southbridge, Ma., U.S.	E14	108
South Brookfield, N.S., Can.	H9	106
South Bruny Island, i., Austl.	N7	70
South Burlington, Vt., U.S.	C13	108
South Carolina, state, U.S.	E10	98
South Channel, strt., Mi., U.S.	E11	110
South Charleston, W.V., U.S.	I5	108
South China Sea, Asia	M7	34
South Coffeyville, Ok., U.S.	C11	116
South Dakota, state, U.S.	C6	98
South East, dept., Bots.	E7	66
South East Cape, c., Austl.	N7	70
South East Point, c., Austl.	L7	70
Southend-on-Sea, Eng., U.K.	J14	8
Southern, dept., Bots.	E7	66
Southern Alps, mts., N.Z.	E3	72
Southern Cross, Austl.	F3	68
Southern Ghāts, mts., India	H4	46
Southern Indian Lake, l., Man., Can.	E13	96
Southern Pines, N.C., U.S.	D7	112
South Esk, stm., Austl.	M7	70
Southey, Sask., Can.	H10	104
South Fabius, stm., Mo., U.S.	C5	114
South Fallsburg, N.Y., U.S.	F12	108
Southfield, Mi., U.S.	H12	110
South Foreland, c., Eng., U.K.	J15	8
South Fork, Co., U.S.	G10	120
South Fort George, B.C., Can.	D12	102
South Fulton, Tn., U.S.	F8	114
Southgate, Mi., U.S.	H12	110
South Georgia, i., S. Geor.	J11	74
South Glamorgan, co., Wales, U.K.	J10	8
South Hadley, Ma., U.S.	E14	108
South Hātia Island, i., Bngl.	I14	44
South Haven, Ks., U.S.	N10	118
South Haven, Mi., U.S.	H9	110
South Heart, stm., Alta., Can.	B18	102
South Henderson, N.C., U.S.	C8	112
South Henik Lake, l., N.W. Ter., Can.	D13	96
South Hero, Vt., U.S.	C13	108
South Hill, Va., U.S.	C8	112
South Holston Lake, res., U.S.	C4	112
South Houston, Tx., U.S.	J11	116
South Indian Lake, Man., Can.	B16	104
Southington, Ct., U.S.	F14	108
South International Falls, Mn., U.S.	B2	110
South Island, i., N.Z.	E2	72
South Kenosha, Wi., U.S.	H8	110
South Lake Tahoe, Ca., U.S.	F6	124
Southland, Tx., U.S.	F5	116
Southlawn, Il., U.S.	C7	114
South Loup, stm., Ne., U.S.	J8	118
South Lyon, Mi., U.S.	H12	110
South Macmillan, stm., Yukon, Can.	E28	100
South Magnetic Pole, Ant.	B7	73
South Medford, Or., U.S.	H3	122
South Miami, Fl., U.S.	N6	112
South Mills, N.C., U.S.	C10	112
South Milwaukee, Wi., U.S.	H8	110
South Molton, Eng., U.K.	J10	8
South Moose Lake, l., Man., Can.	E14	104
South Mountain, mtn., Id., U.S.	H9	122
South Nahanni, stm., N.W. Ter., Can.	D7	96
South Naknek, Ak., U.S.	G16	100
South Nation, stm., Ont., Can.	B11	108
South Negril Point, c., Jam.	E5	94
South Ogden, Ut., U.S.	C5	120
South Orkney Islands, is., B.A.T.	B1	73
South Paris, Me., U.S.	C16	108
South Pass, Wy., U.S.	H17	122
South Pekin, Il., U.S.	J6	110
South Pittsburg, Tn., U.S.	G11	114
South Platte, stm., U.S.	C6	98
South Pole, Ant.	D4	73
South Porcupine, Ont., Can.	B14	110
Southport, Austl.	F10	70
Southport, Eng., U.K.	H10	8
Southport, Fl., U.S.	L11	114
Southport, In., U.S.	C10	114
Southport, N.Y., U.S.	E10	108
Southport, N.C., U.S.	F8	112
South Portland, Me., U.S.	D16	108
South Range, Mi., U.S.	C7	110
South River, Ont., Can.	E16	110
South Rockwood, Mi., U.S.	H12	110
South Sandwich Islands, is., S. Geor.	A2	73
South San Francisco, Ca., U.S.	G3	124
South Saskatchewan, stm., Can.	F8	104
South Shetland Islands, is., B.A.T.	B1	73
South Sioux City, Ne., U.S.	I11	118
South Slocan, B.C., Can.	H17	102
South Spicer Island, i., N.W. Ter., Can.	C17	96
South Superior, Wy., U.S.	C8	120
South Taranaki Bight, N.Z.	C5	72
South Thompson, stm., B.C., Can.	G14	102
South Torrington, Wy., U.S.	I3	118
South Tucson, Az., U.S.	L6	120
South Twillingate Island, i., Newf., Can.	C19	106
South Uist, i., Scot., U.K.	D6	8
South Wabasca Lake, l., Alta., Can.	B21	102
South West Africa see Namibia, ctry., Afr.	F3	58
South West Cape, c., Austl.	N7	70
South West City, Mo., U.S.	F2	114
Southwest Harbor, Me., U.S.	C18	108
Southwest Miramichi, stm., N.B., Can.	F7	106
Southwest National Park, Austl.	N7	70
Southwest Point, c., Bah.	B6	94
South Whitley, In., U.S.	A11	114
South Williamson, Ky., U.S.	B4	112
South Windham, Me., U.S.	D16	108
South Yamhill, stm., Or., U.S.	E2	122
Soutpan, S. Afr.	G8	66
Soutpansberg, mts., Afr.	D9	66
Souvigny, Fr.	F10	14
Sovetsk, Russia	H20	22
Sovetsk, Russia	F7	26
Sovetsk, Russia	F2	26
Sovetskaja Gavan', Russia	H20	28
Sovetskij, Russia	A11	22
Søvik, Nor.	J10	6
Soweto, S. Afr.	F8	66
Soyapango, El Sal.	D5	92
Soyo, Ang.	C2	58
Spa, Bel.	G8	12
Spain (España), ctry., Eur.	G7	4
Spakenburg, Neth.	D7	12
Spalding, Sask., Can.	F10	104
Spalding, Eng., U.K.	I13	8
Spalding, Ne., U.S.	J9	118
Spaniard's Bay, Newf., Can.	E20	106
Spanish, Ont., Can.	D13	110
Spanish Fork, Ut., U.S.	D5	120
Spanish North Africa, dep., Afr.	J6	16
Spanish Peak, mtn., Or., U.S.	F6	122
Spanish Sahara see Western Sahara, dep., Afr.	D4	54
Spanish Town, Jam.	F6	94
Sparkman, Ar., U.S.	I4	114
Sparks, Ga., U.S.	H3	112
Sparks, Nv., U.S.	E6	124
Sparland, Il., U.S.	I6	110
Sparlingville, Mi., U.S.	H13	110
Sparrows Point, Md., U.S.	H10	108
Sparta, Ga., U.S.	F4	112
Sparta, Il., U.S.	D7	114
Sparta, Ky., U.S.	D12	114
Sparta, Mi., U.S.	G10	110
Sparta, N.J., U.S.	F12	108
Sparta, N.C., U.S.	C5	112
Sparta, Tn., U.S.	G11	114
Sparta, Wi., U.S.	G5	110
Spartanburg, S.C., U.S.	E5	112
Sparta see Spárti, Grc.	L6	20
Spárti (Sparta), Grc.	L6	20
Spartivento, Capo, c., Italy	K3	18
Spas-Demensk, Russia	G17	22
Spas-Klepiki, Russia	F23	22
Spassk-Dal'nij, Russia	I18	28
Spátha, Ákra, c., Grc.	N7	20
Spear, Cape, c., Newf., Can.	E21	106
Spearfish, S.D., U.S.	G4	118
Spearman, Tx., U.S.	C5	116
Spearville, Ks., U.S.	N8	118
Spectrum Range, mts., B.C., Can.	H29	100
Spednic Lake, l., N.A.	G6	106
Speedway, In., U.S.	C10	114
Speightstown, Barb.	H15	94
Spello, Italy	G7	18
Spenard, Ak., U.S.	F20	100
Spence Bay, N.W. Ter., Can.	C14	96
Spencer, In., U.S.	C10	114
Spencer, Ia., U.S.	H12	118
Spencer, Ma., U.S.	E15	108
Spencer, Ne., U.S.	I9	118
Spencer, N.C., U.S.	D6	112
Spencer, S.D., U.S.	H10	118
Spencer, Tn., U.S.	G11	114
Spencer, W.V., U.S.	I5	108
Spencer, Wi., U.S.	F5	110
Spencer, Cape, c., Austl.	J2	70
Spencer, Cape, c., N.B., Can.	G8	106
Spencer Gulf, b., Austl.	J2	70
Spencerville, Oh., U.S.	G2	108
Spences Bridge, B.C., Can.	G13	102
Spenser Mountains, mts., N.Z.	E4	72
Sperryville, Va., U.S.	I8	108
Speyer, Ger.	F8	10
Speyside, Trin.	I14	94
Spezia see La Spezia, Italy	E4	18
Spicer, Mn., U.S.	F13	118
Spickard, Mo., U.S.	B3	114
Spiez, Switz.	E8	13
Spijkenisse, Neth.	F5	12
Spillimacheen, stm., B.C., Can.	F18	102
Spillville, Ia., U.S.	G4	110
Spinazzola, Italy	I11	18
Spincourt, Fr.	C12	14
Spindale, N.C., U.S.	D5	112
Spirit Lake, Id., U.S.	C9	122
Spirit Lake, Ia., U.S.	H12	118
Spirit River, Alta., Can.	B16	102
Spiritwood, Sask., Can.	E7	104
Spiro, Ok., U.S.	G2	114
Spirovo, Russia	D17	22
Spišská Nová Ves, Czech.	G20	10
Spitsbergen, i., Sval.	B2	24
Spittal an der Drau, Aus.	I13	10
Spitz, Aus.	G15	10
Split, Cro.	F11	18
Split, Cape, c., N.S., Can.	G9	106
Split Lake, l., Man., Can.	B18	104
Spluga, Passo della (Splügenpass), Eur.	E11	13
Splügen, Switz.	E11	13
Spofford, Tx., U.S.	J6	116
Spoği, Lat.	E9	22
Spokane, Wa., U.S.	C8	122
Spokane, stm., U.S.	C7	122
Spoleto, Italy	G7	18
Spoon, stm., Il., U.S.	B6	114
Spooner, Wi., U.S.	E4	110
Spornoje, Russia	E22	28
Spotsylvania, Va., U.S.	I9	108
Sprague, Man., Can.	I19	104
Sprague, Wa., U.S.	C8	122
Sprague, stm., Or., U.S.	H4	122
Spratly Islands, is., Asia	D5	38
Spray, Or., U.S.	F6	122
Spray Lakes Reservoir, res., Alta., Can.	G19	102
Spremberg, Ger.	D14	10
Spring, stm., U.S.	E3	114
Spring, stm., Ar., U.S.	F5	114
Springbok, S. Afr.	G3	66
Spring City, Tn., U.S.	D2	112
Spring City, Ut., U.S.	E5	120
Springdale, Newf., Can.	C17	106
Springdale, Ar., U.S.	F2	114
Springdale, S.C., U.S.	F5	112
Springdale, Ut., U.S.	G4	120
Springdale, Wa., U.S.	B8	122
Spring Dale, W.V., U.S.	B6	112
Springe, Ger.	C9	10
Springer, N.M., U.S.	C2	116
Springerville, Az., U.S.	J7	120
Springfield, N.S., Can.	H9	106
Springfield, Co., U.S.	N5	118
Springfield, Fl., U.S.	L11	114
Springfield, Ga., U.S.	G5	112
Springfield, Il., U.S.	C7	114
Springfield, Ky., U.S.	E11	114
Springfield, Ma., U.S.	E14	108
Springfield, Mn., U.S.	G13	118
Springfield, Mo., U.S.	E3	114
Springfield, Oh., U.S.	H3	108
Springfield, Or., U.S.	F2	122
Springfield, S.C., U.S.	F5	112
Springfield, S.D., U.S.	I10	118
Springfield, Tn., U.S.	F10	114
Springfield, Vt., U.S.	D14	108
Springfontein, S. Afr.	H7	66
Spring Garden, Guy.	D13	84
Spring Glen, Ut., U.S.	E6	120
Spring Green, Wi., U.S.	G5	110
Spring Grove, Mn., U.S.	G4	110
Spring Grove, Pa., U.S.	H10	108
Springhill, N.S., Can.	G9	106
Springhill, La., U.S.	I3	114
Spring Hill, Tn., U.S.	G10	114
Spring Hope, N.C., U.S.	D8	112
Springhouse, B.C., Can.	F12	102
Spring Lake, N.C., U.S.	D8	112
Spring Mountains, mts., Nv., U.S.	H10	124
Springs, S. Afr.	F9	66
Springsure, Austl.	E8	70
Springtown, Tx., U.S.	G9	116
Springvale, Austl.	D4	70
Springvale, Me., U.S.	D16	108
Spring Valley, Ca., U.S.	L9	124
Spring Valley, Il., U.S.	I6	110
Spring Valley, Mn., U.S.	G3	110
Spring Valley, N.Y., U.S.	F12	108
Spring Valley, Wi., U.S.	F3	110
Springview, Ne., U.S.	I8	118
Springville, Al., U.S.	I10	114
Springville, Ca., U.S.	H7	124
Springville, Ia., U.S.	H4	110
Springville, N.Y., U.S.	E8	108
Springville, Ut., U.S.	D5	120
Sproat Lake, l., B.C., Can.	H9	102
Spruce, stm., Sask., Can.	E9	104
Spruce Brook, Newf., Can.	D15	106
Spruce Grove, Alta., Can.	D21	102
Spruce Knob, mtn., W.V., U.S.	I7	108
Spruce Lake, Sask., Can.	E5	104
Spruce Mountain, mtn., Az., U.S.	J4	120
Spruce Mountain, mtn., Nv., U.S.	D11	124
Spruce Pine, Al., U.S.	H9	114
Spruce Pine, N.C., U.S.	D4	112
Spruce Woods Provincial Park, Man., Can.	I15	104
Spur, Tx., U.S.	F6	116
Spurfield, Alta., Can.	B20	102
Spurger, Tx., U.S.	L2	114
Spuzzum, B.C., Can.	H13	102
Spy Hill, Sask., Can.	H13	104
Squally Channel, strt., B.C., Can.	D5	102
Squamish, B.C., Can.	H11	102
Squamish, stm., B.C., Can.	G11	102
Squatec, Que., Can.	E5	106
Squaw Cap Mountain, mtn., N.B., Can.	E7	106
Squaw Peak, mtn., Mt., U.S.	C11	122
Squaw Rapids, Sask., Can.	E11	104
Squaw Rapids Dam, Sask., Can.	E11	104
Squilax, B.C., Can.	G15	102
Squinzano, Italy	I13	18
Squire, W.V., U.S.	B5	112
Srbija (Serbia), state, Yugo.	F4	20
Srbobran, Yugo.	D3	20
Sredinnyj chrebet, mts., Russia	F24	28
Sredna Gora, mts., Bul.	G8	20
Sredneje Kujto, ozero, l., Russia	I22	6
Srednekolymsk, Russia	D22	28
Srednerusskaja vozvyšennost', plat., Russia	G5	26
Srednesibirskoje ploskogorje, plat., Russia	D13	28
Śrem, Pol.	C17	10
Srê Moăt, Camb.	H9	40
Sremska Mitrovica, Yugo.	E3	20
Sremski Karlovci, Yugo.	D3	20
Sretensk, Russia	G15	28
Sri Jayawardenepura (Kotte), Sri L.	I5	46
Srīkākulam, India	C7	46
Sri Kālahasti, India	F5	46
Sri Lanka, ctry., Asia	H11	42
Srīnagar, India	C6	44
Srīrampur, India	C3	46
Srīrangam, India	G5	46
Şrīvilliputtūr, India	H4	46
Środa Wielkopolski, Pol.	C17	10
Staaten, stm., Austl.	C8	68
Staaten River National Park, Austl.	C8	68
Stachanov, Ukr.	H5	26
Stacyville, Ia., U.S.	G3	110
Stade, Ger.	B9	10
Staden, Bel.	G3	12
Stadl-Paura, Aus.	G13	10
Stadskanaal, Neth.	B10	12
Stadt Haag, Aus.	G14	10
Staffelstein, Ger.	E11	10
Stafford, Eng., U.K.	I11	8
Stafford, Ks., U.S.	N9	118
Stafford, Va., U.S.	I9	108
Staffordshire, co., Eng., U.K.	I11	8
Stafford Springs, Ct., U.S.	F14	108
Staicele, Lat.	D7	22
Staines, Eng., U.K.	J13	8
Stalden, Switz.	F8	13
Stalheim, Nor.	K10	6
Stalingrad see Volgograd, Russia	H6	26
Stalowa Wola, Pol.	E22	10
Stambaugh, Mi., U.S.	D7	110
Stamford, Austl.	C5	70
Stamford, Ct., U.S.	F13	108
Stamford, N.Y., U.S.	E12	108
Stamford, Tx., U.S.	G7	116
Stamford, Lake, res., Tx., U.S.	F7	116
Stamps, Ar., U.S.	I3	114
Stanaford, W.V., U.S.	J5	108
Stanardsville, Va., U.S.	I8	108
Stanberry, Mo., U.S.	B2	114
Standard, Alta., Can.	F22	102
Standard, Ak., U.S.	D20	100
Standerton, S. Afr.	F9	66
Standish, Mi., U.S.	G12	110
Stanfield, Az., U.S.	L5	120
Stanfield, Or., U.S.	E6	122
Stanford, Ky., U.S.	B2	112
Stanford, Mt., U.S.	C15	122
Stanhope, Ia., U.S.	H2	110
Stanislaus, stm., Ca., U.S.	G5	124
Stanke Dimitrov, Bul.	G7	20
Stanley, N.B., Can.	F7	106
Stanley, Falk. Is.	G5	78
Stanley, N.C., U.S.	D5	112
Stanley, N.D., U.S.	C5	118
Stanley, Va., U.S.	I8	108
Stanley, Wi., U.S.	F5	110
Stanley Reservoir, res., India	G4	46
Stanleyville see Kisangani, Zaire	A5	58
Stanovoj chrebet, mts., Russia	F17	28
Stanovoje nagorje (Stanovoy Mountains), mts., Russia	F14	28
Stans, Switz.	E9	13
Stanthorpe, Austl.	G9	70
Stanton, Ia., U.S.	J12	118
Stanton, Ky., U.S.	B3	112
Stanton, Mi., U.S.	G10	110
Stanton, Ne., U.S.	J10	118
Stanton, N.D., U.S.	D6	118
Stanton, Tn., U.S.	G7	114
Stanton, Tx., U.S.	G5	116
Stantonsburg, N.C., U.S.	D9	112
Stanwood, Wa., U.S.	B3	122
Staples, Mn., U.S.	E13	118
Stapleton, Al., U.S.	L9	114
Stapleton, Ne., U.S.	J7	118
Star, Ms., U.S.	J6	114
Star, N.C., U.S.	D7	112
Stará Boleslav, Czech.	E14	10
Starachowice, Pol.	D21	10
Staraja Russa, Russia	C14	22
Staraja Toropa, Russia	E14	22
Staraja Ušica, Ukr.	A11	20
Staraja Vičuga, Russia	D24	22
Stara Pazova, Yugo.	E4	20
Stara Planina (Balkan Mountains), mts., Eur.	G8	20
Stara Zagora, Bul.	G9	20
Starbuck, Man., Can.	I17	104
Starbuck, Mn., U.S.	F12	118
Starbuck, Wa., U.S.	D7	122
Star City, Sask., Can.	F10	104
Star City, Ar., U.S.	I5	114
Star City, In., U.S.	B10	114
Stargard Szczeciński (Stargard in Pommern), Pol.	B15	10
Stargo, Az., U.S.	K7	120
Starica, Russia	E17	22
Starke, Fl., U.S.	J4	112
Starkville, Ms., U.S.	I8	114
Starnberg, Ger.	G11	10
Starnberger See, l., Ger.	H11	10
Starobin, Bela.	I10	22
Starodub, Russia	I15	22
Starogard Gdański, Pol.	B18	10
Staroje Selo, Bela.	F12	22
Staroje Ustje, Russia	H24	22
Starokazačje, Ukr.	C13	20
Staroseslavino, Russia	H23	22
Starožilovo, Russia	G22	22
Staryje Dorogi, Bela.	H11	22
Staryje Popel'uchi, Ukr.	A12	20
Staryj Oskol, Russia	G5	26
Staryj Sambor, Ukr.	F22	10
Stassfurt, Ger.	D11	10
Staszów, Pol.	E21	10
State Center, Ia., U.S.	H2	110
State College, Pa., U.S.	G9	108
State Line, Ms., U.S.	K8	114
Stateline, Nv., U.S.	F6	124
Statenville, Ga., U.S.	I3	112
State Road, N.C., U.S.	C6	112
Statesboro, Ga., U.S.	G5	112
Statesville, N.C., U.S.	D6	112
Staunton, Il., U.S.	C7	114
Staunton, Va., U.S.	I7	108
Stavanger, Nor.	L9	6
Stave Lake, l., B.C., Can.	H12	102
Stavely, Alta., Can.	G21	102
Stavnoje, Ukr.	G22	10
Stavropol', Russia	H6	26
Stawell, Austl.	K5	70
Stawell, stm., Austl.	C5	70
Stawiszyn, Pol.	D18	10
Stayner, Ont., Can.	F15	110
Stayton, Or., U.S.	F3	122
Steamboat Mountain, mtn., Wy., U.S.	C8	120
Steamboat Springs, Co., U.S.	D10	120
Stearns, Ky., U.S.	C2	112
Stebbins, Ak., U.S.	E13	100
Steckborn, Switz.	C10	13
Steele, Mo., U.S.	F7	114
Steele, N.D., U.S.	E8	118
Steeleville, Il., U.S.	D7	114
Steelville, Mo., U.S.	E5	114
Steepbank, stm., Alta., Can.	B3	104
Steephill Lake, l., Sask., Can.	C11	104
Steep Rock, Man., Can.	G16	104
Stefansson Island, i., N.W. Ter., Can.	B11	96
Steffisburg, Switz.	E8	13
Steiermark, state, Aus.	H15	10
Stein, Switz.	C8	13
Steinach, Aus.	H11	10
Steinbach, Man., Can.	I18	104
Steinhausen, Nmb.	C4	66
Steinkjer, Nor.	I12	6
Steksovo, Russia	F26	22
Stella, Ne., U.S.	K12	118
Stellaquo Indian Reserve, B.C., Can.	C10	102
Stellarton, N.S., Can.	G11	106
Stellenbosch, S. Afr.	I4	66
Stenay, Fr.	C12	14
Stendal, Ger.	C11	10
Stende, Lat.	D5	22
Stepanakert, Azer.	J7	26
Stephen, Mn., U.S.	C11	118
Stephens, Ar., U.S.	I3	114
Stephens, Port, b., Austl.	I10	70
Stephens City, Va., U.S.	H8	108
Stephens Island, i., B.C., Can.	C4	102
Stephens Lake, res., Man., Can.	B19	104
Stephenson, Mi., U.S.	E8	110
Stephenville, Newf., Can.	D15	106
Stephenville, Tx., U.S.	G8	116
Stephenville Crossing, Newf., Can.	D15	106
Stepn'ak, Kaz.	G12	26
Sterkstroom, S. Afr.	H8	66
Sterling, Ak., U.S.	F19	100
Sterling, Co., U.S.	K4	118
Sterling, Il., U.S.	I6	110
Sterling, Ks., U.S.	M9	118
Sterling, Mi., U.S.	F11	110
Sterling, Ne., U.S.	K11	118
Sterling, Ok., U.S.	E8	116
Sterling City, Tx., U.S.	H6	116
Sterlington, La., U.S.	J4	114
Sterlitamak, Russia	G9	26
Stettin see Szczecin, Pol.	B14	10
Stettler, Alta., Can.	E22	102
Steubenville, Oh., U.S.	G6	108
Stevenson, Al., U.S.	H11	114
Stevenson, Wa., U.S.	E4	122
Stevenson Lake, l., Man., Can.	E18	104
Stevens Pass, Wa., U.S.	C4	122
Stevens Point, Wi., U.S.	F6	110
Stevens Village, Ak., U.S.	C20	100
Stevensville, Mi., U.S.	H9	110
Stevensville, Mt., U.S.	D11	122
Stewardson, Il., U.S.	C8	114
Stewart, B.C., Can.	B5	102
Stewart, Mn., U.S.	F1	110
Stewart, stm., Yukon, Can.	E25	100
Stewart Island, i., N.Z.	G1	72
Stewarton, Scot., U.K.	F9	8
Stewartstown, Pa., U.S.	H10	108
Stewartsville, Mo., U.S.	C2	114
Stewart Valley, Sask., Can.	H7	104
Stewartville, Mn., U.S.	G3	110
Stewiacke, N.S., Can.	G10	106
Steynsburg, S. Afr.	H7	66
Steyr, Aus.	G14	10
Steytlerville, S. Afr.	I7	66
Stickney, S.D., U.S.	H9	118
Stif, Alg.	B13	62
Stigler, Ok., U.S.	D11	116
Stikine, stm., N.A.	H29	100
Stikine Ranges, mts., B.C., Can.	G29	100
Stilbaai, S. Afr.	J5	66
Stilfontein, S. Afr.	F8	66
Stilís, Grc.	K6	20
Still, Alg.	C13	62
Stillhouse Hollow Lake, res., Tx., U.S.	H9	116
Stillmore, Ga., U.S.	G4	112
Stillwater, B.C., Can.	H10	102
Stillwater, Mn., U.S.	E3	110
Stillwater, Ok., U.S.	C9	116
Stillwater, stm., Mt., U.S.	E16	122
Stillwell, Ok., U.S.	G2	114
Stimson, Mount, mtn., Mt., U.S.	B12	122
Stînca-Costești, Lacul (vodochranilišče Kostešty-Stynka), res., Eur.	B11	20
Stinking Water Creek, stm., Ne., U.S.	K6	118
Ştinnett, Tx., U.S.	D5	116
Štip, Mac.	H6	20
Stirling, Alta., Can.	H22	102
Stirling, Ont., Can.	F18	110
Stirling, Scot., U.K.	E10	8
Stirling City, Ca., U.S.	E4	124
Stirrat, W.V., U.S.	B4	112
Stittsville, Ont., Can.	E20	110
Stockach, Ger.	H9	10
Stöckalp, Switz.	E9	13
Stockbridge, Ga., U.S.	F2	112
Stockbridge, Mi., U.S.	H11	110
Stockdale, Tx., U.S.	J9	116
Stockerau, Aus.	G16	10
Stockett, Mt., U.S.	C14	122
Stockholm, Swe.	L16	6
Stockton, Al., U.S.	L9	114
Stockton, Ca., U.S.	G4	124

Name | Map Ref. | Page

Stockton, Il., U.S. H5 110
Stockton, Ks., U.S. L8 118
Stockton, Mo., U.S. E3 114
Stockton, Ut., U.S. D4 120
Stockton [-on-Tees], Eng., U.K. G12 8
Stockton Plateau, plat., Tx., U.S. I4 116
Stockton Reservoir, res., Mo., U.S. E3 114
Stockton Springs, Me., U.S. C18 108
Stockville, Ne., U.S. K7 118
Stodolišče, Russia G15 22
Stœng Trêng, Camb. H8 40
Stoke-on-Trent, Eng., U.K. H11 8
Stolac, Bos. F12 18
Stolbcy, Bela. H9 22
Stolberg, Ger. E6 10
Stolbovoj, ostrov, i., Russia C19 28
Stolp see Słupsk, Pol. A17 10
Stoneboro, Pa., U.S. F6 108
Stonefort, Il., U.S. E8 114
Stone Harbor, N.J., U.S. H12 108
Stonehenge, Austl. E5 70
Stone Indian Reserve, B.C., Can. F11 102
Stone Mountain, Ga., U.S. F2 112
Stoner, B.C., Can. D12 102
Stoneville, N.C., U.S. C7 112
Stonewall, Man., Can. H17 104
Stonewall, La., U.S. J3 114
Stonewall, Ms., U.S. J8 114
Stonewall, Ok., U.S. E10 116
Stoney Creek, Ont., Can. G15 110
Stonington, Il., U.S. C7 114
Stonington, Me., U.S. C18 108
Stony, stm., Mn., U.S. C4 110
Stony Creek Indian Reserve, B.C., Can. D10 102
Stony Indian Reserve, Alta., Can. F20 102
Stony Lake, l., Man., Can. E13 96
Stony Plain, Alta., Can. D20 102
Stony Plain Indian Reserve, Alta., Can. D21 102
Stony Point, Mi., U.S. I12 110
Stony Point, N.C., U.S. D5 112
Stony Rapids, Sask., Can. E11 96
Storby, Fin. K16 6
Storkerson Bay, b., N.W. Ter., Can. B8 96
Storkerson Peninsula, pen., N.W. Ter., Can. B11 96
Storlien, Swe. J13 6
Storm Bay, b., Austl. N7 70
Storm Lake, Ia., U.S. I12 118
Stormsrivier, S. Afr. I6 66
Stornoway, Scot., U.K. C7 8
Storožinec, Ukr. A9 20
Storrs, Ct., U.S. F14 108
Storthoaks, Sask., Can. I13 104
Storuman, Swe. I15 6
Story, Wy., U.S. F19 122
Story City, Ia., U.S. H2 110
Stoughton, Sask., Can. I11 104
Stoughton, Ma., U.S. E15 108
Stoughton, Wi., U.S. H6 110
Stout Lake, l., Ont., Can. F20 104
Stover, Mo., U.S. D4 114
Stow, Oh., U.S. F5 108
Stowe, Vt., U.S. C14 108
Stowell, Tx., U.S. M2 114
Stoyoma Mountain, mtn., B.C., Can. H13 102
Stradeč', Bela. J6 22
Stradella, Italy D4 18
Strahan, Austl. N6 70
Strakonice, Czech. F13 10
Stralsund, Ger. A13 10
Strand, S. Afr. J4 66
Strangford Lough, l., N. Ire., U.K. G8 8
Stranraer, Scot., U.K. G8 8
Strasbourg, Sask., Can. G10 104
Strasbourg, Fr. D14 14
Strasburg, Co., U.S. L3 118
Strasburg, N.D., U.S. E7 118
Strasburg, Oh., U.S. G5 108
Strasburg, Pa., U.S. H10 108
Strasburg, Va., U.S. I8 108
Stratford, Ont., Can. G15 110
Stratford, N.Z. C5 72
Stratford, Ca., U.S. H6 124
Stratford, Ct., U.S. F13 108
Stratford, Ia., U.S. H2 110
Stratford, Ok., U.S. E10 116
Stratford, Tx., U.S. C4 116
Stratford, Wi., U.S. F5 110
Stratford-upon-Avon, Eng., U.K. I12 8
Strathalbyn, Austl. J3 70
Strathclair, Man., Can. H14 104
Strathclyde, prov., Scot., U.K. F8 8
Strathcona Provincial Park, B.C., Can. H9 102
Strathlorne, N.S., Can. F12 106
Strathmore, Alta., Can. F21 102
Strathmore, Ca., U.S. H6 124
Strathroy, Ont., Can. H14 110
Stratton, Co., U.S. L5 118
Stratton, Me., U.S. B16 108
Stratton, Ne., U.S. K6 118
Straubing, Ger. G12 10
Strausberg, Ger. C13 10
Strawberry, stm., Ar., U.S. F5 114
Strawberry, stm., Ut., U.S. D6 120
Strawberry Mountain, mtn., Or., U.S. F7 122
Strawberry Point, Ia., U.S. H4 110
Strawn, Tx., U.S. G8 116
Streatham, B.C., Can. D8 102
Streator, Il., U.S. I7 110
Streeter, N.D., U.S. E8 118
Streetman, Tx., U.S. H10 116
Streetsboro, Oh., U.S. F5 108
Streetsville, Ont., Can. G16 110
Strel'na, Russia B13 22
Strenči, Lat. D8 22
Stresa, Italy D3 18
Strešin, Bela. I13 22
Streymoy, i., Faer. Is. D8 6b
Strickland, stm., Pap. N. Gui. m15 68a
Strimón (Struma), stm., Eur. I7 20
Strobel, Arg. G8 80
Strogonof Point, c., Ak., U.S. H15 100
Stromboli, Isola, i., Italy K10 18
Strome, Alta., Can. E22 102
Stromeferry, Scot., U.K. D8 8
Stromness, Scot., U.K. C10 8
Stromsburg, Ne., U.S. J10 118
Strömsund, Swe. J14 6
Strong, Ar., U.S. I4 114
Strong, stm., Ms., U.S. J7 114
Strong City, Ks., U.S. M11 118
Stronghurst, Il., U.S. J5 110
Stroud, Austl. I9 70
Stroud, Ok., U.S. D10 116
Stroudsburg, Pa., U.S. G11 108
Struer, Den. M11 6
Struga, Mac. H4 20
Strugi-Krasnyje, Russia C12 22
Strum, Wi., U.S. F4 110
Struma (Strimón), stm., Eur. H7 20
Strumica, Mac. H6 20
Strunino, Russia E21 22
Struthers, Oh., U.S. F6 108
Stryj, Ukr. H2 26
Stryker, Oh., U.S. F2 108
Strzegom, Pol. E16 10
Strzelce Opolskie, Pol. E18 10
Strzelecki Creek, stm., Austl. G4 70
Strzelin, Pol. E17 10
Stuart, Fl., U.S. L6 112
Stuart, Ia., U.S. J13 118
Stuart, Ne., U.S. I8 118
Stuart, Va., U.S. C6 112
Stuart, stm., B.C., Can. C10 102
Stuart Lake, l., B.C., Can. C10 102
Stuarts Draft, Va., U.S. A7 112
Studen Kladenec, jazovir, res., Bul. H9 20
Stuie, B.C., Can. E8 102
Stull, stm., Can. D22 104
Stull Lake, l., Can. D22 104
Stupart, stm., Man., Can. C21 104
Stupino, Russia G21 22
Sturgeon, Mo., U.S. C4 114
Sturgeon, stm., Sask., Can. E8 104
Sturgeon, stm., Mi., U.S. E11 110
Sturgeon Bay, Wi., U.S. F8 110
Sturgeon Bay, b., Man., Can. F17 104
Sturgeon Falls, Ont., Can. D16 110
Sturgeon Lake, l., Alta., Can. B17 102
Sturgeon Lake, l., Ont., Can. C24 104
Sturgeon Lake Indian Reserve, Alta., Can. B17 102
Sturgeon Lake Indian Reserve, Sask., Can. E8 104
Sturgeon Landing, Sask., Can. D13 104
Sturgis, Sask., Can. G12 104
Sturgis, Ky., U.S. E9 114
Sturgis, Mi., U.S. I10 110
Sturgis, Ms., U.S. I7 114
Sturgis, S.D., U.S. G4 118
Sturtevant, Wi., U.S. H8 110
Sturt National Park, Austl. G4 70
Sturt Stony Desert, des., Austl. G4 70
Stutterheim, S. Afr. I8 66
Stuttgart, Ger. G9 10
Stuttgart, Ar., U.S. H5 114
Stykkishólmur, Ice. B2 6a
Styx, stm., Al., U.S. L9 114
Suaçuí Grande, stm., Braz. E7 79
Suaita, Col. D6 84
Suakin Archipelago, is., Sud. H10 60
Su'ao, China J8 34
Suapure, stm., Ven. D9 84
Suaqui Grande, Mex. C5 90
Subačius, Lith. F7 22
Subansiri, stm., Asia F16 44
Subarnarekha, stm., India I12 44
Subata, Lat. E8 22
Subiaco, Italy H8 18
Sublette, Ks., U.S. N7 118
Subotica, Yugo. C3 20
Suca, Eth. N10 60
Sucarnoochee, stm., U.S. J8 114
Suceava, Rom. B10 20
Suceava, co., Rom. B9 20
Sucha [Beskidzka], Pol. F19 10
Süchbaatar, Mong. A8 30
Suchiapa, stm., Mex. I13 90
Súchil, Mex. F8 90
Suchiniči, Russia G18 22
Suchitepéquez, dept., Guat. C3 92
Suchitoto, El Sal. D5 92
Suchodol'skij, Russia H21 22
Suchona, stm., Russia E6 26
Suchotinka, Russia I24 22
Suchou see Suzhou, China E11 30
Suchoverkovo, Russia E18 22
Suchumi, Geor. I6 26
Sucio, stm., Col. D4 84
Sucker Creek Indian Reserve, Alta., Can. B18 102
Sucre, Bol. H9 82
Sucre, Col. C5 84
Sucre, Ec. H2 84
Sucre, state, Ven. B11 84
Sucre, dept., Col. C5 84
Sucúa, Ec. I3 84
Sucuaro, Col. E8 84
Sucunduri, stm., Braz. B12 82
Sucuriú, stm., Braz. F3 79
Sud, Canal du, strt., Haiti E8 94
Suda, Russia B20 22
Sudan, Tx., U.S. E4 116
Sudan (As-Sūdān), ctry., Afr. E7 56
Sudan, reg., Afr. F9 54
Sudañez, Bol. H9 82
Sudbury, Ont., Can. D14 110
Suddie, Guy. D13 84
Sudeten see Sudety, mts., Eur. E16 10
Sudety, mts., Eur. E16 10
Sudislavl', Russia D24 22
Sudogda, Russia F23 22
Sud-Ouest, Pointe du, c., Que., Can. C10 106
Suduroy, i., Faer. Is. E8 6b
Sue, stm., Sud. N5 60
Sueca, Spain F11 16
Suez, Gulf of see Suways, Khalīj as-, b., Egypt C7 60
Suez see As-Suways, Egypt C7 60
Suez Canal see Suways, Qanāt as-, Egypt C7 60
Sufaynah, Sau. Ar. C2 47
Suffield, Alta., Can. H3 104
Suffield, Canadian Forces Base, mil., Alta., Can. H3 104
Suffolk, Va., U.S. C10 112
Suffolk, co., Eng., U.K. I15 8
Sufu see Kashi, China D2 30
Sugar, stm., U.S. H6 110
Sugar, stm., N.H., U.S. D14 108
Sugar City, Id., U.S. G14 122
Sugarcreek, Pa., U.S. F7 108
Sugar Grove, Va., U.S. C5 112
Sugar Hill, Ga., U.S. E2 112
Sugar Island, i., Mi., U.S. D11 110
Sugar Land, Tx., U.S. J11 116
Sugarloaf Mountain, mtn., Me., U.S. B16 108
Sugarloaf Point, c., Austl. I10 70
Suggi Lake, l., Sask., Can. D12 104
Suggi, stm., Russia E23 28
Suhār, Oman B10 47
Suhl, Ger. E10 10
Suhr, Switz. D9 13
Suiá-Miçu, stm., Braz. A2 79
Suichuan, China I3 34
Suide, China D9 30
Suifenhe, China C13 30
Suihua, China B12 30
Suining, China E8 30
Suipacha, Arg. H9 80
Suiping, China B2 34
Suippes, Fr. C11 14
Suixian, China D2 34
Suiyangdian, China C1 34
Suizhong, China C8 32
Šuja, Russia K24 6
Šuja, Russia E24 22
Sujāngarh, India G6 44
Sujiatun, China B11 32
Sukabumi, Indon. j13 39a
Sukagawa, Japan J15 36
Sukch'ŏn, N. Kor. D13 32
Sukhothai, Thai. F5 40
Sukkozero, Russia E4 26
Sukkur, Pak. G3 44
Sukumo, Japan O7 36
Sukunka, stm., B.C., Can. B13 102
Sul, Baía, b., Braz. D14 80
Sul, Canal do, strt., Braz. D9 76
Sula, Kepulauan, is., Indon. F8 38
Sulaco, stm., Hond. B7 92
Sulaimān Range, mts., Pak. F3 44
Sulawesi (Celebes), i., Indon. F7 38
Sulaymān, Birak (Solomon's Pools), hist., Isr. Occ. E4 50
Sulechów, Pol. C15 10
Sulejówek, Pol. C21 10
Sulima, S.L. H4 64
Sulingen, Ger. C8 10
Sulitelma, mtn., Eur. H15 6
Sullana, Peru A1 82
Sulligent, Al., U.S. I8 114
Sullivan, Il., U.S. C8 114
Sullivan, In., U.S. C9 114
Sullivan, Mo., U.S. D5 114
Sullivan Lake, l., Alta., Can. E23 102
Sully, Fr. E9 14
Sulmona, Italy G8 18
Sulphur, Yukon, Can. E25 100
Sulphur, La., U.S. L3 114
Sulphur, Ok., U.S. E10 116
Sulphur, stm., Alta., Can. D16 102
Sulphur, stm., U.S. I2 114
Sulphur Springs, Tx., U.S. F11 116
Sulphur Springs Valley, val., Az., U.S. M7 120
Sultan, Wa., U.S. C4 122
Sultānpur, India G10 44
Sulu Archipelago, is., Phil. D7 38
Sululta, Eth. M10 60
Sulūq, Libya B5 56
Sulu Sea, Asia D6 38
Sulzbach-Rosenberg, Ger. F11 10
Sumampa, Arg. E7 80
Sumas, Wa., U.S. A3 122
Sumatera (Sumatra), i., Indon. F3 38
Sumatra see Sumatera, i., Indon. F3 38
Sumayh, Sud. K6 60
Sumba, Faer. Is. E8 6b
Sumba, i., Indon. G7 38
Sumbawa, i., Indon. G6 38
Sumbawa Besar, Indon. G6 38
Sumbawanga, Tan. C6 58
Sumbay, Peru F6 82
Sumbe, Ang. D2 58
Šumber, Mong. B8 30
Sumbilla, Spain B10 16
Sumbuya, S.L. H4 64
Sümeg, Hung. I17 10
Šumen, Bul. F10 20
Šumenep, Indon. J16 39a
Šumerl'a, Russia F7 26
Šumgait, Azer. I7 26
Šumicha, Russia F10 26
Šumilino, Bela. F12 22
Sumisu-jima, i., Japan E15 30
Sumiswald, Switz. D8 13
Summerfield, Fl., U.S. J4 112
Summerfield, N.C., U.S. C7 112
Summerford, Newf., Can. C19 106
Summerland, B.C., Can. H15 102
Summerside, P.E.I., Can. F10 106
Summersville, Mo., U.S. E5 114
Summersville, W.V., U.S. I6 108
Summerton, S.C., U.S. F6 112
Summertown, Tn., U.S. G9 114
Summerville, Ga., U.S. E1 112
Summerville, S.C., U.S. F6 112
Summit, Ms., U.S. K6 114
Summit, S.D., U.S. F10 118
Summit Lake, B.C., Can. C12 102
Summit Mountain, mtn., Nv., U.S. E9 124
Summit Peak, mtn., Co., U.S. G10 120
Sumner, Ia., U.S. H3 110
Sumner, Ms., U.S. I6 114
Sumner, Wa., U.S. C3 122
Sumoto, Japan M9 36
Šumperk, Czech. F16 10
Sumprabum, Burma A4 40
Sumrall, Ms., U.S. K7 114
Šumšu, ostrov, i., Russia G23 28
Sumter, S.C., U.S. F6 112
Sumy, Ukr. G4 26
Sumzom, China F17 44
Sun, stm., Mt., U.S. C13 122
Suna, stm., Russia J23 6
Sunan, N. Kor. D13 32
Sunbright, Tn., U.S. C2 112
Sunburst, Mt., U.S. B14 122
Sunbury, Austl. K6 70
Sunbury, N.C., U.S. C10 112
Sunbury, Oh., U.S. G4 108
Sunbury, Pa., U.S. G10 108
Sunchales, Arg. F8 80
Sunch'ang, S. Kor. H15 32
Sunchild Indian Reserve, Alta., Can. E19 102
Suncho Corral, Arg. D7 80
Sunch'ŏn, N. Kor. D13 32
Sunch'ŏn, S. Kor. I15 32
Sun City, Az., U.S. K4 120
Suncook, N.H., U.S. D15 108
Suncook, stm., N.H., U.S. D15 108
Sunda, Selat, strt., Indon. G4 38
Sundance, Wy., U.S. G3 118
Sundarbans, reg., Asia J13 44
Sunda Strait see Sunda, Selat, strt., Indon. G4 38
Sundown, Tx., U.S. F4 116
Sundre, Alta., Can. F20 102
Sundridge, Ont., Can. E16 110
Sundsvall, Swe. J15 6
Sunflower, Ms., U.S. I6 114
Sunflower, Mount, mtn., Ks., U.S. L5 118
Sungaipenuh, Indon. F3 38
Sungai Petani, Malay. L6 40
Sunjiabu, China E7 34
Sunjikāy, Sud. K5 60
Sunland Park, N.M., U.S. L10 120
Sunnybrae, N.S., Can. G11 106
Sunnynook, Alta., Can. F23 102
Sunnyside, Newf., Can. E20 106
Sunnyside, Ut., U.S. E6 120
Sunnyside, Wa., U.S. D5 122
Sunnyslope, Alta., Can. F21 102
Sunnyvale, Ca., U.S. G3 124
Sun Prairie, Wi., U.S. G6 110
Sunray, Tx., U.S. C5 116
Sunrise, Wy., U.S. B12 120
Sunrise Manor, Nv., U.S. H10 124
Sunset, La., U.S. L4 114
Sunset, Tx., U.S. F9 116
Sunset Country, reg., Austl. J4 70
Sunset Heights, Tx., U.S. H4 116
Sunset Prairie, B.C., Can. B14 102
Sunshine, Austl. K6 70
Suntrana, Ak., U.S. E20 100
Suntu, Eth. M9 60
Sun Valley, Id., U.S. G11 122
Sunwapta, stm., Alta., Can. E17 102
Sunyani, Ghana H8 64
Sunzom, China F6 30
Suojarvi, Russia J23 6
Suonenjoki, Fin. J20 6
Supachuy, Bol. H9 82
Supamo, stm., Ven. D11 84
Supe, Eth. M8 60
Superior, Az., U.S. K5 120
Superior, Mt., U.S. C11 122
Superior, Ne., U.S. K9 118
Superior, Wi., U.S. D3 110
Superior, Laguna, b., Mex. I12 90
Superior, Lake, l., N.A. C8 110
Suphan Buri, Thai. G6 40
Suponevo, Russia H17 22
Sup'ung-chŏsuji, res., Asia C13 32
Sūq ash-Shuyūkh, Iraq F9 48
Sūq'at al-Jamal, Sud. K4 60
Suqian, China B7 34
Sūq Suwayq, Sau. Ar. I5 48
Suquṭrā (Socotra), i., Yemen G5 42
Ṣūr (Tyre), Leb. B4 50
Ṣūr, Oman C11 47
Sura, stm., Russia G7 26
Surabaya, Indon. J16 39a
Surakarta, Indon. J15 39a
Sūrat, India J5 44
Surat Thani (Ban Don), Thai. J5 40
Suraž, Bela. F13 22
Suraž, Russia H15 22
Surdulica, Yugo. G6 20
Sûre (Sauer), stm., Eur. I9 12
Surendranagar, India I4 44
Suretka, C.R. H12 92
Surf City, N.J., U.S. H12 108
Surfers Paradise, Austl. G10 70
Surgoinsville, Tn., U.S. C4 112
Surgut, Russia E6 28
Suriāpet, India D5 46
Surigao, Phil. D8 38
Surin, Thai. G7 40
Suriname, ctry., S.A. C7 76
Suring, Wi., U.S. F7 110
Sūrmaq, Iran F12 48
Surprise, Az., U.S. K4 120
Surprise Valley, val., U.S. C5 124
Surrency, Ga., U.S. H4 112
Surrey, N.D., U.S. C6 118
Surrey, co., Eng., U.K. J13 8
Surry, Va., U.S. B10 112
Sursee, Switz. D9 13
Surt, Libya B4 56
Surt, Khalīj, b., Libya B4 56
Surtsey, i., Ice. C3 6a
Sürüç, Tur. C5 48
Surumu, stm., Braz. F12 84
Susa, Italy D2 18
Susaki, Japan N8 36
Susanino, Russia C24 22
Susanville, Ca., U.S. D5 124
Susch, Switz. E13 13
Šušenskoje, Russia G16 26
Sušice, Czech. F13 10
Susitna, Ak., U.S. F19 100
Susitna, stm., Ak., U.S. E19 100
Susoh, Indon. M4 40
Susquehanna, Pa., U.S. F11 108
Susquehanna, stm., U.S. H10 108
Susques, Arg. B5 80
Sussex, N.B., Can. G8 106
Sussex, N.J., U.S. F12 108
Sussex, Va., U.S. C9 112
Sussex, East, co., Eng., U.K. K14 8
Susuman, Russia E21 28
Susurluk, Tur. J12 20
Susuzmüsellim, Tur. H11 20
Sutherland, S. Afr. I5 66
Sutherland, Ia., U.S. I12 118
Sutherland, Ne., U.S. J6 118
Sutherland, stm., B.C., Can. C9 102
Sutherlin, Or., U.S. G2 122
Sutlej (Satluj) (Langqên), stm., Asia F4 44
Sutter, Ca., U.S. E4 124
Sutter Creek, Ca., U.S. F5 124
Sutton, Ak., U.S. F20 100
Sutton, Ne., U.S. K10 118
Sutton, W.V., U.S. I6 108
Sutton in Ashfield, Eng., U.K. H12 8
Suttons Bay, Mi., U.S. F10 110
Sutton West, Ont., Can. F16 110
Suttor, stm., Austl. C7 70
Suurbraak, S. Afr. J5 66
Suure-Jaani, Est. C8 22
Suva, Fiji H24 2
Suvainiškis, Lith. E8 22
Suvorov, Russia G19 22
Suvorovo, Ukr. D12 20
Suwa, Eth. G2 47
Suwa, Japan K13 36
Suwałki, Pol. A22 10
Suwannee, stm., U.S. J3 112
Suwannee Lake, l., Man., Can. B14 104
Suwanose-jima, i., Japan R4 37b
Ṣuwayliḥ, Jord. D5 50
Suways, Khalīj as- (Gulf of Suez), b., Egypt C7 60
Suways, Qanāt as- (Suez Canal), Egypt C7 60
Suwŏn, S. Kor. F15 32
Suxi, China F9 34
Suxian, China B5 34
Suyo, Peru J2 84
Suzak, Kaz. I11 26
Suzdal', Russia E23 22
Suzhou (Soochow), China D9 34
Suzigou, China C11 32
Suzuka, Japan M11 36
Sval'ava, Ukr. A6 20
Svalbard, dep., Eur. B2 24
Svappavaara, Swe. H17 6
Svataj, Russia D22 28
Sv'atoj Nos, mys, c., Russia G26 6
Sv'atoj Nos, mys, c., Russia C20 28
Svay Riĕng, Camb. I8 40
Svėdasai, Lith. F8 22
Svelgen, Nor. K9 6
Svelvik, Nor. L12 6
Sven', Russia H17 22
Švenčionėliai, Lith. F9 22
Švenčionys, Lith. F9 22
Sverdlovsk see Jekaterinburg, Russia F10 26
Sverdlovsk, Ukr. H5 26
Sverdrup, ostrov, i., Russia C13 26
Svetlogorsk, Bela. I12 22
Svetlogorsk, Russia G3 22
Svetlograd, Russia H6 26
Svetlyj, Russia G3 22
Svetogorsk, Russia K21 6
Svilajnac, Yugo. E5 20
Svilengrad, Bul. H10 20
Svindal, Nor. L10 6
Svir', Bela. G9 22
Svir', stm., Russia A16 22
Svirsk, Russia G12 28
Svir'stroj, Russia A16 22
Svisloč', Bela. B24 10
Svisloč', Bela. H7 22
Svištov, Bul. F9 20
Svobodnyj, Russia G17 28
Svolvær, Nor. G14 6
Swain Reefs, rf., Austl. C10 70
Swainsboro, Ga., U.S. G4 112
Swakop, stm., Afr. D2 66
Swakopmund, Nmb. D2 66
Swan, stm., Can. F14 104
Swan, stm., Alta., Can. B19 102
Swan, stm., Mn., U.S. C2 110
Swan, stm., Mt., U.S. C12 122
Swanee see Suwannee, stm., U.S. J3 112
Swan Hill, Austl. J5 70
Swan Hills, Alta., Can. C19 102
Swan Hills, hills, Alta., Can. C19 102
Swan Islands see Santanilla, Islas, is., Hond. F3 94
Swan Lake, Man., Can. I16 104
Swan Lake, Mt., U.S. C12 122
Swan Lake, l., Man., Can. F14 104
Swan Lake, l., Ont., Can. D23 104
Swannanoa, N.C., U.S. D4 112
Swanquarter, N.C., U.S. D10 112
Swan Range, mts., Mt., U.S. C12 122
Swan River, Man., Can. F13 104
Swansboro, N.C., U.S. E9 112
Swansea, Austl. N8 70
Swansea, Wales, U.K. J10 8
Swansea, S.C., U.S. F5 112
Swanton, Oh., U.S. F3 108
Swanton, Vt., U.S. C13 108
Swanville, Mn., U.S. E1 110
Swartz Creek, Mi., U.S. H12 110
Swarzędz, Pol. C17 10
Swasey Peak, mtn., Ut., U.S. E3 120
Swatow see Shantou, China L5 34
Swaziland, ctry., Afr. G6 58
Swea City, Ia., U.S. H13 118
Sweden (Sverige), ctry., Eur. C11 4
Swedish Knoll, mtn., Ut., U.S. E5 120
Swedru, Ghana I9 64
Sweeny, Tx., U.S. J11 116
Sweet Briar, Va., U.S. B7 112
Sweet Grass Indian Reserve, Sask., Can. F6 104
Sweet Home, Or., U.S. F3 122
Sweet Home, Tx., U.S. J9 116
Sweet Springs, Mo., U.S. D3 114
Sweetwater, Tn., U.S. D2 112
Sweetwater, Tx., U.S. G6 116
Sweetwater, stm., Wy., U.S. H18 122
Swellendam, S. Afr. J5 66
Swepsonville, N.C., U.S. C7 112
Świdnica (Schweidnitz), Pol. E16 10
Świdnik, Pol. D22 10
Świdwin, Pol. B15 10
Świebodzice, Pol. E16 10
Świebodzin, Pol. C15 10
Świecie, Pol. B18 10
Swift Current, Sask., Can. H7 104
Swift Current Creek, stm., Sask., Can. H7 104
Swifton, Ar., U.S. G5 114
Swilly, Lough, b., Ire. F6 8
Swinburne, Cape, c., N.W. Ter., Can. B13 96
Swindle Island, i., B.C., Can. E6 102
Swindon, Eng., U.K. J12 8
Świnoujście (Swinemünde), Pol. B14 10
Switzerland, ctry., Eur. F9 4
Swords Range, mts., Austl. C4 70
Sycamore, Ga., U.S. H3 112
Sycamore, Il., U.S. I7 110
Sycamore, Oh., U.S. G3 108
Sycan, stm., Or., U.S. H4 122
Syčovka, Russia F17 22
Sydenham, Ont., Can. F19 110
Sydney, Austl. I9 70
Sydney, N.S., Can. F13 106
Sydney Lake, l., Ont., Can. H20 104
Sydney Mines, N.S., Can. F13 106
Syke, Ger. C8 10
Sykesville, Md., U.S. H10 108
Sykesville, Pa., U.S. F8 108
Syktyvkar, Russia E8 26
Sylacauga, Al., U.S. I10 114
Sylhet, Bngl. H14 44
Sylt, i., Ger. A8 10
Sylva, N.C., U.S. D3 112
Sylvan Grove, Ks., U.S. L9 118
Sylvan Hills, Ar., U.S. H4 114
Sylvania, Ga., U.S. G5 112
Sylvania, Oh., U.S. F3 108
Sylvan Lake, Alta., Can. E20 102
Sylvan Lake, l., Alta., Can. E20 102
Sylvester, Ga., U.S. H3 112
Sylvester, Tx., U.S. G6 116
Sylvester, Mount, hill, Newf., Can. D18 106
Sylvia, Ks., U.S. N9 118
Syntul, Russia F24 22
Synžereja, Mol. B12 20
Syracuse, In., U.S. A11 114
Syracuse, Ks., U.S. N6 118
Syracuse, Ne., U.S. K11 118
Syracuse, N.Y., U.S. D10 108
Syracuse see Siracusa, Italy L10 18
Syrdarja, Uzb. I11 26
Syrdarja (Syr Darya), stm., Asia H10 26
Syria (As-Sūrīyah), ctry., Asia B2 42
Syriam, Burma F4 40
Syrskij, Russia I22 22
Sysert', Russia F10 26
Syzran', Russia G7 26
Szabolcs-Szatmár-Bereg, co., Hung. G22 10
Szamos (Someș), stm., Eur. B6 20
Szamotuły, Pol. C16 10
Szarvas, Hung. I20 10
Szczecin (Stettin), Pol. B14 10
Szczecinek (Neustettin), Pol. B16 10
Szczeciński, Zalew (Oderhaff), b., Eur. B14 10
Szczuczyn, Pol. B22 10
Szczytno, Pol. B21 10
Szechwan see Sichuan, prov., China E7 30
Szécsény, Hung. G19 10
Szeged, Hung. I20 10
Szeghalom, Hung. H21 10
Székesfehérvár, Hung. H18 10
Szekszárd, Hung. I18 10
Szentendre, Hung. H19 10
Szentes, Hung. I20 10
Szentgotthárd, Hung. I16 10
Szerencs, Hung. G21 10
Szob, Hung. H18 10
Szolnok, Hung. H20 10
Szombathely, Hung. I16 10
Szprotawa, Pol. D15 10
Szubin, Pol. B17 10

T

Tabacal, Arg. B6 80
Tabaco, Phil. O20 39b
Tabacundo, Ec. G3 84
Tabalosos, Peru B3 82
Tabarka, Tun. M3 18
Tabas, Iran E14 48
Tabasará, stm., Pan. I13 92
Tabasco, state, Mex. I13 90
Tabas Masīnā, Iran E16 48
Tabatinga, stm., Braz. D7 79
Tabelbala, Alg. C6 54
Taber, Alta., Can. H22 102
Tabla, Niger E11 64
Table Bay, b., S. Afr. I4 66
Table Mountain, mtn., Newf., Can. E14 106
Table Rock, Ne., U.S. K11 118
Table Rock Lake, res., U.S. F3 114
Tabligbo, Togo H10 64
Taboco, stm., Braz. I14 82
Taboga, Pan. I15 92
Tábor, Czech. F14 10
Tabor, Ia., U.S. K12 118
Tabor, S.D., U.S. I10 118
Tabora, Tan. C6 58
Tabor City, N.C., U.S. E8 112
Tabou, I.C. I6 64
Tabrīz, Iran B9 48
Tabūk, Sau. Ar. G4 48
Tacámbaro de Codallos, Mex. H9 90
Tacaná, Guat. B2 92
Tacaná, Volcán, vol., N.A. B2 92
Tacañitas, Arg. E7 80
T'ačev, Ukr. A7 20
Taché, Lac, l., N.W. Ter., Can. D8 96
Tacheng, China B3 30
Tachiataš, Uzb. I9 26
Tachie, stm., B.C., Can. C10 102
Tachikawa, Japan L14 36
Táchira, state, Ven. D6 84
Tachov, Czech. F12 10
Tachtamygda, Russia G16 28
Taciuã, Lago, stm., Braz. J12 84
Tacna, Peru H6 82
Tacna, Az., U.S. L3 120
Tacna, dept., Peru G6 82
Tacoma, Wa., U.S. C3 122
Taconic Range, mts., U.S. E13 108
Taco Pozo, Arg. C7 80
Tacotalpa, stm., Mex. I13 90
Tacuarembó, Ur. F11 80
Tacuarembó, stm., Ur. F11 80
Tacuarí, stm., Ur. G11 80
Tacuatí, Para. B10 80
Tacuparé, Cachoeira, wtfl, Braz. A14 82
Tacutu (Takutu), stm., S.A. F12 84
Tademaït, Plateau du, plat., Alg. F12 62
Tādepallegūdem, India D6 46
Tadía, Ciénaga de, l., Col. D4 84
Tadjemout, Alg. H12 62
Tadjoura, Dji. F9 56
Tadoule Lake, l., Man., Can. E13 96
Tadoussac, Que., Can. D4 106
Tādpatri, India E5 46
Tadzhikistan see Tajikistan, ctry., Asia J12 26
T'aebaek-sanmaek, mts., Asia F16 32
Taech'ŏn, S. Kor. G14 32
Taedong, N. Kor. D13 32
Taegu, S. Kor. H16 32
Taegwan, N. Kor. C13 32
T'aein, S. Kor. H14 32
Taejŏn, S. Kor. G15 32
Ta'erwan, China D2 34
Tafalla, Spain C10 16
Tafas, Syria C6 50
Tafassâsset, Oued, val., Afr. D8 54
Tafiré, I.C. G7 64
Tafí Viejo, Arg. D6 80
Tafraoute, Mor. F6 62
Taft, Ca., U.S. I6 124
Taft, Ok., U.S. D11 116
Taft, Tx., U.S. L9 116
Taganrog, Russia F15 4
Tagawa, Japan N5 36
Tagaytay, Phil. N19 39b
Taghit, Alg. E9 62
Tagish Lake, l., Can. G27 100
Taguatinga, Braz. B5 79
Taguke, China E3 30
Taguke, China D11 44
Tagula Island, i., Pap. N. Gui. B10 68
Tagus (Tejo) (Tajo), stm., Eur. F3 16
Tah, Sebkha, l., Afr. G4 62
Tahakopa, N.Z. G2 72
Tahala, Mor. C8 62
Tahanaoute, Mor. E7 62
Tahart, Alg. I13 62
Tahat, mtn., Alg. I13 62
Tahifet, Alg. I13 62
Tahiryuak Lake, l., N.W. Ter., Can. B10 96
Tahiti, i., Fr. Poly. J25 126
Tahkuna neem, c., Est. B5 22
Tāhlāb (Tālāb), stm., Asia G17 48
Tahlequah, Ok., U.S. D12 116
Tahoe, Lake, l., U.S. E5 124
Tahoe City, Ca., U.S. E5 124
Tahoe Lake, l., N.W. Ter., Can. B11 96
Tahoe Valley, Ca., U.S. F5 124
Tahoka, Tx., U.S. F5 116
Tahoua, Niger D12 64
Tahquamenon, stm., Mi., U.S. D10 110
Tahsis, B.C., Can. H8 102
Ṭahṭā, Egypt D6 60
Tahtsa Lake, l., B.C., Can. D7 102
Tahtsa Peak, mtn., B.C., Can. D7 102
Tahuamanu, stm., S.A. D7 82
Tahuna, Indon. E8 38
Tai'an, China G5 32
Taibai Shan, mtn., China D2 32
T'aichung, Tai. K9 34
Taif see Aṭ-Ṭā'if, Sau. Ar. D2 47
Taihang Shan, mts., China D9 30
Taihape, N.Z. C5 72
Taihe, China B4 34
Tai Hu, l., China D9 34
Taijiang, China A10 40
Taikkyi, Burma F3 40
Tailai, China B11 30
Tailem Bend, Austl. J3 70
T'ainan, Tai. L9 34
Tainaron, Akra, c., Grc. M6 20
Taining, China I6 34
Taiobeiras, Braz. C7 79
T'aipei, Tai. J10 34
T'aipeihsien, Tai. J10 34
Taiping, China M2 34
Taiping, Malay. L6 40
Taishun, China H8 34
Taitao, Península de, pen., Chile F1 78
Taitouying, China C7 32

Name	Map Ref.	Page
T'aitung, Tai.	M10	34
Taiwan (T'aiwan), ctry., Asia	G11	30
Taiwan Strait, strt., Asia	K8	34
Taixian, China	C9	34
Taixing, China	C9	34
Ṭaiyiba, Isr.	D4	50
Taiyuan, China	D9	30
Taizhou, China	C8	34
Ta'izz, Yemen	H4	47
Tajerouine, Tun.	N3	18
Tajga, Russia	F9	28
Tajgonos, mys, c., Russia	E24	28
Tajikistan, ctry., Asia	J12	26
Tajimi, Japan	L12	36
Tajique, N.M., U.S.	J10	120
Tajitos, Mex.	B3	90
Tajmura, stm., Russia	E17	26
Tajmyr, ozero, l., Russia	C18	26
Tajmyr, poluostrov, pen., Russia	B18	26
Tajšet, Russia	F11	28
Tajumulco, Volcán, vol., Guat.	B3	92
Tak, Thai.	F5	40
Takāb, Iran	C9	48
Takachu, Bots.	D5	66
Takahashi, Japan	M8	36
Takahe, Mount, mtn., Ant.	C11	73
Takaka, N.Z.	D4	72
Takakkaw Falls, wtfl, B.C., Can.	F18	102
Takamatsu, Japan	M9	36
Takaoka, Japan	K12	36
Takapuna, N.Z.	B5	72
Takasaki, Japan	K14	36
Takatsuki, Japan	M10	36
Takayama, Japan	K12	36
Takefu, Japan	L11	36
Takenake, China	C9	44
Takengon, Indon.	L4	40
Take-shima, i., Japan	Q5	37b
Take-shima (Tok-to), is., Asia	J6	36
Tākestān, Iran	C10	48
Takêv, Camb.	I8	40
Takhli, Thai.	G6	40
Takijuk Lake, l., N.W. Ter., Can.	C10	96
Takikawa, Japan	D16	36a
Takla Lake, l., B.C., Can.	B9	102
Takla Landing, B.C., Can.	B9	102
Taklimakan Shamo, des., China	D3	30
Takrouna, Tun.	M5	18
Taku, stm., N.A.	G28	100
Takua Pa, Thai.	J5	40
Taku Glacier, Ak., U.S.	G27	100
Takum, Nig.	H14	64
Takutu (Tacutu), stm., S.A.	F13	84
Takysie Lake, B.C., Can.	D9	102
Tala, Mex.	G8	90
Tala, Ur.	H11	80
Talagang, Pak.	D5	44
Talagante, Chile	G3	80
Talamanca, Cordillera de, mts., C.R.	H11	92
Talara, Peru	J2	84
Talas, Kyrg.	I12	26
Talasea, Pap. N. Gui.	m17	68a
Talata Mafara, Nig.	E13	64
Talaud, Kepulauan, is., Indon.	E8	38
Talavera de la Reina, Spain	F7	16
Talawdī, Sud.	L6	60
Talbot Lake, l., Man., Can.	D15	104
Talbotton, Ga., U.S.	G2	112
Talbragar, stm., Austl.	I8	70
Talca, Chile	H3	80
Talcahuano, Chile	I2	80
Talchichitle, Isla, i., Mex.	E5	90
Talco, Tx., U.S.	F11	116
Taldom, Russia	E20	22
Taldy-Kurgan, Kaz.	H13	26
Talent, Or., U.S.	H3	122
Tālesh, Iran	C10	48
Talgar, Kaz.	I13	26
Taliabu, Pulau, i., Indon.	F7	38
Talica, Russia	F10	26
Talickij Čamlyk, Russia	I23	22
Talihina, Ok., U.S.	E11	116
Taliouine, Mor.	E7	62
Tali Post, Sud.	O6	60
Talish Mountains (Kūhhā-ye Ṭavālesh, mts., Asia	B10	48
Tal'ka, Bela.	H11	22
Talkeetna, Ak., U.S.	E19	100
Talladega, Al., U.S.	I10	114
Tall 'Afar, Iraq	C7	48
Tallah, Egypt	C6	60
Tallahassee, Fl., U.S.	I2	112
Tallahatchie, stm., Ms., U.S.	I6	114
Tallangatta, Austl.	K7	70
Tallapoosa, Ga., U.S.	F1	112
Tallapoosa, stm., U.S.	J10	114
Tallassee, Al., U.S.	J11	114
Tallinn, Est.	B7	22
Tall Kalakh, Syria	D4	48
Tallmadge, Oh., U.S.	F5	108
Tallula, Il., U.S.	C7	114
Tallulah, La., U.S.	J5	114
Talmage, Ca., U.S.	E2	124
Talmage, Ne., U.S.	K11	118
Tal'menka, Russia	G14	26
Talmont, Fr.	F5	14
Talo, mtn., Eth.	L9	60
Taloga, Ok., U.S.	C8	116
Talpa, Tx., U.S.	H7	116
Talsi, Lat.	D5	22
Taltal, Chile	C3	80
Taltapin Lake, l., B.C., Can.	C9	102
Taltson, stm., N.W. Ter., Can.	D10	96
Talwood, Austl.	G8	70
Tama, Arg.	F5	80
Tama, Ia., U.S.	I3	110
Tamacuarí, Pico, mtn., S.A.	G10	84
Tamadjert, Alg.	H14	62
Tamalameque, Col.	C6	84
Tamale, Ghana	G9	64
Tamana, Japan	O5	36
Tamaná, Cerro, mtn., Col.	E4	84
Tamanaco, stm., Ven.	C10	84
Tamaniquá, Braz.	I10	84
Tamano, Japan	M8	36
Tamanquaré, Ilha, i., Braz.	H10	84
Tamapatz, Mex.	G10	90
Tamaqua, Pa., U.S.	G11	108
Tamar, stm., Austl.	M7	70
Támara, Col.	E6	84
Tamarac, stm., Mn., U.S.	C10	118
Tamaroa, Il., U.S.	D7	114
Tamarugal, Pampa del, pl., Chile	I7	82
Tamási, Hung.	I18	10
Tamaské, Niger	D12	64
Tamaulipas, state, Mex.	F10	90
Tamaya, stm., Peru	C4	82
Tamazula, Mex.	E6	90
Tamazula de Gordiano, Mex.	H8	90
Tamazulapan del Progreso, Mex.	I11	90
Tamazunchale, Mex.	G10	90
Tambacounda, Sen.	E3	64
Tamba Dabatou, Gui.	F4	64
Tāmbaram, India	F6	46
Tambelan, Kepulauan, is., Indon.	N9	40
Tamberías, Arg.	F4	80
Tambo, Austl.	E7	70
Tambo, Peru	E4	82
Tambo, stm., Austl.	K7	70
Tambo, stm., Peru	G6	82
Tambo, stm., Peru	D5	82
Tamboara, Braz.	G2	79
Tambo Grande, Peru	A1	82
Tambohorano, Madag.	P20	67b
Tambopata, stm., S.A.	E7	82
Tambor, C.R.	H9	92
Tamboritha, Mount, mtn., Austl.	K7	70
Tamboryacu, stm., Peru	H5	84
Tambov, Russia	I24	22
Tambura, Sud.	O4	60
Tamchaket, Maur.	C4	64
Tame, Col.	D7	84
Tameapa, Mex.	E6	90
Tameghza, Tun.	C14	62
Tamel Aike, Arg.	F2	78
Tamelelt, Mor.	E7	62
Tamenghest, Alg.	I13	62
Tamenghest, Oued, val., Alg.	I11	62
Tamiahua, Mex.	G11	90
Tamiahua, Laguna de, b., Mex.	G11	90
Tamiami Canal, Fl., U.S.	N5	112
Tamil Nādu, state, India	G5	46
Tamiš (Timiș), stm., Eur.	D4	20
Tamitatoala, stm., Braz.	B2	79
Tam Ky, Viet.	G10	40
Tamms, Il., U.S.	E7	114
Tamnum, Yemen	G7	47
Tampa, Fl., U.S.	L4	112
Tampa Bay, b., Fl., U.S.	L4	112
Tampaón, stm., Mex.	G10	90
Tampere, Fin.	K18	6
Tampico, Mex.	F11	90
Tampico, Il., U.S.	I6	110
Tampin, Malay.	M7	40
Tam Quan, Viet.	G10	40
Tamri, Mor.	E6	62
Tamsagbulag, Mong.	B10	30
Tamsalu, Est.	B9	22
Tamshiyacu, Peru	J6	84
Tamsweg, Aus.	H13	10
Tamworth, Austl.	H9	70
Tamyang, S. Kor.	H14	32
Tana, Chile	H7	82
Tana (Teno), stm., Eur.	F20	6
Tana, Lake, l., Eth.	K9	60
Tanabe, Japan	N10	36
Tanabi, Braz.	F4	79
Tanacross, Ak., U.S.	E23	100
Tanahbala, Pulau, i., Indon.	O5	40
Tanahmasa, Pulau, i., Indon.	O5	40
Tanami Desert, des., Austl.	C5	68
Tan An, Viet.	I9	40
Tanana, Ak., U.S.	D18	100
Tanana, stm., Ak., U.S.	D19	100
Tananarive see Antananarivo, Madag.	Q22	67b
Tancheng, China	I6	32
Tanchoj, Russia	G13	28
Tanch'ŏn, N. Kor.	C16	32
Tancítaro, Pico de, mtn., Mex.	H8	90
Tānda, India	G10	44
Tandaltī, Sud.	K6	60
Tandil, Arg.	I9	80
Tandou Lake, l., Austl.	I5	70
Tanega-shima, i., Japan	Q6	37b
Tan Emellel, Alg.	G15	62
Taneytown, Md., U.S.	H9	108
Tanezrouft, des., Afr.	D6	54
Tanga, Tan.	C7	58
Tangail, Bngl.	H13	44
Tangainony, Madag.	S22	67b
Tangalla, Sri L.	I6	46
Tanganyika, Lake, l., Afr.	C5	58
Tangarana, stm., Peru	I5	84
Tangcun, China	J2	34
Tanger (Tangier), Mor.	C8	62
Tangermünde, Ger.	C11	10
Tanggou, China	B7	34
Tanggu, China	D5	32
Tanggula Shan, mts., China	D13	44
Tangier, N.S., Can.	H11	106
Tangier, Va., U.S.	B11	112
Tangier see Tanger, Mor.	C8	62
Tangipahoa, stm., U.S.	K6	114
Tangjiagou, China	E6	34
Tangjin, S. Kor.	G14	32
Tangra Yumco, l., China	E12	44
Tangsanying, China	B5	32
Tangshan, China	D6	32
Tanguiéta, Benin	F10	64
Tangxian, China	E2	32
Tanimbar, Kepulauan, is., Indon.	G9	38
Taninges, Fr.	F13	14
Tanjiafang, China	G6	32
Tanjiang, China	K5	34
Tanjungbalai, Indon.	M5	40
Tanjungpandan, Indon.	F4	38
Tanjungpinang, Indon.	N8	40
Tanjungselor, Indon.	E6	38
Tānk, Pak.	D4	44
Tan Kena, Alg.	G15	62
Tännàs, Swe.	J13	6
Tanner, Al., U.S.	H10	114
Tanner, Mount, mtn., B.C., Can.	H16	102
Tannu-Ola, chrebet, mts., Asia	G10	28
Tannūrah, Ra's, c., Sau. Ar.	H11	48
Tano, stm., Afr.	I8	64
Tânout, Niger	D14	64
Tanquinho, Braz.	A9	79
Tanshui, Tai.	J10	34
Tánsin, Isla de, i., Hond.	B11	92
Tánsin, Laguna de, b., Hond.	B11	92
Ṭanṭā, Egypt	B6	60
Tan-Tan, Mor.	F5	62
Tantoyuca, Mex.	G10	90
Tanuku, India	D6	46
Tanyang, S. Kor.	G16	32
Tanzania, ctry., Afr.	C6	58
Tao, stm., China	E7	30
Taochong, China	D7	34
Tao'er, stm., China	B11	30
Taolakepa, China	D11	44
Taoling, China	E7	34
Taormina, Italy	L10	18
Taos, Mo., U.S.	D4	114
Taos, N.M., U.S.	H11	120
Taos Pueblo, N.M., U.S.	H11	120
Taoudenni, Mali	I8	62
Taounate, Mor.	C8	62
Taoura, Alg.	M3	18
Taourirt, Mor.	C9	62
Taoussa, Mali	C9	64
Taoyuan, China	J6	34
Tapa, Est.	B8	22
Tapacari, Bol.	G8	82
Tapachula, Mex.	J13	90
Tapah, Malay.	L6	40
Tapaje, stm., Col.	F3	84
Tapajós, stm., Braz.	D7	76
Tapalqué, Arg.	I8	80
Tapanahony, stm., Sur.	C7	76
Tapauá, Braz.	A10	82
Tapauá, stm., Braz.	A9	82
Tapejara, Braz.	E12	80
Tapera, Braz.	E12	80
Taperas, Bol.	G11	82
Taperoá, Braz.	B9	79
Tapes, Braz.	F13	80
Tapeta, Lib.	H5	64
Taphan Hin, Thai.	F6	40
Tāpi, stm., India	B2	46
Tapiche, stm., Peru	A5	82
Taping (Daying), stm., Asia	B4	40
Tapiraí, Braz.	E5	79
Tāplejungg, Nepal	G12	44
Tapoa, stm., Afr.	E11	64
Tapolca, Hung.	I17	10
Tappahannock, Va., U.S.	B10	112
Tappen, N.D., U.S.	E8	118
Tappi-zaki, c., Japan	F15	36
Tappo, Ghana	F8	64
Tapurucuara, Braz.	H10	84
Taqāṭu' Hayyā, Sud.	H9	60
Taquara, Braz.	E13	80
Taquaras, Ponta das, c., Braz.	D14	80
Taquari, Braz.	D2	79
Taquari, Braz.	E13	80
Taquari, stm., Braz.	E13	80
Taquari, stm., Braz.	H13	82
Taquari, Pantanal do, sw., Braz.	H13	82
Taquaritinga, Braz.	F4	79
Taquaruçu, stm., Braz.	F2	79
Tar, stm., N.C., U.S.	D9	112
Tara, Austl.	F9	70
Tara, Russia	F6	28
Taraba, stm., Nig.	G9	54
Tarabine, Oued ti-n-, val., Afr.	J14	62
Tarabuco, Bol.	H9	82
Ṭarābulus (Tripoli), Leb.	D3	48
Ṭarābulus (Tripoli), Libya	B3	56
Ṭarābulus (Tripolitania), hist. reg., Libya	B3	56
Tarago, Austl.	J8	70
Taraira (Traíra), stm., S.A.	H8	84
Tarakan, Indon.	E6	38
Taraklija, Mol.	D12	20
Taranaki, Mount see Egmont, Mount, mtn., N.Z.	C4	72
Tarancón, Spain	E8	16
Taranto, Italy	I12	18
Taranto, Golfo di, b., Italy	I12	18
Tarapacá, Col.	I8	84
Tarapoto, Peru	B3	82
Taraquá, Braz.	G8	84
Tarare, Fr.	G11	14
Tarariras, Ur.	H10	80
Tarāsa Dwīp, i., India	J2	40
Tarascon, Fr.	J8	14
Tarascon, Fr.	I11	14
Tarat, Alg.	G15	62
Tarata, Bol.	G8	82
Tarata, Peru	G6	82
Tarauacá, Braz.	C6	82
Tarauacá, stm., Braz.	B6	82
Tarawa, atoll, Kir.	H21	126
Tarawera, N.Z.	C6	72
Tarazona, Spain	D10	16
Tarazona de la Mancha, Spain	F10	16
Tarbagataj, chrebet, mts., Asia	H8	28
Tarbes, Fr.	I7	14
Tarboro, N.C., U.S.	D9	112
Tarbū, Libya	C4	56
Tarcento, Italy	C8	18
Tarcoola, Austl.	F6	68
Tardajos, Spain	C8	16
Tardoki-Jani, gora, mtn., Russia	H19	28
Taree, Austl.	H10	70
Tärendö, Swe.	H18	6
Tarentum, Pa., U.S.	G7	108
Ṭarfā', Ra's aṭ-, c., Sau. Ar.	F3	47
Ṭarfā', Wādī aṭ-, val., Egypt	G1	48
Ṭarfaya, Mor.	G4	62
Targhee Pass, U.S.	F14	122
Târgovište, Bul.	F10	20
Targuist, Mor.	C8	62
Tarhjijt, Mor.	F6	62
Tarhūnah, Libya	B3	56
Tari, Pap. N. Gui.	G11	38
Táriba, Ven.	D6	84
Tarifa, Spain	I6	16
Tarifa, Punta de, c., Spain	I6	16
Tarija, Bol.	I9	82
Tarija, dept., Bol.	I9	82
Tarīm, Yemen	F6	47
Tarim, stm., China	C3	30
Tarim Pendi, China	A9	44
Taritatu, stm., Indon.	F10	38
Tarka, Niger	D13	64
Tarkastad, S. Afr.	I8	66
Tarkio, Mo., U.S.	B1	114
Tarkio, stm., U.S.	K12	118
Tarkwa, Ghana	I9	64
Tarlac, Phil.	N19	39b
Tarm, Den.	N11	6
Tarma, Peru	D4	82
Tarn, dept., Fr.	I9	14
Tärnaby, Swe.	I14	6
Tarn-et-Garonne, dept., Fr.	H8	14
Tarnobrzeg, Pol.	E21	10
Tarnów, Pol.	E21	10
Tarnowskie Góry, Pol.	E18	10
Taroom, Austl.	E8	70
Taroudant, Mor.	E6	62
Tarpon Springs, Fl., U.S.	K4	112
Tarqui, Peru	H5	84
Tarra, stm., Ven.	C6	84
Tarrafal, C.V.	k16	64a
Tarrafal, C.V.	m17	64a
Tarragona, Spain	D13	16
Tarraleah, Austl.	N7	70
Tarrant City, Al., U.S.	I10	114
Tàrrega, Spain	D13	16
Tarsus, Tur.	C3	48
Tartagal, Arg.	E9	80
Tartagal, Arg.	B7	80
Tartu, Est.	C9	22
Ṭarṭūs, Syria	D3	48
Tarumirim, Braz.	E8	79
Tarusa, Russia	G20	22
Tarutino, Ukr.	C13	20
Tarutung, Indon.	M5	40
Tarvisio, Italy	C8	18
Tarvo, stm., S.A.	F11	82
Tarzan, Tx., U.S.	G5	116
Tašauz, Turk.	I9	26
Tasejeva, stm., Russia	F16	26
Tasejevo, Russia	F16	26
Taseko, stm., B.C., Can.	F11	102
Taseko Lakes, l., B.C., Can.	F11	102
Taseko Mountain, mtn., B.C., Can.	F11	102
Tashi Gang Dzong, Bhu.	G14	44
Ṭashk, Daryācheh-ye, l., Iran	G12	48
Tashkent see Taškent, Uzb.	I11	26
Tasikmalaya, Indon.	J14	39a
Taškent, Uzb.	I11	26
Taškepri, Turk.	J10	26
Tasman Bay, b., N.Z.	D4	72
Tasmania, state, Austl.	H9	68
Tasmania, i., Austl.	N7	70
Tasman Peninsula, pen., Austl.	N7	70
Tasman Sea, Oc.	L19	126
Tăşnad, Rom.	B6	20
Tassara, Niger	C12	64
Tassialouc, Lac, l., Que., Can.	E18	96
Taštagol, Russia	G9	28
Tastiota, Mex.	C4	90
Tata, Hung.	H18	10
T'at'a, vulkan, vol., Russia	C21	36a
Tatabánya, Hung.	H18	10
Tataouine, Tun.	D16	62
Tatarbunary, Ukr.	D13	20
Tatarka, Bela.	H11	22
Tatarlar, Tur.	H10	20
Tatarsk, Russia	F7	28
Tatarskij proliv, strt., Russia	H20	28
Tatar Strait see Tatarskij proliv, strt., Russia	H20	28
Tate, Ga., U.S.	E2	112
Tate, stm., Austl.	A6	70
Tathlina Lake, l., N.W. Ter., Can.	D9	96
Tatitlek, Ak., U.S.	F21	100
Tatla Lake, B.C., Can.	F10	102
Tatla Lake, l., B.C., Can.	F10	102
Tatlayoko Lake, B.C., Can.	F10	102
Tatlayoko Lake, l., B.C., Can.	F10	102
Tatlow, Mount, mtn., B.C., Can.	F11	102
Tatnam, Cape, c., Man., Can.	E14	96
Tatrang, China	A11	44
Tatta, Pak.	H2	44
Tatuk Lake, l., B.C., Can.	D10	102
Tatum, N.M., U.S.	F3	116
Tatum, Tx., U.S.	J2	114
Tatvan, Tur.	B7	48
Taubaté, Braz.	G6	79
Tauberbischofsheim, Ger.	F9	10
Taučik, Kaz.	I8	26
Tauini, stm., Braz.	G13	84
Taulabé, Hond.	C7	92
Taumarunui, N.Z.	C5	72
Taum Sauk Mountain, mtn., Mo., U.S.	E6	114
Taunay, Braz.	I13	82
Taung, Boph.	F7	66
Taungdwingyi, Burma	D3	40
Taunggyi, Burma	D4	40
Taungup, Burma	E3	40
Taunton, Eng., U.K.	J10	8
Taunton, Ma., U.S.	F15	108
Taupo, N.Z.	C6	72
Taupo, Lake, l., N.Z.	C5	72
Tauragė, Lith.	F5	22
Tauranga, N.Z.	B6	72
Taurianova, Italy	K11	18
Tauripampa, Peru	E3	82
Taurisma, Peru	F5	82
Tauroa Point, c., N.Z.	A4	72
Taurus Mountains see Toros Dağları, mts., Tur.	H14	4
Tauste, Spain	D10	16
Tavaí, Para.	D11	80
Tavanasa, Switz.	E11	13
Tavares, Fl., U.S.	K5	112
Tavda, Russia	F11	26
Tavda, stm., Russia	F10	26
Tavernes de Valldigna, Spain	F11	16
Tavernier, Fl., U.S.	N6	112
Tavira, Port.	H4	16
Tavistock, Ont., Can.	G15	110
Tavolžan, Kaz.	G13	26
Tavor, Har (Mount Tabor), mtn., Isr.	C4	50
Tavoy see Dawei, Burma	G5	40
Tavşanlı, Tur.	J13	20
Tawakoni, Lake, res., Tx., U.S.	G10	116
Tawas City, Mi., U.S.	F12	110
Ṭawīlah, Juzur, is., Egypt	H2	48
Ṭawkar, Sud.	H9	60
Taxco de Alarcón, Mex.	H10	90
Taxisco, Guat.	C4	92
Taxkorgan, China	D2	30
Tay, stm., Yukon, Can.	E28	100
Tay, stm., Scot., U.K.	E10	8
Tayabamba, Peru	C3	82
Taylor, B.C., Can.	A14	102
Taylor, Az., U.S.	J6	120
Taylor, Ar., U.S.	I3	114
Taylor, Ne., U.S.	J8	118
Taylor, Tx., U.S.	I9	116
Taylor, Mount, mtn., N.M., U.S.	I9	120
Taylors, S.C., U.S.	E4	112
Taylorsville, In., U.S.	C11	114
Taylorsville, Ky., U.S.	D11	114
Taylorsville, Ms., U.S.	K7	114
Taylorsville, N.C., U.S.	D5	112
Taylorville, Il., U.S.	C7	114
Taymā', Sau. Ar.	H5	48
Taymouth, N.B., Can.	F7	106
Taymyr Peninsula see Tajmyr, poluostrov, pen., Russia	B12	28
Tay Ninh, Viet.	I9	40
Tayoltita, Mex.	E7	90
Tayside, prov., Scot., U.K.	E10	8
Taytay, Phil.	C6	38
Tayyārah, Sud.	K6	60
Taz, stm., Russia	D8	28
Taza, Mor.	C8	62
Tazenakht, Mor.	E7	62
Tazewell, Tn., U.S.	C3	112
Tazewell, Va., U.S.	B5	112
Tazin, stm., Can.	D10	96
Tazin Lake, l., Sask., Can.	E11	96
Tazovskaja guba, b., Russia	D7	28
Tazovskij poluostrov, pen., Russia	D13	26
Tazrouk, Alg.	I14	62
Tazumal, hist., El Sal.	D5	92
Tazungdām, Burma	F17	44
Tbessa, Alg.	C15	62
Tbilisi, Geor.	I6	26
Tchamba, Togo	G10	64
Tchaourou, Benin	G11	64
Tchefuncta, stm., La., U.S.	L6	114
Tchentlo Lake, l., B.C., Can.	B9	102
Tchériba, Burkina	E8	64
Tchesinkut Lake, l., B.C., Can.	C9	102
Tchetti, Benin	H10	64
Tchibanga, Gabon	B2	58
Tchien, Lib.	G5	54
Tchin-Tabáradene, Niger	D12	64
Tchula, Ms., U.S.	I6	114
Tczew, Pol.	A18	10
Teá, stm., Braz.	H10	84
Teaca, Rom.	C8	20
Teacapan, Mex.	F7	90
Teague, Tx., U.S.	H10	116
Te Anau, Lake, l., N.Z.	F1	72
Teano, Italy	H9	18
Teapa, Mex.	I13	90
Te Awamutu, N.Z.	C5	72
Teba, Spain	I7	16
Tebicuary, stm., Para.	D10	80
Tebicuary-Mí, stm., Para.	D10	80
Tebingtinggi, Indon.	M5	40
Tebingtinggi, Pulau, i., Indon.	N7	40
Tébourba, Tun.	M4	18
Téboursouk, Tun.	M4	18
Tecalitlán, Mex.	H8	90
Tecamachalco, Mex.	H11	90
Tecate, Mex.	A1	90
Teche, Bayou, stm., La., U.S.	L5	114
Techirghiol, Rom.	E12	20
Techlé, W. Sah.	J3	62
Tecklenburg, Ger.	C7	10
Tecomán, Mex.	H8	90
Tecopa, Ca., U.S.	I9	124
Tecpan de Galeana, Mex.	I9	90
Tecpán Guatemala, Guat.	C3	92
Tecuala, Mex.	F7	90
Tecuamburro, Volcán, vol., Guat.	C4	92
Tecuci, Rom.	D11	20
Tecumseh, Mi., U.S.	H12	110
Tecumseh, Ne., U.S.	K11	118
Tecumseh, Ok., U.S.	D10	116
Tedžen, Turk.	J10	26
Tedžen (Harīrūd), stm., Asia	C16	48
Teec Nos Pos, Az., U.S.	H7	120
Teeli, Russia	G16	26
Tees, stm., Eng., U.K.	G12	8
Teesside see Middlesbrough, Eng., U.K.	G12	8
Teeswater, Ont., Can.	F14	110
Tefé, Braz.	I10	84
Tefé, stm., Braz.	D5	76
Tefé, Lago, l., Braz.	I10	84
Tegal, Indon.	J14	39a
Tegelen, Neth.	F9	12
Tegernsee, Ger.	H11	10
Tegina, Nig.	F13	64
Tegucigalpa, Hond.	C7	92
Teguise, Spain	N27	17b
Tehachapi, Ca., U.S.	I7	124
Tehachapi Pass, Ca., U.S.	I7	124
Tehamiyam, Sud.	H9	60
Tehek Lake, l., N.W. Ter., Can.	D13	96
Téhini, I.C.	G8	64
Tehrān, Iran	D11	48
Tehrathum, Nepal	G12	44
Tehuacán, Mex.	H11	90
Tehuantepec, Golfo de, b., Mex.	J12	90
Tehuantepec, Istmo de, Mex.	I12	90
Teide, Pico de, mtn., Spain	O24	17b
Teixeira Pinto, Gui.-B.	E3	64
Teixeira Soares, Braz.	C13	80
Tejamén, Mex.	E7	90
Tejkovo, Russia	E23	22
Tejo see Tagus, stm., Eur.	F3	16
Tejupan, Punta, c., Mex.	H8	90
Tejupilco de Hidalgo, Mex.	H9	90
Tekamah, Ne., U.S.	J11	118
Tekapo, Lake, l., N.Z.	E3	72
Tekax, Mex.	G15	90
Tekeli, Kaz.	I13	26
Tekeze, stm., Afr.	F8	56
Tekirdağ, Tur.	I11	20
Tekoa, Wa., U.S.	C8	122
Tekonsha, Mi., U.S.	H11	110
Te Kuiti, N.Z.	C5	72
Tela, Hond.	B7	92
Tela, Bahía de, b., Hond.	B7	92
Télagh, Alg.	C10	62
Tel Aviv-Yafo, Isr.	D3	50
Telde, Spain	O25	17b
Telechany, Bela.	I8	22
Telefomin, Pap. N. Gui.	G11	38
Telegraph Cove, B.C., Can.	G8	102
Telegraph Creek, B.C., Can.	H29	100
Telemark, co., Nor.	L11	6
Telembí, stm., Col.	G4	84
Telén, Arg.	I6	80
Telenešty, Mol.	B12	20
Teleorman, co., Rom.	F8	20
Telertheba, Djebel, mtn., Alg.	H14	62
Telescope Peak, mtn., Ca., U.S.	H8	124
Telfs, Aus.	H11	10
Telica, stm., Hond.	C8	92
Telica, Volcán, vol., Nic.	E8	92
Telkwa, B.C., Can.	C7	102
Telkwa, stm., B.C., Can.	C7	102
Tell City, In., U.S.	E10	114
Teller, Ak., U.S.	D11	100
Tellicherry, India	G3	46
Tellico, stm., U.S.	D2	112
Tellico Plains, Tn., U.S.	D2	112
Tello, Col.	F5	84
Telluride, Co., U.S.	G9	120
Tel Megiddo (Armageddon), hist., Isr.	C4	50
Tel Mond, Isr.	D3	50
Telok Anson, Malay.	L6	40
Teloloapan, Mex.	H10	90
Telpaneca, Nic.	D8	92
Telšiai, Lith.	F5	22
Telti, Italy	I4	18
Teltow, Ger.	C13	10
Tema, Ghana	I10	64
Temagami, Lake, l., Ont., Can.	C15	110
Temax, Mex.	G15	90
Tembenči, stm., Russia	D11	28
Temblador, Ven.	C11	84
Tembleque, Spain	F8	16
Temecula, Ca., U.S.	K8	124
Temera, Mor.	D7	62
Temirtau, Kaz.	G12	26
Témiscamie, Lac, l., Que., Can.	A1	106
Témiscouata, Lac, l., Que., Can.	E5	106
Temora, Austl.	J7	70
Temosachic, Mex.	C6	90
Tempe, Az., U.S.	K5	120
Temperance, Mi., U.S.	I12	110
Tempio Pausania, Italy	I4	18
Tempisque, stm., C.R.	G9	92
Temple, Ok., U.S.	E8	116
Temple, Tx., U.S.	H9	116
Templeton, stm., Austl.	C3	70
Templin, Ger.	B13	10
Tempoal, stm., Mex.	G10	90
Tempoal de Sánchez, Mex.	G10	90
Tempy, Russia	E20	22
Temr'uk, Russia	H5	26
Temuco, Chile	J2	80
Tena, Ec.	H4	84
Tenabo, Mex.	G14	90
Tenaha, Tx., U.S.	K2	114
Tenakee Springs, Ak., U.S.	H27	100
Tenāli, India	D6	46
Tenasserim, Burma	H5	40
Tendaho, Eth.	F9	56
Tende, Col de, Eur.	H14	14
Ten Degree Channel, strt., India	J2	40
Tenente Marques, stm., Braz.	D11	82
Tenente Portela, Braz.	D12	80
Ténéré, des., Niger	E9	54
Tenerife, i., Spain	O24	17b
Ténès, Alg.	B11	62
Teng'aopu, China	B10	32
Tengchong, China	B5	40
Tenggara, Nusa (Lesser Sunda Islands), is., Indon.	G7	38
Tengiz, ozero, l., Kaz.	G11	26
Tengtian, China	H4	34
Tengtiao (Na), stm., Asia	C7	40
Tengxian, China	H5	32
Teniente Rodolfo Marsh, sci., B.A.T.	B1	73
Tenino, Wa., U.S.	D3	122
Tenkāsi, India	H4	46
Tenke, Zaire	D5	58
Tenkiller Ferry Lake, res., Ok., U.S.	D11	116
Tenkodogo, Burkina	F9	64
Ten Mile Lake, l., Newf., Can.	A17	106
Tennant Creek, Austl.	C6	68
Tennessee, state, U.S.	D9	98
Tennessee, stm., U.S.	D9	98
Tennille, Ga., U.S.	G4	112
Teno, Chile	H3	80
Teno (Tana), stm., Eur.	F20	6
Tenosique, Mex.	I14	90
Tenryū, Japan	M12	36
Tensas, stm., La., U.S.	K5	114
Tensed, Id., U.S.	C9	122
Ten Sleep, Wy., U.S.	F18	122
Tenterfield, Austl.	G10	70
Ten Thousand Islands, is., Fl., U.S.	N5	112
Teocaltiche, Mex.	G8	90
Teodelina, Arg.	H8	80
Teófilo Otoni, Braz.	D8	79
Teo Lakes, l., Sask., Can.	G5	104
Teotihuacán, hist., Mex.	H10	90
Tepalcatepec, Mex.	H8	90
Tepeaca, Mex.	H11	90
Tepehuanes, Mex.	E7	90
Tepehuanes, stm., Mex.	E7	90
Tepeji de Ocampo, Mex.	H10	90
Tepelenë, Alb.	I4	20
Tepi, Eth.	N8	60
Tepic, Mex.	G7	90
Teplice, Czech.	E13	10
Teplovo, Russia	F25	22
Tepoca, Bahía, b., Mex.	B3	90
Tepoca, Punta, c., Mex.	C3	90
Tepopa, Cabo, c., Mex.	C3	90
Téra, Niger	D10	64
Tera, stm., Spain	D6	16
Teramo, Italy	G8	18
Terang, Austl.	L5	70
Terborg, Neth.	E9	12
Terbuny, Russia	I21	22
Terceira, i., Port.	k21	62a
Tercero, stm., Arg.	G7	80
Terechovka, Bela.	I14	22
Tereida, Sud.	L6	60
Terek, stm., Russia	I7	26
Terence Bay, N.S., Can.	H10	106
Terenino, Russia	G16	22
Terenos, Braz.	F1	79
Teresina, Braz.	E10	76
Teresópolis, Braz.	G7	79
Terespol, Pol.	C23	10
Teresva, Ukr.	A7	20
Terhorne, Neth.	B8	12
Teribe, stm., N.A.	H12	92
Terlingua, Tx., U.S.	J3	116
Termas de Río Hondo, Arg.	D6	80
Termez, Uzb.	J11	26
Termini Imerese, Italy	L8	18
Términos, Laguna de, b., Mex.	H14	90
Termoli, Italy	G10	18
Ternate, Indon.	E8	38
Ternberg, Aus.	H14	10
Ternej, Russia	H19	28
Terneuzen, Neth.	F4	12
Terni, Italy	G7	18
Ternopol', Ukr.	H3	26
Ternovka, Ukr.	A13	20
Teror, Spain	O25	17b
Terpenija, mys, c., Russia	H20	28
Terpenija, zaliv, b., Russia	H20	28
Terra Alta, W.V., U.S.	H7	108
Terra Bella, Ca., U.S.	I6	124
Terrace, B.C., Can.	C6	102
Terrace Bay, Ont., Can.	B8	110
Terracina, Italy	H8	18
Terral, Ok., U.S.	F9	116
Terralba, Italy	J3	18
Terra Nova Lake, l., Newf., Can.	D19	106
Terra Nova National Park, Newf., Can.	D20	106
Terra Rica, Braz.	G2	79
Terra Roxa, Braz.	C12	80
Terra Santa, Braz.	I14	84
Terrassa, Spain	D14	16
Terrebonne Bay, b., La., U.S.	M6	114
Terre Haute, In., U.S.	C9	114
Terrell, Tx., U.S.	G10	116
Terrell Hills, Tx., U.S.	J8	116
Terrenceville, Newf., Can.	E19	106
Terror Point, c., B.C., Can.	D5	102
Terry, Ms., U.S.	J6	114
Terry, Mt., U.S.	E2	118
Terry Peak, mtn., S.D., U.S.	G4	118
Terschelling, i., Neth.	B7	12
Teruel, Col.	F5	84
Teruel, Spain	E10	16
Terzaghi Dam, B.C., Can.	G12	102
Tésa, Hung.	G18	10
Teša, Russia	F25	22
Tesalia, Col.	F5	84
Tešanj, Bos.	E2	20
Tes-Chem (Tesijn), stm., Asia	A5	30
Tescott, Ks., U.S.	L10	118
Teseney, Eth.	J9	60
Tesijn (Tes-Chem), stm., Asia	B6	30
Teslić, Bos.	E1	20
Teslin, Yukon, Can.	F28	100
Teslin, stm., Can.	F27	100
Teslin Lake, l., Can.	F28	100
Tesouras, stm., Braz.	C3	79
Tesouro, Braz.	D2	79
Tessala, Monts du, mts., Alg.	J11	16
Tessalit, Mali	A10	64
Tessaoua, Niger	E13	64
Tessenderlo, Bel.	F7	12
Tessy-sur-Vire, Fr.	D5	14
Testour, Tun.	M4	18
Tesuque, N.M., U.S.	I11	120
Tetachuck Lake, l., B.C., Can.	D9	102
Tetagouche, stm., N.B., Can.	E8	106
Tete, Moz.	E6	58
Tête-à-la-Baleine, Que., Can.	B14	106
Tête-Jaune-Cache, B.C., Can.	E15	102
Tétépisca, Lac, l., Que., Can.	A4	106
Teterow, Ger.	B12	10
Tetlin, Ak., U.S.	E23	100
Tetlin Lake, l., Ak., U.S.	E23	100
Teton, Id., U.S.	G14	122
Teton, stm., Mt., U.S.	C14	122
Tetonia, Id., U.S.	G14	122
Teton Range, mts., Wy., U.S.	G15	122

Name — Map Ref. — Page

Têtouan, Mor. C8 62
Tetovo, Mac. G4 20
Teuco, stm., Arg. C8 80
Teulada, Italy K3 18
Teulada, Capo, c., Italy K3 18
Teúl de González Ortega, Mex. G8 90
Teulon, Man., Can. H17 104
Teutopolis, Il., U.S. C8 114
Teuva, Fin. J17 6
Tevere (Tiber), stm., Italy G7 18
Teverya (Tiberias), Isr. C5 50
Tevli, Bela. I7 22
Texada Island, i., B.C., Can. H10 102
Texarkana, Ar., U.S. I2 114
Texarkana, Tx., U.S. I2 114
Texas, Austl. G9 70
Texas, state, U.S. E7 98
Texas City, Tx., U.S. J12 116
Texel, i., Neth. B6 12
Texhoma, Ok., U.S. C5 116
Texico, N.M., U.S. E3 116
Texline, Tx., U.S. C3 116
Texoma, Lake, res., U.S. F10 116
Teyateyaneng, Leso. G8 66
Teywarah, Afg. D1 44
Teziutlán, Mex. H11 90
Tezpur, India G15 44
Tezzeron Lake, l., B.C., Can. C10 102
Tha-anne, stm., N.W. Ter., Can. D13 96
Thabana-Ntlenyana, mtn., Leso. G9 66
Thabazimbi, S. Afr. E8 66
Thai Binh, Viet. D9 40
Thailand (Prathet Thai), ctry., Asia B3 38
Thailand, Gulf of, b., Asia I6 40
Thai Nguyen, Viet. D8 40
Thal, Pak. D4 44
Thala, Tun. N3 18
Thale, Ger. D11 10
Thalfang, Ger. F6 10
Thalia, Tx., U.S. F7 116
Thalwil, Switz. D10 13
Thamar, Jabal, mtn., Yemen H4 47
Thames, N.Z. B5 72
Thames, stm., Eng., U.K. J12 8
Thamesford, Ont., Can. G14 110
Thamesville, Ont., Can. H14 110
Thāna, India C2 46
Thanbyuzayat, Burma G4 40
Thang Binh, Viet. G10 40
Thanh Hoa, Viet. E8 40
Thanh Pho Ho Chi Minh (Saigon), Viet. I9 40
Thanjāvūr, India G5 46
Thann, Fr. E14 14
Thar Desert (Great Indian Desert), des., Asia F4 44
Thargomindah, Austl. G5 70
Thar Nhom, Sud. N6 60
Tharrawaddy, Burma F3 40
Thásos, i., Grc. I8 20
Thatcher, Az., U.S. L7 120
Thaton, Burma F4 40
Thaungdut, Burma B3 40
Thaungyin, stm., Asia F5 40
Thaya (Dyje), stm., Eur. G15 10
Thayer, Ks., U.S. N12 118
Thayer, Mo., U.S. F5 114
Thayetmyo, Burma E3 40
Thazi, Burma D4 40
Thealka, Ky., U.S. B4 112
Thebes, Il., U.S. E7 114
Thebes, hist., Egypt E7 60
Thebes see Thívai, Grc. K7 20
The Coteau, hills, Sask., Can. G7 104
The Dalles, Or., U.S. E4 122
Thedford, Ne., U.S. J7 118
The English Companys Islands, is., Austl. B7 68
The Everglades, sw., Fl., U.S. M6 112
The Fens, reg., Eng., U.K. I14 8
The Fishing Lakes, l., Sask., Can. H11 104
The Flat Tops, mts., Co., U.S. D9 120
The Hague see 's-Gravenhage, Neth. E5 12
The Key Indian Reserve, Sask., Can. G12 104
The Little Minch, strt., Scot., U.K. D7 8
Thelon, stm., N.W. Ter., Can. D12 96
The Lynd, Austl. B6 70
The Minch, strt., Scot., U.K. C8 8
Thenia, Alg. B12 62
Theniet el Hadd, Alg. C12 62
Theodore, Austl. E9 70
Theodore, Sask., Can. G12 104
Theodore, Al., U.S. L8 114
Theodore Roosevelt Lake, res., Az., U.S. K5 120
Theólogos, Grc. I8 20
The Pas, Man., Can. E13 104
The Rajah, mtn., Alta., Can. D16 102
The Rand see Witwatersrant, reg., S. Afr. E8 66
Theresa, N.Y., U.S. C11 108
Thermaïkós Kólpos, b., Grc. I6 20
Thermopilai, hist., Grc. K6 20
Thermopolis, Wy., U.S. A8 120
Thermopylae see Thermopílai, hist., Grc. K6 20
The Rock, Austl. J7 70
Thesiger Bay, b., N.W. Ter., Can. B8 96
The Sound, strt., Eur. N13 6
Thessalía, hist. reg., Grc. J6 20
Thessalon, Ont., Can. D12 110
Thessaloníki (Salonika), Grc. I6 20
Thetford-Mines, Que., Can. A15 108
The Valley, Anguilla E13 94
The Wash, b., Eng., U.K. I14 8
Thibaudeau, Man., Can. A20 104
Thibodaux, La., U.S. M6 114
Thicket Portage, Man., Can. C17 104
Thief, stm., Mn., U.S. C11 118
Thief River Falls, Mn., U.S. C11 118
Thielsen, Mount, mtn., Or., U.S. G3 122
Thiene, Italy D6 18
Thiers, Fr. G10 14
Thiès, Sen. D1 64
Thiesi, Italy I3 18
Thika, Kenya B7 58
Thimphu, Bhu. G13 44
Thingvellir, Ice. B3 6a
Thingvellir National Park, Ice. B3 6a
Thionville, Fr. C13 14
Thíra, i., Grc. M9 20
Thiruvārūr, India G5 46
Thistle Island, i., Austl. J2 70
Thívai (Thebes), Grc. K7 20
Thlewiaza, stm., N.W. Ter., Can. D13 96
Thoa, stm., N.W. Ter., Can. D11 96
Thohoyandou, Venda D10 66
Thoi Binh, Viet. J8 40
Thomas, Ok., U.S. D8 116

Thomas, W.V., U.S. H7 108
Thomasboro, Il., U.S. B8 114
Thomas Lake, l., Man., Can. A18 104
Thomaston, Al., U.S. J9 114
Thomaston, Ct., U.S. F13 108
Thomaston, Ga., U.S. G2 112
Thomaston, Me., U.S. C17 108
Thomasville, Al., U.S. K9 114
Thomasville, Ga., U.S. I3 112
Thomasville, N.C., U.S. D6 112
Thom Lake, l., Man., Can. C18 104
Thomlinson, Mount, mtn., B.C., Can. B7 102
Thompson, Man., Can. C17 104
Thompson, Ia., U.S. G2 110
Thompson, stm., B.C., Can. G13 102
Thompson, stm., U.S. C3 114
Thompson Falls, Mt., U.S. C10 122
Thompson Pass, Ak., U.S. F22 100
Thompsonville, Mi., U.S. F10 110
Thomsen, stm., N.W. Ter., Can. B9 96
Thomson, Ga., U.S. F4 112
Thomson, Il., U.S. I5 110
Thomson, stm., Austl. E5 70
Thomson Lake, res., Sask., Can. I8 104
Thon Buri, Thai. H6 40
Thongwa, Burma F4 40
Thonon-les-Bains, Fr. F13 14
Thonotosassa, Fl., U.S. K4 112
Thonze, Burma F3 40
Thorburn, N.S., Can. G11 106
Thoreau, N.M., U.S. I8 120
Thorhild, Alta., Can. C21 102
Thorial, Sud. M5 60
Thornapple, stm., Wi., U.S. E4 110
Thornbury, Ont., Can. F15 110
Thorndale, Tx., U.S. I9 116
Thorne, stm., Ont., Can. D23 104
Thornton, Ar., U.S. I4 114
Thornton, Co., U.S. E12 120
Thornton, Tx., U.S. H10 116
Thorntonville, Tx., U.S. H4 116
Thorp, Wi., U.S. F5 110
Thorsby, Alta., Can. D20 102
Thorsby, Al., U.S. J10 114
Thorsteinson Lake, l., Man., Can. A17 104
Thouars, Fr. F6 14
Thousand Lake Mountain, mtn., Ut., U.S. F5 120
Thousand Oaks, Ca., U.S. J7 124
Thrace, hist. reg., Eur. H10 20
Thrakikón Pélagos, Grc. I8 20
Three Fingered Jack, mtn., Or., U.S. F4 122
Three Forks, Mt., U.S. E14 122
Three Hills, Alta., Can. F21 102
Three Hummock Island, i., Austl. M6 70
Three Lakes, Wi., U.S. E6 110
Three Mile Plains, N.S., Can. H9 106
Three Oaks, Mi., U.S. I9 110
Three Pagodas Pass, Asia G5 40
Threepoint Lake, l., Man., Can. C16 104
Three Rivers, Mi., U.S. I10 110
Three Rivers, Tx., U.S. K8 116
Three Sisters, S. Afr. H6 66
Three Sisters, mtn., Or., U.S. F4 122
Three Springs, Austl. E3 68
Throat, stm., Ont., Can. G21 104
Throckmorton, Tx., U.S. F7 116
Thu Dau Mot, Viet. I9 40
Thule, Grnld. B13 86
Thun, Switz. E8 13
Thunder Bay, Ont., Can. B6 110
Thunder Bay, b., Ont., Can. B6 110
Thunder Bay, b., Mi., U.S. F12 110
Thunder Bay, stm., Mi., U.S. E12 110
Thunderbolt, Ga., U.S. G5 112
Thunder Creek, stm., Sask., Can. H8 104
Thunder Hills, hills, Sask., Can. D8 104
Thunersee, l., Switz. E8 13
Thung Song, Thai. J5 40
Thur, stm., Switz. C10 13
Thurgau, state, Switz. C11 13
Thüringen, state, Ger. D11 10
Thüringer Wald, mts., Ger. E10 10
Thurmont, Md., U.S. H9 108
Thursday Island, Austl. B8 68
Thurso, Scot., U.K. C10 8
Thurston Island, i., Ant. C11 73
Thusis, Switz. E11 13
Thwaites Iceberg Tongue, Ant. C11 73
Thyolo, Mwi. E7 58
Tia Juana, Ven. B7 84
Tianchang, China C8 34
Tiandong, China C9 40
Tianfanjie, China F5 34
Tianjiazhen, China F4 34
Tianjin (Tientsin), China D5 32
Tianjin Shi, China D10 30
Tianjun, China D6 30
Tianlin, China B9 40
Tianmen, China E2 34
Tianshui, China E8 30
Tiantai, China F10 34
Tiantou, China I4 34
Tianxiyang, China I7 34
Tianzhu, China D7 30
Tianzhuang, China J2 34
Tibagi, Braz. C13 80
Tibaji, stm., Braz. B13 80
Tibasti, Sarīr, des., Libya D4 56
Tibbie, Al., U.S. K8 114
Tibe, Eth. M9 60
Tiber see Tevere, stm., Italy G7 18
Tibesti, mts., Chad D4 56
Tibet see Xizang Zizhiqu, prov., China E3 30
Tibiri, Niger E13 64
Tiburón, Cabo, c. C4 84
Tiburón, Isla, i., Mex. C3 90
Tiča, jazovir, res., Bul. F10 20
Tice, Fl., U.S. M5 112
Tichît, Maur. B5 64
Tichmenevo, Russia C21 22
Tichoreck, Russia H6 26
Tichvin, Russia B16 22
Ticino, state, Switz. F10 13
Ticino, stm., Eur. D3 18
Tickfaw, La., U.S. L6 114
Tickfaw, stm., U.S. L6 114
Ticonderoga, N.Y., U.S. D13 108
Ticul, Mex. G15 90
Tide Lake, l., Alta., Can. H3 104
Tidikelt, pl., Alg. G11 62
Tidioute, Pa., U.S. F7 108
Tidjikja, Maur. B4 64
Tidore, Indon. E8 38
Tiekou, China F9 32
Tieli, China B12 30
Tieling, China A11 32
Tielt, Bel. F3 12
Tielutou, China H4 34
Tiémé, I.C. G6 64
T'ienchung, Tai. L9 34
Tien Shan, mts., Asia C3 30

Tientsin see Tianjin, China D5 32
Tie Plant, Ms., U.S. I7 114
Tierra Amarilla, Chile D3 80
Tierra Amarilla, N.M., U.S. H10 120
Tierra Blanca, Mex. H11 90
Tierra del Fuego, Isla Grande de, i., S.A. G3 78
Tierralta, Col. C4 84
Tieshanguan, China L2 34
Tietê, Braz. G5 79
Tietê, stm., Braz. F3 79
Tif, Alg. G11 62
Tiffany Mountain, mtn., Wa., U.S. B6 122
Tiffin, Oh., U.S. F3 108
Tifton, Ga., U.S. H3 112
Tiftona, Tn., U.S. D1 112
Tighennif, Alg. C11 62
Tigil', Russia F23 28
Tiglid, Mor. F5 62
Tignall, Ga., U.S. F4 112
Tignish, P.E.I., Can. F9 106
Tigre, Col. F8 84
Tigre, stm., Peru J5 84
Tigre, stm., Ven. C11 84
Tigre, Cerro, mtn., C.R. I11 92
Tigris (Dicle) (Dijlah), stm., Asia F9 48
Tiguabos, Cuba D7 94
Tiguentourine, Alg. G15 62
Tihāmah, pl., Asia H4 48
Tihert, Alg. C11 62
Tihuatlán, Mex. G11 90
Tijamuchi, stm., Bol. F9 82
Tijesno, Cro. F10 18
Tijuana, Mex. A1 90
Tijucas do Sul, Braz. C14 80
Tijucas, Braz. D14 80
Tijuco, stm., Braz. E4 79
Tikal, hist., Guat. I15 90
Tiko, Cam. I14 64
Tikrīt, Iraq D7 48
Tikša, Russia I23 6
Tikšeozero, ozero, l., Russia H22 6
Tilarán, C.R. G10 92
Tilbalakan, Laguna, b., Hond. B10 92
Tilburg, Neth. E7 12
Tilbury, Ont., Can. H13 110
Tilcara, Arg. B6 80
Tilden, Il., U.S. D7 114
Tilden, Ne., U.S. I10 118
Tilden, Tx., U.S. K8 116
Tilemsès, Niger D12 64
Tilemsi, Vallée du, val., Mali B10 64
Tilhar, India G8 44
Tilimsen, Alg. C10 62
Tilisarao, Arg. G6 80
Tillaberi, Niger D10 64
Tillamook, Or., U.S. E2 122
Tillanchāng Dwīp, i., India J2 40
Tilley, Alta., Can. G23 102
Tillia, Niger C11 64
Tillmans Corner, Al., U.S. L8 114
Tillson, N.Y., U.S. F12 108
Tillsonburg, Ont., Can. H15 110
Tilpa, Austl. H6 70
Tilrhemt, Alg. D12 62
Tilton, Il., U.S. B9 114
Tilton, N.H., U.S. D15 108
Tiltonsville, Oh., U.S. G6 108
Timā, Egypt D6 60
Timaná, Col. G5 84
Timane, stm., Para. I12 82
Timanskij kr'až, mtn., Russia D7 26
Timaru, N.Z. F3 72
Timbedgha, Maur. C5 64
Timber Lake, S.D., U.S. F6 118
Timbío, Col. F4 84
Timbó, Braz. D14 80
Timbo, Lib. I5 64
Timboon, Austl. L5 70
Timbuktu see Tombouctou, Mali C8 64
Timétrine, Mali B9 64
Timeu Creek, stm., Alta., Can. C20 102
Timgad, hist., Alg. C14 62
Timimoun, Alg. F11 62
Timinar, Sud. H6 60
Timir'azevskij, Russia F14 26
Timirist, Râs, c., Maur. B1 64
Timiș, co., Rom. D5 20
Timiș (Tamiš), stm., Eur. D5 20
Timișoara, Rom. D5 20
Timmendorfer Strand, Ger. A10 10
Timmins, Ont., Can. B14 110
Timmonsville, S.C., U.S. E7 112
Timms Hill, hill, Wi., U.S. E5 110
Timor, i., Indon. G8 38
Timor Sea J16 126
Timotes, Ven. C7 84
Timoudi, Alg. F10 62
Timpson, Tx., U.S. K2 114
Tims Ford Lake, res., Tn., U.S. G10 114
Tinaca Point, c., Phil. D8 38
Tinaco, Ven. C8 84
Tinah, Khalīj aț-, b., Egypt F2 48
Tinaja, Punta, c., Peru G5 82
Ti-n-Amzi, val., Afr. B12 64
Tinaquillo, Ven. C8 84
Tindivanam, India F5 46
Tindouf, Alg. G6 62
Tindouf, Hamada de, reg., Afr. F6 62
Tindouf, Sebkha de, pl., Alg. G7 62
Tineo, Spain B5 16
Tinga, mtn., Afr. M2 60
Tingha, Austl. G9 70
Tinghert, Hamādat (Plateau du Tinghert), plat., Afr. F15 62
Tinghert, Plateau du (Hamādat Tinghert), plat., Afr. F15 62
Tingo de Saposoa, Peru B3 82
Tingo María, Peru C3 82
Tingri, China F12 44
Tingsiqiao, China F3 34
Tingvoll, Nor. J11 6
Tinharé, Ilha de, i., Braz. B9 79
Tinh Bien, Viet. I8 40
Tinkisso, stm., Gui. F5 64
Tinniswood, Mount, mtn., B.C., Can. G11 102
Tinnoset, Nor. L11 6
Tinogasta, Arg. E5 80
Tínos, Grc. L9 20
Tínos, i., Grc. L9 20
Tinquipaya, Bol. H9 82
Tinrhir, Mor. E8 62
Tinsley, Ms., U.S. J6 114
Tinsukia, India G16 44
Tintagel, B.C., Can. C9 102
Tintere, Cerro, mtn., S.A. J8 82
Tintina, Arg. D7 80
Ti-n-Zaouatene, Alg. B11 64
Tio, Eth. G2 47
Tioga, N.D., U.S. C5 118
Tioga, Pa., U.S. F9 108
Tioga, stm., U.S. F9 108
Tiojala, Fin. K18 6
Tioman, Pulau, i., Malay. M8 40
Tionesta, Pa., U.S. F7 108

Tionesta Creek, stm., Pa., U.S. F7 108
Tior, Sud. N6 60
Tioro, Selat, strt., Indon. F7 38
Tioughnioga, stm., N.Y., U.S. E10 108
Tipitapa, Nic. E8 92
Tippecanoe, stm., In., U.S. A10 114
Tipperary, Ire. I5 8
Tipperary, co., Ire. I5 8
Tipton, Ca., U.S. H6 124
Tipton, In., U.S. B10 114
Tipton, Ia., U.S. I4 110
Tipton, Mo., U.S. D4 114
Tipton, Ok., U.S. E7 116
Tiptonville, Tn., U.S. F7 114
Tip Top Mountain, mtn., Ont., Can. B10 110
Tiputini, stm., Ec. H4 84
Tīra, Isr. D3 50
Tiradentes, Braz. F6 79
Tīrān, i., Sau. Ar. H3 48
Tīrān, Maḍīq, strt. D8 60
Tiran, Strait of see Tīrān, Maḍīq, strt. D8 60
Tiranë, Alb. H3 20
Tirano, Italy C5 18
Tiraque, Bol. G9 82
Tiraspol', Mol. H3 26
Tirat Karmel, Isr. C3 50
Tirat Ẓevi, Isr. D5 50
Tîrgoviște, Rom. E9 20
Tîrgu Bujor, Rom. D11 20
Tîrgu-Cărbunești, Rom. E7 20
Tîrgu Jiu, Rom. D7 20
Tîrgu Mureș, Rom. C8 20
Tîrgu-Neamț, Rom. B10 20
Tîrgu Ocna, Rom. C10 20
Tîrgusor, Rom. E12 20
Tirich Mīr, mtn., Pak. B4 44
Tirilye, Tur. I12 20
Tiriro, Gui. F5 64
Tîrnăveni, Rom. C8 20
Tírnavos, Grc. J6 20
Tirol, state, Aus. H10 10
Tiros, Braz. E6 79
Tiroungoulou, Cen. Afr. Rep. M2 60
Tirschenreuth, Ger. F12 10
Tiruchchirāppalli, India G5 46
Tiruchengodu, India G4 46
Tiruliai, Lith. F6 22
Tirunelveli, India H4 46
Tirupati, India F5 46
Tiruppattūr, India F5 46
Tiruppur, India G4 46
Tiruvannāmalai, India F5 46
Tiruvottiyūr, India F6 46
Tisa (Tisza), stm., Eur. C4 20
Tisdale, Sask., Can. F10 104
Tishomingo, Ms., U.S. H8 114
Tishomingo, Ok., U.S. E10 116
Tisisat Falls, wtfl, Eth. L9 60
Tīsīyah, Syria D6 50
Tiskilwa, Il., U.S. I6 110
Tisma, Nic. E8 92
Tissemsilt, Alg. C11 62
Tīsta, stm., Asia G13 44
Tisza (Tisa), stm., Eur. C4 20
Tiszaföldvár, Hung. I20 10
Tiszafüred, Hung. H20 10
Tiszavasvári, Hung. H21 10
Tit, Alg. I13 62
Titaf, Alg. G10 62
Titicaca, Lago, l., S.A. F7 82
Titograd, Yugo. G3 20
Titonka, Ia., U.S. G11 110
Titova Mitrovica, Yugo. G4 20
Titovo Užice, Yugo. F3 20
Titov Veles, Mac. H5 20
Titov vrh, mtn., Mac. G4 20
Titran, Nor. J11 6
Tittabawassee, stm., Mi., U.S. G11 110
Tittmoning, Ger. G12 10
Titule, Zaire H6 56
Titusville, Fl., U.S. K6 112
Titusville, Pa., U.S. F7 108
Tivoli, Italy H7 18
Tivoli, Tx., U.S. K10 116
Tiwāl, Wādī, val., Afr. L2 60
Tizimín, Mex. G15 90
Tizi-Ouzou, Alg. B13 62
Tiznados, stm., Ven. C9 84
Tiznit, Mor. F6 62
Tjolotjo, Zimb. B8 66
Tlacotalpan, Mex. H12 90
Tlacotepec, Mex. I10 90
Tlahualilo de Zaragoza, Mex. D8 90
Tlalixtaquilla, Mex. I10 90
Tlalnepantla, Mex. H10 90
Tlaltenango de Sánchez Román, Mex. G8 90
Tlapaneco, stm., Mex. I10 90
Tlapeng, Bots. D5 66
Tlaquepaque, Mex. G8 90
Tlaxcala [de Xicoténcatl], Mex. H10 90
Tłuszcz, Pol. C21 10
Toabré, stm., Pan. I14 92
Toachi, stm., Ec. H3 84
Toahayaná, Mex. D6 90
Toamasina, Madag. Q23 67b
Toano, Va., U.S. B10 112
Toast, N.C., U.S. C6 112
Toay, Arg. I6 80
Toba, Japan M11 36
Toba, Mali F6 64
Toba, stm., B.C., Can. G10 102
Toba, Danau, l., Indon. M5 40
Tobacco, stm., Mi., U.S. G11 110
Tobacco Plains Indian Reserve, B.C., Can. H19 102
Tobago, i., Trin. I14 94
Toba Inlet, b., B.C., Can. G10 102
Toba Kākar Range, mts., Pak. E3 44
Tobas, Arg. E7 80
Toba Tek Singh, Pak. E5 44
Tobejuba, Isla, i., Ven. C12 84
Tobelo, Indon. E8 38
Tobercurry, Ire. G5 8
Tobermory, Austl. F5 70
Tobermory, Ont., Can. E14 110
Tobermory, Scot., U.K. E8 8
Tobias, Ne., U.S. K10 118
Tobin Lake, l., Sask., Can. E11 104
Tobique, stm., N.B., Can. E6 106
Tobol, Kaz. G10 26
Tobol, stm., Asia F11 26
Tobol'sk, Russia F11 26
Tobré, Benin F11 64
Tobruk see Tubruq, Libya A2 60
Tobyhanna, Pa., U.S. F11 108
Tocantinía, Braz. E9 76
Tocantinópolis, Braz. E9 76
Tocantins, stm., Braz. D9 76
Tocantins, stm., Braz. A13 82
Tocantinzinho, stm., Braz. C4 79
Toccoa, Ga., U.S. E3 112
Toccoa (Ocoee), stm., U.S. E2 112
Tochcha Lake, l., B.C., Can. C9 102
Tochigi, Japan K14 36
Tochtamyš, Taj. B6 44
Toco, Chile B4 80
Tocoa, Hond. B8 92

Toconao, Chile B4 80
Tocopilla, Chile B3 80
Tocuco, stm., Ven. C6 84
Tocumwal, Austl. J6 70
Tocuyo, stm., Ven. B8 84
Tocuyo de la Costa, Ven. B8 84
Todi, Italy G7 18
Todos Santos, Bol. G9 82
Todos Santos, Mex. F4 90
Todos Santos, Bahía, b., Mex. B1 90
Todtnau, Ger. H7 10
T'oejo, N. Kor. D15 32
Tofield, Alta., Can. D22 102
Tofino, B.C., Can. H9 102
Togiak, Ak., U.S. G14 100
Togian, Kepulauan, is., Indon. F7 38
Togo, ctry., Afr. G7 54
Togučin, Russia F14 26
Togwotee Pass, Wy., U.S. G15 122
Tohnya, Sud. N5 60
Toiyabe Range, mts., Nv., U.S. E8 124
Tokanui, N.Z. G2 72
Tokara-rettō, is., Japan R4 37b
Tokar'ovka, Russia J24 22
Tokat, Tur. A4 48
Tokelau, dep., Oc. G1 2
Tokmak, Kyrg. I13 26
Toko Range, mts., Austl. D3 70
Tokoroa, N.Z. C5 72
Toksook Bay, Ak., U.S. F12 100
Toksovo, Russia A13 22
Tokuno-shima, i., Japan T3 37b
Tokushima, Japan M9 36
Tokuyama, Japan M6 36
Tōkyō, Japan L14 36
Tokyo Bay see Tōkyō-wan, b., Japan L14 36
Tōkyō-wan, b., Japan L14 36
Tokzār, Afg. C2 44
Tolé, Pan. I13 92
Toledo, Bol. H8 82
Toledo, Braz. C12 80
Toledo, Col. D6 84
Toledo, Spain F7 16
Toledo, Il., U.S. C8 114
Toledo, Ia., U.S. I3 110
Toledo, Oh., U.S. F3 108
Toledo, Or., U.S. F2 122
Toledo Bend Reservoir, res., U.S. K3 114
Tolentino, Italy F8 18
Tolga, Alg. C13 62
Toliara, Madag. S20 67b
Tolima, dept., Col. F5 84
Tolima, Nevado del, mtn., Col. E5 84
Toljatti, Russia G7 26
Tolleson, Az., U.S. K4 120
Tolloche, Arg. C7 80
Tolmačovo, Russia C12 22
Tolmezzo, Italy C8 18
Tolna, Hung. I18 10
Tolna, co., Hung. I18 10
Tolo, Teluk, b., Indon. F7 38
Toločin, Bela. G12 22
Tolongoina, Madag. R22 67b
Tolono, Il., U.S. C8 114
Tolosa, Spain B9 16
Tolstoj, mys, c., Russia F23 28
Toltén, Chile D2 78
Tolú, Col. C5 84
Toluca, Il., U.S. I6 110
Toluca, Nevado de, vol., Mex. H10 90
Toluca [de Lerdo], Mex. H10 90
Tolwa, Sud. N7 60
Tom', stm., Russia F8 28
Tomah, Wi., U.S. G5 110
Tomahawk, Wi., U.S. E6 110
Tomakomai, Japan E16 36a
Tomar, Port. F3 16
Tomás Barrón (Eucaliptus), Bol. G8 82
Tomás Gomensoro, Ur. F10 80
Tomašpol', Ukr. A12 20
Tomaszów Lubelski, Pol. E23 10
Tomaszów Mazowiecki, Pol. D20 10
Tomatlán, Mex. H7 90
Tomave, Bol. I8 82
Tomazina, Braz. G4 79
Tombador, Serra do, plat., Braz. D13 82
Tomball, Tx., U.S. I11 116
Tombe, Sud. O6 60
Tombigbee, stm., U.S. K8 114
Tombos, Braz. F7 79
Tombouctou (Timbuktu), Mali C8 64
Tombstone, Az., U.S. M6 120
Tombstone Mountain, mtn., Yukon, Can. D25 100
Tombua, Ang. E2 58
Tom Burke, S. Afr. D9 66
Tomé, Chile I2 80
Tomelloso, Spain F8 16
Tomini, Teluk, b., Indon. F7 38
Tominian, Mali E7 64
Tommot, Russia F17 28
Tomo, stm., Col. E8 84
Tompkins, Newf., Can. E14 106
Tompkins, Sask., Can. H6 104
Tompkinsville, Ky., U.S. F11 114
Tom Price, Austl. D3 68
Tomra, Nor. J10 6
Toms, stm., N.J., U.S. G12 108
Tomsk, Russia F8 28
Toms River, N.J., U.S. H12 108
Tonalá, Mex. I13 90
Tonantins, Braz. I9 84
Tonantins, stm., Braz. I8 84
Tonasket, Wa., U.S. B6 122
Tonawanda, N.Y., U.S. E8 108
Tonbridge, Eng., U.K. J14 8
Tondano, Indon. E7 38
Tønder, Den. N11 6
Tondoro, Nmb. A4 66
Tonekābon, Iran C11 48
Tonga, Sud. M6 60
Tonga, ctry., Oc. H1 2
Tongaat, S. Afr. G10 66
Tonganoxie, Ks., U.S. L12 118
Tongcheng, China D5 34
Tongchengzha, China D7 34
Tongchuan, China D8 30
Tonggou, China B13 32
Tongguan, China E9 30
Tongguan, China G1 34
Tonghai, China B7 40
Tonghe, China C1 34
Tonghua, China B13 32
Tongjosŏn-man, b., N. Kor. D16 32
Tongli, China C11 30
Tongling, China E6 34
Tongmu, China E3 34
Tongnae, S. Kor. H17 32
Tongo, Austl. H5 70
Tongobory, Madag. S21 67b
Tongoy, Chile F3 80
Tongren, China F8 30
Tongsa Dzong, Bhu. G14 44
Tongshi, China H5 32
Tongtai, China C9 34

Tongtian, stm., China D17 44
Tongtianheyan, China E5 30
Tongue, Scot., U.K. C9 8
Tongue, stm., U.S. E19 122
Tongue, stm., N.D., U.S. C10 118
Tongue, stm., Tx., U.S. F6 116
Tongxian, China D4 32
Tongyu, China C11 30
Tongzhaipu, China C1 34
Tongzi, China F8 30
Tonica, Il., U.S. I6 110
Tonj, Sud. N5 60
Tonk, India G6 44
Tonkawa, Ok., U.S. C9 116
Tonkin, Gulf of, b., Asia D10 40
Tônlé Sab, Bœng, l., Camb. H8 40
Tonle Sap see Tônlé Sab, Bœng, l., Camb. H8 40
Tonneins, Fr. H7 14
Tonnerre, Fr. E10 14
Tönning, Ger. A8 10
Tōno, Japan H16 36
Tonopah, Nv., U.S. F8 124
Tonosí, Pan. D2 84
Tonota, Bots. C8 66
Tønsberg, Nor. L12 6
Toobeah, Austl. G8 70
Tooele, Ut., U.S. D4 120
Toompine, Austl. F6 70
Toomsboro, Ga., U.S. G3 112
Toosey Indian Reserve, B.C., Can. F12 102
Tootsi, Est. C7 22
Toowoomba, Austl. F9 70
Topawa, Az., U.S. M5 120
Topeka, Ks., U.S. L12 118
Topia, Mex. E6 90
Topki, Russia F9 28
Topko, gora, mtn., Russia F19 28
Topley, B.C., Can. C8 102
Toplița, Rom. C9 20
T'oploje, Russia H20 22
Topol'čany, Czech. G18 10
Topolobampo, Mex. E5 90
Topolog, Rom. E12 20
Topozero, ozero, l., Russia I22 6
Toppenish, Wa., U.S. D5 122
Topsham, Me., U.S. D17 108
Tor, Eth. N7 60
Toraya, Peru F5 82
Torbat-e Heydarīyeh, Iran D15 48
Torbat-e Jām, Iran D16 48
Torbay, Newf., Can. E21 106
Torbay see Torquay, Eng., U.K. K10 8
Torbejevo, Russia G26 22
Torbino, Russia C15 22
Torbrook, N.S., Can. H9 106
Torch, stm., Sask., Can. E11 104
Torch Lake, l., Mi., U.S. E10 110
Tordesillas, Spain D6 16
Töre, Swe. I18 6
Torez, Ukr. H5 26
Torgau, Ger. D13 10
Torino (Turin), Italy D2 18
Toriparu, Braz. D2 79
Torit, Sud. H7 56
Tormentine, Cape, c., N.B., Can. F10 106
Tornado Mountain, mtn., Can. H20 102
Torneälven (Tornionjoki), stm., Eur. H18 6
Torngat Mountains, mts., Can. E20 96
Tornillo, Tx., U.S. M10 120
Tornio, Fin. I19 6
Tornionjoki (Torneälven), stm., Eur. H19 6
Tornquist, Arg. J7 80
Toro, Spain D6 16
Toro, Cerro, mtn., Mex. H7 90
Torodi, Niger E10 64
Törökszentmiklós, Hung. H20 10
Torola, stm., N.A. D6 92
Toroni, Nevado, mtn., S.A. H7 82
Toronto, Ont., Can. G16 110
Toronto, Ks., U.S. N12 118
Toronto, Oh., U.S. G6 108
Toronto, S.D., U.S. G11 118
Toropec, Russia E14 22
Tororo, Ug. A6 58
Toroșlar, mts., Tur. H14 4
Torošino, Russia D11 22
Torotoro, Bol. H9 82
Torpy, stm., B.C., Can. D14 102
Torquay, Sask., Can. I11 104
Torquay, Eng., U.K. K10 8
Torrance, Ca., U.S. K7 124
Torrance Lake, l., Man., Can. A16 104
Torre del Campo, Spain H8 16
Torredonjimeno, Spain H8 16
Torrejón de Ardoz, Spain E8 16
Torrelavega, Spain B7 16
Torremaggiore, Italy H10 18
Torremolinos, Spain I7 16
Torrens, Lake, l., Austl. H2 70
Torrens Creek, Austl. C6 70
Torrent, Arg. E10 80
Torrent, Spain F11 16
Torreón, Mex. E8 90
Torreperogil, Spain G8 16
Torres, Braz. E14 80
Torres de Alcalá, Mor. J7 16
Torres Strait, strt., Oc. B8 68
Torrevella, Spain H11 16
Torridon, Scot., U.K. D8 8
Torriglia, Italy E4 18
Torrijos, Spain F7 16
Torrington, Ct., U.S. F13 108
Torrington, Wy., U.S. I3 118
Torrinha, Braz. G4 79
Torrox, Spain I8 16
Tors Cove, Newf., Can. E21 106
Tórshavn, Faer. Is. D8 6b
Tortola, i., Br. Vir. Is. E12 94
Tórtolas, Cerro de las, mtn., S.A. E4 80
Tortoli, Italy J4 18
Tortona, Italy E3 18
Tortosa, Spain E12 16
Tortue, stm., Que., Can. B8 106
Tortue, Île de la, i., Haiti D8 94
Tortuguero, stm., C.R. G11 92
Tortuguero, Parque Nacional, C.R. G11 92
Toruń, Pol. B18 10
Torunos, Ven. C7 84
Torup, Swe. M13 6
Tõrva, Est. C8 22
Toržok, Russia E17 22
T'osan, N. Kor. E14 32
Tosa-shimizu, Japan O7 36
Tosa-wan, b., Japan N8 36
Toscana (Tuscany), prov., Italy F5 18
Toscano, stm., Mex. H8 90
Tosno, Russia B13 22
T'osovo-Netyl'skij, Russia C14 22
T'osovskij, Russia C13 22
Tostado, Arg. E8 80
Tõstamaa, Est. C7 22
Tostón, Spain O26 17b
Totagatic, stm., Wi., U.S. D4 110
Totana, Spain H10 16
Toteng, Bots. C6 66

Name	Map Ref.	Page
Tôtes, Fr.	C8	14
Tot'ma, Russia	B25	22
Totness, Sur.	E14	84
Totonicapán, Guat.	C3	92
Totonicapán, dept., Guat.	B3	92
Totora, Bol.	G9	82
Totora, Bol.	G7	82
Totoras, Arg.	G8	80
Totos, Peru	E4	82
Tototlán, Mex.	G8	90
Tottenham, Austl.	I7	70
Tottenham, Ont., Can.	F16	110
Tottori, Japan	L9	36
Touba, I.C.	G6	64
Toubkal, Jebel, mtn., Mor.	E7	62
Touchwood Hills, hills, Sask., Can.	G10	104
Touchwood Lake, l., Alta., Can.	C23	102
Touchwood Lake, l., Man., Can.	D19	104
Toudaogou, China	A17	32
Tougan, Burkina	E8	64
Touggourt, Alg.	D13	62
Toukoto, Mali	E5	64
Toul, Fr.	D12	14
Touliu, Tai.	L9	34
Toulnustouc, stm., Que., Can.	C5	106
Toulnustouc Nord-Est, stm., Que., Can.	A6	106
Toulon, Fr.	I12	14
Toulon, Il., U.S.	I6	110
Toulouse, Fr.	I8	14
Tounan, Tai.	L9	34
Toungoo, Burma	E4	40
Touques, stm., Fr.	C7	14
Touraine, Que., Can.	B11	108
Tourakom, Laos	E7	40
Tourcoing, Fr.	B10	14
Tournai (Doornik), Bel.	G3	12
Tourndo, Oued, val., Afr.	I16	62
Tournus, Fr.	F11	14
Tou Rout, Viet.	F9	40
Tours, Fr.	E7	14
Tousside, Pic, mtn., Chad	D4	56
Toustain, Alg.	M3	18
Toutle, stm., Wa., U.S.	D3	122
Toutuohe, China	D5	34
Touwsrivier, S. Afr.	I5	66
Tovar, Ven.	C7	84
Tovarkovskij, Russia	H21	22
Tow, Tx., U.S.	I8	116
Towanda, Ks., U.S.	N11	118
Towanda, Pa., U.S.	F10	108
Tower, Mn., U.S.	C3	110
Tower City, N.D., U.S.	E10	118
Tower City, Pa., U.S.	G10	108
Tower Hill, Il., U.S.	C8	114
Town and Country, Wa., U.S.	C8	122
Towner, N.D., U.S.	C7	118
Townsend, Mt., U.S.	D14	122
Townsend, Mount, mtn., Austl.	K8	70
Townshend Island, i., Austl.	D9	70
Townsville, Austl.	B7	70
Towrzī, Afg.	E1	44
Towson, Md., U.S.	H10	108
Toxkan, stm., China	C2	30
Toyah, Tx., U.S.	H3	116
Toyama, Japan	K12	36
Toyama-wan, b., Japan	K12	36
Toyohashi, Japan	M12	36
Toyokawa, Japan	M12	36
Toyonaka, Japan	M10	36
Toyosaka, Japan	J14	36
Toyota, Japan	L12	36
Tozeur, Tun.	D15	62
Trabiju, Braz.	G4	79
Trabzon, Tur.	G15	4
Tracadie, N.B., Can.	E9	106
Tracy, Que., Can.	A13	108
Tracy, Ca., U.S.	G4	124
Tracy, Mn., U.S.	G12	118
Tracy City, Tn., U.S.	G11	114
Trade Lake, l., Sask., Can.	C11	104
Tradewater, stm., Ky., U.S.	E9	114
Traer, Ia., U.S.	H3	110
Trafalgar, Cabo, c., Spain	I5	16
Traiguén, Chile	J2	80
Trail, B.C., Can.	H17	102
Traíra (Taraira), stm., S.A.	H8	84
Traíras, stm., Braz.	C4	79
Trakai, Lith.	G7	22
Tralee, Ire.	I4	8
Trammel, Va., U.S.	B4	112
Tramore, Ire.	I6	8
Tramping Lake, l., Sask., Can.	F6	104
Trancas, Arg.	D6	80
Trancoso, Port.	E4	16
Tranebjerg, Den.	N12	6
Trang, Thai.	K5	40
Trangahy, Madag.	Q21	67b
Trangie, Austl.	I7	70
Trani, Italy	H11	18
Tranqueras, Ur.	F11	80
Transantarctic Mountains, mts., Ant.	D9	73
Transkei, ctry., Afr.	H9	66
Transylvania, hist. reg., Rom.	C7	20
Transylvanian Alps see Carpații Meridionali, mts., Rom.	D8	20
Trapani, Italy	K7	18
Traralgon, Austl.	L7	70
Trasacco, Italy	H8	18
Trasimeno, Lago, l., Italy	F7	18
Trás-os-Montes, hist. reg., Port.	D4	16
Trat, Thai.	H7	40
Traun, Aus.	G14	10
Traun, stm., Aus.	G14	10
Traunstein, Ger.	H12	10
Travellers Lake, l., Austl.	I5	70
Traverse, Lake, l., U.S.	F11	118
Traverse Bay, b., Man., Can.	H18	104
Traverse City, Mi., U.S.	F10	110
Travers Reservoir, res., Alta., Can.	G22	102
Tra Vinh, Viet.	J9	40
Travis, Lake, res., Tx., U.S.	I8	116
Travnik, Bos.	E12	18
Trbovlje, Slo.	C10	18
Třebíč, Czech.	F15	10
Trebinje, Bos.	G2	20
Trebisacce, Italy	J11	18
Trebišov, Czech.	G21	10
Treble Mountain, mtn., B.C., Can.	B5	102
Treblinka, Pol.	C22	10
Trecate, Italy	D3	18
Treene, stm., Ger.	A9	10
Tregosse Islets, is., Austl.	A9	70
Tregubovo, Russia	C14	22
Tréguier, Fr.	D3	14
Treherne, Man., Can.	I16	104
Treinta y Tres, Ur.	G11	80
Trélazé, Fr.	E6	14
Trelew, Arg.	E3	78
Trelleborg, Swe.	N13	6
Tremblant, Mont, mtn., Que., Can.	A12	108
Trembleur Lake, l., B.C., Can.	C9	102
Tremedal, Braz.	C8	79
Tremont, Il., U.S.	J6	110
Tremont, Pa., U.S.	G10	108
Tremonton, Ut., U.S.	C4	120
Trempealeau, Wi., U.S.	F4	110
Trempealeau, stm., Wi., U.S.	F4	110
Trenčín, Czech.	G18	10
Trenel, Arg.	H6	80
Trenque Lauquen, Arg.	H7	80
Trent, stm., Eng., U.K.	H13	8
Trente et un Milles, Lac des, l., Que., Can.	A11	108
Trentino-Alto Adige, prov., Italy	C6	18
Trento, Italy	C6	18
Trenton, N.S., Can.	G11	106
Trenton, Ont., Can.	F18	110
Trenton, Fl., U.S.	J4	112
Trenton, Ga., U.S.	E1	112
Trenton, Ky., U.S.	F9	114
Trenton, Mo., U.S.	B3	114
Trenton, Ne., U.S.	K6	118
Trenton, N.J., U.S.	G12	108
Trenton, N.C., U.S.	D9	112
Trenton, Tn., U.S.	G8	114
Trenton, Tx., U.S.	F10	116
Trent see Trento, Italy	C6	18
Trentwood, Wa., U.S.	C8	122
Trepassey, Newf., Can.	F20	106
Trepassey Bay, b., Newf., Can.	F20	106
Tres Algarrobos, Arg.	H7	80
Tres Árboles, Ur.	G10	80
Tres Arroyos, Arg.	J8	80
Três Corações, Braz.	F6	79
Três Coroas, Braz.	E13	80
Três de Maio, Braz.	D11	80
Tres Esquinas, Col.	G5	84
Três Fronteiras, Braz.	F3	79
Tres Isletas, Arg.	D8	80
Três Lagoas, Braz.	F3	79
Tres Lomas, Arg.	I7	80
Três Marias, Reprêsa de, res., Braz.	E6	79
Tres Montosas, mtn., N.M., U.S.	J9	120
Tres Palos, Laguna, b., Mex.	I10	90
Três Passos, Braz.	D12	80
Tres Picos, Cerro, mtn., Arg.	J8	80
Três Pontas, Braz.	F6	79
Tres Puntas, Cabo, c., Arg.	F3	78
Tres Puntas, Cabo, c., Guat.	B6	92
Três Ranchos, Braz.	E5	79
Três Rios, Braz.	G7	79
Tres Ríos, C.R.	H11	92
Tres Vírgenes, Volcán de las, vol., Mex.	D3	90
Tres Zapotes, hist., Mex.	H12	90
Treuchtlingen, Ger.	G10	10
Treuenbrietzen, Ger.	C12	10
Treviglio, Italy	D4	18
Treviso, Italy	D7	18
Trevorton, Pa., U.S.	G10	108
Trévoux, Fr.	G11	14
Trezevant, Tn., U.S.	F8	114
Triabunna, Austl.	N7	70
Triánda, Grc.	M12	20
Triangle, Va., U.S.	I9	108
Triángulos, Arrecífes, rf., Mex.	G13	90
Tribugá, Ensenada de, b., Col.	E4	84
Tribune, Sask., Can.	I11	104
Tribune, Ks., U.S.	M6	118
Tribune Channel, strt., B.C., Can.	G8	102
Tricase, Italy	J13	18
Trichardt, S. Afr.	F9	66
Trichūr, India	G4	46
Triduby, Ukr.	A14	20
Trier, Ger.	F6	10
Trieste, Italy	D8	18
Trigal, Bol.	H9	82
Triglav, mtn., Slo.	C8	18
Trigueros, Spain	H5	16
Tríkala, Grc.	J5	20
Trikhonís, Límni, l., Grc.	K5	20
Trikora, Puncak, mtn., Indon.	F10	38
Trilby, Fl., U.S.	K4	112
Trimont, Mn., U.S.	H13	118
Trin, Switz.	E11	13
Trincheras, Mex.	B4	90
Trincomalee, Sri L.	H6	46
Trindade, Braz.	D4	79
Trindade, i., Braz.	G12	74
Třinec, Czech.	F18	10
Trinidad, Bol.	F9	82
Trinidad, Col.	E7	84
Trinidad, Cuba	D5	94
Trinidad, Hond.	C6	92
Trinidad, Co., U.S.	N3	118
Trinidad, Tx., U.S.	G10	116
Trinidad, Ur.	G10	80
Trinidad, i., Trin.	I14	94
Trinidad, Isla, i., Arg.	J8	80
Trinidad and Tobago, ctry., N.A.	I14	94
Trinity, Newf., Can.	D20	106
Trinity, Tx., U.S.	I11	116
Trinity, stm., Ca., U.S.	D2	124
Trinity, stm., Tx., U.S.	I12	116
Trinity Bay, b., Newf., Can.	E20	106
Trinity Bay, b., Tx., U.S.	J12	116
Trinkat Island, i., India	J2	40
Trinkitat, Sud.	H9	60
Trino, Italy	D3	18
Trion, Ga., U.S.	E1	112
Tripoli, Ia., U.S.	H3	110
Trípolis, Grc.	L6	20
Tripolis, hist., Tur.	L13	20
Tripoli see Ṭarābulus, Leb.	D3	48
Tripoli see Ṭarābulus, Libya	B3	56
Tripp, S.D., U.S.	H10	118
Tripura, state, India	I14	44
Triquet, Lac, l., Que., Can.	B14	106
Tristan da Cunha Group, is., St. Hel.	L5	52
Tristao, Îles, is., Afr.	F2	64
Triste, Golfo, b., Ven.	B8	84
Triumph, La., U.S.	M7	114
Trivandrum, India	H4	46
Trnava, Czech.	G17	10
Trochu, Alta., Can.	F21	102
Trogir, Cro.	F11	18
Troia, Italy	H10	18
Troick, Russia	G10	26
Troickoje, Ukr.	B14	20
Troicko-Pečorsk, Russia	E9	26
Troina, Italy	L9	18
Troisdorf, Ger.	E7	10
Trois-Pistoles, Que., Can.	D4	106
Trois-Rivières, Que., Can.	A14	108
Trojan, Bul.	G8	20
Trojekurovo, Russia	H22	22
Trollhättan, Swe.	L13	6
Trombetas, stm., Braz.	H14	84
Tromelin, Île, i., Reu.	E10	58
Trompsburg, S. Afr.	H7	66
Troms, co., Nor.	G16	6
Tromsø, Nor.	G16	6
Trona, Ca., U.S.	I8	124
Tronador, Monte, mtn., S.A.	E2	78
Troncoso, Mex.	F8	90
Trondheim, Nor.	J12	6
Troon, Scot., U.K.	F9	8
Tropas, Rio das, stm., Braz.	B13	82
Tropea, Italy	K10	18
Trophy Mountain, mtn., B.C., Can.	F15	102
Tropic, Ut., U.S.	G4	120
Tropojë, Alb.	G4	20
Troškūnai, Lith.	F7	22
Trosna, Russia	I18	22
Trost'anec, Ukr.	A13	20
Trotwood, Oh., U.S.	H2	108
Trou-du-Nord, Haiti	E8	94
Troup, Tx., U.S.	G11	116
Trout, La., U.S.	K4	114
Trout, stm., N.W. Ter., Can.	D8	96
Trout Creek, Mi., U.S.	D6	110
Trout Creek Pass, Co., U.S.	F11	120
Trout Lake, l., B.C., Can.	G17	102
Trout Lake, l., N.W. Ter., Can.	D8	96
Trout Lake, l., Ont., Can.	G21	104
Trout River, Newf., Can.	C15	106
Troutville, Va., U.S.	B7	112
Trouville [-sur-Mer], Fr.	C7	14
Trowbridge, Eng., U.K.	J11	8
Troy, Al., U.S.	K11	114
Troy, Id., U.S.	D9	122
Troy, In., U.S.	E10	114
Troy, Ks., U.S.	L12	118
Troy, Mo., U.S.	D6	114
Troy, Mt., U.S.	B10	122
Troy, N.H., U.S.	E14	108
Troy, N.Y., U.S.	E13	108
Troy, N.C., U.S.	D7	112
Troy, Oh., U.S.	G2	108
Troy, Pa., U.S.	F10	108
Troy, Tn., U.S.	F7	114
Troy, Tx., U.S.	H9	116
Troy, hist., Tur.	J10	20
Troyes, Fr.	D11	14
Troy Peak, mtn., Nv., U.S.	F10	124
Trstenik, Yugo.	F5	20
Truax, Sask., Can.	I10	104
Trubč'ovsk, Russia	I16	22
Truchas, N.M., U.S.	H11	120
Truchas Peak, mtn., N.M., U.S.	I11	120
Truckee, Ca., U.S.	E5	124
Truckee, stm., U.S.	E6	124
Trujillo, Col.	E4	84
Trujillo, Hond.	B8	92
Trujillo, Peru	C2	82
Trujillo, Spain	F6	16
Trujillo, Ven.	C7	84
Trujillo, state, Ven.	C7	84
Truk Islands, is., Micron.	H19	126
Truman, Mn., U.S.	H13	118
Trumann, Ar., U.S.	G6	114
Trumansburg, N.Y., U.S.	E10	108
Trumbull, Ct., U.S.	F13	108
Trundle, Austl.	I7	70
Truro, N.S., Can.	G10	106
Truscott, Tx., U.S.	F7	116
Trust Territory of the Pacific Islands, dep., Oc.	F23	2
Truth or Consequences (Hot Springs), N.M., U.S.	K9	120
Trutnov, Czech.	E15	10
Tryon, Ne., U.S.	J7	118
Tryon, N.C., U.S.	D4	112
Trzcianka, Pol.	B16	10
Trzebież, Pol.	B14	10
Trzebinia, Pol.	E19	10
Tsacha Lake, l., B.C., Can.	D10	102
Tsarabaria, Madag.	N23	67b
Tsaratanana, Madag.	P22	67b
Tsaratanana, Massif du, mts., Madag.	O23	67b
Tsau, Bots.	C6	66
Tsaukaib, Nmb.	F2	66
Tsavo, Kenya	B7	58
Tsaydaychuz Peak, mtn., B.C., Can.	D8	102
Tsayta Lake, l., B.C., Can.	B9	102
Tsekanyani, Bots.	B8	66
Tsévié, Togo	H10	64
Tshabong, Bots.	F6	66
Tshane, Bots.	E5	66
Tshangalele, Lac, l., Zaire	D5	58
Tshela, Zaire	B2	58
Tshesebe, Bots.	C8	66
Tshidilamolomo, Boph.	E7	66
Tshikapa, Zaire	C4	58
Tshofa, Zaire	C5	58
Tshukudu, Bots.	D6	66
Tshwaane, Bots.	D6	66
Tsiafajavona, mtn., Madag.	Q22	67b
Tsianaloka, Madag.	Q21	67b
Tsihombe, Madag.	T21	67b
Tsilmamo, Eth.	N8	60
Tsimilofo, Madag.	T21	67b
Tsimpsean Indian Reserve, B.C., Can.	C4	102
Tsineng, Boph.	F6	66
Tsingtao see Qingdao, China	G8	32
Tsinjomitondraka, Madag.	O22	67b
Tsiribihina, stm., Madag.	Q21	67b
Tsiroanomandidy, Madag.	Q22	67b
Tsitondroina, Madag.	R22	67b
Tsitsutl Peak, mtn., B.C., Can.	E9	102
Tsivory, Madag.	T22	67b
Tsobis, Nmb.	B3	66
Tsomo, stm., Afr.	H8	66
Tsoying, Tai.	M9	34
Tsu, Japan	M11	36
Tsuchiura, Japan	K15	36
Tsugaru-kaikyō, strt., Japan	F15	36a
Tsumeb, Nmb.	B3	66
Tsumis Park, Nmb.	D3	66
Tsumkwe, Nmb.	B5	66
Tsuni see Zunyi, China	F8	30
Tsuruga, Japan	L11	36
Tsuruoka, Japan	I14	36
Tsushima, is., Japan	M4	36
Tsushima-kaikyō (Eastern Channel), strt., Japan	N4	36
Tsuyama, Japan	L9	36
Tua Chau, Viet.	D7	40
Tual, Indon.	G9	38
Tuam, Ire.	H5	8
Tuamotu, Îles, is., Fr. Poly.	J26	126
Tuanfeng, China	E3	34
Tuanlin, China	D7	32
Tuanwang, China	G8	32
Tuapse, Russia	I5	26
Tubac, Az., U.S.	M5	120
Tuba City, Az., U.S.	H5	120
Tubarão, Braz.	E14	80
Tübingen, Ger.	G9	10
Ṭubruq (Tobruk), Libya	A2	60
Tucacas, Ven.	B8	84
Tucacas, Punta, c., Ven.	B8	84
Tucano, Braz.	F11	76
Tucava, stm., Bol.	H12	82
Tuchengzi, China	C12	32
Tuchola, Pol.	B17	10
Tuckerman, Ar., U.S.	G5	114
Tuckerton, N.J., U.S.	H12	108
Tučkovo, Russia	F19	22
Tucson, Az., U.S.	L6	120
Tucumã, mth., Braz.	J9	84
Tucumán, prov., Arg.	D6	80
Tucumcari, N.M., U.S.	D3	116
Tucunuco, Arg.	F4	80
Tucupido, Ven.	C10	84
Tucupita, Ven.	C11	84
Tucuruí, Braz.	D9	76
Tudcum, Arg.	F4	80
Tudela, Spain	C10	16
Tudmur (Palmyra), Syria	D5	48
Tudu, Est.	B9	22
Tugaske, Sask., Can.	H8	104
Tug Fork, stm., U.S.	A4	112
Tugidak Island, i., Ak., U.S.	H17	100
Tuichi, stm., Bol.	F8	82
Tuineje, Spain	O26	17b
Tujmazy, Russia	G8	26
T'ukalinsk, Russia	F12	26
Tukangbesi, Kepulauan, is., Indon.	G7	38
Tuktoyaktuk, N.W. Ter., Can.	B28	100
Tuktoyaktuk Peninsula, pen., N.W. Ter., Can.	B29	100
Tukums, Lat.	D6	22
Tula, Mex.	F10	90
Tula, Russia	G20	22
Tulancingo, Mex.	G10	90
Tulare, Ca., U.S.	H6	124
Tulare, S.D., U.S.	G9	118
Tularosa, N.M., U.S.	K10	120
Tularosa, stm., N.M., U.S.	K8	120
Tularosa Valley, N.M., U.S.	L10	120
Tulbagh, S. Afr.	I4	66
Tulcán, Ec.	G4	84
Tulcea, Rom.	D12	20
Tulcea, co., Rom.	D12	20
Tule, stm., Nic.	F10	92
Tule, stm., Ca., U.S.	H6	124
Tulelake, Ca., U.S.	C4	124
Tulemalu Lake, l., N.W. Ter., Can.	D13	96
Tule Valley, val., Ut., U.S.	E3	120
T'ul'gan, Russia	G9	26
Tuli, Zimb.	C9	66
Tulia, Tx., U.S.	E5	116
Tuling, China	J7	34
Ṭūlkarm, Isr. Occ.	D4	50
Tullahoma, Tn., U.S.	G10	114
Tullamore, Austl.	I7	70
Tullamore, Ire.	H6	8
Tulle, Fr.	G8	14
Tullibigeal, Austl.	I7	70
Tulln, Aus.	G16	10
Tullos, La., U.S.	K4	114
Tullus, Sud.	L3	60
Tully, Austl.	A6	70
Tuloma, stm., Russia	G23	6
Tulsa, Ok., U.S.	C11	116
Tulsequah, B.C., Can.	E6	96
Tuluá, Col.	E4	84
Tuluksak, Ak., U.S.	F14	100
Tulum, Mex.	G16	90
Tulum, hist., Mex.	G16	90
Tulumayo, stm., Peru	D4	82
Tulun, Russia	G12	28
Tulungagung, Indon.	K15	39a
Tuma, Russia	F23	22
Tuma, stm., Nic.	D10	92
Tumaco, Col.	G3	84
Tumaco, Rada de, b., Col.	G3	84
Tumatumari, Guy.	E13	84
Tumba, Lac, l., Zaire	B3	58
Tumbarumba, Austl.	J8	70
Tumbes, Peru	I2	84
Tumbes, dept., Peru	F2	84
Tumbes (Puyango), stm., S.A.	I2	84
Tumble Mountain, mtn., Mt., U.S.	E15	122
Tumbler Ridge, B.C., Can.	B14	102
Tumbotino, Russia	F26	22
Tumby Bay, Austl.	J2	70
Tumča, stm., Eur.	H21	6
Tumen, China	A17	32
T'umen', Russia	F11	26
Tumen (Tuman-gang), stm., Asia	A18	32
Tumeremo, Ven.	D12	84
Tumiritinga, Braz.	E8	79
Tumkūr, India	F4	46
Tummo, Libya	D3	56
Tumos, stm., Afr.	D2	66
Tumpat, Malay.	K7	40
Tumsar, India	B5	46
Tumuc-Humac Mountains, mts., S.A.	C7	76
Tumut, Austl.	J8	70
Tumwater, Wa., U.S.	C3	122
Tunago Lake, l., N.W. Ter., Can.	C32	100
Tunari, Cerro, mtn., Bol.	G8	82
Tunas de Zaza, Cuba	D5	94
Tunaydah, Egypt	E5	60
Tunçbilek, Tur.	J13	20
Tunduru, Tan.	D7	58
Tundža, stm., Eur.	G10	20
T'ung, stm., Russia	E16	28
Tungabhadra Reservoir, res., India	E4	46
Tungaru, Sud.	L6	60
Tungkang, Tai.	M9	34
Tungla, Nic.	D10	92
Tungsha Tao (Pratas Island), i., Tai.	G10	30
Tungshih, Tai.	K9	34
Tungsten, N.W. Ter., Can.	F30	100
Tungurahua, prov., Ec.	H3	84
Tuni, India	D7	46
Tunia, stm., Col.	G6	84
Tunica, Ms., U.S.	H6	114
Tunis, Tun.	M5	18
Tunis, Golfe de, b., Tun.	L5	18
Tunisia (Tunisie), ctry., Afr.	B8	54
Tunja, Col.	E6	84
Tunkás, Mex.	G15	90
Tunkhannock, Pa., U.S.	F11	108
Tunnel Hill, Ga., U.S.	E1	112
Tunnelton, W.V., U.S.	H7	108
Tuntutuliak, Ak., U.S.	F13	100
Tununak, Ak., U.S.	F12	100
Tunungayualok Island, i., Newf., Can.	E20	96
Tunuyán, Arg.	G4	80
Tunuyán, stm., Arg.	G5	80
Tunxi, China	F7	34
Tuo, stm., China	E7	30
Tuocheng, China	K4	34
Tuokusidawan Ling, mtn., China	B11	44
Tuolumne, Ca., U.S.	G5	124
Tuolumne, stm., Ca., U.S.	G5	124
Tupã, Braz.	F3	79
Tupaciguara, Braz.	E4	79
Tupana, stm., Braz.	J12	84
Tupanciretã, Braz.	E12	80
Tuparro, stm., Col.	E8	84
Tupelo, Ms., U.S.	H8	114
Tupelo, Ok., U.S.	E10	116
Tupinambarana, Ilha, i., Braz.	I14	84
Tupi Paulista, Braz.	F3	79
Tupiraçaba, Braz.	C4	79
Tupiza, Bol.	I9	82
Tupper, B.C., Can.	B14	102
Tupper Lake, N.Y., U.S.	C12	108
Tupungato, Arg.	G4	80
Tupungato, Cerro, mtn., S.A.	G4	80
Túquerres, Col.	G4	84
Tura, India	H14	44
Tura, stm., Russia	F10	26
Turabah, Sau. Ar.	D2	47
Ṭurayf, Sau. Ar.	F5	48
Turbaco, Col.	B5	84
Turbacz, mtn., Pol.	F20	10
Turbat, Pak.	I17	48
Turbo, Col.	C4	84
Turda, Rom.	C7	20
Turdej, Russia	H21	22
Turek, Pol.	C18	10
Turfan Depression see Turpan Pendi, depr., China	C4	30
Turfan see Turpan, China	C4	30
Turgaj, Kaz.	H10	26
Turgaj, stm., Kaz.	H10	26
Turgajskaja ložbina, val., Kaz.	G10	26
Turgajskoje plato, plat., Kaz.	G10	26
Turginovo, Russia	E19	22
Turgoš, Russia	B18	22
Turgutlu, Tur.	K11	20
Türi, Est.	C8	22
Turia, stm., Spain	F11	16
Turimiquire, Cerro, mtn., Ven.	B11	84
Turin, Alta., Can.	H22	102
Turinsk, Russia	F10	26
Turin see Torino, Italy	D2	18
Turka, Ukr.	F23	10
Turkestan, Kaz.	I11	26
Túrkeve, Hung.	H20	10
Turkey, Tx., U.S.	E6	116
Turkey (Türkiye), ctry., Asia	H15	4
Turkey, stm., Ia., U.S.	H4	110
Turkey Creek, stm., Ne., U.S.	K10	118
Turkish Republic of Northern Cyprus see Cyprus, North, ctry., Asia	H14	4
Turkmenistan, ctry., Asia	I9	26
Turkmeniya see Turkmenistan, ctry., Asia	I9	26
Turks and Caicos Islands, dep., N.A.	D9	94
Turks Island Passage, strt., T./C. Is.	D9	94
Turks Islands, is., T./C. Is.	D9	94
Turku (Åbo), Fin.	K18	6
Turley, Ok., U.S.	C11	116
Turlock, Ca., U.S.	G5	124
Turmalina, Braz.	D7	79
Turnagain, stm., B.C., Can.	G31	100
Turnagain Arm, b., Ak., U.S.	F20	100
Turneffe Islands, is., Belize	I16	90
Turner, Mt., U.S.	B17	122
Turner, Or., U.S.	F3	122
Turners Falls, Ma., U.S.	E14	108
Turner Valley, Alta., Can.	G20	102
Turnhout, Bel.	F6	12
Türnitz, Aus.	H15	10
Turnor Lake, l., Sask., Can.	B6	104
Turnu-Măgurele, Rom.	F8	20
Turon, Ks., U.S.	N9	118
Turpan, China	C4	30
Turpan Pendi, depr., China	C4	30
Turquino, Pico, mtn., Cuba	E6	94
Turrell, Ar., U.S.	G6	114
Turrialba, C.R.	H11	92
Turrialba, Volcán, vol., C.R.	G11	92
Turriff, Scot., U.K.	D11	8
Turrubares, Cerro, mtn., C.R.	H10	92
Turtle, stm., Man., Can.	G15	104
Turtle, stm., Ont., Can.	I22	104
Turtle Creek, N.B., Can.	G9	106
Turtle-Flambeau Flowage, res., Wi., U.S.	D5	110
Turtleford, Sask., Can.	E6	104
Turtle Lake, N.D., U.S.	D7	118
Turtle Lake, Wi., U.S.	E3	110
Turtle Lake, l., Sask., Can.	E6	104
Turtle Mountain, hill, Man., Can.	I14	104
Turtle Mountain Provincial Park, Man., Can.	I14	104
Turu, stm., Russia	D12	28
Turuchan, stm., Russia	D9	28
Turvo, Braz.	E14	80
Turvo, stm., Braz.	D3	79
Turvo, stm., Braz.	F4	79
Tusas, Rio, stm., N.M., U.S.	H10	120
Tuscaloosa, Al., U.S.	I9	114
Tuscany see Toscana, prov., Italy	F5	18
Tuscarora Mountain, mtn., Pa., U.S.	G9	108
Tuscarora Mountains, mts., Nv., U.S.	D9	124
Tuscola, Il., U.S.	C8	114
Tuscola, Tx., U.S.	G7	116
Tuscumbia, Al., U.S.	H9	114
Tuscumbia, Mo., U.S.	D4	114
Tuskegee, Al., U.S.	J11	114
Tustumena Lake, l., Ak., U.S.	F19	100
Tutajev, Russia	D22	22
Tutang, China	F5	34
Tuticorin, India	H5	46
Tutóia, Braz.	D10	76
Tutrakan, Bul.	E10	20
Tuttle, N.D., U.S.	D8	118
Tuttle, Ok., U.S.	D9	116
Tuttle Creek Lake, res., Ks., U.S.	L11	118
Tutupaca, Volcán, vol., Peru	G6	82
Tutwiler, Ms., U.S.	H6	114
Tuurun-Poorin lääni, prov., Fin.	K18	6
Tuvalu, ctry., Oc.	G24	2
Ṭuwayq, Jabal, mts., Sau. Ar.	D4	47
Tuxford, Sask., Can.	H9	104
Tuxpan, Mex.	G7	90
Tuxpan, Mex.	G11	90
Tuxtepec, Mex.	H11	90
Tuxtla Gutiérrez, Mex.	I13	90
Tuy, stm., Ven.	B9	84
Tuy An, Viet.	H10	40
Tuyen Quang, Viet.	D8	40
Tuy Hoa, Viet.	H10	40
Tuz Gölü, l., Tur.	H14	4
Ṭūz Khurmātū, Iraq	D8	48
Tuzla, Bos.	E2	20
Tuzly, Ukr.	D14	20
Tver' (Kalinin), Russia	E18	22
Tweed, Ont., Can.	F18	110
Tweed Heads, Austl.	G10	70
Tweedsmuir Provincial Park, B.C., Can.	D8	102
Twee Rivieren, S. Afr.	F5	66
Twelve Mile Lake, l., Sask., Can.	I8	104
Twentynine Palms, Ca., U.S.	J9	124
Twillingate, Newf., Can.	C19	106
Twin Bridges, Mt., U.S.	E13	122
Twin City, Ga., U.S.	G4	112
Twin Falls, Id., U.S.	H11	122
Twin Lakes, Ga., U.S.	I3	112
Twin Lakes, Wi., U.S.	H7	110
Twinsburg, Oh., U.S.	F5	108
Twin Valley, Mn., U.S.	D11	118
Twisp, Wa., U.S.	B5	122
Twitya, stm., N.W. Ter., Can.	D30	100
Twofold Bay, b., Austl.	K8	70
Two Harbors, Mn., U.S.	C4	110
Two Hills, Alta., Can.	D23	102
Two Medicine, stm., Mt., U.S.	B13	122
Two River Lake, l., Ont., Can.	E23	104
Two Rivers, Wi., U.S.	F8	110
Tybee Island, Ga., U.S.	G6	112
Tychy, Pol.	E18	10
Tye, Tx., U.S.	G7	116
Tygh Valley, Or., U.S.	E4	122
Tyler, Mn., U.S.	G11	118
Tyler, Tx., U.S.	G11	116
Tylertown, Ms., U.S.	K6	114
Tym, stm., Russia	E8	28
Tyndall, S.D., U.S.	I10	118
Tyndinskij, Russia	F16	28
Tyne, stm., Eng., U.K.	G11	8
Tynemouth, Eng., U.K.	F12	8
Týn nad Vltavou, Czech.	F14	10
Tyonek, Ak., U.S.	F19	100
Tyre see Ṣūr, Leb.	B4	50
Tyrma, Russia	G18	28
Tyrone, Ok., U.S.	C5	116
Tyrone, Pa., U.S.	G8	108
Tyrrell, Lake, l., Austl.	J5	70
Tyrrhenian Sea (Mare Tirreno), Eur.	I7	18
Tytuvėnai, Lith.	F6	22
Ty Ty, Ga., U.S.	H3	112
Tzaneen, S. Afr.	D10	66
Tzucacab, Mex.	G15	90
U		
Uatumã, stm., Braz.	I13	84
Uaupés (Vaupés), stm., S.A.	G9	84
Uaxactún, hist., Guat.	I15	90
Ubá, Braz.	F7	79
Ubaitaba, Braz.	C9	79
Ubangi (Oubangui), stm., Afr.	H10	54
Ubatã, Braz.	C9	79
Ubaté, Col.	E6	84
Ubatuba, Braz.	G6	79
Ubayyiḍ, Wādī al-, val., Asia	B11	60
Ube, Japan	N6	36
Úbeda, Spain	G8	16
Uberaba, Braz.	E5	79
Uberaba, stm., Braz.	E4	79
Uberaba, Lagoa, l., S.A.	G13	82
Uberlândia, Braz.	E4	79
Ubiaja, Nig.	H13	64
Ubly, Mi., U.S.	G13	110
Ubon Ratchathani, Thai.	G8	40
Ubundu, Zaire	B5	58
Ucacha, Arg.	G7	80
Uč-Adži, Turk.	B17	48
Ucayali, dept., Peru	C4	82
Ucayali, stm., Peru	A4	82
Uchi Lake, Ont., Can.	G22	104
Uchiura-wan, b., Japan	E15	36a
Uchiza, Peru	C3	82
Uchoa, Braz.	F4	79
Ucholovo, Russia	H23	22
Uchta, Russia	E8	26
Uchtoma, Russia	A21	22
Uckermark, reg., Ger.	B13	10
Ucluelet, B.C., Can.	I9	102
Ucon, Id., U.S.	G14	122
Uda, stm., Russia	G18	28
Udagamandalam, India	G4	46
Udaipur, India	H5	44
Udall, Ks., U.S.	N10	118
Udamalpet, India	G4	46
Udaquiola, Arg.	I9	80
Udaypur, Nepal	G12	44
Udbina, Cro.	E10	18
Uddevalla, Swe.	L12	6
Udgīr, India	C4	46
Udine, Italy	C8	18
Udoml'a, Russia	D18	22
Udon Thani, Thai.	F7	40
Udskaja guba, b., Russia	G19	28
Udupi, India	F3	46
Udžary, Azer.	A9	48
Ueckermünde, Ger.	B14	10
Ueda, Japan	K13	36
Uelzen, Ger.	C10	10
Ueno, Japan	M11	36
Uetersen, Ger.	B9	10
Ufa, Russia	G9	26
Uffenheim, Ger.	F10	10
Ufra, Turk.	A12	48
Ugab, stm., Nmb.	C1	66
Ugāle, Lat.	D5	22
Uganda, ctry., Afr.	A6	58
Ughaybish, Sud.	L6	60
Ugie, S. Afr.	H9	66
Uglegorsk, Russia	H20	28
Uglič, Russia	D21	22
Uglovka, Russia	C16	22
Ugodskij Zavod, Russia	F19	22
Ugoma, mtn., Zaire	B5	58
Ugra, Russia	G17	22
Uh (Už), stm., Eur.	G22	10
Uha-dong, N. Kor.	C13	32
Uherské Hradiště, Czech.	F17	10
Uherský Brod, Czech.	F17	10
Uhlenhorst, Nmb.	D3	66
Uhlman Lake, l., Man., Can.	B16	104
Uhrichsville, Oh., U.S.	G5	108
Uíge, Ang.	C3	58
Ŭijŏngbu, S. Kor.	F15	32
Ŭiju, N. Kor.	C12	32
Uil, stm., Kaz.	H8	26
Uinebona, stm., Ven.	E11	84
Uinta, stm., Ut., U.S.	D6	120
Uinta Mountains, mts., Ut., U.S.	D6	120
Ŭisŏng, S. Kor.	G16	32
Uitenhage, S. Afr.	I7	66
Uithoorn, Neth.	D6	12
Uj, stm., Asia	G10	26
Ujandina, stm., Russia	D20	28
Ujar, Russia	F16	26
Ujarrás, hist., C.R.	H11	92
Ujemskij, Russia	I27	6
Újfehértó, Hung.	H21	10
Uji-guntō, is., Japan	P4	37b
Ujiji, Tan.	B5	58
Ujjain, India	I6	44
'Ujmān, U.A.E.	B9	47
Ujungkulon National Park, Indon.	J12	39a
Ujungpandang, Indon.	G6	38
Ukiah, Ca., U.S.	E2	124
Ukiah, Or., U.S.	E7	122
Ukmergė, Lith.	F7	22
Ukraine, ctry., Eur.	H3	26
Ulaanbaatar, Mong.	B8	30
Ulaangom, Mong.	B5	30
Ulan, Austl.	I8	70
Ulan Bator see Ulaanbaatar, Mong.	B8	30
Ulang, stm., Nic.	C11	92
Ulan-Ude, Russia	G13	28
Ułazów, Pol.	E23	10
Ulchin, S. Kor.	G17	32
Ulcinj, Yugo.	H3	20

Name | Map Ref. | Page

Ulco, S. Afr. G7 66
Ulcumayo, Peru D4 82
Uldz, stm., Asia H14 28
Ulen, Mn., U.S. D11 118
Ulhāsnagar, India C2 46
Uliastaj, Mong. B6 30
Uljanovka, Russia B13 22
Uljanovka, Ukr. A14 20
Uljanovsk, Russia G7 26
Ulla, Bela. F12 22
Ulladulla, Austl. J9 70
Ullapool, Scot., U.K. D8 8
Ullin, Il., U.S. E7 114
Ulm, Ger. G10 10
Ulm, Mt., U.S. C14 122
Ulmarra, Austl. G10 70
Ulongué, Moz. D6 58
Ulrum, Neth. B9 12
Ulsan, S. Kor. H17 32
Ulster, hist. reg., Eur. G6 8
Ultraoriental, Cordillera (Serra do Divisor), mts., S.A. C5 82
Ulu, Russia E17 28
Ulúa, stm., Hond. B6 92
Ulubey, Tur. K13 20
Ulukışla, Tur. C3 48
Ulungur, stm., China B4 30
Ulungur Hu, l., China B4 30
Uluru National Park, Austl. E6 68
Ulverstone, Austl. M7 70
Ulysses, Ks., U.S. N6 118
Ulysses, Ne., U.S. J10 118
Ulzë, Alb. H3 20
Umán, Mex. G15 90
Uman', Ukr. H4 26
Umari, stm., Braz. B9 82
Umarkot, Pak. H3 44
Umatilla, Fl., U.S. K5 112
Umatilla, Or., U.S. E6 122
Umatilla, stm., Or., U.S. E6 122
Umbertide, Italy F7 18
Umboi Island, i., Pap. N. Gui. m16 68a
Umbrail, Pass, Eur. E13 13
Umbria, prov., Italy G7 18
Umbuzero, ozero, l., Russia H24 6
Umeå, Swe. J17 6
Umfreville Lake, l., Ont., Can. H20 104
Umfuli, stm., Zimb. A9 66
Umhlanga Rocks, S. Afr. G10 66
Umkomaas, S. Afr. H10 66
Umm al-Birak, Sau. Ar. C1 47
Umm al-Qaywayn, U.A.E. B9 47
Umm al-Qittayn, Jord. D7 50
Umm Badr, Sud. J4 60
Umm Dabbī, Sud. J6 60
Umm Dhibbān, Sud. J5 60
Umm Digulgulaya, Sud. L3 60
Umm Durmān (Omdurman), Sud. J7 60
Umm el Fahm, Isr. C4 50
Umm Jamālah, Sud. L5 60
Umm Kaddādah, Sud. K4 60
Umm Kuwaykah, Sud. K7 60
Umm Lajj, Sau. Ar. I4 48
Umm Mirdi, Sud. H7 60
Umm Qantur, Sud. J6 60
Umm Qaṣr, Iraq F9 48
Umm Quṣayr, Jord. E5 50
Umm Ruwābah, Sud. K6 60
Umm Sayyālah, Sud. J6 60
Umm Shalīl, Sud. L2 60
Umm Shutūr, Sud. N7 60
Umm Walad, Syria C5 50
Um'ot, Russia G25 22
Um'ot, Russia I25 22
Umpqua, stm., Or., U.S. G2 122
Umred, India B5 46
Umreth, India I5 44
Ŭmsŏng, S. Kor. G15 32
Umtata, Transkei H9 66
Umtentweni, S. Afr. H10 66
Umuahia, Nig. I13 64
Umuarama, Braz. G2 79
Umzinto, S. Afr. H10 66
Una, Braz. C9 79
Unadilla, Ga., U.S. G3 112
Unadilla, N.Y., U.S. E11 108
Unadilla, stm., N.Y., U.S. E11 108
Unaí, Braz. D5 79
Unalakleet, Ak., U.S. E14 100
Unalaska, Ak., U.S. J11 100
Unare, stm., Ven. C10 84
'Unayzah, Sau. Ar. H7 48
'Unayzah, Jabal, mtn., Asia E5 48
'Unayzah, Jabal, mtn., Jord. G5 50
Uncia, Bol. H8 82
Uncompahgre, stm., Co., U.S. F9 120
Uncompahgre Peak, mtn., Co., U.S. F9 120
Uncompahgre Plateau, plat., Co., U.S. F8 120
Underwood, N.D., U.S. D6 118
Undva nina, c., Est. C4 22
Uneča, Russia I15 22
Uneiuxi, stm., Braz. H10 84
Ungarie, Austl. I7 70
Ungava, Péninsule d', pen., Que., Can. E18 96
Ungava Bay, b., Can. E19 96
Unggi, N. Kor. A18 32
União, Braz. D10 76
União da Vitória, Braz. D13 80
União dos Palmares, Braz. E11 76
Unicoi, Tn., U.S. C4 112
Unimak Island, i., Ak., U.S. I12 100
Unimak Pass, strt., Ak., U.S. I12 100
Unini, stm., Braz. H12 84
Unión, Arg. H6 80
Unión, C.R. I11 92
Unión, Para. C10 80
Union, Ia., U.S. H2 110
Union, La., U.S. L6 114
Union, Ms., U.S. J7 114
Union, Mo., U.S. D5 114
Union, N.J., U.S. G12 108
Union, Or., U.S. E8 122
Union, S.C., U.S. E5 112
Union, Wa., U.S. C2 122
Union, W.V., U.S. B6 112
Union Bay, B.C., Can. H10 102
Union City, Ga., U.S. F2 112
Union City, In., U.S. B11 114
Union City, Mi., U.S. H10 110
Union City, Oh., U.S. G2 108
Union City, Pa., U.S. F7 108
Union City, Tn., U.S. F7 114
Unión de Reyes, Cuba C4 94
Unión de Tula, Mex. H7 90
Union Gap, Wa., U.S. D5 122
Union Grove, Wi., U.S. H7 110
Union Park, Fl., U.S. K5 112
Union Point, Ga., U.S. F3 112
Union Springs, Al., U.S. J11 114
Union Springs, N.Y., U.S. E10 108
Uniontown, Al., U.S. J9 114
Uniontown, Ky., U.S. E9 114
Uniontown, Pa., U.S. H7 108
Unionville, Mi., U.S. G12 110
Unionville, Mo., U.S. B3 114
Unipouheos Indian Reserve, Alta., Can. E4 104
United, Pa., U.S. G7 108
United Arab Emirates (Al-Imārāt al-'Arabīyah al-Muttaḥidah), ctry., Asia E5 42
United Arab Republic see Egypt, ctry., Afr. C7 56
United Kingdom, ctry., Eur. E7 4
United States, ctry., N.A. D7 98
Unity, Sask., Can. F5 104
Universal City, Tx., U.S. J8 116
University, Ms., U.S. H7 114
University City, Mo., U.S. D6 114
University Park, N.M., U.S. L10 120
University Park, Tx., U.S. G10 116
Unjha, India I5 44
Unna, Ger. D7 10
Uno, Canal Numero, Arg. I10 80
Ŭnp'a, N. Kor. E13 32
Unquillo, Arg. F6 80
Ŭnsan, N. Kor. D14 32
Unterterzen, Switz. D11 13
Unterwalden, state, Switz. E9 13
Unuli Horog, China C14 44
Unža, Russia C27 22
Unža, stm., Russia D26 22
Uozu, Japan K12 36
Upala, C.R. G9 92
Upano, stm., Ec. I3 84
Upata, Ven. C11 84
Upemba, Lac, l., Zaire C5 58
Upham, N.D., U.S. C7 118
Upía, stm., Col. E6 84
Upington, S. Afr. G5 66
Upire, stm., Ven. B8 84
Upland, Ne., U.S. K9 118
Upleta, India J4 44
Upolu, i., W. Sam. J22 126
Upolu Point, c., Hi., U.S. q18 125a
Upper Arlington, Oh., U.S. G3 108
Upper Arrow Lake, l., B.C., Can. G17 102
Upper Blackville, N.B., Can. F8 106
Upper Darby, Pa., U.S. H11 108
Upper Demerara-Berbice, prov., Guy. D13 84
Upper Fraser, B.C., Can. C13 102
Upper Goose Lake, l., Ont., Can. G22 104
Upper Hat Creek, B.C., Can. G13 102
Upper Humber, stm., Newf., Can. C16 106
Upper Iowa, stm., U.S. G4 110
Upper Island Cove, Newf., Can. E20 106
Upper Klamath Lake, l., Or., U.S. H4 122
Upper Lake, Ca., U.S. E3 124
Upper Liard, Yukon, Can. F30 100
Upper Manitou Lake, l., Ont., Can. I22 104
Upper Musquodoboit, N.S., Can. G11 106
Upper Red Lake, l., Mn., U.S. C13 118
Upper Sandusky, Oh., U.S. G3 108
Upper Sheila, N.B., Can. E9 106
Upper Takutu-Upper Essequibo, prov., Guy. F13 84
Upper Windigo Lake, l., Ont., Can. F23 104
Uppsala, Swe. L15 6
Upsala see Uppsala, Swe. L15 6
Upstart, Cape, c., Austl. B7 70
Upton, Ky., U.S. E11 114
Upton, Wy., U.S. G3 118
Uquia, Cerro, mtn., Ven. C11 84
Urabá, Golfo de, b., Col. C4 84
Uracoa, Ven. C11 84
Uraj, Russia E10 26
Ural, stm., Asia H8 26
Uralla, Austl. H9 70
Ural Mountains see Ural'skije gory, mts., Russia E9 26
Ural'sk, Kaz. G8 26
Ural'skije gory (Ural Mountains), mts., Russia E9 26
Urana, Austl. J7 70
Urandangi, Austl. C3 70
Urandi, Braz. C7 79
Urangan, Austl. E10 70
Urania, La., U.S. K4 114
Uranium City, Sask., Can. E11 96
Urariá, Paraná, mth., Braz. I14 84
Uraricaá, stm., Braz. F11 84
Uraricoera, Braz. F12 84
Uraricoera, stm., Braz. F12 84
Ura-T'ube, Taj. J11 26
Uravan, Co., U.S. F8 120
Urawa, Japan L14 36
Urbana, Ar., U.S. I4 114
Urbana, Il., U.S. B8 114
Urbana, Mo., U.S. E3 114
Urbana, Oh., U.S. G3 108
Urbandale, Ia., U.S. A3 114
Urbania, Italy F7 18
Urbino, Italy F7 18
Urcos, Peru E6 82
Urdinarrain, Arg. G9 80
Uré, Col. D5 84
Urečje, Bela. I11 22
Urén, stm., C.R. H11 92
Ureña, Ven. D6 84
Ures, Mex. C4 90
Urfa, Tur. C5 48
Urgenč, Uzb. I10 26
Ürgüp, Tur. B3 48
Uri, state, Switz. E10 13
Uriah, Al., U.S. K9 114
Uriah, Mount, mtn., N.Z. E3 72
Uribante, stm., Ven. D7 84
Uribe, Col. F5 84
Uribia, Col. B6 84
Urich, Mo., U.S. D2 114
Urique, Mex. D6 90
Urique, stm., Mex. D6 90
Urituyacu, stm., Peru J5 84
Urla, Tur. K10 20
Urmia see Orūmīyeh, Iran C8 48
Uroševac, Yugo. G5 20
Urrao, Col. D4 84
Ursa, Il., U.S. B5 114
Ursel'skij, Russia E21 22
Urtigueira, Braz. C13 80
Uru, Braz. C4 79
Uruaçu, Braz. C4 79
Uruana, Braz. C4 79
Uruapan del Progreso, Mex. H8 90
Urubamba, Peru E5 82
Urubamba, stm., Peru D5 82
Urubaxi, stm., Braz. H10 84
Urubu, stm., Braz. I14 84
Urucará, Braz. H13 84
Urucu, stm., Braz. J10 84
Uruçuca, Braz. C9 79
Urucuia, stm., Braz. D6 79
Urucurituba, Braz. I14 84
Uruguaiana, Braz. E10 80
Uruguay, ctry., S.A. C5 78
Uruguay (Uruguai), stm., S.A. G10 80
Urumchi see Ürümqi, China C4 30
Ürümqi, China C4 30
Urundel, Arg. B6 80
Urup, ostrov, i., Russia H22 28
Urupá, stm., Braz. D10 82
Urupadi, stm., Braz. J14 84
Urupês, Braz. F4 79
Ur'upinsk, Russia G6 26
Urussanga, Braz. E14 80
Urutaí, Braz. D4 79
Urutaú, Arg. C7 80
Uržum, Russia F8 26
Usa, Japan N6 36
Usa, stm., Russia D9 26
Ušači, Bela. F11 22
Uşak, Tur. K13 20
Ušaki, Russia B13 22
Usakos, Nmb. D2 66
Usedom, i., Eur. A14 10
'Usfān, Sau. Ar. D1 47
Ushant see Ouessant, Île d', i., Fr. D1 14
'Ushayrah, Sau. Ar. D2 47
Ushuaia, Arg. G3 78
Usingen, Ger. E8 10
Usk, B.C., Can. C6 102
Usk, Wa., U.S. B8 122
Uslar, Ger. D9 10
Usman', Russia I22 22
Usolje-Sibirskoje, Russia G12 28
Usoro, Nig. I13 64
Uspallata, Arg. G4 80
Uspanapa, stm., Mex. I12 90
Ussuri (Wusuli), stm., Asia B13 30
Ussurijsk, Russia I18 28
Ustaritz, Fr. I5 14
Ust'-Barguzin, Russia G13 28
Ust'-Cil'ma, Russia D8 26
Ust'-Čorna, Ukr. A7 20
Ust'-Dolyssy, Russia E12 22
Uster, Switz. D10 13
Ust'-Ilimskoje vodochranilišče, res., Russia F18 26
Ústí nad Labem, Czech. E14 10
Ústí nad Orlicí, Czech. F16 10
Ust'-Išim, Russia F12 26
Ustje, Russia D22 22
Ustka, Pol. A16 10
Ust'-Kamčatsk, Russia F24 28
Ust'-Kamenogorsk, Kaz. H8 28
Ust'-Katav, Russia G9 26
Ust'-Koksa, Russia G15 26
Ust'-Kut, Russia F13 28
Ust'-Luga, Russia B11 22
Ust'-Nera, Russia E20 28
Uštobe, Kaz. H13 26
Ust'-Omčug, Russia E21 28
Ust'-Ordynskij, Russia G12 28
Ust'uckoje, Russia C18 22
Ust'urt, plato, plat., Asia I9 26
Ust'-Usa, Russia D9 26
Ust'užna, Russia C19 22
Usu, China C3 30
Usulután, El Sal. D6 92
Usumacinta, stm., N.A. I14 90
Usumun, Russia G17 28
Utah, state, U.S. D4 98
Utah Lake, l., Ut., U.S. D5 120
Utapi, Nmb. A2 66
Utashinai, Japan D17 36a
Ute, Ia., U.S. I12 118
Utembo, stm., Ang. E4 58
Utena, Lith. F8 22
Utete, Tan. C7 58
Uthai Thani, Thai. G6 40
Utiariti, Braz. E12 82
Utica, Ks., U.S. M7 118
Utica, Mi., U.S. H12 110
Utica, Ms., U.S. J6 114
Utica, Ne., U.S. K10 118
Utica, N.Y., U.S. D11 108
Utica, Oh., U.S. G4 108
Utiel, Spain F10 16
Utikoomak Lake Indian Reserve, Alta., Can. B19 102
Utikuma Lake, l., Alta., Can. B19 102
Utila, Hond. A8 92
Utila, Isla de, i., Hond. A8 92
Utinga, stm., Braz. B8 79
Utique, Tun. L5 18
Uto, Japan O5 36
Utopia, Tx., U.S. J7 116
Utorgoš, Russia C13 22
Utrecht, Neth. D7 12
Utrecht, S. Afr. F10 66
Utrecht, prov., Neth. D7 12
Utrera, Spain H6 16
Utsunomiya, Japan K14 36
Uttaradit, Thai. F6 40
Uttar Pradesh, state, India G9 44
Utuado, P.R. E11 94
Uudenmaan lääni, prov., Fin. K19 6
Uusikaupunki (Nystad), Fin. K17 6
Uvá, Braz. C3 79
Uvá, stm., Col. F8 84
Uvalda, Ga., U.S. G4 112
Uvalde, Tx., U.S. J7 116
Uvarovići, Bela. I13 22
Uvarovka, Russia F18 22
Uvarovo, Russia J25 22
Uvat, Russia F11 26
Uvinza, Tan. C6 58
Uvira, Zaire B5 58
Uvs nuur, l., Asia A5 30
Uwajima, Japan N7 36
Uwayl, Sud. M4 60
'Uwaynāt, Jabal al-, mtn., Afr. D5 56
Uxbridge, Ont., Can. F16 110
Uxmal, hist., Mex. G15 90
Uyuni, Bol. I8 82
Uyuni, Salar de, pl., Bol. I8 82
Už (Uh), stm., Eur. G22 10
Užava, Lat. D4 22
Uzbekistan, ctry., Asia I10 26
Uzboj, stm., Turk. B13 48
Uzda, Bela. H10 22
Uzdin, Yugo. D4 20
Užgorod, Ukr. H2 26
Uzlovaja, Russia H21 22
Uzunköprü, Tur. H10 20
Užur, Russia F9 28
Užventis, Lith. F5 22

V

Vääksy, Fin. K19 6
Vaala, Fin. I20 6
Vaalserberg, mtn., Neth. G9 12
Vaalwater, S. Afr. E9 66
Vaanta (Vanda), Fin. K19 6
Vaasa (Vasa), Fin. J17 6
Vaasan lääni, prov., Fin. J18 6
Vabalninkas, Lith. F7 22
Vabkent, Uzb. A18 48
Vác, Hung. H19 10
Vaca, Bol. H10 82
Vača, Russia F25 22
Vacacaí, stm., Braz. F11 80
Vacaria, Braz. E13 80
Vacaria, stm., Braz. D7 79
Vacaria, stm., Braz. F1 79
Vacaville, Ca., U.S. F4 124
Vaccarès, Étang de, b., Fr. I11 14
Vach, stm., Russia E7 28
Vache, Île à, i., Haiti E8 94
Vachš, stm., Taj. J11 26
Vacoas, Mrts. V18 67c
Vadino, Russia F16 22
Vadodara, India I5 44
Vado Ligure, Italy E3 18
Vaduz, Liech. E16 14
Vaga, stm., Russia E6 26
Vagaj, Russia F11 26
Vågåmo, Nor. K11 6
Vágar, i., Faer. Is. D8 6b
Váh, stm., Czech. G17 10
Vaiden, Ms., U.S. I7 114
Vaihingen, Ger. G8 10
Väike-Maarja, Est. B9 22
Vail, Co., U.S. E10 120
Vail, Ia., U.S. I12 118
Vailly-sur-Aisne, Fr. C10 14
Vaiņode, Lat. E4 22
Vajgač, ostrov, i., Russia C9 26
Valais (Wallis), state, Switz. F7 13
Valašské Meziříčí, Czech. F17 10
Valatie, N.Y., U.S. E13 108
Valcheta, Arg. E3 78
Valdagno, Italy D6 18
Valdai Hills see Valdajskaja vozvyšennost', hills, Russia D15 22
Valdaj, Russia D16 22
Valdajskaja vozvyšennost', hills, Russia D16 22
Valdelândia, Braz. C3 79
Valdemārpils, Lat. D5 22
Valdepeñas, Spain G8 16
Valders, Wi., U.S. F8 110
Valdés, Península, pen., Arg. E4 78
Val-des-Bois, Que., Can. B11 108
Valdese, N.C., U.S. D5 112
Valdéz, Ec. G3 84
Valdez, Ak., U.S. F21 100
Val-d'Isère, Fr. G13 14
Valdivia, Chile D2 78
Valdivia, Col. D5 84
Valdobbiadene, Italy D7 18
Val-d'Oise, dept., Fr. C9 14
Valdosta, Ga., U.S. I3 112
Vale, Or., U.S. G8 122
Valemount, B.C., Can. E15 102
Valença, Braz. B9 79
Valença, Braz. G7 79
Valença, Port. C3 16
Valençay, Fr. E8 14
Valence, Fr. H11 14
Valencia, Hond. C9 92
València, Spain F11 16
Valencia, Ven. B8 84
València, prov., Spain F11 16
València, Golf de, b., Spain F12 16
Valencia, Lago de, l., Ven. B9 84
Valencia de Alcántata, Spain F4 16
Valenciennes, Fr. B10 14
Valentine, Ne., U.S. I7 118
Valentine, Tx., U.S. I2 116
Valenza, Italy D3 18
Valera, Ven. C7 84
Valga, Est. D9 22
Valiente, Península, pen., Pan. C2 84
Valiente, Punta, c., Pan. H13 92
Valier, Il., U.S. D7 114
Valier, Mt., U.S. B13 122
Valjevo, Yugo. E3 20
Valka, Lat. D9 22
Valkininkas, Lith. G7 22
Valladolid, Ec. J3 84
Valladolid, Mex. G15 90
Valladolid, Spain D7 16
Vallauris, Fr. I14 14
Valldal, Nor. J10 6
Valle, Lat. E7 22
Valle, Spain B7 16
Valle, dept., Hond. D7 92
Vallecitos, N.M., U.S. H10 120
Valle d'Aosta, prov., Italy D2 18
Valle de Guanape, Ven. C10 84
Valle de la Pascua, Ven. C9 84
Valle del Cauca, dept., Col. F4 84
Valle de Olivos, Mex. D6 90
Valle de Santiago, Mex. G9 90
Valle de Zaragoza, Mex. D7 90
Valledupar, Col. B6 84
Valle Edén, Ur. F10 80
Vallegrande, Bol. H9 82
Valle Hermoso, Arg. F6 80
Valle Hermoso, Mex. E11 90
Vallehermoso, Spain O23 17b
Vallejo, Ca., U.S. F3 124
Vallenar, Chile E3 80
Valles Caldera, crat., N.M., U.S. I10 120
Valletta, Malta N9 18
Valley, Al., U.S. J11 114
Valley, Ne., U.S. J11 118
Valley, stm., Man., Can. G14 104
Valley Bend, W.V., U.S. I7 108
Valley Center, Ks., U.S. N10 118
Valley City, N.D., U.S. E10 118
Valley Falls, Ks., U.S. L12 118
Valley Farms, Az., U.S. L5 120
Valleyfield, Newf., Can. C20 106
Valley Head, Al., U.S. H11 114
Valley Head, W.V., U.S. I6 108
Valley Mills, Tx., U.S. H9 116
Valley of the Kings, hist., Egypt E7 60
Valley Springs, S.D., U.S. H11 118
Valley Station, Ky., U.S. D11 114
Valleyview, Alta., Can. B17 102
Valley View, Tx., U.S. F9 116
Valliant, Ok., U.S. E11 116
Vallimanca, Arroyo, stm., Arg. H8 80
Vallorbe, Switz. E5 13
Valls, Spain D13 16
Val-Marie, Sask., Can. I7 104
Valmaseda, Spain B8 16
Valmeyer, Il., U.S. D6 114
Valmiera, Lat. D8 22
Valognes, Fr. C5 14
Valongo, Port. D3 16
Vālpārai, India G4 46
Valparaíso, Braz. F3 79
Valparaíso, Chile G3 80
Valparaiso, Fl., U.S. L10 114
Valparaiso, In., U.S. A9 114
Valparaiso, Ne., U.S. J11 118
Valparaíso, prov., Chile G3 80
Valréas, Fr. H11 14
Vals, Tanjung, c., Indon. G10 38
Valsbaai, b., S. Afr. J4 66
Valsetz, Or., U.S. F2 122
Valtimo, Fin. J21 6
Valujki, Russia G5 26
Valverde del Camino, Spain H5 16
Van, Tur. B7 48
Van, Tx., U.S. G11 116
Van Alstyne, Tx., U.S. F10 116
Vananda, B.C., Can. H10 102
Van Buren, Ar., U.S. G2 114
Van Buren, Mo., U.S. F5 114
Vanč, Taj. J12 26
Vanceboro, Me., U.S. B19 108
Vanceburg, Ky., U.S. I3 108
Vancleave, Ms., U.S. L8 114
Vancouver, B.C., Can. H11 102
Vancouver, Wa., U.S. E3 122
Vancouver, Cape, c., Austl. G3 68
Vancouver, Cape, c., Ak., U.S. F12 100
Vancouver, Mount, mtn., N.A. F25 100
Vancouver Island, i., B.C., Can. H9 102
Vancouver Island Ranges, mts., B.C., Can. H9 102
Vandalia, Il., U.S. D7 114
Vandalia, Mo., U.S. C5 114
Vandalia, Oh., U.S. H2 108
Vandekerckhove Lake, l., Man., Can. A13 104
Vanderbijlpark, S. Afr. F8 66
Vanderbilt, Mi., U.S. E11 110
Vanderbilt, Tx., U.S. K10 116
Vandergrift, Pa., U.S. G7 108
Vanderhoof, B.C., Can. C10 102
Vanderlin Island, i., Austl. C7 68
Vandervoort, Ar., U.S. H2 114
Van Diemen Gulf, b., Austl. B6 68
Vändra, Est. C8 22
Vanegas, Mex. F9 90
Vänern, l., Swe. L13 6
Vänersborg, Swe. L13 6
Vangaindrano, Madag. S22 67b
Van Gölü, l., Tur. B7 48
Vangsnes, Nor. K10 6
Vanguard, Sask., Can. I7 104
Van Horn, Tx., U.S. H2 116
Van Horne, Ia., U.S. H3 110
Vanier, Ont., Can. B11 108
Vanimo, Pap. N. Gui. F11 38
Vanino, Russia H20 28
Vāniyambādi, India F5 46
Vankleek Hill, Ont., Can. B12 108
Van Lear, Ky., U.S. B4 112
Vanndale, Ar., U.S. G6 114
Vannes, Fr. E4 14
Van Ninh, Viet. H10 40
Van Rees, Pegunungan, mts., Indon. F10 38
Vanrhynsdorp, S. Afr. H4 66
Vansant, Va., U.S. B4 112
Vansittart Island, i., N.W. Ter., Can. C16 96
Vanskoje, Russia C19 22
Vanstadensrus, S. Afr. G8 66
Vanua Levu, i., Fiji J21 126
Vanuatu, ctry., Oc. H24 2
Van Vleck, Tx., U.S. J11 116
Van Wert, Oh., U.S. G2 108
Vanzylsrus, S. Afr. F6 66
Vapn'arka, Ukr. A12 20
Var, dept., Fr. I13 14
Var, stm., Fr. I13 14
Varakļāni, Lat. E9 22
Varallo, Italy D3 18
Vārānasi (Benares), India H10 44
Varangerfjorden, Nor. G22 6
Varangerhalvøya, pen., Nor. F21 6
Varaždin, Cro. C11 18
Varazze, Italy E3 18
Varberg, Swe. M13 6
Vardaman, Ms., U.S. I7 114
Vardar (Axiós), stm., Eur. H6 20
Vardø, Nor. F22 6
Varegovo, Russia D22 22
Varel, Ger. B8 10
Varela, Arg. H5 80
Varėna, Lith. G7 22
Vareš, Bos. E2 20
Varese, Italy D3 18
Varginha, Braz. F6 79
Varjão, Braz. D4 79
Varkaus, Fin. J20 6
Värmlands Län, co., Swe. L13 6
Varna, Bul. F11 20
Värnamo, Swe. M14 6
Varnsdorf, Czech. E14 10
Varnville, S.C., U.S. G5 112
Várpalota, Hung. H18 10
Värska, Est. D10 22
Várzea, Rio da, stm., Braz. D12 80
Várzea da Palma, Braz. D6 79
Várzea Grande, Braz. F13 82
Varzeão, Braz. C14 80
Vas, co., Hung. H16 10
Vasalemma, Est. B7 22
Vasilevičí, Bela. I12 22
Vasiliká, Grc. I7 20
Vasiljevskij Moch, Russia D18 22
Vasiljevskoje, Russia E24 22
Vaskelovo, Russia A13 22
Vaškovci, Ukr. A11 20
Vaškovcy, Ukr. A9 20
Vaslui, Rom. C11 20
Vaslui, co., Rom. C11 20
Vass, N.C., U.S. D7 112
Vassar, Mi., U.S. G12 110
Västerås, Swe. L15 6
Västerbottens Län, co., Swe. I15 6
Västernorrlands Län, co., Swe. J15 6
Västervik, Swe. M15 6
Västmanlands Län, co., Swe. L15 6
Vasto, Italy G9 18
Vas'ugan, stm., Russia F13 26
Vas'uganje, sw., Russia F7 28
Vasvár, Hung. H16 10
Vatan, Fr. E8 14
Vathí, Grc. L10 20
Vatican City (Città del Vaticano), ctry., Eur. H7 18
V'atka, stm., Russia F8 26
Vatnajökull, ice., Ice. B5 6a
Vatneyri, Ice. B2 6a
Vatomandry, Madag. Q23 67b
Vatra Dornei, Rom. B9 20
V'atskije Pol'any, Russia F8 26
Vättern, l., Swe. L14 6
Vaucluse, dept., Fr. H12 14
Vaucouleurs, Fr. D12 14
Vaud, state, Switz. E6 13
Vaughan, Ont., Can. G16 110
Vaughn, N.M., U.S. J11 120
Vaupés, ter., Col. G7 84
Vaupés (Uaupés), stm., S.A. G7 84
Vauréal, Chute, wtfl, Que., Can. C11 106
Vauvert, Fr. I11 14
Vauxhall, Alta., Can. G22 102
Vavatenina, Madag. P23 67b
Vavoua, I.C. H6 64
Växjö, Swe. M14 6
Vazante, Braz. E5 79
Vazante Grande, stm., Braz. H13 82
V'azemskij, Russia H18 28
V'az'ma, Russia F17 22
V'azniki, Russia E25 22
Veazie, Me., U.S. C18 108
Veblen, S.D., U.S. F10 118
Vecht, stm., Eur. C9 12
Vechta, Ger. C8 10
Vecsés, Hung. H19 10
Vedea, Rom. E8 20
Vedia, Arg. H8 80
Veedersburg, In., U.S. B9 114
Veendam, Neth. B10 12
Veenendaal, Neth. D8 12
Vega, Tx., U.S. D4 116
Veghel, Neth. E8 12
Vegreville, Alta., Can. D22 102
Veguita, N.M., U.S. J10 120
Veinticinco de Mayo, Arg. H8 80
Veinticinco de Mayo, Arg. H4 80
Veinticinco de Mayo, Ur. H10 80
Veintiocho de Mayo, Ec. I3 84
Veintisiete de Abril, C.R. G9 92
Veisiejai, Lith. G6 22
Vejer de la Frontera, Spain I6 16
Vejle, Den. N11 6
Velardeña, Mex. E8 90
Velas, Cabo, c., C.R. G9 92
Velázquez, Ur. H11 80
Velbert, Ger. D7 10
Velddrif, S. Afr. I4 66
Velden, Ger. G12 10
Veldhoven, Neth. F7 12
Velet'ma, Russia F25 22
Vélez, Col. D6 84
Velez de la Gomera, Peñón de, i., Sp. N. Afr. J7 16
Vélez-Málaga, Spain I7 16
Vel'gija, Russia C16 22
Velhas, Rio das, stm., Braz. D6 79
Velikaja, stm., Russia E26 28
Velikaja Kosnica, Ukr. A12 20
Velikaja Michajlovka, Ukr. B13 20
Velika Morava, stm., Yugo. E5 20
Velika Plana, Yugo. E5 20
Velikij Ber'oznyj, Ukr. G22 10
Velikije Luki, Russia E13 22
Velikij Ust'ug, Russia E7 26
Velikodvorskij, Russia F23 22
Veliko Gradište, Yugo. E5 20
Velikoje, Russia D22 22
Velikoploskoje, Ukr. B13 20
Veliko Tărnovo, Bul. F9 20
Vélingara, Sen. F4 54
Velíž, Russia F14 22
Velletri, Italy H7 18
Vellore, India F5 46
Velma, Ok., U.S. E9 116
Velp, Neth. D8 12
Vel'sk, Russia E6 26
Velten, Ger. C13 10
Velva, N.D., U.S. C7 118
Venaco, Fr. G4 18
Venadillo, Col. E5 84
Venado, Isla del, i., Nic. F11 92
Venado Tuerto, Arg. G8 80
Venâncio Aires, Braz. E12 80
Vence, Fr. I14 14
Venceslau Braz, Braz. G4 79
Venda, ctry., Afr. D10 66
Venda Nova, Port. D4 16
Vendas Novas, Port. G3 16
Vendée, dept., Fr. F5 14
Vendeuvre-sur-Barse, Fr. D11 14
Vendičany, Ukr. A11 20
Vendôme, Fr. E8 14
Venecia, C.R. G10 92
Veneto, prov., Italy G18 14
Venev, Russia G21 22
Venezia (Venice), Italy D7 18
Venezuela, ctry., S.A. B5 76
Venezuela, Golfo de, b., S.A. B7 84
Vengerovo, Russia F13 26
Veniaminof, Mount, mtn., Ak., U.S. H15 100
Venice, Fl., U.S. L4 112
Venice, La., U.S. M7 114
Venice, Gulf of, b., Eur. D8 18
Venice see Venezia, Italy D7 18
Vénissieux, Fr. G11 14
Venlo, Neth. F9 12
Venosa, Italy I10 18
Vent, Aus. I10 10
Ventanas, Ec. H3 84
Ventersdorp, S. Afr. F8 66
Venterstad, S. Afr. H7 66
Ventimiglia, Italy F2 18
Ventspils, Lat. D4 22
Ventuari, stm., Ven. E9 84
Ventura, Ca., U.S. J6 124
Venus, Fl., U.S. L5 112
Venustiano Carranza, Mex. I13 90
Venustiano Carranza, Mex. H8 90
Venustiano Carranza, Bahía, b., Mex. H16 90
Venustiano Carranza, Presa, res., Mex. D9 90
Vera, Arg. E8 80
Veracruz, state, Mex. H12 90
Veracruz [Llave], Mex. H11 90
Veraguas, prov., Pan. I13 92
Veranópolis, Braz. E13 80
Verāval, India J4 44
Verbania, Italy D3 18
Verbilki, Russia E20 22
Verbovskij, Russia F25 22
Vercelli, Italy D3 18
Vercel [-Villedieu-le-Camp], Fr. E13 14
Verchn'aja Inta, Russia D10 26
Verchn'aja Salda, Russia F10 26
Verchn'aja Tajmyra, stm., Russia C11 28
Verchn'aja Troica, Russia D20 22
Verchn'aja Tura, Russia F9 26
Verchnedneprovskij, Russia G16 22
Verchnedvinsk, Bela. F10 22
Verchnemulomskoje vodochranilišče, res., Russia G22 6
Verchnevil'ujsk, Russia E16 28
Verchnij Baskunčak, Russia H7 26
Verchnij Ufalej, Russia F10 26
Verchojansk, Russia D18 28
Verchojanskij chrebet, mts., Russia D17 28
Verchoturje, Russia F10 26
Verchovje, Russia I20 22
Vercors, reg., Fr. H12 14
Verde, stm., Braz. C4 79
Verde, stm., Braz. D5 79
Verde, stm., Braz. D3 79
Verde, stm., Braz. E3 79
Verde, stm., Braz. E4 79
Verde, stm., Braz. F2 79
Verde, stm., Braz. E13 82
Verde, stm., Braz. E12 82
Verde, stm., Mex. G8 90
Verde, stm., Para. B9 80
Verde, stm., S.A. F11 82
Verde, stm., Az., U.S. K5 120
Verde, Arroyo, stm., Bol. E8 82
Verde, Cape, c., Bah. C7 94
Verde Grande, stm., Braz. C7 79
Verden, Ger. C9 10
Verden, Ok., U.S. D8 116
Verde Pequeno, stm., Braz. C7 79
Verdi, Nv., U.S. E6 124
Verdigre, Ne., U.S. I9 118
Verdigris, stm., U.S. C11 116
Verdinho, stm., Braz. D3 79
Verdon, Ne., U.S. K12 118
Verdun, Que., Can. B13 108
Verdun, Fr. I8 14
Verdun-sur-le-Doubs, Fr. F12 14
Verdun-sur-Meuse, Fr. C12 14
Vereeniging, S. Afr. F8 66
Veregin, Sask., Can. G12 104
Vereja, Russia F19 22
Veremejki, Bela. H14 22
Vereščagino, Russia F8 26
Vergara, Ur. G12 80
Vergennes, Vt., U.S. C13 108
Verín, Spain D4 16

Name | Map Ref. | Page

Veriora, Est. C10 22
Veríssimo, Braz. E4 79
Verkhoyansk see Verchojansk, Russia D18 28
Vermejo, stm., N.M., U.S. H12 120
Vermelho, stm., Braz. C3 79
Vermette Lake, l., Sask., Can. C5 104
Vermilion, Alta., Can. D24 102
Vermilion, Oh., U.S. F4 108
Vermilion, stm., Alta., Can. E3 104
Vermilion, stm., Il., U.S. I7 110
Vermilion, stm., La., U.S. M4 114
Vermilion, stm., Mn., U.S. B3 110
Vermilion Bay, Ont., Can. I21 104
Vermilion Bay, b., La., U.S. M4 114
Vermilion Lake, l., Ont., Can. H22 104
Vermilion Lake, l., Mn., U.S. C3 110
Vermilion Pass, Can. F18 102
Vermillion, S.D., U.S. I11 118
Vermillion, stm., S.D., U.S. H11 118
Vermont, Il., U.S. B6 114
Vermont, state, U.S. C12 98
Vernal, Ut., U.S. D7 120
Vernayaz, Switz. F7 13
Verndale, Mn., U.S. E12 118
Verner, Ont., Can. D15 110
Verneuil, Fr. D7 14
Vernon, B.C., Can. G15 102
Vernon, Fr. C8 14
Vernon, Al., U.S. I8 114
Vernon, Ct., U.S. F14 108
Vernon, Fl., U.S. L11 114
Vernon, In., U.S. D11 114
Vernon, Tx., U.S. E7 116
Vernon, Ut., U.S. D4 120
Vernonia, Or., U.S. E2 122
Vernon River, P.E.I., Can. F11 106
Verny, Fr. C13 14
Vero Beach, Fl., U.S. L6 112
Véroia, Grc. I6 20
Verona, Ont., Can. F19 110
Verona, Italy D6 18
Verona, Ms., U.S. H8 114
Verona, Wi., U.S. H6 110
Verónica, Arg. H10 80
Verrettes, Haiti E8 94
Versailles, Fr. D9 14
Versailles, Il., U.S. C6 114
Versailles, In., U.S. C11 114
Versailles, Ky., U.S. D12 114
Versailles, Mo., U.S. D4 114
Versailles, Oh., U.S. G2 108
Veršino-Darasunskij, Russia G15 28
Vert, Cap, c., Sen. D1 64
Verte, Île, i., Que., Can. D4 106
Vertientes, Cuba D5 94
Vertou, Fr. E5 14
Verviers, Bel. G8 12
Vervins, Fr. C10 14
Vescovato, Fr. G4 18
Vesjegonsk, Russia C20 22
Vesoul, Fr. E13 14
Vespasiano, Braz. E7 79
Vesta, C.R. H11 92
Vest-Agder, co., Nor. L10 6
Vestavia Hills, Al., U.S. I10 114
Vesterålen, is., Nor. G14 6
Vestfjorden, Nor. H14 6
Vestfold, co., Nor. L12 6
Vestmannaeyjar, Ice. C3 6a
Vesuvio, vol., Italy I9 18
Vesuvius see Vesuvio, vol., Italy I9 18
Veszprém, Hung. H17 10
Veszprém, co., Hung. H17 10
Vésztő, Hung. I21 10
Vetluga, Russia F7 26
Vetralla, Italy G7 18
Vetrino, Bela. F11 22
Vetrișoaia, Rom. C12 20
Vetschau, Ger. D14 10
Veurne (Furnes), Bel. F2 12
Vevay, In., U.S. D11 114
Vevey, Switz. F6 13
Vézelise, Fr. D13 14
Viacha, Bol. G7 82
Viadana, Italy E5 18
Viadutos, Braz. D12 80
Viale, Arg. F8 80
Viamão, Braz. F13 80
Viamonte, Arg. G7 80
Vian, Ok., U.S. D12 116
Viana, Braz. D9 76
Viana do Alentejo, Port. G3 16
Viana do Castelo, Port. D3 16
Viangchan (Vientiane), Laos F7 40
Viangphoukha, Laos D6 40
Viareggio, Italy F5 18
Vibank, Sask., Can. H11 104
Viborg, Den. M11 6
Viborg, S.D., U.S. H10 118
Vibo Valentia, Italy K11 18
Vibraye, Fr. D7 14
Viburnum, Mo., U.S. E5 114
Vic (Vich), Spain D14 16
Vícam, Mex. D4 90
Vicco, Ky., U.S. B3 112
Vic-en-Bigorre, Fr. I7 14
Vicente Guerrero, Mex. F8 90
Vicente López, Arg. H9 80
Vicente Noble, Dom. Rep. E9 94
Vicenza, Italy D6 18
Viceroy, Sask., Can. I9 104
Vichada, dept., Col. E8 84
Vichada, stm., Col. E8 84
Vichadero, Ur. F11 80
Vichigasta, Arg. E5 80
Vichuquén, Chile H2 80
Vichy, Fr. F10 14
Vici, Ok., U.S. C7 116
Vicksburg, Mi., U.S. H10 110
Vicksburg, Ms., U.S. J6 114
Vico, Fr. L23 15a
Viçosa, Braz. F7 79
Victor, Id., U.S. G14 122
Victor, Ia., U.S. I3 110
Victor, Mt., U.S. D11 122
Victor, Lac, l., Que., Can. B12 106
Victor Harbor, Austl. J3 70
Victoria, Arg. G8 80
Victoria, Cam. I14 64
Victoria, B.C., Can. I11 102
Victoria, P.E.I., Can. F10 106
Victoria, Chile J2 80
Victoria, Gren. H14 94
Victoria (Xianggang), H.K. M3 34
Victoria, Malay. D6 38
Victoria, Sey. B11 58
Victoria, Ks., U.S. M8 118
Victoria, Tx., U.S. K9 116
Victoria, Va., U.S. C8 112
Victoria, state, Austl. G9 68
Victoria, stm., Austl. C6 68
Victoria, stm., Newf., Can. D17 106
Victoria, Lake, l., Afr. B6 58
Victoria, Lake, l., Austl. I4 70
Victoria, Mount, mtn., Burma D2 40
Victoria, Mount, mtn., Pap. N. Gui. A9 68
Victoria Beach, Man., Can. H18 104
Victoria Falls, Zimb. A7 66
Victoria Falls, wtfl, Afr. A7 66
Victoria Harbour, Ont., Can. F16 110
Victoria Island, i., N.W. Ter., Can. B10 96
Victoria Lake, res., Newf., Can. D16 106
Victoria Land, reg., Ant. C8 73
Victoria Nile, stm., Ug. H7 56
Victoria Peak, mtn., Belize I15 90
Victoria Peak, mtn., B.C., Can. G8 102
Victoria River Downs, Austl. C6 68
Victoria Strait, strt., N.W. Ter., Can. C12 96
Victoriaville, Que., Can. A15 108
Victoria West, S. Afr. H6 66
Victorica, Arg. I6 80
Victorino, Ven. F9 84
Victorino de la Plaza, Arg. I7 80
Victorville, Ca., U.S. J8 124
Vičuga, Russia D24 22
Vicuña, Chile F3 80
Vicuña Mackenna, Arg. G6 80
Vidalia, Ga., U.S. G4 112
Vidalia, La., U.S. K5 114
Vidal Ramos, Braz. D14 80
Vidauban, Fr. I13 14
Videira, Braz. D13 80
Vidigueira, Port. G4 16
Vidin, Bul. F6 20
Vidisha, India I7 44
Vidlica, Russia K23 6
Vidor, Tx., U.S. L2 114
Vidzeme, hist. reg., Lat. D8 22
Vidzy, Bela. F9 22
Viechtach, Ger. F12 10
Viedma, Arg. E4 78
Viedma, Lago, l., Arg. F2 78
Viejo, Cerro, mtn., Peru J3 84
Viekšniai, Lith. E5 22
Viella, Spain C12 16
Vienna, Ga., U.S. G3 112
Vienna, Il., U.S. E8 114
Vienna, Md., U.S. I11 108
Vienna, Mo., U.S. D5 114
Vienna, S.D., U.S. G10 118
Vienna, W.V., U.S. H5 108
Vienna see Wien, Aus. G16 10
Vienne, Fr. G11 14
Vienne, dept., Fr. F7 14
Vienne, stm., Fr. E7 14
Vientiane see Viangchan, Laos F7 40
Vieques, P.R. E12 94
Vieques, Isla de, i., P.R. E12 94
Vierfontein, S. Afr. F8 66
Viersen, Ger. D6 10
Vierwaldstättersee, l., Switz. D9 13
Vierzon, Fr. E9 14
Viesca, Mex. E8 90
Viesīte, Lat. E8 22
Vieste, Italy H11 18
Vietnam, ctry., Asia B4 38
Viet Tri, Viet. D8 40
Vieux-Fort, Que., Can. A16 106
Vieux Fort, St. Luc. H14 94
Vievis, Lith. G7 22
Vieytes, Arg. H10 80
Vigan, Phil. M19 39b
Vigeland, Nor. L10 6
Vigevano, Italy D3 18
Vigneulles-lès-Hattonchâtel, Fr. D12 14
Vignola, Italy E6 18
Vigo, Spain C3 16
Vihowa, Pak. E4 44
Viitasaari, Fin. J19 6
Vijāpur, India I5 44
Vijayawāda, India D6 46
Vijosë (Aóös), stm., Eur. I4 20
Viking, Alta., Can. D23 102
Vikna, i., Nor. C10 4
Vikramasingapuram, India H4 46
Vila da Ribeira Brava, C.V. k16 64a
Vila de Manica, Moz. B11 66
Vila do Bispo, Port. H3 16
Vila Fontes, Moz. A12 66
Vilafranca del Penedès, Spain D13 16
Vila Gomes da Costa, Moz. E11 66
Viļaka, Lat. D10 22
Vilama, Laguna de, l., Arg. B5 80
Vila Machado, Moz. B12 66
Vilanculos, Moz. D12 66
Viļāni, Lat. E9 22
Vila Nova de Foz Côa, Port. D4 16
Vila Nova de Gaia, Port. D3 16
Vilanova i la Geltrú, Spain D13 16
Vila Novo de Ourém, Port. F3 16
Vila Paiva de Andrada, Moz. B12 66
Vila Real, Port. D4 16
Vila Real de Santo António, Port. H4 16
Vilar Formoso, Port. E5 16
Vila Velha, Braz. F8 79
Vila Velha de Ródão, Port. F4 16
Vila Verde, Port. D3 16
Vîlcea, co., Rom. E8 20
Vilejka, Bela. G9 22
Vilelas, Arg. D7 80
Vilhelmina, Swe. I15 6
Vilhena, Braz. E11 82
Viljandi, Est. C8 22
Viljoenskroon, S. Afr. F8 66
Vilkaviškis, Lith. G6 22
Vil'kickogo, ostrov, i., Russia C13 26
Vil'kickogo, proliv, strt., Russia B18 26
Vilkija, Lith. F6 22
Vilkovo, Ukr. D13 20
Villa Abecia, Bol. I9 82
Villa Aberastain, Arg. F4 80
Villa Alemana, Chile G3 80
Villa Ana, Arg. E9 80
Villa Ángela, Arg. D8 80
Villa Atamisqui, Arg. E7 80
Villa Atuel, Arg. H5 80
Villa Bella, Bol. D9 82
Villa Berthet, Arg. D8 80
Villa Bruzual, Ven. C8 84
Villa Cañás, Arg. H8 80
Villacañas, Spain F8 16
Villa Carlos Paz, Arg. F6 80
Villacarrillo, Spain G8 16
Villa Castelli, Arg. E4 80
Villach, Aus. I13 10
Villacidro, Italy J3 18
Villa Comaltitlan, Mex. B2 92
Villa Concepción del Tío, Arg. F7 80
Villa Constitución, Arg. G8 80
Villada, Spain C7 16
Villa de Arista, Mex. F9 90
Villa de Arriaga, Mex. G9 90
Villa de Cos, Mex. F8 90
Villa de Cura, Ven. B9 84
Villa del Carmen, Arg. G6 80
Villa del Rosario, Arg. F7 80
Villa del Rosario, Arg. F10 80
Villa de María, Arg. E7 80
Villa de Nova Sintra, C.V. m16 64a
Villa de San Antonio, Hond. C7 92
Villa de San Francisco, Hond. C8 92
Villa de Soto, Arg. F6 80
Villadiego, Spain C7 16
Villa Dolores, Arg. F6 80
Villa Elisa, Arg. G9 80
Villa Flores, Mex. I13 90
Villa Florida, Para. D10 80
Villafranca de los Barros, Spain G5 16
Villafranca di Verona, Italy D5 18
Village, Ok., U.S. D9 116
Villa General Roca, Arg. G5 80
Villagrán, Mex. E10 90
Villa Grove, Il., U.S. C8 114
Villaguay, Arg. F9 80
Villa Guerrero, Mex. H10 90
Villa Guillermina, Arg. E9 80
Villa Hayes, Para. C10 80
Villahermosa, Mex. I13 90
Villa Hernandarias, Arg. F9 80
Villa Hidalgo, Mex. G8 90
Villa Huidobro, Arg. H6 80
Villaines-la-Juhel, Fr. D6 14
Villa Insurgentes, Mex. E4 90
Villa Iris, Arg. J7 80
Villa Juárez, Mex. D5 90
Villa Krause, Arg. F4 80
Villa Larca, Arg. G6 80
Villaldama, Mex. D9 90
Villalonga, Arg. D4 78
Villa Mainero, Mex. E10 90
Villa María, Arg. G7 80
Villa María Grande, Arg. F9 80
Villa Martín, Bol. I8 82
Villa Matoque, Arg. C7 80
Villa Mazán, Arg. E5 80
Villa Media Agua, Arg. F4 80
Villa Mercedes, Arg. F4 80
Villamontes, Bol. I10 82
Villa Nueva, Arg. G7 80
Villa Nueva, Arg. G4 80
Villanueva, Col. B6 84
Villa Nueva, Guat. C4 92
Villanueva, Hond. B6 92
Villanueva, Mex. F8 90
Villa Nueva, Nic. E8 92
Villanueva, N.M., U.S. I11 120
Villanueva de Córdoba, Spain G7 16
Villanueva de la Serana, Spain G6 16
Villanueva del Río y Minas, Spain H6 16
Villa Ocampo, Arg. E9 80
Villa Ojo de Agua, Arg. E7 80
Villa Oliva, Para. D10 80
Villa Oropeza, Bol. H9 82
Villapinzón, Col. E6 84
Villa Quinteros, Arg. D6 80
Villa Ramírez, Arg. G8 80
Villarcayo, Spain C8 16
Villa Regina, Arg. J5 80
Villa Reynolds, Arg. G6 80
Villa Rica, Ga., U.S. F2 112
Villa Rivero, Bol. G9 82
Villarrica, Chile D2 78
Villarrica, Col. F5 84
Villarrica, Para. C10 80
Villarrobledo, Spain F9 16
Villas, N.J., U.S. H12 108
Villa Sandino, Nic. E10 92
Villa San José, Arg. G9 80
Villa San Martín, Arg. E6 80
Villa Santa, Montaña, mtn., Hond. C8 92
Villa Santo Domingo, Mex. F9 90
Villasayas, Spain D9 16
Villa Serrano, Bol. H9 82
Villasimius, Italy J4 18
Villasor, Italy J3 18
Villa Tunari, Bol. G9 82
Villa Unión, Arg. E4 80
Villa Unión, Arg. E7 80
Villa Unión, Mex. C9 90
Villa Unión, Mex. F6 90
Villa Valeria, Arg. H6 80
Villavicencio, Col. E6 84
Villaviciosa, Spain B6 16
Villa Viscarra, Bol. G9 82
Villazón, Bol. J9 82
Villa Zorraquín, Arg. F9 80
Villé, Fr. D14 14
Villedieu, Fr. D5 14
Villefort, Fr. H10 14
Villefranche, Fr. G11 14
Villena, Spain G11 16
Villeneuve-d'Aveyron, Fr. H9 14
Villeneuve-Saint-Georges, Fr. D9 14
Villeneuve-sur-Lot, Fr. H7 14
Ville Platte, La., U.S. L4 114
Villers-Bocage, Fr. C9 14
Villers-Bocage, Fr. C6 14
Villersexel, Fr. E13 14
Villerupt, Fr. C12 14
Ville-Saint-Georges see Saint-Georges, Que., Can. A16 108
Villeta, Col. E5 84
Villeurbanne, Fr. G11 14
Villiers, S. Afr. F9 66
Villingen-Schwenningen, Ger. G8 10
Villisca, Ia., U.S. K13 118
Vilna, Alta., Can. C23 102
Vilnius, Lith. G8 22
Vilshofen, Ger. G13 10
Vil'uj, stm., Russia E16 28
Vil'ujsk, Russia E16 28
Vil'ujskoje vodochranilišče, res., Russia E20 26
Vimianzo, Spain B2 16
Vimoutiers, Fr. D7 14
Vimperk, Czech. F13 10
Vina, Ca., U.S. E3 124
Vina, stm., Cam. G9 54
Viñac, Peru E4 82
Viña del Mar, Chile G3 80
Vinalhaven, Me., U.S. C18 108
Vinaròs, Spain E12 16
Vincennes, In., U.S. D9 114
Vincennes Bay, b., Ant. B6 73
Vincent, Al., U.S. I10 114
Vinces, Ec. H3 84
Vinchina, Arg. E4 80
Vinchos, Peru E4 82
Vindhya Range, mts., India I7 44
Vinegar Hill, mtn., Or., U.S. F7 122
Vine Grove, Ky., U.S. E11 114
Vineland, N.J., U.S. H11 108
Vinemont, Al., U.S. H10 114
Vineyard Haven, Ma., U.S. F16 108
Ving Ngün, Burma C5 40
Vinh, Viet. E8 40
Vinh Long, Viet. I8 40
Vinita, Ok., U.S. C11 116
Vinkovci, Cro. D2 20
Vinnica, Ukr. H3 26
Vinogradov, Ukr. A7 20
Vinson Massif, mtn., Ant. C12 73
Vinton, Ia., U.S. H3 110
Vinton, La., U.S. L3 114
Vinton, Va., U.S. B7 112
Viny, Russia C15 22
Viola, Il., U.S. I5 110
Viola, Wi., U.S. G5 110
Violín, Isla, i., C.R. I11 92
Vipiteno, Italy C6 18
Vipos, Arg. D6 80
Virac, Phil. C7 38
Virac, Phil. M19 39b
Viradouro, Braz. F4 79
Virago Sound, strt., B.C., Can. C2 102
Viramgām, India I5 44
Viranşehir, Tur. C5 48
Virbalis, Lith. G5 22
Virden, Man., Can. I14 104
Virden, Il., U.S. C7 114
Virden, N.M., U.S. L7 120
Vire, Fr. D6 14
Virelles, Bel. H5 12
Vîrfurile, Rom. C6 20
Virgem da Lapa, Braz. D7 79
Virgil, Ks., U.S. N11 118
Virgilina, Va., U.S. C8 112
Virgin, stm., U.S. H2 120
Virgin Gorda, i., Br. Vir. Is. E12 94
Virginia, S. Afr. G8 66
Virginia, Il., U.S. C6 114
Virginia, Mn., U.S. C3 110
Virginia, state, U.S. D11 98
Virginia Beach, Va., U.S. C11 112
Virginia City, Mt., U.S. E14 122
Virginia City, Nv., U.S. E6 124
Virginia Falls, wtfl, N.W. Ter., Can. F32 100
Virginiatown, Ont., Can. B16 110
Virgin Islands, dep., N.A. E12 94
Virginópolis, Braz. E7 79
Virgolândia, Braz. E7 79
Virŏchey, Camb. H9 40
Virojoki, Fin. K20 6
Viroqua, Wi., U.S. G5 110
Virovitica, Cro. D12 18
Virrat, Fin. J18 6
Virtaniemi, Fin. G21 6
Vîrtopu, Rom. E7 20
Virtsu, Est. C6 22
Virú, Peru C2 82
Virudunagar, India H4 46
Virungu, Zaire C5 58
Viru-Nigula, Est. B9 22
Vis, Cro. F11 18
Vis (Fish), stm., Nmb. E3 66
Vis, Otok, i., Cro. F11 18
Visalia, Ca., U.S. H6 124
Visayan Sea, Phil. C7 38
Visby, Swe. M16 6
Viscount, Sask., Can. G9 104
Viscount Melville Sound, strt., N.W. Ter., Can. B11 96
Visé (Wezet), Bel. G8 12
Višegrad, Bos. F3 20
Viseu, Port. E4 16
Vishākhapatnam, India D7 46
Vislinskij zaliv, b., Eur. A19 10
Visnagar, India I5 44
Viso, Monte, mtn., Italy E2 18
Visoko, Bos. F2 20
Visokoi Island, i., S. Geor. A2 73
Visp, Switz. F8 13
Visselhövede, Ger. C9 10
Vista, Ca., U.S. K8 124
Vista Alegre, Arg. J4 80
Vista Flores, Arg. G4 80
Vistula see Wisła, stm., Pol. A18 10
Vita, Man., Can. I18 104
Vita, stm., Col. E8 84
Vitarte, Peru E3 82
Vitebsk, Bela. F13 22
Viterbo, Italy G7 18
Vitichi, Bol. I9 82
Viti Levu, i., Fiji J21 126
Vitim, stm., Russia F14 28
Vítor, Peru G6 82
Vitor, stm., Peru G5 82
Vitória, Braz. G10 74
Vitória, Braz. F8 79
Vitoria (Gasteiz), Spain C9 16
Vitória da Conquista, Braz. C8 79
Vitré, Fr. D5 14
Vitry-le-François, Fr. D11 14
Vittangi, Swe. H17 6
Vitteaux, Fr. E11 14
Vittel, Fr. D12 14
Vittoria, Italy M9 18
Vittorio Veneto, Italy D7 18
Viver, Spain F11 16
Vivi, stm., Russia D17 26
Vivian, La., U.S. J3 114
Vivoratá, Arg. I10 80
Vivorillo, Cayos, is., Hond. B11 92
Vizcaíno, Desierto de, des., Mex. D3 90
Vize, Tur. H11 20
Vize, ostrov, i., Russia B13 26
Vizianagaram, India C7 46
Vižnica, Ukr. A9 20
Vizzini, Italy L9 18
Vlaardingen, Neth. E5 12
Vladikavkaz, Russia I6 26
Vladimir, Russia E23 22
Vladimirskij Tupik, Russia F16 22
Vladivostok, Russia I18 28
Vlasenica, Bos. E2 20
Vlasotince, Yugo. G6 20
Vlieland, i., Neth. B7 12
Vlissingen (Flushing), Neth. F4 12
Vlonë see Vlorë, Alb. I3 20
Vlorë, Alb. I3 20
Vlorës, Gji i, b., Alb. I3 20
Vltava, stm., Czech. F14 10
Vnukovo, Russia F20 22
Voca, Tx., U.S. H7 116
Vochtoga, Russia C24 22
Vodlozero, ozero, l., Russia J25 6
Vodňany, Czech. F14 10
Vogelsberg, mts., Ger. E9 10
Voghera, Italy E4 18
Vohenstrauss, Ger. F12 10
Vohibinany, Madag. Q23 67b
Vohilava, Madag. R23 67b
Vohimarina, Madag. N24 67b
Vohipeno, Madag. S22 67b
Võhma, Est. C8 22
Void, Fr. D12 14
Voinjama, Lib. G5 64
Voiron, Fr. G12 14
Voitsberg, Aus. H15 10
Voj-Vož, Russia E8 26
Volary, Czech. G13 10
Volcán, Arg. B6 80
Volcán, Pan. C1 84
Volcano, Hi., U.S. r18 125a
Volcán Poás, Parque Nacional, C.R. G10 92
Volchov, Russia B15 22
Volchov, stm., Russia B15 22
Volčje, Ukr. F22 10
Volga, Russia D21 22
Volga, Ia., U.S. H4 110
Volga, S.D., U.S. G11 118
Volga, stm., Russia H7 26
Volgino, Russia C16 22
Volgo-Baltijskij kanal, Russia L26 6
Volgodonsk, Russia H6 26
Volgograd (Stalingrad), Russia H6 26
Volgogradskoje vodochranilišče, res., Russia H7 26
Volkach, Ger. F10 10
Völkermarkt, Aus. I14 10
Völklingen, Ger. F6 10
Volkovysk, Bela. H7 22
Volksrust, S. Afr. F9 66
Volockaja, Russia A25 22
Volodarsk, Russia E26 22
Volodarskoje, Kaz. G11 26
Vologda, Russia B22 22
Vologda, stm., Russia B22 22
Volokolamsk, Russia E18 22
Volontirovka, Mol. C13 20
Vólos, Grc. J6 20
Volosovo, Russia B12 22
Volot, Russia D13 22
Volovec, Ukr. A7 20
Volovo, Russia H21 22
Voložin, Bela. G9 22
Vol'sk, Russia G7 26
Volta, Lake, res., Ghana H9 64
Volta Blanche (White Volta), stm., Afr. F6 54
Volta Noire (Black Volta), stm., Afr. F6 54
Volta Redonda, Braz. G6 79
Volta Rouge, stm., Afr. F9 64
Volterra, Italy F5 18
Voltri, Italy E3 18
Volyně, Czech. F13 10
Volžsk, Russia F7 26
Volžskij, Russia H6 26
Vonda, Sask., Can. F8 104
Vondrozo, Madag. S22 67b
Vopnafjörður, Ice. B6 6a
Vorarlberg, state, Aus. H9 10
Vorau, Aus. H15 10
Vorden, Neth. D9 12
Vorder-Grauspitz, mtn., Eur. D12 13
Vorderrhein, stm., Switz. E10 13
Vordingborg, Den. N12 6
Vorga, Russia H15 22
Voriai Sporádhes, is., Grc. J7 20
Vorkuta, Russia D10 26
Vormsi, i., Est. B6 22
Vorob'jovo, Russia B23 22
Vorochta, Ukr. A8 20
Voronež, Russia G5 26
Voronkovo, Mol. B13 20
Voronovo, Bela. G8 22
Voropajevo, Bela. F10 22
Voroshilovsk see Stavropol', Russia H6 26
Vorošilovgrad see Lugansk, Ukr. H5 26
Vorpommern, hist. reg., Ger. B13 10
Vorsma, Russia F26 22
Võrtsjärv, l., Est. C9 22
Võru, Est. D10 22
Vosges, dept., Fr. D13 14
Vosges, mts., Fr. D14 14
Voskresensk, Russia F21 22
Voskresenskoje, Russia B20 22
Voskresenskoje, Russia D20 22
Voss, Nor. K10 6
Vostočno-Sibirskoje more (East Siberian Sea), Russia C23 28
Vostočnyj Sajan, mts., Russia G11 28
Vostok, sci., Ant. C6 73
Votkinsk, Russia F8 26
Votuporanga, Braz. F4 79
Voulou, Cen. Afr. Rep. M2 60
Vouziers, Fr. C11 14
Voves, Fr. D8 14
Voyageurs National Park, Mn., U.S. B3 110
Vože, ozero, l., Russia K26 6
Vožega, Russia A23 22
Voznesensk, Ukr. H4 26
Voznesenskoje, Russia G25 22
Vraca, Bul. F7 20
Vrådal, Nor. L11 6
Vrancea, co., Rom. D10 20
Vrangel'a, ostrov, i., Russia C28 28
Vranje, Yugo. G5 20
Vrbas, Yugo. D3 20
Vrede, S. Afr. F9 66
Vredenburg, S. Afr. I3 66
Vredenburgh, Al., U.S. K9 114
Vredendal, S. Afr. H4 66
Vreed en Hoop, Guy. D13 84
Vrin, Switz. E11 13
Vrindāvan, India G7 44
Vrondádhes, Grc. K10 20
Vršac, Yugo. D5 20
Vryburg, S. Afr. F7 66
Vryheid, S. Afr. F10 66
Vsetín, Czech. F17 10
Vsevidof, Mount, mtn., Ak., U.S. J10 100
Vtoryje Levyje Lamki, Russia H24 22
Vukovar, Cro. D3 20
Vulcan, Alta., Can. G21 102
Vulcan, Rom. D7 20
Vulcan, Mi., U.S. E8 110
Vulkanešty, Mol. D12 20
Vung Tau, Viet. I9 40
Vuohijärvi, Fin. K20 6
Vuoksenniska, Fin. K21 6
Vuotso, Fin. G20 6
Vuyyūru, India D6 46
Vyborg, Russia A11 22
Vyborgskij zaliv, b., Russia A11 22
Vyčegda, stm., Russia E7 26
Vygoniči, Russia H17 22
Vygozero, ozero, l., Russia J24 6
Vyksa, Russia F25 22
Vypolzovo, Russia D16 22
Vyrica, Russia B13 22
Vyša, Russia H25 22
Vyšgorodok, Russia D11 22
Vyškov, Czech. F17 10
Vyškov, Russia I14 22
Vyšnij Voločok, Russia D17 22
Vysock, Russia A11 22
Vysoké Tatry, mts., Eur. F20 10
Vysokiniči, Russia G19 22
Vysokogornyj, Russia G19 28
Vysokoje, Bela. I6 22
Vysokoje, Russia E17 22
Vysokovsk, Russia E19 22
Vyšší Brod, Czech. G14 10
Vytegra, Russia E5 26

W

Wa, Ghana F8 64
Waal, stm., Neth. E7 12
Waao, China B8 40
Wabag, Pap. N. Gui. G11 38
Wabamun, Alta., Can. D20 102
Wabamun Indian Reserve, Alta., Can. D20 102
Wabamun Lake, l., Alta., Can. D20 102
Wabana, Newf., Can. E21 106
Wabasca, Alta., Can. A21 102
Wabasca, stm., Alta., Can. E9 96
Wabasca Indian Reserve, Alta., Can. B21 102
Wabash, In., U.S. B11 114
Wabash, stm., U.S. E9 114
Wabasha, Mn., U.S. F3 110
Wabasso, Fl., U.S. L6 112
Wabasso, Mn., U.S. G12 118
Wabeno, Wi., U.S. E7 110
Wabigoon Lake, l., Ont., Can. I22 104
Wabowden, Man., Can. D16 104
Wąbrzeźno, Pol. B18 10
W.A.C. Bennett Dam, B.C., Can. A12 102
Waccamaw, stm., U.S. F8 112
Wachapreague, Va., U.S. B11 112
Wacissa, Fl., U.S. I3 112
Waco, Tx., U.S. H9 116
Waconda Lake, res., Ks., U.S. L9 118
Waconia, Mn., U.S. F2 110
Wacouno, stm., Que., Can. A8 106
Wad Al-Ḥaddād, Sud. K7 60
Wad Bandah, Sud. K4 60
Wad Ban Naqa, Sud. I7 60
Waddenzee, Neth. B7 12
Waddington, N.Y., U.S. C11 108
Waddington, Mount, mtn., B.C., Can. F9 102
Wade, Mount, mtn., Ant. D9 73
Wadena, Sask., Can. G11 104
Wadena, Mn., U.S. E12 118
Wädenswil, Switz. D10 13
Wadesboro, N.C., U.S. E6 112
Wad Ḥāmid, Sud. I7 60
Wadham Islands, is., Newf., Can. C20 106
Wadhams, B.C., Can. F7 102
Wādī as-Sīr, Jord. E5 50
Wādī Ḥalfā', Sud. G6 60
Wadley, Al., U.S. I11 114
Wadley, Ga., U.S. G4 112
Wad Madanī, Sud. J7 60
Wadowice, Pol. F19 10
Wadsworth, Nv., U.S. E6 124
Wadsworth, Oh., U.S. F5 108
Waegwan, S. Kor. H16 32
Waelder, Tx., U.S. J9 116
Wafang, China B6 32
Wafrah, Kuw. G10 48
Wageningen, Neth. E8 12
Wageningen, Sur. E14 84
Wager Bay, b., N.W. Ter., Can. C15 96
Wagga Wagga, Austl. J7 70
Wagin, Austl. F3 68
Waging am See, Ger. H12 10
Wagner, S.D., U.S. H9 118
Wagoner, Ok., U.S. D11 116
Wagon Mound, N.M., U.S. C2 116
Wągrowiec, Pol. C17 10
Waha, Libya C4 56
Wāh Cantonment, Pak. D5 44
Wahiawa, Hi., U.S. p15 125a
Wahoo, Ne., U.S. J11 118
Wahpeton, N.D., U.S. E11 118
Wahran (Oran), Alg. C10 62
Waialua, Hi., U.S. p15 125a
Waianae, Hi., U.S. p15 125a
Waiau, N.Z. E4 72
Waiblingen, Ger. G9 10
Waidhofen an der Thaya, Aus. G15 10
Waidhofen an der Ybbs, Aus. H14 10
Waigeo, Pulau, i., Indon. F9 38
Waihi, N.Z. B5 72
Waikato, stm., N.Z. C5 72
Waikerie, Austl. J3 70
Wailuku, Hi., U.S. q17 125a
Waimate, N.Z. F3 72
Waimea, Hi., U.S. p15 125a
Wainganga, stm., India C6 46
Waingapu, Indon. G7 38
Waini, stm., Guy. D13 84
Wainwright, Alta., Can. E24 102
Wainwright, Ak., U.S. A14 100
Waipara, N.Z. E4 72
Waipukurau, N.Z. C6 72
Wairoa, N.Z. C6 72
Waitara, N.Z. C5 72
Waite Park, Mn., U.S. E1 110
Waitsburg, Wa., U.S. D7 122
Waiuku, N.Z. B5 72
Wajima, Japan J11 36
Waka, Eth. N9 60
Waka, Tx., U.S. C5 116
Wakarusa, In., U.S. A10 114
Wakarusa, stm., Ks., U.S. M12 118
Wakaw, Sask., Can. F9 104
Wakaw Lake, l., Sask., Can. F9 104
Wakayama, Japan M10 36
WaKeeney, Ks., U.S. L8 118
Wakefield, Ks., U.S. L10 118
Wakefield, Ne., U.S. I11 118
Wakefield, R.I., U.S. F15 108
Wakefield, Va., U.S. C10 112
Wake Forest, N.C., U.S. D8 112
Wake Island, dep., Oc. E24 2
Wakema, Burma F3 40
Wakeman, stm., B.C., Can. F8 102
Wake Village, Tx., U.S. I2 114
Wakita, Ok., U.S. C9 116
Wakkanai, Japan B16 36a
Wakonda, S.D., U.S. H10 118
Waku Kundo, Ang. D3 58
Wałbrzych (Waldenburg), Pol. E16 10
Walcha, Austl. H9 70
Walcheren, i., Neth. E4 12
Walcott, B.C., Can. C8 102
Walcott, Ia., U.S. I5 110
Walcott, N.D., U.S. E11 118
Wałcz, Pol. B16 10
Wald, Switz. D10 13
Waldbillig, Lux. I9 12
Waldeck, Ger. D9 10
Walden, Co., U.S. D10 120
Walden, N.Y., U.S. F12 108
Walden Ridge, mtn., Tn., U.S. G11 114
Waldheim, Sask., Can. F8 104
Waldkirchen, Ger. G13 10
Waldmünchen, Ger. F12 10
Waldo, B.C., Can. H19 102
Waldo, Ar., U.S. I3 114
Waldoboro, Me., U.S. C17 108
Waldorf, Md., U.S. I10 108
Waldport, Or., U.S. F1 122
Waldron, Sask., Can. H12 104
Waldron, Ar., U.S. H2 114
Waldron, In., U.S. C11 114
Waldron, Mi., U.S. I11 110
Waldshut, Ger. H8 10
Waldviertel, reg., Aus. G15 10
Walenstadt, Switz. D11 13
Wales, Ak., U.S. D10 100
Wales, ter., U.K. I10 8
Wales Island, i., B.C., Can. C4 102
Wales Island, i., N.W. Ter., Can. C15 96
Walgett, Austl. H8 70
Walgreen Coast, Ant. C11 73
Walhachin, B.C., Can. G14 102
Walhalla, N.D., U.S. C10 118
Walhalla, S.C., U.S. E3 112
Walker, Ia., U.S. H4 110
Walker, Mn., U.S. C1 110
Walker, stm., Nv., U.S. E7 124
Walker, Lac, l., Que., Can. B6 106
Walker Lake, l., Man., Can. D18 104
Walker Lake, l., Nv., U.S. F7 124
Walkersville, Md., U.S. H9 108
Walkerton, Ont., Can. F14 110

Name — Map Ref. — Page

Walkerton, In., U.S. A10 114
Walkertown, N.C., U.S. C6 112
Walkerville, Mt., U.S. D13 122
Wall, S.D., U.S. H5 118
Wallace, Id., U.S. C10 122
Wallace, Ne., U.S. K6 118
Wallace, N.C., U.S. E9 112
Wallaceburg, Ont., Can. H13 110
Wallachia, hist. reg., Rom. E8 20
Wallangarra, Austl. G9 70
Wallaroo, Austl. I2 70
Walla Walla, Wa., U.S. D7 122
Waller, Tx., U.S. I11 116
Wallingford, Ct., U.S. F14 108
Wallingford, Vt., U.S. D14 108
Wallis, Tx., U.S. J10 116
Wallis and Futuna, dep., Oc. G1 2
Wallisellen, Switz. D10 13
Wall Lake, Ia., U.S. I12 118
Wallowa, Or., U.S. E8 122
Wallowa, stm., Or., U.S. E8 122
Wallowa Mountains, mts., Or., U.S. E8 122
Walls, Ms., U.S. H6 114
Wallula, Lake, res., U.S. D7 122
Walnut, Il., U.S. I6 110
Walnut, Ia., U.S. A1 114
Walnut, Ks., U.S. N12 118
Walnut, Ms., U.S. H8 114
Walnut, N.C., U.S. D4 112
Walnut, stm., Ks., U.S. N10 118
Walnut Cove, N.C., U.S. C6 112
Walnut Grove, Mn., U.S. G12 118
Walnut Grove, Ms., U.S. J7 114
Walnut Ridge, Ar., U.S. F6 114
Walnut Springs, Tx., U.S. G9 116
Walpeup, Austl. J5 70
Walpole, N.H., U.S. D14 108
Walsenburg, Co., U.S. G12 120
Walsh, Alta., Can. I4 104
Walsh, Co., U.S. N5 118
Walsrode, Ger. C9 10
Walterboro, S.C., U.S. G6 112
Walter F. George Lake, res., U.S. H1 112
Walters, Ok., U.S. E8 116
Waltershausen, Ger. E10 10
Waltersville, Ms., U.S. J6 114
Walthall, Ms., U.S. I7 114
Waltham, Ma., U.S. E15 108
Walthill, Ne., U.S. I11 118
Walton, N.S., Can. G9 106
Walton, In., U.S. B10 114
Walton, Ky., U.S. I2 108
Walton, N.Y., U.S. E11 108
Walvisbaai (Walvis Bay), S. Afr. D2 66
Walvis Bay see Walvisbaai, S. Afr. D2 66
Walworth, Wi., U.S. H7 110
Wamba, Nig. G14 64
Wamba, stm., Afr. C3 58
Wamego, Ks., U.S. L11 118
Wampsville, N.Y., U.S. D11 108
Wampú, Hond. B9 92
Wampú, stm., Hond. B9 92
Wampum, Pa., U.S. G6 108
Wamsutter, Wy., U.S. I18 122
Wanaaring, Austl. G6 70
Wanaka, N.Z. F2 72
Wanamingo, Mn., U.S. F3 110
Wan'an, China I3 34
Wanbi, Austl. J4 70
Wanblee, S.D., U.S. H6 118
Wanchese, N.C., U.S. D11 112
Wandering, stm., Alta., Can. B22 102
Wando, S. Kor. I14 32
Wandoan, Austl. F8 70
Wanette, Ok., U.S. E9 116
Wanfoxia, China C6 30
Wanganui, N.Z. C5 72
Wangaratta, Austl. K7 70
Wangary, Austl. J1 70
Wangdu Phodrang, Bhu. G13 44
Wanghu, China D1 32
Wanghuzhuang, China E5 32
Wangjiang, China E5 34
Wangpan Yang, b., China E11 30
Wangsi, China E4 32
Wangtuan, China F10 32
Wangzhong, China H4 32
Wangzhuangbu, China D1 32
Wanham, Alta., Can. B16 102
Wani, India B5 46
Wanigela, Pap. N. Gui. A9 68
Wanipigow, stm., Can. G19 104
Wānkāner, India I4 44
Wanli, China D9 34
Wanne-Eickel, Ger. D7 10
Wanneroo, Austl. F3 68
Wanxian, China E8 30
Wanzai, China G3 34
Wanzleben, Ger. C11 10
Wapakoneta, Oh., U.S. G2 108
Wapanucka, Ok., U.S. E10 116
Wapato, Wa., U.S. D5 122
Wapawekka Hills, hills, Sask., Can. D10 104
Wapawekka Lake, l., Sask., Can. D10 104
Wapella, Sask., Can. H12 104
Wapello, Ia., U.S. I4 110
Wapesi Lake, l., Ont., Can. H22 104
Wapisu Lake, l., Man., Can. C15 104
Wapiti, stm., Can. B15 102
Wappingers Falls, N.Y., U.S. F13 108
Wapsipinicon, stm., U.S. I5 110
Wapus Lake, l., Sask., Can. B12 104
Waqqāṣ, Jord. C5 50
War, W.V., U.S. B5 112
Warangal, India C5 46
Waratah, Austl. M6 70
Warbreccan, Austl. E5 70
Warburg, Ger. D9 10
Warburton, Austl. K6 70
Warburton Bay, b., N.W. Ter., Can. D10 96
Warburton Creek, stm., Austl. E7 68
Ward, stm., Austl. E7 70
Ward Cove, Ak., U.S. B3 102
Warden, Wa., U.S. D6 122
Wardha, India B5 46
Wardha, stm., India C5 46
Wardlow, Alta., Can. G23 102
Wardner, B.C., Can. H19 102
Ware, Ma., U.S. E14 108
Ware, stm., Ma., U.S. E14 108
Waregem, Bel. G3 12
Wareham, Eng., U.K. K11 8
Wareham, Ma., U.S. F16 108
Waremme (Borgworm), Bel. G7 12
Waren, Ger. B12 10
Warendorf, Ger. D7 10
Ware Shoals, S.C., U.S. E4 112
Wargla, Alg. E13 62
Warialda, Austl. G9 70
Warin Chamrap, Thai. G8 40
Warkworth, Ont., Can. F18 110
Warman, Sask., Can. F8 104
Warmbad, Nmb. G4 66
Warmbad, S. Afr. E9 66
Warminster, Eng., U.K. J11 8
Warminster, Pa., U.S. G11 108
Warm Springs, Ga., U.S. G2 112
Warm Springs, Mt., U.S. D13 122
Warm Springs, Or., U.S. F4 122
Warm Springs, Va., U.S. A7 112
Warm Springs, stm., Or., U.S. E4 122
Warner, Alta., Can. H22 102
Warner, N.H., U.S. D15 108
Warner, Ok., U.S. D11 116
Warner Lakes, l., Or., U.S. H6 122
Warner Mountains, mts., U.S. C5 124
Warner Peak, mtn., Or., U.S. H6 122
Warner Robins, Ga., U.S. G3 112
Warnes, Arg. H8 80
Warnes, Bol. G10 82
Warpath, stm., Man., Can. F16 104
Warracknabeal, Austl. K5 70
Warr Acres, Ok., U.S. D9 116
Warragul, Austl. L6 70
Warrego, stm., Austl. G6 70
Warrego Range, mts., Austl. E7 70
Warren, Austl. H7 70
Warren, Ar., U.S. I4 114
Warren, Il., U.S. H6 110
Warren, Mi., U.S. H12 110
Warren, Mn., U.S. C11 118
Warren, Oh., U.S. F6 108
Warren, Pa., U.S. F7 108
Warren Point, c., N.W. Ter., Can. B28 100
Warrens, Wi., U.S. F5 110
Warrensburg, Mo., U.S. D3 114
Warrensburg, N.Y., U.S. D13 108
Warrenton, S. Afr. G7 66
Warrenton, Ga., U.S. F4 112
Warrenton, Mo., U.S. D5 114
Warrenton, N.C., U.S. C8 112
Warrenton, Or., U.S. D2 122
Warrenton, Va., U.S. I9 108
Warri, Nig. I12 64
Warrington, Fl., U.S. L9 114
Warrior, Al., U.S. I10 114
Warrnambool, Austl. L5 70
Warroad, Mn., U.S. C12 118
Warsaw, Il., U.S. J4 110
Warsaw, In., U.S. A11 114
Warsaw, Ky., U.S. D12 114
Warsaw, Mo., U.S. D3 114
Warsaw, N.Y., U.S. E8 108
Warsaw, N.C., U.S. E8 112
Warsaw, Oh., U.S. G4 108
Warsaw, Va., U.S. B10 112
Warsaw see Warszawa, Pol. C21 10
Warspite, Alta., Can. C22 102
Warszawa (Warsaw), Pol. C21 10
Warta, stm., Pol. C15 10
Wartburg, Tn., U.S. C2 112
Wartburg, hist., Ger. E10 10
Wartrace, Tn., U.S. G10 114
Warud, India B5 46
Warunta, Laguna de, l., Hond. B10 92
Warwick, Austl. G10 70
Warwick, Que., Can. B15 108
Warwick, Eng., U.K. I12 8
Warwick, R.I., U.S. F15 108
Warwick Channel, strt., Austl. B7 68
Warwickshire, co., Eng., U.K. I12 8
Wasaga Beach, Ont., Can. F15 110
Wasagu, Nig. F12 64
Wasatch Plateau, plat., Ut., U.S. E5 120
Wasatch Range, mts., Ut., U.S. D5 120
Wascana Creek, stm., Sask., Can. H10 104
Wasco, Ca., U.S. I6 124
Wasco, Or., U.S. E5 122
Waseca, Mn., U.S. F2 110
Wasekamio Lake, l., Sask., Can. B6 104
Washademoak Lake, l., N.B., Can. G8 106
Washburn, Il., U.S. J6 110
Washburn, N.D., U.S. D6 118
Washburn, Wi., U.S. D5 110
Washburn Lake, l., N.W. Ter., Can. B11 96
Washicoutai, Que., Can. B13 106
Washington, D.C., U.S. I9 108
Washington, Ga., U.S. F4 112
Washington, Il., U.S. J6 110
Washington, In., U.S. D9 114
Washington, Ia., U.S. I4 110
Washington, Ks., U.S. L10 118
Washington, Ky., U.S. I3 108
Washington, La., U.S. L4 114
Washington, Mo., U.S. D5 114
Washington, N.C., U.S. D9 112
Washington, Pa., U.S. G6 108
Washington, Tx., U.S. I10 116
Washington, Ut., U.S. G3 120
Washington, Va., U.S. I8 108
Washington, state, U.S. B2 98
Washington, Mount, mtn., N.H., U.S. C15 108
Washington Court House, Oh., U.S. H3 108
Washington Island, Wi., U.S. E9 110
Washington Island, i., Wi., U.S. E9 110
Washington Terrace, Ut., U.S. C5 120
Washita, stm., U.S. E10 116
Washow Bay, b., Man., Can. G18 104
Washtucna, Wa., U.S. D7 122
Wasilków, Pol. B23 10
Wasilla, Ak., U.S. F20 100
Waskada, Man., Can. I14 104
Waskaganish, Que., Can. F17 96
Waskahigan, stm., Alta., Can. C17 102
Waskaiowaka Lake, l., Man., Can. B18 104
Waskatenau, Alta., Can. C22 102
Waskesiu Lake, l., Sask., Can. E8 104
Waskom, Tx., U.S. J2 114
Waspam, Nic. C11 92
Waspuk, stm., Nic. C10 92
Wassen, Switz. E10 13
Wassenaar, Neth. D5 12
Wasseralfingen, Ger. G10 10
Wasserbillig, Lux. I10 12
Wasserburg am Inn, Ger. G12 10
Wass Lake, l., Man., Can. E19 104
Wassou, Gui. F3 64
Wassy, Fr. D11 14
Watampone, Indon. F7 38
Watapi Lake, l., Sask., Can. C5 104
Waterberg, Nmb. C3 66
Waterberg Plateau Park, Nmb. C3 66
Waterbury, Ct., U.S. F13 108
Waterbury, Vt., U.S. C14 108
Waterdown, Ont., Can. G16 110
Wateree, stm., S.C., U.S. F6 112
Wateree Lake, res., S.C., U.S. E6 112
Waterford, Ont., Can. H15 110
Waterford, Ire. I6 8
Waterford, Ca., U.S. G5 124
Waterford, Pa., U.S. F7 108
Waterford, Wi., U.S. H7 110
Waterford, co., Ire. I6 8
Waterhen, stm., Sask., Can. D6 104
Waterhen Lake, l., Man., Can. F15 104
Waterhen Lake, l., Sask., Can. D6 104
Waterloo, Bel. G5 12
Waterloo, Ont., Can. G15 110
Waterloo, Que., Can. B14 108
Waterloo, Al., U.S. H8 114
Waterloo, Il., U.S. D6 114
Waterloo, Ia., U.S. H3 110
Waterloo, N.Y., U.S. E10 108
Waterloo, Wi., U.S. G7 110
Waterman, Il., U.S. I7 110
Waterproof, La., U.S. K5 114
Watersmeet, Mi., U.S. D6 110
Waterton, stm., N.A. H21 102
Waterton-Glacier International Peace Park, N.A. B12 122
Waterton Lakes National Park, Alta., Can. H21 102
Watertown, N.Y., U.S. D11 108
Watertown, S.D., U.S. G10 118
Watertown, Wi., U.S. G7 110
Water Valley, Ms., U.S. H7 114
Waterville, N.S., Can. G9 106
Waterville, Ks., U.S. L11 118
Waterville, Me., U.S. C17 108
Waterville, Mn., U.S. F2 110
Waterville, Oh., U.S. F3 108
Waterville, Wa., U.S. C5 122
Watervliet, N.Y., U.S. E13 108
Watford, Ont., Can. H14 110
Watford City, N.D., U.S. D4 118
Wathaman, stm., Sask., Can. A11 104
Wathaman Lake, l., Sask., Can. B11 104
Wathena, Ks., U.S. L13 118
Watino, Alta., Can. B17 102
Watkins Glen, N.Y., U.S. E10 108
Watkinsville, Ga., U.S. F3 112
Watling Island see San Salvador, i., Bah. B7 94
Watonga, Ok., U.S. D8 116
Watonwan, stm., Mn., U.S. G13 118
Watrous, Sask., Can. G9 104
Watrous, N.M., U.S. I12 120
Watseka, Il., U.S. J8 110
Watson, Sask., Can. F10 104
Watson Lake, Yukon, Can. F30 100
Watsontown, Pa., U.S. F10 108
Watsonville, Ca., U.S. H4 124
Wattens, Aus. H11 10
Wattenscheid, Ger. D7 10
Wattenwil, Switz. E8 13
Watts Bar Lake, res., Tn., U.S. D2 112
Watts Mills, S.C., U.S. E4 112
Wattwil, Switz. D11 13
Watubela, Kepulauan, is., Indon. F9 38
Watzmann, mtn., Ger. H12 10
Waubay, S.D., U.S. F10 118
Wauchope, Austl. H10 70
Wauchula, Fl., U.S. L5 112
Wauconda, Wa., U.S. B6 122
Waugh, Man., Can. I19 104
Waugh Mountain, mtn., Id., U.S. E11 122
Waukaringa, Austl. I3 70
Waukegan, Il., U.S. H8 110
Waukesha, Wi., U.S. G7 110
Waukomis, Ok., U.S. C9 116
Waukon, Ia., U.S. G4 110
Waunakee, Wi., U.S. G6 110
Wauneta, Ne., U.S. K6 118
Waupaca, Wi., U.S. F6 110
Waupun, Wi., U.S. G7 110
Waurika, Ok., U.S. E9 116
Wausa, Ne., U.S. I10 118
Wausau, Wi., U.S. F6 110
Wausaukee, Wi., U.S. E8 110
Wauseon, Oh., U.S. F2 108
Wautoma, Wi., U.S. F6 110
Wauwatosa, Wi., U.S. G7 110
Wauzeka, Wi., U.S. G5 110
Wave Hill, Austl. C6 68
Waveland, Ms., U.S. L7 114
Waverly, Al., U.S. J11 114
Waverly, Il., U.S. C7 114
Waverly, Ia., U.S. H3 110
Waverly, Ks., U.S. M12 118
Waverly, Mn., U.S. E2 110
Waverly, Mo., U.S. C3 114
Waverly, Ne., U.S. K11 118
Waverly, N.Y., U.S. E10 108
Waverly, Oh., U.S. H4 108
Waverly, Tn., U.S. F9 114
Waverly, Va., U.S. B9 112
Waverly Hall, Ga., U.S. G2 112
Wavre (Waver), Bel. G6 12
Wāw, Sud. N4 60
Wawa, Ont., Can. C11 110
Wawa, Sud. G6 60
Wawa, stm., Nic. C11 92
Wāw al-Kabīr, Libya C4 56
Wawanesa, Man., Can. I15 104
Wawota, Sask., Can. I12 104
Waxahachie, Tx., U.S. G10 116
Waxhaw, N.C., U.S. E6 112
Wayabula, Indon. E8 38
Waycross, Ga., U.S. H4 112
Wayland, Ia., U.S. I4 110
Wayland, Ky., U.S. B4 112
Wayland, Mi., U.S. H10 110
Wayland, N.Y., U.S. E9 108
Waylyn, S.C., U.S. G7 112
Wayne, Alta., Can. F22 102
Wayne, Mi., U.S. H12 110
Wayne, Ne., U.S. I10 118
Wayne, N.J., U.S. G12 108
Wayne, Ok., U.S. E9 116
Wayne, W.V., U.S. I4 108
Wayne City, Il., U.S. D8 114
Waynesboro, Ga., U.S. F4 112
Waynesboro, Ms., U.S. K8 114
Waynesboro, Pa., U.S. H9 108
Waynesboro, Tn., U.S. G9 114
Waynesboro, Va., U.S. A8 112
Waynesburg, Oh., U.S. G5 108
Waynesburg, Pa., U.S. H6 108
Waynesville, Il., U.S. B7 114
Waynesville, Mo., U.S. E4 114
Waynesville, N.C., U.S. D4 112
Waynoka, Ok., U.S. C8 116
Wāzah Khwāh, Afg. D3 44
Wāzin, Libya E16 62
Wazīrābād, Pak. D6 44
We, Pulau, i., Indon. L3 40
Weagamow Lake, l., Ont., Can. F23 104
Weatherford, Ok., U.S. D8 116
Weatherford, Tx., U.S. G9 116
Weatherly, Pa., U.S. G11 108
Weaubleau, Mo., U.S. E3 114
Weaver, Al., U.S. I11 114
Weaver Lake, l., Man., Can. F18 104
Weaverville, Ca., U.S. D3 124
Weaverville, N.C., U.S. D4 112
Webb, Sask., Can. H6 104
Webb, Ms., U.S. I6 114
Webb City, Mo., U.S. E2 114
Webber Lake, l., Man., Can. D20 104
Webbwood, Ont., Can. D14 110
Weber, stm., Ut., U.S. D5 120
Weber, Mount, mtn., B.C., Can. B6 102
Weber City, Va., U.S. C4 112
Weberi Bekera, Eth. M10 60
Webster, Alta., Can. B16 102
Webster, Fl., U.S. K4 112
Webster, Ma., U.S. E15 108
Webster, S.D., U.S. F10 118
Webster, Wi., U.S. E3 110
Webster City, Ia., U.S. H2 110
Webster Springs, W.V., U.S. I6 108
Weda, Indon. E8 38
Weddell Sea, Ant. B1 73
Wedderburn, Austl. K5 70
Wedel, Ger. B9 10
Wedge Mountain, mtn., B.C., Can. G12 102
Wedgeport, N.S., Can. I8 106
Wedowee, Al., U.S. I11 114
Wedweil, Sud. M4 60
Wedza, Zimb. B10 66
Weed, Ca., U.S. C3 124
Weedsport, N.Y., U.S. D10 108
Weedville, Pa., U.S. F8 108
Weems, Va., U.S. B10 112
Weenen, S. Afr. G10 66
Weeping Water, Ne., U.S. K11 118
Weert, Neth. F8 12
Weesp, Neth. D7 12
Wee Waa, Austl. H8 70
Węgrów, Pol. C22 10
Wei, stm., China E8 30
Weiden in der Oberpfalz, Ger. F12 10
Weifang, China G7 32
Weihai, China F10 32
Weilburg, Ger. E8 10
Weilheim, Ger. H11 10
Weimar, Ger. E11 10
Weimar, Tx., U.S. J10 116
Weinan, China E8 30
Weiner, Ar., U.S. G6 114
Weinfelden, Switz. C11 13
Weinheim, Ger. F8 10
Weipa, Austl. B8 68
Weippe, Id., U.S. D10 122
Weir, Ks., U.S. N13 118
Weir, Ms., U.S. I7 114
Weir, stm., Austl. F9 70
Weir, stm., Man., Can. B21 104
Weir River, Man., Can. B20 104
Weirsdale, Fl., U.S. K5 112
Weirton, W.V., U.S. G6 108
Weisburd, Arg. D7 80
Weiser, Id., U.S. F9 122
Weiser, stm., Id., U.S. F9 122
Weishan (Xiazhen), China I5 32
Weishancheng, China C2 34
Weisner Mountain, mtn., Al., U.S. H11 114
Weissenburg, Switz. E7 13
Weissenburg in Bayern, Ger. F10 10
Weissenfels, Ger. D11 10
Weisshorn, mtn., Switz. F8 13
Weisskugel (Palla Bianca), mtn., Eur. E14 13
Weiss Lake, res., U.S. E1 112
Weitou, China K7 34
Weitra, Aus. G14 10
Weiz, Aus. H15 10
Weizhen, China F2 32
Weizhou Wan, b., Asia K7 34
Wejherowo, Pol. A18 10
Wekusko Lake, l., Man., Can. D15 104
Welaka, Fl., U.S. J5 112
Welch, Ok., U.S. C11 116
Welch, Tx., U.S. G4 116
Welch, W.V., U.S. B5 112
Welcome, Mn., U.S. H13 118
Welcome, S.C., U.S. E4 112
Weldon, Sask., Can. E9 104
Weldon, Il., U.S. B8 114
Weldon, N.C., U.S. C9 112
Weldon, stm., U.S. B3 114
Weldona, Co., U.S. K4 118
Weleetka, Ok., U.S. D10 116
Welkite, Eth. M9 60
Welkom, S. Afr. F8 66
Welland, Ont., Can. H16 110
Welland, stm., Ont., Can. G16 110
Wellborn, Fl., U.S. I4 112
Wellborn, Tx., U.S. I10 116
Wellesley Islands, is., Austl. A3 70
Wellesley Lake, l., Yukon, Can. E25 100
Wellfleet, Ma., U.S. F16 108
Wellington, Austl. I8 70
Wellington, Ont., Can. G18 110
Wellington, N.Z. D5 72
Wellington, S. Afr. I4 66
Wellington, Eng., U.K. I11 8
Wellington, Co., U.S. D11 120
Wellington, Ks., U.S. N10 118
Wellington, Mo., U.S. C3 114
Wellington, Oh., U.S. F4 108
Wellington, Tx., U.S. E6 116
Wellington, Ut., U.S. E6 120
Wellington, Isla, i., Chile F2 78
Wellington Bay, b., N.W. Ter., Can. C11 96
Wellington Channel, strt., N.W. Ter., Can. A14 96
Wellington Station, P.E.I., Can. F9 106
Wellman, Ia., U.S. I4 110
Wellman, Tx., U.S. F4 116
Wells, B.C., Can. D13 102
Wells, Mi., U.S. E8 110
Wells, Mn., U.S. G2 110
Wells, Nv., U.S. C11 124
Wells, N.Y., U.S. D12 108
Wells, Tx., U.S. K2 114
Wellsboro, Pa., U.S. F9 108
Wellsburg, Ia., U.S. H3 110
Wellsburg, W.V., U.S. G6 108
Wellsford, N.Z. B5 72
Wells Gray Provincial Park, B.C., Can. E15 102
Wells Lake, l., Man., Can. A13 104
Wells-next-the-Sea, Eng., U.K. I14 8
Wellston, Oh., U.S. H4 108
Wellston, Ok., U.S. D9 116
Wellsville, Ks., U.S. M12 118
Wellsville, Mo., U.S. C5 114
Wellsville, N.Y., U.S. E9 108
Wellsville, Oh., U.S. G6 108
Wellsville, Ut., U.S. C5 120
Wellton, Az., U.S. L2 120
Wels, Aus. G14 10
Welsford, N.B., Can. G7 106
Welsh, La., U.S. L4 114
Welwitschia, Nmb. C2 66
Wembley, Alta., Can. B15 102
Wenatchee, Wa., U.S. C5 122
Wenatchee, stm., Wa., U.S. C5 122
Wenatchee Mountains, mts., Wa., U.S. C5 122
Wenchow see Wenzhou, China G9 34
Wendell, Id., U.S. H11 122
Wendell, N.C., U.S. D8 112
Wenden, Az., U.S. K3 120
Wendeng, China F10 32
Wendo, Eth. N10 60
Wendover, Ut., U.S. D2 120
Wengyang, China G9 34
Wengyuan, China K3 34
Wenling, China G10 34
Wenlock, stm., Austl. B8 68
Wenona, Il., U.S. I6 110
Wenshan, China C8 40
Wentworth, Austl. J4 70
Wentworth, N.C., U.S. C7 112
Wentworth, S.D., U.S. H11 118
Wenzhou, China G9 34
Werda, Bots. E6 66
Werdau, Ger. E12 10
Werder, Ger. C12 10
Werdohl, Ger. D7 10
Were Ilu, Eth. L10 60
Werl, Ger. D7 10
Wernigerode, Ger. D10 10
Werra, stm., Ger. E10 10
Werribee, Austl. K6 70
Werris Creek, Austl. H9 70
Wertheim, Ger. F9 10
Wertingen, Ger. G10 10
Wesel, Ger. D6 10
Weser, stm., Ger. B8 10
Weskan, Ks., U.S. M6 118
Weslaco, Tx., U.S. M9 116
Wesley, Ia., U.S. G2 110
Wesleyville, Newf., Can. C20 106
Wesleyville, Pa., U.S. E6 108
Wessel, Cape, c., Austl. B7 68
Wessel Islands, is., Austl. B7 68
Wessington, S.D., U.S. G9 118
Wessington Springs, S.D., U.S. G9 118
Wesson, Ms., U.S. K6 114
West, Ms., U.S. I7 114
West, Tx., U.S. H9 116
West, stm., Vt., U.S. D14 108
West Alexandria, Oh., U.S. H2 108
West Allis, Wi., U.S. G7 110
Westbank, B.C., Can. H15 102
West Bank, hist. reg., Isr. Occ. E4 50
West Bay, N.S., Can. G12 106
Westbay, Fl., U.S. L11 114
West Bay, b., Tx., U.S. J12 116
West Bend, Ia., U.S. I13 118
West Bend, Wi., U.S. G7 110
West Bengal, state, India I12 44
West Blocton, Al., U.S. I9 114
Westbourne, Man., Can. H16 104
West Branch, Ia., U.S. I4 110
West Branch, Mi., U.S. F11 110
Westbridge, B.C., Can. H16 102
Westbrook, Me., U.S. D16 108
Westbrook, Mn., U.S. G12 118
Westbrook, Tx., U.S. G5 116
West Burlington, Ia., U.S. J4 110
West Butte, mtn., Mt., U.S. B14 122
Westby, Mt., U.S. C3 118
Westby, Wi., U.S. G5 110
West Caicos, i., T./C. Is. D8 94
West Carlisle, Tx., U.S. F5 116
West Channel, mth., N.W. Ter., Can. B27 100
West Chester, Pa., U.S. H11 108
Westchester Station, N.S., Can. G10 106
Westcliffe, Co., U.S. F11 120
West Columbia, S.C., U.S. F5 112
West Columbia, Tx., U.S. J11 116
West Concord, Mn., U.S. F3 110
West Des Moines, Ia., U.S. I2 110
West Elk Mountains, mts., Co., U.S. F9 120
West Elk Peak, mtn., Co., U.S. F9 120
West End, Bah. A5 94
West End, Ar., U.S. H4 114
West End, N.C., U.S. D7 112
Westerlo, Bel. F6 12
Westerly, R.I., U.S. F15 108
Western, Ne., U.S. K10 118
Western, stm., Austl. D5 70
Western Australia, state, Austl. E4 68
Western Channel, strt., Asia I16 32
Western Desert see Gharbīyah, Aṣ-Ṣaḥrā' al-, des., Egypt D4 60
Western Ghāts, mts., India D2 46
Western Isles, prov., Scot., U.K. D6 8
Westernport, Md., U.S. H7 108
Western Sahara, dep., Afr. D4 54
Western Samoa, ctry., Oc. G1 2
Western Shore, N.S., Can. H9 106
Westerschelde, est., Neth. F4 12
Westerstede, Ger. B7 10
Westerville, Oh., U.S. G4 108
West Falkland, i., Falk. Is. G4 78
West Fargo, N.D., U.S. E11 118
Westfield, Il., U.S. C8 114
Westfield, In., U.S. B10 114
Westfield, Ma., U.S. E14 108
Westfield, N.J., U.S. G12 108
Westfield, N.Y., U.S. E7 108
Westfield, Pa., U.S. F9 108
Westfield, Wi., U.S. G6 110
West Fiord, N.W. Ter., Can. A14 96
West Fork, Ar., U.S. G2 114
West Frankfort, Il., U.S. E8 114
Westgate, Austl. F7 70
West Glacier, Mt., U.S. B12 122
West Glamorgan, co., Wales, U.K. J10 8
West Hamlin, W.V., U.S. I4 108
West Hartford, Ct., U.S. F14 108
Westhaven, Ca., U.S. C1 124
West Haven, Ct., U.S. F14 108
West Helena, Ar., U.S. H6 114
Westhoff, Tx., U.S. J9 116
Westhope, N.D., U.S. C6 118
West Ice Shelf, Ant. B5 73
West Indies, is. E9 94
West Jefferson, N.C., U.S. C5 112
West Jefferson, Oh., U.S. H3 108
West Jordan, Ut., U.S. D5 120
West Kettle, stm., B.C., Can. H15 102
West Kingston, R.I., U.S. F15 108
West Lafayette, In., U.S. B10 114
West Lafayette, Oh., U.S. G5 108
Westlake, La., U.S. L3 114
West Laramie, Wy., U.S. C11 120
West Lebanon, In., U.S. B9 114
West Liberty, Ia., U.S. I4 110
West Liberty, Ky., U.S. B3 112
West Liberty, Oh., U.S. G3 108
Westlock, Alta., Can. C21 102
West Lorne, Ont., Can. H14 110
Westmeath, co., Ire. H6 8
West Melbourne, Fl., U.S. K6 112
West Memphis, Ar., U.S. G6 114
West Mifflin, Pa., U.S. G7 108
Westminster, Co., U.S. E11 120
Westminster, Md., U.S. H10 108
Westminster, S.C., U.S. E3 112
West Monroe, La., U.S. J4 114
Westmont, Pa., U.S. G8 108
Westmoreland, Ks., U.S. L11 118
Westmoreland, Tn., U.S. F10 114
Westmorland, Ca., U.S. K10 124
West Nicholson, Zimb. C9 66
West Nishnabotna, stm., Ia., U.S. K12 118
Weston, Co., U.S. G12 120
Weston, Id., U.S. H14 122
Weston, Mo., U.S. C2 114
Weston, Ne., U.S. J11 118
Weston, Oh., U.S. F3 108
Weston, Or., U.S. E7 122
Weston, W.V., U.S. H6 108
Weston-super-Mare, Eng., U.K. J11 8
West Orange, Tx., U.S. L3 114
Westover, Tn., U.S. G8 114
Westover, W.V., U.S. H7 108
West Palm Beach, Fl., U.S. M6 112
West Paris, Me., U.S. C16 108
West Pensacola, Fl., U.S. L9 114
Westphalia, Ks., U.S. M12 118
West Plains, Mo., U.S. F5 114
West Point, Ca., U.S. F5 124
West Point, Ga., U.S. G1 112
West Point, Ia., U.S. J4 110
West Point, Ky., U.S. E11 114
West Point, Ms., U.S. I8 114
West Point, Ne., U.S. J11 118
West Point, N.Y., U.S. F13 108
West Point, Va., U.S. B10 112
West Point, c., Austl. J2 70
West Point, c., P.E.I., Can. F9 106
West Point Lake, res., U.S. F1 112
Westport, Newf., Can. C17 106
Westport, N.S., Can. H7 106
Westport, Ont., Can. F19 110
Westport, N.Z. D3 72
Westport, Ct., U.S. F13 108
Westport, In., U.S. C11 114
Westport, Or., U.S. D2 122
Westport, Wa., U.S. D1 122
West Portsmouth, Oh., U.S. I3 108
West Prairie, stm., Alta., Can. B18 102
West Richland, Wa., U.S. D6 122
West Road, stm., B.C., Can. D11 102
West Rutland, Vt., U.S. D13 108
West Sacramento, Ca., U.S. F4 124
West Saint Marys, stm., N.S., Can. G11 106
West Saint Modeste, Newf., Can. A17 106
West Salem, Il., U.S. D8 114
West Salem, Oh., U.S. G4 108
West Salem, Wi., U.S. G4 110
West Shoal Lake, l., Man., Can. H17 104
West Siberian Plain see Zapadno-Sibirskaja ravnina, pl., Russia E13 26
West Slope, Or., U.S. E3 122
West Spanish Peak, mtn., Co., U.S. G12 120
West Sussex, co., Eng., U.K. K13 8
West Terre Haute, In., U.S. C9 114
West Union, Ia., U.S. H4 110
West Union, Oh., U.S. I3 108
West Union, W.V., U.S. H6 108
West Unity, Oh., U.S. F2 108
West Valley, Mt., U.S. D12 122
West Valley City, Ut., U.S. D5 120
West Vancouver, B.C., Can. H11 102
Westville, N.S., Can. G11 106
Westville, In., U.S. A10 114
Westville, Ok., U.S. G2 114
West Virginia, state, U.S. D10 98
West-Vlaanderen, prov., Bel. F2 12
West Warwick, R.I., U.S. F15 108
West Webster, N.Y., U.S. D9 108
Westwego, La., U.S. M6 114
Westwold, B.C., Can. G15 102
Westwood, Ca., U.S. D4 124
Westwood Lakes, Fl., U.S. N6 112
West Wyalong, Austl. I7 70
West Yellowstone, Mt., U.S. F14 122
Wetar, Pulau, i., Indon. G8 38
Wetaskiwin, Alta., Can. E21 102
Wete, Tan. C7 58
Wethersfield, Ct., U.S. F14 108
Wetiko Hills, hills, Can. D22 104
Wetmore, Ks., U.S. L12 118
Wet Mountains, mts., Co., U.S. F11 120
Wetteren, Bel. F4 12
Wetumka, Ok., U.S. D10 116
Wetumpka, Al., U.S. J10 114
Wetzikon, Switz. D10 13
Wetzlar, Ger. E8 10
Wewahitchka, Fl., U.S. I1 112
Wewak, Pap. N. Gui. k15 68a
Wewoka, Ok., U.S. D10 116
Wexford, Ire. I7 8
Wexford, co., Ire. I7 8
Weyakwin Lake, l., Sask., Can. D8 104
Weyauwega, Wi., U.S. F7 110
Weyburn, Sask., Can. I11 104
Weymouth, N.S., Can. H7 106
Weymouth, Eng., U.K. K11 8
Weymouth, Ma., U.S. E16 108
Whakatane, N.Z. B6 72
Whangarei, N.Z. A5 72
Wharton, Tx., U.S. J10 116
Wharton, W.V., U.S. J5 108
Wharton Lake, l., N.W. Ter., Can. D13 96
Whataroa, N.Z. E3 72
What Cheer, Ia., U.S. I3 110
Whatley, Al., U.S. K9 114
Whatshan Lake, l., B.C., Can. G16 102
Wheatland, Ca., U.S. E4 124
Wheatland, Ia., U.S. I5 110
Wheatland, Wy., U.S. B12 120
Wheatley, Ont., Can. H13 110
Wheatley, Ar., U.S. H5 114
Wheaton, Il., U.S. A8 114
Wheaton, Md., U.S. H9 108
Wheaton, Mn., U.S. F11 118
Wheat Ridge, Co., U.S. E11 120
Wheeler, Ms., U.S. H8 114
Wheeler, Tx., U.S. D6 116
Wheeler, stm., Que., Can. E19 96
Wheeler, stm., Sask., Can. A9 104
Wheeler Lake, res., Al., U.S. H9 114
Wheeler Peak, mtn., Ca., U.S. F6 124
Wheeler Peak, mtn., Nv., U.S. F11 124
Wheeler Peak, mtn., N.M., U.S. H11 120
Wheeling, W.V., U.S. G6 108
Wheelwright, Arg. G8 80
Wheelwright, Ky., U.S. B4 112
Whidbey Island, i., Wa., U.S. B3 122
Whigham, Ga., U.S. I2 112
Whitakers, N.C., U.S. C9 112
Whitbourne, Newf., Can. E20 106
Whitby, Ont., Can. G17 110

Name — Map Ref. — Page

Whitchurch-Stouffville, Ont., Can. G16 110
White, Ga., U.S. E2 112
White, S.D., U.S. G11 118
White, stm., B.C., Can. G19 102
White, stm., N.A. E24 100
White, stm., U.S. H5 114
White, stm., U.S. H7 118
White, stm., U.S. D7 120
White, stm., Az., U.S. K6 120
White, stm., In., U.S. D9 114
White, stm., Nv., U.S. G11 124
White, stm., Vt., U.S. D14 108
White, stm., Wi., U.S. D5 110
White Bay, b., Newf., Can. B17 106
White Bear Indian Reserve, Sask., Can. I12 104
White Bear Lake, Mn., U.S. E2 110
Whitebear Lake, l., Sask., Can. G6 104
White Bluff, Tn., U.S. F9 114
White Butte, mtn., N.D., U.S. E4 118
Whitecap Lake, l., Man., Can. B19 104
White Castle, La., U.S. L5 114
White City, Ks., U.S. M11 118
White Cliffs, Austl. H5 70
White Cloud, Mi., U.S. G10 110
Whitecourt, Alta., Can. C19 102
White Deer, Tx., U.S. D5 116
White Earth, stm., N.D., U.S. C5 118
Whiteface, Tx., U.S. F4 116
Whiteface, stm., Mn., U.S. C3 110
Whiteface Mountain, mtn., N.Y., U.S. C13 108
Whitefield, N.H., U.S. C15 108
Whitefish, Mt., U.S. B11 122
Whitefish, stm., Mi., U.S. E8 110
Whitefish Bay, Wi., U.S. G8 110
Whitefish Bay, b., Ont., Can. I20 104
Whitefish Bay, b., N.A. D11 110
Whitefish Lake, l., Alta., Can. C23 102
Whitefish Lake, l., Man., Can. C21 104
Whitefish Lake, l., N.W. Ter., Can. D11 96
White Fish Lake Indian Reserve, Alta., Can. C23 102
Whitefish Point, Mi., U.S. D11 110
Whitefish Point, c., Mi., U.S. D10 110
White Fox, Sask., Can. E10 104
White Fox, stm., Sask., Can. E10 104
White Gull Creek, stm., Sask., Can. E10 104
White Hall, Ar., U.S. H4 114
White Hall, Il., U.S. C6 114
Whitehall, Mi., U.S. G9 110
Whitehall, Mt., U.S. E13 122
Whitehall, N.Y., U.S. D13 108
Whitehall, Wi., U.S. F4 110
White Haven, Pa., U.S. F11 108
Whitehorse, Yukon, Can. F27 100
White House, Tn., U.S. F10 114
Whitehouse, Tx., U.S. G11 116
White Island, i., N.W. Ter., Can. C16 96
White Lake, S.D., U.S. H9 118
White Lake, Wi., U.S. E7 110
White Lake, l., La., U.S. M4 114
Whitelaw, Alta., Can. A16 102
Whitemark, Austl. M8 70
White Mountain, Ak., U.S. D13 100
White Mountain Peak, mtn., Ca., U.S. G7 124
White Mountains, mts., U.S. G7 124
White Mountains, mts., N.H., U.S. C15 108
Whitemouth, Man., Can. I19 104
Whitemouth, stm., Man., Can. I19 104
Whitemouth Lake, l., Man., Can. I19 104
Whitemud, stm., Man., Can. H15 104
White Nile (Al-Bahr al-Abyad), stm., Sud. L7 60
White Oak, Tx., U.S. J2 114
White Pass, N.A. G27 100
White Pigeon, Mi., U.S. I10 110
White Pine, Mi., U.S. D6 110
White Pine, Tn., U.S. C3 112
White Plains, N.Y., U.S. F13 108
White Plains, N.C., U.S. C6 112
White River, Ont., Can. B10 110
Whiteriver, Az., U.S. K7 120
White River, S.D., U.S. H7 118
White River Junction, Vt., U.S. D14 108
White Rock, B.C., Can. H12 102
Whiterocks, stm., Ut., U.S. D7 120
White Russia see Belarus, ctry., Eur. H11 26
Whitesail Lake, l., B.C., Can. D7 102
White Salmon, Wa., U.S. E4 122
White Salmon, stm., Wa., U.S. E4 122
Whitesand, stm., Sask., Can. G12 104
Whitesboro, Tx., U.S. F10 116
Whitesburg, Ky., U.S. B4 112
White Sea see Beloje more, Russia D5 26
White Settlement, Tx., U.S. G9 116
Whiteshell Provincial Park, Man., Can. I19 104
White Springs, Fl., U.S. I4 112
White Stone Lake, l., Man., Can. B17 104
White Sulphur Springs, Mt., U.S. D15 122
White Sulphur Springs, W.V., U.S. B6 112
Whitesville, Ky., U.S. E10 114
Whitesville, W.V., U.S. J5 108
Whiteswan Lakes, l., Sask., Can. D9 104
Whiteville, N.C., U.S. E8 112
Whiteville, Tn., U.S. G7 114
White Volta (Volta Blanche), stm., Afr. F6 54
Whitewater, Ks., U.S. N10 118
Whitewater, Mt., U.S. B18 122
Whitewater, Wi., U.S. H7 110
Whitewater, stm., U.S. C11 114
Whitewater, stm., Mo., U.S. E7 114
Whitewater Baldy, mtn., N.M., U.S. K8 120
Whitewater Lake, l., Man., Can. I14 104
Whitewood, Austl. C5 70
Whitewood, Sask., Can. H12 104
Whitewood, S.D., U.S. G4 118
Whitewright, Tx., U.S. F10 116
Whithorn, Scot., U.K. G9 8
Whiting, Ia., U.S. I11 118
Whiting, Ks., U.S. L12 118
Whiting, Wi., U.S. F6 110
Whitley City, Ky., U.S. C2 112
Whitman, Ma., U.S. E16 108
Whitmire, S.C., U.S. E5 112
Whitney, Ont., Can. E17 110
Whitney, Tx., U.S. H9 116
Whitney, Lake, res., Tx., U.S. H9 116
Whitney, Mount, mtn., Ca., U.S. H7 124
Whitney Point, N.Y., U.S. E11 108
Whitsunday Island, i., Austl. C8 70
Whittemore, Ia., U.S. H13 118
Whittemore, Mi., U.S. F12 110
Whittier, Ak., U.S. F20 100
Whittier, N.C., U.S. D3 112
Whittle, Cap, c., Que., Can. B13 106
Whittlesea, Austl. K6 70
Whittlesea, Ciskei I8 66
Whitwell, Tn., U.S. G11 114
Wholdaia Lake, l., N.W. Ter., Can. D12 96
Whyalla, Austl. I2 70
Whycocomagh, N.S., Can. G12 106
Wiarton, Ont., Can. F14 110
Wiau Lake, l., Alta., Can. B23 102
Wiawso, Ghana H8 64
Wibaux, Mt., U.S. E3 118
Wichita, Ks., U.S. N10 118
Wichita, stm., Tx., U.S. E8 116
Wichita Falls, Tx., U.S. F8 116
Wichita Mountains, mts., Ok., U.S. E8 116
Wick, Scot., U.K. C10 8
Wickenburg, Az., U.S. K4 120
Wickett, Tx., U.S. H4 116
Wickham, Cape, c., Austl. L5 70
Wickliffe, Ky., U.S. F7 114
Wicklow, co., Ire. I7 8
Wicklow Mountains, mts., Ire. H7 8
Widen, W.V., U.S. I6 108
Widerøe, Mount, mtn., Ant. C3 73
Wiehl, Ger. E7 10
Wiek, Ger. A13 10
Wieliczka, Pol. F20 10
Wielkopolska, reg., Pol. D17 10
Wieluń, Pol. D18 10
Wien (Vienna), Aus. G16 10
Wiener Neustadt, Aus. H16 10
Wienerwald, mts., Aus. G16 10
Wieprz, stm., Pol. D22 10
Wierden, Neth. D10 12
Wiergate, Tx., U.S. K3 114
Wiesbaden, Ger. E8 10
Wieselburg, Aus. G15 10
Wiesloch, Ger. F8 10
Wietze, Ger. C9 10
Wigan, Eng., U.K. H11 8
Wiggins, Co., U.S. K3 118
Wiggins, Ms., U.S. L7 114
Wigtown, Scot., U.K. G9 8
Wijalpurā, Nepal G11 44
Wil, Switz. D11 13
Wilber, Ne., U.S. K11 118
Wilberforce Falls, wtfl, N.W. Ter., Can. C11 96
Wilbur, Wa., U.S. C7 122
Wilburton, Ok., U.S. E11 116
Wilcannia, Austl. H5 70
Wilcox, Sask., Can. H10 104
Wilcox, Ne., U.S. K8 118
Wilcox, Pa., U.S. F8 108
Wildcat Hill, hill, Sask., Can. E12 104
Wilder, Id., U.S. G9 122
Wildersville, Tn., U.S. G8 114
Wildhaus, Switz. D11 13
Wildhay, stm., Alta., Can. D17 102
Wildnest Lake, l., Sask., Can. C12 104
Wildon, Aus. I15 10
Wild Rice, stm., Mn., U.S. D11 118
Wild Rice, stm., N.D., U.S. E10 118
Wildrose, N.D., U.S. C4 118
Wild Rose, Wi., U.S. F6 110
Wildwood, Alta., Can. D19 102
Wildwood, N.J., U.S. I12 108
Wilhelm, Mount, mtn., Pap. N. Gui. m15 68a
Wilhelmina Gebergte, mts., Sur. F14 84
Wilhelminakanaal, Neth. E7 12
Wilhelmina Peak see Trikora, Puncak, mtn., Indon. F10 38
Wilhelmshaven, Ger. B8 10
Wilhelmstal, Nmb. C3 66
Wilkerson Pass, Co., U.S. E11 120
Wilkes-Barre, Pa., U.S. F11 108
Wilkesboro, N.C., U.S. C5 112
Wilkes Land, reg., Ant. C7 73
Wilkie, Sask., Can. F6 104
Will, Mount, mtn., B.C., Can. H30 100
Willacoochee, Ga., U.S. H3 112
Willamette, stm., Or., U.S. E3 122
Willamina, Or., U.S. E2 122
Willandra Billabong Creek, stm., Austl. I6 70
Willapa, stm., Wa., U.S. D2 122
Willapa Bay, b., Wa., U.S. D1 122
Willard, Mo., U.S. E3 114
Willard, N.M., U.S. J10 120
Willard, Oh., U.S. F4 108
Willard, Ut., U.S. C4 120
Willard, Punta, c., Mex. C3 90
Willcox, Az., U.S. L7 120
Willcox Playa, l., Az., U.S. L7 120
Willemstad, Neth. Ant. H10 94
William "Bill" Dannelly Reservoir, res., Al., U.S. J9 114
William Lake, l., Man., Can. E15 104
Williams, Az., U.S. I4 120
Williams, Ca., U.S. E3 124
Williams, Ia., U.S. H2 110
Williams, Mn., U.S. C13 118
Williams, stm., Austl. C4 70
Williams Bay, Wi., U.S. H7 110
Williamsburg, Ia., U.S. I3 110
Williamsburg, Ky., U.S. C2 112
Williamsburg, Pa., U.S. G8 108
Williamsburg, Va., U.S. B10 112
Williams Lake, B.C., Can. E12 102
Williams Lake Indian Reserve, B.C., Can. E12 102
Williamson, N.Y., U.S. D9 108
Williamson, W.V., U.S. B4 112
Williamsport, Newf., Can. B17 106
Williamsport, In., U.S. B9 114
Williamsport, Pa., U.S. F9 108
Williamston, Mi., U.S. H11 110
Williamston, N.C., U.S. D9 112
Williamston, S.C., U.S. E4 112
Williamstown, Ky., U.S. I2 108
Williamstown, Ma., U.S. E13 108
Williamstown, N.J., U.S. H12 108
Williamstown, Vt., U.S. C14 108
Williamstown, W.V., U.S. H5 108
Williamsville, Il., U.S. C7 114
Willich, Ger. A13 14
Willimantic, Ct., U.S. F14 108
Willingboro, N.J., U.S. G12 108
Willingdon, Alta., Can. D22 102
Willingdon, Mount, mtn., Alta., Can. F18 102
Willis, Tx., U.S. I11 116
Willisau, Switz. D9 13
Willis Group, is., Austl. C10 68
Willis Island, i., Newf., Can. D20 106
Williston, S. Afr. H5 66
Williston, Fl., U.S. J4 112
Williston, N.D., U.S. C4 118
Williston, S.C., U.S. F5 112
Williston Lake, res., B.C., Can. A10 102
Willisville, Il., U.S. E7 114
Willits, Ca., U.S. E2 124
Willmar, Mn., U.S. F12 118
Willmore Wilderness Provincial Park, Alta., Can. D15 102
Willoughby, Oh., U.S. F5 108
Willoughby, Cape, c., Austl. J3 70
Willow, Ak., U.S. F19 100
Willow, stm., Alta., Can. B20 102
Willow, stm., B.C., Can. D12 102
Willow, stm., Mn., U.S. D2 110
Willow, stm., Wi., U.S. E3 110
Willowbrook, Sask., Can. G12 104
Willow Bunch, Sask., Can. I9 104
Willow Bunch Lake, l., Sask., Can. I9 104
Willow City, N.D., U.S. C7 118
Willow Creek, Ca., U.S. D2 124
Willow Creek, Mt., U.S. E14 122
Willow Creek, stm., Alta., Can. G20 102
Willowick, Oh., U.S. F5 108
Willow Lake, S.D., U.S. G10 118
Willow Lake, l., N.W. Ter., Can. D9 96
Willowlake, stm., N.W. Ter., Can. D8 96
Willowmore, S. Afr. I6 66
Willow River, B.C., Can. C12 102
Willows, Ca., U.S. E3 124
Willow Springs, Mo., U.S. F5 114
Wills, Lake, l., Austl. D5 68
Willshire, Oh., U.S. G2 108
Wills Point, Tx., U.S. G10 116
Willunga, Austl. J3 70
Wilmar, Ar., U.S. I5 114
Wilmer, Al., U.S. L8 114
Wilmer, Tx., U.S. G10 116
Wilmette, Il., U.S. H8 110
Wilmington, Austl. I3 70
Wilmington, De., U.S. H11 108
Wilmington, Il., U.S. I7 110
Wilmington, N.C., U.S. E9 112
Wilmington, Oh., U.S. H3 108
Wilmington, Vt., U.S. E14 108
Wilmore, Ky., U.S. B2 112
Wilmot, Ar., U.S. I5 114
Wilmot, S.D., U.S. F11 118
Wilsall, Mt., U.S. E15 122
Wilson, Austl. I3 70
Wilson, Ar., U.S. G6 114
Wilson, Ks., U.S. M9 118
Wilson, La., U.S. L5 114
Wilson, N.Y., U.S. D8 108
Wilson, N.C., U.S. D9 112
Wilson, Ok., U.S. E9 116
Wilson, Tx., U.S. F5 116
Wilson, stm., Austl. F4 70
Wilson, stm., Or., U.S. E2 122
Wilson, Cape, c., N.W. Ter., Can. C16 96
Wilson, Mount, mtn., Ca., U.S. J7 124
Wilson, Mount, mtn., Co., U.S. G9 120
Wilson, Mount, mtn., Nv., U.S. F11 124
Wilson Lake, res., Al., U.S. H9 114
Wilson Lake, res., Ks., U.S. M9 118
Wilsons Beach, N.B., Can. H7 106
Wilsons Promontory, c., Austl. L7 70
Wilsonville, Ne., U.S. K7 118
Wilton, Me., U.S. C16 108
Wilton, N.H., U.S. E15 108
Wilton, N.D., U.S. D7 118
Wilton, Wi., U.S. G5 110
Wiltshire, co., Eng., U.K. J12 8
Wiluna, Austl. E4 68
Wimapedi, stm., Man., Can. C15 104
Wimauma, Fl., U.S. L4 112
Wimberley, Tx., U.S. I8 116
Wimbledon, N.D., U.S. D9 118
Winagami Lake, l., Alta., Can. B18 102
Winamac, In., U.S. A10 114
Winburg, S. Afr. G8 66
Winchendon, Ma., U.S. E14 108
Winchester, Ont., Can. B11 108
Winchester, Eng., U.K. J12 8
Winchester, Id., U.S. D9 122
Winchester, Il., U.S. C6 114
Winchester, In., U.S. B12 114
Winchester, Ky., U.S. B2 112
Winchester, N.H., U.S. E14 108
Winchester, Tn., U.S. G10 114
Winchester, Va., U.S. H8 108
Wind, stm., Yukon, Can. D27 100
Wind, stm., Wy., U.S. G17 122
Windber, Pa., U.S. G8 108
Wind Cave National Park, S.D., U.S. H4 118
Winder, Ga., U.S. F3 112
Windermere, B.C., Can. G19 102
Windfall, Alta., Can. C18 102
Windhoek, Nmb. D3 66
Windigo, stm., Ont., Can. E23 104
Windigo Lake, l., Ont., Can. F23 104
Windischgarsten, Aus. H14 10
Wind Lake, Wi., U.S. H7 110
Windom, Mn., U.S. H12 118
Windom Peak, mtn., Co., U.S. G9 120
Windorah, Austl. E5 70
Window Rock, Az., U.S. I7 120
Wind River Peak, mtn., Wy., U.S. H16 122
Wind River Range, mts., Wy., U.S. G16 122
Windsor, Austl. I9 70
Windsor, Newf., Can. D18 106
Windsor, N.S., Can. H9 106
Windsor, Ont., Can. H12 110
Windsor, Que., Can. B14 108
Windsor, Eng., U.K. J13 8
Windsor, Ca., U.S. F3 124
Windsor, Co., U.S. D12 120
Windsor, Ct., U.S. F14 108
Windsor, Il., U.S. C8 114
Windsor, Mo., U.S. D3 114
Windsor, N.C., U.S. D10 112
Windsor, Vt., U.S. D14 108
Windsor, Va., U.S. C10 112
Windsor Forest, Ga., U.S. H5 112
Windsor Locks, Ct., U.S. F14 108
Windthorst, Tx., U.S. F8 116
Windward Islands, is., N.A. H14 94
Windward Passage, strt., N.A. E7 94
Windy Lake, l., Sask., Can. D12 104
Windy Peak, mtn., Co., U.S. F10 120
Windy Peak, mtn., Wa., U.S. B6 122
Winefred, stm., Alta., Can. C4 104
Winefred Lake, l., Alta., Can. B24 102
Winejok, Sud. M4 60
Winfield, Alta., Can. E20 102
Winfield, Al., U.S. I9 114
Winfield, Ia., U.S. I4 110
Winfield, Ks., U.S. N11 118
Winfield, Mo., U.S. D6 114
Winfield, W.V., U.S. I5 108
Wing, N.D., U.S. D7 118
Wingate, N.C., U.S. E6 112
Wingene, Bel. F3 12
Wingham, Austl. H10 70
Wingham, Ont., Can. G14 110
Wingo, Ky., U.S. F8 114
Winifred, Mt., U.S. C16 122
Winifreda, Arg. I6 80
Winisk, Ont., Can. E15 96
Winisk, stm., Ont., Can. F15 96
Winisk Lake, l., Ont., Can. F15 96
Wink, Tx., U.S. H3 116
Winkana, Burma G5 40
Winkelman, Az., U.S. L6 120
Winkler, Man., Can. I17 104
Winlaw, B.C., Can. H17 102
Winlock, Wa., U.S. D3 122
Winneba, Ghana I9 64
Winnebago, Il., U.S. H6 110
Winnebago, Mn., U.S. G1 110
Winnebago, Ne., U.S. I11 118
Winnebago, stm., Ia., U.S. G2 110
Winnebago, Lake, l., Wi., U.S. F7 110
Winneconne, Wi., U.S. F7 110
Winnemucca, Nv., U.S. D8 124
Winner, S.D., U.S. H8 118
Winnetka, Il., U.S. H8 110
Winnett, Mt., U.S. C17 122
Winnfield, La., U.S. K4 114
Winnibigoshish, Lake, l., Mn., U.S. C1 110
Winnie, Tx., U.S. M2 114
Winnipeg, Man., Can. I17 104
Winnipeg, stm., Can. H18 104
Winnipeg, Lake, l., Man., Can. F17 104
Winnipeg Beach, Man., Can. H18 104
Winnipegosis, Man., Can. G15 104
Winnipegosis, Lake, l., Man., Can. F14 104
Winnipesaukee, Lake, l., N.H., U.S. D15 108
Winnsboro, La., U.S. J5 114
Winnsboro, S.C., U.S. E5 112
Winnsboro, Tx., U.S. G11 116
Winnsboro Mills, S.C., U.S. E5 112
Winona, Ks., U.S. L6 118
Winona, Mi., U.S. D7 110
Winona, Mn., U.S. F4 110
Winona, Ms., U.S. I7 114
Winona, Mo., U.S. E5 114
Winona Lake, In., U.S. A11 114
Winooski, Vt., U.S. C13 108
Winooski, stm., Vt., U.S. C14 108
Winschoten, Neth. B11 12
Winside, Ne., U.S. I10 118
Winslow, Az., U.S. I6 120
Winslow, Me., U.S. C17 108
Winsted, Ct., U.S. F13 108
Winsted, Mn., U.S. F1 110
Winston, Fl., U.S. K4 112
Winston, Or., U.S. G2 122
Winston-Salem, N.C., U.S. C6 112
Wintego Lake, l., Sask., Can. C12 104
Winter, Wi., U.S. E4 110
Winter Garden, Fl., U.S. K5 112
Winter Harbor, Me., U.S. C18 108
Winter Harbour, B.C., Can. G6 102
Winterhaven, Ca., U.S. L11 124
Winter Haven, Fl., U.S. K5 112
Wintering, stm., N.D., U.S. D7 118
Wintering Lake, l., Man., Can. C17 104
Winter Island, i., N.W. Ter., Can. C16 96
Winter Park, Fl., U.S. K5 112
Winter Park, N.C., U.S. E9 112
Winterport, Me., U.S. C18 108
Winters, Ca., U.S. F4 124
Winters, Tx., U.S. H7 116
Winterset, Ia., U.S. I1 110
Winterthur, Switz. C10 13
Winterton, Newf., Can. E20 106
Winterville, Ga., U.S. F3 112
Winterville, Ms., U.S. I5 114
Winterville, N.C., U.S. D9 112
Winthrop, Ia., U.S. H4 110
Winthrop, Me., U.S. C17 108
Winthrop, Mn., U.S. F1 110
Winthrop Harbor, Il., U.S. H8 110
Winton, Austl. D5 70
Winton, N.Z. G2 72
Winton, N.C., U.S. C10 112
Wipperfürth, Ger. D7 10
Wirāṭanagar, Nepal G12 44
Wīrgañj, Nepal G11 44
Wirral, pen., Eng., U.K. H10 8
Wirraminna, Austl. H2 70
Wiscasset, Me., U.S. C17 108
Wisconsin, state, U.S. C9 98
Wisconsin, stm., Wi., U.S. G5 110
Wisconsin, Lake, res., Wi., U.S. G6 110
Wisconsin Dells, Wi., U.S. G6 110
Wisconsin Rapids, Wi., U.S. F6 110
Wisdom, Mt., U.S. E12 122
Wise, Va., U.S. C4 112
Wishart, Sask., Can. G10 104
Wishek, N.D., U.S. E8 118
Wishram, Wa., U.S. E5 122
Wisła, stm., Pol. A18 10
Wismar, Ger. B11 10
Wismar, Guy. D13 84
Wisner, La., U.S. K5 114
Wisner, Ne., U.S. J11 118
Wissembourg, Fr. C14 14
Wister, Ok., U.S. H2 114
Wisznice, Pol. D23 10
Witbank, S. Afr. E9 66
Witbooisvlei, Nmb. E4 66
Witchekan Lake, l., Sask., Can. E7 104
Withlacoochee, stm., U.S. I3 112
Witjira National Park, Austl. E7 68
Witless Bay, Newf., Can. E21 106
Witrivier, S. Afr. E10 66
Witsand, S. Afr. J5 66
Witt, Il., U.S. C7 114
Witten, Ger. D7 10
Wittenberg, Ger. D12 10
Wittenberg, Wi., U.S. F6 110
Wittenberge, Ger. B11 10
Wittenburg, Ger. B11 10
Wittenoom, Austl. D3 68
Wittingen, Ger. C10 10
Wittlich, Ger. F6 10
Wittmund, Ger. B7 10
Wittstock, Ger. B12 10
Witwatersrant, reg., S. Afr. E8 66
Witzputz, Nmb. F3 66
Wiwa Creek, stm., Sask., Can. H7 104
Wiżajny, Pol. A22 10
Włocławek, Pol. C19 10
Włoszczowa, Pol. E19 10
Woburn, Ma., U.S. E15 108
Wodonga, Austl. K7 70
Wohlen, Switz. D9 13
Wohlthat Mountains, mts., Ant. C3 73
Woi, Sud. N6 60
Woking, Alta., Can. B16 102
Woking, Eng., U.K. J13 8
Wolbach, Ne., U.S. J9 118
Wolcott, In., U.S. B9 114
Wolcott, N.Y., U.S. D10 108
Wolcottville, In., U.S. A11 114
Wolf, stm., U.S. G7 114
Wolf, stm., Ks., U.S. L12 118
Wolf, stm., Ms., U.S. L7 114
Wolf, stm., Wi., U.S. F7 110
Wolfach, Ger. G8 10
Wolf-Bay, Que., Can. B13 106
Wolf Creek, Mt., U.S. C13 122
Wolf Creek, Or., U.S. H2 122
Wolf Creek Lake, res., Ks., U.S. M12 118
Wolf Creek Pass, Co., U.S. G10 120
Wolfeboro, N.H., U.S. D15 108
Wolfe City, Tx., U.S. F10 116
Wolfen, Ger. D12 10
Wolfenbüttel, Ger. C10 10
Wolfenden, Mount, mtn., B.C., Can. G7 102
Wolfforth, Tx., U.S. F4 116
Wolfhagen, Ger. D9 10
Wolf Lake, Mi., U.S. G9 110
Wolf Lake, l., Alta., Can. C24 102
Wolf Lake, l., Yukon, Can. F29 100
Wolf Point, Mt., U.S. B20 122
Wolfratshausen, Ger. H11 10
Wolfsberg, Aus. I14 10
Wolfsburg, Ger. C10 10
Wolfville, N.S., Can. G9 106
Wolgast, Ger. A13 10
Wolhusen, Switz. D9 13
Wollaston, Islas, is., Chile H3 78
Wollaston Lake, l., Sask., Can. E12 96
Wollaston Peninsula, pen., N.W. Ter., Can. C9 96
Wollemi National Park, Austl. I9 70
Wollogorang, Austl. A2 70
Wollongong, Austl. J9 70
Wolmaransstad, S. Afr. F8 66
Wołomin, Pol. C21 10
Wolseley, Sask., Can. H11 104
Wolseley, S. Afr. I4 66
Wolsey, S.D., U.S. G9 118
Wolsztyn, Pol. C16 10
Wolvega, Neth. C9 12
Wolverhampton, Eng., U.K. I11 8
Wolverine, Mi., U.S. E11 110
Wondai, Austl. F9 70
Wonderland, Ca., U.S. D4 124
Wonewoc, Wi., U.S. G5 110
Wŏnju, S. Kor. F15 32
Wonosobo, Indon. J14 39a
Wonotobo Vallen, wtfl, Sur. E14 84
Wŏnsan, N. Kor. D15 32
Wonthaggi, Austl. L6 70
Wood, S.D., U.S. H7 118
Wood, stm., B.C., Can. E16 102
Wood, stm., Sask., Can. I8 104
Wood, stm., Ne., U.S. K8 118
Wood, stm., Wy., U.S. G16 122
Wood, Mount, mtn., Yukon, Can. F24 100
Woodall Mountain, hill, Ms., U.S. H8 114
Wood Bay, b., N.W. Ter., Can. B30 100
Woodbine, Ga., U.S. I5 112
Woodbine, Ia., U.S. J12 118
Woodbine, N.J., U.S. H12 108
Woodbridge, Va., U.S. I9 108
Woodburn, Or., U.S. E3 122
Woodbury, Ct., U.S. F13 108
Woodbury, Ga., U.S. G2 112
Woodbury, N.J., U.S. H11 108
Woodbury, Tn., U.S. G10 114
Woodenbong, Austl. G10 70
Woodfibre, B.C., Can. H11 102
Woodhull, Il., U.S. I5 110
Wood Islands, P.E.I., Can. G11 106
Woodlake, Ca., U.S. H6 124
Wood Lake, Ne., U.S. I7 118
Wood Lake, l., Sask., Can. C11 104
Woodland, Ca., U.S. F4 124
Woodland, Ga., U.S. G2 112
Woodland, Me., U.S. B19 108
Woodland, N.C., U.S. C9 112
Woodland Park, Co., U.S. F11 120
Woodlawn, Ky., U.S. E8 114
Wood Mountain, mtn., Sask., Can. I8 104
Wood Mountain Indian Reserve, Sask., Can. I8 104
Woodridge, Man., Can. I18 104
Wood River, Il., U.S. D6 114
Wood River, Ne., U.S. K9 118
Woodroffe, stm., Austl. C2 70
Woodroffe, Mount, mtn., Austl. E6 68
Woodrow, N.C., U.S. D9 112
Woodruff, Az., U.S. J6 120
Woodruff, S.C., U.S. E4 112
Woodruff, Wi., U.S. E6 110
Woods, Lake, l., Austl. C6 68
Woods, Lake of the, l., N.A. B13 118
Woodsboro, Tx., U.S. K9 116
Woodsfield, Oh., U.S. H5 108
Woods Hole, Ma., U.S. F16 108
Woodside, Austl. L7 70
Woodson, Tx., U.S. F7 116
Woodstock, N.B., Can. F6 106
Woodstock, Ont., Can. G15 110
Woodstock, Il., U.S. H7 110
Woodstock, N.Y., U.S. E12 108
Woodstock, Vt., U.S. D14 108
Woodstock, Va., U.S. I8 108
Woodsville, N.H., U.S. C14 108
Woodville, N.Z. D5 72
Woodville, Al., U.S. H10 114
Woodville, Fl., U.S. I2 112
Woodville, Ga., U.S. F3 112
Woodville, Ms., U.S. K5 114
Woodville, Oh., U.S. F3 108
Woodville, Tx., U.S. L2 114
Woodward, Ia., U.S. I2 110
Woodward, Ok., U.S. C7 116
Woody, stm., Can. F14 104
Woody Head, c., Austl. G10 70
Woody Island, Ak., U.S. H18 100
Woolgoolga, Austl. H10 70
Woolmarket, Ms., U.S. L8 114
Woomera, Austl. H2 70
Woonsocket, R.I., U.S. E15 108
Woonsocket, S.D., U.S. G9 118
Woorabinda, Austl. E8 70
Wooramel, stm., Austl. E3 68
Wooster, Oh., U.S. G5 108
Worb, Switz. E8 13
Worcester, S. Afr. I4 66
Worcester, Eng., U.K. I11 8
Worcester, Ma., U.S. E15 108
Worden, Mt., U.S. E17 122
Wörgl, Aus. H12 10
Work Channel, strt., B.C., Can. C4 102
Workington, Eng., U.K. G10 8
Worksop, Eng., U.K. H12 8
Workum, Neth. C7 12
Worland, Wy., U.S. F18 122
Wormerveer, Neth. D6 12
Worms, Ger. F8 10
Wortham, Tx., U.S. H10 116
Worthing, Eng., U.K. K13 8
Worthington, In., U.S. C10 114
Worthington, Mn., U.S. H12 118
Worthington, Oh., U.S. G3 108
Worthington Peak, mtn., Nv., U.S. C10 124
Woudrichem, Neth. E7 12
Wounded Knee, S.D., U.S. H5 118
Wounta, Nic. D11 92
Wounta, Laguna de, b., Nic. D11 92
Wouw, Neth. E5 12
Wowan, Austl. D9 70
Woy Woy, Austl. I9 70
Wrangel Island see Vrangel'a, ostrov, i., Russia C28 28
Wrangell, Ak., U.S. H28 100
Wrangell, Cape, c., Ak., U.S. J1 101a
Wrangell, Mount, mtn., Ak., U.S. E22 100
Wrangell Island, i., Ak., U.S. H28 100
Wrangell Mountains, mts., Ak., U.S. F23 100
Wrath, Cape, c., Scot., U.K. C8 8
Wray, Co., U.S. K5 118
Wreck Reef, rf., Austl. D11 70
Wrens, Ga., U.S. F4 112
Wrentham, Alta., Can. H22 102
Wrexham, Wales, U.K. H10 8
Wright, Mount, mtn., Mt., U.S. C13 122
Wright City, Mo., U.S. D5 114
Wright City, Ok., U.S. E11 116
Wright Patman Lake, res., Tx., U.S. I2 114
Wrightson, Mount, mtn., Az., U.S. M6 120
Wrightstown, Wi., U.S. F7 110
Wrightsville, Ga., U.S. G4 112
Wrightsville Beach, N.C., U.S. E9 112
Wrightwood, Ca., U.S. J8 124
Wrigley, N.W. Ter., Can. E33 100
Wrigley, Tn., U.S. G9 114
Wrocław (Breslau), Pol. D17 10
Wrong Lake, l., Man., Can. F18 104
Wrottesley, Cape, c., N.W. Ter., Can. B8 96
Wroxton, Sask., Can. G13 104
Września, Pol. C17 10
Wu, stm., China F8 30
Wucheng, China B2 34
Wuchin see Changzhou, China E10 30
Wuchuan, China D11 40
Wudian, China D1 34
Wudinna, Austl. I1 70
Wudu, China E7 30
Wugang, China F9 30
Wugong Shan, mts., China H2 34
Wuhai, China D8 30
Wuhan, China E3 34
Wuhu, China D7 34
Wuhua, China L4 34
Wuhuanchi, China A9 32
Wuji, China E2 32
Wujiang, China D9 34
Wukari, Nig. H14 64
Wuliang Shan, mts., China B6 40
Wum, Cam. H15 64
Wunnummin Lake, l., Ont., Can. F15 96
Wun Rog, Sud. M5 60
Wunstorf, Ger. C9 10
Wuping, China J5 34
Wuppertal, Ger. D7 10
Wuppertal, S. Afr. I4 66
Würenlingen, Switz. C9 13
Würzburg, Ger. F9 10
Wurzen, Ger. D12 10
Wushan, China E8 30
Wusheng, China F8 34
Wushenqi, China D8 30
Wuskwatim Lake, l., Man., Can. C16 104
Wusong, China D10 34
Wutai, China D9 30
Wutai Shan, mtn., China D1 32
Wutangjie, China F11 34
Wutongqiao, China F7 30
Wuustwezel, Bel. F6 12
Wuvulu Island, i., Pap. N. Gui. F11 38
Wuwei, China D7 30
Wuwei, China D6 34
Wuxi (Wuhsi), China D9 34
Wuyi Shan, mts., China I5 34
Wuyuan, China C8 30
Wuzhi Shan, mtn., China E10 40
Wuzhong, China D8 30
Wuzhou (Wuchow), China C11 40
Wyaconda, Mo., U.S. B5 114
Wyaconda, stm., Mo., U.S. B5 114
Wyalusing, Pa., U.S. F10 108
Wyandotte, Mi., U.S. H12 110
Wyandra, Austl. F6 70
Wyangala, Lake, res., Austl. I8 70
Wyatt, Mo., U.S. F7 114
Wycheproof, Austl. K5 70
Wye, stm., U.K. J11 8
Wyeville, Wi., U.S. F5 110
Wykoff, Mn., U.S. G3 110
Wylie, Tx., U.S. F10 116
Wylie, Lake, res., U.S. D5 112
Wymark, Sask., Can. H7 104
Wymore, Ne., U.S. K11 118
Wyndham, Austl. C5 68
Wyndmere, N.D., U.S. E10 118
Wynndel, B.C., Can. H18 102
Wynne, Ar., U.S. G6 114
Wynnewood, Ok., U.S. E9 116
Wynniatt Bay, b., N.W. Ter., Can. B10 96
Wynona, Ok., U.S. C10 116
Wynot, Ne., U.S. I10 118
Wynyard, Austl. M6 70
Wynyard, Sask., Can. G10 104
Wyocena, Wi., U.S. G6 110
Wyodak, Wy., U.S. G2 118
Wyoming, Ont., Can. H13 110
Wyoming, Il., U.S. I6 110
Wyoming, Ia., U.S. H4 110
Wyoming, Mi., U.S. H10 110
Wyoming, state, U.S. C5 98
Wyong, Austl. I9 70
Wysokie Mazowieckie, Pol. C22 10
Wyszków, Pol. C21 10
Wytheville, Va., U.S. C5 112

X

Xaclbal, stm., N.A. B3 92
Xaidulla, China B8 44
Xainza, China E4 30
Xai-Xai, Moz. E11 66
Xalapa, Mex. H11 90
Xam (Chu), stm., Asia E8 40
Xambrê, stm., Braz. G2 79
Xam Nua, Laos D8 40
Xan (San), stm., Asia G9 40
Xangongo, Ang. E3 58
Xánthi, Grc. H8 20
Xanxerê, Braz. D12 80
Xapecó, stm., Braz. D12 80
Xapuri, Braz. D7 82
Xapuri, stm., Braz. D7 82
Xar Moron, stm., China C10 30
Xàtiva (Játiva), Spain G11 16
Xau, Lake, pl., Bots. C7 66

Name | Map Ref. | Page

Xavantina, Braz. F2 79
Xaxim, Braz. D12 80
Xcalak, Mex. H16 90
X-Can, Mex. G16 90
Xenia, Il., U.S. D8 114
Xenia, Oh., U.S. H3 108
Xertigny, Fr. D13 14
Xeruã, stm., Braz. B7 82
Xhumo, Bots. C7 66
Xi, stm., China G9 30
Xiagaixin, China C5 40
Xiagezhuang, China G8 32
Xiahe, China D7 30
Xiamen (Amoy), China K7 34
Xiamen Gang, b., Asia K7 34
Xi'an (Sian), China E8 30
Xianfeng, China J6 34
Xiang, stm., China F9 30
Xiangcheng, China B2 34
Xiangfan, China E9 30
Xianggongshi, China G2 34
Xiangheguan, China B2 34
Xiangkhoang, Laos E7 40
Xiangkhoang, Plateau de, plat., Laos E7 40
Xiangride, China D6 30
Xiangtan, China H1 34
Xianinggang, China G1 34
Xianju, China G9 34
Xianxian, China E4 32
Xianyou, China J7 34
Xiaodanyang, China D7 34
Xiaogan, China E2 34
Xiaogushan, China D11 32
Xiao Hinggan Ling, mts., China B12 30
Xiaoji, China C8 34
Xiaojiang, China J3 34
Xiaolan, China M2 34
Xiaolipu, China G4 32
Xiaoshan, China E9 34
Xiaoshi, China H5 34
Xiaoshixiang, China E5 34
Xiaoxi, China J4 34
Xiapu, China I9 34
Xiapu, China H3 34
Xiaying, China F7 32
Xibu, China D7 34
Xichang, China F7 30
Xicoténcatl, Mex. F10 90
Xié, stm., Braz. G9 84
Xielipuke, China E10 44
Xigaotun, China C10 32
Xigazê, China F13 44
Xihua, China B3 34
Xijialong, China C7 40
Xikouxu, China J6 34
Xiliao, stm., China C11 30
Ximiao, China C7 30
Xin'an, China I5 34
Xinavane, Moz. E11 66
Xinba, China I7 32
Xincheng, China J3 34
Xindian, China F2 32
Xindukou, China B6 40
Xing'an, China F9 30
Xingcheng, China C8 32
Xinghua, China C8 34
Xingkai Hu (ozero Chanka), l., Asia B13 30
Xinglong, China C5 32
Xingtai, China F2 32
Xingu, stm., Braz. D8 76
Xinguan, China B7 34
Xingyi, China B8 40
Xinhe, China F3 32
Xinhua, China F9 30
Xinhui, China M2 34
Xining, China D7 30
Xinjiaji, China G4 32
Xinjiang, China D9 30
Xinjiang Uygur Zizhiqu (Sinkiang), prov., China C3 30
Xinle (Dongchangshou), China E2 32
Xinmin, China A10 32
Xinshi, China E9 34
Xinwen (Suncun), China H5 32
Xinxian, China D3 34
Xinxiang, China H1 32
Xinxing, China M1 34
Xinyang, China C3 34
Xinzao, China L2 34
Xinzhangzi, China C5 32
Xiongjiachang, China A3 40
Xipamanu (Chipamanu), stm., S.A. D7 82
Xiping, China B3 34
Xique-Xique, Braz. F10 76
Xisha Qundao (Paracel Islands), is., China B5 38
Xishu, China G1 32
Xitole, Gui.-B. F2 64
Xiuyan, China C11 32
Xixian, China C3 34
Xiyou, China F7 32
Xizang Zizhiqu (Tibet), prov., China E3 30
Xizhou, China F10 34
Xochicalco, hist., Mex. H10 90
Xochistlahuaca, Mex. I10 90
Xuancheng, China E7 34
Xuanhua, China C3 32
Xuchang, China A2 34
Xueao, China F10 34
Xuecheng, China I5 32
Xuji, China D5 34
Xun, stm., China G9 30
Xushui, China D3 32
Xuwen, China D11 40
Xuyong, China F8 30
Xuzhou (Süchow), China A6 34

Y

Yaan, China E7 30
Yablis, Nic. C11 92
Yablonovy Range see Jablonovyj chrebet, mts., Russia G14 28
Yacambu, Parque Nacional, Ven. C8 84
Yacaré Norte, Riacho, stm., Para. B9 80
Yaco, Bol. G8 82
Yaco (Iaco), stm., S.A. D6 82
Yacuiba, Bol. J10 82
Yacuma, stm., Bol. E8 82
Yacyretá, Isla, i., Para. D10 80
Yādgīr, India D4 46
Yadkin, stm., N.C., U.S. D6 112
Yadkinville, N.C., U.S. C6 112
Yad Mordekhay, Isr. E3 50
Yadong, China F4 30
Yafran, Libya B3 56
Yağcılar, Tur. J12 20
Yagoua, Cam. F10 54
Yagradagzê Shan, mtn., China C16 44
Yaguachi Nuevo, Ec. I3 84
Yaguajay, Cuba C5 94
Yaguala, stm., Hond. B8 92
Yaguará, Col. F5 84
Yaguaraparo, Ven. B11 84
Yaguarí, Ur. F11 80
Yaguarón (Jaguarão), stm., S.A. G12 80
Yaguas, stm., Peru I7 84
Yahara, stm., Wi., U.S. H6 110
Yahk, B.C., Can. H18 102
Yahongqiao, China D5 32
Yahualica, Mex. G8 90
Yai, Khao, mtn., Asia H5 40
Yainax Butte, mtn., Or., U.S. H4 122
Yaizu, Japan M13 36
Yakima, Wa., U.S. D5 122
Yakima, stm., Wa., U.S. D6 122
Yako, Burkina E8 64
Yakobi Island, i., Ak., U.S. G26 100
Yakoma, Zaire H5 56
Yaku-shima, i., Japan Q5 37b
Yakutat, Ak., U.S. G25 100
Yakutat Bay, b., Ak., U.S. G24 100
Yakutsk see Jakutsk, Russia E17 28
Yala, Thai. K6 40
Yalahau, Laguna, b., Mex. G16 90
Yale, B.C., Can. H13 102
Yale, Mi., U.S. G13 110
Yale, Ok., U.S. C10 116
Yale, Mount, mtn., Co., U.S. F10 120
Yalgoo, Austl. E3 68
Yalinga, Cen. Afr. Rep. N2 60
Yalleroi, Austl. E6 70
Yalobusha, stm., Ms., U.S. I7 114
Yalong, stm., China E6 30
Yalova, Tur. I13 20
Yalta see Jalta, Ukr. I4 26
Yalu (Amnok-kang), stm., Asia C12 32
Yamagata, Japan I15 36
Yamaguchi, Japan M6 36
Yamba, Austl. G10 70
Yambio, Sud. H6 56
Yambrasbamba, Peru A3 82
Yamdena, Pulau, i., Indon. G9 38
Yamethin, Burma D4 40
Yamia, Niger E15 64
Yamma Yamma, Lake, l., Austl. F4 70
Yamoussoukro, I.C. H7 64
Yampa, Co., U.S. D10 120
Yampa, stm., Co., U.S. D8 120
Yamparaez, Bol. H9 82
Yamsay Mountain, mtn., Or., U.S. H4 122
Yamuna, stm., India H9 44
Yamzho Yumco, l., China F14 44
Yanac, Austl. K4 70
Yanacachi, Bol. G8 82
Yanagawa, Japan N5 36
Yanahuara, Peru G6 82
Yanai, Japan N7 36
Yanam, India D7 46
Yan'an, China D8 30
Yanaoca, Peru F6 82
Yanbuʿ al-Baḥr, Sau. Ar. I5 48
Yanbutou, China F4 34
Yanceyville, N.C., U.S. C7 112
Yanchang, China D9 30
Yancheng, China B9 34
Yanchi, China D8 30
Yanco, Austl. J7 70
Yandev, Nig. H14 64
Yandoon, Burma F3 40
Yanfolila, Mali F5 64
Yangcun, China L3 34
Yangguanpu, China C4 34
Yangjia, China I7 32
Yangjiang, China G9 30
Yangkoushi, China G7 34
Yangliuqing, China D5 32
Yanglousi, China F2 34
Yangon (Rangoon), Burma F4 40
Yangp'yŏng, S. Kor. F15 32
Yangquan, China F1 32
Yangsan, S. Kor. H17 32
Yangshuling, China B6 32
Yangtze see Chang, stm., China E10 30
Yangxiaodian, China D5 34
Yangyang, S. Kor. E16 32
Yangzhou, China C8 34
Yanheying, China C7 32
Yanji, China A17 32
Yankdŏk, N. Kor. D14 32
Yankeetown, Fl., U.S. J4 112
Yankton, S.D., U.S. I10 118
Yanliumiao, China C5 34
Yanna, Austl. F7 70
Yanqi, China C4 30
Yanqing, China C3 32
Yanque, Peru F6 82
Yanṭā, Leb. A5 50
Yantabulla, Austl. G6 70
Yantai (Chefoo), China F9 32
Yantian, China H3 34
Yanzhou, China H4 32
Yao, Japan M10 36
Yaopi, China I2 34
Yaoundé, Cam. H9 54
Yaoya, stm., Nic. D10 92
Yapacaní, Bol. G9 82
Yapacani, stm., Bol. G9 82
Yapen, Pulau, i., Indon. F10 38
Yapeyú, Arg. E10 80
Yappar, stm., Austl. B4 70
Yaʿqūb, Sud. K3 60
Yaque del Norte, stm., Dom. Rep. E9 94
Yaqui, stm., Mex. C5 90
Yaracuy, state, Ven. B8 84
Yaraka, Austl. E6 70
Yarbasan, Tur. K12 20
Yardea, Austl. I1 70
Yarí, stm., Col. H6 84
Yarīm, Yemen G4 47
Yaring, Thai. K6 40
Yaritagua, Ven. B8 84
Yarkand see Shache, China A7 44
Yarkant (Yarkand), stm., China D2 30
Yarlung see Brahmaputra, stm., Asia G15 44
Yarmouth, N.S., Can. I7 106
Yarmouth, Me., U.S. D16 108
Yarmūk, Nahr al-, stm., Asia C5 50
Yarram, Austl. L7 70
Yarraman, Austl. F9 70
Yarrawonga, Austl. K7 70
Yarumal, Col. D5 84
Yashiro-jima, i., Japan N7 36
Yasothon, Thai. G8 40
Yass, Austl. J8 70
Yasuní, stm., Ec. H5 84
Yata, Bol. E8 82
Yata, stm., Bol. D9 82
Yatakala, Niger D10 64
Yatesboro, Pa., U.S. G7 108
Yates Center, Ks., U.S. N12 118
Yates City, Il., U.S. J5 110
Yathkyed Lake, l., N.W. Ter., Can. D13 96
Yatsushiro, Japan O5 36
Yaṭṭah, Isr. Occ. F4 50
Yatuá, stm., Ven. G9 84
Yauca, Peru F4 82
Yauca, stm., Peru F4 82
Yauco, P.R. E11 94
Yauli, Peru D3 82
Yaupi, Ec. I4 84
Yauri, Peru F6 82
Yautepec, Mex. H10 90
Yauyos, Peru E4 82
Yavarí (Javari), stm., S.A. D4 76
Yavarí Mirim, stm., Peru J6 84
Yavaros, Mex. D5 90
Yavatmāl, India B5 46
Yavero, stm., Peru E5 82
Yaví, Cerro, mtn., Ven. E10 84
Yavita, Ven. F9 84
Yaviza, Pan. C4 84
Yavne, Isr. E3 50
Yawatahama, Japan N7 36
Yaxchilán, hist., Mex. I14 90
Yaxian, China E10 40
Yayuan, China B14 32
Yazd, Iran F13 48
Yazmān, Pak. F4 44
Yazoo, stm., Ms., U.S. J6 114
Yazoo City, Ms., U.S. J6 114
Ybbs an der Donau, Aus. G15 10
Ybycuí, Para. D10 80
Ye, Burma G4 40
Yecheng, China B7 44
Yech'ŏn, S. Kor. G16 32
Yecla, Spain G10 16
Yécora, Mex. C5 90
Yeelanna, Austl. J1 70
Yegros, Para. D10 80
Yehud, Isr. D3 50
Yei, stm., Sud. N6 60
Yekaterinburg see Jekaterinburg, Russia F10 26
Yela Island, i., Pap. N. Gui. B10 68
Yelarbon, Austl. G9 70
Yele, S.L. G4 64
Yélimané, Mali D4 64
Yellow, stm., U.S. L10 114
Yellow, stm., In., U.S. A10 114
Yellow, stm., Ia., U.S. G4 110
Yellow, stm., Wi., U.S. E3 110
Yellow Grass, Sask., Can. I10 104
Yellowhead Pass, Can. E16 102
Yellow see Huang, stm., China D10 30
Yellowknife, N.W. Ter., Can. D10 96
Yellowknife, stm., N.W. Ter., Can. D10 96
Yellow Medicine, stm., Mn., U.S. G12 118
Yellow Sea (Huang Hai), Asia B11 34
Yellowstone, stm., U.S. B5 98
Yellowstone Falls, wtfl, Wy., U.S. F15 122
Yellowstone Lake, l., Wy., U.S. F15 122
Yellowstone National Park, Wy., U.S. F15 122
Yellowstone National Park, U.S. F15 122
Yellville, Ar., U.S. F4 114
Yelvertoft, Austl. C3 70
Yelwa, Nig. F12 64
Yemaotai, China A10 32
Yemassee, S.C., U.S. G6 112
Yemen (Al-Yaman), ctry., Asia F3 42
Yenangyaung, Burma D3 40
Yen Bai, Viet. D8 40
Yenda, Austl. J7 70
Yende Millimou, Gui. G4 64
Yendéré, Burkina F7 64
Yendi, Ghana G9 64
Yengisar, China D2 30
Yeniköy, Tur. J12 20
Yenisey see Jenisej, stm., Russia D15 26
Yenshuichen, Tai. L9 34
Yeola, India B3 46
Yeoval, Austl. I8 70
Yepachic, Mex. C5 90
Yeppoon, Austl. D9 70
Yerba Buena, Montaña, mtn., Hond. C7 92
Yerevan see Jerevan, Arm. I6 26
Yerington, Nv., U.S. F6 124
Yermasóyia, Cyp. D2 48
Yermo, Ca., U.S. J9 124
Yerupaja, Nevado, mtn., Peru D3 82
Yerushalayim (Al-Quds) (Jerusalem), Isr. E4 50
Yesa, Embalse de, res., Spain C10 16
Yesan, S. Kor. G14 32
Yeşilhisar, Tur. B3 48
Yeso, N.M., U.S. E2 116
Yeste, Spain G9 16
Yetman, Austl. G9 70
Yetti, reg., Afr. G7 62
Ye-u, Burma C3 40
Yeu, Île d', i., Fr. F4 14
Yexian, China B2 34
Ygatimí, Para. C11 80
Yguazú, stm., Para. C11 80
Yhú, Para. C11 80
Yi, stm., Ur. G10 80
Yi'an, China B12 30
Yiannitsá, Grc. I6 20
Yibin, China F7 30
Yicanghe, China C9 34
Yichang, China E9 30
Yichun, China B12 30
Yichun, China F9 30
Yidu, China G6 32
Yifag, Eth. K9 60
Yijiangzhen, China E7 34
Yilan, China B12 30
Yiliang, China B7 40
Yinchuan, China D8 30
Ying, stm., China C5 34
Yingcheng, China E2 34
Yingde, China K2 34
Yingkou, China C10 32
Yingtan, China G6 34
Yingtian, China G1 34
Yining, China C3 30
Yinzhan'ao, China L2 34
Yirba Muda, Eth. N10 60
Yirga Alem, Eth. N10 60
Yirol, Sud. N6 60
Yirwa, Sud. N4 60
Yishan, China B10 40
Yishui, China H6 32
Yíthion, Grc. M6 20
Yitulihe, China A11 30
Yiwu, China F9 34
Yiyang, China F9 30
Ylivieska, Fin. I19 6
Ymir, B.C., Can. H17 102
Yoakum, Tx., U.S. J9 116
Yockanookany, stm., Ms., U.S. J7 114
Yoco, Ven. B11 84
Yocona, stm., Ms., U.S. H7 114
Yogyakarta, Indon. J15 39a
Yoho National Park, B.C., Can. F18 102
Yoichi, Japan D15 36a
Yojoa, Lago de, l., Hond. C7 92
Yŏju, S. Kor. F15 32
Yokkaichi, Japan M11 36
Yokohama, Japan L14 36
Yokosuka, Japan L14 36
Yokote, Japan H15 36
Yola, Nig. G9 54
Yolaina, Serranías de, mts., Nic. F10 92
Yolombó, Col. D5 84
Yom, stm., Thai. F6 40
Yonago, Japan L8 36
Yŏnan, N. Kor. F14 32
Yoncalla, Or., U.S. G2 122
Yonezawa, Japan J15 36
Yŏngam, S. Kor. I14 32
Yongamp'o, N. Kor. D12 32
Yong'an, China J6 34
Yŏngan, N. Kor. B17 32
Yongchang, China F8 34
Yŏngch'ŏn, S. Kor. E15 32
Yŏngch'ŏn, S. Kor. H16 32
Yongdeng, China D7 30
Yongding, China K5 34
Yongding, stm., China K5 34
Yŏngdŏk, S. Kor. G17 32
Yŏngdong, S. Kor. G15 32
Yongfeng, China H4 34
Yonghŭng, N. Kor. D15 32
Yŏngju, S. Kor. G16 32
Yongkang, China G9 34
Yŏngmi-dong, N. Kor. D13 32
Yongren, China F7 30
Yŏngsanp'o, S. Kor. I14 32
Yongshan, China F7 30
Yŏngwŏl, S. Kor. F16 32
Yongxin, China I3 34
Yŏngyn, N. Kor. D13 32
Yonkers, N.Y., U.S. G13 108
Yonne, dept., Fr. E10 14
Yopal, Col. E6 84
York, Austl. F3 68
York, Eng., U.K. H12 8
York, Al., U.S. J8 114
York, Ne., U.S. K10 118
York, N.D., U.S. C8 118
York, Pa., U.S. H10 108
York, S.C., U.S. E5 112
York, stm., Que., Can. D9 106
York, stm., Va., U.S. B10 112
York, Cape, c., Austl. B8 68
York, Kap, c., Grnld. B13 86
Yorke Peninsula, pen., Austl. J2 70
York Factory, Man., Can. A22 104
York Sound, strt., Austl. B5 68
Yorkton, Sask., Can. G12 104
Yorktown, Tx., U.S. K9 116
Yorktown, Va., U.S. B10 112
Yorkville, Il., U.S. I7 110
Yorkville, N.Y., U.S. D11 108
Yoro, Hond. B7 92
Yoro, Mali D8 64
Yoro, dept., Hond. B7 92
Yoron-jima, i., Japan T3 37b
Yosemite National Park, Ca., U.S. G6 124
Yosemite National Park, Ca., U.S. G6 124
Yos Sudarso, Pulau, i., Indon. G10 38
Yŏsu, S. Kor. I15 32
Yotausito, Bol. G10 82
Yotvata, Isr. I4 50
You, stm., China G8 30
Youbou, B.C., Can. I10 102
Young, Austl. J8 70
Young, Sask., Can. G9 104
Young, Az., U.S. J6 120
Young, Ur. G10 80
Younghusband Peninsula, pen., Austl. K3 70
Youngstown, Alta., Can. F23 102
Youngstown, Fl., U.S. I1 112
Youngstown, N.Y., U.S. D7 108
Youngstown, Oh., U.S. F6 108
Youngsville, La., U.S. L5 114
Youngsville, N.C., U.S. C8 112
Youngsville, Pa., U.S. F7 108
Yountville, Ca., U.S. F3 124
Youssoufia, Mor. D6 62
Youxi, China I7 34
Youyang, China F8 30
Yozgat, Tur. B3 48
Ypacaraí, Para. C10 80
Ypané, stm., Para. B10 80
Ypé Jhú, Para. B11 80
Ypres (Ieper), Bel. G2 12
Ypsilanti, Mi., U.S. H12 110
Yreka, Ca., U.S. C3 124
Ystad, Swe. N13 6
Ytambey, stm., Para. C11 80
Yu, stm., China C10 40
Yuʿalliq, Jabal, mtn., Egypt F2 48
Yuan, stm., China F9 30
Yüanlin, Tai. L9 34
Yuanling, China F9 30
Yuanmou, China B6 40
Yuba, stm., Ca., U.S. E4 124
Yuba City, Ca., U.S. E4 124
Yūbari, Japan D16 36a
Yubdo, Eth. M8 60
Yucaipa, Ca., U.S. J8 124
Yucatán, state, Mex. G15 90
Yucatán, Canal de, strt., N.A. D2 94
Yucatan Peninsula (Península de Yucatán), pen., N.A. H15 90
Yucca, Az., U.S. J2 120
Yucca Valley, Ca., U.S. J9 124
Yuci, China D9 30
Yuecheng, China C3 34
Yueyang, China F2 34
Yugoslavia (Jugoslavija), ctry., Eur. G11 4
Yukarıbey, Tur. J11 20
Yukon, Ok., U.S. D9 116
Yukon, prov., Can. D5 96
Yukon, stm., N.A. m19 98a
Yukon, stm., N.A. E14 100
Yukon Flats, sw., Ak., U.S. C21 100
Yukou, China C5 32
Yüli, Tai. L10 34
Yulin, China D8 30
Yulin, China C11 40
Yuma, Az., U.S. L2 120
Yuma, Co., U.S. K5 118
Yuma, Bahía de, b., Dom. Rep. E10 94
Yumare, Ven. B8 84
Yumbel, Chile I2 80
Yumbo, Col. F4 84
Yumen, China D6 30
Yuna, stm., Dom. Rep. E9 94
Yuncheng, China D9 30
Yungas, reg., Bol. F8 82
Yungay, Chile I2 80
Yungay, Peru C3 82
Yunhe, China G8 34
Yunnan, prov., China F7 30
Yunta, Austl. I3 70
Yunxian, China E9 30
Yura, Peru G6 82
Yurimaguas, Peru A3 82
Yuriria, Mex. G9 90
Yuriria, Laguna de, l., Mex. G9 90
Yuruarí, stm., Ven. D12 84
Yurubi, Parque Nacional, Ven. B8 84
Yurumanguí, stm., Col. F4 84
Yusala, Laguna, l., Bol. F8 82
Yuscarán, Hond. D8 92
Yushan, China B2 34
Yü Shan, mtn., Tai. L9 34
Yushu, China E6 30
Yutian, China B9 44
Yuty, Para. D10 80
Yuwangcheng, China D3 34
Yuxian, China A2 34
Yuyao, China E10 34
Yvelines, dept., Fr. D8 14
Yverdon, Switz. E6 13
Yvetot, Fr. C7 14

Z

Zabajkal'sk, Russia H15 28
Žabari, Yugo. E5 20
Zabarjad, Jazīrat, i., Egypt F9 60
Zabīd, Yemen G3 47
Žabinka, Bela. I7 22
Žabje, Ukr. A8 20
Ząbkowice Śląskie, Pol. E16 10
Žabljak, Yugo. F3 20
Zābol, Iran F16 48
Zābolī, Iran H16 48
Zabolotov, Ukr. A9 20
Zabory, Russia F15 22
Zabré, Burkina F9 64
Zabrze (Hindenburg), Pol. E18 10
Zacapa, Guat. C5 92
Zacapa, dept., Guat. B5 92
Zacapu, Mex. H9 90
Zacatecas, Mex. F8 90
Zacatecas, state, Mex. F8 90
Zacatecoluca, El Sal. D6 92
Zacatlán, Mex. H11 90
Zacharovo, Russia G22 22
Zachary, La., U.S. L5 114
Zachmet, Turk. C17 48
Zacoalco de Torres, Mex. G8 90
Zacualpa, Guat. B4 92
Zacualtipan, Mex. G10 90
Zaculeu, hist., Guat. B3 92
Zadar, Cro. E10 18
Zadetkyi Kyun, i., Burma J5 40
Zadonsk, Russia I21 22
Zafer Burnu, c., N. Cyp. D3 48
Zafīr, U.A.E. C8 47
Zafra, Spain G5 16
Żagań, Pol. D15 10
Žagare, Lith. E6 22
Zaghouan, Tun. M5 18
Zagnanado, Benin H11 64
Zagnitkov, Ukr. A12 20
Zagora, Mor. E8 62
Zagreb, Cro. D10 18
Zāgros, Kūhhā-ye, mts., Iran E9 48
Žagubica, Yugo. E5 20
Zagyva, stm., Hung. H20 10
Zahana, Alg. J11 16
Zāhedān, Iran G16 48
Zaḥlah, Leb. A5 50
Záhony, Hung. G22 10
Zahrān, Sau. Ar. F3 47
Zaire (Zaïre), ctry., Afr. B4 58
Zaïre see Congo, stm., Afr. C2 58
Zaječar, Yugo. F6 20
Zajkany, Mol. B11 20
Zajsan, Kaz. H14 26
Zajsan, ozero, l., Kaz. H14 26
Zakamensk, Russia G12 28
Zákas, Grc. I5 20
Zākhū, Iraq C7 48
Zákinthos, Grc. L4 20
Zákinthos, i., Grc. L4 20
Zakīyah, Syria B6 50
Zakopane, Pol. F19 10
Zala, Eth. N9 60
Zala, co., Hung. I16 10
Zalaegerszeg, Hung. I16 10
Zalalövő, Hung. I16 10
Zalanga, Nig. F15 64
Zalaszentgrót, Hung. I17 10
Zalău, Rom. B7 20
Zalegošč', Russia I19 22
Zaleščiki, Ukr. A9 20
Zalesje, Russia C19 22
Zalim, Sau. Ar. C3 47
Zalingei, Sud. K2 60
Zaltbommel, Neth. E7 12
Žaltyr, Kaz. G11 26
Zama, Ms., U.S. J7 114
Zamakh, Yemen F5 47
Zambezi (Zambeze), stm., Afr. E6 58
Zambia, ctry., Afr. D5 58
Zamboanga, Phil. D7 38
Zambrano, Col. C5 84
Zambrów, Pol. B22 10
Zamfara, stm., Nig. E12 64
Zamora, Ec. J3 84
Zamora, Spain D6 16
Zamora, stm., Ec. I3 84
Zamora-Chinchipe, prov., Ec. J3 84
Zamora de Hidalgo, Mex. H8 90
Zamość, Pol. E23 10
Zamuro, Punta, c., Ven. B8 84
Zana, hist., Alg. C14 62
Zanaga, Congo B2 58
Zandvoort, Neth. D6 12
Zandvoort, Circuit Autorace, Neth. D6 12
Zanesville, Oh., U.S. H4 108
Zangasso, Mali E7 64
Zanggezhuang, China F8 32
Zanjān, Iran C10 48
Zanjón, Arg. D6 80
Zanjón, stm., Arg. F4 80
Žannetty, ostrov, i., Russia B23 28
Zanthus, Austl. F4 68
Zanzibar, Tan. C7 58
Zanzibar, i., Tan. C7 58
Zaokskij, Russia G20 22
Zaostrovje, Russia A16 22
Zaouiet Azmour, Tun. M6 18
Zaouiet el Mgaïz, Tun. M5 18
Zaoxi, China E8 34
Zaozhuang, China I5 32
Zaoz'ornyj, Russia F10 28
Zap, N.D., U.S. D6 118
Zapadnaja Dvina, Russia E15 22
Zapadnaja Dvina (Daugava), stm., Eur. F10 22
Zapadno-Sibirskaja ravnina, pl., Russia E13 26
Zapadnyj Sajan, mts., Russia G10 28
Zapala, Arg. J3 80
Zapata, Tx., U.S. M7 116
Zapata, Península de, pen., Cuba C4 94
Zapatera, Isla, i., Nic. F9 92
Zapatoca, Col. D6 84
Zapatosa, Ciénaga de, l., Col. C6 84
Zapl'usje, Russia C12 22
Zapol'arnyj, Russia G22 6
Zapolje, Russia C12 22
Zapopan, Mex. G8 90
Zaporožje, Ukr. H5 26
Zapotillo, Ec. J2 84
Zaprudn'a, Russia E20 22
Zara, Tur. B4 48
Zaragoza, Col. D5 84
Zaragoza, Mex. B6 90
Zaragoza, Mex. C9 90
Zaragoza, Mex. F10 90
Zaragoza, Spain D11 16
Zarajsk, Russia G21 22
Zarand, Iran F14 48
Zarasai, Lith. F9 22
Zárate, Arg. H9 80
Zarautz, Spain B9 16
Zaraza, Ven. C10 84
Zarcero, C.R. G10 92
Zard Kūh, mtn., Iran E11 48
Zarečnyj, Russia D25 22
Zarembo Island, i., Ak., U.S. H28 100
Zarghūn Shahr, Afg. D3 44
Zaria, Nig. F13 64
Žarkovskij, Russia F15 22
Žarma, Kaz. H14 26
Zarqāʾ, Nahr az-, stm., Jord. D5 50
Zarrīn Shahr, Iran E11 48
Zarubino, Russia C16 22
Zaruma, Ec. I3 84
Zarumilla, Peru I2 84
Żary (Sorau), Pol. D15 10
Žaryn', Russia H16 22
Zarzaïtine, Alg. F15 62
Zarzal, Col. E4 84
Zarzis, Tun. D16 62
Zāskār Mountains, mts., Asia D7 44
Zaslavl', Bela. G10 22
Zastavna, Ukr. A9 20
Zastron, S. Afr. H8 66
Zatišje, Ukr. B13 20
Zavalje, Ukr. A14 20
Zavalla, Tx., U.S. K2 114
Zavidovići, Bos. E2 20
Zavitinsk, Russia G17 28
Zavodovski Island, i., S. Geor. J12 74
Zavolžje, Russia E26 22
Zavolžsk, Russia D25 22
Zavoronežskoje, Russia I23 22
Zawiercie, Pol. E19 10
Zawiyat Shammās, Egypt B4 60
Zaza, stm., Cuba D5 94
Zaza, Presa, res., Cuba D5 94
Zazafotsy, Madag. S22 67b
Zbiroh, Czech. F13 10
Zduńska Wola, Pol. D18 10
Zealandia, Sask., Can. G7 104
Zearing, Ia., U.S. H2 110
Zeballos, B.C., Can. H8 102
Zebila, Ghana F9 64
Zebulon, Ga., U.S. F2 112
Zebulon, N.C., U.S. D8 112
Zeebrugge, Bel. F3 12
Zeehan, Austl. M6 70
Zeeland, Mi., U.S. H9 110
Zeeland, N.D., U.S. F8 118
Zeeland, prov., Neth. F4 12
Zeerust, S. Afr. E8 66
Zefat (Safad), Isr. C5 50
Žege, Eth. L9 60
Zehdenick, Ger. C13 10
Zeigler, Il., U.S. E7 114
Zeil, Mount, mtn., Austl. D6 68
Zeist, Neth. D7 12
Zeitz, Ger. D12 10
Zeja, Russia G17 28
Zeja, stm., Russia G17 28
Zejskoje vodochranilišče, res., Russia G17 28
Zelaya, dept., Nic. E10 92
Zele, Bel. F5 12
Żelechów, Pol. D21 10
Zelenoborskij, Russia H23 6
Zelenogorsk, Russia A12 22
Zelenograd, Russia E20 22
Zelenogradsk, Russia G3 22
Železnodorožnyj, Russia G4 22
Železnodorožnyj, Russia E8 26
Železnogorsk, Russia I18 22
Železnogorsk-Ilimskij, Russia F12 28
Zelienople, Pa., U.S. G6 108
Zell, Ger. E7 10
Zella-Mehlis, Ger. E10 10
Zell am See, Aus. H12 10
Zel'onodol'sk, Russia F7 26
Zelów, Pol. D19 10
Želudok, Bela. H7 22
Zel'va, Bela. H7 22
Zelzate, Bel. F4 12
Zemcy, Russia E15 22
Zemetčino, Russia H25 22
Zémio, Cen. Afr. Rep. G6 56
Zemmour, reg., Afr. H4 62
Zempoala, hist., Mex. H11 90
Zemst, Bel. G5 12
Zendeh Jān, Afg. D16 48
Zeneta, Sask., Can. H12 104
Zenica, Bos. E1 20
Zenon Park, Sask., Can. E11 104
Zephyr, Tx., U.S. H8 116
Zephyrhills, Fl., U.S. K4 112
Zeravšan, stm., Asia J11 26
Zerbst, Ger. D12 10
Žerdevka, Russia J24 22
Zermatt, Switz. F8 13
Zernez, Switz. E13 13
Zernograd, Russia H6 26
Zeulenroda, Ger. E11 10
Zeven, Ger. B9 10
Zevenaar, Neth. E9 12
Zevenbergen, Neth. E6 12
Zeytindağ, Tur. K11 20
Zgierz, Pol. D19 10
Zhagenasongduo, China D16 44
Zhanggezhuang, China G7 32
Zhangjiakou (Kalgan), China C2 32
Zhangjinhe, China E1 34
Zhangmutou, China M3 34
Zhangping, China J6 34
Zhangtaizi, China B11 32
Zhangye, China D7 30
Zhangzhou (Longxi), China K6 34
Zhanjiang, China D11 40
Zhanjiaqiao, China F2 34
Zhao'an, China L6 34
Zhaoqing, China G9 30
Zhaotong, China F7 30
Zhaoyuan, China F8 32
Zhapu, China E10 34
Zhaxigang, China D8 44
Zhdanov see Mariupol', Ukr. H5 26
Zhegu, China F14 44
Zhejiang (Chekiang), prov., China F11 30
Zhengding, China E2 32
Zhengguo, China L2 34
Zhengyangguan, China C5 34
Zhengzhou, China E9 30
Zhenjiang, China C8 34
Zhenping, China E9 30
Zhentoushi, China G2 34
Zhenxing, China A12 32
Zhenyuan, China F8 30
Zhidoi, China E5 30
Zhierling, China C2 32
Zhixia, China F8 34
Zhob, Pak. E3 44
Zhob, stm., Pak. E3 44
Zhongba, China F3 30
Zhongbu, China G6 34
Zhongdian, China F6 30

Name	Map Ref.	Page
Zhongheying, China	C7	40
Zhongmeihe, China	D5	34
Zhongning, China	D8	30
Zhongsha, China	I5	34
Zhongshan (Shiqizhen), China	M2	34
Zhongxiang, China	D1	34
Zhoucun, China	G5	32
Zhouning, China	H8	34
Zhoushan Qundao, is., China	E11	34
Zhoushuizi, China	E9	32
Zhuge, China	G6	32
Zhugouzhen, China	C2	34
Zhujiang Kou, est., Asia	M2	34
Zhulanbu, China	J4	34
Zhumadian, China	C3	34
Zhuotian, China	J5	34
Zhuoxian, China	D3	32
Zhushan, China	E9	30
Zhutian, China	G6	34
Zhuya, China	G6	32
Zhuzhou (Chuchow), China	H2	34
Zi, stm., China	F9	30
Žiar nad Hronom, Czech.	G18	10
Zibo (Zhangdian), China	G6	32
Zicavo, Fr.	M24	15a
Ziegenhain, Ger.	E9	10
Zielona Góra (Grünberg), Pol.	D15	10
Zierikzee, Neth.	E4	12
Ziesar, Ger.	C12	10
Žiežmariai, Lith.	G7	22
Ziftā, Egypt	B6	60
Žigalovo, Russia	G13	28
Zigong, China	F7	30
Ziguinchor, Sen.	E1	64
Zihuatanejo, Mex.	I9	90
Zikejevo, Russia	H17	22
Zikhron Ya'aqov, Isr.	C3	50
Žilina, Czech.	F18	10
Žilino, Russia	G4	22
Zillah, Libya	C4	56
Zillah, Wa., U.S.	D5	122
Zillertaler Alpen, mts., Eur.	I11	10
Žiloj, ostrov, i., Azer.	A11	48
Žil'ovo, Russia	G21	22
Zilupe, Lat.	E11	22
Zilwaukee, Mi., U.S.	G12	110
Zima, Russia	G12	28
Zimapán, Mex.	G10	90
Zimbabwe, ctry., Afr.	E5	58
Zimnicea, Rom.	F9	20
Zinal, Switz.	F8	13
Zinder, Niger	E14	64
Zingwanda, Sud.	N4	60
Zion, Il., U.S.	H8	110
Zion National Park, Ut., U.S.	G3	120
Zionsville, In., U.S.	C10	114
Zionz Lake, l., Ont., Can.	G23	104
Zipaquirá, Col.	E5	84
Ziqlāb, Wādī, val., Jord.	C5	50
Žitkoviči, Bela.	I10	22
Žitkovo, Russia	A12	22
Žitomir, Ukr.	G3	26
Zittau, Ger.	E14	10
Zitundo, Moz.	F11	66
Ziway, Lake, l., Eth.	M10	60
Ziwuji, China	C4	34
Ziyun, China	F8	30
Žizdra, Russia	H17	22
Zizhong, China	F7	30
Žižica, Russia	E14	22
Zlatar, Cro.	C11	18
Zlatica, Bul.	G8	20
Zlatoust, Russia	F9	26
Zlín, Czech.	F17	10
Zlīṭan, Libya	B3	56
Žlobin, Bela.	I13	22
Złotoryja, Pol.	D15	10
Złotów, Pol.	B17	10
Zlynka, Russia	I14	22
Zmeinogorsk, Russia	G14	26
Zmi'ovka, Russia	I19	22
Znamenka, Ukr.	H4	26
Znamensk, Russia	G4	22
Znamenskoje, Russia	F12	26
Znamenskoje, Russia	F6	28
Znob'-Novgorodskoje, Ukr.	I16	22
Znojmo, Czech.	G16	10
Žodino, Bela.	G11	22
Zofingen, Switz.	D8	13
Zogno, Italy	D4	18
Zolfo Springs, Fl., U.S.	L5	112
Zollikofen, Switz.	D7	13
Zollikon, Switz.	D10	13
Zolotkovo, Russia	F24	22
Zolotuchino, Russia	I19	22
Žoltyje Vody, Ukr.	H4	26
Žolymbet, Kaz.	G12	26
Zomba, Mwi.	E7	58
Zonguldak, Tur.	G14	4
Zonza, Fr.	M24	15a
Zorgo, Burkina	E9	64
Zorita, Spain	F6	16
Zorkul', ozero, l., Asia	B5	44
Zorritos, Peru	I2	84
Zouar, Chad	D4	56
Zouérat, Maur.	I4	62
Zouping, China	G5	32
Zourma, Burkina	F9	64
Žovten', Ukr.	B14	20
Zrenjanin, Yugo.	D4	20
Zriba, Tun.	M5	18
Zuata, stm., Ven.	C10	84
Zubcov, Russia	E17	22
Zubova Pol'ana, Russia	G25	22
Zuénoula, I.C.	H6	64
Zuera, Spain	D11	16
Ẓufār, reg., Oman	F9	47
Zug, Switz.	D10	13
Zug, state, Switz.	D10	13
Zugdidi, Geor.	I6	26
Zugersee, l., Switz.	D10	13
Zugspitze, mtn., Eur.	H10	10
Zuiderzee see IJsselmeer, Neth.	C7	12
Zuid-Holland, prov., Neth.	D6	12
Zujevka, Russia	F8	26
Žukovka, Russia	H16	22
Žukovskij, Russia	F21	22
Zulia, state, Ven.	B6	84
Zulia, stm., S.A.	C6	84
Zulueta, Cuba	C5	94
Zululand, hist. reg., S. Afr.	F10	66
Zumba, Ec.	J3	84
Zumbo, Moz.	E6	58
Zumbro, stm., Mn., U.S.	F3	110
Zumbrota, Mn., U.S.	F3	110
Zungeru, Nig.	G13	64
Zungur, Nig.	G14	64
Zuni, N.M., U.S.	I8	120
Zuni, stm., U.S.	J7	120
Zunyi, China	F8	30
Zuodeng, China	C9	40
Zuoz, Switz.	E12	13
Zūq Muṣbīh, Leb.	A5	50
Zurayghiṭ, Sau. Ar.	H6	48
Zurich, Ont., Can.	G14	110
Zurich, Neth.	B7	12
Zürich, Switz.	D10	13
Zürich, state, Switz.	D10	13
Zürichsee, l., Switz.	D10	13
Zuru, Nig.	F12	64
Zutphen, Neth.	D9	12
Zuwārah, Libya	B3	56
Zuwayzā, Jord.	E5	50
Zvenigorod, Russia	F19	22
Zvishavane, Zimb.	C10	66
Zvolen, Czech.	G19	10
Zvornik, Bos.	E3	20
Zweibrücken, Ger.	F7	10
Zweisimmen, Switz.	E7	13
Zwettl, Aus.	G15	10
Zwickau, Ger.	E12	10
Zwiesel, Ger.	F13	10
Zwijndrecht, Neth.	E6	12
Zwolle, Neth.	C9	12
Zwolle, La., U.S.	K3	114
Zymoetz, stm., B.C., Can.	C6	102
Zyr'anovsk, Kaz.	H8	28
Żyrardów, Pol.	C20	10
Żywiec, Pol.	F19	10